OXFORD ECONOMIC ATLAS OF THE WORLD

FOURTH EDITION

PREPARED BY
THE CARTOGRAPHIC DEPARTMENT OF THE CLARENDON PRESS

ADVISORY EDITOR
D. B. JONES, INSTITUTE OF ECONOMICS AND STATISTICS,
UNIVERSITY OF OXFORD

OXFORD UNIVERSITY PRESS
1972

Oxford University Press, Ely House, London W.1

GLASGOW NEW YORK TORONTO MELBOURNE WELLINGTON
CAPE TOWN IBADAN NAIROBI DAR ES SALAAM LUSAKA ADDIS ABABA
DELHI BOMBAY CALCUTTA MADRAS KARACHI LAHORE DACCA
KUALA LUMPUR SINGAPORE HONG KONG TOKYO

FIRST EDITION 1954
SECOND EDITION 1959
THIRD EDITION 1965
FOURTH EDITION 1972

Compiled, drawn and photomechanically processed by
The Cartographic Department of the Clarendon Press

Printed in Great Britain,
maps by Cook, Hammond and Kell, Ltd, London
gazetteer and statistical supplement at the University Press, Oxford

ACKNOWLEDGEMENTS

We acknowledge with gratitude the co-operation and assistance given by numerous government bodies and statistical agencies, national trade associations, and private companies throughout the world. Some individuals and organizations deserving special mention are listed here.

Aluminium Federation, Birmingham, U.K.
Prof. J. S. Anderson, Dept. of Inorganic Chemistry, University of Oxford
Anglo American Corporation of South Africa Ltd., Johannesburg
Anglo American International (U.K.) Ltd., London
Dr. J. H. Appleton, Dept. of Geography, University of Hull, U.K.
K. W. Ashberry, British Rail
G. R. Bamber, Editor of *Water Power*, London
Dr. L. M. Bechelli, Division of Communicable Diseases, W.H.O., Geneva
Dr. P. Beckett, Dept. of Soil Science, University of Oxford
D. P. Bickmore, Royal College of Art, London
N. Bittner, Special Committee for Machinery, O.E.C.D., Paris
Prof. G. E. Blackman, Dept. of Agricultural Science, University of Oxford
Board of Trade Library, London
Bodleian Library, University of Oxford
T. A. Boley, Electricity Council, London
K. E. Boome, International Road Federation, Geneva
British Man-Made Fibres Federation
British Paper and Board Makers' Association, London
Dr. D. G. Browning, School of Geography, University of Oxford
Dr. L. J. Bruce-Chwatt, Division of Malaria Eradication, W.H.O., Geneva
Prof. J. H. Burnett, Dept. of Agricultural Science, University of Oxford
Cadbury Schweppes Ltd., Birmingham, U.K.
A. A. L. Caesar, Dept. of Geography, University of Cambridge
J. Cashman, Lloyd's, London
Prof. S. B. Cohen, Dept. of Geography, Clark University, Worcester, Massachusetts
Commodities Division, Commonwealth Secretariat, London
Miss P. Cook, Medical Research Council, London
S. G. Cooper, International Civil Aviation Organization, Montreal
Cyanamid International, Wayne, New Jersey
P. A. Delafield, British Association of Synthetic Rubber Manufacturers Ltd., London
Dr. A. J. Duggan, Wellcome Institute, London
Economist Intelligence Unit, London
D. B. Evans, British Bureau of Non-ferrous Metal Statistics, Birmingham, U.K.
Dr. B. E. F. Fender, Dept. of Inorganic Chemistry, University of Oxford
R. Fountain, British Aircraft Corporation, Weybridge, U.K.
Prof. J. Gottmann, School of Geography, University of Oxford
Guildhall Library, London
J. Guthrie-Brown, Sir Alexander Gibb and Partners, London
R. Hankinson, International Planned Parenthood Federation, London
G. W. Hemy, Crosfield Chemicals, Warrington, U.K.
T. V. Hill, Intelligence Dept., Lloyd's, London
K. E. Hunt, Institute of Agricultural Economics, University of Oxford
M. C. Hyde, Editor of *Chemical Age*, London
Imperial Tobacco Group Limited, London
Institute of Commonwealth Studies Library, University of Oxford
Institute of Economics and Statistics, University of Oxford
A. Jeffery, International Synthetic Rubber Co. Ltd., Southampton
D. G. Jones, British Sulphur Corporation Ltd., London
W. G. G. Kellett, Rubber Growers' Association, London
A. La Spada, International Tin Council, London
Lead Development Association, London
Dr. M. J. M. Leask, Dept. of Physics, University of Oxford

J. J. MacGregor, Dept. of Forestry, University of Oxford
G. B. Masefield, Dept. of Agricultural Science, University of Oxford
Miss M. McAfee, United Nations Library, London
Mineral Resources Division, Institute of Geological Sciences, London
   W. A. Campbell, Dr. R. S. Collins, R. A. Healing, D. E. Highley, D. S. Paterson, Dr. D. Slater, I. A. Thomas, A. H. J. Todd, Dr. D. C. Turner
Ministry of Agriculture, Fisheries and Food, London
Ministry of Overseas Development, London
National Coal Board, London
Natural Rubber Producers' Research Association, Welwyn Garden City, U.K.
   P. W. Allen, Dr. L. Mullins
Miss B. Needham, Textile Council, Manchester, U.K.
N. G. Osman, International Sugar Organization, London
Overseas Activities Section, Electricity Council, London
Overseas Development Institute Ltd., London
Dr. E. R. Oxburgh, Dept. of Geology, University of Oxford
Pan American Coffee Bureau, New York
J. H. C. Patten, School of Geography, University of Oxford
M. L. Pearl, Iron and Steel Institute, London
L. Perk Vlaanderen, Secretariat of the International Rubber Study Group, London
B. A. Proctor, Economic Intelligence Dept., Barclays Bank Ltd., London
Railway Technical Centre Library, Wilmorton, U.K.
Reed Paper and Board (U.K.) Ltd., London
C. I. M. Reekie, Unilever Ltd., London
Rhodes House Library, University of Oxford
G. B. Richardson, Faculty of Social Studies, University of Oxford
G. R. Robinson, British Computer Society Library, London
Dr. J. S. Rollett, University Computing Laboratory, Oxford
Royal Automobile Club, Croydon, U.K.
Royal School of Mines Library, Imperial College, London
Royal Society for the Prevention of Accidents, London
A. E. Schreck, U.S. Bureau of Mines, Washington, D.C.
J. Slater, Mathematical Institute, University of Oxford
Dr. E. B. Smith, Dept. of Physical Chemistry, University of Oxford
C. G. Smith, School of Geography, University of Oxford
Dr. A. M. Stewart, Faculty of Medicine, University of Oxford
Dr. M. M. Sweeting, School of Geography, University of Oxford
E. J. Taaffe, Dept. of Geography, Ohio State University, Columbus
Unigate Limited, London
United Kingdom Atomic Energy Authority, London
United Nations Statistical Office, New York
Dr. B. B. Waddy, Ross Institute of Tropical Medicine, London
Dr. K. Warren, School of Geography, University of Oxford
G. Weber, Editor of *Oil and Gas Journal*, Tulsa, Oklahoma
J. Weinthal, Society of Motor Manufacturers and Traders Ltd., London
Wellcome Institute, London
Westminster Commercial Reference Library, London
Wool Industry Bureau of Statistics, Bradford, U.K.
Zinc Development Association, London

For technical assistance:
Church Army Press & Supplies Ltd., Oxford
William Clowes & Sons Ltd., Beccles
Cook, Hammond & Kell Ltd., London
Fairey Surveys Ltd., Maidenhead
David L. Fryer & Co., Henley-on-Thames
S. Glossop & Sons Ltd., Cardiff
Oxford Litho Plates Ltd., Oxford

CONTENTS

IV

SUBJECT INDEX

INTRODUCTION

The **arrangement** of the atlas has two main parts: maps grouped into thirteen sections, and the Statistical Supplement arranged in alphabetical order by country.

The maps include eight sections based on commodity groups, one introductory section of physical geography and summary maps, and four sections providing background information on demography, disease, social and political factors, and communications.

The maps and Supplement are complementary and should be used together. The maps provide a world view of any topic while the Supplement gives precise statistics for each country, showing the relative importance of any commodity in the country's economy.

The atlas is in series with the Oxford Regional Economic Atlases, which deal separately and in much greater detail with *Western Europe, North America, Africa, the U.S.S.R. and Eastern Europe,* and the *Middle East and North Africa.* The regional atlases contain larger scale topographic and economic maps, and they have maps of commodities which are important regionally but not on a world scale. The world map shows the world distribution pattern of all the more important commodities, industries and resources; in this edition these are supplemented by larger scale treatment of congested areas on each map.

For the economic maps, **commodities** were chosen mainly on the basis of their importance in world trade, with the minimum value being U.S.$100,000. Exceptionally, commodities that would not on their own have qualified for inclusion have been added expressly to increase the usefulness of maps of other associated commodities. Demographic and other non-economic topics were chosen on the basis of their relevance to economics taking into account the availability of information, the feasibility of mapping it, and the validity of the maps which would result.

Most maps are based on the **period** 1963-5. Comparative statistics for 1953-5 are given in tabular form, both accompanying the maps and in the Statistical Supplement. However, where industries were changing rapidly, and if there were more recent data available for the whole world, more up-to-date information was used, and comparative statistics for 1963-5 and 1953-5 added where possible. In some instances it was difficult to obtain data as recent even as 1963-5, particularly for China P.R. Where earlier information was considered likely to affect significantly the validity of the map its date is given.

Major **sources** of information are listed. Whenever possible statistics were obtained from international bodies for maximum comparability. Often, however, such data do not exist, and many of the statistics were obtained from national associations and statistical offices and from private companies and individuals. Others who have been advisers on collection and presentation of data are listed in the acknowledgements.

Detailed **data** for most maps have been adjusted to standard estimates of statistics on a national basis. These estimates were supplied for all countries by organizations collecting statistics on an international level, such as the United Nations, the Food and Agriculture Organization, the United States Bureau of Mines, and the Institute of Geological Sciences.

Data for each topic are presented whenever possible in statistically significant numerical categories. Exceptionally they were available only in predetermined categories, or in insufficient detail for this to be done. Most maps give an indication of the range of the statistics by stating the minimum values involved; many give maximum values as well.

Symbols are centred on the point to which they refer. The point indicated by a sector or a semi-circle is the centre of the circle of which it is a part. Symbols representing the total production of a region or province are located on the main area of production when this is known, and the location may therefore differ from the geographic centre of the region as given in the gazetteer. Symbols representing the total production of scattered centres may be placed in a box to avoid confusion with symbols for specific centres. The location of the boxed symbol does not necessarily indicate the centre of the producing area which it represents.

Insets have been used to show at a larger scale the more congested areas of the world maps; they are normally positioned just below the main map, but are occasionally on adjoining pages.

The **projection** is a modified Gall which is not an equal area projection. However, distortion of area is excessive only in polar and near-polar latitudes where economic activity is minimal. To reduce still further the effect of distortion, the method of representing data by areal shading has been little used except where the base to which the data apply. Approximate equatorial scale, on both maps and the insets, is given only as a basis for comparison between them and, in broad terms, with other maps of which the reader has knowledge. It is not appropriate to use the scale to measure distances.

The international **boundaries** used are those which existed in 1965. They have been compiled from U.N. Boundary Commission and other geographic reports and from large scale topographic maps. The internal divisions of Australia, Brazil, Canada, China P.R., the U.S.A. and the U.S.S.R. are also shown because these countries cover such large areas.

The atlas is presented in metric **units.** However, although data in the metric system formed the basis for the environment maps, data in the English system of inches, degrees Farenheit, etc, were used in the agriculture notes. In these two cases therefore, data are given in both systems. Since original data of this nature are to some extent approximate, conversion from one system to the other has also been approximate.

Certain **standard symbols** have been used in statistical tables throughout the atlas:

*	estimate	—	nil, negligible
...	not applicable	NA, na	data not available

Standard symbols have also been used on the maps themselves. On dot distribution maps countries which are known to produce the commodity in significant quantities, but for which detailed data are not available, have been shaded. On maps of industry, known centres of production for which detailed statistics are not available are indicated by a cross.

For most commodities mapped there are also tables listing the leading producing countries and the percentage of total world production for which they were responsible. In some instances this information is given for two or more associated commodities in one table. Although not all countries included in such composite tables were leading producers of all the commodities, their ratings for all commodities are given. For this reason, the ratings of the leading producers are emphasized by backing them with grey rectangles. A rating which is not grey-backed is not therefore among the leaders; its presence is incidental for that commodity and there is at least one other country whose production of that commodity is higher, although its production of none of the commodities is high enough to warrant its inclusion in the table. Some countries have more than one of these, and the few names used in the atlas which might not be immediately identifiable with other versions are listed below, along with some of the alternatives. Here and elsewhere, the word Republic as part of a country name has been abbreviated to R.

China P.R.	People's Republic of China/Mainland China/China
Congo D.R.	Democratic Republic of the Congo/Congo (Kinshasa)/Zaire
Congo R.	Republic of the Congo/Congo (Brazzaville)
Germany D.R.	German Democratic Republic/East Germany
Germany F.R.	Federal Republic of Germany/West Germany
Irish R.	Republic of Ireland/Eire
North Korea	Democratic People's Republic of Korea
South Korea	Republic of Korea
Taiwan	Nationalist China/Formosa
U.A.R.	Egypt
North Vietnam	Democratic Republic of Vietnam
South Vietnam	Republic of Vietnam

All **other names** are in the forms used in the countries concerned (transliterated into the Roman alphabet where applicable). In countries with two or more official languages, the nationally recommended version is used. If a place name has a well-known English version which is not clearly recognizable from the vernacular form, the English is normally added in parenthesis. The spelling and locations of most place names have been taken from the United States Board on Geographic Names publications; a fuller list of sources accompanies the gazetteer.

Names in upright type indicate specific places. Names in italic type indicate administrative and other statistical regions, areas around towns, and geographical features. The letter (a) in parenthesis after a name in italic type indicates that a town name has been used as a means of identifying either a producing centre which can be located only in relation to the nearest populated place, or the amalgamation of small centres represented by one symbol. Geographical features are further differentiated by letters in parenthesis following their names as follows:

b	bay	h	hill(s), ridge	pen	peninsula
bn	basin	i	island	pl	plain, plateau
cl	canal	l	loch(s), lake(s),		uplands
ct	coast		lagoon(s)	pt	point
d	deposit	m	mountain range,	r	river
dt	desert		mountain(s)	s	sea
e	estuary	o	oasis	st	straits
f	fjord	p	pass		

used. Data have been adjusted for maximum comparability, for example by excluding transport costs.

Commodities and commodity groups used are found in the 'Standard International Trade Classification, Revised' U.N. Statistical Papers, Series M, No. 34. They were selected according to the availability of data and of space on the map and the relevance to the rest of the map.

The flows have been drawn schematically, no attempt being made to follow actual routes. Those to and from Europe have been grouped according to whether the link is with a country in Southern, NE. or NW. Europe, or in Scandinavia. Those to and from countries of North Africa, the Middle East, and the Caribbean have been similarly grouped. Otherwise, two or more flows have been amalgamated only where they originate from, or are destined for, the same country. In all cases the identity of individual flows is preserved.

The width of each flow represents the value of that link. The scale used for value varies from map to map according to the range to be shown and the space available. The precise value of each flow, in U.S. $ millions, is given. If provenance and/or destination are not clear, this information is also given. Where necessary, flows are represented in boxes in which provenance is stated, and destination and value are treated in the same manner as on the map.

Details of precise value, and provenance and destination where necessary, are given by labelling individual or grouped flow lines, for example:

E TO D(6) F(4) GB(3)

indicating exports from Spain to Germany F.R., France and the U.K. valued at $6 million, $4 million and $3 million, respectively.

The international automobile registration letters, as established by the International Conventions of 1926 and 1949, have been used. Those countries not included among them have been assigned appropriate letters. A complete list of the letters used appears below; those countries not given official registration letters by the Conventions are asterisked.

A	Austria	LI	Libya*
AUS	Australia	MA	Morocco
B	Belgium	MEX	Mexico
BR	Brazil	MS	Mauritius
BS	Bahamas	N	Norway
CDN	Canada	NA	Netherlands Antilles
CGO	Congo D.R.	NIC	Nicaragua
CH	Switzerland	NIG	Niger
CPR	China P.R.*	NL	Netherlands
CS	Czechoslovakia	P	Portugal
CY	Cyprus	PA	Panama
D	Germany F.R.*	PAK	Pakistan
DE	Germany D.R.*	PL	Poland
DK	Denmark	PTM	Malaysia
DZ	Algeria	R	Romania
E	Spain	RA	Argentina
EAU	Uganda	RCH	Chile
EC	Ecuador	RF	Réunion*
ES	El Salvador*	RI	Indonesia
ET	U.A.R.	RL	Lebanon
F	France	RNR	Zambia
FJ	Fiji*	S	Sweden
GB	U.K.	SA	Saudi Arabia*
GH	Ghana	SF	Finland
GR	Greece	SGP	Singapore
HK	Hong Kong	SU	U.S.S.R.
I	Italy	SUD	Sudan
IL	Israel	T	Thailand
IND	India	TN	Tunisia
IR	Iran	TR	Turkey
IRL	Irish R.	TT	Trinidad/Tobago
IRQ	Iraq	USA	U.S.A.
JA	Jamaica	VNS	South Vietnam*
KS	South Korea*	WAN	Nigeria
KWT	Kuwait	YU	Yugoslavia
L	Luxembourg	ZA	South Africa

When centres of activity are so close together that there is insufficient space to name all of them individually without ambiguity, one of three courses has been adopted. Where two names refer to a single symbol, the names are placed one after the other, that of the larger centre first, and joined by a stroke (/). Where two symbols are named together the individual names are placed one after the other, that of the larger symbol first, and joined by an ampersand (&). Where more than two symbols are involved, their names have been placed in a box and grouped according to size, with a horizontal line separating names of different sized symbols. The names of the largest symbol size are first, followed by other size groups in descending order. Within each size group the names are arranged according to the position of the symbols, not by size within that category. Boxes containing names of more than one type of symbol may include spots of colour or other indicators to assist the assigning of names to symbols.

Trade flow mapped in this atlas is defined as the value of trade in one direction between a pair of countries. The flows shown for different commodities (or groups of associated commodities) are the few largest which, taken together, account for much of world trade in each commodity or group and, individually are appreciably larger than the hundreds of much smaller flows making up the balance. They vary considerably in number for different commodities. They are essentially bilateral links and, although they are the most important ones, they do not necessarily involve all major exporters or importers.

Trade tables accompanying the maps list the major exporters and importers with their percentage of world trade, and the Statistical Supplement gives absolute figures for total exports and imports for every country (where data are available).

The source of the data is the United Nations Statistical Office Data Bank (International Trade Statistics Centre). Data were obtained for 60 reporting countries which together accounted for over 90% of total world trade in each commodity in 1966, excluding trade within the bloc of countries with centrally-planned economies. Wherever possible, data were based on both imports and exports as reported by two trading partners but, where only one partner was a reporting country, only its imports or exports have been

Political Units

Political units

Boundaries (1965)
—— International
—— Internal

Names (1970)

Mexico — Country names (in the anglicized form)

OHIO — Major administrative divisions (in the vernacular form, transliterated where necessary)

For complete forms of U.S.A. state abbreviations see the introduction to the gazetteer

Modified Gall Projection
Equatorial Scale 1:88 Million approx.

© Oxford University Press

On the economic maps in the atlas the internal boundaries shown in the U.S.S.R. are those of the economic regions which form the basis for that country's statistical reports. Some of these economic regions are subdivisions of the S.S.R.s; others comprise several small S.S.R.s. The divisions are:

S.S.R.: *Economic Region*
Rossiyskaya (R.S.F.S.R.): *Severo-Zapad, Tsentr, Volgo-Vyatsk, Tsentralno-Chernozem, Povolzhsk, Severo-Kavkaz, Ural, Zapadno-Sibir', Vostochno-Sibir', Dal'nevostock*
Ukrainskaya: *Donetsko-Pridneprovsk, Yugo-Zapad, Yuzhnyy*
Uzbekskaya, Kirgizskaya, Tadzhikskaya, Turkmenskaya: *Sredneazia*
Litovskaya, Latviyskaya, Estonskaya, Kaliningradskaya (Oblast'): *Pribaltika*
Armyanskaya, Gruzinskaya, Azerbaydzhanskaya: *Zakavkaz*²

The S.S.R.s of Kazakh, Belorossiya and Moldavia are coincident with the economic regions of the same name.

¹On all economic maps the S.S.R. boundaries are shown.
²On all economic maps the boundary for the economic region only is shown.

On some economic maps in the atlas data have been reported for first order administrative divisions and for their sub-divisions, most of which are too small to be shown on a world map of this scale. Examples of these are: the provinces, states, departments, etc. of most countries; the counties of the U.S.A., which are subdivisions of the states; and the prefectures (ken) of Japan, which are subdivisions of the islands. Occasionally regional names have been used in reference to clearly defined physical units such as the Red Basin of Szechwan (Ssu-ch'uan Pen-i), the North European Plain and the Ganges Plain, or to areas unified by their economic activity, such as the Corn Belt (of the U.S.A. and Canada), the Maize Triangle (of South Africa) and the Ruhr (the major industrial conurbation of Germany F.R.).

The Federation of Rhodesia and Nyasaland comprised the states of Zambia and Malawi (both of which became independent in 1964) and Rhodesia (which declared its independence in 1965).

Indo-China comprised the states of Laos (1949), Cambodia (1953), North Vietnam (1954) and South Vietnam (1954), which became independent in the years shown.

Spanish West Africa retains only the province of Spanish Sahara. Ifni was returned to Morocco in 1968.

French West Africa comprised the sovereign states of Guinea (which became independent in 1958), Ivory Coast, Togo, Niger, Dahomey, Senegal, Mali (formerly the territory of French Sudan) Mauritania and Upper Volta, all of which became independent in 1960.

French Equatorial Africa comprised the states of Central African Republic (formerly the territory of Ubangi Shari), the Republic of the Congo (formerly the territory of Middle Congo), Chad and Gabon, all of which became independent in 1960.

The Federation of Malaysia, which came into being in 1963, comprised the Federation of Malaya, the State of Singapore and the colonies of North Borneo (renamed Sabah) and Sarawak. In 1965 Singapore seceded from the Federation and became an independent sovereign state.

Country name changes (1950–1970)

PRESENT NAME	FORMER NAME	YEAR OF CHANGE
Botswana	Bechuanaland	1966
Burundi	Ruanda-Urundi	1962
Cameroun	Cameroun Republic (Fr.)/Southern Br. Cameroons	1961
Congo, Democratic Republic of the	Belgian Congo	1960
Equatorial Guinea	Spanish Guinea¹	1968
French Territory of the Afars and the Issas	French Somaliland	1967
Ghana	Gold Coast/Trusteeship Territory of Togoland	1957
Guyana	British Guiana	1966
Lesotho	Basutoland	1966
Malagasy Republic	Madagascar	1960
Malawi	Nyasaland	1964
Malaysia	Malaya/Sabah/Sarawak	1963
Oman	Muscat & Oman	1970
Rhodesia	Southern Rhodesia	1965
Rwanda	Ruanda-Urundi	1962
Somali Republic	Br. Somaliland/Somalia	1960
Southern Yemen	Federation of South Arabia	1967
Tanzania	Tanganyika/Zanzibar	1964
United Arab Republic	Egypt	1958
Zambia	Northern Rhodesia	1964

¹incl. Fernando Po and Rio Muni

SCALE 1:44 MILLION 1 CM. TO 440 KM.

VII

Environment

The economic activity of any area and the degree to which it has been developed are influenced to some extent by the prevalent physical conditions and the resources available. However, the nature of man's activity is also influenced by such social and economic factors as his technical knowledge and skills, cultural preferences, the efficiency of his systems of communication, world demand for commodities and local and national policies. These may override physical conditions.

The majority of the maps in this section present those components of the physical environment which most influence human activities. The last three maps of the section give a general summary of the ways in which man has responded to his environment, information which is presented in detail in the sections following.

Climate, rock type, relief, soil, vegetation and geomorphic processes acting on the land are all important components of man's environment. In any one area the landscape represents the complex interaction of all these factors through time, together with the effect of human activity which itself is an integral part of the environment and of its development. Man's activity has led to an alteration of many characteristics of the landscape as it was before his appearance, and to a disturbance of the interrelations between the elements of the environment. The extent to which this has occurred has varied through time, depending to a large extent on his need for materials and his technical understanding and abilities.

Since early in his history man has played a major role in altering the vegetation cover of a large portion of the earth's surface. Vast areas of forest have been cleared to provide land for crop cultivation and wood for building, fuel, and other uses. Changes in the vegetation have caused a disruption of the balance which existed between the different elements of the environment. Soils, for example, are more subject to erosion without the protection afforded by the vegetation, and changes in the hydrological cycle have also been initiated. The alteration of the vegetation pattern is but one example of the part man has played in fashioning his environment. Urbanization, industrialization and mining are all responsible for changes of various kinds.

More efficient use of resources, becoming ever more necessary as population growth increases the pressure on existing resources, is an important factor in economic development. Man's ability to modify his environment and to use it so as to increase its economic potential has improved as his knowledge and technical skills have advanced. This modification of the environment is exemplified by the development of irrigation schemes and the use of wind breaks, glass-houses and smudge pots in order to make climatic conditions more favourable for crops; the use of organic and inorganic fertilizers to increase the productivity of the soil; selective breeding of crops and of animals; and development of new methods of overcoming the problems posed by permafrost. Furthermore the increase in the extent and efficiency of the communications system makes possible the economic development of areas where such development has been for a long time impossible or uneconomic because of their inaccessibility.

It is important to note that for all these activities a knowledge of the physical characteristics of the environment is vital. Further development of resources will depend on an increased understanding both of the nature of the individual elements which make up the environment and of their interrelationships.

Lack of knowledge of the working of the environment, together with pressure on resources, has often led to indiscriminate and careless exploitation, resulting in the destruction or depletion of resources, pollution and the dereliction of land.

There is an increasing realization of the importance of conserving the earth's natural resources and minimizing the disruption of the environment. This involves not only the rehabilitation of those areas which have suffered through exploitation (for example by reafforestation and improvement of farming techniques) but also the employment of conservation measures concurrently with economic development, to ensure that areas at present unspoilt will remain so. Conservation requires careful and efficient planning, based on thorough knowledge of every aspect of the environment.

Pressure/Winds

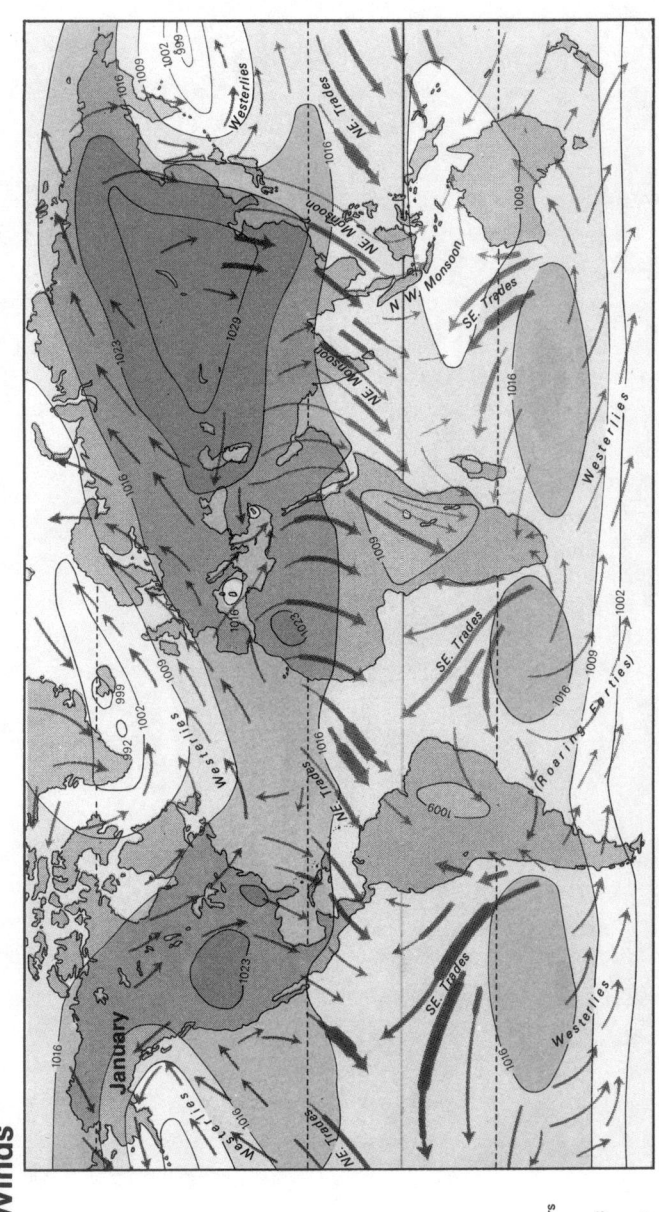

January

July

Atmospheric pressure

In.	Millibars
30.2	1 023
30.0	1 016
29.8	1 009

1 029 mb (30.4 in.).
1 002 mb (29.6 in.).
999 mb (29.5 in.) isobars are also shown

Prevailing winds

Arrows indicate wind direction. The heavier the arrow the more regular (constant) the direction of the wind.

Temperature/Ocean currents

January

July

Actual temperature

°F	°C
90	32
70	21
50	10
30	-1
0	-18

Ocean currents

cold
warm

Frost Incidence

Frost-free period

Number of days with minimum temperature above 0°C (32°F)

- 60
- 90
- 120
- 150
- 180
- 210
- 240
- 270

Summer frosts may occur where frost-free period is less than 90 days

No summer frosts where frost-free period is more than 90 days

Frosts occur in some years only

Absence of frosts

Boundaries of frost probability

- 100%
- 50%

Modified Gall Projection

Equatorial Scale 1 : 88 Million approx.

Date Line

Arctic Circle

Tropic of Cancer

Equator

Tropic of Capricorn

© Oxford University Press

Permafrost (perennially frozen ground) occurs extensively in Canada, Alaska and the U.S.S.R. It can be differentiated into 3 main zones: (a) continuous permafrost, where very little land is unfrozen and where permafrost may reach depths over 600 m. (approx 2 000 ft.); (b) discontinuous permafrost, where scattered patches of unfrozen land occur; and (c) sporadic permafrost, where patches of permafrost occur in a generally unfrozen area. Overlying permafrost is an 'active' layer of rock or soil which thaws in summer and freezes in winter. Permafrost creates both technical and financial problems for economic development. Melting of permafrost due to heat from buildings may lead to flooding and land subsidence, thus necessitating the careful siting of buildings and the use of effective insulation. Similarly, roads, railways, bridges, dams, sewerage and water-supply systems are affected by flooding, slumping and freezing, and maintenance is costly. Mining operations are hindered by the hardness of the ground, the thawing of permafrost in mine shafts and the formation of ice on machines. Agriculture is virtually negligible where permafrost near the ground surface limits the amount of soil available for plant growth. Also, apart from restrictions imposed by flooding and slumping, it is especially affected by the poorly developed soils and short growing season which are found in permafrost zones.

Plants vary quite considerably in their tolerance to low temperature conditions; some are killed when temperatures approach or reach freezing point whereas others can withstand such conditions although growth is negligible. In general, all plant activity is extremely low when temperatures are at or near freezing point and plant growth is not of economic significance when temperatures are below 4°C (approx. 40°F). The accompanying small world map indicates those areas where the mean monthly temperature is below 4°C for part or all of the year.

The length of the frost-free period gives a general indication of the length of the growing season and hence the suitability of different areas for the production of various crops. It may also serve to indicate whether double cropping is possible during the year. The length of the frost-free period is not, however, the only criterion for determining whether an area is suitable for the production of a particular crop. Other conditions may be equally important,

including the following: light intensity; photo-period (number of daylight hours), for example in temperate rice growing areas; day and night temperature intensities, for example in the production of tomatoes; and water regime.

In some areas, where the occurrence of frosts threatens crops which are otherwise suited to the area, protective measures may be employed to avoid losses. Fruit crops are particularly susceptible to frosts, especially at blossom time. Consequently in some fruit growing areas, particularly the citrus groves of Florida and California, the use of smudge pots to create smoke palls, or of oil heaters, combats damaging frosts. The spreading of straw and mulch over vegetable crops is another method of frost protection. Also, advances are being made in the development of crops which mature in a shorter, but favourable growing season, so permitting the extension of crop production in such areas as Alaska, Northern Canada and Siberia.

1

Permafrost zones

North America

SCALE 1:72/MILLION

U.S.S.R.

SCALE 1:76 MILLION

Data for Mongolia P.R. not available

- Continuous permafrost
- Discontinuous permafrost

Sporadic permafrost and permafrost in mountain areas outside discontinuous zone excluded

Mean January and July temperatures

Mean monthly temperatures

- below 4°C (40°F) throughout the year
- below 4°C for part of the year
- above 4°C throughout the year

July 4°C   Jan. 4°C

July 4°C   Jan. 4°C

SCALE 1:352 MILLION

Mean Annual Precipitation

2

© Oxford University Press

Modified Gall Projection
Equatorial Scale 1: 88 Million approx.

Isohyet intervals

mm.	ins. (approx.)
3000	120
2000	100
1500	80
1000	60
750	40
500	30
250	20
100	10
	4

Potential evaporation (evapotranspiration)

Potential evaporation from the land surface
mm. per year

	mm.
	2 500
	2 000
	1 500
	1 000
	600
	200

data not available for highland areas and continental ice sheets

SCALE 1:352 MILLION, 1CM. TO 3 520KM.

Potential evaporation (P.E.) is the moisture loss that could occur if an unlimited supply of water were available. It often differs greatly from actual evaporation, especially in hot deserts where water transfer rate is far less than the rate at which evaporation could occur under the prevailing climatic conditions. Knowledge of P.E. is valuable for determining the irrigation requirements of an area, but problems may arise in areas of high P.E. where water added to the land is rapidly evaporated, leading to increased soil salinity which may be harmful to crops.

Precipitation data for selected stations (1931–60 av.)[1]

For each station altitude is given in metres and mean annual precipitation in millimetres.

Rochambeau (airport), French Guiana — Alt.9 m. — 3744 mm.

Prince George, Canada — Alt.676 m. — 626 mm.

Regina, Canada — Alt.574 m. — 394 mm.

Montréal (Dorval), Canada — Alt.30 m. — 971 mm.

Montréal and Bulawayo 1941–60 av.

Phoenix, U.S.A. — Alt.337 m. — 183 mm.

Little Rock, U.S.A. — Alt.81 m. — 1236 mm.

Rosario, Argentina — Alt.27 m. — 991 mm.

Lima (Limatambo), Peru — Alt.155 m. — 36 mm.

Moskva, U.S.S.R. — Alt.156 m. — 575 mm.

Irkutsk, U.S.S.R. — Alt.485 m. — 458 mm.

Berlin (Tempelhof), Germany — Alt.50 m. — 556 mm.

Hulwân, U.A.R. — Alt.141 m. — 25 mm.

Bergen (Fredriksberg), Norway — Alt.44 m. — 1958 mm.

Kew, U.K. — Alt.5 m. — 594 mm.

Kumasi, Ghana — Alt.293 m. — 1465 mm.

Perpignan, France — Alt.48 m. — 639 mm.

Bulawayo, Rhodesia — Alt.1 345 m. — 589 mm.

Valentia Island, Ireland — Alt.14 m. — 1398 mm.

Athínai, Greece — Alt.107 m. — 402 mm.

Brisbane, Australia — Alt.41 m. — 1 092 mm.

Tōkyō, Japan — Alt.6 m. — 1563 mm.

Perth, Australia — Alt.60 m. — 889 mm.

Bombay (Colaba), India — Alt.11 m. — 2 078 mm.

Seasonal Climates

Seasonal climates

This classification comprises eleven basic climatic types. Nine types are classified according to the temperature characteristics of summer and winter and two additional types are distinguished where aridity is the dominant influence.

Middle latitude climates are further subdivided according to seasonal temperature range. Tropical and certain subtropical climates are further subdivided according to the duration of wet and dry seasons.

A total of twenty-six climatic types thus occurs. The extent of each type is shown on the map and the boundaries are extended over the oceans. In addition to this, regions where rainfall occurs predominantly in winter are indicated.

Summer and winter temperature characteristics

Summers are classified according to the mean temperature of the warmest month and designated 0, 1, 2 or 3.

		MEAN TEMPERATURE OF THE WARMEST MONTH
0	No summer	6°C (43°F) and under.
1	Very cool summer	6°-10°C (43°-50°F)
2	Cool summer	10°-20°C (50°-68°F)
3	Full summer	over 20°C (68°F)

Winters are classified according to the mean temperature of the coldest month and designated 0,1 or 2.

		MEAN TEMPERATURE OF THE COLDEST MONTH
0	No winter	over 13°C (55°F)
1	Mild winter	2°-13°C (36°-55°F)
2	Cold winter	below 2°C (36°F)

Combinations of summer and winter conditions are used to indicate climatic types. These are shown on land areas by colour and on sea areas by figures, in which case the digit for summer is always given first. Thus 02 indicates no summer, cold winter.

Combinations of summer and winter conditions

Colour	Summer	Winter
	No summer	Cold winter
	Cool summer	No winter
	Very cool summer	Cold winter
	Full summer	Cold winter
	Very cool summer	Mild winter
	Full summer	Mild winter
	Cool summer	Cold winter
	Full summer	No winter
	Cool summer	Mild winter

Duration of wet and dry seasons

For areas 30 and 31 only

a All months rainy
   i.e. with over 50 mm. (2 in.) rainfall

b Rainy season predominant
   8-11 months with over 50 mm.

c Rainy and dry seasons approx. equal
   5, 6 or 7 months with over 50 mm.

d Dry season predominant
   1-4 months with over 50 mm.

Winter rain regions

(- · - · -) Boundary of region where rainfall occurs predominantly in winter

Seasonal temperature range

For areas 21, 22 and 32 outside the tropics

1 Oceanic
   Seasonal range under 12°C (22° F)

2 Sub Continental
   Seasonal range 12°-24°C (22°-43°F)

   Continental
   Seasonal range 24°-36°C (43°-65°F)

3 Very Continental
   Seasonal range 36°-48°C (65°-86°F)

4 Extremely Continental
   Seasonal range over 48°C (86°F)

Arid climates

Arid

Arid climates are those climates in middle and low latitudes in which no month receives as much as 50 mm. (2 in.) rainfall.

Extremely arid

Extremely arid climates are perennially rainless with no more than 2.5 mm. (0.1 in.) rainfall per month for at least 10 months of the year.

Classification devised by Professor D.L. Linton

Equatorial Scale 1: 88 Million approx.

Modified Gall Projection

© Oxford University Press

Mean monthly temperatures for January and July (1931–60)

Selected stations *(with altitude in metres)*

	Jan.		July				Jan.		July	
	°C	°F	°C	°F			°C	°F	°C	°F
Coppermine (0)	-28.6	-19	9.3	49		Chicago (190)	-3.3	26	24.3	76
Verkhoyansk (137)	-46.8	-52	15.7	60		New York (16)	0.9	34	24.9	77
Winnipeg (240)	-17.7	0	20.2	68		Sydney (42)	21.9	71	12.3	54
Moskva (156)	-9.9	14	19.0	66		Rosario (27)	23.8	75	9.9	50
Berlin (50)	-0.5	31	19.4	67		Rio de Janeiro (27)	21.0	75	10.3	51
Reykjavik (16)	-0.4	31	11.2	52		Pretoria (1400)¹	26.0	79	20.8	69
Kew (5)	4.2	40	17.6	64		Kumasi (293)¹	25.2	77	24.2	76
Hobart (54)	16.3	61	7.8	46		Madras (16)	24.5	76	30.7	87
Quito (2812)	13.0	55	12.9	55		New Delhi (216)¹	14.3	58	31.2	88
Tōkyō (6)	3.7	39	25.1	77		Phoenix (337)	10.4	51	32.9	91

Temperatures decrease with increasing altitude at a rate of about 2°C (3.6°F) for every 300m. (1 000 ft). Location, season and time of day all influence the actual rate.
¹1941–90   ²1961–80

3

Relief

4

Modified Gall Projection
Equatorial Scale 1:88 Million approx.

Relief

Relief

	METRES
Land	
Highest point: Mt. Everest	8 848
Lowest point: Shores of the Dead Sea	-392
Average height	840
Oceans and seas	
Greatest known depth: Marianas Trench	11 022
Average depth	3 808

Area

	MILLION SQ. KM
Land	149
Water surface	361
Total	510
of which: Ice sheets and glaciers	16

SCALE 1:29 MILLION

SCALE 1:29 MILLION

SCALE 1:29 MILLION
10M. TO 290 KM

ICE CAPS

feet	metres
16 500	5 000
13 200	4 000
9 900	3 000
6 600	2 000
3 300	1 000
1 650	500
660	200
0	0 sea level
660	200
6 600	2 000
13 200	4 000
16 500	5 000
23 100	7 000

Arctic Circle

Tropic of Cancer

Equator

Tropic of Capricorn

Soil

Soil classification

This map shows the general distribution of soils, classified into orders and sub-orders. Only the most extensive areas of orders and the dominant sub-orders, are shown. Great groups, which are further divisions of sub-orders, are not shown but are referred to in the key under 'Soils of mountain areas'. The boundaries between the map units are generalized and the composition of a unit can be expected to vary from one part of the world to another. The nomenclature is systematic. Order names end in sol, (L. solum, soil), for example Entisol and contain a formative element which also occurs as the final syllable of the sub-order names, for example Aquent. Other elements used in the names give some indication of soil characteristics. These are:

alb   L. albus, white; soils with a bleached eluvial horizon
and   From Ando soils; soils from vitreous parent materials
aqu   L. aqua, water; soils that are wet for long periods
arg   L. argilla, clay; soils with a horizon of clay accumulation
bor   Gk. boreas, northern; cool soils
cry   Gk. kryos, icy cold; cold soils
hum   L. humus, earth; presence of organic matter
ochr   Gk. ochros, pale; soils with little organic matter
orth   Gk. orthos, true; common or typical
psamm   Gk. psammos, sand; sandy soils
rend   From Rendzina; soils with a high carbonate content
torr   L. torridus, hot and dry; soils of very dry climates
ud   L. udus, humid; soils of humid climates
umbr   L. umbra, shade; dark colours reflect much organic matter
ust   L. ustus, burnt; soils of dry climates with summer rains
xer   Gk. xeros, dry; soils of dry climates with winter rains

Entisols
Weakly developed soils

E1   **Aquents**   Seasonally or perennially wet
E2   **Orthents**   Loamy or clayey texture; often shallow to bedrock
E3   **Psamments**   Sand or loamy sand texture

Vertisols
Grumusols

Soils with a high content of active clays which swell when wet and shrink and develop deep, wide cracks when dry. Usually have a moderate to high nutrient status, but may be difficult to manage.

V1   **Uderts**   Usually moist, with cracks open less than 90 cumulative days in the year
V2   **Usterts**   Dry and cracked more than 90 cumulative days in the year

Inceptisols
Moderately developed soils

Soils with some horizons of pedogenic alteration, or concretion of weathering products, but no horizons of redistributed materials commonly possibly of silica, or carbonates. Usually moist; base supply usually medium to high. May support a variety of crops.

I1   **Andepts**   Soils containing amorphous or allophanic clay, often associated with volcanic ash and/or pumice
I2   **Aquepts**   Seasonally or perennially wet
I3   **Ochrepts**   Soils with thin, light-coloured surface horizons
I4   **Tropepts**   Continuously warm or hot
I5   **Umbrepts**   Dark surface horizons; medium to low base supply

Aridisols
Desert or saline soils

Soils with pedogenic horizons, which contain little organic matter or nitrogen, and are usually dry for more than 6 months in the year. Many areas salts accumulate on or near the soil surface to form crusts or hardpans. Since their nutrient content, excepting nitrogen, is often high, these soils can be productive with irrigation, but are vulnerable to salt accumulation.

D1   **Aridisols**   Undifferentiated
D2   **Argids**   Soils with horizons of clay accumulation (U.S.A.)

Mollisols
Brown forest, chernozem and chestnut soils

Soils with dark, organic-rich surface horizons, high base supply and which are either usually moist or usually dry. They have a better organic status and structure than spodosols and are less acidic. With adequate lime and fertilizer, they will support the continued production of a variety of crops.

M1   **Albolls**   Soils with a seasonally perched water table
M2   **Borolls**   Cool or cold
M3   **Rendolls**   Soils with subsurface accumulations of calcium carbonate, but no clay
M4   **Udolls**   Temperate or warm; usually moist
M5   **Ustolls**   Temperate to hot; dry more than 90 cumulative days in the year
M6   **Xerolls**   Cool to warm; dry in winter and continuously dry for more than 60 days in summer

Spodosols
Podsols of high latitudes

Soils with subsurface accumulations of amorphous materials (mainly iron and aluminium oxides); usually moist or wet, and generally strongly leached (therefore poor in mineral elements); acid and almost structureless, in upper layers. Can be agriculturally productive with the addition of lime and fertilizer.

S1   **Spodosols**   Undifferentiated
S2   **Aquods**   Seasonally wet
S3   **Humods**   Soils with subsurface accumulation of organic matter
S4   **Orthods**   Soils with subsurface accumulation of organic matter, iron and aluminium

Alfisols
Podsolic soils of middle latitudes and degraded grassland soils

Soils with grey to brown surface horizons, sub-surface clay accumulation and a medium to high base supply. They have a better organic status and structure than spodosols and are less acidic. With adequate lime and fertilizer, they will support the continued production of a variety of crops.

A1   **Boralfs**   Cool
A2   **Udalfs**   Temperate to hot, and usually moist
A3   **Ustalfs**   Temperate or warm; dry more than 90 cumulative days in the year
A4   **Xeralfs**   Cool to warm; dry in winter and continuously dry for more than 60 days in summer

Ultisols
Strongly weathered or podsolic soils of middle to low latitudes

Soils with subsurface horizons of clay accumulation and low base supply; usually moist and usually low in organic matter. Lower horizons may contain iron concretions. Natural agricultural capacity not high, but can be productive with fertilization and good management.

U1   **Aquults**   Seasonally wet
U2   **Humults**   Temperate or warm; moist all of the year; high content of organic matter
U3   **Udults**   Temperate to hot; usually moist
U4   **Ustults**   Warm or hot; dry more than 90 cumulative days in the year

Oxisols
Strongly weathered soils of middle to low latitudes (laterites, latosols)

Soils with pedogenic horizons that are mixtures principally of kaolin, hydrated oxides and quartz and are low in weatherable materials. Humus breakdown is rapid and the soils are usually deep and porous. They require fertilization to support continued crop production.

O1   **Orthox**   Hot and nearly always moist
O2   **Ustox**   Warm or hot; dry for long periods, but moist for a period of more than 90 days in the year

Histosols
Bog and peat soils

Wet organic soils. Slow rates of decay lead to the accumulation of peat or raw humus.

Soils of mountain areas

Soils with various temperature and moisture regimes. Altitude, aspect, steepness of slope and relief cause soils to vary greatly within short distances, and vertical zonation is common. In many places soils are absent.

X1   Cryic great groups of Entisols, Inceptisols and Spodosols
X2   Boralfs and cryic great groups of Entisols and Inceptisols
X3   Udic great groups of Alfisols, Entisols and Ultisols; Inceptisols
X4   Ustic great groups of Alfisols, Inceptisols, Mollisols and Ultisols
X5   Xeric great groups of Alfisols, Entisols, Inceptisols, Mollisols and Ultisols
X6   Torric great groups of Entisols; Aridisols
X7   Ustic and cryic great groups of Alfisols, Entisols, Inceptisols and Mollisols; ustic great groups of Ultisols; cryic great groups of Spodosols
X8   Aridisols; toric and cryic great groups of Entisols; cryic great groups of Spodosols and Inceptisols

Areas where soils are largely absent

Icefields and rugged mountains

Modified Gall Projection
Equatorial Scale 1:88 Million approx.

The map is based on "Soil Classification. A Comprehensive System. 7th Approximation" (U.S. Department of Agriculture, Soil Conservation Service, 1960 and 1967)

© Oxford University Press

Soil erosion is a natural and continual process which is normally balanced by soil-forming processes so that the basic character of a soil is maintained. At the same time, however, the rate of erosion has been greatly accelerated resulting in the removal of part or all of the soil within a relatively short time. Thus, many areas have become either useless for cultivation or else very costly to cultivate due to the large amounts of fertilizer required. Only in those areas where the most fertile horizons are low down in the soil profile can the removal of the upper layers be beneficial, and it may therefore be induced. Accelerated erosion is usually initiated when the equilibrium of an environment is disturbed through human interference, for example by the clearing of land for cultivation, overcultivation or overstocking of sloping land, and the cultivation of steep slopes without terracing. Once the soil has lost its protective covering of vegetation and its surface has been broken up by ploughing, it is less able to withstand erosion, and rapid stripping of material by wind and by water (for example sheetwash and gullying) may result. The actual rate of erosion depends on the type of soil, the climatic conditions, and the relief. Attempts are now being made to prevent further destruction and to reclaim land which has suffered extensive erosion. Conservation measures include the use of more suitable crop rotations, strip cropping, contour ploughing, terracing and destocking and a return to either forest or pasture, of land which has proved unsuitable for cultivation.

5

Rural Land Use/Vegetation

© Oxford University Press

Modified Gall Projection
Equatorial Scale 1:88 Million approx.

Rural land use/vegetation

Arable and mixed farming land (intensive farming)

Grazing land (incl. marginal farmed land)

Rice land (farmed land where paddy is the predominant crop)

Other irrigated land (irrigated areas in dry lands where paddy is not dominant)

Coniferous forest

Mixed coniferous and deciduous forest

Deciduous forest

Equatorial forest

Tropical woodland and grassland

Marsh or bog

Sand desert

Other desert

High altitude wasteland, tundra and ice cap areas

Land use/vegetation divisions of major regions

Each circle area is proportional to the total area of the region

Arable land

Meadow and pasture

Forested land

Built-on areas, waste-land and other land

Proportions of arable land under various crops (1963/4) are expressed as percentages, for example Wheat *18*

Africa

Millet/Sorghum *10* Maize(corn) *5*
Wheat *3* Other cereals *4*
Oilseeds *4* Cotton *1* Pulses *1*

Asia

(Crop percentages are for Asia excl. China P.R.)

Rice *24* Wheat *11*
Other cereals *18* Oilseeds *9*
Pulses *6* Cotton *3*

U.S.S.R.

(Crop percentages are for sown area)

Wheat *28* Barley *9*
Other cereals *16* Potatoes *3*
Sugar beet *2* Cotton *2*

U.S.A. and Canada

(Incl. Greenland, Bermuda, St. Pierre and Miquelon)

Wheat *13* Maize(corn) *11*
Oats *6* Other cereals *6*
Oilseeds *9* Cotton *3*

Latin America

Maize(corn) *21* Wheat *8*
Other cereals *10* Oilseeds *4*
Pulses *6* Cotton *6*

Oceania

Wheat *19* Oats *4*
Other cereals *4* Sugar cane *1*
Potatoes *0.3* Oilseeds *0.3*

Europe

Wheat *18* Barley *9*
Other cereals *20* Potatoes *6*
Pulses *4* Sugar beet *2*

Predominant Economies

Modified Gall Projection   Equatorial Scale 1: 88 Million approx.

© Oxford University Press

Employment categories for selected countries 1966[1] (percentage of employed population)

Countries (left to right): Canada, U.S.A., Mexico, Argentina, U.K., France, Germany F.R., Romania[1], U.S.S.R.[1], Kenya, South Africa, India, Indonesia, Japan, Australia

Scale: 0, 10, 20, 30, 40, 50, 60, 70, 80, 90, 100

Legend:
- AGRICULTURE, FORESTRY, FISHING AND HUNTING
- MINING AND QUARRYING
- MANUFACTURING
- CONSTRUCTION
- POWER WATER AND SANITARY SERVICES
- COMMERCE
- TRANSPORT STORAGE AND COMMUNICATION
- SERVICES
- OTHERS

* Estimate
[1] Or latest available data pre-1966

Predominant economies

- Little or no economic activity
- Nomadic herding
- Hunting, gathering, fishing and primitive cultivation
- Shifting and marginal cultivation
- Commercial forestry
- Extensive grazing or stock raising

- Subsistence agriculture: rice dominant
- Subsistence agriculture: rice unimportant
- Subsistence agriculture: mixed crop and livestock
- Mediterranean agriculture
- Plantation crops
- Specialized horticulture

- Other commercial crops: grain dominant
- Commercial agriculture: mixed crop and livestock
- Dairy farming
- Manufacturing and service industries
- Isolated industrial centres
- Mining and extractive industries (1965)

Arctic Circle

Tropic of Cancer

Equator

Tropic of Capricorn

Date Line

7

Economic Geology

© Oxford University Press

Modified Gall Projection
Equatorial Scale 1: 88 Million approx.

Economic geology

Tectonic regions

Stable blocks

- Ancient shields (folded and metamorphosed Pre-Cambrian rocks)
- Sedimentary cover on ancient shields

Fold belts later than Pre-Cambrian

- Regions of Palaeozoic folding (Caledonian and Hercynian)
- Troughs of sediments derived from erosion of Palaeozoic fold belts
- Depressions in Caledonian fold belts containing late Palaeozoic deposits
- Sedimentary cover on Palaeozoic folded rocks
- Regions of post-Palaeozoic folding (mainly Tertiary)
- Troughs of sediments derived from erosion of Mesozoic and Tertiary fold belts
- Sediment filled depressions within Mesozoic and Tertiary fold belts

Extrusive and intrusive igneous rocks

- Post-Palaeozoic lava fields
- Post-Palaeozoic granitoid intrusions
- Principal volcanic islands

Continental shelf/ocean shallows

- Represented approximately by those areas lying between 0 and 200 m. below sea level

Pleistocene glaciation

- Approximate limit of maximum extent of Pleistocene glaciation

Minerals (major areas)

Worked mineral deposits

- ○ gold, silver, lead, zinc, copper[1]
- □ iron
- ◇ bauxite
- ◁ tin
- ▽ uranium
- △ manganese
- ⊠ nickel
- ⊡ chrome
- ◆ diamond
- ▶ asbestos
- ◖ mica
- ⬙ potash
- ⬗ phosphates
- ◤ sulphur
- ▲ pyrites
- titanium

Fossil fuels

- FIELD / BASIN Coal and lignite
- Crude oil fields (incl oil shales)
- Natural gas fields

[1] These ores are grouped together as two or more occur frequently in association

---

There is great variation in the nature and origin of mineral deposits, and the major types are outlined as follows:

Magmatic deposits result from the crystallization of minerals directly from magma (molten rock). Deposits of economic significance are found where concentration of a particular mineral occur in the rocks formed from the magma. These deposits are mainly associated with basic igneous rocks and include platinum, magnetite, chromite, copper and nickel.

Pegmatitic deposits are formed from residual magmatic fluids which remain after the major part of a magma body has crystallized. These residual fluids commonly penetrate fissures either in the main body of the igneous mass, or in the surrounding country rock. These fluids are rich in water which leads to the growth of large crystals. Pegmatitic deposits are usually profitable to work and include mica, beryl, tungsten, tin and molybdenum.

Metamorphic deposits include new minerals formed when pre-existing minerals have been exposed to intense heat and pressure in the processes known as metamorphism. Some existing mineral deposits may have been enriched. Asbestos and many important iron deposits are metamorphic in origin.

Metasomatic deposits result from the complete or partial replacement of pre-existing minerals by new mineral matter through the action of circulating waters, which either originate in cooling igneous bodies or come from higher levels in the earth's crust. Certain deposits of iron, lead and zinc are examples.

Sedimentary deposits result from the accumulation of material by processes of sedimentation. They include coal (which is derived from an accumulation of plant material), salt deposits and some iron deposits.

Placer deposits are concentrations of mineral particles which have been removed by weathering from the parent rock, transported and eventually deposited by streams. The point of deposition of the mineral particles is determined largely by their specific gravity and therefore particles of one type of mineral are deposited in the same area. Placer deposits are important sources of tin, gold and diamonds. Ancient placer deposits form the source of much of South Africa's gold.

Weathering deposits are derived from the alteration of minerals by weathering processes. Bauxite, for example, is formed when weathering causes the removal of silica from feldspars (important constituent minerals of igneous rocks).

Crude oil and natural gas deposits occur either in 'traps' produced by the folding of porous and non-porous sedimentary rocks as a result of earth movements, or in association with salt domes (as in the U.S. Gulf coast). The exact origin of oil is not known, but it has been ascertained that it contains compounds that must have come from living matter once inhabiting a shallow, calm, tropical sea.

Earthquakes / volcanoes

Principal earthquake zones (1961-9)

- Areas with a high frequency of earthquakes
- Areas with a lower frequency of earthquakes

Volcanoes

- ▲ Active volcanoes

Volcanoes which have shown no major activity during this century have been omitted.

Most earthquake zones coincide with active volcanic districts, but this is not always so. All volcanoes occur in tectonic fault zones in which tensional forces have caused fissuring of the crust.

SCALE 1:392 MILLION

The map gives a general indication of the distribution of worked mineral deposits and their relationship with the structure of the earth's crust. Only the major areas of worked deposits of a selection of minerals are indicated. A more complete representation of mineral production is given by the mineral maps.

It is important to note that lack of mineral workings does not necessarily indicate lack of deposits. Some areas remain unworked either because of insufficient knowledge of the geology or inaccessibility of deposits, or because the deposits are uneconomical to work given present day levels of technology.

Cereals/Potatoes

Barley p.10
Maize-Corn p.10
Rice p.11
Wheat p.12
Nutrition p.20
Potatoes p.11

For individual country data see Statistical Supplement

Cereals include those members of the grain family which have starchy edible seeds; the most common being rice, wheat, barley, oats, maize, sorghums and some millets. Potatoes, though not a cereal, are mapped in this section because they are a starch-producing crop and possess similar dietary properties. Cereals have been grown throughout historical times, and every major civilization has been founded on them as the principal source of food. It was largely owing to their cultivation that settled communities were formed. Cereals and potatoes are still the world's basic foods.

The pre-eminence of cereals as a foodstuff is partly explained by the ease with which they can be produced, stored and transported. They yield more food, both in bulk and in nutritive value, per unit of land and labour than most other crops. This is why they are so vital to large communities crowded on small areas. Also, cereals provide the basis for man's diet, either in direct human consumption, or as a food for animals producing meat, milk, eggs and fats. As living standards rise, consumption of cereals per head at first rises with them; but, after a point, more expensive and attractive food is sought, and direct consumption begins to decline.

Wheat ranks as the leading bread grain. Rye predominates for bread-making only in East Europe and the U.S.S.R. Elsewhere rye is mainly an animal feed, and as such the least important of feed grains. Whereas wheat is the bread grain of the temperate zones, rice is the principal grain of, and, indeed, the principal food, of the warmer humid areas, especially in Asia. That continent grows and consumes about nine-tenths of the world's rice.

As a source of human food potatoes rival wheat and rice. In terms of potential dry matter potatoes yield more per hectare than wheat. Potatoes are grown in vast quantities in Europe, the U.S.A. and the U.S.S.R., and they are a main item of the diet of hundreds of millions. Oats and barley are grown usually to provide food for livestock; but, by volume of output, the most important animal feed grain is maize, of which the United States produces almost half the total.

Other cereals are grown primarily as subsistence crops. These include millets and sorghums which are major food crops in India and Africa, and are grown for animal consumption in the U.S.A. or as forage crops in Europe and elsewhere. Cassava (manioc) is a starch-producing crop occurring in most tropical countries especially in South America; allied crops are sweet potatoes and yams.

Data for oats, rye, millets and sorghums, sweet potatoes and yams are given in the statistical index but are not mapped.

Although cereals are chiefly consumed in the form of grain or processed products there are other important applications, particularly the brewing of beer from barley or in Africa from sorghum. All cereals are used in varying degrees for the distillation of potable spirits and industrial alcohols.

World production of grains has greatly expanded in the past 100 years to keep pace with the growth of population and with rising living standards. Although the extension of grain areas, notably in North America, partly accounts for the expansion of output, increases in yield have had a far greater effect. These have resulted from the breeding of more productive strains, the use of nitrogenous and other fertilizers, the control of diseases and pests, the spraying of crops with weed killers and continual improvement in cultivation and harvesting. Naturally, it is in highly-developed countries and where scarcity of farm land in relation to population encourages intensive farming methods that the biggest returns are obtained. Yield, therefore, varies considerably; during 1963-5 wheat yields ranged from 0.56 metric tons per hectare in Africa to 4.42 metric tons per hectare in the Netherlands. The tables below indicate the relative importance of cereals and other starchy foods in the national average diet of selected countries.

Wheat (S.I.T.C. no. 041)

Production: 260 093 700 met. tons 1963-5 av. / 157 900 000 1953-5 av.
Percentage exported: 19% 1963-5 av. / 16% 1953-5 av.
Imports: 47 145 100 met. tons 1963-5 av. / 24 848 000 1953-5 av.
Exports: 48 156 200 met. tons 1963-5 av. / 25 743 700 1953-5 av.

Imports	1963-5 av.	1953-5 av.	Exports	1963-5 av.	1953-5 av.
U.S.S.R.	12	—	U.S.A.	39	28
India	11	11	Canada	25	30
China P.R.	11	—	Australia	12	10
U.K.	9	19	France	12	8
Japan	7	8	U.S.S.R.	5	3
Brazil	5	5	Mexico	1	—
Poland	4	2	Sweden	1	1
Germany F.R.	4	10	Others	14	26
Others	37	51			
	100	100		100	100

Barley (S.I.T.C. no. 043)

Production: 104 450 000 met. tons 1963-5 av. / 63 933 000 1953-5 av.
Percentage exported: 7% 1963-5 av. / 9% 1953-5 av.
Imports: 7 039 700 met. tons 1963-5 av. / 5 445 400 1953-5 av.
Exports: 7 154 900 met. tons 1963-5 av. / 5 542 300 1953-5 av.

Imports	1963-5 av.	1953-5 av.	Exports	1963-5 av.	1953-5 av.
Germany F.R.	28	16	France	28	1
Italy	19	15	U.S.A.	19	15
U.S.S.R.	16	2	U.S.S.R.	16	2
Spain	8	—	Canada	10	33
Japan	6	13	Australia	5	9
Poland	6	—	Argentina	4	4
Czechoslovakia	5	9	Syria	4	5
Denmark	4	4	Others	14	26
Others	43	65			
	100	100		100	100

Rice (S.I.T.C. no. 042)

Production: 256 652 000 met. tons 1963-5 av. / 185 900 000 1953-5 av.
Percentage exported: 3% 1963-5 av. / 3% 1953-5 av.
Imports: 7 270 300 met. tons 1963-5 av. / 4 555 000 1953-5 av.
Exports: 7 412 000 met. tons 1963-5 av. / 4 717 000 1953-5 av.

Imports	1963-5 av.	1953-5 av.	Exports	1963-5 av.	1953-5 av.
Indonesia	10	5	Thailand	24	25
Malaysia	10	11	Burma	20	29
India	9	8	China P.R.	18	13
Ceylon	7	9	U.A.R.	10	6
Hong Kong	6	6	Cambodia	6	4
Philippines	5	1	Taiwan	6	2
U.S.S.R.	3	7	Pakistan	5	1
Cuba	3	4	S. Vietnam	3	NA
Germany F.R.	2	2	Italy	1	4
Others	38	26	Others	9	12
	100	100		100	100

Potatoes (S.I.T.C. no. 054.1)

Production: 288 080 000 met. tons 1963-5 av. / 163 233 300 1953-5 av.
Percentage exported: 1% 1963-5 av. / 1% 1953-5 av.
Imports: 3 318 100 met. tons 1963-5 av. / 1 975 000 1953-5 av.
Exports: 3 359 300 met. tons 1963-5 av. / 2 084 300 1953-5 av.

Imports	1963-5 av.	1953-5 av.	Exports	1963-5 av.	1953-5 av.
Germany F.R.	16	8	Poland	19	5
Czechoslovakia	11	—	Netherlands	19	24
U.K.	10	12	France	12	11
Italy	9	12	Italy	7	8
Spain	6	3	Belg./Lux.	6	9
France	6	3	Canada	6	6
Germany D.R.	4	6	Spain	6	1
Hungary	4	—	Morocco	3	7
U.S.A.	3	3	U.K.	3	4
Others	27	49	Others	19	30
	100	100		100	100

Rye (S.I.T.C. no. 045.1)

Production: 32 832 000 met. tons 1963-5 av. / 19 800 000 1953-5 av.
Percentage exported: 3% 1963-5 av. / 6% 1953-5 av.
Imports: 904 100 met. tons 1963-5 av. / 1 546 700 1953-5 av.
Exports: 888 300 met. tons 1963-5 av. / 1 546 000 1953-5 av.

Imports	1963-5 av.	1953-5 av.	Exports	1963-5 av.	1953-5 av.
Netherlands	20	20	U.S.S.R.	38	28
Poland	15	26	U.S.A.	22	4
Germany D.R.	14	10	Canada	14	19
Germany F.R.	10	8	Argentina	4	32
Sweden	9	2	Turkey	4	3
Czechoslovakia	5	4	Denmark	5	1
Norway	5	4	France	3	1
Finland	5	6	Netherlands	2	2
Belg./Lux.	5	13	Romania	2	1
U.S.A.	3	—	Czechoslovakia	1	1
Others	9	21	Others	3	12
	100	100		100	100

Oats (S.I.T.C. no. 045.2)

Production: 46 296 000 met. tons 1963-5 av. / 50 800 000 1953-5 av.
Percentage exported: 3% 1963-5 av. / 2% 1953-5 av.
Imports: 1 370 800 met. tons 1963-5 av. / 1 459 000 1953-5 av.
Exports: 1 433 800 met. tons 1963-5 av. / 1 436 700 1953-5 av.

Imports	1963-5 av.	1953-5 av.	Exports	1963-5 av.	1953-5 av.
Germany F.R.	30	6	Australia	23	8
Italy	12	3	Canada	22	48
Netherlands	11	14	U.S.A.	21	23
Switzerland	10	8	Argentina	13	9
Denmark	6	4	Sweden	6	7
China P.R.	5	7	Netherlands	6	2
Belg./Lux.	4	44	France	3	1
U.S.A.	2	2	Germany F.R.	2	1
U.K.	2	6	U.S.S.R.	2	1
Finland	1	2	Denmark	1	4
Others	13	9	Others	1	12
	100	100		100	100

Maize-Corn (S.I.T.C. no. 044)

Production: 221 111 000 met. tons 1963-5 av. / 152 700 000 1953-5 av.
Percentage exported: 10% 1963-5 av. / 3% 1953-5 av.
Imports: 21 908 100 met. tons 1963-5 av. / 5 285 200 1953-5 av.
Exports: 22 806 200 met. tons 1963-5 av. / 5 309 300 1953-5 av.

Imports	1963-5 av.	1953-5 av.	Exports	1963-5 av.	1953-5 av.
Italy	19	3	U.S.A.	56	50
U.K.	16	27	Argentina	13	22
Japan	14	5	South Africa	6	8
Germany F.R.	9	10	Thailand	6	1
Netherlands	9	10	France	4	2
Belg./Lux.	3	8	U.S.S.R.	3	1
France	3	6	Brazil	2	1
Canada	2	2	Others	9	14
Others	25	29			
	100	100		100	100

Millets/Sorghums

Production: 77 237 000 met. tons 1963-5 av. / 62 533 000 1953-5 av.
Percentage exported: 5% 1963-5 av. / 2% 1953-5 av.
Imports: 4 066 900 met. tons 1963-5 av. / 1 000 300 1953-5 av.
Exports: 3 998 600 met. tons 1963-5 av. / 1 126 700 1953-5 av.

Imports	1963-5 av.	1953-5 av.	Exports	1963-5 av.	1953-5 av.
Japan	72	68	U.S.A.	72	68
Belg./Lux.	15	11	Argentina	15	11
U.K.	3	4	South Africa	3	4
Germany F.R.	3	4	Sudan	3	4
Israel	1	3	Morocco	1	3
Poland	1	—	Netherlands	1	—
Others	5	13	Australia	1	—
			Others	5	13
	100	100		100	100

Consumption of principal food commodities[1] (1960 - 3 av.)

(Kg. per capita)

Selected countries	CEREALS	STARCHY ROOTS	SUGAR	NUTS/ PULSES	VEGE-TABLES	FRUIT	MEAT	EGGS	FISH	MILK FAT	MILK PROTEIN	FAT
Turkey	223	39	17	13	105	89	14	2	3	4	4	8
Romania	196	66	13	9	62	44	35	5	2	5	5	5
Afghanistan	174	—	3	—	23	27	13	1	NA	4	4	1
Japan	149	69	16	16[3]	90	26	8	8	27	1	1	5
Ethiopia	149	19	2	19	13	2	27	—	—	3	3	5
Uganda	68[2]	NA										
Poland	146	221	31	2	92	16	54	8	4	7	7	10
Guatemala	141	8[2]	26	9	39	28	12	2	—	1	2[4]	3
India	140	11	18	23	3	18	2	—	1	3	3	4[4]
Israel	116	38	32	10	112	142	40	20	7	4	5	18
Brazil	109	149	40	30	8	112	28	3	3	2	2	8
Finland	107	111	40	2	15	44	34	11	11	12	12	20
France	98	99	29	6	142	64	78	11	7	6	7	22
Switzerland	96	69	43	5	75	162	60	10	4	9	7	20
Argentina	91	88	35	4	48	80	100	8	2	4	3	16
Australia	84	47	50	6	64	104	109	12	5	7	7	15
U.K.	81	98	49	5	58	55	74	15	10	8	8	23
U.S.A.	66	206	50	5	99	101	96	19	5	8	9	21
Colombia	65	476[5]	13	27	12	45	36	3	1	2	2	4
Uganda	61	13	27	17	23	7	10	1	4	1	1	2
Dominican R.	57	124[6]	21	23	23	220	19	4	3	3	3	4

Percent of total calorie intake derived from cereals/starches

Selected countries	1961-4 av.	1951-4 av.
Malagasy R.	86[7]	NA
Afghanistan	82	NA
Bolivia	72[8]	NA
Ethiopia	71	NA
Turkey	71	NA
Uganda	70[8]	NA
Guatemala	68[8]	NA
Japan	68	78
India	68	69
Romania	68	NA
Yugoslavia	64	NA
Israel	64	73
South Africa	58	59
Poland	55	NA
Brazil	51	51
Colombia	50	NA
Israel	42	55
Finland	40	NA
France	40	44
Argentina	39	40
Switzerland	37	48
Australia	33	38
U.K.	30	36
Denmark	29	35
U.S.A.	24	26

[1] At the retail level [2] Incl. plantains [3] Incl. soya bean preparations in terms of soya bean [4] Incl. butter [5] Incl. plantains [6] Incl. plantains [7] Excl. butter [8] Incl. milk for making butter Data for 1959

Both cereals and starchy roots contain large amounts of carbohydrates but are relatively poor in proteins and other essential nutrients. Thus the proportion of calories derived from them gives an approximate idea of the nutritional value of the diet as a whole. The lower the proportion of these foods in the diet, the higher generally would be the proportion of the more nutritious foods. However, the nutritive value of the diet is influenced not only by this proportion but also by the precise nature of the foods comprising the group of cereals and starchy roots as well as the nutrients provided by the rest of the foods in the diet. Nevertheless, this indicator has the merit of simplicity, and since in almost all countries cereals and starchy roots are staples of diet, it is fairly widely applicable.

Cereals contribute more than any other food group to the energy value and protein content of diets. Starchy roots generally provide the cheapest source of energy. Sugar consists entirely of carbohydrates and is thus a source only of energy. Pulses and nuts are nutritionally important, being a source of energy, protein, some minerals and B-complex vitamins. Fruit and vegetables provide many essential minerals and vitamins. Products of animal origin provide high-quality protein and are a rich source of essential nutrients. Cereals and starchy roots are commonly known as 'staple foods'; pulses, fruit, vegetables and foods of animal origin are known as 'protective foods' because of their high nutritional quality.

Barley/Maize-Corn

(1963–5 av.)[1]

One dot represents 100 000 met. tons

• barley • maize

Major trade flows (1966)

Commodity   S.I.T.C. no.

BARLEY (UNMILLED) 043
MAIZE-CORN (UNMILLED) 044

Value ($ U.S.)

0.b mm represents increments of $50 million

—— UNDER $25 MILLION   VALUE IN $ MILLIONS
($ MILLIONS)
480
250
50

Data for China P. R. 1952-6 av.

Modified Gall Projection   Equatorial Scale 1 : 88 Million approx.

Barley production

104 450 700 met. tons 1963-5 av.[1]
63 933 000 1953-5 av.[1]

	1963-5 av.	1953-5 av.
	PERCENTAGE	
U.S.S.R.	22	18
U.S.A.	8	12
U.K.	7	4
France	7	4
Canada	4	8
Denmark	4	3
Germany F.R.	3	3
Turkey	3	5
India	2	5
Others	40	56
	100	100

¹ Excl. China P. R.

Barley yield

Selected countries

(metric tons per hectare)

	1963-5 av.
Netherlands	3.88
Denmark	3.90
U.K.	3.65
Germany F.R.	3.11
France	2.94
Czechoslovakia	2.20
U.S.A.	2.07
Canada	1.83
Turkey	1.28
U.S.S.R.	1.11
India	0.82
World average	1.49

Maize-corn production

221 111 000 met. tons 1963-5 av.[1]
152 700 000 1953-5 av.[1]

	1963-5 av.	1953-5 av.
	PERCENTAGE	
U.S.A.	44	53
U.S.S.R.	5	...³
Brazil	5	5
Mexico	4	3
Romania	3	4
Yugoslavia	3	2
South Africa	2	2
Argentina	2	2
India	2	1
Others	30	28
	100	100

¹ Excl. China P.R.

Maize-corn yield

Selected countries

(metric tons per hectare)

	1963-5 av.
Canada	4.71
Yugoslavia	4.28
U.S.A.	2.47
U.S.S.R.	2.25
Romania	1.86
Argentina	1.71
Brazil	1.28
South Africa	1.15
Mexico	1.09
India	1.00
Philippines	0.69
World average	2.20

INTRA-EUROPEAN TRADE
PROVENANCE — DESTINATION
France   D (81)
France   D (63) B-L (27) CH (22) NL (1?)
Netherlands   D (19)
U.K.   D (3)

Barley has the shortest growing season of all cereals and when spring-sown can be grown further north, at higher altitudes, and in more arid regions than any other cereal. The requirements for malting barley differ from those for barley for direct consumption. Where autumn-sown crops are exposed to mild winters, or where the soil in the spring still retains much of the moisture due to winter precipitation, barley for food purposes can withstand hot arid—but not humid—conditions in the heading and post-heading stage; malting barley demands cooler conditions in the ripening phase. Barley is a crop of both the woodland and grassland climax, and is specific in its soil requirements; it demands good drainage and relatively fertile soils without acid conditions.

In most countries barley is used more for animal feeding than for direct human consumption. But some higher-grade barley is used in the malting industry for beer and to a small extent for the production of whisky and of industrial alcohol.

Most crops are grown with 25–40 in. (650–1 000 mm.) annual rainfall but there must be adequate water available during mid-seasonal growth. Maize grows on a wide range of soils provided there is a high availability of mineral nutrients, especially nitrogen, in the later phases of vegetative growth.

Selective cross-breeding has resulted in hybrids that are more uniform and productive. Yields have been raised 20–50%, and in 1960, 96% of the maize-sown area in the U.S.A. was planted with hybrid strains. There is a diversity of types of maize suitable for cultivation in most tropical to warm temperate areas of the world. Maize is an important subsistence crop in Asia and Africa, but most of the maize entering international trade is as a livestock feed. Large quantities are converted into compound feeding stuffs or used as a source of glucose, starch, oil, dextrins, alcohol and breakfast foods.

Maize is susceptible to frost, thus the length of frost-free periods limits distribution. Optimum grain yields result when the growing period is at least 140 days and the mean summer tempera-tures are approximately 75°F (24°C) by day, 57°F (14°C) by night.

Varieties differ in their temperature requirement; early-maturing types will succeed when the summer temperature is approxi-mately 66°F (19°C), or less if the growing season is cool but long.

© Oxford University Press

Rice/Potatoes

Modified Gall Projection Equatorial Scale 1: 88 Million approx.

One dot represents 100 000 met. tons

- rice
- potatoes

© Oxford University Press

Date Line

Ssu-ch'uan Pen-ti (Red Basin of Szechwan)

Ganges Valley

Irrawaddy Delta

Mekong Delta

Djawa (Java)

Tropic of Cancer

Equator

Tropic of Capricorn

Arctic Circle

USA TO VNS (03)

PAK TO SU (20)

INTRA-EUROPEAN TRADE

PROVENANCE	DESTINATION		
	B/L (7)		
France	D (15)	B/L (10)	
Netherlands			

Rice/Potatoes (1963-5 av.)

Rice production

256 652 000 met. tons 100 000 met.
185 900 000 1953-5 av. tons

Major trade flows (1966)

Commodity : S.I.T.C. no.

	1963-5 av.	1953-5 av.
	PERCENTAGE	
China P.R.	33	35
India	21	22
Pakistan	7	7
Japan	6	7
Thailand	5	4
Indonesia	4	4
Burma	3	3
Brazil	3	2
S. Vietnam	2	N/A*
Others	16	N/A
	100	100

*Excl. U.S.S.R. *Vietnam data not divided

RICE (FRESH)

POTATOES [FRESH POTATOES] SWEET POTATOES

Value ($ U.S.)
0.5 mm represents increments of $20 million

VALUE IN $ MILLIONS

UNDER $20 MILLIONS

Rice yield

Selected countries
(metric tons per hectare)

	1963-5 av.
Spain	6.17
Japan	5.02
Taiwan	3.64
S. Vietnam	2.04
Indonesia	1.79
Pakistan	1.69
Burma	1.66
Brazil	1.57
India	1.49
China P.R.	1.15*
World average	2.06

*Data for 1956-8

Potato production

288 080 000 met. tons
162 233 000 1953-5 av.*

	1963-5 av.	1953-5 av.
	PERCENTAGE	
U.S.S.R.	29	...
Poland	16	19
Germany F.R.	7	15
France	4	10
Germany D.R.	4	9
U.K.	4	6
Spain	2	5
Czechoslovakia	2	5
Others	30	29
	100	100

*Excl. U.S.S.R.

Potato yield

Selected countries
(metric tons per hectare)

	1963-5 av.
Netherlands	29.33
Germany F.R.	25.07
U.K.	23.07
U.S.A.	22.17
France	18.37
Germany D.R.	17.43
Poland	16.03
Australia	14.33
Czechoslovakia	12.37
Spain	11.73
U.S.S.R.	9.90
World average	12.20

11

(19°C). Unlike other cereals, rice can tolerate very high temperatures combined with high humidities. Rich alluvial soils with an impervious subsoil are best, but other soils are suitable as long as they can hold the irrigation or flood water.

Until recently the highest yields of rice have been obtained in the warm temperate zones with a Mediterranean type of climate. However, yields in the tropics should be substantially increased following the introduction of new varieties bred at the International Rice Research Institute in the Philippines.

The high productivity of rice coupled with its ability to maintain good yields under a system of continuous cultivation have contributed to its historical position as the staple food of millions of people in Asia. Unfortunately milled rice (the form in which it is usually eaten) is a deficient diet.

Only about 5% of the world's rice enters into trade. The bulk of this trade is carried on within the Asiatic continent.

Rice growing does extend beyond areas shown on the map, but reliable statistics for such areas are not available.

also a source of industrial alcohol and potable spirits, especially in East Europe and the U.S.S.R.

Rice is normally grown in standing water for most of the growth cycle, while other requirements are high temperature and, for maximum yields, high light intensities. Varieties of 'upland' rice can be cultivated without irrigation or flooding as long as the rainfall is heavy and very frequent, such as 60 in. (1 500 mm.) minimum during the season in the Philippines. In the warm temperate zones the limits of production are associated with the length of the frost-free period combined with minimal temperatures during germination, vegetative growth and ripening; varieties differ in these requirements but the minimal limits for the phases are 64°–68°F (18°–20°C), 72°–75°F (22°–24°C) and 66°F

Potatoes require a long cool growing season with adequate moisture throughout. Growth starts at about 45°F (7°C); if mean maximum temperatures exceed 64°F (18°C) yields are lower. High temperatures combined with high humidity lead to attacks of 'blight'. Where the springs are mild but the summers hot, the less productive early-maturing types are cultivated. These can also be grown in the extreme north of Europe, where the season is short but the days long. Potatoes, like rye, can be grown in exposed acid sands; the best soils are loams or silts, with a good content of organic matter. A high level of mineral nutrients is needed and heavy applications of fertilizers normally give economic returns.

Under good conditions the potato can produce more food per hectare than any of the cereals. This was an important factor in the rapid increase in population in NW. Europe in the nineteenth century. Today in East and Central Europe the potato is the staple food for millions of people. In some parts of Europe as much as 40% of the crop may be fed to livestock. Potatoes are

Wheat

Modified Gall Projection   Equatorial Scale 1 : 88 Million approx.   © Oxford University Press

Map labels: Arctic Circle · Tropic of Cancer · Equator · Tropic of Capricorn · Ukraine · Punjab · Pampa

Wheat (1963-5 av.)

One dot represents 100 000 met. tons

Wheat production

260 093 670 met. tons 1963-5 av.
157 900 000 1953-5 av.¹

Major trade flows (1966)

Commodity: S.I.T.C.no.

WHEAT [PNCJ, SPLI]AMES[UN] : 041

Values ($ U.S.)
0.5mm represents increments of $60 million

	($ MILLIONS)
780	
540	
300	
60	

VALUE IN $ MILLIONS

Wheat production

	1963-5 av.	1953-5 av.¹
	PERCENTAGE	
	1963-5 av.	1953-5 av.¹
U.S.S.R.	24	...
U.S.A.	13	18
China P.R.	9	14
France	7	8
Canada	5	6
India	5	6
Turkey	4	5
Italy	4	5
China P.R.	3	5
Australia	3	4
Argentina	3	4
Others	26	33
	100	100

¹Data for 1952
²Excl. U.S.S.R.

Wheat production by region

(million metric tons)

	1934-8 av.	1948-52 av.	1955	1965
World¹	129	140	158	205
Europe²	43	41	49	67
N. America	27	44	44	39
Latin America	7	8	10	15
Middle East	9	8	10	10
China P.R.	23	18	23	26
Africa	2	3	4	4
Oceania	3	4	5	7
U.S.S.R.	38	NA	NA	61

¹Excl. U.S.S.R.
²Incl. U.S.S.R.

Wheat yield

Selected countries

(metric tons per hectare)

	1963-5 av.
Netherlands	4.42
U.K.	4.04
France	3.03
U.A.R.	2.72
Czechoslovakia	2.37
U.S.A.	1.74
Argentina	1.57
Australia	1.24
Turkey	1.13
U.S.S.R.	0.91
China P.R.	0.87
World average	1.21

Wheat is a basic food for human consumption within the temperate zones. It ranks with rice as the most important of all crops. Three-quarters of the crop is autumn-sown. Spring sowing is practised where winters are too cold for autumn-sown crops. Rainfall requirements are normally from 10-25 in. (250-640 mm), but at the lower end of this scale fallowing in alternate years may be necessary. Wheat requires warm moist conditions for its early growth and a minimum temperature of 60°F (15.5°C) for ripening the grain. The normal growth period for spring wheat is about 90 days but with new varieties or in high latitudes may be shorter. Wheat is hardy but will not tolerate extreme cold. The northern limit corresponds with the May isotherm of 50°F (10°C). High temperature and humidity in the growing period also inhibit wheat growing — the limit in the U.S.A. is a mean temperature of 68°F (20°C) and annual rainfall above 50 in. (1 250 mm). A recent development has been the breeding in Mexico and elsewhere of short high-yielding varieties suitable for the tropics. Wheat is associated with a grassland, and more rarely a woodland,climate, and is most productive on black earths and medium-textured soils with reasonable drainage.

Hard wheats are the best bread-making varieties, and are grown where the climate ensures rapid maturity, i.e. in countries such as the U.S.A., Canada, Argentina and Australia. Britain and some other countries grow the softer wheat with more moisture for biscuits and cakes, and import hard wheat, which may be mixed with home-grown soft wheat, for bread-making. Wheat is also used for alcohol production.

Wheat is one of the most widely grown cereals and has become a major world export commodity. About 21% of production enters world trade. Some European and Asiatic countries are partly dependent on imports, while one of the bigger wheat consumers, the U.K., relies on supplies from overseas for almost two-thirds of its requirements. In contrast the U.S.A., Canada, Argentina and Australia rely on exporting about half of their production and wheat exports are an important source of foreign currency.

The U.S.S.R. is a traditional exporter of wheat, in 1961 accounting for 12% of total world exports. By 1965, this had fallen to 3%, and the U.S.S.R. had become the world's largest importer accounting for 13% of total world imports of wheat. In the mid-fifties this position was held by the U.K., but now both India and China P.R. besides the U.S.S.R. import more than the U.K. which is 4th on the world scale, Japan following closely in 5th place. High U.S.A. wheat production. About 21% of production enters world trade.

The U.S.A. accounts for 12% of the world's wheat exports which came from North America, the bulk of this exported through Montreal, New York and Vancouver. Ice blocks the St.Lawrence River and prevents shipments from Montreal during the first three months of the year, but due to the St. Lawrence Seaway more wheat can be shipped while the river is ice-free. Exports from the southern hemisphere, mainly Argentina and Australia, while smaller, are still important, particularly as the crop is harvested at a different time; importers thus receive a more regular supply than would otherwise be possible, and need store less wheat for a shorter time.

Because of the great importance of wheat in world trade there have been, since 1949, a series of International Wheat Agreements to counteract the vagaries of a wholly free market. The fifth International Wheat Agreement came into force in July 1962. The international price limits of meeting concern to the agreement, fixed in advance by buyers and sellers and impose on both the obligation to maintain a minimum volume of trade at these prices; if exporters' prices rise above the 'ceiling', importers are released from their percentage of quotas. Particular agreements also exist in the domestic markets.

strains, which are earlier maturing or resistant to insect and disease attacks, are continually being developed. selective weed killers, fertilizers to improve yields and prevent soil exhaustion, soil conservation to avoid recurrences of the 'dust-bowl' of the American Midwest, and ever-growing efficiency in sowing and harvesting have all combined to result in higher yields per unit area sown. Further increases in world production are likely to result more from improvement in yield than in extension of sown area.

Improved transport played an important part in this development: the introduction of grain elevators and devices for mechanical handling, extension of the railway network, and the building of ocean-going ships able to make rapid crossings of the Atlantic. This revolution in transport brought the new wheat lands in distant continents within reach of importing countries and so stimulated further production and trade. But the great increase in output since then has been due to modern science and farming technology. New and more resistant

International trade in beverages, tobacco, sugar and chocolate (1963-5 av.)

Tobacco (S.I.T.C. no. 121)

Production 4 383 000 met. tons 1963-5 av.; 3 297 000 1953-5 av.[1]

	1963-5 av.	1953-5 av.
U.S.A.	24	36
Rhodesia[2]	12	NA
Bulgaria	9	3*
India	7	5
Greece	7	8
Turkey	6	10
Brazil	6	4
Philippines	3	1
Others	26	NA
	100	100

Exports[3] 944 700 met. tons 1963-5 av.; 641 000 1953-5 av.

Percentage exported 22% 1963-5 av.; 19% 1953-5 av.

Imports[1] 934 000 met. tons 1963-5 av.; 608 000 1953-5 av.

	1963-5 av.	1953-5 av.
U.K.	15	24
Germany F.R.	14	10
U.S.S.R.	12	8*
U.S.A.	8	8
France	6	6
Netherlands	5	6
Spain	4	4
Belg./Lux.	3	1
Germany D.R.	3	NA
Others	31	34
	100	100

Coffee (S.I.T.C. no. 071.1)

Production 4 090 300 met. tons 1963-5 av.; 2 607 000 1953-5 av.[1]

	1963-5 av.	1953-5 av.
Brazil	33	41
Colombia	13	19
Ivory Coast	7	NA
Uganda	5	3
Angola	5	3
El Salvador	4	3
Guatemala	3	2
Mexico	3	2
Indonesia	3	2
Others	24	NA
	100	100

Exports[3] 2 892 100 met. tons 1963-5 av.; 1 973 000 1953-5 av.

Percentage exported 71% 1963-5 av.; 76% 1953-5 av.

Imports[1] 2 933 000 met. tons 1963-5 av.; 1 970 000 1953-5 av.

	1963-5 av.	1953-5 av.
U.S.A.	46	59
Germany F.R.	9	5
France	8	9
Italy	4	4
Sweden	3	3
Netherlands	3	3
Canada	3	2
U.K.	2	2
Belg./Lux.	2	2
Others	20	14
	100	100

Cocoa (cacao) (S.I.T.C. no. 072.1)

Production 1 303 800 met. tons 1963-5 av.; 795 000 1953-5 av.

Percentage exported 87% 1963-5 av.; 92% 1953-5 av.

	1963-5 av.	1953-5 av.
Ghana	38	30
Nigeria	20	13
Ivory Coast	10	NA
Brazil	7	16
Cameroon	6	8
Ecuador	3	3
Equatorial Guinea	3	2
Dominican R.	3	2
New Guinea	—	—
Others	10	NA
	100	100

Exports[3] 1 134 900 met. tons 1963-5 av.; 737 700 1953-5 av.

Imports[1] 1 104 700 met. tons 1963-5 av.; 730 000 1953-5 av.

	1963-5 av.	1953-5 av.
U.S.A.	28	34
Germany F.R.	13	10
Netherlands	10	8
U.S.S.R.	6	2
France	6	3
Italy	4	3
Japan	3	1
Spain	3	—
Others	20	14
	100	100

Chocolate and chocolate products (S.I.T.C. no. 073.0)

Imports 148 100 met. tons 1963-5 av.; 80 000 1952-6 av.

Exports 161 300 met. tons 1963-5 av.; 90 900 1952-6 av.

Exports:

	1963-5 av.	1952-6 av.
Netherlands	27	50
U.K.	19	20
Germany F.R.	16	7
Belgium	10	7
Switzerland[7]	7	4
France	5	4
U.S.A.	3	2
Italy	2	3
Canada	2	—
Sweden	1	—
Denmark	1	—
Others	3	3
	100	100

Imports:

	1963-5 av.	1952-6 av.
U.K.[8]	27	68
Germany F.R.	23	8
U.S.A.	10	3
France	7	6
Belgium	6	7
Netherlands	4	5
Canada	4	—
Denmark	2	2
Sweden	2	1
Austria	2	—
Hong Kong	8	—
Others	—	—
	100	100

Tea (S.I.T.C. no. 074.1)

Production 1 112 200 met. tons 1963-5 av.; 645 000 1953-5 av.

Exports[3] 613 900 met. tons 1963-5 av.; 490 000 1953-5 av.

	1963-5 av.	1953-5 av.
Ceylon	35	33
India	34	41
China P.R.[4]	10	10
Indonesia	5	5
Kenya	4	1
U.K.[5]	4	7*
Taiwan	3	2
Malawi	2	1*
Argentina	2	—
Others	8	11
	100	100

Percentage exported 55% 1963-5 av.; 76% 1953-5 av.

Imports[11] 613 600 met. tons 1963-5 av.; 465 000 1953-5 av.

	1963-5 av.	1953-5 av.
U.K.	41	48
U.S.A.	10	10
U.S.S.R.	5	5
Australia	4	5
U.A.R.	4	1
Canada	4	4
Iraq	3	2
South Africa	3	1*
Irish R.	3	2
Others	24	22
	100	100

Sugar (S.I.T.C. no. 061.1, 2)

Production[9] 59 133 900 met. tons 1963-5 av.; 38 289 000 1953-5 av.

Exports[11] 18 134 600 met. tons 1963-5 av.; 13 496 000 1953-5 av.

Percentage exported 31% 1963-5 av.; 35% 1953-5 av.

	1963-5 av.	1953-5 av.
Cuba	24*	35
Australia	6	5
Philippines	5	5
France	5	5
Taiwan	4*	5*
U.S.S.R.	4	3
Dominican R.	3	3
Mauritius	3	4
South Africa	3	1
Others	41	34
	100	100

Imports[11] 17 637 700 met. tons 1963-5 av.; 13 370 700 1953-5 av.

	1963-5 av.	1953-5 av.
U.S.A.	20	28
U.K.	13	19
U.S.S.R.	10	9
Japan	9	8
Canada	4	3*
China P.R.	2*	—
France	2	—
Italy	2	3
Iran	2	2
Others	36	35
	100	100

Cocoa (cacao) consumption — Selected countries (kg. per capita) (1963-5 av.)

	1963-5 av.
Switzerland	3.4
Netherlands	2.5
U.S.A.	2.2
New Zealand	1.8
U.K.	1.8
Australia	1.4
Iceland	1.0
Av. of available countries	0.4

Tea consumption — Selected countries (kg. per capita)

	1963-5 av.
U.K.	4.2
Irish R.	4.0
Libya	2.9
Australia	2.6
Ceylon	1.4
Japan	0.8
Chile	0.7
Israel	0.5
India	0.4
U.S.S.R.	0.3
Norway	0.1
Italy	0.05
Ghana	0.01
Av. of available countries	0.6

Beverages, Tobacco and Sugar

For individual country data see Statistical Supplement

All these crops, except tobacco and sugar beet, are grown mainly for export to economically advanced countries, and even tobacco is important in world trade. In varying degrees the beverages act as stimulants, and all are wanted for taste and flavour rather than nutritive value. Equally they all come more or less within the category of semi-luxuries, the amounts consumed being dependent on the prosperity of the consumer.

Tea has the distinction of being the world's principal and cheapest beverage. Although more expensive by unit weight than coffee, it is more economical in use. Yet, outside China and Japan, where green tea is grown, the tea-drinking habit was comparatively unknown until about 150 years ago. Cultivation of black tea in India and Ceylon, nowadays the chief exporters, is of still more recent origin. India did not begin commercial production before about 1830. Ceylon, where tea dramatically superseded coffee after its destruction by disease, followed forty years later. In both countries the tea industries were initially financed and developed by British enterprise. Britain still is dominant in world tea trade, as well as being the largest consumer of imported tea.

The demand for tea is inelastic—fairly small change in supply causes a big change in price. An international agreement aimed at restricting output in order to stabilize prices lapsed in 1955 when heavy demand in the immediate post-war years. But with increased world production due to develop with higher yielding strains of tree in the Asian countries, has declined from the record 1954 level.

Coffee has been the flavour of stimulating effect, began to gain wider popularity from the seventeenth century onwards, first in the famous coffee houses of Britain and Continental Europe, later in the houses of the well-to-do. Though no longer a luxury, coffee is still more expensive than tea when made up into a beverage. The U.S.A. is the largest single coffee consuming country but per capita consumption is highest in Sweden.

Production is concentrated in Latin America which grows almost 70% of the world crop. African and Far Eastern production is increasing and in 1965 made up 25% and 5% of the world production respectively. Brazil accounted for about 58% of Latin American production in 1965; compared with 68% pre-war; Colombian and Mexican production is substantially higher than pre-war.

Coffee exports are important in that they provide many of the developing countries with an invaluable source of foreign exchange. For example, Colombia, coffee accounts for almost 68% of all exports. Coffee ranks amongst the most important traded commodities in the world. In terms of volume it is relatively small but in value it accounts for 1.2% of all commodity exports and represents 1.2% of total international trade. In recent years the volume of coffee exported has risen considerably.

The demand for coffee is also inelastic, and the history of production is characterized by a series of surpluses and shortages. For example, as a result of over-production in the 1930's about four million tons of coffee had to be destroyed in Brazil. An International Coffee Agreement has played an important role in stabilizing world trade by the restriction of exports and the avoidance of cyclical shortages and surpluses.

It seems probable that in the next few years there will be a relative coffee shortage. Stocks have been declining as consumption has exceeded production in the past few years, and in addition to this, disastrous frosts destroyed many trees in Brazil in July, 1969. Until the new trees planted begin to bear fruit an increase in production will depend on improved farming methods and greater use of fertilizer.

Cocoa (cacao) which is produced mainly in West Africa and South America is usually included with the beverages. As a beverage, however, it has far less stimulating effect than either tea or coffee. Its main use is in the manufacture of chocolate.

The main constituent of chocolate is cocoa-butter, which is extracted from the bean, while the rest of the cocoa is made. Chocolate is one of the most appetizing and most nutritious of foods. Its manufacture is a complex process and one of the world's major industrial enterprises.

There has been considerable expansion in production since the beginning of the century and this has had an important effect on the economies of several countries, especially Ghana. In 1900, 78% of world cocoa production was from the Americas (mainly Brazil and Ecuador) and the West Indies, but by 1959 Ghana alone was producing more than the whole of the Americas.

World consumption of cocoa has exceeded production in the last few years, and demand has doubled in the last 15 years and is continuing to increase. Higher standards of living are partly responsible for the rise in demand, and the need to meet it has necessitated more intensive research and the use of new methods. More intensive production is required rather than simply an increase in acreage, and the use of insecticides, fungicides and higher yielding strains of tree are important in this respect.

Much trade in cocoa is handled by cocoa marketing boards which protect farmers from fluctuations in world market prices and also provide financial support for research and development. An International Cocoa Agreement acceptable to both producers and consumers has not yet been formulated. The aim of such an Agreement would be to stabilize world prices and encourage production and consumption.

Without **sugar**, the palatability and, therefore, the use of tea, coffee and cocoa would be greatly diminished. But not only does sugar add taste to drink and food: it is itself a major foodstuff. All countries with high living standards consume sugar in large quantities, though elsewhere it is frequently beyond the means of millions. The great expansion in sugar consumption was made possible by the development of low-cost production in sugar cane countries, which provide almost all of the sugar entering international trade.

Many of these countries are excessively dependent on sugar growing. Most of the Caribbean Islands and Mauritius can be said to have "one crop economies" although attempts are now being made at a measure of diversification. The low prices of the 1930's affected them very severely; demand was high immediately post-war, but after 1951 supply began to exceed demand and an International Sugar Agreement was set up in 1953 to stabilize the world free market price of raw sugar through the operation of a system of export quotas. New agreements have since emerged and the latest came into operation from the beginning of 1969.

The Commonwealth Sugar Agreement imposes quotas on Commonwealth countries. By far the larger part of world sugar consumption is traded subject to protective measures, subsidies or preferential arrangements extended by governments.

Sugar was first extracted from beet by a German chemist in 1747 but commercial development dates from the Napoleonic wars, when sugar supplies to continental Europe were cut off by the British naval blockade. European governments have since protected beet sugar partly because it takes a valuable place in the rotation of crops; since 1880 beet has been the principal source of sugar consumed in Europe.

As a stimulant **tobacco** exceeds even coffee and tea in importance. At least as early as the first century B.C. the smoking of tobacco was practised by the Mayan Indians of Central America. It was introduced to other parts of the world by early explorers (especially the Spanish), and commercial trading in tobacco on an international basis dates from the mid-sixteenth century when a demand for it was being created in several countries. The spread of smoking (which was at first a luxury enjoyed only by the rich) and the consequent increase in demand for tobacco necessitated an increase in production. Existing plantations were therefore extended and new ones established. Tobacco farming began in Europe in the late sixteenth century.

Tobacco is usually heavily taxed and the vast sums spent on tea, coffee and cocoa combined. Tobacco has been taxed in Britain since 1590 when Queen Elizabeth I introduced a duty on tobacco imported into England. In 1969 tobacco provided 8% (£1 105 millions) of the U.K. government's revenue.

In recent years the relationship between smoking and respiratory disease, notably lung cancer, has been the subject of much research. In some countries cigarette packets are now required to carry a note warning people that cigarette smoking may be hazardous to health.

Consumption of beverages and tobacco (1963-5 av.)

Coffee — Selected countries (kg. per capita)

	1962-4 av.
Sweden	11.5
Switzerland	9.9
U.S.A.	7.0
Brazil	5.5
France	4.6
Colombia	3.7
Algeria	2.6
U.K.	1.4
Australia	1.1
South Africa	0.8
Japan	0.7
Congo D.R.	0.2
Thailand	0.1
Av. of available countries	2.3

Tobacco — Selected countries (kg. per adult 15 yrs. and over)

	1963-5 av.
Canada	4.5
U.S.A.	4.5
Netherlands	4.0
Switzerland	3.8
Australia	3.4
Iceland	3.0
U.K.	2.9
Germany F.R.	2.8
France	2.3
Japan	2.3
South Africa	2.0
Brazil	1.7
Portugal	1.2
India	0.8
Av. of available countries	2.6

Tobacco production

374 000 met. tons 1963-5 av.; 277 000 1953-5 av.

	'000 MET. TONS 1963-5 av.	1953-5 av.
Bulgaria	115	NA
U.S.A.	78	93
France	18	19
Netherlands	16	16
South Africa	14	10
S. Korea	11	10
Germany F.R.	9	4
Norway	5	3

Cigar production

World total not available

	MILLIONS 1963-5 av.	1953-5 av.
U.S.A.	8 062	5 637
Germany F.R.	3 970	4 692
Netherlands	1 883	1 713
Germany D.R.	1 844	NA
Colombia	652	499
U.K.	476	531
Canada	461	119
Cuba	455	245
Belgium	366	105
Spain	350	592

Cigarette production

2 198 000 million 1963-5 av.; 1 401 000 million 1953-5 av.

	PERCENTAGE 1963-5 av.	1953-5 av.
U.S.A.	25	26
U.S.S.R.	13	14
U.K.	5	8*
Germany F.R.	4	3*
Brazil	3	3*
Japan	3	2
Poland	2	2
France	2	1
India	2	1
Others	33	30
	100	100

*Estimate **1953 only Excluding U.S.S.R. Centrifugal sugar Unmanufactured (raw basis) Raw and refined (raw basis) Beans, raw or roasted Coffee, green or roasted Coffee, green or roasted, and coffee substitutes containing coffee Excluding trade between continental U.S.A. and Hawaii and Puerto Rico Re-exports Including milk crumb Including filled chocolate since 1954 Excl. China P.R. and N. Korea Incl. cigarillos for most countries Incomplete world total Where reported by weight a conversion factor of 1 million cigarettes per metric ton was used Sales 1954 only Excl. Brazil Cigarillos included with cigars Consumption of cocoa beans and cocoa products in terms of beans

Sugar

Modified Gail Projection • Equatorial Scale 1:88 Million approx.

© Oxford University Press

14

Sugar cane/beet
Production (1963-5 av.)

One dot represents 20 000 met. tons of centrifugal sugar.[1]

• SUGAR CANE   • SUGAR BEET

Consumption (1963-5 av.)

(kg. sugar per capita per year)

a	51 & OVER
b	31 - 50
c	11 - 30

0-10

DATA N A

[1] Raw value: i.e. 92% net sucrose content. [2] Letters are used where shading cannot be shown.

Major trade flows (1966)

Commodity : S.I.T.C. no.[1]

RAW SUGAR (CANE & BEET) : 061.1
REFINED SUGAR : 061.2

Value ($ U.S.)
0.5mm represents increments of $20 million

($ MILLIONS)
260
180
100
20

36 VALUE IN $ MILLIONS

[1] S.I.T.C. = STANDARD INTERNATIONAL TRADE CLASSIFICATION

Centrifugal sugar

59 133 934 met. tons 1963-5 av.
38 289 000 1953-5 av.

	PERCENTAGE	
	1963-5 av.	1953-5 av.
U.S.S.R.	13	.9
Cuba	8	13
U.S.A.	8	8
Brazil	6	5
India	5	4
France	4	4
China P.R.	3	2
Australia	3	3
Mexico	3	2
Others	47	50
	100	100

Centrifugal sugar : beet

25 639 872 met. tons 1963-5 av.
15 532 000 1953-5 av.

	PERCENTAGE	
	1963-5 av.	1953-5 av.
U.S.S.R.	30	22
U.S.A.	11	11
France	9	10
Germany F.R.	7	8
Poland	6	7
Italy	4	5
Czechoslovakia	3	6
U.K.	3	5
Germany D.R.	3	5
Others	24	21
	100	100

Centrifugal sugar : cane

33 494 062 met. tons 1963-5 av.
22 757 000 1953-5 av.

	PERCENTAGE	
	1963-5 av.	1953-5 av.
Cuba	14	21
Brazil	11	9
India	9	6
U.S.A.	6	7
Australia	6	5
Mexico	6	4
Philippines	5	5
China P.R.	5	3
South Africa	4	3
Others	34	37
	100	100

Sugar consumption

Selected countries

(kg. centrifugal sugar per capita)

	1963-5 av.
Cuba	61
Australia	60
U.K.	54
U.S.A.	47
Argentina	39
U.S.S.R.	38
France	34
Colombia	21
Algeria	20
Greece	16
India	6
China P.R.	3
Nigeria	1
World average	16

Sugar cane is essentially a perennial plant of the tropics and highest yields are obtained when frequent heavy rainfall is interspersed with bright sunshine. Under these conditions the rate of sugar accumulation in the stem of the mature plant is highest. The crop is generally ready for harvesting after 12–24 months. If frost shortens the season, as in Louisiana, the crop is cut when immature and the sugar yield is lower. The minimum annual rainfall requirement is about 50–65 in. (1 250–1 650 mm.) and in many areas the crop is irrigated.

Raw sugar is derived from sugar cane and sugar beet (which has been grown commercially in Europe since about 1870). The raw sugar is first extracted from the cane and beet and then refined to produce white sugar. Beet pulp and cane molasses are valuable by-products; both are used for cattle-feed, and molasses is also used in the production of rum and alcohol. Much of the cane sugar is exported raw, whereas beet sugar is generally refined and consumed in the countries which produce it. In the twentieth century production has sometimes tended to exceed demand.

Sugar beet demands a temperate climate, a long growing season, (preferably 5 – 6 months),a regular supply of water, long days, and high light intensities. In the autumn it requires either a dry period or cool nights to check growth and thereby accelerate sugar accumulation in the roots. The highest yield is obtained when the crop is irrigated, or the annual rainfall is more than 25 in. (650mm.), and the summer temperature ranges around 60°–70°F (15.5°–21°C). Sugar beet is usually grown on medium to light soils; the drainage must be good and the nutrient status high.

Temperature requirement varies according to species. In general growth is slow below 59°F (15°C) and active only above 70°F (21°C). Plants regenerate after the first harvest but such 'ratoon' crops have a lower sugar yield. Sugar cane will grow in a variety of soils but the best are deep soils which are well drained but retain moisture. A high level of fertility, particularly application of fertilizer, particularly nitrogen, is necessary for maximum production. Given suitable conditions of soil and climate, sugar cane can be grown on the same land for several years.

Coffee

Coffee is mainly obtained from two species of tree, *Coffea arabica*, which grows from 3 300-6 600 ft. (1 000-2 000m.) and is most widely cultivated, and *C. robusta*, which grows from sea level to 1 000m. The trees require a deep, rich, well-drained soil and an annual rainfall of 60-120in. (1 500-3 000mm.) is most favourable for cultivation. They will not tolerate frost or long periods of direct heat. Harvesting is carried out by hand and a large labour force is needed. Coffee beans are the seeds inside the fruits (or 'cherries') and extraction involves either drying alone, or more commonly washing and drying. After grading the beans are then stored or exported.

SCALE 1:176 MILLION 1 CM TO 1760 KM.

Major trade flows (1966)

Commodity: S.I.T.C. no.

COFFEE (GREEN/ROASTED) : 071.1
COFFEE EXTRACTS/ESSENCES : 071.3

Value ($ U.S.)
0.5mm. represents increments of $60 million ($ MILLIONS)
540 300 60
UNDER $30 MILLION
VALUE IN $ MILLIONS 50

Production (1963-5 av.)
One dot represents 5 000 metric tons

Major producers	BRAZIL	COLOMBIA	IVORY COAST	UGANDA	OTHERS	MET. TONS WORLD
			PERCENTAGE			
1963-5 av.	37	12	6	5	40	4 090 300
1953-5 av.	45	14	4¹	2	35	2 607 000

¹This figure is for former French West Africa of which Ivory Coast was a part

Cocoa/Tea

Cocoa (cacao) is a tropical forest crop which flourishes in a hot, rainy uniform climate with a mean annual temperature of at least 70°F (21°C) and a well distributed rainfall of at least 50in. (1 250mm.). It is normally grown under shade trees, but this is not essential for established plantations. Cultivation is mainly in the hands of peasant farmers.
Tea is a perennial crop which grows best where monthly maximum temperatures range from 70°-84°F (21°-29°C), annual rainfall is at least 50in. (1 250mm.) and the soils acid, well-drained and porous. It will grow at heights of up to 8 000ft. (2 440m.). In the tropics harvesting is mainly by hand, and only the tops of young shoots are plucked.

© Oxford University Press
Modified Gall Projection SCALE 1:176 MILLION 1 CM TO 1760 KM

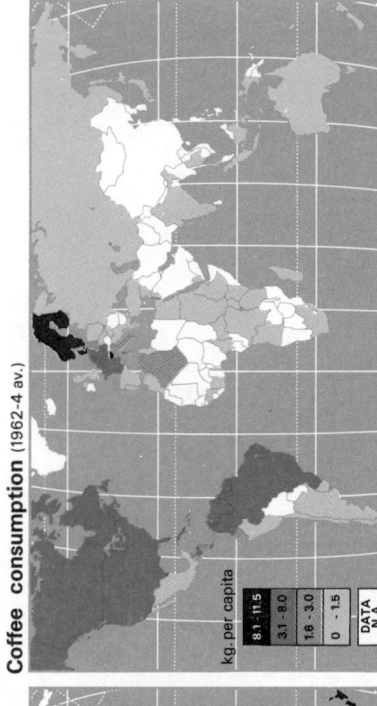

Major trade flows (1966)

Commodity: S.I.T.C. no.

TEA : 074.1 | COCOA : 072
CHOCOLATE/PRODUCTS : 073

Value ($ U.S.)
0.5mm. represents increments of $40 million ($ MILLIONS)
360 200 40
UNDER $20 MILLION
VALUE IN $ MILLIONS 77

Production (1963-5 av.)
One dot represents 5 000 metric tons
cocoa •   tea •

Cocoa Major producers	GHANA	NIGERIA	BRAZIL	IVORY COAST	OTHERS	'000 MET. TONS WORLD
			PERCENTAGE			
1963-5 av.	36	18	9	9	28	1 303.8
1953-5 av.	28	13	19	8*	32	795

Tea	INDIA	CEYLON	CHINA P.R.	INDONESIA	OTHERS	WORLD
			PERCENTAGE			
1963-5 av.	33	20	14*	2*	25	1 112.3
1953-5 av.	44	25	14*	6	23	656

*Estimate *Former French West Africa

15

Tobacco

The tobacco plant originated in tropical America, but can tolerate climates ranging from the humid tropical to the dry temperate: it grows best where temperature and water supply are fairly constant, the atmosphere is humid and the soil well-drained and rich in nitrogen and potassium. The type of tobacco, the climate and soil conditions and the way in which the leaves are processed and dried (curing) all affect the flavour of the tobacco. After curing the tobacco is sold to the manufacturer and may be stored up to two years before being used in the production of cigarettes, cigars, pipe and chewing tobacco and snuff. Tobacco is grown in many countries, though mostly only on a small scale and for local consumption.

SCALE 1:176 MILLION 1 CM TO 1760 KM.

Major trade flows (1966)

Commodity: S.I.T.C. no.

TOBACCO (UNMANUFACTURED) : 121

Value ($ U.S.)
0.5mm. represents increments of $40 million ($ MILLIONS)
520 360 200 40
UNDER $20 MILLION
VALUE IN $ MILLIONS 88

Production (1963-5 av.)
One dot represents 5 000 metric tons

Major producers	U.S.A.	CHINA P.R.	INDIA	BRAZIL	U.S.S.R.	OTHERS	MET. TONS WORLD
			PERCENTAGE				
1963-5 av.	22	10	8	5	4	51	4 383 000
1953-5 av.	30	11	8	4	...¹	47	3 297 000¹

¹Excluding U.S.S.R.

Tobacco consumption (1962-4 av.)
kg. per adult (15 yrs. and over)
3.6-4.5
2.5-3.5
1.5-2.4
0 -1.4
DATA N A
SCALE 1:92 MILLION

Cocoa consumption (1963-5 av.)
kg. per capita
2.1- 3.4
0.6- 2.0
0.1- 0.5
0 - 0.09
DATA N A
SCALE 1:92 MILLION

Coffee consumption (1963-5 av.)
kg. per capita
8.1-11.5
3.1- 8.0
1.6- 3.0
0 - 1.5
DATA N A
SCALE 1:92 MILLION

Tea consumption (1963-5 av.)
kg. per capita
3.6- 4.2
1.1- 3.5
0.09- 1.0
0 - 0.08
DATA N A
SCALE 1:92 MILLION

Consumption of cocoa beans and cocoa products in terms of beans

Fruit

The cultivation of fruit has been carried on in one form or another for many thousands of years. Certainly figs, dates, olives, and bananas have been cultivated for at least 4 000 years, and citrus fruit, apples, pears, plums and apricots for half that time. Cultivation of soft fruit, such as raspberries, gooseberries, currants, etc., is of comparatively recent origin.

More recently, demand for fruit has been further stimulated by the appreciation of the medical value of vitamin C and of the importance of many fruits as a source of this vitamin.

Commercial fruit growing has led to the development of special methods of preserving and marketing its products. Canning and drying have been long established, but a recent development is the production of 'fresh frozen' fruits. Soft fruit is particularly suited to being frozen, and an increasing amount is being processed in this way. The expansion of trade has been assisted by developments in transport and refrigeration, which now make it possible for costly fruit to be shipped cheaply across the world and to arrive at its destination in good condition.

Pears are widely cultivated in the temperate zones of both the northern and southern hemispheres. Of a total world production of 5 587 000 met. tons, 1963-5 av., Italy produced 18% China P.R. 15% the U.S.A. 9%, France 7% Germany F.R. 7% and Japan 6%. Turkey, Australia and Argentina are also significant producers, and Germany F.R., the U.K. and France are the major importers. The distribution of pear production is similar to that of apples. Pineapples grow throughout the tropics. Total recorded world production, 1963-5 av., was 3 264 000 met. tons of which Hawaii produced 29% Venezuela 12% West Malaysia 10% Thailand 9% Brazil 9% and Ghana 7% A large proportion of trade production is canned.

The date palm thrives best in a sunny and arid environment where a low relative humidity is maintained. Total world date production, 1963-5 av., was 1 825 000 met. tons of which the U.A.R. produced 21% Iraq 18% Iran 16% Saudi Arabia 15% and Algeria 6% India, China P.R., Germany D.R. and the U.S.S.R. are the main importers. World fig production, 1963-5 av., was 1 489 000 met. tons of which Portugal produced 24% Italy 18% Turkey 14% Spain 10% and Greece 8%

The tomato is a native fruit of South and Central America but is cultivated in the open in the warm temperate zones during the frost-free periods; it has also become a major greenhouse product. Total world production, 1963-5 av., was 18 697 000 met. tons of which the U.S.A. produced 26% Italy 16% Spain 7% and the U.A.R. 6%

Citrus fruit consumption (1963/4)

	ISRAEL	LEBANON	GREECE	ARGENTINA	U.S.A.	BRAZIL	CANADA	SWITZERLAND	AUSTRALIA	GERMANY F.R.	SPAIN	U.K.	JAPAN	SOUTH AFRICA	WORLD
Total ('000 metric tons)	212	89	346	837	5191	2115	515	138*	256	1 206	668	789	1 077	178	22 818*
Kg. per capita	89*	46	41	39	28	28	27	24*	24	21	21	15	11	11	10*¹,³

*Estimate ¹Excl. China P.R. ²Average

International trade in fruit (1963-5 av.)

Apples (S.I.T.C. no. 051.4)

Production
19 071 700 met. tons 1963-5 av.
13 667 000 1953-5 av.

Percentage exported
9% 1963-5 av.
6% 1953-5 av.

Exports
1 740 810 met. tons 1963-5 av.
754 330 1953-5 av.

Imports
1 709 900 met. tons 1963-5 av.
754 330 1953-5 av.

	PERCENTAGE 1963-5 av.	1953-5 av.		PERCENTAGE 1963-5 av.	1953-5 av.
Italy	26	28	Germany F.R.	31	35
Argentina	12	7	U.K.	14	20
Australia	8	10	U.S.S.R.	8	—
Hungary	7	2	France	8	4
France	6	9	Germany D.R.	6	4
U.S.A.	6	4	Austria	3	3
China P.R.	5	—	Czechoslovakia	3	1
South Africa	5	2	Belg./Lux.	3	5
Netherlands	4	11	Sweden	4	4
Canada	4	5	Brazil	2	2
Others	18	22	Finland	2	2
	100	100	Others	20	20
				100	100

Bananas (S.I.T.C. no. 051.3)

Production
21 840 000 met. tons 1963-5 av.
11 200 000 1953-5 av.

Percentage exported
20% 1963-5 av.
25% 1953-5 av.

Exports
4 408 970 met. tons 1963-5 av.
2 968 000 1953-5 av.

Imports
4 211 430 met. tons 1963-5 av.
2 944 330 1953-5 av.

	PERCENTAGE 1963-5 av.	1953-5 av.		PERCENTAGE 1963-5 av.	1953-5 av.
Ecuador	35	57	U.S.A.	29	35
Costa Rica	7	12	Germany F.R.	7	12
Honduras	9	9	France	10	10
Panama	8	10	U.K.	10	14
Brazil	8	1	Japan	6	—
Colombia	5	7	Italy	5	2
Jamaica	4	5	Argentina	4	6
Taiwan	4	6	Canada	4	12
Cameroun	4	1	Netherlands	3	NA
Ivory Coast	3	NA	Others	23	NA
Others	12	11		100	100
	100	100			

Citrus fruit (S.I.T.C. no. 051.1.2)

Production
24 971 000 met. tons 1963-5 av.
17 467 000 1953-5 av.

Percentage exported
17% 1963-5 av.
16% 1953-5 av.

Exports
4 150 570 met. tons 1963-5 av.
2 800 000 1953-5 av.

Imports
4 186 040 met. tons 1963-5 av.
2 770 000 1953-5 av.

	PERCENTAGE 1963-5 av.	1953-5 av.		PERCENTAGE 1963-5 av.	1953-5 av.
Spain	26	26	Germany F.R.	26	25
Italy	12	12	France	12	13
Israel	12	9	U.K.	12	19
Morocco	10	10	Canada	6	9
South Africa	9	15	Netherlands	6	6
U.S.A.	7	8	Sweden	4	6
Algeria	5	8	U.S.A.	3	8
Brazil	4	—	Others	18	—
Lebanon	3	—		100	100
Greece	2	—			
Others	11	12			
	100	100			

Grapes (S.I.T.C. no. 051.5)

Production
50 859 700 met. tons 1963-5 av.
39 433 000 1953-5 av.

Percentage exported
2% 1963-5 av.
1% 1953-5 av.

Exports
824 320 met. tons 1963-5 av.
310 000 1953-5 av.

Imports
798 760 met. tons 1963-5 av.
287 000 1953-5 av.

	PERCENTAGE 1963-5 av.	1953-5 av.		PERCENTAGE 1963-5 av.	1953-5 av.
Italy	24	19	Germany F.R.	29	35
Bulgaria	23	24	Canada	13	9
U.S.A.	20	17	U.S.S.R.	13	2
Spain	11	14	U.K.	7	13
Romania	6	—	Czechoslovakia	5	2
France	6	4	Germany D.R.	4	6
South Africa	4	6	Switzerland	4	4
Hungary	3	NA	Poland	3	NA
Afghanistan	3	4	Sweden	3	3
Yugoslavia	2	NA	Austria	2	3
Others	8	NA	Others	14	17
	100	100		100	100

Apple production data for the U.S.S.R. are not available.

Regions of commercial apple production are limited by the danger of winter frost injury coupled with the need for winter cooling prior to budbreak and blossoming in the spring. Well-distributed rainfall of 20-40 in. (500-1 000 mm) is necessary, but in drier areas irrigated crops can be grown. Local topography is important in determining the degree of risk to blossom and young fruit from late spring frost. Other limiting factors are those affecting the 'finish' and quality of dessert apples; the link between climate and disease, for example high summer humidity and scab in England; and adequate storage and transport facilities. Dessert and cooking apples are most important but some are produced for cider. Bananas (incl. plantains) are grown in most humid tropical areas; often plantains are an important subsistence crop. Extensive plantations in Central America are sited on well-drained and aerated sandy to medium clay loams, usually in rain-forest alluvial regions with a well-distributed rainfall of at least 80 in. (2 000 mm.) In drier areas supplementary irrigation may be practised. Diverse soils and localities may be used, provided high fertility can be maintained.

SCALE 1:176 MILLION 1 CM TO 1 760 KM.

Major trade flows (1966)

Commodity : S.I.T.C. no.
APPLES : 051.4
BANANAS : 051.3

Value ($ U.S.)
0.5mm represents increments of $20 million
180 / 100 / 20 — UNDER $10 MILLION / $ MILLIONS
41

Production (1963-5 av.)

One dot represents 20 000 metric tons

• apples • bananas

Major producers

	FRANCE	ITALY	U.S.A.	GERMANY F.R.	JAPAN	U.K.	OTHERS	WORLD MET. TONS⁴
Apples 1963-5 av.	18	15	12	8	6	3	38	19 071 700
1953-5 av.	30	7	4	3	4	—	30	13 667 000

	BRAZIL	ECUADOR¹	INDIA	VENEZUELA	PAKISTAN	OTHERS	WORLD
Bananas 1963-5 av.	20	13	12	6	—	44	21 840 000
1953-5 av.	34	5	17	—	—	NA	11 200 000

¹Exports only ⁴Excl. U.S.S.R.

Apples/Bananas

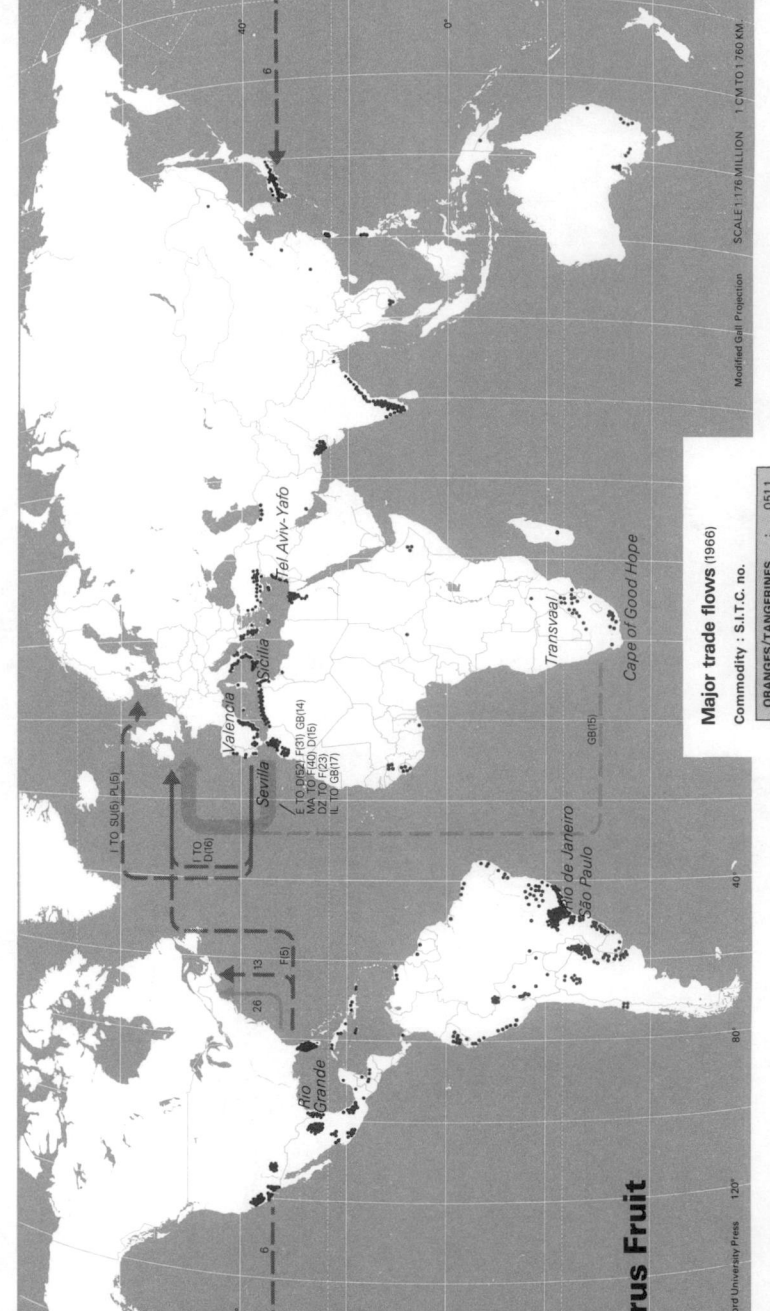

Citrus includes eight species of the *Rutaceae* family varying in characteristics and commercial importance. The lime and citron are tropical and frost-susceptible, while the hardiest, the Seville orange, can tolerate several degrees of frost. Average temperature limits are 40°F (4.5°C) in the coldest month with 70-75°F (21-24°C) for most of the summer. Where citrus is grown in the tropics the temperature may reach 120°F (49°C). Citrus tolerates a wide range of rainfall and extensive irrigation may be practised. Most non-alkaline, well-drained soils are suitable. In 1965 the main producers were: of oranges, the U.S.A. (24%) and Brazil (12%); of lemons and limes, the U.S.A. (21%) and Italy (20%); and of grapefruit, the U.S.A. (75%) and Israel (7%).

© Oxford University Press Modified Gall Projection SCALE 1:176 MILLION 1 CM TO 1 760 KM.

Major trade flows (1966)

Commodity : S.I.T.C. no.
ORANGES/TANGERINES : 051.1
OTHER CITRUS FRUIT : 051.2

Value ($ U.S.)
0.5mm represents increments of $40 million
360 / 200 / 40 — UNDER $20 MILLION / $ MILLIONS
26

Production (1963-5 av.)

One dot represents 20 000 metric tons

Major producers

	U.S.A.	SPAIN	ITALY	BRAZIL	JAPAN	INDIA	OTHERS	WORLD MET. TONS
Citrus 1963-5 av.	28	9	8	7	6	5	37	24 971 000
1953-5 av.	42	8	7	6	3	4	30	17 467 000

Citrus Fruit

Grapes

Grapes can be grown in many parts of the temperate zone, but considerations of quality or the type of product restrict the localities of commercial cultivation. Conditions for growth vary with the species of vine and the nature of the rootstock. All European vines are descended from one species, *Vitis vinifera*. Vines require a good supply of water in the vegetative phase and dry sunny weather during ripening and harvesting; high summer temperatures of about 65°-72°F (18.5°-22°C) for a prolonged period are inimical. At least 80% of the world's grapes are grown for wine. The North African muscat is grown primarily for dessert, while the U.S.A., Turkey, Greece, Australia and Iran produce large quantities of raisins or sultanas.

SCALE 1:176 MILLION 1 CM. TO 1760 KM.

Production data for Afghanistan and Iraq are not available

Production (1963-5 av.)
One dot represents 20 000 metric tons

Major trade flows (1966)
Commodity : S.I.T.C. no.
FRESH GRAPES : 0515

Value ($ U.S.)
0.5mm. represents increments of $10 million
17 VALUE IN $ MILLIONS
UNDER $5 MILLION

Major producers	ITALY	FRANCE	SPAIN	U.S.A.	U.S.S.R.	TURKEY	OTHERS	WORLD
	PERCENTAGE							MET. TONS
1963-5 av.	19	19	9	6	6	6	35	50 859 700
1953-5 av.	22	23	8	7	..¹	5	35	39 433 000

¹excl. U.S.S.R.

Wine

Wine results from the fermentation of grape juice by naturally occurring yeasts. Wine can be produced economically in the northern hemisphere between lats. 30°-50° and in the southern hemisphere between lats. 30°-45°. Wines are classified according to strength and appearance. Table wines contain between 8-14% ethyl-alcohol, those with a higher alcohol content being grown in regions with much sun during the ripening period. Fortified wines, such as Sherry, are those in which spirits, usually brandy, have been added to increase the alcoholic content to 18-21%. Aromatic wines, such as Vermouths and Dubonnet, are fortified wines to which herbs and spices have been added.

SCALE 1:176 MILLION 1 CM. TO 1760 KM.

Production (1963-5 av.)
One dot represents 200 000 hectolitres

Major trade flows (1966)
Commodity : S.I.T.C. no.
WINE OF FRESH GRAPES : 112.1

Value ($ U.S.)
0.5mm. represents increments of $30 million
31 VALUE IN $ MILLIONS
UNDER $15 MILLION

Major producers	ITALY	FRANCE	SPAIN	ARGENTINA	ALGERIA	PORTUGAL	OTHERS	WORLD
	PERCENTAGE							'000 HECTO-LITRES
1963-5 av.	23	23	11	7	5	5	26	274 666
1953-5 av.	24	27	9	6	8	5	21	225 473

▲ European wine areas

Each dot represents the production of 200 000 hectolitres of wine, located in the major wine-grape areas of each province.
The names form a selection of wine-producing centres which are usually settlements but occasionally wine names although some places, such as Barsac and Chablis, have obviously given their names to many well-known wines.

¹Area around the volcano

SCALE 1:29 MILLION 1 CM. TO 290 KM.

Consumption of alcoholic beverages (1966)

Wine

litres per capita
46 - 120
16 - 45
6 - 15
0 - 5
DATA N.A.

Beer

litres per capita
96 - 140
51 - 95
21 - 50
5 - 20
DATA N.A.

SCALE 1:352 MILLION 1 CM. TO 3520 KM.

Spirit (100% proof)

litres per capita
2.5 -3.24
1.75-2.49
1.25-1.74
0.5 -1.24
DATA N.A.

Total alcohol (100% proof)

litres per capita
12.5 - 19
6.5 -12.4
3.5 - 6.4
1.5 - 3.4
DATA N.A.

SCALE 1:352 MILLION 1 CM. TO 3520 KM.

© Oxford University Press.

The consumption maps for wine and beer are based upon the total volume of the drink consumed. Total alcohol and spirit consumption maps are based upon the volume adjusted to show the consumption of 100% proof potable total alcohol and spirit.

The wine and beer data may be recalculated on the same basis by assuming an average alcohol content of 12% for wine and 5% for beer. It should be noted that the true range of individual figures is quite high; a Rhine wine may have an average alcohol content of 10% while that of a Sherry may be 18%.

Data for South Africa exclude Bantu-produced alcohol. No data are available for much of Latin America and most of Africa and Asia although much non-commercial brewing and distilling, both legal and illegal, are known to exist. Data for the U.S.S.R. are estimated.

Vegetable Oilseeds and Oils

Groundnuts p.19 Soya Beans p.19
Rapeseed p.19 Sunflower Seed p.19

For individual country data see Statistical Supplement

It is estimated that in recent years vegetable oils have accounted for just under three-fifths of the total world supply of fats and oils. World production of the main vegetable oil crops, in oil equivalent, mounted from 14 million tons in 1939 to 21.5 million tons in 1960 and to 39.6 million tons in 1968.

With animal fats lagging behind the growth of world population, more and more vegetable oils have been consumed as food; their use in paints, varnishes, lubricants, synthetic fabrics and other manufactures has also been expanded. Valuable by-products remain after extracting the oil from the seed, which can be used as livestock feed, as fertilizer, or, with soya beans, as protein-meal for human consumption.

As prosperity increases, the consumption of vegetable oils rises; more fats are added to the diet and more technical uses are discovered for oilseed products as industry advances. In 1960-2 consumption of fat varied from 1.1 kg. per capita in the Malagasy Republic to 35.9 kg. per capita in Denmark. Consumption of fats and oils also expands with population growth. From 1850 to 1990 the population of Western Europe about doubled. In the same period the consumption of vegetable oils quadrupled, owing partly to population growth, partly to the swift rise of living standards.

The increasing demand could not be met by the traditional forms and sources of fats. The Dutch butter producers, the Jurgens, were therefore forced to supply an edible fat made from flour, milk and suet, which was called margarine by its inventor Hippolyte Mège Mouriès. But this margarine had relied on a solid animal fat, and until Crosfield invented in 1909 a method of making liquid vegetable oils solid by hydrogenation, and until refining processes were introduced, the enormous potentialities of tropical oils for producing a cheap edible fat lay unrealized.

In 1965 world output of margarine was over two-and-a-half times as great as in 1938, although the rate of increase in world production recently has been considerably slower than in the 1951-4 period. The United States is the largest producer, and with the progressive removal of restrictions and a price ratio in favour of margarine, consumption has risen steadily at the expense of butter. In 1965, in the U.S.A. consumption of margarine was 4.4 kg. per capita while that of butter was 2.8 kg. per capita. Corresponding figures for the U.K. are 5.4 kg. and 8.7 kg. per capita.

Since the development of hydrogenation and refining processes the demand for oilseed products greatly expanded, both for making margarine and for industrial products including soap and cattle cake. Palm oil production in West Africa and copra production in the Pacific Islands became increasingly profitable and new methods of crushing enable more and better quality oil to be extracted from the seed. For example, by traditional methods the Nigerian can extract only about 45% of the oil from the pericarp of the oil palm fruit, with a hand press about 65% while in a mechanized mill some 85-90% of the available oil is extracted.

Since 1945 the patterns of world trade in oils and oilseeds have been radically altered. Wartime shortages, higher consumption in the producing countries, and a tendency to crush the seed within the producing country have all left a lasting mark. The last world war, for instance, cut off imports into America of the Chinese soya bean and of copra from Indonesia and the Philippines. This resulted in the expansion of oilseed crops in the U.S.A. Acreages of groundnuts, cottonseed, linseed, and particularly soya beans, rose. Tung trees were planted to supply the valuable drying oil which was formerly obtained only from China P.R. Mechanical harvesting was used for all these crops.

Also the substitution of one vegetable oil for another, as a result of improvements in processing, enabled margarine producers to use the oils of soya beans, groundnuts or cottonseed according to their availability, just as it allowed different oils to be used from their former exclusive reliance on linseed oil and tung oil.

In this way the U.S.A., which before the war was a heavy importer of most of the major oilseeds, is now increasingly a net exporter; in the period 1958-60 nearly 25% of the total domestic production was exported, though some of this was for charitable purposes. Although world production has risen, world trade has remained at the same level. Increased world demand has been met by growing the oilseeds best suited to local conditions and consuming them locally.

Since the 1940's vegetable oils have encountered strong competition from growing world output of synthetic chemical products and animal and marine fats. With the expanding production of synthetic detergents in the U.K., other West European countries, the U.S.A. and Canada, the use of vegetable oils in soap has tended to decline. In the U.S.A. where this trend has been particularly marked, oil consumption in soap averaged only 66 000 metric tons between 1963-65 compared with 242 000 metric tons in 1938. The rise of detergents has done much to allay fears of a long term shortage of oils and fats. In addition synthetic resins are now used in paint, and new surface coatings have begun to replace industrial oils.

The increased use of lard and marine oils in the manufacture of margarine, particularly in the U.K., is seen in the following figures. In 1954 they accounted for 16.6% of the total oils and fats used for margarine in the U.K., by 1965 the proportion had risen to 62.5% Corresponding figures for the U.S.A., where 75% of margarine production is from soya bean oil, are 1.4% and 5.4%.

Despite these facts the demand for oilseeds is certain to increase. In the foreseeable future the need for edible fats and oils can only be met by oil-bearing plants. While synthetics make further inroads on the use of vegetable oils in soap and in industry, food is the major use; with rising living standards and a growing world population consumption will continue to rise. In many of the developing countries consumption of fat is below the level required for a balanced diet.

International trade in vegetable oilseeds and oils (1963-5 av.)

Soya beans/Soya bean oil (S.I.T.C. no. 221.4/421.2)

Production (beans): 33 543 000 met. tons 1963-5 av. / 19 467 000 1953-5 av.
Percentage exported (beans): 18% 1963-5 av. / 9% 1953-5 av.[1]

Exports Beans: 6 155 300 met. tons 1963-5 av.* / 1 734 000 1953-5 av.

PERCENTAGE	1963-5 av.	1953-5 av.
U.S.A.	90	80
China P.R.*	8	14
Canada	1	1
Others	1	5
	100	100

Imports Beans: 5 999 500 met. tons 1963-5 av. / 1 616 000 1953-5 av.

PERCENTAGE	1963-5 av.	1953-5 av.
Japan	28	36
Germany F.R.	21	19
Canada	7	11
Others	44	34
	100	100

Oil (exports): 685 100 met. tons 1963-5 av. / 78 800 1953-5 av.

	1963-5 av.	1953-5 av.
U.S.A.	79	49
Denmark	6	2
Israel	3	—
Others	12	49
	100	100

Oil (imports): 620 900 met. tons 1963-5 av. / 80 200 1953-5 av.

	1963-5 av.	1953-5 av.
Spain	6	—
Pakistan	12	—
Turkey	6	—
Others	68	100*
	100	100

Groundnuts[3]/Groundnut oil (S.I.T.C. no. 221.1/421.4)

Production (nuts): 10 860 500 met. tons 1963-5 av. / 8 003 300 1953-5 av.[1]
Percentage exported (nuts): 13% 1963-5 av. / 12% 1953-5 av.[1]

Exports Nuts: 1 443 700 met. tons 1963-5 av. / 937 000 1953-5 av.

PERCENTAGE	1963-5 av.	1953-5 av.
Nigeria	42	41
Senegal	15	23*
Sudan	10	3
Others	32	33
	100	100

Imports Nuts: 1 392 300 met. tons 1963-5 av. / 929 000 1953-5 av.

PERCENTAGE	1963-5 av.	1953-5 av.
France	35	33
U.K.	10	39
Italy	9	2
Others	46	26
	100	100

Oil (exports): 401 000 met. tons 1963-5 av. / 270 700 1953-5 av.

	1963-5 av.	1953-5 av.
Senegal	31	34*
Nigeria	20	10
India	11	27
Others	38	29
	100	100

Oil (imports): 425 200 met. tons 1963-5 av. / 248 600 1953-5 av.

	1963-5 av.	1953-5 av.
France	34*	34
U.K.	13	15
Spain	11	—
Others	42	51
	100	100

Sunflower seed/Sunflower seed oil (S.I.T.C. no. 221.8/421.6)

Production (seed): 7 558 700 met. tons 1963-5 av. / 1 683 000 1953-5 av.
Percentage exported (seed): 3% 1963-5 av. / 3% 1953-5 av.[1]

Exports Seed: 230 100 met. tons 1963-5 av. / 102 900 1953-5 av.

PERCENTAGE	1963-5 av.	1953-5 av.
U.S.S.R.	42	52
Bulgaria	34	6
Hungary	18	35
Others	6	7
	100	100

Imports Seed: 217 500 met. tons 1963-5 av. / 90 400 1953-5 av.

PERCENTAGE	1963-5 av.	1953-5 av.
Germany D.R.	32	4*
Italy	29	3
Germany F.R.	14	31
Others	25	62
	100	100

Oil (exports): 293 900 met. tons 1963-5 av. / 31 800 1953-5 av.

	1963-5 av.	1953-5 av.
U.S.S.R.	71	55*
Romania	12	21
Hungary	7	24
Others	10	45
	100	100

Oil (imports): 297 900 met. tons 1963-5 av. / 28 900 1953-5 av.

	1963-5 av.	1953-5 av.
Germany D.R.	22	27
Germany F.R.	20	21
Cuba	12*	—
Others	46	79
	100	100

Linseed/Linseed oil (S.I.T.C. no. 221.5/422.1)

Production (seed): 3 490 000 met. tons 1963-5 av. / 2 630 000 1953-5 av.
Percentage exported (seed): 17% 1963-5 av. / 15% 1953-5 av.[1]

Exports Seed: 599 000 met. tons 1963-5 av. / 391 000 1953-5 av.

PERCENTAGE	1963-5 av.	1953-5 av.
Canada	60	39
U.S.A.	20	32
Belg./Lux.	15	2
Others	5	27
	100	100

Imports Seed: 572 800 met. tons 1963-5 av. / 390 000 1953-5 av.

PERCENTAGE	1963-5 av.	1953-5 av.
U.K.	21	7
Japan	17	13
France	13	30
Others	49	50
	100	100

Oil (exports): 276 200 met. tons 1963-5 av. / 372 500 1953-5 av.

	1963-5 av.	1953-5 av.
Argentina	79	46
Uruguay	7	8
U.S.A.	4	27
Others	10	19
	100	100

Oil (imports): 292 100 met. tons 1963-5 av. / 357 900 1953-5 av.

	1963-5 av.	1953-5 av.
Germany F.R.	25	23
U.K.	15	17
U.S.S.R.	10	11
Others	50	39
	100	100

Palm kernels/Palm kernel oil (S.I.T.C. no. 221.3/422.4)

Production (kernels): 1 049 700 met. tons 1963-5 av. / 963 000 1953-5 av.
Percentage exported (kernels): 64% 1963-5 av. / 83% 1953-5 av.

Exports Kernels: 667 500 met. tons 1963-5 av. / 802 000 1953-5 av.

PERCENTAGE	1963-5 av.	1953-5 av.
Nigeria	61	55
Sierra Leone	8	6*
Dahomey	6	10*
Others	25	27
	100	100

Imports Kernels: 666 900 met. tons 1963-5 av. / 802 000 1953-5 av.

PERCENTAGE	1963-5 av.	1953-5 av.
U.K.	31	47
Germany F.R.	19	16
Netherlands	19	11
Others	31	26
	100	100

Oil (exports): 81 400 met. tons 1963-5 av. / 61 300 1953-5 av.

	1963-5 av.	1953-5 av.
Congo D.R.	44	40*
Netherlands	24	17
U.K.	9	31
Others	23	10
	100	100

Oil (imports): 83 400 met. tons 1963-5 av. / 50 700 1953-5 av.

	1963-5 av.	1953-5 av.
U.S.A.	46	44
Germany F.R.	18	27
Italy	10	10
Others	26	29
	100	100

Copra/Coconut oil (S.I.T.C. no. 221.2/422.3)

Production (kernels): 3 307 200 met. tons 1963-5 av. / 2 900 000 1953-5 av.
Percentage exported (kernels): 46% 1963-5 av. / 50% 1953-5 av.

Exports Kernels: 1 513 000 met. tons 1963-5 av. / 1 448 300 1953-5 av.

PERCENTAGE	1963-5 av.	1953-5 av.
Philippines	61	53
Indonesia	9	20
New Guinea	4	5
Others	26	22
	100	100

Imports Kernels: 1 401 500 met. tons 1963-5 av. / 1 446 000 1953-5 av.

PERCENTAGE	1963-5 av.	1953-5 av.
U.S.A.	18	21
Germany F.R.	18	10
Netherlands	9	9
Others	55	55
	100	100

Oil (exports): 447 700 met. tons 1963-5 av. / 333 100 1953-5 av.

	1963-5 av.	1953-5 av.
Philippines	48	40
Ceylon	21	26
Netherlands	8	11
Others	23	43
	100	100

Oil (imports): 462 400 met. tons 1963-5 av. / 329 100 1953-5 av.

	1963-5 av.	1953-5 av.
U.S.A.	40*	19
Germany F.R.	11	17
U.K.	10	10
Others	39	54
	100	100

*Estimate. [1]Ex-shell basis. [2]Belgian Congo. [3]French West Africa (incl. Dahomey, Ivory Coast, Niger, Senegal, Upper Volta and Mali).

Vegetable oils

('000 met. tons)

	EXTRACTION RATE[1]	PRODUCTION[2] 1963-5 av.	PRODUCTION[2] 1953-5 av.	EXPORTS[3] 1963-5 av.	EXPORTS[3] 1953-5 av.	IMPORTS[3] 1963-5 av.	IMPORTS[3] 1953-5 av.	MAJOR EXPORTERS 1963-5
Edible								
Soya bean oil	18%	6 038	3 504	685	79	621	80	U.S.A., Denmark
Groundnut oil	46%[a]	4 996	3 682	401	271	425	249	Senegal, Nigeria
Cottonseed oil	18%	3 881	2 472	272	239	286	180	U.S.A., Sudan
Sunflower oil	35%	2 646	589	294	32	298	29	U.S.S.R., Bulgaria
Rapeseed oil	38%	1 669	900	59	32	50	30	Germany F.R., France
Olive oil		1 411	1 080	168	114	183	124	Spain, Tunisia
Sesame oil	48%	784	861	NA	NA	NA	NA	NA
Edible/Industrial								
Coconut oil	64%	2 117	1 856	462	328	448	333	Philippines, Ceylon
Palm oil		1 326	1 110	564	578	553	574	Nigeria, Malaysia
Palm kernel oil	48%	504	462	81	61	83	51	Congo D.R.,[b] Netherlands
Industrial								
Linseed oil	34%	1 187	894	276	372	292	358	Argentina, Uruguay
Castor oil	45%	323	194	149	69	141	67	Brazil, India
Tung oil		1 050	107	43	59	43	56	China P.R., Argentina

*Estimate. [1]Average yield from commercial sources. [2]Oil equivalent of oilseed where extraction rate is given. [3]Traded oil. [a]Ex-shell groundnut extraction rate.

Groundnuts

The groundnut is grown where there is a growing season of at least four months with mean temperatures of about 80°F (26.5°C) for most of the period. Much of the crop is cultivated in regions with 40 in. (1 000 mm.) or more annual rainfall although seasonal rainfall may be as low as 20-30 in. (500-750 mm.), and a dry period during harvesting is necessary. In Africa and Asia groundnuts are an important subsistence crop; since the buried pods are collected by hand they can be grown on soils unsuitable for mechanical harvesting due to their heavy texture or liability to compaction. The highest quality kernels are produced on fertile light soils. Groundnuts are a valuable source of edible oil, and the meal is used as animal feed.

Major trade flows (1966)

Commodity: S.I.T.C.no.

GROUNDNUTS/PEANUTS (GREEN): 2211
GROUNDNUT/PEANUT OIL : 421.4

Value ($U.S.)
0.5mm represents increments of $40 million
($ MILLIONS)
360 / 200 / 40
UNDER $20 MILLION
52 — VALUE IN $ MILLIONS

Production (1963-5 av.)
One dot represents 20 000 metric tons (in shell)

	PERCENTAGE						MET.TONS
	INDIA	CHINA P.R.	NIGERIA	SENEGAL	U.S.A.	OTHERS	WORLD
1963-5 av.	32	14	9	7	6	32	15 515 000
1953-5 av.	34	23	8	8	6	21	11 433 000¹

¹Excl. U.S.S.R.

Soya Beans

Soya beans can be grown under a wide range of conditions, but the selection of the variety is essential since varieties differ markedly in their environmental requirements such as the length of day which initiates flowering. In general the climatic conditions demanded are similar to those of maize (corn). Fertile well-drained soils are the most productive but a wide range are tolerated depending on the variety. The seedlings of some varieties are susceptible to frost, and low night temperatures of about 55°F (13°C) greatly retard development. The plants can tolerate short droughts when past the seedling stage, but a relatively even distribution of rainfall during the growth cycle is needed. The oil is used as an edible oil for margarine or as a drying oil for paint-making. The residual meal is a valuable source of protein for animal or human consumption.

Major trade flows (1966)

Commodity: S.I.T.C.no.

SOYA BEANS (EXCL. FLOUR+MEAL): 2211A
SOYA BEAN OIL : 421.2

Value ($U.S.)
0.5mm represents increments of $40 million
($ MILLIONS)
360 / 200 / 40
UNDER $20 MILLION
85 — VALUE IN $ MILLIONS

Production (1963-5 av.)
One dot represents 20 000 metric tons

	PERCENTAGE					MET.TONS
	U.S.A.	CHINA P.R.	BRAZIL	U.S.S.R.	OTHERS	WORLD
1963-5 av.	61	33	1	1	4	33 543 000
1953-5 av.	46	47	1	...	6	19 467 000¹

¹Excl. U.S.S.R.

SCALE 1:176 MILLION   1 CM TO 1 760 KM.

Rapeseed

There are four main types of rape plant, two of which are sown in spring and two sown in autumn. The life-cycle of the spring-sown varieties may be very short, minimum about 75 days, while the more productive autumn sown types are grown where winters are not severe. They are adapted to temperate conditions and in the sub-tropics are grown in the cool season. The water requirements vary with type of plant, although the rape is often grown where annual rainfall is less than 20 in. (500 mm.). Soils may vary considerably; neutral fertile soils with high nitrogen content are best. Rapeseed oil is mainly used for edible purposes, although it also has specialized industrial uses.

INTRA-EUROPEAN TRADE

PROVENANCE	DESTINATION
France	N(L2) D(1)
Germany F.R.	A(1)
Hungary	

Major trade flows (1966)

Commodity: S.I.T.C.no.

RAPE,COLZA 6 MUSTARD OILS : 421.7

Value ($U.S.)
0.5mm represents increments of $5 million
UNDER $2.5 MILLION
4 — VALUE IN $ MILLIONS

Production (1963-5 av.)
One dot represents 20 000 metric tons

	PERCENTAGE							MET.TONS
	INDIA	CHINA P.R.	CANADA	POLAND	PAKISTAN	FRANCE	OTHERS	WORLD
1963-5 av.	28	25	8	8	7	5	19	4 392 300
1953-5 av.	18	56	—	NA	6	2	NA	5 000 000¹

¹Excl. U.S.S.R.

SCALE 1:176 MILLION   1 CM TO 1 760 KM.

Sunflower Seed

The sunflower is an extremely adaptable species; the same variety has been grown successfully in the tropics and at latitude 50°N with a July temperature of 68°F (20°C). Much of the crop is grown where the annual rainfall is less than 20 in. (500 mm.), but greater rainfall gives yields as long as there is a dry period during the later stages of ripening. A wide range of soils of moderate fertility is used. In some areas large-scale production is limited by the supply of pollinating insects. In the major centres of production the heads are mechanically harvested and threshed but elsewhere hand collection is common. Sunflower seed oil can be used for margarine or salad oil and the residue can be made into cattle cake.

The U.S.S.R. and the countries of Eastern Europe are major exporters of sunflower seed oil but trade flow data for these countries are not available

INTRA-EUROPEAN TRADE

PROVENANCE	DESTINATION
Germany F.R.	CH(1)
Hungary	
Romania	D(3) A(1)

Major trade flows (1966)

Commodity: S.I.T.C.no.

SUNFLOWER SEED OIL : 421.6

Value ($U.S.)
0.5mm represents increments of $5 million
($ MILLIONS)
45 / 25
UNDER $2.5 MILLION
7 — VALUE IN $ MILLIONS

Production (1963-5 av.)
One dot represents 20 000 metric tons

	PERCENTAGE						MET.TONS
	U.S.S.R.	ARGENTINA	ROMANIA	BULGARIA	YUGOSLAVIA	OTHERS	WORLD
1963-5 av.	69	7	7	5	3	9	7 558 700
1953-5 av.	...	27	NA	NA	7	NA	1 683 000¹

¹Excl. U.S.S.R.

SCALE 1:176 MILLION   1 CM TO 1 760 KM.

Modified Gall Projection

© Oxford University Press

Nutrition

20

Basic food crops

Production
areas of production of selected crops

(One dot: 100 000 metric tons)   (One dot: 20 000 metric tons)

Rice, Wheat, Corn,   Cassava, Yams,   Sugar (beet & cane)
Barley, Rye,   Potatoes   Bananas (incl. plantains)
Millet, Teff   Other Fruit

Consumption
estimated domestic consumption from national
production of those crops shown

(calories per capita per day)

| 1 660-1 220 | 1 220-750 | 750-450 | 450-160 | DATA NA |

Modified Gall Projection   Equatorial Scale 1:88 Million approx.

For each country are shown per capita domestic consumption and areas of
production for one or more basic food crop. The crops selected are those
carbohydrates which contribute the highest number of calories per capita of
any home-grown crop. Selection has been based on national averages, and
does not take account of regional or other variations; for example, rice is the
basic crop shown for Pakistan, but if shown regionally rice would probably remain the
basic crop for East Pakistan although wheat would probably be more important for West Pakistan.

A further crop is shown for a country if its contribution to the national
average caloric intake is at least 75% of that of the first crop selected.
When this occurs, the consumption category is based on the aggregate for
both crops; for example, in Brazil rice provides 394 calories per capita per
day and corn 302 (76.7% of the rice). Both crops are mapped and calorific
intake is given as 696 calories per capita per day.

In general there are two methods
employed in increasing food production. The first is to improve the
existing methods of husbandry at a
minimal cost. The second, which is
used to raise the levels of yield
further, entails the breeding and
selection of seeds or crops best
fitted to the environment coupled
with the efficient use of fertilizers,
pesticides and farm mechanization. Increased productivity of the
agrarian labour force is also a requirement. In some areas a high
level of mechanization is essential
to ensure that the crops are sown
and harvested at the right times, as
in the Canadian wheat belt. In
other regions where, as a conse-
quence of industrialization, farm
workers must be paid high wages,
mechanization is essential to keep

down costs of production. Tractors
are only a part of mechanization
but the following table gives an
idea of one aspect of the labour-
mechanization balance.

	Agrarian labour as % of total	Tractors per arable 10 000 ha.
Cambodia	80.9	—[1]
India	72.9	2
Bulgaria	64.1	133
Ghana	58.0	25
Brazil	61.6	21
Peru	49.7	25
Jordan	35.3	13
U.S.S.R.	35.2	67
Kenya	35.2	36
Japan	26.9	29
New Zealand	14.4	1 096
Netherlands	10.7	1 115
U.S.A.	6.2	250
U.K.	5.1	508

[1]Three tractors per 1 000 000 ha.

Fat levels per capita
Selected countries
(grammes per day)

	1961-3 av.
New Zealand	157.2
U.S.A.	143.4
Argentina	142.7
Greece	109.1
Uganda	88.1
Japan	39.0
Iraq	36.3
Bolivia	35.5
India	28.2
Malagasy R.	26.6
	16.8

Estimated calories per capita per day

| 3 480-3 000 | 3 000- | 2 800- | 2 600- | 2 200- | 2 000- | 2 000- | 1 780 | N A |

Estimated protein per capita (gm. per day)

| 86-110 | 75-86 | 66-76 | 56-66 | 38-56 | N A |

Estimated minimum calorie
requirement to avoid
malnutrition, by region

Europe[1]	2 590
North America	2 590
Latin America	2 410
Middle East	2 400
Africa	2 340
Asia[2]	2 300

Estimated gm. per day of
protein available, by region

North America	93
Europe[1]	88
Middle East	76
Latin America	67
Africa	61
Asia[2]	56

[1]Incl. U.S.S.R.   [2]Incl. China P.R.

© Oxford University Press

Livestock/Livestock Products

For individual country data see Statistical Supplement

Man uses livestock for food, power and sport. Food from livestock – meat, eggs and dairy products – is eaten mainly by those with a high standard of living. Livestock is used for power largely in developing areas, where the ox ploughing or drawing a cart is a familiar sight. The most important use of animals for sport is horse racing.

Food from livestock is generally expensive when compared, for example, with cereals. Man can obtain up to ten times as many calories by eating a crop instead of the livestock products which would result from feeding beasts off land on which crops can be grown for human consumption. But the raising of livestock is not always at the expense of grains for human consumption, since much grazing land is unsuitable for cultivation, and good husbandry often requires a rotation which includes grass or fodder crops.

The output of meat and dairy products could be greatly increased in many countries by proper management. It can also be raised by careful breeding and by controlling disease, which in a normal year causes the loss of about 15% of the total output of livestock in the U.K. The world total of livestock has increased substantially since 1945 but at a rate sufficient only to keep pace with growing population. Numbers of livestock per head of population are shown in the table below.

Cattle. In Europe most of the cattle are of breeds good for producing both milk and beef, for which the relatively high local standard of living provides a ready demand. Grazing land is usually limited, and cattle are therefore often kept in courts or yards and fed largely on farm by-products and root crops grown for them on mixed farms. In winter they are generally kept warm in sheds so as to economize on feed. In the Western U.S.A., Australia and Argentina cattle can usually be grazed on open range, and it is possible to graze both beef types that are raised. A large part of the beef production of Australia, Argentina and New Zealand is refrigerated and exported. In India the climate is more suitable for Zebu or humped cattle, which are used primarily as a source of milk and as draught animals, although the hides are also valuable and important in international trade.

In the more industrialized countries great progress has been made not only in the care and feeding of animals but also in improving the quality of the herds. This is done by breeding from registered stock and by the use of artificial insemination, which greatly extends the influence of the best bulls. Beef steers, which used to be slaughtered for market in eighteen months, can now often be fattened when four to six years old, can now often be slaughtered for market in eighteen months. In Europe since 1945 milk and beef yields per animal have been rising by about two per cent per annum. Milk marketing has been improved by the development of the canning and dehydrating industries, which enable large quantities of milk to be stored and transported over long distances.

Sheep and Goats. Most sheep are raised for wool and meat; the merino yields a particularly fine wool, and crossbreds are superior for meat. Although both meat and wool must be produced together, it is possible to vary the proportion in which they are supplied by varying the breeds or the age at which the animals are killed.

Although wool and meat are by far the most important products, sheep are raised chiefly for their skins in some countries and in parts of Southern Europe cheese is made from their milk. Milk is also the chief product of goats raised in European countries, although elsewhere meat and hides are usually most important. The Angora goat, a native of the Turkish steppes but now also reared in the U.S.A., South Africa, Lesotho and elsewhere, is the source of mohair, used in plushes, linings and carpets. Sheep can normally be left to graze in open pasture; goats, unless they are tethered, eat the bark and branches of trees and shrubs.

Poultry. More people keep poultry than any other type of livestock; production is highest in North America, but there are large numbers in other countries, notably India and China P.R. Most chickens are kept for egg production, usually on general farms and often with free range, but there are also intensive producers using battery or deep-litter systems. The specialist systems sell the birds after one year's laying. Since 1945 a broiler industry has grown up in North America and Europe producing birds for meat only.

The use of incubators enables numbers to be increased cheaply and rapidly and production levels to be maintained throughout the year. Marketing difficulties have been reduced in some countries by co-operatives and by egg preservation and deep freezing of dressed birds. Chickens are the most common poultry, but ducks are raised for eggs and meat in many countries; geese and turkeys, which are widely distributed, are mainly kept for meat.

Equines. Horses, ponies, donkeys and mules are used mainly as draught or pack animals, but their hides are valuable, and in some countries their meat and milk are also valued. In more industrialized countries animals are being replaced by motor vehicles; in the U.S.A. the number of horses has fallen by over 80% since 1939. Camels, while not equines, serve much the same purpose.

Pigs. Pigs are normally kept on mixed farms where they can be fed cheaply on farm by-products or coarse grains. In Denmark, for example, the Landrace pig, which has been carefully bred to produce bacon economically, is fed on barley and the skim milk left over from butter-making. Pigs eat less and fatten more quickly if warm and dry, and this helps to cover the high capital cost of the buildings which are essential for housing them during the winter in northern countries.

It takes about four months to fatten a pig for pork, and rather longer for bacon. The breeding cycle can be completed in six months, and pigs normally litter 8-10, so it is possible to increase the supply of pigmeat rapidly. This causes large cyclical fluctuations, when scarcity of pigs, resulting in high prices, alternates with abundance, which lowers prices.

Livestock population

	LIVESTOCK PER CAPITA 1963-5 av.	1953-5 av.	TOTAL LIVESTOCK 1963-5 av.	1953-5 av.	CATTLE[1] 1963-5 av.	1953-5 av.	CAMELS/HORSES 1963-5 av.	1953-5 av.	SHEEP 1963-5 av.	1953-5 av.	PIGS 1963-5 av.	1953-5 av.
	HEAD				MILLION HEAD							
Oceania	14.5	12.7	246	190	26	22	1	1	217	165	2	2
South America	2.6	2.9	415	361	170	145	27	26	148	145	70	45
Africa	1.4	1.6	416	348	128	102	24	20	258	222	6	4
Central America	1.3	1.2	102	68	47	28	12	9	22	18	21	13
U.S.A./Canada	1.0	1.1	215	200	117	105	3	6	33	35	62	54
Europe[2]	0.9	0.9	395	368	118	106	14	21	147	151	116	90
U.S.S.R.	1.3	1.2	290	247	87	61	10	16*	139	128	54	42
Asia[3]	0.7	0.7	730	598	365	301	19	18	305	255	41	24
China P.R.*	0.6	0.4	429	259	90	63	21	21	120	79	198	96
World	1.0	1.0	3 238	2 639	1 148	933	131	138	1 389	1 198	570	370

*Estimate [1] Including buffaloes [2] Excluding the U.S.S.R. [3] Excluding China P.R.

International trade in livestock/livestock products (1963-5 av.)

Bovine cattle (S.I.T.C. no. 001.1)

Production: 1 030 730 300 head (1963-5 av.); 842 333 000 (1953-5 av.)
Percentage exported: 0.4% (1963-5 av.); 0.2% (1953-5 av.)
Imports: 3 948 700 head (1963-5 av.); 1 801 000 (1953-5 av.)
Exports: 4 016 800 head (1963-5 av.); 1 845 700 (1953-5 av.)

Exports	1963-5 av.	1953-5 av.
Irish R.	17	25
Mexico	12	4
Canada	9	3
Denmark	7	19
Others	55	49
	100	100

Butter (S.I.T.C. no. 023)

Production: 4 813 300 met. tons (1963-5 av.); 3 418 000 (1953-5 av.)
Percentage exported: 14% (1963-5 av.); 14% (1953-5 av.)
Imports: 687 400 met. tons (1963-5 av.); 442 700 (1953-5 av.)
Exports: 660 100 met. tons (1963-5 av.); 484 000 (1953-5 av.)

Exports	1963-5 av.	1953-5 av.
New Zealand	27	31
Denmark	16	28
Australia	14	12
U.S.S.R.	7	—
Others	36	29
	100	100

Imports	1963-5 av.	1953-5 av.
U.K.	65	67
Germany D.R.	5	3*
Italy	5	—
Germany F.R.	3	4
Others	22	24
	100	100

Eggs[4] (S.I.T.C. no. 025.01)

Production: 14 629 900 met. tons (1963-5 av.); 10 120 000 (1953-5 av.)
Percentage exported: 3% (1963-5 av.); 4% (1953-5 av.)
Imports: 345 700 met. tons (1963-5 av.); 367 300 (1953-5 av.)
Exports: 370 000 met. tons (1963-5 av.); 393 700 (1953-5 av.)

Exports	1963-5 av.	1953-5 av.
Netherlands	29	29
Poland	11	5
China P.R.	10	7*
Belg./Lux.	9	1
Denmark	8	26
Others	33	32
	100	100

Imports	1963-5 av.	1953-5 av.
Germany F.R.	40	39
Italy	11	6
Hong Kong	11	6
U.S.S.R.	7	4
Switzerland	7	4
Others	24	41
	100	100

Milk and cream[1] (S.I.T.C. no. 022)

Production: 331 603 000 met. tons (1963-5 av.); 226 033 000 (1953-5 av.)
Percentage exported: 3% (1963-5 av.); 2% (1953-5 av.)
Imports: 9 969 000 met. tons (1963-5 av.); 3 471 000 (1953-5 av.)
Exports: 11 320 000 met. tons (1963-5 av.); 4 288 000 (1953-5 av.)

Exports	1963-5 av.	1953-5 av.
U.S.A.	46	41
Netherlands	14	23
France	8	1
New Zealand	7	11
Germany F.R.	25	24
	100	100

Imports	1963-5 av.	1953-5 av.
Netherlands	10	1
U.K.	9	17
Japan	7	3
Venezuela	4	5*
Others	70	74
	100	100

Cheese and curd (S.I.T.C. no. 024)

Production: 5 217 700 met. tons (1963-5 av.); 2 812 000 (1953-5 av.)
Percentage exported: 11% (1963-5 av.); 14% (1953-5 av.)
Imports: 572 800 met. tons (1963-5 av.); 374 300 (1953-5 av.)
Exports: 576 100 met. tons (1963-5 av.); 392 000 (1953-5 av.)

Exports	1963-5 av.	1953-5 av.
Netherlands	20	23
Denmark	16	24
France	14	15
Italy	10	5
Others	40	33
	100	100

Imports	1963-5 av.	1953-5 av.
U.K.	26	37
Germany F.R.	22	16
Italy	11	6
Belg./Lux.	6	9
Others	35	32
	100	100

Meat of swine (S.I.T.C. no. 011.3/012.1)

Production: 30 669 000 met. tons (1963-5 av.); 17 723 000 (1953-5 av.)
Percentage exported (pork): 1% (1963-5 av.); 1% (1953-5 av.)
Imports Pork: 377 000 met. tons (1963-5 av.); 130 300 (1953-5 av.)
Exports Pork: 354 200 met. tons (1963-5 av.); 141 000 (1953-5 av.)

Exports (pork)	1963-5 av.	1953-5 av.
Denmark	21	24
Netherlands	21	4
Yugoslavia	11	4
U.S.A.	10	2
Canada	5	13
Others	32	48
	100	100

Imports (pork)	1963-5 av.	1953-5 av.
France	22	12
Germany F.R.	22	16
Italy	8	2
U.K.	7	—
Belg./Lux.	6	—
Others	35	70
	100	100

Bacon exports: 435 300 met. tons (1963-5 av.); 369 700 (1953-5 av.)

Exports (bacon)	1963-5 av.	1953-5 av.
Denmark	69	61
Poland	12	15*
Irish R.	6	2
U.S.A.	3	7
Netherlands	2	10
Others	8	5
	100	100

Bacon imports: 434 600 met. tons (1963-5 av.); 348 300 (1953-5 av.)

Imports (bacon)	1963-5 av.	1953-5 av.
U.K.	91	89
U.S.A.	1	2
Canada	1	1
Hong Kong	6	9
Others	—	—
	100	100

Meat of bovine animals[7] (S.I.T.C. no. 011.1)

Production: 32 641 000 met. tons (1963-5 av.); 22 160 000 (1953-5 av.)
Percentage exported: 5% (1963-5 av.); 3% (1953-5 av.)
Imports: 1 452 100 met. tons (1963-5 av.); 516 700 (1953-5 av.)
Exports: 1 506 300 met. tons (1963-5 av.); 564 300 (1953-5 av.)

Exports	1963-5 av.	1953-5 av.
Argentina	29	24
Australia	19	25
New Zealand	8	12
Uruguay	6	5
Others	38	34
	100	100

Imports	1963-5 av.	1953-5 av.
U.S.A.	24	2
U.K.	23	61
Italy	18	7
Germany F.R.	8	2
Others	27	28
	100	100

Meat of sheep and goats[2] (S.I.T.C. no. 011.2)

Production: 5 942 000 met. tons (1963-5 av.); 4 140 000 (1953-5 av.)
Percentage exported: 9% (1963-5 av.); 10% (1953-5 av.)
Imports: 519 000 met. tons (1963-5 av.); 386 700 (1953-5 av.)
Exports: 525 400 met. tons (1963-5 av.); 406 700 (1953-5 av.)

Exports	1963-5 av.	1953-5 av.
New Zealand	69	66
Australia	17	15
Argentina	5	15
Irish R.	3	1
Others	6	3
	100	100

Imports	1963-5 av.	1953-5 av.
U.K.	67	90
Japan	11	—
U.S.A.	5	—
Greece	4	—
Others	13	10
	100	100

Meat (S.I.T.C. no. 011, 012, 013)

Net imports	'000 METRIC TONS 1963-5 av.	1953-5 av.
Europe	659	417
U.S.S.R.	9	...
North America*	919	706
Asia	1 587	1 123

Net exports	'000 METRIC TONS 1963-5 av.	1953-5 av.
South America	1 223	767
Oceania	298	86
Africa	142	76
Asia	81	41
		15
Total	1 744	970

Types traded — Fresh, chilled and frozen: 3 367 000 met. tons (1963-5 av.); 1 260 000 (1953-4 av.)

	1963-5 av.	1953-4 av.
Beef	45	41
Mutton/lamb	16	33
Pork	10	10
Poultry and others	29	16
	100	100

Prepared and canned: 1 063 000 met. tons (1963-5 av.); 1 092 000 (1953-4 av.)

	1963-5 av.	1953-4 av.
Bacon*	41	43
Canned meat and preparations	56	52
Others	3	5
	100	100

*Estimate [1] Incl. condensed, evaporated and dried milk [2] Milk equivalent [3] From cows [4] In the shell [5] From hens [6] Excl. U.S.S.R. [7] Fresh, chilled and frozen [8] Incl. ham and other dried, salted and smoked pigmeat *Incl. Central America

Cattle

Cattle (1963–5 av.)

Distribution One dot represents 100,000 head

Major trade flows (1966)

Commodity: S.I.T.C.no.

BOVINE CATTLE INCL. BUFFAL.(001.1)

MEAT OF BOVINE CATTLE (011.1)

DAIRY PRODUCTS/EGGS (02)

Value ($ U.S.)
0.5mm represents increments of $40 million

Modified Gall Projection   Equatorial Scale 1:88 Million approx.

INTRA-EUROPEAN TRADE

PROVENANCE	DESTINATION
France	
Irish R.	
Hungary	
Netherlands	

Cattle population
1 030 730 300 head 1963-5 av.
842 333 000 1953-5 av.

PERCENTAGE

	1963-5 av.	1953-5 av.
India	18	NA
U.S.A.	10	11
U.S.S.R.	8	7
Brazil	8	7
China P.R.	6	5
Argentina	6	5
Pakistan	3	4
Mexico	3	3
Ethiopia	2	NA
Others	38	NA
	100	100

Milk production (from cows)
331 603 000 met. tons 1963-5 av.
226 033 000 1953-5 av.

PERCENTAGE

	1963-5 av.	1953-5 av.
U.S.A.	19	NA
U.S.S.R.	17	24
Germany F.R.	6	7
Poland	4	4
U.K.	4	5
India	3	NA
Italy	3	3
Canada	3	3
Netherlands	2	3
Others	39	NA
	100	100

Milk yield per milk cow
Selected countries
(kg. per annum)

	1963-5 av.
Netherlands	4156
Japan	3971
Denmark	3783
U.K.	3711
Germany F.R.	3571
S. Korea	3558
U.S.A.	3033
France	2795
U.S.S.R.	1667
Chile	1606
Peru	680
Pakistan	421
Uganda	284

Cheese production
5 217 700 met. tons 1963-5 av.
2 812 000 1953-5 av.

PERCENTAGE

	1963-5 av.	1953-5 av.
U.S.A.	20	29
France	10	11
U.S.S.R.	9	NA
Italy	7	11
Germany F.R.	7	9
Netherlands	4	NA
U.A.R.	4	6
Poland	4	2
Argentina	3	4
Others	32	NA
	100	100

Butter production
4 813 300 met. tons 1963-5 av.
3 418 000 1953-5 av.

PERCENTAGE

	1963-5 av.	1953-5 av.
U.S.S.R.	21	12
U.S.A.	13	21
Germany F.R.	10	10
France	9	9
New Zealand	5	6
Australia	4	5
Germany D.R.	4	NA
Poland	3	3
Canada	3	NA
Others	28	27
	100	100

Beef & veal production[1]
32 532 000 met. tons 1963-5 av.
22 847 000 1953-5 av.[2]

PERCENTAGE

	1963-5 av.	1953-5 av.
U.S.A.	26	29
U.S.S.R.	13	...
Argentina	7	8
China P.R.	6	NA
France	5	6
Brazil	4	5
Germany F.R.	3	3
Australia	3	2
Others	36	NA
	100	100

[1] From indigenous animals only
[2] Excl. U.S.S.R.

Hides & skins (cattle & buffalo)
Major producers
('000 metric tons)

	1963-5 av.	1953-5 av.
Brazil	183	47
Germany F.R.	106	84
U.K.	89	70
Mexico	59	NA
Poland	40	NA
Uruguay	36	36
Yugoslavia	26	NA
Netherlands	22	16
New Zealand	21	19
Belgium	19	10
Japan	19	

Two distinct types of cattle exist—European cattle, found mainly in temperate zones; and Zebu, or humped cattle, in the tropics. The former thrive best in areas where mean monthly temperatures are below 64°F (18°C), while the latter thrive best at temperatures above 70°F (21°C). Cattle are kept primarily for milk, meat or work, or for any combination of these purposes. Work cattle are found mainly in the tropics, Southern Europe and Asia, while in the U.S.A., Argentina, Uruguay and Australia there are large numbers of pure beef cattle. Specialized dairy farming tends to occur near densely populated areas with a high standard of living, and is most important in NE. U.S.A. and NW. Europe. In the U.S.A., and to some extent the U.K., specialized dairy breeds are important. In most of Europe dual-purpose milk-beef types predominate. In general the size of the cattle in any area depends on environmental and nutritional conditions. In areas of high rainfall where soils are leached of calcium and phosphorus, the native breeds of cattle are usually small, whereas in arid areas they are large. From prehistoric times man in his migrations has tended to bring his own native breeds with him, and the present distribution of the different breeds throughout the world reflects this general pattern, although there are exceptions.

Sheep/Pigs

Sheep/pigs (1963–5av.)

Distribution One dot represents 100 000 head
sheep
pigs

Major trade flows (1966)

Commodity: S.I.T.C.no.

Modified Gall Projection
Equatorial Scale 1:88 Million approx.

© Oxford University Press

23

Sheep population

1 030 418 700 head 1963-5 av.
871 000 000 1953-5 av.

	PERCENTAGE 1963-5 av.	1953-5 av.
Australia	16	15
U.S.S.R.	13	13
China P.R.	6	5
New Zealand	5	4
Argentina	4	6
India	4	NA
South Africa	4	4
Turkey	3	3
Iran	3	NA
Others	42	NA
	100	100

Goat population

368 613 000 head 1963-5 av.
327 000 000 1953-5 av.

	PERCENTAGE 1963-5 av.	1953-5 av.
India	18	NA
China P.R.	15	12
Turkey	6	6
Nigeria	6	NA
Ethiopia	5	NA
Brazil	4	3
Iran	4	NA
Mexico	3	2
Pakistan	3	1
Others	36	NA
	100	100

Pig population

569 366 000 head 1963-5 av.
370 133 000 1953-5 av.

	PERCENTAGE 1963-5 av.	1953-5 av.
China P.R.	35	26
U.S.A.	10	13
Brazil	10	9
U.S.S.R.	10	11
Germany F.R.	3	4
Mexico	2	3
Poland	2	3
France	2	4
Germany D.R.	2	1
Others	24	26
	100	100

Wool production (clean basis)

1 507 000 met. tons 1963-5 av.
1 060 000 1953-5 av.

	PERCENTAGE 1963-5 av.	1953-5 av.
Australia	30	37
U.S.S.R.	14	10
New Zealand	14	13
Argentina	7	10
South Africa	4	5
U.K.	4	4
Iran	3	5
Uruguay	3	NA
China P.R.	3	2
Others	18	23
	100	100

Meat production[1] (1965)

Mutton/lamb
5 923 000 met. tons

	PERCENTAGE
U.S.S.R.	14
Australia	10
China P.R.	9
New Zealand	8
India	7
U.S.A.	5
U.K.	4
Iran	3
Ethiopia	3
Argentina	3
Others	23
	100

Pork
31 453 000 met. tons

	PERCENTAGE
China P.R.	30
U.S.A.	16
U.S.S.R.	10
Germany F.R.	6
Poland	6
France	4
U.K.	3
Denmark	3
Germany D.R.	2
Brazil	2
Others	21
	100

[1] From indigenous animals only

Sheep are raised primarily either for meat or for wool, though in many countries dual-purpose animals are common. In Southern Europe another minor product is cheese made from ewe-milk. Fine Merino comes from areas of low rainfall. Medium crossbred is produced where the rainfall is higher and the pasturage better and here the dual-purpose animal is often kept. Coarse carpet wool is associated with 'hill' sheep. Australia is the chief producer of Merino wool, though important quantities come also from South Africa and to some extent from Argentina. Considerable amounts of lamb are produced in New Zealand and the U.S.A. Of minor economic importance in some parts of Africa and the Middle East are the fat-tailed and fat-rumped sheep.

The distribution of pigs is based mainly on food supply and not climate; they are often kept in buildings, and so protected from the rigours of northern winters. The pig converts perishable by-products into human food—in Denmark and New Zealand from the butter and cheese-making industries, in Germany and Poland from small potatoes, in Canada and Australia from shrivelled grain unsuitable for milling. The maize growing areas of the 'corn belt' of America and S.E. Europe also support large numbers and tend to produce a lard type. The pig (especially the Chinese and Bantu type) is also a scavenger, and converts into food substances otherwise unfit for human consumption. The main products are pork, bacon and lard.

Trade in meat of sheep/goats is, by value, three times that of live sheep/goats. There are no particularly predominant flows of the latter and trade is mainly among the countries of the Middle East and Eastern Europe. The main flows (which account for 11% of total trade) in live sheep/goats are from Iran and Kuwait to Greece.

Trade in meat of pigs is, by value, four times that of live pigs. The main flows (which account for 40% of total trade) in live pigs are from China P.R. to Hong Kong and from Denmark to Germany F.R.

Forest Products

Forests   p. 25   Paper   p. 25

For individual country data see Statistical Supplement

Forests cover about 4 100 million hectares, 30% of the world's land surface. Their extent is just greater than the total agricultural area. Broadleaved forests are the more widespread, yet coniferous forests are of far greater industrial use and much more heavily cut. In 1963-5, 55% of total fellings were absorbed by industry; the rest was used as firewood. Sawlogs and veneer logs are the chief industrial uses taking 40% of total fellings in 1963-5. The largest single user is the pulp and paper industry, based on the coniferous forest belt of the northern hemisphere.

Conifers predominate in cool temperate climates; the northern limits are independent of the severity of the winter but require mean July temperatures of over 50°F (10°C). Where similar conditions prevail in mountainous regions conifers are dominant even in the tropics, but although in a more favourable environment conifers give way to hardwoods, they are not completely eliminated except in the wet tropics. The coniferous forest is tolerant of low rainfall but typically experiences a heavy snowfall. *Temperate hardwoods* are the principal trees where the mean annual temperature lies between 40°-65°F (4.5-18.5°C), frosts together with varying amounts of snow occur during the winter, and the annual rainfall exceeds 20 in. (500 mm.) A few hardwoods, such as birch, extend northwards or upwards almost as far as the conifers.

Tropical hardwoods are limited to regions which are frost-free and receive annually more than 20 in. (500 mm.) of rain. A reasonably distributed annual rainfall of at least 80 in. (2 000 mm.) is necessary for full development, but good timber may be produced with only 30 in. (750 mm.) falling during four months. If the precipitation is between 20-30 in. (500-750 mm.), the resulting small trees are only useful for special purposes. The mean annual temperature is normally over 75°F (24°C) and the coldest month not below 60°F (15.5°C).

Paper (and paperboard) is made from cellulose fibre usually obtained from wood. The main types of wood used are pine, spruce, poplar and aspen, but the use of harder woods such as beech and chestnut is extending. It is sometimes made from other fibres such as those derived from waste paper, cotton, linen, jute, hemp, straw, bagasse, esparto grass and papyrus (from which paper gets its name). There are two main methods of treating woodpulp. It can either be ground into pulp by mechanical milling under a flow of water, or reduced to small pieces and treated with chemicals which remove most of the lignin and other non-cellulose material. Pulp made in this way is stronger and superior in quality to that made by the mechanical method. Pulp derived from other fibrous materials is always made by the second (chemical) method. The pulp is drawn on to a continuous belt. As the fibres dry they adhere together to form the paper, which is finally wound on to reels. Cheap types of printing paper, like newsprint, are made from a mechanical or part mechanical pulp. Other printing and writing papers are usually made from chemical woodpulp, though a pulp with a high cotton rag or esparto grass content is used for fine grade book papers where special characteristics are required. For strong wrapping papers and packaging boards pure woodpulp (mechanical or chemical) is used, but for the cheaper types waste paper pulp is most frequently used.

Woodpulp can be treated to make the resultant paper and board waterproof, fire proof and resistant to acids. It can be beaten out to make the paper totally transparent. Once it is made, the paper can be coated with various substances. The coating most frequently used is china clay which gives the paper an extra smooth surface suitable for printing.

In this way paper and board can be made to suit many different applications from household and facial tissues to filter paper and insulating board; from book papers to building boards. This means that paper and board can successfully replace other materials such as wood, cloth, glass and metals. The rate of paper consumption per capita is regarded as a reliable indicator of national standards of living, with more affluent nations using more paper.

International trade in forest products (1963-5 av.)

Softwood[1] (S.I.T.C. no. 242.2/243.2)

Production[1]: 955 087 700 cu. metres 1963-5 av.; 734 953 000 1953-5 av.
Exports[2]: 82 401 000 cu. metres 1963-5 av.; 47 281 000 1953-5 av.
Percentage exported: 9% 1963-5 av.; 6% 1953-5 av.
Imports[2]: 80 781 000 cu. metres 1963-5 av.; 47 256 000 1953-5 av.

Exports:

	PERCENTAGE 1963-5 av.	1953-5 av.
Canada	31	34
U.S.S.R.	19	5
Sweden	11	16
U.S.A.	9	6
Finland	9	12
Austria	6	11
Romania	3	2
Brazil	3	3
Czechoslovakia	2	1
Poland	2	NA
Others	6	9
	100	100

Imports:

	PERCENTAGE 1963-5 av.	1953-5 av.
U.S.A.	25	25
U.K.	24	25
Germany F.R.	9	9
Japan	8	1
Italy	7	6
Netherlands	6	7
France	3	3
Germany D.R.	3	2
Canada	2	2
Denmark	2	2
Others	19	22
	100	100

Hardwood[1] (S.I.T.C. no. 242.3/243.3)

Production[1]: 978 419 300 cu. metres 1963-5 av.; 576 570 000 1953-5 av.
Exports[2]: 27 733 000 cu. metres 1963-5 av.; 10 990 000 1953-5 av.
Percentage exported: 3% 1963-5 av.; 2% 1953-5 av.
Imports[2]: 27 065 000 cu. metres 1963-5 av.; 9 998 000 1953-5 av.

Exports:

	PERCENTAGE 1963-5 av.	1953-5 av.
Philippines	24	22
Sabah	12	4
Ivory Coast	7	NA
Malaya	5	4
Gabon	4	NA
Sarawak	4	9
France	4	1
Romania	4	6
Ghana	4	4
Nigeria	3	4
Others	28	19
	100	100

Imports:

	PERCENTAGE 1963-5 av.	1953-5 av.
Japan	32	16
Germany F.R.	8	8
U.K.	7	17
Italy	5	4
France	5	14
U.S.A.	4	9
Singapore	3	4
Netherlands	2	4
Canada	2	6
Belg./Lux.	2	3
Others	27	NA
	100	100

Wood pulp[1,4] (S.I.T.C. no. 251.2, 6, 7, 8, 9)

Production[1]: 74 381 700 met. tons 1963-5 av.; 42 473 300 1953-5 av.
Exports[2]: 12 132 000 met. tons 1963-5 av.; 6 767 000 1953-5 av.
Percentage exported: 16% 1963-5 av.; 16% 1953-5 av.
Imports[2]: 12 023 300 met. tons 1963-5 av.; 6 649 000 1953-5 av.

Exports:

	PERCENTAGE 1963-5 av.	1953-5 av.
Sweden	28	33
Canada	27	29
Finland	17	17
U.S.A.	11	6
Norway	7	10
U.S.S.R.	2	1
Austria	2	NA
South Africa	6	NA
	100	100

Imports:

	PERCENTAGE 1963-5 av.	1953-5 av.
U.K.	24	29
U.S.A.	22	29
Germany F.R.	9	7
France	8	7
Italy	7	10
Japan	4	4
Netherlands	4	3
Austria	2	—
Others	20	11
	100	100

Paper[1] (S.I.T.C. no. 641)

Production[1]: 75 362 000 met. tons 1963-5 av.; 40 700 000 1953-5 av.
Exports[2]: 6 716 000 met. tons 1963-5 av.; 2 667 000 1953-5 av.
Percentage exported: 9% 1963-5 av.; 7% 1953-5 av.
Imports[2]: 6 446 700 met. tons 1963-5 av.; 2 546 700 1953-5 av.

Exports:

	PERCENTAGE 1963-5 av.	1953-5 av.
Finland	22	17
Sweden	21	22
U.S.A.	18	14
Netherlands	6	11
Norway	6	8
Canada	5	4
Italy	5	5
Austria	3	3
Japan	3	7
Others	15	16
	100	100

Imports:

	PERCENTAGE 1963-5 av.	1953-5 av.
Germany F.R.	19	9
U.K.	16	22
France	6	2
Belg./Lux.	6	4
Netherlands	6	5
Italy	3	2
Denmark	3	3
U.S.A.	3	7
Others	37	46
	100	100

Newsprint[1] (S.I.T.C. no. 641.1)

Production[1]: 16 086 000 met. tons 1963-5 av.; 10 600 000 1953-5 av.
Exports[2]: 8 442 700 met. tons 1963-5 av.; 6 227 000 1953-5 av.
Percentage exported: 52% 1963-5 av.; 55% 1953-5 av.
Imports[2]: 8 412 300 met. tons 1963-5 av.; 6 163 000 1953-5 av.

Exports:

	PERCENTAGE 1963-5 av.	1953-5 av.
Canada	72	81
Finland	12	7
Sweden	5	3
Norway	3	3
U.S.S.R.	1	—
New Zealand	1	2
U.S.A.	1	1
Austria	1	1
Chile	1	—
Others	3	4
	100	100

Imports:

	PERCENTAGE 1963-5 av.	1953-5 av.
U.S.A.	64	74
U.K.	14	16
Germany F.R.	6	5
Australia	3	3
Argentina	2	1
Denmark	1	1
India	1	1
France	1	1
Brazil	1	1
Others	13	10
	100	100

Use of softwood and hardwood (1963-5 av.)

SOFTWOOD 955 087 700 cu. metres
HARDWOOD 978 419 300 cu. metres

Production	SOFTWOOD PERCENTAGE	HARDWOOD PERCENTAGE
Sawlogs, veneer logs for sleepers	53	18
Pulpwood and pitprops	22	4
Other industrial wood	8	6
Fuelwood (incl. wood for charcoal)	17	72
	100	100

Proportion of land area forested

Figures in brackets indicate percentages of regional land area[3]

	FOREST	ARABLE	PERMANENT MEADOW	OTHER	TOTAL[2]
	MILLION HECTARES				
South America	911 (51)	75 (4)	309 (17)	485 (28)	1 780
U.S.S.R.	880 (39)	230 (10)	370 (17)	760 (34)	2 240
North America[10]	810 (33)	256 (11)	364 (15)	997 (41)	2 427
Africa	727 (24)	254 (8)	398 (13)	1 644 (54)	3 023
Asia[9]	449 (26)	450 (26)	152 (9)	690 (40)	1 741
Europe[11]	137 (28)	90 (18)	35 (7)	279 (57)	493
Oceania	77 (9)	114 (23)	460 (54)	178 (21)	853
China P.R.	178 (18)	109 (11)	612 (63)	—	976
World	4 070 (30)	1 461 (11)	2 521 (19)	5 481 (40)	13 533

Production of forest products (1963-5 av.)

Softwood removals[1,8]

955 087 700 cu. metres 1963-5 av.; 734 953 000 1953-5 av.

	PERCENTAGE 1963-5 av.	1953-5 av.
U.S.S.R.	32	32
U.S.A.	23	27
Canada	6	6
China P.R.	6*	5
Sweden	4	5
Japan	4	4
Finland	3	2
Brazil	2*	2
Germany F.R.	2	2
Others	15	13
	100	100

Hardwood removals[1,8]

978 419 300 cu. metres 1963-5 av.; 576 570 000 1953-5 av.

	PERCENTAGE 1963-5 av.	1953-5 av.
Brazil	14	16
U.S.A.	12*	9
Indonesia	9	11
China P.R.	7*	—
India	7	5
Nigeria	3*	4
Japan	3	4
France	3	4
Colombia	3	1
Others	44	49
	100	100

Paper production[1,6]

75 362 000 met. tons 1963-5 av.; 40 700 000 1953-5 av.

	PERCENTAGE 1963-5 av.	1953-5 av.
U.S.A.	39	45
Japan	16	8
Germany F.R.	7	8
U.K.	7	—
U.S.S.R.	5	4
China P.R.	4*	—
France	4	4
Canada	3*	—
Sweden	3*	—
Others	12	20
	100	100

Wood pulp production[1,6]

74 381 700 met. tons 1963-5 av.; 42 473 300 1953-5 av.

	PERCENTAGE 1963-5 av.	1953-5 av.
U.S.A.	40	45
Canada	16	20
Sweden	8	—
Finland	7	—
Japan	7	—
U.S.S.R.	4	—
Norway	3*	—
Germany F.R.	2	—
France	2	—
Others	12	10
	100	100

Newsprint production[1]

16 086 000 met. tons 1963-5 av.; 10 600 000 1953-5 av.

	PERCENTAGE 1963-5 av.	1953-5 av.
Canada	41	51
U.S.A.	12	11
Japan	6	5
Finland	5	6
U.K.	5	6
Sweden	4	4*
U.S.S.R.	4	3
France	3	—
China P.R.	2*	—
Others	15	12
	100	100

Timber (1963-5 av.)

Modified Gall Projection

Removals (million cu. metres)[1]

Circle sizes: 81 AND OVER; 27-81; 9-27; 3-9; 0.5-1

Roundwood

Type: SOFTWOOD (CONIFEROUS) / HARDWOOD (BROADLEAVED)

Use: INDUSTRIAL / FUELWOOD

SCALE 1:76 MILLION   1 CM TO 760 KM
SCALE 1:40 MILLION

Total removals

	NORTH AMERICA	ASIA	U.S.S.R.	EUROPE[3]	BRAZIL	CHINA P.R.	OTHERS	WORLD[2] MILLION CUBIC METRES
1963-5 av.	23	18	17	7	7	11	11	1 934
1953-5 av.	23	18	16	8	7	8	13	1 312

	NORTH AMERICA	U.S.S.R.	U.S.A.	BRAZIL	AFRICA[1]	SOUTH AMERICA[2]	PACIFIC
1963-5 av.	19	16	7	46	51	11	11
1953-5 av.	23	37	8	18	7	11	12

© Oxford University Press

Paper

Production centres (1965)

Annual output ('000 met. tons)
- 400 & OVER
- 200 – 400
- 100 – 200
- 50 – 100

+ Data not available but reported to be in at least the smallest category

Forests

Predominant types
- BROADLEAVED
- CONIFEROUS
- MIXED

Modified Gall Projection
Equatorial Scale 1:88 Million approx.

Major trade flows (1966)

Commodity : S.I.T.C.no.
- PAPER (PAPERBOARD) 641
- PAPER PRODUCTS - 642

Value($U.S.)
0.5mm represents increments of $40 million

Paper production

	met. tons 1963-5 av.	
91 422 000		
51 247 000		

	PERCENTAGE	
	1963-5 av.	1953-5 av.
U.S.A.	39	46
Canada	10	13
Japan	8	4
U.K.	5	6
Germany F.R.	4	4
U.S.S.R.	4	3
France	3	3
Finland	3	2
China P.R.	3	—
Others	21	18
	100	100

*Excl. China P. R.

Value($U.S.)
($MILLIONS)
- 680
- 520
- 360
- 200
- 40
- 77 UNDER $20 MILLION
- VALUE IN $ MILLIONS

SCALE 1:29 MILLION 1 CM TO 290 KM

© Oxford University Press

25

26

Fish/Fish Products

Fish   p. 27

For individual country data see Statistical Supplement

In general fish feed on minute organisms in sea water, called plankton, or the small invertebrates (and/or other fish) which themselves feed on plankton. The productivity of the oceans in these organisms varies with climatological, physiological and oceanographical conditions, and the number of fish and other large sea animals is directly dependent on the fertility of the water. On the whole the open ocean of the tropics is less productive than the open ocean of higher latitudes. However there are some regions in the tropics which show a marked fertility, where the upwelling currents, such as the Humboldt current off the coast of Peru, bring the deeper, richer water to the surface and encourage a high rate of production, sometimes even exceeding the productivity of the Antarctic.

The marine fisheries are of two kinds, pelagic and demersal. Pelagic fisheries exploit fish living near the surface (herring) while demersal fisheries exploit fish feeding on the bottom-living invertebrate animals found in the shallow regions of seas (cod) and in coastal waters (shrimps).

Successful commercial fishing requires large shoals of fish of one species, numerous enough to withstand regular exploitation, within economic distances of markets. The areas most heavily fished at present are the commercial fishing grounds shown on the map, although almost all other coastal areas are fished to some extent. The fertile tropical waters are, as yet, only exploited for tuna, which is also caught in coastal waters.

Fish is a rich source of protein, and could become a valuable addition to the diet of many undernourished peoples. With modern technology more distant grounds, such as those of the North Atlantic and Arctic, have been fished, and markets further inland have been penetrated. But demand is still limited by a lack of taste for fish in many countries and by inadequate technical resources in others. Developing countries find it hard to provide trained crews and the large and costly trawlers needed for modern ocean fishing, and the marketing of fresh fish presents special difficulties.

Not only is demand very variable, but there are daily and seasonal variations in supply and fresh fish is extremely perishable. It is therefore necessary to have expensive facilities for the rapid distribution of fresh fish and for preserving what cannot be sold immediately by freezing, salting, smoking, drying or canning. Some fish are also used to make oils, meals, glues and fertilizers. Preserving and processing give the trade some protection from violent fluctuations in the price of fresh fish, and sometimes provide the main market, as with the canning of salmon and sardines and the manufacture of oil and meal from South African pilchards, the American menhaden and the Peruvian anchovy.

The following table shows the relative importance of various species in total world catch.

Catch by species[1]

	51 340 000 met tons 1963-5 av.	27 470 000 1953-5 av.
		PERCENTAGE
		1963-5 av.	1953-5 av.
Herring, sardine, anchovy		33	23
Freshwater fish[2]/diadromous fish		13	14
Cod, hake, haddock		12	16
Mullet, jack, sea bass etc.		10	11
Molluscs		5	6
Tuna, bonito, mackerel etc.		5	6
Crustacea/other invertebrates		2	3
Flounder, halibut, sole		2	1
Salmon, trout, smelt		1	1
Shark, ray etc.		1	1
Aquatic animals and plants		1	—
Unsorted/unidentified		15	14
		100	100

[1]Excl. whales   [2]Excl. salmon, trout, smelt

industry. The salmon is caught in the rivers to which it returns to spawn after it has spent two or more years in the sea. The Pacific salmon usually dies after spawning. Pollution of rivers has severely affected catches in many countries and rivers have to be restocked periodically. In Canada artificial salmon pools have been constructed.

The main centres of the sturgeon fishing industry are the U.S.S.R. and the U.S.A. where the meat is either canned or fresh-frozen. The sturgeon, fished for both its meat and roe (from which caviar is made) is found from Scandinavia to the Mediterranean and from the St. Lawrence to the Gulf of Mexico. It has been greatly depleted by over-fishing.

Fishing in the North American Great Lakes and in British Columbia exploits the salmon trout. Another economically important fish is the Lake Whitefish of Canada and the U.S.A.

Commercial breeding of carp, a fish originally indigenous to Asia, is widespread in Europe and Asia. It has also been introduced into North America, where an annual catch of some 15 000 tons comes largely from the Mississippi River basin.

Pond and lake breeding of fish is practised in many countries to increase supplies of protein foods. In the U.S.S.R., Israel, China P.R. (where fish culture goes back to 2000 B.C.), Hungary, Italy, the Netherlands, Denmark, Czechoslovakia (where fish culture began in the sixteenth century), India, Malaya and the U.S.A. mainly carp and eel are bred. Fish meal is used as a cheap means of feeding and fattening the fish.

Whales are widely distributed in both hemispheres and generally migrate to tropical waters during the winter and into higher latitudes during the summer. It is during the summer feeding period that they are taken, mainly in the Antarctic. Overfishing is a danger as whales breed slowly compared with fish. To combat this the International Whaling Commission decides the number to be killed in the Antarctic from year to year. Processing of whales today is almost entirely carried out on factory ships, which form part of the whaling fleets.

Freshwater fishing is an important sector of the fishing industry. The most important fish caught in freshwater is the salmon. The Atlantic salmon is found on both sides of the North Atlantic, while the Pacific salmon species, chum, pink and red salmon, are found from northern Japan to Alaska and southwards as far as San Francisco Bay, California. Red and pink salmon are mainly used in the canning

Catch by species (1965)

Selected countries

	FRESHWATER[1]	SALMON SMELT TROUT	STURGEON	FLOUNDER HALIBUT	COD HAKE HADDOCK	HERRING SARDINE ANCHOVY	MULLET JACK SEA BASS	TUNA BONITO MACKEREL	SHARK RAY	CRUSTACEA	MOLLUSCS	OTHERS	TOTAL
Peru	80.0	0.2	—	—	—	7 256.8	28.5	78.5	7.6	0.6	4.6	5.2	7461.9
Japan	59.9	184.5	—	216.3	781.0	494.4	1 455.0	1 396.7	66.9	134.2	1 138.1	980.7	6,907.7
U.S.S.R.	807.0	153.2	16.8	158.8	1 380.8	1 347.3	881.6	36.5	3.7	49.3	NA	NA	5099.9
U.S.A.	90.2	158.4	0.5	106.9	168.6	841.1	159.9	257.8	7.2	283.1	646.9	3.7	2,724.3
Norway	0.5	219.2	—	23.7	648.0	1 089.2	161.0	23.5	32.2	14.4	10.8	84.8	2307.3
Spain	10.7[1]	1.8	—	14.1	475.0	250.2	88.0	97.9	11.4	17.9	109.3	84.8	1,341.5
India	517.6	—	—	1.8	5.5	359.8	207.3	17.5	31.4	79.7	0.3	22.0	1 331.3
Canada	37.6	75.0	0.2	126.7	414.4	385.3	63.8	3.3[1]	0.4	20.8	89.4	31.2	1 262.3
Iceland	—	49.7	—	9.8	330.0	762.9	—	6.9	0.4	4.6	0.2	3.4	1 199.0
U.K.	0.8	2.6	—	63.9	701.8	161.3	32.8	139.7	24.7	13.3	14.5	28.3	1,047.3
Denmark	3.5	14.3	—	61.1	210.3	350.2	26.4	6.9	1.5	6.9	18.3	28.1	840.8
Chile	—	—	—	0.3	106.0	481.6	425.6	36.5	0.4	24.5	36.7	7.2	708.5
Philippines	80.7	—	—	4.7	—	95.9	—	54.0	NA	22.9	10.0	NA	685.7
South Africa	0.1	—	—	1.8	87.0	412.7	—	17.9	0.5	8.4	1.8	30.6	663.9
Mexico	3.9	—	—	0.3	—	30.8	32.9	—	5.1	62.2	40.9	62.4	256.4
Greece	12.0	—	—	1.8	4.1	30.7	21.3	5.7	4.4	2.8	4.9	36.3	124.0
Australia	0.6	—	—	0.1	—	0.7	24.1	11.2	4.8	17.9	18.5	1.7	79.6
Ghana	2.0	—	—	1.7	—	7.8	29.3	11.0	4.8	—	4.0	11.9	72.5

[1]Excl. salmon, smelt, trout, sturgeon   [1]Incomplete data   [1]Mackerel only

---

International trade in fish/fish products

(1963-5 av.)

Aquatic animal oils and fats

Production

	721 000 met. tons 1963-5 av.[1]	
	697 000 met. tons 1953	
		PERCENTAGE
		1963-5	1953
Peru		19	NA
Japan		18	5
U.S.A.		12	13
Iceland		11	6
Norway		9	34
South Africa[1]		7	9
U.S.S.R.		6	NA
Denmark		5	NA
Germany F.R.		2	NA
Others		11	NA
		100	100

Exports

	697 000 met. tons 1963-5 av.	
	371 200 1953	
		PERCENTAGE
		1963-5 av.	1953
U.K.		23	28
Germany F.R.		16	35
Netherlands		12	4
Norway		9	4
U.S.A.		5	5
France		5	3
U.S.S.R.		4	NA
Denmark		4	NA
Others		16	NA
		100	100

Imports

	769 000 met. tons 1963-5 av.	
	586 400 1953	
		PERCENTAGE
		1963-5 av.	1953
			(97% 1963-5 av.)
			(NA 1953-5 av.)

[1]Incl. South West Africa

Whale oil

Production[3]

	379 200 met. tons 1963-5 av.	
	464 300 1953-5 av.	

Exports

Specific export data are not available but the major producers in both 1963-5 and 1953-5 were Norway and Japan. In 1953-5 Norway exported mostly to the U.K. and Japan to Germany F.R. By 1963-5 both had extended their markets to include other countries of Western Europe, and Japan also exported to China P.R. The other major producer of whale oil in 1963-5, the U.S.S.R., retained the whole of its production for domestic consumption.

[3]Incl. sperm oil

Fish/Fish products

(S.I.T.C. no. 03)

Production

	51 330 000 met. tons 1963-5 av.	
	27 470 000 1953-5 av.	
		PERCENTAGE
		1963-5 av.
Peru		25
Japan		9
Norway		8
South Africa		6
Denmark		6
Canada		5
Sweden		4
U.S.S.R.		4
Others		26
		100

Exports

	5 912 000 met. tons 1963-5 av.	
	Data for 1953-5 av. not available	

Imports

	5 912 000 met. tons 1963-5 av.	
	Data for 1953-5 av. not available	

Percentage exported

	12% 1963-5 av.	
	NA 1953-5 av.	

Percentage exported

	97% 1963-5 av.	
	NA 1953-5 av.	

Imports

	5 888 000 met. tons 1963-5 av.	
	NA 1953-5 av.	
		PERCENTAGE
		1963-5 av.
U.S.A.		15
Germany F.R.		13
U.K.		12
France		5
Netherlands		5
Italy		4
Denmark		3
Belg./Lux.		3
Japan		3
Others		35
		100

Types of fish and products traded

	1963-5 av.	
	2 457 000 met. tons	
		PERCENTAGE
	1963-5	1950-3 av.
		13
Aquatic animal meals and solubles	38	13
Fresh and frozen fish	26	22
Aquatic animal oils and fats	12	23
Canned fish and preparations	9	11
Dried, salted and smoked fish	9	21
Crustacea and molluscs	5	7
Canned crustacea and molluscs	1	3
	100	100

Whale oil production[3]

	1963-5 av.	
	5 806 000 met. tons	
		PERCENTAGE

Major producers	JAPAN	U.S.S.R.	NORWAY	SOUTH AFRICA	OTHERS	WORLD MET. TONS
1963-5 av.	40	31	11	4	14	379 200
1953-5 av.	14	9	34	7	34	464 300

[1]Fish oil   [3]Incl. sperm oil

Marine catch (by region)

	44 770 000 met. tons 1963-5 av.	
	23 900 000 1953-5 av.	

	PACIFIC					ATLANTIC					INDIAN OCEAN		MEDITERRANEAN/ BLACK SEA
	N.	CENTRAL	SW.	E. CENTRAL	W. CENTRAL	NW.	NE.	CENTRAL	SW.	E. CENTRAL	W.	E.	
1963-5 av.	11	3	1	19	2	8	19	1	1	4	3	2	3
1953-5 av.	12	24	2	1	10	37	4	2	3	2	3		3

Freshwater catch

	6 570 000 met. tons 1963-5 av.	
	3 570 000 1953-5 av.	
		PERCENTAGE
		1963-5 av.	1953-5 av.
Asia		70	56
Africa		14	14
U.S.S.R.		11	21
Europe		3	3
South America		2	3
North America			3
		100	100

Fishing

Fishing

Fishing grounds
- commercial
- other

Type
- Trawling (shrimps, prawns, etc.)
- Trawling (cod, flatfish, sea bream, etc.)
- Purse-seine (herring, anchovy, tuna, etc.)
- over exploited

Regional catch (1963-5 av.) (met. tons)
- 0.05 MILLION
- 1 MILLION

World fishing map showing North Pacific, East Central Pacific, West Central Pacific, SW Pacific, SE Pacific, NW Atlantic, NE Atlantic, West Central Atlantic, East Central Atlantic, SW Atlantic, SE Atlantic, West Indian Ocean, East Indian Ocean, and continents. Tuna grounds marked; Africa, Europe, Asia, U.S.S.R., North America, South America labelled. Mediterranean Sea, Black Sea shown.

Fish

Fish (1963–5 av.)

Landings (000 metric tons)

- 1801–3400
- 601–1800
- 181–600
- 61–180
- 16–60
- 0–15
- DATA NOT AVAILABLE

Modified Gall Projection
Equatorial Scale 1:88 Million approx.

Landings represent the weight of the cleaned or processed fish at the time of landing. Catches represent the live weight equivalent of landings.

Major trade flows (1966)

Commodity: S.I.T.C. no.¹ 03

FISH/PREPARATIONS	($ MILLIONS)
Value ($U.S.) 0.5mm represents increments of $ 30 million	390
	270
	150
	30
	UNDER $15 MILLION
	VALUE IN $ MILLIONS

---- 17

¹ S.I.T.C. = STANDARD INTERNATIONAL TRADE CLASSIFICATION

Fish catches

51 340 000 met. tons 1963–5 av.
27 470 000 1953–5 av.

	PERCENTAGE	
	1963–5 av.	1953–5 av.
Peru	15	1
Japan	13	17
U.S.S.R.	9	8
U.S.A.	5	10
Norway	3	7
India	2	3
Canada	2	3
Spain	2	3
Indonesia	1	2
Others	48	46
	100	100

27

© Oxford University Press

Fibres/Textiles

For individual country data see Statistical Supplement

The manufacture of textiles in their various forms is one of the world's leading industries, and in many of the less-industrialized countries is the biggest single source of industrial employment. Textiles are manufactured from natural fibres, man-made fibres or mixtures of both. Natural fibres are still by far the most important, but man-made fibres now make up about 30% of world consumption, as shown below.

Consumption of fibres (kg. per capita)

	1938	1954-6	1959-61	1964-6
Cotton	2.9	3.3	3.4	3.2
Wool	0.4	0.5	0.5	0.6
Cellulosic fibre	0.4	0.8	0.9	0.8
Non-cellulosic fibre	—	0.1	0.2	0.6

Coir is a soft, water-resistant fibre found between the outer husk of the coconut and the shell of the inner kernel. It is of three main types: bristle fibre; curl, tow or mattress fibre; and mat fibre, used in ropes, twinings and matting. The only important producers are India, Ceylon, which exports mainly fibre.

Kapok is the floss obtained from the pods of the kapok tree, cultivated in Java and to a lesser degree in other parts of Indonesia, India, Pakistan, Ceylon, Ecuador, Indo-China and other tropical areas. It is very light, resilient, moisture-proof and is used in bedding, upholstery, in thermal and sound insulation and as a substitute for cork.

Hemp is found between the bark and the pith in the stem of the *Cannabis sativa* plant found in humid regions within the temperate zone, where the mid-season temperatures average between 60°F (15.5°C) and 80°F (26.5°C), and the frost-free period exceeds four months. Moist soils, rich in organic matter, are the most suitable especially if they are calcareous. Hemp fibre is used mainly for small cordage.

Agave fibres are used primarily in cordage industries. Abaca (Manila hemp) is a strong, hard fibre with a natural resistance to wind, rain, sun and rubbing, making abaca rope particularly useful as marine hawser. It is obtained from *Musa textilis*, a species of banana, grown in the Philippines and Central America under warm humid conditions. Sisal is the most widely used substitute for abaca, although used more for twine than for rope. It is particularly drought resistant and is grown in the dry tropical climates of East Africa, Brazil, Haiti and Java. Henequen, a soft fibre, is similar to sisal, although it is not so strong and is used mostly for inferior twines. It is grown in Cuba and Mexico.

Some flax plants are grown for fibre, others primarily for linseed, though they yield fibre as a by-product. From this fibre a variety of linen goods are produced for domestic and industrial use, but demand is declining, partly as a result of substitution. Jute is vital to the world food economy because it is a cheap material readily converted into sacking for agricultural produce. Yet only two countries, India and Pakistan, grow it to any extent. Jute, sisal, abaca and hemp, with their specialized industrial uses, do not seriously compete with cotton, wool and man-made fibres.

Cotton is unsurpassed for sheer volume of output and versatility in use among fibres. The U.A.R. produces the finest long staple cotton but the greatest production is of cheap, medium staple in the U.S.A. India produces mainly the coarse and short varieties. Cotton demands a long hot growing season but is grown under a wide range of annual rainfall. Best results are obtained when the period of maturation coincides with a dry period. The summer isotherm of 77°F (25°C) and a 200-day frost-free period are the economic limits of cultivation in the U.S.A., although the rainfall variation is 23-60 in. (600-1 500 mm). After cotton has been picked, the seed is separated from the fibre (ginning), crushed to extract oil, and the residue used as cattle feed. The fibres are pressed into bales and subsequently made into a wide range of products from light cloth to heavy tarpaulins.

Wool gives warmth without weight and will absorb water without feeling wet and is thus an important fibre in the clothing industry. There are two types of wool yarn: worsted, where the fibres are combed parallel and tightly spun to form a firm smooth yarn used to make worsted cloth; and woollen, where the fibres lie in all directions and result in a soft, fuzzy yarn used to make blankets and woollen cloth.

Man-made fibres, in contrast to the older fibres, are produced mainly from materials readily available in Western Europe and North America. They are of two main origins. Regenerated fibres, of which the principal example is viscose rayon, derive from vegetable or animal materials in which the physical or chemical form has been changed. Synthetic fibres, such as nylon, polyester or glass fibres, are built up from chemical or mineral constituents. Thus there is a very close relationship between the synthetic fibre industry and the chemical industry.

Fibres are, for the most part, grown for the **textile industries**, of which the cotton industry is by far the largest and most widely spread; cotton manufacturing often appears in the earliest stages of industrialization, particularly in cotton growing areas. The British, West European and Japanese industries can obtain cotton only from imports, and a highly organized market for raw cotton has grown up, with New Orleans, Memphis, New York, Alexandria and Liverpool as the main centres. In Japan and the U.S.A. the bulk of cotton cloth comes from integrated concerns which both spin and weave. Elsewhere this vertical integration is much less marked, despite the existence of large combines.

The wool industry produces both woollens made from new wool to shoddy (i.e. re-manufactured fibres), and worsteds which use only new wool. In many countries, the wool industry was originally based on domestic raw materials, but this is no longer true of the world's major producers. Much of the raw wool entering world trade is sold by auction in London and Sydney. The silk industry, heavily concentrated in Japan, has suffered severely from first rayon and then nylon, which has come to displace silk in the manufacture of high-grade hosiery for women. The rapid development of man-made fibres is breaking down some of the traditional distinction between the cotton and wool textile industries; mixtures of such fibres with either wool or cotton are becoming increasingly common.

International trade in yarns/textiles (1963-5 av.)

Cotton yarn[1]

Production: 8 131 000 met. tons 1963-5 av.; 6 958 000 1953-5 av.
Percentage exported: 3% 1963-5 av.; 2% 1953-5 av.

Exports: 231 900 met. tons 1963-5 av.; 123 700 1953-5 av.

PERCENTAGE	1963-5 av.	1953-5 av.
U.A.R.	14	7
Pakistan	10	10
Italy	9	7
Belgium	7	18
Others	60	65
	100	100

Imports: 205 000 met. tons 1963-5 av.; 101 300 1953-5 av.

PERCENTAGE	1963-5 av.	1953-5 av.
Germany F.R.	14	5
Netherlands	5	13
U.K.	8	4
Belgium	7	2
Others	63	76
	100	100

Cotton cloth

Production: 5 500 800 met. tons 1963-5 av.; 3 440 900 1953-5 av.
Percentage exported: 13% 1963-5 av.; 15% 1953-5 av.

Exports: 786 200 met. tons 1963-5 av.; 525 000 1953-5 av.

PERCENTAGE	1963-5 av.	1953-5 av.
Japan	18	21
India	8	16
China P.R.*	8	...
Hong Kong	59	60
Others		
	100	100

Imports: 735 100 met. tons 1963-5 av.; 488 100 1953-5 av.

PERCENTAGE	1963-5 av.	1953-5 av.
U.K.	13	9
U.S.A.	9	2
Indonesia	5	12
Hong Kong	6	3
Others	68	78
	100	100

*Excl. China P.R.

Wool yarn[3]

Production: 1 880 700 met. tons 1963-5 av.; 1 366 600 1953-5 av.
Percentage exported: 6% 1963-5 av.; 4% 1953-5 av.

Exports: 104 800 met. tons 1963-5 av.; 56 000 1953-5 av.

PERCENTAGE	1963-5 av.	1953-5 av.
France	24	32
Belgium	24	21
U.K.	14	22
Italy	11	4
Others	27	21
	100	100

Imports: 96 500 met. tons 1963-5 av.; 51 100 1953-5 av.

PERCENTAGE	1963-5 av.	1953-5 av.
Germany F.R.	35	26
Netherlands	13	17
Belgium	7	5
Denmark	5	4
Others	40	48
	100	100

Woven wool fabrics[2,5]

Production: 685 100 met. tons 1963-5 av.; 256 800 1953-5 av.
Percentage exported: 18% 1963-5 av.; 32% 1953-5 av.

Exports: 125 500 met. tons 1963-5 av.; 83 000 1953-5 av.

PERCENTAGE	1963-5 av.	1953-5 av.
Italy	45	33
U.K.	18	35
Belgium	8	4
Japan	8	9
Others	20	19
	100	100

Imports: 99 600 met. tons 1963-5 av.; 57 400 1953-5 av.

PERCENTAGE	1963-5 av.	1953-5 av.
Germany F.R.	27	9
U.S.A.	11	10
Netherlands	9	3
U.K.	9	12
France	44	57
Others		
	100	100

*Worsted and woollen

International trade in fibres (1963-5 av.)

Cotton lint[1] (S.I.T.C. no. 263)

Production: 11 493 000 met. tons 1963-5 av.; 7 367 000 1953-5 av.
Percentage exported: 33% 1963-5 av.; 33% 1953-5 av.

Exports: 3 766 400 met. tons 1963-5 av.; 2 549 000 1953-5 av.

PERCENTAGE	1963-5 av.	1953-5 av.
U.S.A.	27	28
U.S.S.R.	10	4
Mexico	10	11
U.A.R.	8	12
Others	45	45
	100	100

Imports: 3 738 800 met. tons 1963-5 av.; 2 553 300 1953-5 av.

PERCENTAGE	1963-5 av.	1953-5 av.
Japan	19	19
Germany F.R.	8	11
France	7	11
U.K.	6	13
Others	60	48
	100	100

Flax[4] (S.I.T.C. no. 265.1)

Production: 666 100 met. tons 1963-5 av.; 247 000 1953-5 av.
Percentage exported: 64% 1963-5 av.; 49% 1953-5 av.

Exports: 426 400 met. tons 1963-5 av.; 121 300 1953-5 av.

PERCENTAGE	1963-5 av.	1953-5 av.
Netherlands	34	18
France	29	5
Belg./Lux.	22	70
Others	15	7
	100	100

Imports: 408 100 met. tons 1963-5 av.; 121 700 1953-5 av.

PERCENTAGE	1963-5 av.	1953-5 av.
Belg./Lux.	62	12
U.K.	11	35
France	5	9
Others	22	44
	100	100

Abaca-Manila hemp[7] (S.I.T.C. no. 265.5)

Production: 116 700 met. tons 1963-5; 130 000 1953-5 av.
Percentage exported: 97% 1963-5 av.; 94% 1953-5 av.

Exports: 113 600 met. tons 1963-5 av.; 122 000 1953-5 av.

PERCENTAGE	1963-5 av.	1953-5 av.
Philippines	93	87
Malaysia	4	2
Others	3	11
	100	100

Imports: 107 400 met. tons 1963-5 av.; 118 000 1953-5 av.

PERCENTAGE	1963-5 av.	1953-5 av.
U.S.A.	28	35
Japan	28	26
U.K.	16	14
Others	28	25
	100	100

Hemp (S.I.T.C. no. 265.2)

Production: 336 500 met. tons 1963-5 av.; 346 700 1953-5 av.
Percentage exported: 12% 1963-5 av.; 16% 1953-5 av.

Exports: 41 200 met. tons 1963-5 av.; 55 500 1953-5 av.

PERCENTAGE	1963-5 av.	1953-5 av.
India	26	17
Yugoslavia	20	27
Hungary	11	...
Others	36	53
	100	100

Imports: 36 600 met. tons 1963-5 av.; 55 700 1953-5 av.

PERCENTAGE	1963-5 av.	1953-5 av.
Italy	20	27
Germany F.R.	12	21
U.K.	12	...
Others	46	50
	100	100

Wool[3] (S.I.T.C. no. 262.1/262.2)

Production: 1 507 000 met. tons 1963-5 av.; 1 060 000 1953-5 av.
Percentage exported: 59% 1963-5 av.; 69% 1953-5 av.

Exports: 895 500 met. tons 1963-5 av.; 732 000 1953-5 av.

PERCENTAGE	1963-5 av.	1953-5 av.
Australia	43	41
New Zealand	19	19
Argentina	8	10
South Africa	7	8
Others	21	22
	100	100

Imports: 934 900 met. tons 1963-5 av.; 722 000 1953-5 av.

PERCENTAGE	1963-5 av.	1953-5 av.
U.K.	19	31
Japan	15	7
U.S.A.	8	16
France	10	14
Others	46	32
	100	100

Jute[5] (S.I.T.C. no. 264)

Production: 3 283 000 met. tons 1963-5 av.; 1 833 000 1953-5 av.
Percentage exported: 26% 1963-5 av.; 53% 1953-5 av.

Exports: 856 300 met. tons 1963-5 av.; 974 300 1953-5 av.

PERCENTAGE	1963-5 av.	1953-5 av.
Pakistan	89	98
India	3	—
Belg./Lux.	5	2
Others	3	—
	100	100

Imports: 983 300 met. tons 1963-5 av.; 961 700 1953-5 av.

PERCENTAGE	1963-5 av.	1953-5 av.
U.K.	13	15
France	10	10
Belg./Lux.	10	8
Others	67	67
	100	100

Sisal/Henequen[7] (S.I.T.C. no. 265.4)

Production: 871 500 met. tons 1963-5 av.; 536 700 1953-5 av.
Percentage exported: 71% 1963-5 av.; 86% 1953-5 av.

Exports: 622 300 met. tons 1963-5 av.; 460 700 1953-5 av.

PERCENTAGE	1963-5 av.	1953-5 av.
Tanzania	34	34
Brazil	22	15
Kenya	10	8
Others	34	42
	100	100

Imports: 600 000 met. tons 1963-5 av.; 443 300 1953-5 av.

PERCENTAGE	1963-5 av.	1953-5 av.
U.S.A.	15	34
U.K.	12	15
France	10	8
Others	63	43
	100	100

Silk[8] (S.I.T.C. no. 261)

Production: 32 400 met. tons 1963-5 av.; 24 000 1953-5 av.
Percentage exported: 36% 1963-5 av.; 29% 1953-5 av.

Exports: 11 700 met. tons 1963-5 av.; 7 000 1953-5 av.

PERCENTAGE	1963-5 av.	1953-5 av.
Japan	26	65
China P.R.*	18	16
U.S.S.R.	13	...
Others	43	19
	100	100

Imports: 11 900 met. tons 1963-5 av.; 6 000 1953-5 av.

PERCENTAGE	1963-5 av.	1953-5 av.
Italy	30	51
U.S.A.	25	2
Japan	13	...
Others	32	42
	100	100

Non-cellulosic fibres

Production: 1 692 000 met. tons 1963-5 av.; 205 900 1953-5 av.
Percentage exported: 17% 1963-5 av.; NA 1953-5 av.

Exports: 282 700 met. tons 1963-5 av.; *Data for 1953-5 av. not available*

PERCENTAGE	1963-5 av.	1953-5 av.
Germany F.R.	16	9
U.S.A.	15	7
Italy	14	6
France	8	...
Others	47	...
	100	100

Imports: 258 900 met. tons 1963-5 av.; *Data for 1953-5 av. not available*

PERCENTAGE	1963-5 av.	1953-5 av.
U.K.	16	...
Germany F.R.	13	...
Belgium	7	...
France	6	...
U.S.A.	6	...
Others	64	...
	100	100

Cellulosic fibres

Production: 3 227 900 met. tons 1963-5 av.; 2 065 900 1953-5 av.
Percentage exported: 18% 1963-5 av.; 13% 1953-5 av.

Exports: 574 400 met. tons 1963-5 av.; 269 000 1953-5 av.

PERCENTAGE	1963-5 av.	1953-5 av.
Germany F.R.	18	16
Japan	17	20
Italy	13	9
U.K.	8	9
France	8	7
Others	35	...
	100	100

Imports: 447 500 met. tons 1963-5 av.; 145 700 1953-5 av.

PERCENTAGE	1963-5 av.	1953-5 av.
U.S.S.R.	13	...
U.S.A.	11	32
China P.R.	10	...
Germany F.R.	7	12
South Africa	7	4
Others	52	52
	100	100

Footnotes: [1] Estimate. [2] Excl. China P.R., U.S.S.R. and Eastern Europe. [3] Clean basis. [4] Fibre, tow and waste. [5] Incl. kenaf. [6] 1963-5 data for raw cotton other than linters. [7] Incl. other agave fibres. [8] Raw. *Excl. China P.R.

Wool Yarn

Wool yarn (1965)

Production centres — spindles installed

- ● Major — 100 000 AND OVER
- ● Secondary — 50 001 – 100 000
- ● Minor — 10 001 – 50 000
- + Data not available but reported to be at least a minor production centre

Sheep
One dot represents 100 000 head of sheep

Major trade flows (1966)
Commodity: S.I.T.C.no.

Value ($ U.S.)
0.5mm represents increments of $20 million

Modified Gall Projection
Equatorial Scale 1: 88 Million approx.

© Oxford University Press

Wool spindles

Number installed, end of year
(in thousands)

	1965	1955
U.K.	3897	4971
Italy	1700	1608
Japan	1700	1779
U.S.A.	1223	1768
France	1191	2124
Germany F.R.	1042	1201
Spain	560	589
Poland	554	NA
Belgium	485	777
Argentina	375	NA

Wool yarn production

1 860 700 met. tons 1963-5 av.
1 366 400 1953-5 av.

	PERCENTAGE	
	1963-5 av.	1953-5 av.
U.K.	14	18
U.S.S.R.	13	17
U.S.A.	13	23
Italy	9	NA
Japan	8	6
France	8	9
Germany F.R.	6	8
Belgium	3	3
Poland	3	4
Others	23	NA
	100	100

29

Flax/Jute

Production (1963-5 av.)
One dot represents 5 000 metric tons
- flax
- jute (including kenaf)

Major trade flows
Commodity : S.I.T.C.no.

| FLAX,FLAX TOW,WASTE | : 265.1 |
| JUTE | : 264 |

JUTE WOVEN FABRICS

Value ($ U.S.)
0.5mm represents increments of $20 million

Flax fibre production (1966)
666 100 met. tons 1963-5 av.
247 000 1953-5 av.[1]

| | PERCENTAGE | |
	1963-5 av.	1953-5 av.[1]
U.S.S.R.	59	44
France	11	15
Poland	8	21
Belgium	6	15
Netherlands	5	16
Czechoslovakia	3	NA
U.K.	1	NA
Others	7	NA
	100	100

[1] Excl. U.S.S.R.

Jute production[1]
3 283 000 met. tons 1963-5 av.
1 833 000 1953-5 av.[2]

| | PERCENTAGE | |
	1963-5 av.	1953-5 av.[2]
India	39	44
Pakistan	33	46
China P.R.	12	...[3]
Thailand	6	...[3]
Brazil	2	1
U.S.S.R.	2	NA
Nepal	1	NA
Others	5	NA
	100	100

[1] Incl. kenaf [2] Excl. China P.R. [3] Only kenaf

Natural and synthetic rubber

Natural rubber is primarily derived from the bast tissues just underneath the bark of the tree, *Hevea brasiliensis*. When a shallow incision is made in the bark (tapping) a white viscous juice, latex (which is 60% water) flows out. This is collected and processed in one of two ways: either the juice is taken direct to the factory where the water is largely removed by a centrifuge to produce concentrated latex—see later—or acid is added to encourage coagulation of the rubber particles and partial separation of the water. This coagulum is further processed to remove dirt followed by mechanical pressure and drying. *Hevea*, a native of the Amazon was first introduced into Ceylon, Indonesia and Malaya in the 1870's. The subsequent rapid expansion of the planted areas arose from the tremendous demand for rubber for the new motor industry. Few commodities have ever achieved so fast a pre-eminent place amongst the world's key raw materials. The great growth of natural rubber output in this century can be ascribed to a variety of factors. The introduction of *Hevea* required the clearance of indigenous forests and therefore the input of much capital which lead to the development of large estates with well-organized systems of production. Secondly, by breeding and selection, the application of chemicals to prolong the latex flow and advances in the techniques of tapping, and other plantation practices, yields of rubber have been greatly increased. More recently improved methods of processing have led to the production of more closely standardized grades of rubber. In Malaysia and Indonesia the production of rubber by smallholders has been encouraged and today world output is roughly equally divided between estates and smallholdings.

Industrial application of rubber began only in the early nineteenth century with the work of Hancock on rubber processing and the introduction by Mackintosh of a patented process for waterproofing cloth. Later the discovery of vulcanization by Goodyear opened up a whole new range of end products, above all the invention by Dunlop of the pneumatic tube and the production of rubber tyres.

In 1948 more than 90% of the world supply was natural rubber; today over 60% is synthetic, made mainly from hydrocarbon monomers produced by the petro-chemical industry. Such chemicals can also be obtained from other sources such as coal.

The synthetic rubber industry, which began in Germany in the 1930's was developed in the U.S.A. in the early 1940's and also in the U.S.S.R. In the 1950's a wider spread still to the newer producing countries, particularly Japan. Synthetic production during World War II enabled the U.S.A. to meet its growing world demand for synthetic rubber products and for tyres in particular, when

supplies of natural rubber were disrupted. Since then further increases in production have helped both to meet rising demand and to steady the prices of an essential raw material which in the past had fluctuated wildly.

Today natural rubber's share of world consumption is declining although its actual rate of consumption is still increasing. In many applications, and these include tyre production, the best characteristics in a product are obtained by blending synthetic and natural rubbers or by using different rubbers in different parts such as the treads and sidewalls of tyres. Because of the specific properties of polymers the emergence of SMR (Standard Malaysian Rubber)—a technically specified natural rubber—reflects the industry's awareness that its customers require consistent quality.

Of all consumers of both natural and synthetic rubber the motor industry is the largest. Over 50% of all rubber used goes into tyres. But tyres are not the only outlet for rubber in the automotive industry; it has been estimated that there are approximately 300 components made of rubber in a car.

Latex

In addition to the concentration of the latex by a centrifuge, ammonia or other preservatives are added to suppress the activities of micro-organisms during shipment abroad and storage in bulk. Latex is employed in the manufacture of foam rubber used extensively for cushions, upholstery and mattresses. It is also used in paper/fabric coating and for dipped goods, such as surgeons' gloves.

Very large quantities of natural and synthetic latices are currently being used by the carpet industry; firstly as primary backing to tufted carpets and secondly in the form of spread foam, as either attached or separate foam underlays, adding that touch of luxury to the product.

Styrene/Butadiene Synthetic rubber (SBR) is the chief general purpose synthetic rubber and slightly more specialized in their use.
For example Butyl rubber holds air and gases well, resists heat and the harmful effects of acids, and is thus used in the manufacture of inner tubes, and linings for tubeless tyres. Cis-Polyisoprene rubber is very much like natural rubber and is used mainly for tyres. Polychloroprene rubber resists the normally harmful effects of oxygen, sunlight, oil and petrol (gasoline) and is therefore used for the manufacture of gasoline hose, insulation for wires and cables used in conjunction with oil, and gaskets for sealing against gas and oil. Nitrile rubbers have a high resistance to gasoline, grease, oil, wax and solvents and are also heat-resistant to 349°F (176°C). These are used for paper and leather products. Polysulphide rubber resists chemical ageing, air, sunlight and the normally harmful effects of grease so is used for lining gasoline hoses, printing plates and rollers. Polyurethane also resists age and heat and withstands stresses and pressures so that it outlasts natural rubber. Silicone rubber can be used at temperatures ranging from −130°F to 707°F (−90°C to 375°C) and is therefore used for seals, gaskets and components for jet planes and machinery exposed to high temperatures. Other uses for synthetic rubbers are footwear, floor coverings, belting and waterproof clothing.
Polybutadiene's resistance to abrasion and low temperatures has enabled it to establish for itself a very important role in tyre technology, and it is currently branching out successfully into many other applications, not least of which is the reinforcement of plastics materials. Lastly, Ethylene/Propylene rubbers may prove to be the fastest growing rubber polymer of the next decade.

Flax fibre and linseed seed are obtained from selected types of a common parent. Their environment and soil criteria are somewhat similar, but for the production of fibre the requirements are more exacting. The quality of the fibre in the stems is highest under moist, cool conditions, [59°-64°F (15°-18°C) in July] and well drained, fertile soils. In warmer and drier areas dual purpose varieties are grown and the shorter fibres (tow) can be obtained from linseed straw. Thus although U.S.S.R. grows 59% of the world's output, more favourable conditions in Western Europe give higher yields and superior quality flax so that the Netherlands, France and Belgium are the main exporters. Although nylon is now largely replacing it in rope production, flax is still used to make fine linen and thread.

Jute fibres are derived from the stems of two closely related tropical species of the genus *Corchorus*. Both are tall annuals (3-4 metres) the stems of which are harvested within 3 or 4 months of planting, while the plants are flowering. *Corchorus* requires flooding, hot moist conditions and soils of high fertility. It also demands much hand labour. Jute is used mainly for making cheap, strong sacks and burlap, but also for twine, tarpaulin, carpets and linoleum backing. Although there has been a considerable increase in the world production of packable commodities over the last 20 years, the relative increase in the production of jute goods has been very small. This is mainly due to modern methods of bulk carrying and only partly to the use of synthetics.

Natural rubber
Production (1963-5 av.)
One dot represents 5 000 metric tons

Synthetic rubber
Producing capacity (met.tons) (1969)

OVER 260 000 / 160 000-260 000 / 60 000-160 000 / 60 000 & UNDER
+ capacity unknown
+ plant under construction
o plant under construction / ultimate capacity unknown

Major trade flows (1968)
Commodity: S.I.T.C.no. (Brussels no.)

| NATURAL RUBBER | : 231.1 (40.01) |
| SYNTHETIC RUBBER | : 231.2 (40.02) |

Value ($ U.S.)
0.5mm represents increments of $20 million

Natural rubber production
2 957 000 met. tons 1970*
2 252 200 1963-5 av.
1 843 000 1953-5 av.

| | PERCENTAGE | | |
	1970*	1963-5 av.	1953-5 av.
Malaysia[1]	44	40	36
Indonesia	26	29	40
Thailand	9	9	6
Ceylon	5	5	5
Others	16	17	13
	100	100	100

*Estimates [1] Incl. Singapore

Reclaimed rubber production
374 396 met. tons 1968
403 700 1963-5 av.
378 100 1953-5 av.

| | PERCENTAGE | | |
	1968	1963-5 av.	1953-5 av.
U.S.A.	70	70	79
Germany F.R.	9	11	9
U.K.	9	11	9
Brazil	4	3	2
Australia	4	2	NA
Canada	4	3	18[1]
	100	100	100

Synthetic rubber production
4 770 000 met. tons 1970*
2 925 000 1963-5 av.
927 000 1953-5 av.

| | PERCENTAGE | | |
	1970*	1963-5 av.	1953-5 av.
U.S.A.	50	60	89
Japan	11	11	—
U.K.	6	5	5
France	6	5	1
Germany F.R.	5	5	—
Canada	6	7	10
Netherlands	NA	3	—
Italy	3	4	—
Brazil	1	1	—
Others	8	7	17
	100	100	100

*Data for 1970 is based on estimates and excludes Eastern Europe

Natural rubber imports
2 743 335 met. tons 1968
2 443 970 1963-5 av.
2 118 000 1953-5 av.

| | PERCENTAGE | | |
	1968	1963-5 av.	1953-5 av.
U.S.A.	19	18	30
U.S.S.R.	12	10	10
Japan	9	8	4
China P.R.	7	8	13
U.K.	7	6	7
Germany F.R.	5	6	7
France	NA	4	3
Malaysia	5	4	3
Italy	4	4	3
Others	8	7	17
	100	100	100

*Excl. U.S.S.R. and some minor producers
*Data for 1970 is based on estimates and excludes Eastern Europe

Natural rubber exports
2 494 403 met. tons 1968
2 478 730 1963-5 av.
2 116 000 1953-5 av.

| | PERCENTAGE | | |
	1968	1963-5 av.	1953-5 av.
Malaysia	45	43	44
Indonesia	29	27	33
Thailand	10	8	6
Ceylon	10	6	5
Others	10	18	12
	100	100	100

Synthetic rubber trade
('000 met. tons)

	Imports	Exports
1968	880	1 034
1963-5 av.	635	751[1]

[1] U.S.A., Canada and Netherlands.... 66%

Rubber consumption

Figures in brackets indicate percentages used in tyres and tyre products, where known.

| | Natural | | Synthetic | |
	1960	1970*	1970*	1960
World	2098	2947	4643	1832
U.S.A.	486 (68)	589	2179	1096 (62)
Japan	169 (46)	269	460	62 (35)
Germany F.R.	148 (51)	194	298	118 (63)
U.K.	183 (46)	193	259	92 (54)
France	129 (53)	140	230	53 (46)
Italy	75 (60)	110	190	57 (68)
U.S.S.R.[1]	193	254	5	13
Canada	36 (69)	53	128	57 (68)
India	50	100	37	18
Brazil	49	40	82	28
Australia	41	42	52	28
Czechoslovakia	NA	46	36	NA
Sweden	NA	26	53	18[1]
Others	NA	891	634	NA

*Estimates [1] Data refers to imports

growth the soil should be deep, fertile, well drained and not alkaline, although the application of fertilizers allows the use of otherwise unsuitable soils. Above 300 metres *Hevea* is liable to attack by the fungus *Oidium*, and in Central and South America the establishment of plantations has been greatly hampered by the leaf blight disease *Dothidella ulei*.

Cotton Yarn

Production centres — spindles installed
- Major — 200 000 and over
- Secondary — 100 000 - 200 000
- Minor — 25 000 - 100 000
- + Data not available but reported to be at least a minor production centre

Cotton lint
One dot represents 100 000 met. tons of cotton lint production.

Major trade flows (1966)
Commodity: S.I.T.C.no.

INTRA-EUROPEAN TRADE
PROVENANCE: Belg./Lux.
DESTINATION
N.(32)

COTTON YARN (AND THREAD) 651.3/4
COTTON CLOTH (NOT MADE UP) 652.1/2

Value ($U.S.)
0.5mm represents increments of $20 million
VALUE IN $ MILLIONS
51

Cotton yarn production (1966)
8 131 000 met. tons 1963-5 av.
6 968 000 1953-5 av.

	PERCENTAGE	
	1963-5 av.	1953-5 av.
U.S.A.	23	24
U.S.S.R.	16	14
India	11	10
Japan	6	6
Germany F.R.	5	5
France	4	4
Pakistan	3	1
U.K.	3	5
Italy	2	2
Others	27	29
	100	100

Cotton spindles
Number installed, end of year
130 495 000 1965
103 400 000 1955*

	PERCENTAGE	
	1965	1955
U.S.A.	15	22
India	12	11
Japan	10	8
U.S.S.R.	10	NA
China P.R.	9	NA
Germany F.R.	4	6
U.K.	3	11
Italy	3	5
France	3	7
Others	31	NA
	100	100

*Excl. China P.R.
*Excl. U.S.S.R.

Modified Gall Projection
Equatorial Scale 1: 88 Million approx.
© Oxford University Press

This map shows ring spindles installed for spinning cotton and cotton blend yarn as of 1965.

31

Man-made fibres

Japan (A)

N. America (B)

Europe (C)

SCALE 1:29 MILLION 1 CM TO 290 KM

© Oxford University Press

---

rayon and acetate filament yarn was of the viscose type. Rayon can be produced as continuous filament ready for weaving or as staple cut into short lengths which subsequently can be spun into yarn.

Textile glass fibre is glass in the form of fine threads twisted into yarns and cords and subsequently woven into cloth and tape. These threads can be finer than human hair and may look and feel like silk. The fibres are stronger than steel and will not burn, stretch, rot or fade.

Total production of man-made fibre in 1965 was 5 389 000 metric tons, 62% of which was cellulosic fibre. Non-cellulosic production was over two-thirds as large as rayon production and increasing rapidly. 1968 producing capacity was more than double the actual 1965 production and sixteen times that of 1955.

The main types of non-cellulosic fibre are:
1. Nylon (Polyamide), based on coal, petroleum and castor oil;
2. Acrylic (Acrilan, Courtelle, Orlon, etc.);
3. Polyester (Terylene, Dacron, etc.);
4. Other fibres such as Vinyl, Azlon, Olefin, Saran, Spandex, Vinyon, Alginate and TFE-fluorocarbon.

In 1965 of a total of 2 050 700 metric tons produced, 50% was nylon, 22% was polyester and 20% was acrylic and modacrylic. Rayon is regenerated cellulose, (viscose or cuprammonium depending on the process of manufacture). Acetate and triacetate are cellulose acetate. In 1965 76% of the world output of acetate.

Cotton lint

Production (1963-5 av.)

One dot represents 5000 met. tons

Major trade flows (1966)

Commodity: COTTON
S.I.T.C. No.

Value ($U.S.)
0.5mm. represents increments of $20 million

COTTON: 263

VALUE IN $ MILLIONS
200 · 100 · 20

SCALE 1:176 MILLION   1 CM TO 1760 KM

Cotton statistics

		U.S.A	U.S.S.R	CHINA P.R.	INDIA	BRAZIL	MEXICO	PAKISTAN	TURKEY	JAPAN	GERMANY F.R.	OTHERS	WORLD
		PERCENTAGES UNLESS OTHERWISE STATED											MET. TONS
Lint consumption	1963-5 av.	18	14	12	11	3	5	1	1	7	3	26	10 737 000
production	1963-5 av.	44	...	10	10	5	5	5	4	—	—	15	7 367 000*
	1953-5 av.												
Yield kg. per hectare	1963-5 av.	583	740	261	131	217	649	687	263	452	—	—	NA
Seed production	1963-5 av.	26	17	11	10	6	5	5	4	—	—	19	21 285 000
	1953-5 av.	41	...	11	11	6	5	5	2	—	—	19	13 733 000*

*Excl. U.S.S.R.

Man-made fibres

Production centres (1967)

Fibre types
- Cellulosic
  acetate, triacetate & viscose etc.
- Non-cellulosic (Synthetic)
  nylon, polyester, acrylic, etc.
- ▲ Textile glass fibre
- ★ All of the above

Major trade flows (1966)

Trade flows in synthetic and regenerated yarn are predominantly intra-European although flows within Asia and North America are also important. The main flows are from the Netherlands to Germany, and from Japan to S. Korea.

SCALE 1:176 MILLION   1 CM TO 1760 KM

Modified Gall Projection

Man-made yarn/staple

		U.S.A	JAPAN	U.S.S.R	GERMANY F.R.	U.K.	ITALY	GERMANY D.R.	FRANCE	POLAND	NETHERLANDS	CANADA	OTHERS	WORLD
Major producers					PERCENTAGE									MET. TONS
Cellulosic	1963-5 av.	20	15	9	9	7	6	5	4	2	2	2	19	3 227 903
	1953-5 av.	26	14	4	10	9	6	6	4	...	...	2	14	2 065 904
Non-cellulosic	1963-5 av.	39	19	3	8	7	6	1	1	1	2	3	7	1 692 063
	1953-5 av.	67	5	...	6	3	4	1	1	...	1	3	9	205 856

Energy

Large supplies of energy are a vital adjunct to our present way of life. The process of industrialization which has improved living standards for the people of many countries, requires a plentiful energy source. Between 1958 and 1968 world consumption of energy rose almost continuously both absolutely and on a per capita basis.

Energy sources are normally classified into two categories: primary and secondary. Primary fuels are those which occur naturally such as coal, crude oil, natural gas, peat, wood and dung. Whilst the last three of these are important sources of energy in certain countries, such as India, available data on consumption are poor and, with the occasional exception of peat, they are rarely included in official statistics. Three other primary fuels are hydro, nuclear and geothermal energy which are used to produce the secondary fuel, electricity. Other secondary fuels are manufactured gas, various manufactured solid fuels and refined oil products.

The distribution of energy sources throughout the world is governed by geological and geographical factors. However the pattern of production differs from that of consumption because the consumption of energy is linked with stages of economic development. North America is able to produce approximately enough energy from its own resources, Western Europe has to import over half of its consumption, since in 1968 Western Asia exported twelve times its own total energy consumption, principally in the form of oil. The world balance of energy production and consumption is shown on the table below.

Energy production and consumption

In kg. per capita of coal equivalent (1963-5 av.)

	PRODUCTION	CONSUMPTION
North America[1]	8 032	8 732
Western Asia[2]	5 765	469
Caribbean America[3]	2 962	939
Oceania	2 297	3 416
Western Europe	1 702	2 980
U.S.S.R./China P.R./ Eastern Europe	1 467	1 392
Africa	527	270
Other America[4]	362	569
Far East	198	306
World average	1 572	1 543

[1]Mainly Canada and U.S.A.
[2]Mainly Middle East
[3]Incl. Caribbean Islands, Central America, Colombia and Venezuela
[4]South America excl. Colombia and Venezuela

Until the end of the 1960's solid fuel had been the major energy source for the world. However by 1968 this position had been taken over by liquid fuels. Third was natural gas which has grown rapidly in importance, whilst nuclear and geothermal energy accounted for only 2% of world consumption.

In absolute terms, world-wide consumption of solid fuel has increased, but it has declined in certain areas and countries. In most areas, the decrease in the share of energy consumption held by solid fuel has occurred since the beginning of the 1950's, although in North America, which has large indigenous oil and gas resources, it started much earlier. The increasing importance of liquid fuels has been due partly to the rapid growth in transport, where liquid fuels have a captive market, and partly to substitution for solid fuel. This substitution has been caused both by technical factors which enable liquid fuel to be used more easily than solid fuel and also by a favourable price ratio. Because of the ease of transport by pipeline or tanker, the growth of liquid fuel consumption has occurred in practically all countries, whereas

natural gas use has been concentrated in countries with indigenous sources. Although the share of hydro and nuclear electricity has remained fairly static over many years, increasing numbers of nuclear power stations are now being planned throughout the world.

There are three main types of **coal** which, in descending order of thermal value, are anthracite, bituminous coal and lignite (or brown coal). The coal reserves of the world are extremely large and those that have been measured could supply several hundred times the present annual consumption. About 60% of the world reserves are believed to lie in the U.S.S.R. with about another 15% in both the U.S.A. and China P.R.

Most coal is obtained from deep mines as opposed to open-cast mines where only a thin layer of top soil needs to be removed to expose the coal seams. In industrialized countries, the most easily worked seams have already been mined and consequently strenuous efforts are being made to mechanize production in deep mines in order to make it economic to extract coal from seams in geologically difficult conditions. The great bulk of all the coal mined is either burnt directly as a fuel or is converted into other solid fuels such as coke. Only certain types of bituminous coal have the correct coking qualities, and the major buyer of such coals is the steel industry. When coking coals are heated in a sealed oven with little air, the volatile matter is driven off and the coke, mainly fixed carbon, remains. Coke is an essential material in steel-making as it is used in the blast furnaces which smelt the iron ore.

About 1¼ tons of coal are needed to produce 1 ton of coke, and the volatile matter driven off in the carbonization process can itself be used for heating purposes. This gas may be used in the steel works or added to town (coal) gas supplies. It can also be used for manufacturing certain chemicals such as dyes, detergents and plastics. In industrial countries the principal uses of coal burnt directly are electricity production, steam raising in industry and domestic heating. Coal may also be used to produce synthetic gasoline (petrol) and this, together with the underground gasification of coal, may provide new markets for coal in the future.

Crude oil varies considerably in composition and appearance both between countries and between fields in a country. The major impurity is sulphur, in various compound forms, which is released as sulphur dioxide when the oil is burnt. With increasing concern about air pollution, those oils with a low sulphur content, notably from North Africa, are becoming more valuable. The most important refined oil products are gasoline and fuel oils, the former being used for transport and the latter mainly for providing heat in, for example, industrial furnaces. Only about 10% of oil consumption is used for non-energy purposes.

Over the last 30 years, there has been a steady movement of oil refining away from the producing areas to the consuming areas. This movement has been due to both economic and strategic factors. As oil consumption has increased, the cost of shipping crude oil and building medium size refineries close to the demand centres has become less than that of putting large refineries on the oilfields and shipping refined products. From the strategic viewpoint, the increasing importance of oil in the consuming countries meant that supply disruptions were increasingly

serious, but home-based refineries can be adjusted to take crude oil from alternative supply sources. In addition, the producing countries have realized the value of what is, in many cases, their only natural asset and their ability to dictate, within limits, their own supply terms. The Organization of Petroleum Exporting Countries (OPEC) has been formed to increase their bargaining power through the presentation of a united front.

Natural gas occurs both alone and in conjunction with oil, and its principal component is methane. Much of the natural gas occurring with oil is burnt at the point of production because of the difficulty of transporting it to the consuming areas. However pipeline development in the United States in the 1920's and 1930's led to natural gas taking an increasing share of the energy market there. The rising world-wide demand for energy has increased exploration, and new reserves of natural gas have been found so that proved reserves now total about half those of oil. Technical developments are making it economic to liquefy natural gas and transport it in refrigerated tankers to other countries, and several inter-country pipelines are under construction.

Natural gas must, like oil, be produced from wells at a steady rate in order to obtain the maximum percentage of the reserves but, unlike oil, it cannot easily be stored. In order to meet fluctuations in demand either liquefied gas storage tanks are used or the gas is pumped into naturally occurring underground reservoirs. Natural gas is non-toxic, virtually free of sulphur and has a calorific value twice that of coal gas. Being sulphur-free, it can be used for direct process heating in industry without affecting the product, so it has a premium value over oil. However for general use in steam raising it must compete directly on price. Whilst the bulk of the natural gas is used by industry, a large proportion also goes into the domestic market for heating and cooking. The availability of natural gas has supplanted coal or oil in the town gas industry, as the higher calorific value doubles the capacity of the existing assets and the price is usually very much lower than that of manufactured gas. Particularly in the U.S.A., natural gas has been identified with 'total energy' schemes whereby all the energy requirements in an establishment are supplied by the one fuel. A gas-driven engine connected to a generator provides the electrical requirements and the exhaust heat from the engine is used, together with more gas if necessary, to supply the heating requirements. Whilst the thermal efficiency of such schemes is high, the increased capital cost remains a barrier to their widespread adoption.

Electricity is a versatile and refined fuel capable of providing services such as lighting, heating and motive power with great flexibility. Throughout the world, its importance in the energy market has increased very rapidly. Although the overland transmission of electricity is relatively simple, so that few undersea connections have been built owing to technical difficulties. Two factors which put constraints on the type of plant used and hence on the final selling price of the fuel are that it is not economically feasible to store electricity in large quantities and that the majority of electricity is produced from other primary fuels through a conversion process which is only about 30% efficient. In order to

eliminate the remaining heat large quantities of cooling water are used so plants are sited on rivers, lakes or the coast.

For many decades, the demand for electricity has increased by over 7% per annum and growth rates much higher than this are occurring in those countries beginning a period of industrialization. Out of a total world production of over 4 200 000 million kilowatt hours in 1968, 26% was supplied by the primary sources of hydro, geothermal and nuclear energy and the remainder by the conversion of the other primary fuels. In any particular area, the choice of fuel to generate electricity is mainly a function of the relative capital costs of the various types of plant, the expected future cost and availability of the various fuels, the existing generating system and the expected growth in electrical load. Although the capital costs of hydro and nuclear generating plants are high, in relation to fossil-fuel fired ones, their running costs are very low. As the capital costs of fossil-fuel fired plant burning either coal, oil, gas or peat are very similar, the choice between them depends mainly on the local cost and availability of each fuel.

Hydro-electric schemes use a flow of water from a river, which may be retained by a dam, to drive turbines which in turn drive electricity generators. Although in some countries nearly all the electricity is generated this way, the hydro-electric share of world production has been decreasing. The cheapest sites have already been developed, and the relative economics have changed in favour of fossil-fuel fired power stations. However the world potential for hydro-electricity is basically untapped. In many cases, the hydro-electric plant is only part of a general irrigation scheme so that the resource, water, can have more than one use. Given favourable conditions it is also possible to make use of the energy in the tides, and one such scheme is in operation on the Rance estuary in Northern France. Another variant which is being developed is pumped storage, where water is pumped to a high-level reservoir when the electrical load on the system is low and is then re-

leased at peak times to generate electricity in the normal way.

Geothermal energy is unimportant on a world scale, being only about half of one percent of hydro generation, but power stations based on steam wells are operating in such countries as the United States, New Zealand, Iceland, Mexico and Italy.

Nuclear energy arises from the heat generated by the fission of uranium atoms. In natural uranium the component isotope U_{235}, which represents only 0.7% of the metal, is fissile and emits neutrons. When the nucleus of a U_{235} atom is struck by a neutron the atom splits into two, releasing more neutrons which in turn strike other nuclei and hence sustain a chain reaction. This heat can be transferred by a coolant and, through heat exchangers, used to raise steam for turbines. In order to slow down the speed of the neutrons to make the chain reaction sustainable and controllable a moderator is needed. Three types have been developed and are in commercial use. The United States has concentrated on light water moderated and cooled systems, Canada and Sweden on heavy water moderator and coolant and France and the U.K. on the gas-cooled, graphite-moderated system.

An important aspect of nuclear reactors is that some of the non-fissile uranium isotope U_{238} is converted into plutonium, which is fissile. A prototype reactor, using plutonium, is being built in the U.K. with liquid sodium as the coolant. Another fissile isotope is U_{233}, and it is possible that this could be bred from thorium. A more remote possibility is that the fusion of two separate nuclei, which also produces large quantities of heat, could be used to produce electricity. However this process has yet to be handled successfully even in the laboratory.

Nuclear power plants are still relatively new, and the oldest commercial plant is far from retirement so the technical problems of dealing with the safety of obsolete radio-active plant have still to be tackled in practice. Small experimental reactors have, of course, been dismantled satisfactorily.

The future development of the various energy industries is part of a complex economic process. Many of the decisions taken by a particular industry react on the others both nationally and internationally and on society as a whole by, for example, the resulting impact on the landscape, water resources and the atmosphere. Although techniques are being developed to attempt to quantify these 'external' effects a substantial amount of subjective judgement must still be used in order to balance the conflicting requirements that exist.

Most electricity is not used directly, but it is an integral part of industrialized society because of the widespread use of lighting, electric motors, communications and countless other devices. One direct use of electricity is in electro-chemistry including the manufacture of chlorine and ozone, the manufacture of aluminium from its oxide and in copper refining. Electricity can also be used directly in the fabrication of components by electro-discharge techniques either induced magnetically or through a fluid. Such techniques are being used in the U.S.A. in the aerospace industry. Machining can also be done electrically either by electrochemical corrosion, spark erosion or glow discharge techniques. Material cutting, which is difficult by mechanical methods at high speeds, can also be done electrically by electron beams, lasers or plasmas. Paint deposition on variable contour surfaces can be aided electrically by the use of electrostatic fields.

The use of electricity in the transport industry is also expanding. The advantages of electric traction on the railways, given heavily used lines, are being increasingly realized and even higher speed travel is promised by the hovertrain which can be driven by a newly developed linear type of electric motor. Electric vehicles are at present confined to short distance service operations because of the energy storage limitations of the lead-acid battery. However the potential advantages of electric vehicles have led to battery research throughout the world and several experimental batteries are under consideration.

Production and consumption of fuel and energy (1963-5 av.)

Million metric tons coal equivalent

	Solid fuel[1,2]	Liquid fuel[3]	Natural gas[1,2]	H.E.P./ Nuclear energy
World totals				
Production	2 225	1 865	871	107
Consumption	2 218	1 783	865	107

Regional totals: North America[4], Caribbean America[5], Other America[6], Western Asia[7], Far East, Oceania, Africa, Western Europe, Eastern Europe/U.S.S.R./China P.R.

[1]External trade in coke and manufactured gas is subtracted from the consumption of the exporting country and added to that of the importing country. [2]Mainly coal and lignite but incl. peat where important. [3]incl. wood and dung [4]Canada, U.S.A., Greenland and St. Pierre/Miquelon [5]incl. Colombia and Venezuela [6]South America excl. Colombia and Venezuela [7]Bahrain, Cyprus, Iran, Iraq, Israel, Jordan, Kuwait, Lebanon, Neutral Zone, Qatar, Saudi Arabia, Southern Yemen, Syria, Trucial Oman, Turkey and Yemen

Natural gas

Fields

gas producing areas

Reserves (proven, as of 1st July,1968)

OVER 5 000 000   million cubic metres

2 000 000–5 000 000
800 000–2 000 000
200 000–600 000
90 000–200 000
45 000–90 000
0–45 000

Symbols are located on the major regions and named accordingly.
Underlining of names indicates that reserves are found predominantly in association with crude oil;
e.g. *Mereenie* : *Amza*

Annual movements (1967)

where international trade is below 500 million cu. metres
Thereafter every additional 500 million cu. metres is shown by 0.5 mm. width, thus
represents 1 000 million cu.m.

major internal movements (not quantified)

planned internal and international movements

L.N.G. Liquified Natural Gas movements

□ liquefaction plants

■ centres of distribution and/or consumption

Modified Gall Projection
Equatorial Scale 1 : 88 Million approx.

© Oxford University Press

Insets for this map follow the Oil Refining map

Natural gas, which is composed almost entirely of hydrocarbons, (of which methane is the most important), may occur alone or alongside oil reserves. 'Associated gas' is that which is found dissolved with crude oil and which must therefore be produced with it. Thus gas production rates, in this case, depend on oil output, although excess gas may be flared off if no market can be found for it. Regions from which gas alone can be produced economically yield 'non-associated gas'. Many of the world's important gas fields are in this category. Total 'proven' reserves at the end of 1968 were 37 715 976 million cubic metres. Although this great quantity of gas is known to exist, its use has been limited in some instances, such as the Middle East, by the cost of long distance transport to the major consuming markets. Although natural gas consumption has shown a spectacular growth rate over the past forty years and now provides approximately one-fifth of total world energy consumption, its use until quite recently has been restricted to those consuming centres which are within economical piping distance of reserves. Thus, the U.S.A. and the U.S.S.R. between them account for 85% of total consumption, the U.S.A. alone accounting for 65%. This pattern is now showing signs of change. The more recent discovery of reserves of non-associated gas in the North Sea, the Netherlands, Algeria, Australia and many other countries and the development of new transport techniques, has meant the emergence of the great energy market of Europe as a market for gas. Other regions and countries have also become gas markets in recent years. Natural gas can be liquefied by cooling it to –258°F (–161°C) when it is known as L.N.G. (Liquefied Natural Gas). L.N.G. occupies only 1/600th of its previous volume, thus transport in specially insulated tankers is possible. L.N.G. links have been established between Arzew (Algeria) and Canvey Island (U.K.) and Le Havre (France), between Alaska and Japan and between Libya and Italy and Spain. Other L.N.G. movements are in the active planning or construction phase. The propane and butane elements of natural gas can also be stripped out and are then known as L.P.G. (Liquefied Petroleum Gas). When liquefied they occupy only 1/250th of their original volume, and can be stored and shipped in relatively small quantities economically. L.P.G. supply links between Kuwait, Saudi Arabia, Iran and Japan already exist; there are also links between Venezuela and Brazil and Argentina, and other trans-ocean movements are projected. At present the percentage of total energy requirements met by natural gas varies greatly from 34% in the U.S.A. and 17% in the U.S.S.R. to 5% in France. It is estimated that Europe as a whole will meet some 11% of her energy demand with natural gas by 1975, although of course the percentage will be higher in certain individual countries, for example the Netherlands.

Natural gas 'proven' reserves
(as of 1st July, 1968)

37 626 000 million cu. metres

	1967	1965	1955
	PERCENTAGE		
Eastern Europe/China	25	24	
U.S.S.R.			
North America	25	22	
U.S.A.	17		
Middle East		8	
Iran			
Kuwait			
Saudi Arabia	13	3	
Africa			
Algeria	11	11	
Western Europe		2	
Netherlands			
U.K.			
Latin America	5	4	
	100	100	100

Natural gas production

821 650 million cubic metres 1967
704 130 million 1965
300 450 million 1955

	1967	1965	1955
	PERCENTAGE		
U.S.A.	63	65	69
U.S.S.R.	16	18	3
Canada	2	2	1
Romania	2	2	1
Mexico	2	1	1
Italy	1	1	1
Venezuela	1	1	1
Netherlands	1		
France			
Others	4	3	3
	100	100	100

Natural gas consumption

816 720 million cubic metres 1967
700 730 million 1965
(equivalent data for 1955 not available)

	1967	1965
	KG. PER CAPITA	PERCENTAGE
U.S.A.	697	64	66
U.S.S.R.	208	19	18
Canada	47	4	4
Romania	25	2	2
Mexico	19	2	2
Italy	12	1	1
Venezuela	10	1	1
France	8	1	1
Netherlands	8		
Others		5	5
		100	100

Natural gas exports

21 640 million cubic metres 1967
15 180 million 1965
1 279 million 1955

	1967	1965	1955
	PERCENTAGE		
Canada	66	75	25
U.S.A.	8	5	69
Mexico	7	10	
U.S.S.R.	6	3	
Algeria	5		
Netherlands	5		
Afghanistan	1	1	
Romania	1	1	
Others	1	1	6
	100	100	100

Natural gas imports

21 940 million cubic metres 1967
15 120 million 1965
1 257 million 1955

	1967	1965	1955
	PERCENTAGE		
U.S.A.	73	85	25
Canada	7	3	25
Poland	5	3	44
France	3	1	
Belg./Lux.	2	1	
Germany F.R.	2	1	
Mexico	2	2	
Czechoslovakia	1	2	
Others	2	2	6
	100	100	100

Crude Oil

Producing areas

◢ major ◁ minor ≡ oilshale

Reserves ('proven' as of 1st July,1968)

million barrels

40 000 AND OVER
17 500–40 000
4 500–17 500
900–4 500
350–900
under 350

Kapuni underlining indicates condensate reserves only

Symbols are located on the major regions

Annual movements (1967)

← where movement is below 45 million barrels

Thereafter every additional 90 million barrels is shown by 0.5 mm. width, thus: ▬ represents 180 million barrels

▪— major tanker terminals

One barrel of crude oil (world average gravity) is equal to 0.137 metric tons.

Modified Gall Projection
Equatorial Scale 1: 88 Million approx.

© Oxford University Press

Crude oil 'proven' reserves (1st July 1968)

453 526 million barrels

PERCENTAGE 59

Middle East	
South West Iran	17
Kuwait	15
Iran	12
East Europe/China	12
U.S.S.R.	10
Africa	8
Libya	7
North America	9
U.S.A.	7
Latin America	7
Venezuela	3
Asia Pacific	2
Indonesia	—
Europe	—

Crude oil production (1967)

13 063 million barrels 1967
11 237 million 1965
6 423 million 1955

	PERCENTAGE		
	1967	1965	1955
U.S.A.	26	26	39
U.S.S.R.	16	16	8
Venezuela	10	12	12
Saudi Arabia	7	7	5
Iran	7	6	5
Kuwait	6	6	6
Libya	6	4	—
Iraq	4	4	4
Algeria	2	2	1
Others	16	16	24
	100	100	100

Crude oil exports

5 932 million barrels 1967
4 865 million 1965
1 855 million 1955

	PERCENTAGE		
	1967	1965	1955
Venezuela	16	18	35
Saudi Arabia	13	13	15
Iran	13	11	3
Kuwait	13	15	21
Libya	10	9	3
U.S.S.R.	7	6	13
Algeria	4	4	1
Canada	2	2	1
Others	15	12	11
	100	100	100

Crude oil imports

5 942 million barrels 1967
4 869 million 1965
1 862 million 1955

	PERCENTAGE		
	1967	1965	1955
Japan	13	10	3
Italy	11	10	11
U.K.	11	9	11
France	9	9	10
Germany F.R.	9	9	3
U.S.A.	7	6	17
Neth. Antilles	7	5	9
Netherlands	4	4	5
Canada	2	3	5
Others	30	30	23
	100	100	100

Insets for this map follow the Oil Refining map

Crude oil and natural gas occur either in 'traps' produced by the juxtaposition of porous and non-porous sedimentary rocks as a result of earth movements or in association with salt domes (as in the U.S. Gulf coast). The exact origin of oil is not known but it has been ascertained that it contains compounds that must have come from living matter, once inhabiting a shallow, calm tropical sea.

'Proven' crude oil reserves at mid-year 1968 were sufficient for 35 years at present consumption rates. They are defined as the amount which technically (geologically and with present engineering skill) it is estimated can be recovered from known oil reservoirs. This may represent as little as 25% of the total oil in a field. With improved methods this figure ultimately may be doubled. A century has passed since the drilling of the first oil well, yet only 5% of the world has been thoroughly searched for oil deposits. It is estimated that 73 000 million barrels await discovery under the continental shelves, and at depths of up to 1 000 feet which, together with that to be found on land will eventually put total reserves at a minimum of 3 650 000 million barrels.

As oil deposits are generally far from the industrial consumers, the greatest portion of cargo carried by the world merchant fleet. High levels of demand and the need, in conditions of extreme competition exacerbated by world-wide inflation, for cheaper transport has resulted in the development of the 'super tanker'. At the end of 1968 two 312 000 ton tankers were in operation, four more were under construction, and one of 370 000 tons was on order.

In Western Europe and Japan the demand for fuel oils and middle distillates—nowadays for domestic as well as industrial purposes— is the chief feature. At present nearly 80% of all organic chemicals produced originate from petroleum feedstocks.

Unlike coal, the principal sources of oil occur outside the industrial consumer countries, in the Middle East, S.E. Asia, Latin America and Africa. However, the U.S.A. remains the largest single producer of oil, producing 26% of the world output with only 8% of total reserves. The countries of the Middle East together also produce 28% of the world total yet have 62% of total proven reserves.

Fear of overdependence upon the Middle East has been an incentive to exploration elsewhere and has led to important discoveries of new oil-bearing regions. The most important feature of the last 10 years has been the rapid increase in production by North Africa, especially Libya, which is by far the most important producer in the area and which now surpasses Iraq in total production.

In addition some 2 628 000 million barrels are estimated to lie in the deposits of tar sands and oil shales of the world, the most important being the Athabasca tar sands of Alberta in Canada, the Orinoco tar belt in Venezuela and the Green River shale deposits of the U.S.A. There are also deposits of 'condensate', a liquid/hydrocarbon mixture which may be recovered from some non-associated reservoirs, i.e. those only economically productive for natural gas.

Oil Refining

© Oxford University Press

Oil refineries (1968)

Crude oil capacity by producing centre
'000 barrels per stream day

- 400 & OVER
- 270 – 400
- 180 – 270
- 105 – 180
- 19 – 105
- 6 – 19
- UNDER 6

Associated petro-chemicals

Major trade flows (1966)

Commodity : S.I.T.C. no.²

CRUDE	33
PETROLEUM REFINED BY-PRODUCTS	

0.5mm represents increments of $150 million

Value ($U.S.)

VALUE IN $ MILLIONS

Trade flow shows only major trading partners, not total trade

²S.I.T.C. = STANDARD INTERNATIONAL TRADE CLASSIFICATION

Modified Gall Projection
Equatorial Scale 1:88 Million approx.

Petroleum is composed of hydrogen and carbon. Many different combinations of these two elements occur within the crude oil. Each gives special characteristics to the different fractional parts of petroleum. Some are valuable products in themselves, for example gasoline and kerosene; others must be changed before they can be used. A refinery separates and then refines these parts, converting crude oil into useful products.

Separation is done by distillation based on the fact that different hydrocarbons vaporize and cool at different temperatures. This is known as fractional distillation. Conversion is achieved through cracking, which is either by heating under pressure causing the oil to decompose and the larger molecular constituents to break down to smaller, lighter ones (thermal cracking) or by placing in contact with a catalyst (catalytic cracking). Polymerization is the reverse of this process, combining the smaller molecular parts to form heavy oils. Alkylation is the combining of gaseous hydrocarbons into a liquid state suitable for gasoline. Hydrogenation is a process whereby the addition of extra hydrogen to heavy oils (which are hydrogen deficient) produces light oils. Reforming (thermal and catalytic) produces aromatics (benzene, toluene and xylene) the basis for the petro-chemical industry.

The location of refineries is greatly dependent upon logistic considerations both economic and strategic. The reduction in unit costs of transportation which has resulted from the development of ever-larger crude oil carriers has permitted a shift of location away from the centres of oil production to those of oil consumption—a trend which both large and small current governments have encouraged. Because of the need of deep water facilities and abundant supplies of cooling water, the rule has been for refineries to be located on the coast. Recently, however, Europe has seen refineries located inland in the industrial areas such as the Saar, Ruhr and Bavaria, where the volumetric increase in demand has been greatest. This has only been possible since the development of air-cooling and long-distance, large diameter, pipeline systems, which run overland to the refineries from the ports of discharge, large: Rotterdam, Wilhelmshaven, Marseilles, Genoa and Trieste.

Refining capacity may be expressed in barrels per stream day which represents the out-turn when periods of shutdown for maintenance and so forth have been allowed for. Barrels per calendar day is another measure used and may be calculated either on the capacity at the end of the year or by averaging capacity over the year. To convert from barrels per stream day multiply by 0.9.

Insets for this map are on the following page

Refined oil fuel imports¹

5 671 020 barrels per calendar day 1967
5 010 092 1965
2 783 628 1955

	PERCENTAGE		
	1967	1965	1955
U.S.A.	26	25	19
U.K.	13	9	8
Germany F.R.	7	7	2
Japan	6	6	2
Sweden	6	6	5
Netherlands	3	3	3
Singapore	3	3	2
Others	37	39	59
	100	100	100

¹Gasoline, kerosene and fuel oil only

Refined oil fuel exports¹

6 203 233 barrels per calendar day 1967
5 585 916 1965
2 850 303 1955

	PERCENTAGE		
	1967	1965	1955
Venezuela	17	23	16
Neths. Antilles	12	13	27
U.S.S.R.	8	8	4
Italy	7	6	4
Trinidad/Tobago	6	5	3
Netherlands	4	4	5
France	4	4	4
U.K.	3	3	2
Others	39	32	32
	100	100	100

¹Gasoline, kerosene and fuel oil only

Refined oil fuel consumption¹

31 310 430 barrels per calendar day 1967
27 074 740 1965
16 046 860 1955

	KG. PER CAPITA	PERCENTAGE		
		1967	1965	1955
U.S.A.	2 649	36	38	45
U.S.S.R.	790	13	13	8
Japan	930	6	5	1
Germany F.R.	1 274	6	5	1
U.K.	1 288	5	5	7
Canada	2 670	5	4	3
France	1 036	4	4	3
Italy	1 003	4	3	1
Others		23	24	36
		100	100	100

¹Gasoline, kerosene and fuel oil only

Refined oil fuel production¹

34 454 000 barrels per calendar day 1967
29 874 000 1965
14 914 000 1955

	PERCENTAGE		
	1967	1965	1955
U.S.A.	30	31	49
U.S.S.R.	13	13	9
Japan	6	4	1
Italy	5	4	1
Germany F.R.	4	4	1
France	4	4	3
Venezuela	4	4	4
Others	30	32	27
	100	100	100

¹Gasoline, kerosene and fuel oil only

Refining capacity (end 1968)

44 911 000 barrels per stream day

	PERCENTAGE
North America	30
U.S.A.	28
Western Europe	28
Italy	6
U.K.	5
Germany F.R.	5
France	5
Eastern Europe/China	14
U.S.S.R.	12
Latin America	11
Venezuela	3
Asia Pacific	10
Japan	6
Middle East	5
Africa	2

Natural Gas

Persian Gulf

SCALE 1:29 MILLION   1 CM. TO 290 KM.

Europe/N. Africa

L.N.G.

SCALE 1:29 MILLION   1 CM. TO 290 KM.

Natural gas

Fields (proven as of 1st July 1968)

Reserves (proven as of 1st July 1968)

million cubic metres

OVER 6 000 000
2 000 000–6 000 000
600 000–2 000 000
200 000–600 000
60 000–200 000
20 000–60 000
UNDER 20 000

gas producing areas

Underlined names indicate 'associated' gas

Annual movements (1967)

where international trade is below 500 million cu.m.
represents 1 000 million cu.m. international trade

major internal movements
planned internal and international movements (not quantified)

L.N.G.   Liquefied Natural Gas movements
liquefaction plants
centres of distribution and/or consumption

Crude Oil

Persian Gulf

SCALE 1:29 MILLION   1 CM. TO 290 KM.

Europe/N. Africa

TO JAPAN

SCALE 1:44 MILLION   1 CM. TO 440 KM.

Crude oil

Producing areas (proven as of 1st July 1968)
major   minor   oilshale

Reserves (proven as of 1st July 1968)
million barrels

40 000 AND OVER
17 500–40 000
4 500–17 500
800–4 500
350–800
UNDER 350

Annual movements (1967)
million barrels

where movement is below 45 million barrels
represents 180 million barrels

major tanker terminals

One barrel of crude oil (world average gravity) is equal to 0.137 metric tons

Symbols are located on the major regions

Oil Refining

Japan

Yokkaichi, Wakayama, Sakai, Shimotsu, Kainan, Umaokoshi—

SCALE 1:29 MILLION   1 CM. TO 290 KM.

N. Europe

Gelsenkirchen, Dinslaken, Neuenkamp, Wesseling, Mannheim, Mülheim, Abwessen

Pernis, Antwerpen, Rotterdam, Gent, Dunkerque, Amsterdam, Oostvoorne, Rozenburg

Grangemouth, Ardrossan, Sydenham, Stanlow, Eastham, Ellesmere Port, Teesside, Trafford Park

Speyer, Karlsruhe, Mannheim, Reichstett, Strasbourg

Vern-sur-Seiche, Donges

Gonfreville-l'Orcher, Le Petit-Couronne, Port-Jérôme, N.D.-de-Gravenchon

SCALE 1:29 MILLION   1 CM. TO 290 KM.

S. Europe

Neuchâtel, Collombey

Villasanta, Rho, Milano, Sannazaro, Vanuzzo, Como

Cremona, Mantova, Cortemaggiore, Fornovo di Taro

La Mède, Berre-l'Étang, Fos-sur-Mer, Frontignan

Café de Lavéra—

SCALE 1:29 MILLION   1 CM. TO 290 KM.

Persian Gulf

SCALE 1:29 MILLION   1 CM. TO 290 KM.

N. America

Whiting, East Chicago, Lemont, Lockport, Hammond

St. Paul Park & Pine Bend

Wood River, Hartford, East St. Louis—

Bradford, Warren, Rouseville, Farmers Valley, Reno, Franklin, Emlenton, Karns City

Bayonne, Westville, Bayonne, Sewaren

Marcus Hook, Philadelphia, Delaware City, Linden

Port Credit, Clarkson, Oakville

West Branch, Bay City, Alma, Corunna

Paulsboro, Westville, Bayonne, Sewaren

Baytown, Beaumont, Lake Charles, Nederland, Sweeny

Westlake, Port Neches, Pasadena

SCALE 1:29 MILLION   1 CM. TO 290 KM.

Oil refineries (1968)

Crude oil refining capacity by producing centre
'000 barrels per stream day

400 AND OVER
270
180
105
19
UNDER 6   —   6 — 19

Associated petro-chemicals

Petro-chemicals are derived from petroleum 'feed-stock'—crude oil and natural gas. The primary products, ethylene, ethylene, ammonia and aromatic hydro-carbons, are the 'building blocks' for many other petro-chemicals, including organic monomers and polymers, synthetic resins, plastics, synthetic rubber and fibres.

In 1945 of a total world production of 1 million tons of organic chemicals very little originated from petroleum. In 1965 79% of the 34 million tons produced were petro-chemicals.

Petro-chemicals were first produced in the U.S.A. The U.S.A. has long been the largest producer of petro-chemicals but the shift of oil refining into the consumer markets of Western Europe post-1945 paved the way for the development of a major petro-chemical industry. Now Japan and Australia are developing their own refining complexes and the oil producing areas of the Middle East and Caribbean have similar aims.

37

© Oxford University Press

Hydro-electric Power

Hydro-electric power

Dams with associated power plants of capacity shown. Where dams share a power plant the symbol refers to the power plant.

Plant capacity (megawatts)

BUILT 1965

UNDER CONSTRUCTION/PROPOSED BEFORE 1970

200 – 500	500 – 1 000	1 000 – 3 500
3 500 AND OVER		

La Rance : Tidal power plant

+ Capacity data not available but believed to be at least 200 MW

Where several dams together form one river system this is named in CAPITALS with the individual dam names following, for example
ACHELOÖS: Kremastá and Kastrákion

Total installed capacity by region
(1963-5 av. in megawatts)

30 000 AND OVER	200 – 500
10 000 – 30 000	50 – 200
3 500 – 10 000	0 – 50
1 000 – 3 500	NIL

DATA NA

H.E.P. installed capacity

202 200 MW 1963-5 av.¹
95 698 1963-5 av.¹

	PERCENTAGE	
	1963-5 av.	1963-5 av.¹
U.S.A.	21	25
U.S.S.R.	11	5
Canada	10	11
Japan	8	9
Italy	7	10
France	6	8
Sweden	4	5
Norway	4	5
Switzerland	4	4
Others	25	19
	100	100

¹Excl. China P.R.

H.E.P. production

839 679 million kWh 1963-5 av.¹
440 330 million 1963-5 av.¹

	PERCENTAGE	
	1963-5 av.	1963-5 av.¹
U.S.A.	22	26
Canada	13	16
U.S.S.R.	9	5
Japan	9	10
Norway	5	5
France	5	5
Sweden	5	7
Italy	3	2
Brazil	24	19
Others		
	100	100

¹Excl. China P.R.

Modified Gall Projection
Equatorial Scale 1 : 88 Million approx.

Hydro-electric power production (1963-5 av.)

thousand million

100 & OVER	
45 – 100	
5 – 45	
1 – 5	
0 – 1	NIL

DATA NA

39

© Oxford University Press

SCALE 1:22 MILLION
SCALE 1:53 MILLION 1 CM TO 530 KM.
SCALE 1:350 MILLION 1 CM TO 3 500 KM.

Uranium/Rare Earths/Nuclear Energy

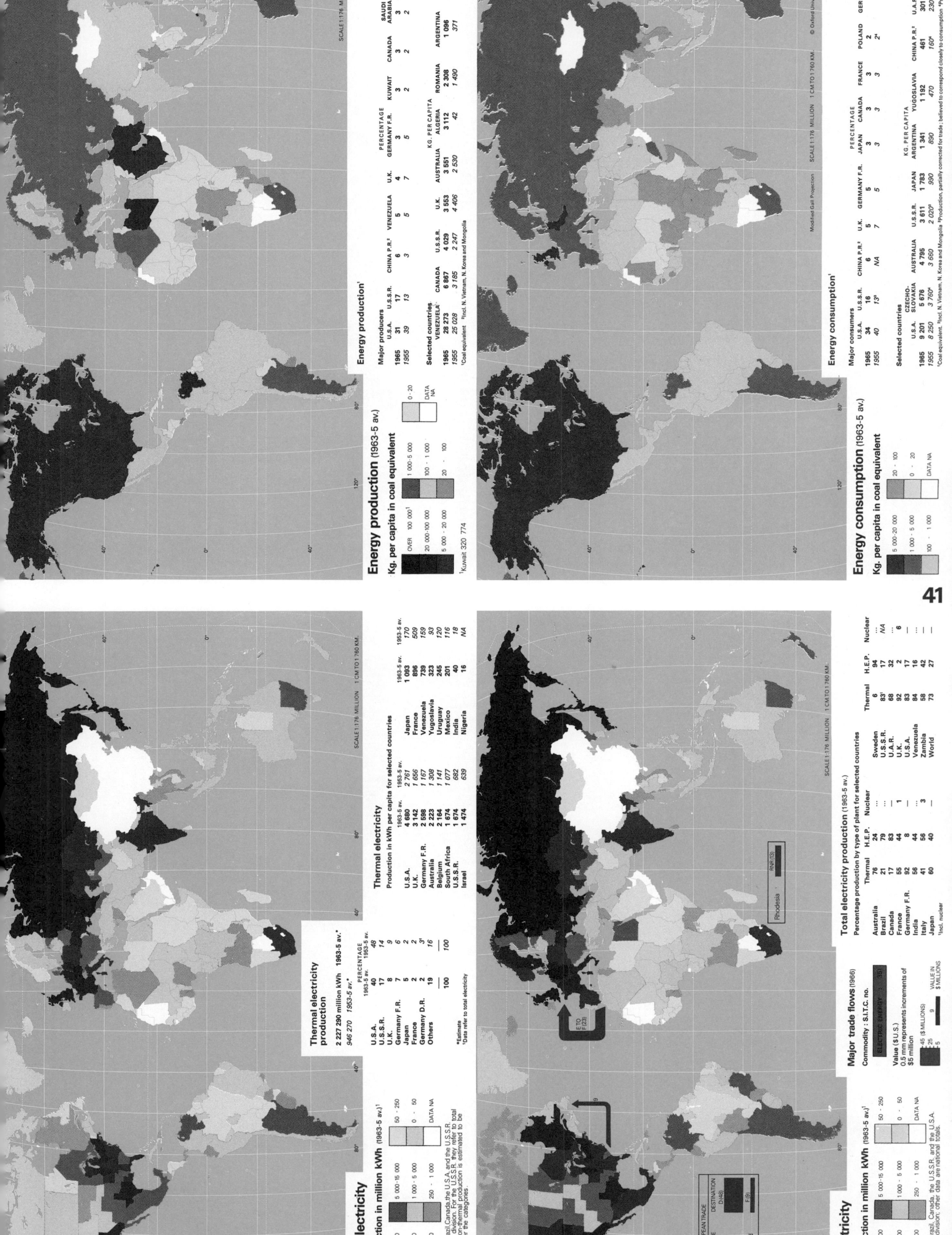

Thermal electricity

Thermal electricity production

2 227 230 million kWh 1963-5 av.[*]
946 270 1953-5 av.[*]

PERCENTAGE

	1953-5 av.	1963-5 av.[*]
U.S.A.	40	48
U.S.S.R.	17	14
Germany F.R.	8	9
U.K.	7	6
Japan	5	6
France	2	2
Germany D.R.	2	3[*]
Others	19	16
	100	100

[*]Estimate
[1]Data refer to total electricity

Annual production in million kWh (1963-5 av.)[1]
OVER 100 000
45 000-100 000
15 000-45 000
5 000-15 000
1 000-5 000
250-1 000
50-250
0-50
DATA NA

[1]Data for Australia, Brazil, Canada, the U.S.A. and the U.S.S.R. are by administrative division. For the U.S.S.R. they refer to total electricity; however, non-thermal production is estimated to be not so high as to alter the categories.

SCALE 1:176 MILLION   1 CM TO 1 760 KM.

Thermal electricity

Production in kWh per capita for selected countries

	1963-5 av.	1953-5 av.
U.S.A.	4 680	2 761
U.K.	3 142	1 656
Germany F.R.	2 598	1 167
Australia	2 223	1 308
Belgium	2 164	1 141
South Africa	1 674	1 077
U.S.S.R.	1 674	682
Israel	1 474	639
Japan	1 093	170
France	896	509
Venezuela	739	159
Yugoslavia	323	93
Uruguay	245	120
Mexico	201	116
India	40	18
Nigeria	16	NA

Total electricity

Annual production in million kWh (1963-5 av.)[1]
OVER 100 000
45 000-100 000
15 000-45 000
5 000-15 000
1 000-5 000
250-1 000
50-250
0-50
DATA NA

[1]Data for Australia, Brazil, Canada, the U.S.S.R. and the U.S.A. are by administrative division; other data are national totals.

SCALE 1:176 MILLION   1 CM TO 1 760 KM.

Rhodesia

Total electricity production

Percentage production by type of plant for selected countries

	Thermal	H.E.P.	Nuclear			Thermal	H.E.P.	Nuclear
Australia	76	24	...		Sweden	6	94	...
Brazil	21	79	...		U.S.S.R.	83[1]	17	...
Canada	17	83	...		U.A.R.	68	32	...
France	55	44	1		U.S.A.	83	17	1
Germany F.R.	92	8	...		Venezuela	84	16	...
India	56	44	...		Zambia	58	42	...
Italy	56	41	3		World	73	27	6
Japan	60	40	...					

[1]incl. nuclear

Major trade flows (1966)

Commodity : S.I.T.C. no.
ELECTRIC ENERGY 351

Value ($U.S.)
0.5 mm represents increments of $5 million

INTRA-EUROPEAN TRADE
PROVENANCE DESTINATION
Austria D(48)
Switzerland F(9)

VALUE IN $ MILLIONS
45 26 9 5

ETO F(23)

Energy production (1963-5 av.)

Kg. per capita in coal equivalent
OVER 100 000[1]
20 000-100 000
5 000-20 000
1 000-5 000
100-1 000
20-100
0-20
DATA NA

Kuwait 320 774

SCALE 1:176 MILLION   1 CM TO 1 760 KM.

Energy production[1]

Major producers

MILLION MET. TONS
		PERCENTAGE				
	U.S.A.	U.S.S.R.	CHINA P.R.[2]	VENEZUELA	U.K.	GERMANY F.R.
1965	31	17	6	5	5	3
1955	39	13	3	5	7	5

	ALGERIA	ROMANIA	KUWAIT	CANADA	SAUDI ARABIA	POLAND	INDIA	CHINA P.R.	OTHERS	WORLD
1965	3	2	3	3	3	2	850	480	23	5 327
1955	5	3	2	2		3	103	166	19	3 295

Selected countries

KG. PER CAPITA
	VENEZUELA	CANADA	U.S.S.R.	U.K.	AUSTRALIA	ALGERIA	ROMANIA	ARGENTINA	INDIA	CHINA P.R.
1965	28 273	6 867	4 029	4 406	3 551	3 112	2 308	1 096	850	480
1955	25 028	3 785	2 247		2 530	42	1 490	371	103	166

[1]Coal equivalent. [2]Incl. N. Vietnam, N. Korea and Mongolia

Energy consumption (1963-5 av.)

Kg. per capita in coal equivalent
5 000-20 000
1 000-5 000
100-1 000
20-100
0-20
DATA NA

Major consumers

MILLION MET. TONS
		PERCENTAGE							
	U.S.A.	U.S.S.R.	CHINA P.R.[2]	GERMANY F.R.	U.K.	JAPAN	FRANCE	CANADA	POLAND	GERMANY D.R.
1965	34	16	6	5	5	5	3	3	2	2
1955	40	13[1]	NA	5	7		3	3	2[1]	2[1]

	OTHERS	WORLD
1965	21	5 223
1955	NA	3 426

Selected countries

KG. PER CAPITA
	U.S.A.	CZECHO-SLOVAKIA	U.S.S.R.	AUSTRALIA	JAPAN	YUGOSLAVIA	ARGENTINA	U.A.R.	INDIA	CHINA P.R.[2]	NIGERIA	WORLD AVERAGE
1965	9 201	5 676	3 611	4 795	1 783	1 192	1 341	301	172	461	44	1 604
1955	8 250	3 760[*]	2 020[*]	3 660	990	470	890	230	120	160[*]	40	1 290

[1]Coal equivalent. [2]Incl. N. Vietnam, N. Korea and Mongolia. [*]Production, partially corrected for trade, believed to correspond closely to consumption. [*]Production data

Modified Gall Projection
© Oxford University Press
SCALE 1:176 MILLION   1 CM TO 1 760 KM.

Iron/Steel

Iron and steel are the commonest, as well as the cheapest, of the metals. They provide a basic material for a host of secondary industries, including mechanical engineering, constructional engineering, motors, hardware and hollow-ware, shipbuilding, and also railways and collieries.

Historically, the industry has usually arisen where iron ore and coking coal were found in proximity and where there was a demand for iron and steel products. Typical examples abound in Britain, in England, South Wales and the Ruhr. The American steel industry, however, with the growth in importance of the Lake Superior iron ore fields, has become less concentrated on the coalfields and more dependent on sites close to its markets and where the ores are lowest, leading to development of lakeside steel centres. In Japan and increasingly in other countries the industry depends on seaborne ore. Once the industry is established in a particular location, there is a strong tendency for it to remain and develop there.

Iron was not used by man until long after such metals as copper and its alloy, bronze, which gave the name to the Bronze Age which preceded the Iron Age. Pure iron is too soft for use in implements, and until engines and railways were built there was no great need for iron.

The principal ores are haematite (Fe_2O_3), magnetite (Fe_3O_4), limonite ($2Fe_2O_3.3H_2O$), siderite or chalybite ($FeCO_3$). Magnetite and haematite are the richest, with about 72% iron; haematite about 70%, limonite about 60% and siderite about 48%. These theoretical percentages are never attained in the iron ore deposits, even the best and most productive magnetite ores of Kiruna and Gällivare, in Northern Sweden, are never attained in the iron ore deposits. Limonite deposits are of secondary origin, and siderite deposits may be of primary or of secondary origin.

Broadly, only the rich ores (over 50% Fe) enter international trade, though an understandable exception is the export of lean Lorraine ore from France to Germany and Belgium/Luxembourg. Newly-developed fields are changing the established pattern of iron ore production. The U.S.A. is taking increasing amounts from Canada, with the development of the Labrador deposits, as well as from the newer Venezuelan, Brazilian and Liberian fields. The U.S.S.R. has become a major exporter since the war; other relatively new exporters are China P.R., Chile, Peru and Australia. Most iron ore business is done on the basis of long-term contracts as the investment involved is so large. New ports for major iron and steel firms to have a financial interest in iron mines and to build special ore-carrying vessels and dock facilities.

of ore fines and the pelletization of inferior ores made it possible to utilize low-iron content home ores.

Blast furnace efficiency was also improved by developments in design, better refractory linings, and reduced coke consumption. As a result, *in the best practices throughout the world*, the average iron content of metallic bearing materials charged into the blast furnace increased from about 52% Fe in 1950 to over 60% Fe in 1965; the raw iron ore part of the burden decreased from about eight-tenths of the charge in 1950 to about one-third in 1965. The downward trend of tons of total blast furnace burden per ton of hot metal pig iron produced continued, about 3.3 tons being required to produce one ton of pig iron in 1950 whereas in 1965 only about 2.4 tons of burden materials including coke were required. The production rate was much increased, rising from the typical large blast furnace of 1950-1955 which produced about 1 500 tons a day to a production of about 2 750 tons a day from the largest units in 1965.

In foundries the molten iron is poured into moulds to make cast iron products, such as pipes, railway chairs, parts of machinery and of internal combustion engines, etc. Though hard and strong, cast iron is generally brittle and incapable of being rolled, forged or drawn, as steel can be. Indeed, steel is remarkably versatile, being worked into such diverse products as girders, rails, bars, plates, sheets, strip, tinplate, tubes and wires, besides various castings and forgings. It has virtually eliminated wrought iron and is replacing cast iron in some uses.

Ore is smelted in the blast furnace to produce pig iron, which generally carries impurities, mainly 4% of carbon and smaller amounts of phosphorus, sulphur, silicon and manganese. There were considerable advances in iron-making and in the efficiency of the blast furnace in the period 1950-1965. Coal cleaning, coal pulverization, and scientific blending permitted the use of previously unsuitable coals for the manufacture of coke. Exploration and exploitation of substantial deposits of high-iron content ore, particularly in South America, Canada, Africa and Australia, and their shipment by very large carriers to the major steel producers provided a valuable source of good quality raw material, while the improved sintering

making process may take from 8 to 20 hours. By contrast, the Bessemer converter (*acid* Bessemer process invented by Henry Bessemer in 1856 and *basic* process about twenty years later by Thomas and Gilchrist) generally has a capacity of 25 to 50 tons and uses molten iron almost exclusively, air being blown through the molten metal (no fuel being used) and refining being completed in 12-15 minutes. The basic Bessemer ('Thomas') process was most important in France, Belgium and Luxembourg, being the only suitable process to deal with the high phosphoric irons produced by the local ores. The Bessemer process producing great quantities of cheap mild steel provided material for much of the industrial advance throughout the world in the nineteenth century and displaced wrought iron as the chief constructional material.

Its dominance was in turn gradually challenged by the rise of the open-hearth process which took the lead in production in Britain in 1891 and in the U.S.A. in 1908. The crucible process (invented by Huntsman in 1740) has universally declined, especially since the end of World War I and the emergence of the electric processes mainly used to make alloy and other special steels and used with particular advantage in areas of cheap electric power (see table below showing major innovations). With the availability of low-cost high purity oxygen after World War II, the lead of basic open hearth process began to be threatened. Various hearth steel-making processes have been developed and have achieved rapid application. Chief among these is the Linz-Donawitz process (named from

two neighbouring Austrian towns where the process was originally developed) abbreviated to the 'L-D' process and also known as 'BOF' and 'BOP' after basic oxygen process or furnace. In its operation, a stream of oxygen of more than 99.5% purity is directed by a lance onto a bath consisting of blast furnace hot metal and scrap iron coolant. As in the Bessemer process no fuel is required. A normal blowing time is about 25 minutes and several increases in furnace size have taken place in the years between 1954 and 1965, rising in many places from 35 tons per heat to 150-ton heats. With fast blowing and charging, production rates of the order of 300 to 400 tons an hour have been achieved; there is no doubt that these proportions will grow and that in time the process will displace the open hearth.

The replacement boom after World War II and the demand resulting from the Korean War led to increased production up to 1952. Since then there have been three periods of lower world production, in 1952, 1954, and 1957-58, caused mainly by reductions in North American output. By 1959 output had recovered and 1960 showed a 13% increase over the previous year. Since then production has constantly increased. World crude steel

production exceeded 400 million tons for the first time in 1964 and during the decade ending in 1965 almost doubled with an average annual increase of over 20 million tons. From the end of World War II to 1965 there were appreciable changes in the world distribution of iron- and steel-making plants, as is indicated in the figures for the U.S.A., whose share of world steel production has fallen from about one-half to one-quarter in this time, and for Japan where output has risen from 7½ to about 40 million tons in the decade 1955-1965. By 1965, however, over three-quarters of the world steel capacity was still concentrated in seven countries: the U.S.A., the U.S.S.R., Japan, Germany F.R., the U.K., France and Italy. The major technical changes that have most profoundly affected the iron and steel industry in just over one hundred years are summarized in the following table.

Major iron/steel industry innovations

Periods of development and application	
1856-1880	Bessemer pneumatic steel-making
	Thomas Gilchrist basic process
	Siemens-Martin open hearth steel-making
1910-1930	Stainless steel
	Universal rolling mill
	By-product coke ovens
	Electric arc steel-making
	Continuous hot strip mill
	Agglomeration of flue dust and fine ores
1946-1965	Oxygen steel-making
	Continuous casting
	Vacuum degassing
	Pelletization

Estimated crude steel consumption and production
Selected countries — KG. PER CAPITA

	AUSTRALIA	BELG./LUX.	BRAZIL	CANADA	GERMANY F.R.	INDIA	JAPAN	SOUTH AFRICA	SPAIN	SWEDEN	U.K.	U.S.A.	U.S.S.R.	VENEZUELA
Consumption 1965	514	330	39	531	540	16	294	210	194	424	424	656	376	138
1955	333	292	26	322	410	7	82	138	50	402	367	620	225	116
Production 1965	480	1 404	37	466	648	13	420	184	111	611	505	613	395	78
1955	243	995	21	261	425	5	106	112	45	293	393	643	208	—

International trade in iron ore, iron and steel (1963-5 av.)

Iron ore[1]

Production: 586 600 000 met. tons 1963-5 av. / 340 716 000 1953-5 av.*
Exports: 194 888 800 met. tons 1963-5 av. / 77 548 000 1953-5 av.
Percentage exported: 33% 1963-5 av. / 23% 1953-5 av.*

Exports	PERCENTAGE 1963-5 av.	1953-5 av.		Imports	PERCENTAGE 1963-5 av.	1953-5 av.
Canada	15	10		U.S.A.	21	22
U.S.S.R.	12	11		Germany F.R.	18	17
Sweden	12	17		Japan	17	6
France	11	15		Belg./Lux.	11	11
Venezuela	8	7		U.K.	9	16
Liberia	8	2		Poland	5	5
India	6	2		Czechoslovakia	5	5
Brazil	5	2		Italy	5	3
Others	25	32		Others	9	15
	100	100			100	100

Pig iron/Ferro-alloys

Production: 311 366 000 met. tons 1963-5 av. / 173 362 000 1953-5 av.*
Exports: 8 254 000 met. tons 1963-5 av. / 3 592 000 1953-5 av.
Percentage exported: 3% 1963-5 av. / 2% 1953-5 av.*

Exports	PERCENTAGE 1963-5 av.	1953-5 av.		Imports	PERCENTAGE 1963-5 av.	1953-5 av.
U.S.S.R.	27	—		Japan	27	13
Germany F.R.	10	13		U.S.A.	10	10
Norway	10	6		Italy	9	6
South Africa	8	8		Germany D.R.	8	19
Canada	7	6		U.K.	6	6
France	6	6		Germany F.R.	6	5
Germany D.R.	5	5		Belg./Lux.	5	9
Belg./Lux.	5	9		Poland	5	9
Rhodesia	3	2		Sweden	3	2
Others	22	39		Others	22	39
	100	100			100	100

Iron and steel scrap

Production data not available
Percentage exported: 1% 1963-5 av. / 1% 1953-5 av.

Exports: 13 185 000 met. tons 1963-5 av. / 4 988 000 1953-5 av.*
Imports: 5 732 000 met. tons 1963-5 av. / 1 711 000 1953-5 av.

Exports	PERCENTAGE 1963-5 av.	1953-5 av.		Imports	PERCENTAGE 1963-5 av.	1953-5 av.
U.S.A.	49	43		Italy	22	14
Germany F.R.	12	12		France	13	10
France	11	11		Argentina	10	22
U.S.S.R.	3	1		Spain	8	7
Canada	3	3		Hungary	7	3
Netherlands	3	3		Germany F.R.	6	7
India	3	3		Pakistan	5	3
Others	16	24		Belg./Lux.	4	10
	100	100		Others	25	24
					100	100

Steel

Production: 428 044 000 met. tons 1963-5 av. / 242 792 000 1953-5 av.*
Exports: 4 751 000 met. tons 1963-5 av. / 1 977 000 1953-5 av.
Imports: 13 069 000 met. tons 1963-5 av. / 5 891 000 1953-5 av.

Exports	PERCENTAGE 1963-5 av.	1953-5 av.		Imports	PERCENTAGE 1963-5 av.	1953-5 av.
Germany F.R.	22	14		Japan	33	19
U.S.S.R.	13	9		Italy	30	27
Belg./Lux.	10	22		Germany F.R.	9	7
U.K.	7	6		Canada	6	3
France	10	7		France	4	3
Japan	8	7		Mexico	4	7
Canada	6	5		Spain	3	3
India	4	10		U.S.A.	10	30
Others	20	20		Others	1	1
	100	100			100	100

*Estimate   [1]Including pyrites

In the U.K. the chief consumers of steel are the construction and engineering industries (19%) and the motor vehicles industry (16%). In the U.S.A. the automobile industry consumes 28% of construction 17% and containers 12%.

Steel is made from pig iron by removing much of the carbon, as well as the phosphorus and sulphur. The addition of various ferro-alloys, which is required for the production of alloy steels, which are in growing demand as a result of the invention of the gas turbine (which requires for its blades a steel which can withstand extremely high temperatures) and of other engineering advances.

Different steel-making processes are used according to the quality of the pig iron and the melting charge and the nature of the required product. Until the late 1960's, the most important in Britain and the U.S.A. was the open hearth (Siemens-Martin) process. Here a proportion of scrap is used with the pig iron. The furnaces vary greatly in size with capacities up to 350 tons or more, and the steel-

About 75% of the world's steel production comes from the highly industrialized areas of the U.S.A., Western Europe and Japan – where most of it is also converted into various manufactures, such as motor vehicles etc. The table below shows further steel production data for selected countries.

In the U.S.A. the industry is largely concentrated on the Northern Appalachian coalfield around Pittsburgh (its original location), but more recent expansion has tended to take place on the lake shores (Chicago, Detroit, Cleveland) at the trans-shipment plants have also been built on the eastern seaboard, at such sites as Sparrows Point. The British industry is widely dispersed on inland and coastal sites, all with access to good coal. With the gradual exhaustion of most of its rich ore deposits, the U.K. imports nearly half of its ore requirements, mainly from Sweden, Canada and Venezuela. The industry is based on Ruhr, Belgian and French coal and on the local lean ores.

By 1965 the U.S.S.R., Eastern Europe and China P.R. accounted for one-third of crude steel output. The U.S.S.R. was the major producer of this group with a fivefold increase over the immediate pre-war level, and China P.R. ranked seventh in world production with the greatest rate of increase in the period since 1958.

In 1959 Japan overtook France to become the fifth world producer, due to very large additions to capacity in 1957, and by 1965 she was third in world production. For an historical representation of world steel production see the diagram below.

Crude steel and pig iron
World production 1880-1967[1]

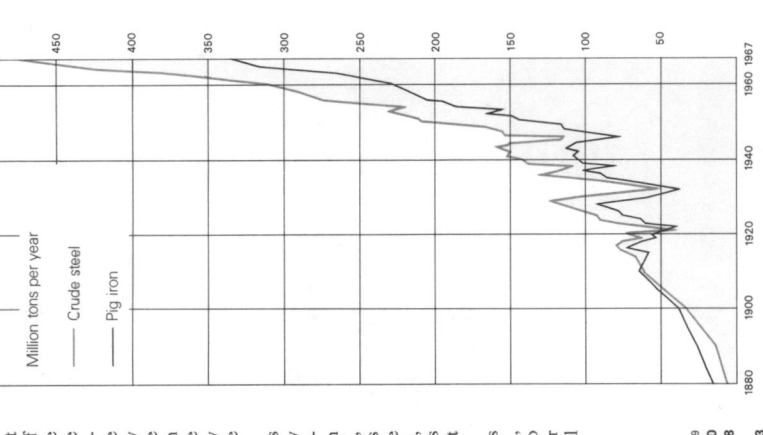

Million tons per year — Crude steel / Pig iron

[1] Excl. China P.R. whose estimated production for 1955 and 1965 in million met. tons, was as follows: pig iron, 3.7 and 19; steel, 2.9 and 15

Crude steel production
Selected countries

	1955	1960	1965	1969
	MILLION MET. TONS			
U.S.A.	106.2	90.1	119.3	128.0
U.K.	20.1	24.7	27.4	26.8
European Coal & Steel Community	52.5	72.8	86.0	107.3
India	1.7	3.3	6.4	6.5
U.S.S.R.	45.3	65.3	91.0	110.2
Japan	9.5	22.5	41.1	82.2

Iron Ore/Steel

43

Non-ferrous Minerals and Metals

Aluminium	p. 45	Tin	p. 45
Bauxite	p. 47	Zinc	p. 46
Copper	p. 47	Lead	p. 47

For individual country data see Statistical Supplement

The ability to extract metals from the ores in which the earth's crust abounds marked one of man's most important steps towards civilization. Some of the earth's mineral resources remain unexploited today, notably those in the sea and under the polar ice-caps and other deposits which are too small for mining to be profitable. Nevertheless, production of the major non-ferrous metals is widespread throughout the world and the five most important metals—aluminium, copper, lead, zinc and tin—play a vital part in the world economy.

Aluminium

Aluminium is the most abundant metallic element, forming 8% of the earth's crust. Although aluminium can be obtained from many common rocks, bauxite is the only important ore, consisting of hydrated aluminium oxides together with impurities of iron, silicon, and titanium oxides. Bauxite deposits are formed on or near the earth's surface through humid tropical weathering of rocks containing aluminium silicates.

Alumina (aluminium oxide) is produced by the reaction of caustic soda on bauxite dissolving out the alumina which is then precipitated and roasted in a kiln to produce a white powder. The production of aluminium metal from alumina by smelting requires great amounts of electricity, which accounts for the industry being established where there is cheap hydro-electric power available. Aluminium has many valuable properties which have encouraged its use. It is the lightest of the major metals, weighing only about one-third as much as steel, copper or zinc, and a quarter as much as lead. It is second only to copper as a heat and electricity conductor, and it reflects light and radiant heat well. It also has a strong resistance to corrosion. World consumption has grown during the past 25 years at a faster rate than any of the other major metals, initially as a result of the growth of the aircraft industry. The applications for aluminium have steadily widened, and more recently its use in the building and electrical industries has grown considerably.

Copper

Copper, the oldest of the major metals, is produced in over 50 countries and this number will rise during coming years as new mines come into operation in Mauritania, Indonesia, Malaysia and Bougainville Island. At present the four major production areas account for 80% of total world mine production. They are listed below with their 1969 production statistics.

	'000 MET. TONS
North America (U.S.A. and Canada)	1 901
African Copper Belt (Zambia and Congo)	1 084
Western Andes (Chile and Peru)	887
Urals and Kazakhstan, U.S.S.R.	875

Products made of copper or containing copper components are used in every country in the world. As copper is malleable and ductile and has a high electrical conductivity, over 50% of world consumption is in the electrical and allied industries. Copper's ability to withstand corrosion leads to its use in shipbuilding and construction, as does its capacity for forming strong and easily worked alloys, such as bronze and brass, many of which are also used in general engineering and the motor industry. Most copper ore is concentrated, smelted and refined in the countries in which it is produced, although there are some important exceptions to this. At present, for example, the whole of the rapidly expanding production by the Philippines is shipped in the form of concentrates to the U.S.A. and Japan while part of the smelter production of the Congo D.R., South Africa, Zambia, Chile and Peru is exported for refining in other countries.

Since one of copper's greatest virtues is its durability, it is possible to recover considerable quantities of copper from scrap materials. "Secondary" copper recovered in this way accounts for 40% of total world copper consumption.

In 1967 Chile, Congo D.R., Peru and Zambia, who between them produce a third of world mine output held a conference at Lusaka, Zambia, and formed the Conseil Intergouvernemental des Pays Exportateurs de Cuivre, known as CIPEC.

Lead and Zinc

Lead and zinc ores are very often found together and contain important quantities of silver and gold. For producing the metals by the electrolytic and well established thermal processes, the ores must be treated to yield separate lead and zinc concentrates. The Imperial Smelting process, which uses a blast furnace can, however, produce both metals from mixed concentrates. Zinc and lead are widely distributed throughout the world, and Canada, Australia, the U.S.A. and U.S.S.R. are the biggest producers. The chief source of lead is galena (lead sulphide, PbS) but some is also found as cerussite ($PbCO_3$) formed by the oxidation of galena. The main use of lead is in storage batteries (used in motor vehicles), which takes about 30% of world production. Other important uses are for sheathing electric power cables; for anti-knock compounds to adjust the octane rating of petrol; as building materials in the form of sheet and pipe; for solders and other alloys such as printing metal and for paint pigments and other compounds such as ceramic glazes. Lead also has a wide range of miscellaneous uses, including shielding for radio-active materials, shot and bullet rod for ammunition, foil and seals for packaging, balance weights.

The chief source of zinc is the mineral sphalerite or zinc blende (ZnS), but smithsonite ("calamine", $ZnCO_3$) and various silicates which are formed by the action of air and water on zinc blende are important in some parts of the world. Nearly a half of the world's annual zinc production is used to protect steel products in the form of galvanized and other zinc coatings. Brass, an alloy with copper, is another very important use, and special high purity zinc alloyed with 4% aluminium and a little magnesium is pressure diecast on a very large scale to produce components of cars, household equipments, hardware etc. Zinc sheet and strip are important building materials and zinc compounds are used in the manufacture of rubber, paints and ceramic goods.

Tin

Most of the world's tin deposits occur as cassiterite (SnO_2), either in alluvial deposits, for example in Malaysia and Nigeria, where it is recovered mainly by dredging and gravel pumps, or as veins and lodes, for example in Bolivia, where it is mined by conventional methods. Because it is unusually malleable and resists corrosion, it is largely used in the making of tin plate for the canning industry. With the development of electrolytic methods of tin plating, in which the coating of tin is very thin, the quantity of tin used per ton of tinplate has decreased but a greater amount of tin plate is being produced. Other uses include alloys (such as whitemetal, bronze and gunmetal), solder and tin oxide and tin powders.

International trade in non-ferrous minerals and metals¹ (1963-5 av.)

Copper ore/Copper metal

Exports — Ore (731 000 met. tons 1963-5 av. / 381 000 1953-5 av.)
	1963-5 av.	1953-5 av.
Philippines	37	20*
Cyprus	28	28
Canada	12*	11
Chile	5	8
Peru	3	3
Others	15	52
	100	100

Exports — Metal (3 720 000 met. tons 1963-5 av. / 2 046 000 1953-5 av.)
	1963-5 av.	1953-5 av.
Zambia	18	18*
Chile	15	18
U.S.A.	10	12
Belg./Lux.	9	8
Congo D.R.	8*	11
Others	40	33
	100	100

Imports — Ore (967 000 met. tons 1963-5 av. / 549 000 1953-5 av.)
	1963-5 av.	1953-5 av.
Japan	63	28
Germany F.R.	15	28
Sweden	9	8
Norway	6	6*
U.S.A.³	2	19
Others	5	32
	100	100

Imports — Metal (3 576 000 met. tons 1963-5 av. / 1 783 000 1953-5 av.)
	1963-5 av.	1953-5 av.
Germany F.R.	16	14
U.K.	15	21
U.S.A.	13	26
Belg./Lux.	10	8
France	8	8
Others	38	30
	100	100

Tin ore/Tin metal

Exports — Ore (73 000 met. tons 1963-5 av. / 121 000 1953-5 av.)
	1963-5 av.	1953-5 av.
Indonesia	29	38
Bolivia¹	29	25
Thailand¹	19	9
Congo D.R.	11*⁴	15
Argentina	3*	—
Others	9	13
	100	100

Exports — Metal (144 000 met. tons 1963-5 av. / 147 000 1953-5 av.)
	1963-5 av.	1953-5 av.
Malaysia	52	47
Netherlands	7	19
U.K.	7	8
Nigeria	7	6
China P.R.*	6	3
Others	19	23
	100	100

Imports — Ore (103 000 met. tons 1963-5 av. / 153 000 1953-5 av.)
	1963-5 av.	1953-5 av.
U.K.	44	40
Netherlands	20	24
Malaysia	11	8
Germany F.R.	8	7
Belg./Lux.	7	—
Others	10	18
	100	100

Imports — Metal (149 000 met. tons 1963-5 av. / 140 000 1953-5 av.)
	1963-5 av.	1953-5 av.
U.S.A.	28	48
Japan	10	4
Germany F.R.	9	5
France	6	6
U.K.	6	1
Others	40	36
	100	100

Zinc ore/Zinc metal

Exports — Ore (1 908 000 met. tons 1963-5 av. / 1 520 000 1953-5 av.)
	1963-5 av.	1953-5 av.
Canada²	22	29
Mexico	16	25
Peru²	15	15
Sweden	13	30
Finland	9	3
Others	41	53
	100	100

Exports — Metal (1 073 000 met. tons 1963-5 av. / 884 000 1953-5 av.)
	1963-5 av.	1953-5 av.
U.S.A.	19	33
U.K.	17	23
Germany F.R.	11	6
Italy	6	5
Netherlands	6	6
Others	41	37
	100	100

Imports — Ore (637 000 met. tons 1963-5 av. / 430 000 1953-5 av.)
	1963-5 av.	1953-5 av.
Belg./Lux.	22	27
France	21	20
Germany F.R.	19	30
U.S.A.²	10	4
Japan	9	3
Others	19	16
	100	100

Imports — Metal (1 132 000 met. tons 1963-5 av. / 936 000 1953-5 av.)
	1963-5 av.	1953-5 av.
Australia	19	20
Mexico	17	8
Canada	12	24
U.S.S.R.	7	4
Peru	4	7
Others	44	38
	100	100

Lead ore/Lead metal¹⁰

Exports — Ore (619 000 met. tons 1963-5 av. / 392 000 1953-5 av.)
	1963-5 av.	1953-5 av.
Morocco	20	27
Australia	15*	10
Peru	19	16
South West Africa²	7	3
Sweden	38	38
Others		
	100	100

Exports — Metal (1 277 000 met. tons 1963-5 av. / 765 000 1953-5 av.)
	1963-5 av.	1953-5 av.
Canada	16	20
Belg./Lux.	15	8
U.S.A.	12	24
India	7	4
U.S.S.R.	6	6
Australia	44	38
	100	100

Imports — Ore (1 073 000 met. tons 1963-5 av. / 884 000 1953-5 av.)
	1963-5 av.	1953-5 av.
U.S.A.	19	33
U.K.	17	23
Germany F.R.	11	6
Italy	6	5
Netherlands	6	6
Others	41	37
	100	100

Bauxite ore¹¹/Aluminium

Exports — Ore (18 378 000 met. tons 1963-5 av. / 10 416 000 1953-5 av.)
	1963-5 av.	1953-5 av.
Jamaica	33*	19
Surinam	21	31
Guyana	8*	21
Greece	6	4
Yugoslavia	5	5
Others	27	20
	100	100

Exports — Metal (2 291 000 met. tons 1963-5 av. / 944 000 1953-5 av.)
	1963-5 av.	1953-5 av.
Canada	28	49
U.S.A.	14	17
Norway	11	6
France	9	4*
U.S.S.R.	14	8
Others	29	33
	100	100

Imports — Ore (17 610 000 met. tons 1963-5 av. / 9 387 000 1953-5 av.)
	1963-5 av.	1953-5 av.
U.S.A.	60	52
Canada	10	28¹³
Germany F.R.	9	11
Japan	9	—
U.S.S.R.	3*	—
Others	9	6
	100	100

Imports — Metal (2 090 000 met. tons 1963-5 av. / 868 000 1953-5 av.)
	1963-5 av.	1953-5 av.
U.S.A.	23	30
U.K.	17	25
Germany F.R.	11	6
Belg./Lux.	8	6
Italy	9	4*
Others	23	16
	100	100

Annual consumption of major non-ferrous metals

Selected countries (1963-5 av.)

'000 MET. TONS	COPPER	TIN	LEAD	ZINC	ALUMINIUM
U.S.A.	1 679	61¹²	966	1 099	2 576
U.S.S.R.	749	30	319	323	858*
U.K.	612	22	301	276	341
Germany F.R.	539	13	258	312	363
Japan	412	18	150	321	256
France	276	11⁵	162	190	247
Italy	208	6	93	102	125
China P.R.	120	15	71	80	88
Australia	92	5	56	102	67*
India	69	4	42	60	63
Mexico	34	1	53	20	18
Poland	—	3	55	112	56
World	5 800	229	2 800	3 900	6 000

Metal production

Copper (5 230 000 met. tons 1963-5 av.* / 3 081 000 1953-5 av.*)
	1963-5 av.	1953-5 av.
U.S.A.	24	30
U.S.S.R.	12	11
Zambia	12	12*
Chile	11	12*
Canada	11	7
Japan	7	6
Germany F.R.	6	8
Congo D.R.	6	8
Peru	3	1
Others	14	11
	100	100

Tin (197 000 met. tons 1963-5 av.* / 197 000 1953-5 av.*)
	1963-5 av.	1953-5 av.
Malaysia	39	35
China P.R.*	13	5
Indonesia	11	12
Bolivia	11	12
Netherlands	9	14
Nigeria	7	6
Belgium	6	8
Thailand	5	7
Others	13	9
	100	100

Lead (2 520 000 met. tons 1963-5 av.* / 1 959 000 1953-5 av.*)
	1963-5 av.	1953-5 av.
U.S.A.	15	22
U.S.S.R.*	13	13
Australia	11	12
Mexico	7	11
Canada	6	7
Germany F.R.	4	6
Yugoslavia	4	4
Japan	4	4
Belgium	4	4
Others	32	22
	100	100

Zinc (3 727 000 met. tons 1963-5 av.* / 2 501 000 1953-5 av.*)
	1963-5 av.	1953-5 av.
U.S.A.	15	22
U.S.S.R.*	11	10
Japan	9	8
Canada	8	8
Belgium	6	8
Poland	4	6
Australia	4	7
France	4	4
Germany F.R.	4	4
Others	23	22
	100	100

Aluminium (5 843 000 met. tons 1963-5 av.* / 2 805 000 1953-5 av.*)
	1963-5 av.	1953-5 av.
U.S.A.	39	46
U.S.S.R.*	12	13
Canada	12	19
France	5	5
Japan	5	4
Norway	4	4
Germany F.R.	4	4
Italy	2	2
China P.R.*	2	—
Others	14	8
	100	100

*Estimate ¹Incl. alloys, scrap and salts ²Metal content of ore *Estimate ¹Incl. Rhodesia *Estimate ¹Incl. copper-gold-silver concentrate ²Incl. burnt cupreous pyrites ³Excl. Cu content of cement copper and cupreous pyrites ⁴Excl. cuprous pyrites ⁵Incl. copper-nickel matte ⁶Incl. copper-lead-silver-gold ore ⁷Incl. blister and electrolytic copper ⁸Incl. tin-silver ore ⁹Incl. Pb content of base bullion ¹⁰Incl. Rwanda and Burundi ¹¹Incl. bauxite ¹²Primary and secondary tin ¹³Incl. alumina ¹⁴Incl. cryolite ¹⁵Imports from Greece only ¹⁶Incl. Saar ¹⁷Oceania

Copper/Tin

Copper/Tin

Production (1963–5 av in metric tons)

Copper mines — metal content of concentrates

Tin mining areas — metal content of ore

Processing (1965 output capacity in '000 met. tons)

Major trade flows (1966)
Commodity: S.I.T.C. no.

COPPER ORE/MATTE/ CONCENTRATES : 2831	TIN ORE/ CONCENTRATES : 2833
COPPER METAL : 682 (WORKED/UNWORKED)	TIN METAL : 687 (WORKED/UNWORKED)

Copper ore production[1]		
4 883 000 met. tons 1963–5 av.*		
2 891 000 1953–5 av.*		
	PERCENTAGE	
	1963–5 av.	1953–5 av.
U.S.A.	24	29
U.S.S.R.	15	11
Zambia	13	12
Chile	12	13
Canada	9	8
Congo D.R.	6	7
Peru	4	1
Japan	2	2
Australia	2	1
Others	13	13
	100	100

*Estimate 'Metal content

Tin ore production[1]		
198 000 met. tons 1963–5 av.*		
193 000 1953–5 av.*		
	PERCENTAGE	
	1963–5 av.	1953–5 av.
Malaysia	31	37
China P.R.*	13	6
Bolivia	12	16
U.S.S.R.*	10	5
Thailand	9	5
Indonesia	7	18
Nigeria	5	4
Congo D.R.	4	2
Australia	2	1
Others	6	6
	100	100

*Estimate 'Metal content

Where mine or mining area and processing centre are coincident the locational name is underlined for example, *McGill* or *Baia Mare*

Modified Gall Projection
Equatorial Scale 1 : 88 Million approx.

© Oxford University Press

45

Lead / Zinc

Production (1963–5 av.)

Type **Size**

LEAD

ZINC

'000 met. tons metal content

Production data not available

× LEAD AND ZINC

× LEAD   + ZINC

Processing (refining 1965)

Type **Size**

LEAD

ZINC

'000 met. tons metal output capacity

Refining capacity data not available

× LEAD   × ZINC

Cadmium is recovered as a by-product of zinc and, to a much lesser extent, lead and copper processing. The largest producers, in order, are the U.S.A., the U.S.S.R., Japan and Canada. They produced 71% of the estimated total of 12 150 met. tons of cadmium metal recovered 1963–5 av. This metal was recovered from domestic or imported ores.

Major trade flows (1966)

Commodity :   S.I.T.C. no.

ZINC ORES/CONCENTRATES	283.5
ZINC METAL (WORKED/UNWORKED) : 686	
LEAD METAL (WORKED/UNWORKED) : 685	
LEAD ORES/CONCENTRATES	283.4

Value ($U.S.)

0.5 mm represents increments of $10 million

UNDER $5 MILLION

VALUE IN $ MILLIONS

© Oxford University Press

Lead production[1]

	1963–5 av.	1953–5 av.[*][ii]
	2 583 000 met. tons	**2 029 000**
	PERCENTAGE	
	1963–5 av.	1953–5 av.
Australia	15	14
U.S.S.R.	13	10
U.S.A.	10	15
Canada	8	11
Mexico	6	6
Peru	4	4
Yugoslavia	4	NA
China P.R.	4	NA
Bulgaria	4	4
Others	29	100
	100	100

[*]Estimate   [i]Content of ore

Zinc production[1]

	1963–5 av.	1953–5 av.[*][ii]
	3 997 500 met. tons	**2 736 700**
	PERCENTAGE	
	1963–5 av.	1953–5 av.
Canada	16	13
U.S.A.	13	17
U.S.S.R.	11	9
Australia	9	9
Mexico	6	6
Japan	5	4
Peru	4	4
Poland	4	4
Italy	3	4
Others	27	25
	100	100

[*]Estimate   [i]Content of ore   [ii]Excl. Czechoslovakia, Romania & N.Vietnam

SCALE 1:29 MILLION   1 CM. TO 290 KM.

SCALE 1:29 MILLION   1 CM. TO 290 KM.

SCALE 1:29 MILLION   1 CM. TO 290 KM.

Equatorial Scale 1: 88 Million approx.

Modified Gall Projection

Bauxite (and Aluminium)/Titanium

© Oxford University Press

Modified Gall Projection
Equatorial Scale 1 : 88 Million approx.

47

Bauxite/titanium

Production (1963-5 av.)

Bauxite

('000 met. tons)

- 3000 AND OVER
- 1000-3000
- 500-1000
- 250-500
- 100-250
- 1-100

Titanium

- MAJOR CENTRE
- MINOR CENTRE

+ Production data not available

Processing (1965)

Bauxite

- REFINING (ALUMINA)
- SMELTING (ALUMINIUM)

Names underlined when refining and smelting coincident

('000 met. tons output capacity)

- 3000 AND OVER
- 900-3000
- 600-900
- 300-600
- 180-300
- 90-180
- 30-90
- 1-30

× Refining capacity data not available

Bauxite production

	1963-5 av. '000 met. tons	PERCENTAGE 1963-5 av.	1953-5 av.
	33 830 000 met. tons 1963-5 av.*		
	15 783 000 1953-5 av.*		
Jamaica	23	13
U.S.S.R.*	13	6
Surinam	12	21
Guyana	8	15
France	7	8
Guinea	5	—
U.S.A.	5	11
Hungary	4	8
Yugoslavia	4	4
Others	19	14
	100	100

Aluminium production

	1963-5 av.	1953-5 av.
	5 843 000 met. tons 1963-5 av.*	
	2 805 000 1953-5 av.*	
U.S.A.	39	46
U.S.S.R.*	14	13
Canada	12	19
France	5	4
Japan	4	2
Norway	4	2
Germany F.R.	4	4
Italy	2	2
China P.R.*	2	—
Others	14	8
	100	100

*Estimate

Titanium production[1]

	1963-5 av.	1953-5 av.
	2 482 000 met. tons 1963-5 av.*	
	1 185 000 1953-5 av.*	
U.S.A.	35	43
Australia	21	11
Canada	18	7
Norway	11	12
Malaysia*	5	4
Finland	5	4
Spain	2	—
Others	3	22
	100	100

*Estimate
[1]Ilmenite and rutile
*Exports

Major trade flows (1966)

Commodity: S.I.T.C. no.

BAUXITE/ALUMINIUM CONCENTRATES : 283.3	
ALUMINIUM METAL (WORKED/UNWORKED) : 684	

Value($U.S.)

0.5mm represents increments of \$20 million

VALUE ($ U.S.)

S.I.T.C. = STANDARD INTERNATIONAL TRADE CLASSIFICATION

SCALE 1:29 MILLION 1CM TO 290 KM

Other Minerals

Ferro-alloys are used to make various types of steels with physical and mechanical properties which would not otherwise be obtainable.

Manganese is used principally as a cleanser in the manufacture of steel, where it acts as a deoxidizer and desulphurizer. Steels containing about 1% manganese are employed for structural work and for rails; steels of 12% manganese have high tensile strength and resistance to abrasion for use in rock-crushers, sprockets, railway points and crossings, etc. The compounds of manganese are important in the production of disinfectants and batteries.

About 45% of the world's production of **nickel** is used in steels, either alone or in combination with chromium, manganese, or other metals. Stainless steel is the most important single resultant product, followed by high nickel alloys and plating and constructional steels. Nickel steels are less than 6% nickel have high strength, ductility and toughness suitable for automobile and aircraft construction, and heavy machinery, and in the dairying industries where its resistance to corrosion makes it a valuable material for containers and machinery parts in contact with liquids. Aircraft parts, warship superstructures, armour-plating and rifle barrels are also frequently made from it. Nickel alloys with 45%–85% nickel are used in sub-marine cable sheathing, radio transformers, and telephone and telegraph relay parts. About half the world's production of nickel comes from Canada's Sudbury district, although production in the U.S.S.R. is rising.

Chromium is obtained from chromite found in chrome ore. Stainless chromium - nickel steel has many uses in electrical and marine engineering, and in the dyeing and dairying industries where its resistance to corrosion makes it a valuable material for containers and machinery parts in contact with liquids. Aircraft parts, warship superstructures, armour-plating and rifle barrels are also frequently made from it. Chrome ore is used as a refractory (in the form of bricks, cements, and plasters) in constructing furnaces, and the metal and its salts are employed in the electrical industry.

Tungsten steels are used principally for high-speed machine tools and cutting instruments. Tungsten carbide, one of the hardest materials available, is widely used in cutting tools, drill bits and machine parts. Tungsten alloys are used in jet engines, rockets, and missiles. Tungsten also forms the filament in electric light bulbs. The chief sources of tungsten are the minerals wolframite, $(Fe, Mn)WO_4$, and scheelite, $CaWO_4$.

Cobalt, when alloyed, is very hard and resistant to high temperatures and is used in cutting tools. Cobalt alloys are used in jet engines and in the production of atomic energy. Cobalt is magnetic, it is a component of it, has medicinal uses and the radio-active isotope can be used in radio-therapy. Almost all the world's cobalt is obtained as a by-product from complex ores worked chiefly for the other metals they contain.

By far the most important use of **molybdenum** is as an alloy in steel, particularly for stainless and high-speed steels. Molybdenum can be used as a substitute for tungsten in the manufacture of high-speed steels, only half as much molybdenum as tungsten being required; this is strategically important as about half the world's production of tungsten comes from China P.R. Molybdenum is used for increasing strength and creep resistance of steel at high temperatures. A small amount of molybdenum is used as a metal, especially for high-temperature purposes, and some is used in chemicals, pigments and catalysts and for improving lubricants. MoS_2, but the balance of world production is a by-product, mainly of copper and tungsten mining.

Vanadium produces about 1% of the grain of steel and imparts strength, toughness, resistance to impact and abrasion, and makes it easier to machine and weld. Steel with up to 1% vanadium is used in construction and engineering, in springs, forging, and uses involving high stresses. It is used instead of, platinum as a catalyst in sulphuric acid manufacturing, and the salts are used in paints, dyes and insecticides. Much ferrovanadium is produced and used as well as vanadium oxide, these being the two vendable products of vanadium ore besides the metal.

There are many other minerals of great economic and industrial importance of which only a few are shown on the maps in this section.

Mercury has many unique properties, being liquid at room temperature, with high electrical conductivity, high density, chemical stability and uniform volume expansion. The principal uses are in electrical apparatus, agriculture, pharmaceuticals, etc. The electrolytic preparation of chlorine and caustic soda. Almost all the world's mercury is obtained from the red sulphide mineral cinnabar, HgS, but a little native metal occurs. With surface mining, ore with about 1.5 kg. of mercury per ton is an economic proposition, but with underground methods the proportion must be about 4.5 kg. per ton.

Zirconium is mainly used in nuclear reactors, being corrosion-resistant, especially in water at high temperatures, and absorbing very few neutrons. It is also used in the chemical industry, due to its resistance to corrosion by acids and alkalis. Zirconium is also used in the electrical industry, being readily machined, in porcelain manufacture and as a de-oxidizing agent in steel-making. Almost all zirconium is derived from the two minerals zircon, $ZrSiO_4$, (itself a valuable refractory much used in foundries and aluminium furnaces), and baddeleyite, ZrO_2. Zircon is found with ilmenite, rutile and monazite in beach sands; baddeleyite is found in stream gravels in Brazil.

Magnesium is recovered from seawater, natural brine and the rocks dolomite and magnesite. It is alloyed with aluminium and lithium to produce a light, strong, workable metal suitable for aircraft, vehicles, spacecraft and marine applications. It is also used in the reduction of uranium. Magnesium minerals are used extensively in the metallurgical and chemical industries. Magnesite, although very important in the production of basic refractories, is being replaced as a source of magnesium compounds and metal by the seawater-magnesia processes. Magnesium salt deposits are exploited by the chemical industry.

The most important source of **beryllium** is the mineral beryl, $Be_3Al_2Si_6O_{18}$, which contains only about 5% beryllium. Except for a few sporadic occurrences, deposits containing beryl are rarely workable for that mineral unless it is associated with other useful minerals. Large low-grade deposits of bertrandite, $Be_4Si_2O_7(OH)_2$, have recently been discovered and may eventually become the main source of beryllium. A major use is in alloys with copper; about 2% of beryllium in copper greatly increases the tensile strength and durability of the metal. The alloy is especially suitable for aircraft in electrical devices, motion-picture cameras, aircraft under-carriage springs, etc. Pure beryllium is mainly used in X-ray tube windows and with radium as a source of neutrons. The future of the metal now depends largely on its use in nuclear energy projects and in the aerospace industry.

Antimony is not normally used by itself, but is commonly alloyed with lead in battery plates, cable sheathings, and sulphuric acid-resistant sheet and pipe. It is also used in making bearing-metal solder and low-melting-point alloys. Type-metal is basically a lead-antimony-tin alloy, and antimony enters into the composition of Britannia metal and some pewters. Some of the antimony salts are important in the chemical industry, in making paints and enamels, and in treating textiles to make them flameproof. Potential uses in electronics are numerous. The metal is derived chiefly from stibnite, Sb_2S_3, which is usually found in association with the ores of other metals, especially mercury.

The principal use of **titanium** in recent years is in the form of titanium oxide, TiO_2, as a white paint pigment of truly remarkable opacity, which is rapidly replacing lithopone, white lead and zinc oxide in paints. Titanium oxide is used also in toilet preparations, linoleum and rubber. The metal has high resistance to corrosion, is very light and strong and can be substituted for aluminium, making it very important in the aircraft and chemical industries. The metal is used in making the alloys of ferrotitanium and ferrocarbon-titanium; and titanium carbide has beneficial effects in the manufacture of chromium steels. An alloy of titanium carbide and molybdenum carbide is used for extra-hard cutting tools. The minerals ilmenite, $FeTiO_3$, and rutile, TiO_2, are the chief sources of titanium. The "black sands" of certain sea and lake beaches yield part of the world's supply of titanium, the most productive beach deposits being on the eastern coast of Australia. This region is especially important for rutile production.

Cadmium is a relatively rare element recovered as a by-product of zinc and, to a much lesser extent, lead and copper production from ores associated with zinc. Since the only significant cadmium mineral, greenockite, CdS, never occurs as a separate mineral in sufficient quantities to be workable, greater production of cadmium can be achieved only by increased output of zinc or improved methods of recovery. More than half the supply is consumed in protective coatings for iron and steel. A considerable amount of cadmium is used in alloys for electricity transmission cables, storage batteries, type founding metal and solders. It can also be used for fission control in nuclear reactors. Cadmium is also used for low friction bearings and in cadmium salts and compounds, used principally in pigments for stable oil, water and ceramic colours.

Notes relating to **diamonds**, **asbestos**, and **mica** can be found with the maps.

Precious metals, including gold, silver and the platinum group, have important industrial, as well as decorative and monetary, uses.

The principal use of **gold** is as the standard for monetary systems in the form of coinage or as ingots of the metal (bullion). Gold is also used as a conductor in the electronics industry, and in dental and other alloys. An important use of gold is in jewellery, for which it is too soft when pure. Most of the world's gold is obtained from 'native gold', or the yellow metallic mineral which is rarely pure, almost invariably containing some silver. In the past production was from surface gold-bearing gravels, but for several decades the main source has been deep mines, such as those in the Witwatersrand goldfield in South Africa.

About 80% of the world consumption of the **silver** (excl. the U.S.S.R., Eastern Europe and China P.R., for whom no data are available) is by art and industry. Monetary use has a decreasing proportion, as newer coins use less silver or none at all. Silver has increasing industrial uses, particularly in the fields of photography, electrical engineering, and electronics. The principal mineral source of the metal is argentite, Ag_2S; it also occurs naturally in metallic form. Most of the world's production is as a by-product of argentiferous lead, zinc and copper ores or of gold ores.

The **platinum** group metals, including osmium, rhodium, iridium, ruthenium, palladium and platinum, are particularly important in the chemical, petroleum, glass and electronics industries. Considerably more palladium than platinum is used in industry; however, the total value of the platinum used is the greater. Platinum is a catalyst in the petrochemical industry, particularly important as a catalyst in the conversion of ammonia to nitric acid. Platinum group metals are used in glass manufacture and glass seals and in thermo-couples. A thin coating of platinum gives protection against oxidation and corrosion at high temperatures particularly useful in jet and missile technology. Production of platinum in South Africa is from ore mined primarily for its platinum content. In Canada platinum metal is produced as a by-product of nickel production. In Colombia and the U.S.A. platinum production is from placer deposits.

Asbestos is a fibrous mineral which, due to its properties, is an invaluable material for many types of industry. It is resistant to heat, fire, rot, friction and corrosion, is a poor conductor of electricity and sound, and most varieties possess a high tensile strength, similar to that of steel. The uses of asbestos are many and varied, including a wide range of fireproof and building materials. Of the different types of asbestos, chrysotile, which accounts for over 90% of world production, is commercially the most valuable and is used for such commodities as fireproof clothing, brake linings and asbestos cement. Amphibole fibres (crocidolite, amosite and anthophyllite) are harsher and are used for building and thermal insulating materials.

Mica is also a valuable industrial mineral on account of its properties, which include perfect cleavage, flexibility, elasticity, infusibility, low thermal conductivity, transparency and, in particular, high dielectric strength. Muscovite, the most important kind is found in workable quantities in coarse-grained granite pegmatites, and much of the world's supply of high grade sheet muscovite is from India. It is used for electric condensers and in telephones, dynamos and domestic heating equipment. Another variety, phlogopite, is used in commutators; ground mica, largely from waste, is used as a powder in paint and for coating and filler in roofing and rubber material. Synthetic mica is now being produced.

Diamonds

Diamond occurs in a type of basic igneous rock known as Kimberlite and in gravels derived from it by weathering. It is the hardest of all known substances, is resistant to chemicals, can withstand great pressure, and is therefore a valuable industrial material, used principally as a cutting or abrasive agent. Other diamonds, metal, rock and concrete can all be cut by diamond. It is also used in dies for drawing very fine wire, and in optical and precision instruments. Diamonds suitable for gem-stones (dark or flawed varieties) are used in industry, either as whole diamonds or in fragmented form. Synthetic diamonds are now being manufactured and help meet the rising demand for industrial diamonds.

SCALE 1:176 MILLION 1 CM TO 1,760 KM.

Natural diamonds
Production (1963–5 av. in metric carats)

Symbols: 10,000,000 AND OVER; 1,000,000; 100,000; 10,000; 1,000–100,000

% GEM (APPROX.)
A ALLUVIAL DIAMONDS M MARINE DIAMONDS
▲ INDUSTRIAL P PIPE DIAMONDS

Synthetic diamonds
● Non-quantified production centre

Major producers — Natural diamonds

	CONGO D.R.	CONGO R.[1]	SOUTH AFRICA	GHANA	U.S.S.R.	OTHERS	WORLD '000 MET. CARATS
			PERCENTAGE				
Total 1963–5 av.	38	15	12	7	7	17	37 155
1953–5 av.	62	NA	13	11	—	17	20 692
Industrial 1963–5 av.	46	17	9	9	11	8	29 895
1953–5 av.	72	NA	10	10	—	8	16 906
Gem 1963–5 av.	3	4	25	2	11	55	7 260
1953–5 av.	15	NA	26	14	—	NA	3 786

*Estimate [1] Estimated exports

For some countries accurate production figures are not available as smuggling is common. In these cases official export figures have been used for these which are indicated by underlining the symbol names.

Asbestos/Mica

SCALE 1:176 MILLION 1 CM TO 1,760 KM.

Asbestos
Production (1963–5 av. in metric tons)

Symbols: 80,000–800,000; 8,000–80,000; 800–8,000; 100–800

Type: CHRYSOTILE CROCIDOLITE ANTHOPHYLLITE AMOSITE

Mica
Production areas (1963–5 av.)
● MAJOR ● MINOR UNSPECIFIED

Major producers

Asbestos	CANADA	U.S.S.R.	SOUTH AFRICA	RHODESIA	OTHERS	WORLD MET. TONS
			PERCENTAGE			
1963–5 av.	46	27	7	6	15	2 709 000*
1953–5 av.	56	22	6	5	11	1 563 700*

Mica (incl. scrap)	U.S.A.	INDIA[1]	U.S.S.R.	SOUTH AFRICA	OTHERS	WORLD
			PERCENTAGE			
1963–5 av.	70	23		3	5	149 200*
1953–5 av.	75	17		2	5	101 500*

*Estimate [1] Re-exports (Excl. China P.R., N Korea, Romania, U.S.S.R.)

Raw mica is not produced in Norway. Scrap is milled and re-exported, largely from India.

© Oxford University Press

Mercury / Zirconium / Magnesium / Beryl

Major producers

(PERCENTAGE)	AUSTRALIA	ARGENTINA	BRAZIL	CANADA	CHINA P.R.	INDIA	ITALY	NORWAY	SENEGAL	SPAIN	U.S.S.R.	U.S.A.	OTHERS	WORLD (MET. TONS)
Mercury 1963-5 av.					10*		22			28	14†	7	19	8 850*
1953-5 av.					NA		30			23	7*	10	NA	6 030*
Zirconium 1963-5 av.	98					...						1	1	204 730*
1953-5 av.	91					...						...	NA	43 350*
Magnesium (primary) 1963-5 av.				6				15			21*	47	6	152 530*
1953-5 av.				5				4			35*	50	6	135 770*
Beryl 1963-5 av.	2	2	28			8					19*	4	31	5 380*
1953-5 av.	2	12	23			6						8	NA	7 500*

*Estimate. †Excl. U.S.A., U.S.S.R. & India. ¹Production in the U.S.A. ²Production by U.S.A. was 53% of that by Australia; comparable 1963-5 data NA. ³Former French West Africa.

SCALE 1:44 MILLION · 1 CM TO 440 KM

Manganese / Nickel / Antimony / Chrome ore

Major producers

(PERCENTAGE)	BOLIVIA	BRAZIL	CANADA	CHINA P.R.	CUBA	INDIA	NEW CALEDONIA	PHILIPPINES	RHODESIA	SOUTH AFRICA	U.S.S.R.	OTHERS	WORLD (MET. TONS)
Manganese ore (high grade: 30% Mn & over)* 1963-5 av.		8*		6*		9†		11		9	44*	24	16 043 250*
1953-5 av.		2		NA		17		15		7	44*	6	10 474 960*
Nickel 1963-5 av.			55		6*		11		NA	7	21*	6	391 900*
1953-5 av.			83		7		8			7	...	NA	175 690*
Antimony (content of ore) 1963-5 av.	15			25*		1			11	21	10*	28	59 450*
1953-5 av.	14			27*		1				27	...	36	39 920*
Chromite (chrome) 1963-5 av.						1	2	2	11	20	30*	34	4 384 730*
1953-5 av.						2		2	12	18	15*	34	3 538 020*

*Estimate. †Percent Mn varies by country; all above 30% except U.S.S.R. (grade NA). ‡Incl. Goa. §Excl. U.S.S.R.

SCALE 1:76 MILLION · 1 CM TO 760 KM

Tungsten / Cobalt / Molybdenum / Vanadium

Major producers

(PERCENTAGE)	CANADA	CHILE	CHINA P.R.	CONGO D.R.	FINLAND	S. KOREA	MOROCCO	SOUTH AFRICA	SOUTH WEST AFRICA	U.S.S.R.	U.S.A.	OTHERS	WORLD (MET. TONS)
Tungsten (concentrates & ores: 60% WO₃ basis) 1963-5 av.	2		35*			9				19*	12	23	57 910*
1953-5 av.			24*			7				10*	17	38	72 270*
Cobalt 1963-5 av.	9			49	11		10			8	2*	11	16 030*
1953-5 av.	9			67	NA		6				5		12 640*
Molybdenum (in ores & concentrates) 1963-5 av.	4*	4	4*							13*	69	2	45 430*
1953-5 av.		4									91	4	29 570*
Vanadium (in ores & concentrates) 1963-5 av.								17	15		56		7 280*
1953-5 av.									16		79	5	3 590*

*Estimate. ¹Incl. Rwanda and Burundi. ²Excl. U.S.S.R., China P.R. and Eastern Europe.

SCALE 1:176 MILLION · 1 CM TO 1 760 KM

Ferro-alloy and other minerals

Producing districts¹ (1963-5 av.)

	MAJOR	MINOR
Cinnabar (Mercury)	◁	◁
Zirconium minerals	○	○
Magnesium minerals	○	○
Beryl	▷	▷
Manganese minerals	□	□
Nickel minerals	◇	◇
Antimony minerals	▽	▽
Chrome ore	▽	▽
Tungsten minerals	◇	◇
Cobalt minerals	◇	◇
Molybdenum minerals	⬡	⬡
Vanadium minerals	○	○

Trade in ferro-alloy minerals

Nickel The major sources of the ore in world trade are Canada and New Caledonia; metal is exported by Canada, Norway and the U.K. Chief importers of ores, matte and other nickel-bearing raw materials are Japan, the U.K., Norway and France.

Tungsten Most is traded in the form of ores and concentrates. The chief exporters of these are Australia, Bolivia, S. Korea and China P.R.; they are imported mainly by the U.S.A., Germany F.R. and the U.K. The U.K. exports two-thirds of the ferro-tungsten reported in international trade data; Sweden is the major importer. Tungsten metal is exported by Germany F.R., the U.S.A. and France.

Molybdenum The U.S.A. and Chile are the major exporters, mainly in the form of ores and concentrates. Chief exporters of ferro-molybdenum are the U.S.S.R., the U.S.A. and France. Molybdenum is imported by Germany F.R., the U.K., Japan and France.

Cobalt The Congo D.R. is the largest exporter; Zambia and Morocco are also major exporters. Main importers are France, the U.S.A., the U.K. and Japan.

Vanadium The U.S.A., South West Africa and Finland are principal exporters; France, Belgium/Luxembourg and Italy are the major importers.

Manganese ore exports

7 106 670 met. tons 1963-5 av.
5 237 630 1953-5 av.

	PERCENTAGE 1963-5 av.	1953-5 av.
India	21	18
U.S.S.R.	20	14
South Africa	17	13
Brazil	14	12
Gabon	10	30
Others	18	33
	100	100

Manganese ore imports

7 623 700 met. tons 1963-5 av.
4 417 460 1953-5 av.

	PERCENTAGE 1963-5 av.	1953-5 av.
U.S.A.	43	37
Japan	11	10
France	8	12
Germany F.R.	7	6
U.K.	6	11
Others	25	27
	100	100

Chrome ore exports

3 166 850 met. tons 1963-5 av.
2 297 160 1953-5 av.

	PERCENTAGE 1963-5 av.	1953-5 av.
U.S.S.R.	21	7
South Africa	20	21
Philippines	17	21
Rhodesia	14	16
Turkey	10	23
Others	18	12
	100	100

Chrome ore imports

3 015 520 met. tons 1963-5 av.
2 389 590 1953-5 av.

	PERCENTAGE 1963-5 av.	1953-5 av.
U.S.A.	43	70
Japan	11	2
Germany F.R.	8	8
U.K.	7	6
France	6	3
Others	25	11
	100	100

Transport Industries

Shipbuilding

The distribution of the shipbuilding industry shows the predominance of Europe, where there is a long history of shipbuilding, and of Japan, which has always had a traditional industry but which in this century has made such progress that in 1970 she launched almost half of the world's tonnage.

The most dramatic event in modern shipbuilding has been the increase in size of the largest ships constructed. In 1963 the largest ship launched in the world was 58 000 gross registered tonnage (G.R.T.). In 1968 the largest ship launched was 150 000 G.R.T. and in 1970 54 ships (of which 30 were built in Japan) each exceeded 100 000 G.R.T. All but one of these were oil tankers. These giant ships, too large to transit the Suez Canal fully laden, have considerable economic advantage over smaller ones on long sea voyages. Closure of Suez in 1967, therefore, by denying to smaller tankers the shorter route for oil from the Persian Gulf to Europe, effectively accelerated the demand for the supertanker.

Sizes of ships launched (1966)

'000 G.R.T.	Total	PERCENTAGE
Total number of ships launched	2 561	
of which tankers	210	
'000 G.R.T. size		
0.1 — 1	61	30
1 — 4	14	12
4 — 8	8	4
8 — 15	9	4
15 — 25	5	33
25 — 50	5	16
50 & above	2	1
	100	100

¹Excl. ships of less than 100 G.R.T.

Bulk carriers, which transport chiefly ore or grain, are an important part of world shipping fleets. In 1970 they formed 28% of all merchant tonnage launched, compared with 46% for oil tankers. This type of ship has now emulated the oil tanker in size. There are orders in hand for single purpose bulk carriers of 80 000 G.R.T. while the combination type ore/bulk/oil carrier ship is now of the 140 000 G.R.T. size.

General cargo ships are being replaced by the new fast container ships which average about 27 000 G.R.T. as compared to a maximum size of about 14 000 G.R.T. for a conventional cargo liner. Container ships are also growing in size and there are now orders in hand for fully refrigerated container ships of 40 000 G.R.T. If container ships are generally adopted on established routes, the number of ships needed to deal with the general cargo trade could be greatly reduced. For example, before the introduction of container ships nearly 100 conventional cargo ships carried the regular trade between Australia and the U.K. It has been said that, in theory, 9 container ships would be capable of carrying 80% of this trade.

Large passenger ships are rarely built nowadays; the *Queen Elizabeth 2* could well be the last of the great passenger liners. There is a continuing demand for smaller passenger ships which are used for or for holiday cruises. The demand for small ships of quality, such as coasters and fishing vessels, will always remain. Many of these are built in shipyards with a production too small to appear on the shipbuilding map. These small shipbuilding places are particularly numerous along the coast of Norway and on the waterways of the Netherlands, but they exist in smaller shipbuilding countries such as Peru, Pakistan, Angola and Greece. Ships have traditionally been custom built but this is

now changing and series, or standard, shipbuilding is the foremost factor influencing shipbuilding today. This method can be used for ships of any size, including the giant tankers. During the building of a series, the benefits of mass prefabrication become evident and costs per ton gradually decrease.

Most shipbuilding industries are to some extent assisted by their own governments, because of their value to the country's economy and because of the social problems which the closure of a shipyard can cause. Government protection is even greater in the young industries of developing countries. Here, costs of production are high because complex parts and equipment must be imported from a distance. Thus prices of new ships built in Brazil, for example, are between 25% and 40% above world average. The main importing countries are those with large merchant fleets; such countries may also have important shipbuilding industries of their own. Liberia provides a 'flag of convenience' offering special privileges for shipowners.

The pattern of naval shipbuilding differs considerably from that of merchant shipbuilding. The leading producers are the two great military powers, the U.S.A. and the U.S.S.R., and the industry seems to be of importance also in China. New naval ships are normally supplied by a country's own industry, and imported only by those countries which have insufficient shipbuilding industries.

Motor vehicles

Motor vehicles, in particular motor cars, are now recognized as an essential part of modern industrial life, and the motor vehicle industry has become one of the major indicators of industrial and economic advance. Its effect on the economy is difficult to determine, but it is estimated that 10% of the U.K.'s industrial production depends either directly or indirectly on vehicle manufacture and the effect on other European countries is probably much greater. The importance of the motor industry to industrial growth lies in the vast number of associated industries which supply and service it, some of these being metal manufacturing, glass, rubber and plastics. Motor vehicle production necessitates the development of roads, servicing, parts and fuel supply stations. Some countries, such as the U.S.S.R., have in the past been unwilling or unable to invest in this kind of development and the motor industry, particularly private vehicle production, has been held back.

In both Europe and North America it is the production of private cars which forms the most important part of total vehicle production. In 1969 the U.S.A. produced 8 224 327 private vehicles and 1 980 719 commercial vehicles whereas the U.S.S.R. produced 293 600 private vehicles and 974 100 commercial vehicles. In developing countries the mechanization of agriculture plus the overriding initial requirement of road transport for carrying goods, creates a demand for commercial vehicles which is sustained until further developments in other forms of transport produce a levelling off of demand.

In most developing countries the motor car is still very much a luxury, but as industrialization takes place demand increases and new markets emerge. Recognizing these new markets, motor manufacturers are now breaking away from their national origins and building new factories or setting up new companies wherever it is most profitable or convenient to do so. The experience of Belgium shows in a dramatic form the way in which this process is occurring all over the world. Belgium's output of

motor vehicles increased from 216 000 in 1960 to 475 000 in 1965 and to 766 896 in 1969 yet there is no domestic manufacturer; every plant is owned, or licensed, by one of the big American or European companies. Even small, newly independent countries are establishing their own motor vehicle industry; for example, Trinidad, where the market is so small that the Rootes, Ford and British Leyland Motor Corporation dealers have joined to run a co-operative plant. The waiving of the 25% import duty on completed cars is just sufficient to offset the extra cost of assembling in Trinidad instead of in the U.K. This arrangement of assembly plant is an advantage not only to the companies involved but also to the host country, particularly to developing nations where lack of sufficient technical knowledge and foreign currency and, frequently, high tariff barriers on imports of foreign goods are partially circumvented by part assembly of European and American manufactured components. The next step, already taken in Brazil, is to move to full-scale production. Assembly plant has now been established in countries such as Chile, Argentina, Venezuela, Ghana, South Africa, South Korea, India and Australia. In order to make full use of cheaper labour in developing countries, some big manufacturers are beginning to sub-contract to plants in countries such as Mexico where, for example, a Volkswagen factory is producing spare parts which are exported to Germany and to the U.S.A. Some countries are assembling vehicles not only for home consumption but also for re-export to a third market.

The increasingly wider distribution of the industry has meant that the U.S.A. no longer produces more than half of the total world output of cars. This is due in part to an increase in assembly plant throughout the world but more particularly to increased production from countries such as Italy, Germany F.R., and Japan, whose industry had its beginning some years after that of the U.S.A. The Japanese industry more than doubled its production between 1960 and 1965 and increased it almost tenfold from 481 551 in 1960 to 4 674 340 in 1969. Japan is now proving to be a serious competitor on the American market.

Although the percentage of two car families in Europe has risen from 1.9% in 1963 to 6.3% in 1969, demand in the established markets of Northwestern Europe and North America is beginning to level off and the industry is seeking new markets, apart from the building of assembly plant, have centred on the two rapidly advancing areas of Southern Europe and Asia.

Just as social and economic changes affect the *demand* for motor vehicles, so too they affect the *type* of vehicle produced. In the Western world increased congestion in cities has produced a demand for a smaller more manoeuvrable car. Competition from foreign imports of smaller cars has forced the U.S.A. to design and produce smaller cars for their home market, which forms 95% of American vehicle sales.

A question now beginning seriously to affect the motor vehicle industry is that of pollution from poisonous exhaust fumes. If traffic congestion and air pollution in cities continue to increase, drastic solutions will have to be sought and those alternatives already submitted could seriously affect the motor industry. Alternatives, such as monorail systems and overhead railways, could completely change the present demand for private motor vehicles.

Japan where conditions are more favourable for their use than in the U.S.A. These are even more powerful than the new diesels, averaging between 3 000 and 5 000 h.p. Since the end of the first world war alternative means of transport have cut the amount of passenger traffic handled by the railways in the U.S.A. and Western Europe.

There is considerable surplus capacity for the production of railway vehicles, both locomotives and trailers (including self-powered cars). This is caused not only by the growth of other forms of transport but also by the growth of production centres in the developing countries, who consequently import less; by the growth of railway workshops which do work formerly done by private producers; and by gross fluctuations in demand. As a result of this some firms producing railway vehicles have diversified whilst others have merged or closed down completely.

The distribution of the aircraft industry is complex. Many companies own a number of plants in different locations and also sub-contract the assembly of important parts of aircraft, such as the wings, to other companies, not necessarily in the same country. Like the motor industry the aircraft industry draws on other industries for the supply of such things as tyres, special glass, and electrical equipment. It is also important to realize that many aircraft manufacturers, whether of air-frames or of aero-engines, are also engaged in space technology.

Railways

In the OECD countries output of railway vehicles reached peaks in the years 1955-63 which have never since been surpassed. In many of the developed countries the industry has actually been declining in more recent years. Output, however, is not the sole measure of the importance of the industry. According to an estimate made for the OECD countries the industry accounts for only 5% of the total output of the transport industries (other figures are: road vehicles 61%; aircraft 25%; ships and boats 9%) but these railway vehicles carry an estimated 40% of internal freight traffic and 25% of passenger traffic. Another important consideration is that the diesel locomotives which are now being produced are more powerful than those they replace.

In the U.S.A. diesels of 1 200 – 1 400 h.p. are now being replaced by diesels of 2 000 – 3 000 h.p. Electric locomotives are favoured in Europe and

the U.S.S.R.

Aircraft

The aircraft industry is divided into two distinct sections, the military and the civil. Both types of aircraft production are important and both types of aircraft are exported, but statistics relating to the production and trade of military aircraft are classified. Some countries, of which Sweden is an example, produce only military aircraft but many countries produce both, and many advances in civil aviation have been a direct result of research conducted for military purposes.

The cost of developing a new aircraft from drawing-board to operational readiness is very high and for this reason is often subsidized to a considerable extent by governments. The aircraft industry is, therefore, particularly vulnerable to changes in government or in government policy. The U.S.A. has far more resources available for research into new aircraft than any individual country of Europe and some attempts have been made within Europe to answer American competition by co-operative ventures. A famous example of this is the Anglo-French supersonic airliner Concorde. A similar aeroplane is being developed in the U.S.S.R. and is expected to be in service before Concorde. Another recent development, pioneered in the U.S.A., is the very large airliner, the so-called jumbo-jet, carrying more than 300 passengers, which is already in commercial service.

During the 1960's production of civil airliners increased partly because of an increase in the number of passengers and the amount of freight to be transported and partly because of a widespread change from piston-engined aircraft to faster and more powerful jet aeroplanes. The replacement of piston-engined aircraft by jets is still far from complete but the proportion of piston-engined planes in the fleets of I.C.A.O.¹ countries has declined both absolutely and proportionally from 4 178 (91%) in 1958 to 3 069 (52%) in 1966 and to 1 995 (27%) in 1970. The changeover is not likely ever to reach 100% unless

¹International Civil Aviation Organization which has 120 member states, excluding China P.R.

economic considerations are sacrificed to prestige because some routes are too short to justify the use of jets.

The production of light aircraft for business or pleasure is increasing and, being relatively simple, is carried out in some countries such as Argentina and Brazil which do not produce larger aircraft though the largest growth has been in the U.S.A. where the number of light aircraft produced rose from less than 7 000 to almost 16 000 between 1962 and 1966.

The distribution of the aircraft industry is complex. Many companies own a number of plants in different locations and also sub-contract the assembly of important parts of aircraft, such as the wings, to other companies, not necessarily in the same country. Like the motor industry the aircraft industry draws on other industries for the supply of such things as tyres, special glass, and electrical equipment. It is also important to realize that many aircraft manufacturers, whether of air-frames or of aero-engines, are also engaged in space technology.

Railways

In the OECD countries output of railway vehicles reached peaks in the years 1955-63 which have never since been surpassed. In many of the developed countries the industry has actually been declining in more recent years. Output, however, is not the sole measure of the importance of the industry. According to an estimate made for the OECD countries the industry accounts for only 5% of the total output of the transport industries (other figures are: road vehicles 61%; aircraft 25%; ships and boats 9%) but these railway vehicles carry an estimated 40% of internal freight traffic and 25% of passenger traffic. Another important consideration is that the diesel locomotives which are now being produced are more powerful than those they replace.

In the U.S.A. diesels of 1 200 – 1 400 h.p. are now being replaced by diesels of 2 000 – 3 000 h.p. Electric locomotives are favoured in Europe and the U.S.S.R.

International trade in transport equipment[1]

Merchant ships[2,3]

	Exports[2,3]		Imports	
	G.R.T. 7 132 031		G.R.T. 7 132 031	
	Data for 1953-5 av. not available		Data for 1953-5 av. not available	
		PERCENTAGE		**PERCENTAGE**
		1966		1966
Japan		56	Norway	32
Sweden		11	Liberia	25
Germany F.R.		8	U.S.S.R.	11
U.K.		4	Greece	7
Poland		4	Netherlands	5
Germany D.R.		3	Romania	2
Yugoslavia		2	Poland	1
Denmark		2	Others	18
Others		10		100
		100		

¹International Civil Aviation Organization which has 120 member states, excluding China P.R.

Aircraft

	Exports		Imports	
	$1 827 million 1963-5 av.		$1 085 million 1963-5 av.	
	$908 million 1953-5 av.		$727 million 1953-5 av.	
	PERCENTAGE			**PERCENTAGE**
	1963-5 av.	1953-5 av.		1963-5 av.	1953-5 av.
U.S.A.	55	82*	Germany F.R.	11	16
U.K.	9	12*	Canada	10	—
Netherlands	8*	3*	U.S.A.	10	—
Canada	8*	—	Netherlands	7	2
France	7*	—	Australia	6	2
Belg./Lux.	4	—	Japan	6	1
Italy	4	1	Belg./Lux.	5	5
Germany F.R.	3	—	France	5	5
Others	2	2	Others	39	68
	100	100		100	100

Railway vehicles

	Exports		Imports	
	$724 million 1963-5 av.		$518 million 1963-5 av.	
	$400 million 1953-5 av.		$332 million 1953-5 av.	
	PERCENTAGE			**PERCENTAGE**
	1963-5 av.	1953-5 av.		1963-5 av.	1953-5 av.
Germany D.R.	19	5*	U.S.S.R.	30*	5*
Germany F.R.	18	28	Argentina	9	9
U.S.A.	13	15	Pakistan	6	6*
Poland	10*	—	Mexico	6	—
Czechoslovakia	6	—	South Africa	5	7
U.K.	6	7	Brazil	4	30
Japan	5	30	Italy	3	—
Brazil	3	—	Indonesia	3	—
Italy	3	—	Others	30	78
Others	14	22		100	100
	100	100			

Motor vehicles

	Exports		Imports	
	$7 985 million 1963-5 av.		$7 600 million 1963-5 av.	
	$3 350 million 1953-5 av.		$2 369 million 1953-5 av.	
	PERCENTAGE			**PERCENTAGE**
	1963-5 av.	1953-5 av.		1963-5 av.	1953-5 av.
Germany F.R.	27	14	U.S.A.	11	3
U.K.	22	39	Canada	10	14
U.S.A.	19	27	Belg./Lux.	6	5
France	13	7	Netherlands	6	3
Italy	6	3	Sweden	4	5
Belg./Lux.	4	1	Germany F.R.	4	7
Japan	3	—	France	4	7
Sweden	3	1	Australia	4	7
Others	6	14	Others	52	58
	100	100		100	100

¹Total of available countries. ²Export data from the U.S.S.R. and China P.R. are not available. *Figures for individual countries within the British Commonwealth are only available when they cross the frontier after purchase or sale abroad. ³Incl. second-hand aircraft purchased or sold abroad. ⁴Excl. ships of less than 100 G.R.T. ⁵Incl. second-hand aircraft when bought new. ⁶ᵗʰ Railway carriages, wagons and parts. ⁷Locomotives and railway materials.

51

Shipbuilding

52

Tonnage completed per year[1]

Merchant ships

Gross registered tons (G.R.T.) in thousands

(showing main types as share of total tonnage)

ABOVE 300 | 151–300 | 51–150
11–25
26–50

(colour shows type of ship with largest share of tonnage)

The figures by the names show
First, in light type, the average number of ships completed, 1963–5.
Second, in heavier type, the average gross registered tonnage completed, 1963–5, in thousands.

+ Data not available

Ships of under 100 G.R.T. are excluded

OIL TANKERS
GENERAL CARGO

BULK CARRIERS
OTHER SHIPS

Naval ships

Displacement tons, in thousands

e.g. Philadelphia   ABOVE 20

Bremerton   11 – 20

Hamburg   6 – 10

● Indicates location

○ Data not available

Non-combat naval ships are included

Modified Gall Projection
Equatorial Scale 1: 88 Million approx.

1. Although ships are allocated to the year of completion they are not necessarily allocated to the place of completion. They are always shown as having been built at the place where the hull was constructed before launching.

2. Bulk carriers are especially designed for handling bulk cargoes such as ore or grain.

3. 'General cargo' includes cargo ships of at least 2000 G.R.T. and with a capacity of less than 100 passengers.

4. 'Other ships' are mainly fishing or passenger ships or small cargo ships.

5. 'Other ships' may include one or more type of ship with too small a share of total tonnage to be shown separately as a distinct sector.

1963-5 data for merchant shipbuilding in the U.S.S.R. are incomplete

© Oxford University Press

Merchant ships completed[1]

	1963-5 av. G.R.T.	1954-5 av.
10 771 997 G.R.T. 1963-5 av.[3,3]		
5 208 487 G.R.T. 1954-5 av.[4]		

| | PERCENTAGE | |
	1963-5 av.	1954-5 av.
Japan	34	10
Sweden	10	10
U.K.	10	27
Germany F.R.	9	18
France	4	6
Italy	4[2]	4
U.S.S.R.	24	25
Others	24	25
	100	100

[1] Excl. ships below 100 G.R.T.
[2] Excl. China P.R. U.S.S.R. figure incomplete
[3] Excl. China P.R.
[4] Excl. China P.R. Germany D.R. & U.S.S.R.

Ships and boats (S.I.T.C. no. 735)

Total value of exports
$1 964 million 1963-5 av.

| | PERCENTAGE |
	1963-5 av.
Japan	27
Sweden	13
Germany F.R.	11
Netherlands	6
Norway	6
France	5
Poland	5
U.K.	5
Denmark	4
U.S.A.	3
Others	15
	100

Inset A (Europe)

Glasgow/Clydebank Port 13 138
Glasgow/Greenock 13 138
Newcastle/Wallsend 15 161
Sunderland 18 230
Middlesbrough/Haverton Hill 5 78
Belfast 4 90
Barrow 3 35
Birkenhead 3 42
Cork 1 25
Brest
Saint-Nazaire 6 204
Nantes 9 33
Le Trait 3 23
Dunkerque 3 78
Bordeaux 7 12
Bilbao 25 44
El Ferrol del Caudillo 13 23
Gijón 2 10
Port-de-Bouc 2 18
La Seyne 339 3 111
Vigo 47 19
La Ciotat 4 58
Livorno
La Spezia 4 58
Genova 5 119
Venezia 6 27
San Marco 1 41
Montfalcone 4 76
Rijeka 5 69
Pula 6 57
Ancona 5 31
Split 7 84
Budapest 1 12
København 6 73
Malmö 7 224
Landskrona 7 150
Lindö 2 72
Oskarshamn 4 13
Gdańsk 20 190
Gdynia 13 28
Szczecin 8 49
Rostock 15 42
Wismar 4 26
Lübeck 10 69
Warnemünde
Stralsund 16 39
Hamburg 45 262
Bremen/Vegesack 18 177
Emden 11 101
Amsterdam 6 46
Hoboken 3 51 &
Vlissingen 4 30 (Flushing)
Rotterdam/Schiedam 6 43
Rozenburg 2 40
Alblasserdam 3 30
Krimpen a/d IJssel 5 24

Inset B (Japan)

Yokohama/Tsurumi 15 347
Kure 25 240
Hiroshima 45 135
Imabari 47 55
Tōkyō 11 176
Shiba 1 24
Aioi 13 424
Shimizu 82 91
Kōbe 17 374
Yokosuka 12 84
Nagoya 8 51
Ōsaka 33 194
Saebo 5 136
Tamano 11 266
Nagasaki 26 450
Inno-shima 14 279

Main map labels

Komsomol'sk-na-Amure
Hakodate 9 43
Shang-hai
Lü-ta (Dairen)
Kuang-chou (Canton)
Vishakhapatnam 2 14
Whyalla 2 16
Severodvinsk
Leningrad 17 222
Gor'kiy
Nikolayev 4 45
Kherson 4 45
Galati 5 14
Varna 5 17
Castellammare di Stabia 3 28
Palermo 2 17
Valencia 4 12
Sevilla 1 25
Cádiz 6 34
Turku 17 74
Rauma 9 34
Helsinki 4 14
Fredrikstad 6 45
Oslo 3 14
Moss 3 11
Uddevalla 8 182
Göteborg 26 604
Tønsberg 3 36
Horten 1 13
Kragerø 2 11
Stavanger 2 82
Leirvik 3 71
Bergen 5 43
Haugesund 4 23
Rio de Janeiro 24
Bremerton
Seattle
Mare Island
San Diego 2 20
Lauzon 12 51
Sorel 4 18
Port Weller 2 14
Montréal 2 14
Collingwood 3 35
Groton
Bath
Portsmouth 6 Quincy 2 32
Brooklyn
Philadelphia
Camden
Chester 3 42
Sparrows Point 4 85
Newport News 1 31
Pascagoula 3 32
Avondale 4 43

Railway Vehicles

54

Railway vehicles
Average number assembled per year 1963–5

Powered

	Electric	Diesel and diesel-electric
LOCOMOTIVES		
RAILCARS		

Higher categories increase by units of 100

| 1 | 101–200 | 51–100 | 26–50 | 11–25 |

Locomotives of under 100 h.p. are excluded

e.g. **3** shows production of 301–400

Non-powered rolling stock

●	500
●	501–
●	1,001–
●	2,000
● ABOVE	2,000
	101–500

+ Data not available (specialized locomotive production shown in the appropriate colour)

* Estimate

Railway vehicles (number produced)

Locomotives

9 250 1963–5 av.[1]
5 551 1953–4 av.[2]

	PERCENTAGE	
	1963–5 av.	1953–4 av.
U.S.S.R.	23	18
U.S.A.	16	30*
Germany F.R.	11	13
U.K.	8	21
Germany D.R.	6	...*
Czechoslovakia	6	17
Others	30	...
	100	100

[1]Estimated from 24 major producers excluding China P.R.
[2]11 countries only

Railway vehicles (S.I.T.C. no. 731)

Total value of exports[1]
$724 million 1963–5 av.[2]

	PERCENTAGE	
	1963–5 av.	
Germany D.R.	19	
U.S.A.	18	
Germany F.R.	13	
Poland[3]	10	
Czechoslovakia[3]	9	
U.K.	7	
Japan	5	
Italy	5	
Others	14	
	100	

[1]Estimated from 24 major producers excluding China P.R.
[2]20 countries only
[3]Freight & passenger cars only

Modified Gall Projection
Equatorial Scale 1: 88 Million approx.

© Oxford University Press

Major trade flows (1966)

Commodity: S.I.T.C.no.	
RAILWAY VEHICLES	: 731

Value ($ U.S.)
0.5 mm represents increments of $10 million

A trade flow is defined as trade in one direction only between any two countries. This indicates major trading partners but not

Motor Vehicles

Motor vehicles

Type

PRODUCTION — COMMERCIAL VEHICLES / PRIVATE VEHICLES — ASSEMBLY

Country totals (1963-5 av.)

Each quadrant has a radius (in mm.) equal to half the square root of the number of vehicles (in thousands) produced or assembled by type, for example

100000

△ Less than 6 200 vehicles produced or assembled

Country total not available

Production centres

○ Known production and/or assembly centres

Number of vehicles produced or assembled per '000 population (1963-5 av.)

OVER	40	40		25
25	10	10		1
1	0.1	0.1		UNDER 0.1

Major trade flows (1966)

Commodity: S.I.T.C. no.

ROAD MOTOR VEHICLES 732

Value ($ U.S.)
0.5 mm. represents increments of $100 million

VALUE IN $ MILLIONS

Trade flow is defined as trade in one direction between two countries. This indicates major trading partners but not necessarily major traders.

INTRA-EUROPEAN TRADE

PROVENANCE	DESTINATION
Belg./Lux.	D (233) I (146)
France	B (145) E (80) I (137)
Germany F.R.	B (207) F (200) A (143) N (181) CH (114)

Modified Gall Projection
Equatorial Scale 1: 88 Million approx.

© Oxford University Press

Motor vehicle production

Private vehicles		
17 460 000 units	1963-5 av.	
9 013 000	1953-5 av.	
	PERCENTAGE	
	1963-5 av.	1953-5 av.
U.S.A.	47	72
Germany F.R.	15	6
U.K.	10	8
France	8	5
Italy	6	4
Canada	3	4
Japan	3	1
U.S.S.R.	2	1
Others	5	1
	100	100

Commercial vehicles		
4 893 000 units	1963-5 av.	
2 293 000	1953-5 av.	
	PERCENTAGE	
	1963-5 av.	1953-5 av.
U.S.A.	32	51
Japan	23	5
U.S.S.R.	12	13
U.K.	9	12
France	5	7
Germany F.R.	5	5
Canada	2	4
Brazil	1	—
Italy	1	2
Others	10	2
	100	100

Estimated number of vehicles in use

Selected countries

	PER '000 POPULATION			
	Private		Commercial	
	1965	1955	1965	1955
U.S.A.	385	314	73	64
New Zealand	271	170	61	53
Canada	269	187	69	62
Australia	255	146	77	71
Sweden	232	88	18	16
France	196	69	45	30
U.K.	170	69	33	23
Germany F.R.	158	36	15	22
Kuwait	123	N/A	46	N/A
Austria	109	27	41	9
Italy	106	18	13	8
Netherlands	104	25	19	11
South Africa	63	42	16	12
Venezuela	44	24	19	14
Argentina	41	18	26	14
Israel	30	10	16	10
Spain	25	5	12	3
Japan	22	2	44	3
Mexico	18	10	9	8
Brazil	14	6	12	6
Morocco	12	11	5	4
Kenya	8	4	4	4
Poland	8	1	6	3
Colombia	7	6	5	5
Philippines	5	2	6	3
India	1	1	1	—

55

SCALE 1:22 MILLION   1 CM. TO 220 KM.

SCALE 1:22 MILLION   1 CM. TO 220 KM.

Fertilizer Minerals

© Oxford University Press

SCALE 1:176 MILLION 1 CM. TO 1760 KM. Modified Gall Projection

SCALE 1:152 MILLION 1 CM. TO 1520 KM.

Sulphur production

Native sulphur

	8 960 000 met. tons 1963-5 av.*	
	6 500 000 1953-5 av.*	
	PERCENTAGE	
	1963-5 av.	1953-5 av.
U.S.A.	22	27
Mexico	18	9
U.S.S.R.	11	24*
Poland	4	21*
Japan	3	—
China P.R.	1*	3
Italy	1	—
Others	40	16
	100	100

*Estimate *Crude sulphur

Recovered sulphur

	5 297 000 met. tons 1963-5 av.*	
Data for 1953-5 not available		
	PERCENTAGE	
	1963-5 av.	1953-5 av.
Canada	29	NA
France	28	NA
U.S.A.	11	NA
U.S.S.R.	8	NA
China P.R.	3	NA
Germany D.R.	2	NA
Germany F.R.	2	NA
Spain	2	NA
Iran	1	NA
Others	7	NA
	100	

Pyrites[1]

	9 400 000 met. tons 1963-5 av.*	
	6 300 000 1953-5 av.*	
	PERCENTAGE	
	1963-5 av.	1953-5 av.
Japan	19	17
U.S.S.R.	18	15
Spain	11	9
Italy	7	6
China P.R.	6	9*
Cyprus	4	6
U.S.A.	4	6
Norway	4	5
Portugal	3	5
Others	24	NA
	100	100

*Estimate [1]Sulphur equivalent

Consumption of fertilizer nutrients N, K₂O and P₂O₅ (1964/5)

Met. tons per 1000 ha. arable land	
250 - 584	
50 - 100	
10 - 50	
1 - 10	
DATA N A	

economic importance, such as those of China P.R. and North Vietnam also have large reserves. Morocco, the U.S.A., the U.S.S.R., Tunisia and Nauru Island are the main exporters of phosphate rock. Japan, France, Germany F.R., Italy, the U.K., Canada and Australia are the main importers.

About 90% of world potash production is employed as a fertilizer in agriculture and horticulture, but until early this century the principal uses of potash were in dyeing and tanning and for making glass, porcelain, soap, matches and explosives. Most of the world's mineral potash fertilizer comes from salt beds, formed in past geological times when the evaporation of sea water in enclosed but extensive basins resulted in the accumulation of saline residues containing the chlorides and sulphates of potassium. Some of these now form deposits of great

most productive deposits are those formed in the cap-rocks overlying great plug-like intrusions of rock salt, such as those along the U.S. Gulf Coast in the vicinity of Beaumont, Texas and Port Sulphur, Louisiana. Apart from the 'native' sulphur already mentioned, 'recovered' sulphur accounts for nearly 50% of world sulphur production. It is derived primarily from natural gas and oil refinery gases. Sulphur is also obtained in considerable quantities by roasting pyrite (iron pyrites), FeS₂. This mineral is frequently found in copper mines. The U.S.A., Mexico, France, Canada and Poland are the principal exporters of sulphur; this group of five countries is significant as being major exporters of elemental sulphur. The U.K., Australia and India are the chief importers.

Fertilizer minerals

Producing districts (1969)

Annual production capacity in '000 met. tons

Phosphates (phosphate rock)
- OVER 500
- 100 - 500
- OVER 100

Potash (K₂O)
- OVER 100

Sulphur
- OVER 100

Pyrites (sulphur equivalent)
- OVER 100

Major trade flows (1966)

Commodity: S.I.T.C.no.

PHOSPHATES[1]/FERTS./MATERIALS	: 271.3
	: 561.3
POTASSIC SALTS/FERTS./MATERIALS	: 271.4
	: 561.3
SULPHUR/IRON PYRITES (unexpected)	: 274

Value (\$ U.S.)
- 0.5mm represents increments of \$10 million
  - 90
  - 50
  - 10
  - 22 VALUE IN \$ MILLIONS
- (\$5 MILLION)

Trade flow is defined as trade in one direction between two countries. This indicates major trading partners but not necessarily major traders.
[1]Natural minerals

The use of artificial fertilizers, in areas which also have a high standard of cultivation and adequate water supply, increases crop yield. The contents of plant nutrients in fertilizers are measured by N (nitrogen), P₂O₅ (phosphorus pentoxide) and K₂O (potassium oxide), although the fertilizers do not contain them in those particular chemical combinations.

The main use of phosphate deposits is as a source of fertilizers. The two principal varieties and sources of natural phosphates are: (1) rock phosphates such as phosphorite, phosphatic limestone, guano and bone-beds and (2) the mineral apatite, 3Ca₃P₂O₈CaF₂. The U.S.A. and the U.S.S.R. are more or less self-sufficient in phosphates, but most European countries have to import large amounts from the rich deposits of North Africa and the

islands of the Pacific and Indian Oceans. China P.R. and North Vietnam also have large reserves. Morocco, the U.S.A., the

Potash[1] production

	12 450 000 met. tons 1963-5 av.*	
	6 560 000 1953-5 av.*	
	PERCENTAGE	
	1963-5 av.	1953-5 av.
U.S.A.	22	17
U.S.S.R.	17	9
Germany F.R.	17	24
Germany D.R.	15	21*
France	14	16
Canada	7	—
Spain	3	3
Israel	2	—
Others	3	—
	100	100

*Estimate *K₂O equivalent

Phosphate[1] production

	56 571 000 met. tons 1963-5 av.*	
	29 380 000 1953-5 av.*	
	PERCENTAGE	
	1963-5 av.	1953-5 av.
U.S.A.	41	44
U.S.S.R.	20	15
Morocco	17	16
Tunisia	5	4
Nauru Is.	3	—
N. Vietnam	2*	7
China P.R.	1	—
Senegal	1	—
Togo	1	—
Others	9	14
	100	100

*Estimate [1]Rock [2]Exports

Manufacturing Industries

For individual country data see Statistical Supplement

The manufacturing industries as they are known in the industrialized nations today may be said to have begun with the invention of the water frame for cotton spinning in 1769. This machine was too big to be used in the home so its adoption marked the beginning of the factory system. Of the manufacturing industries which are of importance today only textiles and pottery have continued right through from the early days of the industrial revolution. Many new light industries have started and become important since then. Some of these important newer industries, including computers and electrical engineering, have been the direct result of scientific research. One particular scientific breakthrough, the synthesis of urea from inorganic substances, has been important in the development of the chemical industry, but even more important has been the development of the petroleum industry.

Petro-chemicals are made from the by-products of petroleum refining, and these constitute a very important part of the chemicals industry. Industry repays its debt to science by the manufacture of ever more sophisticated scientific instruments.

The manufacturing industries offer a growth potential to the developing countries because one or more of them can often be developed in areas where the raw materials, the technical skill, or the financial

resources for the development of heavy industry are lacking but where centuries of skill in domestic crafts can be used as the basis of a manufacturing industry. Too rapid industrialization can bring many problems to a developing country. Urban areas become overcrowded and unemployment is caused by the change from cottage industry to factory industry. Even the most labour intensive industry is less labour intensive than simple agriculture and concealed under-employment on the land becomes overt unemployment in the factories.

The cement industry is a particularly interesting example of the role of industry in development. The basis of cement is lime which is widely available, and the manufacture of cement is relatively cheap and straightforward. When it is made into concrete, cement gives a building material which is strong and durable as well as being fireproof and watertight. Cement is also extremely costly to transport and for this reason, as well as for those stated above, the cement industry is very widely spread and may even be one of the first signs that a country is beginning to industrialize. The beer industry is also very widespread, much more so than the statistics for the commercial industry would suggest. Beer does not travel well and therefore there is little trade in it but

more important is the fact that most beer is produced only for local consumption and much of it is never even bottled and labelled.

The chemical industry is both one of the most important and also one of those which has a large potential for growth because there is no immediate danger of a decline in the petroleum industry which serves it and which spends a considerable sum on research and development. Chemicals are important in every aspect of life; providing fertilizers, drugs, paint, and plastics among many other things. In the industrialized nations the major factor influencing the further development of the manufacturing industries is the relatively high cost of labour. The cost of labour is one of the factors which favours the employment of women in these industries. The garments industry and the electronics industry both employ more women than men, thus making use of their temperament and dexterity while paying into the labour force many women who would not otherwise be wage earners. An increasingly greater emphasis is also being given to automation which uses computer-controlled machines. In industrialized countries the future development of new manufacturing industries is likely to be the result of advances in scientific research.

Beer

Production (1963-5 av.)

'000 hl.
- OVER 8000
- 3001 - 8000
- 1001 - 3000
- 250 - 1000

Production centre

Production by region or country

Major trade flows (1966)

Commodity: S.I.T.C.no.

| | | 112 |

Value (\$ U.S.)
- 0.5mm represents increments of \$5 million
  - 25 VALUE IN \$ MILLIONS
  - 5

Beer production

	429 259 000 hl. 1963-5 av.*	
	322 167 000 1953-5 av.*	
	PERCENTAGE	
	1963-5 av.	1953-5 av.
U.S.A.	25	33
Germany F.R.	13	10
U.K.	10	12
U.S.S.R.	6	6
France	4	3
Others	42	36
	100	100

*Estimate

SCALE 1:176 MILLION 1 CM. TO 1760 KM.

SCALE 1:25 MILLION 1 CM. TO 250 KM.

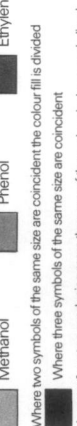

Chemicals I

Benzene/Phthalic Anhydride

Benzene/phthalic anhydride

Production centres (1970)

'000 metric tons capacity

- 601 - 1000
- 301 - 600
- 101 - 300
- 31 - 100
- 0 - 30

Under construction/planned

+ Data not available

Benzene

Phthalic anhydride

Where two symbols of the same size are coincident the colour fill is divided

Where a centre producing more than one of these chemicals are underlined

SCALE 1:1176 MILLION 1 CM TO 1760 KM.

SCALE 1:22 MILLION 1 CM TO 220 KM.

Methanol/Phenol/Ethylene

Methanol/phenol/ethylene

Production centres (1970)

'000 metric tons capacity

- 601 - 1000
- 301 - 600
- 101 - 300
- 31 - 100
- 0 - 30

Under construction/planned

+ Data not available

Methanol

Phenol

Ethylene

Where two symbols of the same size are coincident the colour fill is divided

Where three symbols of the same size are coincident

Names of centres producing more than one of these chemicals are underlined

Major trade flows (1966)

Commodity:	S.I.T.c. no.	Value ($ U.S.)
METHYL ALCOHOL (METHANOL)	512.21	
PHENOLS/PHENOL ALCOHOL	512.27	

0.5 mm. represents increments of $3 million

VALUE IN ($ MILLIONS)	UNDER $15 MILLION

SCALE 1:176 MILLION 1 CM TO 1760 KM. © Oxford University Press

Modified Gall Projection

U.S.S.R.

58

Sulphuric Acid

© Oxford University Press

SCALE 1:176 MILLION   1 CM TO 1 760 KM.

Modified Gall Projection

Major trade flows

All but one of the top eleven trade flows in 1966 were intra-European, the fourth largest flow, from Canada to the U.S.A. The largest flow, valued at about $1.6 millions, was from Italy to Greece.

Sulphuric acid
Production centres (1970)

'000 met. tons capacity

| 2 001 & OVER |
| 1 001 – 2 000 |
| 601 – 1 000 |
| 301 – 600 |
| 101 – 300 |
| 31 – 100 |
| 0 – 30 |
| + × DATA NA |

○ UNDER CONSTRUCTION/ PLANNED

SCALE 1:29 MILLION   1 CM TO 290 KM.

59

Chemicals II

Heavy Inorganics

Estimated total U.S.S.R. production capacity for sodium hydroxide in 1965 was 2 450 000 tons and for sodium carbonate was 3 000 000 tons.

INTRA-EUROPEAN TRADE

| PROVENANCE | DESTINATION |

SCALE 1:29 MILLION   1 CM TO 290 KM.

SCALE 1:176 MILLION   1 CM TO 1 760 KM.

Heavy inorganics
Production centres (1970)

'000 tons capacity

| 2 001 & OVER |
| 1 001 – 2 000 |
| 601 – 1 000 |
| 301 – 600 |
| 101 – 300 |
| 31 – 100 |
| 0 – 30 |
| + × DATA NA |

○ UNDER CONSTRUCTION/ PLANNED

CHLORINE
SODIUM HYDROXIDE
SODIUM CARBONATE

Where two symbols of the same size coincide the colour fill is divided

Where three symbols of the same size coincide more than one of these chemicals are produced

Names of centres producing more than one of these chemicals are underlined

0.5mm. represents increments of 5 million

Major trade flows (1966)

Commodity: S.I.T.C. no.

Value ($U.S.)

| CHLORINE | 513.21 | UNDER $2.5 MILLION |
| SODIUM CARBONATE | 514.28 | $5 MILLION |

Chemicals III

Synthetic Rubbers

Plastics/Fibres

Synthetic rubbers

Synthetic rubber monomers and
Carbon Black, much of which is
used to reinforce synthetic rubber

Production centres (1970)

'000 met. tons capacity

601 - 1000
300 - 600
101 - 300
31 - 100
0.0 - 30

+ Under construction/planned

Data not available

Styrene
Butadiene
Carbon Black

Where two symbols of the same size are
coincident the colour fill is divided.
Names of centres producing more than
one of these chemicals are underlined.

Major trade flows (1966)

Commodity : S.I.T.C. no.

STYRENE : 512.11
CARBON BLACK : 513.27

Value ($U.S.)
0.5 mm. represents increments of
$4 million
($ MILLIONS)

VALUE IN
$ MILLIONS
20   6
4

Plastics/fibres

Production centres (1970)

'000 met. tons capacity

601 - 600
301 - 600
101 - 300
31 - 100
0.0 - 30

+ Under construction/planned

Data not available

Polyvinyl chloride (PVC)
Polyamides (NYLON)
Polyethylene

Where two symbols of the same size are
coincident the colour fill is divided.
Where three symbols of the same
size are coincident.
Names of centres producing more than one
of these chemicals are underlined.

Major trade flows (1966)

Commodity : S.I.T.C. no.

PLASTICS : 581.2/581.3

Value ($ U.S.)
0.5 mm. represents increments of
$40 million
($ MILLIONS)

VALUE IN
$ MILLIONS
200   80
40

SCALE 1 : 176 MILLION
1 CM TO 1760 KM.

SCALE 1 : 22 MILLION
1 CM TO 220 KM.

Chemicals IV

Ammonia

Urea/Nitric Acid

Computers

Modified Gall Projection   Equatorial Scale 1:88 Million approx.

© Oxford University Press

62

Computers (as at 1st March, 1970*)

Number installed

OVER 5 250
(U.S.A. 43 000)

2 251—5 250

281—2 250

51—250

11—50

1—10

DATA NA

Type of user

EDUCATION

FINANCE

GOVERNMENT

MANUFACTURING

OTHER

Investment in computers
($ U.S. per capita)

30 AND OVER

15 — 30

5 — 15

1 — 5

UNDER 1

Production centres

● Location (not quantified)

Production centres include both assembly and component manufacturing facilities. Those shown represent locations of producers responsible for 95% of computer output. Data for smaller producers were not available at time of publication.

Computers installed

U.S. $18 698 million 1970*
Total value

	PERCENTAGE 1970
U.S.A.	45
U.K.	9
Japan	7
Germany F.R.	6
France	5
U.S.S.R.	5
Canada	4
China P.R.	3
Italy	2
Switzerland	2
Others	12
	100

*Estimate as of 1st March

SCALE 1:29 MILLION 1 CM. TO 290 KM.

Installation of computers not only increases efficiency but also induces basic changes within enterprises and institutions. Computers are faster and thus have a greater productive capacity than humans; they are universal in their ability to process information.

Computer operations can be simply described: a computer accepts information from outside as input, combines this, according to the rules of a program which is stored in its memory, with information already received and stored, and returns information to its environment as output.

The input and output devices (peripherals), arithmetic and control circuits and the memory (central processor) form the 'hardware' of the computer. The instructions or programs which set the system to work are known as the 'software'. Computers lack the ability to think or reason for themselves. Their efficiency, ability and accuracy depend on the state of the art and science of programming as well as on the speed and memory capacity of the computer.

Up to the mid-1960's the main change in computers was in the growth of the power of the central processor. Whilst this is continuing more effort has since been made to improve on and from methods of passing information to and from the computer. The use of remote terminals utilizing the power of one central processor, visual display units enabling a user to 'converse' with the computer, and the technique of time sharing where the computer can be working on more than one problem at once, will all extend the role of the computer in the 1970's. The future development of computer-based information services using these tools will mean that the computer will become a significant factor not only in commerce and industry, but also in society as a whole.

The ability of the computer to make calculations which were previously laboriously made manually has not always been well received. Some developing countries have restricted their use because of the unemployment problems that they might cause.

Top Firms

U.S.A. 1957

U.S.A. 1967

The largest industrial corporations in the U.S.A. 1967 (top 30 ranked by sales)

RANK 1967	COMPANY	HEADQUARTERS	SALES (Million $ U.S.)	ASSETS (Million $ U.S.)
1	General Motors	Detroit	20 026	13 273
2	Standard Oil (N.J.)	New York	13 266	15 197
3	Ford Motor	Detroit	10 516	7 967
4	General Electric	New York	7 741	5 347
5	Chrysler	Detroit	6 213	3 855
6	Mobil Oil	New York	5 772	6 224
7	I.B.M.	Armonk, N.Y.	5 345	5 599
8	Texaco	New York	5 121	7 163
9	Gulf Oil	Pittsburgh	4 202	6 458
10	U.S. Steel	New York	4 006	5 606
11	Western Electric	New York	3 711	2 953
12	Standard Oil (Calif.)	San Francisco	3 298	5 310
13	Du Pont (E.I.) de Nemours	Wilmington, Del.	3 102	3 071
14	Shell Oil	New York	3 073	3 421
15	McDonnell Douglas	St. Louis	3 014	2 084
16	Radio Corp. of America	New York	2 934	1 366
17	Standard Oil (Ind.)	Chicago	2 918	4 058
18	Westinghouse Electric	Pittsburgh	2 901	2 075
19	Boeing	Seattle	2 880	2 030
20	Swift	Chicago	2 835	758
21	International Tel. & Tel.	New York	2 761	2 961
22	Goodyear Tire & Rubber	Akron, Ohio	2 638	2 083
23	General Tel. & Electronics	New York	2 622	5 431
24	Bethlehem Steel	Bethlehem, Pa.	2 594	3 084
25	Union Carbide	New York	2 546	3 088
26	International Harvester	Chicago	2 542	1 812
27	Proctor & Gamble	Cincinnati	2 439	1 483
28	North American Rockwell	Los Angeles	2 438	1 144
29	Eastman Kodak	Rochester, N.Y.	2 392	2 233
30	Lockheed Aircraft	Los Angeles	2 335	881

SCALE 1:44 MILLION 1 CM TO 440 KM

The largest industrial corporations in the U.S.A. 1957 (top 30 ranked by sales)

RANK 1957	COMPANY	HEADQUARTERS	SALES (Million $ U.S.)	ASSETS (Million $ U.S.)
1	General Motors	Detroit	10 990	7 498
2	Standard Oil (N.J.)	New York	7 830	8 712
3	Ford Motor	Detroit	5 771	3 348
4	U.S. Steel	New York	4 414	4 373
5	General Electric	New York	4 336	2 361
6	Chrysler	Detroit	3 565	1 497
7	Socony Mobil Oil	New York	2 976	3 105
8	Gulf Oil	Pittsburgh	2 730	3 241
9	Bethlehem Steel	Bethlehem, Pa.	2 604	2 260
10	Swift	Chicago	2 542	545
11	Western Electric	New York	2 480	1 329
12	Texas Co.	New York	2 344	929
13	Standard Oil (Ind.)	Chicago	2 010	2 535
14	Westinghouse Electric	Pittsburgh	2 009	1 401
15	Du Pont (E.I.) de Nemours	Wilmington, Del.	1 964	2 756
16	Armour	Chicago	1 936	443
17	Shell Oil	New York	1 765	1 407
18	Standard Oil (Calif.)	San Francisco	1 657	2 246
19	Boeing Airplane	Seattle	1 651	1 021
20	General Dynamics	New York	1 563	571
21	National Dairy Products	New York	1 432	554
22	Goodyear Tire & Rubber	Akron, Ohio	1 422	929
23	Union Carbide	New York	1 395	1 456
24	Sinclair Oil	New York	1 251	1 481
25	North American Aviation	Los Angeles	1 244	350
26	United Aircraft	E. Hartford, Conn.	1 233	451
27	Republic Steel	Cleveland	1 227	980
28	International Harvester	Chicago	1 171	752
29	Radio Corp. of America	New York	1 171	752
30	Firestone Tire & Rubber	Akron, Ohio	1 159	780

SCALE 1:44 MILLION 1 CM TO 440 KM

Outside the U.S.A. 1967

Modified Gall Projection © Oxford University Press SCALE 1:176 MILLION 1 CM TO 1 760 KM

Outside the U.S.A. 1957

SCALE 1:176 MILLION 1 CM TO 1 760 KM

The largest industrial companies outside the U.S.A. (top 30 ranked by sales)

RANK 1967	COMPANY	1957 HEADQUARTERS	SALES (Million $ U.S.)	ASSETS (Million $ U.S.)	1967 HEADQUARTERS	SALES (Million $ U.S.)	ASSETS (Million $ U.S.)
1	Royal Dutch/Shell	s'Gravenhage	7 377	6 512	s'Gravenhage	8 376	12 870
2	Unilever	London	3 415	1 909	London	5 560	3 271
3	British Petroleum	London	2 220	1 356	London	2 974	4 686
4	I.C.I.	London	1 850	764	London	2 692	4 014
5	Imperial Tobacco	London	1 650	962			
6	British-American Tobacco	London	1 244	1 036			
7	Philips' Gloeilampenfabrieken Eindhoven	Eindhoven	1 150	157	Eindhoven	2 439	2 736
8	Nestlé	Vevey	836	988	Vevey	2 334	4 064
9	Fried. Krupp	Essen	817	N A	Milano	2 092	4 463
10	Distillers Corp.—Seagrams	Montréal	800	647	München	1 984	1 406
11	Hawker Siddeley	London	746	499	Torino	1 911	1 511
12	Cie Française des Pétroles	Paris	730	403	Tōkyō	1 796	415
13	Mannesmann	Düsseldorf	714	253	Tōkyō	1 749	2 097
14	British Motor	London	667	476	Frankfurt	1 651	2 463
15	Gelsenkirchener Bergwerks-A.G. Essen	Essen	650	672	Duisburg	1 650	1 495
16	Guttehoffnungshütte	Oberhausen	647	295	Paris	1 519	632
17	Gallaher	London	643	524	Stuttgart	1 491	735
18	Vickers	London	599	N A	Leverkusen	1 459	1 424
19	Fiat	Torino	571	289	Kitakyūshū	1 376	2 032
20	Tube Investments	Birmingham	568	469	Paris	1 343	788
21	Volkswagenwerk	Wolfsburg	560	1 019	London	1 320	1 815
22	Courtaulds	London	560	279	London	1 308	884
23	Phoenix-Rheinrohr	Berlin	537	525	Roma	1 295	1 019
24	Renault	Paris	531	402	Birmingham	1 273	3 037
25	Canada Packers	Toronto	515	211	Wolfsburg	1 259	1 598
26	Ford Motor	Dagenham	482	88	Yokohama	1 258	1 318
27	A.E.G.	Berlin	465	368	Ludwigshafen	1 258	1 621
28	Toyota Motor				Tōkyō	1 233	1 106
29	Krupp-Konzern				Aichi-ken	465	368
30	Finsider				Genova	462	279

63

Outside the U.S.A. 1957

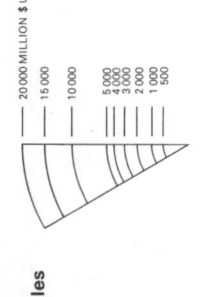

This map has been compiled from Fortune Magazine's lists of the 'Top 500 U.S. Industrials' and 'Top 200 Industrials Outside the U.S.'. To be eligible for inclusion, companies must have derived at least 50% of their sales from manufacturing and/or mining. Sales of subsidiaries are included when they are consolidated.

Figures have been converted into U.S. dollars at official exchange rates. For British companies, whose financial year ended after the devaluation of the pound in November 1967, sales have been converted to $ U.S. using an exchange rate that represents the whole financial year. Total assets, shown in the tables, have been converted at the exchange rate prevailing at the end of each company's financial year.

As sales and assets may be assessed by various methods, close comparisons between figures are inadvisable, particularly between U.S. firms and those in the rest of the world. The classification of firms into six groups is somewhat arbitrary. Many firms are diversified into a wide range of industries other than their original ones, and in these cases they have been classified according to their main products. There is also a trend towards multi-national companies such as Royal Dutch/Shell and Unilever who are both owned jointly by Britain and the Netherlands.

Sales are not the only yardstick for assessing a company's size or economic success. High sales, even when coupled with high assets, do not necessarily produce high profits. For instance, in 1967 the National Coal Board (N.C.B.) registered sales of U.S. $2 439 million, placing them fifth in Fortune's ranking; yet their net profit was only U.S. $958 000, lower than any firm in the top 120.

SCALE 1:44 MILLION 1 CM TO 440 KM

Top firms

Sales

- 20000 MILLION $ U.S.
- 15000
- 10000
- 5000
- 3000
- 2000
- 1000
- 500

Industry

- Petroleum and products
- Chemicals, fibres and rubber
- Motors, aircraft and shipbuilding
- Iron, steel and coal
- Electricals, electronics and engineering
- Foodstuffs, tobacco, drinks, etc.

Demography

For individual country data see Statistical Supplement

The development of world population

That the future stability and welfare of the world as a whole is closely linked to the changes in the numbers of its people has long been widely recognized. Recent increases in population are striking for the short period over which they have taken place; the predicted future growth for its enormous size and speed of development.
The following diagram illustrates population increase from 1800.

Many of the figures on which it is based are estimates; the world-wide taking of accurate and regular censuses has still to be completely achieved, and totals for the nineteenth century, as for some developing countries today, must be regarded with reserve. It is from about 1650, in Western Europe at least, that the beginnings of the sudden spurt of population growth can be traced. Undoubtedly this growth was closely connected with the industrial and scientific revolutions of the eighteenth and nineteenth centuries; it was also involved with important associated economic, social and political changes. Three centuries ago most of the world had, by the standards of today, a near stationary population, the result of a high and erratic death rate cancelling a high but fluctuating birth rate. In this situation probably half the children died before reaching the age of ten or twelve; 50% of the population was under 20 and expectation of life was short for most. There were perhaps 500–600 million people in the world in 1650, at least a half of these being in East and SE. Asia, a proportion close to that found today; the concentration of population here over a long period is one of the primary features of the distribution of the earth's people. Over the 300 years since, the situation has been dramatically altered, although with many regional differences in the rate and timing of advance. A five-fold multiplication between 1650 and 1950 has been the result.

Until about 1900 this growth was moderate and restricted to parts of Europe and Asia; population was advancing at a rate by which the world total doubled about every century. From 1900 onwards all over the world the rate of increase has dramatically altered; the population will soon be doubling in 30 or 40 years. In the early modern period scattered and inaccurate sources make it difficult to decide whether it was rising fertility, declining mortality or a combination of both that aided the sudden acceleration in Europe: today mortality rates continue to fall there, albeit very slowly, but they have declined much faster in the developing countries in recent years. The differences in mortality are thus beginning to vanish under the impetus of world-wide changes in standards of public health and hygiene.

Expectation of life for the developing countries still, of course, falls below the 67–72 years at birth to be found for most men and women in Europe and North America. It ranges between 30 and 60 on average. This in itself represents a great and ever-growing improvement on the situation before the days of the world-wide spread of scientific medicine and higher standards of sanitation, when the expectation of life reached only about 30 years. It is thus the astonishing fertility of the peoples of most of Africa, Asia and Latin America which, tied to their falling death rates, allows a clear distinction to be drawn between "developing" and "developed" countries in a demographic sense; they represent, at the moment, two separate population types.

It is to be expected that mortality will continue to fall: any decrease in the rate of population growth in the last few decades and its projected future developments must come through an induced decline in the birth rate.

The rates of recent growth in different areas vary widely. In the period 1920–1960 the population of Latin America grew by 135% of South Asia by 85% and of East Asia by about 45%. This last figure is the most uncertain of all owing to the lack of reliable demographic information emanating from the giant country of China P.R. Europe as a whole, on the other hand, reached only a 40% increase.

The divergence between the growth rates of the two major population types naturally affects their relative size within the world total. There has been and will continue to be an increase in the share of the developing countries at the expense of the more developed, such as Europe, the U.S.S.R., North America, Japan, Australia, New Zealand, and parts of temperate South America and South Africa, whose portion has dropped from 35% to 30% in recent years, and which may fall below 20% by the year 2000. At present the population of the developing countries is increasing at an annual rate of 1.5–3.5% save in those with a still high mortality rate; the equivalent rate for most developed countries is between 0.5–1.0%. The expected increase over the next decade is shown in the table below.

Forecast of population increase 1970–1980

PERCENTAGE

Latin America	34	North America	15
Africa	30	East Asia	14
South Asia	28	U.S.S.R.	13
Oceania	21	Europe	6

If fertility remains high and constant in the developing nations, however, or declines no faster than it did in the West from the nineteenth century, unmanageable increases in population could result. Africa's great advances in population could be still to come, although that of Latin America which began in the 1920's shows signs of levelling off, as it does in some parts of Asia. The pressing problem is the length of time that will be taken for the fall in birth rates now apparently beginning in island and peninsular countries around the edge of the Asian mainland to spread effectively through the one and a half billion (1 500 000 000) people on the continent. Some regions, especially in Asia itself, start out with population numbers and densities greatly in excess of those in the West at the beginning of its rapid growth, so the increase of people and the resulting pressure on resources and agricultural land will be far, far greater. Furthermore, the West's period of advance was paralleled by a rapidly expanding industrial economy which was able to support more and more people at ever higher standards of living. This is certainly not the case in most developing countries, where there is no guarantee that even Western style industrialization and economic advance a similar fall in net population growth will occur in the same way.

The probability is of a world population of 7000 million by the end of the millenium with the peak still to come; and of the total doubling and quadrupling thereafter with frightening speed according to some projections. Past experience has often shown these to be underestimates, although on the other hand, projections for France and the U.S.A. in recent years have proved to be overestimates. This presents two great problems: the limitation of fertility to reduce births and the feeding of the natural increase that does occur.

Much more is known today about birth control than during the great period of European population growth, and so perhaps fertility decline can be initiated at an earlier stage of demographic development. The post-war period in particular has seen great advances in the techniques and effectiveness of birth control devices; the lowering of their cost and the efforts of many national and international agencies have spread their use throughout the developing world in various forms.

The degree of acceptance by the indigenous populations of different countries has varied, and ratios of effectiveness have often been rather low: indeed a high proportion of unplanned conceptions even in Europe in recent years has occurred despite the use of contraceptive devices. In some developing countries the proportion of women of childbearing age practising birth control is still only about 10%. The problems therefore concern semi-educated and economically advanced peoples with different social standards; but it is though that the modifying effect on population must come from within. This is necessary in order to establish productive capacity and to meet the demands not only of more mouths to feed but of eventually rising living standards. Agricultural advances, when achieved will also undoubtedly eventually lead, with growing efficiency, to the economic redundancy of much of the already underemployed agricultural sector. These people will increasingly look to industry and to the city for employment and place of residence.

Certainly it is unlikely that there will be any solution found to problems of overpopulation in large scale migration. There will probably never again be movements on the scale of the great transatlantic exodus of European peoples to the new world of the Americas, and to a lesser extent Australia and New Zealand; such a mass transfer of people was probably the biggest in human history. Recent movement into the new lands of Siberia and of China P.R. is probably considerable, but lack of reliable information makes this difficult to quantify. Since the sixteenth century it is estimated that over 75 million people have emigrated to the new lands, at least 45 million of these going to Anglo-America. Besides re-distributing population, such movements led to the opening up of new regions and the adoption of more productive agricultural techniques, bringing about an enormous increase in the world's production of foodstuffs.

There have been few recent examples of large population increases due to long range international migration, except perhaps the doubling of Israel's size between 1948 and 1951 when the natural rate of increase was only moderate. Political and national considerations have led to the closing of many former channels of migration; the level of intake into the U.S.A. has dropped to between 250 000 and 350 000 per year, and that country and others like Canada and Australia are now very selective in the choice of their new nationals.

On the other hand, shorter distance and less permanent movements may be expected to increase as barriers to the free movement of labour drop in response to the organization of units like the European Economic Community; for example, some of the industries of Germany F.R., France and Belgium depend on a regular supply of workers from Italy. As a whole, the Southern European countries of Italy, Spain, Portugal, Yugoslavia and Greece have suffered a net loss of about 300 000 a year since 1945, with fewer crossing the Atlantic as European opportunities began to open. The effects of such relatively small movements on the density and distribution of world population is, however, likely to remain slight.

But such movements of foodstuffs are only a temporary palliative for developing countries like India and Pakistan. These are unquestionably over-populated in terms both of agricultural land and employment opportunities. In such areas the impetus must come from within.

The problems therefore concern semi-educated and economically advanced peoples with different social standards; but it is though that the modifying effect on population programmes that the modifying effect on population must come, unless catastrophic losses through famine and epidemic disease take their toll. These last dangers are under twin-pronged attack by improvements in medical and agricultural practice.

A true 'agricultural revolution' in a modern sense is still awaited in many parts of the developing world, as new techniques and crops are uncertainly and sometimes unsuccessfully tried in an attempt to meet increasing population pressure on the availability of foodstuffs. Food supply is unlikely to present any great problem in future years in the developed and industrialized countries. A number of these, the U.S.A., Canada, Australia and New Zealand, have great agricultural resources, and surpluses of staples like grain are often produced. Some is exported to such countries as the U.K. or Germany F.R., whose dense industrial populations are partially dependent on imported foodstuffs. Such produce is often more difficult to redistribute in times of need to the developing countries themselves. The social habits of the people often resist the introduction of new foodstuffs, political problems are sometimes difficult to overcome, even though Canada, for example, has sent vast shipments of grain to China P.R. in some recent years.

Increasing urbanization of the world's population

By far the most marked characteristic of today's accelerating world population growth is its very great rate of urbanization. The increase in the total is associated with an ever continuing shift towards employment in non-agricultural activities. Similarly, parallel with the spread of popular education, material and cultural aspirations are undergoing continuing transformation while social relationships may be altering within an urban framework. These are some of the changes, amongst many others, marking the last century or so, which part in response and part in stimulation to urbanization act as a total mechanism which pushes the process into an ever increasing upward spiral. Indeed the very character of urbanity itself has undergone much change in recent decades because of the shifts from manufacturing to service and higher level activities. Entire regions are now affected by this change, for example much of the NE. seaboard of the U.S.A. has been identified as one continuous urban agglomeration, megalopolis. Others can be seen perceptibly growing around the Great Lakes, in Western Europe (the Rhine-Ruhr axis, for example) and in Japan. The conurbation stretching between Kobe and Tokyo is now merging imperceptibly into "Tokaido." With the great increase in the number of urban activities and attributes and their ever widening diffusion it is doubtful whether the traditional division of the world's population into rural and urban components is any longer valid, at least for many developed countries. This trend is likely to continue in the future throughout the developing countries, and to be undoubtedly the most important change in the future life style of the world's burgeoning population.

Urbanization, with even the possible development of a true world city, may in the long term retard the growth of population which is actually being tackled in the short term by the spread of birth control. Much evidence, admittedly largely drawn from already industrialized Western society which may not necessarily provide generally applicable principles, exists to suggest that levels of fertility are invariably lower in more urbanized societies. This has been attributed to higher levels of income and education, as well as to a greater variety of types of employment opportunity for women found in cities. Rising aspirations have historically led to smaller families. Indeed the very way of life in a city environment may have a profound psychological effect on attitudes to fertility as it does on other matters of individual as well as mass behaviour. Even if this limiting effects on the growth of the human population are found in the future to apply on a world-wide scale, the time that this will take will inevitably be long.

In recent years the most conspicuous rates of urbanization have been experienced in Asia and Latin America; but, growing from 200 million to 450 million in the 40 years up to 1960, the urban population of the developed Western world has more than doubled and may do so again by the end of the century. In the same period, the urban population of the developing world has quadrupled to over 300 million; it is likely to quadruple again to about 1 500 million by the year 2000. The ever changing relationships of "urban" and "rural" populations in the developing and developed countries is illustrated in the table below.

Despite the increasing momentum of urbanization in both parts of the populated world nearly half of the increase up to the year 2000 is estimated to be going to take place in what are still conventionally described as rural and small town sectors of the population, and about half of this will occur in an already overcrowded South Asia struggling with the twin problems of sometimes near starvation and the difficulties of initiating true industrial advance.

Comparison of the world's urban and rural population 1920–2000

YEAR	MILLIONS TOTAL POPULATION	PERCENTAGE OF WORLD TOTAL DEVELOPED REGIONS URBAN	RURAL	TOTAL	DEVELOPING REGIONS URBAN	RURAL	TOTAL
1920	1 860	11	25	36	4	60	64
1940	2 295	13	23	36	5	59	64
1960	2 991	18	15	33	10	57	67
1980	4 318	15	12	27	16	57	73
2000	6 112	15	9	24	23	53	76

Estimated world population

In millions 1800–1970

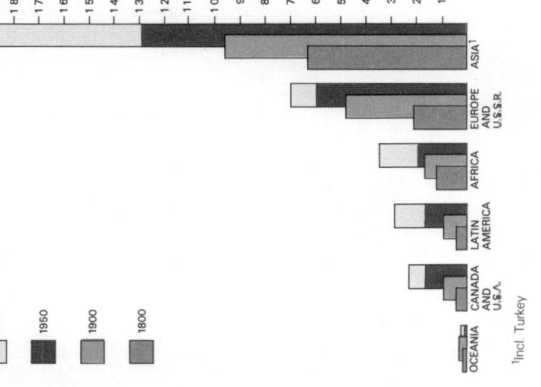

OCEANIA · CANADA AND U.S.A. · LATIN AMERICA · AFRICA · EUROPE AND U.S.S.R.* · ASIA†

*Incl. Turkey

1800 1900 1950 1970

Population I

Modified Gall Projection   Equatorial Scale 1: 88 Million approx.   © Oxford University Press

Population distribution

Towns of at least
100 000 population

OVER 10 000 000
7 500 001 – 10 000 000
5 000 001 – 7 500 000
2 500 001 – 5 000 000

1 000 001 – 2 500 000
500 001 – 1 000 000
250 001 – 500 000
100 001 – 250 000

One dot per 100 000 population
outside the towns shown

Population statistics for selected countries

Latest census available in 1968

	BURMA	NIGERIA	SAUDI ARABIA	YUGO-SLAVIA	CHINA P.R.	INDIA	INDO-NESIA	ALGERIA	PHILIP-PINES	PARAGUAY	TURKEY	POLAND	U.S.S.R.	SOUTH AFRICA	MEXICO	TAIWAN	SWEDEN	GERMANY F.R.	FRANCE	IRAQ	U.A.R.	BRAZIL	ISRAEL	U.S.A.	NETHER-LANDS	U.K.	JAPAN	CANADA	ARGENTINA	AUSTRALIA
Total population (thousands)	16 823	55 670	6 990	18 549	582 603	435 512	96 319	12 102	27 088	1 817	31 391	29 776	208 827	15 994	34 923	13 383	7 766	53 977	46 520	8 262	25 984	70 119	2 183	179 323	11 462	52 709	98 270	18 238	23 031	11 541
Population density (persons/sq. km.)[1]	38	67	3	78	75	156	74	5	116	5	42	102	11	15	23	365	17	233	91	19	31	10	129	21	375	226	270	2	8	2
Percentage urbanized	7	9	9	9	10	10	10	14	15	17	19	23	24	27	28	29	31	32	34	34	35	36	41	45	47	49	50	52	57	63
Size of largest urban agglomeration (thousands)	821	665	225	585	6 900	4 903	2 907	903	1 402	305	2 052	1 261	6 507	1 153	3 353	1 155	1 262	2 191	7 369	1 745	4 220	5 383	390	11 410	1 048	7 914	11 005	2 437	7 000	2 445

[1] 1967

65

Population II

1850

1920

1960

1980

66

SCALE 1:176 MILLION   1 CM TO 1 760 KM.

© Oxford University Press   Modified Gall Projection

Population (historical distribution)

National population totals
(in millions)

0.1—1.0

thereafter, population approximately equals [r × ²⁄₃]², where r is the radius of the circle in millimetres

Thus:

144

64

4

Regional totals

Data not available

Annual average rate of population change
(percentage)

3.0 AND OVER

3

1.5 — 3

0.75 — 1.5

0 — 0.75

DATA N A

Decrease shown by heavy black line around colour

Population pyramids (% of population in each ten-year age group)

These pyramids show the structure of the population of selected countries in terms of age and sex. They are based on ten-year age groups up to the age of 80. The difference in age structures between nations is largely a result of their level of development. Thus Ghana, India and Venezuela have very large 0-9 age groups and a low number of older people. On the other hand, the U.K. and France do not have a constant number of people in each age group, up to 60, signifying lower birth-rate and better medical standards. The pyramids also show that although more males than females are born, the females tend to live longer, as seen clearly in the U.K.

Ghana (1960)

Venezuela (1965)[1]

Germany D.R. (1964)[1]

U.S.S.R. (1959)

France (1964)

U.S.A. (1960)

England and Wales (1961)

Japan (1965)

India (1961)

[1]Data for Germany D.R. and Venezuela, undifferentiated above the age of 70

Population by region

	PERCENTAGE OF WORLD TOTAL		
	1920	1960	1980
Europe	17.6	14.2	11.2
U.S.S.R.	8.3	7.2	6.5
North America	6.2	6.7	6.1
Latin America	4.8	7.1	8.8
East Asia[1]	29.7	26.5	24.4
South Asia	25.2	28.7	32.0
Africa	7.7	9.1	10.5
Oceania	0.5	0.5	0.5

[1]East Asia : China P.R., Japan, Taiwan, Korea, Mongolia, Hong Kong, Macao, Ryukyu Is.

This series of maps is intended to show the accelerating growth of the world's population since 1850 and its expected increase in the immediate future.

In 1850 the total population was about 1 000 million compared with the present figure of 3 500 million, and precise information about the population was scarce. At that time only a few nations had carried out national censuses. Most of the figures are based upon rough estimates made by various organizations and individuals. A large majority of the population lived in South and East Asia, where the agriculture-based economy was very similar to that found in many areas of the region today. It was only in Western Europe and North America that industrialization was leading to diversification in the employment of the labour force, making censuses more important for social planning.

By 1920 statistical information had improved considerably and only in tropical Africa and parts of the Middle East was there still an almost complete lack of demographic data. Thus, a general pattern of population distribution could be seen, major concentrations being in South and East Asia and Europe, with the U.S.A. having the fastest rate of increase (1850-1920) mainly because of large-scale immigration. This came first from

North and West Europe, and then, at the end of the nineteenth century and the beginning of the twentieth century, from South and East Europe, until the introduction of immigration restrictions, particularly after 1924.

The population distribution in 1960 was similar to that in 1920. It is estimated that the world population increased by 473 millions during the 1950's. If current growth rates are maintained, the world population would be 7 000 million by the end of the century, and 12 000 million by 2030. Latin America showed the fastest rate of increase (1920-60). Other areas of rapid increase were a result of exceptional political situations, such as the creation of Israel as a Jewish state in 1948, and emigration from the Chinese mainland to Taiwan and Hong Kong after the revolution in 1949.

The forecast rates of increase (1960-80), based when possible on the 'medium' population projections of the 'UN Report on World Population Prospects as Assessed in 1963' are similar to those of 1920-60. Central America has particularly high growth rates while Europe has a low rate of increase, having reached a stable demographic equilibrium of low birth and death rates.

Population III

Modified Gall Projection   Equatorial Scale 1: 88 Million approx.

© Oxford University Press

Urban change

In those cities of at least 100 000 population at the last census

Size at last census shown by graded circles

OVER 10 000 000
7 500 001–10 000 000
5 000 001–7 500 000
2 500 001–5 000 000

1 000 001–2 500 000
500 001–1 000 000
200 001–500 000
100 001–200 000

Percentage change in previous decade shown by colour

0–5%
5–15%
15–30%
30–60%
60–120%
OVER 120%
DATA NA

decreases shown by black line around colour

cities below 100 000 population at the beginning of the decade shown by open circles because data on change are not available

It must be noted that data on change are applied only to those cities which had 100 000 population at the beginning of the decade, and are shown as percentages over the 10 years, p%.

To convert to an average annual rate, r% p.a., use the compound interest formula:

$$r = \left(100 \times \sqrt[10]{\frac{p+100}{100}}\right) - 100$$

SCALE 1:22 MILLION   1 CM TO 220 KM

Population IV

Life expectation at birth[1]

Rate per thousand population (1963-5 av.)

65 & OVER	55 – 65	40 – 55
UNDER 40		
DATA NA		

One dot to 100 000 population

[1] Data based on latest available national censuses and in say be as early as 1940

Increases in life expectation at birth

		AGE			
		1900-10	1920-30	1947-49	1966
Netherlands	Male	51	62	69	71
	Female	53	64	72	76
Japan	Male	44	45[1]	50[2]	68
	Female	45	47	54[2]	74
India	Male	23	27	32[3]	42[4]
	Female	23	27	32[3]	41[4]

[1] 1928-30 [2] 1947 [3] 1941-50 [4] 1961 [5] 1960 latest available

Expectation of life at birth is calculated on the average number of years of life which would be expected for males and females, when born in a particular period of time, if they continue to be subject to the same mortality conditions as existed in that particular period of time. It is important to reach separate figures for males and females, since generally throughout the world women have a longer life expectation than men and it is only in a very few countries, of those for which data are available, that the reverse is true; these include India, Pakistan, Ceylon, Cambodia and Upper Volta. Central Africa is the area of lowest life expectancy in the world.

Here, as in other areas of low life expectancy, the figure is rising rapidly as a direct result of a falling general mortality rate. This will, in turn, bring about an increased birth rate since more women will live throughout all their possible childbearing years. Consequently, in the developing nations the number of elderly, unproductive persons will rise as well as the number of young persons. A severe strain will be placed upon the developing economies as more persons need to be employed and supported, necessitating an ever-increasing capital investment, which the nations concerned are finding difficult to maintain.

SCALE 1:176 MILLION 1 CM. TO 1760 KM.

ALGERIA	Algerian 36	Non-Algerian 63
GUINEA 27		
GABON	Male 25	Female 45
BRAZIL	Male 39.3	Female 45.5

SOUTH AFRICA		NA
African		
Asiatic	Male	55.8
	Female	54.8
Coloured	Male	44.8
	Female	47.8
White	Female	64.6
	Male	70.1

| NETHERLANDS | Male 71 | Female 75.9 |

RHODESIA		
African	50.0	
European	Male 66.9	Female 74.0

| AUSTRALIA | Male 67.9 | Female 74.2 |

Infant mortality

Number of deaths of infants under one year of age per thousand live births which occurred during the same period (1963-5 av.)

100 & OVER	60 – 100
30 – 60	UNDER 30
DATA NA	

One dot to 100 000 population

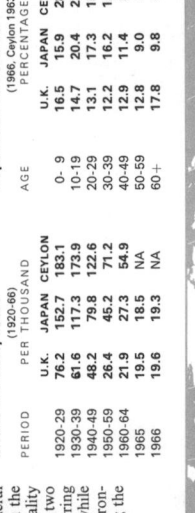

There is a close connection between infant mortality and the general mortality rate; a drop in the former will result in a substantial fall in the latter, since infant mortality is an important quantitative part of mortality rates in general. Deaths during the first year of life can be divided into two major causes differing in importance with time from birth. Those occurring during the first month after birth are primarily due to genetic causes, while the majority in the remaining eleven months are the result of the environment. The latter are far easier to control, and most work in reducing the rates of infant mortality is being done in this sphere.

SCALE 1:176 MILLION 1 CM TO 1760 KM.

Infant mortality rates

			PER THOUSAND	
PERIOD	U.K.	JAPAN	CEYLON	
1920-29	76.2	152.7	183.1	
1930-39	61.6	117.3	173.9	
1940-49	48.2	79.8	122.6	
1950-59	26.4	45.2	71.2	
1960-64	21.9	27.3	54.9	
1965	19.5	18.5	NA	
1966	19.6	19.3	NA	

Population structures

(1966, Ceylon 1963)

AGE	PERCENTAGE		
	U.K.	JAPAN	CEYLON
0 – 9	16.5	15.9	28.9
10-19	14.7	20.4	22.3
20-29	13.1	17.3	15.5
30-39	12.2	16.2	12.6
40-49	12.9	11.4	8.7
50-59	12.8	9.0	5.9
60+	17.8	9.8	6.1

SCALE 1:176 MILLION 1 CM TO 1760 KM.

| SWEDEN 14.3 |
| NETHERLANDS 15.1 |
| MAURITANIA 188 |
| CHAD 160 |

| PAKISTAN 145.6 |

ZAMBIA	NA
African	
Asiatic	
European 25.0

MALAWI	NA
African	3.9
Asiatic	NA
European	NA

RHODESIA	NA
African	49.7
Asiatic	
Coloured	40.2
European	19.3

SOUTH WEST AFRICA	
African	105.2
White	34.4

SOUTH AFRICA	NA
African	69.4
Asiatic	
Coloured	127.7
White	30.9

Crude death rate

Rate per thousand population (1963-5 av.)

18 & OVER	12 – 18
6 – 12	UNDER 6
DATA NA	

One dot to 100 000 population

There are many difficulties in obtaining accurate mortality statistics. A major problem is the variation among countries in the basis of tabulation. If registration is by date of occurrence or by date of registration. If registration is delayed internationally comparable data will not be produced, especially since the number of events registered may vary due to temporary incentives to encourage registration. There is also a real danger of excluding the deaths of infants who died before registration of their births. Large areas of Latin America, North Africa, the Middle East and Asia are particularly suspect.

Although death rates are still high in many developing nations, great advances are being made with the introduction of advanced medical methods such as in the campaign to fight malaria in Ceylon which started in 1946. The rapidly falling death rates, which are linked with medical technology and socio-political organization, are not matched by equally declining birth rates, which are more responsive to cultural conditions.

Ceylon Death rates

1921-25	27.0
1940-44	19.7
1946	19.8
1948	12.9
1955	10.8
1965	8.1

SCALE 1:176 MILLION 1 CM TO 1760 KM.

| PAPUA | NA |
| Indigenous | 2.4 |

| NEW GUINEA | NA |
| Indigenous | |
| Non-indigenous 3.9 |

| UGANDA | NA |
| African | |
| Non-African 2.6 |

| KENYA | NA |
| African | |
| Non-African 5.2 |

ZAMBIA	NA
African	19.6
Asiatic	3.5
European 4.2

MALAWI	NA
African	5.0
Asiatic	
European 3.3

RHODESIA	NA
African	
Asiatic	7.5
Coloured	5.9
European 6.4

SOUTH WEST AFRICA	NA
African	
Coloured	7.7
White	6.8

SOUTH AFRICA	NA
African	
Asiatic	7.7
Coloured	15.3
White	9.1

Deaths in pregnancy and childbirth

Number of deaths of women in pregnancy and childbirth per million babies born alive (1962-4)

2000 & OVER	1000 – 2000
500 – 1000	UNDER 500
DATA NA	

One dot to 100000 population

Like all mortality rates, the number of deaths caused by complications of pregnancy and childbirth are falling. Several factors responsible for this reduction are commonly affecting all forms of mortality. There is the general spread of health facilities which now reach an ever-growing proportion of the population. Public measures are being taken to produce general improvements in the environment, such as water purification schemes, better sewage disposal, vaccinations, and the use of chemicals in large-scale drives against certain diseases. Also, public awareness of mother and child, which are linked with fertility, marriage and childbirth.

health hazards has increased, and individuals are making correspondingly greater efforts to protect themselves. All this has been made possible by an increase in the real income per capita, enabling people to live at higher socio-economic levels: better food and housing making for stronger resistance to disease. However, deaths in maternity are still high in certain developing areas since the introduction of more advanced medical science is hampered by traditional customs and taboos often harmful to the mother and child, which are linked with fertility, marriage and childbirth.

SCALE 1:176 MILLION 1 CM TO 1760 KM.

Modified Gall Projection

© Oxford University Press

| THAILAND 3 772 |
| CEYLON 2 864 |
| SWEDEN 197 |
| URUGUAY 1967-9 data |
| CHILE 2 973 |

SOUTH AFRICA	NA
African	
Asiatic	1 621
Coloured	1 837
White	531
1959-61 data	

Population V

SCALE 1:176 MILLION 1 CM TO 1 760 KM.

Population growth rates

Percentage annual growth (1963-7 av.)

| 3 & OVER | 2 - 3 | 1 - 2 | UNDER 1 |

DATA N.A.

One dot to 100'000 population

Growth per year	Population doubles in
3%	23½ yrs
2%	35 yrs
1%	70 yrs

Data for much of Asia, Africa, Latin America and Oceania are of dubious reliability.

For some years now economists and others have been disturbed by the rate of population growth. Prior to the nineteenth century this growth was almost undetectable, and surpluses from Western Europe could be absorbed by 'New Lands', a movement which started as early as the sixteenth century. Now the pressures are much greater.

In many countries a high rate of growth is combined with a low income especially in parts of Africa, Asia and Latin America. New methods of agriculture can help where finance, land and initiative are available; however in many countries changes in the social framework must take place if such methods are to flourish. Much has been achieved by these new methods already in the attempt to increase world food supplies. The spread of modern birth control entails many social adjustments but is certainly one of the most important means now widely available of arriving at a balance between population and food supply. These maps serve to indicate in a small way the need for, and progress of, family planning throughout the world in 1968.

Crude birth rate

Annual rate per '000 (1963-5 av. or latest available data pre-1963)

| 40 & OVER | 30 - 40 | 20 - 30 | 5 - 20 |

DATA N.A.

One dot to 100'000 population

Data for much of Asia, Africa, Latin America and Oceania are of dubious reliability. Comparison between any countries should be treated with care. The extent and type of survey, variation in basis and year of data will all affect the rate.

GUYANA — Amerindians 46.3, Others 40.7

SOUTH WEST AFRICA — White 24.0, Coloured 56.6, African N.A.

SOUTH AFRICA — White 23.4, Coloured 46.2, Asiatic 32.7, African N.A.

RHODESIA — European 19.4, Coloured 36.9, Asiatic 33.4, African 48.1

MALAWI — European 27.9, Asiatic 50.2, African N.A.

KENYA — Non-African 28.4, African 50.0

UGANDA — Non-African 26.7, African 42.0

NEW GUINEA — Indigenous N.A., Non-indigenous 33.8

PAPUA — Indigenous N.A., Non-indigenous 29.7

Growth rates

	AFRICA	ASIA	EUROPE	N. AMERICA	LAT. AMERICA	OCEANIA	U.S.S.R.	WORLD
Population (millions) 1950	222	1 381	392	166	163	13	180	2 517
1960	318	1 868	449	217	253	18	233	3 356
Av. annual birth rate (‰) 1960-66	46	38	18	22	41	26	22	34
Av. annual death rate (‰) 1960-66	23	18	10	9	13	11	7	16
Av. rate of population increase (%) 1960-66	2.3	2.3	0.9	1.5	2.8	2.1	1.4	1.9

SCALE 1:176 MILLION 1 CM TO 1 760 KM.

Development of family planning

As indicated by the level of national and international co-operation in 1968

Countries which have:
- Membership of I.P.P.F.[1]
- Government effective programme
- Family planning association[2]
- Government commitment only
- Some degree of anti-contraceptive legislation
- Data not available

[1]International Planned Parenthood Federation
[2]Not shown if already a member of I.P.P.F.

An effective government family planning programme may be assumed to reach 10% or more of eligible women: this category excludes countries with high contraceptive practice but without a government policy.

Government commitment to provide family planning services may be *either* as a health measure or as a means of slowing population growth. In Europe it means that legislation has been passed to encourage the use of contraception; for example, Danish doctors must give advice after child birth or abortion.

It should be noted that the anti-contraceptive legislation may be by-passed in some countries, such as Canada and the Netherlands. However it is still significant as it affects *government* involvement in family planning.

Contraceptive practice

Percentage of eligible females using effective contraceptive measures in 1968

| 30 & OVER | 10 - 30 | 5 - 10 | 0 - 5 |

DATA N.A.

One dot to 100'000 population

Effective contraceptive measures are *here*[1] defined as:—
a Barrier methods
b Intra-uterine devices
c Oral method—'the pill'
d Rhythm method—if teaching supplied
e Sterilization
Eligible females are defined as those aged 15-45 years.
[1]Coitus interruptus and abortion may be as effective a control in many cases.

African statistics are fairly reliable; it is known that contraceptive practice is very low. Latin America is mainly Roman Catholic, hence figures are virtually non-existent. The estimates shown are based on manufacturers' figures, social surveys, etc. Data for the Caribbean and North America are most reliable. Estimates for Asia are quite well supported, notable exceptions being former Indo-China and the Middle East. China P.R., Mongolia, N. Vietnam and N. Korea are omitted as, although there is no evidence, contraceptive practice may be quite high, especially in China P.R. and N. Vietnam. Oceania and Europe are considered to be reasonable estimates. The map does not show the wide variations in urban and rural areas.

© Oxford University Press   Modified Gall Projection   SCALE 1:176 MILLION 1 CM TO 1 760 KM.

Migrations

These maps are based on data from the International Travel Statistics published by the International Union of Official Travel Organisations (I.U.O.T.O.). Most of the countries which provided data used the I.U.O.T.O. definition of a tourist—'a temporary visitor staying at least 24 hours in the country visited and the purpose of whose journey can be classified under one of the following headings:
a) leisure (recreation, holiday, health, study, religion, sport)
b) business, family, mission, meeting.'

The rapid growth in the number of tourists in recent years is a result of higher socio-economic levels; in particular an annual leave of absence and a wage level high enough to permit a holiday. Thus most tourists come from Western Europe and North America, and since intercontinental holidays are, as yet, rare, these are also the main centres of the tourist industry.

SCALE 1:176 MILLION   1 CM TO 1 760 KM.

Tourists (1964-5 av.)

Annual number of foreign tourists per 100 000 residents

OVER 30 000
10 001-30 000
1 001-10 000
0-1 000
DATA N.A.

Countries whose annual number of foreign tourists per 100 000 residents is over 75 000

Monaco	349 000
Bermuda	346 200
Bahamas	331 300
Kuwait	115 500
Luxembourg	115 100
Switzerland	97 700
Austria	86 900

Annual number of tourist arrivals (in millions)

OVER 10
10
5
1
0.5
0.1
0.05
0.01
0.005 & UNDER

One dot to 100 000 residents

© Oxford University Press

Modified Gall Projection

SCALE 1:176 MILLION   1 CM TO 1 760 KM.

Hong Kong

Bermuda

Barbados

Tourism, besides being of sociological interest, is also of growing economic importance. Nationally, the major factor is the difference between expenditure and receipts. In some countries there is a substantial gain of foreign capital (Spain and Italy annually gain almost $1 000 million each) while in others, the loss of capital through tourism is a major concern as in the U.S.A. and Germany F.R. which each year lose $1 200 and $700 million respectively.

Tourism may affect the development of particular regions, for it provides the capital and also the incentive for development, in order to attract more tourists. Not only is better accommodation provided, but also new communication systems and other physical and social amenities, such as more advanced water supplies, helping to alter the nature of the region's economy.

Tourism (1964-5 av.)

Receipts from foreign tourists and expenditures by residents abroad in million $U.S.

RECEIPTS EXPENDITURES

OVER 2 000 —
1 001-2 000 — 50
501-1 000 — 21
51-100 — 11
— 0-10

Where one or both semicircles are missing, the relevant data are not available

---

SCALE 1:176 MILLION   1 CM TO 1 760 KM.

Emigration (1963-5 av.)

This map is based on the annual number of long-term emigrants from each country, that is, the number of residents leaving a country for a period longer than one year. The value of the data for both emigration and immigration is restricted by a number of factors. International comparability is limited since even when frontier checks are numerically accurate, the definitions and categories used in such checks vary widely. These records are based on the stated intentions of travellers, who may change their plans. Also clandestine movements, known to occur across certain frontiers, escape statistical recording.

Morocco, Uganda, New Guinea, Papua include short-term immigrants leaving.
Jamaica—data exclude movements to other parts of the West Indies.
Germany F.R.—data exclude movements to Germany D.R.
U.K.—data for intercontinental migrants using ships sailing between the U.K. and places outside Europe.
Scandinavia—data exclude all movements between the five countries of the Nordic passport zone.
Israel—data for declaring long-term emigrants only; other long-term emigrants were estimated to be about 6 000 in 1965.

Annual rate of long-term emigrants per 100 000 residents

OVER 750
101-750
26-100
0-25
DATA N.A.

Countries whose annual rate of long-term emigrants per 100 000 residents is over 1 000

Luxembourg	2 878
Malta	2 434
Jamaica	2 368
Brunei	2 005
Papua	1 399
Aden	1 228
Greece	1 208

Annual number of long-term emigrants

OVER 250 000
50 001-250 000
10 001-50 000
2 501-10 000
501-2 500
1-500

One dot to 100 000 population

SCALE 1:176 MILLION   1 CM TO 1 760 KM.

Immigration (1963-5 av.)

This map is based on the annual number of long-term immigrants to each country, that is, the number of non-residents (nationals and aliens) intending to remain for longer than one year.

Barbados, Ceylon, Fiji Is., Grenada, Jamaica, Kenya, Luxembourg, Morocco, Singapore, South Africa, South West Africa, Tanzania, Uganda, Zambia—data include short-term immigrants, that is, non-residents intending to exercise, for a period of one year or less, an occupation remunerated from within the country.

Germany F.R.—movements from Germany D.R. excluded.
Scandinavia—data exclude all movements between the five countries of the Nordic passport zone.
Spain—data for intercontinental movements only.
U.K.—data for intercontinental movements using ships sailing between the U.K. and places outside Europe.
U.S.A.—data represent aliens admitted for the first time for permanent residence and alien residents returning after one year or more abroad.
France—over 50% of immigrants are Algerian workers.

Annual rate of long-term immigrants per 100 000 residents

OVER 750
101-750
26-100
0-25
DATA N.A.

Countries whose annual rate of long-term immigrants per 100 000 residents is over 1 000

Grenada	9 066
Luxembourg	3 580
Papua	2 044
Israel	1 930
Singapore	1 543
Australia	1 422
New Zealand	1 349
Germany F.R.	1 117

Annual number of long-term immigrants

OVER 250 000
50 001-250 000
10 001-50 000
2 501-10 000
501-2 500
1-500

One dot to 100 000 population

Fatal Accidents

Modified Gall Projection   Equatorial Scale 1: 88 Million approx.

© Oxford University Press

Motor vehicles in use (1963–5 av. in thousands)

SCALE 1:263 MILLION
1 CM 10.3 1020 KM

| 85–256 |
| 7.401– |
| 11.800 |
| 2.601– |
| 7.400 |
| 601– |
| 2.600 |
| 51– |
| 600 |
| 0–50 |
| DATA N A |

Fatal accidents (1963–4 av. for age group 15–64)

Number of accident deaths

| 57 009 (U.S.A.) |
| 45 247 (U.S.A.) |
| 17 001–27 000 |
| 7 001–17 000 |
| 3 501–7 000 |
| 1 501–3 500 |
| 501–1 500 |
| 0–500 |

Type of accident

MOTOR VEHICLE

OTHER

Accident deaths per 100 000 population

| 64–77 |
| 49–63 |
| 34–48 |
| 15–33 |
| DATA N A |

Sex of victims

MALE

FEMALE

71

The annual toll of accidents throughout the world, whether in industry, the home, on the roads, or any other area of human activity, is constantly rising. The cost in human life, misery and money is enormous, and in spite of the most prolonged efforts to counteract the trend, there seems to be no really effective way of preventing this lamentable waste. Education, training and legislation help, but the effects are difficult to measure and many think that a high proportion of accidents arise from human inadequacies which cannot entirely be covered by these approaches. Obviously, where hazards exist there will always be a proportion of casualties; it is also generally accepted that the majority of accidents are preventable, so the waste in human life and the suffering caused by unnecessary risk-taking are made all the more pronounced.

In the United States the cost of all accidents in 1969 was estimated at $25 000 million. In that year the number of working days lost through injuries at work in the United States was 245 million. In Great Britain in an average year 22 million working days are lost through industrial injuries compared with 5 million for industrial disputes. The most effective controls can perhaps be operated in industry where statutory legislation in the factory ensures a certain basic protection. But carelessness, neglect and lack of proper instruction and supervision still lead to a high proportion of industrial accidents. Accidents in the home in Great Britain account for 7 500 deaths a year, with a further

120 000 casualties being admitted to hospital. Another 1.5 million attend casualty out-patient departments. In an average year in Great Britain fatal home accidents exceed those on the road, but in the United States the fatal home accident figure is about half the road fatality total. It is estimated in Britain that the cost of each personal-injury accident on the road is about £400. In spite of vehicle tests, tyre regulations, research into driver behaviour and constant propaganda, the casualty rate is rising.

Accidents of all kinds are the fourth leading cause of death (following heart disease, cancer and strokes) in the United States. Further, in the United States accidents of all kinds are the leading cause of death for the 1–37 age-group.

The international comparability of statistics on accidents is limited by the lack of published data and the variation in definition of the terms employed. For example, in some countries an accident is considered fatal if the victim dies many months after its occurrence; in other countries death must occur at the time of the accident or within a few hours. Also, many countries include in occupational accident statistics those injuries or deaths which occur in commuting to and from work. These differences in data collection do not alter the fact that accidents have important consequences in economic, as well as human, terms.

Disease

The present world pattern of disease distribution broadly reflects economic conditions rather than aspects of the physical or biological environments. In developing countries infectious diseases are still rife, and malnutrition and intestinal parasites affect large sections of the population, sapping energy and stunting ability. These are mostly conditions of known origin (typhoid, cholera, smallpox, rabies, plague, malaria, tuberculosis and kwashiakor) which could be greatly reduced in frequency and almost eliminated as they have been elsewhere in the world, if only sufficient money could be devoted to raising the level of nutrition and sanitation and to implementing the necessary programmes of vaccination and control of insect vectors.

In the economically more prosperous countries, where the control of infections and malnutrition has largely been achieved, the major hazards are now the degenerative conditions such as cancer and heart disease which for the most part affect the older age groups but which even so reduce by twenty or thirty years the potential lives of the majority of those affected. Mental sickness has also become a major health problem and many deaths and disabilities are caused by accidents, especially accidents involving motor vehicles.

Within the broad economic framework the detailed distribution of individual diseases is determined by a complex of environmental and social factors. Climate and topography affect the distribution of the vectors which carry sleeping sickness, onchocerciasis and schistosomiasis and, as these require warm temperatures for their survival, the infectious diseases which they transmit add to the burden of disease in the developing world.

As the environmental or social conditions change so, too, does the characteristic pattern of disease. Very valuable epidemiological information can be gained by studying morbidity and mortality among the migrant communities of the world. Black Americans have a disease pattern which is far more similar to that of white Americans than to present day inhabitants of Africa, thus stressing the importance of environment rather than genetic constitution in the development of most diseases. However, recent migrants retain the disease pattern of their original community for a period of time after immigration, sometimes for as long as several generations if major cultural customs such as diet are maintained or followed in the new environment. A good example of this are the Asian inhabitants of Africa who are of Indian origin and who show differences both from local Africans because they have continued their own cultural traditions in relatively closed communities, and from Indians in India because they have for the most part improved their standard of living after migration to Africa.

recorded. The maps which show the distribution of doctors and the availability of hospital beds in the section on medical care can therefore also be used as an index of the reliability of data shown in the disease maps. A further indication is given by the proportion of all deaths ascribed to 'senility or unknown causes', which varies in the selected countries shown in the table below from 0.6% in Canada to 22.3% in the U.A.R.

Various indices have been used to measure disease frequency. The most informative is the *incidence rate* which is based on the number of new cases developing each year, but it is also possible to measure the total number of people affected at a given point in time (to give a *prevalence* rate) or the number of deaths caused by a disease (to give a *mortality* rate). The prevalence and mortality rates reflect not only the frequency of a disease but also its duration and the extent to which it can be treated and cured and so are artificially lowered in countries which have highly developed medical services. However they are generally easier to study than incidence since mortality statistics are routinely collected by many governments and since prevalence can be measured in a specially organized study on a single day instead of over a period of months or years.

Certain infectious diseases are notifiable by international agreement so that their spread can be controlled and it has therefore been possible to map incidence for cholera, sleeping sickness and malaria. It must be remembered though that in countries where these diseases are most frequent the medical services are very poorly staffed and that a case can be only notified if the disease has first come to the notice of a doctor. The incidence in the high frequency areas is therefore only a minimal estimate of the true frequency.

Research interest in the unsolved problems of cancer aetiology has led many countries to establish cancer registries which record each new case as it is diagnosed. It has therefore also been possible to base the cancer maps largely on incidence data. Where only mortality figures are available an adjustment has been made for each specific type of cancer to allow for the probable difference between the incidence and mortality rates from the average difference observed in countries for which data are available.

The bronchitis, tuberculosis and heart disease maps are based on mortality figures. For bronchitis the death rates indicate the pattern of regional variation but greatly underestimate the extent of the disease. In parts of NE. England, for example, a survey of the population indicated that one in six women is affected by chronic bronchitis. The number who actually die from the disease is very much lower. The condition generally lasts many years and it is estimated that about one-third of sufferers are incapacitated from their normal occupation for over one month every year.

For tuberculosis the mortality figures are affected by the availability of treatment in different countries. They fail to distinguish therefore between the situation in Denmark where very few cases occur and the situation in Britain where the frequency of air-borne infection is such that new cases still develop but where the disease is controlled by treatment and mortality is again very low.

The leprosy map is based on prevalence rates estimated from various W.H.O. investigations. The estimates are for the most part based on the number

spent on such medical treatment in the developed world since the scientific advances of the past century and a half (vaccination and chemotherapy in medicine and anaesthetics and antiseptics in surgery) showed an ideal of physical well-being in which the discomfort of disease need not be accepted as a normal part of life. This is reflected in the fact that nations such as the U.K. or the U.S.A. spend almost 100 times as much per capita per annum maintaining their health as some developing countries. Paradoxically, epidemiological research is beginning to suggest that much of this expenditure perhaps need not have been incurred because it seems that many of the diseases of economic prosperity are themselves caused by the way of life that such prosperity permits or demands. Heart disease, appendicitis, varicose veins, diabetes, lung cancer and bowel cancer are all very common in Western society but are practically unknown in rural communities of Asia and Africa.

Obviously all disease places an economic burden on a community but in choosing the diseases to map for an economic atlas it was decided to concentrate mainly on those which attack the adult population and thus impose the particular economic burden of loss of efficiency and loss of working hours among a country's labour force. Some were chosen as typical of the developing world, — tuberculosis, sleeping sickness, malaria, cholera and leprosy. Others such as heart disease, bronchitis and cancer play a similar role in economically developed communities.

The choice of diseases mapped has also been determined partly by the availability of data. Conditions such as bilharzia and syphilis could not be considered for inclusion because no adequate statistics are available. The principal source of data has been the various reports of the World Health Organization supplemented by cancer registry material for the cancer maps. A more detailed source list can be found in the section of sources at the end of the atlas.

The large areas on the maps indicating lack of medical care in the world reflect the very uneven distribution of medical care in the world. In much of Asia and Africa there is less than one doctor to every 100 000 inhabitants, compared with over one per 1 000 in much of Western Europe and America, and under these circumstances the fact of death, let alone the cause, often goes un-

Iron and zinc deficiencies occur in areas of drier climate, for example parts of the U.A.R. or Iran, where lack of rainfall prevents the cultivation of an adequate range of foodstuffs and where there is an excessive loss of essential elements through heavy sweating. Geology is an important factor in the distribution of diseases such as goitre and cretinism which are due to iodine deficiency and which are

common in limestone areas of recent mountain ranges such as the Swiss Alps. Geology may also play a part in the occurrence of coronary heart disease, which in several areas of the world shows a clear association with the hardness of the drinking water.

With other diseases the causative factors seem to lie more in the social and cultural environments. Both cigarette smoking which is a major cause of lung cancer, and air pollution which has a contributory effect, are features of a man-made environment. Deaths from liver cirrhosis are common in France as a result of high alcohol intake. Cancer of the mouth is far more common in India than in other parts of the world, apparently from the habit of chewing a quid of tobacco and lime wrapped in betel leaves.

The origin of most degenerative diseases is still unknown, but the marked geographical variation in frequency which many display suggests that, as with the examples given above, some environmental factor is involved in their development and that they could therefore be prevented. At present all that is possible against most degenerative disorders is curative or palliative treatment after the symptoms of disease have appeared. Enormous sums of money have been

various suspected factors involved in the development of bronchitis (domestic and industrial air pollution, cigarette smoking, cold and humidity and industrial hazards such as dust from mining activities) have only been disentangled by detailed studies within national territories and not by broad comparisons between countries. However detailed information of this kind is routinely available only for a very few countries and most of the maps published here have had to be based on national figures. Where figures for different ethnic groups are available they have been included. The importance of this kind of breakdown is clear from the example of tuberculosis in South Africa, where the death rate per million varies from 1436 for Coloureds (non-African) to 295 for Asians and 61 for Whites.

this is of less importance because comparisons are largely being made within the areas where life expectation is still low.

Standards of diagnosis, especially on death certificates, tend to vary not only between countries but also between different sectors of the population in the same country. They are generally least good among the elderly where symptoms are ascribed simply to 'senility' without a more detailed investigation. The level of mis-diagnosis varies from country to country, and for this reason it is advisable to restrict comparisons of frequency to persons under the age of sixty-five.

The maps for heart disease, bronchitis and cancers of the lung, stomach and breast have been drawn for the age group 35-64 partly for this reason and partly because relatively few cases in adults occur under this lower age limit. The map for liver cancer has been drawn for the age group 15-44 because, although primary liver cancer continues to occur with increasing frequency in older people, tumours of other sites commonly metastasize to the liver and, at older ages, it is difficult to distinguish primary from secondary growths in the cancer statistics. However, liver cancer is also distinctive in occurring at younger ages than is common for the other tumours mapped here.

For malaria, cholera, tuberculosis and sleeping sickness, in keeping with the policy of mapping diseases which cause death and disability in people who are normally economically active, an attempt was made to calculate the frequency rates for the age span of the working population. However, the data were nowhere good enough to permit such refinement and crude rates had to be used instead.

In calculating disease rates it is necessary to take account not only of the number of persons affected but also of the size and structure of the population at risk. For a disease with such marked geographical variation as cholera a simple dot map of cases would give a fairly clear picture of the world distribution, but in order to distinguish more subtle variation it is necessary to relate the number of cases to the total population so that the disease map is not merely a pale reflection of population density.

The simplest allowance is to divide the total number of cases by the total population in which they occur. This gives a measure known as a *crude* disease rate. However many diseases show a sharp rise in frequency with age and where this occurs it is essential to make allowance also for the age structure of the population at risk. For example, many old people retire to the south coast of England and for this reason a town in that area, such as Bournemouth, appears to have a higher crude death rate than a town elsewhere in the country, such as Bradford. If the death rates at each age of life (age specific death rates) were compared, Bournemouth would appear the healthier town at all ages but the crude death rate is inflated by the elderly structure of the population at risk.

If the number of people in each age group is known in each area (and preferably also the local age specific disease rates) the statistical procedure of 'age standardization' can be applied to the frequency rates for specific diseases, and it then becomes possible to compare the disease experience of the 'young' countries of the developing world with that of Western Europe where the expectation of life is so much greater. Heart disease, bronchitis and many types of cancer all become increasingly frequent at older ages, and age standardized incidence and mortality rates have been mapped for these diseases. Only with 'age standardization' did it become apparent that cancer was not specifically a disease of economically developed countries but that it occurred almost as frequently among the middle aged and elderly of Africa and Asia.

Data which are adequate for age standardization are not available for all the diseases mapped here, but

The World Health Organization, from whose reports most of the data for the maps of disease and medical care have been drawn, is one of the specialized agencies of the United Nations. It came into being in 1948 and through its organization the public health authorities and medical professions of more than 100 countries exchange knowledge and experience and collaborate in an effort to improve the level of health throughout the world.

The speed of modern travel has so shrunk distances that diseases can be carried thousands of miles within a few hours. Without an effective world system of epidemic control no community would be really safe and dramatic changes could occur in the world pattern of disease distribution. One of the major roles of W.H.O. is to broadcast daily epidemic bulletins from Geneva of the appearance in any new area of the world of the pestilential diseases, or of outbreaks of conditions such as influenza or polio, and to lay down and revise international regulations for quarantine, inoculations and vaccinations.

The purpose of drawing maps of disease, and the ultimate aim of research by organizations such as W.H.O. and the various national medical institutions, is to understand better the causes of each disease so that the distribution patterns which the maps show can be destroyed. The present series of maps indicate the situation at one point in time; the more quickly they become out of date because of diminishing frequencies the better for the health of mankind.

Most of the data published by the World Health Organization are given at a national level, but incidence and mortality rates calculated on this basis can disguise wide regional differences within a country. Disease boundaries rarely coincide with national boundaries, and for a proper understanding of the different causative factors which may play a part in the development of any disease it is usually necessary to study the frequency in more limited sectors of the population and therefore in smaller areas, or in different occupational, social class or ethnic groups. The relative importance of the

Causes of death as a percentage of total deaths (1966)

Selected countries

(figures in brackets indicate G.N.P. per capita in $ U.S.)

	W.H.O. I.C.D. NUMBER	U.A.R. (160)	PHILIPPINES (160)	PORTUGAL (380)	MEXICO (470)	CHILE (470)	SINGAPORE (570)	JAPAN (860)	ISRAEL (1160)	ENGLAND/ WALES (1620)[2]	FRANCE (1730)	CANADA (2240)	SWEDEN (2270)
Tuberculosis	B1, B2	0.7	11.9	2.7	2.3	3.9	5.4	3.0	0.5	0.4	1.2	0.5	0.4
Other infective or parasitic diseases	B3-B17	1.2	6.2	1.2	6.1	3.3	1.1	0.8	0.8	0.4	0.6	0.4	0.3
Malignant neoplasms	B18	1.4	3.0	10.6	3.7	9.9	12.8	16.4	18.1	19.2	19.4	17.9	18.9
Diabetes mellitus	B20	0.3	0.3	0.8	1.0	0.6	0.9	0.9	0.7	0.8	1.6	1.7	1.7
Vascular lesions affecting the central nervous system	B22	0.6	2.0	15.8	2.3	5.6	7.2	25.7	12.6	14.0	12.1	10.4	11.7
Heart disease	B24-28	6.9	4.4	14.4	3.6	8.7	11.0	12.3	32.6	31.3	18.8	36.1	35.8
Influenza	B30	0.0	0.8	0.5	1.2	1.5	0.2	0.1	0.1	0.7	0.6	0.4	0.2
Pneumonia	B31	2.2	15.1	8.1	13.1	14.6	7.7	3.2	1.9	6.3	1.8	3.6	5.0
Bronchitis	B32	8.5	5.7	2.8	2.8	0.9	1.4	0.8	0.6	5.7	0.4	0.9	0.6
Ulcer of stomach and duodenum	B33	0.1	1.1	0.8	0.5	0.5	0.5	1.3	0.8	0.7	0.3	0.6	0.9
Gastritis, duodenitis, enteritis and colitis	B36	32.5	7.6	4.6	9.6	5.9	2.0	1.2	0.7	0.5	0.1	0.4	0.4
Cirrhosis of the liver	B37	0.0	0.5	3.1	2.0	3.2	1.0	1.5	0.8	0.3	3.3	0.9	0.7
Deliveries and complications of pregnancy, childbirth and the puerperium	B40	0.3	0.8	0.2	0.3	0.9	0.3	0.2	0.2	0.0	0.1	0.1	0.0
Congenital malformations	B41	0.1	0.7	0.6	0.8	0.8	1.5	0.7	1.9	0.8	0.7	1.5	0.7
Birth injuries and diseases of the newborn and early infancy	B42-44	11.1	8.6	4.6	12.3	13.9	7.7	2.1	4.3	1.5	1.6	3.4	1.2
Senility and ill-defined or unknown causes	B45	22.3	11.0	15.6	18.2	5.9	17.9	8.5	3.3	0.8	13.0	0.6	1.0
Motor vehicle accidents	BE47	0.0	0.2	1.5	0.7	1.5	2.5	2.7	1.7	1.3	2.3	3.6	1.8
All other accidents	BE48	2.8	2.9	2.7	4.1	5.8	2.8	3.7	3.1	2.1	4.3	4.0	2.8
Suicide	BE49	0.0	0.1	0.8	0.1	0.6	1.8	2.2	0.1	0.9	1.5	1.1	2.0
Homicide and operations of war	BE50	0.0	1.4	0.1	1.9	0.2	0.2	0.2	0.1	0.1	0.1	0.1	0.1
Others		9.0	15.7	8.5	13.3	11.0	14.0	12.4	14.2	12.2	16.2	11.7	13.8

[2] Average for U.K. including Northern Ireland and Scotland

World Health Organization International Classification of Diseases 7th edition Geneva 1955

Disease I

Heart disease

Mortality from arteriosclerotic heart disease is highest in the economically more developed English-speaking communities with the white population of the U.S.A. at the forefront followed by the Asian, white and coloured populations of South Africa, and by Australia, Canada, New Zealand, the U.K. and Ireland. The only non-English-speaking country with an exceptionally high incidence is Finland. The rest of North and West Europe has rates a little lower than those in England and Wales, but the total variations between the U.S.A. and the lowest of these countries (Spain and Iceland) is only about threefold. (The mortality in France is apparently exceptionally low for Western Europe but it may be that this represents a national difference in diagnostic practice.)

In developing countries, though little statistical evidence is available, the total mortality from cardiovascular disease is known to be very small (even allowing for the much younger age structure of the population). This has led to the suggestion that the white race has a genetic pre-disposition to heart disease, but such a hypothesis is belied by the evidence from America and South Africa where negroes and Asians have a rate very much higher than is common in most of Africa or in India.

A diet rich in sugar, fats or refined carbohydrates, the psychological stresses of modern urban society and lack of exercise have all been suggested as possible causes of heart disease. Any or all of these may be in some way involved, but at present the specific cause is unknown.

USA 365

SOUTH AFRICA	
White	279
Coloured	205
Asian	314
African	NA

SCALE 1:176 MILLION 1 CM TO 1760 KM.

Heart disease[1]
Average annual age standardized death rate per 100 000 in the age group 35-64 for 1961 or 1962

- 140 & over
- 70 - 140
- 35 - 70
- 2 - 35
- DATA NA

One dot to 100 000 population

[1] WORLD HEALTH ORGANIZATION (WHO) INTERNATIONAL CLASSIFICATION OF DISEASE NUMBER 420-422

Tuberculosis

Tuberculosis in man is caused either by the human or the bovine type of tubercle bacillus (mycobacterium tuberculosis). The human type is spread by the cough spray and expectoration of sufferers, the bovine type by infected milk from cows with udder tuberculosis. Pulmonary tuberculosis which is principally a disease of adults, is the most prevalent form of tuberculosis and is almost all of the human type. Bovine tuberculosis mainly affects children. Wherever possible the figures mapped are for pulmonary tuberculosis because of the incapacity which it causes among the adult working population. The mode of transmission is such that pulmonary tuberculosis is most common in conditions of poverty and overcrowding, and it is thus more common in towns than in rural areas.

In industrialized societies it has tended to reach a peak in the early stages of industrialization. In England and Wales from 1780 to 1800 the mortality rate is estimated to have reached 1 000 per 100 000 and to have declined steadily since, apart from a sharp increase during the two world wars. Although tuberculosis has been known in the world since earliest history, lack of communications formerly limited its spread. Large areas were free until it was introduced by the infected, economically developed nations. It then spread with devastating severity in Africa, Asia and South America where there was no protection from acquired immunity. BCG vaccination can now give a considerable measure of protection and tuberculosis can also be cured by treatment with drugs.

PHILIPPINES 148

NEW ZEALAND 1958-9	
Maori	43
Non-Maori	4

USA 1957-9	
Non-white	16
White	5

SOUTH AFRICA	
White	6
Coloured	144
Asian	30
African	NA

SCALE 1:176 MILLION 1 CM TO 1760 KM.

Tuberculosis[1]
Average annual age standardized death rate per 100 000 in the age group 15-64 for 1961-3

- 60 & over
- 30 - 60
- 10 - 30
- 1 - 10
- DATA NA

One dot to 100 000 population

[1] WHO INTERNATIONAL CLASSIFICATION OF DISEASE NUMBER 001-008

Bronchitis

Bronchitis occurs either as an isolated acute attack in which the symptoms of cough and expectoration of mucus are exaggerations of the normal mechanisms for clearing the throat or as a chronic disease in which long-standing inflammation of the bronchi causes permanent injury and serious disablement. Onset of chronic bronchitis is commonest after the age of thirty and the average duration is over twenty-five years. The most striking feature of the regional distribution is that the mortality in the British Isles is about thirty times greater than in the U.S.A. and five or six times greater than in most of Western Europe. Within England and Wales it is largely a disease of poor, overcrowded urban areas. The most important

causative factor seems to be air pollution and in particular pollution from domestic chimneys rather than from industrial sources. However, the problem is most probably aggravated in Britain by the natural climatic conditions. Certainly attacks in individuals suffering from chronic bronchitis are precipitated by damp, cold weather and by fog. The disease also occurs quite commonly among South American Indians who sleep with very little shelter at high altitudes where the cold and damp towards dawn are considerable. As might be expected in a disease so clearly associated with air pollution, smokers are far more prone to bronchitis than non-smokers.

MAURITIUS 24

SOUTH AFRICA	
White	5
Coloured	13
Asian	12
African	NA

SCALE 1:176 MILLION 1 CM TO 1760 KM.

Bronchitis[1]
Average annual age standardized death rate per 100 000 in the age group 15-64 for 1961-3

- 17.5 & over
- 7.5 - 17.5
- 2.5 - 7.5
- 0.5 - 2.5
- DATA NA

One dot to 100 000 population

[1] WHO INTERNATIONAL CLASSIFICATION OF DISEASE NUMBER 500-502

Sleeping sickness

African trypanosomiasis (sleeping sickness) occurs in humans and animals infected by the protozoa trypanosome which is transmitted by the blood-sucking tsetse fly (glossina spp.), an insect found only in the African continent. In man the disease is characterized initially by fever and intense headache and secondarily by wasting and somnolence as the central nervous system is affected. Untreated, it is fatal in about 90% of cases, but the widespread epidemics in man which used to occur and which led to the abandonment of large areas of fertile land following tsetse infestation have largely been controlled. However, trypanosomiasis also has a high fatality among domestic animals, and this has had a crippling effect on the

agricultural development of much of Africa. In affected areas stockraising is impracticable, diet is badly lacking in animal protein and cultivation is severely restricted because of the lack of draught animals. The disease is most typical of sparsely settled savanna woodland with 30-60 in. (750-1 500 mm.) of rain a year and poor soils. In drier areas it is found mainly near rivers and lakes. It can be controlled by clearing the bush, by killing game animals which are also affected, and by spraying the favoured resting sites of the fly. In South America another variety of trypanosomes causes an infection known as Chagas disease. Unlike African trypanosomiasis it is rarely fatal.

GAMBIA 68
PORT GUINEA 56
GUINEA 27
IVORY COAST 26
EQ.GUINEA 34
GABON 29

© Oxford University Press   Modified Gall Projection   SCALE 1:176 MILLION 1 CM TO 1760 KM.

Sleeping sickness[1]
Average annual incidence rate per 100 000 population for 1960-4

- 10.5 & over
- 5.5 - 10.5
- 0.5 - 5.5
- 0 - 0.5
- DATA NA

One dot to 100 000 population

MAIN DISTRIBUTION OF TSETSE FLY

[1] WHO INTERNATIONAL CLASSIFICATION OF DISEASE NUMBER 121

73

Malaria I[1]

Labels on map: GREECE 13 702 · IRAQ 13 404 · CEYLON 36 932 · CAPE VERDE IS. 10 109 · MAURITIUS 13 195 · MALAGASY R. 18 580 · SOUTH VIETNAM 70 · BRUNEI 190 · WEST IRIAN 367

Malaria is caused by parasites, protozoa of the genus *plasmodium*, which multiply in the blood stream where they attack and destroy red blood cells. The resulting anaemia and accompanying bouts of fever are extremely debilitating and account for an enormous loss of work potential in the tropical and sub-tropical areas where malaria is still endemic. However, adults in endemic areas have acquired a degree of immunity from repeated attack in endemic areas; children, after weaning, have no such immunity and the death rate up to the age of two may be as high as 50 %. The malaria parasites are transmitted from one human being to another by the bite of the female anopheline mosquitoes, of which over sixty species are recognized as vectors of human malaria. The majority of these thrive

where temperatures and humidity are high, but the climatic limits are broad [a summer temperature not falling below 60°F (15.5°C) with rainfall and drainage such as to give stretches of stagnant or slow moving water in which the mosquitoes can breed], and malaria has been recorded as far north as 60°N. Seasonal variation in the intensity of malarial infection follows closely the distribution of rainfall. Malaria transmission is perennial only in an equatorial belt (from about 10°N to 10°S) where it is possible for the mosquito vector to breed throughout the year. Outside this belt the occurrence varies from regular seasonal outbreaks to occasional disastrous epidemics. This map shows the extent of the disease before the introduction of any major control or eradication programme.

Average annual incidence rate per 100 000 for 1944–6

4 000 & over	5 – 85
900 – 4 000	0 – 5
85 – 900	DATA NA

One dot to 100 000 population

COUNTRIES WITH ERADICATION PROGRAMMES IN 1965

[1] WORLD HEALTH ORGANIZATION (WHO) INTERNATIONAL CLASSIFICATION OF DISEASE NUMBER 110–117

Malaria II[1]

Labels on map: SENEGAL 10 446 · PORT GUINEA 10 979 (P) · NIGERIA 734 (P) · EQ. GUINEA 17 404 · SÃO TOMÉ · PRINCIPE 11 503 (P) · GABON 15 659 · CONGO R. 14 612 · ANGOLA 3 439 (P) · NEW HEBRIDES 16 592

Programmes to control malaria have concentrated mainly on attacking the mosquito vectors. If the number can be reduced and held at a low level for several years, malaria will die out from the control area. The mosquito population may subsequently increase but there will be no infection to be spread. Early measures were directed at the mosquito breeding grounds either by draining swamps, by spraying stretches of water with oil or by destroying larvae with chemicals. Later such cheaper insecticides such as DDT were developed which would kill adult mosquitoes, and which would remain effective for several months after being sprayed on the house walls where the mosquitoes normally rest

after biting. As the mosquitoes developed resistance to various insecticides, it became necessary to shift the emphasis from "malaria control" to "malaria eradication". So far, however, only the richer countries have successfully carried out eradication programmes. Malaria has now disappeared from Europe, North America and the U.S.S.R. It is still an enormous problem throughout Africa from Rhodesia to the Sahara and in much of S.E. Asia. A major obstacle to control in poorer areas is the large number of immigrants, either traditional pastoralists or families seeking a higher standard of living in the towns, who are liable to reintroduce the disease into areas from which it has been cleared.

Incidence rate per 100 000 for 1966

4 000 & over	5 – 85
900 – 4 000	0 – 5
85 – 900	DATA NA

(P) 'Prevalence rate'

One dot to 100 000 population

[1] WHO INTERNATIONAL CLASSIFICATION OF DISEASE NUMBER 110–117

Cholera[1]

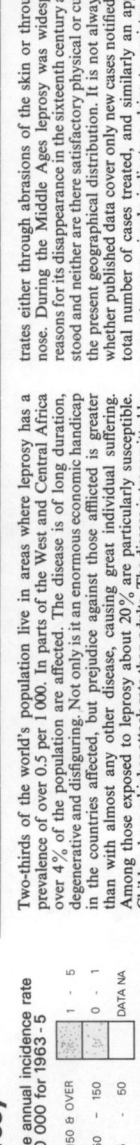

Cholera is an acute intestinal disease which is spread directly from person to person by water contaminated by infected sewage. The disease has been endemic in India since the beginning of recorded society, and during the nineteenth century it several times exploded in epidemic waves which spread almost throughout the world following the routes of traders, pilgrims, and soldiers. The fatality among untreated cases is 50 or 60% but only about 10% in treated cases. The disease predominates in children in endemic areas, but in newly invaded areas where there is no acquired immunity it attacks all ages. With improved sanitation and with the establishment of quarantine stations there has been no epidemic of cholera in the Americas during the present century and

none in Europe since 1923. There was an isolated outbreak in Egypt in 1947 and since then the disease has also disappeared from Africa. Two strains of cholera exist, the Classical and El Tor. Up to 1960 classical cholera had retreated to its original endemic foci in India and a few neighbouring territories, and El Tor was endemic only in Sulawesi Island in Indonesia. During the last decade Classical Cholera has increased in India and El Tor has spread to entirely new areas as far west as the Persian Gulf and as far north as Soviet Uzbekistan. In most countries so far there have only been sporadic outbreaks but with rapidly expanding populations and the attendant threat of overcrowding, cholera could again spread disastrously, especially in developing areas.

Average annual incidence rate per 100 000 for 1963–5

10 & over	1 – 5
5 – 10	0 – 1

DATA NA

One dot to 100 000 population

[1] WHO INTERNATIONAL CLASSIFICATION OF DISEASE NUMBER 043

Leprosy[1]

Labels on map: GAMBIA 488 · UPPER VOLTA 280 · IVORY COAST 275

Two-thirds of the world's population live in areas where leprosy has a prevalence of over 0.5 per 1 000. In parts of the West and Central Africa over 4% of the population are affected. The disease is of long duration, degenerative and disfiguring. Not only is it an enormous economic handicap in the countries affected, but prejudice against those afflicted is greater than with almost any other disease, causing great individual suffering. Among those exposed to leprosy about 20% are particularly susceptible. Children have a higher attack rate than adults. The disease is transmitted by direct person to person contact in which the *mycobacterium leprae* penetrates either through abrasions of the skin or through the mucosa of a nose. During the Middle Ages leprosy was widespread in Europe. The reasons for its disappearance in the sixteenth century are not properly understood and neither are there satisfactory physical or cultural explanations for the present geographical distribution. It is not always possible to ascertain whether published data cover only new cases notified during the year or the total number of cases treated, and similarly an apparent increase within a country may simply indicate a drive to register and treat more cases. International comparisons of frequency are therefore only very approximate.

Average annual incidence rate per 100 000 for 1963–5

150 & over	1 – 5
50 – 150	0 – 1
5 – 50	DATA NA

One dot to 100 000 population

[1] WHO INTERNATIONAL CLASSIFICATION OF DISEASE NUMBER 060

SCALE 1:176 MILLION   1 CM TO 1 760 KM.

Modified Gall Projection   © Oxford University Press

Disease III

Breast cancer[1]

Average annual age standardized incidence rate per 100 000 females in the age group 35-64

90 AND OVER	30 – 60
60 – 90	0 – 30
	DATA N.A.

One dot to 100 000 population

U.S.A. *Hawaii*
Caucasian 133.1
Hawaiian 109.2
Japanese 50.9

Kingston 62.9

Ibadan 41.4

HONG KONG 41.4

SINGAPORE 18.9

Bombay 44.5

Kyadondo 21.8

RHODESIA
Bulawayo
African 26.1

Lourenço Marques 10.2

SOUTH AFRICA *Natal*
African 23.5
Indian 40.8

SOUTH AFRICA *Cape*
African 123.5
Indian 55.9
African 38.1

Johannesburg
Bantu 25.1

SOUTH AFRICA
White 100.6
Coloured 66.1
African N.A.

Incidence rates are estimated from mortality rates for all except these countries: Canada, Chile, Denmark, England/Wales, Finland, Iceland, India, Israel, Jamaica, Mozambique, New Zealand, Nigeria, Norway, Puerto Rico, Rhodesia, Singapore, Sweden, Uganda, U.S.A.(Hawaii). U.S.S.R. data are based on towns within the republics

[1]WORLD HEALTH ORGANIZATION (WHO) INTERNATIONAL CLASSIFICATION OF DISEASE NUMBER 170

Cancer of the breast in women occurs most commonly in Canada and the United States. From this area of high incidence it shows a steady reduction in frequency eastward across the northern hemisphere through Western and Central Europe and into Central Asia. The incidence in India and the Far East is also much lower than in Western Europe or America. To a certain extent the world pattern reflects the situation in Britain where breast cancer occurs more commonly among women in the higher socio-economic groups but there are some notable exceptions, in particular the high incidence in whites and non-whites in the U.S.A. and the high frequency in Colombia in South America. There is some tendency for cancer of the breast to run in families, but genetic factors cannot explain the geographical variation; the difference in frequency between Africans in Africa and non-whites in America, or between the Japanese in Hawaii and in Japan, points strongly to some social or environmental influence. Fertility and prolonged lactation are associated with lower incidence but recent work suggests that age at first pregnancy may be a more decisive factor. Between the ages of twenty-five and fifty there is a sharp increase in the incidence of cancer of the breast after which the rate of increase with age slows down. Many other tumours show a continued progressive rise in frequency with age, and the shape of the age curve for cancer of the breast may indicate that the carcinogenic agent ceases to be active after a number of years, possibly at the time of the menopause.

Liver cancer[1]

Average annual age standardized incidence rate per 100 000 males in the age group 15-44

6 AND OVER	0.5 – 1
1 – 6	0 – 0.5
	DATA N.A.

One dot to 100 000 population

[1]WHO INTERNATIONAL CLASSIFICATION OF DISEASE NUMBER 155

NETHERLANDS
Friesland 0.2
's Gravenhage
Rotterdam

Slovenia 0.1

U.S.A.
New York (Exc) 0.1
New York City 0.4
Connecticut

U.S.A. *Hawaii*
Caucasian 0.0
Hawaiian 0.5
Japanese 1.4

St. Andrews/ 2.0
Kingston

Cali 0.7

Ibadan 10.2

Kyadondo 6.5

RHODESIA
Bulawayo
African 14.1

Lourenço Marques 164.6

SOUTH AFRICA *Natal*
African 13.4
Indian 0.7

SOUTH AFRICA *Cape*
African 0.0
Coloured 0.0
African 16.3

Johannesburg
Bantu 10.2

SINGAPORE
Chinese 4.1

Primary liver cancer is the most consistently common tumour in Africa south of the Sahara, representing almost everywhere over 10% of all malignant tumours diagnosed in men and a substantial, though lower, proportion of tumours in women. By contrast it is almost unknown in Western Europe and North America. The highest recorded incidence is in Lourenço Marques, Mozambique, where it represents over half of cancer of all sites and where the incidence in men aged 20–44 is as high as lung cancer in England among men twenty years older. The range of frequency between Lourenço Marques and Canada, Scandinavia or England is about a thousand-fold whereas the world-wide variation in cancer of the lung is only forty-fold and in stomach cancer thirty-fold. Within Africa south of the Sahara there seems to be only about a five-fold variation. A possible clue to the aetiology of primary liver cancer was the discovery that aflatoxin, a product of the mould *aspergillus flavus* commonly found in the tropics on stored crops such as groundnuts and cereals, was highly toxic to the livers of turkeys and was capable of producing a high incidence of liver cancer in experimental animals. Much work is being done to see whether a relationship between aflatoxin and liver cancer exists in man. The research would be greatly facilitated if it were possible to establish an area of genuinely lower frequency in Africa.

Lung cancer[1]

Average annual age standardized incidence rate per 100 000 males in the age group 35-64

120 AND OVER	30 – 60
60 – 120	0 – 30
	DATA N.A.

One dot to 100 000 population

U.S.A. *Hawaii*
Caucasian 67.5
Hawaiian 69.0
Japanese 22.1

U.S.A.
White 70.1
Non-white 60.9

Kingston 27.9

Ibadan 3.1

SCOTLAND 154.3

Bombay 21.5

Kyadondo 19

RHODESIA
Bulawayo
African 86.6

Lourenço Marques 7.8

SOUTH AFRICA *Natal*
African 85.9
Indian 27.3

SOUTH AFRICA *Cape*
White 78.2
Coloured 68.2
African 41.1

Johannesburg
Bantu 17.9

HONG KONG 50.8

SINGAPORE
Chinese 24.6

Incidence rates are estimated from mortality rates for all except these countries: Canada, Chile, Denmark, England/Wales, Finland, Iceland, India, Israel, Jamaica, Mozambique, New Zealand, Nigeria, Norway, Puerto Rico, Rhodesia, Singapore, Sweden, Uganda, U.S.A.(Hawaii). U.S.S.R. data are based on towns within the republics

[1]WHO INTERNATIONAL CLASSIFICATION OF DISEASE NUMBER 162/163

Like bronchitis, cancer of the lung is more common in Britain than anywhere else in the world. However, the difference between Britain and other countries is less pronounced than with bronchitis since lung cancer is also common in Central and Eastern Europe, the U.S.S.R. and the U.S.A. Incidence is slightly less in Canada, Australia and among the white population of South Africa, and considerably less in Scandinavia, South America and Asia. In East and West Africa it is virtually unknown, but among Africans in urban Zambia and South Africa it has become one of the more commonly diagnosed tumours. Wherever the disease is now common it has become so only in the last thirty or forty years and there is considerable evidence that this is due to an increase in cigarette smoking. Everywhere the increase in incidence has been greater among men than women, but in Britain in recent years the female incidence has started to increase faster than the male, probably reflecting the time-lag before smoking became widely acceptable for women. The geographical distribution is not wholly explained by the number of cigarettes smoked, and it may be that cigarette smoking is more harmful to tissue already affected by some agent such as air pollution. However, studies of the length of butt discarded or the number of puffs taken from each cigarette indicate national differences in the exposure levels from cigarette smoking.

Stomach cancer[1]

Average annual age standardized incidence rate per 100 000 males in the age group 35-64

120 AND OVER	40 – 80
80 – 120	0 – 40
	DATA N.A.

One dot to 100 000 population

[1]WHO INTERNATIONAL CLASSIFICATION OF DISEASE NUMBER 157

R.S.F.S.R. 172.3

U.S.A.
White 14.8
Non-white 35.6

Kingston 40.2

Ibadan 21.9

Bombay 16.6

Kyadondo 6.6

RHODESIA
Bulawayo
African 21.2

Lourenço Marques 47

SOUTH AFRICA *Natal*
African 19.5
Indian 28.8

SOUTH AFRICA *Cape*
White 44.6
Coloured 101.5
African 23.0

Johannesburg
Bantu 19.4

SOUTH AFRICA
White 36.2
Coloured 79.0
African N.A.

HONG KONG 36.8

SINGAPORE
Chinese 29.5

Incidence rates are estimated from mortality rates for all except these countries: Canada, Chile, Denmark, England/Wales, Finland, Iceland, India, Israel, Jamaica, Mozambique, New Zealand, Nigeria, Norway, Puerto Rico, Rhodesia, Singapore, Sweden, U.S.A.(Hawaii). U.S.S.R. data are based on towns within the republics

The highest recorded incidence of stomach cancer is in Japan, but it is very common also throughout Central Soviet Asia. From there the incidence declines steadily westward to a much lower level in North America. The Japanese population of Hawaii have far less stomach cancer than the Japanese in Japan, which strongly suggests an environmental influence. Stomach cancer is unusual among tumours in that there has been a general reduction in mortality in recent years, especially in Europe and North America. This has led to the suggestion that carcinogenic agents could be produced by the deterioration of stored foodstuffs, which has largely been checked in the West with the widespread introduction of refrigeration and better methods of food preservation.

SCALE 1:176 MILLION   1 CM TO 1 760 KM.

Modified Gall Projection   © Oxford University Press

Medical Care

The type of health service available to any individual is determined by the social history and present wealth of his country. Almost all governments have now taken responsibility for organizing some aspects of medical care, but there may also be a confused mixture of private medicine, compulsory and voluntary insurance schemes, industrial health clinics, philanthropic institutions and traditional remedies provided by local healers.

For example, in Iran compulsory insurance schemes provide benefits up to 6% of the population and in Yugoslavia to 98%. In Peru and Costa Rica employers play an important part in the provision of medical care. In Jamaica beds in private hospitals and clinics accounted for 5% of the total in the country; in Cyprus 38%. In East Africa herbalists supplement western medicine to some extent, while in Pakistan there are an estimated 50 000 ayurvedic practitioners compared with only 3 300 western trained doctors.

The great variety of authorities responsible for organizing and financing medical care in different countries make valid international comparisons of the actual level of care very difficult. The three indices mapped here (the proportion of doctors and hospital beds relative to the total population and the expenditure per capita on health services by public institutions) give some idea of the world situation, but they give no indication, for example, of whether the majority of doctors are in public service or private practice, or of whether the hospital bed is in a fully equipped western teaching hospital or in a corrugated iron mission hut where the doctor is desperately short even of such simple necessities as cottonwool and aspirins. There is also great variation between countries in the proportion of beds devoted to different specialist services. In the U.K. and Finland 31% of time in hospital is spent in general hospitals; in Ceylon and Chile the proportion is over 70%. In the U.K. and the U.S.A. 45% of all bed-days are spent in psychiatric hospital while in Yugoslavia and Czechoslovakia the proportion is only 10%.

The figures mapped for public health expenditure are for 'indirect' payments (that is, payments by governments, employers, insurers and charities) because details of 'direct' payments (private expenditure by the patient) are very difficult to obtain. Estimates of total expenditure have been made for a few countries and are presented in the table below. Among high-income countries it is not those which rely most heavily on government financing that allocate the highest proportion of their resources to health services.

There is obviously no relationship between the level of medical care available and the health needs of a country, but given the very uneven distribution of resources there is also very little systematic knowledge about the optimum use of available funds so as best to solve local health problems. In part this results from lack of detailed knowledge about patterns of morbidity and mortality in developing countries, and faced with this lack of data W.H.O. is at present organizing research programmes to investigate in depth the real medical needs of communities in developing areas. In part it results from a natural desire on the part of governments in poorer countries to copy the best facilities of western medicine and to build, for example, a lavishly equipped medical school in the capital city when the needs of the majority of people might be better served by improving the network of rural clinics. Some adjustments to local conditions are being made. For example, the loss of medical manpower through doctors seeking employment abroad has reached such serious proportions in some developing countries that governments are beginning to concentrate resources more on the training of semi-skilled medical assistants who will be able to contribute more to solving the health problems of their own people.

In part the lack of knowledge about the best use of resources results from ignorance as to what is genuinely best for the patient. There can for example be no sound medical reason why the average length of stay in maternity hospitals is 5½ days in the U.S.A. and Israel, 8 days in Finland and over 9 days in Yugoslavia. Most wealthy countries have increased their health expenditure in recent years and if the present trends continue there will be countries which before the end of the century spend over 10% of their gross national product on medical services. This results partly from the scientific advances of medicine with the introduction of more expensive drugs and equipment and partly from the expectation by patients of better personal care in hospital and in the home. These services can be provided only by more nurses, more medical social workers and more domiciliary helps, and all such ancillary help is very expensive to provide in countries with a high material standard of living.

Total annual expenditure on health services
Including direct payments by recipients (early 1960s)

	Current/capital expenditure as a percentage of G.N.P.	Current expenditure $U.S. per capita	Direct payments by recipients as a percentage of current payments
Israel	6.3	90	27
Canada	6.0	108	36
U.S.A.	5.8	163	48
Chile	5.6	37	57
Sweden	5.4	4	22
Australia	5.2	74	39
Yugoslavia	5.0	12	6
Netherlands	4.8	56	33
Finland	4.8	48	40
France	4.4	72	10
Federation of Rhodesia and Nyasaland	4.2	6	39
U.K.	4.2	58	14
Ceylon	4.0	94	38
Czechoslovakia	3.6	37	7
Kenya	3.5	3	51
Tanganyika	2.5	2	32

In evaluating figures on health expenditure it is essential to take into consideration differences in wage structure. In countries where doctors have incomes well above average a higher proportional expenditure is inevitable. This applies both to high income countries such as the U.S.A. and to low income countries with particularly wide discrepancies in personal earnings. It also means that in terms of the actual services provided the differences between countries may not be so great as they appear from the figures of per capita expenditure. Hospital treatment accounts for two-thirds of the money spent on personal health in the U.S.A., Sweden and Australia, compared in the U.S.A. or Sweden to 87% in Taiwan and 95% in Senegal. Even so, many African countries are relatively better provided with

capital (development) expenditure. The proportion of the total devoted to capital costs varies widely between countries and from year to year since capital expenditure can be more easily reduced or postponed in times of economic stress. In the years shown here the proportion varies from over 20% in Swaziland and Hong Kong to 4% in the U.K. Over 90% of both current and capital expenditure in most countries is spent on personal health care; the remainder is spent on items such as public health education, research and training of doctors. Hospital treatment accounts for two-thirds of the money spent on personal health in the U.S.A., Sweden and Australia, compared with about one-half in Yugoslavia, Poland, Israel and France.

Public health expenditure (1966)[1]

Annual expenditure per capita in $U.S.

70 & OVER	1 – 5
50 – 70	0 – 1
30 – 50	DATA N.A.
20 – 30	
10 – 20	
5 – 10	

[1] Or latest available previous data

The number of people served by one doctor varies from 410 in Israel or 480 in the U.S.S.R. to 97 000 in Rwanda. In most European countries the number is less than 1 000 and in most African countries south of the Sahara it is over 10 000. The actual discrepancies are even more marked than is indicated by the national figures since in all countries there is a tendency for doctors to work in cities rather than rural areas, partly because specialist facilities are concentrated there and partly because they themselves prefer the amenities of living in an urban area. In a poorer country this can result in over half the total doctors working in a single town. In Senegal, for example, in 1966, 69% of all doctors in the country were working in Dakar. Inevitably this means that over vast tracts of

rural territory each doctor may serve well over 100 000 persons. Many countries which are large in area have a Flying Doctor service, but this can help only very few people unless sophisticated communications systems are widely developed. In more prosperous countries there are still serious regional differences in the distribution of doctors. Most of the counties of SE. England have fewer than 500 people per doctor while in many northern counties the number is over 1 000. Some countries try to overcome this problem by requiring young doctors to work in remote areas for a period immediately following their training; others attempt, by providing incentive payments within a state system of medicine, to encourage doctors to work in rural or poor urban areas.

Physicians (1960–5 av.)

Number of people per physician

UNDER 1000	8000 – 18000
1000 – 4000	18000 & OVER
4000 – 8000	DATA N.A.

One dot to 100 000 population

SCALE 1:176 MILLION   1 CM TO 1 760 KM.

hospital places than with doctors. In Europe and North America there are generally 5 to 10 hospital beds to each doctor; in most African countries the number is between 20 and 70. This reflects the fact that, whereas in a country such as England approximately half the doctors are in general practice without direct responsibility for hospital beds, in Africa south of the Sahara almost all trained doctors are working in hospitals. In the poorer countries of Asia doctors and hospital places tend to be equally scarce. The actual number of beds is only a very approximate guide to the standard of hospital service available because so much depends on the staffing and resources of the various units.

The number of hospital beds available divides the world in the same way as the ratio of doctors to population—a crude division into rich and poor nations. In most developed countries there is one hospital bed to every hundred or so people; in Afghanistan the number of people to a hospital bed is over 8 000 and in East Pakistan over 10 000. The cost of hospital care is used for "indirectly" (see Medical Care introduction above) in most countries but in terms of yearly per capita national income in some countries this varies from 13%, in Taiwan and 95% in Senegal.

Hospital beds (1962–6 av.)

Number of people per hospital bed

UNDER 150	800 – 1600
150 – 250	1600 & OVER
250 – 800	DATA N.A.

One dot to 100 000 population

SCALE 1:176 MILLION   1 CM TO 1 760 KM.

SCALE 1:176 MILLION   1 CM TO 1 760 KM.   Modified Gall Projection   © Oxford University Press

Income

Modified Gall Projection
Equatorial Scale 1:88 Million approx.

Gross national product per capita (1966)

$ U.S.

A	2000 & OVER
B	1000 – 2000
C	500 – 1000
D	200 – 500
E	0 – 200
	DATA N A

One dot represents 100 000 population
¹G.N.P. shown by letters for very small areas

The table to the right is based on data from a survey of 120 countries by the U.S. Arms Control and Disarmament Agency. The amount spent on public health and education may be augmented by varying amounts of private spending, depending on the extent to which these services are provided by governments or supported by the private sector. The expenditure of even a small percentage of G.N.P. for military purposes is a burden to developing countries, whose limited capital resources could be otherwise invested in projects which would aid long-term growth and raise the standard of living.

G.N.P. per capita (1966)

Selected countries

	$U.S.
U.S.A.	3 526
Sweden	2 270
Australia	1 940
France	1 730
U.K.	1 620
Germany D.R.	1 220
Israel	1 160
U.S.S.R.	890
Japan	860
Romania	650
South Africa¹	550
Mexico	470
Peru	320
Brazil	240
India	90
Nigeria	80

¹Incl. South West Africa

Comparative public expenditure of G.N.P. (1966)

REGION AND COUNTRY	G.N.P. '000 MILLION $U.S.	PUBLIC EXPENDITURE PERCENTAGE OF G.N.P. Military	Education	Health
North America	800.9	8.1	4.7	1.7
U.S.A.	747.6	8.5	4.6	1.6
Europe	1 037.3	7.4	5.6	3.2
European NATO	468.6	4.6	4.0	1.3
Warsaw Pact	473.5	NA	7.6	5.9
U.S.S.R.	(357.0)	NA	8.6	6.9
Other Europe	92.2	3.1	3.7	2.2
Latin America	102.4	2.1	2.4	1.6
Far East	218.7	4.3	3.7	0.7
China P.R.	80.0	8.1	3.5	0.4
Japan	97.5	1.0	4.2	0.1
South Asia	54.2	3.5	2.4	0.4
India	36.9	4.0	2.7	0.5
Middle East	24.8	7.5	4.0	2.4
Africa	42.5	2.5	2.8	1.2
Oceania	30.6	3.9	3.3	1.6
World	2 311.1	6.9	4.8	2.3

Gross national product (G.N.P.) is a way of measuring the total value of a country's production. G.N.P. per capita is more or less equivalent to average income. There are many problems in measuring and comparing G.N.P. for different countries. For example, the centrally planned economies only measure 'material product' which, unlike G.N.P., excludes the production of many services (such as commerce, public transport and government). In this map adjustments have been made in an attempt to produce comparable G.N.P. figures for as many countries as possible, but there is no perfect way of comparing the value of production in countries where tastes and consumption patterns are completely different.

Per capita G.N.P. figures also fail to show the distribution of income. Both rich and poor countries have some areas which are vastly richer than others, although these contrasts are often most pronounced in poor countries. Poor countries also generally have greater proportional differences in incomes between the rich and the poor, irrespective of regional differences.

No conceptual or statistical problems can, however, hide the enormous variation in per capita G.N.P. between countries. This income gap between the very rich and very poor countries is tending to increase, not decrease. The East European countries generally have lower per capita incomes than the developed Western group, but are catching them up because of their higher growth rates.

Average annual percentage change in per capita income¹ (1960-4)

6 & OVER	
4.0 – 6.0	
2.0 – 4.0	
0 – 2.0	
DECREASE	
DATA N A	

SCALE 1:850 MILLION
1CM. TO 8 500 KM

Average annual rate of increase in 'real'¹ per capita income (1960-4)

Selected countries

	PERCENTAGE
Japan	9.7
Romania	8.2
Israel	6.5
U.S.S.R.	4.8
Sweden	4.7
France	3.8
South Africa	3.5
Peru	3.4
Mexico	3.0
U.S.A.	2.7
Australia	2.6
U.K.	2.6
Nigeria	2.5
Germany D.R.	2.4
Brazil	1.5
India	0.7

¹At constant market prices

¹In real terms

77

Education

First / second level education 1955[1]

Percentage of 5-19 year-olds enrolled in schools

- 85 AND OVER
- 65 – 85
- 45 – 65
- 25 – 45
- UNDER 25
- DATA N.A.

One dot to 100 000 population   [1]Adjusted

The school enrolment figures on which these maps are based have been compiled on the principle of enrolment figures in all types of school related to the estimated population figures of 5-19 year olds and adjusted to minimize the effect of differences in the national school systems. It should be emphasized that these ratios can be regarded only as indicators of the development of education at the first and second levels for a given country, and they should be treated with great caution in international comparisons. Education at the first level is taken as 'basic instruction in the tools of

learning' which continues for about 6 years in most countries, where it may be compulsory unless there is no suitable school within reach and may also be free. In some countries secondary education is an alternative to primary, or they may overlap, but normally the second level of education provides general or specialized instruction for a pupil who has had at least four years schooling at the first level. From 1950-1966 total enrolment at this level increased by 70% and 154% respectively.

Third level education

Number of students per 100 000 population (1963-5 av.)

- 1000 – 3000
- 760 – 1000
- 360 – 760
- 60 – 360
- UNDER 60
- DATA N.A.

One dot to 100 000 population

Percentage of students who are female (1965)

- 40 – 55
- 30 – 39
- 20 – 29
- 10 – 19
- UNDER 10

Education at the third level has as a pre-requisite successful completion of education at the second level or evidence of attainment at the second level of education equivalent. From 1950-1965 the enrolment at the third level of education increased by 216%; the estimated world enrolment in 1950 being 6.5 millions, in 1960 11.5 millions and in 1965 18 millions. During this time the total population increase was 31%. Education at this level comprises all types of institution, public or private, which are concerned with higher education—whether they grant degrees or not—

including universities, higher technical colleges, teacher training colleges (except those included at the second level of education) and theological colleges. As far as possible the figures include part-time students but exclude those taking correspondence courses (except in the U.S.S.R. and Hungary). Where there are no figures available for a locality it may mean that third level education is undertaken in another country; some or all of the third level students in many countries may be attending educational institutions abroad.

SCALE 1:176 MILLION 1 CM TO 1760 KM.

First / second level education 1963-4 av.[1]

Percentage of 5-19 year-olds enrolled in schools

- 85 AND OVER
- 65 – 85
- 45 – 65
- 25 – 45
- UNDER 25
- DATA N.A.

One dot to 100 000 population   [1]Adjusted

Education programmes at both first and second levels in developing countries are frequently hampered by shortages of money, equipment and teachers, and in some cases there is great dependence on outside help to supply teaching assistance. Poor communications are another hindrance to the spread of education, but in many areas increased educational development has been encouraged by increased mechanization of industry and farming bringing greater demands by employers for educational attainment.

The second level of education may include teacher training, but teachers

trained at this level may often be restricted to pre-school, first level or vocational teaching; some countries (such as Israel and Colombia) include all teacher training with their second level of education figures. In Argentina, where there is high enrolment for third level education, 81% of the teachers training at the second level are women, but in Ethiopia and Liberia, where third level enrolment is low, only 10% and 6% of those training at the second level are women, suggesting that there may be a correlation between the education level of women and the overall enrolment for third level education.

SCALE 1:176 MILLION 1:CM TO 1760 KM.

Teachers / literacy

Increase in number of teachers

Percentage increase for all levels by area (1950-65)[1]

- 200 – 260
- 150 – 199
- 100 – 149
- 60 – 99
- UNDER 50
- DATA N.A.

Number at all levels per '000 population by area (1965)[1]

- 10 – 12
- 8 – 10
- 5 – 8
- 2.5 – 5
- UNDER 2.5
- DATA N.A.

One dot to 100 000 population

Annual increase in adult literacy[2]

Percentage of annual adult population increase by area (1950-60)[1]

- 100 AND OVER
- 80 – 99
- 40 – 86
- 20 – 39
- UNDER 20

Adult literacy is here defined as the ability both to read and to write at the age of 15 years. Where the increased number of adult literates is equal to the increase in adult population the percentage increase in adult literacy is 100; where the increase exceeds 100% illiteracy is being overcome; where it is below 100% education is falling behind population increase.

[1]As used by UNESCO   [2]World average 86.6%

Modified Gall Projection   © Oxford University Press   SCALE 1:176 MILLION 1:CM TO 1760 KM.

Employment

Population (latest census)

TOTAL / ECONOMICALLY ACTIVE

42 PERCENTAGE ECONOMICALLY ACTIVE

Red and green outlines are used to differentiate between ethnic groups where data are available (see note).

Modified Gall Projection
Equatorial Scale 1:88 Million approx.

Economic activity[1]

GROUP A U.N. GROUP 0   Agriculture, forestry, fishing and hunting

GROUP B U.N. GROUPS 1-4   Manufacturing, construction, mining and quarrying

GROUP C U.N. GROUPS 4   Commerce

GROUP D U.N. GROUPS 5,7,8   Services, including electricity, gas, water, sanitary services, transport, etc.

GROUP E U.N. GROUPS 9   Others (see note), including the above categories when too small to show separately

[1] Based on data from the United Nations International Labour Office 'Yearbook of Labour Statistics 1966'

The data presented refer to the economically active population, i.e., to the total of employed persons. This excludes students, women occupied solely in domestic duties, retired persons and dependents. The treatment of such groups as armed forces, inmates of institutions, occupants of reservations, persons seeking work for the first time, seasonal and part-time workers varies between countries.

The comparability of the data is further hampered by differences in methods of collection and tabulation. Definitions of economic activity also vary, as does the minimum age at which the term can apply. For example, the extent to which family workers, who assist in family enterprises, are included amongst the 'economically active' varies from country to country. The employment groupings are also subject to some inconsistency. However, none of these dissimilarities is so great that the value of the map is seriously impaired.

The nine United Nations employment groups have been reallocated into five main employment categories to simplify representation. Where the right-hand semi-circle is empty, data on the division of labour are not available. Where data on the percentage economically active are unavailable, a black tone is printed over that country.

Group E (United Nations Group 9) consists of the economically active population which cannot be categorized according to groups A-D. Where the unemployed are not classified according to their last job, they are frequently included under group E, as are those seeking work for the first time. Group E also includes any groups of A-D, which would be too small to be shown as distinct sectors.

In Algeria, Rhodesia and South Africa, superimposed symbols facilitate a comparison between the economic activities of different ethnic groups. In Algeria the green circle represents Europeans and the red circle non-Europeans. In Rhodesia the green circle represents non-Africans and the red circle Africans, and in South Africa, the green circle represents 'whites' and the red circle 'non-whites'.

It is significant to note the dependence upon primary industries (agriculture, fishing etc.) in developing countries. These countries are characterized by small service industries and little commerce.

Secondary industries (such as manufacturing) and tertiary industries (services) develop as a country becomes more industrialized —Canada, the U.S.A. and the U.K. have noticeably large service industries.

When developed countries have large agricultural industries these are often so highly mechanized that they employ comparatively few people, as in the U.S.A., Canada and Australia. Therefore, it should be emphasized that the sectors refer to the numbers employed in each category and not the financial importance of the industries in that category.

SCALE 1:44 MILLION   1 CM TO 440 KM.

© Oxford University Press

79

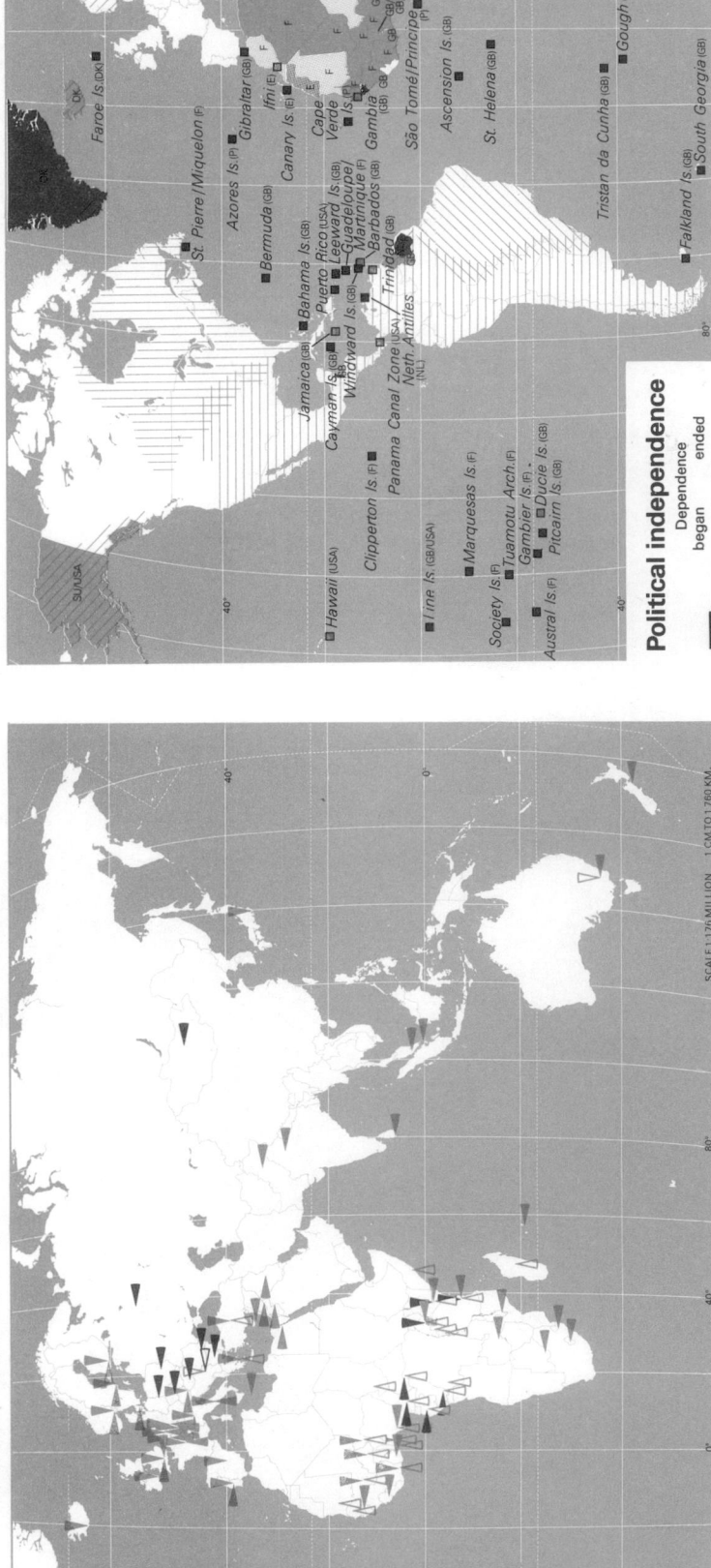

Government structure (1965)

Sovereign states
- Hereditary head of state
- Federal republic (incl. Swiss confederation)
- Republic (incl. States of Spain, Yemen and Kuwait)
- Socialist republic (incl. People's Republic, Socialist Federal Republic, Federation of Soviet Republics)

Non-sovereign states
- Overseas province or department and other non-sovereign areas (incl. associate states, territories and British colonies)

Between 1965 and 1970 several countries saw a change in their type of government structure. British Guiana (now Guyana), Bechuanaland (now Botswana), Basutoland (now Lesotho) and Barbados all became independent members of the Commonwealth in 1966. Mauritius and Swaziland attained this status in 1968. Rhodesia unilaterally declared independence in November 1965. South Arabia was declared the Southern Yemen People's Republic in 1967. Constantine II fled Greece after failing to restore civilian and democratic government in 1967. Spain plans to have the monarchy reinstated.

Political instability[1] (1945–70)

Number of unconstitutional changes in governmental leadership since 1945 (or year of independence if later)[2]

1	2	3 OR MORE

1 Criteria were military and political coups, abdication under pressure, elimination of opposition parties and suspension of constitution.
2 Only states independent before 1965 are included

SCALE 1:176 MILLION   1 CM TO 1760 KM.

© Oxford University Press   Mollweide Gall Projection

Political independence

	Dependence	
	began	ended
	before 1900	not before 31st Dec. 1970
	after 1900	1930–70
	before 1900	1900–30
	after 1900	

Colonial status and political dependence vary in form and degree, so that precise comparison of status is difficult. Furthermore, the nature of transition to independence also varies from a sudden violent overthrow of colonial rule to the final deliberate acknowledgement of an independence which has been complete in all but name for decades. The map shows the spread of political independence, defined here as the attainment of self-government by an area, or its merging with a larger independent state of which it becomes an integral part. Military occupation and changes of boundary resulting from major wars have been excluded from consideration. In addition, areas which achieved their independence before 1900 have been included.

Areas colonized by 1763

Colonizing nation
- Britain
- Spain
- Others
- Germany
- Portugal

Incl. only colonization of overseas territories. Excl. Ottoman, Chinese and Russian land empires.

Suzerain nation

A	Austria
AUS	Australia
B	Belgium
CPR	China P.R.
D	Germany
DK	Denmark
E	Spain
ET	Egypt
GB	Britain
I	Italy
J	Japan
NL	Netherlands
NZ	New Zealand
P	Portugal
SU	U.S.S.R.
TR	Turkey
USA	United States
ZA	South Africa

Political / defence blocs

Membership of multilateral organizations (1969)
- Arab League
- OAS (Organization of American States)
- OAU (Organization of African Unity)
- OCAM (Afro-Malagasy Common Organization)
- CENTO (Central Treaty Organization)
- Warsaw Pact
- NATO (North Atlantic Treaty Organization)
- SEATO (South East Asia Treaty Organization)

The Arab League, formed in 1945, has as its aim the re-integration of the Arab community, by providing a basis for political and cultural co-operation. Similarly the more recently formed Organization of African Unity (1963) has as its chief objective the furtherance of African solidarity and unity. The Organization of American States (1948) differs in that it aims at mutual co-operation starting from a geographic basis as a framework. It includes the U.S.A. as a member along with the majority of Latin American nations. The North Atlantic Treaty Organization (1949), the South-East Asia Treaty Organization (1954) and the Central Treaty Organization (previously the Baghdad Pact 1955) are all collective defence agreements with a regional basis. NATO is particularly concerned with the peaceful settlement of disputes in the North Atlantic and Mediterranean areas. SEATO provides for collective security action in SE. Asia and the SW. Pacific. CENTO deals with disputes and political or economic problems in the general area of its member states. The Warsaw Pact (1955) is a mutual defence agreement signed by the U.S.S.R. and most East European countries.

Apart from regional political groupings, the United Nations organization, an international peace-keeping body with membership covering most of the world, has been in existence since 1945.

SCALE 1:176 MILLION   1 CM. TO 1760 KM.

Economic / trading blocs

Membership of multilateral organizations (1969)
- LAFTA (Latin American Free Trade Association)
- COMECON or CMEA (Council for Mutual Economic Aid)
- COMECON Associate Member
- Arab Common Market
- UDEAC (L'Union Douanière Economique de l'Afrique Centrale)
- UDEAO (L'Union Douanière des Etats de l'Afrique de l'Ouest)
- EEC (European Economic Community)
- EEC Associate Member
- EEC Associate Member
- CACM (Central American Common Market)
- CARIFTA (Caribbean Free Trade Association)
- East African Community
- EFTA (European Free Trade Association)
- EFTA Associate Member
- Commonwealth
- OECD (Organization for Economic Co-operation and Development)
- OECD Associate Member

The main regional economic groupings in the world are indicated above, but several more broadly based economic agreements also exist, in close relationship to the main United Nations organization. The General Agreement on Tariffs and Trade, (GATT 1948), with 76 full members by 1969, lays down regulations and controls on world trade. Notably absent are many developing countries especially in Latin America and the Middle East. Also in existence are the International Monetary Fund, (IMF), aiming at promoting international monetary co-operation; the International Bank for Reconstruction and Development, (World Bank), which provides capital to facilitate investment and economic development; and the closely affiliated International Finance Corporation, (IFC), which supplements World Bank activities.

SCALE 1:176 MILLION   1 CM TO 1760 KM.

Direction of Trade

Direction of trade (1966)

IMPORTS   EXPORTS

Value of trade (million $U.S.)

30 000 & OVER
20 000 — 30 000
10 000 — 20 000
5 000 — 10 000
2 000 — 5 000
1 200 — 2 000
700 — 1 200
300 — 700
100 — 300

□ UNDER 100¹

Provenance of imports/destination of exports

U.S.A.
CANADA
U.K.
EEC
OTHER EUROPE
AUSTRALIA, NEW ZEALAND SOUTH AFRICA
JAPAN
LATIN AMERICA & THE CARIBBEAN
MIDDLE EAST
OTHER AFRICA
OTHER ASIA
CENTRALLY PLANNED ECONOMIES
OTHERS

When a country's imports and exports are in the same category and above $100 million, but that country has a trade surplus or balance of at least 10%, this name is underlined.
Other Europe excludes the East European states of COMECON and includes Turkey and Yugoslavia. The Middle East includes Cyprus, Iran, Iraq, Israel, Jordan, Lebanon, Syria, the U.A.R. and the Arabian Peninsula States. Other Africa refers to the African continent excluding South Africa and the U.A.R. The Centrally Planned Economies refers to the Sino-Soviet bloc, including Albania, Bulgaria, China P.R., Cuba, Czechoslovakia, Germany D.R., Hungary, Mongolia P.R., North Korea, North Vietnam, Poland, Romania and the U.S.S.R. For every country 'Others' refers to countries not elsewhere specified, such as Greenland. However for each country 'Others' also includes those categories too small to be shown separately.

¹For this category only the largest provenance and/or destination of trade is shown.

Modified Gall Projection
Equatorial Scale 1 : 88 Million approx.

This map includes trade in 'visible' commodities only; it excludes trade in 'invisibles', such as banking, insurance, shipping and tourism, which play a significant role in the trading pattern and balance of payments of countries such as the U.K., Switzerland, Liberia and Greece.

© Oxford University Press

Total value of world trade (1966) $419 200 million

Proportion accounted for by selected countries and groups of countries (see legend for colour code)

PERCENTAGE
0   25   50   75   100

Trading patterns of selected trade blocs (1966)

EEC¹

Total value of trade $106 492 million
Internal trade 43%
External trade 57%
Imports $30 881 million
Exports $29 426 million

	PERCENTAGE IMPORTS	EXPORTS
EFTA	25	36
U.S.A.	20	14
Other Africa²	14	9
Middle East	9	5
LAFTA	8	6
COMECON	6	6
Other Europe	4	8
Others	14	16
	100	100

¹Includes Belgium, France, Germany F.R., Italy, Luxembourg and Netherlands
²Excludes U.A.R. and South Africa

EFTA¹

Total value of trade $65 738 million
Internal trade 24%
External trade 76%
Imports $27 640 million
Exports $22 673 million

	PERCENTAGE IMPORTS	EXPORTS
EEC	40	34
U.S.A.	13	14
COMECON	6	6
Other Africa³	5	4
LAFTA	5	4
Other Europe	4	5
Middle East	4	5
Others	22	23
	100	100

¹Includes Austria, Denmark, Norway, Portugal, Sweden, Switzerland and Finland (associate member)
³Excludes U.A.R. and South Africa

COMECON¹,²

Total value of trade $41 826 million
Internal trade 61%
External trade 39%
Imports $9 048 million
Exports $8 320 million

	PERCENTAGE IMPORTS	EXPORTS
EEC	27	25
EFTA	21	21
Other Sino-Soviet bloc	11	14
Other Europe	7	10
Other Asia³	7	6
Others	26	24
	100	100

²Estimated
¹Includes Bulgaria, Czechoslovakia, Germany D.R., Hungary, Mongolia P.R., Poland, Romania and U.S.S.R.
³Excludes Japan

LAFTA¹

Total value of trade $18 252 million
Internal trade 10%
External trade 90%
Imports $7 232 million
Exports $9 163 million

	PERCENTAGE IMPORTS	EXPORTS
U.S.A.	50	36
EEC	22	23
EFTA	12	12
Other Latin America	1	10¹
Others	15	19
	100	100

¹Includes Argentina, Bolivia, Brazil, Chile, Colombia, Ecuador, Mexico, Paraguay, Peru, Uruguay and Venezuela
¹Three-fifths of which was Venezuela exports to Netherlands Antilles

CACM¹

Total value of trade $1 778 million
Internal trade 20%
External trade 80%
Imports $756 million
Exports $674 million

	PERCENTAGE IMPORTS	EXPORTS
U.S.A.	51	44
EEC	19	29
Japan	8	13
EFTA	6	—
Other Latin America	3	1
Others	13	13
	100	100

¹Includes Costa Rica, El Salvador, Guatemala, Honduras and Nicaragua

SCALE 1:29 MILLION   1 CM TO 290 KM

81

Foreign Aid/Trade

Most developing countries are trying to raise incomes by investing more in agriculture, industry and economic infrastructure such as roads and ports. They must maintain or increase social expenditure on education and health, and in many cases political independence has led to a greatly increased military expenditure. This leads to two 'gaps' —firstly between the revenue governments can raise from domestic taxation and savings, and the expenditures to which they are committed; and secondly, a gap between export earnings and import requirements. Foreign aid helps to fill these two gaps.

In general aid is a far more important factor to the recipient countries than to the donor countries. Few donor countries contribute as much as one per cent of their G.N.P. yet this can play a vital part in the development programmes of the recipient countries.

Unfortunately aid is not always given in ways that produce the greatest benefit to recipient countries. Donor countries prefer to give aid directly rather than through international organizations and, not unnaturally, tend to give it in ways that lead to the greatest political advantages, and the least economic sacrifices.

Thus aid is often 'tied' to imports from the donor country, which may be more expensive or technically less suitable than similar goods from other sources; or it may be 'tied' to projects which are attractive to the donor country, sometimes resulting in unnecessary prestige projects.

'Food aid' may stave off famine, but is often a convenient way for the donor to dispose of surplus stocks and can, in the process, damage the development of food and agricultural industries of the recipient country. Construction projects may be tied to contractors from the donor country, with the result that much of the 'aid' immediately flows back to the donor country, even when local firms could have done the work. Technical assistance (skilled personnel) is invariably tied to personnel from the donor countries. Various estimates suggest that if all forms of 'tying' were abandoned, the real value of aid to recipients would rise by at least fifty per cent.

Another factor reducing the value of 'aid' is that, despite the name, much consists of loans at various rates of interest. Some are merely commercial loans from suppliers of equipment, guaranteed by the government of the donor country. In other cases 'soft' loans are given with low interest rates and long repayment periods. However, combined debt repayment and interest payments from recipients to donors now make up about 19% of the gross outflow of aid.

Donors also concentrate their aid on countries within their 'sphere of influence' or where they have important commercial investments. This can be a powerful weapon to influence economic and political policies of recipient countries.

United Nations, but donors are unwilling to relinquish the political influence their aid carries with it.

Some of the deficiencies in the official aid programmes are compensated for by investment from private companies. In 1968 of the total net disbursements to developing countries, investment by private companies accounted for over 40%. Developing nations offer tax benefits and other inducements in an effort to offset the fears of foreign investors that their industries might be nationalized and confiscated. Many of these drawbacks would be remedied if more aid was given through international agencies like the

The larger and more developed a country, the greater is the range of goods it can produce efficiently within its nation's boundaries with less reliance on trade. This depends more on its having a wide range of industries than on its having extensive natural resources. Thus, the U.S. and the U.S.S.R. both have very low dependence on trade, but even Japan with meagre natural resources but high G.N.P. has fairly low trade dependence. The picture is less clear for developing countries. A few (India and Pakistan) have large enough populations to support a wide range of industries, despite very low per capita incomes, and have low dependence on trade. The majority, however, have smaller and less sophisticated economies, and have to import most manufactured goods, which they pay for by exporting primary products. For countries rich in primary products this can lead to very high dependence on trade, which ties their economic growth to the primary products needs of the developed countries. Many developing countries have therefore tried to increase their economic growth by reducing dependence

on trade through industrialization. Paradoxically this may initially lead to greater dependence on trade, since more primary products have to be exported to pay for imports of plant and equipment. A few resource-poor areas (Singapore) have achieved high dependence on trade based on exports of manufactured goods, whilst some countries have low dependence on trade simply because they lack potential exports. Policies to reduce trade dependence for political or strategic reasons, or in response to balance of payments problems and demands for protection by domestic producers, also have an impact. However this can be offset by attempts to increase trade within trade blocs. Although not included in this map, it is important to remember that 'invisible' trade in services like tourism, shipping, insurance, or the profits on investment has the same economic role as 'visible' trade in goods. Some countries specialize in exports of such services (Liberia and Greece in shipping; Switzerland and Lebanon in financial services), and to this extent their dependence on trade is underestimated.

Net official aid receipts per capita in $U.S. (1966-8 av.)

- 24 & OVER
- 9 - 24
- 6 - 9
- 3 - 6
- UNDER 3
- DATA NA OR NOT APPLICABLE

SCALE 1:176 MILLION   1 CM TO 1 760 KM.

Net official aid receipts as a percentage of G.N.P. (1966-8 av.)

- 14.0 - 35.0
- 7.0 - 14.0
- 4.4 - 7.0
- 1.8 - 4.4
- UNDER 1.8
- DATA NA OR NOT APPLICABLE

SCALE 1:176 MILLION   1 CM TO 1 760 KM.

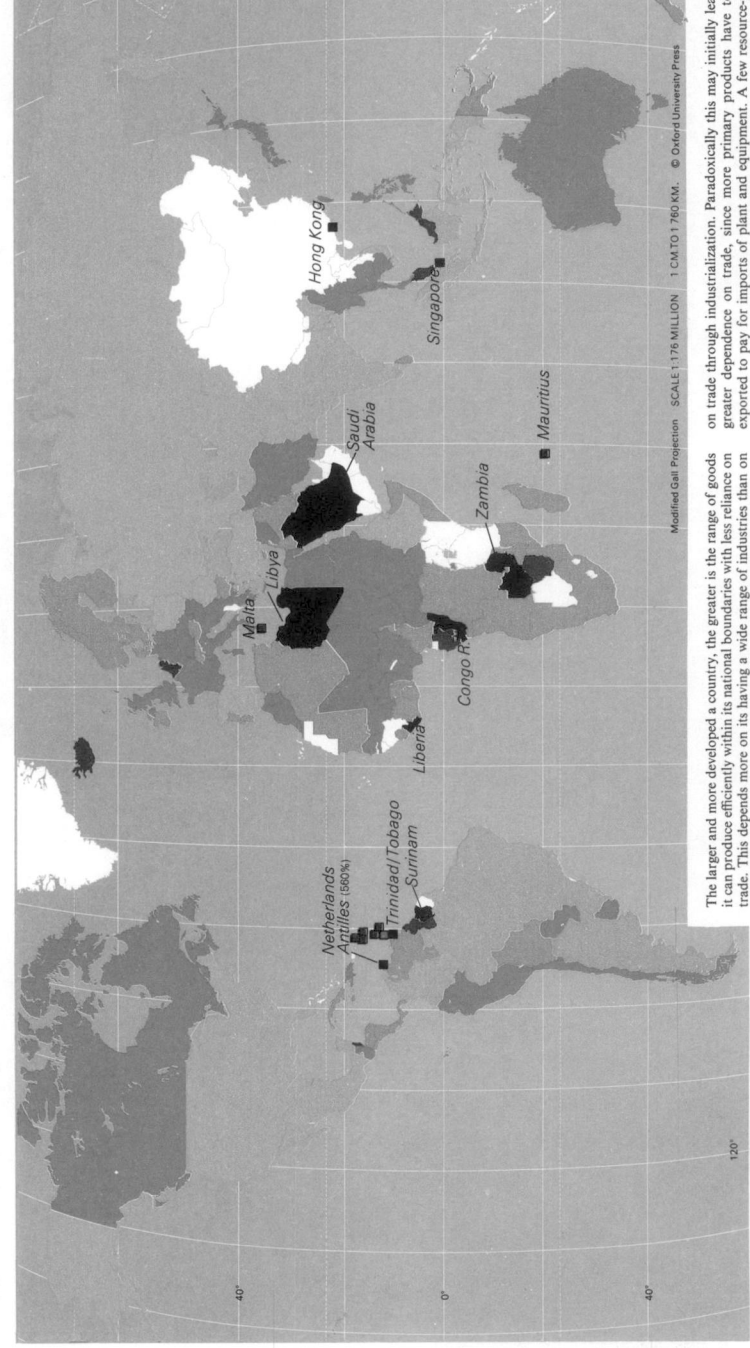

International trade as a percentage of G.N.P. (1965)

- 100 & OVER
- 70 - 100
- 40 - 70
- 20 - 40
- 5 - 20
- DATA NA

'Exports plus imports

Modified Gall Projection   SCALE 1:176 MILLION   1 CM TO 1 760 KM.   © Oxford University Press

Foreign aid from agencies and O.E.C.D. countries² (1983-5 av.)

Diameter of circle in mm. equals half the square root of the total aid in million $U.S.

For example

100   400

Total aid from each donor region divided in proportion to the amount given by the following donor countries:

- FRANCE
- U.S.A.
- OTHER O.E.C.D.
- GERMANY F.R.
- CANADA
- MULTILATERAL AGENCIES
- U.K.
- JAPAN
- UNDIFFERENTIATED

Total aid from each donor country divided in proportion to the amount given to the following recipient regions:

- AFRICA
- EUROPE
- OTHER/UNALLOCATED
- AMERICA
- OCEANIA
- ASIA
- MULTILATERAL AGENCIES

SCALE 1:176 MILLION   1 CM TO 1 760 KM.

¹Net flow of total official financial resources. Incl. money donations by governments as bilateral aid or through multilateral agencies. Incl. repayment of loans but not interest paid on loan. Excl. aid from the U.S.S.R. and China P.R. (roughly estimated to be $350 million in 1966). Excl. unofficial, but private, aid or investment and aid in non-monetary form.

²Incl. Austria, Belgium, Canada, Denmark, France, Germany F.R., Greece, Iceland, Irish R., Italy, Japan, Luxemburg, Netherlands, Norway, Portugal, Spain, Sweden, Switzerland, Turkey, U.K., and

Mass Communications

Newspapers[1] (1962-4 av.[2])

Total circulation (in '000's)

Circulation of newspapers per '000 population

450 & OVER	100 - 200	UNDER 10
300 - 450	10 - 100	4
200 - 300		

10 000 - 75 000
5 000 - 10 000
1 000 - 5 000
100 - 1 000
UNDER 4

[1] Daily [2] Or latest available previous data
Data are available only for selected newspapers for the following countries: Australia, China, Costa Rica, Cuba, Honduras, India, Israel, Libya, Morocco, Nigeria, Panama, Syria, Venezuela. Data for the U.S.A. include only English language and for Canada only English and French language newspapers.

SCALE 1:176 MILLION   1 CM. TO 1 760 KM.

SCALE 1:44 MILLION   1 CM. TO 440 KM.

In recent years increased competition from radio and television has forced the press, particularly in industrialized countries, to consolidate and/or diversify in order to compete more strongly for the advertising revenue which forms its major source of income. However, the transitory nature of radio and television signals, and the need for detailed and local information in more permanent form, have enabled the press to continue expanding despite increased competition.

Telephones (1966)

Total number installed (in '000's)[1]

98 000
10 000 - 50 000
5 000 - 10 000
1 000 - 5 000
100 - 1 000
10 - 100
1 - 10
UNDER 1

Number of telephones per '000 population

450 & OVER	100 - 200	UNDER 10
300 - 450	10 - 100	10
200 - 300		

[1] Or latest available for Albania (1959), China P.R. (1948)

SCALE 1:176 MILLION   1 CM. TO 1 760 KM.

SCALE 1:44 MILLION   1 CM. TO 440 KM.

Telephone conversations[1] (1966)

	AV. NUMBER PER CAPITA
U.S.A.	648
Sweden	585
Australia	194
Italy	157
U.K.	136
Brazil	103
South Africa	100
Mexico	47
Ghana	4

[1] For selected countries

Telephones installed (1966)

	ARGENTINA	JAPAN	SOUTH AFRICA	SPAIN	U.K.	U.S.A.
Business[1]	42	68	54	66	54	28
Residence[1]	58	32	46	34	46	72
Ext. & P.B.X.[1]	22	27	34	37	44	39
Increase 1957-1966	32	330	65	156	58	64

PERCENTAGE

[1] Percentage of country total [2] Extension and Private Branch Extension

Radio/Television (1963-5 av.)

Total number of licences issued or receivers in use (in '000's)

☐ Television   ○ Radio

25 000 - 75 000
219 000
5 000 - 25 000
1 000 - 5 000
100 - 1 000
100 - 200
10 - 100
UNDER 10

Number of licences issued or receivers in use per '000 population

450 & OVER[1]	200 - 300	10 - 100
300 - 450	100 - 200	UNDER 10

[1] U.S.A. 1140 radio receivers per '000 population

SCALE 1:176 MILLION   1 CM. TO 1 760 KM.

SCALE 1:44 MILLION   1 CM. TO 440 KM.

Mail (1963-5 av.)

Total number of letters sent or received (in millions)

DOMESTIC   FOREIGN
◖ Received
◗ Sent

Undivided circles represent total foreign and domestic mail

66 000
5 000 - 20 000
1 000 - 5 000
500 - 1 000
100 - 500
50 - 100
10 - 50
1 - 10
UNDER 1

Domestic and foreign[2] mail per capita

200 & OVER	100 - 150	10 - 50
150 - 200	50 - 100	UNDER 10

[1] Or latest available previous data   [2] Total foreign mail

SCALE 1:176 MILLION   1 CM. TO 1 760 KM.

SCALE 1:44 MILLION   1 CM. TO 440 KM.

Modified Gall Projection

© Oxford University Press

Surface Communications I

84

Surface communications I

Ports (1963-5 av.)

Net registered tons entered (millions)

○ 50 - 75
○ 25 - 50
○ 15 - 25
○ 1 - 15
○ UNDER 1

Gross registered tons entered (millions)

△ 50 - 90
△ 25 - 50
△ 15 - 25
△ 1 - 15
△ UNDER 1

• Data not available

Predominant cargoes

Percentage of tonnage by type of cargo

	60% AND OVER	60% AND OVER
Tanker		Tanker/Passenger
Passenger		Tanker/Other
Other		Passenger/Other

No cargo predominant

Data not available

Railways¹

Density (km. of track per '000 sq. km. area)²

	110+ very dense network
	65 - 110 dense network
	25 - 65 moderately dense network
	5 - 25 sparse network
	0 - 5 very sparse network

railway routes (indicated only where the density of track is under 25 km. per '000 sq. km. area)

¹ Latest available data in 1970

² Compiled on a national basis except in the U.S.S.R. (economic regions), Canada (provinces), the U.S.A.

© Oxford University Press

Modified Gall Projection

Equatorial Scale 1: 88 Million approx.

SCALE 1:29 MILLION 1 CM. TO 290 KM.

Surface Communications II

Modified Gall Projection   Equatorial Scale 1:88 Million approx

© Oxford University Press

Surface communications II

Roads

— Principal roads

Shipping

In tons per mile on 10th March 1967

Gross registered tons per nautical mile

— 1 - 40

— 40 - 400

— 800 - 1 000

Thereafter every 200 tons is shown by 0.5 mm. thus

• Ports

Data for total shipping movements are based on a one in three sample of the 15 000 ships in *Lloyd's Shipping Index*, of which only 2 500 were at sea on the 10th March 1967. The length of the voyages was calculated and the data adjusted to produce the number of tons per mile for each route.

The sample used gives an indication of the relative density of traffic at sea at a particular point in time, but it was not large enough to include all the ports, nor to indicate their relative importance.

The routes shown should not be regarded as precise shipping lanes since they have to a certain extent been generalized: the route followed will vary, according to climatic and other conditions.

Shipping movements along inland waterways have not been shown although they are important in some areas. Particularly in the U.S.A. and Canada (for example the Great Lakes and the Mississippi) and in NW. Europe (for example the Rhine/Rhône Waterway).

Communication and transport have become synonymous as terms for expressing the interaction between people and places. This interaction between resources, production and distribution in developed and developing industrial economies demands efficient means of conveying people and materials between countries and continents. Efficiency in this field is gauged by the time, effort and cost involved.

The desire to increase efficiency has led to technological improvements, particularly in the transport of raw materials, which are complicating the problem of defining communications. For example, crude oil, gasoline and natural gas are transported thousands of miles in pipelines, one of the longest of which extends 1 800 miles from the Urals to Eastern Europe. Also, improve-

ments in the transport of electricity via national and international grid systems have greatly decreased the quantity of coal transported to small, localized generating stations. Despite the increasing complexity of communications networks certain principles and patterns may still be discerned both on a national and on a world scale.

On an international level the main forms of transport are low-cost, time-consuming shipping, particularly suited to carrying bulk freight; and relatively high-cost, time-saving air services, which are particularly suited to carrying passengers and freight with a high value : weight ratio. Shipping routes, air control and terminal procedures have been standardized by international agreement. Problems of traffic control and safety of vessels

and aircraft in international waters or air space are discussed by the countries involved, for example the decision to ease congestion in the English Channel by instituting one-way shipping lanes.

The main concern of these two forms of transport is to improve efficiency, in particular the cutting of running costs, by technological improvements which increase carrying capacity ('supertankers' and 'jumbo-jets'), which further mechanize terminal procedures (containerization and automated cargo terminals) and which cut travelling time (supersonic jets).

On a national rather than on an international level, the problems facing both freight and passenger transport systems vary considerably from country to country and even within a national framework. The

priorities in development between states, regions and provinces may vary as much as between nations. In the developing countries of Asia, Africa and South America, the new and expanding industries take priority over passenger requirements when transport systems are planned. The primary aim is to provide a basic network to link resources with industry and distribution points. This leaves vast areas still relying on primitive methods of transport.

In the highly developed industrial conurbations of North America, Western Europe and, more recently, Japan the means of surface transport have evolved into highly complex systems of road, rail, sea and air communications, each inter-acting and competing with the others in transporting both freight and passengers.

In contrast to developing nations the initial network connecting resources, production centres and distribution areas has already been established, and the problem being faced now is to keep the system operating under increased pressure from the growth and redistribution of industry, urban expansion, increasing ownership of private cars and the changing pattern of work and leisure activity.

These last two factors are particularly important as the provision of adequate road services, particularly in urban areas, is one of the greatest problems facing road transport planners. In 1890 an average American travelled 200 miles a year away from his home community; now the average is 4 000 miles a year, 3 600 of these by motor car. As more road systems

land area has already been given over to road systems, yet congestion still remains.

The use of road systems depends to a great extent on individuals. This makes road traffic control more difficult than, for example, air traffic control where flights are scheduled and planned to connect with other flights both on a national and on an international basis. Control of road traffic is further complicated by the nature of road networks which are so closely tied to other transport networks, acting as feeder routes to and from air, sea and rail terminals. This dependence of one transport system upon another creates a communications system which, in order to operate effectively, must respond as a unit to the changing demands and pressures placed upon it.

are built so more people are drawn to use them and thus congestion begins, leading to new plans to provide for this increased usage. It is this circle which transport planners are finding increasingly difficult to break.

The benefit to users in the increased efficiency of jet air services, inter-state highways, motorways and express train services will be lost unless more viable solutions can be found to channel both passengers and freight through the urban terminal centres. Japan sees the solution in overhead trans-city motor-ways, whereas the U.S.S.R. is looking ahead to high speed underground railways. Monorail systems and helicopter services have also been the object of experimentation, in an attempt to by-pass traditional trans-city road and rail networks. In some American cities 30-40% of the

85

Surface Communications III

Europe

Surface communications III

Shipping

In tons per mile of route
on 10th March 1967

Gross registered tons per nautical mile

	1 – 40
	40 – 400
	800 – 1 000

Thereafter every 200 tons is shown
by 0.5mm. width, thus

---- COMPLETED BY THE END OF 1970
········ UNDER CONSTRUCTION / PLANNED

● Ports

Motorways

Dual carriage, two or more lane roads with limited access and curves and gradients designed for fast¹ motor traffic.

---- COMPLETED BY THE END OF 1970
········ UNDER CONSTRUCTION / PLANNED

Data for the U.S.A. represent the situation at the end of 1966. Over 90% of the network shown is the Interstate Highway System which is scheduled for completion by the end of 1972.

¹ excl. urban motorway systems

North America/Caribbean

Western U.S.A.

Japan

SCALE 1:29 MILLION   1 CM. TO 290 KM.

SCALE 1:29 MILLION   1 CM. TO 290 KM.

SCALE 1:29 MILLION   1 CM. TO 290 KM.

SCALE 1:29 MILLION

Motorways are, in the broadest sense, a special class of road designed to carry a greater density of heavier traffic at higher speeds than ordinary roads. They are essentially unstandardized because, until the 1950s, construction was very limited throughout the world, and some motorways make use of existing roads by improving them to motorway standards and linking them into the new system. The definition of motorways used in these maps has resulted in the omission of some major highways, such as the Yugoslav 'autoput', which might elsewhere be termed motorways. Otherwise, the maps show all the inter-urban motorway systems of the world, excluding two small stretches: in Ghana from Accra to Tema, and in Australia from Sydney to Newcastle (planned). Also not shown are the complex intra-urban motorway networks found in many cities around the world. Motorways are safer and more efficient than ordinary roads in moving goods and people from place to place. Thus,

they encourage industry to move away from crowded urban centres by making development areas more accessible. However, their usefulness, especially in the transport of freight, is constrained by the limited nature of the networks. The great expansion of motorway construction on a national, rather than an international, level. Motorway financing is a major problem, especially in urban areas where land costs are high. It has been said that the supply of roads has created an unmanageable demand for them, and that at an economic price should be put on time and freedom of movement by requiring vehicle users to pay for the roads they use. Some motorways and bridges do use a system of tolls to make them self-financing, but most are financed by local and national authorities, who may obtain part of these funds from fuel and other taxes paid by motorists. The non-monetary costs of motorways – their accompanying noise, pollution and disrupted countryside – are borne by society as a whole.

Air Communications 1

In order to avoid further congestion the 120 airports in the U.S. which have fewer than 100-300 flights per week have been omitted.

Modified Gall Projection
Equatorial Scale 1: 88 Million approx.

Airports (1969/1970)
Number of incoming flights per week
(scheduled services only)

25600 AND OVER

12800 – 25600

6400 – 12800

3200 – 6400

1600 – 3200

800 – 1600

400 – 800

100 – 400

Where several airports serve one city their combined traffic is shown by one symbol which is given the city name, for example the New York symbol represents traffic data for John F. Kennedy International Airport, La Guardia Airport and Newark Airport.

© Oxford University Press

‡ Tri-City Airport serves Bristol, Kingsport and Johnson City

SCALE 1:22 MILLION
1 CM TO 220 KM

SCALE 1:22 MILLION
1 CM TO 220 KM

SCALE 1:22 MILLION
1 CM TO 220 KM

Air Communications II

Jet flights to New York, London, Moskva and Tōkyō during April 1970 (from cities of one million population in 1966)

New York

- Non-stop flights
- Stopping flights
- City of arrival

West Berlin stopping, as shown
East Berlin no jet flight

SCALE 1:352 MILLION

London

- Non-stop flights
- Stopping flights
- City of arrival

West Berlin non-stop, as shown
East Berlin stopping

SCALE 1:352 MILLION

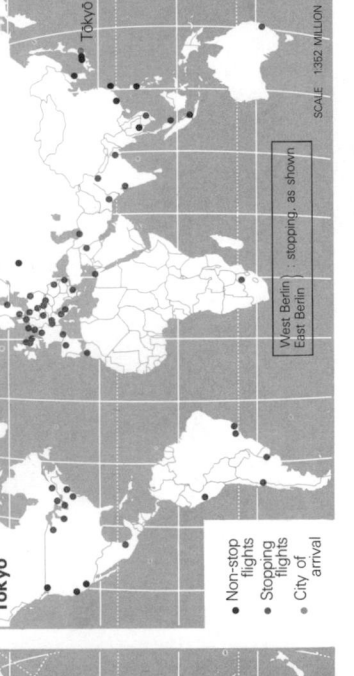

Tōkyō

- Non-stop flights
- Stopping flights
- City of arrival

West Berlin stopping, as shown
East Berlin no jet flight

SCALE 1:352 MILLION

Moskva

- Non-stop flights
- Stopping flights
- City of arrival

West Berlin stopping, as shown
East Berlin non-stop, as shown

SCALE 1:352 MILLION

Cities of one million population in 1966

Ahmadābād
Al Iskandarīyah
Al Qāhirah (Cairo)
Amsterdam
Anaheim
Athínai
Atlanta
Baghdād
Baku
Baltimore
Bangalore
Barcelona
Belo Horizonte
Berlin (East & West)
Birmingham (U.K.)
Bogotá
Bombay
Boston
Bruxelles
Bucureşti
Budapest
Buenos Aires
Buffalo
Calcutta
Caracas
Casablanca
Ch'eng-tu
Chicago
Ch'ing-tao
Chung-ch'ing
Cincinnati
Ciudad de México
Cleveland
Dallas
Denver
Detroit
Djakarta
Gor'ky
Guadalajara
Ha-erh-pin
Hamburg
Hong Kong
Houston
Hsi-an
Hyderābād
Indianapolis
İstanbul
Johannesburg
Kānpur
Kansas City
Khar'kov
Kiev
Kitakyūshū
Kōbe
København
Krung Thep (Bangkok)
Kyōto
Kuang-chou (Canton)
La Habana
Lahore
Leeds
Leningrad
Lima
Liverpool
London
Los Angeles
Lü-ta
Madras
Madrid
Manchester
Manila
Miami
Milano
Milwaukee
Minneapolis/St. Paul
Montevideo
Montréal
Moskva
München
Nagoya
Nan-ching
Napoli
Newark
New Orleans
New York
Novosibirsk
Ōsaka
Paris
Paterson
Pei-p'ing
Philadelphia
Pittsburgh
Pusan
Praha
Recife
Rio de Janeiro
Roma
Rotterdam
Sai Gon
St. Louis
San Bernardino
San Diego
San Francisco
Santiago
São Paulo
Seattle
Shang-hai
Shen-yang
Singapore
Sodi
Stockholm
Surabaja
Sydney
T'ai-pei
T'ai-yüan
Tashkent
Tehrān
Tien-ching
Tōkyō
Toronto
Warszawa
Washington
Wien
Wu-han
Yokohama

Non-stop jet connections (April 1970)

One connection per day for five or more days each week between cities of one million population[1]

- Cities of one million population

Molltweide Gall Projection   SCALE 1:176 MILLION   1 CM. TO 1760 KM

[1] in 1966

Intra-North American non-stop jet connections

SCALE 1:29 MILLION   1 CM. TO 290 KM

European non-stop jet connections

SEATTLE

MONTRÉAL

TORONTO
NEW YORK
CHICAGO

MONTRÉAL

NEW YORK
TORONTO
LOS ANGELES
CHICAGO
BOSTON
MONTRÉAL

NEW YORK
MONTRÉAL

PHILADELPHIA
MIAMI
WASHINGTON
MONTRÉAL

NEW YORK

BOSTON

CHICAGO
NEW YORK

NEW YORK

NEW YORK

RIO DE JANEIRO

TEHRĀN

KARACHI

CAIRO

CAIRO

CAIRO

CASABLANCA

SCALE 1:29 MILLION   1 CM. TO 290 KM

© Oxford University Press

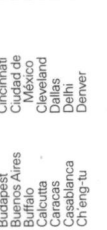

Travel times by jet from New York, London, Moskva, Tōkyō during April 1970

Hours of travelling time including transfer time where no direct flight is scheduled

For times greater than one day the number of hours (to the nearest hour) is shown

Standard time 1970

Numbers indicate hours ahead or behind GMT (Greenwich Mean Time)

International Date Line

Areas where legal time is less or more than one hour different from the adjacent zone

HOURS FROM GMT

Afghanistan	+4.5
Australia (South Australia/ Northern Territory)	+9.5
Burma	+6.5
Canada (Newfoundland)	−3.5
Guyana	−3.75
India/Nepal/Ceylon	+5.5
Iran	+3.5
Liberia	−0.75
Surinam	−3.5
Singapore/Malaya	+7.5

The standard time system is based on the division of the world's surface into 24 zones of 15° (1 hour) of longitude, each using the mean (solar) time of the central meridian of the zone. This system is applied with modifications, principally to allow political or economic regions to maintain the same time. The time used in each country, whether it is the time of the theoretical zone or a modification of it, is fixed by law and is known as 'standard time'. For economic reasons certain countries adjust their standard time for part of the year, usually the summer (Daylight Saving Time), advancing it by an hour or some other amount of time. Where such deviations operate throughout the year that time is considered to be 'standard time'. In the U.S.S.R. standard times are one hour in advance of the theoretical zone times.

New York

London

Moskva

Tōkyō

SCALE 1:176 MILLION 1 CM. TO 1760 KM.

Modified Gall Projection   SCALE 1:176 MILLION 1 CM. TO 1760 KM.

© Oxford University Press

Standard Time

−11 −10 −9 −8 −7 −6 −5 −4 −3 −2 −1 GMT +1 +2 +3 +4 +5 +6 +7 +8 +9 +10 +11 +12

SOURCES

Environment

Academy of Sciences U.S.S.R./Main Administration of Geodesy Cartography, S.G.C. U.S.S.R. (Moskva 1964):
Fiziko-Geograficheskiy Atlas Mira
K. H. W. Klages (New York 1942):
Ecological Crop Geography
C. Embleton & C. A. M. King (London 1968):
Glacial & Periglacial Geomorphology
Times Newspapers Ltd. (London)/John Bartholomew & Son Ltd. (Edinburgh):
The Times Atlas of the World, Comprehensive Edition 1967
World Meteorological Organization (Geneva):
Climatological Normals (Clino) for Climat and Climat Ship Stations for the Period 1931–1960 (WMO/OMM—No. 117. TP.52)
WMO/OMM No. 9. TP.4 Volume A Stations
Prof. D. L. Linton, Dept. of Geography, University of Birmingham, U.K.
U.S. Dept. of Agriculture, Soil Conservation Service (Hyattsville, Maryland):
Soil Map of the World based on Soil Classification, A Comprehensive System, 7th Approximation
G. T. Trewartha, A. H. Robinson, and E. H. Hammond (New York 1967):
Physical Elements of Geography
International Association of Agricultural Economists, Istituto Geografico de Agostini, S.p.A. (Novara 1970):
World Atlas of Agriculture
Haack (Leipzig 1969):
Weltatlas
Food and Agriculture Organization (Roma):
Production Yearbook 1964
Clarendon Press (Oxford):
Oxford Regional Economic Atlas of the United States and Canada
A. Holmes (London 1965):
Principles of Physical Geology
Rand McNally & Company (Chicago 1964):
Goode's World Atlas
J. H. Paterson (London 1970):
North America
International Labour Organization (Geneva):
Yearbook of Labour Statistics
H. F. Gregor (Princeton 1963):
Environment and Economic Life
U.S. Dept. of Commerce, Environmental Science Services Administration (Washington, D.C.):
World Seismicity 1961–9

Crops

Food and Agriculture Organization (Roma):
Production Yearbook 1956, 1966
Trade Yearbook 1955, 1957, 1966
Cocoa Statistics Vol. 12 1969
Unilever Ltd., Economics and Statistics Dept. (London):
World Oils and Fats Statistics 1963/1966 and 1964/1967
International Tea Committee (London):
Annual Bulletin of Statistics 1969
United Nations (New York):
Statistical Yearbook 1957, 1967, 1968
Compendium of Social Statistics 1967
Tobacco Research Council (London):
Research Paper 6 (Ed. 2)
International Sugar Organization (London):
Sugar Yearbook 1966, 1968
Alexis Lichine (London 1967):
Encyclopaedia of Wines and Spirits
Hugh Johnson (London 1966):
Wine
U.S. Dept. of Agriculture (Washington, D.C.):
The World Food Budget 1970
James Lambe (London 1967):
Rich World, Poor World
International Coffee Organization (London):
World Coffee Requirements, 1953–75
Produktschap voor Gedistilleerde Dranken (Schiedam):
Hoevel Alcoholhoudende Dranken Worden er in de Wereld Gedronken

Livestock

F.A.O. (Roma):
Production Yearbook 1955, 1956, 1966
Trade Yearbook 1955, 1957, 1966

Forestry and Fishing

F.A.O. (Roma):
Yearbook of Fishery Statistics 1966
Yearbook of Forest Products Statistics 1965, 1966
Production Yearbook 1964
U.N. (New York):
Statistical Yearbook 1956, 1966
Commonwealth Economic Committee (London):
Vegetable Oils and Oilseeds 1968
J. A. Gulland, Fishery Resources and Exploitation Division of the F.A.O. (Roma)

Admark Publishing Co. Ltd. (London):
Paper Makers' and Merchants' Directory of all Nations 1966
S. C. Phillips and Co. Ltd. (London):
Phillips' Paper Trade Directory of the World 1965

Fibres and Textiles

F.A.O. (Roma):
Production Yearbook 1955, 1957, 1966
Trade Yearbook 1955, 1957, 1966
U.N. (New York):
Statistical Yearbook 1956, 1966
Thomas Skinner & Co. Ltd. (London):
Skinner's Wool Trade Directory of the World 1965–1966
Skinner's Cotton and Man-Made Fibres Directory of the World 1967
Textile Economics Bureau, Inc. (New York):
Textile Organon 1956, 1965, 1966
Rubber and Plastics Age (London):
Technical and Marketing Data
International Rubber Study Group (London):
Rubber Statistical Bulletin 1966
International Synthetic Rubber Co. Ltd. (Southampton)
International Cotton Advisory Committee (Washington, D.C.):
Cotton—World Statistics Oct. 1967
Comité International de la Rayonne et des Fibres Synthétiques (Paris):
CIRFS 1967

Energy

U.N. (New York):
World Energy Supplies 'Statistical Papers' Series J, Nos. 3, 11, 12
Statistical Yearbook 1956, 1966, 1967
The Petroleum Publishing Co. (Tulsa, Oklahoma):
International Petroleum Encyclopedia 1969
Oil and Gas Journal
Petroleum Information Bureau (London):
Publications of production by region
International Commission on Large Dams (Paris):
World Register of Dams
Institute of Geological Sciences (London):
Statistical Summary of the Mineral Industry 1952–1957, 1962–1967
Mineral Resources Division
Radiogeology and Rare Minerals Unit

U.S. Department of the Interior (Washington, D.C.):
Bureau of Mines, Minerals Yearbook 1956, 1965, 1966
Vol. II Mineral Fuels
Vol. III Area Reports: Domestic
Vol. IV Area Reports: International
N.T.P. Business Journals Ltd. (London):
Nuclear Engineering International Jan/Feb 1971

Minerals and Metals

Institute of Geological Sciences (London):
Statistical Summary of the Mineral Industry 1952–1957, 1962–1967
Mineral Resources Division
U.S. Dept. of the Interior (Washington, D.C.):
Bureau of Mines, Minerals Yearbook 1956, 1965, 1966
Vol. I Metals and Minerals
Vol. III Area Reports: Domestic
Vol. IV Area Reports: International
American Bureau of Metal Statistics (New York):
Year Book 1963–1965
Metal Bulletin Ltd. (London):
Iron and Steel Works of the World 1965
British Iron and Steel Federation, Intelligence Dept. (London)
Alluminio, Direzione, Redazione e Publicita (Milano):
Alluminio
A.M.M.I. S.p.A. (Roma):
Non Ferrous Metals and Ferroalloys
Metallgesellschaft Aktiengesellschaft (Frankfurt am Main):
Metal Statistics 1958–1967
The British Bureau of Non-ferrous Metal Statistics (Birmingham, U.K.):
World Non-ferrous Metal Statistics 1968
Thomas Skinner & Co. Ltd. (London):
Skinner's Mining Yearbook 1963–1969
International Tin Council (London):
Statistical Year Book 1964
Minerais et Métaux 1965
Asbestos Information Committee (London)
Industrial Diamond Information Bureau (London)

Society and Politics

International Labour Organization (Geneva):
Yearbook of Labour Statistics 1966
U.N. (New York):
Yearbook of National Accounts Statistics 1965
UNESCO Statistical Yearbook 1965–1968
Yearbook of International Trade Statistics
Statistical Yearbook 1964–1967
International Monetary Fund (Washington, D.C.):
Direction of Trade Annual 1963–7
International Bank for Reconstruction and Development (Washington, D.C.):
World Bank Atlas
American Telephone and Telegraph Company (New York):
The World's Telephones 1967
O.E.C.D. (Paris):
Development Assistance Efforts and Policies 1968 and 1969
Macmillan & Co. Ltd. (London):
The Statesman's Year Book
Europa Publications Limited (London):
Europa Year Book
P. Robson (London 1968):
Economic Integration in Africa
Cambridge University Press (London 1970):
The New Cambridge Modern History Atlas
J. Wreford Watson (London 1968):
North America, Its Countries and Regions
G. Pendle (London 1968):
A History of Latin America

Surface and Air Communications

Macmillan & Co. Ltd. (London):
The Statesman's Year Book
Kultura (Budapest):
Cartactual
Lloyd's (London):
Shipping Index
Register of Shipping
Voyage Supplement
Maritime Atlas
Dr. B. J. Turton, Dept. of Geography, University of Keele, U.K.
Thomas Skinner & Co. Ltd. (London):
ABC World Airways Guide April 1970
Reuben H. Donnelly Corp. (Oak Brook, Illinois):
Official Airline Guide
International Edition, Sept. 1969
North American Edition, March 1970

Bulletin
Vol. 28: J. Ford, 'Distribution of Vectors of African Pathogenic Trypanosomes' and
Vol. 34: L. M. Bechelli & V. M. Domingues, 'The Leprosy Problem in the World'
Second and Third Reports on the World Health Situation
Public Health Papers
No. 32: B. Abel-Smith, 'An International Study of Health Expenditure'
World Health Magazine
U.N. (New York):
Demographic Yearbook 1966
International Leprosy Association (Washington, D.C.):
International Journal of Leprosy
J. May (New York 1958):
Ecology of Human Disease
American Society of Tropical Medicine and Hygiene (Baltimore, Maryland):
American Journal of Tropical Medicine and Hygiene
A. H. Gale (London 1959):
Epidemic Diseases
American Public Health Association (New York 1960):
Control of Communicable Diseases in Man
Ross Institute Records (London)
T. H. Davey and W. P. H. Lightbody (London 1961):
The Control of Diseases in the Tropics
E. Rodenwalt (Hamburg 1952–7):
World Atlas of Epidemic Diseases
U.I.C.C., International Union Against Cancer (Berlin 1966):
R. Doll, P. Payne, J. Waterhouse (eds.), *Cancer Incidence in Five Continents*
Dept. of Public Health, University School of Medicine (Sendai, Japan 1966):
Segi, Mitsuo, et al., *Cancer Mortality for Selected Sites in 24 Countries*
British Journal of Cancer (Vol. 23, 1969):
R. Doll, *The Geographical Distribution of Cancer*
Nuffield Provincial Hospitals Trust, 1967:
R. Doll, *Epidemiology of Cancer*
R. M. Prothero (London 1965):
Migrants and Malaria

Transport Industries

Sampson Low, Marston & Co. (Great Missenden, U.K.):
Jane's World Railways
Jane's All the World's Aircraft
Transport and Technical Publications Ltd. (London):
Railway Directory and Yearbook 1967/1968
Organization for Economic Co-operation and Development (Paris):
The Engineering Industries in North America, Europe and Japan 1966/67
Railway Age (New York):
Railway Age Statistical Review 1962–1965
International Civil Aviation Organization (Montréal)
American Aviation Publications (Washington, D.C.):
American Aviation
Lloyd's (London):
Register of Ships 1967/8
Annual Summary of Merchant Ships Launched in the World 1953–1955 and 1964–1966
U.N. (New York):
Statistical Yearbook 1957, 1967
Yearbook of International Trade Statistics 1965
Repertoire International de l'Industrie Automobile 1965
Society of Motor Manufacturers and Traders Ltd. (London):
Motor Industry of Great Britain
Automobile Club of Italy:
World Car Club

Manufacturing Industries

CEMBUREAU, The European Cement Association (Malmö, Sweden):
World Cement Directory
U.N. (New York):
Statistical Yearbook 1957, 1966, 1968
Computer Consultants Limited (Llandudno, U.K.):
European Computer Survey 1968/9
European Computer Users' Handbook 1964
British Commercial Computer Digest 1963
The British Sulphur Corporation Limited (London)
U.S. Dept. of the Interior (Washington, D.C.):
Bureau of Mines, Minerals Yearbook
Vol. I Metals and Minerals

F.A.O. (Roma):
Fertilizers—An Annual Review of World Production, Consumption and Trade 1966
European Chemical News (London):
'Chemical Product Data' 1969
'Chemical Plant Data' 1969
Verlag für Internationale Wirtschaftsliteratur GmbH. (Zürich):
International Brewers' Directory and Soft Drink Guide 1965
William Reed Ltd. (London):
The Brewers Journal
Modern Brewery Age (Stamford, Connecticut):
Blue Book 1968
Time, Inc. (Chicago):
The Fortune Directory of the 500 Largest U.S. Industrial Corporations 1957 and 1967
The Fortune Directory of the 200 Largest Industrial Companies Outside the U.S. 1957 and 1967

Demography

U.N. (New York):
Demographic Yearbook
Report on World Population Prospects, as Assessed in 1963
Statistical Yearbook 1967
International Planned Parenthood Federation (London)
International Union of Official Travel Organizations (London):
International Travel Statistics
World Health Organization (Geneva):
Statistics Annual Vol. I, 1962, 1963, 1964
Third Report on the World Health Situation 1961–1964

Disease

World Health Organization (Geneva):
Epidemiological and Vital Statistics Reports
Statistics Annual 1957–1966
Epidemiological Assessment on the Status of the World Health
Malaria—Official Records of the World Health Organization No. 118
Official Records of the W.H.O. No. 127
W.H.O. Chronicle

GAZETTEER

The gazetteer lists more than eight thousand names of populated places, specific sites (such as mines or dams), physical features and administrative divisions which are named on the maps. It does not list country names.

The gazetteer uses the vernacular form of all place names, transliterated into the Roman alphabet where appropriate, according to the system used by the United States Board on Geographic Names. Where the vernacular form of a name may be unfamiliar to English-speaking readers and there is a common English form, this English form is given as a cross-reference. Entries for places recently renamed also may include a cross-reference to the previous name. For each place the name used is a de facto representation of the situation at the time of the compilation of the gazetteer and does not imply any political comment or bias.

The names in the gazetteer are arranged in alphabetical order taking no account of diacritical marks or letters not found in the Roman alphabet. Names which begin St. or Ste. are alphabetized as though written out in full. Names beginning Le, La, Les, Los, etc. are alphabetized under the pronoun. Names which have had to be abbreviated on the maps are written out in full in the gazetteer and alphabetized accordingly.

Any name which is not that of a populated place is followed by a description in italic type except that where the descriptive term forms part of the name it is italicized but not repeated. No distinction of size is made in respect of administrative divisions; but the counties of the U.S.A., the names of which are not familiar, are described simply as Co. Every entry is identified by the name of the country in which it is to be found, and entries for places in the U.S.A. are further specified by their state location.

Wherever possible co-ordinates have been given to the nearest minute, enabling entries to be located on maps at any scale. The majority of such co-ordinates have been taken from a printed source as specified below but in some cases, particularly for dams and mines, they have been plotted for this atlas (as accurately as possible) from less authoritative maps. Regions or physical features which are not well defined have not been located with such precision. References to large geographical or administrative areas are generalized, and each refers to the approximate centre of the area. The co-ordinates given for large areas will not, therefore, necessarily coincide with the position of a symbol on a map. The same is true of the co-ordinates given for rivers which refer always to the location of the mouth of the river.

Each entry is followed by a list of all the pages on which the name occurs. Where a name occurs on an inset map, rather than on the main world map, this is indicated by the use of a capital letter which corresponds to the letter of the inset on which the name occurs.

Sources. The gazetteers of official standard names which are published by the United States Board on Geographic Names have been taken as authoritative for both the location of places and the spelling of place names for all countries with the following major exceptions:

Algeria	New Zealand
Canada	Nigeria
Cyprus	Peru
Czechoslovakia	Philippines
Greece	Poland
India	South Africa
Irish Republic	Switzerland
Israel	U.K.
Netherlands	U.S.A.

For all of these the *Index-Gazetteer of the World* published by The Times Publishing Company Ltd., has been taken as authoritative for the location of places and, supplemented where appropriate by national atlases, has been used as the major source for spellings. The U.S.B.G.N. gazetteer for Morocco appeared too late to be used as an authority on spellings but has been used for locations. Moroccan names are spelt as in the Atlas du Maroc published by the Comité de Géographie du Maroc.

The Comprehensive edition of the *Atlas of the World*, published by The Times Newspapers Ltd., and the *International Atlas* published by Rand McNally and Co. (George Philip & Son Ltd. in the U.K.), have also been used extensively.

Of the many atlases and maps which have been consulted during the preparation of this gazetteer, the following are the most important and most frequently used:

The National Atlases of Canada and Czechoslovakia
Pergamon Press: *Pergamon World Atlas*
Touring Club Italiano: *Atlante Internazionale del T.C.I.*
Rand McNally & Co.: *International World Atlas*
Clarendon Press: *The Atlas of Britain*
Kartográfiai Vállalat Budapest: *Képes Politikai és Gazdasági Világatlasz*
Columbia University Press: *The Columbia Lippincott Gazetteer of the World*
Kultura: *Cartactual*
National and State road maps
The Petroleum Publishing Co.: *International Petroleum Encyclopedia*
George Philip & Son Ltd.: *Geographical Digest* (used particularly to verify name changes)

Generic terms. The following generic terms in foreign languages appear in the gazetteer. English equivalents are taken from the U.S.B.G.N. gazetteers.

Term	Meaning
Basseyn (*Russian*)	basin
Berg (*German*)	hill, mountain
Birkat (*Arabic*)	lake, marsh
Bukit (*Indonesian*)	hill, mountain, peninsula
Bîr (*Arabic*)	port
Cerro(s) (*Spanish*)	hill(s), mountain(s)
Deresi (*Turkish*)	stream
Ghar (*Pakistani*)	mountain(s), mountain range
Gora, Gory (*Russian*)	mountain, mountains
Guba (*Russian*)	bay
Ho (*Spanish*)	lake, stream
Jabal, Jbel, Djebel (*Arabic*)	hill(s), mountain(s)
Jazireh (*Persian*)	island
Khalij (*Arabic*)	gulf
Khao (*Thai*)	hill, mountain
Khrebet (*Russian*)	mountains, mountain range
Khuan (*Thai*)	dam
Ko (*Thai*)	island, peninsula, point
Kuh (*Persian*)	hill(s), mountain(s)
Ling (*Chinese*)	hill(s), mountain(s), pass
Lough (*Gaelic*)	lake
Marsá (*Arabic*)	anchorage, bay
Misaki (*Japanese*)	peninsula
Morro (*Portuguese*)	hill(s), mountain(s)
Ostov, Ostova (*Russian*)	island(s)
Oya (*Ceylonese*)	stream
Pegunungan (*Indonesian*)	mountains, mountain range
P'en-ti (*Chinese*)	basin
Pereval (*Russian*)	mountain pass
Poluostrov (*Russian*)	peninsula
Pulau (*Indonesian*)	island, reef
Río (*Spanish*)	river, stream
Serra (*Portuguese*)	mountain range
Shima (*Japanese*)	island(s)
Sierra (*Spanish*)	hill(s), mountain(s)
Stena (*Yugoslav*)	mountain
Tanjong (*Malay*)	point
Wâdî (*Arabic*)	stream, irrigation canal
Wâhat (*Arabic*)	oasis
Yama (*Japanese*)	hill, mountain(s)

Abbreviations. The abbreviations listed below have been used in the gazetteer.

Abbr.	Meaning
admin.	administrative division
Ala.	Alabama
arch.	archipelago
Arg.	Argentina
Ariz.	Arizona
Ark.	Arkansas
Austl.	Australia
Calif.	California
Cent. Af. R.	Central African Republic
China P.R.	The People's Republic of China
Co.	County
Colo.	Colorado
Congo D.R.	Democratic Republic of the Congo
Congo R.	Republic of the Congo
Conn.	Connecticut
Czech.	Czechoslovakia
Del.	Delaware
Den.	Denmark
Dom. R.	Dominican Republic
Eng.	England
Fla.	Florida
Fr. Guiana	French Guiana
Ga.	Georgia (U.S.A.)
G.D.R. / Germany D.R.	German Democratic Republic
G.F.R. / Germany F.R.	Federal Republic of Germany
Ice.	Iceland
Ill.	Illinois
Ind.	Indiana
Indon.	Indonesia
Irish R.	Irish Republic
is.	island or islands
Kans.	Kansas
Ky.	Kentucky
La.	Louisiana
Malagasy R.	Malagasy Republic
Mass.	Massachusetts
Md.	Maryland
Mich.	Michigan
Minn.	Minnesota
Miss.	Mississippi
Mo.	Missouri
Mont.	Montana
Mor.	Morocco
mtn.(s)	mountain(s)
N.C.	North Carolina
N.D.	North Dakota
Nebr.	Nebraska
Neths.	Netherlands
Nev.	Nevada
N.H.	New Hampshire
N.J.	New Jersey
N. Korea	North Korea
N. Mex.	New Mexico
N.Y.	New York
Okla.	Oklahoma
Oreg.	Oregon
Pa.	Pennsylvania
pen.	peninsula
pt.	point
reg.	region
R.I.	Rhode Island
riv.	river
S. Africa	South Africa
S. Vietnam	South Vietnam
S.C.	South Carolina
S.D.	South Dakota
S.S.R.	Sovietskaya Sotsialisticheskaya Respublika
St. Maarten	Sint Maarten
Tenn.	Tennessee
Thai.	Thailand
U.A.R.	United Arab Republic
U.S.A.	United States of America
U.S.S.R.	Union of Soviet Socialist Republics
Va.	Virginia
Vt.	Vermont
Wash.	Washington
Wis.	Wisconsin
W. Va.	West Virginia
Wyo.	Wyoming
Yugo.	Yugoslavia

A

Name	Lat	Long	Page(s)
Aachen: Germany F.R.	50 46 N	6 06 E	32C, 38B, 54B
Aalst: Belgium	50 56 N	4 02 E	31B
Aathal: Switzerland	47 20 N	8 46 E	37A, 37G, 59, 60, 67, 84
Ābādān: Iran	30 20 N	48 16 E	38
Abakan: U.S.S.R.	53 43 N	91 26 E	27D
Ābashiri: Japan	44 01 N	144 17 E	38
Åbenrå: Denmark	55 02 N	9 26 E	84C
Aberdeen: Miss., U.S.A.	33 49 N	88 34 W	60B
Aberdeen: S.D., U.S.A.	45 28 N	98 30 W	27C, 67, 87
Aberdeen: Scotland	57 10 N	2 04 W	62
Aberfoyle Creek: stream, Austl.	51 24 N	147 48 E	50
Abertawe see Swansea: Wales			57C
Aberthaw: Wales	51 24 N	3 23 W	57C
Abilene: Texas, U.S.A.	32 27 N	99 45 W	67, 84, 87
Abitibi: river, Canada	49 52 N	81 29 W	29, 52, 58, 67
Åbo see Turku: Finland			57C
Aboño: Spain	43 34 N	5 43 W	57C
Abshiron: region, U.S.S.R.			50
Abū Tulu, Jabal: hill, Sudan			43
Abū Za'bal: U.A.R.	30 16 N	31 28 E	59
Acajutla: El Salvador	13 36 N	89 50 W	36, 59, 61, 84
Acapulco de Juárez: Mexico	16 51 N	99 55 W	87
Acari: Peru	15 25 S	74 37 W	43
Accra: Ghana	5 33 N	0 21 W	55, 67, 87
Accrington: England	53 46 N	2 21 W	31B
Achinsk: U.S.S.R.	56 10 N	90 30 E	38, 47, 57
Achisay: U.S.S.R.	43 35 N	68 53 E	46, 49
Acme: N.C., U.S.A.	34 20 N	78 11 W	59B, 59F
Acton: Mass., U.S.A.	42 28 N	71 26 W	43, 59, 60
Ada: Okla., U.S.A.	34 47 N	96 41 W	57A
Adamawa: Turkey	37 01 N	35 16 E	61
Ad Dawhah: Qatar	25 16 N	51 27 E	37A
Addis Ababa: Ethiopia	9 03 N	38 42 E	30A
Adelaide: Australia	34 56 S	138 36 E	31, 34, 36, 67, 87

Name	Lat	Long	Page(s)
Aden: Southern Yemen	12 50 N	45 03 E	38
Adler: U.S.S.R.	43 26 N	39 56 E	43
Adoni: India	15 38 N	77 16 E	87
Adriatic Sea: Europe	43 00 N	15 00 E	31C
Aetsä: Finland	61 18 N	22 42 E	84
Agadir: Morocco	30 26 N	9 36 W	27, 84
Agaro: U.S.S.R.	55 19 N	38 00 E	50
Ågesta: Sweden	59 14 N	18 08 E	59F
Agricola: Fla., U.S.A.	27 30 N	81 50 W	34
Agua Grande: region, Brazil	11 30 S	38 00 W	43
Aguaylia: Peru	8 35 S	74 40 W	43
Agudo, Morro: hill, Brazil	21 45 N	47 28 W	57
Ahlen: Germany F.R.	51 45 N	7 55 E	58D, 61D
Ahvaz: Iran	31 19 N	48 42 E	38
Aichi-ken: admin., Japan	35 03 N	137 15 E	55, 60C, 63
Aiken: S.C., U.S.A.	33 34 N	81 44 W	32B
Aintree: England	53 29 N	2 57 W	32C, 60D
Aioi: Japan	34 48 N	134 28 E	52B
Air: plateau, Niger	18 00 N	8 00 E	45
Airvault: France	46 50 N	0 09 W	53B
Aiud: Romania	46 18 N	23 43 E	57C
Aizu-Shimodate: Japan	36 18 N	140 00 E	59G
Ajka: Hungary	47 06 N	17 33 E	17
Ajmer: India	26 29 N	74 38 E	46C
Ajo: Ariz., U.S.A.	32 22 N	112 53 W	55A
A'kan-chen: China P.R.	24 24 N	103 09 E	45A
Akchatau: U.S.S.R.	47 59 N	74 00 E	48
Akershus: admin., Norway	60 15 N	11 14 E	45D, 46C
Akhan-Gharan: U.S.S.R.	39 43 N	140 07 E	57
Akita: Japan	39 43 N	140 07 E	57
Akita-ken: admin., Japan	40 00 N	140 30 E	57E, 46C, 58C, 59G, 61C, 84D
'Akko (Acre): Israel	32 55 N	35 04 E	43, 59, 60
Akola: India	20 43 N	77 00 E	87
Akosombo: dam, Ghana	6 16 N	0 04 E	55
Akranes: Iceland	64 18 N	22 01 W	39
Akron: Ohio, U.S.A.	41 04 N	81 31 W	30A, 63, 67A, 87B
Aksu: Turkey	37 04 N	31 09 E	67
Aktyubinskaya Oblast': admin., U.S.S.R.	50 17 N	57 10 E	49
Akyab: Burma	20 09 N	92 55 E	48C
Akzhal: U.S.S.R.	49 13 N	81 25 E	49

Name	Lat	Long	Page(s)
Alabama: admin., U.S.A.	33 00 N	38 00 W	38
Alagoas: admin., Brazil	9 00 S	36 00 W	61A
Alam, Marsa al: anchorage, U.A.R.	25 05 N	34 54 E	35
Alamo: Mexico	27 01 N	101 01 W	48
Alamogordo: U.S.A.	32 54 N	105 57 W	49A
Alapayevsk: U.S.S.R.	57 52 N	61 42 E	38B
Al 'Aqabah (Aqaba): Jordan	29 32 N	35 00 E	27, 35, 38
Alarup: Albania	40 51 N	20 48 E	45
Alaska: admin., U.S.A.	65 00 N	153 00 W	59, 84
Albacete: Spain	38 58 N	1 51 W	45
Albania	41 08 N	20 04 W	31C, 87C
Albany: Australia	35 02 N	117 53 E	31A, 87C, 87B
Albany: Ga., U.S.A.	31 35 N	84 10 W	40C, 67A, 59, 61
Albany: N.Y., U.S.A.	42 40 N	73 49 W	37A, 59, 61
Alberta: admin., Canada	54 00 N	113 00 W	31A
Alborg: Denmark	57 03 N	9 50 E	27
Al Burqān: region, Kuwait	28 58 N	47 58 E	32C
Albuquerque: U.S.A.	35 05 N	106 39 W	52A
Alcalá de Henares: Spain	40 29 N	3 22 W	54C
Alcázar de San Juan: Spain	39 24 N	3 12 W	35, 37C
Alcoa: Tenn., U.S.A.	35 47 N	84 00 W	32C, 60
Aldan: U.S.S.R.	58 44 N	125 22 E	54
Aldeadávila: dam, Spain	41 13 N	6 44 W	47
Aleksandrovac: Yugoslavia	43 37 N	21 03 E	49A
Aleksandrovsk-Sakhalinskiy: U.S.S.R.	50 54 N	142 10 E	49
Aleksin: U.S.S.R.	54 29 N	37 10 E	17
Alençon: France	48 25 N	0 05 E	57, 87
Alençon: France	48 25 N	0 05 E	31A
Aleppo see Ḥalab: Syria			38
Aleisund: Norway	62 28 N	6 12 E	17
Alexander City: Ala., U.S.A.	32 57 N	86 00 W	57
Alexandria see Al Iskandarīyah			
Alfeld: Germany F.R.	51 59 N	9 49 E	31A
Al Fuhays: Jordan			25C
Algarrobo: Chile			43
Alger: Algeria	36 50 N	3 00 E	27B, 36, 58
Al Hadīthah: Iraq			17, 59H, 67, 84A, 87
Al Ḥallūfah, Jabal: hill, Tunisia			37G
Alhandra: Portugal	38 57 E	9 09 W	46B
Al Ḥindīyah: Iraq			87C
Al Hoceima: Morocco	35 14 N	3 56 W	56
Alicante: Spain	38 21 N	0 29 W	27B
Alipur: Pa., U.S.A.	40 38 N	80 16 W	17
Ali Ghelii: Somali Republic			27B
Al Iskandarīyah (Alexandria): U.A.R.	31 13 N	29 54 E	27, 29, 36, 84B
Alivérion: Greece	38 24 N	24 02 E	25C
Al Jīzah (Giza): U.A.R.	30 01 N	31 13 E	47
Aljustrel: Portugal	37 52 N	8 10 W	56
Al Khurṭūm (Khartoum): Sudan	15 36 N	32 32 E	27B, 36, 58
Al Kuwayt (Kuwait): Kuwait	29 20 N	47 59 E	84B, 87
Al Lādhiqīyah: Syria	35 31 N	35 47 E	47
Allahabad: admin., India	25 27 N	81 50 W	31B
Allahabad: India	25 27 N	81 50 E	27B
Allegheny River: dam, Pa., U.S.A.	41 50 N	79 01 W	39
Allentown: Pa., U.S.A.	40 37 N	75 30 W	55B, 67A, 87B
Allen, Lough: lake, Irish R.	54 08 N	8 08 W	29B
Alloa: Scotland	56 07 N	3 49 W	30A
Alms Point: Conn., U.S.A.	41 04 N	72 12 W	35, 47
Alma: Mich., U.S.A.	43 23 N	84 40 W	47
Alma-Ata: U.S.S.R.	43 15 N	76 57 E	50, 31
Almadén: Spain	38 46 N	4 50 W	37H, 47B
Al Maḥallah al Kubrā: U.A.R.	30 59 N	31 10 E	31B
Al Maks: U.A.R.	25 31 N	30 30 E	27B
Almásfüzitő: Hungary	47 43 N	18 16 E	25D, 57B
Al Mawṣil: Iraq	36 21 N	43 08 E	29, 31, 32, 34, 67, 87
Almeden: Idaho, U.S.A.	44 10 N	116 45 W	58D
Almelo: Netherlands	52 21 N	6 40 E	27B
Almería: Spain	36 50 N	2 27 W	
Alpena: Mich., U.S.A.	45 04 N	83 27 W	
Alpena: river, region, G.F.R.	48 05 N	11 56 W	
Al Qāhirah (Cairo): U.A.R.	30 03 N	31 15 E	
Al Qal'ah al Jardā': Tunisia	35 40 N	8 35 E	
Al Quṣayr (Quseir): U.A.R.	26 06 N	34 17 E	
Alsdorf: Germany F.R.	50 53 N	6 10 E	

Name	Lat	Long	Page(s)
Alsen: N.Y., U.S.A.	42 11 N	73 55 W	57B
Altamira: Mexico	22 24 N	97 55 W	30, 59
Altenessen: Germany F.R.	51 29 N	7 00 E	37F, 58D
Altenrhein: Switzerland	47 28 N	9 30 N	39
Alto Anchicaya: Colombia	3 46 N	77 10 W	48, 50
Alto Ligonha: Mozambique	15 31 S	38 16 N	49A
Altona: Australia	37 52 S	144 50 E	38B
Alverca: Portugal	38 54 N	9 02 W	61
Al Wahṭāṭ al Baḥrīyah: region, U.A.R.	28 57 E	28 57 E	43
Alwaye: India	10 06 N	76 25 E	31C, 40, 47, 59
Amagasaki: Japan	34 43 N	135 25 E	55, 58C
Amakusa-shima-jima: is., Japan	32 20 N	130 05 E	38C
Amalfi: Italy	40 38 N	14 36 E	31C
Amalner: India	21 01 N	75 09 E	31C
Amapá: Brazil	2 03 N	51 05 W	45
Amarante: Portugal	41 16 N	8 05 W	37A, 59, 61
Amarillo: Texas, U.S.A.	35 14 N	101 50 W	6H
Ambarès-et-la Grave: France	44 55 N	0 29 W	31C
Ambarnath: India	19 11 N	73 11 E	58D
Ambasamudram: India	8 45 N	77 27 E	36
Amberg: Germany F.R.	49 27 N	11 52 E	36
Ambes, Bec d': point, France	45 03 N	0 37 W	27B
Ambindrakrakema: Malagasy Republic	25 02 S	46 23 E	40
Amboasary: Malagasy R.	25 02 S	46 23 E	40
Amboenemo: Malagasy R.	22 45 S	47 20 W	
Americana: Brazil	22 45 S	47 20 W	55A, 62A
Amersfoort: Netherlands	52 09 N	5 23 E	59A
Amherstburg: Canada	42 06 N	83 06 W	48D
Amiandos: Cyprus	34 55 N	32 51 E	67D
Amiens: France	49 54 N	2 18 E	67, 87
'Ammān (Rabbah): Jordan	31 57 N	35 56 E	32, 84
Amoy see Hsia-men: China P.R.	24 27 N	118 05 W	
Ampa: region, Brunei	5 00 N	114 56 E	27B
Amritsar: India	31 35 N	74 54 E	
Amsterdam: Netherlands	52 21 N	4 54 E	

Name	Lat	Long	Page(s)
Amsterdam: N.Y., U.S.A.	42 56 N	74 12 W	30B, 37B, 37F
Amuay: Venezuela	11 47 N	70 15 W	52A, 56A, 58H,
Amvrosiyevka: U.S.S.R.	47 47 N	38 30 E	59H, 62A, 67B,
Anaco: Venezuela	9 27 N	64 28 W	84C, 87D, 32B
Anaco: Mexico	46 30 N	122 42 W	29A, 32B
Anacortes: Wash., U.S.A.	48 30 N	122 42 W	31
Anadyr': U.S.S.R.	64 45 N	177 50 E	57
Anaheim: Calif., U.S.A.	33 50 N	117 55 W	46A, 59
Anápolis: Brazil	16 20 S	48 58 W	37A
Anchieta: Brazil	20 48 S	40 39 W	83A
Anchorage: Alaska, U.S.A.	61 10 N	149 54 W	46, 49
Ancón: Ecuador	2 20 S	80 52 W	46, 49
Ancona: Italy	43 38 N	13 30 E	88
Andalgalá: Argentina	27 36 S	66 19 W	84, 87
Andean Highland: region, Peru	13 00 S	72 01 W	52A, 84A
Anderson: Alaska, U.S.A.	64 30 N	149 18 W	45
Andhra Pradesh: admin., India	16 00 N	79 00 E	31A, 32B, 60B
Andoain: Spain	43 13 N	2 01 W	45
Andrade: Brazil	21 38 N	42 39 N	32C, 60D
Andrychów: Poland	49 52 N	19 21 E	31
Andūjar, Kūh: mtn., Iran	34 30 N	66 19 W	
An-fu: China P.R.	27 35 S	114 37 E	58G, 60C
Angara: river, U.S.S.R.	58 06 N	94 00 E	61
Angaston: Australia	34 30 S	139 01 E	35, 57
Angat: dam, Philippines	14 55 N	121 01 E	31B
Angers: France	47 28 N	0 33 W	46B
Anglesea: Australia	38 25 N	144 10 E	31
Angleur: Belgium	50 35 N	5 36 E	17, 62A
Angostura: Mexico	41 16 N	102 41 W	46B
Angren: U.S.S.R.	40 59 N	70 12 E	35
Anguilin, Kūh: mtn., Iran	28 44 N	51 18 E	57, 61
Ar Ruṣayfah (Riyadh): Saudi Arabia	24 44 N	46 48 E	50D
Animas: Bolivia	21 30 S	67 30 W	49
Ankara: Turkey	39 56 N	32 52 E	35
Ankleswar: India	21 30 N	30 38 E	59H, 84A
Annaba: Algeria	36 55 N	7 47 E	56
Annaka: Japan	36 21 N	138 54 E	46C
Annecy: France	45 54 N	6 07 E	49
Annex Kleinsee: mine, S. Africa	29 35 N	17 04 W	25A, 31A, 59B
Anniston: Ala., U.S.A.	33 40 N	85 50 W	84
Annonay: France	45 14 N	4 40 E	43, 46, 55, 67
An-shan: China P.R.	41 07 N	122 57 E	53B
Ansty: England	52 27 N	1 24 W	39
Anta: Brazil	22 03 S	42 39 W	84B
Antalya: Turkey	36 53 N	30 42 E	
Antananarivo (Tananarive): Malagasy Republic			67, 87
Antioch: Calif., U.S.A.	38 01 N	31 E	65, 84
Antioquia: admin., Colombia	6 10 N	75 30 W	27, 67
Antofagasta: Chile	23 39 S	70 24 W	

Name	Lat	Long	Page(s)
Antrim: Northern Ireland	54 43 N	6 13 W	32C, 60
Antung see Tan-tung: China P.R.	40 08 N	124 24 E	25, 32
Aalst: admin., Belgium	51 13 N	4 24 E	56A
Antwerpen (Anvers): Belgium	51 13 N	4 25 E	30B, 37D, 37F, 45, 55A, 58D, 58H, 59D, 59H, 60D, 60H, 61H, 67B, 84C
Anvers see Antwerpen: Belgium			
An Xuyen: region, S. Vietnam	9 00 N	105 05 E	27
An-yang: China P.R.	36 05 N	114 21 E	43
Anyang-ni: South Korea	37 23 N	126 55 E	32A, 60
Anzhero-Sudzhensk: U.S.S.R.	56 07 N	86 00 E	38
Aomori: Japan	40 49 N	141 00 E	27D, 67
Aomori: admin., Japan	40 45 N	141 00 E	50
Aosta: Italy	45 43 N	7 19 E	43B
Aouam: Jbel: hill, Morocco	33 10 N	4 40 W	46, 49
Apache Co.: Ariz., U.S.A.	35 30 N	109 30 W	40A, 50A
Apaxco de Ocampo: Mexico	19 59 N	99 10 W	84
Apeldoorn: Netherlands	52 13 N	5 57 E	25C
Apollo: Pa., U.S.A.	40 34 N	79 34 W	40C
Appalachian Mountains, North: mtns., Maine, U.S.A.	45 00 N	70 00 W	50
Appingedam: Netherlands	53 18 N	6 52 E	25C
Aqaba see Al 'Aqabah: Jordan	29 32 N	35 00 E	46, 49A
Aracaju: Brazil	10 55 S	37 04 W	67
Arad: Romania	46 11 N	21 19 E	37B, 54
Aragua de Maturin: Venezuela	9 58 N	63 29 W	50
Arakaka: Guyana	7 35 N	60 07 W	50
Aransas Pass: Texas, U.S.A.	27 55 N	97 10 W	60G
Ararat: U.S.S.R.	39 50 N	44 42 E	57
Aratu: Brazil	12 54 S	38 25 W	62A
Arauco: admin., Chile	37 50 S	73 15 W	38
Arcachon: France	44 39 N	1 10 W	27B
Archangel see Arkhangel'sk: U.S.S.R.			
Arcola: Italy	44 07 N	9 54 E	25, 67, 84
Arcos: Brazil	20 17 S	45 32 W	37H
Ardal: Norway	61 14 N	7 48 E	47
Ard as Suwaydā': region, Syria	32 52 N	36 43 W	37A
Ardee: Irish Republic	53 52 N	6 33 W	31
Ardlethan: Australia	34 21 S	146 54 E	37J
Ardmore: Okla., U.S.A.	34 11 N	97 08 W	37F, 84C
Ardrossan: Scotland	55 39 N	4 49 W	58
Arecibo: Puerto Rico	18 28 N	66 43 W	29, 32, 67
Arequipa: Peru	16 25 S	71 32 W	53B
Arezzo: admin., Italy	43 27 N	11 15 E	53B
Arezzo: Italy	43 27 N	11 53 E	38B
Argentuil: France	48 57 N	2 15 E	54B, 67, 84C
Argenteuil: France	48 57 N	2 15 E	27, 55, 84
Århus: Denmark	56 09 N	10 13 E	27
Arhbar: Morocco	34 00 N	4 39 W	47A
Arica: Chile	18 29 S	70 20 W	49A
Ariège: admin., France	43 00 N	1 30 E	47A
Arizona: admin., U.S.A.	34 00 N	112 00 W	27, 38
Arizpe: Mexico	30 20 N	110 10 W	37J
Arkadelphia: Ark., U.S.A.	34 07 N	93 06 W	25, 67, 84
Arkalyk: U.S.S.R.	50 13 N	66 49 E	61D, 61H
Arkansas: admin., Kans., U.S.A.	35 00 N	94 00 W	36
Arkansas City: Kans., U.S.A.	37 03 N	97 02 W	56
Arkhangel'sk (Archangel): U.S.S.R.	64 34 N	40 32 E	53
Arklow: Irish Republic	52 48 N	6 09 W	38C
Armavir: U.S.S.R.	45 00 N	41 08 E	38
Arnao: Spain	43 35 N	5 58 W	48
Arnett: Okla., U.S.A.	36 06 N	99 46 W	37J, 59, 59A
Arnhem: Netherlands	52 00 N	5 53 E	30, 35, 37B, 37D, 37D
Arnprior: Canada	45 26 N	76 24 W	61, 84A
Arnsberg: G.F.R.	51 24 N	8 03 E	48
Arnstadt: region, G.F.R.	50 51 N	10 57 E	38
Arroyo Grande: Calif., U.S.A.	35 08 N	120 34 W	43
Ar Ruṣayfah: Jordan	32 01 N	36 02 E	32, 60, 61, 84B
Artëm: U.S.S.R.	43 22 N	132 13 E	87C
Artëmovskiy: U.S.S.R.	57 21 N	61 54 E	54B
Artesia: N. Mex., U.S.A.	32 51 N	104 24 W	45D, 47B
Arvida: Canada	48 26 N	71 11 W	32
Arzew: Algeria	35 50 N	0 19 W	
Asahigawa: Japan	43 46 N	142 22 E	
Asahi-mura: admin., Japan	38 33 N	140 12 E	
Asbestos: U.S.S.R.	57 01 N	61 28 W	
Asem, Bukit: hill, Indonesia	3 45 S	103 46 N	
Asha: U.S.S.R.	55 00 N	57 16 E	
Ashdod: Israel	31 45 N	34 40 E	
Asheville: N.C., U.S.A.	35 35 N	82 35 W	
Ashford: England	51 09 N	0 52 E	
Ashio: Japan	36 38 N	139 27 E	
Ashkelon: Israel	31 40 N	34 33 E	

93

	°	′		°	′		Page(s)
Ashkhabad: U.S.S.R.	37	57	N	58	23	E	29, 31, 67
Ashland: Ky., U.S.A.	38	28	N	82	40	W	43A
Ashtabula: Ohio, U.S.A.	41	53	N	80	47	W	59A, 60B, 60F
Ashton: R.I., U.S.A.	41	56	N	71	26	W	32B
Asia, Central: reg., U.S.S.R.	42	14	N	73	00	E	34, 38
Asientos: Mexico	22	13	N	102	06	W	59A
Asmara: Ethiopia	15	20	N	38	58	E	87
Asprópirgos: Greece	38	03	N	23	36	E	37J, 57, 59D
Assam: admin., India	26	00	N	92	00	E	84
Assemini: Italy	39	18	N	9	04	E	57, 35, 38, 59
As Samāwah: Iraq	31	18	N	45	17	E	58, 59D
As Sidar: Libya	30	37	N	18	29	E	56
Assonet: Mass., U.S.A.	41	48	N	71	04	W	60B
As Sukhayrah: Tunisia	34	17	N	10	06	E	37B
As Suways (Suez): U.A.R.	29	58	N	32	33	E	37D, 84

	°	′		°	′		Page(s)
Baar: Switzerland	47	12	N	8	32	E	31B
Babelsberg: Germany D.R.	52	24	N	13	06	E	54B
Bacău: admin., Romania	46	40	N	26	40	E	38B
Bacău: Romania	46	34	N	26	54	E	29, 37B
Bacchus Marsh: Australia	37	41	S	144	27	E	39
Bachelor Lake: Canada	49	30	N	76	30	W	49
Backnang: Germany F.R.	48	57	N	9	26	E	55A
Bacolod: Philippines	10	38	N	122	58	E	87
Bacon's Castle: Va., U.S.A.	37	10	N	76	40	W	40C
Badacsony: hill, Hungary	46	48	N	17	30	E	37B

	°	′		°	′		Page(s)
Bankstown: Australia	33	55	S	151	02	E	53
Ban Sang: admin., Thailand	13	45	N	100	15	E	53
Banská Bystrica: Czech.	48	45	N	19	07	E	57C
Bantry Bay: Irish Republic	51	41	N	9	52	W	37D
Banzart (Bizerte): Tunisia	37	17	N	9	52	E	37D
Bao: dam, Spain	42	13	N	7	10	W	39
Barauni: India	25	28	N	86	12	E	39
Barbate de Franco: Spain	36	12	N	5	55	W	49
Barber: N.J., U.S.A.	40	32	N	74	16	W	59A
Barberton: Ohio, U.S.A.	41	02	N	81	37	W	59
Barberton: South Africa	25	48	S	31	03	E	87
Barcelona: admin., Spain	41	40	N	2	00	E	40C
Barcelona: Spain	41	23	N	2	11	E	37B, 49

	°	′		°	′		Page(s)
Bayreuth: Germany F.R.	49	57	N	11	35	E	31B
Bayswater: Australia	37	35	S	145	16	E	32, 59, 60
Baytown: Texas, U.S.A.	29	43	N	94	59	W	30A, 37I, 58A, 58E, 59F, 60G
Beas: dam, India	31	57	N	75	50	E	39
Beatrice: Nebr., U.S.A.	40	17	N	96	45	W	61A, 61E
Beauharnois: Canada	45	18	N	73	52	W	47, 59A
Beaumont: dam, Canada	47	33	N	72	44	W	39B
Beaumont: Texas, U.S.A.	30	04	N	94	06	W	30A, 37I, 56, 58A, 60A, 61B, 61E

Name	Lat	Long	Page(s)
Bergen: Norway	60 23 N	5 20 E	2, 27C, 29, 31, 52,
Bergheim: Germany F.R.	50 58 N	6 39 E	87
Bergisch Gladbach: G.F.R.	50 59 N	7 08 E	29B
Berguslavka: U.S.S.R.	56 12 N	87 12 E	49
Berkeley: England	51 42 N	2 27 W	40B
Berlin: G.D.R./G.F.R.	52 31 N	13 24 E	2, 3, 32C, 55A, 63A, 67B, 87
Berlin: N.H., U.S.A.	44 27 N	71 13 W	59A
Berneo: Spain	43 26 N	2 43 W	
Bernburg: Germany D.R.	51 47 N	11 44 E	57B
Bernkastel-Kues: G.F.R.	49 55 N	7 04 E	
Beroun: Czechoslovakia	49 58 N	14 05 E	31B
Berre-l'Étang: France	43 28 N	5 11 E	30B, 37H, 58H, 60H
Berrima: Australia	34 29 S	150 20 E	57
Besana in Brianza: Italy	45 42 N	9 17 E	39B
Besançon: France	47 15 N	6 02 E	32C, 60D
Besessen: Ala., U.S.A.	49 30 N	87 00 W	54
Bessel: Pa., U.S.A.	40 59 N	80 31 W	57B
Besshi: Japan	33 52 N	133 10 E	59H
Bessines-sur-Gartempe: France	46 06 N	1 22 E	40B
Bethany: Okla., U.S.A.	35 30 N	97 37 W	
Bethal: South Africa	26 27 S	29 28 E	49
Bethel: Md., U.S.A.	39 07 N	75 35 W	62
Bethlehem: Pa., U.S.A.	40 36 N	75 22 W	43A, 57B, 63
Bethpage: N.Y., U.S.A.	40 46 N	73 28 W	
Betioky: admin., Malagasy R.	23 45 S	44 25 E	40C
Beverly: Mass., U.S.A.	42 35 N	70 52 W	32B
Beverly: N.J., U.S.A.	40 03 N	74 55 W	57
Bezau: island, Switzerland	38 05 N	58 12 E	40B
Bezons: France	48 56 N	2 13 E	32C, 58D
Bhakra: India	31 24 N	76 41 E	
Bhandara: India	21 10 N	79 41 E	31C
Bhatinda: India	21 46 N	74 40 E	
Bhilwara: admin., India	25 23 N	74 32 E	43, 59
Bhiwani: India	28 47 N	76 10 E	48
Bhopal: India	23 17 N	77 20 E	67
Biache-Saint-Vaast: France	50 18 N	2 57 E	29
Bibis: Germany F.R.	49 41 N	8 27 E	40B
Białystok: Poland	53 08 N	23 08 E	57C
Bicaz: Romania	46 54 N	26 04 W	49
Bicol: river, Philippines	13 44 N	123 08 E	31
Biddeford: Maine, U.S.A.	43 29 N	70 30 W	55A
Biel: Switzerland	47 09 N	7 16 E	29
Biella: Italy	45 34 N	8 03 E	29C
Bielsko-Biała: Poland	49 50 N	19 04 W	25A
Big Island: Va., U.S.A.	37 33 N	79 24 W	37I, 58A, 60G, 61B
Big Rock Point: Mich., U.S.A.	45 22 N	85 11 W	27, 38
Big Spring: Texas, U.S.A.	32 15 N	101 30 W	40
Bihar: admin., India	25 00 N	86 00 W	38
Bijni Munji: mtns., Romania			50
Bikin: U.S.S.R.	46 48 N	134 16 E	
Bikita: Rhodesia	20 06 N	31 41 E	49
Bilbao: Spain	43 15 N	2 58 W	31C
Bilbino: U.S.S.R.	68 03 N	166 20 E	55A
Bilimora: India	20 45 N	73 00 E	29C
Billingham: England	54 36 N	1 17 W	40A
Billings: Mont., U.S.A.	45 47 N	108 30 W	45
Billiton Co.: N.D., U.S.A.	47 00 N	103 10 W	
Billiton see Belitung: island, Indonesia			43B
Bilston: England	52 34 N	2 05 W	50C
Bindura: Rhodesia	17 18 N	31 19 E	49
Binangonan: Philippines	14 28 N	121 11 E	31
Bingham Canyon: U.S.A.	40 32 N	112 09 W	67A, 87B
Bingham, Utah, U.S.A.	42 06 N	112 55 W	40B
Binh Thuan: admin., South Vietnam	11 00 N	108 00 E	57C
Binsfeldhammer: G.F.R.	50 45 N	6 15 E	
Bintan, Pulau: island, Indonesia	1 04 N	104 30 E	43B
Birch, U.S.S.R.	29 28 N	30 40 W	47
Birkenhead: England	53 24 N	3 02 W	27
Birmingham: Ala., U.S.A.	33 30 N	86 55 W	43, 57B, 54B, 63B, 67B, 87C
Birmingham: England	52 30 N	1 50 W	37B, 54B, 55A, 63A, 63B, 67B,
Birobidzhan: U.S.S.R.	48 48 N	132 57 E	31
Birsacrosse: France	46 24 N	118 24 W	50A
Bishop: Calif., U.S.A.	37 25 N	95 40 W	59E
Bissett: Canada	51 01 N	95 40 W	39C
Bissina: Italy	44 35 N	10 20 E	17
Bistrița: Romania	47 09 N	24 30 W	47D, 60D
Bitterfeld: Germany D.R.	51 38 N	12 19 E	53B
Bitterwell: England	52 28 N	1 13 W	37H
Bizerte see Banzart: Tunisia	37 17 N	9 52 E	

Name	Lat	Long	Page(s)
Blachownia Śląska: Poland	50 24 N	18 18 E	58D, 58H, 60D
Blackburn: England	53 45 N	2 29 W	31B
Black Hills: C.D., U.S.A.	44 00 N	104 00 W	45, 50
Blackpool: England	53 50 N	3 03 W	87
Blackwell: Okla., U.S.A.	36 47 N	97 18 W	48
Blagnac: France	43 38 N	1 24 E	53B
Blagoveshchensk: U.S.S.R.	50 16 N	127 32 E	32C
Blair Athol: Australia	22 42 S	147 33 E	67
Blanes: Spain	41 41 N	2 48 E	32C
Blantyre: Malawi	15 47 S	35 00 E	67
Blaubeuren: Germany F.R.	48 24 N	9 47 E	67
Bleiberg-Kreuth: Austria	46 38 N	13 38 E	46B
Blida: Algeria	36 30 N	2 50 E	
Bloemfontein: South Africa	29 07 S	26 14 E	54, 67
Bloomfield: Conn., U.S.A.	41 50 N	72 44 W	37I, 58F
Blue Island: Ill., U.S.A.	41 40 N	87 42 W	40A
Bluewater: N. Mex., U.S.A.	35 16 N	107 58 W	27, 84
Bluff: New Zealand	46 38 N	168 21 W	61B
Blumenau: Brazil	26 55 S	49 04 W	39
Bly: island, U.S.A.	26 47 S	80 05 W	39
Boa Esperança: dam, Brazil	6 45 S	43 33 W	39
Boca Raton: Fla., U.S.A.	26 22 N	80 05 W	23B, 31B
Bocholt: Germany F.R.	51 50 N	6 36 E	23B, 58D
Bochum: Germany F.R.	51 29 N	7 12 E	59H
Bochum-Riemke: G.F.R.	51 30 N	7 12 E	
Bodaybo: U.S.S.R.	57 51 N	114 10 E	32A, 60C
Bodø: Norway	67 18 N	14 23 E	25A
Bôfu: Japan	34 03 N	131 34 E	67, 87
Bogalusa: La., U.S.A.	30 46 N	89 53 W	57A
Bogotá: Colombia	4 36 N	74 05 W	46B
Bogotol: U.S.S.R.	56 10 N	89 35 E	47
Boguchan: U.S.S.R.	58 23 N	97 29 E	39
Böhlen: Germany D.R.	51 11 N	13 18 E	37F
Bohunice: Czechoslovakia	49 51 N	16 39 E	40
Bohus: Sweden	48 30 N	12 40 E	62A
Boigny: France	47 55 N	2 01 E	
Boise: Idaho, U.S.A.	43 35 N	116 12 W	45, 39
Bois Noirs Les: mtns., France	45 45 N	3 45 E	36, 54
Boksitogorsk: U.S.S.R.	59 29 N	33 51 E	38
Bolan: deposit, Pakistan	29 45 N	67 23 E	29C
Boletice nad Labem: Czech.	50 44 N	14 12 E	45, 59
Boliden: Sweden	64 52 N	20 15 E	39C
Bolivar: admin., Venezuela	7 00 N	63 23 W	17
Bolivar, Cerro: mtn., Venezuela	7 28 N	63 25 W	43B
Bollene: France	44 17 N	4 43 E	58D, 60G
Bologna: Italy	44 30 N	11 20 E	57C
Bolsena: Italy	42 38 N	11 59 E	37D
Bolton: England	53 35 N	2 26 W	38B
Bolzano: Italy	46 31 N	11 22 E	50
Bombay: India	18 56 N	72 51 E	53B
Bomi Hills: Liberia	6 54 N	10 50 W	39A
Bonanza: Oreg., U.S.A.	42 11 N	121 24 W	61B
Bong Range: mines, Liberia	6 48 N	10 26 W	35
Bonner Springs: Kans., U.S.A.	39 04 N	94 53 W	46
Bonney Terre: Mo., U.S.A.	37 56 N	90 34 W	59F, 61B
Bonnie: Fla., U.S.A.	43 14 N	0 17 W	39A
Bonny: N. Mex., U.S.A.	60 24 N	25 40 E	45A
Boone: Nigeria	52 08 N	7 25 E	35
Booté: Brazil	45 20 N	7 30 W	61B
Boquira: Brazil	53 51 N	9 00 E	57D
Borås: Sweden	1 00 N	114 00 E	27, 48, 61
Bordeaux: France	58 24 N	33 55 E	25, 38
Bordes: France (Porvoo): Finland	41 40 N	20 45 W	40B
Borger: Texas, U.S.A.	46 14 N	16 10 E	59D, 61H
Borghorst: Germany F.R.	45 08 N	18 01 E	47B
Borgofranco d'Ivrea: Italy	44 15 N	17 50 W	37H
Borgo San Dalmazzo: Italy	53 31 N	120 00 E	38B
Borneo see Kalimantan: island, Indonesia	48 24 N	18 26 E	50
Borovichi: U.S.S.R.	40 19 N	27 48 W	59E
Borralha: Portugal	46 14 N	16 01 W	49
Borsod: Hungary	45 08 N	18 02 E	59D, 60H
Borssele: Netherlands	44 15 N	4 18 W	58D, 61D
Bosanska Krupa: Yugoslavia	53 15 N	120 00 E	53
Bosanski Brod: Yugoslavia	15 15 N	25 20 E	57
Bosanski Petrovo Selo: Yugo.	22 52 N	4 18 W	25D
Bosna i Hercegovina: admin., Yugoslavia	30 32 N	64 42 W	

Name	Lat	Long	Page(s)
Bou Beker: Morocco	34 30 N	1 48 W	46
Bouches-du-Rhône: admin., France	43 30 N	5 00 E	38B
Bogie: Algeria	44 08 N	104 22 W	17
Bouguenais: France	47 11 N	1 37 W	53B
Bou Khadra, Djebel: mtn., Algeria	35 45 N	8 00 E	43
Boulder: Colo., U.S.A.	40 02 N	105 10 W	50A, 62
Boulder Co.: Colo., U.S.A.	40 00 N	105 10 W	49B
Boulogne-sur-Mer: France	50 43 N	1 37 W	27C
Bourges: France	47 05 N	2 24 E	32B, 58B
Bourlamaque: Canada	48 05 N	77 56 W	53B, 53C
Bou Skour: Morocco	30 56 N	6 18 W	49
Boussens: France	43 11 N	0 58 E	45
Bowden: Australia	51 58 N	114 14 E	57C, 59D
Bowen: Australia	20 01 S	148 14 E	36
Bowen Island: Australia	35 16 N	107 28 E	48
Boyer: Australia	27 29 S	168 01 W	40A
Brabant: admin., Belgium	50 47 N	4 31 E	56A
Bradenton: Fla., U.S.A.	27 29 N	82 33 W	29, 87
Bradford: England	53 48 N	1 45 W	61B
Bradwell: England	51 48 N	0 54 W	39
Braga: Portugal	41 33 N	8 26 W	37I
Brainerd: Minn., U.S.A.	46 21 N	94 10 W	32C, 59D, 84
Bralorne: Canada	50 46 N	122 51 W	48
Brampton: Canada	43 41 N	79 46 W	55A
Brandenburg: Germany D.R.	52 24 N	12 33 E	43B
Brandon: Canada	49 50 N	99 57 W	58F
Brandon: Miss., U.S.A.	32 16 N	89 59 W	36, 59
Brani, Pulau: island, Singapore	1 15 N	103 50 E	57A
Brantford: Canada	43 09 N	80 17 W	45C
Brasília: Brazil	15 47 S	47 55 W	29, 38C, 37H, 57C
Brașov: Romania	45 38 N	25 35 E	
Bratislava (Pressburg): Czechoslovakia	48 10 N	17 08 E	37I, 43A, 57B, 58D, 59E, 67A,
Bratsk: dam, U.S.S.R.	56 05 N	101 48 E	87B
Bratsk: U.S.S.R.	56 17 N	101 55 E	31B, 55A, 60D, 87
Braubach: Germany F.R.	50 17 N	7 46 E	40
Braunschweig: Germany F.R.	52 16 N	10 32 E	57B
Brazeau: dam, Romania	52 56 N	115 28 W	37C
Brazzaville: Congo Republic	4 16 S	15 17 E	49
Brea: Calif., U.S.A.	33 55 N	117 54 W	
Brebach: Germany F.R.	49 13 N	7 03 E	37H, 58
Breda: Netherlands	51 35 N	4 46 E	61
Bredy: U.S.S.R.	52 26 N	60 21 E	58D
Bremen: admin., Germany F.R.	53 05 N	8 50 E	67B
Bremen: Germany F.R.	53 05 N	8 48 E	56A
Bremen: Ohio, U.S.A.	39 43 N	82 26 W	43B, 52A, 55,
Bremerhaven: Germany F.R.	53 33 N	8 35 W	58, 59, 60, 62, 67,
Bremerton: Wash., U.S.A.	48 21 N	122 40 W	53B, 57C, 58D,
Brennilis: France	48 21 N	3 51 W	59D, 67, 84A, 84C
Brescia: Italy	45 33 N	10 15 E	50
Brest: France	48 23 N	4 29 W	27C, 60H
Brest: U.S.S.R.	52 06 N	23 42 E	60H
Brevik: Norway	60 04 N	81 59 W	40B
Brewster: Ohio, U.S.A.	40 43 N	81 59 W	55A, 59D
Bria: Central African Republic	6 32 N	21 59 W	52A, 59H, 67B
Bridgeport: Conn., U.S.A.	41 12 N	73 12 W	57
Bridgeport: N.J., U.S.A.	39 48 N	75 21 W	54A
Bridgeport: Pa., U.S.A.	40 06 N	75 20 W	
Bridge River: Canada	50 50 N	122 12 W	53A, 55B, 67A
Bridgeville: Pa., U.S.A.	40 22 N	80 06 W	29A
Bridgman: Mich., U.S.A.	41 57 N	86 32 W	58B
Briey-Thionville, Bassin Ferrifère de: deposit, France			40C
Brighton: Trinidad	49 15 N	6 00 E	43B
Brignoud: France	45 15 N	5 54 E	36
Brimsdown: England	51 41 N	0 01 E	
Brindisi: Italy	40 40 N	17 56 E	37D, 58D, 58H,
Brisbane: Australia	27 30 S	153 01 E	59D, 60, 60H
Bristol: England	51 27 N	2 35 W	37D, 58H, 59D,
Bristol: Pa., U.S.A.	40 06 N	74 52 W	46
Bristol: R.I., U.S.A.	41 41 N	71 16 W	40B
Britannia Beach: Canada	49 38 N	123 11 W	45, 46
British Columbia: admin., Canada	54 00 N	125 00 W	
Brixham: England	50 24 N	3 30 W	16C, 27
Brixlegg: Austria	47 25 N	11 53 E	45
Brno: Czechoslovakia	49 10 N	16 39 E	29C
Broach: India	21 42 N	73 02 E	31C
Broadmeadows: Australia	37 40 N	141 26 E	31
Broken Hill: admin., Zambia	30 35 N	81 56 W	46, 46, 49, 50
Broken Hill: Australia	31 58 S	141 27 E	25D
Broken Hill: Zambia	15 15 N	28 27 E	50B
Bromsgrove: England	52 20 N	1 56 W	57
Brookfield: Canada	22 52 S	6 18 W	25D
Brooklyn: Canada	49 04 N	64 42 W	

Name	Lat	Long	Page(s)
Brooklyn: N.Y., U.S.A.	40 30 N	73 55 W	32B, 52, 56
Brough: England	54 32 N	0 36 W	53B
Brownlee: Czechoslovakia	50 46 N	116 59 W	31B
Brownlee: dam, Idaho, U.S.A.	44 36 N	87 00 W	39A
Brownsville: Ala., U.S.A.	25 54 N	97 30 W	40
Brownsville: Nebr., U.S.A.	40 23 N	96 49 W	40
Bruck an der Mur: Austria	47 25 N	15 17 E	40
Brugg: Switzerland	47 29 N	8 13 E	61B, 84
Bruhagen: Norway	63 02 N	8 45 E	40
Brunei: Brunei	4 53 N	114 56 E	87
Brunsbüttelkoog: Germany F.R.	53 54 N	9 08 E	
Brunswick: Ga., U.S.A.	31 09 N	81 30 W	59B
Bruxelles: admin., Belgium	50 50 N	4 20 E	59B
Bruxelles: Belgium	50 50 N	4 20 E	29B, 31B, 37B, 87D
Bryansk: U.S.S.R.	53 15 N	34 22 E	55A, 67B,
Brzezie: Poland	50 09 N	12 07 E	61D, 54, 57
Bua: Sweden	57 14 N	12 07 W	27D
Bucaramanga: Colombia	7 08 N	73 09 W	67, 87
Bucelas: Portugal	38 54 N	9 07 W	84
Buchanan: Liberia	5 53 N	10 03 W	45, 46, 49
Buchans: Canada	48 49 N	56 53 W	
Buckeye: Ariz., U.S.A.	44 26 N	26 06 E	29, 31, 54, 87
Buckingham: Canada	45 35 N	75 24 W	48
Bucksport: Maine, U.S.A.	44 35 N	68 47 W	25D
București (Bucharest): Romania	44 26 N	26 06 E	25D
Bucharest see București: Romania			36
Budapest: Hungary	47 30 N	19 05 E	29, 31, 54, 87, 55A, 54B, 59D, 59H, 87
Budel: Netherlands	51 17 N	5 35 E	46B
Buenaventura: Colombia	3 53 N	77 04 W	57A
Buenos Aires: Argentina	34 36 S	58 27 W	45C
Buffalo: N.Y., U.S.A.	42 52 N	78 55 W	27, 84
Buffelsfontein: South Africa	26 52 S	26 39 E	39
Buffington: Ind., U.S.A.	41 38 N	87 25 W	57B
Bū Ḥaṣaḥ: hill, Abu Dhabi	23 34 N	53 37 W	37C
Buhemba: Tanzania	1 46 S	34 05 E	49
Buhwa Mountain: Rhodesia	20 38 S	30 30 E	39
Bukachacha: U.S.S.R.	52 59 N	116 55 E	39
Bukhtarma: dam, U.S.S.R.	49 36 N	83 48 E	39
Bukit Asem: hill, Indonesia	4 16 S	103 46 E	43
Bukoba: Tanzania	1 35 S	31 30 E	50
Bukuka: U.S.S.R.	51 11 N	116 55 E	2, 49, 67
Bulawayo: Rhodesia	20 09 S	28 36 E	48
Buller: New Zealand	41 44 N	171 44 W	48
Bulolo River: New Guinea	7 08 S	146 40 E	
Bultfontein: mine, South Africa	27 03 S	25 48 E	57
Bulwer: island, Australia	27 23 S	153 08 E	84
Bumburi: region, Kenya	4 00 S	39 43 E	57B
Bunbury: Australia	33 20 S	115 38 E	40B
Bundaberg: Australia	24 51 S	152 21 E	57C
Bunnell: Fla., U.S.A.	29 28 N	81 16 W	55
Buñol: Spain	39 25 N	0 47 W	57
Burbach: Germany F.R.	49 41 N	7 13 W	57C
Burbank: Calif., U.S.A.	34 10 N	118 21 W	53
Burdwan: India	23 15 N	87 52 E	17, 30, 54, 58,
Bureinsk: deposit, U.S.S.R.	51 15 N	133 00 E	58D, 60D, 60H,
Burgas: Bulgaria	42 30 N	27 28 W	84B
Burghausen: Germany F.R.	48 10 N	12 50 E	37F, 58H, 59D,
Burgos: Spain	42 20 N	3 41 W	60D
Burjasot: Spain	21 18 N	76 08 W	38B
Burlington: N.J., U.S.A.	40 03 N	0 25 W	31C
Burlington: Vt., U.S.A.	44 29 N	73 14 W	40C, 60B
Burnaby: Australia	41 09 N	145 55 S	26, 87B
Burnpur: India	23 40 N	86 55 E	45, 54
Burnside: La., U.S.A.	30 05 N	90 55 W	47A, 59F
Burnt Island: N.C., U.S.A.	35 56 N	82 15 W	47
Burntisland: Scotland	56 03 N	3 15 W	
Burqān, Al: region, Kuwait	28 58 N	47 30 W	29, 32, 32C, 67
Bursa: Turkey	40 11 N	29 04 E	27, 84B
Bûr Safd (Port Said): U.A.R.	31 16 N	32 14 E	36, 84
Bûr Sûdân (Port Sudan): Sudan	19 37 N	37 14 E	25C, 31B
Bury: England	53 36 N	2 17 W	59D, 84D, 87
Busalla: Italy	44 34 N	8 57 E	59D, 61D
Busan see Pusan: South Korea			35
Bussi sul Tirino: Italy	42 12 N	13 49 E	
Busto Arsizio: Italy	45 37 N	8 51 E	45
Butler Co.: Ala., U.S.A.	31 45 N	86 43 W	54
Butte Co.: Idaho, U.S.A.	43 40 N	113 10 W	45A
Butte: Mont., U.S.A.	46 00 N	112 32 W	45
Butterworth: Malaysia	5 24 N	100 24 E	45C
Butuan: Philippines	8 56 N	125 31 E	67
Bydgoszcz: Poland	53 10 N	18 00 E	58H
Bystré: Czechoslovakia	49 01 N	21 32 E	57C

95

Name	Lat	Long	Page(s)
Cabangaan: Philippines	14 53 N	120 13 E	48
Cabedelo: Brazil	6 58 S	34 50 W	84
Cabinet Gorge: dam, Idaho, U.S.A.	48 06 N	116 02 W	39A
Cabo: Brazil	8 17 S	35 02 W	30
Cabo Bassa: dam, Mozambique	15 30 S	33 00 E	
Cachoeira Dourada: dam, Brazil	18 30 S		27B, 52, 84A
Cádiz: Spain	36 32 N	6 18 W	67B
Caen: France	49 11 N	0 22 W	
Cagayan de Oro: Philippines	8 29 N	124 40 E	49
Cagayan: river, Philippines	18 17 N	121 38 E	87
Cagliari: admin., Italy	39 30 N	8 45 E	37H, 57C, 58H, 59D, 60
Cagliari: Italy	39 13 N	9 07 E	
Cairns: Australia	16 55 S	145 46 E	84, 87
Cairo see Al Qāhirah: U.A.R.	30 03 N	31 15 E	29, 31, 32, 34, 67
Cajamarca: admin., Peru	6 15 S	78 50 W	46, 49
Calais: France	50 57 N	1 50 E	25C
Calbuco: Germany D.R.	41 46 S	11 46 E	84C
Calcutta: India	22 35 N	88 21 E	25, 31, 55, 58, 59, 67, 84, 87
Caldera: Chile	27 04 S	70 50 W	
Calder Hall Atomic Energy Station: England	54 23 N	3 32 W	40B
Caletones: Chile	34 06 S	70 27 W	
Calgary: Canada	51 05 N	114 05 W	36, 56, 59, 61, 67, 87
Calhoun: Tenn., U.S.A.	35 13 N	84 45 W	25A
Cali: Colombia	3 27 N	76 31 W	25, 60, 67, 87
Calicut (Kozhikode): India	11 15 N	75 49 E	67
Calima II: dam, Colombia	3 56 N	76 31 W	16, 17, 27, 35
Callao: Peru	12 05 S	77 08 W	39
Callide: Australia	24 19 S	150 28 E	27, 27A, 56, 59, 61, 67, 84
Caltanissetta: Italy	37 29 N	14 04 E	
Calumet: Canada	45 40 N	74 42 W	56
Calvert Island: Canada	51 30 N	128 00 W	57C
Calvados-d'Adda: Italy	45 40 N	9 38 E	43B
Calvert City: Ky., U.S.A.	37 02 N	88 22 W	40C
Calverton: N.Y., U.S.A.	40 55 N	72 46 W	53A
Camaguey: Cuba	21 23 N	77 55 W	
Camargo: Brazil	23 23 N	51 51 W	40B
Camas: Wash., U.S.A.	45 35 N	122 26 W	25
Camas Co.: Idaho, U.S.A.	43 35 N	115 00 W	25
Camayenne: Guinea	9 32 N	13 41 W	43
Cambambe: dam, Angola	9 32 N	14 30 E	34
Camberley: region, India	51 21 N	0 45 W	32C
Camborne: England	50 27 N	5 18 W	
Cambridge: Minn., U.S.A.	45 34 N	93 11 W	62
Cambridge: Ark., U.S.A.	35 57 N	75 06 W	38B
Camden: N.J., U.S.A.	39 57 N	75 06 W	38B, 49A, 50A
Camden: S.C., U.S.A.	34 16 N	80 37 W	48
Camiri: Bolivia	20 03 N	63 31 W	49A
Camopi: Bolivia	15 43 S	69 21 W	50B
Campana: Argentina	34 10 S	58 57 W	40B, 50
Campbellpore: Pakistan	33 46 N	72 22 E	38
Camperdown: Scotland	56 28 N	2 58 W	67
Campinas: Brazil	22 54 S	47 05 W	60
Campine see Kempenland: region, Belgium	51 10 N	5 20 E	23
Campo Durán: Argentina	22 14 S	63 42 W	25A, 59B
Campo Grande: Brazil	20 26 S	54 38 W	37J, 43A, 67A, 87B
Campo Santo: Argentina	24 40 S	65 05 W	
Campton: Ky., U.S.A.	37 44 N	83 35 W	25A
Cam Ranh: South Vietnam	11 54 N	109 12 E	48
Canaan: N.Y., U.S.A.	42 25 N	73 30 W	
Canal du Centre: canal, Belgium	50 27 N	4 06 E	32B, 60B
Cananea: Mexico	30 57 N	110 18 W	48
Canandaigua: France	12 49 S	75 03 W	49A
Canas: Mexico	22 40 N	102 42 E	50B
Canastra: Brazil	20 15 N	46 34 W	50B
Canavieiras: Brazil	15 41 S	38 57 W	40B, 50
Canberra: Australia	35 18 S	149 08 E	67, 87
Candeias: Brazil	12 40 S	38 33 W	60
Candela: Italy	41 08 N	15 31 E	49A
Candelaria: Mexico	18 11 N	91 12 W	50B
Çanakkale: Turkey	40 09 N	26 24 E	40B, 50
Cankiri: admin., France	40 48 N	34 36 E	38
Canterbury: admin., New Zealand	44 20 S	171 20 E	25A, 59B
Canterbury Plains: New Zealand	43 45 S	171 45 E	25, 32, 55, 57, 59, 60
Canton: N.C., U.S.A.	35 33 N	82 50 W	37J, 43A, 67A
Canton: Ohio, U.S.A.	40 48 N	81 23 W	87B
Canton see Kuang-chou: China P.R.	23 07 N	113 15 E	
Canvey Island: England	51 32 N	0 35 E	37B

Name	Lat	Long	Page(s)
Cao Bang: admin., North Vietnam	22 40 N	106 15 E	45
Cape Breton Island: Canada	46 00 N	60 30 W	36
Cape Girardeau: Mo., U.S.A.	37 19 N	89 31 W	57B
Capel: Australia	33 34 S	115 33 E	40, 50
Cape of Good Hope: admin., South Africa	31 00 S	23 00 E	16, 17
Cape Town: South Africa	33 56 S	18 28 E	27, 29, 36, 67, 84
Capitán Bermúdez: Argentina	32 49 S	60 43 W	87
Capivari-Cachoeira: dam, Brazil	25 23 S	48 59 W	60
Capreol: Canada	46 43 N	80 56 W	43A
Capri: island, Italy	40 33 N	14 13 E	17
Capuava: Brazil	23 56 S	46 55 W	58, 59, 56, 57, 60, 67, 87
Caracas: Venezuela	10 30 N	66 55 W	
Caracoles: Bolivia	16 59 S	67 24 W	48D
Carangola: Brazil	20 44 S	42 02 W	40A
Carapito: Venezuela	41 30 N	107 00 W	84C
Cardiff: Wales	51 30 N	3 13 W	43B, 54B, 67B
Carignan: France	44 48 N	0 29 W	87
Carillon: dam, Canada	45 34 N	74 21 W	39B
Carlentini: France	10 08 N	63 06 W	58D, 58H, 60II
Carloforte: Italy	39 08 N	8 18 E	61D, 80B, 58H
Carlsbad: Calif., U.S.A.	33 09 N	117 21 W	62
Carlstadt: N.J., U.S.A.	40 49 N	74 05 W	62
Carmaux: France	44 01 N	2 09 E	60D
Carnarvon: Australia	24 56 S	113 37 E	60D
Carnello: Italy	41 41 N	13 41 E	48
Carnot: Cent. Af. R.	4 56 N	15 52 E	61D, 61H
Carolina: South Africa	26 05 S	30 07 E	48
Carolusberg: South Africa	29 38 S	17 53 E	57
Carrara: Italy	44 05 N	10 06 E	61D, 58H, 60D,
Carrickfergus: Northern Ireland	54 43 N	5 49 W	32C
Carrington: England	53 26 N	2 24 W	32C, 60D
Carrizo Springs: Texas, U.S.A.	28 33 N	99 54 W	37J
Carson City: Mich., U.S.A.	43 11 N	84 50 W	37J
Cartagena: Colombia	10 25 N	75 32 W	45B
Cartagena: Spain	37 36 N	0 59 W	84A
Carteret: N.J., U.S.A.	40 35 N	74 14 W	
Carters: dam, Ga., U.S.A.	34 37 N	84 51 W	25D
Cartago: Costa Rica	9 50 N	83 56 W	
Carupano: Venezuela	10 40 N	63 13 W	60G
Carville: La., U.S.A.	30 10 N	91 06 W	57, 67, 84, 87
Casablanca: Morocco	33 39 N	7 35 W	55
Cascavel: Brazil	4 07 S	38 14 W	55
Caseros: Argentina	34 36 S	58 33 W	27A
Casma: Peru	9 30 S	78 18 W	32C
Casoria: Italy	40 54 N	14 17 E	48
Casper: Wyo., U.S.A.	42 50 N	106 20 W	17
Cassinga: Angola	15 08 S	16 05 E	46
Cassiar: Canada	59 15 N	129 49 W	32C, 60D
Cassis: France	43 13 N	5 32 E	58H, 61H
Castaño Viejo: Argentina	30 59 S	69 34 W	36, 58H,
Castelaccio: Italy	40 42 N	16 30 E	27B, 37D, 46B,
Castellammare di Stabia: Italy	40 42 N	14 29 E	49, 59H, 61H,
Castellanza: Italy	45 37 N	8 54 E	84A
Castellón de la Plana: Spain	39 59 N	0 02 W	
Castillejo: Spain	39 51 N	3 44 W	61D
Castle Donington: England	52 51 N	1 19 W	87
Castleford: Scotland	53 44 N	1 21 W	62
Castle Hayne: N.C., U.S.A.	34 21 N	77 54 W	61D
Castlereagh: Northern Ireland	54 35 N	5 54 W	57
Castrop-Rauxel: Germany F.R.	51 33 N	7 19 E	57, 59H, 84A
Catania: Italy	37 31 N	15 06 E	57
Catanzaro: Italy	38 54 N	16 35 E	57C
Catavi: Bolivia	18 24 S	66 40 W	25A
Catawba: S.C., U.S.A.	34 51 N	80 57 W	37J, 58B
Catlettsburg: Ky., U.S.A.	38 24 N	82 37 W	49B
Catorce: Mexico	23 40 N	100 50 W	57B
Catron Co.: N. Mex., U.S.A.	34 00 N	108 30 W	57C
Catskill: N.Y., U.S.A.	42 14 N	73 52 W	36
Cauldon: England	53 03 N	1 54 W	60
Cauquenes: Chile	35 58 S	72 19 W	60
Cavite: Philippines	14 30 N	120 54 E	48
Cawnpore see Kanpur: India	26 27 N	80 14 E	48
Caxias: Brazil	4 50 S	43 21 W	36
Caxito: Angola	8 35 S	13 38 W	61F
Cayenne: French Guiana	4 55 N	52 18 W	60, 67
Cayo Guam, Rio: river, Cuba	22 12 S	74 54 W	48
Ceará: admin., Brazil	5 00 S	39 00 W	27
Cebu: Philippines	10 17 N	123 46 E	38
Cebu: island, Philippines	10 15 N	123 40 E	67, 84
Cedar Bayou: Texas, U.S.A.	29 41 N	94 56 W	58E, 60A
Cedar Rapids: Iowa, U.S.A.	41 59 N	91 39 W	87B
Cedar Springs: Ga., U.S.A.	31 10 N	85 03 W	25A
Cedral: Mexico	23 48 N	100 44 W	49A
Celebes see Sulawesi: island, Indonesia	2 00 S	121 00 E	27, 50

Name	Lat	Long	Page(s)
Çelik: Turkey	40 33 E		38
Celje: Yugoslavia	46 14 N	15 16 E	46B, 59H
Cellino: region, Italy	42 35 N	13 50 E	37B
Cement City: Mich., U.S.A.	42 07 N	84 18 W	57B
Cementon: Pa., U.S.A.	40 42 N	75 31 W	57B
Cengio: Italy	44 23 N	8 12 E	29A
Centerdale: R.I., U.S.A.	41 50 N	71 30 W	58H
Central Asia: reg., U.S.S.R.	40 00 N	73 00 E	54A
Central, Ill., U.S.A.	38 32 N	89 08 W	49
Central Region: admin., Ghana			17
Central Valley of Chile see Vaca Longitudinal: valley, Chile	36 00 S	72 00 W	
Centre Atomique de Marcoule: France	44 08 N	4 42 E	40D
Centre/Mons: region, Belgium	50 25 N	3 55 E	38B
Ceres: South Africa	33 23 S	19 19 E	31B
Céroux-Mousty: Belgium	50 40 N	4 31 E	37H
Cërrik: Albania	41 02 N	19 59 E	27A
Cerro Azul: Peru	13 05 S	76 29 W	43
Cerro Bolivar: mtn., Venezuela	7 25 N	66 01 W	45
Cerro Chorolque: mtn., Bolivia	20 56 S	76 15 W	49A
Cerro de Pasco: Peru	10 43 S	100 49 W	49A
Cerro Iticamul: mtn., Argentina	22 13 N	54 20 W	45
Cerro Largo: admin., Uruguay	32 20 S	54 00 W	31B
Cerro Maggiore: Italy	45 36 N	8 57 E	45
Cerro Potosi: mtn., Bolivia	19 37 S	65 45 W	31B
Cesano Maderno: Italy	45 30 N	9 08 E	32C, 60D
Ceská Skalice: Czechoslovakia	50 24 N	16 03 E	11B
Cevennes: France	44 10 N	3 48 E	50
Chacarilla: Bolivia	17 48 N	68 19 W	60D
Chacras de Coria: Argentina	33 00 S	68 52 E	48
Chagan-Uzun: U.S.S.R.	50 06 N	88 22 E	60
Chagres: Chile	30 00 S	70 58 W	45
Chaibassa: India	22 31 N	85 53 W	50
Chalatpata: Bolivia	18 54 S	67 49 W	50
Chalchihuites: Mexico	23 29 N	103 53 W	49A
Chalchuapa: El Salvador	14 00 N	89 41 W	17
Chalmette: La., U.S.A.	29 57 N	89 58 W	37J, 47A, 58A
Chalon-sur-Saône: France	46 47 N	4 51 E	17, 32C
Chambéry: France	45 34 N	5 56 E	17
Chambishi: Zambia	12 40 S	28 03 E	45B
Champagnier: France	45 06 N	5 43 E	30B
Champagnole: France	46 45 N	5 55 E	57C
Champaign: Ill., U.S.A.	40 07 N	88 14 W	67A, 87B
Chancay: Peru	11 36 S	77 14 W	27A
Chandler: Ariz., U.S.A.	33 18 N	111 49 W	61
Chandraghona: Pakistan	22 23 N	92 06 W	43
Ch'ang-chiang: China P.R. (Yangtze Basin)	30 00 N	109 01 E	60G
Changhang: South Korea	31 48 N	125 21 E	57, 67, 84, 87
Chang-hua: Taiwan	36 12 N	126 45 E	55
Ch'ang-lo-chieh: China P.R.	24 06 N	120 32 E	55
Ch'ang-p'u: China P.R.	28 30 N	114 14 E	27A
Ch'ang-sha: China P.R.	28 12 N	112 58 E	32C
Ch'ang-shou: China P.R.	29 50 N	107 04 W	48
Changsu-ri: South Korea	35 39 N	127 37 E	17
Channelview: Texas, U.S.A.	29 46 N	95 26 W	46
Chanute: Kans., U.S.A.	37 41 N	95 27 W	57A
Chapais: Canada	49 47 N	74 52 E	57
Chapel Cross: England	55 05 N	3 15 W	45, 49
Charcas: Mexico	23 53 N	101 07 W	40B
Charleroi: Belgium	50 25 N	4 26 W	46, 49A
Charleston: S.C., U.S.A.	32 48 N	79 58 W	38B, 67B
Charleston: Tenn., U.S.A.	35 17 N	84 44 W	59F, 67, 84, 87C
Charleston: W. Va., U.S.A.	38 22 N	81 39 W	25A, 53, 58B
Charlotte: N.C., U.S.A.	35 03 N	80 50 W	58F, 59E, 67A,
Charlottesville: Va., U.S.A.	38 02 N	121 44 E	87C
Charvaksskaya: dam, U.S.S.R.	41 35 N	69 54 E	30A, 60B, 87C
Chascomús: Argentina	35 34 S	78 34 W	39
Chasse: France	45 35 N	4 48 E	87C
Chassong: dam, North Korea	41 15 N	126 32 E	39
Château-Pape: France	44 09 N	4 50 E	39
Châteauneuf-du-Pape: France	44 03 N	4 52 E	61H
Châtillon: N.Y., U.S.A.	42 22 N	73 36 W	39
Chattanooga: Tenn., U.S.A.	35 02 N	85 18 W	25D
Chauk: Burma	20 53 N	94 49 E	32C
Chaun: South Korea	37 32 N	128 00 E	32C
Chauny: France	49 37 N	3 13 W	32A, 30A, 31A,
Chavantes: dam, Brazil	49 20 S	49 43 W	32B, 30A, 57B,
Chaykovskiy: U.S.S.R.	56 47 N	54 09 W	58A, 60B, 61B,
Cheboksarskaya: dam, U.S.S.R.	56 08 N	46 52 E	61E, 87C
Chedde: France	45 55 N	6 43 W	45, 49
Chelan: dam, Wash., U.S.A.	47 50 N	120 30 W	50
Chełm: Poland	51 08 N	23 29 E	58D
Cheltenham: England	51 54 N	2 04 W	39
Chelyabinsk: U.S.S.R.	55 10 N	61 24 E	84, 37B
Chembur: India	19 03 N	72 54 E	67

Name	Lat	Long	Page(s)
Chemnitz see Karl-Marx-Stadt: Germany D.R.	50 50 N	12 55 E	29C, 31B
Chemor: Malaysia	4 43 N	101 07 E	57
Cheng-chou: China P.R.	34 45 N	113 40 E	50
Ch'eng-te: China P.R.	40 58 N	117 53 E	50
Ch'eng-tu: China P.R.	30 40 N	104 04 E	25, 61, 67
Cherbourg: France	49 39 N	1 39 W	27C, 84C
Cherdoyak: U.S.S.R.	48 48 N	84 00 E	45
Cheremkhovo: U.S.S.R.	53 09 N	103 05 E	38, 67
Cherepovets: U.S.S.R.	59 08 N	37 54 E	43
Cherkassy: U.S.S.R.	49 26 N	32 04 E	32C, 60, 61
Chernigov: U.S.S.R.	51 30 N	31 18 E	29, 32C
Cherokee: Ala., U.S.A.	34 45 N	87 59 W	31
Cherokee Co., Ga., U.S.A.	34 13 N	84 29 W	61B, 61E
Cherry Creek: Nev., U.S.A.	39 54 N	114 53 W	48
Chesapeake: Va., U.S.A.	36 50 N	76 15 W	50, 50A
Cheshire, Lancashire and: region, England	53 30 N	2 30 W	43B
Cheshunt: England	51 43 N	0 02 W	56A
Chester: England	53 12 N	2 54 W	55A
Chester: Pa., U.S.A.	39 50 N	75 23 W	46B, 53B
Chester: S.C., U.S.A.	34 43 N	81 14 W	25D, 52
Chesterfield: England	53 15 N	1 25 W	32B
Cheswold: Del., U.S.A.	39 13 N	75 36 W	58H, 59D, 59H
Cheyenne: Wyo., U.S.A.	41 08 N	104 50 W	30A
Chia-mu-ssu: China P.R.	46 50 N	130 21 E	36, 37J, 61
Chiang-hsi (Kiangsi): admin., China P.R.	28 00 N	116 00 E	25
Chiang Mai: Thailand	18 47 N	98 59 E	50D
Chiapas: Bolivia	17 40 S	68 19 W	98
Chiao-men: China P.R.	22 35 N	113 05 E	25
Chiao-ho: China P.R.	33 00 S	127 13 E	38C
Chiao-tso: China P.R.	35 15 N	113 13 E	38C
Chiatura: U.S.S.R.	42 43 N	43 18 E	50
Chiavari: Italy	44 19 N	9 19 E	50B
Chia-wang: China P.R.	34 27 N	117 27 E	38C
Chiba: Japan	35 36 N	140 07 E	35, 36, 37E, 43D, 47C, 52B, 58C, 58G, 59C, 60C, 60E, 61C, 61G
Chibougamau: Zambia	49 56 N	74 24 W	45, 49
Chibuluma: Zambia	12 43 S	28 07 E	3, 25, 25D, 34, 43A, 55, 56,
Chicago: Ill., U.S.A.	41 50 N	87 45 W	58D, 59I, 63, 67A, 84, 87B
Chicago Heights: Ill., U.S.A.	41 31 N	87 39 W	54A
Ch'i-ch'i-ha-erh (Tsitsihar): China P.R.	35 59 N	139 05 E	43D, 46C, 57D
Chichoki Mallian: Pakistan	47 22 N	123 57 E	25, 54, 67
Chicken Creek: Alaska, U.S.A.	31 42 N	74 05 W	38
Chiclayo: Peru	64 04 N	142 00 W	49
Chicoutimi: Canada	6 47 S	79 47 W	67
Chief Joseph: dam, Wash., U.S.A.	48 26 N	71 04 W	84
Chigirishima: Japan	48 04 N	119 43 W	39A
Chih-chiang: China P.R.	34 22 N	132 40 E	46C
Chihuahua: admin., Mexico	45 18 N	130 58 E	38
Chihuahua: Mexico	28 38 N	106 05 W	25, 32, 34, 49A
Chikugo: Japan	33 15 N	130 27 E	61, 67
Chilca: Peru	12 33 S	76 41 W	38C
Childersburg: Ala., U.S.A.	33 16 N	86 21 W	32B, 59F
Chi-lin (Kirin): admin., China P.R.	43 00 N	126 00 E	50
Chi-lin (Kirin): China P.R.	43 51 N	126 33 E	25, 36, 43, 49, 61
Chillicothe: Ohio, U.S.A.	38 20 N	83 00 W	25D
Chi-lung: Taiwan	15 12 S	121 44 E	60, 84
Chilwa, Lake: Malawi	42 18 N	78 34 W	27
Chimbote: Peru	9 04 S	69 36 E	27, 27A
Chimkent: U.S.S.R.	42 18 N	69 36 E	31, 46, 57
Chimney Rock Hollow: dam, Okla., U.S.A.	36 15 N	95 10 W	39
Chi-nan (Tsinan): China P.R.	36 40 N	117 00 E	43, 55, 61
Ch'in-chou: China P.R.	21 57 N	108 37 E	50D
Chinghai see Hsi-ning: China P.R.	41 07 N	121 06 E	40
Ch'ing-hai: China P.R.	36 37 N	101 46 E	29, 43, 67
Ch'ing-hsing: China P.R.	39 56 N	116 24 E	50D, 61C
Ch'ing-tao (Tsingtao): China P.R.	25 07 N	121 51 E	59G, 61C, 61G
Chinon: France			47, 84
Chinsura: India	47 10 N	0 15 E	45, 49
Chippis: Switzerland	46 17 N	7 33 E	50
Chirchik: U.S.S.R.	41 29 N	69 35 E	17, 40B
Chiren: Bulgaria	43 36 N	23 40 E	31
Chirkeyskaya: dam, U.S.S.R.	42 30 N	46 50 E	47B
Chisimaio: Somali Republic	0 22 S	42 30 E	34, 37B
Chita: U.S.S.R.	52 03 N	113 30 E	84, 67
Chita-Hantō: pen., Japan	34 50 N	136 53 E	60E

Name	Lat	Long	Page(s)
Dehra Dun: India	30 19 N	78 03 E	67
Dehra-on-Son: India	24 45 N	84 11 E	49
Dekin, U.S.A.	39 35 N	76 00 W	27
Delaware City: Del., U.S.A.	45 23 N	75 36 W	60F
Delfzijl: Netherlands	53 19 N	6 56 E	47, 59D
Delhi: India	28 40 N	77 14 E	31, 67, 87
Delinesti: Romania	45 23 N	22 05 E	50B
Delmar see Georgetown: Guyana	6 46 N	58 10 W	27, 47, 67, 84, 87
Demirci: Turkey	40 20 N	33 13 E	38
Demir Kapija: Yugoslavia	41 25 N	22 15 E	57B
Demopolis: Ala., U.S.A.	32 30 N	87 50 W	43B
Den Haag see 's Gravenhage: Netherlands	52 05 N	4 16 E	63A, 63B
Denver: Colo., U.S.A.	39 45 N	105 00 W	36, 37J, 55, 59, 62, 67, 87
Denver City: Texas, U.S.A.	32 58 N	102 50 W	59E
Depue: Ill., U.S.A.	41 19 N	89 20 W	59E
Deputatskiy: U.S.S.R.	69 18 N	139 54 E	45
Dera Ghazi Khan: admin., Pakistan	29 50 N	70 15 E	40
Derby: England	52 55 N	1 30 W	53B, 54B
Deresi Uzulmez: river, Turkey	41 08 N	31 49 E	38
Derince: Turkey	40 46 N	27 52 W	84B
Derrio: Spain	43 18 N	2 53 W	59D
Des Moines: Iowa, U.S.A.	41 35 N	93 35 W	57, 87B
De Soto: Kans., U.S.A.	38 57 N	94 57 W	59E
Dessau: Germany D.R.	51 50 N	12 15 E	54B
Destilería Chachapoyas: Arg.	24 45 S	65 03 W	61
Detroit: Mich., U.S.A.	42 23 N	83 05 W	25D, 34, 37J, 43A, 48, 55B, 59E, 62, 63, 58B, 59E, 64, 87B
Deutz: Germany F.R.	50 56 N	6 59 E	55A
Devils Slide: Utah, U.S.A.	41 04 N	111 31 W	61H
Devnya: Bulgaria	43 13 N	27 33 E	50
Devoll: region, Albania	40 49 N	20 25 E	84
Devonport: Australia	41 11 N	146 21 E	57A
Devrek: Turkey	41 14 N	31 57 W	38
Dewas: India	23 04 N	76 05 E	29B
Dewsbury: England	53 42 N	1 38 W	46
Dhahran:	47 59 N	86 32 E	59B
Dhanbad: India	23 47 N	86 30 E	47
Dhistomon: Greece	38 57 N	22 40 E	50B
Dhomokos: Greece	39 07 N	22 40 E	31C
Dhulia: India	20 52 N	74 50 E	60
Diablo Canyon: Calif., U.S.A.	35 16 N	120 47 W	39B
Diavata: region	40 40 N	69 06 W	60
Dickey: dam, Maine, U.S.A.	47 05 N	69 06 W	17
Didiran: U.S.A.	51 59 N	139 00 E	39
Dieblich: Germany F.R.	50 20 N	7 31 E	84A
Diego-Suarez: mtn., Algeria	49 17 N	2 06 E	84
Diepholz: Germany F.R.	52 36 N	8 22 E	84B
Dieppe: France	49 56 N	1 05 E	54B
Dieuze: France	48 49 N	6 43 E	27C, 84C
Diez de Octubre: Mexico	24 44 N	104 39 W	49A
Differdange: Luxembourg	49 32 N	5 53 E	43B
Digboi: India	27 24 N	95 34 E	36
Dijon: France	47 19 N	5 03 E	39
Dike Creek: dam, Texas, U.S.A.	33 08 N	97 10 W	39B
Dila, Bela: mtn., India	48 31 N	21 21 E	43B, 61D
Dillingen: Germany F.R.	49 21 N	6 44 E	38, 59H
Dimashq (Damascus): Syria	33 30 N	36 15 E	87
Dimitrovgrad: Bulgaria	42 03 N	25 36 E	50
Dimmitt: Texas, U.S.A.	34 33 N	102 20 W	40B
Dinant: Belgium	50 15 N	125 30 E	27
Dinagat: is., Philippines	10 12 N	125 30 E	31C
Dingle: Irish Republic	52 08 N	10 15 W	27C
Dinslaken: Germany F.R.	51 35 N	6 44 E	55A
Diredawa: Ethiopia	9 35 N	41 50 E	84
Dixon: Ill., U.S.A.	41 52 N	89 30 W	37F, 58D
Divriği: Turkey	39 23 N	38 07 E	38
Djakarta: Indonesia	6 10 S	106 48 E	67
Djawa Barat, Daerat Tingkat i: admin., Indonesia	7 00 S	107 00 E	61
Djebel Bou Khadra: mtn., Algeria	35 45 N	8 00 E	43
Djebel Ouenza: mtns., Algeria	35 57 N	8 06 W	34, 37B
Djema de M'Rirt: Morocco	33 10 N	6 03 E	47B
Djember: admin., Indonesia	8 15 S	113 45 E	57
Derissa: Tunisia	35 51 N	8 38 E	61A
Djokjakarta see Jogjakarta: Indonesia	7 48 S	110 22 E	38
Dneprodzerzhinsk: U.S.S.R.	48 31 N	34 35 E	39
Dnepropetrovsk: U.S.S.R.	48 29 N	34 59 E	49
Dobresti: Romania	46 51 N	22 18 E	50
Dobrovat: U.S.S.R.	54 42 N	32 41 E	57
Dodge City: Kans., U.S.A.	37 45 N	100 02 W	55A
Dodurga: Turkey	40 52 N	34 50 E	38

Name	Lat	Long	Page(s)
Doel: Belgium	51 19 N	4 16 E	40B
Dok-um: South Korea	34 55 N	126 35 E	49
Dolinsk: U.S.S.R.	47 21 N	142 48 E	25
Dolisie: Congo Republic	4 12 S	12 41 E	49
Dolni Dubnik: admin., Bulgaria	43 24 N	24 26 E	37D
Domat (Ems): Switzerland	46 51 N	9 28 E	32C, 60D, 61D
Dombarovskiy: U.S.S.R.	50 46 N	59 32 E	49
Dombasle-sur-Meurthe: France	48 38 N	6 21 E	48
Dominguez: Calif., U.S.A.	33 50 N	118 13 W	59D
Donnarvet: Sweden	60 00 N	15 27 E	59
Donaldsonville: La., U.S.A.	30 05 N	91 00 W	43
Donauwörth: Germany F.R.	48 43 N	10 48 E	61B, 61E
Doncaster: England	53 32 N	1 07 W	59, 54B
Donetsk: U.S.S.R.	48 00 N	37 48 E	43C
Donetskiy Basseyn: basin, U.S.S.R.	48 30 N	38 30 E	32C
Donges: France	47 18 N	2 04 W	38
Donora: Pa., U.S.A.	40 11 N	79 54 W	37F, 58D
Don Otto: Argentina	25 26 S	66 20 W	40
Doornhoek: South Africa	28 30 S	28 50 E	45
Dorchester: Canada	45 54 N	64 32 W	60
Dordrecht: Netherlands	51 48 N	4 40 E	61B
Doringbaai: bay, South Africa	31 48 S	18 15 E	53B
Dormagen: Germany F.R.	51 06 N	6 50 E	27
Dorogomilovo: U.S.S.R.	55 45 N	37 34 E	50D, 58H, 59D, 60D, 61H
Dortmund: Germany F.R.	51 31 N	7 27 E	58
Dothan: Ala., U.S.A.	31 12 N	85 25 N	43B, 58D, 60H, 61H
Douai: France	4 03 N	9 42 E	59F, 87C
Douaria: Tunisia	48 06 N	9 11 E	27, 56, 67, 84
Douarnenez: France	31 44 N	4 20 W	43
Douglas: Ariz., U.S.A.	44 44 N	69 34 W	40C
Douglas: Point, Canada	35 20 N	81 35 W	37J
Douglasville: Ga., U.S.A.	35 26 N	84 45 W	37D
Douleb: region, Tunisia	33 00 S	9 05 W	40
Dounreay: Scotland	53 08 N	2 50 E	54A
Douro: river	41 08 N	1 19 E	61D
Douro Valley: Portugal	40 01 N	8 14 E	84A
Dover: England	40 08 N	75 43 W	32B, 62
Downey: Calif., U.S.A.	33 28 N	79 29 W	53A
Downingtown: Pa., U.S.A.	44 19 N	24 06 E	57
Downsview: Canada	59 44 N	10 15 E	25B
Dow Rüd: Iran	45 03 N	13 45 E	25C, 60D
Drammen: Norway	59 44 N	49 23 E	35C
Drava: river, Europe	45 33 N	10 08 W	32C
Dresden: Germany D.R.	53 46 N	10 27 E	47
Drighlington: England	43 52 N	72 30 W	40A
Drnis: Yugoslavia	43 50 N	6 21 W	59A
Drocourt: France	55 37 N	118 52 W	87
Drogheda: Irish Republic	45 22 N	11 42 E	60
Drummondville: Canada	52 09 N	2 09 E	60, 61, 67, 87
Drütte: Germany F.R.	49 18 N	0 57 E	29B
Dryden: Canada	53 18 N	6 15 W	43B, 84C
Dublin: Irish Republic	25 18 N		57
Du Bois: Pa., U.S.A.	41 06 N	78 46 W	54A
Dubová: Czechoslovakia	48 49 N	19 26 E	54A
Dubrava: Czechoslovakia	42 31 N	19 30 E	50, 50B
Dubuque: Iowa, U.S.A.	42 31 N	90 41 W	59E
Duisburg: Germany F.R.	51 26 N	6 45 E	43B, 46B, 59H
Dukhan: Qatar	25 25 N	50 50 E	37C
Duluth: Minn., U.S.A.	51 50 N	92 10 W	37D
Dumas: Texas, U.S.A.	35 51 N	101 57 W	43A, 57, 84, 87
Dum Dum: India	22 37 N	88 25 N	35
Dumya (Damietta): admin., U.A.R.	31 20 N	31 45 E	54
Dunaújváros: Hungary	46 00 N	18 55 E	43B
Dunbar: Scotland	56 00 N	2 30 W	57
Duncan: Canada	48 46 N	123 40 W	25
Duncan: Okla., U.S.A.	34 30 N	97 57 W	84C
Dundalk: Irish Republic	43 16 N	6 24 W	57B
Dundee: Scotland	55 35 N	4 36 W	32C
Dundonald: Scotland	55 35 N	87 00 W	40C
Dune Acres: Ind., U.S.A.	45 52 S	170 30 E	87
Dunedin: New Zealand	54 31 N	6 46 W	32C
Dungannon: Northern Ireland	51 57 N	0 58 E	40B
Dungeness: England	51 03 N	2 22 E	84C
Dunkirk see Dunkerque: France			
Dunkwa: Ghana Republic	5 58 N	1 47 W	49
Duque de Caxias: Brazil	22 47 S	43 18 W	27C
Durack Range: mtns., Australia	16 50 N	127 40 E	30
Durango: admin., Mexico	24 50 S	104 50 W	84C
Durban: South Africa	31 00 N		29, 56, 59, 67, 84, 87
Durg: admin., India	22 00 N	81 10 E	32C
Durgapur: India	23 30 N	87 20 E	40B
Durham, England	54 50 N	1 34 W	84C

Name	Lat	Long	Page(s)
Durham, Northumberland and: region, England	55 00 N	2 00 W	56A
Durnstein: Austria	48 23 N	15 31 E	17
Durrës: Albania	41 19 N	19 26 E	59H
Düsseldorf: Germany F.R.	51 13 N	6 46 E	25C, 55A, 58D, 58H, 87D
Dutoitspan: mine, South Africa	28 48 S	24 48 E	56A
Dwarka: India	22 15 N	69 03 E	57
Dworshak: dam, Idaho, U.S.A.	46 31 N	116 16 W	39A
Dyushambe: U.S.S.R.	38 38 N	68 48 E	31, 57, 67
Dzerzhinsk: U.S.S.R.	56 15 N	43 24 E	59, 60
Dzerzhinsk: U.S.S.R.	48 22 N	61 12 E	58, 49
Dzhezkazgan: U.S.S.R.	47 53 N	67 27 E	45, 57
Dzhida: U.S.S.R.	50 41 N	116 03 E	50
Dzhirgalan: U.S.S.R.	51 27 N	79 02 E	38
Dzialoszyn: Poland	51 06 N	18 50 E	57C
E			
Eagle Co.: Colo., U.S.A.	39 40 N	106 30 W	46, 49B
Eagle Mountain: Calif., U.S.A.	33 50 N	115 30 W	43
Easley: S.C., U.S.A.	34 50 N	82 34 W	37B
Easington: England	54 45 N	0 00 W	31A
East Anglia: region, England	52 45 N	1 00 E	14
East Broughton: Canada	46 14 N	71 05 W	48
East Chicago: Ind., U.S.A.	41 38 N	87 27 W	37J, 43A
East Dubuque: Ill., U.S.A.	42 30 N	90 37 W	61A
Eastern Counties: region, Eng.	52 15 N	0 15 E	56A
Eastern Visayas: is., Philippines	11 30 N	125 00 W	49
East Fishkil: N.Y., U.S.A.	41 33 N	73 47 W	62
Eastham: England	53 19 N	2 58 W	37F
East Hartford: Conn., U.S.A.	41 46 N	72 38 W	53A, 63
East Kilbride: Scotland	55 46 N	4 10 W	37, 31, 55, 67, 84, 87
East London: South Africa	33 00 S	27 54 E	27, 31, 32C, 55, 60
East Midlands: region, England	53 30 N	1 15 E	38B, 37D, 56A
East Rochester: N.Y., U.S.A.	43 05 N	77 30 W	54A
Enka: N.C., U.S.A.	35 30 N	82 34 W	37J, 46, 59E
East St. Louis: Ill., U.S.A.	38 35 N	90 04 W	48
East Sayan Region: U.S.S.R.	54 00 N	98 00 E	50
Ébange: France	49 19 N	6 08 E	57C
Ebensee: Austria	47 47 N	3 12 W	84
Eberlare: dam, Austria	47 10 N	11 50 E	43B
Ebetsu: Japan	43 07 N	141 34 E	59D
Eboli: Italy	49 49 N	6 25 E	39C
Eola: La., U.S.A.	31 54 N	92 12 W	25
Epe: Germany F.R.	52 13 N	7 03 E	32C, 60D
Épernay: France	49 03 N	3 58 E	32C
Erdington: England	52 31 N	1 54 W	47
Erwitte: Germany F.R.	45 32 N	8 05 W	40A
Erzgebirge (Krušné Hory): Germany D.R.	50 25 N	13 00 E	59A
Erzincan: Turkey	44 17 N	44 25 E	87
Erfurt: Germany D.R.	50 59 N	11 02 E	59
Erie: Pa., U.S.A.	42 07 N	80 05 W	60, 61, 67, 87

Name	Lat	Long	Page(s)
Ellesmere Port: England	53 17 N	2 54 W	25, 25B, 37F, 55A, 60H
Elliot Lake: Canada	46 24 N	82 41 W	40C
Ellweiler: Germany F.R.	49 37 N	7 09 E	40B
Elmira: Canada	43 36 N	80 24 W	59E, 59E, 87B
Elmira Heights: N.Y., U.S.A.	42 08 N	76 49 W	55B
El Mochito: Honduras	14 49 N	88 07 W	46, 49
El Palito: Venezuela	10 29 N	68 07 W	36
El Paso: Venezuela	8 01 N	62 38 W	43
El Paso: Texas, U.S.A.	31 45 N	106 30 W	37J, 45A, 57, 67, 87
El Puerto de Santa María: Spain	36 36 N	6 13 W	17
El Romeral: Chile	29 43 N	71 15 W	43
El Salvador: Chile	26 10 S	69 24 W	59
El Segundo: Calif., U.S.A.	33 56 N	118 25 W	45, 49, 50, 36, 58, 60
Els Monjos: Spain	41 19 N	1 40 E	57C
El Soldado: Chile	32 42 S	71 05 W	58
El Toño: Chile	29 27 S	71 33 W	43
Elwood: Ill., U.S.A.	41 23 N	88 06 W	59E
Elworth: England	53 08 N	2 22 W	59D
Ely: England	52 24 N	0 16 E	36, 50, 50A
Emarese: Italy	45 43 N	7 41 E	54B
Emba: region, U.S.S.R.	47 00 N	54 00 E	35
Embsen: Germany F.R.	53 11 N	7 13 E	61H
Emden: Germany F.R.	53 22 N	7 13 E	37F, 52A, 84C
Emery Co.: Utah, U.S.A.	39 00 N	110 45 W	40A
Emlenton: Pa., U.S.A.	41 12 N	79 43 W	37J
Emmenbrücke: Switzerland	47 04 N	8 17 E	60D
Emmer-Compascuum: Neths.	52 49 N	7 03 E	60D
Empress: Canada	50 56 N	110 01 W	60
Ems see Domat: Switzerland	46 51 N	9 28 E	32C, 60D, 61D
Encruzilhada do Sul: Brazil	30 32 S	52 31 W	50
Endako: Canada	54 04 N	125 03 W	50
Engel: U.S.S.R.	51 30 N	46 07 E	29, 31, 32C, 55, 60
Engels: Okla., U.S.A.	35 32 N	82 38 W	32B, 60B
Enkafala: Ethiopia	14 10 N	40 00 E	35
Ennigerloh: Germany F.R.	51 50 N	8 01 E	57C
Enschede: Netherlands	52 13 N	6 54 E	31B, 67B
Ensenada: Argentina	34 55 S	57 55 W	60
Ensenada: Mexico	31 52 N	116 37 W	49B, 84
Entebbe: Uganda	0 05 N	32 29 E	87
Enugu: Nigeria	6 20 N	7 29 E	38, 67
Eola: La., U.S.A.	31 54 N	92 12 W	60G
Epe: Germany F.R.	52 13 N	7 03 E	31B
Épernay: France	49 03 N	3 58 E	47
Erdington: England	52 31 N	1 54 W	17
Ereğli: Turkey	41 17 N	31 25 E	43
Erevan see Yerevan: U.S.S.R.	40 11 N	44 30 E	30, 47, 48, 60
Erfurt: Germany D.R.	50 59 N	11 02 E	29C, 67B
Erganl: Turkey	38 17 N	39 46 E	45, 59
Erie: Pa., U.S.A.	42 07 N	80 05 W	25D, 43A, 54A, 58H, 61D
Erkenschwick: Germany F.R.	51 38 N	7 15 E	60D
Erkner: Germany D.R.	52 25 N	13 45 E	55B
Erraguene: dam, Algeria	36 40 N	5 26 E	39
Erwitte: Germany F.R.	36 09 N	82 25 W	40C
Erzgebirge (Krušné Hory): Germany D.R.	51 37 N	13 11 E	57C
Esashi: Japan	50 18 N	143 25 N	40B
Esbjerg: Denmark	44 50 N	29 29 E	31
Escanaba: Mich., U.S.A.	45 45 N	87 05 W	27C, 32C, 84C
Esch-sur-Alzette: Luxembourg	49 30 N	5 59 E	25D
Escombreras: Spain	37 34 N	0 57 W	43B
Escuintla: Guatemala	14 18 N	90 47 W	36, 61D
Esfahan: Iran	32 40 N	51 38 E	36
Esholt: England	53 51 N	1 43 W	59H
Eskifjördur: Iceland	65 04 N	14 01 W	25
Eskilstuna: Sweden	59 22 N	16 30 E	55
Eskişehir Kazasi: admin., Turkey			
Eskişehir Vilâyeti: admin., Turkey	39 50 N	30 40 E	50B
Elevsis: Greece	37 51 N	96 52 W	48
Essonnes: Portugal	48 35 N	2 28 E	62A
Esteras: Portugal	43 43 N	8 34 W	61D
Estonskaya S.S.R.: admin., U.S.S.R.	50 40 N	102 02 W	56
Esmeralda: dam, Colombia	5 42 N	73 19 W	39
Espanola: Canada	43 45 N	81 46 W	59A
Esperanza: Ariz., U.S.A.	46 15 N	81 04 W	45A
Espirito Santo: admin., Brazil	32 21 N	111 55 E	27, 47
Essaouira: Morocco	31 30 N	9 47 W	27, 84
Essen: Germany F.R.	51 27 N	7 01 E	46B, 54B, 55A, 58D
Es' Sider: Libya	30 40 N	18 16 E	84
Estreito: dam, Brazil	20 03 S	49 18 W	49
Étel: France	1 29 S	11 35 E	49
Etobicoke: Canada	47 39 N	79 30 W	55A
Étampes: France	35 20 N	84 30 W	60B
Etten: Netherlands	36 03 N	37 31 E	32C
Etter: Texas, U.S.A.	36 03 N	102 00 W	61B, 61E

This page is a gazetteer index of place names, each with geographic coordinates (latitude and longitude in degrees and minutes) and page reference(s). The entries are arranged in six columns across the page.

Place	Lat	Long	Page(s)
Goldsworthy, *Mount*: Austl.	20 21 S	119 32 E	43
Golfito: Costa Rica	8 38 N	83 10 N	84
Golzau: Germany D.R.	51 20 N	12 05 N	38F
Gonen: U.S.S.R.	31 00 N	14 E	—
Gonfreville-l'Orcher: France	49 30 N	0 14 E	—
Gônome: Japan	37 44 N	140 28 E	31
Goodnews Bay: Alaska, U.S.A.	59 06 N	161 58 W	49
Gora Kachkanar: *mtn.*, U.S.S.R.	58 47 N	59 23 E	61F
Gorakhpur: India	26 45 N	83 23 E	—
Gora Tyuya-Muyun: *mtn.*, U.S.S.R.	40 25 N	72 12 E	50
Goražde: Yugoslavia	43 40 N	18 59 E	58H
Gordon: *dam*, Australia	42 35 S	146 24 E	39
Gordonsbaai: *bay*, South Africa	34 10 S	18 52 E	27
Goregaon: India			32
Gorham: U.S.A.			25D
Gori: Italy			31
Gor'kiy: U.S.S.R.			32D
Gor'kiy: *dam*, U.S.S.R.			39
Gorlice: Poland	49 40 N	21 09 E	—
Gorodok: U.S.S.R.	52 23 N	103 17 E	50
Gorzów Wielkopolski: Poland	51 54 N	15 12 N	32C
Goslar: Germany F.R.	51 55 N	10 26 N	46B
Gosselies: Belgium	50 28 N	4 27 N	53B
Göteborg: Sweden	57 43 N	11 58 E	25B, 27C, 29, 31, 37B, 58, 67, 84C, 87
Govora: Romania	45 04 N	24 14 E	59D
Gowganda: Canada	47 39 N	80 46 W	49
Goylarisquizga: Peru	10 45 N	76 26 N	38, 60D
Gozzano: Italy	45 45 N	8 26 N	32C
Gracesputi: *mine*, South Africa	30 00 N	23 43 E	60D
Grafton: Mass., U.S.A.	42 13 N	71 40 W	47A, 59B
Grama: U.S.A.			43
Grand Canyon: U.S.A.			39A
Grand Co.: Utah, U.S.A.			40A
Grand-Couronne: France			25C, 61D, 61H
Grand Dixence: *dam*, Switzerland			39C
Grande Maison: *dam*, France			25
Grande Falls: Canada			87
Grand Fork: N.D., U.S.A.			49
Grand-Lahou: Ivory Coast			50
Grand'Mere: Canada			3F
Grand Rapids: Canada			67A, 87B, 58H, 60, 84C
Grand Rapids: Mich., U.S.A.			30B, 37F
Grangemouth: Scotland			25C, 61H
Grängesberg: Sweden			84
Granite City: Ill., U.S.A.			55A, 45, 46A, 87
Greatham: England			43B
Great Falls: Mont., U.S.A.			56
Great Salt Lake: Utah, U.S.A.			62
Great Valley: Pa., U.S.A.			25D, 87B
Green Bay: Wis., U.S.A.			57C
Greencastle: Australia			27D
Greencastle: Irish Republic			29B
Greeneville: Germany D.R.			57C
Gretz: Germany F.R.			32C
Grenoble: France			61H
Gresik: Indonesia			57C, 60D
Greve: Italy			31B
Greven: Germany F.R.			47B
Grevenbroich: Germany F.R.			29
Greystone: R.I., U.S.A.			31A
Grimsby: England			25C, 27C, 30B
Grindavik: Iceland	63 50 N	22 26 W	27

Place	Lat	Long	Page(s)
Griqualand, West: *region*,	28 40 S	23 30 W	48
Gröditz: Africa	8 38 N	13 27 E	47B
Gröditz: Germany D.R.	51 30 N	12 00 N	38B
Grodno: U.S.S.R.	53 41 N	23 50 N	25C
Grodziec: Poland	52 12 N	19 04 E	67D
Gronau: Germany F.R.	52 12 N	7 02 E	60D
Groningen: admin., Neths.	53 15 N	6 35 E	57
Grono: Switzerland	46 15 N	9 09 E	29B, 31B
Groote Eylandt: *island*, Austl.	14 00 S	136 40 E	37B
Grossauheim: Germany F.R.	50 06 N	8 57 E	84A
Groszowice: Poland	50 38 N	17 57 E	59H, 84C
Groton: Conn., U.S.A.	41 28 N	72 05 W	48
Groves: Texas, U.S.A.	29 57 N	93 55 W	67B
Groznyy: U.S.S.R.	43 40 N	45 42 E	57D, 67C
Grums: Sweden	59 20 N	13 06 E	50
Grünbach: Austria	47 47 N	15 59 E	60H
Grünstadt: Rheinish-Westphalen S.S.R.: *admin.*, U.S.S.R.	42 00 N	43 30 E	57C

Place	Lat	Long	Page(s)
Hazaribagh: India	24 00 N	85 23 E	48
Hazlehurst: Ga., U.S.A.	31 53 N	82 34 W	32B
Hebronville: Mass., U.S.A.	41 54 N	71 18 W	58
Hedaru: Tanzania		37 54 E	48
Heerlen: Netherlands	50 53 N	5 59 E	58D
Heide: Germany F.R.	54 12 N	9 06 E	37F, 58D, 58H
Heidebreck *see* Kędzierzyn: Poland			61D
Heidelberg: South Africa	50 20 N	18 12 E	61D
Hei-lung-chiang: admin., China	49 08 N	9 13 E	49
Heinola: Finland	48 00 N	128 00 E	55A
Heilbronn: Germany F.R.	61 13 N	26 02 E	49
Heishan: China P.R.	41 40 N	122 03 E	25B
Helena: Ark., U.S.A.	34 30 N	90 35 W	61B, 61E
Heliopolis *see* Miṣr al Jadīdah: U.A.R.	30 06 N	31 20 E	53
Hells Canyon: *dam*, Oreg., U.S.A.	45 18 N	116 37 W	39A
Helmsted: Germany F.R.	36 31 N	120 09 W	59, 61
Helsinki: Finland	61 10 N	24 58 E	38B
Hematite: Mo., U.S.A.	48 10 N	90 29 W	52, 54, 55, 58, 84, 87
Höming: France	48 47 N	6 57 E	40C
Henderson: Germany F.R.	53 42 N	115 00 W	57C
Hemmoor: Nev., U.S.A.	52 16 N	11 46 E	57C
Hengelo: Netherlands	52 16 N	6 12 E	31B, 32C
Henningsdorf: Germany D.R.	68 00 N	13 13 W	43B, 54B
Henningsvaer: Norway	41 07 N	89 23 N	60B
Henry: Ill., U.S.A.		96 00 W	50
Henry's Knob: *mtn.*, S.A., U.S.A.	38 08 N	144 26 E	47
Hérault: France	43 40 N	3 21 E	38B, 47B
Herbeton: Australia	17 24 S	145 23 E	45
Hercules: Calif., U.S.A.	38 01 N	122 17 W	45
Hermosillo: Mexico	34 25 N	110 58 N	27
Hernani: Spain	43 16 N	1 58 W	49A, 67
Heroya: Norway	59 08 N	9 34 E	59D, 60D
Herrenwyk: Germany F.R.	53 54 N	10 48 E	50, 58, 59, 60, 61
Herstal: Belgium	50 40 N	5 38 E	45
Herten: Netherlands	51 11 N	5 59 E	53B
Hessen: admin., Germany F.R.	50 30 N	9 15 E	59D
Heysham: England	54 02 N	2 54 W	38B, 56A, 58D
			37F, 40B, 58H, 61D, 61H

Place	Lat	Long	Page(s)
Hibi: Japan	34 27 N	133 55 E	—
Hickok: Kans., U.S.A.	37 34 N	101 45 W	60G
Hicksville: N.Y., U.S.A.		73	55
Hidalgo: Co., N. Mex., U.S.A.	32 00 N	108 30 W	38C
Hidalgo del Parral: Mexico	26 56 N	105 40 W	57D
Hendelaencina: Spain	41 05 N	3 00 W	—
Highland *Valley*: Canada		121 20 W	49
High Mountain Sheep: *dam*, Idaho, U.S.A.	45 45 N	116 50 W	39A
Higüero, *Punta*: *point*, Puerto Rico	18 21 N	67 16 W	40
Hikone: Japan	34 15 N	136 15 E	29D, 57D
Hikoshima: Japan	34 00 N	130 57 E	46C
Hillerød: Denmark	55 56 N	12 19 E	55
Hillington: Scotland	55 48 N	4 15 W	60D
Hilo: Hawaii, U.S.A.	19 44 N	155 05 W	43
Himeji: Japan	34 49 N	134 42 E	61C
Himi: Japan	36 51 N	136 59 E	61
Hindiya Barrage: Iraq	32 44 N	44 18 E	57
Hindley Green: England	53 31 N	2 33 W	57
Hindubāgh: Pakistan	30 54 N	67 45 E	32C
Hinganghat: India	20 32 N	78 52 E	31C
Hinkley Point *Atomic Energy Station*: England	51 12 N	3 09 W	40B
Hinode: Japan	34 44 N	139 34 E	57D
Iinojosa: *dam*, Spain	40 59 N	6 47 W	39
Hirakud: *dam*, India	21 32 N	83 55 N	50
Hirasawa: Japan	35 44 N	137 08 N	37F
Hirase: Japan		36 44 N	50
Hirohata: Japan	34 48 N	134 38 E	43D, 58C, 59G, 61C
Hirose: Japan	35 31 N	67 45 E	50
Hiroshima: Japan	20 32 N	132 27 E	31C
Hirtshals: Denmark	57 35 N	9 58 E	40B
Hissar: India	29 10 N	75 45 N	27C
Hitachi: Japan	36 10 N	140 39 E	45D, 54C, 57D, 59G
Hiyama: Japan	40 10 N	140 07 E	50
Hobbs: N. Mex., U.S.A.	42 55 N	103 40 W	59, 60D
Hoboken: Belgium	21 42 N	4 21 E	46B, 52A
Höchst: Germany F.R.	50 06 N	8 33 E	58H, 59D, 60D, 61H
Hoedjesbaai: *bay*, S. Africa	32 18 N	92 42 W	25A
Hof: Germany F.R.	50 19 N	11 55 E	27
Höganäs: Sweden	56 12 N	12 34 E	43B, 49
Ho-hsien: China P.R.	36 35 N	111 44 E	50D, 38C

Place	Lat	Long	Page(s)
Halifax: England	53 44 N	1 52 W	29B
Halimba: Hungary		12 00 N	47B
Halle: admin., Germany D.R.	51 30 N	12 00 E	38B
Hallein: Austria	47 41 N	13 06 E	25C, 67D
Hällekis: Sweden	36 49 N	10 18 E	60D
Halq al Wādi: Tunisia	53 13 N	6 35 E	57
Hälsingborg: Sweden	61 30 N	17 00 E	84A
Hälsingland: *reg*, Sweden	14 00 S	132 05 N	59H, 84C
Hamada: Japan	50 38 N	17 44 E	48
Hamamatsu: Japan	24 42 N	137 00 E	67B
Hamilah, Jabal: *mtn.*, U.A.R.	55 33 N	10 00 N	27D, 57D, 67C
Hamble: England			50
Hamburg: admin., G.F.R.			50
Hamburg: Germany F.R.			53B
			56A
			27C, 32C, 37B, 37F, 45, 46, 52A, 53B, 55A, 58H, 59H, 60H, 67B, 84C, 87

Place	Lat	Long	Page(s)
Hämeenlinna: Finland	61 00 N	24 27 N	55
Hamel: Minn., U.S.A.	45 03 N	93 30 W	62
Hamgyông-pukto: admin., North Korea	41 45 N	129 50 E	38C
Hamhŭng: North Korea	39 54 N	127 32 E	59
Ha-mi: China P.K.	42 48 N	64 48 W	38, 43
Hamilton: Bermuda	43 15 N	79 50 W	29, 31, 43A, 54A, 55A, 59A, 59E, 60F, 67A, 84
Hamilton: Canada	39 49 N	84 24 W	25D, 59E, 67A
Hamina: Finland	60 34 N	27 12 E	25B
Hammerfest: Norway	70 40 N	23 42 E	—
Hammond: Ind., U.S.A.	41 37 N	87 30 W	87
Hana: Hawaii, U.S.A.	40 15 N	155 59 W	45D
Hanasaki-Misaki: *pen.*, Japan	40 11 N	145 36 E	27D
Hanawa: Japan	40 11 N	140 47 E	45D
Hancock: Mich., U.S.A.	30 45 N	88 34 W	45
Hanford: Calif., U.S.A.	36 15 N	119 39 W	59
Hang-chou: China P.R.	30 15 N	120 10 E	36
H.nghq: Malaysia	58 08 N	22 08 E	25
Han-K'ou: China P.R.	30 35 N	114 16 E	43
Hannibal: Mo., U.S.A.	39 42 N	91 20 W	57, 61E
Hannover: Germany F.R.	52 22 N	9 43 E	55A, 56, 59D, 67B, 87D, 87

Place	Lat	Long	Page(s)
Ha Noi: North Vietnam	21 02 N	105 51 E	67
Hao-pi: China P.R.	41 24 N	114 13 E	38C
Harajuku: Japan	35 54 N	139 21 E	57D
Harbin *see* Ha-erh-pin: China P.R.			—
Harding *Valley*: Canada	45 45 N	126 39 E	25, 32, 67
Haren: Belgium	45 03 N	103 30 W	29C
Harleyville: S.C., U.S.A.	45 30 N	4 22 N	40A
Harlingerode: Germany F.R.	61 00 N	22 08 N	53B
Harmony: South Africa	28 06 S	2 54 E	45, 59
Harnes: France	42 35 N	2 51 W	27C
Haro: Spain	62 52 N	6 57 N	27C
Haroya: *island*, Norway	51 17 N	76 54 N	27B
Harrisburg: Pa., U.S.A.	40 17 N	19 25 N	39
Harspränget: dam, Sweden	66 52 N	18 49 N	39
Harstad: Norway	68 48 N	16 00 N	27
Hart Co.: Ga., U.S.A.	34 18 N	30 26 E	48
Hartbeestfonteinn U.South Africa	26 52 S	28 39 E	40
Hassi-Messaoud: Algeria	31 52 N	90 46 W	40B
Hassi-R'Mel: Algeria	32 52 N	42 42 W	87B
Hastings: Nebr., U.S.A.	40 37 N	98 00 W	37J
Hatfield: England	52 25 N	0 13 W	48
Hathras: India	27 36 N	78 02 N	25A, 40
Hatton: England	52 10 N	5 52 N	57
Haugesund: Norway	59 25 N	5 10 E	27C, 52
Hauts-de-Seine: *admin.*, France	48 50 N	2 10 E	53B
Havana *see* La Habana: Cuba	23 08 N	82 22 W	87
Havant: England	50 51 N	0 59 W	62A
Haverhill: Mass., U.S.A.	25 40 N	81 20 W	48
Haverton Hill: England	54 36 N	1 14 W	57F, 58F
Havre: France	19 30 N	155 30 W	52A
Hawarden: Wales	35 24 S	2 47 N	58D
Hawick: Scotland	55 26 N	19 08 W	58H
Hawthorne: Calif., U.S.A.	33 54 N	156 47 W	29B
Hayden: Ariz., U.S.A.	33 01 N	111 44 E	45A, 59

The page is a multi-column gazetteer index. Each entry lists a place name followed by latitude (degrees, minutes, N/S), longitude (degrees, minutes, E/W) and page reference(s).

Right-hand columns (…–J):

Place	Lat			Long			Page(s)
İzmit: Turkey	40	46	N	29	55	E	25, 36, 58, 59, 60
Izumrud: U.S.S.R.	57	05	N	61	23	E	50
Izvoru Muntelui: *dam,* Romania	46	57	N	26	06	E	39

J

Place	Lat			Long			Page(s)
Jabal Abū Tulu: *hill,* Sudan	11	41	N	28	40	E	43
Jabal al Ḥallūfah: *hill,* Tunisia	36	40	N	10	25	E	46B
Jabal al Jallūd: Tunisia	36	46	N	10	13	E	57
Jabal Ḥamāṭah: *mtn.,* U.A.R.	24	12	N	35	00	E	50
Jabal Sīdī 'Abd ar Raḥmān: *ridge,* Tunisia	23	30	N	30	00	E	47
Jablonec nad Nisou: Czech.	36	47	N	10	44	E	37B
Jabłonowo: Poland	50	22	N	12	55	E	55A
Jachymov: Czechoslovakia	50	22	N	12	55	E	40B
Jacksonville: Fla., U.S.A.	30	20	N	81	40	W	61B, 87C
Jacksonville: Ill., U.S.A.							25A, 32B, 40, 47, 50, 67, 84, 87C
Jacobs: South Africa	29	53	S	31	00	E	29
Jacupiranga: Brazil							56
Jacurici: *dam,* Brazil	10	51	S	39	43	W	39
Jadotville *see* Likasi: Congo D.R.							
Jaduguda: India	10	59	S	26	44	E	45, 67
Jaén: *admin.,* Spain							85
Jaffa *see* Yafo: Israel							40
Jaffna: Ceylon							46B
Jagersfontein: *mine,* S. Africa	29	45	S	25	28	E	84
Jahrom: Iran							48
Jajce: Yugoslavia							39
Jämnagar: India	42	20	N	17	30	W	59D
Jämsänkoski: Finland							60
Jämtland: Sweden							25B
Janesville: Wis., U.S.A.							43, 54, 59
Janja Lipa: Yugoslavia							55
Japla: India							37B
Jarocin: Czechoslovakia							43A
Jarrahdale: Australia							31B
Jarrie: France							47
Jasenova: Yugoslavia							50, 59D
Jasło: Poland							37F
Jasso: Mexico							57
Java *see* Djawa: *Is.,* Indon.	7	30	S				10, 11, 27
Jaykaynagar: India	23	05	N	87	01	E	47
Jazīreh-ye Khārk: *island,* Iran							37C, 56
Jebba: *dam,* Nigeria	33	09	N	5	39	W	39
Jeddah *see* Juddah: Saudi Arabia							
Jedlicze: Poland	21	30	N	39	23	E	36, 67, 84, 87
Jefferson City: Mo., U.S.A.	38	33	N	92	10	W	87B
Jefferson Co.: Mont., U.S.A.	46	20	N	107	49	W	40A, 59
Jeffrey City: Wyo., U.S.A.	50	55	N	15	45	E	25C, 32C
Jelenia Góra: Poland	47	24	N	11	47	E	54B
Jemeppe: Belgium	34	17	N	6	08	W	38
Jenbach: Austria	33	41	N	2	07	W	17
Jerada: Morocco	49	13	N	74	04	W	87
Jerez de la Frontera: Spain	46	27	N	14	04	E	67A
Jersey: *island,* Channel Is.							43B
Jersey City: N.J., U.S.A.	5	59	N	116	04	E	84, 87
Jesenice: U.S.S.R.	36	08	N	68	01	E	38
Jesselton *see* Kota Kinabalu: Malaysia	33	09	N	5	39	W	31, 45
Jhimpir: Pakistan	34	14	N	16	51	E	41, 50
Ji-H. Kerr: *dam,* Va., U.S.A.	21	36	N	81	50	W	31
Jiva Ugenti: Czechoslovakia	38	13	N	43	48	W	34
Joal: Senegal	34	58	N	82	56	W	39
Joanna: S.C. U.S.A.	37	50	N	3	21	W	59D
João Monlevade: Brazil							67
João-Tablón: *region,* Colombia	5	59	N	110	22	E	29, 31, 49, 54, 55, 56, 67, 87
Jocasse: *dam,* S.C., U.S.A.	36	10	S	87	01	E	39A
Jódar: Spain	14	01	N	78	56	W	32B
Jogjakarta (Djokjakarta): Indonesia	34	21	N	9	31	E	43
Johannesburg: South Africa	41	32	N	88	05	W	43A, 54A, 67A
John Day: *dam,* Oreg., U.S.A.	55	05	N	24	17	E	58B, 58F, 59E, 67A
Johnsonville: S.C., U.S.A.	57	47	N	14	11	E	61H
Johore: *admin.,* Malaysia	32	03	N	34	45	E	47A
Joliet: Ill., U.S.A.	57	51	N	13	14	E	55
Jonava: U.S.S.R.	18	51	N	88	52	W	61A, 61E, 87C
Jones Mill: Ark., U.S.A.	17	20	N	96	29	W	16, 17
Joplin: Mo., U.S.A.	32	03	N	34	45	E	34
Joppa: Ill., U.S.A.	35	58	N	5	14	E	45, 50
Joppa *see* Yafo: Israel							60
Jos: Nigeria	18	00	N	92	30	W	34
José Colomo: *region,* Mexico	34	54	S	58	00	W	
José Hernández: Argentina	39	40	N	113	00	W	49B
Jos Plateau: Nigeria	40	30	W				48
Juab Co.: Utah, U.S.A.	38	25	N	27	09	E	
Juàziero: Brazil							

Name	Lat	Long	Page(s)
Juddah (Jeddah): Saudi Arabia	21 30 N	39 12 E	36, 67, 84, 87
Juiz de Fora: Brazil	21 45 S	43 20 W	31
Julianehaab: Greenland	60 45 N	46 00 W	84
Jullundur: India	31 18 N	75 40 E	40B
Junagadh: admin., India	21 32 N	70 32 E	47
Jundiaí: Brazil	23 10 S	46 52 W	58
Juneau: Alaska, U.S.A.	58 20 N	134 20 W	87
Junín: admin., Peru	11 30 S	75 00 W	46, 49
Jupiá: dam, Brazil	20 48 S	51 40 W	31
Jurançon: France	43 18 N	0 23 W	17
Jyoban: Japan	37 00 N	141 00 E	38

K

Name	Lat	Long	Page(s)
Kaanapali: Hawaii, U.S.A.	20 56 N	156 42 W	87
Kandos: Australia	32 51 S	149 58 E	61
Kanev: dam, U.S.S.R.	49 44 N	31 28 E	57
Kangming: South Korea	37 44 N	128 54 E	39
Kannapolis: N.C., U.S.A.	35 30 N	80 36 W	38C
Kano: Nigeria	12 00 N	8 31 E	31A
Kanpur (Cawnpore): India	26 27 N	80 14 E	29, 31, 32, 53, 61F
Kansas City: Kans., U.S.A.	39 05 N	94 37 W	29, 31, 38
Kansas City: Mo., U.S.A.	39 02 N	94 33 W	37J
Kansay: U.S.S.R.	40 30 N	69 41 E	32B, 43, 55, 87B
Kansk: U.S.S.R.	56 13 N	95 41 E	31, 38
Kansko-Achinskii Basseyn: basin, U.S.S.R.	55 15 N	90 50 E	38
Kao-hsiung: Taiwan	22 38 N	120 17 E	47, 57, 58, 59C, 60, 61, 67, 84
Kapsan-ip: North Korea	41 05 N	128 18 E	34, 35
Kapuni: region, New Zealand	39 30 S	174 20 E	25D
Kapuskasing: Canada	49 25 N	82 26 W	39
Karababa: dam, Turkey	37 25 N	38 42 E	31
Karabanovo: U.S.S.R.	56 19 N	38 42 E	45
Karabash: U.S.S.R.	55 30 N	60 14 E	45
Karabük: Turkey	41 12 N	32 37 E	50B
Karaburun: admin., Turkey	38 37 N	26 28 E	58, 60, 61, 67, 84, 57
Karachi: Pakistan	24 52 N	67 03 E	57
Karadag: U.S.S.R.	40 16 N	49 36 E	67
Karaganda: U.S.S.R.	49 50 N	73 10 E	61
Karagandinskiy Ugol'nyy Basseyn: basin, U.S.S.R.	50 00 N	73 00 E	38
Karakaya: dam, Turkey	38 16 N	39 10 E	39
Karama see Ko-la-ma-i: China P.R.			
Karamzor: U.S.S.R.	45 30 N	84 55 E	35
Karatsu: Japan	33 27 N	129 58 E	46
Karhula: Finland	60 31 N	26 57 E	27D, 38C
Kariba: Lake, Rhodesia	16 30 S	28 00 E	25B
Kariba: dam, Rhodesia	16 31 S	28 45 E	39
Karibib: South West Africa	21 59 S	15 51 E	57D
Karita: Japan	33 33 N	130 59 E	25B
Karkar: Afghanistan	36 15 N	68 35 E	
Karkur: India	27 04 N	94 52 E	29C, 31B
Karl-Marx-Stadt (Chemnitz): Germany D.R.	50 50 N	12 55 E	25
Karlsborg: Sweden	65 48 N	14 24 E	84C
Karlshamn: Sweden	56 11 N	14 52 E	37F
Karlsruhe: Germany F.R.	49 01 N	8 24 E	57C
Karlstad: Sweden	59 24 N	13 30 E	37J
Karlstadt: Germany F.R.	49 57 N	9 41 W	48
Karnobat: Bulgaria	42 40 N	27 00 E	40
Karonje: mtn., Rwanda	2 10 S	29 20 E	40
Kars: Turkey	40 37 N	43 05 E	57B
Karsdorf: Germany D.R.	51 17 N	11 39 E	57B
Kartal: Turkey	40 53 N	29 11 E	50
Kasekelesa: Congo D.R.	10 53 S	24 56 E	45
Kashabowie: Canada	48 40 N	90 26 W	39
Kāshān: Iran	33 59 N	51 29 E	57
Kashima: Japan	35 30 N	133 01 E	46B

Name	Lat	Long	Page(s)
Kashiwazaki: Japan	37 22 N	138 33 E	37E
Kaspi: admin., Guinea	41 N	44 25 E	47
Kassan, Île: island, Guinea	9 02 N	13 45 W	
Kassandra: peninsula, Greece	40 06 N	23 25 E	46B
Kassel: Germany F.R.	51 19 N	9 29 E	54B, 55A
Kastoría: Yugoslavia	43 23 N	16 25 E	60D
Kastóri: Greece	40 23 N	22 36 E	39
Kastrup: Denmark	55 38 N	12 39 E	25D
Kasumi: Japan	35 39 N	134 37 E	58D
Katanga: Congo D.R.	8 00 S	26 00 E	49, 50, 57
Katanga-Oriental: admin., Congo D.R.	7 40 S	27 06 E	45
Katav-Ivanovsk: U.S.S.R.	54 45 N	58 12 E	49
Katmandu: Nepal	27 42 N	85 19 E	57
Katowice: Poland	50 15 N	18 59 E	46B, 87
Katsuura: Japan	35 08 N	140 18 E	38B
Katsuyama: Japan	33 37 N	135 56 E	27D
Katukurunda: Ceylon	6 30 N	79 58 E	40
Kaufbeuren: Germany F.R.	47 53 N	10 37 E	31B
Kaunakakai: Hawaii, U.S.A.	21 05 N	157 02 W	25D
Kaunas: U.S.S.R.	54 54 N	23 54 E	39C
Kauttua: Finland	61 06 N	22 09 E	87
Kavalla: Greece	40 56 N	24 24 E	61H, 84B
Kawaguchi: Hawaii, U.S.A.	19 55 N	155 59 W	29D, 56
Kawagumo: stream, Zambia	15 30 N	27 30 E	57D
Kawashin: Congo D.R.	12 55 S	28 45 E	84D
Kawaguchi: Japan	35 49 N	139 43 E	58C
Kawakami: Japan	34 30 N	136 14 E	45C
Kawambwa: Rhodesia	18 10 S	26 41 E	47C
Kambare: U.S.S.R.	53 10 N	26 38 E	39
Kambove: Congo D.R.	10 52 S	26 38 E	45
Kamen: Germany F.R.	51 36 N	7 40 E	58D
Kamensk-Ural'skiy: U.S.S.R.	56 28 N	61 54 E	32
Kameoka: Japan	35 00 N	135 34 E	47
Kamii: Bolivia	42 43 N	81 18 W	87
Kami-Nakaze: Japan	36 14 N	139 26 E	57D
Kamioka: Japan	36 16 N	140 07 E	47
Kamloops: Canada	50 39 N	120 24 W	46C, 59G
Kamo: U.S.S.R.	40 35 N	45 08 E	36
Kampen-Lintfort: Germany F.R.	51 30 N	6 33 E	31
Kampumbu: stream, Zambia	12 55 N	30 45 E	31
Kananga (Luluabourg): Congo D.R.	5 54 S	22 25 E	67
Kanazawa: Japan	36 34 N	136 39 E	67C
Kanchanaburi: Thailand	14 08 N	99 06 E	46
Kandahar: Afghanistan	31 35 N	65 47 E	45
Kandalaksha: U.S.S.R.	67 09 N	32 25 E	47
Kandili: Turkey	41 21 N	31 30 E	38

Name	Lat	Long	Page(s)
Kandla: India	23 00 N	70 10 E	61
Kandos: Australia	32 51 S	149 58 E	39
Kanev: dam, U.S.S.R.	49 44 N	31 28 E	39
Kangning: South Korea	37 44 N	128 54 E	38C
Kannapolis: N.C., U.S.A.	35 30 N	80 36 W	31A
Kano: Nigeria	12 00 N	8 31 E	31
Kanpur (Cawnpore): India	26 27 N	80 14 E	29, 31, 32, 53, 61F
Kansas City: Kans., U.S.A.	39 05 N	94 37 W	37J
Kansas City: Mo., U.S.A.	39 02 N	94 33 W	46, 49
Kansay: U.S.S.R.	40 30 N	69 41 E	32B, 43, 55, 87B
Kansk: U.S.S.R.	56 13 N	95 41 E	31, 38
Kansko-Achinskii Basseyn: basin, U.S.S.R.	55 15 N	90 50 E	38
Kao-hsiung: Taiwan	22 38 N	120 17 E	47, 57, 58, 59C, 60, 61, 67, 84
Kapsan-ip: North Korea	41 05 N	128 18 E	34, 35, 25D
Kapuni: region, New Zealand	39 30 S	174 20 E	39
Kapuskasing: Canada	49 25 N	82 26 W	31, 32, 59, 60
Karababa: dam, Turkey	37 25 N	38 42 E	27, 87
Karabanovo: U.S.S.R.	56 19 N	38 42 E	49, 50
Karabash: U.S.S.R.	55 30 N	60 14 E	40B
Karabük: Turkey	41 12 N	32 37 E	32A
Karaburun: admin., Turkey	38 37 N	26 28 E	38C
Karachi: Pakistan	24 52 N	67 03 E	37E
Karadag: U.S.S.R.	40 16 N	49 36 E	39
Karaganda: U.S.S.R.	49 50 N	73 10 E	25B
Karagandinskiy Ugol'nyy Basseyn: basin, U.S.S.R.	50 00 N	73 00 E	47
Karakaya: dam, Turkey	38 16 N	39 10 E	31C
Karamay see Ko-la-ma-i: China P.R.			57
Karamzor: U.S.S.R.	45 30 N	84 55 E	25
Karatsu: Japan	33 27 N	129 58 E	39
Karhula: Finland	60 31 N	26 57 E	45C
Kariba: Lake, Rhodesia	16 30 S	28 00 E	29D, 32A, 59G
Kariba: dam, Rhodesia	16 31 S	28 45 E	27
Karibib: South West Africa	21 59 S	15 51 E	25D, 87
Karita: Japan	33 33 N	130 59 E	49, 50
Karkar: Afghanistan	36 15 N	68 35 E	40B
Karkur: India	27 04 N	94 52 E	32A
Karl-Marx-Stadt (Chemnitz): Germany D.R.	50 50 N	12 55 E	38C
Karlsborg: Sweden	65 48 N	14 24 E	37E
Karlshamn: Sweden	56 11 N	14 52 E	45C
Karlsruhe: Germany F.R.	49 01 N	8 24 E	27, 48, 61
Karlstad: Sweden	59 24 N	13 30 E	32C, 54
Karsdorf: Germany D.R.	51 17 N	11 39 E	
Kartal: Turkey	40 53 N	29 11 E	20 30 E

Name	Lat	Long	Page(s)
Kazakh: U.S.S.R.	41 05 N	45 22 E	29
Kazakhskaya S.S.R.: admin., U.S.S.R.	48 00 N	68 00 E	27, 43, 56
Kazan': U.S.S.R.	55 45 N	49 08 E	30, 36, 53, 58, 60
Kazanlǔk: Bulgaria	42 37 N	25 24 E	31
Kazincbarcika: Hungary	48 15 N	20 38 E	60D, 61H
Kdyně: Czechoslovakia	49 24 N	13 03 E	29C
Kearny: N.J., U.S.A.	40 46 N	74 09 W	58B
Keban: dam, Turkey	38 49 N	38 45 E	39
Kechoula: region, Morocco	31 50 N	9 34 W	34, 37B
Kedah: admin., Malaysia	6 00 N	100 40 E	43
Kedzierzyn (Heidebreck): Poland	50 20 N	18 12 E	61D, 61H
Keflavik: Iceland	64 01 N	22 34 W	29B
Keighley: England	53 52 N	1 52 E	32C
Kelberg: Germany F.R.	48 55 N	11 52 E	46A, 50, 59
Kellerbach: Germany F.R.	51 04 N	8 32 E	58H, 60D
Kellogg: Idaho, U.S.A.	47 32 N	116 06 W	39
Kemano: dam, Canada	53 31 N	127 56 W	57, 61, 67
Kemerovo: U.S.S.R.	55 20 N	86 05 E	38B
Kempenland (Campine): region, Belgium	51 10 N	5 20 E	31B
Kempten: Germany F.R.	47 43 N	10 19 E	53, 59
Kinesthma: U.S.S.R.	26 05 N	28 14 E	38
Kenadsa: Algeria	31 35 N	2 26 W	34, 36, 61
Kenai: Alaska, U.S.A.	60 35 N	151 19 W	38
Kendrylyk: U.S.S.R.	47 35 N	85 12 E	38
Kenitra see Mina Hassan Tani: Morocco	34 20 N	6 34 W	50
Kennewick: Wash., U.S.A.	46 13 N	119 08 W	36, 43, 45, 50
Kenney: dam, Canada	53 38 N	124 59 W	67
Kenogami: Canada	48 26 N	71 16 W	57C
Kenora: Canada	49 47 N	94 26 W	37G
Kenosha: Wis., U.S.A.	42 34 N	87 50 W	27D, 38B
Kent: admin., England	51 12 N	0 40 E	38A
Kentucky: admin., U.S.A.	37 30 N	85 00 W	27, 34, 35, 38A
Keonjhar: admin., India	22 00 N	85 36 E	43, 50
Keowee: S.C., U.S.A.	34 48 N	82 50 W	27
Kerala: admin., India	10 40 N	76 30 E	67A
Kerch': U.S.S.R.	45 22 N	36 28 E	43, 50
Kerki: Turkes.	37 53 N	65 15 W	37G
Kermānshāh: Iran	34 19 N	47 04 E	48
Kerr, J.H.: dam, Va., U.S.A.	36 35 N	78 16 W	45C
Kershaw: S.C., U.S.A.	34 33 N	80 36 W	27D
Kesang: Malaysia	2 07 N	102 30 W	61B
Kesennuma: Japan	38 54 N	141 35 E	56
Ketona: Ala., U.S.A.	33 34 N	86 41 W	36
Kettle: dam, Canada	56 21 N	94 43 W	36
Kevin: Mont., U.S.A.	48 44 N	111 58 W	40C
Kew: England	51 29 N	0 18 W	27
Kewaunee: Wis., U.S.A.	44 27 N	87 31 W	36, 57, 67
Keystone: dam, Pa., U.S.A.	40 37 N	79 35 W	
Khabarovsk: U.S.S.R.	48 30 N	135 06 E	37C, 37G
Khalij as Suways (Gulf of Suez): region, U.A.R.	28 24 N	33 27 E	35, 43, 45, 50
Khalkis: Greece	38 28 N	23 36 E	57C
Khānaqin: Iraq	34 21 N	45 22 E	37G
Khanh Hoa: admin., South Vietnam	12 36 N	109 00 E	27
Khangat al Hajjaj: Tunisia	36 37 N	10 25 E	50
Khao Luang: mtn., Thailand	8 32 N	99 40 E	39B
Khapcheranga: U.S.S.R.	49 42 N	112 24 E	47C
Kharanor: U.S.S.R.	50 20 N	116 40 E	27
Khārk, Jazireh-ye: island, Iran	29 15 N	50 19 E	37C, 56
Khar'kov: U.S.S.R.	50 00 N	36 15 E	53, 54, 57, 67
Khartoum see Al Khurtūm: Sudan	15 35 N	32 32 E	31, 67, 87
Khaydarken: U.S.S.R.	39 57 N	71 20 E	31, 52
Kherson: U.S.S.R.	46 38 N	32 38 E	87
Khor-al-Amaya: Iraq	29 47 N	48 41 E	57
Khost: Pakistan	67 37 N	67 35 E	38
Khotan see Ho-t'ien: China P.R.			
Khouribga: Morocco	32 54 N	6 57 W	29
Khrusni Inyy: U.S.S.R.	44 21 N	135 06 E	56
Khulna: Pakistan	22 48 N	89 33 E	45
Khumara: Japan	43 50 N	92 35 E	39
Khurays: region, Saudi Arabia	24 55 N	48 05 E	84
Khiabakari: Tanzania	1 46 S	34 02 E	34, 37A
Kianga-Moura: region, Austl.	24 40 S	150 05 E	38
Kiangsi-see Chiang-hsi: admin., China P.R.			
Kibre Mengist: Ethiopia	5 52 N	39 00 E	50, 50D
Kidd Zohar: region, Israel	31 00 N	35 00 E	49
Kiddermaster: England	52 23 N	2 14 W	29B
Kidderminster: England	46 46 N	35 00 E	34
Kidsgrove: England	53 05 N	2 14 W	87B
Kiel: Germany F.R.	54 20 N	10 08 E	62A
Kien Giang: admin., S. Vietnam	10 00 N	105 15 E	84C
Kierunavaara: mtn., Sweden	38 45 N	20 12 E	43

Name	Lat	Long	Page(s)
Koblenz: Germany F.R.	50 21 N	7 36 E	67B
Kobuta: Pa., U.S.A.	40 41 N	80 19 W	60F
Kochav-Helez-Bror: region, Israel	31 36 N	34 39 E	37C
Kōchi: Japan	33 33 N	133 33 E	57D, 67C, 87
Kochi-ken: admin., Japan	33 30 N	133 30 E	45
Ko-chu: China P.R.	24 23 N	103 09 E	45
Kodarma: India	24 28 N	85 35 E	38B
Kōfu: Japan	35 39 N	138 33 E	58D
Koflach: Austria	47 04 N	15 05 E	67C
Kohala: Yugoslavia	35 39 N	6 06 E	61
Kohima: India	50 50 N	27 15 E	36, 61
Kohtla-Järve: U.S.S.R.	59 24 N	27 15 E	36, 61
Kokand: U.S.S.R.	40 30 N	70 57 E	
Kokkola (Gamlakarleby): Finland	63 50 N	23 07 E	56, 59, 61
Kokomo: Ind., U.S.A.	38 45 N	86 09 W	55B
Koksan-gun: admin., N. Korea	38 45 N	126 49 E	59C
Kokura: Japan	33 53 N	130 52 E	38
Kola: U.S.S.R.	18 30 N	73 00 E	47
Kola-Yangak: U.S.S.R.			
Kolaka (Karamal): China P.R.	45 30 N	84 55 E	35
Kolar: admin., India	13 08 N	78 08 E	31B
Kolberg: dam, Austria	47 51 N	12 04 E	39C
Kolhapur: India	16 42 N	74 19 E	31C, 67
Köln (Cologne): G.F.R.	50 56 N	6 57 E	37E, 55A, 58H, 60H, 67B, 87D
Köln-Kalk: Germany F.R.			61H
Kolomna: U.S.S.R.	50 55 N	7 00 E	54, 57
Kolskiy Poluostrov: pen., U.S.S.R.	55 05 N	38 47 E	
Kolwezi: Congo D.R.	67 20 N	37 00 E	40, 50
Kolyvan': U.S.S.R.	10 43 S	82 34 E	49
Komarovo: U.S.S.R.	53 48 N	31 00 E	50G
Komatsu: Japan	36 24 N	136 27 E	45, 46, 49
Kombat: South West Africa	16 12 N	18 16 E	38B
Komló: admin., Hungary			
Kompong Son (Sihanoukville): Khmer Rep.	10 38 N	103 30 E	36, 84
Komsomol'sk-na-Amure: U.S.S.R.	50 35 N	137 02 E	36, 43, 45, 52, 57, 67
Kona Mill: Hawaii, U.S.A.	19 32 N	155 58 W	67
Kondopoga: U.S.S.R.	62 12 N	34 17 E	25
Königsberg see Kaliningrad: U.S.S.R.			
Konomai: Japan	54 43 N	20 30 E	25, 54B, 84C
Konongo: Ghana	6 37 N	1 13 W	49
Konosha: Japan	48 32 N	37 43 E	59G
Konstantinovka: U.S.S.R.	16 08 N	123 45 E	43C, 46
Koolan Island: Australia	30 49 S	119 36 E	38
Koolyanobbing Range: mtns., Australia			
Koombana Bay: Australia	45 33 N	15 44 E	40
Koper: Yugoslavia	59 17 N	5 07 E	27C
Kopervik: Norway	55 07 N	61 37 E	45C
Kopeysk: U.S.S.R.	59 31 N	16 00 E	55, 57, 61
Köping: Sweden	60 00 N	14 30 E	56, 49
Kopparberg: admin., Sweden	49 36 N	18 07 E	39C
Koppies: dam, South Africa	18 48 N	82 41 E	53
Koprivnice: Czechoslovakia	66 05 N	13 50 E	46
Kops: dam, Austria	37 56 N	22 55 E	17, 59H
Koraput: India	54 54 N	140 23 E	32A, 59C, 67C
Korgen: Norway	54 51 N	61 23 E	48
Korinthos (Corinth): Greece	45 09 S	28 16 E	40, 46
Koriyama: Japan	62 05 N	140 38 E	48
Korkino: U.S.S.R.	40 19 N		45B, 46C, 49, 59G
Korkut: Yugoslavia	54 07 N	37 33 E	43
Korogwe: Tanzania	33 02 N	89 36 W	45C
Korsnäs: admin., Finland	48 43 N	21 14 E	25B, 84
Kortrijk (Courtrai): Belgium	38 06 N	85 55 W	57B
Kosaya Gora: U.S.S.R.	43 35 N	20 52 E	49
Kosciusko: Miss., U.S.A.	42 53 N	20 52 E	38B, 59H
Košice: Czechoslovakia	42 49 N	23 13 E	51, 32, 60, 61
Kosmosdale: Ky., U.S.A.	25 11 N	75 58 E	25B
Kosovo I Metohija: admin., Yugoslavia	5 59 N	116 04 E	84, 87
Kosovska Mitrovica: Yugo.	62 33 N	77 33 E	45C
Kossou: dam, Ivory Coast	33 02 N	80 32 E	43
Kostinbrod: Bulgaria	60 15 N	15 07 E	31C
Kota: India	22 16 N	72 55 E	60
Kota Kinabalu (Jesselton): Malaysia	17 25 N	161 22 E	49
Kozaki: Japan	34 48 N	137 22 E	32A

Name	Lat	Long	Page(s)
Kozhikode see Calicut: India			
Kozloduy: Bulgaria	11 15 N	75 45 E	67
Kozhu: Turkey	43 47 N	23 44 E	40
Krabi: Thailand	41 26 N	98 55 E	38
Israel	8 04 N	99 01 E	48, 52
Kragujevac: admin., Japan	44 01 N	19 55 E	43B
Kragujevac: Yugoslavia	50 04 N	19 57 E	54B
Kraków: Poland	50 03 N	20 43 E	37F
Krakowskie: admin., Poland	50 26 N	20 01 E	30, 58H, 59H, 60H
Kralievo: Yugoslavia	50 14 N	14 19 E	57C
Kralupy: Czechoslovakia	49 59 N	19 21 E	43C, 57
Králův Dvůr: Czechoslovakia	63 09 N	10 00 E	39
Kramatorsk: U.S.S.R.	45 02 N	86 00 E	38
Krasno: Czechoslovakia	36 24 N	139 37 E	57D
Krasnodar: U.S.S.R.	51 16 N	15 08 E	25B
Krasnogvardeyskiy: U.S.S.R.	57 23 N	62 08 E	59H
Krasnokamsk: U.S.S.R.	58 04 N	55 48 E	47
Krasnoturinsk: U.S.S.R.	58 23 N	60 12 E	
Krasnoufimsk: U.S.S.R.	60 01 N	57 03 E	45, 47
Krasnovodsk: U.S.S.R.	40 00 N	53 00 E	40A
Krasnoyarsk: dam, U.S.S.R.	55 52 N	80 29 E	27C
Krasnoyarsk: U.S.S.R.	56 01 N	92 50 E	29D, 55, 60C
Krasnyy Sulin: U.S.S.R.	47 54 N	40 03 E	57
Kremasta: dam, Greece	38 55 N	6 34 E	45
Kremenchug: dam, U.S.S.R.	49 04 N	32 26 E	29, 36, 54, 55
Kremenchug: U.S.S.R.	49 04 N	33 25 E	17
Krems an der Donau: Austria	48 25 N	15 36 E	29C
Křešice: U.S.S.R.	50 43 N	14 15 E	57
Krichev: U.S.S.R.	51 15 N	31 35 E	52A
Krishna: India	16 30 N	80 30 E	57
Krishnanagar: India	23 30 N	88 03 E	
Kristiansand: Norway	58 10 N	7 45 E	27C, 45
Kristiansund: Norway	63 07 N	7 57 E	
Krivoy Rog: U.S.S.R.	47 55 N	33 17 E	29C
Krnov: Czechoslovakia	50 05 N	17 40 E	45, 50B, 56
Krompachy: Czechoslovakia	48 55 N	20 52 E	45, 50C, 56
Krugersdorp: South Africa	26 06 S	27 45 E	43
Krumovo: Bulgaria	42 16 N	24 37 E	87
Krung Thep (Bangkok): Thai.	13 45 N	100 31 E	67, 84, 87
Krušné Hory see Erzgebirge: mtns., Germany D.R.			
Kuala Lumpur: Malaysia	3 10 N	101 42 E	45C, 47
Kuala Lumpur: admin., Malaysia	3 14 N	101 40 E	40B
Kuang-chou (Canton): China P.R.	23 07 N	113 15 E	
Kuang-hsi: admin., China P.R.	24 00 N	109 00 E	25, 43, 47, 50D, 52
Kuang-tung: admin., China P.R.	23 00 N	113 00 E	52, 55, 57, 59, 60
Kubikenborg: Sweden	62 23 N	17 21 E	58
Kubiki: region, Japan	37 08 N	138 05 W	47
Kubong: South Korea	36 34 S	126 53 E	37E
K'u-ch'e: China P.R.	41 43 N	82 54 E	49
Kuching: Malaysia	1 33 N	110 20 E	31B
Kudamatsu: Japan	34 00 N	131 52 E	84, 87
Kuei-yang: China P.R.	26 35 N	106 40 E	37E
Kufstein: Austria	47 13 N	12 10 E	57C, 58H, 59D
Kūh Angūrān: mtn., Iran	53 53 N	9 35 E	31B
Kukës: Albania	42 05 N	20 24 E	57C
Kuldja see I-ning: China P.R.	44 00 N	81 20 E	50B
Kulim: admin., Malaysia	7 50 S	110 39 E	67
Kulon Progo: admin., Indon.	36 08 N	139 23 W	45C
Kumagaya: Japan	6 27 N	3 24 E	2, 3, 49
Kumano: U.S.S.R.	33 02 N	85 02 E	38
Kumba: Cameroon	41 44 N	21 40 E	39
Kumertau: U.S.S.R.	22 15 N	81 30 E	38
Kumhari: India	35 10 N	81 00 E	57
Kunda: U.S.S.R.	7 40 N	76 30 E	39
Kunitomi: Japan	35 48 N	140 30 E	46, 59G
Kunovice: Czechoslovakia	42 45 N	29 25 E	27, 45, 56, 57, 67
Kunsan: South Korea	23 04 N	102 41 E	53
Kuorevesi: Finland	35 56 N	130 43 E	84D
Kurashiki: Japan	61 56 N	24 43 E	32A, 55
Kurday: U.S.S.R.	34 35 N	133 46 E	49
Kürdzhali: Bulgaria	43 45 N	75 00 E	46B
Kure: Japan	41 38 N	25 22 E	43D, 52B
Kurgan: U.S.S.R.	34 14 N	132 34 E	38
Kurgali: Australia	55 26 N	65 18 E	55, 36, 60
Kurobegawa: Japan	36 55 N	141 05 E	
Kuroki: Japan	36 35 N	132 34 E	58C, 58G, 59G, 67
Kurski: U.S.S.R.	5 59 N	36 12 E	29, 33C, 67
Kursk: U.S.S.R.	51 42 N	36 12 E	35, 27D, 38, 59G, 67
Kuruman: admin., S. Africa	27 28 S	23 28 E	
Kushiro: Japan	42 58 N	144 23 E	67
Kushk: Iran	31 50 N	55 45 E	46
Kushmurun: U.S.S.R.	52 27 N	64 36 E	38, 47

Name	Lat	Long	Page(s)
Kushtia: Pakistan	23 55 N	89 07 E	31
Kusinsky Zavod: U.S.S.R.	55 21 N	59 24 E	47
Kuskokwim River: Alaska, U.S.A.	61 30 N	86 00 E	
Kütahya: Turkey	39 25 N	63 59 E	38
Kutaisi: U.S.S.R.	42 15 N	42 40 E	59H
Kutina: Yugoslavia	45 29 N	16 46 E	60H, 61H
Kuvasay: U.S.S.R.	45 25 N	17 53 E	17
Kuwait see Al Kuwayt: Kuwait	50 14 N	4 11 E	25
Kuvshinovo: U.S.S.R.	57 02 N	34 12 E	56, 67, 84, 87
Kuybyshev: U.S.S.R.	53 12 N	50 09 W	30, 36, 58, 60, 61, 67
Kuznetskiy Basseyn: basin, U.S.S.R.	54 00 N	86 00 E	38
Kuzuu: Japan	36 31 N	139 37 E	57D
Kvarnsveden: Sweden	51 16 N	15 08 E	25B
Kwaadmechelen: Belgium	51 06 N	5 08 E	59H
Kwakwani: Guyana	58 04 N	58 04 W	47
Kwangtung: dam, China P.R.	40 15 N	115 48 E	
Kyle Co.: U.S.A.	57 17 N	5 43 W	36, 47, 59, 61
Kyle of Lochalsh: Scotland	1 30 N	80 29 E	27C
Kyonre: India	23 47 N	135 45 E	57
Kyoga, Lake: Uganda	35 00 N	135 30 E	43B
Kyōto: Japan	51 56 N	135 00 E	50
Kyōto-fu: admin., Japan	51 42 N	10 40 E	45
Kyshtym: U.S.S.R.	55 42 N	60 34 E	38
Kyzyl: U.S.S.R.	40 16 N	72 08 E	38
Kyzyl-Kiya: U.S.S.R.			

Column 4 (L)

Name	Lat	Long	Page(s)
L			
La Angostura: Bolivia	19 57 S	62 58 W	59
La Barasse: France	43 17 N	5 28 E	47B
La Bassée: France	50 32 N	2 48 E	61D, 61H
La Bâthie: dam, France	45 38 N	6 31 E	33C
La Blancha: Spain	43 43 N	2 48 W	37J
La Calera, U.S.A.	32 47 N	91 02 W	57
La Calera: Chile	4 37 N	74 04 W	57
Lac Allard: Canada	50 53 N	8 29 E	27B
La Calle: Algeria	36 53 N	8 29 E	47
La Ceiba: Honduras	46 57 N	86 50 W	87
La Chapelle-Largeau: France	47 00 N	0 50 W	40B
La Ciotat: France	42 49 N	5 36 E	35
La Cira: Colombia	7 00 N	73 47 W	43A
Lackawanna: N.Y., U.S.A.	48 22 N	78 00 W	50
Lacorne: Canada	43 10 N	2 01 E	52A
La Coruña: admin., Spain	42 06 S	65 37 W	47B
La Coruña: Spain	43 22 N	8 23 W	50
La Couronne: France	45 37 N	0 06 E	27B, 36, 37D, 38, 47, 61, 61D, 67, 84, 60H
Lacq: France	43 23 N	0 38 W	57C
Ladner: Canada	49 06 N	91 04 W	37B, 56, 58D, 58H, 59H, 60H
La Dorada: Colombia	5 27 N	74 40 W	58
Ladysmith: South Africa	28 34 S	29 47 E	36
Lae: New Guinea	6 44 S	147 00 E	31
Lafarge: France	44 31 N	4 41 E	87
Lafayette: La., U.S.A.	30 12 N	92 01 W	40B
La Felguera: Spain	43 18 N	5 41 W	57C
Lagenthal: Switzerland	47 13 N	7 48 E	61D
Lägerdorf: Germany F.R.	53 53 N	9 35 E	31B
Lago Agrio: region, Ecuador	0 00 N	76 30 W	57C
Lago de Maracaibo: lake, Venezuela	9 40 N	71 30 W	35
Lagos: Nigeria	6 27 N	3 28 E	34, 35, 56
La Grange: Ga., U.S.A.	33 02 N	85 02 E	39C
La Grange: Ill., U.S.A.	41 49 N	87 52 W	32B
La Grave: France	45 03 N	6 18 E	57C
La Habana (Havana): Cuba	23 08 N	82 22 W	25, 35, 36, 67, 84
Lahore: Pakistan	31 35 N	74 18 E	67, 87
L'Aigle: dam, France	45 11 N	2 15 E	39
La Jolla: Calif., U.S.A.	32 50 N	117 16 W	62
Lake Albert: lake, Africa	1 40 N	31 00 E	30A, 37J, 57A, 58A, 59B, 59F, 60A, 60G, 61E, 87C
Lake Bangweulu: lake, Zambia	11 05 S	29 45 E	49B
Lake Charles: La., U.S.A.	30 13 N	93 13 W	47
Lake Co.: Colo., U.S.A.	39 15 N	106 30 W	27
Lakehurst: N.J., U.S.A.	40 01 N	74 19 W	59, 84
Lake Kariba: lake, Africa	17 00 S	28 00 E	49
Lake Khangiti: lake, Tanzania	1 04 S	34 30 E	45
Lakeland: Fla., U.S.A.	28 03 N	81 57 W	40
Lake Malawi see Lake Nyasa: lake, Africa	12 00 S	34 30 E	48
Lake Malombe: lake, Malawi	14 38 S	35 15 E	38
Lake Mweru: lake, Africa	9 00 S	28 45 E	39
Lake Nyasa (Lake Malawi): lake, Africa	12 00 S	34 30 E	38B
Lake Oswego: Oreg., U.S.A.	45 25 N	122 42 W	45A
Lake Rukwa: lake, Tanzania	8 00 S	32 25 E	32C

Column 5 (Lavradio)

Lavradio

Name	Lat	Long	Page(s)
Laketon: Ind., U.S.A.	40 58 N	85 49 W	37J
Lake Victoria: lake, Africa	1 00 S	33 00 E	47
Lake Woollaston: lake, Canada	58 15 N	103 20 W	47
Lakheri: India	25 34 N	101 25 W	57
Lakki: Japan	23 34 N	78 30 W	57
La Libertad: Peru	2 14 S	80 57 W	49
La Louvière: France	48 39 N	4 15 E	36
La Madeleine: France	48 39 N	3 00 W	43B
La Mancha: plain, Spain	32 04 S	18 20 E	59D, 61D, 61H
Lambertshaai: South Africa	38 55 N	22 26 E	17
La Mède: France	38 19 N	40 54 E	37H
La Motte: Canada	20 50 N	156 55 W	61H
Lamia: Greece			50
Lamu: Kenya			84
Lanai City: Hawaii, U.S.A.	53 30 N	2 30 W	87
Lancashire and Cheshire: region, England	54 03 N	2 48 E	56A
Lancaster: England	36 00 N	103 41 E	32C
Lan-chou: China P.R.	40 00 N	10 34 E	30
Landeck: Austria	44 00 N	117 00 W	40A
Landes: admin., France	55 52 N	12 50 E	38B
Landskrona: Sweden	33 00 N	10 20 E	27, 56
Langebaan: South Africa	51 56 N	10 20 E	30B
Langelsheim: Germany F.R.	47 13 N	7 48 E	37B
Langensalza: admin., G.D.R.	64 49 N	3 44 E	61H
Langenbrugge: Belgium	21 23 N	20 15 E	25C
Langwa: Burma	43 08 N	96 11 E	45
Lannemezan: France			35
L'Anse: Mich., U.S.A.	46 45 N	88 27 W	61H
Lansing: Mich., U.S.A.	29 00 N	85 34 W	25D
Lanzhot: Czechoslovakia	22 30 N	13 00 W	55B, 67A, 87B
Lao Cai: North Vietnam	11 36 N	16 58 E	27
Laoca Ho: river, China P.R.	10 10 N	75 54 W	36
La Palice: France		1 13 W	45, 46, 50, 59
La Pampilla: Peru	16 30 S	68 00 W	61D, 61H
La Paz: admin., Bolivia	24 41 N	68 09 W	36
La Paz: Bolivia	34 55 S	100 43 W	49
La Paz: Mexico	24 10 N	110 18 W	49A
La Paz: Mexico	26 59 N	105 02 W	87
La Plata: Argentina	41 05 N	95 55 W	45
La Porte: Nebr., U.S.A.	30 46 N	28 11 E	32, 36, 58, 84
Lappeenranta: Finland	61 04 N	28 11 E	61A, 61E
La Pra: France	42 05 N	65 37 W	60A
La Quiaca: Argentina	37 11 N		57
L'Aquila: admin., Italy	40 10 N	10 10 W	50
Larache: Morocco	48 17 N	79 44 W	27B
La Rance: dam, France	48 31 N	2 02 E	49
Laredo: Spain	46 47 N	122 35 W	57C
L'Argentière-la-Bessée: France	44 47 N	6 33 E	46B
La Rioja: admin., Argentina	30 00 N	67 00 W	40
La Rioja: region, Spain	42 20 N		57C
La Robla: Spain	46 10 N	5 37 W	27C
La Rochelle: France	24 25 S	1 09 W	27, 40B, 55A, 84
La-sa (Lhasa): China P.R.	47 13 N	7 48 E	29
La Seyne-sur-Mer: France	43 06 N	6 29 E	47B
La Soups: France	44 20 N	5 53 E	52A
Las Palmas: admin., Canary Is.	28 28 N	14 20 W	57C
Las Palmas de Gran Canaria: Canary Is.	28 06 N	15 24 W	16
La Spezia: Italy	44 07 N	9 50 E	27, 59, 61, 84, 37B, 37H, 46B, 52A, 84A
Lastourville: Gabon	0 49 S	12 42 E	49
Las Ventanas: Chile	32 44 S	71 29 W	87A
Latina: Italy	41 28 N	12 52 E	45
Lathrop: Calif., U.S.A.	37 48 N	121 17 W	59, 61
Lauta: Germany D.R.	51 28 N	14 04 E	39D
Lautenthal: Germany F.R.	38 07 S	147 13 E	25D
Lauzon: Canada	47 29 N	72 48 W	39B
Laval: France	57 00 N	25 00 E	27
La Vallita: dam, Mexico	45 40 N	108 46 W	84
Lavantal: valley, Austria	46 40 N	14 50 E	38B
Lavender: Ariz., U.S.A.	48 48 N	4 47 E	45A
La Voulte-sur-Rhône: France	38 40 N	9 03 W	32C
Lavradio: Portugal			61, 61D

Column 1 (Lávrion ...) — *Page(s)*

Lávrion: Greece
La Wantzenau: France
Lawrence: Kans., U.S.A.
Lawrence: Mass., U.S.A.
Lawrenceville: Ill., U.S.A.
Lawton: Okla., U.S.A.
Leavesden: England
Le Bouchet: France
Lebanon Co.: Pa., U.S.A.
Lechința: Romania
Le Creusot: France
Leeds: England
Leesville: dam, Va., U.S.A.
Le Genevray: France
Leghorn see Livorno: Italy
Legnago: Italy
Legnano: Italy
Legnica: Poland
Le Grand-Quevilly: France
Le Havre: France
Leicester: England
Leigh: England
Leigh Creek: river, Australia
Leinster: region, Irish Republic
Leipzig: admin., Germany D.R.
Leipzig: Germany D.R.
Leith: Scotland
Le Lardin: France
Le Mans: France
Lemhi Co.: Idaho, U.S.A.
Lemona: Spain
Lemont: Ill., U.S.A.
Le Moyne: Ala., U.S.A.
Lend: Austria
Lendava: Yugoslavia
Lengerich: Germany F.R.
Leninabad: U.S.S.R.
Leninakan: U.S.S.R.
Leningorsk: U.S.S.R.
Leninsk-Kuznetskiy: U.S.S.R.
Leninskoye: U.S.S.R.
Lenin, V.I.: dam, (Dnepr), U.S.S.R.
Lenin, V.I.: dam, (Volga), U.S.S.R.
Lenzing: Austria
Leominster: Mass., U.S.A.
León: Mexico
León: admin., Spain
Leopoldville see Kinshasa: Congo D.R.
Le Palais: France
Lepanto-Péonne: France
Le Petit-Couronne: France
Le Pont-de-Claix: France
Le Port: Réunion
Lequeitio: Spain
Lérida: admin., Spain
Lerma: Mexico
Lerwick: Scotland
Les Bois Noirs: mtns., France
L'Escaupont: France
Leskovac: Yugoslavia
Leticia: Colombia
Letchworth: England
Le Touquet-Paris-Plage: France
Le Trait: France
Letsi: dam, Sweden
Leuna: Germany D.R.
Levanger: Norway
Leverkusen: Germany F.R.
Levikha: U.S.S.R.
Levskigrad: Bulgaria
Lewis and Clark Co.: Mont., U.S.A.
Lewiston: Idaho, U.S.A.
Lewiston: Maine, U.S.A.
Lexington: Ky., U.S.A.
Lexington: N.C., U.S.A.
Leydsdorp: South Africa
Lezo: Spain
Liao-ning: admin., China P.R.

Column 2 (Liao-yüan ...) — *Page(s)*

Liao-yüan: China P.R.
Libby: dam, Mont., U.S.A.
Liberdade: Brazil
Libreville: Gabon
Li-chiang: China P.R.
Lichtenburg: South Africa
Lidcombe: Australia
Liège (Luik): Belgium
Liepāja: U.S.S.R.
Liestal: Switzerland
Liguria: admin., Italy
Lihue: Hawaii, U.S.A.
Likasi (Jadotville): Congo D.R.
Likino: U.S.S.R.
Lilla Edet: Sweden
Lille: France
Lillebonne: France
Lima: admin., Peru
Lima: Ohio, U.S.A.
Lima: Peru
Limassol: Cyprus
Limbe: Malawi
Limburg: dam, Austria
Limburg: admin., Belgium
Limburg: Southern: region, Netherlands
Lime: Oreg., U.S.A.
Limerick: Irish Republic
Limhamn: Sweden
Limni: Cyprus
Limón: Costa Rica
Limoux: France
Limpias: Spain
Linares: Spain
Lincoln: Nebr., U.S.A.
Lincoln Co.: Nev., U.S.A.
Lincolnton: N.C., U.S.A.
Lindale: Ga., U.S.A.
Linden: N.J., U.S.A.
Lindö: Denmark
Lingamakki: dam, India
Lingen: Germany F.R.
Linköping: Sweden
Linne: Netherlands
Linz: Austria
Lionel: Australia
Lipetsk: U.S.S.R.
Lipis: admin., Malaysia
Lisas, Point: Trinidad
Lisboa: Portugal
Li-shu: admin., China P.R.
Lisichansk: U.S.S.R.
Lisnaskea: Northern Ireland
Listerhill: Ala., U.S.A.
Lithgow: Australia
Litoměřice: Czechoslovakia
Litovskaya S.S.R.: admin., U.S.S.R.
Little Bay: Canada
Little Goose: dam, Wash., U.S.A.
Little Heath: England
Little Rock: Ark., U.S.A.
Litvinov: Czechoslovakia
Liu-chou: China P.R.
Liu-shu-tun: China P.R.
Liu-tao-wan: China P.R.
Liu-tu: Taiwan
Livermore Falls: Maine, U.S.A.
Liverpool: England
Livorno (Leghorn): Italy
Lixhe: Belgium
Ljubljana: Yugoslavia
Ljuboten: Yugoslavia
Llandarcy: Wales
Llancery: England/Wales
Llanwern: Wales
Llavallol: Argentina
Llolleo: Chile
Lloyd: Angola
Lloydminster: Canada
Lobitos: Peru
Lobito: Angola
Lochaber: Scotland
Lo-ch'ang: China P.R.
Lockport: Ill., U.S.A.
Lock Haven: Pa., U.S.A.
Lockwood: Czechoslovakia
Lod: Israel

Column 3 (Lodève ...) — *Page(s)*

Lodève: France
Lodosa: Spain
Łódź: Poland
Loffa River: Liberia
Loire: admin., France
Logroño: Spain
Lomas: Peru
Lommel: Belgium
London: admin., Austria
London: Canada
London: England
London: region, England
Londonderry: Northern Ireland
London, North West: region, England
Londrina: Brazil
Lone Star: Texas, U.S.A.
Long Beach: Calif., U.S.A.
Long Itchington: England
Longview: Texas, U.S.A.
Longview: Wash., U.S.A.
Longwy: France
Loos: France
Lorain: Ohio, U.S.A.
Loreto: France
Los Angeles: Calif., U.S.A.
Los Bronces: Chile
L'Oseraie: France
Lossiemouth: Scotland
Lostock Gralam: England
Lot: Belgium
Loudonville: Ohio, U.S.A.
Lough Allen: lake, Irish Rep.
Loughborough: England
Louisiana: admin., U.S.A.
Louisville: Ky., U.S.A.
Louisville: Nebr., U.S.A.
Lourdes: France
Lourenço Marques: Mozambique
Louvroil: France
Loveland: Colo., U.S.A.
Lovosice: Czechoslovakia
Lowell: Vt., U.S.A.
Lower Granite: dam, Wash., U.S.A.
Lower Monumental: dam, Wash., U.S.A.
Lowestoft: England
Lowland: Tenn., U.S.A.
Lo-yang: China P.R.
Lozère: admin., France
Loznica: Yugoslavia
Lozovaya: U.S.S.R.
Luanda: Angola
Luang, Khao: mtn., Thailand
Luanshya: Zambia
Lubaczów: Poland
Luban: Poland
Lübbecke: Germany F.R.
Lubbock: Texas, U.S.A.
Lübeck: Germany F.R.
Lublin: Poland
Lubmin: Germany D.R.
Luboń: Poland
Lubudi: Congo D.R.
Lubumbashi (Elisabethville): Congo D.R.
Lucenec: Czechoslovakia
Luchana: Spain
Lüdenscheid: Germany F.R.
Lüderitz: South West Africa
Ludhiana: India
Ludwigshafen: Germany F.R.
Lueders: Texas, U.S.A.
Luena: Congo D.R.
Lufkin: Texas, U.S.A.
Lugones: Spain
Luik see Liège: Belgium
Luilo: Congo D.R.
Luino: Italy
Luján de Cuyo: Argentina
Lukavac: Yugoslavia
Luke: Md., U.S.A.

Column 4 (Luleå ...) — *Page(s)*

Luleå: Sweden
Luling: La., U.S.A.
Lülsdorf: Germany F.R.
Luluabourg see Kananga: Congo D.R.
Lumberton: N.C., U.S.A.
Lunda: admin., Angola
Lundazi: Zambia
Lünebach: Germany F.R.
Lünersee: dam, Austria
Lunéville: France
Lung-yen: China P.R.
Lupa: river, Tanzania
Lupeni: Rhodesia
Lusaka: Zambia
Lu-ta (Dairen): China P.R.
Luton: England
Lutong: Malaysia
Lutopia: Philippines
Lütry: Switzerland
Lützkendorff: Germany D.R.
Luxembourg: Luxembourg
Luzon: is., Philippines
L'vov: U.S.S.R.
L'vovsko-Volynskiy Basseyn: basin, U.S.S.R.
Lyallpur: Pakistan
Lyanger: U.S.S.R.
Lyaskelya: U.S.S.R.
Lydd: England
Lydenburg: South Africa
Lyell, Mount: Australia
Lynchburg: Va., U.S.A.
Lynn: Mass., U.S.A.
Lynn Lake: Canada
Lyon: France
Lyons Falls: N.Y., U.S.A.
Lysanovka: U.S.S.R.
Lysekil: Norway
Lyssva: U.S.S.R.
Lytton: Australia

M

Ma-an-shan: China P.R.
Maastricht: Netherlands
Mabini: Philippines
McAdenville: N.C., U.S.A.
Macagua-Caroni: dam, Venezuela
Macalders: Kenya
McAllen: Texas, U.S.A.
McCormick: dam, Canada
McCormick: S.C., U.S.A.
Macedonia see Makedonija: admin., Yugoslavia
Maceió: Brazil
Macerata: Italy
Machachi: New, U.S.A.
Machi: basin, Pakistan
Macherla: India
Machias: Maine, U.S.A.
McIntosh: Ala., U.S.A.
Machów: Poland
Mackay: Australia
Mackenzie: Guyana
McKinley Co.: N. Mex., U.S.A.
McMurray: Canada
McNary: dam, Wash./Oreg., U.S.A.
Macon: France
Macon: Ga., U.S.A.
McPherson: Kans., U.S.A.
Mactan: Philippines
Mactaquac: dam, Canada
Madawaska: Maine, U.S.A.
Madhya Pradesh: admin., India
Ma'din, Wādi al: stream, India
Madison: Wis., U.S.A.
Madison Co.: Mont., U.S.A.
Madras: India
Madras see Tamilnadu: admin., India
Madrid: Spain
Madukarai: India
Madura: Island, Indonesia
Madurai: India
Mae Mo: Thailand
Mae Sariang: admin., Thailand
Magadan: U.S.S.R.
Magallanes: admin., Chile
Magenta: Italy

Name	Lat	Lon	Page(s)
Magheramorne: Northern Ireland	54 50 N	5 49 W	57C
Magma: Ariz., U.S.A.	33 10 N	111 29 W	45A
Magna: Utah, U.S.A.	40 43 N	112 06 W	59
Magnitogorsk: U.S.S.R.	53 27 N	59 04 E	43, 57, 61, 67
Magog: Canada	45 18 N	72 09 W	31
Maguechic: Mexico	28 21 N	107 40 W	49A
Maharashtra: admin., India	20 N	76 E	27, 38
Mahavelli Oya: river, Ceylon	7 20 N	81 40 E	39
Mahwah: N.J., U.S.A.	41 06 N	74 57 E	55B
Maidstone: England	51 17 N	0 32 E	25, 25C
Maiduguri: Nigeria	11 53 N	13 16 E	50B
Maine-et-Loire: admin., France	47 30 N	0 30 W	43B
Mainz: Germany F.R.	50 00 N	8 15 E	32B, 61, 61A
Maipú: Chile	33 31 S	70 46 W	57C, 62A
Maitland: Canada	44 38 N	75 37 W	84D
Maize Triangle: reg., S. Africa	30 30 S	25 00 E	45
Maizuru: Japan	35 27 N	135 21 E	10
Majdanpek: Yugoslavia	44 25 N	21 56 E	27
Majunga: Malagasy Republic	15 43 S	46 19 E	45
Makarwal Kheji: Pakistan	32 53 N	71 09 E	38
Makasar: Indonesia	5 07 S	119 24 E	27, 67, 84
Makedonija (Macedonia): admin., Yugoslavia	41 50 N	22 00 E	38B, 48
Makeyevka: U.S.S.R.	48 02 N	37 58 E	43C
Makhachkala: U.S.S.R.	43 00 N	47 30 E	31, 57, 67
Makiyama: Japan	33 31 N	130 52 E	59C
Makkah (Mecca): Saudi Arabia	21 27 N	39 49 E	40
Makkokui: Japan	31 16 N	130 19 E	40
Makurazaki: Japan	31 16 N	130 19 E	40
Málaga: Spain	36 43 N	4 25 W	27D, 31, 46B, 57, 61D, 61H, 87
Malagueño: Argentina	31 28 S	64 22 W	57
Malang: Indonesia	48 09 N	78 09 E	49
Malaric: Canada			27
Malawi, Lake see Nyasa, Lake: Africa			40
Malibu Beach: Calif., U.S.A.	12 00 S	34 30 E	55
Mallemort: France	43 44 N	118 35 E	27
Malmberget: Sweden	67 10 N	20 40 E	43
Malmö: Sweden	55 36 N	13 00 E	55A
Malombe, Lake: Malawi	14 38 S	35 12 E	40B
Måløy: Norway	61 56 N	5 07 E	32
Malpaso: dam, Mexico	17 03 N	93 40 W	61, 67, 84
Malton: Canada	43 42 N	79 39 W	32
Maluku (Moluccas): island, Indonesia	2 00 S	128 00 E	27
Malvern Link: England	52 56 N	3 01 E	55A
Malvesi: river, U.S.S.R.	48 22 N	16 14 E	40B
Mammol: Italy	41 38 N	16 05 E	43A
Managua: Nicaragua	12 08 S	86 17 E	48
Manakara: Malagasy Republic	22 08 S	48 01 E	
Manakenina: dam, New Zealand	45 35 S	167 08 E	36, 67, 84
Manapouri: dam, New Zealand	45 35 S	167 32 E	84
Manapparai: India	10 36 N	78 27 E	40
Manassas: Va., U.S.A.	38 45 N	77 28 W	31C
Manaus: Brazil	3 08 S	60 01 W	36, 67, 84, 87
Manchester: England	53 30 N	2 15 W	31B, 37B, 53B, 62A, 84C, 31, 67A
Manchester: N.H., U.S.A.	42 59 N	71 28 W	35
Manchester: Germany see China P.R.			87B
Man-chou-li: China P.R.	49 36 N	117 25 E	39B
Manchuria: reg., China P.R.	44 00 N	125 00 E	39B
Mandalay: Burma	22 00 N	96 05 E	38
Mandan: N.D., U.S.A.	46 50 N	100 54 W	67
Mandioli: Congo D.R.	1 11 S	23 35 E	50B
Manila: Philippines	14 36 N	120 59 E	31, 55, 62, 67, 67, 84, 87
Manipur: admin., India	25 00 N	94 00 E	27
Manitoba: admin., Canada	54 00 N	97 00 W	27
Manitowadge: Canada	49 08 N	85 49 W	31, 32
Manizales: Colombia	5 04 N	75 32 W	61D, 61H
Mannersdorf: Austria	47 58 N	16 36 E	32C
Mannheim: Germany F.R.	49 29 N	8 28 E	45, 50
Manningtree: England	51 57 N	1 04 E	43
Manono: Congo D.R.	6 18 S	27 25 E	40A
Mano River: Liberia	6 56 N	11 31 W	67

Name	Lat	Lon	Page(s)
Manresa: Spain	41 44 N	1 50 E	56
Mansfield: Germany D.R.	51 33 N	11 28 E	32
Mansfield: Ohio, U.S.A.	40 46 N	82 31 W	84
Manta: Ecuador	0 59 S	80 44 W	36
Mantaro River: dam, Peru	12 10 S	74 32 W	17
Mantes-la-Jolie: France	48 59 N	1 43 E	25B
Mantos Blancos: Chile	23 25 S	70 05 W	48
Mantova (Mantua): Italy	45 09 N	10 48 E	17
Mantua see Mantova: Italy			17, 48
Mapimí: Mexico	25 49 N	103 51 W	59
Maputo: Nigeria	36 46 N	10 14 E	58
Maracaibo, Lago de: lake, Venezuela	9 40 N	71 30 W	59A, 37E, 58C, 67A, 37E, 58C
Maracay: Venezuela	10 15 N	67 28 W	67C, 61C, 67C, 87
Marampa: Sierra Leone	8 41 N	12 28 W	45, 46, 49
Maranhão: admin., Brazil	5 00 S	45 00 W	32A, 37E, 58C
Marcaim: India	15 31 N	73 52 E	57D
Marcona: Peru	15 10 S	75 02 W	45
Marchienne-au-Pont: Belgium	50 24 N	4 23 E	87
Marcoule, Centre Atomique de: France	44 08 N	4 42 E	58
Marcq-en-Baroeul: France	50 50 N	3 05 E	40, 50
Marcus Hook: Pa., U.S.A.	39 50 N	75 25 W	46, 49
Mar del Plata: Argentina	38 00 S	57 33 W	43
Mare Island: Calif., U.S.A.	38 04 N	122 15 W	49A
Marganets: U.S.S.R.	47 41 N	34 40 E	62
Margherita: Italy	45 48 N	67 05 E	61
Mari: region, Pakistan	31 28 S	67 45 E	48, 87
Maria Juana: Argentina	31 41 S	61 44 W	
Mariager Fiord: bay, Denmark	56 41 N	10 00 E	50
Mariara: Brazil	20 23 S	49 23 W	
Maribor: Yugoslavia	46 33 N	15 39 E	45
Maricopa Co.: Ariz., U.S.A.	33 33 N	112 15 W	59
Mariel: Cuba	23 02 N	82 52 W	57, 54B, 55A
Marienau: France	49 11 N	6 52 E	48
Mariestad: Sweden	58 43 N	13 51 E	29C, 54B, 55A
Marietta: Ga., U.S.A.	33 57 N	84 34 W	58H
Marietta: Ohio, U.S.A.	39 26 N	81 27 W	25B
Marifu: Japan	34 23 N	132 20 E	30A
Mariposa Co.: Calif., U.S.A.	37 30 N	119 58 W	37E
Maritsa-Iskok: basin, Bulgaria	42 07 N	25 38 E	53B
Marly: France	51 39 N	7 05 E	38B
Marmora: Canada	50 20 N	3 33 W	30B, 58D, 58H, 59D, 60D, 60H
Marowijne: river, Surinam	4 00 N	56 00 W	43A
Marquette Range: deposit, Mich., U.S.A.	46 35 N	87 25 W	43A
Marrero: La., U.S.A.	31 49 N	90 06 W	17, 67
Marsa al 'Alam: anchorage, U.A.R.	25 05 N	34 54 E	25A
Marsa el Brega see Qasr al Burayqah: Libya			48
Marseille: France	30 25 N	19 34 E	36, 37B, 37D, 84
Marseilles: Ill., U.S.A.	41 20 N	88 42 W	84A, 37B, 47B
Marshall Co.: W. Va., U.S.A.	39 50 N	80 30 W	55
Marsh Hat: U.S., Bahamas	26 32 N	77 03 W	59E
Martigny-Bourg: Switzerland	60 00 N	7 03 E	80F
Martigny-Ville: Switzerland	46 06 N	7 04 E	80C
Martin: Czechoslovakia	49 05 N	18 55 E	59D
Martinsburg: W. Va., U.S.A.	39 28 N	77 59 W	47B
Martins Creek: Pa., U.S.A.	40 47 N	75 12 W	22C
Martinsville: Va., U.S.A.	36 43 N	79 53 W	36, 59
Martorell: Spain	41 28 N	1 56 E	57B
Marv Dasht: plain, Iran	29 50 N	52 40 E	59D, 60D
Marviken: Sweden	58 34 N	16 51 E	40
Maryborough: Australia	37 03 S	143 46 E	40
Mary Kathleen: dam, Australia	20 44 S	140 01 E	38
Maryland: admin., U.S.A.	39 00 N	76 45 W	40
Maryneal: Texas, U.S.A.	32 14 N	100 26 W	57A
Marysville: Australia	37 31 N	145 45 E	59
Masan: Italy	44 31 N	11 12 E	25
Masz: Italy	45 49 N	11 10 E	25
Masegawa: dam, Japan	36 03 N	137 10 E	9D
Mashaba: Rhodesia	20 03 S	30 29 E	48
Mashhad (Meshed): Iran	36 16 N	59 36 E	27
Masjed Soleymán: Iran	31 59 N	49 18 E	53B
Mason City: Iowa, U.S.A.	43 10 N	93 15 W	57B
Masqat (Muscat): Muscat and Oman	23 37 N	58 38 E	45
Massachusetts: admin., U.S.A.	42 00 N	72 00 W	84
Massa Marittima: Italy	43 03 N	10 53 E	27
Massawa: Ethiopia	15 37 N	39 28 E	84
Massuda: Japan	34 40 N	131 51 E	84
Matadi: Congo D.R.	5 49 S	13 27 E	32A

Name	Lat	Lon	Page(s)
Matamoros: Mexico	25 53 N	97 30 W	62
Matanzas: Cuba	23 03 N	81 35 W	32
Matarani: Peru	17 00 S	72 07 W	84
Mataripe: Brazil	12 41 S	38 27 E	36
Mataró: Spain	41 32 N	2 27 E	17
Matfors: Sweden	62 21 N	17 02 E	25B
Matheson: Canada	48 33 N	80 28 W	48
Matías de Gálvez: Guatemala	15 42 N	88 37 W	84
Mato Grosso: admin., Brazil	17 03 N	9 40 E	17
Matola-Rio: Mozambique	16 00 S	36 00 W	59
Matrahville: Australia	33 57 S	151 14 E	84
Matsue: Japan	35 27 N	133 04 E	59, 58
Matsuyama: Japan	33 50 N	132 45 E	59A, 37E, 58C, 59C, 61C, 67C, 87
Mattagami: Canada	49 47 N	77 38 W	32A, 37E, 58C
Matzen: Austria	33 24 N	31 51 E	45
Mavrovouni: Cyprus	35 06 N	97 09 E	50
Mawchi: Burma	18 49 N	97 09 E	50
Mayagüez: Puerto Rico	18 12 N	67 09 W	87
Maydown: Northern Ireland	54 59 N	7 19 W	58
Mayli-Say: U.S.S.R.	41 17 N	72 24 E	40, 50
Mayo District: Canada	63 30 N	136 00 W	46, 49
Mayurbhanj: admin., India	21 50 N	86 30 E	43
Maywood: Ill., U.S.A.	41 51 N	87 48 W	62
Mazapil: Mexico	24 38 N	101 34 W	49A
Mazar-i-Sharif: Afghanistan	36 43 N	67 05 E	61
Mazaruni-Potaro: admin., Guyana	6 00 N	59 30 W	48, 87
Mazatlán: Mexico	23 13 N	106 25 W	84, 87
Mazatzal Mountains: Ariz., U.S.A.	34 00 N	111 30 W	50
Mazingarbe: France	50 28 N	2 42 E	58H, 60H, 61H
Mazra'eh Mazâre': Iran	38 36 N	47 03 E	45
Mazul'skiy: U.S.S.R.	61 44 N	93 09 E	59
Mbao: Senegal	15 44 N	16 31 W	59
Mbeya: Tanzania	8 54 S	33 27 E	61
Mbuji-Mayi (Bakwanga): Congo D.R.	6 09 S	23 36 E	48
Mead: Wash., U.S.A.	47 45 N	117 20 W	47
Meadow Brook: W. Va., U.S.A.	41 38 N	80 10 W	46
Meadville: Pa., U.S.A.			32B
Mecca see Makkah: Saudi Arabia			
Mechanicville: N.Y., U.S.A.	42 27 N	73 42 W	67
Mechelen: Belgium	51 02 N	4 28 E	59A, 55A
Mecsek: mtns, Hungary	46 10 N	18 18 E	29B
Medan: Indonesia	3 35 N	98 35 E	67
Medellín: Colombia	6 15 N	75 35 W	29, 31, 32, 60, 67, 84
Meden Rudnik: Bulgaria	42 27 N	27 24 E	45
Medford: Oreg., U.S.A.	42 20 N	122 52 W	87
Medgidia: Romania	44 15 N	28 17 E	57C
Medias: Romania	46 10 N	24 21 E	17
Medicine Hat: Canada	50 03 N	110 41 W	59, 61
Mednogorsk: U.S.S.R.	51 24 N	57 37 E	45
Medveddyegorsk: U.S.S.R.	62 55 N	34 28 E	45
Meerut: India	29 00 N	77 42 E	31
Megalópolis: Greece	37 24 N	22 08 E	38
Meggen: Germany F.R.	51 08 N	8 04 E	56
Meknès: Morocco	33 53 N	5 37 W	11
Medina del Campo: Spain	41 18 N	4 55 W	27, 49, 67
Medina del Campo: Spain			67, 84, 87
Mekong Delta: South Vietnam	10 00 N	106 20 E	49A
Melbourne: Australia	37 50 S	145 00 E	25D, 87B
Melbourne: Fla., U.S.A.	28 04 N	80 38 W	43A
Melchor Ocampo: Mexico	44 51 N	101 39 W	39
Meldal: Norway	63 03 N	9 41 E	61D, 61H
Melekeng: Conn., U.S.A.	41 09 N	72 10 W	37J
Melk: Austria	48 14 N	15 20 W	61
Melton: England	16 20 N	0 53 E	46, 60
Melton Mowbray: England	52 46 N	0 53 W	32
Melun: France	48 32 N	2 40 E	61
Memaliaj: Albania	40 20 N	19 58 E	29B
Memphis: Tenn., U.S.A.	35 10 N	90 00 W	53C
Mendoza: admin., Argentina	32 53 S	68 30 W	53B
Mendoza: Argentina	32 53 S	68 50 W	57B
Menominee Range: deposit, Mich., U.S.A.	45 07 N	87 37 W	57C
Mequinenza: dam, Spain	41 22 N	0 17 E	45
Merano: Italy	45 01 N	11 09 E	39
Meraux: La., U.S.A.	29 54 N	89 55 W	43
Merced: Calif., U.S.A.	37 17 N	120 29 W	40A
Mercedes: Argentina	34 39 S	59 27 W	67
Mercedes: Argentina	33 40 S	65 28 W	23
Merefa: region, Australia	38 39 S	144 40 E	
Mergui: Burma	12 26 N	98 36 E	
Mérida: Mexico	20 58 N	89 36 W	
Mérignac: France	44 50 N	0 36 E	
Merone: Italy	45 47 N	9 15 E	
Merritt: Canada	36 48 N	124 38 E	
Mersin: Turkey	23 37 N	92 50 W	
Mesabi Range: deposit, Minn., U.S.A.	47 30 N	92 50 W	
Mesa Co.: Colo., U.S.A.	43 03 N	108 30 W	
Meshed see Mashhad: Iran	15 17 N	74 57 E	
Mesopotamia Argentina: reg., Argentina	30 00 S	58 00 W	23

Name	Lat	Lon	Page(s)
Messaure: dam, Sweden	66 40 N	20 21 E	39
Messina: Italy	38 11 N	15 34 E	17, 84A
Messina: South Africa	22 23 S	30 00 E	45
Metaline Falls: Wash., U.S.A.	25 43 N	68 01 E	57
Meting: Pakistan	24 43 N	68 01 E	38
Mettupalayam: India	11 18 N	76 57 E	32
Mettur: India	11 33 N	77 51 E	47, 60
Metuchen: N.J., U.S.A.	40 33 N	74 23 W	32B
Metz: France	49 08 N	6 10 E	55A, 67B
Meurthe-et-Moselle: admin., France			56A
Mexican Hat: Utah, U.S.A.	48 35 N	6 10 E	40A, 59
Mexico City see Ciudad de México: Mexico	37 10 N	109 54 W	
Mexía: Yugoslavia	19 24 N	99 09 W	25, 29, 31, 32, 34, 45, 55, 56, 57, 59, 61, 62, 67, 87
Miami: Ariz., U.S.A.	46 31 N	14 52 E	56A
Miami: Fla., U.S.A.	33 24 N	110 54 W	45A
Miami: Rhodesia	25 45 N	29 46 E	46B
Miänwäli: admin., Pakistan	16 40 S	80 15 W	57, 67, 87C
Miao-li: Taiwan	32 10 N	71 30 E	57
Miass: U.S.S.R.	24 34 N	120 49 E	60, 61
Mibladene: Morocco	54 59 N	60 06 E	55
Miboro: dam, Japan	32 46 N	4 38 W	46
Mica: dam, Canada	36 48 N	136 55 E	39D
Micheville: France	51 30 N	87 48 W	39
Michigan: admin., U.S.A.	49 28 N	13 16 E	43B
Michigan City: Ind., U.S.A.	41 43 N	85 00 W	54A
Middlebrough: Ohio, U.S.A.	40 35 N	86 54 E	57B
Middletown: Conn., U.S.A.	54 32 N	81 11 W	52A, 58D, 84C
Middle Yenisei: dam, U.S.S.R.	39 11 N	7 39 W	58F, 59A, 60F
Midland: Mich., U.S.A.	65 20 N	84 13 E	25D, 43A, 58B
Midland: Pa., U.S.A.	43 38 N	84 14 W	58
Midland: Texas, U.S.A.	40 38 N	80 28 W	30A, 40C, 59A, 60F
Midland Junction: Australia	32 00 N	102 00 W	61A
Midlands: region, England	31 54 S	116 00 E	43A
Midlands, East: region, England	52 30 N	1 00 W	87C
Midlands, West: region, England	52 30 N	2 30 W	54
Midlothian: Texas, U.S.A.	41 38 N	80 10 W	56A
Midono: Japan	35 37 N	137 39 E	37D, 38B, 56A
Midvale: Utah, U.S.A.	40 37 N	111 55 W	38B
Miena: Poland	50 18 N	21 25 E	57A
Miena: Australia	43 15 N	146 44 E	39D
Miguel Hidalgo: dam, Mexico	26 28 N	108 35 W	46
Miguel Burnier: Brazil	20 26 S	43 47 W	44 E
Mihama: Japan	33 24 N	135 06 E	53
Mihaylovka: U.S.S.R.	50 03 N	43 15 E	58D
Mikkaichi: Japan	36 52 N	137 00 E	39
Milano: Italy	45 28 N	9 12 E	29, 31, 32C, 37B, 37H, 43B, 55B, 58D, 58H, 60H, 60H, 87D
Milazzo: Italy	38 13 N	15 14 E	55
Mile End: Australia	34 56 S	138 35 E	27C, 37D, 37F,
Milford Haven: Wales	51 44 N	5 07 W	58D, 84C
Mill City: Nev., U.S.A.	40 42 N	118 03 W	50A
Millhaven: Canada	44 15 N	76 55 W	60B
Millinocket: Maine, U.S.A.	45 39 N	68 43 W	25D
Millstone Point: Conn., U.S.A.	41 19 N	72 10 W	43B
Milnerton: Bolivia	34 05 S	68 00 W	40C
Milnerton: South Africa	16 20 S	69 00 W	50
Milwaukee: Wis., U.S.A.	43 03 N	87 56 W	36, 56, 57B, 58B, 67A, 84
Miná' 'Abd Allah: Kuwait	29 01 N	48 10 E	87G
Miná' al Ahmadí: Kuwait	29 04 N	48 02 E	37C, 37G
Mina Hassan Tani (Kenitra): Morocco			
Minamata: Japan	34 20 N	6 34 W	27B, 59G
Minas: Indonesia	32 13 N	130 24 E	59G, 60C, 61C, 61G
Minas de Matahambre: Cuba	22 35 N	0 50 N	35
Minas Gerais: admin., Brazil	18 00 S	101 01 E	45
Miná' Su'úd: Neutral Zone	28 48 N	44 00 W	27, 40, 46, 48, 49
Minatitlán: Mexico	17 59 N	94 31 W	37G
Mindanao: is., Philippines	7 30 N	125 00 E	45, 49, 50
Mineral Co.: Colo., U.S.A.	37 47 N	106 50 W	36, 58, 59, 61
Mineral Co.: Nev., U.S.A.	38 30 N	118 00 W	27, 49
Mineral Park: admin., Australia	34 00 N	114 02 W	49B
Mingechaur: U.S.S.R.	40 45 N	47 03 E	50
Miniera di Monteponi: Italy	39 18 N	8 24 E	50, 50A
Minis: Romania	46 08 N	21 36 E	39
Minkébú: Gabon	1 46 N	12 48 E	46B
Minneapolis: Minn., U.S.A.	45 00 N	93 15 W	17
Minnesota: admin., U.S.A.	46 00 N	94 00 W	25, 31, 34, 55, 56, 62, 67, 87B
Minsk: U.S.S.R.	53 54 N	27 34 E	27
Minusinsky Ugol'nyy Basseyn: basin, U.S.S.R.	53 35 N	91 20 E	34, 37B, 55
Mira: Portugal	39 32 N	8 43 W	38

N

Column 1 (Neustadt)

Name	Lat	Long	Page(s)
Neustadt an der Donau: G.F.R.	48 48 N	11 46 E	37F
Neuves-Maisons: France	48 37 N	6 06 E	43B
Neville Island: Pa., U.S.A.	40 30 N	80 13 W	57C
Nev'yansk: U.S.S.R.	57 30 N	60 13 E	55B
Newark: N.J., U.S.A.	40 44 N	74 11 W	57
Newark: Ohio, U.S.A.	40 03 N	82 25 W	59E
New Bedford: Mass., U.S.A.	41 38 N	70 55 W	37I, 38B
New Bern: N.C., U.S.A.	35 05 N	77 04 W	87C
Newberry: S.C., U.S.A.	34 17 N	81 37 W	59H
New Brunswick: Texas, U.S.A.	29 43 N	98 09 W	31A
New Brunswick: admin., Canada	47 00 N	66 00 W	31
Newcastle: Australia	32 55 S	151 45 E	27
Newcastle: Ind., U.S.A.	39 56 N	85 23 W	38
Newcastle: Wyo., U.S.A.	43 51 N	104 14 W	55B
Newcastle-upon-Tyne: England	54 59 N	1 35 W	55
New Cornelia: Ariz., U.S.A.	32 23 N	112 50 W	37H
New Delhi: India	28 15 S	77 13 E	37B
New Era: South Africa	26 16 S	28 24 E	62A, 84C, 87
Newfoundland: admin., Canada	52 00 N	56 00 W	45A
Newhall: Calif., U.S.A.	34 23 N	118 33 W	3
New Jersey: admin., U.S.A.	40 00 N	74 30 W	32
New Johnsonville: Tenn., U.S.A.	36 00 N	87 56 W	48
Newlyn: England	50 06 N	5 34 W	50
New Martinsville: W. Va., U.S.A.	39 39 N	80 52 W	27
New Mexico: admin., U.S.A.	35 00 N	106 00 W	27C
Newnan: Ga., U.S.A.	33 23 N	84 48 W	61E
New Orleans: La., U.S.A.	30 00 N	90 03 W	27, 38, 48
Newport: England/Wales	51 35 N	3 00 W	38B, 56A
Newport: Ky., U.S.A.	39 05 N	84 27 W	38B
Newport News: Va., U.S.A.	36 59 N	76 26 W	50B
Newport Pagnell: England	52 05 N	0 44 W	54
Newry: Northern Ireland	54 11 N	6 20 W	59C
New South Wales: admin., Australia	33 00 S	146 00 E	47C, 61C, 61G
Newton-le-Willows: England	54 17 N	1 40 W	60C, 61C, 61G
New Westminster: Canada	26 11 S	122 58 W	67C, 84D
New York: admin., U.S.A.	43 09 N	75 30 W	34, 35
New York: N.Y., U.S.A.	40 40 N	74 00 W	58G, 61C, 59G
Neyveli: India	11 36 N	79 26 E	57D
Ngwenya: mtn., Swaziland	26 11 S	31 05 E	55
Niagara: dam, Canada	43 09 N	79 04 W	55
Niagara Falls: N.Y., U.S.A.	43 07 N	79 03 W	45D
Niagara Falls: N.Y., U.S.A.	43 06 N	79 04 W	17, 52, 57C, 84
Nicaro: Cuba	20 42 N	75 33 W	36, 43
Nice: France	43 42 N	7 15 E	50B
Nichinan: Japan	31 33 N	131 23 E	43B, 47B
Nicosia: Cyprus	35 11 N	33 23 E	14, 31
Niedersachsen: admin., G.F.R.	48 36 N	12 00 W	47
Nienstein: Germany F.R.	49 55 N	8 30 E	40C
Nièvre: admin., France	47 00 N	3 44 W	40C
Niger: admin., Turkey	5 00 N	6 00 E	29B
Niger Delta: Nigeria	5 00 N	5 00 E	43
Nihongi: Japan	34 39 N	136 40 W	32A, 58G, 59C, 60C
Niigata: Japan	37 55 N	139 03 E	60B
Niigata-ken: admin., Japan	37 30 N	139 00 E	39
Niihama: Japan	33 58 N	133 16 E	

Column 2 (Nizhniy Tagil)

Name	Lat	Long	Page(s)
Nizhniy Tagil: U.S.S.R.	57 55 N	59 57 E	43, 49, 54, 57, 67
Nizhnyaya Salda: U.S.S.R.	58 05 N	60 43 E	43
Nizhnyaya Tunguska: dam, U.S.S.R.			
Nkalago: Nigeria	65 48 N	88 04 E	39
Nkana-Kitwe: Zambia	6 23 N	28 15 E	57
Noboka: Japan	12 49 S	7 48 E	45B
Nocara: Italy	32 35 N	131 40 E	32A, 59C, 59G, 60C, 61C, 61G
Noginsk: U.S.S.R.	40 06 N	16 29 E	67C
Nölbinnae: South Korea	55 51 N	38 27 E	59H
Noranda: Canada	43 22 N	0 36 W	31, 43
Norco: La., U.S.A.	48 16 N	128 09 E	47B
Nord: admin., France	30 01 N	79 03 W	48
Nordic Mi.: Canada	55 00 N	116 30 E	45, 46, 49, 56
Nordrhein-Westfalen: admin., Germany F.R.	47 00 N	17 20 E	37I, 58E
Norfolk: Va., U.S.A.	46 19 N	82 43 W	38B, 56A
Norfolk: Va., U.S.A.	51 30 N	0 30 E	40C
Noril'sk: U.S.S.R.	36 54 N	76 18 W	56A
Norman Wells: Canada	69 20 N	88 06 E	55, 57B, 59E, 67, 87C
Normetal: Canada	65 19 N	126 46 W	67
Norrköping: Sweden	65 08 N	79 22 W	36
Norseman: Australia	33 18 N	92 40 W	37I
Northampton: England	58 36 N	16 11 E	57
Northam: Ga., U.S.A.	32 12 S	121 45 E	29
North Anna: Va., U.S.A.	52 14 N	0 54 W	49
North Australian Mountains: Main	40 40 N	75 23 W	67B
North Bay: Canada	37 48 N	77 25 W	40C
North Carolina: admin., U.S.A.	45 00 N	70 00 W	50
North China Plain: China P.R.	46 20 N	80 00 W	61
North Dakota: admin., U.S.A.	38 00 N	117 00 W	27
Northern Territory: admin., Australia	20 00 S	134 00 E	19, 31
North European Plain: Europe	53 44 N	16 00 W	27, 38
North Ferriby: England	42 43 N	0 31 W	14, 23
Northfield: Ill., U.S.A.	41 23 N	87 46 W	45
Northfleet: England	51 27 N	0 20 E	58B
North Haven: Conn., U.S.A.	41 23 N	72 52 W	57C
North Italian Plain: Italy	45 00 N	9 00 E	53A
North Miami: Fla., U.S.A.	25 53 N	80 10 W	54W
North Shields: England	55 01 N	1 26 W	32B
North Stradbroke Island: Austl.	27 35 S	153 28 E	27C
North Tonawanda: N.Y., U.S.A.			40
Northumberland: admin., Eng.	43 02 N	78 54 W	37I
Northumberland and Durham: region, England	55 00 N	2 00 W	38B
North Vancouver: Canada	49 59 N	123 05 W	56A
North West London: region, England			59
Northwest Territories: admin., Canada	51 35 N	0 15 W	53B

Column 3 (Nueva Segovia / O)

Name	Lat	Long	Page(s)
Nueva Segovia: admin., Nicaragua	13 40 N	86 10 W	50
Nuevitas: Bahía de: bay, Cuba	21 30 N	77 12 W	43
Nuevo Casas Grandes: Mexico	30 25 N	107 55 W	49A
Numazu: Japan	35 05 N	138 52 E	27D
Nünchritz: Germany D.R.	51 18 N	13 24 E	59H
Nurek: dam, U.S.S.R.	37 01 N	68 16 E	39
Nurnberg see Nürnberg: Germany F.R.			
Nürnberg (Nuremberg): G.F.R.	49 27 N	11 05 E	32C, 54B, 67B
Nusa Tenggara Barat: admin., Indonesia	8 50 S	117 30 E	27
Nyasa, Lake (Lake Malawi): Africa	12 00 S	34 30 E	58H
Nyborg: Denmark	55 19 N	10 48 W	37H
Nye Co.: Dev., U.S.A.	38 00 N	116 30 W	32B, 60D
Nyergesujfalu: Hungary	47 00 N	18 30 E	37F, 37H
Nyírád: Hungary	47 00 N	17 21 E	45
Nyírbogdány: Hungary	48 03 N	21 53 E	36, 37F, 58
Nylund: Sweden	65 00 N	18 37 E	32A
Nynäshamn: Sweden	58 54 N	17 57 E	
Nyogawa: Japan	33 56 N	133 05 E	

O

Name	Lat	Long	Page(s)
Oahe: dam, S.D., U.S.A.	44 25 N	100 23 W	39
Oak Harbor: Ohio, U.S.A.	41 31 N	83 10 W	40C
Oakland: Calif., U.S.A.	37 50 N	122 15 W	84A, 87A
Oakville: Canada	43 27 N	79 41 W	37I, 55A
Oaxaca: admin., Mexico	17 00 N	96 30 W	40
Oban: Scotland	56 25 N	5 29 W	58C
Oberhausen-Holten: Germany G.F.R.	51 33 N	6 48 E	60D, 61D, 61H
Oberbolzer: South Africa	26 20 S	27 10 E	49
Oberkassel: Germany F.R.	48 15 N	14 00 E	56A
Oberösterreich: admin., Austria	50 02 N	8 35 E	53B
Oberursel: Germany F.R.	49 58 N	8 35 E	45
Obluch'ye: U.S.S.R.	55 05 N	131 05 E	47B
Obninsk: U.S.S.R.	36 37 N	36 00 E	49A
Ophthalmia Range: mtns., Australia	23 17 S	119 30 E	25
Obourg: Belgium	50 28 N	4 06 E	40B
Obrigheim: Germany F.R.	49 21 N	15 41 E	31B
Obrovac: Yugoslavia	50 16 N	86 18 E	59D
Obuasi: Ghana	6 15 N	1 40 W	32
Ocampo: Mexico	28 11 N	108 22 W	27D, 29D
Ocampo: Mexico	22 50 N	102 21 W	32A
Ocean Falls: Canada	52 24 N	127 40 W	
Ocho Ríos: Jamaica	18 25 N	77 11 E	
Ocna Mureş: Romania	46 23 N	23 46 E	67
Ocotlán: Mexico	20 21 N	102 46 W	57B
Odawara: Japan	35 15 N	139 10 E	67B
Odda: Norway	60 04 N	6 33 E	58H
Odendaalsrus: South Africa	27 52 S	26 42 E	47, 38A
Odense: Denmark	55 24 N	10 23 E	67
Odenton: Md., U.S.A.	39 05 N	76 41 W	30A, 37I, 57, 60A
Odessa: Texas, U.S.A.	31 50 N	102 23 W	60G, 61B, 61B
Odessa: U.S.S.R.	46 28 N	30 44 E	17, 35, 55, 84
Offenburg: Germany F.R.	48 29 N	7 56 E	31B
Ofuna: Japan	8 23 N	141 32 E	34, 35
Ogaki: Japan	35 04 N	136 37 E	34A, 30C
Ogbomosho: Nigeria	32 49 N	4 11 E	27D, 32A
Oglesby: Ill., U.S.A.	41 16 N	89 02 W	67
Ogrodzieniec: Poland	50 27 N	19 31 E	57B
Ohe: Japan	44 15 N	133 25 E	84
Ohio: admin., U.S.A.	40 15 N	82 45 W	58H
Oildale: Calif., U.S.A.	35 25 N	119 00 W	47
Oissel: France	49 20 N	1 06 E	31B, 37H, 55A, 58H, 61A, 61D, 61H
Oita: Japan	33 14 N	131 36 E	43
Oita-ken: admin., Japan	33 15 N	131 30 E	27, 38
Oji: Japan	34 59 N	135 37 W	61
Ojos Negros: Spain	40 44 N	1 30 W	43B
Okay: Ark., U.S.A.	35 52 N	95 04 E	
Okayama: Japan	34 39 N	133 55 E	
Okazaki: Germany F.R.	34 57 N	137 10 E	
Oker: Germany F.R.	51 54 N	10 28 E	
Oka: U.S.S.R.	54 43 N	37 48 E	
Okinawa: island, Ryukyu Is.	26 20 N	128 00 E	
Oklahoma City: Okla., U.S.A.	35 28 N	97 30 W	
Okmulgee: Okla., U.S.A.	35 38 N	95 59 W	
Okulovka: U.S.S.R.	58 22 N	33 18 E	
Okutadami: dam, Japan	36 54 S	139 15 E	
Ölafsjordur: fjord, Norway	37 54 N	60 17 W	
Olavarría: Argentina	36 55 N	60 20 W	
Olazaguitia: Spain	52 19 N	2 07 W	
Oldenzaal: Netherlands	52 19 N	6 56 E	
Oldham: England	53 33 N	2 07 W	
Old Hickory: Tenn., U.S.A.	36 15 N	86 39 W	
Olean: N.Y., U.S.A.	42 05 N	78 26 W	
Olenegorsk: U.S.S.R.	68 09 N	33 18 E	
Oleum: Calif., U.S.A.	37 58 N	122 13 W	

Column 4 (Ostend)

Name	Lat	Long	Page(s)
Olivais: Portugal	38 46 N	9 06 W	61D
Olkusz: Poland	50 16 N	19 33 E	46B
Olney: England	61 29 N	115 33 E	48
Olstoppen: region, Norway	64 30 N	23 30 W	39
Oltenia: region, Romania	44 30 N	23 30 E	38B
Olympia: Wash., U.S.A.	36 30 N	122 52 E	56
Omachi: Japan	41 15 N	137 52 E	47C
Omaha: Nebr., U.S.A.		96 00 W	46, 56, 62, 67, 87B
Omaruru: South West Africa	21 28 S	15 56 E	45
Omdurman see Umm Durmān: Sudan			67
Omine: Japan	15 38 N	32 30 E	30, 57D, 60C
Omi: Japan	37 01 N	137 48 E	45D
Omori: Japan	35 50 N	141 04 E	38
Omsk: U.S.S.R.	55 00 N	73 12 E	38, 31, 36, 60, 67
Omuta: Japan	63 22 N	153 48 E	58C, 58G, 59C, 59G, 60E, 60E, 61C
Omuta: Japan	33 02 N	130 27 E	27D, 45D, 58G, 59G, 61C
Onagawa: Japan	38 26 N	141 27 E	38
Onahama: Japan	36 57 N	140 54 E	27B
Ondárroa: Spain	43 19 N	114 18 E	30, 37H, 58, 59H, 60H
Oneşti see Gheorge Gheorghiu-Dej: Romania	46 15 N	26 45 E	57D
Onoda: Japan	33 59 N	131 11 E	27
Ontario: admin., Canada	51 00 N	85 00 W	49C
Ontario: Calif., U.S.A.	34 04 N	117 38 W	40C
Ontonagan Co.: Mich., U.S.A.	46 50 N	89 20 W	49
Ookvesart: Suriname	2 38 S	55 14 W	45, 50
Oostende (Ostend): Belgium	51 13 N	2 55 E	27C, 87D
Oost-Vlaanderen: admin., Belgium	51 00 N	3 45 E	56A
Oostvoorne: Netherlands	51 55 N	4 06 E	37F
Ootsi: Botswana	25 00 S	25 30 E	50, 50C
Opava: Czechoslovakia	49 58 N	17 55 E	29C
Opelika: Ala., U.S.A.	32 39 N	85 26 W	31A
Opole: Poland	50 40 N	17 56 E	43
Opp: Ala., U.S.A.	31 16 N	86 18 W	57C
Oppu: Japan	40 45 N	140 30 E	46C
Oputo: Romania	30 03 N	110 30 W	49A
Oradea: Romania	47 03 N	21 55 E	47B
Oran: Algeria	35 45 N	0 38 W	29, 31, 57, 84A
Orange: Calif., U.S.A.	33 48 N	117 51 W	32A, 58F, 60A
Orange: N.J., U.S.A.	40 47 N	74 15 W	57A, 58F, 60A
Orange: Texas, U.S.A.	30 05 N	93 43 W	60G
Orange Free State: admin., South Africa	28 00 S	27 00 E	38, 49
Ordu: admin., Turkey	40 59 N	37 30 E	27
Ordzhonikidze: U.S.S.R.	43 00 N	44 40 E	46
Orebro: Sweden	59 17 N	15 13 E	25B
Oregon: admin., U.S.A.	44 00 N	121 00 W	25
Oregon City: Oreg.: U.S.A.	45 21 N	122 36 W	25
Orekhovo-Zuyevo: U.S.S.R.	55 49 N	38 59 E	29, 34
Orenburg: U.S.S.R.	51 45 N	55 06 E	57C
Orange-Sainte-Sophie: France	49 00 N	1 04 E	27, 38
Orissa: admin., India	20 00 N	84 00 E	27, 38
Orito: region, Colombia	0 45 N	77 00 W	67
Orizaba: Mexico	18 51 N	97 06 W	67, 38
Orlando: Fla., U.S.A.	28 33 N	81 21 W	67, 87C
Orlická Přehradní Nádrž: dam, Czechoslovakia	47 55 N	1 54 E	55A
Orléans: France			
Orne: admin., France	49 31 N	14 09 E	39
Ornans: France	48 40 N	0 05 E	43B
Ornskoldsvik: Sweden	63 18 N	18 43 E	59
Oro Grande: Calif., U.S.A.	34 36 N	117 20 W	56
Oron: Israel	30 55 N	35 01 E	57
Oroville: Calif., U.S.A.	39 26 N	121 31 W	59A
Orrington: Maine, U.S.A.	44 42 N	58 49 W	43, 50, 57, 67
Orsk: U.S.S.R.	51 12 N	58 04 E	58D
Ortuella: Spain	62 23 N	77 48 E	25B
Oruro: Bolivia	18 40 S	67 30 W	67
Oruro: Bolivia	18 00 S	67 00 W	55A
Orvieto: Italy	42 43 N	12 07 E	87B
Osaka: Japan	34 40 N	135 30 E	55, 87B, 40, 52, 56, 59, 67, 84
Osarizawa-kōzan: Japan	40 11 N	140 45 E	45
Oasco: Brazil	23 32 S	46 46 W	52A
Oschatz: Germany D.R.	51 18 N	13 10 E	32C
Osaka: Japan	44 01 N	142 07 E	67
Oshawa: Canada	43 53 N	78 51 W	55A
Oshkosh: Wis., U.S.A.	44 01 N	88 32 W	87A
Oskarshamn: Sweden	57 16 N	16 25 E	52A
Oskarström: Sweden	59 55 N	10 45 E	52, 56, 59, 67, 84, 84D, 87
Oslo: Norway	52 16 N	8 03 E	31B, 43B, 58D
Ostend see Oostende: Belgium	51 13 N	2 55 E	27C, 87D

This page is a gazetteer index of place names with latitude/longitude coordinates and page reference columns, arranged in six vertical columns. Representative entries (name : description — coordinates — page references):

- Ostinovskaya: *dam*, U.S.S.R. — 61 23 N 89 45 E — 39
- Ostrava: Czechoslovakia — 49 50 N 18 25 E — 37F, 43B, 59H
- Ostravsko-Karvinská: *basin*, Czechoslovakia — 49 50 N 18 28 E — 38B
- Östringen: Germany F.R. — 49 13 N 8 43 E — 32C, 60D
- Ostrov Sakhalin: *is.*, U.S.S.R. — 51 00 N 143 00 E — 43
- Ostrowiec: N.Y., U.S.A. — 50 28 N 26 11 W — 45
- Oswego: N.Y., U.S.A. — 43 27 N 76 31 W — 30B, 58H, 59D, 60H, 61H
- Oświęcim: Poland — 50 02 N 19 11 E — 43
- Ōta: Japan — 36 18 N 139 22 E — 29D
- Otago: *admin.*, New Zealand — 44 45 S 169 10 E — 87
- Otake: Japan — 34 12 N 132 13 E — 32A, 58G, 60C
- Otanmäki: *hill*, Finland — 64 08 N 27 06 E — 27D, 67, 84
- Otaru: Japan — 43 13 N 141 00 E — 50
- Ojosundu: South West Africa — 29 50 S 17 51 E — 29B
- Otley: Portugal — 53 54 N 17 32 E — 53
- Otumco de Coronado: Mexico — 49 12 N 75 25 N — 25D, 34, 62, 67, 87

Column "P" heading:

P

- Paarl: South Africa — 33 45 S 18 58 E — 31, 60
- Pacasmayo: Peru — 7 27 S 79 33 W — 27A
- Pachuca de Soto: Mexico — 20 07 N 98 44 W — 49A
- Pacolet Mills: S.C., U.S.A. — 34 54 N 81 43 W — 31A
- Padang: Indonesia — 0 57 S 100 21 E — 67
- Padang Jawa: Malaysia — 3 05 N 101 29 E — 59, 61
- Padova (Padua): Italy — 45 25 N 11 53 E — 57C, 58D

(Additional columns list names continuing through "Pampa" / "Pamplona" in column one and through "Peixoto" / "Peking see Pei-p'ing" in the central columns, and through "Point Tupper: Canada" in the right-hand column. Sample right-column entries:)

- Pietersburg: South Africa — 28 41 S 26 35 E — 49
- Pieve Vergente: Italy — 46 00 N 8 16 E — 61D
- Pihuamo: Mexico — 19 15 N 103 23 W — 43
- Pikalevo: U.S.S.R. — 34 41 N 04 E — 31A
- Pilar: Argentina — 31 27 S 61 15 W — 47, 57, 59
- Pilbara: Australia — 21 15 S 118 11 W — 58, 61
- Pimentel: Peru — 5 20 N 112 N — 45A, 50A
- Pinal Co.: Ariz., U.S.A. — 32 40 N 111 30 W — 32
- Pine Bend: Minn., U.S.A. — 44 20 N 92 00 W — 37J, 61A, 61E
- Pine Bluff: Ark., U.S.A. — 34 13 N 92 00 W — 25A, 59B
- Pine Creek: Australia — 13 49 S 131 49 E — 40
- Pine Falls: Canada — 50 35 N 96 15 W — 25
- ...
- Plymouth: N.C., U.S.A. — 35 33 N 76 46 W — 25A, 59B
- Plzeň: admin., Czechoslovakia — 49 45 N 13 25 E — 54A
- Plzeň: Czechoslovakia — 49 45 N 13 25 E — 56A
- Pocatello: Idaho, U.S.A. — 42 53 N 112 26 W — 43B, 54B
- ...
- Point Pleasant: W. Va., U.S.A. — 38 53 N 82 09 W — 61
- Point Tupper: Canada — 45 37 N 61 25 W — 59

(This page is a dense alphabetical gazetteer index. Each entry lists a place name, its latitude (° ′ N/S), its longitude (° ′ E/W), and the map page(s) on which it appears. The entries are reproduced below in reading order, column by column, with coordinates transcribed as best-effort readings.)

Name	Lat	Long	Page(s)
Polevskoy: U.S.S.R.	56 26 N	60 11 E	43
Pöllinc: Austria	46 44 N	14 24 E	38B
Polica: Poland	53 34 N	14 35 E	59H
Polignac *Basin*: Algeria	27 00 N	6 00 E	35
Polk City: Fla., U.S.A.	28 11 N	81 51 W	59F
Polk Co.: Tenn., U.S.A.	35 10 N	84 30 W	49
Polotsk: U.S.S.R.	55 29 N	28 47 E	36, 58, 60
Polpaico: Chile	33 09 S	70 54 W	57
Polpinskaya: U.S.S.R.	53 14 N	34 27 E	56
Polunochnoye: U.S.S.R.	60 52 N	60 25 E	50
Polyphyton: *dam*, Greece	40 10 N	21 40 E	39
Pomigliano d'Arco: Italy	40 54 N	14 23 E	53
Pomona: Calif., U.S.A.	34 03 N	117 45 W	56
Pomona: Calif., U.S.A.	40 58 N	74 04 W	37I, 58, 60G
Pomeroy: France	48 01 N	6 00 E	17
Ponca: Puerto Rico, U.S.A.	11 56 N	66 11 W	31C
Pondicherry: *admin.*, India	11 56 N	79 50 E	40
Pondicherry: India	11 59 N	79 50 E	40
Ponta da Fruta: Brazil	20 31 S	40 16 W	31C
Ponte Nossa: Italy	45 52 N	9 53 E	46B
Pontevedra: Spain	42 26 N	8 38 W	45
Pontianak: Indonesia	0 02 S	109 20 E	45
Pont-Rouge: Canada	46 45 N	71 42 W	55B
Pontypool: England/Wales	51 43 N	3 02 W	25D
Poona see Pune: India	18 34 N	73 58 E	32C, 60D
Poopó: U.S.S.R.	44 23 N	36 21 E	32C
Porbandar: India	21 40 N	69 40 E	31C
Porcupine: Canada	48 30 N	81 10 W	49
Pori: Finland	61 29 N	21 47 E	25B, 31, 45
Pori amar: Venezuela	10 57 N	63 51 W	87
Poronaysk: U.S.S.R.	49 13 N	143 07 E	50
Poros: Greece	34 15 N	23 28 E	57
Port Alberni: Canada	49 11 N	124 49 W	39
Port Alfred: Canada	48 20 N	70 54 W	25, 84
Port Angeles: Wash., U.S.A.	48 06 N	123 26 W	84
Port Arthur: Canada	48 27 N	89 12 W	84
Port Arthur: Texas, U.S.A.	29 55 N	93 56 W	52A
Port Augusta: Australia	32 30 S	137 46 E	84
Portile de Fier (Iron Gate): Romania	44 41 N	22 31 E	39
Portimão: Portugal	37 08 N	8 32 W	38B, 60H
Port-Jérôme: France	49 28 N	0 32 E	60G

Name	Lat	Long	Page(s)
Portovelo: Ecuador	3 43 S	79 39 W	43
Porto Tesme: Italy	39 12 N	8 24 E	38B
Porto Piru: Australia	33 12 S	138 00 E	59H
Port Radium: Canada	66 04 N	118 00 W	35
Port Robinson: Canada	43 02 N	79 13 W	59F
Port Said see Būr Saʿīd: U.A.R.	31 16 N	32 18 E	49
Port St. Joe: Fla., U.S.A.	29 49 N	85 19 W	45
Port-Saint-Louis-du-Rhône: France	43 23 N	4 48 E	57
Portsmouth: Dominica	15 35 N	61 28 W	84A
Portsmouth: England	50 48 N	1 05 W	25B, 67B
Portsmouth: N.H., U.S.A.	43 03 N	70 47 W	52
Portsmouth: Ohio, U.S.A.	38 45 N	82 59 W	43A, 58B
Portsmouth: Va., U.S.A.	36 50 N	76 20 W	84
Port Stanley: Falkland Is.	51 42 S	57 52 W	84
Port Sudan see Būr Sūdān: Sudan	19 37 N	37 14 E	36, 84
Port Sulphur: La., U.S.A.	29 29 N	89 42 W	36
Port Swettenham: Malaysia	3 00 N	101 24 E	36, 37F
Port Talbot: Wales	51 36 N	3 47 W	38C, 47
Potenza: Italy	40 39 N	15 48 E	43, 50
Poti: U.S.S.R.	42 08 N	41 40 E	59H, 61D, 61H
Potosi: Bolivia	19 35 S	65 45 W	84
Potosí, Cerro: *mtn.*, Bolivia	19 37 S	65 45 W	50
Potrerillos: Chile	26 26 S	69 29 W	45, 49
Potsdam: Germany D.R.	52 24 N	13 04 E	60B
Pottstown: Pa., U.S.A.	40 15 N	75 38 W	58
Potwin: Kans., U.S.A.	37 57 N	97 01 W	102
Poughkeepsie: N.Y., U.S.A.	41 43 N	73 56 W	56
Povoa-sul-Loire: France	44 55 N	4 43 E	55
Vale, Ireland			
Povolzhye: U.S.S.R.	53 09 N	49 00 E	56
Powell Co.: Mont., U.S.A.	46 40 N	113 00 W	58
Powell River: Canada	49 54 N	124 34 W	84
Poza Rica: Mexico	20 33 N	97 27 W	50B
Pozharevo: Bulgaria	42 45 N	24 07 E	38B
Poznański: *admin.*, Poland	52 25 N	16 53 E	38B
Pozzuoli: Italy	40 49 N	14 07 E	57C
Prachovice: Czechoslovakia	49 28 N	15 38 E	31B, 37B, 53, 54B,
Prachuap Khiri Khan: Thai.	11 49 N	99 48 E	87
Prague see Praha: Czechoslovakia	50 05 N	14 25 E	56A
Praha (Prague): Czechoslovakia	50 05 N	14 25 E	55A, 87
Praia: Cape Verde Is.	14 55 N	23 31 W	40C
Prairie Island: Minn., U.S.A.	44 45 N	92 36 W	32C
Prat del Llobregat: Spain	41 20 N	2 06 E	32C
Prato: Italy	43 52 N	11 06 E	58D, 58H
Pratteln: Switzerland	47 32 N	7 41 E	46B
Pravdinsk: U.S.S.R.	56 32 N	43 34 E	55A
Prayon: Belgium	50 35 N	5 40 E	59H
Premier: *mine*, South Africa	25 42 S	28 30 E	45
Přemriz: Czechoslovakia	49 28 N	17 00 E	31B, 32C, 37B,
Přerov: Czechoslovakia	49 28 N	17 27 E	60D, 87
Prescot: England	53 26 N	2 48 W	45
Preslav: Bulgaria	43 10 N	26 49 E	54A
Pressburg see Bratislava: Czech.	48 10 N	17 08 E	31B, 32C, 53B, 55A
Prestea: Ghana	5 26 N	2 09 W	2, 36, 59
Preston: England	53 46 N	2 42 W	48
Pretoria: South Africa	25 45 S	28 12 E	39A
Pribilof Is.: Alaska, U.S.A.	57 00 N	170 00 W	48
Pribol'ski *region*, U.S.S.R.	57 51 N	56 15 E	2, 36, 59
Pribram: Czechoslovakia	49 42 N	14 02 E	40
Priest Rapids: *dam*, Wash., U.S.A.	46 39 N	119 55 W	59, 84
Prilep: Yugoslavia	41 20 N	21 32 E	38, 59D,
Primorsky Kray: *reg.*, U.S.S.R.	45 00 N	135 00 E	59H, 60H, 61D,
Prince Edward Island: Canada	46 30 N	63 00 W	61H
Prince George: Canada	53 55 N	122 49 W	84
Prince Rupert: Canada	54 19 N	130 20 W	60D
Princeton: Ind., U.S.A.	38 21 N	87 33 W	84
Princeton: W. Va., U.S.A.	37 23 N	81 06 W	39
Priolo Gargallo: Italy	37 09 N	15 11 E	59H

Name	Lat	Long	Page(s)
Providence: R.I., U.S.A.	41 50 N	71 25 W	29A, 36, 59A, 67A, 87B
Prudhoe Bay: Alaska, U.S.A.	71 30 N	157 00 W	25, 57A, 61B
Pryor: Okla., U.S.A.	36 19 N	95 19 W	38B, 59H
Ptolemaïs: Greece	40 32 N	21 42 E	27A
Pucallpa: Peru	8 21 S	74 41 W	43, 47
Pucusana: Peru	12 35 S	76 47 W	29B
Pudozhga: Ceylon	6 19 N	80 32 E	32
Pudsey: England	53 48 N	1 40 W	31, 58, 60, 67
Puebla de Zaragoza: Mexico	19 03 N	98 12 W	37D
Pueblo: Colo., U.S.A.	38 17 N	104 38 W	37H, 57, 58, 60
Puente de García Rodríguez: Spain			25D
Puerto Cabezas: Nicaragua	14 02 N	83 24 W	49
Puerto Cortés: Honduras	15 48 N	87 56 W	57
Puerto de Pasajes: Spain	43 20 N	1 56 W	40
Puerto Galván: Argentina	38 45 N	62 18 W	31C
Puerto La Cruz: Venezuela	10 13 N	64 38 W	67, 87C
Puerto Leguizamo: Colombia	0 12 S	74 46 W	67
Puertollano: Spain	38 41 N	4 07 W	62, 87C
Puerto Madryn: Argentina	42 46 S	65 03 W	45, 49
Puerto Montt: Chile	41 28 S	72 57 W	31
Puerto Ordaz: Venezuela	8 16 N	62 44 W	47
Puerto Vallarta: Mexico	20 37 N	105 15 W	40
Puglia: Italy	41 15 N	16 15 E	57
Puglia: *admin.*, Italy	41 15 N	16 15 E	40
Pula: Yugoslavia	44 52 N	13 50 E	48
Pulau Bintan: *island*, Indonesia	1 05 N	104 30 E	32C, 54B, 84C
Pulau Brani: *island*, Singapore	0 30 S	104 25 E	45C
Pulau Singkep: *island*, Indonesia	0 30 S	104 25 E	47
Pulawy: Poland	51 25 N	21 59 E	61D, 61H
Pulgaon: India	20 40 N	78 22 E	31C
Pulmoddai: Ceylon	8 57 N	80 59 E	32
Punchbowl: Australia	33 56 S	151 03 E	54C
Pune (Poona): India	18 34 N	73 58 E	47B
Punjab: *admin.*, India	30 50 N	75 00 E	50, 27
Punjab: *admin.*, Pakistan	30 00 N	72 00 W	46, 49
Puno: Peru	15 50 S	70 00 W	27, 84
Punta Arenas: Chile	53 09 S	70 55 W	34, 36, 84
Punta Cardón: Venezuela	11 38 N	70 14 W	40
Punta Higüero: *point*, Puerto Rico	18 22 N	67 16 W	37G, 37G
Puntarenas: Costa Rica	9 58 N	84 50 W	37C, 37G
Purfleet: England	51 29 N	0 15 E	47, 50
Pusan (Busan): South Korea	35 06 N	129 03 E	67
Putumayo: *admin.*, Colombia	0 30 N	75 30 W	25C
Puy-de-Dôme: *admin.*, France	45 40 N	3 00 E	31, 32, 84D, 87
Pyatigorsk: U.S.S.R.	44 01 N	43 05 E	38B
Pyaye: Burma	19 15 N	95 06 E	34
Pyhäsalmi: Finland	63 41 N	25 59 E	46, 49
P'yŏngan: North Korea	40 00 N	125 00 E	38C
Pyshma: U.S.S.R.	56 56 N	63 13 E	45

Column 4 (Q and R sections)

Name	Lat	Long	Page(s)
Q			
Qābis: Tunisia	33 53 N	10 07 E	61
Qafsah: Tunisia	34 25 N	8 48 E	27
Qaṣr al Burayqah (Marsa el Brega): Libya	30 25 N	19 34 E	31, 36, 67
Qayyârah: Iraq	35 48 N	43 14 E	37G
Qomi: Malta	35 39 N	14 28 W	32
Québec: Canada	52 00 N	71 15 W	25D, 57, 67, 84, 87
Queen Charlotte *Islands*: Canada	53 00 N	132 00 W	43
Queensland: *admin.*, Australia	23 00 N	145 00 E	27, 47, 50
Queenstown: Australia	42 05 S	145 33 E	45
Quelimane: Mozambique	17 51 S	36 51 E	84
Que Que: Rhodesia	18 55 S	29 49 E	43, 50C, 61
Questa: N. Mex., U.S.A.	36 43 N	105 36 W	50A
Quezon City: Philippines	14 39 N	121 01 E	67
Quiberon: France	47 29 N	3 07 W	27
Quillota: Chile	32 53 S	71 16 W	32, 36, 56
Quilon: *admin.*, India	8 53 N	76 38 W	25
Quilmes: Argentina	34 43 S	58 16 W	84
Quincy: Ill., U.S.A.	39 55 N	91 24 W	40C
Quincy: Mass., U.S.A.	42 14 N	71 00 W	45
Quirke Lake: Canada	46 29 N	82 33 W	84
Quito: Ecuador	0 13 S	78 31 W	50
Quixeramobim: Brazil	5 12 S	39 17 W	50
Qutdligssat: Greenland	70 00 N	53 00 W	38
Qyteti Stalin: Albania	40 48 N	19 55 E	37H
R			
Rabat: Morocco	34 02 N	6 51 W	17
Rabaul: New Guinea	4 12 S	152 12 E	84

Column 5 (R section — guide word Reims)

Name	Lat	Long	Page(s)
Rabbah see 'Ammān: Jordan			
Radcliff: Ky., U.S.A.	31 57 N	35 56 E	67, 87
Radcliffe: Austria	46 48 N	85 57 W	50B
Radom: Poland	53 34 N	13 43 W	59H
Radford: Va., U.S.A.	32 18 S	140 40 W	40
Radium Hill: Australia	40 04 N	0 20 W	53B, 53C
Radlett: England	23 32 N	75 20 W	62
Radnor: Pa., U.S.A.	36 55 N	80 32 W	32
Ragedara: Ceylon	19 03 N	86 10 W	40
Raghunathpur: India	38 17 N	14 36 E	57B
Ragland: Ala., U.S.A.	36 55 N	14 44 W	37H, 57, 58, 60
Ragusa: Italy	16 02 N	74 17 W	25D
Ragusa: *admin.*, Italy	44 21 S	146 26 E	57
Raichur: *admin.*, India	46 21 S	77 36 E	31C
Railway: N.J., U.S.A.	27 00 N	84 35 E	27, 56
Railton: Australia	22 18 N	84 43 E	67
Rainier: Oreg., U.S.A.	35 46 N	34 52 E	62, 87C
Rajapalaiyam: India	31 55 N	34 52 E	45, 49
Rajasthan: *admin.*, India	28 48 N	79 03 E	31
Rajgāngpur: India	1 22 N	104 16 E	47
Rajkot: India	24 58 N	75 38 E	40
Raleigh: N.C., U.S.A.	21 36 N	69 40 E	57
Ramla: Israel	56 28 N	10 03 E	32C, 54B, 84C
Rammels-berg: *mtn.*, G.F.R.	26 10 N	85 00 E	48
Rampur: India	33 20 N	80 00 E	31, 67, 84, 87
Ramuiia, Tanjong: *point*, Malaysia	16 47 N	96 10 E	36
Ranaghat: India	23 25 N	47 17 E	45C
Ranavav: India	9 58 N	98 38 E	47B
Ranchi: *admin.*, India	48 13 N	13 03 E	40
Randers: Denmark	33 20 N	12 43 E	31B
Randfontein: South Africa	47 14 N	8 50 E	
Randolph Co.: Ala., U.S.A.	28 24 N	48 33 E	37C, 37G
Rangely: Colo., U.S.A.	31 44 N	18 34 E	37D, 37G
Rangoon: Burma	37 16 N	50 25 E	47, 50
Ranomena: Malagasy R.	17 00 N	89 25 E	67
Ranong: Thailand	45 40 N	129 03 E	43
Ranshofen: Austria	66 27 N	15 57 W	27
Ranstad: Sweden	61 08 N	21 30 E	52
Rapel: *dam*, Chile	50 01 N	8 27 E	37F, 58H, 60H
Rapla: U.S.S.R.	44 06 N	145 12 E	43
Rapperswil: Switzerland	22 28 N	85 01 E	27D
Ra's al Khafjī: *point*, Neutral Zone	47 14 N		30B, 35, 37D,
Ra's al Unūf: Libya			57C, 58H,
Rashid: United Arab Republic			37F, 59D, 60H, 61D,
Rasht: Iran	37 16 N	48 33 E	61H, 84A
Rat Buri: Thailand	13 30 N	99 48 E	
Ratnagiri: *admin.*, India	17 00 N	73 30 E	58D
Raub: *region*, Malaysia	3 47 N	101 51 E	
Raufarhöfn: Iceland	66 27 N	15 57 W	31, 36, 67
Rauma: Finland	61 08 N	21 30 E	27, 32, 60
Raunheim: Germany F.R.	50 01 N	8 27 E	45A
Rausu: Japan	44 06 N	145 12 E	47, 50
Raurkela: India	22 16 N	85 01 E	57B
Ravenna: Italy	44 25 N	12 12 E	49A
Ravenna: *admin.*, Italy	44 25 N	12 12 E	53B
Ravenscraig: Scotland	55 57 N	4 47 W	31, 58, 60, 67, 84,
Ravensthorpe: Australia	33 35 S	120 02 E	87
Rävliden: Sweden	65 04 N	18 29 E	45
Räwalpindi: Pakistan	33 40 N	73 04 E	31, 36, 67
Rawson: Argentina	43 19 S	65 06 W	27, 32, 60
Raychikhinsk: U.S.S.R.	49 46 N	129 25 E	45A
Razdolinsk: U.S.S.R.	58 25 N	94 37 E	38
Razo: *admin.*, Spain	43 17 N	8 43 W	47, 50
Reading: Pa., U.S.A.	40 20 N	75 55 W	57B
Real Morelos: Mexico	26 42 N	107 40 W	49A
Rearsby: England	52 44 N	1 01 W	53B
Recife: Brazil	8 03 S	34 54 W	31, 58, 60, 67, 84,
Recklinghausen: G.F.R.	51 37 N	7 12 E	58D
Recsk: Hungary	47 56 N	20 07 E	46B
Redange-sur-Attert: Luxembourg	49 46 N	5 53 E	43B
Red Basin of Szechwan see Ssu-ch'uan P'en-ti: *basin*, China P.R.			
Redcliffe: Rhodesia	33 00 N	105 00 W	11, 34
Red Deer: Canada	19 00 S	29 49 W	61
Redding: Calif., U.S.A.	52 15 N	122 24 W	57
Redfern: Australia	33 54 S	151 12 E	55
Red Lake: Canada	50 59 N	93 40 W	43, 49
Redruth: England	50 14 N	5 14 W	45
Red Sea: Middle East	20 00 N	38 00 E	27
Redwater: Canada	53 57 N	113 06 W	57A
Redwood: Miss., U.S.A.	32 28 N	90 52 W	57
Redwood Falls: Minn., U.S.A.	44 32 N	95 07 W	40A
Reefton: New Zealand	42 07 S	171 51 E	38
Reeves *Township*: Canada	48 30 N	81 20 W	48
Regensburg: Germany F.R.	49 01 N	12 06 E	67B
Reggio nell'Emilia: Italy	44 42 N	10 38 E	54B
Regina: Canada	50 30 N	104 38 W	2, 36, 67, 87
Reichstett: France	48 39 N	7 45 E	37F
Reims: France	49 15 N	4 02 E	17, 55A, 67B

	Lat.	Long.	Page(s)
Reinosa: Mexico	26 07 N	98 18 W	34, 37I, 58E, 60
Rejowiec: Poland	51 06 N	23 18 E	
Reka Zletovska: river, Yugo.	43 13 N	22 36 E	57C, 59D, 60D
Remac: Canada	49 01 N	117 22 W	46A
Remiremont: France	48 01 N	6 35 E	31B
Renison Bell: Australia	41 48 S	145 25 E	45
Renkum: Netherlands	51 58 N	5 44 E	25C
Rennes: France	48 05 N	1 41 W	55A, 67B
Reno: Nev., U.S.A.	39 32 N	119 49 W	37J
Reno: Pa., U.S.A.	41 26 N	79 46 W	87A
Renory: Belgium	50 36 N	5 33 E	61D
Renton: Wash., U.S.A.	47 29 N	122 11 W	46B
Reșița: Romania	45 18 N	21 53 E	53, 54
Reute: Austria	47 27 N	10 42 E	43B
Revda: U.S.S.R.	56 48 N	59 57 E	
Reyðarfjörður: fjord, Iceland	65 02 N	14 10 W	17
Reykjavík: Iceland	64 09 N	21 58 W	17
Rheinbach: Germany F.R.	50 37 N	6 36 E	37C
Rheine: Germany F.R.	52 17 N	7 27 E	31B
Rheinfelden: Germany F.R.	47 33 N	7 48 E	47B, 59D, 60D
Rheinland-Pfalz: admin., G.F.R.	49 40 N	7 30 F	38B, 56A
Rheinsberg: Germany D.R.	53 06 N	12 53 E	40B
Rheydt: Germany F.R.	51 10 N	6 27 E	29B, 31B
Rho: Italy	45 32 N	9 02 E	30B, 37H, 58D
Rhodes see Ródhos: Island, Greece	33 50 N	151 05 E	58

	Lat.	Long.	Page(s)
Ródhos (Rhodes): is., Greece	36 26 N	28 13 E	17
Rodniki: U.S.S.R.	36 18 N	28 14 E	57C
Roesdare: Belgium	41 15 N	0 21 E	57B
Rolle see Mont-sur-Rolle: Switzerland	50 57 N	3 08 E	40
Roma: Italy	46 11 N	119 17 W	57
Rome: Ga., U.S.A.	37 56 N	122 20 W	25A
Romford: England	28 36 N	6 21 E	32B
Romorantin: France	41 54 N	12 29 E	25A, 32B, 59E,
Rompin: Malaysia			60B, 67A, 87C
Ronaldsway Airport: Isle of Man	34 01 N	85 02 W	50
Rondônia: Brazil	51 35 N	0 11 E	57
Rønnsari: Sweden	47 22 N	1 45 E	25A
Ronse: Belgium	54 04 N	4 33 W	43B
Roodepoort: South Africa	64 40 N	21 16 E	32C
Roolberg: South Africa	26 10 S	27 53 E	43B
Rorschach: Switzerland	24 30 S	49 30 E	43B
Rosario: Argentina	32 57 S		58

	Lat.	Long.	Page(s)
Roseau: Dominica	24 09 N	83 02 E	37H, 52A, 84A
Rosebery: Australia	45 21 N	114 24 W	39
Rosignano Solvay: Italy	41 11 N	11 03 E	37H
Rosignol: Guyana	44 23 N	21 16 E	59D, 60D
Rosmalen: Netherlands	13 30 N	84 24 W	25C
Ross: dam, Wash.	41 44 S	147 45 E	40
Rossarden: Australia	57 15 N	12 07 E	38B
Roskilde: Denmark	55 15 N		40A
Rossing: South West Africa	40 08 N	108 15 W	50
Rossiyskaya Sovietskaya Federativnaya Sotsialistich- eskaya Respublika	20 00 N	74 30 E	39
(R.S.F.S.R.): admin., U.S.S.R.	22 54 S	43 14 W	36, 52, 58, 60, 62
Rostock: Germany D.R.			67, 84, 87

	Lat.	Long.	Page(s)
Rostov-na-Donu: U.S.S.R.	35 00 S	57 50 W	27
Rotem: Belgium	20 05 S	54 04 W	50
Rotherham: England	32 02 S	52 05 W	36, 67, 84
Rotterdam: Netherlands			16
Rottweil: Germany F.R.	26 00 N	98 00 W	27
Roubaix: France			
Rouen: France	45 43 S	36 00 W	27, 38
Round Butte: dam, Oreg., U.S.A.	30 00 S	116 51 W	46A, 49
Rourkela: India	49 46 N	75 46 W	50
Roussillon: France	33 28 S	70 42 W	49
Rovinj: Yugoslavia	32 11 N	54 41 W	49
Rovno: U.S.S.R.	24 24 S	54 06 W	59H
Rowe: Mass., U.S.A.	37 40 N	6 39 W	47B
Rowleysburg: dam, W. Va., U.S.A.	34 12 S	58 18 W	27
Roxburgh: dam, New Zealand	48 10 N	74 44 W	50
Rozel: Turkey	42 48 S	147 20 E	17
Rishra: India	45 35 N	88 21 W	60
Rişnov: Romania	40 58 N	81 09 W	61D, 61H
Rittersgrün: Germany D.R.	40 28 N	121 47 W	25C
Rittman: Ohio, U.S.A.	52 30 N	107 46 W	54A, 58B
River Rouge: Mich., U.S.A.	41 50 N	111 22 W	57, 87A
Riyadh: Saudi Arabia	43 02 N	108 22 W	59
Riyadh see Ar Riyad: Saudi Arabia			
Rize: Turkey	24 38 N	46 43 E	67, 87
Rjukan: Norway	59 52 N	8 34 E	17
Roanne: France	46 02 N	4 04 W	32C
Roanoke: Va., U.S.A.	37 15 N	79 58 W	54A, 57B, 67A, 87C

	Lat.	Long.	Page(s)
Roanoke Rapids: N.C., U.S.A.	36 27 N	77 40 W	25A
Robe: River: Australia	21 19 S	115 40 E	43
Robert H. Saunders: dam, Canada	45 02 N	74 45 W	
Robert Moses: dam, N.Y., U.S.A.	45 00 N	74 50 W	39B
Robertsfors: Sweden	64 11 N	20 51 E	48
Robinson: Ill., U.S.A.	39 00 N	87 43 W	
Rocha: Uruguay	34 29 S	54 22 W	40
Rochambeau: airport, Fr. Guiana	5 00 N	52 22 W	
Rochdale: England	53 36 N	2 09 W	61D, 61H
Roche-la-Molière: France	45 26 N	4 33 W	39
Rochelle: Ill., U.S.A.	41 55 N	89 05 W	39C
Rochester: England	51 23 N	0 31 E	57C
Rochester: Mich., U.S.A.	42 41 N	83 08 W	62
Rochester: Minn., U.S.A.	44 01 N	92 28 W	47A
Rochester: N.Y., U.S.A.	43 12 N	77 37 W	67A, 87B
Rockdale: Texas, U.S.A.	30 40 N	97 00 W	32A, 38, 56, 62, 63, 47A, 87B
Rockhampton: Australia	25 40 S	150 30 E	38, 84, 84, 87
Rock Hill: S.C., U.S.A.	58 03 N	77 48 W	31
Rock Island: dam, Wash., U.S.A.			
Rocklea: Australia	47 21 N	38 50 E	39A
Rockmart: Ga., U.S.A.	27 33 S	29 00 E	55
Rocky Mount: N.C., U.S.A.	34 01 N	85 02 W	32B
Rocky Reach: dam, Wash., U.S.A.	35 56 N	77 48 W	

	Lat.	Long.	Page(s)
Rufisque: Senegal	14 43 N	17 17 E	57
Ruhr: region, Germany F.R.	51 25 N	7 00 E	32C, 38B, 63A, 63B
Rukwa, Lake: Tanzania	8 00 S		27
Rumaylah: Iraq	30 47 N	47 37 E	37C
Rumayian: mtn., Syria	41 11 N	41 58 E	37C
Rumford: R.I., U.S.A.	41 51 N	71 21 W	59E
Rum Jungle: Australia	13 01 S	131 00 E	40, 45, 59
Rumoi: Japan	43 56 N	141 39 E	27D, 38
Rumuekpe: region, Nigeria	5 00 N	6 45 E	34
Runcorn: England	53 20 N	2 44 W	59D, 60D
Rundvik: Sweden	63 32 N	19 26 E	25
Ruse: Bulgaria	43 50 N	25 57 W	37H
Russell: Ky., U.S.A.	38 32 N	82 42 W	55
Russellsville: Ark., U.S.A.	35 17 N	93 06 W	40A
Russelsheim: Germany F.R.	50 00 N	8 25 E	55A
Ruwe: Congo D.R.	25 00 S	27 15 E	49, 50C
Rwinkwavu: Rwanda	1 58 S	30 34 E	45
Ryazan: U.S.S.R.	58 03 N	38 50 E	32C, 36, 57, 67
Rybinsk: U.S.S.R.			31
Rybinsk/Sheksna: dam, U.S.S.R.			
Ryluiísa: U.S.S.R.	58 03 N	38 50 E	39
Rydal: Sweden	57 45 N	29 00 E	57C
Ryōtsu: Japan	34 05 N	12 41 E	31
		138 26 E	27D

S

	Lat.	Long.	Page(s)
Saarbrücken: Germany F.R.	49 14 N	7 00 E	58D
Saarland: admin., G.F.R.	49 45 N	7 00 E	38B, 56A
Sabac: Yugoslavia	41 45 N	19 43 E	46B
Sabadell: Spain	43 06 N	1 24 E	29
Sabangir: dam, India	42 31 N	6 20 E	47B
Sabbione: dam, Italy			39
Sabínánigo: Spain	38 32 N	121 30 W	39C
Sacramento: Calif., U.S.A.	39 15 N	122 00 W	47B, 59D, 60D, 61D, 61H
Sacramento Valley: Calif., U.S.A.			40, 87A
Sadd-el-Aali (Aswan High Dam): dam, U.A.R.	23 56 N	32 53 E	34
Sado: is., Japan	42 38 N	138 25 E	
Sadon: Is., Japan	42 51 N	131 54 E	39
Saeki: Japan	26 48 N	44 44 W	49
Safâjah, Wâdî: stream, U.A.R.	32 30 N	10 17 W	46, 49
Safi: Tunisia	33 06 N	7 37 W	46, 49, 56
Safi: Morocco	35 05 N	31 03 E	27, 59, 84
Safonovo: U.S.S.R.	49 11 N	117 16 W	39
Saganoseki: Japan	43 25 N	83 54 W	45D, 46C, 59G
Saginaw: Mich., U.S.A.	29 03 N	64 06 W	67A, 87B
Sagua la Grande: Cuba	39 41 N	0 16 W	40A, 49B
Sagunto: Spain	34 50 N	77 33 E	31
Saharanpur: India	36 39 N	35 22 E	37C, 37G
Saïda: Algeria	10 45 N	134 40 E	32A
Saïda (Sidon): Lebanon	33 55 N	35 22 E	32A
Saidaiji: Japan	47 00 N	11 08 E	67, 84, 87
Saigon: South Vietnam	46 04 N	6 60 E	25D
Saijō: Japan	46 45 N	71 49 W	47B, 59D, 60D
Ste. Anne de Beaupré: Canada			57
Saint-Auban: France			
Saint-Basile: Canada			
Saint-Benoît-de-Carmaux: France	44 03 N	2 08 E	61H
Saint Boniface: Canada	49 54 N	97 07 W	36
Saint Charles: Mo., U.S.A.	38 48 N	90 30 E	54B
St. Charles Parish: admin., La., U.S.A.			53
Ste.-Croix: Haiti	29 55 N	90 25 W	
St. Croix: island, Virgin Is., U.S.A.	18 25 N	73 09 W	59B
Saint-Égrève: France			47
Saint-Émilion: France	45 14 N	64 45 W	
Saint-Étienne-du-Rouvray: France	44 53 N	0 09 W	36, 87
Saint-Fons: France			57C

	Lat.	Long.	Page(s)
Saint-Guénolé: France	47 49 N	4 22 W	25C
St. Helenabaai: bay, S. Africa	33 24 N	18 05 E	59D, 59H, 60D, 61D, 61H
St. Helens: England			27
St. Helens: Oreg., U.S.A.	45 52 N	122 49 W	27
St. Hyacinthe: Canada			25, 61
Sandouville: France			31
St. Jérôme: Canada	45 17 N	6 21 E	
Saint John: Canada	45 16 N	66 03 W	47B
Saint Johns: Antigua	17 06 N	61 51 W	29
St. John's: Canada	47 34 N	52 41 W	36, 87
Saint-Laurent-de-Blangy: France	50 18 N	2 50 E	67, 84, 87
St. Lawrence: river, Canada	49 00 N	67 00 W	32C, 60D
St. Louis: France	47 35 N	7 33 E	40B
St. Louis: Mich., U.S.A.	43 21 N	84 35 W	47B

	Lat.	Long.	Page(s)
St. Louis: Mo., U.S.A.	38 40 N	90 15 W	32B, 45, 53, 54, 55, 56, 57A, 58B, 63
Saint-Marcet: France	43 12 N	0 45 E	87B
St. Marks: Fla., U.S.A.	30 12 N	84 12 W	37B
St. Mary's: Ga., U.S.A.	30 43 N	81 34 W	57B
St. Mary's: W. Va., U.S.A.	39 24 N	81 13 W	25A
Saint-Menet: France	43 17 N	5 27 E	37J
Saint-Nabord: France	47 07 N	6 35 E	60D
Saint-Nazaire: France	47 17 N	2 12 W	32C, 60D
St. Paul, Minn., U.S.A.	45 00 N	93 00 W	52A, 53B
St. Paul Park: Minn., U.S.A.	44 50 N	93 00 W	25, 55, 56, 62, 87B
St. Pierre-la-Cour: France	48 12 N	1 02 W	57J
Saint-Pourçain-sur-Besbre: France			32C
Saint-Quentin: France	46 23 N	3 39 E	17
Saint-Renan: France	49 51 N	3 17 E	40B
Saint-Sylvestre: France	48 26 N	4 37 W	31B
Ste. Thérèse: Canada	45 38 N	73 50 W	45
St. Thomas: Island, Virgin Is. (U.S.A.)	18 21 N	64 55 W	32B, 55
St. Urbain: Canada	47 35 N	70 33 W	87
Saint-Vulbas: France	45 50 N	5 17 E	40B
Saitama-ken: admin., Japan	34 35 N	139 30 E	55, 58G, 59C, 60C, 60E, 61C
Sakai: Japan		135 28 E	

	Lat.	Long.	Page(s)
Sakai: Japan	35 33 N	139 14 E	27D
Sakata: Japan	38 55 N	139 50 E	38
Sakhalin Ostrov: is., U.S.S.R.	51 00 N	143 30 E	33
Sakoshi: Japan	34 46 N	137 47 E	33A
Salamanca: Mexico	20 34 N	101 12 W	39D
Salamanca: Spain	40 58 N	5 39 W	30, 36, 60, 61
Sala-nod-Vahom: Czech.	48 09 N	17 55 E	59H
Salavat: U.S.S.R.	53 21 N	55 55 E	58, 60, 61
Saldanhabaai: bay, S. Africa	33 00 S	17 56 E	27
Salem: Mo., U.S.A.	11 38 N	78 08 E	31C, 47, 50
Salem: N.J., U.S.A.	39 35 N	75 28 W	59E
Salem: Oreg., U.S.A.	37 38 N	91 34 W	40C
Salerno: Italy	40 41 N	14 47 E	27
Salford: England	53 30 N	2 16 W	57C
Salgótarján: Hungary	48 07 N	19 49 E	38B
Salina: Kans., U.S.A.	38 53 N	97 37 W	31B
Salindres: France	44 10 N	4 10 E	59D
Saline Co.: Ark., U.S.A.	34 40 N	92 35 W	47B, 59H
Salisbury: admin., Rhodesia	17 50 S	31 03 E	47B
Salisbury: N.C., U.S.A.	35 40 N	80 30 W	31A, 32B
Salisbury: Rhodesia	17 50 S	117 16 W	46A
Salmo: Canada	49 11 N	64 06 W	34, 35
Salta: admin., Argentina	25 00 N	65 25 W	34, 35
Salta: Argentina	24 47 S	65 55 W	36, 45, 67, 87
Salt Lake City: Utah, U.S.A.	40 45 N	112 00 W	36, 45, 67, 87
Salt Lake Co.: Utah, U.S.A.	40 45 N	112 00 W	46, 49B
Salto Grande: dam, Argentina	31 14 S	57 55 W	39
Salt River: South Africa	33 56 S	18 28 E	
Salt River Canyon: Ariz., U.S.A.	33 45 N	110 45 W	48
Saltville: Va., U.S.A.	36 52 N	81 48 W	59B
Salvador: Brazil	12 59 S	38 31 W	67, 84, 87
Salvajina: dam, Colombia	4 03 N	74 50 W	4 03 N
Salzgitter: Germany F.R.	52 05 N	10 20 E	43B, 54B
Samanco: bay, Peru	9 30 S	117 00 W	27
Samarinda: Indonesia	0 30 S	117 09 E	25
Sambalpur: India	21 28 N	84 04 E	
Samchŏk-up: admin., South Korea			
Samch'ŏk: South Korea	37 26 N	129 10 E	57D
Samson: Turkey	37 27 N	129 08 E	38C, 59C
San Andreas: Calif., U.S.A.	41 17 N	36 20 W	59H
San Antonio: Texas, U.S.A.	38 10 N	121 01 W	59H
San Bernardino: Calif., U.S.A.	33 35 N	98 30 W	57
San Celoni: Spain	34 04 N	117 18 W	84B
San Cristóbal: Mexico	41 41 N	2 29 W	57
Sandakan: Malaysia	18 23 N	105 33 W	49A
Sandbach: England	5 53 N	118 07 E	49B
Sande: Norway	53 09 N	2 22 W	58
Sandersville: Miss., U.S.A.	59 44 N	10 12 E	87
San Diego: Calif., U.S.A.	31 47 N	89 02 W	25B
Sandhamn: Sweden	32 45 N	117 10 W	55D
Sandsvall: Sweden	59 17 N	18 54 E	40, 52, 53, 87A
Sandouville: France	62 38 N	17 20 E	27C
Sand Springs: Okla., U.S.A.	36 08 N	96 07 W	55A
Sandur: India	15 06 N	76 31 E	49A
Sandusky: Ohio, U.S.A.	41 27 N	82 42 W	59E
San Eduardo: Ecuador	2 12 S	79 56 W	57
San Esteban: dam, Spain	42 25 N	7 40 W	39
San Felipe: Mexico	30 22 N	110 13 W	49A
San Felipe del Progresso: Mexico			
San Fernando: Philippines	19 43 N	99 57 W	84
	16 39 N	120 19 E	49A

	°	'		°	'		Page(s)
Sharon: Pa., U.S.A.	41	16 N		80	30 W		54A
Shasta: *dam*, Calif., U.S.A.	40	37 N		122	28 W		39
Shawinigan: Canada	46	33 N		72	45 W		25D, 31, 47, 59A,
Shawville: Canada	45	36 N		76	30 W		59E
Shchëkino: U.S.S.R.	53	59 N		37	38 E		43A
Shcheÿkovo: U.S.S.R.	55	55 N		38	00 E		38
Shchigry: U.S.S.R.	51	52 N		36	54 E		31
Shebelinka: U.S.S.R.	49	27 N		36	31 E		56
Sheffield: Ala., U.S.A.	53	23 N		87	40 W		34
Sheffield: England				1	30 W		61B, 61E
Sheksna/Rybinsk: *dam*, U.S.S.R.							43B, 58D, 67B

Index entries, column headings: Name | Latitude | Longitude | Page(s)

Name	Lat	Long	Page(s)
Takeo: Japan	33 12 N	130 01 E	60C
Ta Khli: Thailand	15 15 N	100 21 E	84
Takoradi: Ghana	04 53 N	01 45 W	84
Ta-ku Pao: see Po-t'ou			45C
Talaiyuthu: India	09 00 N	98 21 E	84
Talang Akar: Indonesia	03 16 S	103 50 E	55
Talara: Peru	04 38 S	81 18 W	36
Talbingo: dam, Australia	35 36 S	148 18 E	39
Talcahuano: Chile	36 43 S	73 07 W	37
Talladega: Ala, U.S.A.	33 26 N	86 07 W	87C
Tallahassee: Fla, U.S.A.	30 26 N	84 19 W	29, 31A
Tallinn: U.S.S.R.	59 25 N	24 45 E	25, 25B, 31
Talmessi-Meskani: Iran	33 28 N	53 30 E	52B
Tamano: Japan	34 32 N	133 56 E	32A
Tamashima: Japan	34 32 N	133 41 E	36, 84
Tambo de Mora: Peru	13 30 S	76 08 W	27A
Tambov: U.S.S.R.	52 44 N	41 28 E	30, 67
Tamil Nadu (Madras): admin, India	11 00 N	78 15 E	43
Tampa: Fla, U.S.A.	27 58 N	82 38 W	60C
Tampere: Finland	61 30 N	23 45 E	61B, 67, 84, 87C
Tampico: Mexico	22 13 N	97 51 W	55A
Tamworth: England	52 39 N	01 40 W	84D
Tanabe: Japan	33 44 N	135 22 E	
Tananarivo see Antananarivo: Malagasy Republic			27, 38
Tanga: Tanzania	05 07 S	39 05 E	41, 56, 57, 59F
Tanger: Morocco	35 48 N	05 45 W	61B, 67, 84, 87C
Tang-shan (Hopeh): China P.R.	39 38 N	118 11 E	84
Tanjong Ramunia: point, Malaysia	01 22 N	104 16 E	47
Tannu Tuva: reg., U.S.S.R.	53 00 N	96 00 E	25, 32
Tan-tung (Antung): China P.R.	40 06 N	124 25 E	31B
Tanvald: Czechoslovakia	50 46 N	15 19 E	57D
Tao-lin: China P.R.	28 55 N	113 07 E	
Taormina: Italy	37 51 N	15 17 E	17
Tao-yüan: Taiwan	24 59 N	121 15 E	31, 60
Tapajós, Rio: river, Brazil	04 24 S	56 18 W	49
Tarābulus (Tripoli): Lebanon	34 27 N	35 50 E	37C, 37G, 84, 87C
Tarābulus (Tripoli): Libya	32 54 N	13 11 E	61, 67, 84, 87
Tarakohe: New Zealand	40 51 N	172 54 E	57
Taranaki: admin, New Zealand	42 34 S	171 08 E	38C
Taranaku River: New Zealand	39 20 S	174 30 E	37H, 43B, 84A
Taranto: Italy	40 28 N	17 14 E	40
Tarapur Chinchani: India	19 52 N	72 42 E	43B, 57
Tarbela: Pakistan	34 14 N	72 49 E	40
Tarkwa: Ghana	05 18 N	01 59 W	53B
Tarnobrzeg: Poland	50 35 N	21 41 E	57
Tarnos: France	43 32 N	01 29 W	38B
Tarnów: Poland	50 01 N	20 59 E	59H
Taró: Japan	39 44 N	141 58 E	61D, 61H
Tarquinia: Italy	42 15 N	11 45 E	46C
Tarragona: Spain	41 07 N	01 15 E	45
Tarragona: admin, Spain	41 10 N	01 14 E	38C, 57
Tarrant City: Ala, U.S.A.	33 38 N	86 46 W	38B
Tarrasa: Spain	41 34 N	02 00 E	38B
Tarsus: Turkey	36 55 N	34 53 E	32A
Tarui: Japan	40 47 N	07 58 E	43
Tashkent: U.S.S.R.	41 20 N	69 18 E	32, 61, 67, 87
Tashtagol: U.S.S.R.	52 47 N	87 53 E	47, 87
Tasmania: admin, Australia	42 00 S	147 00 E	38B, 84A
Tatui: Brazil	23 21 N	47 51 E	38B
Tatvan: Turkey	38 31 N	42 15 E	49
Ta-t'ung: China P.R.	40 09 N	113 17 E	61
Ta-t'ung (Tsitsihar): China P.R.	47 23 N	123 59 E	37F
Ta-ung: China P.R.	25 30 N	114 45 E	43B, 87
Ta-yü: China P.R.	25 25 N	114 22 E	37G, 57, 59, 60
Chitondzi: Congo Republic	04 33 N	12 00 E	67, 87
Tébessa: Algeria	35 40 N	08 07 E	50B
Tecuci: Romania	45 50 N	27 31 E	
Tegucigalpa: Honduras	14 06 N	87 14 W	
Tehrān: Iran	35 40 N	51 26 E	
Tekeli: U.S.S.R.	44 48 N	78 57 E	
Tekirdağ: Turkey	40 59 N	27 31 E	

Name	Lat	Long	Page(s)
Telamayo: Bolivia	21 08 S	66 19 W	49
Tel Aviv: Israel	32 05 N	34 46 E	59
Telejen-cheia: Romania	45 27 N	25 56 E	84
Tema: Ghana	05 42 N	00 09 E	84
Temangan: Malaysia	05 08 N	102 04 E	38
Temir-Tau: U.S.S.R.	50 05 N	87 28 E	57
Temir Akar: Indonesia	03 08 N	98 51 E	59A
Tempoku: basin, Japan	44 48 N	142 02 E	37
Temse: Belgium	51 08 N	04 13 E	39C
Ténès: Algeria	36 34 N	01 18 E	27B
Tennant Creek: Australia	19 39 S	134 12 E	45, 49
Tennessee: admin, U.S.A.	36 00 N	86 00 W	29, 38A, 46
Tepexi del Oro: Mexico	17 51 S	41 30 W	67
Teplice: Czechoslovakia	50 40 N	13 50 E	46B
Teploozersk: U.S.S.R.	49 00 N	131 05 E	57
Terek: U.S.S.R.	43 30 N	44 11 E	50
Teresa: Brazil	05 05 S	42 49 W	67
Teresina: Brazil	05 09 S	42 49 W	67
Termez: U.S.S.R.	37 14 N	67 16 E	34, 36
Termini Imerese: Italy	37 59 N	13 42 E	59H
Terneuzen: Netherlands	51 20 N	03 49 E	60D, 60H, 60D
Terni-pol': U.S.S.R.	49 34 N	25 59 E	38B, 43B, 60D
Terre Haute: Ind., U.S.A.	39 27 N	87 24 W	61A, 61E, 67A, 84D
Terre-Neuve: Haiti	19 36 N	72 44 W	57, 55B, 58B
Tertre: Belgium	50 40 N	03 48 E	58D, 61D, 61H
Teruel: admin, Spain	40 40 N	01 00 W	59D, 59H
Teslić: Yugoslavia	44 37 N	17 52 E	46, 49
Tessenderlo: Belgium	51 04 N	05 05 E	43
Tetyukhe-Pristan: U.S.S.R.	44 21 N	135 35 E	37J, 45, 58A, 58E, 59F, 60A, 60G
Texada Island: Canada	49 40 N	124 30 W	61B, 84
Texas: admin, U.S.A.	32 00 N	100 00 W	43
Texas City: Texas, U.S.A.	29 23 N	94 55 W	54
Teykovo: U.S.S.R.	56 52 N	40 34 E	37D
Thabazimbi: South Africa	24 24 S	27 28 E	60
Thames Estuary: England	51 31 N	00 31 E	59D
Thames Haven: England	51 30 N	00 30 E	39A
Thana: India	19 14 N	73 02 E	45
Thanjavur: India	10 46 N	79 09 E	
Thann: France	47 49 N	07 05 E	59D
Thaon: France	48 16 N	06 25 E	59H
The Dalles: Oreg., U.S.A.	45 36 N	121 10 W	61D, 61H
Thessaloniki: Greece	40 38 N	22 58 E	46C
Thetford Mines: Canada	46 06 N	71 18 W	
Thévenard: Australia	32 10 S	133 38 E	38
Thionville: France	49 22 N	06 10 E	59B
Thom see Tho	45 55 N	89 20 W	29A
Thompson: Canada	55 45 N	97 54 W	29A
Thorne: England	53 37 N	00 58 W	40C
Thorold: Canada	43 07 N	79 14 W	49
Three Mile Island: Pa., U.S.A.	40 09 N	76 45 W	49
Thuddungra: Australia	34 09 S	148 01 E	49
Thunder Bay: Canada	48 20 S	89 15 W	49
Thursday Island: Australia	10 35 S	142 13 E	35, 36
Tiber: Colombia	08 39 N	72 42 W	45
Tien-ching (Tientsin): China P.R.	39 08 N	117 12 E	25, 29, 31, 43, 55
Tien-ching see Tien-ching: China P.R.			59, 84
Tien-pao-shan: China P.R.	42 57 N	128 57 E	25, 29, 31, 43, 55,
Tientsin see Tien-ching: China P.R.	39 08 N	117 12 E	59, 84
Tierra del Fuego: admin, Arg.	54 00 S	67 00 W	59, 84
Tiflis see Tbilisi: U.S.S.R.	41 48 N	44 48 E	40B
Tigil: U.S.S.R.	57 48 N	158 40 E	57
Tihange: Belgium	50 31 N	05 14 E	38
Tijeras: N. Mex., U.S.A.	35 04 N	106 21 W	38
Tijuana: Mexico	32 32 N	117 01 W	38B
Tikhoretsk: U.S.S.R.	45 51 N	40 09 E	45
Tilburg: Netherlands	51 34 N	05 05 E	45, 46
Tilleur: Belgium	50 37 N	05 30 E	31, 38B
Till Cove: Canada	47 47 N	54 11 W	61D, 61H
Timagami: Canada	47 04 N	80 04 W	45
Timmins: Canada	48 28 N	81 20 W	45, 46
Timna: Israel	29 45 N	35 13 E	31, 38B
Tingha: Australia	29 57 S	151 14 E	87
Tîrgu Mureş: Romania	46 33 N	24 34 E	43B, 87
Tîrnăveni: Romania	46 20 N	24 17 E	59F
Tirunelveli: Wales	08 45 N	77 04 E	67, 87
Tiszapalkonya: Hungary	47 53 N	21 04 E	50B
Titas: region, Pakistan	24 08 N	91 00 E	
Tixkan: Ecuador	02 08 S	78 48 W	

Name	Lat	Long	Page(s)
Tjikotok: Indonesia	07 44 S	106 19 E	49
Tjilanjap: Indonesia	07 44 S	109 00 E	59
Tjirebon: Indonesia	06 44 S	108 34 E	84
Tkibuli: U.S.S.R.	42 21 N	43 00 E	38
Tkvarcheli: U.S.S.R.	42 51 N	41 41 E	38
Tlalnepantla: Mexico	19 00 N	98 59 W	57
Tlaxcala de Xicohténcatl: Mexico	19 19 N	98 14 W	60
Tobata: Japan	33 53 N	130 50 E	58C, 58G, 59G, 60E, 61C
Tobias: region, Angola	09 40 S	12 35 E	34
Toby Creek: Yuruq, Libya	32 05 N	23 59 E	46A
Tocopilla: Chile	22 05 S	70 12 W	84
Töging: Germany F.R.	48 15 N	12 35 E	47B
Tokai: Japan	48 07 N	136 25 E	40
Tokmak: U.S.S.R.	41 35 N	72 42 E	17
Tokogul: dam, U.S.S.R.	34 03 N	131 49 E	57
Toktogul: dam, U.S.S.R.			39
Tokuyama: Japan	34 03 N	131 49 E	32A, 60C, 57D, 58C, 58G, 59C, 60C, 60E, 61C, 84D
Tōkyō: Japan	35 42 N	139 46 E	2, 3, 25, 27D, 29D, 31, 34, 38, 43D, 48, 52B, 53, 55, 56, 59C, 60E, 63, 67, 84, 87B
Toledo: Ohio, U.S.A.	41 40 N	83 35 W	37J, 55B, 58B, 60F, 67B, 84, 87B
Tolland: Conn., U.S.A.	41 52 N	72 22 W	32, 60
Toluca de Lerdo: Mexico	19 17 N	99 40 W	30, 55, 60
Tol'yatti (Savropol'): U.S.S.R.	53 11 N	49 24 E	32
Tomago: Australia	32 50 S	151 44 E	25D
Tomahawk: Wis, U.S.A.	45 27 N	89 42 W	25, 59
Tomakomai: Japan	42 38 N	141 36 E	
Tomaszów Mazowiecka: Poland	51 33 N	20 00 E	29C, 32C
Tōmatsu: Japan	35 15 N	141 55 E	60
Tommot: U.S.S.R.	58 58 N	126 19 E	48
Tom Price, Mount: Australia	22 49 S	117 51 E	43
Tomsk: U.S.S.R.	56 30 N	84 58 E	61, 67
Tonawanda: N.Y., U.S.A.	43 01 N	78 54 W	58B, 58F, 60B
Tongane: South Korea	39 22 N	125 25 E	39
Tongariro: dam, New Zealand	39 07 N	175 39 E	45
Toobeah: Utah, U.S.A.	40 00 N	113 16 W	49B
Topeka: Kans, U.S.A.	39 03 N	95 41 W	49A
Topia: Mexico	25 13 N	106 34 W	17
Topola: Yugoslavia	44 15 N	20 41 E	45, 50
Toquepala: Peru	17 24 S	70 25 W	57C
Toral de los Vados: Spain	42 33 N	06 47 W	50
Torane: New Hebrides	17 39 S	168 21 E	31B, 37B, 43B, 54B, 55A, 63A, 63B, 87D
Torino (Turin): Italy	45 03 N	07 40 E	25D, 29, 34, 55A, 56, 58B, 62, 63, 67A, 87B
Toronto: Canada	43 42 N	79 25 W	59
Tororo: Uganda	0 42 N	34 11 E	30A, 43, 53, 58, 60
Torrance: Calif., U.S.A.	37 36 N	118 35 W	34, 59, 67
Torredonjimeno: Spain	37 46 N	03 57 W	32C, 59D, 60D
Torrelavega: Spain	43 21 N	04 03 W	31B
Torres Vedras: Portugal	39 06 N	09 16 W	29B
Tórshavn: Faeroe Is.	62 00 N	06 46 W	45, 84, 87
Tortiya: Ivory Coast	08 46 N	05 40 W	67, 84A, 87
Toruń: Poland	53 01 N	18 35 E	40A
Torviscosa: Italy	45 45 N	13 18 E	57
Tosa-shimizu: Japan	32 47 N	132 58 E	84
Totoro-ko: Japan	32 31 N	131 41 E	57C, 60D
Tou-fen: Taiwan	24 41 N	120 54 E	52B
Touissit: Morocco	34 29 N	01 49 W	50
Toulouse: France	43 36 N	01 26 E	32A, 40, 57D, 59C, 59G, 61C, 61G, 84D
Toyoha: Japan	43 00 N	141 00 E	46
Toyohashi: Japan	34 46 N	137 23 E	32A, 43D
Toyota: Japan	35 05 N	137 09 E	59G
Tozeur: Tunisia	33 55 N	08 08 E	57F
Trail: Canada	49 04 N	117 40 W	46, 59, 61
Transvaal: admin, S. Africa	24 00 S	30 00 E	39
Tràslövsläge: Sweden	57 04 N	12 16 E	27C
Travancore: admin, India	09 00 N	76 00 E	47, 50
Traverse City: Mich, U.S.A.	44 46 N	85 38 W	87B
Trawsfynydd: Wales	52 55 N	03 55 W	40B
Tredyffrin: Pa. U.S.A.	40 03 N	75 26 W	60H
Trengganu: admin, Malaysia	05 00 N	103 00 E	62
Trento: Italy	46 04 N	11 03 E	58D, 58H

Name	Lat	Long	Page(s)
Trenton: Canada	45 37 N	62 38 W	54
Trenton: Mich, U.S.A.	42 08 N	83 09 W	57J
Trenton: N.J., U.S.A.	40 15 N	74 43 W	30, 32B
Trepça: Yugoslavia	42 55 N	20 50 E	46B, 56
Trés Marias: dam, Brazil	18 15 S	45 15 W	49
Treviso: Italy	45 40 N	12 15 E	59
Tri-City Airport: Tenn., U.S.A.	36 28 N	82 24 W	17
Trident: Mont, U.S.A.	45 58 N	111 25 W	87C
Trier: Germany F.R.	49 45 N	06 38 E	57
Trieste: Italy	45 40 N	13 46 E	17
Trimmelkam: Austria	48 02 N	12 52 E	37H, 57C, 58D, 84A
Trinec: Czechoslovakia	49 41 N	18 18 E	38B
Trino: Italy	45 12 N	08 18 E	40B
Trói Creek: Tarābulus: Lebanon	45 12 N	35 50 E	37C, 37G, 84, 87
Tripoli see Tarābulus: Libya	32 54 N	13 11 E	61, 67, 84, 87
Tripura: admin, India	24 00 N	92 00 E	67
Trivandrum: India	08 41 N	76 57 E	60D
Troisdorf: Germany F.R.	50 49 N	07 10 E	25D, 31, 84
Trois Rivières: Canada	46 21 N	72 34 W	84A
Troitsk: U.S.S.R.	54 06 N	61 35 E	38B
Trollhättan: Sweden	58 16 N	12 18 E	53, 54, 55
Trombay: India	19 01 N	72 58 E	27, 87
Tromsø: Norway	69 40 N	18 58 E	59
Trona: Calif, U.S.A.	35 46 N	117 24 W	56, 67, 84, 87
Trondheim: Norway	63 25 N	10 25 E	
Trondheimsfjorden: fjord, Norway	63 39 N	10 49 E	43, 46
Troódos: Cyprus	34 55 N	32 52 E	32C
Troutdale: Oreg., U.S.A.	45 32 N	122 23 W	50, 50B
Troy: Ind., U.S.A.	38 00 N	86 00 W	47
Trujillo: Peru	08 06 S	79 00 W	67
Tsu: Japan	34 53 N	136 28 E	38C
Tselinograd: U.S.S.R.	51 10 N	71 30 E	56
Tshikapa: Congo D.R.	06 25 S	20 48 E	48
Tsinan see Chi-nan: China P.R.			
Tsingtao see Ch'ing-tao: China P.R.	36 04 N	117 00 E	55, 61
Tsining Shan see Ch'in Ling: mtn., China P.R.			29, 31, 43, 54, 84
Tsitsihar see Ch'i-ch'i-ha-erh: China P.R.	34 00 N	108 00 E	50
Tsu: Japan	47 22 N	123 57 E	25, 54, 67
Tsukumi: Japan	34 43 N	131 52 E	29D, 32A
Tsurusaki: Japan	33 14 N	131 42 E	57D
Tsuruga: Japan	35 39 N	136 04 E	32A, 40, 57D, 59G
Tsurumi Ku: Japan	35 32 N	139 33 E	60C, 84D
Tuba City: Ariz., U.S.A.	36 08 N	111 18 W	52B
Tubruq (Tobruk): Libya	32 05 N	23 59 E	30, 38G, 60C
Tu Chanh Nong Son: South Vietnam	15 43 N	108 01 E	40A, 84
Tucson: Ariz., U.S.A.	32 15 N	110 57 W	36
Tudela-Agüeria: Spain	43 19 N	05 48 W	57C
Tula de Allende: Mexico	20 03 N	99 21 W	32C, 43, 58, 61
Tula: Okla, U.S.A.	36 07 N	95 58 W	57
Tulsa: Pa, U.S.A.	36 07 N	95 58 W	37J, 53, 57A, 58B, 59F, 87C
Tulun: U.S.S.R.	54 35 N	100 33 E	58B, 59F, 59F
Tumaco: Colombia	01 52 N	78 46 W	38
Tumut II: dam, Australia	35 22 S	148 23 E	39
Tuncbilek: Turkey	39 33 N	29 31 E	84
Tundzha: region, Bulgaria	42 30 N	26 34 E	57C, 60D
Tundza-ch'üan: China P.R.	30 56 N	118 01 W	50
Tung-chuan: China P.R.	41 41 N	109 03 W	31B, 37B, 43B, 55A
Tung-hua: China P.R.	41 41 N	125 55 E	63B, 54B, 55A, 55B, 63B, 63B, 87D
Tung-ling: China P.R.	30 56 N	117 48 E	40
Tunhovd: dam, Norway	60 30 N	08 38 W	27
Tunis: N.C., U.S.A.	36 35 N	76 55 W	29, 52, 58, 67
Tunis: Tunisia	36 48 N	10 11 E	61A, 61A, 67, 87
Tuolumne Co.: Calif, U.S.A.	38 00 N	120 00 W	84A, 87
Tura el Hajjārah: U.A.R.	29 58 N	31 16 E	40A
Turbo: Colombia	08 06 N	76 43 W	57
Turgay: U.S.S.R.	49 38 N	63 30 E	57C, 60D
Turin see Torino: Italy	45 03 N	07 40 E	50
Türkali: Turkey	39 24 N	26 26 E	31B, 37B, 43B, 55A
Turkey Point: Fla., U.S.A.	25 26 N	80 19 W	63B, 54B, 55A, 63B, 87D
Turkmenskaya S.S.R.: admin, U.S.S.R.			54B
Turnu Măgurele: Romania	43 45 N	24 52 E	54B
Turnu Severin: Romania	44 38 N	22 40 E	58F, 59E, 60B
Tuscaloosa: Ala, U.S.A.	33 12 N	87 33 W	37J, 59F
Tuscola: Ill., U.S.A.	39 49 N	88 18 W	59F
Tu-shan-tzu: China P.R.	44 20 N	84 51 E	61A
Tuticorin: India	08 48 N	78 10 E	36
Tutunup: Australia	33 40 S	115 35 E	3IC, 59, 60, 84

STATISTICAL SUPPLEMENT

Introduction

THE STATISTICAL SUPPLEMENT gives in tabular form for each country much of the economic data depicted on the maps. Countries are arranged in alphabetical order except that entries for dependent territories (or references to them) follow the entry for the suzerain nation.

Background and summary data on area, population, employment, trade, etc., are given first, in a standard format which is altered only when statistical information is not available. This section is followed by detailed figures for production, exports and imports. Statistics are given for the years 1963–5 and 1953–5 so that the trend of a national economy for this specific period may be studied. Also, the relative importance of various commodities in the economy of a country may be seen even if they are insignificant in the world context. They are arranged in eleven tables which group the statistics for related commodities. These, with references to the relevant map pages, are as follows:

Table		Map pages
1	Cereals	9–12
2	Fruit, etc.	16–17
3	Beverages, Forest Products, etc.	13–15, 24–25
4	Vegetable Oilseeds and Oils	18–19
5	Livestock, Animal Products, etc.	21–23, 26–27
6	Fibres, Textiles, etc.	28–32
7	Fuel and Power	33–41
8	Iron and Steel	42–43
9	Non-ferrous Minerals and Metals	44–50
10	Chemicals and Fertilizers	56, 58–61
11	Industry	51–57

The trade statistics are for either special trade or general trade. Special trade is defined as imports for domestic consumption or improvement and exports of home-produced or processed goods. General trade refers to total imports and total exports including re-exports. Most of the statistics in tables 1–6 are on a general trade basis; however, where imports or exports are known to be, or to include, re-exports, this has been indicated. Tables 7–11 are on a special trade basis unless otherwise stated.

Generally, mention has been made of any commodity known to be produced or traded by a country even where the quantity is not known. For certain commodities, such as cassava, no trade figures are available; in these cases the trade columns have been left blank, and the commodity has been listed only under producing countries. For certain countries, in particular those with centrally planned economies (the Sino-Soviet bloc), production and trade statistics are not always available. The omission of a commodity from the data for one of these countries does not necessarily indicate that the commodity is not a factor in its economy.

Common units, usually in the metric system, have been used wherever possible. The definitions of commodity categories have also been held constant from country to country as far as possible, but statistics for related items are not always available on the same basis. Thus, for example, many production figures for metalliferous ores refer to the weight of the metal content, whereas those for trade refer to the total weight of the ore. Attention is drawn to the Appendix which contains an alphabetical list of the commodities included in the supplement, together with definitions and other relevant information.

117

COUNTRY INDEX

AFGHANISTAN — CENTRAL ASIA

Afghanistan is a constitutional monarchy; parliamentary democracy was established in 1965, and Islamic law abolished. Transit arrangements with Pakistan enable the bulk of trade to be transported through Karachi.

AREA: 657 500 sq. km. (250 000 sq. miles)

LAND USE: (percentage of total)

	1962
Arable and orchard	13.7
Permanent meadow and pasture	4.9
Forest and woodland	2.3
City areas, waste and other land	79.1

POPULATION: 15 751 000 (1967 estimate)
Largest city: KABUL, capital; population: 456 342 (1967)

		Year(s)
Population per physician	22 140	1966
Population per hospital bed	5 810a	1966
School enrolment: age 5–19 years (percentage)	10	1963–4 av.
age over 19 years (per 100 000 population)	22	1963–5 av.

a government hospitals only

EMPLOYMENT AND PRODUCTION
Agriculture (crops and sheep) is the main occupation. There are two cereal crops per annum. Sugar beet, fruit and cotton are grown. Silk, woollen and hair cloth, and carpets are made. Salt, silver, copper, coal, iron, lead, chrome, talc, and precious stones are mined in small quantities.

COMMUNICATIONS

		Year(s)
Motor vehicles in use ('000s): private	9.3	1963–5 av.
commercial	10.5	
Telephones (per '000 urban population)	10.1*	1967
Radio receivers (per '000 population)	12	1963–5 av.
Daily newspapers (per '000 population)	4	1962–3 av.

FINANCE
Currency unit: The afghani

Exchange rates	1965	1960	1957a
Per $ U.S.	79.84b	42.49	23.35
Per £ sterling	223.55	118.97	62.3

		Year
National Income (million $ U.S.)	649	1958
G.N.P. per capita ($ U.S.)	70	1966

a official rate. The market rate was 50 to 55 afghanis per $ U.S. or 140 to 164 afghanis per £ sterling. b free rate.

TRADING

Total trade (in million $ U.S.)	1965
Exports (f.o.b.)	70
Imports (c.i.f.)	131

Main trading partners (percentage of total value)

Exports	1965	Imports	1965
U.S.S.R.	47	U.S.S.R.	25
U.K.	15	U.S.A.	18
Pakistan	13	Germany F.R.	16
India	6	Japan	14
Germany F.R.	4	India	8
		U.K.	7
		Czechoslovakia	2

Distribution of trade (percentage of total value)

Exports	1965	Imports	1965
Crude materials and fuels	50	Loans and grant imports	57
(fur skins) (cotton)	(23)	Manufactured goods	24 (9)
Food	36	(fabrics and clothing)	(16)
(edible nuts; dried, pre-served fruits)	(26)	(machinery and transport equipment)	
Carpets	13	Food	5 (6)
		Fuels	3

PRODUCTION, EXPORTS AND IMPORTS
Years: 1963–5 average and 1953–5 average Units: '000 metric tons unless otherwise indicated

	Production		Exports		Imports	
1. CEREALS, etc.						
Barley	379.3	283.0¹	—	—	—	—
Maize (corn)	717.7		—	—	—	—
Rice	359.7	na	—	—	—	—
Wheat	2 159.7	2 124.0	—	—	78.4*	5.0*¹
2. FRUIT, etc.						
Grapes	20.0¹*	20.0*	1.2*		—	—
Raisins	na	na	16.6*	17.4*	—	—
3. BEVERAGES, FOREST-PRODUCTS, etc.						
Sugar: beet	49.0	30.7*	—	—	42.7*	5.01*
raw	10.0	5.7*	—	—	5.2*	2.4²
Softwood j	686.7*	na	—	—	3.4²	
Hardwood j	4 654.0*	na	—	—	0.31	
Other paper			—	—	0.3²	
4. VEGETABLE OILSEEDS AND OILS						
Cottonseed	80.70	35.00*	13.00*	—	—	—
Linseed seed	na	na	1.89	—	na	
Soya bean oil	na	na		—	na	
5. LIVESTOCK‡, ANIMAL PRODUCTS, etc.						
Cattle d	3 361.7*	2 000¹**				
Goats d	3 500.0*	8 000¹**				
Sheep d	18 268.3*	14 000¹**				
Horses d	145.7*	1951				
Meat† 'A'	18.1	na				
Eggs	336.0*	na	—	—	0.30*	
Milk	na	na	1.8¹	—	—	
Hides/skins	na	na	2.4*	—	3.9*	
Wool	na	3*	0.5*	—	—	

d number in thousands.

	Production		Exports		Imports	
6. FIBRES, TEXTILES, etc.						
Cotton lint	45.7	17.7*	16.9*	9.0	—	—
Silk	5.5*	2.1*	—	—	—	—
Cotton, woven fabrics	na	0.22m	na	—	—	—
Wool, woven fabrics						
7. FUEL AND POWER						
Coal 'A'‡	117	20	—	—	—	—
Electricity h: total	245	10	—	—	—	—
hydro	166¹	10				
thermal	79					
Petroleum, refined	—	—	—	—	—	na
11. INDUSTRY						
Cement	122.0*	—	—*	—	17.0*	—
Electrical engineering a	—	—			1.8	
Motor vehicles a	—	—			3.8	

n million metres. h million kWh. a million $ U.S.

ALBANIA — EUROPE

Albania was occupied by the Italians and Germans from 1939–44. Elections in 1945 resulted in a communist-controlled assembly, and the following year a republic was declared. Albania withdrew from the Warsaw Pact in 1968, severed diplomatic relations with the U.S.S.R. and strengthened her ties with China P.R.

AREA: 28 748 sq. km. (11 101 sq. miles)

LAND USE: (percentage of total)

	1964
Arable and orchard	17.4
Permanent meadow and pasture	25.4
Forest and woodland	43.7
City areas, waste and other land	13.5

POPULATION: 1 965 000 (1967 estimate)
Largest city: TIRANE, capital; population: 156 950 (city proper, 1964)
Total working population: 730 762 (1960)

		Year(s)
Life expectancy at birth (years): male	63.7	1963–4 av.
female	66.8	
Infant mortality (per '000)	86.8	1965
Crude birth rate (per '000)	35.2	1965
Crude death rate (per '000)	9	1965
Population per physician	2 070	1965
Population per hospital bed	170	1966
School enrolment: age 5–19 years (percentage)	107‡	1966
age over 19 years (per 100 000 population)	677	1963–5 av.

EMPLOYMENT AND PRODUCTION
Albania is mainly an agricultural land although the raising of livestock, apart from poultry, has decreased since World War II. Cultivated and forest land is farmed mainly by the state and cooperatives. A third 5-year plan (1961–5) could be fulfilled because China's aid had not made up for the withdrawal of Soviet assistance. The main crops are maize, sugar beet and wheat. Cotton, fruit, tobacco, oats and rice are also grown. An afforestation programme has been undertaken. Mineral wealth is considerable but only oil, lignite, chrome, iron content have recently been located. Large iron deposits with high nickel content have recently been located. Industries are concerned mainly with processing of agricultural products, and making of cement, textiles and paper.

COMMUNICATIONS

		Year(s)
Railway track (km.)	151	1964
Telephones (per '000 urban population)	0.3	1959n
Radio receivers (per '000 population)	51	1963–5n
Television sets (per '000 population)	0.4	1963–5 av.
Daily newspapers (per '000 population)	48.5	1963–4 av.

n latest data available

FINANCE
Currency unit: The lek

Exchange rates	1965q	1960p	1950q
Per $ U.S.	50	50	125
Per £ sterling	140	140	350

		Year(s)
National Income (million $ U.S.)	570n	1966
G.N.P. per capita ($ U.S.)	300*	1966
Rate of increase of G.N.P. per capita	4.1	1960–4 av.

n middle rate. p official rate. q tourist rate

TRADING

Total trade (in million $ U.S.)	1965	1955
Exports (f.o.b.)	na	13
Imports (c.i.f.)	43	43

In 1963 49% of the exports and 59% of the imports were accounted for by China P.R. Eastern European countries took 42% of the exports and supplied 32% of the imports, there being no trade with the U.S.S.R.

PRODUCTION, EXPORTS AND IMPORTS
Years: 1963–5 average and 1953–5 average Units: '000 metric tons unless otherwise indicated

	Production		Exports		Imports	
1. CEREALS, etc.						
Barley	8.0*		—	—	—	—
Maize (corn)	181.3		na		na	
Oats	14.0*		na		na	
Potatoes	30.3*		na		na	
Rice	8.7*		na		na	
Rye	6.0*		na		na	
Wheat	95.3*		na		110.3²	
2. FRUIT, etc.						
Figs	11.3*		na		na	
Grapes	na		na		na	
Olives	29.7*		na		na	
Oranges	2.0		na		na	
Plums	8.7*		na		na	
Wine b	na		na		na	
3. BEVERAGES, FOREST-PRODUCTS, etc.						
Sugar: beet	126.3*		na		na	
raw	14.7		6.0²		9.8²	
Tobacco: leaf	14.3*		7.42*			
products	na		3.0n			
Softwood j	520.0²		na		na	
Hardwood j	1 020.02*		na		na	
Paper	na		na		na	
4. VEGETABLE OILSEEDS AND OILS						
Cottonseed	15.30		na		na	
Olive oil	4.00*		na		na	
5. LIVESTOCK‡, ANIMAL PRODUCTS, etc.						
Chickens d	1 691.0*n		na		na	
Cattle d	412.0		na		na	
dairy cows d	na		na		na	
Goats d	1 146.0		na		na	
Sheep d	1 613.0		na		na	
Pigs d	145.0		na		na	
Meat† 'A'	44.0*		na		na	
'B'	1.6*		na		na	
Cheese	4.0*		3.01		na	
Eggs	3.1*		na		na	
Milk	3.6*		2.5		na	
Hides/skins	80.0*		na		na	
Wool	na		7.0		0.4²	

d incl. ducks, geese and turkeys

	Production		Exports		Imports	
6. FIBRES, TEXTILES, etc.						
Cotton lint	8.0*		—		21.2²	0.3*
Rubber, natural	7.6¹		na		na	
Cotton: yarn	3.4¹		5.5¹		na	
woven fabrics	na		na		na	
Rayon: fibre/yarn	na		na		na	
Wool, woven fabrics	1.0²n		na		110.3²	na
7. FUEL AND POWER						
Coal 'B'‡	143	190				
Coke	na				11	
Electricity h: total	272	80¹				
thermal	186²	30¹				
hydro	86	50¹				
Oil, crude	776	210¹	293		20	
Petroleum, refined	247	90¹				
8. IRON AND STEEL						
Iron ore	na		na			
Pig iron	na		349		2	
9. NON-FERROUS MINERALS AND METALS						
Chrome, ore	305.07m	91.62m	285.37			
Copper: ore	2.54		na		na	
metal	na		2.65		0.11	
Zinc, metal	2.75					
11. INDUSTRY						
Alcoholic beverages b	107.0	na	10.02n		—	
beer b	na					
Cement	136.0*	43.0*	na		20.01*	
Electrical	—	—				
engineering	na		5.92q		—p	

b '000 hectolitres. n wine and cognac only. p excl. trade with other communist countries. q electric motors and radios, number in thousands. j '000 cu. metres of roundwood equivalent. n cigarettes only. h million kWh. m metal content. n million metres.

d number in thousands. na: data not available. — negligible or nil. — not available. * estimate. 2 two year average. 1 one year only. ‡ see appendix. † re-exports.

na: data not available. — negligible or nil. 2 two year average. 1 one year only. * estimate. ‡ see appendix. † re-exports.

ALGERIA

Algeria became independent from French administration in 1962. This followed armed rebellion by the Moslem National Liberation Front (F.L.N.) in 1954, and referenda in France, and referenda in both countries. Within a few years of independence, 80% of the French population had left Algeria.

AREA: 2 466 833 sq. km. (952 198 sq. miles)

LAND USE: (percentage of total)	1954
Arable and orchard	3.1
Permanent meadland and pasture	18.2
Forest and other land	1.4
City areas, waste and other land	77.3

POPULATION: 11 833 126 (1966 census)
Largest city: ALGER (Algiers), capital; population: 943 142 (1966)

Distribution of working population (1954)
Total working population: 3 511 934 [European: 354 510, non-European 3 157 424]

U.N. group no.		Percentage	
		Europeans	Non-Europeans
0	Agriculture, forestry, fishing and hunting	11.1	82.1
1	Mining and quarrying	0.8	0.9
2/3	Manufacturing	17.2	7.9
4	Construction	9.7	1.7
5	Electricity, gas, water and sanitary services	1.2	—
6	Commerce	20.8	3.2
7	Transport, storage and communications	8.8	1.0
8	Services	25.1	2.2
9	Others	5.3	6.5

	Year(s)
Life expectancy at birth (years): Algerians	35	1948
Non-Algerians	63	1955
Infant mortality (per '000): Algerians	86.3*	1965
Non-Algerians	46.2*	1966
Crude birth rate (per '000)	10.1*	1964
Crude death rate (per '000)		1966
Population per physician	8 950	1963
Population per hospital bed	290	1963-4 av.
School enrolment: age 5–19 years (percentage)	53	1963-5 av.
age over 19 years (per 100 000 population)		

COMMUNICATIONS

		Year(s)
Motor vehicles in use ('000s): private	205.7	1963-5 av.
commercial	92.5	1964
Railway track (km)	3 900	
Mail per capita: domestic	11	1963-5 av.
foreign received		
foreign sent	1.2	1964
Telephones (per '000 urban population)	134	1967
Radio licences (per '000 population)	9.1	1963-5 av.
Television sets (per '000 population)		1963-5 av.
Daily newspapers (per '000 population)	24	1961

PRODUCTION, EXPORTS AND IMPORTS

Years: **1963–5** average and 1953–5 average   Units: '000 metric tons unless otherwise indicated

	Production		Exports		Imports	
	1963–5	1953–5 av.				

1. CEREALS, etc.

Barley	449.0	788.3	32.6*[2]	87.2	na	0.6
Maize (corn)	5.3*	11.0[2]	0.7*[1]	0.7	na	3.5
Millets/sorghum	1.7*	12.0			na	0.1†
Oats	29.3	104.0	20.6*	3.6	17.2*	22.9
Potatoes	214.3	247.5[2]	1.8*[2]	88.0	81.4*	5.5
Rice	5.3*	8.0	2.8*[2]	4.7	na	4.7
Rye	na	na				
Sweet potatoes/ yams	7.0*	na				
Wheat	1 358.3	1 249.0	7.8*[1]	26.9	308.4*	43.3

2. FRUIT, etc.

Apples	16.0*	na			5.7*	6.6
Apricots	14.7*	11.5	na	0.6	17.2*	8.8
Bananas			na	3.5		
Dates	110.0*	92.3	20.6*	0.1†	na	0.2
Figs	59.0	93.3		22.9	na	0.1
Grapes	1 684.7*[2]	2 236.3*	1.8*[1]	5.5		
Lemons	15.0	11.0*	2.8*[2]	4.7	1.8	
Olives	153.7*	193.5[2]				
Oranges	409.0	340.3*	200.1*	220.1	0.1*[1]	1.8
Other citrus fruit	4.7	3.7*	3.6*	2.7[2]		
Peaches	10.0*	9.1	na	0.1	2.6*	1.3
Pears	na	na		1.4		2.8
Plums	11.0*	10.5	na	0.7		
Raisins	11.0*	na	na	1.4		1.4
Tomatoes	121.0*	na		0.3		
Wine b	13 106.0	17 311.0	8 102.7*	14 400.0	na	225.7

b '000 hectolitres

PRODUCTION, EXPORTS AND IMPORTS continued

4. VEGETABLE OILSEEDS AND OILS—continued

	Production	Exports	Imports
Palm kernels	—	—	0.20
Palm oil	—	—	1.47
Rape seed	0.47*	—	0.47*
Rapeseed oil	66.34*	—	66.34*
Sesame seed	7.96*	—	7.96*
Soya beans	na	—	3.42
Soya bean oil	na	—	0.27
Sunflower seed oil	4.09	—	4.09
Tung oil	na	—	2.14n
	na	—	1.46[2]p

n incl. maize oil and sunflower oil.   p incl. other minor vegetable oils.

5. LIVESTOCK‡, ANIMAL PRODUCTS, etc.

	Production	Exports	Imports
Chickens d	6 500.0*	—	—
Cattle d	755.3*	—	—
Goats d	2 558.0[2]	0.3	14.1
Sheep d	5 508.3*	—	na
Horses d	117.7	—	29.3*
Pigs d	170.0	0.9	na
Bacon/ham	62.3*	1.0*	0.1*
Meat‡: 'A'	20.7	0.1	5.2*
'B'		0.1	1.6*
Butter	10.0*	0.1	5.6*
Cheese	20.0*	2.3	5.0*
Eggs	17.5	12.4*	1.7*
Fish	285.7*	1.8	2.1
Milk	na	na	98.9*
Hides/skins	na	7.6[1]	1.71
Wool	na	1.1	0.2

d number in thousands.

6. FIBRES, TEXTILES, etc.

	Production	Exports	Imports
Cotton lint	1.0*	—	0.1
Jute	na	2.0	0.4
Rubber, natural	na	—	0.1*
Cotton: yarn	1.7*	—	0.72
woven fabrics	0.3	0.1	3.6[2]
Wool: yarn	na	—	na
woven fabrics	na	0.1	na

7. FUEL AND POWER

	Production	Exports	Imports
Coal 'A'‡	47	na	274
Electricity h: total	1 094		
hydro	313		
thermal	781		
Natural gas i	1 020		
Oil, crude	25 620	24 300	19*n
Petroleum, refined	1 500	740	1 000

h '000 hectolitres.   i million cu. metres.   n incl. coke.

FINANCE

Currency unit: The Algerian dinar (at par with the French franc)

Exchange rates	1961	1954
Per $ U.S.	3.0	
Per £ sterling	16.1	
	1.3	
	79.6	

National Income (million $ U.S.) 2 272 (1964)
G.N.P. per capita ($ U.S.) 220 (1966)

TRADING

Total trade (in million $ U.S.)	1964	1955	1938
Exports (f.o.b.)	727	463	162
Imports (c.i.f.)	703	696	143

Main trading partners (percentage of total value)

Exports	1964	1955	1938
France	78	74	83
Germany F.R.	3	3	2a
Italy	2	3	1
Netherlands	2	1	8
U.K.	2	1	5
Belg./Lux.	1	1	—
Spain	1	1	1

Imports	1965	1955	1938*
France	71	76	75
U.S.A.	4	3	1
U.K.	3	1	2
Ivory Coast.	3	1	na
Italy	3	2	1
Germany F.R.	2	2	1a
Morocco	2	2	5b

a incl. Germany D.R.   b former French Morocco

Distribution of trade (percentage of total value)

Exports	1965	1955	1938*
Petroleum and products	54	40	49
Alcoholic beverages	18	26	19
Food (citrus fruit)	17	(7)	(2)

Imports	1965	1955	1938*
Food	22	19	15
Machinery and transport equipment	15	20	14
Textiles and clothing	14	13	7
Chemicals	8	5	na
Iron and steel	5	6	6
Wood and paper			

A trade agreement was signed with the U.S.S.R. in November 1963 for the exchange of Soviet machinery for Algerian wheat and fruit.

3. BEVERAGES, FOREST PRODUCTS, etc.

	Production	Exports	Imports
Cocoa	—	—	0.3
Coffee	—	—	30.7*n
Sugar: beet	15.0	—	234.2*
raw	1.6	3.7*	na
Tea	—	na	na
Tobacco: raw	6.4*	1.42*n	na
cigarettes	5 585.0x	7 906.0*e r	0.2*[1]n
cigars	3.1	2.4	
tobacco/snuff	51.01*	124.5[2]	315.2*
Softwood j	153.01*	230.5[2]	65.3*
Hardwood j	1*	23.5	1.22
Wood pulp	2*	2	22.01
Newsprint	30.2*	26.55*	25.01
Other paper	14.00*	19.0[2]	13.8[2]

e number in millions.   j '000 cu. metres of roundwood equivalent.   r manufactured tobacco only.

4. VEGETABLE OILSEEDS AND OILS

	Production	Exports	Imports
Castor oil	—	—	0.01
Copra	—	—	0.30
Coconut oil	3.30*	—	0.92[2]
Cottonseed	2.00*	—	—
Cottonseed oil	na	—	3.39
Groundnuts	na	na	11.90
Groundnut oil	1.00*[1]	0.01	8.07
Linseed	na	0.01	8.32
Linseed oil	na	0.67	0.40
Olive oil	23.00*	13.04	0.94
		2.33	1.43

continued

---

8. IRON AND STEEL

	Production	Exports	Imports
Iron ore	1 416m	1 652m	na	211.30
Pig iron	—	—	—	1
Steel ingots/castings	—	—	—	16
Iron/steel scrap	—	56[2]	69	—

m metal content.

9. NON-FERROUS MINERALS AND METALS

	Production	Exports	Imports
Gold k,	na	—	na
bullion/coins, etc.	—	—	244.67
Silver: ore	281.70	55.70	na	2.88
bullion	—	—	0.04
Asbestos: fibre	—	—	3.53
manufactured	—	—	1.85
Aluminium: bauxite	10.16[2]*	0.97*n	0.83[2]*
aluminium	—	—	
Antimony: ore	0.02n	0.24	0.02
metal	—	5.85	0.04
Chrome, metal	—	—	
Copper: ore	1.05m	0.14m	
metal	3.78	—	8.57
Lead: ore	9.40m	9.68m	1.74	0.25
metal	—	11.65	4.04
Magnesium: dolomite	12.00	2.74	
magnesite	na	—	na
Manganese, ore	na	—	0.05
Mercury‡	10.0*	—	1.30
Tin, metal	0.01	—	0.20
Zinc: ore	36.67m	26.61m	na
metal	59.46	43.77	1.88
		0.45	

f metric tons.   k '000 fine troy ounces.   m metal content.   n incl. scrap.

10. CHEMICALS n AND FERTILIZERS

	Production	Exports	Imports
Chemicals	—	—	na
Fertilizers:			
Phosphates	169.0	714.6	9.6
Potash	24.0x	127.6	660.3	18.2
Pyrites	33.6	0.1	10.9
Sulphur	23.7p	na	19.9

n data not available for years 1953–5.   p native.   x sulphur content.

11. INDUSTRY

	Production	Exports	Imports
Aircraft a	—	—	na
Alcoholic beverages	—	—	4.5m
beers	255.0	393.7	
spirits	—	—	0.31
Cement	788.0	595.7	100.0*	15.0*	135.0
Elec. engineering a	340.0*	—	17.8[1]q	24.42
Railway vehicles a	—	37.3	2.3q	2.8
Machine tools a	—	—	0.61	2.62
Motor vehicles: commercial d	2.1p	na	26.21a	36.41a
private d	3.6p	na		

a no. in thousands.   d no. in thousands.   p assembly of imported parts.   q data incomplete.

EUROPE

ANDORRA

Andorra is a neutral co-principality under the joint sovereignty of the French President and the Bishop of Urgel to both of whom the state pays dues.

Tourism, encouraged by the absence of customs duties, is the main source of revenue. The main agricultural products are potatoes, cereals and tobacco. Stockbreeding is also important. Extensive deforestation has decreased former timber resources. The working of rich deposits of iron, alum, lead, slate and stone is handicapped by lack of transport.

EMPLOYMENT AND PRODUCTION

CURRENCY: The French franc and the Spanish peseta

AREA: 465 sq. km. (190 sq. miles)

POPULATION: 14 000 (1967 U.N. estimate)
Capital city: ANDORRA; population: 2 463 (1965)

---

na: data not available.   — negligible or nil.   — not available.   [1] one year only.   [2] two year average.   * estimate.   ‡ see appendix.   † re-exports.

na: data not available.   — negligible or nil.   [1] one year only.   [2] two year average.   * estimate.   ‡ see appendix.   † re-exports.

n wines and spirits

ARABIAN PENINSULAR STATES

SAUDI ARABIA—see page 206
SOUTHERN YEMEN—see page 210

COMMUNICATIONS

		Year(s)
Telephones (per '000 urban population)	4	1967
Radio receivers (per '000 population)	750a	1963–5 av.
Television sets (per '000 population)	59.2	1963–5 av.
Daily newspapers (per '000 population)	58	1958

BAHRAIN

Bahrain is an Arab sheikdom which has special treaty relations with the U.K.

AREA: 598.3 sq. km. (231 sq. miles)

POPULATION: 182 203 (1965 census)

Capital city: AL MANĀMAH; population: 79 098 (1965)

Total working population: 45 479 (1959)

		Year(s)
Population per physician	2 030	1965
Population per hospital bed	240b	1966
School enrolment: age 5–19 years (percentage)	90a	1963–4 av.

a public education only. b government hospitals only.

FINANCE

Currency unit: The Bahrain dinar replaced the Indian (external) rupee in 1965

Exchange rates	1965	1960a
Per $ U.S.	0.357	4.76
Per £ sterling	1.0	13.33

a rupees.

EMPLOYMENT AND TRADE

The standard of living is high in the merchant groups and rapidly rising in the lower social groups. The pearl fishing trade has now declined. Oil was discovered in 1932 and a refinery built, 80% of the oil for which is piped from Saudi Arabia. The free transit of goods for the mainland has encouraged the entrepôt trade, and by 1966 Bahrain was re-exporting 30% of its imports. Bahrain has also an international airport. Imports are food, manufactured goods, building materials, machinery and vehicles.

KUWAIT

Kuwait has long been independent and in 1961 recognition of her sovereignty was re-affirmed by the U.K. Iraqi claims to the territory were made, but British and Arab League forces supported Kuwait's independence. Since 1946 oil concessions have been granted to several oil companies.

AREA: 24 280 sq. km. (9 375 sq. miles) (after partition of the Neutral Zone)

POPULATION: 467 339 (1965 census)

Largest city: AL KUWAYT, capital; population: 295 273 (1961)

Total working population: 95 533 (1961)

		Year(s)
Infant mortality (per '000)	39.8*	1965
Crude birth rate (per '000)	46.2*	1965
Crude death rate (per '000)	6.2*	1965
Accidental deaths (per 100 000 population)		
caused by motor vehicles	61.7*	1967
due to other causes	27.1	1967
Population per physician	810	1965
Population per hospital bed	140	1966
School enrolment: age 5–19 years (percentage)	97	1963–4 av.

COMMUNICATIONS

		Year(s)
Motor vehicles in use ('000s): private	52.1	1963–5 av.
commercial	20.0	1964–5 av.
Mail per capita: domestic	36	
foreign received	26	
foreign sent	6.3	
Telephones (per '000 urban population)	340	1967
Radio receivers (per '000 population)	810	1963–5 av.
Television sets (per '000 population)	115.3	1963–5 av.
Daily newspapers (per '000 population)	28	1964

EMPLOYMENT AND PRODUCTION

Kuwait formerly served as an entrepôt for goods for the interior and the export of hides and wool, and as a pearl fishing centre. Kuwait remains an important entrepôt centre but revenue from oil drilling has enabled her to start on large scale development plans. Some 20% of the oil was refined locally in 1965.

FINANCE

Currency unit: The Kuwait dinar, at par with the pound sterling until 1968, replaced the Indian (external) rupee in 1961.

Exchange rates	1965	1960a
Per $ U.S.	0.357	4.76
Per £ sterling	1.0	13.33

a rupees.

		Year(s)
National Income (million $ U.S.)	1487	1965
G.N.P. per capita ($ U.S.)	3410	1966
Foreign trade (percentage of G.D.P.)	76	1963–5 av.

TRADING

Total trade (in million $ U.S.)	1965	1960
Exports (f.o.b.)	1 250	957
Imports (c.i.f.)	377	242

Main trading partners (percentage of total value)

Exports	1965		Imports	1965
Italy	27		U.S.A.	21
Japan	23		U.K.	16
U.K.	19		Japan	10
France	16		Germany F.R.	9
Netherlands			Italy	5
			China P.R.	3
			Iran	3

Distribution of trade (percentage of total value)

Exports*	1965		Imports	1965
Petroleum	94		Manufactured goods	68
Food	2		(machinery and transport equipment)	(32)
Cigarettes	2		(textiles and clothing)	(12)
Machinery and transport equipment	1		Food	21

OMAN

Oman is an independent sovereign sultanate extending inland to the great desert. The population is very mixed with many Indian merchants. A small tract on the Baluchistan coast was handed over to Pakistan in 1958. Close ties are maintained with the British government.

AREA: 212 000* sq. km. (82 000* sq. miles)

LAND USE: (percentage of total)	1948
Arable and orchard	—
Permanent meadow and pasture	—
Forest and woodland	0.4
City areas, waste and other land	99.6

POPULATION: 565 000 (1967 U.N. estimate)

Capital city: MASQAŢ (Muscat); population: 6 208 (1960)

FINANCE

Currency unit: The riyal Saidi replaced the Indian (external) rupee in 1970. Previously the Maria Theresa dollar and the Indian (external) rupee were circulated. A copper coin, the baiza, is still in use.

Exchange rates in 1958	Maria Theresa dollar	Indian rupee
Per $ U.S.	3.69	4.76
Per £ sterling	10.34	13.33

		Year
National Income (million $ U.S.)	32	1958

LAND USE AND EMPLOYMENT

The only cultivatable area is the 10 mile wide coastal plain. Dates and sugar cane are grown and cattle are reared. Drilling for oil started in 1967. Trade is mainly with India, Pakistan, the U.K. and the Persian Gulf States. In 1964 chief exports were dates, fruit and fish. Imports included cereals, cement and vehicles.

NEUTRAL ZONE

This consists of two areas of desert which were administered jointly by Kuwait and Saudi Arabia until 1966 when they were partitioned between these two states.

Oil production which started in 1954 reached 19 million metric tons in 1965. Exploitation of oil and other natural resources will continue to be shared between Kuwait and Saudi Arabia.

QATAR

Qatar is an independent Arab sheikdom with special treaty relations with the U.K.

AREA: 10 360* sq. km. (4 000* sq. miles)

POPULATION: 75 000 (1967 estimate)

Largest city: AD DAWḤAH (Doha), capital; population: 45 000 (city proper, 1963)

FINANCE

Currency unit: The riyal replaced at par the Indian (external) rupee in 1966

Exchange rates	1968	1958
Per $ U.S.	4.76	4.76
Per £ sterling	11.43	13.33

EMPLOYMENT AND TRADE

The population consists mainly of semi-nomadic tribesmen and Bedouin using the poor grazing. Pearl fishing has declined. Development projects now depend on oil drilling, begun in 1949, on land and off-shore, and a cement factory and prawn freezing plant have been built. A large number of migrant labourers are employed.

TRUCIAL STATES

The Trucial States consist of seven independent Arab sheikdoms which have treaty relations with the U.K. Aid is given by the other independent states of the Persian Gulf.

AREA: 83 660* sq. km. (32 300* sq. miles)

POPULATION: 136 000 (1967 estimate)

Capital city: DUBAYY (Dubai); population: 65 000 (1966)

FINANCE

Currency unit: The riyal replaced at par the Indian (external) rupee in 1966. The Bahrain dinar is also used.

Exchange rates	1968a	1958a
Per $ U.S.	4.76	4.76
Per £ sterling	11.43	13.33

a riyals. b rupees.

EMPLOYMENT AND TRADE

One-tenth of the population is estimated to be nomadic. The main crops are cereals, dates, vegetables, fruit and tobacco. There is a fishing trade and a declining pearl fishing industry. Revenue is derived from customs duties and oil concession payments from Abu Dhabi (since 1962). Dubai has an entrepôt trade and an international airport and Sharjah is an R.A.F. base. The chief exports are oil, dried fish and tobacco. The chief trading partners are the U.K., Japan and India.

YEMEN

In 1958 Yemen federated with the United Arab Republic (a union of Egypt and Syria) to form the United Arab States. Syria broke away in 1961, and later that year Yemen's union with Egypt was terminated.

AREA: 195 000* sq. km. (75 000* sq. miles)

POPULATION: 5 000 000 (1967 U.N. estimate)

Capital city: ŞAN'A'; population: 60 000 (1956)

FINANCE

Currency unit: The silver riyal has replaced at par the Maria Theresa dollar

Exchange rates	1965	1960a	1958a
Per $ U.S.	1.1	1.1	3.69
Per £ sterling	3.08	3.08	10.34

		Year(s)
National Income (million $ U.S.)	180	1958
G.N.P. per capita ($ U.S.)	90	1966

a Maria Theresa dollars.

EMPLOYMENT AND TRADE

Semi-nomadic herding and settled agriculture occupy most of the population, since no crude oil has yet been found. The main products are millet, coffee, cotton, oilseeds, salt and hides. Soviet, Chinese and U.S. aid is received.

PRODUCTION, EXPORTS AND IMPORTS

Years: 1963–5 average and 1953–5 average   Units: '000 metric tons unless otherwise indicated

These data are for the seven states listed above and do not include Saudi Arabia and Southern Yemen.

1. CEREALS, etc.

	Production	Exports	Imports
Barley			20.6*
Maize (corn)			4.2
Millets/sorghum			0.4*
Oats			6.0*
Potatoes	15.7*	3.1[1]‡†	90.0*
Rice			
Wheat	25.0*		18.7*

2. FRUIT, etc.

	Production	Exports	Imports
Apples			2.0*
Bananas			6.1*
Dates	60.0*n	12.9*	24.8*
Grapes		0.1*‡†	0.9*
Lemons			3.6*
Oranges			0.2*
Other citrus fruit			0.1*
Pears			
Raisins			0.6*
Wine b			0.6*

b '000 hectolitres. n Yemen only.

3. BEVERAGES, FOREST PRODUCTS, etc.

	Production	Exports	Imports
Coffee	4.9*	4.1*	2.4*
Sugar, raw	4.4*	9.5*‡†	101.0*
Tobacco: leaf		2.2[1]‡†	4.3*
cigarettes		0.6*‡†	0.6*
Newsprint			3.3
Other paper c			6.2*

c number in millions.

4. VEGETABLE OILSEEDS AND OILS

	Production	Exports	Imports
Copra		2.50*	0.10*
Coconut oil			0.40*
Cottonseed			0.60*
Cottonseed oil			0.60*
Groundnuts			0.40*
Groundnut oil			0.20*
Linseed oil			0.20*
Olive oil			0.30
Palm oil			0.20*
Sesame seed			
Soya bean oil			
Sunflower seed			

5. LIVESTOCK†, ANIMAL PRODUCTS, etc.

	Production	Exports	Imports
Cattle d	1 250.0*	1.7*	na
Goats d	na		na
Sheep d	11 493.3*	145.6*	na
Horses d	3.0*		na
Butter		0.8*	na
Cheese		1.4*	na
Eggs	123.0*	2.5*	na
Milk	75.0*		na
Hides/skins	1.6[1]	49.5*	na
Wool	0.2*		20.2*

d number in thousands.

6. FIBRES, TEXTILES, etc.

	Production	Exports	Imports
Cotton lint n	1.2*		

7. FUEL AND POWER

	Production 1965	Production 1960a	Exports	Imports
Electricity ht:				
Bahrain	137	20[1]	—	na
Kuwait	584	60[1]	—	na
Natural gas i:	1 660		—	na
Oil, crude:				
Bahrain	2 520	1 500[1]	93 017	na
Kuwait	104 320	54 760[1]	15 130	na
Neutral Zone	18 713	5 440[1]	8 410	na
Qatar	8 413		7 810	na
Petroleum, refined:				
Kuwait	10 037	9 440[1]	8 777	127
Neutral Zone	10 887	1 530[1]	6 040	10
Qatar	3 823	190[1]	2 723	37
Trucial States	30			23

h million kWh. i million cu. metres. t thermal.

11. INDUSTRY n

	Production	Exports	Imports
Aircraft a	na		2.5[1]
Beer	na		na
Electrical engineering a	na		42.6[1]
Merchant ships g		2.7†	25.0
Motor vehicles a		2.0†	36.6

a million $ U.S. g '000 G.R.T. n Kuwait only.

na: data not available. — negligible or nil. * estimate. [1] one year only. [2] two year average. ‡ see appendix. † re-exports.

ARGENTINA

Argentina is a republic. The country suffered several years' economic instability due mainly to overemphasis on industrialization and frequent changes in leadership. Some attempt was made in 1957 towards more democratic government, but there was a reversion in 1966, and the president now rules by decree.

AREA: 2 808 602 sq. km. (1 084 120 sq. miles)

LAND USE: (percentage of total)

	1960	1954
Arable and orchard	7.0	10.8
Permanent meadow and pasture	42.6	40.7
Forest and woodland	25.2	32.3
City areas, waste and other land (incl. non-agricultural holdings)	25.2	16.2

POPULATION: 23 031 000 (1967 estimate)
Largest city: BUENOS AIRES, capital: population: 7 000 000* (1960)
Total working population: 7 599 071*

U.N. group no.		Percentage	Year(s)
0	Agriculture, forestry, fishing and hunting	19.2	1960–5 av.
1	Mining and quarrying	0.6	
2/3	Manufacturing	25.2	
4	Construction	5.6	
5	Electricity, gas, water and sanitary services	1.1	
6	Commerce	11.9	
7	Transport, storage and communications	6.3	
8	Services	20.0	
9	Others	10.1	

			Year(s)
Life expectancy at birth (years):	male	63.7	1960–5 av.
	female	69.5	1960–5 av.
Infant mortality (per '000)		58.3*	1965
Crude birth rate (per '000)		22.5*	1960–5 av.
Crude death rate (per '000)		8.5*	1960–5 av.
Accidental deaths		na	
Population per physician		670	1962
Population per hospital bed		160	1965
School enrolment: age 5–19 years (percentage)		74	1963–4 av.
age over 19 years (per 100 000 population)		1038	1963–5 av.

COMMUNICATIONS

			Year(s)
Motor vehicles in use ('000s):	private	809.3	1963–5 av.
	commercial	559	
Railway track (km.)		42 913	1948
Mail per capita:	domestic	41	1963–5 av.
	foreign received	5	
	foreign sent	6.7	
Telephones (per '000 population)		67	1967
Radio receivers (per '000 population)		282	1963–5 av.
Television sets (per '000 population)		65.1	1963–5 av.
Daily newspapers (per '000 population)		155	1959

FINANCE
Currency unit: The peso

Exchange rates	1965a	1960b	1950b	1938b
Per $ U.S.	188.5	82.7	7.5	3.64a
Per £ sterling	528.35	231.95	21.01	16.74

a selling rate. b official rate.

		Year(s)
National Income (million $ U.S.)	16 537	1965
G.N.P. per capita ($ U.S.)	780	1966
Rate of increase of G.N.P. per capita	0.3	1960–4 av.
Foreign trade (percentage of G.D.P.)	15	1963–5 av.

TRADING

Total trade (in million $ U.S.)	1965	1955	1938
Exports (f.o.b.)	1493	929	438
Imports (c.i.f.)	1199	1173	443

Main trading partners (percentage of total value)

Exports	1965	1955	1938	Imports	1965	1955	1938
Italy	16	4	3	U.S.A.	23	13	17
Netherlands	11	11	8	Brazil	14	9	15
U.K.	10	22	33	Germany F.R.	9	6	10d
Brazil	7	14	12d	Italy	7	6	6
Germany F.R.	6	7	8	U.K.	6	6	20
U.S.A.	6	13	na	France	4	4	5
China P.R.	6	na		Japan	4	4	

Distribution of trade (percentage of total value)

Exports	1965	1955	1938*
Food	75	61*	70
(cereals)	(39)	(37)	(45)
(meat and meat preparations)	(22)	(21)	(24)
Crude materials and fuels	13	19*	24
(textile fibre and waste)	(8)	(14)	(11)

Imports	1965	1955	1938*
Manufactured goods	57	54*	na
(machinery and transport equipment)	(25)	(18)	(15)
(iron and steel)	(15)	(16)	(9)
Crude materials and fuels	25	31*	na
(fuels)	(10)	(17)	(16)
Chemicals	11	8	6
Food	6	7	6

d incl. Germany D.R.

PRODUCTION, EXPORTS AND IMPORTS
Years: 1963–5 average and 1953–5 average   Units: '000 metric tons unless otherwise indicated

1. CEREALS, etc.

	Production		Exports		Imports	
Barley	750.0	985.7	293.5	579.1	—	—
Cassava	243.7	304.5²	—	—	—	—
Maize (corn)	4 950.0	3 622.0	2 863.2	1 210.4	—	—
Millets/sorghum	1 391.3	275.0	610.8	36.1	—	—
Oats	730.3	668.0	303.4	330.6	—	—
Rice	1 811.3	1 531.3	6.2	16.3	28.4	9.1
Rye	212.0	182.7	21.6	27.5	—	—
Sweet potatoes/yams	478.3	701.7	70.3	500.3	—	—
Wheat	8 533.3	6 380.0	4 067.1	3 028.8	—	—

2. FRUIT, etc.

	Production		Exports		Imports	
Apples	463.0	286.3	210.6	57.5	—	—
Apricots	12.7	8.8	na	na	—	—
Bananas	69.0	na	na	na	173.6	153.5
Cherries	2.0	na	na	na	—	—
Figs	6.3	4.3²*	na	na	—	—
Grapes	2 345.3	2 007.7	6.2	5.5	0.4	—
Lemons	76.0	66.7				
Olives	68.3	34.0	2.3		6.6	19.1
Oranges	62.0	13.3	0.2			
Other citrus fruit						

continued

PRODUCTION, EXPORTS AND IMPORTS continued

4. VEGETABLE OILSEEDS AND OILS

	Production		Exports		Imports	
Castor seed	5.00	2.74	—	—	0.10	0.19
Castor oil	na	na	—	0.13	1.92	0.73
Coconut oil	240.70	238.30	—	—	0.01	na
Cottonseed	252.96	117.60	1.19	1.83	—	15.78
Cottonseed oil	na	na	0.19	7.00	—	—
Groundnuts	718.67	351.00m	32.92	7.00	—	—
Groundnut oil	na	na	7.09	171.07	—	—
Linseed	9.67	5.00²*	219.02	0.42	0.01	na
Linseed oil			7.43		0.38	0.16
Olive oil	na	na	—	—	na	na
Palm oil			—	—	na	na
Rapeseed			—	—	na	na
Sesame seed	16.70	0.50²	—	—	na	na
Soya beans	569.67	460.67	13.35	7.39	na	na
Sunflower seed			15.45	12.00	na	na
Sunflower seed oil	13.50	12.43	—	—	na	na
Tung oil						

n flax grown for seed only.

5. LIVESTOCK‡, ANIMAL PRODUCTS, etc.

	Production		Exports		Imports	
Chickens d	35 566.7	44 500.0¹				
Cattle d	42 406.0	44 429.5²				
dairy cows d	15 826.0⁰*	na				
Goats d	5 025.0⁰*	na				
Horses d	46 139.3	50 728.0¹	188.6	46.7	4.3	
Pigs d	3 760.3*	5 849.0¹				
Bacon/ham	3 439.0*	3 750.0²	26.7		2.7	
Meat‡ 'A'	2 695.3*	2 159.5	0.6	0.6²	0.3	
Meat 'B'				0.3		
Butter	107.4	58.7n	466.1	208.7		
Cheese	148.3n	57.4²	94.8	25.2		
Eggs	148.7	155.4²	10.4	33.9	1.9	
Fish	168.0	78.4	2.6	3.9	9.0	0.2
Milk	4 784.0	4 828.5²	6.1	11.2		na
Hides/skins	na	na	2.0		1.3	
Wool	105.8*	108.0*	181.7	15.6n		
			72.9	75.9		

d no. in thousands. e no. in millions. n factory produce only.

6. FIBRES, TEXTILES, etc.

	Production		Exports		Imports	
Agaves (sisal etc.)	123.3	124.3	17.1	30.3	2.0	3.5
Cotton lint	1.7*				11.1	2.3
Flax fibre						1.9
Hemp fibre					0.5	12.5
Jute					8.0	26.7
Rubber: natural	1.2		0.1¹		25.4	26.5²
synthetic					2.0	1.2
Silk f	86.2	85.1	na		0.22	1.2
Cotton: yarn	54.9¹	62.1			0.1	0.1
woven fabrics	16.3	11.0	na		1.0	na
Rayon, fibre/yarn						
Non-cellulosic fibre/yarn	na		0.4	0.1²	1.3	na
Wool: yarn	na		0.1		—²	—²
woven fabrics				0.1²	—²	

f metric tons.

7. FUEL AND POWER

	Production		Exports		Imports	
Coal 'A' ‡	303	130			706	1 289
Coke	13 727	6 000¹			51	62
Electricity h: total	1 220	300¹				
hydro	12 507	5 700¹				
thermal	3 790	9811			33	4 130¹
Natural gas i	14 336	4 370¹	40		1 970	3 380¹
Oil, crude	26	7 460¹	707	¹	883	
Petroleum, refined		na				
Uranium f						

f metric tons. h million kWh. i million cu. metres.

8. IRON AND STEEL

	Production		Exports		Imports	
Iron ore	50m	37*m			—	—
Pig iron	574	33			984.0	1 051.0b
Steel ingots/castings	1 182	192	20	na	318.2	456.6*
Iron/steel scrap					149.3*	121.3
Iron/steel products a	43.1d		12		174.0	53.0
	113.2d				15.9	77.7
					131	634

a million $ U.S. m metal content.

9. NON-FERROUS MINERALS AND METALS

	Production		Exports		Imports	
Diamonds					0.04¹a	na
Gold: ore m	na	6.00				
bullion/coins etc.			—	0.13		
Silver: ore m	2 190.70	316.70	386.67	na		
Steel: ore m						8.70
Asbestos: fibre	0.35	0.18¹			12.80	8.70
manufactured	na	0.20			0.02	na
Mica	0.44	0.63	0.10		21.66	0.89
Aluminium: bauxite	na	na			28.35	11.76
aluminium	9.67	0.01m	1.10		0.65	0.47
Antimony: ore	na	na				
metal	0.44	0.87	0.44	0.57		0.01
Beryl	na	na				2.09
Cadmium					0.06	1.80
Chrome, metal						13.40
Cobalt, metal					20.11	na
Copper: ore	4.14m	23.01m	1.34		0.16	0.68
metal	28.21m	18.42			1.10	
Lead: ore	26.37		0.25		4.09	na
metal	98.63				0.47	0.57
Magnesium: dolomite						
magnesite					0.94	2.39
Manganese/salts	17.01	3.73			42.80	0.06
Mercury f	6				0.41	na
Nickel: ore	0.36m	0.11m	1.85n			
metal					1.35	1.73
Tin: ore					5.10	0.96
Titanium minerals	0.12	0.83	0.36	0.40		
Tungsten: ore	27.11m	0.01m				
metal	21.83	19.00*m	26.63	na	1.20	
Vanadium		12.00	1.47	3.38		
Zinc: ore						
metal						

a metric tons. k '000 fine troy oz. m metric tons. n incl. tin-silver ore.

10. CHEMICALS n AND FERTILIZERS

	Production		Exports		Imports	
Organic chemicals:						
Benzene	177.0¹		na		na	na
Butadiene			na		na	2.3
Ethylene					7.6	11.1
Methanol	9.7¹		na		0.9¹	
Phenol			na			
Phthalic anhydride	na				na	
Styrene monomer	na		na		3.4²	
Urea	na				46.7	
Inorganic chemicals:						
Ammonia	6.7¹		na			
Carbon black	10.4		na		108.9	
Chlorine	46.7				12.8	
Nitric acid	5.2¹		—¹			
Sodium carbonate	65.0					
Sodium hydroxide	140.7		0.1²		1.0¹	1.0¹
Sulphuric acid					0.5²	
Plastics:						
Polyamides	18.7¹		4.0¹			
Polyethylene	12.3					
Polyvinyl chloride						
Fertilizers:						
Phosphates	0.4q	na			3.2	
Potash					2.7a	
Sulphur	22.9p	17.2p			164.3	

n data not available for years 1953–5. p native. q guano.

11. INDUSTRY

	Production		Exports		Imports	
Aircraft a					64.4	na
Alcoholic beverages	1 818.0	3 634.0	0.3a		46.4	21.5
beer b	2 822.7	1 745.7	1.7	1.0		
Cement					16.0	1.2
Electrical			3.0		84.3a	19.6a
engineering a						
Locomotives			0.6			
Railway vehicles a	25.0¹					
Machine tools a	8.0		1.23a	na		
Motor vehicles g						
commercial						
private						

a million $ U.S. g '000 G.R.T.

continued

na: data not available. — negligible or nil. — not available. * estimate. * see appendix. ‡ see appendix. † re-exports.

¹ one year only. ² two year average. ² two year average. * estimate. * see appendix. † re-exports.

AUSTRALIA

The Commonwealth of Australia was established in 1901. In 1957 a preferential trade agreement was signed with the U.K., and subsequently reciprocal tariff agreements with various other countries.

AREA: 7 686 900 sq. km. (2 967 909 sq. miles)

LAND USE: (percentage of total)

	1964	1954
Arable and orchard	4.6	2.9
Permanent meadow and pasture	58.1	47.0
Forest and woodland	5.4	5.4
City areas, waste and other land	32.7	44.7

POPULATION: 11 540 764 (1966 census)
Largest city: SYDNEY; population: 2 444 735 (1966)
Capital city: CANBERRA; population: 100 090 (1967)
Total working population: 4 255 096

Distribution of working population (1961)

U.N. group no.		Percentage
0	Agriculture, forestry, fishing and hunting	10.9
1	Mining and quarrying	1.3
2/3	Manufacturing	27.0
4	Construction	8.8
5	Electricity, gas, water and sanitary services	2.2
6	Commerce	19.6
7	Transport, storage and communications	8.6
8	Services	19.6
9	Others	2.0

		Year(s)
Life expectancy at birth (years): male	67.9	1960-2 av.
female	74.2	
Infant mortality (per '000)	18.5a	1965
Crude birth rate (per '000)	19.3	1965
Crude death rate (per '000)	8.8	1965
Accidental deaths (per 100 000 population)	27.8	1965
due to other causes	26.0	1965
Population per physician	720	1965
Population per hospital bed	80b	1966
School enrolment: age 5–19 years (percentage)	90b	1966
age over 19 years (per 100 000 population)	1 109	1966

a excl. pure aborigines. b incl. pre-school and special education.

COMMUNICATIONS

		Year(s)
Motor vehicles in use ('000s): private	2 699.7	1963-5 av.
commercial	859.7	1963-5 av.
Railway track (km)	40 496	1964
Mail per capita: domestic	141	
foreign received	193	1963-5 av.
foreign sent	10	
Telephones (per '000 urban population)	25.8	1966
Radio licences (per '000 population)	212	1963-5 av.
Television licences (per '000 population)	163.1	1963-5 av.
Daily newspapers (per '000 population)	316.5	1962-3 av.

FINANCE

Currency unit: The Australian dollar replaced the Australian pound in 1966 at the rate A$1 to A£0.5.

Exchange rates, for Australian pounds

	1965	1960	1950	1938
Per $ U.S.	0.45	0.45	0.45	0.26
Per £ sterling	1.25	1.25	1.25	1.25

		Year(s)
National Income (million $ U.S.)	18 400	1965
G.N.P. per capita ($ U.S.)	1 840	1966
Rate of increase of G.N.P. per capita	2.6	1960-4 av.
Foreign trade (percentage of G.D.P.)	29	1963-5 av.

TRADING

Trading figures refer to year ending 30th June of year stated

Total trade (in million $ U.S.)

	1965	1955	1938
Exports (f.o.b.)	2 889	1 703	642
Imports (f.o.b.)	3 182	1 884	507

Main trading partners (percentage of total value)

Exports	1965	1955	1938
U.K.	19	37	55
Japan	17	8	7
U.S.A.	10	5	7
New Zealand	6	5	5
China P.R.	6	8	—
France	4	3	2
Italy	3	4	2

Imports	1965	1955	1938
U.K.	26	45	41
U.S.A.	24	12	16
Japan	9	6	4
Germany F.R.	6	4	4d
Canada	4	4	2
France	2	2	1
Indonesia	2	2	1

Distribution of trade (percentage of total value)

Exports	1965	1955	1938*
Crude materials (wool)	40 (30)	53 (46)	43 (33)
Food (cereals)	39 (16)	35 (11)	46 (20)
Manufactured goods (non-ferrous metals)	16 (5)	10 (4)	1 (1)

Imports	1965	1955	1938*
Manufactured goods (machinery and transport equipment)	66 (37)	67 (29)	51 (22)
Crude materials and fuels (petroleum and products)	15 (8)	20 (11)	12 (8)
Chemicals	9	5	6

d incl. Germany D.R.

PRODUCTION, EXPORTS AND IMPORTS

Years: 1963-5 average and 1953-5 average   Units: '000 metric tons unless otherwise indicated

1. CEREALS, etc.

	Production		Exports		Imports	
Barley	1 017.0	845.3	335.3	514.9	—	—
Maize (corn)	153.3	123.3	3.6	13.1	—	—
Millets/sorghum	225.7	143.5a	2.6	66.1	—	—
Oats	1 205.0	696.3	330.1	108.3	—	—
Potatoes	588.0	472.7	11.3	35.0	1.8	—
Rice	143.7	63.7	59.9	35.0	1.1	—
Rye	11.7	12.7	0.4	—	—	—
Sweet potatoes/yams	2.0	6.0¹	—	—	—	—
Wheat	8 677.0	5 100.0	5 585.3	1 490.6	—	—

2. FRUIT, etc.

	Production		Exports		Imports	
Apples	358.7	236.3	141.6	84.7	—	—
Apricots	41.3	32.9	na	na	—	—
Bananas	126.5*	65.0	na	na	—	—
Cherries	8.0*	6.1	na	na	6.1n	4.3²
Coconuts	—	—	—	—	3.8	4.5
Dates	1.0*	1.0²	1.4	1.1	7.1	7.0²
Grapes	615.0	461.1	0.6	0.2	—	—
Lemons	18.7	16.0²	20.4	10.7	29.7	26.7²
Oranges	212.3*	136.0²	na	0.1	9.0*	5.5²
Other citrus fruit	9.0*	5.5²	na	0.1	—	—
Pears	126.0	64.4	28.6	24.1	—	—
Pineapples	85.3	61.7	na	na	2.5	1.50
Plums	27.3	23.4	1.0*	na	—	—
Raisins	95.7	78.0	65.6	63.4	33.15	—
Tomatoes	146.0*	82.0²	—	—	—	—
Wine b	1 730.5³	1 091.0	78.0	57.7	14.75	2.29

b '000 hectolitres. c dessicated. f flax grown for seed only.

3. BEVERAGES, FOREST PRODUCTS, etc.

	Production		Exports		Imports	
Cocoa	na	na	0.1†n	0.1†	11.5	7.9
Coffee	na	na	0.1†n	0.1†	13.1	4.2
Sugar: cane	14 004.7	9 485.0				
raw	1 957.9	1 275.7	1 197.1†	682.2†	0.5	0.1†
Tea	14.6	3.3	0.8†	0.3†	29.7	26.7
Tobacco: leaf raw		19.2a	0.2	—	12.9	19.1
cigarettes/snuff						
Softwood j	20 139.0a	8 449.3a	—	0.9²a	6.5a	5.9a
Hardwood j						
Woodpulp j	1 881.3	232.0	4.0	2.3	970.3	974.0
Newsprint j	428.6	65.0	76.7	105.3	521.4	221.3
Other paper	568.7	219.3		0.1	252.3	162.0
			14.9	6.4	139.3	96.0

a million $ U.S. n no. in millions. j '000 cu. metres of roundwood equivalent.

4. VEGETABLE OILSEEDS AND OILS

	Production		Exports		Imports	
Castor seed	na	na	0.05	0.06	0.10*	3.002*
Castor oil	na	na	0.03	0.501	1.81	1.49
Copra	na	na	—	—	33.09	29.13
Coconut oil	na	na	0.26	—	0.72	—
Cottonseed	20.70	1.00			0.30	0.07
Cottonseed oil					0.94	0.07
Groundnut oil	8.63	10.22			2.52	1.50
Linseed			0.02	0.35	9.50	2.38
Linseed oil	27.67	6.67n			104.46	89.25
Olive oil	na	na			4.68	2.29

PRODUCTION, EXPORTS AND IMPORTS *continued*

4. VEGETABLE OILSEEDS AND OILS — continued

	Production		Exports		Imports	
Palm kernel oil	—		—		0.93	
Palm oil	—		—		3.10	
Rapeseed	—		—		0.40	
Rapeseed oil	—		—		2.10	
Soya beans	—		—		3.28	
Sunflower seed	na		na		4.41	
Tung oil	2.33	1.00²			1.16	1.73

5. LIVESTOCK, ANIMAL PRODUCTS, etc.

	Production		Exports		Imports	
Chickens d	21 103.3*	na				
Cattle d	18 806.7	15 561.7	8.7	4.8		
dairy cows d	11 068.0n	8 932.0				
Goats d	79.0*	na	293.3	na		0.7
Horses d	164 742.7	808.0				
Pigs d	1 523.0	1 162.7	0.1	0.9		
Bacon/ham d	1 689.7*	1 211.7	0.2	0.5		2.0
Meat 'A', 'B'	177.4*	134.1	383.0	202.9		0.2
Butter	206.7	175.3	90.0	56.7		2.9
Cheese	60.3	47.7	33.2	31.9		
Eggs	149.7	15.9	2.5	22.3		42.6
Milk	6 988.0	52.5q	13.1	12.9		na
Fish		16.9	410.1	341.4		0.1
Whale/sperm oil	8.8	5 795m				1.1²
Hides/skins		59.0p	90.5a	42.7a		3.5
Wool	451.2	332.0	387.4	299.0		2.1

a million $ U.S. b from sheep only. m cows and heifers over one year old. n in thousands. q recorded commercial catch only.

6. FIBRES, TEXTILES, etc.

	Production		Exports		Imports	
Abaca	—	—	—	—	—	0.2²
Agaves (sisal etc.)	—	—	—	—	1.0	13.7
Cotton lint	10.7	1.0	—	—	20.5	19.2
Flax fibre	0.2*	2.8	—	—	22.4	1.2
Hemp fibre	—	—	—	—	0.2	1.2
Jute	—	—	—	—	7.0	4.6
Rubber: natural	—	—	—	—	38.0	43.3
synthetic	19.0	—	—	—	16.3	17.1
Silk f	—	—	—	—	0.2	0.1
Cotton: yarn	25.2	17.1n	—	—	2.3	10.2
woven fabrics	6.6*	3.6	0.1²	—	2.3	2.6
Rayon: fibre/yarn	7.0²	2.0	—	—	8.3²	6.5
woven fabrics	3.0	2.5p	—	—	3.5q	4.4
Non-cellulosic fibre/yarn						
Wool: yarn	6.6*	18.8	1.0	0.1	7.4	0.1
woven fabrics	24.0	25.2a	0.1	—	0.5	

f metric tons. n incl. tyre cord. p incl. mixture piece goods. q incl. weight of yarns consumed in weaving. u million square metres.

7. FUEL AND POWER

	Production		Exports		Imports	
Coal 'A', 'B'	27 190	19 580	4 245n	19 560	—	71²
Coke	6 500	10 270	344m	23	10²	6
Electricity k: total	32 494	13 910			15 423	4 850l
hydro	7 783	2 000			1 390	4 290l
thermal	24 710	11 910				
Oil: crude	14 816	4 750l	1 670	180l		
Petroleum, refined	1 994*q	137pq	2 233	123		
Rare earths f	609²	—				
Uranium f						

f metric tons. h million kWh. n incl. a small quantity in bunkers. p monazite content of high-grade concentrates. q metric tons.

8. IRON AND STEEL

	Production		Exports		Imports	
Iron ore	3 898m	2 273m	138	—	286	175.0
Pig iron	4 033	1 862	99	114	27	1
Steel ingots/castings	5 054	2 186	17	65	18	1
Iron/steel scrap	na	na	318	77	177	82
			104	21		

a million $ U.S. m metal content.

9. NON-FERROUS MINERALS AND METALS

	Production		Exports		Imports	
Diamonds	na	na	0.01a	0.02a	0.10*	3.002*
Gold k: ore m	955.00	1 081.00	50.47	12.03	1.81	1.49
bullion etc.	na	na	479.09	993.20	33.09	29.13
Platinum group metals k	—	—	0.46	0.51	0.72	—
Silver k: ore m	3 518.0	1 823.7	3 184.03	1 725.55	0.94	0.07
bullion	—	—	6 792.27	9 673.49	2.52	1.50
Asbestos: fibre k	116.62	5.09	233.84n	34.84n	9.50	2.38
manufactured	na				875.65n	
Mica	na	0.62	56.34np	24.25np	4.68	2.29

a million $ U.S. k metal content.

9. NON-FERROUS MINERALS AND METALS — continued

	Production		Exports		Imports	
Aluminium: bauxite	781.00	5.80	392.78	0.03	11.10	3.31
alumina	136.73	1.27l	—	—	60.82q	na
aluminium	69.90	0.22m	15.70	0.66	9.41	14.00*
Antimony: ore	0.13n	na	—	0.10	0.04	0.77
Beryl	—	0.6	—	0.01	0.50	0.02
Cadmium	0.51	0.09	0.09	0.17	—	
Chrome: ore	0.08n	2.60m	0.38	0.20	19.11	5.22
Cobalt: ore	0.02n	0.01m			3.92	1.52
metal	104.62m	41.67m	15.17m	2.30m	—	0.07²
Copper: ore	82.13	37.14	35.00	8.60	0.09	0.93
metal	388.57m	279.65m	93.59m	41.29	18.98	21.26
Lead: ore	287.13	226.78	248.89l	208.45l	1.13	0.02
metal						
Magnesium: dolomite	240.15	na				na
magnesite	38.80	na	1.23	0.09	32.37	1.46
metal/salts			1.04	0.05	1.04	1.03
Manganese: ore	67.43	36.75	36.22	6.25	60.03	1.54
Mercury f					9.65	1.02
Molybdenum f	6.35n	0.60m		0.07²	69.20	38.70
Nickel: ore					276.40	118.30²
metal	3.49m	1.91m	0.19	0.03m	0.61	na
Tin: ore	2.99	1.87	0.39m	0.32	2.26	1.00
metal			0.02		1.59	0.55
Titanium minerals	518.35	44.42	456.10	47.71	4.30	15.56
metal	1.77	2.42	1.47	2.16	0.03	na
Tungsten: ore					2.04	129.69
metal						1.59
Zinc: ore m	354.02	252.74	134.00	na	na	
metal	191.12	100.18	92.30	40.16	na	
Zirconium minerals	200.93	39.28	201.52	38.74	38.5l	

a million $ U.S. p incl. a small quantity of manufactures. n '000 metric tons. q incl. hydrate. l incl. lead content of base bullion. u sales only.

10. CHEMICALS AND FERTILIZERS

Organic chemicals:

	Production		Exports		Imports	
Benzene	na		na		na	
Butadiene	43.5l				na	
Ethylene	19.8l				na	
Methanol	na				4.8²	
Phenol	64.3		1.9		0.3	
Phthalic anhydride	138.3		1.7		1.3	
Styrene monomer			0.1		38.5l	
Urea						

Inorganic chemicals:

	Production		Exports		Imports	
Ammonia	na		na		4.0	
Carbon black	na					
Chlorine	na		1.9		5.4	
Nitric acid	na				6.8	
Sodium carbonate	16.0l		0.3		1	
Sodium hydroxide	14.0²				10.9	
Sulphuric acid	820.9p	350.9p	815.8p	345.9p	2 101.2	1 185.9
					92.2	23.1

Plastics:

	Production		Exports		Imports	
Polyamides	na		na		4.0	
Polyethylene						
Polyvinyl chloride						

Fertilizers:

	Production		Exports		Imports	
Phosphates	820.9p	350.9p	60.0*q	63.9q	334.3	175.0
Potash	92.8k	95.3x				
Pyrites	na					
Sulphur						

a not available for years 1953-5. p mainly from Christmas Is. q sulphur content of zinc concentrates. t year 1965-6. x sulphur content.

11. INDUSTRY

	Production		Exports		Imports	
Aircraft a	na		—		68.4	17.9
Alcoholic beverages: beer b	91.21n	66.71q	4.7	1.2	11.6a	4.5a
spirits b	3 518.0	823.7		3.8a		
Cement	11 921.0	9 434.3	21.9	26.0	52.3	95.7
Electrical engineering c	na	na	6.4²		167.2	76.8²
Locomotives a	558.01		na	0.3	17.2	
Railway vehicles a	54.0*		na	0.3²	34.8	12.6²
Machine tools a	na					
Merchant ships g	35.0	19.0				
Motor vehicles commercial d	62.9p	52.5q	38.0a	5.4a	290.4a	170.9²a
manufactured d	291.8²					

a million $ U.S. d no. of units. g '000 G.R.T. l 1960/1 figure. m metal content. n '000 hectolitres. p production year 1966/7. q 1960/1 figure. t '000 hectolitres. q incl. assembly of imported parts. † motor vehicle chassis and bodies only.

continued

na: data not available. — negligible or nil. * estimate. ² two year average. ‡ see appendix. † re-exports. ¹ one year only.

AUSTRALIA (TERRITORIES)

PAPUA AND NEW GUINEA

Papua and New Guinea were joined in an administrative union in 1949 as an international trusteeship under Australian administration.

AREA: 461 700 sq. km. (178 300 sq. miles)

LAND USE: (percentage of total)

	1953
Arable and orchard	0.2
Forest and woodland	69.4
City areas, waste and other land	30.4

POPULATION: 2 129 036 (1966 census)
Largest city: PORT MORESBY, capital; population: 42 133 (1966)
Total working population: 80 000 (1964)

		Year
Infant mortality (per '000)	10.2a	1965
Crude birth rate (per '000)	29.0a	1965
Crude death rate (per '000)	3.6	1965
Population per physician	10 040b	1965
Population per hospital bed	120b	1966
School enrolment: age 5–19 years (percentage)	47	1963–4 av.
age over 19 years (per 100 000 population)	47	1963–5 av.

a non-indigenous population only. b Papua only.

COMMUNICATIONS

		Year(s)
Motor vehicles in use ('000s): private	56.7	1965
commercial	5.4	1965
Telephones (per '000 urban population)	0.6	1965

FINANCE
Currency unit: The Australian dollar

		Year
National Income (million $ U.S.)	300*	1966
G.N.P. per capita ($ U.S.)	140	1966

TRADING: PAPUA

Total trade (in million $ U.S.)	1965	1955	1938
Exports (f.o.b.)	10	6	1
Imports (c.i.f.)	37	17	2

Main trading partners (percentage of total value)

Exports	1965	1955		Imports	1965	1955
Australia	76	79		Australia	62	68
U.K.	13	1		U.K.	9	11
Japan	3			Japan	7	8

Distribution of trade (percentage of total value)

Exports	1965a	1956a
Copra/coconut oil	46	47
Rubber	42	47
Crocodile skins	6	na

Imports	1965a	1956a
Manufactured goods (machinery and transport equipment)	59	(27)
(textiles and clothing)	21	(6)
Food	6	6
Chemicals	5	6

TRADING: NEW GUINEA

Total trade (in million $ U.S.)	1965	1938
Exports (f.o.b.)	44	
Imports (c.i.f.)	61	

Main trading partners (percentage of total value)

Exports	1965	1955		Imports	1965	1955
Australia	40	32		Australia	54	61
Germany F.R.	35	60		Japan	10	10
U.K.	7	—		U.K.	8	6
Netherlands	4	1		U.S.A.	6	5
U.S.A.	3	6		Hong Kong	4	10
				Germany F.R.	4	2

Distribution of trade (percentage of total value)

Exports	1965a	1956a
Copra/coconut oil	58	52
Cocoa	20	75
Coffee	10	(25) (19)
Wood		(9)

EAST INDIES

PRODUCTION, EXPORTS AND IMPORTS Units: '000 metric tons unless otherwise indicated
Years: 1963–5 average and 1953–5 average

	Production		Exports		Imports	
1. CEREALS, etc.						
Potatoes	—	—	—	—	0.9	13.1
Rice	—	—	—	—	25.1	
Sweet potatoes/yams	12.7*	8.0			0.1	
Wheat						
2. FRUIT, etc.						
Apples					0.3	
Bananas	1.0*					
Coconuts	643.3*e	0.8			0.1	
Grapes					0.2	
Oranges					1.8	
Wine b						
3. BEVERAGES, FOREST PRODUCTS, etc.						
Cocoa	17.4	1.7*	16.9	0.8		
Coffee	3.3*		6.9			
Sugar, raw					8.4	
Tea					0.3	
Tobacco: leaf					0.5	
products					na	
Softwood j	92.3*	81.0/78.0*			16.1¹	1.5
Hardwood j	3 873.0*		72.3		12.5	na
Paper					na	
j '000 cu. metres of roundwood equivalent.						
4. VEGETABLE OILSEEDS AND OILS						
Copra	113.63	93.30	81.46	72.93		
Coconut oil	na	23.80	7.60	23.80		
Groundnuts	na		1.82	na		
Groundnut oil	1.00*	na			0.06	
Linseed oil	1.0				0.04	0.02
5. LIVESTOCK‡, ANIMAL PRODUCTS, etc.						
Chickens d	17.4*	29.0d			0.8	
Cattle d	31.0	7.4n				
Sheep d	2.0	1.7				
Horses d	1.0	1.0				
Pigs d	4.0	4.6n				

continued

INDIAN OCEAN

COCOS ISLANDS

The Cocos or Keeling Islands were originally incorporated with Singapore but from 1942–6 were temporarily placed under the control of Ceylon. In 1955 they were transferred to the Commonwealth of Australia. Their chief value is as a cable and wireless centre, a civil aviation and marine base, and as a meteorological station.

AREA: 14 sq. km. (5.5 sq. miles)
The islands are thickly covered with coconut palms.
POPULATION: 684 (1966 census)
Total working population: 282

PACIFIC OCEAN

NORFOLK ISLAND

POPULATION: 1 152 (1966 census)
Largest town: KINGSTON
Total working population: 311 (1961)

EMPLOYMENT AND TRADE
The chief products are citrus fruit, bananas and vegetables. Cattle are reared, and a programme of forestry has been undertaken. Tourism is the major industry. Trade, which includes the export of fish, is mainly with Australia.

AREA: 33 sq. km. (13 sq. miles)

LAND USE: (percentage of total)

	1965	1955
Arable and orchard	5.5	5.7
Permanent meadow and pasture	41.7	40.0
Forest and woodland	13.9	11.4
City areas, waste and other land	38.9	42.9

EUROPE

AUSTRIA

Austria was overrun by the Germans in 1938 and liberated in 1945. Sovereignty and independence were not fully recovered until 1955. Austria is a member of the European Free Trade Association.

AREA: 83 849 sq. km. (32 366 sq. miles)

LAND USE: (percentage of total)

	1965	1955
Arable and orchard	20.6	21.1
Permanent meadow and pasture	26.9	27.6
Forest and woodland	37.9	36.2
City areas, waste and other land	14.6	15.1

POPULATION: 7 323 000 (1967 estimate)
Largest city: WIEN (Vienna), capital; population: 1 638 100 (1966)

Distribution of working population (1961)
Total working population: 3 369 815

U.N. group no.		Percentage
0	Agriculture, forestry, fishing and hunting	22.8
1	Mining and quarrying	1.5
2/3	Manufacturing	28.6
4	Construction	9.9
5	Electricity, gas, water and sanitary services	0.9
6	Commerce	10.9
7	Transport, storage and communications	18.3
8	Services	
9	Others	

		Year(s)
Life expectancy at birth (years): male	66.57	1967
female	73.41	1967
Infant mortality (per '000)	23.3	1967
Crude birth rate (per '000)	17.9	1965
Crude death rate (per '000)	13.0	1965
Accidental deaths (per 100 000 population)	74	1965
caused by motor vehicles	24.6	1965
due to other causes	42.9	1966
Population per physician	550	1966
Population per hospital bed	90	1963–4 av.
School enrolment: age 5–19 years (percentage)	69	1964–5 av.
age over 19 years (per 100 000 population)	677	1963–5 av.

COMMUNICATIONS

		Year(s)
Motor vehicles in use ('000s): private	706.8	1963–5 av.
commercial	280.0	1963–5 av.
Railway track (km)	6 601	1964
Mail per capita: domestic	112	1963–5 av.
foreign received	19	1963–5 av.
foreign sent	14.88	1967
Telephones (per '000 urban population)	296	1963–5 av.
Radio licences (per '000 population)	81.37	1963–5 av.
Television licences (per '000 population)	239	1962–4 av.
Daily newspapers (per '000 population)		

FINANCE
Currency unit: The schilling

Exchange rates

	1965	1960	1950	1938
Per $ U.S.	25.89	26.04	21.49	5.41
Per £ sterling	72.57	73.01	60.20	24.89

		Year(s)
National Income (million $ U.S.)	7 035	1965
G.N.P. per capita ($ U.S.)	1150	1966
Rate of increase of G.N.P. per capita	3.5	1960–4 av.
Foreign trade (percentage of G.D.P.)	39	1963–5 av.

TRADING

Total trade (in million $ U.S.)	1965	1960	1955	1937
Exports (f.o.b.)	1 600	699	228	
Imports (c.i.f.)	2100	887	273	

Main trading partners (percentage of total value)

Exports	1965	1955	1937		Imports	1965	1955	1937
Germany F.R.	29	25	15d		Germany F.R.	42	35	16d
Italy	11	17	14		Italy	8	8	3
Switzerland	6	5	3		Switzerland	4	4	5
U.K.	5	5	5		U.K.	4	5	6
U.S.A.	4	4	5		France	4	3	5
Netherlands	4	1	2		Netherlands	3		2

Distribution of trade (percentage of total value)

Exports	1965	1955	1938*
Manufactured goods (machinery and transport equipment)	74	51	(8)
(iron and steel)	(20)	(10)	(15)
(textiles)	(13)	(12)	(17)
Crude materials and fuels (wood)	16	23	(14)
Food	5	5	na
Chemicals	5	3	na

Imports	1965	1955	1938*
Manufactured goods (machinery and transport equipment)	59	43	(4)
(textiles)	(30)	(22)	(5)
Crude materials and fuels	17	17	na
Food	12	19	na

d incl. Germany D.R.

PRODUCTION, EXPORTS AND IMPORTS Units: '000 metric tons unless otherwise indicated

	Production		Exports		Imports	
5. LIVESTOCK‡, ANIMAL PRODUCTS, etc. — *continued*						
Bacon/ham					0.2	
Meat‡: A					1.8	0.72
B					0.3	0.2
Butter					0.4	0.2
Cheese					0.2	
Eggs	0.2*				5.3	na
Milk	na	1.0			5.6	2.4*
n on farms only.						
6. FIBRES, TEXTILES, etc.						
Rubber, natural	5.3		5.1	3.6	93	
7. FUEL AND POWER						
Electricity h: total	75	19				
hydro	51	10				
thermal	24	9				
Petroleum, refined						501
h million kWh.						
9. NON-FERROUS MINERALS AND METALS						
Gold i: ore m	38.30	94.00	39.65	105.59		
bullion/coins etc.						
Platinum group: metals ore	22.30	0.01				
Silver k: ore m			na	54.09		
bullion	na	0.02	na	0.07		
Manganese, ore						
k '000 fine troy oz. m metal content.						
11. INDUSTRY						
Aircraft a					0.5	
Cement						
Electrical engineering a					1.5	11.3
Motor vehicles a					36.3	
a million $ U.S.					3.8	na
					4.3	na

continued

---

na: data not available. — negligible or nil. — negligible or nil. * estimate. * estimate. † re-exports. † re-exports. ‡ see appendix. ‡ see appendix.
1 one year only. 1 one year only. 2 two year average. 2 two year average.

AUSTRIA continued

PRODUCTION, EXPORTS AND IMPORTS continued

10. CHEMICALS AND FERTILIZERS

Organic chemicals:	Production	Exports	Imports
Benzene	na	—	0.5
Butadiene	—	—	na
Ethylene	na	—	2.3
Methanol	na	3.0	1.6
Phenol	na	na	1.8
Phthalic anhydride	na	na	na
Styrene monomer	na	na	na
Urea	na	na	0.9

Inorganic chemicals:			
Ammonia	na	na	1.0
Carbon black	na	1.4	9.2
Chlorine	na	na	0.1
Nitric acid	na	na	na
Sodium carbonate	na	1.0	2.4
Sodium hydroxide	na	0.5	0.4
Sulphuric acid a	208.7	9.1	20.6

Plastics:			
Polyamides	—	—	na
Polyethylene	—	—	14.4
Polyvinyl chloride b	15.7	6.5*	6.7

10. CHEMICALS AND FERTILIZERS—continued

Fertilizers:	Production	Exports	Imports
Phosphates	—	—	233.5 / 27.7
Potash	—	—	305.4 / 117.0
Sulphur	—	39.1†	27.5 / 93.6
n data not available for years 1953–5.	—	—	96.8 / 22.5

11. INDUSTRY

	Production	Exports	Imports
Aircraft a	na	—²	8.4 / na
Alcoholic beverages:			
beer b	3.6	0.6a	8.3a / 1.7a
spirits b	6 655.0 / 4 201.0	—	15.7 / 12.7
Cement	185.0¹n / 456.9¹b	25.0	24.0
Electrical engineering a	3 724.3 / 1 620.3	88.1	18.3²
	270.5² / na	134.0* / na	111.0 / 24.8²
Locomotives c	14.0	8.3	6.0 / 1.9
Railway vehicles a		9.4	1.7² / 7.4²
Machine tools a		21.5a / 12.3a	27.8 / 166.8a / 53.4²a
Motor vehicles:			
commercial d	4.7 / 5.2q		
private d	5.9 / 8.1q		

a no. of units. b '000 hectolitres. c no. of units. d no. in thousands. p 1959–60 figure. q incl. assembly of imported parts. n 1966 figure.

AUSTRIA continued

PRODUCTION, EXPORTS AND IMPORTS
Years: 1963–5 average and 1953–5 average Units: '000 metric tons unless otherwise indicated

1. CEREALS, etc.	Production		Exports		Imports	
Barley	581.7	326.0	0.2	—	220.1	52.1
Maize (corn)	197.7	150.7	1.5	1.7	387.6	332.8
Millets/sorghum	1.7	2.3	—	—	12.2	5.2
Oats	314.3	352.7	—	—	18.7	4.1
Potatoes	3 158.7	3 030.3	7.2	13.4	36.3	30.0
Rice	—	—	—	—	35.8	28.4
Rye	342.0	402.3	—	—	15.1	50.7
Wheat	700.7	500.0	—	—	61.9	266.6

2. FRUIT, etc.						
Apples	368.3	273.0	1.9	1.0	45.1	23.0
Apricots	22.7	8.8	—	—	2.7	8.8
Bananas	—	—	na	1.0	40.2	6.4
Cherries	30.3	25.4	na	na	2.1	
Dates	—	—	—	—	0.5	0.3
Figs	—	—	—	—	na	6.7
Grapes	258.7*	156.0*	—	—²	27.2	12.4
Lemons	—	—	—	—	23.2	30.1
Oranges	—	—	—	—	44.4	30.3
Other citrus fruit	—	—	—	—	1.6	6.1
Peaches	8.3	4.4	—	—	17.8	14.2
Pears	213.3	158.7	—	—	7.7	7.7
Plums	8.5	63.7	—	—	4.8	4.6
Raisins	—	—	—	—	na	na
Tomatoes	11.0	5.0	—	—	na	na
Wine b	1 816.3	1 088.7	20.7	16.7	357.7	85.7

b '000 hectolitres.

3. BEVERAGES, FOREST PRODUCTS, etc.						
Cocoa	na		—		11.3	7.0
Coffee	na		—		16.4	5.0
Sugar: beet	1 918.3	1 280.7	0.1†		na	42.2
raw	297.7	201.7	0.3		0.7	0.4
Tobacco: leaf	0.7	0.7	0.4	0.8	11.1	9.2
cigars	89.0c	77.3c	—		0.7	0.12
cigarettes	10 027.0c	6 910.3c	—			
tobacco/snuff	0.8	1.3	—²		0.7	0.12
Softwood j	4 782.0	5 092.1	120.3	105.8	35.3	4.8
Hardwood j	9 133.0	9 266.3	154.0	153.3	311.9	9.4
Wood pulp	1 464.3	1 465.3	60.7	81.0	39.5	11.0
Newsprint	715.8	490.7	255.7	335.7	0.1	0.1
Other paper	134.0	104.7			5.70	5.6

4. VEGETABLE OILSEEDS AND OILS						
Castor oil	na		—		1.08	0.45
Copra	na		—		1.04	1.35²
Coconut oil	na		—		9.97	2.97n
Cottonseed	na		0.01		0.01	na
Cottonseed oil	na		—		2.54	2.44
Groundnuts	na		—		1.91	na
Groundnut oil	na		—		8.19	2.85
Linseed	na		0.4		0.40	0.13
Linseed oil	na		—		3.87	4.42
Olive oil	na		—		0.44	0.90
Palm kernels	na		—		0.33	na
Palm kernel oil	na		—		1.20	1.36
Palm oil	10.00	8.30	5.05		1.15	0.99
Rapeseed	na		—		1.14	0.60
Rapeseed oil	na		—		5.70	0.36
Sesame seed	na		—		na	na
Soya beans	na		—		na	na
Sunflower seed	3.00		0.73		0.18	0.11
Sunflower seed oil	na		—		11.97	5.46
Tung oil	0.3		—		4.82	2.03

g incl. refined palm kernel oil. j '000 cu. metres of roundwood equivalent.

5. LIVESTOCK†, ANIMAL PRODUCTS, etc.						
Chickens d	10 348.3	6 655.0	—		109.5	21.4
Cattle d	2 366.0	2 317.0	—		1.5	
dairy cows d	1 240.7	1 193.7				
Goats d	121.0	296.3	—		0.7	na
Horses d	108.0	239.0	5.9		11.8	5.9
Pigs d	2 969.0	2 715.7			116.4	62.6
Bacon/ham	465.7	287.0	3.0	1.4	7.7	1.2
Meat† 'A'	46.6	17.6	0.9	0.6	15.2	0.9
Butter	42.3	30.7	1.9	1.0	3.4	1.5
Cheese	44.7	21.7	10.1	2.3	58.2	20.2*
Eggs	85.8	48.0	0.4	0.3*	12.4	13.3
Milk	3 128.7	2 498.7	149.0	2.3²	15.2	5.2
Hides/skins	na					
Wool b	0.3		0.2		21.6	17.2

d no. in thousands.

6. FIBRES, TEXTILES, etc.						
Agaves (sisal etc.)	na	—	0.1†		7.0	2.3
Cotton: lint	na	0.5	0.2	0.2	24.8	21.1
Flax fibre	na	0.5	0.1	0.6	1.9	3.2
Hemp fibre	na		0.3†		5.3	7.0
Jute	na		—		12.0	10.0
Rubber: natural	—		—		15.0	na
synthetic	na		1.1	1.7†	0.3	22.7
Silk f	25.1	21.1	1.1	0.8	5.3	0.7
Cotton: yarn	18.8	13.8	3.5	1.4	7.7	1.7
woven fabrics	64.2	36.7	43.4	13.8	4.9	4.3
Rayon: fibre/yarn	13.3	11.1	7.2	3.9n	2.2	0.3n
Non-cellulosic	0.1		0.7	1.1	9.0	na
Wool: fibre/yarn	7.4	7.4	2.0	0.5	3.3	2.8p
woven fabrics	na					

f metric tons. n spun rayon cloth only. p excl. velvet and woven felt.

7. FUEL AND POWER						
Coal 'A'‡	87	170	—	23	4 435	4 360
'B'‡	2 877	6 620	16	1	108	200
Coke	20 348	9 790¹	180	180¹	946	349
Electricity h: total	13 739	7 200¹	180	150¹		
hydro	6 609	2 590¹				
thermal	1 730	435			810	na
Natural gas i	2 710	3 660¹	—		1 740	330¹
Oil, crude	3 103	2 060¹	—		669u	79u
Petroleum, refined			1 450¹			
Rare earths f			150¹			

f metric tons. h million kWh. i million cu. metres. u incl. uranium salts.

8. IRON AND STEEL						
Iron ore	1 139m	866m	21	93	1 437	847
Pig iron	2 174	1 394	4	363	217	18
Steel ingots/castings	3 121	1 587	6	55	14	8
Iron/steel scrap	na		204	92	102	59
Iron/steel products a	na				60	18

a million $ U.S. m metal content.

9. NON-FERROUS MINERALS AND METALS						
Gold, bullion/coins etc.	na		—		0.56	5.21
Platinum group metals k	73.30	5.00	0.06	1.85	0.02	0.13
Silver: ore m	0.19	na	0.02	0.13		
bullion	1 595.00				3 791.67	491.67
Asbestos: fibre	na		14.01		24.62	8.24
manufactured	na		0.34		7.94	0.16
Mica	na	0.75			0.76	0.17
Aluminium: bauxite	11.18²	18.21	3.08	8.87	18.10	6.54
alumina	15.00m	49.56	59.14	31.70	158.74n	96.32b
aluminium	77.66	0.43m	0.28	0.63	7.94	3.06
Antimony: ore	0.47m	na			0.35	na
metal	0.02	na	0.64	2.05	0.01	0.11
Cadmium: metal	na				46.22	59.07
Chrome: ore	1.66m	2.87m	na	0.45	14.34	6.08
Copper: ore	14.63	9.68	11.39	1.72	0.42	0.01
metal	5.08m	4.96m	3.44	3.61	31.88	14.80
Lead: ore	7.54	11.82			4.56	4.91
metal					13.16	6.88
Magnesium: dolomite					2.92	0.83
magnesite					25.89	0.43
kieserite						
metal/salts					2.17	2.68
Manganese: ore			202.37	224.40	13.71	16.23
metal					20.20	4.39
Mercury f	0.17		0.16	0.04	369.80	20.60
Molybdenum f, f metal					0.35	67.50
Nickel: ore					3.23	0.34
metal					0.72	0.47
Titanium minerals					4.80	1.14
Tin: metal					3.18	0.52
Tungsten: ore	7.09m	0.55	8.22	31.45	0.19	0.16
metal	12.60	6.73	5.50	226.09	12.95	4.86
Zinc: ore					8.44	8.01
metal						

f metric tons. k '000 fine troy oz. m metal content. n hydrate. p calcined.

BAHAMAS
WEST ATLANTIC

The Bahamas, a British colony, was granted internal self-government in 1964.

AREA: 13 950 sq. km. (5 386 sq. miles)

LAND USE: (percentage of total)
Arable and orchard
Permanent meadow and pasture
Forest and woodland
City areas, waste and other land

POPULATION: 144 000 (1967 estimate)
Largest city: NASSAU, capital: population: 80 907 (1963)

Distribution of working population (1963)
Total working population: 51 948

U.N. group no.		Percentage
0	Agriculture, forestry, fishing and hunting	15.5
1	Mining and quarrying	
2/3	Manufacturing	7.6
4	Construction	14.6
5	Electricity, gas, water and sanitary services	1.1
6	Commerce	10.6
7	Transport, storage and communications	6.8
8	Services	39.7
9	Others	4.1

COMMUNICATIONS

		Year
Infant mortality (per '000)	41	1965
Crude birth rate (per '000)	32.6	1965
Crude death rate (per '000)	8.1	1965
Population per physician	1 330	1964
Population per hospital bed	170a	1966
School enrolment: age 5–19 years (percentage)	88	1964
age over 19 years (per 100 000 population)	43	1964

		Year(s)
Motor vehicles in use ('000s): private	15.9	1963–5 av.
commercial	3.4	
Telephones (per '000 urban population)	17.7	1967
Radio receivers (per '000 population)	248	1963–5 av.
Television sets (per '000 population)	28.9	1963–5 av.
Daily newspapers (per '000 population)	110.5	1963–4 av.

a government hospitals only.

FINANCE

Currency unit: The Bahamian dollar replaced the Bahamas pound (at par with the pound sterling) in 1966 at the rate B$1 to £0.35

EMPLOYMENT AND TRADE

Tourism is now the economic mainstay of the islands. Exports consist of pulpwood, salt, cucumbers, crawfish, sponges, and imports are foodstuffs, cars, hardware and clothing, the chief trading partners being the U.S.A., the U.K. and Canada. Industries such as cement, rum distilling and fish processing are developing.

PRODUCTION, EXPORTS AND IMPORTS
Years: 1963–5 average and 1953–5 average Units: '000 metric tons unless otherwise indicated

1. CEREALS, etc.	Production	Exports	Imports
Maize (corn)	na	—	0.3
Oats	na	—	0.1
Potatoes	na	—	2.9
Rice	na	—	4.3

2. FRUIT, etc.			
Apples	—	—	0.5*
Citrus fruit	na	—	—
Wine b	—	—	7.5*

5. LIVESTOCK†, ANIMAL PRODUCTS, etc.			
Cattle d	na	—	0.1
Goats d	na	—	4.4
Sheep d	na	—	0.1
Chickens d	525.0*n	4.76n	45.0²

continued

PRODUCTION, EXPORTS AND IMPORTS, etc.—continued

5. LIVESTOCK†, ANIMAL PRODUCTS, etc.—continued	Production	Exports	Imports
Horses d	na	—	1.0
Pigs d	11.0*	—	3.0
Bacon/ham	70.0¹	—	0.6
Meat† 'A'	na	—	0.5
'B'	na	—	0.3
Butter	—	—	
Cheese	na	—	
Eggs	0.2*	—	
Fish	2.0	1.4	
Milk	1.0	na	

d no. in thousands. n incl. ducks, geese and turkeys.

7. FUEL AND POWER			
Electricity h t	124	30¹	—
Petroleum, refined	na	—	1 520

h million kWh. t thermal.

11. INDUSTRY			
Cement	na	—	na
Merchant ships g	40¹		20.0

g '000 G.R.T.

continued

---

na: data not available. — negligible or nil. — negligible or nil. ¹ one year only. ² two year average. * estimate. † re-exports. ‡ see appendix.

BARBADOS — CARIBBEAN SEA

Barbados achieved full self-government in 1961, and in 1966 became an independent state within the British Commonwealth.

AREA: 430 sq. km. (166 sq. miles)

LAND USE: (percentage of total)

	1960	1955
Arable and orchard	60.5	65.1
Permanent meadow and pasture	9.3	11.6
Forest and woodland	—	—
City areas, waste and other land	30.2	23.3

POPULATION: 246 000 (1967 U.N. estimate)
Largest city: BRIDGETOWN, capital; population: 11 452 (city proper, 1960)
Distribution of working population (1960)
Total working population: 92 200

U.N. group no.		Percentage
0	Agriculture, forestry, fishing and hunting	24.3
1	Mining and quarrying	0.5
2/3	Manufacturing	14.1
4	Construction	9.7
5	Electricity, gas, water and sanitary services	0.9
6	Commerce	15.9
7	Transport, storage and communications	4.8
8	Services a	21.9
9	Others a	7.9

a incl. unemployed and those seeking employment for the first time.

			Year(s)
Life expectancy at birth (years): male	62.7		1959–61 av.
female	67.4		
Infant mortality (per '000)	39.5*		1965
Crude birth rate (per '000)	30.5*		1965
Crude death rate (per '000)	9*		1965
Accidental deaths (per 100 000 population)			
caused by motor vehicles	4.9		1965
due to other causes	20.5		1964
Population per physician	2 560		1966
Population per hospital bed	150		1964
School enrolment: age 5–19 years (percentage)	81a		1963–4 av.
age over 19 years (per 100 000 population)	145		1963–5 av.

a public education only.

COMMUNICATIONS

			Year(s)
Motor vehicles in use ('000s): private	11.6		1963–5 av.
commercial	3.3		
Mail per capita: domestic	22		1964–5 av.
foreign received	30		
foreign sent	14		
Telephones (per '000 population)	74.1		1967
Radio receivers (per '000 population)	174		1963–5 av.
Television sets (per '000 population)	8.3		1963–5 av.
Daily newspapers (per '000 population)	105.7		1962–4 av.

PRODUCTION, EXPORTS AND IMPORTS
Years: 1963–5 average and 1953–5 average   Units: '000 metric tons unless otherwise indicated

1. CEREALS, etc.

	Production	Exports	Imports
Barley	—	—	0.1
Cassava	1.0*	—	na
Maize (corn)	1.0*	—	2.0
Oats	—	—	1.3
Potatoes	—	—	4.7
Rice	—	0.2	7.9
Wheat	—	—	9.3²

2. FRUIT, etc.

	Production	Exports	Imports
Apples	—	—	0.3
Bananas	—	—	0.2
Oranges	1 897.0*	—	1.7
Other citrus fruit	185.7	165.5	160.7	0.1
Wine b	—	—	0.2²
b '000 hectolitres.			

3. BEVERAGES, FOREST PRODUCTS, etc.

	Production	Exports	Imports
Coffee	—	—	0.7
Sugar: cane	1 897.0*		
raw	185.7	170.0	165.5	0.1
Tea	—	—	0.1
Tobacco: leaf	171.0e		0.2
cigarettes			0.2²
Softwood j	—	—	34.3
Hardwood j	—	—	2.6
Newspaper	14.1		0.8
Other paper			1.3
j '000 cu. metres of roundwood equivalent.			

4. VEGETABLE OILSEEDS AND OILS

	Production	Exports	Imports
Castor oil	0.46		0.02
Copra	0.20*		3.51
Coconut oil			0.47
Cottonseed oil			0.03
Groundnuts			0.46²
Linseed			0.01
Linseed oil			0.05
Olive oil			0.01

FINANCE
Currency unit: The East Caribbean dollar

Exchange rates	1965	1960	1950
Per $ U.S.	1.72	1.72	1.72
Per £ sterling	4.8	4.8	4.8

		Year
National income (million $ U.S.)	88	1965
G.N.P. per capita ($ U.S.)	400	1966

TRADING

Total trade (in million $ U.S.)	1965	1960	1938
Exports (f.o.b.)	37	23	7
Imports (c.i.f.)	68	32	10

Main trading partners (percentage of total value)

Exports	1965	1955
U.S.A.	42	42
Canada	11	42
Irish R.	8	40
Trin./Tob.	6	na
St. Lucia	3	4
Dominica	2	na

Imports	1965	1955
U.K.	30	40
U.S.A.	16	16
Canada	12	8
Venezuela	8	6
Trin./Tob.	6	4
Netherlands	3	3
New Zealand	3	2

Distribution of trade (percentage of total value)

Exports	1965	1955
Food (sugar and molasses)	90 (78)	92 (87)
Rum	6	6

Imports	1965	1955
Manufactured goods (machinery and transport equipment) (textiles)	46 (16)	42 (12)
Food (meat and preparations)	27 (6)	30 (na)
Crude materials and fuels (petroleum products)	13 (8)	12 (na)
Chemicals	7	8

PRODUCTION, EXPORTS AND IMPORTS
Years: 1963–5 average and 1953–5 average   Units: '000 metric tons unless otherwise indicated

5. LIVESTOCK‡; ANIMAL PRODUCTS, etc.

	Production	Exports	Imports
Chickens d	329.0* n		
Cattle d	16.0*	13.0¹	
Goats d	17.0*	16.0¹	
Sheep d	39.3*	33.0¹	0.1
Horses d	1.0*		
Pigs d	26.0*	24.0¹	
Butter			2.2
Cheese			1.3
Eggs	1.1*		0.7
Fish	4.0	0.1	0.6
Milk	6.0*	0.6	0.1
Bacon/ham			1.7
Meat†, A¹			18.1
Meat†, B¹			0.3*

d no. in thousands. n incl. ducks, geese and turkeys.

7. FUEL AND POWER

	Production	Exports	Imports
Electricity h†	60		20¹
Natural gas i			2¹
Oil, crudo	30		10¹
Petroleum, refined			30
			307

h million kWh. i million cu. metres. t thermal.

9. NON-FERROUS MINERALS AND METALS

	Production	Exports	Imports
Asbestos			0.03
Aluminium, manufactured			0.07
Copper, metal			0.12
Lead, metal			0.17¹
Tin, metal			0.24
Zinc, metal			0.01
p '000 $ U.S.			

10. FERTILIZERS

	Production	Exports	Imports
Potash	na	1.4 n	5.1

11. INDUSTRY

	Production	Exports	Imports
Spirits	na		na
Cement	na		na
Electrical engineering a			1.3
Motor vehicles a			2.9

a million $ U.S. * rum only.

na: data not available. — negligible or nil. * estimate. † re-exports. ¹ one year only. ² two year average.

BELGIUM — EUROPE

An economic union between Belgium and Luxembourg has been in operation since 1922, apart from the war years 1940–45. The Netherlands joined these two countries to form the Benelux Customs Union in 1948, and in 1960 this was replaced by a full economic union between the three, and membership of the European Economic Community.   Trading figures refer to Belgium and Luxembourg.

AREA: 30 513 sq. km. (11 778 sq. miles)

LAND USE: (percentage of total)

	1965
Arable and orchard	30.7
Permanent meadow and pasture	23.6
Forest and woodland	19.7
City areas, waste and other land	26.0

POPULATION: 9 581 000 (1967 estimate)
Largest city: BRUXELLES (Brussels) capital; population: 1 074 586 (1966)

Distribution of working population (1964)
Total working population: 3 725 700 (incl. armed forces)

U.N. group no.		1965	Percentage
0	Agriculture, forestry, fishing and hunting		5.8
1	Mining and quarrying		2.8
2/3	Manufacturing		33.6
4	Construction		7.6
5	Electricity, gas, water and sanitary services		0.8
6	Commerce		14.8
7	Transport, storage and communications		6.7
8	Services		23.5
9	Others		4.3

			Year(s)
Life expectancy at birth (years): male	67.7		1959–63 av.
female	73.5		
Infant mortality (per '000)	24.1		1965
Crude birth rate (per '000)	16.4		1965
Crude death rate (per '000)	12.1		1965
Accidental deaths (per 100 000 population)			
caused by motor vehicles	24.4		1965
due to other causes	35.8		1965
Population per physician	680		1966
Population per hospital bed	130		1963–4 av.
School enrolment: age 5–19 years (percentage)	110‡		1963–5 av.
age over 19 years (per 100 000 population)	810		

COMMUNICATIONS

			Year(s)
Motor vehicles in use ('000s): private	1 180.7		1963–5 av.
commercial	222.6		
Mail per capita: domestic	4 485		1964
foreign received	227		1963–5 av.
foreign sent	19		
Telephones (per '000 urban population)	20		1967
Radio licences (per '000 population)	325		1963–5 av.
Television licences (per '000 population)	140		1963–5 av.
Daily newspapers (per '000 population)	285		1961

FINANCE
Currency unit: The Belgian franc

Exchange rates	1965a	1960a	1950a	1938b
Per $ U.S.	49.64	49.70	50.12	29.68
Per £ sterling	139.15	139.35	140.40	136.53

	1965	1966	Year(s)
National income (million $ U.S.)	13 302	1965
G.N.P. per capita ($ U.S.)	1 630	1966
Rate of increase of G.N.P. per capita	4.6	1960–4 av.
Foreign trade (percentage of G.D.P.)	74	1963–5 av.

a spot rate. b selling rate.

TRADING (including Luxembourg)

Total trade (in million $ U.S.)	1965	1955	1938
Exports (f.o.b.)	6 382	2 776	730
Imports (c.i.f.)	6 497	2 830	767

Main trading partners (percentage of total value)

Exports	1965	1955	1938
Netherlands	22	21	12
Germany F.R.	22	12	12d
France	12	10	15
U.S.A.	6	9	7
Italy	5	4	1
Switzerland	3	2	3

Imports	1965	1955	1938
Germany F.R.	21	15	11d
Netherlands	15	13	14
France	13	12	14
U.S.A.	8	7	9
Italy	4	3	1
Congo D.R.	3	8	8

Distribution of trade (percentage of total value)

Exports	1965	1955	1938*
Manufactured goods (machinery and transport equipment) (iron and steel)	75 (20)	73 (11)	(7)
Crude materials and fuels	9	9	(14)
Food	9 (18)	14 (24)	4
Chemicals	6	7	8

Imports	1965	1955	1938 (8)
Manufactured goods (machinery and transport equipment) (fuels)	54 (24)	44 (16)	(na)
Crude materials and fuels	25 (9)	33 (10)	(na)
Food	11	13	4
Chemicals	7	5	

d incl. Germany D.R.

PRODUCTION, EXPORTS AND IMPORTS
Years: 1963–5 average and 1953–5 average   Units: '000 metric tons unless otherwise indicated

Production data are for Belgium; data for Luxembourg are given where applicable.   Trade figures apply to Belgium and Luxembourg combined.

1. CEREALS, etc.

	Production	Exports	Imports
Barley	506.0	273.7	28.3	6.7	282.3	472.5
Lux.	20.7	13.3		
Maize (corn)	2.0	10.7	85.6	5.7	756.4	412.0
Millets/sorghum			26.5	2.0	543.5	113.3
Oats	357.3	465.0	1.7	1.6	63.0	107.4
Lux.	74.7	39.0		
Potatoes	1 568.0	2 245.7	188.2	126.4	137.3	120.2
Lux.	34.0	141.0	105.0		
Rice	87.3	133.3	7.6	6.8	39.9	38.6
Rye	119.0	226.0	1.5	5.5	42.1	139.5
Lux.	9.7			
Wheat	848.3	637.3	199.2	3.5	511.6	625.7
Lux.	42.3	40.0		

2. FRUIT, etc.

	Production	Exports	Imports
Apples	165.0	250.0	34.5	41.4	42.9	7.7
Lux.	11.3	na		
Bananas			4.1†	0.8†	70.9	47.1
Cherries	16.3	30.5	2.4	2.7	1.2	1.4
Lux.	1.0*	na		
Dates			0.1†	0.1†	14.7	0.4
Grapes	11.3*	12.7			14.8	10.0
Lux.	20.0*	14.7*		
Lemons			6.1†	0.2†	132.7	110.3
Oranges			0.3†	0.3†	8.3	7.0
Other citrus fruit			na	na		3.6
Peaches	6.7					

2. FRUIT, etc.—continued

	Production	Exports	Imports
Pears	55.0	210.0	11.0	16.4	13.0	4.9
Lux.	1.0*	na		
Plums	16.7	37.3	—	1.8	5.5	1.6
Raisins	2.7	na	—	—		
Tomatoes	74.7		64.3	12.7	873.6	528.7
Wine b		Lux. 141.0	105.0		
b trade in '000 hectolitres.			

3. BEVERAGES, FOREST PRODUCTS, etc.

	Production	Exports	Imports
Cocoa			0.2†	0.2†	15.7	8.7
Coffee			0.8†	1.9†	63.7	48.4
Sugar: beet raw	2 595.3	2 255.7	95.4	135.7	34.0	54.5
	449.9	381.0	2.0	0.2	0.6	0.4
Tea	2.5	3.7	5.6	1.0²	31.2	21.5
Tobacco: leaf	366.0e	105.4e			0.6²	
cigars				
cigarettes	15 188.0e	9 386.0e		
tobacco/snuff			
Softwood j	1 375.0	1 261.7	269.0	130.4	1 638.0	1 034.1
Lux.	7.4	70.0		
Hardwood j	1 156.7	1 050.0	127.3	17.0	587.8	318.4
Lux.	114.3	81.7	12.1	10.0		
Wood pulp	85.1	67.3			230.6	168.7
Newsprint	324.0	246.7	138.0	45.0	71.3	47.0
Other paper	403.0				363.0	104.3
j '000 cu. metres of roundwood equivalent.				continued

na: data not available. — negligible or nil. * estimate. ‡ see appendix. † re-exports. ¹ one year only. ² two year average. e no. in millions. j '000 cu. metres of roundwood equivalent.

continued

PRODUCTION, EXPORTS AND IMPORTS continued

4. VEGETABLE OILSEEDS AND OILS

	Production	Exports	Imports
Castor seed d	na	0.07	2.84
Castor seed d . Lux.	—	3.11	1.91
Castor oil d	na	0.83	32.02
Castor oil d . Lux.	—	0.37†	27.53
Copra d	na	1.40	3.99
Coconut oil d . Lux.	—	4.94	9.65
Cottonseed oil d	na	10.60†	64.38
Cottonseed oil d . Lux.	—	0.82†	3.28
Groundnuts d	na	7.37	16.67
Groundnut oil d	20.33	11.21	84.47
Groundnut oil d . Lux.	19.67	5.01	25.97
Linseed d	na	1.84	29.04
Linseed oil d	na	6.23	0.88
Linseed oil d . Lux.	—	5.43	3.94
Olive oil d	na	—	0.54
Palm kernels d	na	0.13†	24.93
Palm kernel oil d	70	1.49	25.70
Palm oil d	na	5.61†	35.70
Rapeseed d	—	0.74†	0.54
Rapeseed oil d	1.30	0.01	125.70
Soya beans d	na	6.20†	4.44
Soya bean oil d	—	3.98	3.30
Sunflower seed d	na	0.19†	2.16
Sunflower seed oil d	na	—	7.49
Tung oil d	na	—	0.35

5. LIVESTOCK‡, ANIMAL PRODUCTS, etc.

	Production	Exports	Imports
Chickens d	32 805.0	43.1	49.9
Chickens d . Lux.	15 696.7	2.2²	13.3
Cattle d	2 433.0		
Cattle d . Lux.	2 364.7		
dairy cows d . Lux.	161.0		
Goats d . Lux.	25.0		
Sheep d	166.7	18.8	81.8
Sheep d . Lux.	3.0		na
Horses d	124.7		
Horses d . Lux.	11.6		
Pigs d	1 825.0	148.7	25.0
Pigs d . Lux.	100.0	11.1	
Bacon/ham A	478.3	0.7	0.2
Meat‡ A . Lux.	371.7	20.2	40.6
Bacon/ham B	25.7	16.6	25.9
B . Lux.	18.7	2.6	5.5
Butter d	152.5	7.2	8.6
Butter d . Lux.	56.1	—	10.1
Cheese d	32.3p	7.2	33.9
Cheese d . Lux.	13.7p	0.3	3.6
Eggs d	166.5	32.8	0.2
Eggs d . Lux.	2.3	3.3	—
Fish d	60.4q	22.5	184.7
Milk d	3 914.3	378.1	281.4
Milk d . Lux.	194.0	86.3	128.8
Whale/sperm oil d	24.2	—	11.2
Hides/skins d . Lux.	24.2²	18.3²	36.7
Wool d	1.0	17.5	60.6

6. FIBRES, TEXTILES, etc.

	Production	Exports	Imports
Abaca d	—	0.3†	1.7
Agaves (sisal etc.) d	—	4.6†	36.7
Cotton lint d	—	1.4†	84.1
Flax fibre d	39.1*	95.8†	284.1
Hard fibre d . Lux.	38.5	0.1†	261.6
Jute d	—	23.1†	94.7
Rubber: natural d	12.0	1.8†	19.6
synthetic d	—	11.9	22.5²
Silk d	—	34.7†	26.3
Cotton: yarn d	95.5	17.2	14.4
woven fabrics d	81.2	41.4	20.8
Rayon: fibre/yarn d	37.4	15.0	13.0
woven fabrics d	16.6	15.3	14.7
Non-cellulosic fibre/yarn d	7.3	7.8	18.3
Wool: yarn d	63.8	24.8	6.5
woven fabrics d	18.4	11.5	5.0

7. FUEL AND POWER

	Production	Exports	Imports
Coal: A‡	20 837	2 403	7 344
Coal: B	29 920	5 931	3 465
Coke	na	467	231
Coke . Lux.	na	739	3 266
Electricity:h total	20 516		
Electricity:h total Lux.	2 122		
hydro	176		
hydro . Lux.	737		
nuclear	49		
thermal	20 291		
thermal . Lux.	1 385		
Natural gas i	70	—	13 633
Oil, crude	—	—	4 323
Petroleum, refined	11 453	3 217	7
Uranium f	—	1 800¹	—

8. IRON AND STEEL

	Production	Exports	Imports
Iron ore	29m	390	22 225
Iron ore . Lux.	7 976	138	439
Pig iron	7 976	138	439
Pig iron . Lux.	3 974	41	330
Steel ingots/castings	8 476	640	254
Steel ingots/castings . Lux.	4 392	385	74
Iron/steel scrap	na	284	69
Iron/steel products a	na	1 026	187

9. NON-FERROUS MINERALS AND METALS

	Production	Exports	Imports
Diamonds a	264.95‡	89.07‡	255.10	76.54
Gold k	204.00†	123.87†	1 013.33†	413.00
bullion/coins etc.	9 837.00†	3 433.00†	7 218.00†	1 738.33
Silver k, bullion	0.18	0.22†	55.56	33.95
Asbestos: fibre	216.09†	103.91†	1.10	2.54
manufactured	0.18²	0.30†	5.30	1.06
Mica	—	0.01†	11.24p	1.30
Aluminium: bauxite	—	0.30†	11.24p	0.43
alumina	107.33†	27.92†	127.18	31.83
aluminium	1.53†	0.72r†	0.37	0.09
Antimony, metal	0.82²	0.12†	0.35	0.02
Chrome: ore	0.70	—	1.15	0.50
metal	—	0.05	6.05	3.39²
Cobalt, metal	1.35	32.97		
Copper: ore	—	—	2.81	172.51
metal	352.97†	168.19r	366.00	13.28
Lead: ore	—	0.29†	141.56	115.63
metal	77.40	58.87	33.41	22.95
Magnesium: dolomite	—	—	16.24	6.33
metal/salts	499.88	130.75	4.72	2.60
Manganese: ore	0.03	0.22	4.51	17.07
metal	—	—	267.88u	108.62u
Mercury f	4.00†	9.97²	91.32	64.70²
Molybdenum: metal	11.30†	4.80†	95.80	36.00
Nickel, metal	—	—		
Tin: ore	0.68†	0.08†	317.70	114.80
metal	0.68†		7.05	0.62
Titanium minerals	5.65	10.62	3.38	14.49
Tungsten: ore	12.17†	0.15†	9.20w	1.86
metal	—	—	0.05	0.11
Vanadium	0.04†		0.02	0.05
Zinc: ore	0.39†u	—	460.71	464.26
metal	184.78	52.08†	26.03	5.59

a million $ U.S. *f* metric tons. *k* '000 fine troy oz. *n* incl. matte. *p* hydrate. *q* antimony oxide only. *t* incl. re-exports. *u* incl. ferro-manganiferous iron ore. *v* ferro-titanium and titanium oxide only. *w* ferro-vanadium and vanadium oxide. *x* primary magnesium only. *y* incl. calcined.

10. CHEMICALS‡ AND FERTILIZERS

Organic chemicals:

	Production	Exports	Imports
Benzene	46.1	29.8	7.4
Butadiene	na	na	na
Ethylene	na	na	na
Ethanol	na	na	na
Methanol	14.0	5.1p†	7.4p
Phenol	—	0.1	0.8
Phthalic anhydride	30.5²	55.2	1.2
Styrene monomer			6.0
Urea			

n data not available for years 1953–5. *p* incl. phenol salts.

---

10. CHEMICALS‡ AND FERTILIZERS—continued

Inorganic chemicals:

	Production	Exports	Imports
Ammonia	356.6	41.0	2.8
Carbon black	7.52*	3.6	14.0
Carbon black . B	73.0	9.3	0.5
Chlorine	na	2.2	0.9
Nitric acid	226.3	4.9	39.6
Sodium carbonate	58.7	14.4	25.1
Sodium hydroxide	1 357.3	101.6	47.5
Sulphuric acid			

Plastics:

	Production	Exports	Imports
Polyamides	17.7	0.1	5.0
Polyethylene	40.7	11.3	22.1
Polyvinyl chloride		na	12.3

Fertilizers:

	Production	Exports	Imports
Phosphates	19.1*	28.6	1 158.5	385.9
Potash	—	994.2†	1 345.6	1 109.7
Pyrites	—	0.3†	284.1	344.3
Sulphur	4.5q	7.7†	222.8	54.1

n data not available for years 1953–5. *q* recovered.

11. INDUSTRY

	Production	Exports	Imports
Aircraft a	42.0*v	—		
Alcoholic beverages: beer b	11 099.0	92.3	62.0
beer b . Lux.	501.0	1.6	47.5a
spirits b . Lux.	45.61n	1.5a	12.2
Cement	5 487.0†		20.3a
Cement . Lux.	210.0	1 452.3	30.7
Electrical engineering a	549.3²	226.0	278.3
Locomotives c	122.0*	74.8²	80.7²
Railway vehicles a	na	na	na
Machine tools a	24.01	21.9	4.4
Merchant ships g	93.0	6.7²	29.7
Motor vehicles: commercial d	17.8u	31.0	8.0
private d	364.5u	60.5	443.6
		40.8²	115.3²

a '000 hectolitres. *c* no. of units. *d* no. in thousands. *g* '000 G.R.T. *h* U.S. *b* '000 hectolitres. *v* 1960 figure. *n* assembly of imported parts. *p* 1966 figure. *q* 1961 figure. *t* 1961 figure. *u* 1965–7 av.

WESTERN ATLANTIC

BERMUDA

BERMUDA, a British colony, was granted internal self-government in 1968.

AREA: 53.3 sq. km. (20.59 sq. miles)

LAND USE: (percentage of total)

	1964	1950
Arable and orchard	4.0	13.0
Permanent meadow and pasture	4.0	15.0
Forest and woodland	60.0	53.3
City areas, waste and other land	32.0	18.4

POPULATION: 51 000 (1967 estimate)
Largest city: HAMILTON, capital; population: 3 000 (1965)
Total working population: 20 067 (1960)

		Year(s)
Life expectancy at birth (years): male	65.6	1965–6 av.
female	72.4	
Infant mortality (per '000)	30.5	1965
Crude birth rate (per '000)	23.0	1965
Crude death rate (per '000)	7.4	1965
Population per physician	960	1964
Population per hospital bed	110	1963
School enrolment: age 5–19 years (percentage)	99	1963–4 av.

COMMUNICATIONS

		Year(s)
Motor vehicles in use ('000s): private	7.9	1963–5 av.
commercial	1.4	
Mail per capita: domestic	99	1963–5 av.
foreign received	164	
foreign sent	186	
Telephones (per '000 urban population)	45.1a	1967
Radio receivers (per '000 population)	231.6	1963–5 av.
Television sets (per '000 population)	340	1963
Daily newspapers (per '000 population)		1963

a excl. those of armed forces.

FINANCE

Currency unit: The Bermuda dollar replaced the Bermuda pound (at par with the pound sterling) in 1970 at the rate Bermuda $1 to £0.433 (U.S. $1.039).

EMPLOYMENT AND TRADE

The important vegetable trade with the U.S.A. has decreased owing to the imposition of tariffs, and the export of Bermuda cedarwood (juniper) ceased after the severe blight of 1943. Some fruit and concentrated essences are exported, but most foodstuffs have to be imported, as do clothing, fuel and building materials. The economy depends on the tourist trade and the use of the island as an air and naval base. Main trading partners are the U.S.A., the U.K., Canada and the Netherlands Antilles.

PRODUCTION, EXPORTS AND IMPORTS

Years: 1963–5 average and 1953–5 average Units: '000 metric tons unless otherwise indicated

1. CEREALS, etc.

	Production	Exports	Imports
Oats	—	—	1.7²
Potatoes	1.0*	—	7.0²
Rice	—	—	0.3²

2. FRUIT, etc.

	Production	Exports	Imports
Apples	—	—	0.4²
Bananas	1.0*	—	—
Oranges	—	—	0.5²
Raisins	—	1.0	—

b '000 hectolitres.

3. BEVERAGES, FOREST PRODUCTS, etc.

	Production	Exports	Imports
Coffee	—	—	0.1²
Sugar, raw	—	—	2.1²
Tea	—	—	0.1

5. LIVESTOCK‡, ANIMAL PRODUCTS, etc.

	Production	Exports	Imports
Chickens d	1.0*	—	—
Cattle d	—	—	0.4²
Pigs d	—	—	0.7
Bacon/ham	—	—	1.0
Meat‡: A	—	—	2.7²
B	0.5*	—	—

5. LIVESTOCK, ANIMAL PRODUCTS, etc.—continued

	Production	Exports	Imports
Butter	—	—	0.4²
Cheese	—	—	0.2²
Eggs	0.8*n	—	0.6*n
Fish	4.0	—	6.6
Milk	3.0²	—	2.4

n marine fisheries only.

7. FUEL AND POWER

	Production	Exports	Imports
Coal: A‡	—	—	—
Electricity:h‡	134	60¹	1
Petroleum, refined.	—	—	207	100¹

h million kWh. ¹ thermal.

9. NON-FERROUS MINERALS AND METALS

	Production	Exports	Imports
Diamonds a	—	—	0.70
Asbestos a	—	—	0.03
manufactured a	—	—	0.04

a million $ U.S.

continued

---

na: data not available. — negligible or not available. — negligible or nil. ¹ one year only. ² two year average. * estimate. ‡ see appendix. † re-exports.

BHUTAN

Bhutan is an independent, mainly Buddhist, state; some guidance in its external affairs has been given by India since the independence of the latter in 1949. In 1964 the king assumed directrule, but in 1969 a more democratic form of government was introduced.

AREA: 41 400 sq. km. (16 000 sq. miles)

POPULATION: 770 000 (1967 U.N. estimate)
Summer capital: TASHI CHHO DZONG (Thimbu)
Winter capital: PUNAKHA

FINANCE
Currency unit: The Indian rupee (a sterling currency maintained at the value £0.075)

Exchange rates	1965	1960	1955	1938
Per $ U.S.	4.773	4.773	4.775	2.888
National Income (million $ U.S.)			32	(1958)

EMPLOYMENT AND TRADE
Land cultivation is primitive, the main crops being rice, maize, millet; much of the land is under forest. There are small handicraft industries, such as weaving and metalwork. Large deposits of limestone and gypsum have been found. The main exports are timber and grain, trade being mainly with India.

BOLIVIA

The Republic of Bolivia has suffered several years' political and economic instability, the latter aggravated by the lack of diversification, tin being the only important product; in 1962 aid for a development plan was received from the U.S.A. and elsewhere.

AREA: 1 098 580 sq. km. (424 160 sq. miles)

LAND USE: (percentage of total)	1950
Arable and orchard	2.8
Permanent meadow and pasture	10.3
Forest and woodland	42.8
City areas, waste and other land	44.1

POPULATION: 3 801 000 (1967 estimate)
Largest city: LA PAZ, capital: population: 360 329 (city proper, 1965)

Distribution of working population (1950)
Total working population: 1 058 725 (excl. Indian tribes: 87 000*)

U.N. group no.		Percentage
0	Agriculture, forestry, fishing and hunting	63.4
1	Mining and quarrying	4.1
2/3	Manufacturing	10.3
4	Construction	2.4
5	Electricity, gas, water and sanitary services	3.9
6	Commerce	5.4
7	Transport, storage and communications	2.0
8	Services	6.6
9	Others	1.9

		Year(s)
Life expectancy at birth (years): male	49.7	1949–51 av.
female	49.7	
Infant mortality (per '000)	76.5*	1965
Crude birth rate (per '000)	44*	1960–5 av.
Crude death rate (per '000)	21*	1960–5 av.
Population per physician	3160	1966
Population per hospital bed	400	1966
School enrollment: age 5–19 years (percentage)	51	1963–4 av.
age over 19 years (per 100 000 population)	349	1964–5 av.

COMMUNICATIONS
Motor vehicles in use ('000s):		Year(s)
private	13.5	1963–5 av.
commercial	36.1	
Railway track (km.)	3 580.7	1964
Telephones (per '000 urban population)	127	1967
Daily newspapers (per '000 population)	26	1961

FINANCE
Currency unit: The peso Boliviano was introduced in 1963 at the rate 1 peso Boliviano per 1 000 bolivianos

Exchange rates	1965	1960b	1950b	1938b
Per $ U.S.	11.88a	11.885	60.6	30.44
Per £ sterling	33.28	33278	169.75	140.02

		Year(s)
National Income (million $ U.S.)	532	1965
G.N.P. per capita ($ U.S.)	160	1966
Rate of increase of G.N.P. per capita	3.4	1960–4 av.
Foreign trade (percentage of G.D.P.)	36	1963–5 av.

a selling rate. b bolivianos.

TRADING
Total trade (in million $ U.S.)	1965	1955	1938
Exports (f.o.b.)	129	100	27
Imports (c.i.f.)	126	81	19

Main trading partners (percentage of total value)

Exports	1965	1955	Imports	1965	1955
U.K.	45	33	U.S.A.	47	38
U.S.A.	42	60	Japan	13	1
Germany F.R.	5	1	Germany F.R.	12	10
Japan	2	—	Argentina	6	7
Netherlands	2	—	U.K.	6	4
Belg./Lux.	2	—	Netherlands	4	4

Distribution of trade (percentage of total value)

Exports	1962	1955
Non-ferrous ores (tin ore)	98	95 (58)
Imports		
Food	20	26
Machinery and transport equipment	16	14
Fuel	4	4

PRODUCTION, EXPORTS AND IMPORTS
Units: '000 metric tons unless otherwise indicated
Years: 1963–5 average and 1963–5 average

1. CEREALS, etc.	Production		Exports		Imports	
Barley	93.3	44.0[1]				
Cassava	154.0	na				
Maize (corn)	254.7	138.0[1]				
Millets/sorghum						
Oats	13.0	2.0[1]			0.1	0.7
Potatoes	685.0	691.0*			0.1	0.2
Rice	42.0*	29.7*		0.2		6.4
Sweetpotatoes/yams						
Wheat	68.3	46.0[1]			14.4	54.9

2. FRUIT, etc.						
Apples	50.0[1]	50.0*	0.4			
Bananas	9.0*	na			1.6n	
Grapes	40.0*	42.0*				
Lemons	113.3*	137.0*[2]				
Oranges						
Pineapples	2.3*	na			0.1	
Raisins					2.5	
Wine h						

b '000 hectolitres. n incl. pears and quince.

PRODUCTION, EXPORTS AND IMPORTS *continued*

5. LIVESTOCK‡, ANIMAL PRODUCTS, etc.	Production		Exports		Imports	
Chickens d	2 174.3	na				
Cattle d	1 500.0	2 260.0[1*]		1.0[1]		12.0
Goats d	1 483.0	1 229.0*				
Sheep d	6 180.3	6 464.0[1*]				
Pigs d	201.0*	na			0.1	0.3
Meat‡: A	667.0*	509.0*		0.4	0.3	0.4
B	1.0*					
Butter						
Cheese					0.3	
Eggs	4.0*	na			1.7[2]	0.61*
Fish	1.41n			0.91n	45.5	27.5*
Milk	44.3*				0.2	0.3
Wool		3.0*				

d no. in thousands. n excl. subsistence fishing.

6. FIBRES, TEXTILES, etc.	Production		Exports		Imports	
Cotton lint	na	na		0.1*		1.8
Rubber, natural	na	na	2.1		1.7	0.2[2]
Silk f	0.3[2]	na			1.0[2]	
Cotton: yarn	1.1	0.9*			0.41	na
woven fabrics	1.0n	1.4n				
Wool, woven fabrics	na					

f metric tons. m million metres.

7. FUEL AND POWER	Production		Exports		Imports	
Coal' A‡	—	6	—		—	
Electricity h: total	540	220[1]				
hydro	415[2]	210[1]	30			
thermal	125	10[1]	47		13	30[1]
Natural gas i	100	3	3			
Oil, crude	430	350[1]		na[1]		
Petroleum, refined	383	270[1]		20[1]		

h million kWh. i million cu. metres.

9. NON-FERROUS MINERALS AND METALS	Production		Exports		Imports	
Gold k: ore m	125.30	28.00	0.38	18.92	—	—
bullion/coins etc.	na	na	95.63	77.74	—	—
Silver k, ore m			4 598.15	5 894.13	—	—
Asbestos			0.01	0.26	—	—
Antimony, ore m	8.66	8.65	8.65	5.40	—	—
Copper, ore m			4.14	3.87	—	—
Lead: ore m	17.28	20.38	17.92	19.19	—	—
Mercury f	0.55	na	0.02	1.42	—	—
Tin: ore m	2.17		2.80[2]	na	—	—
metal	23.84	31.00	20.73	30.40	—	—
Tungsten, ore m	3.21	0.16	2.74	0.16	—	—
Zinc, ore m	9.13	21.87	9.37	22.73	—	—

f metric tons. k '000 fine troy oz. m metal content.

10. CHEMICALS n AND FERTILIZERS	Production		Exports		Imports	
Chemicals	na				na	
Fertilizers:						
Sulphur	10.1	3.0			10.1	—

n data not available for years 1953–5.

11. INDUSTRY	Production		Exports		Imports	
Beer b	247.0	262.3				2.0
Cement	60.7	35.3			7.3	
Electrical engineering						na
Motor vehicles a					7.8	1.9

a million $ U.S. b '000 hectolitres.

BOTSWANA

Botswana, formerly the British protectorate of Bechuanaland, became a republic within the Commonwealth in 1966, but is still linked to the South African customs union.

AREA: 575 000 sq. km. (222 000 sq. miles)

LAND USE: (percentage of total)	1965
Arable and orchard	0.3
Permanent meadow and pasture	72.2
Forest and woodland and other land	1.7
City areas, waste and other land	25.8

POPULATION: 593 000 (1967 estimate)
Capital city: GABORONE; population: 4 200 (city proper, 1965)

Distribution of working population (1964)
Total working population: 250 678

U.N. group no.		Percentage
0	Agriculture, forestry, fishing and hunting	90.8
1	Mining and quarrying	0.8
2/3	Manufacturing	0.8
4	Construction	1.1
5	Electricity, gas, water and sanitary services	
6	Commerce	1.0
7	Transport, storage and communications	0.9
8	Services	3.9
9	Others	0.5

COMMUNICATIONS
Motor vehicles in use ('000s):		Year(s)
private	1.5	1963–5 av.
commercial	1.7	
Railway track (km.)	640	1964
Telephones (per '000 urban population)	0.4	1967
Radio licences (per '000 population)	8	1963–5 av.

FINANCE
Currency unit: The rand was introduced in 1961 at the rate R1 at £0.5 sterling

Exchange rates	1965	1960a	1955a
Per $ U.S.	0.714	0.357	

		Year
National Income (million $ U.S.)	34*	1966
G.N.P. per capita ($ U.S.)	60	1966

a £ sterling.

EMPLOYMENT, PRODUCTION AND TRADE
Cattle-rearing and dairying are the main occupations; there is little arable farming on account of limited rainfall. Twenty per cent of the male population work on temporary contracts in the mines and industries of South Africa, producing invisible earnings which contribute to the balance of trade. Exports are mainly carcasses and animal products, and small quantities of gold, silver, asbestos and manganese. Large nickel reserves were located in 1969. Imports are mainly cereals, sugar, petroleum products and manufactured goods.

PRODUCTION, EXPORTS AND IMPORTS
Units: '000 metric tons unless otherwise indicated
Years: 1963–5 average and 1963–5 average

1. CEREALS, etc.	Production		Exports		Imports	
Maize (corn)	2.3*	2.0[2]			3.1	50.9
Millets/sorghum	70.0*[1]	22.0[2]			0.3	0.2
					0.2[2]	0.3

3. BEVERAGES, FOREST PRODUCTS, etc.	Production		Exports		Imports	
Hardwood j	878.7*	19.0			0.2[1]	14.4
					4.6[1]	2.3[*1]

j '000 cu. metres of roundwood equivalent.

5. LIVESTOCK‡, ANIMAL PRODUCTS, etc.	Production		Exports		Imports	
Bacon/ham	21.0*	20.0[1*]				
Meat‡: A	3.0	0.2*				
B	0.2*	0.2[2]				
Eggs	3.5*	32.0	na	na		
Fish			na	na		
Milk			na	na		
Hides/skins	0.6[2]	0.6[*p]	na	na		

d no. in thousands. n incl. ducks, geese and turkeys. p from cattle only.

9. NON-FERROUS MINERALS AND METALS	Production		Exports		Imports	
Gold k, ore m	na					
Silver, ore m		1.06				
Asbestos, fibre	1.64	0.82	na	na		
Manganese, ore	15.79		na	na		

k '000 fine troy oz. m metal content.

continued

---

na: data not available. — negligible or nil. * estimate. ‡ see appendix. † re-exports.
1 one year only. 2 two year average.

BRAZIL

SOUTH AMERICA

Brazil is a federal republic with a presidential system similar to that of the U.S.A.

AREA: 8 511 965 sq. km. (3 286 500 sq. miles)

LAND USE: (percentage of total)

	1960	1955
Arable and orchard	3.5	2.3
Permanent meadow and pasture	12.6	12.6
Forest and woodland	60.8	60.8
City areas, waste and other land	23.1	24.3

POPULATION: 85 655 000 (1967 estimate)

Largest city: SÃO PAULO; population: 5 383 000 (city proper, 1967) was estimated to be 200 000.

The new capital, BRASILIA, was inaugurated in 1960. In 1965 the population

Distribution of working population (1960)

U.N. group no.		Percentage
1a	Agriculture, forestry	51.6
2/3	Mining and quarrying, fishing and hunting	8.9
	Manufacturing	8.5
4	Construction	3.5
5b	Electricity, gas, water and sanitary services, and finance	9.9
6b	Commerce (excl. finance)	6.7
7	Transport, storage and communications	4.8
8	Services	12.1

Total working population: 22 651 263* (excl. Indian jungle population)

Life expectancy at birth (years): male / female	39.3 / 45.5	1940-50 av.
Crude birth rate (per '000)	42*	1960-5 av.
Crude death rate (per '000)	11*	1960-5 av.
Accidental deaths (per 100 000 population)	27.2*	1960
caused by motor vehicles	31.1*	1960
due to other causes		
Population per physician	2 290	1960
Population per hospital bed	290	1964
School enrolment: age 5-19 years (percentage)	60	1963-4 av.
age over 19 years (percentage)	184	1964-5 av.

a fishing and hunting are included in group 1 instead of group 6.
b finance is included in group 5 instead of group 6.

COMMUNICATIONS

Motor vehicles in use ('000): private / commercial	998 / 921	1963-5 av.
Railway track (km.)	35 349	1963
Mail per capita: domestic / foreign received / foreign sent	6 / 35 / 8	1963-5 av.
Telephones (per '000 urban population)	1.7	1967
Radio receivers (per '000 population)	95	1963-5 av.
Television sets (per '000 population)	26.5	1963-5 av.
Daily newspapers (per '000 population)	53.5	1962-3 av.

FINANCE

Currency unit: The new cruzeiro was introduced in 1967, equivalent to 1 000 old cruzeiros

Exchange rates

	1965a	1960a	1950a	1938a
Per $ U.S.	2 220	205.10	18.72	16.5
Per £ sterling	6 216	574.28	52.44	75.9

		Year(s)
National Income (million $ U.S.)	17 809	1965
G.N.P. per capita ($ U.S., 1967)	240	1966
Rate of increase of G.N.P. per capita	1.5	1960-3 av.
Foreign trade (percentage of G.D.P.)	13	1963-5 av.

a old cruzeiros

TRADING

Total trade (in million $ U.S.)

	1965	1955
Exports (f.o.b.)	1 595	1 423
Imports (c.i.f.)	1 096	1 307

Main trading partners (percentage of total value)

Exports	1965	1955	1938
U.S.A.	33	47	34
Germany F.R.	9	9	19d
Italy	5	5	2
Netherlands	5	4	4
U.K.	4	4	9
France	4	4	6

Imports	1965	1955	1938*
U.S.A.	30	24	24
Argentina	12	12	12
Germany F.R.	12	7	25d
Venezuela	7	3	na
U.S.S.R.	3	na	na
Japan	3	5	3
France	7	na	(18)

Distribution of trade (percentage of total value)

Exports	1965	1938*
Food (coffee)	62 (44)	75 (45)
Crude materials and fuels (cotton and concentrates)	25 (6)	20 (2)
Manufactured goods	7	1 (10)

Imports	1965	1938*
Food (cereals)	18 (14)	15 (11)
Crude materials and fuels (fuels)	25 (21)	17 na
Chemicals	16	na
Manufactured goods and transport equipment	40 (22)	na (30)

d incl. Germany D.R.

PRODUCTION, EXPORTS AND IMPORTS

Units: '000 metric tons unless otherwise indicated

Years: 1963-5 average and 1953-5 average

1. CEREALS, etc.

	Production 1963-5	1953-5	Exports 1963-5	1953-5	Imports 1963-5	1953-5
Barley	25.3	30.3	—	—	34.2	2.8
Cassava	23 866.0	14 265.7	440.4	30.6	0.4	16.5
Maize (corn)	10 646.0	6 929.7	7.8n	na	11.4	7.0
Millets/sorghum	20.0	13.3	4.9	na	12.1	10.7
Oats	1 226.0	842.7	4.9	na	6.9	22.9
Potatoes	6 555.0	3 637.7	83.1	1.8	17.0	3.2
Rice	17.0	18.3	—	—	—	—
Rye	1 621.7	965.0	—	—	—	—
Sweet potatoes/ yams	540.0	914.7	—	—	2 220.3	1 570.2
Wheat						

n incl. other cereals.

2. FRUIT, etc.

	Production		Exports		Imports	
Apples	11.7	7.7	215.7	209.5	54.1	40.7
Bananas	4 332.7*	3 769.0	0.6	0.3	—	—
Coconuts	508.7n	na	na	na	—	—
Figs	15.0	9.5z	na	na	0.1	—
Grapes	484.3	316.7z	na	na	0.9	5.9
Lemons	44.3	na	0.3	na	—	—
Oranges	133.7	na	3.4	34.2	—	—
Other citrus fruit	2 329.3	1 405.0	—	—	—	—

2. FRUIT, etc.—continued

	Production		Exports		Imports	
Peaches	82.3	44.7¹	na	na	9.0	11.0
Pears	47.0	30.7	na	na	1.6	1.4
Pineapples	285.7	171.0	na	11.5		
Tomatoes	549.0	233.0	na	na	5.4	27.0
Raisins						
Wine b	2.2	740.0*	na	30.6		

b '000 hectolitres. e no. in millions.

3. BEVERAGES, FOREST PRODUCTS, etc.

	Production		Exports		Imports	
Cocoa	116.3	150.0*	78.5	44.7¹	—	1.3
Coffee	1 508.1	1 172.5	958.8	803.5	—	11.0
Sugar: cane	68 658.3	39 863.3	—	—	—	—
raw	3 680.7	2 368.0*	512.1	330.3	—	—
Tea	2.2	0.7	1.7	0.4	9.0	—
Tobacco: leaf	221.8	142.3	53.3	26.7	1.6	0.1²
cigarettes e	58 798.0	na	—	—	5.4	—
Softwood j	2 192.5²	16 805.0²	1 670.0	1 554.8	—	—
Hardwood j	115 975.0²	82 515.0²	126.7	95.1	—	—
Wood pulp	106.3*	62.9*	17.3	na	—	27.0
Newsprint	49.0	na	—	na	—	—
Other paper	516.7*	288.0*	0.1	—	—	—

e no. in millions. j '000 cu. metres of roundwood equivalent.

na: data not available. — negligible or nil. * estimate. 1 one year only. 2 two year average.

PRODUCTION, EXPORTS AND IMPORTS *continued*

4. VEGETABLE OILSEEDS AND OILS

	Production		Exports		Imports	
Castor seed	301.67	164.60	109.51	47.27	—	—
Castor oil	na	na	na	22.41	0.17	—
Coconut oil	na	na	—	—	7.02	3.70
Cottonseed	1 206.00	781.00	1.45	0.02	—	—
Cottonseed oil	423.97	126.00	11.14	—	—	—
Groundnuts	38.67	26.67*m	10.22	—	0.06	—
Linseed oil	na	na	—	—	0.28²	—
Olive oil	—	—	—	—	8.22	6.89
Palm kernels	156.03	74.47p	—	0.01q	—	—
Palm oil	na	na	0.27	—	0.88	—
Rape seed	—	—	—	—	0.02	—
Sesame seed	4.00*	5.00¹*	0.27	0.10	—	—
Soya beans	383.70	114.33	36.25	34.30	—	—
Sunflower seed	na	na	0.04	—	4.38	—
Tung oil	1.2	0.88	1.02	0.13	—	—

n flax grown for seed only. p babassu kernels. q babassu oil.

5. LIVESTOCK‡, ANIMAL PRODUCTS, etc.

	Production		Exports		Imports	
Chickens d	214 059.0	117 966.6	—	—	—	—
Cattle d	80 988.7	58 307.3	4.7	0.1	—	—
Goats d	13 144.0	9 072.7	—	—	—	—
Sheep d	20 876.0	16 855.7	—	—	12.9	5.5
Horses d	8 945.3	7 303.0	—	—	69.2	na
Pigs d	55 972.0	33 064.0	—	—	—	—
Meat: 'A'	2 046.0*	1 582.3	23.0	1.5	3.2	—
'B'	227.6*	31.8	4.1	1.1	0.1	—
Butter	24.0	26.7	—	—	3.7	0.1
Cheese	40.0	33.3n	0.2	0.2*	0.8	—
Eggs	422.3	174.3	2.0	—	25.6	23.0*
Milk	6 239.3	3 443.0	25.4	24.9¹	201.5	30.7
Hides/skins	0.8	na	7.0	4.7		
Whale/sperm oil	189.8	154.4	—	—	—	—
Wool	17.6	16.3	—	—	0.6	0.2

d no. in thousands. n government inspected factory produce only.

6. FIBRES, TEXTILES, etc.

	Production		Exports		Imports	
Agaves (sisal etc.)	223.3	77.7²	138.6	52.6	0.1	—
Cotton: lint	634.7	399.3	211.5	208.2	1.9	0.8
Flax fibre	—	—	0.2†	—	0.4	—
Hemp fibre	—	—	—	—	—	—
Jute	65.3	22.7	6.0	1.4	10.5	12.6
Rubber: natural	26.1	23.5	4.9	5.3	11.0r	—
synthetic	32.7	na	4.5	na	—	—
Silk f	96.7	180.0*	122.7*	na	—	—
Cotton: yarn	106.8n	na	0.9¹	na	—	—
woven fabrics	27.2*	na	2.5²	na	—	—
Rayon, fibre/yarn	41.9	30.6	na	—	0.2	na
Non-cellulosic fibre/yarn	—	—	—	—	0.2	na
Wool, woven fabrics	12.6	19.0p	0.1	—	0.2	na

f metric tons. n São Paulo only. p million metres. r incl. imports for re-export.

7. FUEL AND POWER

	Production		Exports		Imports	
Coal: 'A' ‡	2 270	878	na	15	9.0	1.3
'B'	na	na	na	na	na	11.0
Coke	11 560	na	—	—	1.6	1.4
Electricity h: total	29 030	9 810	—	—	—	—
hydro	28 894	1 750	—	—	—	—
thermal	6 136	na	—	—	—	—
Natural gas i	570	20	—	—	—	—
Oil, crude	4 500	280¹	—	—	5.4	27.0
Petroleum, refined	14 076	3 240¹	5	—	10 480	4 100¹
Rare earths f	594n	na	2 022p	827p	867	5 190¹
Uranium	—	—	—	—	—	4 107q

f metric tons. h million kWh. i million cu. metres. n monazite. p cerium chloride. q radium and radium products, in milligrams.

8. IRON AND STEEL

	Production		Exports		Imports	
Iron ore	10 814n	2 191n	10 243	1 930	23.0	13.0²
Pig iron	2 526	1 030	131	211	—	2.1a
Steel ingots/ castings	2 982	1 138	—	—	—	—
Iron/steel products a	na	na	21	62	—	—

a million $ U.S. m metal content.

9. NON-FERROUS MINERALS AND METALS

	Production		Exports		Imports	
Diamonds	350.00*¹	200.00*¹	—	—	0.36²a	na
Gold k: ore m	143.00	148.00*	—	—	0.68	30.70
bullion/coins etc.	—	—	—	—	—	—
Platinum group metals k†	—	—	—	—	0.35	5.54s
Silver k: ore m	274.30	159.30	—	—	—	—
bullion	—	—	—	—	1 147.00	577.00
Asbestos: fibre	1.23	2.21	—	—	16.23	9.71s
manufactured	—	—	—	—	0.46	0.99i
Mica	1.45	1.72	1.76	0.90	0.02	na
Aluminium: bauxite	152.75	30.51	2.68	1.34	0.85	0.39
alumina	—	—	—	—	1.00p	0.26
aluminium	49.66	na	—	—	22.47	16.56i
Antimony: ore	24.89	na	—	—	0.14	na
metal	—	—	—	—	0.40	0.49i
Beryl	1.50	1.71	1.49	1.59	0.04	0.01
Cadmium: metal	—	—	—	—	na	1.74s
Chrome: ore	14.48m	3.20m	—	—	0.58	na
metal	—	—	—	—	0.03	0.40i
Cobalt, metal	—	—	—	—	0.40	0.16
Copper: ore	2.72m	na	—	—	36.66	30.50
metal	2.50²	na	—	—	—	—
Lead: ore	18.00*m	3.00*m	—	—	8.24	20.72s
metal	12.91	3.12	—	12.93i	—	—
Magnesium: dolomite	343.80	na	—	—	—	—
magnesite	102.89	na	10.02	1.95	na	0.80
kieserite	—	—	—	—	2.34	0.78
Manganese: ore	1 334.05	202.14	913.80	145.68	—	—
metal	—	—	2.42	na	0.04	0.09i
Mercury†	—	—	—	—	93.00	76.00s
Nickel: ore	1.05m	0.05m	—	—	—	—
metal	—	—	—	—	0.54	0.23i
Tin: ore	1.27m	0.18m	—	—	1.71	0.74s
metal	1.88	1.22	—	—	6.70	0.29i
Titanium minerals	8.33	0.15²q	0.52	1.42	—	1.79i
Tungsten minerals	0.44	1.53	—	0.46	—	—
Zinc: ore	1.74m	na	—	—	—	—
metal	—	—	—	—	40.85	22.45
Zirconium minerals	0.46	3.29	—	1.29i	—	—

a million $ U.S. f metric tons. k '000 fine troy oz. l '000 carats. m metal content. n Bahia only. p incl. hydrate. q rutile only. s incl. imports for re-export. t chiefly baddeleyite.

10. CHEMICALS‡ AND FERTILIZERS

Organic chemicals:	Production	Exports	Imports
Benzene	na	—	na
Butadiene	na	—	19.6
Ethylene	na	—	2.6²
Methanol	na	—	0.4¹
Phthalic anhydride	na	—	2.3¹
Styrene monomer	na	—	7.1
Urea	na	—	—
Inorganic chemicals:			
Ammonia	24.5²	0.2²	—
Carbon black	na	—	3.7²
Nitric acid	na	—	—¹
Sodium carbonate	68.7	—	28.9²
Sodium hydroxide	81.0	—	123.9
Sulphuric acid	359.3	—	—
Plastics:			
Polyamides	na	—	0.4
Polyethylene	na	—	2.7
Polyvinyl chloride	18.8²	—	1.2¹
Fertilizers:			
Phosphates	267.6p 67.4*	—	186.1 114.7
Potash	na	—	160.0 69.2
Pyrites	na 5.4q	—	170.1 74.1
Sulphur, native			

a million $ U.S. p incl. apatite. q incl. recovered sulphur.
n data not available for years 1953-5.

11. INDUSTRY

	Production		Exports	Imports	
Aircraft a	—		2.2	23.0	13.0²
Alcoholic beverages beer a	6 701.0		2.0	—	2.1a
Cement	5 420.0	2 400.3	—	21.0*	525.7
Electrical engineering a	—		2.4	64.6	7.0²
Railway vehicles a	31.0¹		—	15.2	18.7
Machine tools a	49.0		—	1.0	na
Merchant ships g	—		2.0a	27.7a	25.1²a
Motor vehicles commercial a	73.0	18.6²n	—		
private a	108.0	4.67n	—		

a million $ U.S. b U.S. g '000 G.R.T. n assembly of imported parts.

na: data not available. — negligible or nil. — not available. * estimate. 1 one year only. 2 two year average. g '000 G.R.T.

BRUNEI

Unlike the other Malay inhabited states, Brunei remained a British protectorate in 1963 at the formation of the Federation of Malaysia.

AREA: 5 800* sq. km. (2 240* sq. miles)

LAND USE: (percentage of total)

	1964
Arable and orchard	11.4
Permanent meadow and pasture	na
Forest and woodland	85.0
City areas, waste and other land	na

POPULATION: 107 000 (1967 U.N. estimate)
Capital city: BANDAR SERI BEGAWAN (Brunei Town); population: 9 702 (city proper, 1960)
Total working population: 24 830

Distribution of working population (1960)

U.N. group no.		Percentage
0		33.5
1	Agriculture, forestry, fishing and hunting	15.1
	Mining and quarrying	15.7
2/3	Manufacturing	13.6
4	Construction	1.1
5	Electricity, gas, water and sanitary services	1.0
6	Commerce	4.0
7	Transport, storage and communications	19.2

		Year(s)
Infant mortality (per '000)	41.0	1965
Crude birth rate (per '000)	41.5	1965
Crude death rate (per '000)	6.6*	1965
Population per physician	4 590	1965
Population per hospital bed	260	1966
School enrolment: age 5–19 years (percentage)	78	1963–4 av.

COMMUNICATIONS

		Year(s)
Motor vehicles in use ('000s): private	4.6	1967
commercial	1.8	
Telephones (per '000 population)	1.9	1963–5 av.
Radio receivers (per '000 population)	92	

FINANCE

Currency unit: The Brunei dollar (at par with the Malayan dollar)

Exchange rates	1955	1960	1965	1938
Per $ U.S.	3.058	3.058	3.063	1.846
Per £ sterling	8.571	8.571	8.571	8.5

		Year
National Income (million $ U.S.)	106	1958
G.N.P. per capita ($ U.S.)	1 330	1966

TRADING

Total trade (in million $ U.S.)

	1955	1960	1965	1938
Exports (f.o.b.)	65	65	99	4
Imports (c.i.f.)	30	36	30	2

Main trading partners (percentage of total value)

Exports	1965
Sarawak	98
Singapore	1

Imports	1965
U.K.	26
U.S.A.	17
Singapore	14
Japan	9
China P.R.	5
Thailand	3
Australia	3

Distribution of trade (percentage of total value)

Exports	1965	1955
Fuels	97	95

Imports	1965	1955
Manufactured goods and transport equipment	65 (35)	68 (23)
Food (cereals)	18 (5)	18 (3)
Chemicals	6	4

PRODUCTION, EXPORTS AND IMPORTS
Years: 1963–5 average and 1953–5 average   Units: '000 metric tons unless otherwise indicated

1. CEREALS, etc.

	Production		Exports		Imports	
Cassava	1.3*	na			0.8²	
Maize (corn)		na			0.2²	
Potatoes	3.3	3.7			7.8*	
Rice	1.0	1.2²				
Sweet potatoes/yams			0.1	2.4²		

2. FRUIT, etc.

	Production		Imports	
Apples			0.2²	
Bananas	8.0*		0.3²	
Coconuts	7.3		0.2²	
Oranges			0.1²	
Wine b			0.2²	

5. LIVESTOCK‡, ANIMAL PRODUCTS, etc.

	Production		Exports		Imports	
Chickens d	178.7	67.7			1.3²	
Cattle d	2.4*	1.0				
Goats d	4.0*	6.7			5.9²	
Pigs d	8.0				0.1²	
Meat‡; 'A'; 'B'					0.1²; 0.3²; 0.8²	
Butter					6.9²	
Eggs	0.3*	0.2²				
Fish	3.8	0.6²		.2		
Milk	na			0.1	7.0	

d no. in thousands.

6. FIBRES, TEXTILES, etc.

	Production		Exports	
Rubber, natural	1.3*		1.3*	1.3

7. FUEL AND POWER

	Production		Exports		Imports	
Electricity i	71t					
Natural gas i	190	68*	53		74	
Oil, crude	3 703	5 310¹	3 643		na	
Petroleum, refined	87		23		10¹	

h million kWh.   i million cu. metres.   t thermal.

9. NON-FERROUS MINERALS AND METALS

	Production		Imports	
Gold k: bullion/coins etc.				
Asbestos: manufactured			45.67²	
			1.34²	

k '000 fine troy oz.

11. INDUSTRY

	Production		Imports	
Aircraft a				
Alcoholic beverages a	0.1²	0.5²	146.9	0.5
Electrical engineering a			0.2²	
Motor vehicles a	2.0²	2.8	1.1	2.1

a million $ U.S.

na: data not available.   — negligible or nil.   ¹ one year only.   ² two year average.   * estimate.   † re-exports.   ‡ see appendix.

BRITISH HONDURAS

British Honduras is a British colony with internal self-government, but the governor, who is appointed by the Crown, retains certain powers as long as the country receives financial aid from the U.K.

AREA: 22 963 sq. km. (8 867 sq. miles)

LAND USE: (percentage of total)

	1964	1953
Arable and orchard	1.4	5.1
Permanent meadow and pasture	0.7	0.6
Forest and woodland	45.8	94.3
City areas, waste and other land	52.1	

POPULATION: 113 000 (1967 estimate)
Largest city: BELIZE; capital: population: 45 572 (1964)
Total working population: 27 006

Distribution of working population (1960)

U.N. group no.		Percentage
0		39.0
1	Agriculture, forestry, fishing and hunting	0.1
	Mining and quarrying	14.1
2/3	Manufacturing	7.0
4	Construction	7.5
5	Electricity, gas, water and sanitary services	4.7
6	Commerce	19.7
7	Transport, storage and communications	
8	Services	
9	Others	7.0

		Year(s)
Life expectancy at birth (years): male	45	1944–8 av.
female	49	
Infant mortality (per '000)	48.5*	1965
Crude birth rate (per '000)	43.7*	1965
Crude death rate (per '000)	6.7*	1965
Population per physician	3 530	1965
Population per hospital bed	210	1966
School enrolment: age 5–19 years (percentage)	92	1963–4 av.
age over 19 years (percentage)	52	1963–5 av.

COMMUNICATIONS

		Year(s)
Motor vehicles in use ('000s): private	1.5	1967
commercial	1.1	1963–5 av.
Telephones (per '000 population)	1.5	1967
Radio receivers (per '000 population)	283	1963–5 av.
Daily newspapers (per '000 population)	55	1962–4 av.

FINANCE

Currency unit: The British Honduras dollar

Exchange rates	1964	1950	1960	1965	1938
Per $ U.S.	1.4	1.42	1.42	1.42	At par
Per £ sterling	4.0	4.0	4.0	4.0	2.8

		Year
National Income (million $ U.S.)	38*	1966
G.N.P. per capita ($ U.S.)	360	1966

TRADING

Total trade (in million $ U.S.)

	1955	1960	1965	1938
Exports (f.o.b.)	6	12	65	3
Imports (c.i.f.)	10	24	30	4

Main trading partners (percentage of total value)

Exports	1965	1955
U.K.	40	29
U.S.A.	35	32
Mexico	6	
Canada	6	3
Jamaica	5	17
Guatemala	1	1

Imports	1965	1955
U.S.A.	37	34
U.K.	32	35
Jamaica	4	4
Canada	4	3
Netherlands	2	4
Japan	2	2
Hong Kong	2	1

Distribution of trade (percentage of total value)

Exports	1965	1938
Food (sugar) (fruit)	65 (33)	(5)
Crude materials (wood)	30 (26)	(12)

Imports	1965	1938
Manufactured goods	58 (25)	(63)
Food (machinery and transport equipment)	22 (25)	(15)
Chemicals	8	(39)

PRODUCTION, EXPORTS AND IMPORTS
Years: 1963–5 average and 1953–5 average   Units: '000 metric tons unless otherwise indicated

1. CEREALS, etc.

	Production		Exports		Imports	
Maize (corn)	3.0*	5.7			0.3	0.3
Potatoes	na				0.7	
Rice	1.7	1.0²			1.6	1.3

2. FRUIT, etc.

	Production		Exports		Imports	
Apples					0.1	
Bananas		na	1.2	0.4		
Coconuts	1.0*e	na	0.3	1.7	0.1	
Grapes	34.7	²			0.1	
Other citrus fruit	9.7	8.0*¹	1.1²	1.0	0.2	
Wine b						

3. BEVERAGES, FOREST PRODUCTS, etc.

	Production		Exports		Imports	
Cocoa	0.1		0.1			
Sugar: cane	281.3*	30.7				
raw	32.8	4.3	31.0	1.3		
Tobacco					0.5	0.1b
Softwood j	52.7*	54.3	8.0	42.4		
Hardwood j	78.7*	53.0	29.9	32.6		
Newsprint					0.1²	0.1
Other paper					0.1	

4. VEGETABLE OILSEEDS AND OILS

	Production		Exports		Imports	
Copra	na	0.17	0.10		0.05²	0.01
Linseed oil						

5. LIVESTOCK‡, ANIMAL PRODUCTS, etc.

	Production		Exports		Imports	
Chickens d	164.0	95.0				
Cattle d	27.7	16.0	0.2			
Goats d	1.0*	2.0	0.1			
Sheep d	2.0*	2.0				0.1
Horses d	4.3*	2.0	1.4			0.1
Pigs d	14.0	27.0			0.4	
Bacon/ham	1.0*				0.5	0.1
Meat‡; 'A'; 'B'					0.1	0.2
Butter					0.2	0.1
Cheese	0.3*	na	0.3		0.1	0.1
Eggs	na	0.5			0.1	
Fish	5.0*	na	0.7		8.9	1.1
Milk						

d no. in millions.

7. FUEL AND POWER

	Production		Imports	
Electricity h	11n			
Petroleum, refined			27	10¹

h million kWh.   n thermal.

11. INDUSTRY

	Production		Imports	
Alcoholic beverages a			0.6²p	2.7
Cement			8.3	
Electrical engineering a			0.8	0.3
Motor vehicles a			0.9	0.2

a million $ U.S.   p beer and spirits.

j '000 cu. metres of roundwood equivalent.   n cigarettes only.   p raw and manufactured tobacco.

na: data not available.   — negligible or nil.   ¹ one year only.   ² two year average.   ³ 1953–5 average.   * estimate.   † re-exports.   ‡ see appendix.

BULGARIA

EUROPE

Bulgaria is a member of Comecon. Formerly a principality, the country was declared a republic in 1946.

AREA: 110 911.5 sq. km. (42 823 sq. miles) (incl. territorial waters)

LAND USE: (percentage of total)

	1965
Arable and orchard.	41.1
Permanent meadow and pasture	11.1
Forest and woodland	32.6
City areas, waste and other land	15.2

POPULATION: 8 226 564 (1965 census, based on 3% sample return)
Largest city: SOFIYA (Sofia), capital; population: 810 300 (1966)
Total working population (1956) 4 150 207

Distribution of working population   Percentage
U.N. group no.
0	Agriculture, forestry, fishing and hunting	64.1
1/2/3	Mining, quarrying and manufacturing	15.9
5	Electricity, gas, water and sanitary services	2.8
4	Construction	3.4
6	Commerce	3.2
7	Transport, storage and communications	3.2
8	Services	9.8
9	Others	0.8

		Year(s)
Life expectancy at birth (years): male	67.8	1960–2 av.
female	71.4	1960–2 av.
Infant mortality (per '000)	30.8	1965
Crude death rate (per '000)	8.3	1965
Accidental deaths (per 100 000 population)	15.2	1965
caused by motor vehicles	7.2	1965
due to other causes		
Population per physician	600	1965
Population per hospital bed	140	1966
School enrolment: age 5–19 years (percentage)	90	1963–4 av.
age over 19 years (per 100 000 population)	1 240	1964–5 av.

COMMUNICATIONS

		Year(s)
Motor vehicles in use ('000s): private	6	1950
commercial	5	1950
Railway track (km.)	5771	1964
Telephones (per '000 urban population)	240	1967
Radio licences (per '000 population)	3.7	
Television licences (per '000 population)	15.2	1963–5 av.
Daily newspapers (per '000 population)	155	1962–4 av.

FINANCE

Currency unit: The lev. (A new lev equivalent to 10 old leva was introduced on 1 January 1962)

Exchange rates	1965a	1960b
Per $ U.S.	1.17	6.8
Per £ sterling	3.20	19.0

a official rate, new leva. b old leva.

		Year(s)
National Income (million $ U.S.)	5 000*	1966
G.N.P. per capita ($ U.S.)	620*	1966
Rate of increase of G.N.P. per capita	5.7	1960–4 av.

TRADING

Total trade (in million $ U.S.)	1965	1955
Exports (f.o.b.)	1 176	236
Imports (f.o.b.)	1 178	250

Main trading partners (percentage of total value)

Exports	1965	1955
U.S.S.R.	52	47
Germany D.R.	9	15
Czechoslovakia	9	11
Germany F.R.	3	3
Poland	3	3
Italy	3	
Yugoslavia	2	1

Imports	1965	1955
U.S.S.R.	50	46
Germany D.R.	7	12
Czechoslovakia	7	11
Germany F.R.	6	5
Poland	4	5
Italy	3	1
Austria	3	

Distribution of trade (percentage of total value)

Exports	1965	1955
Food	36	34*
Crude materials and fuels	25	na
Machinery and transport equipment.	21	na

Imports	1965	1955
Machinery and transport equipment.	44	40*
Crude materials and fuels	37	na
(fuels)	7 (27)	4 (6*)
Food		
Chemicals	6	6*

PRODUCTION, EXPORTS AND IMPORTS
Years: 1963–5 average and 1953–5 average   Units: '000 metric tons unless otherwise indicated

1. CEREALS, etc.	Production		Exports		Imports	
Barley	752.7	na	0.5	na	8.0*	4.6*
Maize (corn)	1 675.3	2.01	120.6	38.2*	80.5	1.8*
Millets/sorghum	9.0*	na	0.3	na	na	—
Oats	128.7	na	na	—	4.6²	—
Potatoes	399.0	na	44.0	na	19.5	—*
Rice	35.3	na	19.6	4.8*	34.4	—
Rye	57.3	na	1.1	8.0*	8.4	—
Wheat	2 310.3	na	14.9	149.6*	250.0	—*

2. FRUIT, etc.	Production		Exports		Imports	
Apples	317.7	2.01	50.1	—	130.6	—
Apricots	32.7	na	na	—	80.8	—
Cherries	46.7	6.11	0.5	—	0.8	—
Dates	—	—	—	—	0.1	—
Grapes	1 133.0	na	189.8	28.1*	3.1	—
Lemons	—	—	—	—	4.0	—
Oranges	—	—	—	—	250.0	—
Peaches	80.3	3.1	1.1	0.6*	0.5	—
Pears	81.0	na	na	0.4*	1.1	—
Plums	203.3	55.9	0.3	—	na	1
Raisins	—	—	—	—	—	1
Tomatoes	724.3	na	945.5	46.0*	24.5	—
Wineb	na	na	na	na	na	—

b '000 hectolitres.

3. BEVERAGES, FOREST PRODUCTS, etc.	Production		Exports		Imports	
Cocoa	—	—	—	—	5.6	—
Sugar: beet	1 638.0	565.3*	—	—	—	—
raw.	211.3	75.7*	3.11	0.2*	146.0*	—
Tea	—	—	—	—	0.5	—
Tobacco: leaf	125.9	29.5*	86.1	21.1*	1.1	1
cigarettes	24 498.0c	8 860.0c	14.6nc	40.3a	—	—
tobacco/snuff	144.6	—	—	—	149.7	—
Sorwoodd	1 165.3b	na	83.0	11.1	—	—
Hardwoodd	4 055.4b	na	79.7	8.7	—	—
Wood pulp	70.1	na	12.4	—	25.6	—
Newsprint	—	—	—	—	21.7	11.01
Wood paper	116.7	6.02*	—	—	26.6	5.91

PRODUCTION, EXPORTS AND IMPORTS continued

6. FIBRES, TEXTILES, etc.	Production		Exports		Imports	
Cotton lint.	14.0	22.0²*	1.0	—	41.6	6.9*
Flax fibre	2.4	na	0.4	—	0.2	2.3
Hemp fibre	5.9	na	0.4	—	1.5	—
Jute	—	—	—	—	6.3	—
Rubber, natural	—	—	—	—	9.4	0.5*
Silk f	180.0	30.0*	73.3	5.3*	4.0	—
Cotton: yarn	58.0	na	na	na	na	na
woven fabrics	32.8	14.8*	4.9²	na	—	na
Rayon: fibre/yarn	1.6	na	na	na	—	na
woven fabrics	—	8.8	na	na	—	na
Wool: yarn	17.4	10.4	—	—	—	—
woven fabricsg	19.3	—	—	—	—	—

f metric tons. g million metres.

7. FUEL AND POWER	Production		Exports		Imports	
Coal i, A	607	290	12	—	1 742	—
B	11 420	9 760	—	—	—	—
Coke	8 709	1 830	—	—	—	—
Electricity h: total	1 852	1 650¹	—	—	312	—
hydro	6 867	1 180	—	—	—	—
thermal						
Natural gas i	—	—	—	—	1 486	na
Oil, crude	187	150¹	40	—	1 420	na
Petroleum, refined.	1 490	201	37	—	—	—

h million kWh. i million cu. metres.

8. IRON AND STEEL	Production		Exports		Imports	
Iron ore	657m	na	12	—	149	—
Pig iron	472	6	147	na	—	—
Steel ingots/castings	508	50	9	—	—	—

m metal content.

9. NON-FERROUS MINERALS AND METALS	Production		Exports		Imports	
Asbestos, fibre	1.27	1.07	—	—	—	—
Cadmium	na	na	—	—	—	—
Chrome	na	na	—	—	—	—
Cobalt.	na	na	—	—	—	—
Copper: ore	20.77m	na	—	—	—	—
metal	22.29	3.18	7.19	—	—	—
Lead: ore	93.39m	10.00¹*m	na	—	—	—
metal	77.42	3.04	na	—	—	—
Manganese, ore	44.16	39.00	na	—	—	—
Zinc: ore	62.79m	na	—	—	—	—
metal	60.16	0.45	na	—	—	—

m metal content.

10. CHEMICALS n AND FERTILIZERS	Production		Exports		Imports	
Organic chemicals:						
Benzene	na		na		na	
Butadiene	na		na		na	
Ethylene	na		na		na	
Methanol	na		na		na	
Phenol	na		na		na	
Phthalic anhydride	na		na		na	
Styrene monomer	na		na		na	
Urea	25.2		na		na	
Inorganic chemicals:						
Ammonia	255.0		na		na	
Carbon black	na		na		na	
Chlorine	na		na		na	
Nitric acid.	424.5		90.6		—	
Sodium carbonate	223.4		12.7		—	
Sodium hydroxide	28.1		na		na	
Sulphuric acid.	292.7		—		—	
Plastics:						
Polyamides	—		—		—	
Polyethylene	—		—		—	
Polyvinyl chloride.	—		—		—	
Fertilizers:						
Phosphates	60.0		—		—	
Pyrites	6.7		—		441.2	
Sulphur, recovered	7.2¹		—		—	

n data not available for years 1953–5.

11. INDUSTRY	Production		Exports		Imports	
Beer b	1 518.0	518.3	41.8a	—	105.0*p	—*p
Spirits b	143.0¹r	na	—	—	—	—
Cement	2 489.0	768.7	715.0¹*p	57.0*p	40.8	0.6¹
Electrical	na	na	na	na	23.0	0.8¹
engineering a	na	na	na	na	8.6	—
Machine tools a						
Merchant ships g						
Motor vehicles a						

a million $ U.S. b '000 hectolitres; trade refers to all alcoholic beverages, in million $ U.S. g '000 G.R.T. p excl. trade with other Comecon countries. r production for home consumption in 1967.

BURMA

SOUTH EAST ASIA

Burma left the British Commonwealth to become an independent republic in 1948.

AREA: 678 000 sq. km. (261 800 sq. miles)

LAND USE: (percentage of total)

	1965	1954
Arable and orchard.	23.4	12.6
Permanent meadow and pasture	0.5	57.7
Forest and woodland	66.8	29.7
City areas, waste and other land	9.3	

POPULATION: 25 811 000 (1967 estimate)
Largest city: RANGOON, capital; population: 821 800 (city proper, 1957)

		Year
Life expectancy at birth (years): male	40.8	1954
female	43.8	1954
Infant mortality (per '000)	109.3*	1965
Crude birth rate (per '000)	47.0*	1965
Crude death rate (per '000)	18.2*	1965
Accidental deaths (per 100 000 population)		
caused by motor vehicles	6.7*	1962
due to other causes	47.0*	1962
Population per physician	11 900	1965
Population per hospital bed	1 030b	1966
School enrolment: age 5–19 years (percentage)		1964
age over 19 years (per 100 000 population)	85	1964

b government hospitals only

COMMUNICATIONS

		Year(s)
Motor vehicles in use ('000s): private	25.6	1963–5 av.
commercial	22.3	1963–5 av.
Railway track (km.)	2 990	1959
Mail per capita: domestic	0.2	1963–5 av.
foreign	0.1	1963–5 av.
Telephones (per '000 urban population)	10	1967
Radio licences (per '000 population)	9	1963–5 av.
Daily newspapers (per '000 population)		1962

FINANCE

Currency unit: The kyat replaced the rupee in 1952

Exchange rates	1960	1958a
Per $ U.S.	4.782	4.775
Per £ sterling	13.378	13.333

		Year(s)
National Income (million $ U.S.)	1 362	1964
G.N.P. per capita ($ U.S.)	60	1966
Rate of increase of G.N.P. per capita	1.9	1960–3 av.
Foreign trade (percentage of G.D.P.)	31	1963–4 av.

EMPLOYMENT AND PRODUCTION

Three-quarters of the population are employed in agriculture or forestry, rice and teak being the chief products. Mineral deposits and oil reserves are considerable. Cement, brick and steel works have been built with the aid of loans from China P.R., Japan, and Germany F.R., and a sugar refinery and H.E.P. plant are also in production.

continued

4. VEGETABLE OILSEEDS AND OILS	Production		Exports		Imports	
Castor seed	—	—	—	—	0.01	—
Castor oil	—	—	0.53	—	0.53	—
Coconut oil	—	—	—	—	0.70	0.40*
Cottonseed	26.30	36.00*	4.00*	—	—	—
Cottonseed oil	na	na	—	—	—	—
Groundnuts	0.70	na	0.86	—	4.28	1.00*
Linseed oil	—	—	2.72	—	2.54	—
Olive oil	—	—	—	—	1.08	—*
Palm kernels	—	—	—	—	1.02	0.06*
Palm oil	—	—	—	—	—	—
Rapeseed	1.30	na	2.25	4.23*	0.03	—
Rapeseed oil	0.20	na	—	1.10*	—	—
Sesame seed	0.30	na	—	—	—	—
Soya beans	343.33	na	78.55	8.43	0.54	—
Sunflower seed	—	—	6.49	0.53*	0.12	—
Sunflower seed oil						
Tung oil						

5. LIVESTOCK‡; ANIMAL PRODUCTS, etc.	Production		Exports		Imports	
Chickens d n	21 591.3	12 874.0				
Cattle d	1 516.7	1 855.0¹				
dairy cows d	621.3*	765.0²*	43.0	—	1.2	—*
Goats d	354.0	7 735.0²*	435.0	na	2.1	na
Sheep d	10 285.0					
Horses d	260.7	468.6	176.1	9.5p	0.2	—
Meat†, B	2 857.0	1 415.0¹	8.9	12.9	9.8	—
Butter.	69.1*	na	2.1	—	0.2	—
Cheese	11.3	na	10.2	0.1*	—	—
Eggs	109.3	na	23.2	10.4	—	—
Fish	13.5	7.2	—	—	21.4	—
Hides/skins	907.7	na	0.8	0.4a	—	—
Milk	14.6²	na	—	—	1.8	0.4
Wool d	13.3	8.0*	—	—	—	—

a million $ U.S. c '000. d no. in millions. i '000 cu. metres of roundwood equivalent. b over 6 months only.
c cigarettes only. d no. in thousands. n incl. ducks, geese and turkeys. p pigs j from state forests only.   continued

na: data not available. — negligible or nil. * estimate. ‡ see appendix. † re-exports.
1 one year only. 2 two year average. 1953–5 average.

BURMA continued

TRADING

Total trade (in million $ U.S.)	1965	1955a	1938ab
Exports (f.o.b.)	225	227	178
Imports (c.i.f.)	247	181	78

Main trading partners (percentage of total value)

Exports	1965	1955a	1938ab	Imports	1965	1955a	1938ab
Philippines	14	na		Japan	29	21	7
Ceylon	10	6	54	China P.R.	11	25	18
India	10	18	1	U.S.A.	9	3	18
Japan	8	18		U.K.	7	5	1
China P.R.	6	7	14	Pakistan	5	3	na
U.S.S.R.	6	8		India	5	18	55
				Netherlands	4	4	3

PRODUCTION, EXPORTS AND IMPORTS

Years: 1965-5 average and 1953-5 average   Units: '000 metric tons unless otherwise indicated

	Production 1965	1955a	Exports 1965	1955a	1938ab	Imports 1965	1955a	1938ab
1. CEREALS, etc.								
Maize (corn)	58.3	32.0²	19.5		24.1			
Millets/sorghum	43.7	na	3.5²		3.3			
Potatoes	53.0	na						
Rice	8 115.3	5 762.7	1 475.6	1 356.9				
Wheat	53.0	4.5²				15.3²		3.2
2. FRUIT, etc.								
Coconuts	50.0¹e		na			7.2	na	7.6
Dates						na		1.9*
Raisins						0.1		
Wine h						0.2		
3. BEVERAGES, FOREST PRODUCTS, etc.								
Sugar: cane (raw)	1 215.3 / 68.3m	1 147.3* / 22.0m						
Tea	44.9	48.6*						
Tobacco: leaf	970.0¹	245.0²						
Cigarettes	3 488.0¹	2 077.0²						
Hardwood j			262.0²	98.4²				
Newsprint						15.0¹	5.8²	
Other paper						14.0¹	12.6²	
4. VEGETABLE OILSEEDS AND OILS								
Castor oil	na		0.04					0.04
Copra	na		na					na
Coconut oil	37.00	39.30*						14.47
Cottonseed	226.30	130.20	6.37					
Groundnuts			17.22					14.49
Groundnut oil			26.47					0.24
Linseed oil			0.29					0.22
Palm oil								
Sesame seed	72.13	41.67						
Soya bean oil			1.00¹q					0.17
Tung oil								
q incl. mustard seed.								
5. LIVESTOCK, ANIMAL PRODUCTS, etc.								
Cattle d	6 053.3	4 706.7						
dairy cows d	1 573.3*	na						
Goats d	523.0	217.3						
Sheep d	139.0	33.0						
Horses d	25.7	14.0						
Pigs d	804.0	482.3						
Meat† 'A'	31.3	9.7						
Butter	5.0*	na				0.2		
Cheese	8.0*	na				0.2		
Eggs	360.0	213.0²						
Fish	260.0	na	5.4	na				
Hides/skins	119.5	193.5²	66.5*					

d no. in thousands. r incl. fish landed in foreign ports, and fish landed in Burma by foreign vessels.

BURUNDI

Burundi, as part of Ruanda-Urundi, was formerly under Belgian trusteeship, until proclaimed an independent constitutional monarchy in 1962. Joint economic arrangements with Rwanda ended two years later. Since a coup in 1966 the president has ruled through the National Revolutionary Council.

AREA: 27 834 sq. km. (10 747 sq. miles)

LAND USE: (percentage of total)	1965
Arable and orchard	37.3
Permanent meadow and pasture	22.6
Forest and woodland	2.5
City areas, waste and other land	37.6

POPULATION: 3 210 090 (1965 census)
Largest city: BUJUMBURA capital; population: 71 000 (1965)

		Year(s)
Life expectancy at birth (years): male	35*	} 1965
female	38.5*	
Infant mortality (per '000)	150*	1965
Crude birth rate (per '000)	46.1	1965
Crude death rate (per '000)	25.6*	1965
Population per physician	56 320	1966
Population per hospital bed	900	1966
School enrolment: age 5–19 years (percentage)	22	1964
age over 19 years (per 100 000 population)	6	1964–5 av.

FINANCE

Currency unit: The Burundi franc

	1965a	1965b*
Exchange rates		
Per $ U.S.	50	107
Per £ sterling	140	300

		Year
National Income (million $ U.S.)	106	1958
G.N.P. per capita ($ U.S.)	50	1966

a official rate; b free rate.

EMPLOYMENT AND TRADE

Subsistence agriculture accounts for well over half the gross national income; recently a fishing industry has developed on Lake Tanganyika. There are a few other small industries: food processing, brewing, cement and textile manufacturing. Trade is mainly with the U.S.A. and the U.K.

No independent production and trade figures are available for Burundi for the years 1963–5. 1953–5 data for Ruanda-Urundi are given under Rwanda.

CAMBODIA

Cambodia, Laos and Vietnam were known as French Indo-China until 1949 when Cambodia became an independent state within the French Union. In 1954 the Geneva Conference arranged for the withdrawal of French forces following the establishment of sovereign independence.

AREA: 181 000* sq. km. (70 000* sq. miles)

LAND USE: (percentage of total)	1965	1954
Arable and orchard	16.2	17.1
Permanent meadow and pasture	0.1	4.9
Forest and woodland, including rough grazing	73.9	34.3
City areas, waste and other land	na	

POPULATION: 6 415 000 (1967 estimate)
Largest city: PHNOM PENH, capital; population: 393 995 (city proper, 1962)
Total working population: 2 560 500

Distribution of working population (1962)

U.N. group no.		Percentage
0	Agriculture, forestry, fishing and hunting	80.9
1	Mining and quarrying	0.1
2/3	Manufacturing	2.8
4	Construction	0.7
5	Electricity, gas, water and sanitary services	0.1
6	Commerce	5.9
7	Transport, storage and communications	7.1
8	Services	1.5
9	Others	

		Year(s)
Life expectancy at birth (years): male	44.2	} 1958–9
female	43.3	
Population per physician	18 760	1965
Population per hospital bed	1 320	1965
School enrolment: age 5–19 years (percentage)	46	1963–4 av.
age over 19 years (per 100 000 population)	79	1963–5 av.

FINANCE

Currency unit: The riel

	1965	1954
Exchange rates		
Per $ U.S.	35.0	35.0
Per £ sterling	98.0	98.0

		Year(s)
National Income (million $ U.S.)	686	1965
G.N.P. per capita ($ U.S.)	120	1966
Rate of increase of G.N.P. per capita	2.3	1960–3 av.

TRADING

Total trade (in million $ U.S.)	1965	1955
Exports (f.o.b.)	105	40
Imports (c.i.f.)	103	48

Main trading partners (percentage of total value)

Exports	1965	1955	Imports	1965	1955
France	29	26	France	20	26a
Singapore	15	8	Japan	17	10
Hong Kong	8	6	China P.R.	14	5
China P.R.	6	5	Philippines	5	1
Japan	5	1	Czechoslovakia	5	
			Germany F.R.	4	1
			Singapore	4	

Distribution of trade (percentage of total value)

Exports	1965	1955	Year(s)
Food (rice)	60	(49)	1964
Crude materials and fuels (rubber)	39	(33)	1967
Imports			
Manufactured goods (machinery and transport equipment)	73	(26)	1963–5 av.
(textiles)		(17)	
Chemicals (medicinal and pharmaceutical products)	12	(6)	1962

a incl. former French overseas territories.

COMMUNICATIONS

		Year(s)
Motor vehicles in use ('000s): private	16.6	} 1963–5 av.
commercial	9.3	
Railway track (km)	385	1964
Telephones (per '000 population)	0.1	1967
Radio receivers (per '000 population)	154	1963–5 av.
Television sets (per '000 population)	na	
Daily newspapers (per '000 population)	8	1962

CAMBODIA — PRODUCTION, EXPORTS AND IMPORTS

	Production 1965	1955	Exports 1965	1955	1938ab	Imports 1965	1955a	1938ab
6. FIBRES, TEXTILES, etc.								
Cotton lint	18.7	20.7*	13.2	18.5				0.1¹
Jute	13.3	na	1.7					
Rubber: natural	8.2	na	8.2	11.2		12.9²		
Silk f						0.1		
Cotton: yarn	5.0²	1.4	2.0†			112.3		186.3
woven fabrics	1.0*					11.0²	6.9	13.5
f metric tons.								
7. FUEL AND POWER								
Coal 'A'‡	7		2†			180		233
Coke						2		8
Electricity h: total	554	180¹						
hydro	258²	—						
thermal	296	180¹						
Natural gas i	na	10						
Oil, crude	580	210¹						
Petroleum, refined	627	170¹				106	40	150¹
h million kWh. i million cu. metres.								
8. IRON AND STEEL								
Iron ore m	2 540²m					39.4 / 21.0	0.4	0.2²h
m metal content.								
9. NON-FERROUS MINERALS AND METALS								
Silver k, ore	1 860.00m	1 762.70m						1 219.87u
Asbestos: fibre	na							
manufactured								
Aluminium						1.21 / 0.20 / 3.38		
Antimony: ore	0.15*m	0.08*m	0.01					
metal	0.15²m		0.37					
Copper: ore	0.37		0.37	2.08		0.26		
metal				10.68				
Lead: ore	19.41m	11.98m	2.08	2.47²				
metal	0.10²	4.27				0.02		
Manganese, ore	na	1.18						
Nickel, metal	0.88		0.45	0.06n				
Tin: ore m	0.56	1.95	0.84					
metal			0.86	2.15i		0.44		
Tungsten, ore	na							
metal								
Zinc: ore	7.83m	5.99m	15.48	31.73				
k '000 fine troy oz. m metal content. n nickel content of speiss. t incl. u bullion.								
10. CHEMICALS n AND FERTILIZERS								
Chemicals	na					na		0.3
Fertilizers:								
Phosphates						0.2		0.4²
Potash						0.7		0.2
Sulphur								57.0
n data not available for years 1953–5.								
11. INDUSTRY								
Aircraft a						0.61	0.41	
Alcoholic beverages a	125.0	54.7	9.0*			70.0*¹		
Cement								
Electrical engineering a						9.1¹¹		7.6²
Railway vehicles a						2.4		6.4
Merchant ships a						8.1¹		5.6²
Motor vehicles a						9.2¹		
a million $ U.S. g '000 G.R.T.								

continued

CAMBODIA continued

PRODUCTION, EXPORTS AND IMPORTS

Years: 1963–5 average and 1953–5 average   Units: '000 metric tons unless otherwise indicated

Note—few data are available for the years 1953 and 1954, so the majority of the figures in italics refer to the year 1955 only.

1. CEREALS, etc.

	Production		Exports		Imports	
Cassava	19.3	na	—	—	—	—
Maize (corn)	175.3		115.0	66.0	—	—
Potatoes	na		—	—	0.2¹	0.2¹
Rice	2 627.3	157.7*	447.4	5.9¹	—	5.2¹
Sweet potatoes/yams	28.0*	39.0¹	—	0.9	—	—
Wheat	na		—	—	—	3.0

2. FRUIT, etc.

	Production		Exports		Imports	
Apples	156.7*	na	—	—	—	0.1¹
Bananas	28.3*	na	—	—	—	—
Coconuts	na		—	—	0.1	0.6¹
Grapes	na		—	—	0.2	0.1¹
Oranges	52.3	12.0²	0.3¹		12.0	0.1¹
Other citrus fruit	8.7*	6.5²	—			
Pineapples	23.0		—			
Raisins						
Wine b					3.0	4.0¹

b '000 hectolitres.   c no. in millions.

3. BEVERAGES, FOREST PRODUCTS, etc.

	Production		Exports		Imports	
Coffee	—	—	—	4.3¹	0.2	0.1¹
Sugar, raw	9.3	5.5²	0.3	0.7¹	6.5	5.4¹
Tea	na		—	—	0.2	0.6¹
Tobacco: leaf	518.7*	416.7	85.0	90.8	0.2	0.2¹
cigarettes						
Wood pulp	—	—	—	—	0.7²	—
Newsprint	1.0		—	—	5.4¹	0.1¹
Other paper	0.7		—	—	1.1¹	0.3
Hardwood j					183	
j '000 cu. metres of roundwood equivalent.						

4. VEGETABLE OILSEEDS AND OILS

	Production		Exports		Imports	
Castor seed	2.33		—			
Copra	5.20		—			
Coconut oil	—	na	—			
Groundnuts	4.00		—			
Groundnut oil	11.66	2.80	—			
Linseed oil	na		—			
Sesame seed	10.10	2.00²	5.30		0.1	
Soya beans	8.00	8.00	6.41		0.1	
Soya bean oil			0.11			
Tung oil			0.06			

5. LIVESTOCK‡, ANIMAL PRODUCTS, etc.

	Production		Exports		Imports	
Chickens d	2 925.0	4 000.0				
Cattle d	1 417.7	853.3	25.2*			0.1²
dairy cows d	445.7	179.7				
Goats d	3.0*	na				
Horses d	4.7	3.0			0.1	0.2¹
Pigs d	822.0	384.7	4.2*	2.1¹		
Meat‡ 'A'	32.0	17.7n				
'B'	8.0*	7.9²				
Butter	2.4*	na	0.2		0.1	
Eggs	162.6	6.3²			0.6¹	
Fish	85.0*	150.0²	1.5		0.1¹	
Milk	0.8²	1.8²	na		0.1¹	
Hides/skins					12.0	11.5¹

d no. in thousands.   n government inspected meat only.

6. FIBRES, TEXTILES, etc.

	Production		Exports		Imports	
Cotton lint	2.3		0.6			0.1¹
Jute	2.0					0.1¹
Rubber, natural	46.8	24.9	45.1	26.2	53.7	16.0¹
Cotton,	na	20.0*	2.0		na	na
woven fabrics f						

f metric tons.

7. FUEL AND POWER

	Production		Exports		Imports	
Electricity h	83				na	1.7
Petroleum, refined			183		na	na

h thermal.

9. NON-FERROUS MINERALS AND METALS

	Production		Exports		Imports	
Gold k: ore m						

k '000 fine troy oz.   m metal content.

11. INDUSTRY

	Production		Exports		Imports	
Aircraft a	1.65		0.10¹		0.12	
Alcoholic beverages a	2.28				0.8	1.7
Cement	0.19	na	0.30¹		1.2	
Electrical	na		—		6.9²	1.9¹
engineering a						
Railway vehicles a	5.30		0.70¹		0.3	
Machine tools a	6.41		3.40¹		0.5	2.9¹
Motor vehicles a	0.06		—		6.5	

a million $ U.S.

CAMEROUN

The Cameroun Federal Republic was formed in 1961 of the French (East) Cameroun and the southern part of the British (West) Cameroons, the northern part electing to join Nigeria. There are separate Assemblies for the East and West zones under a joint National Assembly. Cameroun joined the Equatorial Customs Union in 1966.

All pre-1961 data for West Cameroons refer to the whole of the former British Cameroons.

AREA: 474 000* sq. km. (183 012* sq. miles)

LAND USE: (percentage of total)

	1958 a	1954 b
Arable and orchard	30.2	16.2
Permanent meadow and pasture	6.9	18.5
Forest and woodland	27.7	52.9
City areas, waste and other land	35.2	12.4

a British Cameroons.   b French Cameroun.

POPULATION: 5 740 000 (1967 estimate)

Largest city: DOUALA; population: 200 000* (1965)

Capital city: YAOUNDE; population: 101 000 (city proper, 1965)

		Year(s)
Life expectancy at birth (years): male	34.3 a	1964–5 av.
female	37.2 a	1964–5 av.
Infant mortality (per '000)	137.2* a c	1964–5 av.
Crude birth rate (per '000)	49.9* a c	1964–5 av.
Crude death rate (per '000)	25.7* a	1964–5 av.
Population per physician	33 950	1965
Population per hospital bed	480	1966
School enrolment: age 5–19 years (percentage)	69 d	1964–5 av.
age over 19 years (per 100/000 population)	24	1964–5 av.

a African population only.   c African population only.   d incl. pre-school education.

COMMUNICATIONS

		Year(s)
Motor vehicles in use ('000s): private	15.0	1963–5 av.
commercial	20.7	1963
Railway track (km.)	520	1967
Telephones (per '000 urban population)	0.1*	1962–4 av.
Daily newspapers (per '000 population)	3	

FINANCE

Currency unit: The franc CFA

	1965	1960	1958 b
Exchange rates			
Per $ U.S.	246.85	246.85	210
Per £ sterling	691.18	691.18	590

		Year(s)
National Income (million $ U.S.)	520	1963
G.N.P. per capita ($ U.S.)	110	1966
Foreign trade (percentage of G.D.P.)	36	1963–4 av.

b applies to French Cameroun only.

EMPLOYMENT AND PRODUCTION

The bulk of the population is employed in agriculture, coffee and cacao being the principal products of East Cameroun; recently modernization centres have been set up. Bauxite is mined and, with the development of H.E.P., is refined locally; there are also resources of gold and tin.

continued

WEST AFRICA

TRADING

Total trade (in million $ U.S.)	1965	1955 b	1938 b
Exports (f.o.b.)	139	96	7
Imports (c.i.f.)	153	104	6

Main trading partners (percentage of total value)

Exports	1965	1955 b	Imports	1965 b	1955 b	1938 b
France	48	48	France	58	63	
Netherlands	16	16	Germany F.R.	6	7	
U.S.A.	10	11	U.S.A.	6	4	
Germany F.R.	8	19	Guinea	5	1	
Italy	3	3	Belg./Lux.	4	1	
Belg./Lux.	3	—	Italy	3	na	
Spain	2	2	Japan	3	3	

PRODUCTION, EXPORTS AND IMPORTS

Years: 1963–5 average and 1953–5 average   Units: '000 metric tons unless otherwise indicated

Note—data for 1953–5 refer to East (former French) Cameroun only.

1. CEREALS, etc.

	Production		Exports		Imports	
Cassava	663.4*	601.0				
Maize (corn)	193.7	98.0			3.1	1.8²
Millets/sorghum	399.0*	347.0			0.7	3.8
Potatoes	26.1*	1.7			5.7	
Rice	12.3*	6.0	0.2			
Sweet potatoes/yams	226.3*	148.3			0.2n	

2. FRUIT, etc.

	Production		Exports		Imports	
Apples						
Bananas	140.6*	127.0²b	118.7	74.1		2.3
Coconuts	3.0*	na			9.2	
Pineapples	3.0*	na			1.0	0.9
Wine b			0.2		0.1q	0.12

b '000 hectolitres.   n incl. pears and quince.   p in addition.   q incl. other tobacco products.

3. BEVERAGES, FOREST PRODUCTS, etc.

	Production		Exports		Imports	
Cocoa	84.3	56.7*	72.1	55.4		
Coffee	48.3	10.4	47.5	11.6		2.3
Sugar, raw	0.3*	na	0.4	0.9	9.2	
Tea	3.8*	1.5²	1.1	—	1.0	0.9
Tobacco: cigarettes	744.0c		—	2	0.1q	0.12
Softwood j						1.3²
Hardwood j	5 765.3*	2 262.0²	227.3	105.7²	1.1	
Paper						

e no. in millions.   j '000 cu. metres of roundwood equivalent.   British Cameroons: 86.5².

4. VEGETABLE OILSEEDS AND OILS

	Production		Exports		Imports	
Castor oil	na	na	0.06	—	0.01	0.15²
Copra	na	12.30*	3.37	0.50		
Coconut oil	na	55.30	15.46	na	0.01	0.01
Cottonseed	17.30			6.43	0.27	
Groundnuts	105.93*			0.25	0.18	
Groundnut oil					0.01	
Linseed oil					0.02	
Olive oil						
Palm kernels	23.33*	21.07r	16.63	18.23		
Palm kernel oil			1.02	0.89		
Palm oil	42.96*	na	9.45	0.79		
Sesame seed	2.40	2.10	0.32	0.17	0.50	0.37

r commercial production only.

5. LIVESTOCK‡, ANIMAL PRODUCTS, etc.

	Production		Exports		Imports	
Chickens d	4 436.7*	2 500.0²				
Cattle d	2 436.7*	250.0				0.1
Goats d	1 997.0*	880.0				
Sheep d	1 032.9*	466.7				
Horses d	46.3*	17.0²			0.1	
Pigs d	273.0*	250.0				

continued

Distribution of trade (percentage of total value)

Exports	1965 b	1955 b
Food	55	na
(cocoa)	(27)	(49)
(coffee)	(23)	(14)
Manufactured goods	22	na
(aluminium alloys)	(17)	(na)
Imports		
Manufactured goods	67	na
(machinery and transport equipment)	(28)	(20)
(textiles)	(12)	(12)
Chemicals	13	1
Food	9	10

b French Cameroun only.

5. LIVESTOCK‡, ANIMAL PRODUCTS, etc.—continued

	Production		Exports		Imports	
Meat‡ 'A'	60.0*	14.01n		0.3	0.3	0.2
'B'	3.0*	na			0.1	0.1
Butter					0.2	0.2
Cheese	4.4*	na				
Eggs	57.4	36.5		2.4	2.8	
Milk	77.3	na	0.5*		3.9	3.1*
Hides/skins	na	1.31	1.1	0.92		

d no. in millions.   n government inspected meat only.

6. FIBRES, TEXTILES, etc.

	Production		Exports		Imports	
Cotton lint	17.3	6.0*	16.1	2.5		
Rubber, natural	6.2		6.2	3.2		
Cotton, woven fabrics			—	—	3.4	3.1

7. FUEL AND POWER

	Production		Exports		Imports	
Coal/coke						
Electricity h: total	1 094	201				
hydro	1 051	101				
thermal	43	101				
Petroleum, refined					140	901

h million kWh.

9. NON-FERROUS MINERALS AND METALS

	Production		Exports		Imports	
Gold k: ore m	1.30	1.00	1.03‡	1.03		
bullion, coins etc.					101.34	
Aluminium:						
alumina	51.64		49.04			
aluminium	0.04m	0.09m	0.07	0.12		
Tin, ore		0.08²	—	0.11		
Titanium minerals		2				

k '000 fine troy oz.   m metal content.

10. CHEMICALS n AND FERTILIZERS

	Production		Exports		Imports	
Chemicals	na				na	
Fertilizers:						
Phosphates					4.0	
Potash						

n data not available for years 1953–5.

11. INDUSTRY (see pages 102–117)

	Production		Exports		Imports	
Aircraft a					0.4	0.2
Alcoholic beverages b	415.0		0.3² a		3.9a	4.8a
beer b		1.7				
Cement					91.3	77.3
Electrical					4.9²	28.3²
engineering a	1.1	1.9			1.5	0.8
Railway vehicles a					0.3	
Merchant ships b						
Motor vehicles a		0.1		0.9†	12.0	4.3

a million $ U.S.   b '000 hectolitres.   g '000 G.R.T.

---

na: data not available.   — negligible or nil.   1 one year only.   2 two year average.   * estimate.   ‡ see appendix.   † re-exports.

CANADA

The provinces of Canada were united as a British colony in 1867 and the country was granted complete autonomy as a member of the Commonwealth in 1931. The influence of the French settlers remains, however, particularly in Québec province, where both French and English are official languages.

AREA: 9 976 169 sq. km. (3 851 809 sq. miles)

LAND USE: (percentage of total)

	1961	1951
Arable and orchard	4.2	3.9
Permanent meadow and pasture	2.1	2.2
Forest and woodland	44.4	34.3
City areas, waste and other land	49.3	59.6

POPULATION: 20 014 880 (1966 census)
Largest city: MONTRÉAL; population: 2 436 817 (1966)
Capital city: OTTAWA; population: 494 535 (1966)

Distribution of working population (1966)
Total working population: 7 177 000

U.N. group no.		Percentage
0	Agriculture, forestry, fishing and hunting	7.9
1	Mining and quarrying	1.6
2/3	Manufacturing	23.5
4	Construction	6.2
5	Electricity, gas, water and sanitary services	1.0
6	Commerce	20.3
7	Transport, storage and communications	7.1
8	Services	27.8
9	Others	4.6

		Year(s)
Life expectancy at birth (years): male	68.4	1960–2 av.
female	74.2	
Infant mortality (per '000)	23.6	1965
Crude death rate (per '000)	21.4	1965
Crude birth rate (per '000)	7.6	1965
Accidental deaths (per 100 000 population)		
caused by motor vehicles	25.8	1965
due to other causes	30.2	1965
Population per physician	820	1966
Population per hospital bed	90	1963–4 av.
School enrolment: age 5–19 years (percentage)	82	1963–5 av.
age over 19 years (per 100 000 population)	1 386	1963–5 av.

COMMUNICATIONS

		Year(s)
Motor vehicles in use ('000s): private	5 035.4	1963–5 av.
commercial	1 297	1964
Railway track (km.)	93 713	1963–5 av.
Mail per capita	210	1964
Telephones (per '000 urban population)	507	1967
Radio receivers (per '000 population)	258.1	1963–5 av.
Television sets (per '000 population)	223	1962–3 av.
Daily newspapers (per '000 population)		

PRODUCTION, EXPORTS AND IMPORTS
Years: 1963–5 average and 1953–5 average Units: '000 metric tons unless otherwise indicated

1. CEREALS, etc.

	Production		Exports		Imports	
Barley	4 369.0	5 008.7	689.7	1 816.5		
Maize (corn)	1 259.7	632.3	5.2	22.1	526.8	126.0
Millets/sorghum			8.8	10.2	0.1	0.3
Oats	6 298.3	5 765.3	308.5	684.5	7.0	10.6
Potatoes	2 127.0	1 716.7	187.3	120.5	100.8	44.5
Rice				0.3†	14.8	15.0
Rye	353.3	488.7	126.4	294.3	166.8	199.6
Wheat	17 897.0	12 855.0	12 076.1	6 244.3	57.8	8.5

2. FRUIT, etc.

	Production		Exports		Imports	
Apples	444.7	308.7	63.5	43.8	24.5	14.8
Apricots	3.7	3.7			3.6	3.0
Bananas					158.4	134.7
Cherries	19.7	13.6	na	0.5	na	1.5
Dates					7.0	10.6
Grapes	53.0	40.0	9.6	9.2	100.8	18.6
Lemons					14.8	15.0
Oranges					166.8	199.6
Other citrus fruit					57.8	8.5
Peaches	51.7	60.3	na	0.3†	10.6	9.1
Pears	14.3	18.6	3.3	1.5	23.6	23.9
Plums						
Raisins						
Tomatoes	358.0	na	0.1		139.7	59.7
Wine[b]	na	225.0				

[b] '000 hectolitres

3. BEVERAGES, FOREST PRODUCTS, etc.

	Production		Exports		Imports	
Cocoa						
Coffee						
Sugar: beet	1 126.3	872.7	0.1	0.1	18.7	13.8
cane	148.2	121.7			76.9	46.4
Tea						
Tobacco: leaf	79.0	69.4	27.5	1.2	777.2	592.4
cigars	455.0[a]	245.3[a]	1.1	16.5	21.2	20.7
cigarettes	41 502.0[a]	22 820.3[a]	20.2		1.6	
tobacco/snuff	9.5	12.4		0.54[a]		0.6[2]
Softwood[j]	89 491.0[1]	81 216.7[1]	25 791.0	16 296.2	1 820.3	874.5
Hardwood[j]	7 703.0[1]	8 786.0	751.6	645.2	739.5[2]	332.3
Wood pulp	12 213.3[1]	8 458.7	3 274.5	1 955.3	73.4	46.7
Newsprint	6 555.0[1]	5 414.0	6 113.7	5 037.7	134.3	80.9
Other paper	2 289.3	1 462.0	319.0	99.0		

a million $ U.S. j '000 cu. metres of roundwood equivalent.

4. VEGETABLE OILSEEDS AND OILS

	Production		Exports		Imports	
Castor oil					2.75	2.26
Copra					17.72	13.37
Coconut oil					18.69	12.68
Cottonseed oil					42.89	19.94
Groundnuts					5.67	29.27
Groundnut oil	598.33	346.30	356.97	151.83	0.61	3.16
Linseed			7.49	6.38	0.02	0.73
Linseed oil					1.26	0.09
Olive oil					3.82	1.03
Palm kernel oil					8.70	
Palm oil	335.70	20.00	181.14	11.20*		25.86
Rapeseed	na	na	0.08	18.80*		0.01
Rapeseed oil	181.70	136.33	15.89		438.57	176.77
Soya beans			5.85		14.22	9.76
Sunflower seed	15.00	5.00				
Sunflower seed oil	na	na			1.09	0.14
Tung oil						1.96

continued

FINANCE

Currency unit: The Canadian dollar

Exchange rates

	1965	1960	1950[a]	1938[b]
Per $ U.S.	1.075	0.9962	1.060	1.01
Per £ sterling	3.0131	2.7929	2.969	4.646

		Year(s)
National Income (million $ U.S.)	35 785	1965
G.N.P. per capita ($ U.S.)	2 240	1966
Rate of increase of G.N.P. per capita	3.2	1960–4 av.
Foreign trade (percentage of G.D.P.)	34	1963–5 av.

[a] mean rate. [b] spot and selling rate.

TRADING

Total trade (in million $ U.S.)

	1965	1955	1938
Exports (f.o.b.)	8 109	4 384	844
Imports (c.i.f.)	7 985	4 526	674

Main trading partners (percentage of total value)

Exports	1965	1955	1938	Imports	1965	1955	1938
U.S.A.	58	60	33	U.S.A.	70	73	63
U.K.	14	18	41	U.K.	8	7	18
Japan	3	2	—	Venezuela	3	3	1
U.S.S.R.	2	—	2	Japan	3	1	1
Germany F.R.	1	1	1	Germany F.R.	2	1	1
Australia	1	1	1[d]	France	1	—	1
Netherlands	1	1	4	Italy	1	—	1

Distribution of trade (percentage of total value)

Exports	1965	1955	1938*
Manufactured goods	43	41	na
(machinery and transport equipment)	(15)	(6)	(5)
Crude materials and fuels	(12)	(18)	(14)
(fuels)	33	32	na
Food	18	18	na
(cereals)	(11)	(12)	(16)

Imports	1965	1955	1938*
Manufactured goods	67	60	na
(machinery and transport equipment)	(40)	(33)	(15)
Crude materials and fuels	15	19	na
(fuels)	(7)	(10)	(14)
Food	8	9	na
Chemicals	6	6	10

PRODUCTION, EXPORTS AND IMPORTS continued

5. LIVESTOCK‡, ANIMAL PRODUCTS, etc.

	Production	Exports	Imports
Chickens[d]	67 531.7 65 779.1		
Cattle[d]	11 560.7 9 258.0	52.9	15.1
cows[d]	5 612.3 4 734.0[n]		
Goats[d]	17.0[n] na	na	29.3
Sheep[d]	878.0[1] 168.0[n]	13.8	
Horses[d]	426.3 895.0		0.1
Bison/ham	5 307.0 5 129.7[n]	5.5	4.7
Meat[1], B	1 295.3 1 009.0	4.0	4.4
	421.3*	38.0	6.3
Butter	161.7 151.0	22.1	5.4
Cheese	101.7 45.7	8.7	7.6
Eggs	292.3 252.4	13.5	0.2
Milk	1 223.6[p] 972.2[p]	1.0	7.3
Wool	8 363.3 7 663.0	334.8	3.3
Hides/skins[a]	2.9 na	415.9	30.6
Whale/sperm oil	na na		23.0
Fish	1.6 2.0	15.8[2]	27.8
		0.9	26.9

[d] no. in thousands. [n] on farms only. [p] incl. fish, except tuna, landed in foreign ports. [s] incl. re-exports.

6. FIBRES, TEXTILES, etc.

	Production	Exports	Imports
Abaca (sisal etc.)			1.6 2.8
Cotton: lint	0.1	40.5 25.5
Flax fibre	0.3	95.8 100.7
Hemp fibre		0.2
Jute	0.1	2.4
Rubber: natural	196.2 91.9	0.6 43.3 45.4
synthetic		1.2[1] 65.0[2] 26.7
Silk[r]		129.5 23.7
Cotton: yarn	78.8 66.8	4.5 6.0
woven fabrics	36.9* 32.3	6.2 6.0
Rayon: fibre/yarn	48.3 32.3	7.0[r]
woven fabrics	17.5 9.5	3.9
Non-cellulosic		
fibre/yarn	31.2 5.8	2.5 7.5
woven fabrics	10.5[2] 11.9[1]	0.5 2.1
Wool: yarn		4.8
woven fabrics		1.0

[f] metric tons. [q] incl. spun yarn. [r] incl. synthetic piece goods. [s] incl. [t] excl. blankets.

7. FUEL AND POWER

	Production	Exports	Imports
Coal‡, 'A'	8 330 11 360	1 085	13 596
'B'	593 2 080	366	18 736
Coke	1 133 862	12	2
Electricity[h]: total	133 862 75 030	116	294
hydro	111 413 70 610		
nuclear	116		
thermal	22 286 4 420	287	316
Natural gas[i]	36 610 3 518	10 860	
Oil, crude	39 960 17 590	13 520	20 350 5 700
Petroleum, refined	41 807 23 410	857	2 010 12 400
Rare earths[p][u]			4 670[1]
Uranium[t]	5 149[f] 1 762[1][q]	82 262[u]	327[n] 529[u]

[f] metric tons. [h] million kWh. [i] million cu. metres. [p] thorium and cerium salts only. [q] 1956 figure. [r] radium and compounds. [t] radium only. [u] '000 $ U.S.

8. IRON AND STEEL

	Production	Exports	Imports
Iron ore	18 034[m] 5 015[m]	28 831	3 551
Pig iron	6 059 2 663	546	317
Steel ingots/castings	8 283 3 580	340	12
Iron/steel scrap	na na	413	765
Iron/steel products[a]	na na	199	290

[a] million $ U.S. [m] metal content.

9. NON-FERROUS MINERALS AND METALS

	Production	Exports	Imports
Diamonds[a]	3 814.70 4 321.00	2 634.06[1]	9.86
Gold‡: bullion/coins etc.	399.01 344.01	503.15[c] 0.13	14.25
Platinum group metals[k]	30 553.30 29 133.70	227.58[2] 21.65[a]	557.14[1]
Silver‡: ore[m]	na na	10 003.65 6 244.24	na
bullion	7 026.0 3 715.0	11 827.66[l] 15 223.84	13 268.0 9 799.0
Asbestos: fibre		1 167.04 877.67[l] 837.06	1 682.0[m] 1 545.0[p]
manufactured	1 656.1[2]	0.31 0.13	na
Mica	0.44 0.85	4.96[m] 3.35[a]	na
Aluminium: bauxite	na na	2.51 0.06	1 656.2
alumina	na na	0.57[p] 0.53[a]	25.0[1]
aluminium	723.48 519.52	722.9[2] 2 583.65[n]	130.0
Antimony: ore	na na	767.93[2] 3.2	118.1
metal	0.68[m] 0.73[m]	70.29[2] 19.78	601.7
		0.77[1] 0.56[a]	89.7
		0.88	340.9

continued

[a] million $ U.S. [c] no. of units. [d] no. in thousands. [g] '000 G.R.T. [k] '000 hectolitres. [l] 1958/59 figure. [m] metal content. [n] 1965/66 figure. [p] '000 hectolitres. [q] 1965–7 av. [r] excl. parts.

---

9. NON-FERROUS MINERALS AND METALS—continued

	Production	Exports	Imports
Cadmium	1.06 0.62	0.75 0.50	45.06[1] 62.74
Chromium: metal	na		11.71[2] 13.56
Cobalt: ore	1.49[m] 1.08[m]	0.99	13.11
metal	440.49[m] 266.70[m]	0.88 20.96	0.01 0.13
Copper: ore	426.3 895.0	86.03[m] 42.38	na
metal	5 307.0 5 129.7[n]	257.56[1] 156.33	14.36[1] 9.21
Lead: ore[m]	369.56 181.43	1.57[a]	
metal	214.19 185.96	72.90 54.31	2.86[1] 1.23
Magnesium: dolomite	149.04 145.91	102.98 94.99	
magnesite	na na		20.30[2] 8.00
metal/salts	8.58[1] 6.32‡	2.95[1] 4.98[a]	14.49 12.11
Manganese: ore	na na	3.74[a]	1.13[a][u] 0.79[a]
metal	1.07 na		96.97[1] 87.98
Mercury[f]	1 756.00[m] 215.00[m]	2.17 10.37	25.38 4.18
Molybdenum[f]: ore	215.55 145.[2]	2.6	274.00 145.50
metal	0.26 0.22	670.87[1]	
Nickel: ore[m]	444.51[u] 133.03	141.43[s] 85.28	228.30 217.70
Tin: ore[m]	1.41 1.65	0.46 0.21	72.72[2] 2.05
metal			
Titanium minerals	na na	94.87	4.68[2] 4.03
Tungsten: ore		1.68[1]	11.30[2] 30.18
metal			0.29[1] 0.05
Vanadium			0.17 0.04
Zinc: ore	646.52[m] 366.38[m]	333.72[m] 170.37[m]	0.27[2][w]
metal	296.42 230.08	219.22 180.41	10.17[2] na
Zirconium minerals[p]			3.99 5.03
			0.35[1][r] 0.15

[a] million $ U.S. [f] metric tons. [k] '000 fine troy oz. [m] metal content. [n] incl. alumina and cryolite for refining. [p] manufactures. [q] incl. bauxite not for refining. [u] bricks and alloys only. [v] excl. titanium dioxide slag (70% TiO₂). [w] anodes. [x] sales. [y] nickel oxide. [z] excl. scrap.

10. CHEMICALS[n] AND FERTILIZERS

	Production	Exports	Imports
Organic chemicals:			
Benzene	138.5	na	14.4[2]
Butadiene	225.7	na	21.2
Ethylene	na	na	11.4
Methanol	33.5[2]	na	37.3
Phenol	9.3[2]	6.8	na
Phthalic anhydride	na	na	3.3
Styrene monomer	na	na	0.4
Urea	168.0	124.5[2]*	6.3
			3.0[2]
Inorganic chemicals:			
Ammonia	686.0	na	21.2
Carbon black	67.5	na	11.4
Chlorine	489.7	28.1	37.3
Sodium carbonate	573.6[2]		91.0
Sodium hydroxide	588.4	54.2	113.8
Sulphuric acid	2 009.2		4.1
Plastics:			
Polyamides	82.0	21.2	na
Polyethylene	24.1	2.4	12.6
Polyvinyl chloride	na		18.6
Fertilizers:			
Phosphates	900.1[1]	0.9[1] 144.3[2]	1 336.1 547.2
Potash	179.5	272.7	85.7 130.1
Pyrites[x]	1 544.2[q]	26.4*[n][q]	
Sulphur		1 092.7 3.2	139.8 315.3

[n] data not available. [q] K₂O content. [r] data for years 1953–5. [x] recovered sulphur. [y] sulphur content. [p] shipments.

11. INDUSTRY

	Production	Exports	Imports
Aircraft[a]	456.01*[q]	na	14.4[2]
Alcoholic beverages: beer[b]	13 268.0 9 799.0	148.7 30.9[r]	119.1
spirits[b]	1 682.0[m] 1 545.0[p]	99.7[a] 64.9[a]	106.5 20.2[a]
Cement	7 026.0 3 715.0		28.8[a]
Electrical: engineering[a]	1 656.1[2]	273.7 58.3	35.7 409.3
Locomotives[c]	na	143.8 32.9[2]	367.8 244.5[2]
Railway vehicles[a]	na		
Machine tools[a]	25.0[1] na	11.1	34.1
Merchant ships[g]	130.0 54.0	77.7	38.4
Motor vehicles: commercial[a]		176.8[a] 41.9[2][a]	0.9 na
private[a]			743.4[a] 322.4[m]

[a] million $ U.S. [c] no. of units. [d] no. in thousands. [g] '000 G.R.T. [m] metal content. [n] 1965/66 figure. [p] '000 hectolitres. [q] 1965–7 av. [r] excl. parts.

na: data not available. — negligible or nil. * estimate. ‡ see appendix. [1] one year only. [2] two year average. [d] no. in thousands.

CEYLON

INDIAN OCEAN

Ceylon became an independent republic within the British Commonwealth in 1948.

AREA: 65 610 sq. km. (25 332 sq. miles)

LAND USE: (percentage of total)

	1965
Arable and orchard	28.6
Cultivated pasture	0.2
Forest and woodland	50.7
City areas, waste and other land	20.5

POPULATION: 11 741 000 (1967 estimate)
Largest city: COLOMBO; capital; population: 510 947 (city proper, 1963)
Total working population: 2 983 109

Distribution of working population (1953)

U.N. group no.		Percentage
0	Agriculture, forestry, fishing and hunting	53.1
1	Mining and quarrying	0.4
2/3	Manufacturing	10.2
4	Construction	1.9
5	Electricity, gas, water and sanitary services	0.2
6	Commerce	8.2
7	Transport, storage and communications	3.5
8	Services	16.3
9	Others	

		Year(s)
Life expectancy at birth (years): male / female	61.9 / 61.4	1962
Infant mortality (per '000)	53.2	1965
Crude birth rate (per '000)	33.1	1965
Crude death rate (per '000)	8.2	1965
Accidental deaths (per 100 000 population)	1.4	1965
due to motor vehicles	27.5	1965
due to other causes	5 820	1966
Population per physician	320a	1966
Population per hospital bed	81b	1963-4 av.
School enrolment: age 5-19 years (percentage)		
age over 19 years (per 100 000 population)	120c	1963-5 av.

a government hospitals only. b includes correspondence courses. c excludes teacher-training and technical colleges.

COMMUNICATIONS

		Year(s)
Motor vehicle in use ('000s): private	82.6	1963-5 av.
commercial	36.5	
Mail per capita: domestic	1484	1964
foreign received	1	
foreign sent	0.4	1963-5 av.
Telephones (per '000 urban population)	38	1967
Radio licences (per '000 population)	35	1964
Daily newspapers (per '000 population)		

FINANCE

Currency unit: The rupee

Exchange rates

	1965a	1960	1950	1938
Per $ U.S.	4.788	4.762	4.775	2.888
Per £ sterling	13.33	13.33	13.33	13.33

		Year(s)
National Income (million $ U.S.)	1 458	1965
G.N.P. per capita ($ U.S.)	150	1966
Rate of increase of G.N.P. per capita	0.4	1960-4 av.
Foreign trade (percentage of G.D.P.)	46	1963-5 av.

a selling rate

TRADING

Total trade (in million $ U.S.)

	1965	1955	1938
Exports (f.o.b.)	409	407	104
Imports (c.i.f.)	310	307	86

Main trading partners (percentage of total value)

Exports	1965	1955	1938
U.K.	18	21	21
China P.R.	17	17	—
U.S.A.	8	5	7
Japan	8	—	—
U.S.S.R.	7	na	na
Australia	6	6	na
Burma	5	8	3

Imports	1965	1955	1938
U.K.	26	27	54
China P.R.	9	9	13
U.S.A.	8	9	na
India	8	6	13
Iraq	5	na	na
U.S.S.R.	5	na	na
South Africa	5	4	3

Distribution of trade (percentage of total value)

Exports	1965	1955	1938*
Food	70	70	
(tea)	69		
Crude materials	22 (63)	24 (64)	24 (65)
(rubber)			
Coconut oil	7 (16)	6 (19)	5 (18)

Imports	1965	1955	1938*
Food	41	41	35
(cereals)	37 (17)	38 (12)	40 (21)
Manufactured goods			
machinery and transport equipment	11 (12)	11 (12)	(6)
(textiles and clothing)			(9)
Crude materials and fuel	11	11	15

PRODUCTION, EXPORTS AND IMPORTS Units: '000 metric tons unless otherwise indicated
Years: 1963-5 average and 1953-5 average

1. CEREALS, etc.	Production		Exports		Imports	
	1963-5	1953-5	1963-5	1953-5	1963-5	1953-5
Barley	—	—	—	—	0.3	—
Cassava	354.3	234.3	—	—	—	—
Maize (corn)	10.0	9.0	—	—	2.9	—
Millets/sorghum	20.0*	22.0	—	0.4	—	—
Oats	—	—	—	—	0.2	0.7
Potatoes	4.7*	7.0	—	—	66.3	39.3
Rice	945.7	654.7	0.1	—	530.3*	300.0
Sweet potatoes/yams	60.7	46.7	—	1.5	399.1	0.1n
Wheat	—	—	—	—	0.1n	—

n in addition, milled wheat 224 (1963-5 av.) and 238 (1953-5 av.).

2. FRUIT, etc.	Production	Exports		Imports	
Apples				1.1	
Coconuts	2 486.7e	59.0	65.6	11.0	3.3
Dates					
Pineapples	31.0	0.4	0.4	0.4	0.5
Raisins				0.4	0.3
Wine b				0.5	

3. BEVERAGES, FOREST PRODUCTS, etc.	Production		Exports		Imports	
Cocoa	2.3	2.7*	2.0	2.8		
Coffee	83.7*		4.7			
Sugar: cane, raw	6.7		0.4	4.7	192.1	149.1
Tea	222.2	164.8	212.5	160.2	0.5	1.03

continued

3. BEVERAGES, FOREST PRODUCTS, etc.—continued	Production		Exports	Imports	
Tobacco: leaf	4.1*	3.4*	0.5	0.8	0.7
cigars	1 838.0c	1 492.0e			1.1
cigarettes		4.1			
tobacco/snuff	na	na			
Softwood j					
Hardwood j	250.3	300.0	0.2	2.8	1.6
Wood pulp j				4.8	9.9
Newsprint				12.0	10.2
Other paper	6.3			12.4	10.1

e no. in millions. j '000 cu. metres of roundwood equivalent.

4. VEGETABLE OILSEEDS AND OILS	Production		Exports		Imports	
Castor oil					0.17	0.03
Coconut oil	275.47	249.93	48.13	46.00		
Copra	0.67		96.70	85.29	0.8	—
Cottonseed	2.80				0.01	0.04
Groundnuts					0.04	0.14
Groundnut oil					0.14	0.46
Linseed oil					0.02	0.06
Olive oil					0.27	na
Palm kernel oil					0.26	0.401
Palm oil						
Rapeseed						
Sesame seed	8.13*	6.5²			0.48	0.10

continued

CENTRAL AFRICAN REPUBLIC

The Central African Republic, formerly Oubangi-shari, a territory of French Equatorial Africa, and from 1958 a member state of the French Community, became independent in 1960. The country has been a member of the Equatorial Customs Union since its foundation in 1959.

AREA: 617 000 sq. km. (238 000 sq. miles)

LAND USE: (percentage of total)

	1964
Arable and orchard	9.4
Permanent meadow and pasture	0.2
Forest and woodland	11.9
City areas, waste and other land including rough grazing	78.5

POPULATION: 1 459 000 excl. 28 000 refugees from Sudan (1967 estimate)
Largest city: BANGUI; capital; population: 150 000 (1966)
Total working population: 480 000 (1961)

		Year(s)
Life expectancy at birth (years): male / female	33 / 36	1959-60 av.
Population per physician	33 000	1961
Population per hospital bed	640a	1966
School enrolment: age 5-19 years (percentage)	30	1963-4 av.

a government hospitals only.

COMMUNICATIONS

		Year(s)
Motor vehicles in use ('000s): private	3.1	1963-5 av.
commercial	4.7	1967
Telephones (per '000 population)	0.2*	1963-5 av.
Radio receivers (per '000 population)	19	1962-4 av.
Daily newspapers (per '000 population)	0.3	

FINANCE

Currency unit: The franc CFA

Exchange rates

	1965	1960	1955
Per $ U.S.	246.85	246.85	
Per £ sterling	691.18	691.18	

		Year(s)
National Income (million $ U.S.)	166	1965
G.N.P. per capita ($ U.S.)	110	1966
Foreign trade (percentage of G.D.P.)	35	1963-4 av.

TRADING

Total trade (in million $ U.S.)

	1965	1955
Exports (f.o.b.)	26	16
Imports (c.i.f.)	27	18

Main trading partners (percentage of total value)

Exports	1965
France	38
Israel	22
U.S.A.	13
U.K.	7
Netherlands	6
Italy	4
Yugoslavia	2

Imports	1965
France	60
U.S.A.	6
Germany F.R.	6
U.K.	4
Netherlands	3
Belg./Lux.	3

Distribution of trade (percentage of total value)

Exports	1965
Crude materials and fuels	83 (54)
(diamonds)	
Cotton, (raw cotton)	16 (19)
Food (coffee)	(15)

Imports	1965
Manufactured goods	72
(machinery and transport equipment)	(30)
(textiles)	
Food	11 (14)

PRODUCTION, EXPORTS AND IMPORTS Units: '000 metric tons unless otherwise indicated
Years: 1963-5 average
Note—no data are available for the years 1953-5

1. CEREALS, etc.	Production	Exports	Imports
Cassava	1 000.0*	—	—
Maize (corn)	29.3	—	0.1
Potatoes			0.1
Rice	4.3*	—	0.1
Sweet potatoes/yams	40.0*		

2. FRUIT, etc.	Production	Exports	Imports
Apples			0.1n
Bananas	170.0*		
Lemons	1.0*		
Oranges	11.0*		0.02
Other citrus fruit	5.0*		0.20
Wine b			38.6

3. BEVERAGES, FOREST PRODUCTS, etc.	Production	Exports	Imports
Coffee	10.0*	8.6	
Tea			
Tobacco, leaf	0.5*	0.4	0.1
Hardwood j	1 883.7*	20.5	

j '000 cu. metres of roundwood equivalent.

4. VEGETABLE OILSEEDS AND OILS	Production	Exports	Imports
Cottonseed	19.00*	0.03	
Groundnuts	45.97	1.47	0.02
Groundnut oil	1.23	1.24	
Palm kernels	1.30*		0.20
Palm oil			
Sesame seed	8.53	2.05	

5. LIVESTOCK‡, ANIMAL PRODUCTS, etc.	Production	Exports	Imports
Chickens d	866.7*		
Cattle d	400.0*		
dairy cows d	316.7*		
Goats d	47.0*		
Sheep d	108.0*		
Horses d	10.0		
Pigs d			
Bacon/ham A	8.3		
Meat‡ A			
Butter			
Cheese			
Eggs	5.3*		
Fish	na		
Milk	15.0*		0.1
Hides/skins	0.3²	0.3	

d no. in thousands.

6. FIBRES, TEXTILES, etc.	Production	Exports	Imports
Agaves (sisal etc.)	0.2*	0.1	
Cotton lint	10.0*	9.6	
Rubber, natural		1.0	
Cotton, woven fabrics	4.7n		

n million metres.

7. FUEL AND POWER	Production	Exports	Imports
Electricity h: total	20		
hydro	19		
thermal	1		
Petroleum, refined			23

h million kWh.

9. NON-FERROUS MINERALS AND METALS	Production	Exports	Imports
Diamonds,	443.67l	12.51a	

a million $ U.S. l '000 carats.

10. CHEMICALS AND FERTILIZERS	Production	Exports	Imports
Chemicals			na
Fertilizers: Phosphates			0.3²

11. INDUSTRY	Production	Exports	Imports
Alcoholic beverages			1.0a
beer b	81.0		
Cement			17.0
Electrical engineering a			1.5
Motor vehicles a			3.3

a million $ U.S. b '000 hectolitres.

continued

na: data not available. — negligible or nil. 1 one year only. 2 two year average. * estimate. ‡ see appendix. † re-exports.

CEYLON *continued*

PRODUCTION, EXPORTS AND IMPORTS *continued*

5. LIVESTOCK‡; ANIMAL PRODUCTS, etc.

	Production	Exports	Imports
Chickens d	6 166.0 / 673.7	—	—
dairy cows d	1 781.3 / 1 313.0	—	—
Goats d	568.0 / 518.0	—	0.2
Sheep d	35.0 / 96.0	—	—
Horses d	3.0* / 3.0*	—	—
Pigs d	117.0 / 66.7	—	—
Bacon/ham	18.3 / 20.01 n	—	19.8
Meat† 'A'	2.7*	—	0.1
'B'	na	—	0.3
Butter	—	—	1.0
Cheese	—	—	0.2
Eggs	20.7 / 12.2²	—	1.6
Fish	96.2 / 28.8	0.2	37.8 / 38.9*
Milk	136.7 / 103.5²	0.1	90.9 / 39.5²

d no. in thousands. n government inspected meat only.

6. FIBRES, TEXTILES, etc.

	Production	Exports	Imports
Cotton lint	0.3	—	0.7
Rubber, natural	111.6 / 97.0	103.3	2.3
Cotton: yarn	1.9² / 0.8	—	2.2
woven fabrics	0.8* / 0.8	—	11.2
Rayon, woven fabrics	—	95.8	1.3 p
p incl. synthetic piece goods.			

7. FUEL AND POWER

	Production	Exports	Imports
Electricity h ‡: total	419 / 180 1	—	153
hydro	333² / 130 1	—	—
thermal	86 / 50 1	—	—
Petroleum, refined	507	144	907
Rare earths f / q	537	31 1	960 1

f metric tons. h million kWh. q monazite.

8. IRON AND STEEL

	Production	Exports	Imports
Pig iron	—	—	1
Steel ingots/castings	—	—	2 / 1 1

9. NON-FERROUS MINERALS AND METALS

	Production	Exports	Imports
Diamonds a	—	—	0.27
Gold j	—	—	6.84
Gold/coins etc.	—	—	—
Silver k: ore n	18.00 1	—	18.73
bullion	—	—	— 1
Asbestos: fibre	—	—	9.27
manufactured	—	—	3.09
Aluminium	—	—	0.39
Copper, metal	—	—	3.27
Lead, metal	—	—	0.65
Magnesium, metal	—	—	0.47
dolomite	5.08 1	—	3.58
Tin, metal	—	—	—
Titanium minerals	38.15	—	0.22
Zinc, metal	—	—	—

a million $ U.S. k '000 fine troy oz. m metal content.

10. CHEMICALS n AND FERTILIZERS

	Production	Exports	Imports
Chemicals a	—	—	na
Fertilizers:			
Phosphates	—	—	59.9 / 35.0
Potash	—	—	57.2 / 27.5
Sulphur	—	—	2.9 / 3.2

n data not available for years 1953–5.

11. INDUSTRY

	Production	Exports	Imports
Aircraft a	—	—	1.6 1 / 0.5
Cement	60.0 / 30.9	—	—
Electrical engineering a	78.7 / 79.3	—	196.0 / 119.3
Railway vehicles a	—	—	6.32 / 6.9 1
Merchant ships g	—	—	2.4 1 / 18.0
Motor vehicles a	—	—	11.3 1 / 11.1 1

a million $ U.S. g '000 G.R.T.

b '000 hectolitres.

PRODUCTION, EXPORTS AND IMPORTS

Years: 1963–5 average   Units: '000 metric tons unless otherwise indicated

Note—no data are available for the years 1953–5

1. CEREALS, etc.

	Production	Exports	Imports
Cassava	46.7*	—	—
Maize (corn)	12.0	—	—
Millets/sorghum	835.0*	—	—
Potatoes	32.3	—	0.2
Rice	—	—	0.4
Sweet potatoes/yams	50.0*	—	—
Wheat	3.3	—	0.7

2. FRUIT, etc.

	Production	Exports	Imports
Apples	—	—	0.1 p
Bananas	18.7*	—	0.3
Dates	—	—	0.1
Oranges	—	0.3	—
Wine b	—	—	19.7

b '000 hectolitres. p incl. pears and quince.

3. BEVERAGES, FOREST PRODUCTS, etc.

	Production	Exports	Imports
Tea	—	—	0.8
Hardwood j	2 601.7*	—	12.2²
Newsprint	—	—	na
Other paper	—	—	na

j '000 cu. metres of roundwood equivalent.

4. VEGETABLE OILSEEDS AND OILS

	Production	Exports	Imports
Cottonseed	62.70	—	0.01
Groundnuts	100.30	1.55	—
Groundnut oil	—	—	0.13
Olive oil	na	—	—
Sesame seed	5.00*	0.02	0.01

5. LIVESTOCK‡; ANIMAL PRODUCTS, etc.

	Production	Exports	Imports
Cattle d	4 000.0*	—	—
Goats d	2 750.0*	72.0	—
Sheep d	1 250.0*	24.0	1.2
Horses d	150.0*	—	—
Bacon/ham	248.0*	0.6	—
Meat† 'A'	—	0.1	0.1
Butter	—	—	—
Cheese	na	—	—
Eggs	1.6	—	—
Fish	90.0²	0.3	0.1
Milk	65.0*	0.6	1.9
Hides/skins	0.4	—	—

d no. in thousands.

6. FIBRES, TEXTILES, etc.

	Production	Exports	Imports
Agaves (sisal)	35.0	—	35.7

7. FUEL AND POWER

	Production	Exports	Imports
Electricity h t;	16	—	—
Petroleum, refined	—	—	33

h million kWh. t thermal.

11. INDUSTRY

	Production	Exports	Imports
Alcoholic beverages a	—	—	1.3
Cement	—	—	9.0
Electrical engineering a	—	—	1.6
Motor vehicles a	—	—	2.5

a million $ U.S.

SOUTH AMERICA

CHILE

Chile is one of the more stable South American republics. The balance of the economy depends to a great extent upon the production of copper, but recently some attempt has been made towards diversification, industrialization, and social reform.

AREA: 741 767 sq. km. (286 397 sq. miles)

LAND USE: (percentage of total)

	Year(s)	
Arable and orchard	1965	6.1
Permanent meadow and pasture		13.6
Forest and woodland		27.9*
City areas, waste and other land		52.4*

POPULATION: 8 935 000 (1967 U.N. estimate)
Largest city: SANTIAGO, capital; population: 2 313 720 (1966)

Distribution of working population (1960)
Total working population: 2 388 667

U.N. group no.		Percentage
0	Agriculture, forestry, fishing and hunting	27.7
1	Mining and quarrying	3.8
2/3	Manufacturing	18.0
4	Construction	5.7
5	Electricity, gas, water and sanitary services	10.1
6	Commerce	4.9
7	Transport, storage and communications	22.8
9	Others	6.2

	Year(s)	
Life expectancy at birth (years): male	1952	49.8
female		53.9
Infant mortality (per '000)	1965	101.7
Crude birth rate (per '000)	1960–5 av.	35
Crude death rate (per '000)	1960–5 av.	11.5
Accidental deaths (per 100 000 population)	1964	5.8
caused by motor vehicles	1964	69.1
Population per physician	1965	2 100
Population per hospital bed	1966	260 a
School enrolment: age 5–19 years (percentage)	1963–4 av.	79
age over 19 years (per 100 000 population)	1963–5 av.	444

a government hospitals only.

COMMUNICATIONS

	Year(s)	
Motor vehicles in use ('000s): private	1963–5 av.	90.1
commercial		100.3
Railway track (km.)	1964	8408
Mail per capita: domestic	1961–3 av.	na
foreign received		na
foreign sent		na
Telephones (per '000 population)	1967	3.19
Radio receivers (per '000 population)	1963–5 av.	187
Television sets (per '000 population)	1963–5 av.	5.11
Daily newspapers (per '000 population)	1962–4 av.	118.5

FINANCE

Currency unit: The Chilean escudo was introduced in 1960, equivalent to 1 000 pesos

Exchange rates	1960	1956 b	1938 b
Per $ U.S.	1.053	3.47	31.47
Per £ sterling	2.984	9.71	144.76

	Year(s)	
National income (million $ U.S.)	1960	4 427
G.N.P. per capita ($ U.S.)	1965	510
Rate of increase of G.N.P. per capita	1966	1
a trade rate. b official rate, for pesos.	1963–5 av.	23

TRADING

	Year(s)		
Total trade (in million $ U.S.)	1965	1955	
Exports (f.o.b.)	888	475	
Imports (c.i.f.)	604	376	

Main trading partners (percentage of total value)	1965	1955	1938
Exports U.S.A.	39	43	28
Germany F.R.	11	11	26 d
U.K. Argentina	8	11	4
Netherlands Peru	8	5	6

Distribution of trade (percentage of total value)		
Exports	1965	1938*
Minerals (copper)	90	(49)
Imports	na	
Machinery and transport equipment	34	29
Chemicals	10	4

d includes Germany D.R.

continued

CHAD

Formerly a territory of French Equatorial Africa, and from 1958 a member state of the French Community, Chad became an independent state in 1960. Chad has been a member of the Equatorial Customs Union since its foundation in 1959.

AREA: 1 284 000 sq. km. (496 000 sq. miles)

LAND USE: (percentage of total)

	Year(s)	
Arable and orchard	1962	5.5
Permanent meadow and pasture		35.0
Forest and woodland		12.5
City areas, waste and other land		47.0

POPULATION: 3 410 000 (1967 estimate)
Largest city: FORT-LAMY, capital; population: 99 000 (1964)

Distribution of working population (1961)
Total working population: 1 380 000

U.N. group no.		Percentage
0	Agriculture, forestry, fishing and hunting	82.6
1	Mining and quarrying	0.1
2/3	Manufacturing	0.5
4	Construction	0.5
5	Electricity, gas, water and sanitary services	0.4
6	Commerce	0.2
7	Transport, storage and communications	1.5
9	Others	14.4

	Year(s)	
Life expectancy at birth (years): male		na
female		na
Infant mortality (per '000)	1964	160 a
Crude birth rate (per '000)	1964	45 a
Crude death rate (per '000)	1964	31*
Population per physician	1964	73 330
Population per hospital bed	1966	900
School enrolment: age 5–19 years (percentage)	1963–4 av.	16

a African population.

CENTRAL AFRICA

COMMUNICATIONS

	Year(s)	
Motor vehicles in use ('000s): private	1963–5 av.	2.4
commercial		4.2
Telephones (per '000 urban population)	1967	0.1
Radio receivers (per '000 population)	1962	0.3
Daily newspapers (per '000 population)		—

FINANCE

Currency unit: The franc CFA

Exchange rates	1965	1960
Per $ U.S.	246.85	246.85
Per £ sterling	691.18	691.18

	Year	
National income (million $ U.S.)	1965	192
G.N.P. per capita ($ U.S.)	1963	70
Foreign trade (percentage of G.D.P.)	1963	24

TRADING

	Year(s)	
Total trade (in million $ U.S.)	1965	
Exports (f.o.b.)		27
Imports (c.i.f.)		31

Main trading partners (percentage of total value)	1965	1955
Exports France	45	46
Yugoslavia	12	13
Nigeria	8	
U.K.	6	
Belg./Lux.		
Imports France		
Neths. Antilles		
U.S.A.		
Germany F.R.		
Cameroun		
Belg./Lux.		
Japan		

Distribution of trade (percentage of total value)		
Exports	1965	
Crude materials and fuels (raw cotton)	85	(77)
Food (live animals)	11	(8)
Imports	1965	
Manufactured goods (machinery and transport equipment) (textiles)	55	(21)(11)
Petroleum products	20	
Food	9	
Chemicals	6	

continued

---

na: data not available.   — negligible or nil.   1 one year only.   2 two year average.   * estimate.   ‡ see appendix.   † re-exports.

CHINA, PEOPLE'S REPUBLIC OF

COMMUNICATIONS

			Year(s)
Railway track (km)	31 193		1958
Telephones (per '000 urban population)		12	1947
Radio licences (per '000 population)		0.1a	1958
Television sets (per '000 population)		0.1	1963-5 av.
Daily newspapers (per '000 population)		19a	1955

a latest available figure.

The attempt to create an industrial state has led to an expansion of communications particularly by rail and, in the south, water. A civil air service has been built up since 1949 and China now has three international-standard airports. The radio is much used as a means of propaganda and its ownership is therefore encouraged.

AREA: 9 700 000* sq. km. (3 745 000* sq. miles)

LAND USE: (percentage of total)

	1954
Arable and orchard	11.2
Permanent meadow and pasture	18.2
Forest and woodland	7.9
City areas, waste and other land	62.7

In recent years great emphasis has been placed on afforestation to combat soil erosion and the reclamation of waste land. New techniques of irrigation and flood control have improved the reliability of large areas of fertile land.

POPULATION: 720 000 000 (1967 estimate)

In addition, apart from 13 million in Taiwan, about 16 million Chinese live outside China, the majority in South East Asian countries.
Largest city: SHANG-HAI; population 6 900 000 (city proper, 1957)
Capital city: PEI-P'ING (Peking); population: 4 010 000 (city proper, 1957)

		Year(s)
Infant mortality (per '000)	34*	1957
Crude birth rate (per '000)	34.1*	1957
Crude death rate (per '000)	11*	1957
School enrolment: age 5-19 years (percentage)	58*	1958
age over 19 years (per 100 000 population)	128	1960-2 av.

The death and infant mortality rates have fallen substantially due to the emphasis on public hygiene. The birth rate remains fairly constant since contraception is not popular and the emphasis of birth control propaganda is on late marriage and maternal and infant health rather than prevention of births. Much education is practical and at secondary level is combined with periods of work on the land.

EMPLOYMENT

About 80% of the population is rural and engaged principally in agriculture during the tending season and in local workshop industry during slack times. A feature of employment is the massive numbers engaged in major construction works and local projects built and financed by individual communes.

FINANCE

Currency unit: The yuan

Exchange rates a	1960	1965
Per $ U.S.	2.34	2.34
Per £ sterling	6.859	6.859

a official rates. (1955 figure as quoted by the Bank of China.)

In the first year of communist control the galloping inflation, which had helped to contribute to the downfall of the Nationalist government, was controlled and the financial balance has since remained stable.

TRADING

Total trade (in million $ U.S.)	1960	1965
Exports (f.o.b.)	1647	1736
Imports (c.i.f.)	1491	1642

Main trading partners (percentage of total value)

Exports	1965	1960	Imports	1965	1960
Hong Kong	25	12	Japan	16	...
U.S.S.R.	14	49	U.S.S.R.	13	50
Japan	14	...	Australia	11	1
Cuba	8	...	Canada	7	...
U.K.	5	4	Cuba	7	2
Germany F. R.	4	4	Germany F. R.	6	5
France	3	1	Argentina	5	...
Italy	2	1	U.K.	5	5

The value of foreign trade is only about 4% of China's G.N.P. The majority of China's exports are agricultural raw materials, but the proportion of made-up textiles and light industrial goods is increasing. China has an unfavourable balance of trade only with the major grain exporting countries. A sterling balance is earned through a high level of exports to Hong Kong whence imports are virtually non-existent. Since 1960 trade with all the Comecon countries has declined.

PRODUCTION, EXPORTS AND IMPORTS

Years: 1963-5 average and 1953-5 average Units: '000 metric tons unless otherwise indicated

1. CEREALS, etc.

	Production		Exports		Imports	
Barley	na	12 924*n				205*
Maize (corn)	na	18 812*n	175*	12*		1952*
Millets/sorghum	na	12*	7*			15*
Oats	na	1 557*n	25*	7*		68*
Potatoes	na	18 150*n	724*	289*		92*
Rice	85 000*	65 000*	110*			54*
Sweet potatoes/yams	na	22 635				5 063*
Wheat	23 630*					7*

n 1952-1956 av.

2. FRUIT, etc.

	Production	Exports	Imports
Apples	318*	79*	1*
Bananas	160*	15*	10*
Dates	na	2	3*
Grapes	123*	2	—
Lemons	na	37*	17*
Oranges	na	4*	—
Other citrus fruit	na	15*	—
Pears	831*		
Raisins	na		

Rice is the most extensive food crop in China but maize, sorghum, wheat, barley, and yams also are important crops. Citrus and tropical fruits can be grown in some areas and apples are proving an important crop in Ssu-ch'uan and around Lan-chou.

3. BEVERAGES, FOREST PRODUCTS, etc.

	Production		Exports		Imports	
Cocoa	—	—	—	—		6*
Coffee	—	—	1*	—		
Sugar: beet	3 693*	990¹*	1*	—		
cane	21 670*	8 350²b				
raw (beet)	443¹b	190²*b	305*			2 850¹*
(cane)	1 567*	613*				6 650¹*
Tea	169¹	72¹*	30*	8*	9 100²*	
Tobacco, leaf	443¹	374¹*	9*	15*	2*	

Though China's tea exports have never recovered from the development of tea growing in India and Ceylon, there is sufficient demand from the home market to make tea an important crop. Tobacco also is grown for local use and coffee growing has started on a very small scale.

3. BEVERAGES, FOREST PRODUCTS, etc.—continued

	Production		Exports		Imports	
Softwood j	61 260*		13			16
Hardwood j	72 830*		2*			13
Wood pulp	350*		23			82
Newsprint						1
Other paper	2 567*					

j '000 cu. metres of roundwood equivalent, p in addition, non-centrifugal sugar, 560* (1963-5 av.) and 315* (1953-5 av.).

A new timber industry is developing as a result of the afforestation programme. A great variety of trees is grown in different regions, for the production of wood-oil as well as for timber. Teak is commercially the most important wood.

4. VEGETABLE OILSEEDS AND OILS

	Production		Exports		Imports	
Castor seed	2 313*	1 550²*	10*	23*	2*	6*
Copra						62
Coconut oil			3*		13*	16*
Cottonseed	1 515*	1 993*	31*	47*		
Cottonseed oil			5*			1
Groundnuts			13*		7*	
Linseed						
Linseed oil	1 092*	2 850¹*	2*	16*		
Rapeseed			1*	4*		
Rapeseed oil	360*	650¹*	3*	32*	2*	
Sesame seed	10 923*	9 100²*	464*	249*		
Soya beans						
Sunflower seed						
Tung oil	75*	76*	16*	36*		3*

Rape and sesame are both grown for oil whereas soya beans are grown principally for food, though some oil is extracted.

continued

*na: data not available. — negligible or nil. — not available. * estimate. ‡ see appendix. † re-exports.*

CHILE continued

PRODUCTION, EXPORTS AND IMPORTS

Years: 1963-5 average and 1953-5 average Units: '000 metric tons unless otherwise indicated

1. CEREALS, etc.

	Production		Exports		Imports	
Barley	131.3	82.0	1.2	9.8	—	—
Maize (corn)	193.0	103.0	1.9	3.9	4.0	—
Oats	128.0	104.0	3.4	—	0.1	0.72
Potatoes	768.7	611.7	—	1.6	15.0*	2.0
Rice	86.3	78.0	—	—	269.0	166.8
Rye	14.3	6.7				
Wheat	1 290.3	1 027.0				

2. FRUIT, etc.

	Production		Exports		Imports	
Apples	55.0	31.3*	15.0	8.4	—	—
Apricots	4.0*	na	—	—	—	—
Bananas	na		—	—	30.2*	19.8
Cherries	3.3	na	—	—	—	—
Grapes	670.0*	532.0²	8.7	2.7	0.1	—
Lemons	44.7	26.0*	4.1	2.5	0.2	—
Oranges	41.0	28.3	—	—	—	—
Olives	20.0*	3.01	na	—	—	—
Peaches	40.3*	30.1	na	0.9	—	—
Pears	11.3*	3.7*	2.9	0.8	—	—
Plums	22.7*	na	0.1	0.7	—	—
Tomatoes	61.3*	na	0.1	0.1	—	—
Raisins	0.8*	0.2*n			34	—
Wine b	4 243.0²	3 587.0	82.6	68.3	0.1	—

b '000 hectolitres. n commercial production only.

3. BEVERAGES, FOREST PRODUCTS, etc.

	Production		Exports		Imports	
Cocoa					1.3	1.0
Coffee					8.8	5.8
Sugar: beet raw	686.7	27.3*				
raw	107.1	8.7*			179.1	230.0
Tea					6.4	3.4
Tobacco: leaf	6.2	5.0		0.1	1.1	0.3
cigars e	—	2.0				
cigarettes	6 470.0	7 688.0	90.0	145.3	1.4	6.6
Softwood j	2 506.3	4 794.0¹	35.7	153.1	6.0²	—
Hardwood j	4 168.2	4 728.0¹	16.9²		6.2¹	—
Newsprint	78.3	70.8	46.0²		6.2¹	—
Other paper	89.0*	48.0	—²		4.2¹	—

e no. in millions. j '000 cu. metres of roundwood equivalent.

4. VEGETABLE OILSEEDS AND OILS

	Production		Exports		Imports	
Cocoa	4.00*	4.67			0.34	0.17
Castor seed					0.80	0.03
Copra					0.39	—
Coconut oil					0.09	—
Cottonseed oil					0.02	0.05
Groundnuts					0.02	0.02
Linseed	2.00*	0.50²	0.01		0.21	0.37
Linseed oil					0.21	0.08
Olive oil					1.20	na¹
Palm oil	60.00		0.70²	—¹		
Rapeseed					0.01	0.05
Soya bean oil					0.16	0.05
Sunflower seed	43.67	69.00			12.26	
Sunflower seed oil						

n incl. other minor vegetable oils.

5. LIVESTOCK‡, ANIMAL PRODUCTS, etc.

	Production		Exports		Imports	
Chickens d	3 066.3	963.0²			na	
Cattle d	3 065.3	2 494.7			111.2	35.1
dairy cows d	1 023.0		0.1			
Goats d	1 442.0*	800.0¹			37.6	na
Sheep d	6 483.7*	6 034.3*				
Horses d	541.7*	466.0			8.8	0.2
Pigs d	1 210.0	858.5*	0.9	1.0	4.0	4.4
Meat‡: A	222.4*	168.5²	0.2		0.1	1.1
B	22.2*	7.01				
Butter	5.0	11.0²			na	
Cheese	9.3	na				
Eggs	24.0	32.51*	0.91*		0.3²	na¹
Milk	877.1b	155.0b	120.9		28.9	19.7
Hides/skins	5.7	5.4				
Wool	11.2*	9.3*	1.2q	0.31	2.4q	0.6

a million $ U.S. d no. in thousands. p incl. fish landed by foreign vessels.
q undressed skins only.

6. FIBRES, TEXTILES, etc.

	Production		Exports		Imports	
Cotton lint					1.0*	0.31
Cotton seed	1.0*	0.7	0.1	0.1	3.5	
Flax fibre	3.8*	3.7	0.2	1.0	7.4	3.6
Hemp fibre					4.0	
Jute					292.7	na
Rubber, natural						
Silk f	27.5¹	na				
Cotton: yarn	11.5*	5.8*n	0.01		2.0	na
woven fabrics		na				
Rayon, fibre/yarn	4.7	3.8	0.70²	—¹	1.4	na

continued

*na: data not available. — negligible or nil. 1 one year only. 2 two year average. * estimate. ‡ see appendix. † re-exports. q non-sparkling wines only.*

COLOMBIA

Colombia is one of the more democratically stable republics of South America. Progress has recently been made towards industrialization and diversification to alleviate the problems of a one-product economy.

AREA: 1 138 914 sq. km. (439 735 sq. miles)

LAND USE: (percentage of total)

	1960	1949
Arable and orchard	4.4	2.2
Permanent meadow and pasture	12.8	2.2
Forest and woodland	61.0	30.6
City areas, waste and other land	21.8	4.8

POPULATION: 19 191 000 (1967 estimate)
Largest city: BOGOTA, capital; population: 2 066 131 (city proper, 1967)
Total working population: 3 755 609

Distribution of working population (1951)

U.N. group no.		Percentage
0	Agriculture, forestry, fishing and hunting	53.9
1	Mining and quarrying	1.3
2/3	Manufacturing	12.3
4	Construction	3.5
5	Electricity, gas, water and sanitary services	0.3
6	Commerce	5.4
7	Transport, storage and communications	3.5
8	Services	15.9
9	Others	3.6

		Year(s)
Life expectancy at birth (years): male	44.2	1950–2 av.
female	46.4	1950–2 av.
Infant mortality (per '000)	82.4*	1965
Crude birth rate (per '000)	42.5*	1960–5 av.
Crude death rate (per '000)	13*	1960–5 av.
Accidental deaths (per 100 000 population)	11.4*	1965
caused by motor vehicles	32.4*	1965
Population per physician	2 470	1965
Population per hospital bed	400	1966
School enrolment: age 5–19 years (percentage)	61	1963–4 av.
age over 19 years (per 100 000 population)	207	1963–4 av.

COMMUNICATIONS

		Year(s)
Motor vehicles in use ('000s): private	119.1	1963–5 av.
commercial	104.6	1963–5 av.
Railway track (km.)	3 435	1964
Mail per capita: domestic	3	1959–60 av.
foreign received	0.2	
foreign sent	2.5	1967
Telephones (per '000 urban population)	183	1963–5 av.
Radio receivers (per '000 population)	16.4	1963–5 av.
Television sets (per '000 population)	54	1962–3 av.
Daily newspapers (per '000 population)		

FINANCE

Currency unit: The Colombian peso

Exchange rates	1965a	1960	1950a	1938b
Per $ U.S.	13.51	6.7	2.038	1.755
Per £ sterling	37.728	18.76	5.709	8.073

		Year(s)
National Income (million $U.S.)	4 279	1965
G.N.P. per capita ($ U.S.)	280	1966
Rate of increase of G.N.P. per capita	2.1	1960–3 av.
Foreign trade (percentage of G.D.P.)	18	1963–5 av.

a principal selling rate. b selling rate.

TRADING

	1965	1955	1938
Total trade (in million $ U.S.)			
Exports (f.o.b)	539	580	81
Imports (c.i.f.)	454	669	89

Main trading partners (percentage of total value)

Exports	1965	1955	Imports	1965	1955
U.S.A.	47	74	U.S.A.	47	63
Germany F.R.	12	5	Germany F.R.	11	10
Netherlands	5	1	U.K.	5	4
Trin./Tob.	5	2	Canada	4	3
Spain	4	1	Japan	4	1
U.K.	4	4	Sweden	3	2
Sweden	4	2	Spain	2	—

Distribution of trade (percentage of total value)

Exports	1965	1938
Coffee	64	65
Crude materials and fuels	21	23
Imports		
Manufactured goods	64 (9)	70 (10)
(road motor vehicles)		
Chemicals	16	12
Crude materials and fuels	10	10
Food	5	17

PRODUCTION, EXPORTS AND IMPORTS

Years: **1963–5 average** and **1953–5 average**   Units: '000 metric tons unless otherwise indicated

1. CEREALS, etc.

	Production		Exports		Imports	
Barley	85.7*	50.0²	—		1.9	
Cassava	1 882.0	734.0				
Maize (corn)	1 047.0*	894.3	0.8		1.1	
Millet/sorghum						
Oats					6.8	
Potatoes	827.0*	600.3	1.2	0.6	2.8	
Rice	590.0	297.0	1.1	6.3	6.1	
Sweet potatoes/yams					0.3	
Wheat	110.0* / 107.3*	150.7*		141.5	43.1	

2. FRUIT, etc.

	Production	Exports	Imports
Apples	811.0*	—	0.8
Bananas	15.01*	209.2 / 200.5	
Coconuts			
Grapes			
Raisins			0.1²
Tomatoes	42.3*		0.3
Wine b		0.2¹	6.6 / 9.7

3. BEVERAGES, FOREST PRODUCTS, etc.

	Production		Exports	Imports
Cocoa	16.7	13.7*ⁿ		9.9
Coffee	474.2	404.9*	363.6 / 365.0	
Sugar: cane	13 945.0*			8.8
raw	1 041.0*	260.7*p	58.3 / 10.0	6.4
Tobacco: leaf	50.0	25.0*	12.8 / 4.9	
cigars	17 645.0c	531.3e		0.4
cigarettes	22.1	32.1*		
tobacco/snuff	59.4*	55.1*		
Softwood j	20.0¹	56.0²		
Hardwood j	25 310.0¹	7 612.0²	41.1	
Wood pulp	13.5*²	5.3*		1.1
Newsprint	49.7b			14.5
Other paper	110.0²	15.3	15.9¹ / 30.0	0.2¹ / 0.9

b '000 hectolitres. e no. in millions.

4. VEGETABLE OILSEEDS AND OILS

	Production		Exports	Imports
Castor oil	0.50*	3.00¹	1.9	0.03
Copra	na	na		41.03
Coconut oil	129.30	48.00*		1.71q
Cottonseed	na	294.0¹		0.83
Cottonseed oil	na	1 222.5²		0.45
Linseed oil	0.12	1 824.0¹		0.73
Olive oil	0.55			0.27
Palm oil	0.45			8.54
Rapeseed oil	0.01			
Rapeseed	0.01			
Sesame seed	47.20	10.00¹		
Soya beans	40.70	na		
Soya bean oil	6.21			0.92
Tung oil	0.03²			na

q incl. palm kernel oil.

5. LIVESTOCK‡, ANIMAL PRODUCTS, etc.

	Production		Exports		Imports	
Chickens d	24 166.7*ⁿ	14 690.5²	20.4	2.4	0.2²	
Cattle d	15 191.7*	11 994.0¹				7.9
dairy cows d	5 681.0*	na				
Goats d	388.0*	na			1.5	
Sheep d	1 011.0*	1 222.5²				
Pigs d	2 475.0*	1 824.0¹				0.2
Horses d	1 101.0*					
Meat‡ 'A'	443.3*					
Meat‡ 'B'	476.0c / 17 645.0c	12 767.3e				
Eggs	22.1	32.1*				
Fish	59.4*	55.1*	0.8	0.41*	1.1	
Milk	1 942.0	1 892.0¹			14.1	3.41*
Hides/skins		16.7b			1.2	9.9*
Wool		1.0¹			3.3*	0.9

d no. in thousands. n incl. ducks, geese and turkeys. p in addition, panela, 637 (1963–5 av.) and 567 (1953–5 av.). e no. in millions. j '000 cu. metres of roundwood equivalent.

continued

PRODUCTION, EXPORTS AND IMPORTS continued

5. LIVESTOCK‡, ANIMAL PRODUCTS, etc.

	Production		Exports		Imports	
Chickens d	457 850*ⁿ	na			na	
Cattle d	43 000*	na			na	
Goats d	54 000*	39 590*	55*	32*	na	
Sheep d	54 000*	39 590*	7*	na	na	
Horses d	65 800*	7 220*			na	
Pigs d	198 300*	95 250*	1 634*	493*	na	
Bacon/ham	11 780*				na	
Eggs	na	na	39*	26*	na	
Fish	na	2 237*			na	
Milk	2 790*		1*	—	3*	
Wool	46*	28*	14*	10*	1*	

d no. in thousands. n incl. ducks, geese and turkeys.

The keeping of pigs is encouraged, principally for the production of fertilizer, and other animals are kept for draught purposes. Some sheep are bred for wool. Land which can be cultivated is rarely used for grazing which gives a lower output of calories per acre. Fishing is growing in importance. Sea fishing is becoming mechanized and extending its range, and fresh-water fish ponds are receiving more attention.

6. FIBRES, TEXTILES, etc.

	Production		Exports		Imports	
Agaves (sisal etc.)	1 157*	695²*	—	—	7*	51*
Cotton lint			4*		136*	
Flax fibre			3*	—	—	
Hemp fibre			1*	—	8*	
Jute	390*		3²*	—	47*	53*
Rubber: natural	—	—			136*	
synthetic	—	—			1*	
Silk f	7 500*	4 200*	2 110*	1 133*		
Cotton: yarn						
woven fabrics	488*		67²*			
Rayon, fibre/yarn	na	na	na			
Wool, yarn	na	na	na			

f metric tons.

Silk is the most long-standing of China's textile industries and sericulture is still practised though it is in decline. Cotton growing is increasing.

7. FUEL AND POWER

	Production		Exports	Imports
Coal	270 000 b	190 000 q	na	na
Electricity h,i		10 100		
Oil, crude n	8 687	970	—	186
Petroleum, refined n	7 730	1 270	na	na
Uranium f				

f metric tons. h million kWh. q 1958 figure. t thermal and hydro. b 1967 figure.

China has large resources of coal much of which is easily mined. Oil is also present in considerable quantities though it has only recently been exploited to any extent. Despite great hydro-electric potential most of the electricity is generated thermally because the development costs are less.

8. IRON AND STEEL

	Production		Exports	Imports
Iron ore		5 060*ᵐ		
Pig iron	17 962*	3 235*	na	na
Steel ingots/castings	13 638*	2 284*	na	na

m metal content.

9. NON-FERROUS MINERALS AND METALS

	Production		Exports		Imports	
Gold k, ore m	60	100*	na		na	
Silver k, ore m	800	320*	na		na	
Asbestos, fibre	115*	na	na		na	
Aluminium: bauxite a	406*	na	na		na	
alumina	200*	na	na		na	
aluminium	100	2*p	na		na	
Antimony, ore m	15*	11*	na		na	
Cobalt	na	na	na		na	
Copper: ore m	90*	8*	na		na	
metal	100*	9*	na		na	
Lead: ore m	100*	9*	na		na	
metal	96*	14*	na		na	
Magnesium/salts	na	na	na		na	
Manganese, ore	1 000*	1*g	na		na	
Mercury f	896*	172¹*	na		na	
Molybdenum f, ore	1 500*ᵐ	11*	na		na	
Tin: ore m	26*	10*	9*		na	
metal	26*	18*	5*		na	
Tungsten, ore	100*	9*	na		na	
Zinc: ore m	91*	9*	na		na	
metal	na	na	na		na	

f metric tons. k '000 fine troy oz. m metal content. b Manchuria only. g primary magnesium only.

China has considerable reserves of iron and is beginning to develop a highly sophisticated steel industry. She is also particularly rich in the non-ferrous minerals. Her deposits of antimony, molybdenum, tin, and tungsten may well be the richest in the world, and many other minerals, including mercury are to be found in considerable amounts.

10. CHEMICALS AND FERTILIZERS

	Production		Exports	Imports
Chemicals			na	na
Fertilizers:				
Phosphates	816*	203*	na	na
Potash	na	—	na	na
Pyrites	599*x	na	na	na
Sulphur: native	122*	—	na	na
recovered	132*	—	na	na

x sulphur content.

The production of chemical fertilizers has developed dramatically in the past thirty years in the service of agriculture, but, despite this and the increasing degree of sophistication achieved, China was still the world's largest importer of chemical fertilizers in 1965. The manufacture of plastics began in 1958 and has developed very rapidly to include a wide range of polythene and cellulose products for farming and industrial use.

11. INDUSTRY

	Production		Exports	Imports
Beer b	640*			
Cement	10 500*	4 530p	950* 7*pq	2pq
Machine tools a	80¹			

a million $ U.S. b '000 hectolitres. p incl. North Korea. q excl. trade with other Communist countries.

Both heavy and light industry are growing in importance. Recently the emphasis has been on industry in the service of agriculture. Tractor production is important, as is cement for construction work, and locomotives for transport. As military aircraft are assembled and some manufactured under contract. Chinese ingenuity has led to a very high level of sophistication in electrical engineering.

---

na: data not available. — negligible or nil. * estimate. ‡ see appendix. † re-exports. 1 one year only. 2 two year average.

COLOMBIA continued

PRODUCTION, EXPORTS AND IMPORTS continued

	Production	Exports	Imports
6. FIBRES, TEXTILES, etc.			
Cotton lint . . .	72.0	14.9	4.6 · · 7.8
Flax fibre	—	—	0.1 · 6.2
Rubber: natural	—	—	7.0
Cotton: yarn	5.5²	0.1†	na · 1.7²
woven fabrics	36.9³	1.0¹	1.0 · na
Rayon, fibre/yarn	10.2	3.0	—
Non-cellulosic			1.3 · na
fibre/yarn	1.6	0.2	— · 1.9
Wool: yarn	2.5²	—	—¹ · 0.1
woven fabrics	5.7²	—²	—²

r million metres.

	Production	Exports	Imports
7. FUEL AND POWER			
Coal 'A' ‡	3 090	—	—
Electricity h: total	5 669		
hydro	3 470²		
thermal	2 199²		
Natural gas j	790	—	—
Oil, crude	9 050	4 740	—
Petroleum, refined	3 760	603	30 · 480¹

h million kWh. i million cu. metres.

	Production	Exports	Imports
8. IRON AND STEEL			
Iron ore	na	—	— · 4
Pig iron	204	—	— · 21
Steel ingots/castings	232	—	—

	Production	Exports	Imports
9. NON-FERROUS MINERALS AND METALS			
Gold k: ore m	336.30	na	—
bullion/coins etc.	398.00	320.41	—
Platinum group			
metals k	18.26	28.40	—
Silver k: ore m	117.30		—
bullion	114.00	4.67	0.09
Asbestos: fibre	na	na	9.97 · 577.33
manufactured	na	2.92	1.03 · 6.80
Mica	na	1.64	0.41
Aluminium: bauxite	na	na	0.12
alumina	na	na	6.95 · 8.01
aluminium	na	na	6.04
Antimony, metal	0.26	na	0.03
Chrome: ore m			
metal	0.42 m	na	5.31
Copper, metal			
Lead: ore	na	0.32	2.05 · 5.73
metal			
Magnesium:	6.67	—	3.80 · na
dolomite	0.22	—	0.05 · 0.05
magnesite	na		0.61 · 0.43
metal/salts	—†		

9. NON-FERROUS MINERALS AND METALS—continued

	Production	Exports	Imports
Mercury f	0.60		5.60 · 3.20
Nickel, metal	0.41		0.39 · 0.08
Tin, metal	1.01		0.18 · 0.04
Titanium minerals			1.80 · 0.71
Zinc: ore	0.08 n	0.14	
metal	21.6²		5.42 · 1.63

f metric tons. k '000 fine troy oz. m metal content. n incl. hydrates.

10. CHEMICALS n AND FERTILIZERS

Organic chemicals:	Production	Exports	Imports
Benzene	na	na	na
Butadiene	na	na	na
Ethylene	na	na	na
Methanol	na	na	2.31
Phenol	na	na	na
Phthalic anhydride	na	na	na
Styrene monomer	na		0.31
Urea			
Inorganic chemicals:			
Ammonia	na	na	0.1¹
Carbon black	na	na	5.3²
Chlorine	na	na	na
Nitric acid	na		0.1¹
Sodium carbonate	21.7	na	7.8¹
Sodium hydroxide	24.7	na	2.3¹
Sulphuric acid	121.0		na
Plastics:			
Polyamides	na		na
Polyethylene	na		na
Polyvinyl chloride	na		2.3²
Fertilizers:			
Phosphates	14.5		16.8 · 1.2
Potash			40.3 · 15.4
Sulphur	4.5		2.7 · 0.5

n data not available for years 1953–5.

11. INDUSTRY

	Production	Exports	Imports
Aircraft a			7.5² · 6.2
Alcoholic beverages			1.3² a · 2.9 a
beer b			
Cement	6 672.0		—
Electrical	1 929.7		9.7
engineering a	96.7²	165.7	—
Railway vehicles a		0.4	43.0 · 44.7
Machine tools a			6.4² · 2.8
Merchant ships g			8.6
Motor vehicles:			27.0 · 7.2
commercial d	1.1 p		48.8² a · 67.1 a
private d	0.7 p		

a million $ U.S. b '000 hectolitres. d no. in thousands. g '000 G.R.T.
p assembly of imported parts.

continued

CONGO, DEMOCRATIC REPUBLIC OF THE CENTRAL AFRICA

The former Belgian Congo was granted independence in 1960, but the departure of the Belgian administrators and technicians left a vacuum which the Congolese were not ready to fill. Tribal and regional rivalries led to the collapse of the administration and the breakaway of the province of Katanga, on which the economy of the country largely depended. U.N. intervention restored order and the country was reunited, and a 'people's republic' was declared in 1964. In 1971 the name of the country was officially changed to Zaïre.

AREA: 2 345 409 sq. km. (895 348 sq. miles)

LAND USE: (percentage of total)
	1959	1955
Arable land and orchard	10.0	20.7
Permanent meadow and pasture	20.9	1.0
Forest and woodland	42.7	42.3
City areas, waste and other land	35.4	26.0

POPULATION: 16 353 000 (African population only) (1967 estimate)
Largest city: KINSHASA, formerly Léopoldville, capital: population: 507 868 (city proper, 1966)

Distribution of working population (1955–7 av.)
Total working population: 6 309 941

U.N. group no.		Percentage
0	Agriculture, forestry, fishing and hunting	86.4
1	Mining and quarrying	1.2
2/3	Manufacturing	3.1
4	Construction	2.5
5	Electricity, gas, water and sanitary services	1.3
6	Commerce	1.6
7	Transport, storage and communications	3.1
8	Services	0.8
9	Others	

		Year(s)
Life expectancy at birth (years): male	37.6	1950–2 av.
female	40.0	
Population per physician	31 250	1966
Population per hospital bed	280	1964
School enrolment: age 5–19 years (percentage)	44	1963–4 av.
age over 19 years (per 100 000 population)	18	1963–5 av.

COMMUNICATIONS

		Year(s)
Motor vehicles in use ('000s): private	42.3	1963–4 av.
commercial	32.4	1958
Railway track (km.)	5 174	
Mail per capita: domestic	2.2 a	1958
foreign received	0.9 a	
foreign sent	0.1*	1967
Telephones (per '000 urban population)	13	1963–5 av.
Radio receivers (per '000 population)	1	1962
Daily newspapers (per '000 population)		

a incl. Rwanda and Burundi.

FINANCE

Currency unit: The Congolese franc

Exchange rates	1965 b	Year
Per $ U.S.	180	1964
Per £ sterling	504	1966

		Year
National Income (million $ U.S.)	1 014	1964
G.N.P. per capita ($ U.S.)	60	1966

b devaluation from 65 to 180 francs per $ U.S. took place in 1963.

TRADING

Total trade (in million $ U.S.)	1965	1955 c	1938 c
Exports (f.o.b.)	336	456	52
Imports (c.i.f.)	321	379	37

Main trading partners (percentage of total value)

Exports	1965	1955 c	1938 c
Belg./Lux.	54	52	47
Italy	11	8	8
U.K.	8	8	5 d
France	4	7	6
Germany F.R.	4	4	1
U.S.A.	4	17	2
Netherlands	3	3	

Imports	1965	1955 c	1938 c
Belg./Lux.	33	37	52
U.S.A.	24	19	7
Germany F.R.	8	6	9
Italy	5	4	4
France	5	4	7
U.K.	4	7	2
South Africa	3	4	

Distribution of trade (percentage of total value)

Exports	1965
Copper	62
Other metals	12
Vegetable oils	8
Diamonds	8
Non-ferrous ores and concentrates	7
Coffee	4

Imports	1965
Manufactured goods (machinery and transport equipment)	52
(textiles and clothing)	12
Food (cereals)	17
Chemicals	8
Crude materials and fuels	5

c 1938 and 1955 figures incl. Ruanda-Urundi (Rwanda and Burundi).
d incl. Germany D.R.

PRODUCTION, EXPORTS AND IMPORTS

Years: 1963–5 average and 1953–5 average   Units: '000 metric tons unless otherwise indicated

	Production		Exports		Imports	
	1963–5	1953–5	1963–5	1953–5	1963–5	1953–5
1. CEREALS, etc.						
Barley					0.2	
Cassava	6 171.3³	7 018.7				
Maize (corn)	235.3*	324.7	11.2		55.4	
Millets/sorghum	43.7*	38.5²	0.5 n			
Potatoes	18.0*	14.3	0.3		3.6	
Rice	57.0*	184.7	0.7²		26.9	
Sweet potatoes/yams	293.3³	336.7				
Wheat	2.7*	4.0			0.2	

n may include some oilseeds.

	Production		Exports		Imports	
2. FRUIT, etc.						
Apples					0.4	1.1
Bananas	49.7*	34.3	13.7	24.2		0.4
Grapes					0.1	0.8
Oranges						0.8
Wine b					9.3	72.0

b '000 hectolitres.

	Production		Exports		Imports	
3. BEVERAGES, FOREST PRODUCTS, etc.						
Cocoa	5.6	2.9	5.0	2.9		
Coffee	61.0*	26.8	35.9	37.5		3.0
Sugar: cane	333.3*	168.3 b				37.5
raw	35.9	17.3	4.4	0.5	2.0*²	4.3
Tea	4.9*	0.7	0.1		2.8	3.8
Tobacco	3.0*	0.2			na	768.4 a
cigarettes e	2 808.0	2 686.0	149.0²	203.5	6.6²	5.5
Hardwood j	10 939.5	5 128.3			0.1²	0.8
Wood pulp					1.11	0.8
Newsprint	—*				6.0¹	14.7
Other paper	0.7*					

e no. in millions. q incl. Rwanda and Burundi.
j '000 cu. metres of roundwood equivalent. p from estates only.

	Production		Exports		Imports	
4. VEGETABLE OILSEEDS AND OILS						
Castor seed	1.52					0.03
Castor oil						
Cottonseed	16.70	94.67			1.27	
Cottonseed oil	80.71	126.70	0.08²	0.72	0.11	
Groundnut oil			0.72	0.02	0.38	
Groundnuts	103.27*	118.83 r	2.86¹	6.21	1.20	0.34
Linseed oil					0.01	0.72
Olive oil					0.06	
Palm kernels	196.77	790.67	1.38	73.90	0.01	2.86¹
Palm kernel oil	6.10*	5.23 r	35.85	24.80		
Palm oil			111.06	139.64		
Sesame seed					0.27	
Soya beans	2.00*	0.43			0.10	

r figure possibly incomplete.

	Production		Exports		Imports	
5. LIVESTOCK†, ANIMAL PRODUCTS, etc.						
Chickens d	na		na			3.4
Cattle	1 147.7*	806.7			0.3	
Goats d	2 316.0*	507.0	0.2			0.3
Sheep d	680.5*	537.3			0.3²	
Horses d	1.0*	1.0²				0.1
Pigs d	383.0*	304.3	0.2		10.5	7.1
Bacon/ham					2.2	7.5
Meat† A	2.7*				0.8	1.2
Butter	1.0*				0.1	0.1
Cheese		0.3			0.1	
Eggs	16.0*	na			28.3	7.3
Milk	75.2²	78.4			19.0	
Fish	27.7*	15.0				21.3
Hides/skins	na	0.7	1.3² q			

d no. in thousands. q incl. Rwanda and Burundi.

	Production		Exports		Imports	
6. FIBRES, TEXTILES, etc.						
Agaves (sisal etc.)	0.2*	0.2	0.1	42.6	0.2	
Cotton lint	8.3	47.3	6.1²	4.5		0.1
Rubber, natural	6.7*	9.0	1.9¹	22.2		
Cotton:	na		31.0		na	6.7
woven fabrics	9.4*	72.0*				
Rayon,	na	5.5²			na	2.5
woven fabrics						
f metric tons.						

f metric tons.

	Production		Exports		Imports	
7. FUEL AND POWER						
Coal 'A' ‡	100	480				
Electricity h: total	2 509	1 260				
hydro		1 160				
thermal		100				
Petroleum, refined	na	361 n			158	
Rare earths f	7 t	na	18 200 p	400¹		
Uranium	na	na				

f metric tons. h million kWh. n monazite and bastnaesite.
p radium content only. t monazite only.

	Production		Exports		Imports	
8. IRON AND STEEL						
Pig iron					2	

	Production		Exports		Imports	
NON-FERROUS MINERALS AND METALS						
Diamonds	14 006.67 i	12 747.04 l	19.65 a	19.46 a		
Gold k: ore m	164.70	369.00		371.00		
bullion/coins etc.						
Platinum group metals k	103.27*	0.18¹				
Silver k: ore m	1 371.70	4 529.30				
bullion						
Asbestos, fibre	2.00*				2.23	

a million $ U.S. i '000 carats. k '000 fine troy oz. l '000 carats. m metal content.

continued

---

na: data not available. — negligible or nil. ¹ one year only. ² two year average. * estimate. ‡ see appendix. † re-exports. r from villages only.

na: data not available. — negligible or nil. — negligible or nil. ¹ one year only. ² two year average. * estimate. † re-exports.

t from villages only.

CONGO, DEMOCRATIC REPUBLIC OF THE *continued*

PRODUCTION, EXPORTS AND IMPORTS *continued*

9. NON-FERROUS MINERALS AND METALS—*continued*

	Production	Exports	Imports
Aluminium: bauxite			0.02
alumina			0.07
aluminium			2.84[l]
Bismuth	0.12 0.13q		0.64n
	0.14 0.09	0.46*	0.07
Cadmium			—
Cobalt: ore	7.81m 8.49m		—
metal		8.13[l,p] 260.35p	—[2]
Copper: ore	278.83m 223.36m		—
metal	278.83 223.83	284.00* 229.84	—
Lead: ore	1.26m na		1.18
metal			—
Magnesium: metal			—
metal/salts			1.75
Manganese: ore	319.10 354.44	364.09* 236.06	1.90
metal	6.20m 15.38mq	8.13*[q] 17.65	—
Mercury[f]	1.61 2.78	1.37*[q] 2.64	0.04
Titanium minerals			—
Tungsten: ore	0.22r 1.46q	0.31* 1.24	—
metal	109.41m 92.95m	92.98m 116.36	—
Zinc: ore	55.10 24.59	42.34* 23.01	0.36

f metric tons. m metal content. n exports to U.S.A. only. p incl. cobalt-copper ingots. q incl. Rwanda and Burundi. r incl. tungsten oxide content of tin-tungsten concentrates.

PRODUCTION, EXPORTS AND IMPORTS *continued*

4. VEGETABLE OILSEEDS AND OILS

	Production	Exports	Imports
Castor seed		0.04	0.01
Copra		0.47	—
Groundnuts	7.70*	0.11	0.10
Groundnut oil	na		0.02
Olive oil			—
Palm kernels	7.37	7.22	0.08
Palm kernel oil		0.03	0.05
Palm oil	7.10*	2.64	—

5. LIVESTOCK‡, ANIMAL PRODUCTS, etc.

	Production	Exports	Imports
Cattle[d]	22.3*		—
cows[d]	11.0*		—
Goats[d]	72.0*		—
Sheep[d]	52.0*		—
Pigs[d]	36.0*		0.1
Meat: ‘B’			0.2
Butter			0.2
Cheese			—
Eggs	1.9		5.6
Fish	12.7		3.8
Milk	2.0*	0.1	

d no. in thousands.

6. FIBRES, TEXTILES, etc.

	Production	Exports	Imports
Rubber, natural	0.2*	0.1	—

7. FUEL AND POWER

	Production	Exports	Imports
Electricity[h]: total	42		
hydro	27		
thermal	15		
Oil, thermal	87	83	90[l]
Petroleum, refined			

h million kWh.

9. NON-FERROUS MINERALS AND METALS

	Production	Exports	Imports
Diamonds[l]	5416.30*	na	
Gold[k/m]	3.70	na	
Copper, ore[m]	0.29	na	
Lead, ore[m]	1.77	na	
Tin, ore	0.06m	0.06	0.4
Zinc, ore	4.22m	16.50[l]	2.9

k '000 fine troy oz. l '000 carats. m metal content.

10. CHEMICALS AND FERTILIZERS

Potash—A deposit, thought to be the world's largest, came into production in 1969, and is expected to yield some 500 000 tons per annum when in full production.

11. INDUSTRY

	Production	Exports	Imports
Aircraft[a]			3.6
Alcoholic beverages[b]			1.8
Cement	34.0		50.0
Electrical engineering[a]			
Railway vehicles[a]			5.7
Motor vehicles[a]		0.3	

a million $ U.S. b '000 hectolitres.

CENTRAL AMERICA

COSTA RICA

Costa Rica has been an independent republic since 1821. The population, unlike that of neighbouring countries, is basically of European stock; the land is fertile, and the country economically and politically stable and advanced in the provision of social services.

AREA: 50 900* sq. km. (19 653* sq. miles)

LAND USE: (percentage of total)

	1963	1950
Arable and orchard	12.3	7.0
Permanent meadow and pasture	18.2	12.3
Forest and woodland	58.8	78.2
City areas, waste and other land	10.7	2.5

POPULATION: 1 594 000 (1967 provisional estimate)
Largest city: SAN JOSÉ, capital; population: 349 484 (1966)
Total working population: 395 273 (1963)

Distribution of working population (1963)

U.N. group no.		Percentage
0	Agriculture, forestry, fishing and hunting	49.1
1	Mining and quarrying	0.3
2/3	Manufacturing	11.5
4	Construction	5.9
5	Electricity, gas, water and sanitary services	1.1
6	Commerce	9.8
7	Transport, storage and communications	3.7
8	Services	17.2
9	Others	1.4

		Year(s)
Life expectancy at birth (years): male	61.9	1962–4 av.
female	64.8	
Infant mortality (per '000)	75.0	1965
Crude birth rate (per '000)	45*	1960–5 av.
Crude death rate (per '000)	8.5*	1960–5 av.
Accidental deaths (per 100 000 population) caused by motor vehicles	11.6	1965
due to other causes	31.8	1965
Population per physician	1 200	1967
Population per hospital bed	250	1966
School enrolment: age 5–19 years (percentage)	84[a]	1963–4 av.
age over 19 years (per 100 000 population)	471	1963–5 av.

a excl. private vocational schools; incl. evening courses.

COMMUNICATIONS

		Year(s)
Motor vehicles in use ('000s): private	20.5	1963–5 av.
commercial	10.8	
Railway track (km)	805	1966–7 av.
Telephones (per '000 population)	1.6	1967
Radio receivers (per '000 population)	82	1963–5 av.
Television sets (per '000 population)	22.9	1963–5 av.
Daily newspapers (per '000 population)	77	1964

FINANCE

Currency unit: The colon

Exchange rates	1965[a]	1950[b]	1938
Per $ U.S.	6.62	6.24	5.62
Per £ sterling	18.54	17.48	25.85

		Year(s)
National Income (million $ U.S.)	506	1965
G.N.P. per capita ($ U.S.)	400	1966
Foreign trade (percentage of G.D.P.)	45	1963–5 av.

a export rate. b principal import rate.

TRADING

	1965	1955	1938
Total trade (in million $ U.S.)			
Exports (f.o.b.)	112	81	9
Imports (c.i.f.)	178	87	13

Main trading partners (percentage of total value)

Exports	1965	1955	Imports	1965	1955
U.S.A.	50	55	U.S.A.	40	60
Germany F.R.	12	26	Germany F.R.	10	9
Netherlands	6	3	Japan	10	2
Nicaragua	4	na	France	4	4
El Salvador	4	4	Neths. Antilles	4	1
Guatemala	3	2	U.K.	3	3
Belg./Lux.			Guatemala	3	na

Distribution of trade (percentage of total value)

Exports		1965
Coffee	42	46
Fruit and vegetables (mainly bananas)	26	41
Cattle and beef	5	4
Sugar and preparations	4	1
Fertilizers	3	

Imports		1965
Manufactured goods	67	63
(machinery and transport equipment)	(29)	(27)
Chemicals	18	15
Food	8	13
Mineral fuels	5	6

continued

CONGO, REPUBLIC OF THE

CENTRAL AFRICA

The Republic of the Congo, formerly known as Middle Congo, a territory of French Equatorial Africa, and from 1958 a member state of the French Community, became fully independent in 1960. The Congo has been a member of the Equatorial Customs Union since its foundation in 1959.

AREA: 342 000 sq. km. (132 046 sq. miles)

LAND USE: (percentage of total)

	1963
Arable and orchard	1.8
Permanent meadow and pasture	na
Forest and woodland	47.5
City areas, waste and other land	na

POPULATION: 860 000 (1967 U.N. estimate)
Largest city: BRAZZAVILLE, capital; population: 136 200 (1961/2 census)

		Year(s)
Life expectancy at birth (years): male	37	1960–1 av.
female		
Population per physician	11 640	1966
Population per hospital bed	190	1966
School enrolment: age 5–19 years (percentage)	67	1963–4 av.
age over 19 years (per 100 000 population)	116	1964–5 av.

COMMUNICATIONS

		Year(s)
Railway track (km)	516	1966
Telephones (per '000 urban population)	1*	1963–5 av.
Television sets (per '000 population)	0.4*	1963
Daily newspapers (per '000 population)	0.5	

PRODUCTION, EXPORTS AND IMPORTS Units: '000 metric tons unless otherwise indicated

Note—no data are available for the years 1953–5

	Production	Exports	Imports
1. CEREALS, etc.			
Cassava	783.3*		
Maize (corn)	2.0*		1.1
Potatoes			1.2
Rice	4.0*		
Sweet potatoes/yams	60.0*		
Wheat			9.6
2. FRUIT, etc.			
Apples			0.3[n]
Bananas	5.0*	0.1	
Grapes			0.1
Oranges	2.0*		0.1
Wine[b]		0.1	115.9

b '000 hectolitres. n incl. pears and quince.

FINANCE

Currency unit: The franc CFA

Exchange rates	1965	1960
Per $ U.S.	246.85	246.85
Per £ sterling	691.18	691.18

		Year
National Income (million $ U.S.)	106	1958
G.N.P. per capita ($ U.S.)	120	1966

TRADING

	1965	1960
Total trade (in million $ U.S.)		
Exports (f.o.b.)	47	10
Imports (c.i.f.)	65	43

Main trading partners (percentage of total value)

Exports	1965	Imports	1965
Netherlands	25	France	61
U.K.	23	U.S.A.	6
Germany F.R.	21	Belg./Lux.	6
France	9	Germany F.R.	4
Belg./Lux.	5	Netherlands	3
Israel	3	U.K.	3
South Africa	3	Italy	2

Distribution of trade (percentage of total value)

Exports		1965
Manufactured goods (diamonds)	51	(43)
Crude materials and fuels (hardwood saw and veneer logs)	45	(38)

Imports		1965
Manufactured goods (machinery and transport equipment)	71	(35)
Food	11	
Chemicals	6	
Petroleum products	6	

3. BEVERAGES, FOREST PRODUCTS, etc.

	Production	Exports	Imports
Cocoa	0.8	0.8	
Coffee	0.8*	0.7	
Sugar: cane	323.3*		
raw	28.8		0.1
Tobacco: leaf	0.6*		0.6
cigarettes/snuff	0.6	0.3	
Hardwood[j]	911.0	505.3	
Paper	1 849.0*		3.3

continued

j '000 cu. metres of roundwood equivalent.

---

na: data not available. — negligible or nil. * estimate. 2 two year average. 1 one year only. ‡ see appendix. † re-exports.

COSTA RICA continued

PRODUCTION, EXPORTS AND IMPORTS
Years: 1963–5 average and 1953–5 average Units: '000 metric tons unless otherwise indicated

	Production		Exports		Imports	
1. CEREALS, etc.						
Barley	10.8	9.0*	—	—	—	0.1
Cassava	57.2	30.1*	8.5	—	—	—
Maize (corn)	66.7*	69.5*	—	—	7.3	—
Millets/sorghum	1.3*	3.7*	—	—	0.1	0.12
Rice	17.0*	na	0.2	—	1.8	2.1
Wheat	71.0	35.7*	0.1	0.5	0.4	5.5
2. FRUIT, etc.						
Bananas	506.3	na	29.1	346.9	—	—
Coconuts	5.0*	na	—	—	—	—
Grapes			—	—	—	0.2
Oranges	1.0*	na	—	—	0.52	0.2
Wine b			—	—	2.8	4.3
3. BEVERAGES, FOREST PRODUCTS, etc.						
Cocoa	8.6		8.5	8.6	—	—
Coffee	57.2	63.01	51.3	26.6	—	—
Sugar: cane	1192.7ⁿ		—	—	—	—
Tobacco: leaf	1.3*	3.7*	—	—	0.1	—
cigarettes e	2.01	63.01	—	—	—	0.51
Hardwood j	1996.0*¹	881.0¹	6.62	12.71	1	0.41
Newsprint			—	—	—²	12.13n
Other paper	2.7*²		—	—	4.61	1.72
non-centrifugal sugar 35 (1963–5 av.) and 30 (1953–5 av.)				18.91	3.51
4. VEGETABLE OILSEEDS AND OILS						
Castor oil	1 022.0ⁿ		—	—	0.01	0.02
Coconut oil	2.01	63.01	—	—	0.08	0.03
Cottonseed			0.03	—	1.42	0.27
Cottonseed oil			0.02	—	1.50	0.09
Groundnuts			—	—	0.04	—
Linseed			—	—	0.02	0.07
Linseed oil	7.701		—	—	0.06	0.05
Olive oil			—	—	—	—
Palm kernels	20.00*	1.02p	0.26	—	1.08	—
Palm oil	8.20*	1.462*	0.21	—	0.20	0.11
Soya bean oil			—	—	—	—
5. LIVESTOCK‡, ANIMAL PRODUCTS, etc.						
Chickens d	1886.7*¹	1389.0¹				
Cattle d	1083.7	670.0	11.0	2.6	0.3	0.2
dairy cows d	385.7					
Goats d	2.0*	na				
Sheep d	1.0*	na				
Horses d	101.0*	85.02	6.8	0.51	0.1	—
Pigs d	144.0*	109.02	0.1	—	—	—
Meat‡ 'A'	30.3*	na				
Butter	2.3*p	1.02p	—	—	0.1	0.1
Cheese	37.0*	3.02	—	—	1.4	1.01*
Eggs	3.0	7.0	1.1	—	0.52	14.4
Fish						
Milk	80.0*	146.3p	1.61*	1.61*	5.8	5.62*

b '000 hectolitres. d no. in thousands. e no. in millions. j '000 cu. metres of roundwood equivalent. n in addition, non-centrifugal sugar. p factory produce only. k '000 fine troy oz. m metal content. s incl. imports for re-export.

	Production		Exports		Imports	
6. FIBRES, TEXTILES, etc.						
Abaca	3.1*				—	—
Cotton lint	na	3.7*	—	1.1	—	0.1
Rubber, natural	0.1	4	—	0.1	—	—
Cotton, woven fabrics			—	—	1.71	—
Rayon, woven fabrics			—	—	0.52	—
7. FUEL AND POWER						
Electricity h: total	570	2701				
hydro	492	2401				227
thermal	78	301				1101
Petroleum, refined	—	—	—	—	—	—
9. NON-FERROUS MINERALS AND METALS						
Gold k, ore m	2.30	4.20*	na	na		
Asbestos					0.43	0.09
Aluminium: alumina					0.66	0.09b
manufactured					0.27	12.13n
aluminium					0.10	—
Copper, metal					0.20	—
Lead, metal					1.801	—
Manganese, ore					—	—
Mercury f					—	—
Titanium minerals					0.141	—
10. CHEMICALS n AND FERTILIZERS						
Chemicals			na	na	na	na
Fertilizers:					4.9	—
Potash					0.12	0.1
Sulphur						
11. INDUSTRY						
Aircraft a			na	na	0.2	—
Alcoholic beverages	89.0	45.92			0.6	0.8
beer b	49.3		1.3		1.0a	0.5a
Cement			—	—	63.3	52.3
Electrical engineering a			—	—	10.7	5.02
Machine tools a			—	—	0.3	0.7
Railway vehicles a			—	—	—	0.52
Motor vehicles a			—	—	9.8	5.62

a million $ U.S. b '000 hectolitres.

na: data not available. — negligible or nil. ¹ one year only. ² two year average. * estimate. ‡ see appendix. † re-exports.

CUBA

CARIBBEAN SEA

In 1959 the revolutionary movement led by Dr. Castro overthrew the former dictatorship. Close ties were formed between Cuba and the U.S.S.R. and links with the U.S.A. were severed. Trade with many western countries diminished.

AREA: 114 524 sq. km. (44 206 sq. miles)

POPULATION: 8 033 000 (1967 estimate)
Largest city: LA HABANA (Havana) capital; population: 1 543 900 (1965)

Distribution of working population (1953)
Total working population: 1 972 266

LAND USE: (percentage of total)

	1946
Arable and orchard	17.2
Permanent meadow and pasture	34.0
Forest and woodland	26.1
City areas, waste and other land	22.7

Distribution of working population:

U.N. group no.		Percentage
1	Agriculture, forestry, fishing and hunting	41.5
2/3	Mining and quarrying	0.5
	Manufacturing	16.6
4	Construction	3.3
5	Electricity, gas, water and sanitary services	0.8
6	Commerce	11.5
7	Transport, storage and communications	5.3
8	Services	20.1
9	Others	0.5

			Year(s)
Infant mortality (per '000)	38.4*	35*	1965
Crude birth rate (per '000)	8.5*		1960–5 av.
Crude death rate (per '000)			1960–5 av.
Accidental deaths (per 100 000 population) caused by motor vehicles	10.1*		1965
due to other causes	21.1*		1965
Population per physician	1180		1965
Population per hospital bed	180a		1966
School enrolment: age 5–19 years (percentage)	73		1963–4 av.
age over 19 years (per 100 000 population)	340		1963–5 av.

a government hospitals only.

COMMUNICATIONS

			Year(s)
Railway track (km.)			1965
Motor vehicles in use ('000s): private	162*		1965
commercial	103.7a		1967
Telephones (per '000 urban population)	5976.a		
Radio receivers (per '000 population)	181		1963–5 av.
Television sets (per '000 population)	73.4		1963–5 av.
Daily newspapers (per '000 population)	88		1961

a in addition the large sugar estates operate 12 135 km. of track connecting them with the main lines.

FINANCE
Currency unit: The Cuban peso

Exchange rates	1965	1960	1950	1938
Per $ U.S.	1.0	1.02	1.0	1.02
Per £ sterling	2.8	2.86	2.801	4.692

		Year
National Income (in million $ U.S.)	2 500*	1966
G.N.P. per capita ($ U.S.)	320*	1966

TRADING

Total trade (in million $ U.S.)	1965	1960	1955	1938
Exports (f.o.b.)	686	594	143
Imports (c.i.f.)	866	575	106

PRODUCTION, EXPORTS AND IMPORTS
Years: 1963–5 average and 1953–5 average Units: '000 metric tons unless otherwise indicated

	Production		Exports		Imports	
1. CEREALS, etc.						
Barley	—	—	—	—	48.6*	—²
Cassava	203.3*	na	—	—	153.7*	0.1
Maize (corn)	194.3*	204.7*	11.2	—	0.12	0.7
Millets/sorghum	26.3*	na	—	—	20.3*	1.3
Oats	—	—	3.12	—	41.5*	34.62
Potatoes	87.3*	na	0.3	—	251.8*	186.7
Rice	192.7	171.7*	—	—	422.1*	50.1
Sweet potatoes/yams	276.7*	312.52	—	—		
Wheat	—	—	—	—		
2. FRUIT, etc.						
Apples	—	—	4.8	—	2.0*	4.4
Bananas	63.3	na	0.3	—	—	—
Coconuts	10.01*e	na	—	—	0.7*¹	2.1*
Grapes	—	—	—	—	—	—
Lemons	7.7	57.3*	—	—		
Oranges	84.7	7.7*	3.12	—		
Other citrus fruit	100.0*	87.7*	31.0	—		
Pineapples	108.0*	na	—	—	7.0*	13.0*
Tomatoes						
Wine b						
3. BEVERAGES, FOREST PRODUCTS, etc.						
Cocoa	1.9	42.9	0.6	—	2.5*²	—
Coffee	30.5		1.4	—		
Sugar: cane	41 618.0	43 950.01	0.6*¹	4 756.1		
raw	4 830.9	4 719.3*	12.5*	19.1		0.47s
Tobacco: leaf	50.1	47.6*	1.8	342.7i		197.00
cigarettes	15 941.0e	9 146.0e		238.02q		
tobacco/snuff				367.4¹		
Softwood j	15.01	23.3*	—	—¹	229.02	—
Hardwood j	2 179.0*¹	809.0*	—	25.5*²	41.91	—
Wood pulp			—²	6.0*	17.01	na
Newsprint	6.0*²		—	—	13.21	37.61
Other paper	74.0*²		na	—		
4. VEGETABLE OILSEEDS AND OILS						
Castor oil					na	0.042
Coconut oil					2.181*	2.08*
Cottonseed	8.00*	na	2	—		
Cottonseed oil	10.03	3.97*	—	—	13.612	0.282
Groundnuts					0.50*	2.7
Groundnut oil					2.43*	1.152
Linseed oil					4.071*	6.96*
Olive oil						0.062
Palm oil						0.012
Palm kernel oil						
Soya beans					25.501	—
Soya bean oil					0.551*	2.25*
Sunflower seed oil					35.10*	—
5. LIVESTOCK‡, ANIMAL PRODUCTS, etc.						
Chickens d	7 467.0*n				4.8*	0.4
Cattle d	6 058.7*¹	4 150.01			1.0*	—
Goats d	187.0*	na	—	—		
Sheep d						
Horses d	496.7*n	na	2	—		
Pigs d	1 767.0*¹	1 352.52				
Meat‡ 'A'	235.7*	na				
Butter	4.8*	na	—	—	0.1	0.1
Cheese	4.0*p	2.0*p	—	—	5.5	0.12
Eggs	3.7*p	2.3*p	—	—	4.2*	0.3
Fish	13.5*	na	—	—	1.2*	0.9
Hides/skins	37.4	17.5	0.8	—	34.0	4.2
Milk	1 190.7*n	701.3*	1.61*	—	163.3*	9.31*
						73.4
						2.1

d no. in thousands. e no. in millions. f metric tons. k '000 fine troy oz. m metal content. p factory produce only. q exports to U.S.A. only. s incl. imports for re-export.

	Production		Exports		Imports	
6. FIBRES, TEXTILES, etc.						
Agaves (henequen)	10.0*	11.7*	7.0	—	6.5*	—²
Cotton lint	2.7*	na	na	—	13.9*	6.5*
Jute	—	na	—	—	2.8*	7.9
Rubber, natural	13.92*	9.3	na	—	1.82	1.0*
Cotton: yarn	1.4	na	0.52	—	1.02	5.32
woven fabrics					3.81	na
Rayon, fibre/yarn						
Non-cellulosic fibre/yarn					0.3	na
7. FUEL AND POWER						
Coal 'A' ‡					55	37
Coke	3 336	2 0001			24	23
Electricity h: total	na	201				
hydro	na	1 9801				
thermal	40	501			3 553	4601
Oil, crude	3 566	4401	10	—	1 150	1 7201
Petroleum, refined h million kWh.						
8. IRON AND STEEL						
Iron ore			25	—	26	—
Pig iron						
Iron/steel scrap						
9. NON-FERROUS MINERALS AND METALS						
Gold k, ore m	1.00					
Platinum group						
metals						
Silver k, ore m	197.00					
bullion						
Asbestos						
Aluminium					9.332	9.332
Antimony, metal	367.4¹		81.00	—	6.392	6.392
Chrome, ore	73.22m	39.99	16.40	—	0.142	0.142
Cobalt, ore	16.96m		15.49	—		
Copper, ore	0.66m		5.99*	—	0.01	1.75
metal	0.03m				3.112	0.322
Lead: ore					2.772	
metal					0.182	0.182
Magnesium, ore						
metal/salts					0.64	0.64
Manganese, ore	312.33		75.54	—		
Mercury f	13.16		23.16	—	9.30i	9.30i
Nickel, ore	17.62				0.07s	0.07s
Tin, metal	0.34		0.21	—	0.29	0.29
Zinc: ore						
metal						
10. CHEMICALS n AND FERTILIZERS						
Chemicals			288.52	—		
Fertilizers:						
Potash					39.4	21.9
Pyrites x	13.9*	48.6*			48.52	11.8
Sulphur	1.0*					
11. INDUSTRY						
Aircraft a					9.51	9.51
Manufacturing					1.61a	1.61a
Alcoholic beverages: beer b	973.0	1 189.7			33.3*	178.3
Cement	804.0*	417.3			23.21	9.52
Electrical engineering a					28.0	
Merchant ships a					57.71	35.5
Motor vehicles a						

a million $ U.S. b '000 hectolitres. f metric tons. g '000 G.R.T. x sulphur content.

Main trading partners (percentage of total value)

Exports	1965	1955	1938	Imports	1965	1955	1938
U.S.S.R.	47	6	na	U.S.S.R.	49	na	na
China P.R.	15	na	na	China P.R.	14	na	na
Czechoslovakia	5	2	1	U.K.	6	5	4
Spain	5			Spain	5	5	1
Germany D.R.	3			Czechoslovakia	4	3	1
Bulgaria				Germany D.R.	3	2	4f
Japan				France	2	1	3
				f incl. German F.R.			

Distribution of trade (percentage of total value)

Exports	1964	1955	1938
Sugar	88	80	70*
Tobacco	4	7	9

Imports	1964	1955	1938
Manufactured goods (machinery and transport equipment)	52	na	na
Food	22(31)	(13*)	(12)
Crude materials and fuels (petroleum and products)	14	(8*)	(4)
Chemicals	9	na	na

na: data not available. — negligible or nil. ¹ one year only. ² two year average. * estimate. ‡ see appendix. † re-exports.

continued

CYPRUS

Cyprus, formerly a British colony, became an independent republic in 1960 after pressure by the Greek Cypriots. There followed several years of conflict between the Greek and Turkish factions of the population. The U.N. supplied peace-keeping forces, and in 1968 the two parties met to try to find a more peaceful method of solving their problems. Cyprus remains within the Commonwealth and Britain retains rights to certain service bases.

AREA: 9 251 sq. km. (3 572 sq. miles)

LAND USE: (percentage of total)

	1965	1955
Arable and orchard	46.7	46.9
Permanent meadow and pasture	10.0	10.1
Forest and woodland	18.5	18.5
City areas, waste and other land	24.8	24.5

POPULATION: 614 000 (1967 estimate)
Largest city: NICOSIA, capital; population: 106 000 (1966)

Distribution of working population (1960)
Total working population: 235 358

U.N. group no.		Percentage
0	Agriculture, forestry, fishing and hunting	40.3
1	Mining and quarrying	2.3
2/3	Manufacturing	13.7
4	Construction	8.7
5/8	Services, incl. electricity, gas, water and sanitary services	14.7
7	Commerce	6.9
	Transport, storage and communications	4.1
9	Others	9.3

		Year(s)
Life expectancy at birth (years): male	63.6	1948–50 av.
female	68.8	
Infant mortality (per '000)	24.8*	1965
Crude birth rate (per '000)	24.4*	1965
Crude death rate (per '000)	6.1*	1965
Population per physician	1 320	1965
Population per hospital bed	190	1966
School enrolment: age 5–19 years (percentage)	55a	1963–4 av.
age over 19 years (per 100 000 population)	82	1963–5 av.

a public education only, and excluding Turkish schools.

COMMUNICATIONS

		Year(s)
Motor vehicles in use ('000s): private	31.0	1963–5 av.
commercial	11.5	
Mail per capita: domestic	22	1963–5 av.
foreign received	24.4*	1964–5 av.
foreign sent	25	
Telephones (per '000 urban population)	18	1967
Radio licences (per '000 population)	208	1963–5 av.
Television licences (per '000 population)	17.1	1963–5 av.
Daily newspapers (per '000 population)	180.5	1963–5 av.

FINANCE
Currency unit: The Cyprus pound, at par with the pound sterling

Exchange rates	1965	1960	1950	1938
Per $ U.S.	0.357	0.357	0.357	0.215

	1965		1955
National Income (million $ U.S.)	370		
G.N.P. per capita ($ U.S.)	690		
Rate of increase of G.N.P. per capita	2		
Foreign trade (percentage of G.D.P.)	55		

TRADING

Total trade (in million $ U.S.)	1965	1960	1955
Exports (f.o.b.)	71	52	
Imports (c.i.f.)	148	85	

Main trading partners (percentage of total value)

Exports	1965	1955	Imports	1965	1955
U.K.	31	27	U.K.	33	50
Germany F.R.	27	35	Italy	10	5
Spain	9	na	Germany F.R.	8	4
Netherlands	6	6	France	6	3
U.S.S.R.	5	na	Netherlands	5	3
Italy	4	3	Greece	3	3
Israel	3	1	U.S.A.	3	4

Distribution of trade (percentage of total value)

Exports	1955a	1955a
Food (fruit and vegetables)	48 (37)	30 (16)
Copper ore and concentrates	24 (8)	31
Beverages and tobacco	8	4

Imports		
Manufactured goods (machinery and transport equipment) (textiles and clothing)	59 {24}{11}	64 {26}{11}
Food	16	13
Chemicals	9	6
Petroleum products	6	8

a These are percentages of national exports† which comprised 94% of general exports in 1955.

PRODUCTION, EXPORTS AND IMPORTS Units: '000 metric tons unless otherwise indicated
Years: 1963–5 average and 1953–5 average

	Production		Exports		Imports	
1. CEREALS, etc.						
Barley	97.3	63.3	43.6	13.9		0.6
Maize (corn)		1.02a			17.7	0.8
Millets/sorghum						
Oats	1.7	2.7			9.8	3.6
Potatoes	126.0	67.0	87.0	41.1	3.3	2.3
Rice					3.6	2.3
Wheat	67.0	66.7	156.0	11.0	22.4	38.4
2. FRUIT, etc.						
Apples	4.0	1.0			1.1	0.4
Bananas						
Figs			0.2			
Grapes	96.1	100.0	6.9	5.8		
Lemons	117*	75.0	8.3	2.4		
Oranges	60.0*	33.3	51.9	18.4		
Other citrus fruit	22.0*	8.7	18.3	5.3		
Olives	14.3	10.0				
Raisins	5.8	6.8	5.8			
Tomatoes	12.0	5.7	156.0	94.7		0.1
Wine b	226.7	151.3				

b '000 hectolitres.

	Production		Exports		Imports	
3. BEVERAGES, FOREST PRODUCTS, etc.						
Coffee					1.0	0.4
Sugar, raw					14.3	6.4
Tea	1.5	0.7	0.7		0.1	0.5
Tobacco: leaf			0.7		0.2	0.12
cigars						
cigarettes	618.0c		na	0.7a		
tobacco/snuff						
Softwood j	45.0	41.3	0.2		52.9	64.6
Hardwood j	5.2	7.1			1.9	0.5
Newsprint					1.4	0.4
Other paper					4.9a	2.8*

j '000 cu. metres of roundwood equivalent.
continued

na: data not available. — negligible or nil. * estimate. 1 one year only. 2 two year average. † re-exports.

PRODUCTION, EXPORTS AND IMPORTS continued

	Production		Exports		Imports	
6. FIBRES, TEXTILES, etc.						
Cotton lint		0.7	0.3			
Hemp fibre		0.1				
Rubber, natural					0.2	
Cotton yarn					0.41	
Rayon					0.9	0.9
woven fabrics					0.5n	0.3
Wool, yarn			1*		0.2	

n incl. synthetic piece goods.

	Production	Exports	Imports
7. FUEL AND POWER			
Coal/coke			3
Electricity h i	320		160¹
Petroleum, refined	50		350

h million kWh. i thermal.

	Production	Exports	Imports
8. IRON AND STEEL			
Steel ingots/castings			1

	Production		Exports		Imports	
9. NON-FERROUS MINERALS AND METALS						
Gold k, ore m						
Silver k, bullion						
Asbestos: fibre	15.53	14.06	14.24	13.62	10.28	0.21
manufactured	na	na			60.67	1.07
Aluminium	4.30n				3.84	2.57
Chrome, ore	na		3.24	8.71	0.15a	0.02a
Cobalt, ore	na				0.27	

continued

	Production		Exports		Imports	
9. NON-FERROUS MINERALS AND METALS—continued						
Copper: ore	20.87m	24.24m	24.14	24.24m	0.05	0.08
metal			204.14	4.03	0.07	0.03
Lead, metal						
Magnesium					0.01	
Magnesite, natural						
Manganese, ore	na		0.04		0.01	0.01
Tin, metal					0.06	
Zinc, metal						

k '000 fine troy oz. m metal content.
a million $ U.S.

	Production		Exports		Imports	
10. CHEMICALS n AND FERTILIZERS						
Chemicals					na	
Fertilizers:						
Potash	413.5x	555.2*x			0.4	
Pyrites	859.4				1.7	1.0
Sulphur	813.3					

n data not available for years 1953–5. x sulphur content.

	Production		Exports		Imports	
11. INDUSTRY						
Aircraft a					0.7	
Alcoholic beverages: beet a	54.0		3.4a	1.4a		
spirits b	9.3? p					
Cement	88.7				70.3	85.3
Electrical engineering a					7.1	5.1²
Motor vehicles a					8.5	5.4²

a million $ U.S. b '000 hectolitres. p production for home consumption only, 1967.

CZECHOSLOVAKIA

The Czechoslovak state was broken up for the benefit of Germany, Poland, and Hungary in 1938 and re-established after the war. In 1948 a communist government was formed. A programme of liberalization in 1968 led to Soviet occupation which caused the abandonment of most of the changes planned. Czechoslovakia is a member of Comecon.

AREA: 127 870 sq. km. (49 370 sq. miles)

LAND USE: (percentage of total)

	1965	1948
Arable and orchard	42.1	43.1
Permanent meadow and pasture	13.9	15.9
Forest and woodland	39.2	31.8
City areas, waste and other land		9.2

POPULATION: 14 305 000 (1967 estimate)
Largest city: PRAHA (Prague) capital; population: 1 022 621 (1965)

Distribution of working population (1950)
Total working population: 5 811 724

U.N. group no.		Percentage
0	Agriculture, forestry, fishing and hunting	38.0
1	Mining and quarrying	2.7
2/3	Manufacturing	28.3
4	Construction	0.7
5	Electricity, gas, water and sanitary services	0.5
6	Commerce	8.1
7	Transport, storage and communications	5.8
8	Services	10.7
9	Others	0.6

		Year(s)
Life expectancy at birth (years): male	67.3	1966
female	73.6	
Infant mortality (per '000)	25.5	1965
Crude birth rate (per '000)	16.4	1965
Crude death rate (per '000)	10.0	1965
Accidental deaths (per '000) caused by motor vehicles	15.4	1965
due to other causes	35.8	1965
Population per physician	540	1966
Population per hospital bed	87	1966
School enrolment: age 5–19 years (percentage)	100	1963–4 av.
age over 19 years (per 100 000 population)	1 005	1964–5 av.

COMMUNICATIONS

		Year(s)
Motor vehicles in use ('000s): private	na	1963–5 av.
commercial	134.8	
Railway track (km.)	13 197	1965
Telephones (per '000 urban population)	263	1967
Radio licences (per '000 population)	133.8	1963–5 av.
Television licences (per '000 population)	111.1	1963–5 av.
Daily newspapers (per '000 population)	276.7*	1962–4 av.

FINANCE
Currency unit: The koruna (or crown), which is pegged to the rouble at 1.8 korunas per rouble.

Exchange rates	1965a	1960	1950	1938
Per $ U.S.	7.22	7.22	7.17	na
Per £ sterling	20.22	20.22	20.16	na

		Year(s)
National Income (million $ U.S.)	14 000*	1966
G.N.P. per capita ($ U.S.)	1 010*	1966
Rate of increase of G.N.P. per capita	0.9	1960–4 av.

a buying rate (selling rate: 20.1 per £1). There is also a tourist rate, introduced in 1964, of 44.2 korunas per £1.

TRADING

Total trade (in million $ U.S.)	1965	1956	1937
Exports (f.o.b.)	2 688	1 387	418
Imports (f.o.b.)	2 673	1 186	383

Main trading partners (percentage of total value)

Exports	1965	1956	1937	Imports	1965	1956	1937
U.S.S.R.	38	31	15f	U.S.S.R.	36	33	17f
Germany D.R.	10	10		Germany D.R.	11	8	6
Poland	9	4	2	Hungary	6	6	3
Germany F.R.	5	3	d	Germany F.R.	6	5	2
Hungary	5	3		Bulgaria	3	3	1
Romania	3			Romania	3	3	d

Distribution of trade (percentage of total value)

Exports	1965	1956
Machinery and transport equipment	43	25
Crude materials	25	39
Food	5	6
Imports		
Crude materials	40	54
Machinery and transport equipment	30	13
Food	16	29

d see Germany D.R. f incl. Germany F.R.

PRODUCTION, EXPORTS AND IMPORTS Units: '000 metric tons unless otherwise indicated

	Production		Exports		Imports	
4. VEGETABLE OILSEEDS AND OILS						
Coconut oil					0.02	0.27
Cottonseed oil		1.00				1.03
Groundnuts					na	2.08
Groundnut oil					3.18	0.62
Linseed		0.67		0.53	0.06	0.08
Linseed oil		1.30		0.32	0.01	0.04
Olive oil	2.33		0.10		0.02	na
Palm kernel oil			0.44			0.03
Palm oil	0.10	0.17	0.02		1.44	0.03
Rapeseed					0.51	0.40
Sesame seed					0.81	0.09a
Soya beans					1.17	na
Sunflower seed oil						

	Production		Exports		Imports	
5. LIVESTOCK‡, ANIMAL PRODUCTS, etc.						
Chickens d	1 972.7	962.3				
Cattle d	32.7	35.0¹				
Goats d	206.0	180.0				
Sheep d	391.0	341.0¹				
Pigs d	2.0*	4.0¹			0.1	0.2
Horses d	9.7	7.0				
Bacon/ham					0.1	0.1
Meat: 'A'	5.6*	na			2.7	2.7
'B'					0.1	0.1
Butter	3.0	2.7	0.2		0.4	0.2
Cheese	3.4*	1.1²	0.1		0.8	0.3
Eggs		4.0			0.3²	
Fish	12.3	na			2.2	na
Hides/skins			0.8	0.3²	15.7	5.3
Wool	0.3	na	0.3		16.7	5.3²

d no. in thousands.
continued

na: data not available. — negligible or nil. * estimate. 1 one year only. 2 two year average. ‡ see appendix. † re-exports.

DAHOMEY

Dahomey, formerly a member state of French West Africa, became an independent republic in 1960. Close economic ties have been formed with Togo.

AREA: 115 762 sq. km. (44 696 sq. miles)

LAND USE: (percentage of total)
Arable and orchard . . . .
Permanent meadow and pasture . . .
Forest and woodland . . .
City areas, waste and other land . . .

POPULATION: 2 505 000 (1967 U.N. estimate)
Largest city: COTONOU: population: 109 328 (city proper, 1964)
Capital city: PORTO-NOVO: population: 69 500 (city proper, 1964)
Total working population: 1 110 000* (1960)

		Year(s)
Life expectancy at birth (years)	37.3*	1961
Population per physician	20 090	1962
Population per hospital bed	930a	1962
School enrolment: age 5–19 years (percentage	20	1963–4 av.
age over 19 years (per 100 000 population)	2	1964–5 av.

a government hospitals only.

EMPLOYMENT AND PRODUCTION

The population is mainly employed in agriculture, growing maize, millet and groundnuts. The forests contain oil palms which are profitably utilized. Cotton has been introduced in the north of the country and coffee in the south.

COMMUNICATIONS

		Year(s)
Motor vehicles in use ('000s): private	6.0	1963–5 av.
commercial	4.1	1965
Railway track (km.)	579	1967
Telephones (per '000 urban population)	0.2	1963–5 av.
Radio receivers (per '000 population)	1²	1962–4 av.
Daily newspapers (per '000 population)		

FINANCE

Currency unit: The franc CFA

Exchange rates	1965	1960
Per $ U.S.	246.85	246.85
Per £ sterling	691.18	691.18

		Year
National Income (million $ U.S.)	106	1958
G.N.P. per capita ($ U.S.)	80	1966

TRADING

	1965	1955
Total trade (in million $ U.S.)		
Exports (f.o.b.)	14	16
Imports (c.i.f.)	34	24

Main trading partners (percentage of total value)

Exports	1965		Imports	1965
France	55		France	55
Netherlands	11		Netherlands	5
Italy	9		Germany F.R.	4
U.K.	5		Senegal	3
U.S.A.	3		Belg./Lux.	3
			Nigeria	2

Distribution of trade (percentage of total value)

Exports	1965		Imports	1965
Vegetable oilseeds and oils	62		Manufactured goods	78
Food	78		(textiles)	(21)
			(machinery and transport equipment)	(17)
			Food	14

PRODUCTION, EXPORTS AND IMPORTS

Years: 1963–5 average Units: '000 metric tons unless otherwise indicated
Note.—1953–5 data are not available

1. CEREALS, etc.	Production	Exports	Imports
Cassava	1 171.0*		
Maize (corn)	225.3	0.3²	—
Millets/sorghum	69.3	...¹	0.4²
Rice	1.0*		5.5*
Sweet potatoes/yams	558.7*		

2. FRUIT, etc.	Production	Exports	Imports
Bananas	10.0*		
Coconuts	40.0*¹ᵉ	0.8²	—
Pineapples	3.0*		
Tomatoes	4.3*		24.0²
Wine b.			

3. BEVERAGES, FOREST PRODUCTS, etc.	Production	Exports	Imports
Coffee	1.3*	1.0²	6.7*
Sugar, raw			0.6²
Tobacco: leaf	0.6*	0.3²	0.7
Other products			6.3ⁿ
Hardwood	1 671.7*		
Other paper		0.3²	0.1²

n incl. softwood.

4. VEGETABLE OILSEEDS AND OILS	Production	Exports	Imports
Castor seed			
Copra			
Coconut oil	0.49*		0.1
Groundnuts	1.06²		0.05²
Groundnut oil	2.70*		1.23*
Linseed oil	18.43		4.28
Palm kernels	53.67	41.15	
Palm oil	41.33	11.65	
Soya bean oil			0.01²

5. LIVESTOCK‡, ANIMAL PRODUCTS, etc.	Production	Exports	Imports
Chickens d	4 000.0		
Cattle d	369.7		
Goats d	497.0		
Sheep d	387.0		
Horses d	3.0		
Pigs d	302.0		
Meat†, 'A'	3.0		
Cheese			0.1²
Eggs	14.5		1.3
Fish	23.7	0.2	1.4
Milk	22.3*		47

d no. in thousands.

6. FIBRES, TEXTILES, etc.	Production	Exports	Imports
Cotton: lint	1.0*	1.1¹²	0.1
woven fabrics			1.7

7. FUEL AND POWER	Production	Exports	Imports
Electricity h t	16		
Petroleum, refined.			

h million kWh. t thermal.

11. INDUSTRY	Production	Exports	Imports
Alcoholic beverages a			1.1
Cement			60.0
Electrical engineering a			
Railway vehicles a			1.2
Motor vehicles a			2.3

a million $ U.S.

CZECHOSLOVAKIA continued

PRODUCTION, EXPORTS AND IMPORTS

Years: 1963–5 average and 1953–5 average Units: '000 metric tons unless otherwise indicated

1. CEREALS, etc.	Production		Exports		Imports	
Barley	1 482.7	na	29.2	15.0*	397.7	25.6*
Maize (corn)	478.7	395.5*²	6.8	—	292.4	69.9*
Millets/sorghum	3.7	5.5²	—	*	0.2	0.1*
Oats	698.7	na	—	—	—	—
Potatoes	5 946.7	na	11.9	25.5*	350.3	6.1*
Rye	857.3	885.5²	4.3	6.0*	44.8	5.0*
Wheat.	1 862.3	na	15.0	8.1*	1 262.8	41.0*

2. FRUIT, etc.	Production		Exports		Imports	
Apples	128.3	na	0.5	—	56.0	12.6*
Apricots	17.3	17.3	—	—	8.7	0.3*
Bananas			—	—	0.8	0.1*
Cherries	52.3	82.3	0.12‡	—	39.8	6.6*
Dates			1.12‡	—	24.9	14.1*
Grapes	68.3	63.0*	3.4²‡	—	26.2	12.8
Lemons			1.4†	—	3.6	—
Oranges			—	—	—	—
Other citrus fruit	40.7	na	2.5	1.0*	1.3	—
Pears	184.6	na	—	—	4.7	0.8*
Plums			2.5	na	—	—
Raisins			—	—	—	—
Tomatoes	122.0	na	0.1	na	443.3	74.0*
Wine b.	380.0*					

b '000 hectolitres.

3. BEVERAGES, FOREST PRODUCTS, etc.	Production		Exports		Imports	
Cocoa.			—	—	13.3	2.5
Coffee.			—	—	10.9	3.5*
Sugar: beet	7 051.3	5 400.0*	501.6	106.2*	136.5*	30.5*
raw	888.8	775.7*	2.2	*	1.6	5.0*
Tea	7.3	9.1²			15.8	—
Tobacco: leaf	29.0	56.6	—	—	—	—
cigarettes	18 543.0	15 425.1	—	—	—	—
cigars e	3.4	3.4	0.1*	0.87*	24.63	1.83*
Tobacco/snuff			—	—	—	—
Softwood j	10 016.0	na	1 471.0	681.3	312.3	55.3
Hardwood j	2 706.0	na	8.1	7.3	101.1	33.4
Wood pulp	600.0*	na	—	—	43.3	—
Newsprint	59.7	63.3*	23.0	6.0	4.7	0.96*
Other paper	620.7	367.0*²	50.0	41.0¹	13.7	2.0¹

e no. in millions. j '000 cu. metres of roundwood equivalent.

8. IRON AND STEEL	Production		Exports		Imports	
Iron ore	870.0ⁿ	542ᵐ	na		9 398	3 554
Pig iron	5 647	2 851	—	—	142	—
Steel ingots/castings	8 191	4 370	—	—	—	—

m metal content. n low grade ore.

9. NON-FERROUS MINERALS AND METALS	Production		Exports		Imports	
Silver k, ore m	2 400.00*	1 608.00*	na		24.91	
Asbestos, fibre	na		na			
Aluminium	59.87*	14.18*	na			
Antimony, ore m	2.0*	1.6*	na			
Lead t, ore m	14.15*	8.80*	na			
Magnesium	100.00*ⁿ	na	na			
Manganese, ore	25.05*	24.99*	na		146.65	
Mercury f	0.21	0.20*	na		296.35	
Tin, ore m			na			
Zinc			na			

f metric tons. k '000 fine troy oz. m metal content.

10. CHEMICALS n AND FERTILIZERS	Production		Exports		Imports	
Organic chemicals:						
Benzene	na		na		0.06	*
Butadiene	na		na		4.39	2.30*
Ethylene	na		na		4.88*	0.15*
Methanol	67.0²		na		2.93†	*
Phenol	na		na		23.00	—
Phthalic anhydride	na		na		44.98	0.10*
Styrene monomer	na		na		0.41	—
Urea	na		na		4.42	1.83*

Inorganic chemicals:	Production		Exports		Imports	
Ammonia	na		na		2.11	0.37*
Carbon black	na		na		3.73	0.99*
Chlorine	na		na		22.63	1.15*
Nitric acid	60.8		na		2.16	—
Sodium carbonate	145.0		na		2.83	—
Sodium hydroxide	850.3		na		7.61	0.83*
Sulphuric acid.			na		27.57	0.96*
					27.97	3.00*
					1.02	—

Plastics:	Production		Exports		Imports	
Polyamides	na		na			
Polyethylene	na		4.2		4.2	9.1*
Polyvinyl chloride	26.2		na			

Fertilizers:	Production		Exports		Imports	
Potash	140.2		na		18.6*	17.2*
Pyrites x	na		na		0.1	17.2*
Sulphur			na		67.3	1.0*

x sulphur content. n data not available for years 1953–5.

4. VEGETABLE OILSEEDS AND OILS	Production		Exports		Imports	
Castor seed	na	na	—	—	4.42	4.9*
Castor oil	na	na	—	—	14.2	1.7*
Copra	na	na	—	—	2.4	1.7*
Coconut oil	na	na	—	—	137.4	1.6*
Cottonseed	na	na	—	—	40.3†	—
Groundnuts	na	na	—	—	21.3†	4.3*
Groundnut oil	16.33	na	2.53	0.10*	21.3†	4.3*

Linseed oil	na	na	1.00²	—	56.2	—
Olive oil	na	na	1.94	—	8.4	—
Palm kernels	53.70	na	—	—	3.0	0.1*
Palm kernel oil	na	na	0.61	0.01*	0.1	0.3*
Palm oil	na	na	—	—	3.4	0.3*
Rapeseed	na	na	—	—	4.4	—
Rapeseed oil	na	na	—	—	1.0	—
Sesame seed	na	na	—	—	17.9	—
Soya beans	na	na	—	—	—	—
Soya bean oil	na	na	—	—	—	—
Sunflower seed	3.33	na	—	—	—	—
Sunflower seed oil	59.7	63.3*	—	—	—	—
Tung oil	na	na	0.24	—	—	—

5. LIVESTOCK‡, ANIMAL PRODUCTS, etc.	Production		Exports		Imports	
Chickens d	27 581.0	20 629.0	na		na	na
Cattle d	4 474.3	4 061.5²	na		na	na
dairy cows d	2 291.3	na			na	na
Goats d	576.0	na	0.2		0.2	—
Sheep d	539.7	1 017.0²	na		na	na
Horses d	228.3	562.0	na		na	na
Pigs d	5 960.0	4 472.5²	56.2		320.1*	na
Bacon/ham			8.4		120.2	na
Meat†, 'A'	665.0*	na	3.0		196.1	na
Butter	66.0	na	0.1		na	na
Cheese	80.0	40.0*p	3.4	403.0¹	155.0*†	250.0¹*
Eggs	137.0	87.2²	4.4		na	na
Fish	10.4q	6.5	1.0		64.7a	na
Milk	3 740.7	3 392.5²⁴	17.9		43.6a	na

d no. in thousands. p factory production only. q excl. catches in rivers by state fish farm organizations. r from cattle production only.

6. FIBRES, TEXTILES, etc.	Production		Exports		Imports	
Agaves (sisal etc.).	na	na	—	—	103.7	21.1*
Cotton lint	22.7	na	0.5*†	—	—	3.7*
Hemp fibre	5.1	na	—	—	16.0*	3.6*
Jute						continued

DENMARK

Denmark is a kingdom; the legislative power lies jointly with the king and the 'Folketing' (parliament) in which the Faeroe Islands and Greenland are both represented. Denmark is a member of the European Free Trade Association.

AREA: 43 031 sq. km. (16 611 sq. miles)

LAND USE: (percentage of total)	1965	1955
Arable and orchard	62.9	63.5
Permanent meadow and pasture	7.5	9.1
Forest and woodland	9.3	10.2
City areas, waste and other land	20.3	17.2

POPULATION: 4 767 597 (1965 census)
Largest city: KØBENHAVN (Copenhagen), capital; population: 1 377 605 (1965)
Total working population: 2 093 631

Distribution of working population (1960)	Percentage
U.N. group no.	
1 Agriculture, forestry, fishing and hunting	17.5
2/3 Mining and quarrying	0.6
Manufacturing	28.5
4 Construction	7.2
5 Electricity, gas, water and sanitary services	0.6
6 Commerce	15.0
7 Transport, storage and communications	7.2
8 Services	
9 Others	21.7

			Year(s)
Life expectancy at birth (years): male	70.1	74.7	1965-6 av.
female			
Infant mortality (per '000)	18.7		1965
Crude birth rate (per '000)	18.0		1965
Crude death rate (per '000)	10.1		1965
Accidental deaths (per 100 000 population)			
caused by motor vehicles	21.9	30.3	1965 / 1966
Population per physician	750		1966
Population per hospital bed	85		1963-4 av.
School enrolment: age 5–19 years (percentage)	110		1963-5 av.
age over 19 years (per 100 000 population)	911		1963-5 av.

COMMUNICATIONS		Year(s)
Motor vehicles in use ('000s): private	674.5	1963-5 av.
commercial	227.8	1964
Railway track (km.)	4 020	
Mail per capita: foreign received	10	1963-5 av.
foreign sent	9	
Telephones (per '000 urban population)	29.1	1967
Radio licences (per '000 population)	342	1963-5 av.
Television licences (per '000 population)	214	1963-5 av.
Daily newspapers (per '000 population)	344	1962-4 av.

FINANCE

Currency unit: The krone

Exchange rates	1965	1960	1950	1938
Per $ U.S.	6.89	6.906	6.91	4.83
Per £ sterling	19.3	19.345	19.37	22.22

		Year(s)
National Income (million $ U.S.)	7 861	1965
G.N.P. per capita ($ U.S.)	1 830	1965
Rate of increase of G.N.P. per capita	4.1	1966
Foreign trade (percentage of G.D.P.)	51	1960-4 av. / 1963-5 av.

TRADING

Total trade (in million $ U.S.)	1965	1960	1955	1938
Exports (f.o.b.)	2 320		1 072	335
Imports (c.i.f.)	2 822		1 179	354

Main trading partners (percentage of total value)				
Exports	1965	1960	1955	1938
U.K.	22		33	56
Germany F.R.	17		17	20 d
Sweden	17		7	5
U.S.A.			7	3
Norway	6		4	4
Italy	4		4	3
France	3		2	1

Distribution of trade (percentage of total value)				
Exports	1965	1960	1955	1938*
Food	46		66	69
(pigs, bacon, etc.)		(13)	(19)	(25)
(dairy produce and eggs)		(10)	(25)	(36)
(cattle and beef)		(6)	(7)	(4)
Manufactured goods	38	(22)	24	na
(machinery and transport equipment)	8		5	(13)
Crude materials and fuels				

Imports	1965	1960	1955	1938
Manufactured goods	58	(25)	44	na
(machinery and transport equipment)	20	(25)	30	(10)
Crude materials and fuels				na
(mineral fuels, etc.)	11	(11)	16	(14)
Food	9		7	11
Chemicals				7

d incl. Germany D.R.

PRODUCTION, EXPORTS AND IMPORTS

Years: 1963-5 average and 1953-5 average Units: '000 metric tons unless otherwise indicated

1. CEREALS, etc.	Production		Exports		Imports	
Barley	3 808.0	2 141.7	186.0	169.7	345.2	210.5
Maize (corn)	—	—	0.3	0.9	148.2	22.5
Millets/sorghum	—	—	—	5.7	124.4	43.7
Oats	757.3	828.7	20.6	23.2	76.7	60.4
Potatoes	1 161.3	1 755.0	54.2	0.5	6.5	6.7
Rice	—	—	6.5	5.7	9.4	110.5
Rye	292.0	266.0	27.8	—	18.1	226.2
Wheat	533.0	276.3	57.9	26.9		

2. FRUIT, etc.	Production		Exports		Imports	
Apples	188.7	185.0	11.1	22.7	9.3	28.3
Bananas	—	—	0.1	—	32.1	—
Cherries	10.0*	6.8	0.2	—	0.8	1.0
Dates	—	—	—	—	0.8	2.5
Grapes	—	—	0.2	—	9.2	4.5
Lemons	—	—	0.5	0.1	6.8	30.9
Oranges	—	—	²	—	42.1	0.8
Other citrus fruit	—	—	0.1	2	3.2	
Pears	20.7*	18.3	—	0.1	2.3	
Plums	14.3*	13.6	—	—	—	
Raisins	—	—	—	—	3.6	4.0
Tomatoes	18.7	16.3n	0.1	—	—	
Wine b	—	—	3.8	—	167.1	96.3

3. BEVERAGES, FOREST PRODUCTS, etc.	Production		Exports		Imports	
Cocoa	—	—	—	—	4.4	2.8
Coffee	—	—	0.3†	—	50.4	26.0
Sugar, beet	2 545.0	2 067.7	107.5	30.1	29.4	0.5
raw	341.4	303.3*	—	—	1.5	1.2
Tea						

continued

3. BEVERAGES, FOREST PRODUCTS, etc.—continued	Production		Exports		Imports	
Tobacco: leaf	—	—	0.4†	—	14.6	10.0
cigars	314.0c	214.0c	na	—	1.1	0.5²
cigarettes	6 941.0c	4 532.7c	na	2	1 731.0	1 776.8
tobacco/snuff j	3.3	3.5	33.6	2.8	269.7	61.9
Softwood j	920.7	930.5²	134.0	34.4	111.3	82.0
Hardwood j	894.3	990.5²	23.0	2.5	113.0	62.7
Wood pulp	35.7	6.0*	17.6		209.3	84.6
Newsprint	—	0.21				
Other paper	197.7*	118.0*				

j '000 cu. metres of roundwood equivalent.

4. VEGETABLE OILSEEDS AND OILS	Production		Exports		Imports	
Castor oil	—	—	0.43	—	0.48	0.34
Copra	—	—	—	—	34.72	52.17
Coconut oil	na	na	0.04†	1.16	0.80	0.23
Cottonseed	—	—	—	—	0.44	6.80²
Cottonseed oil	na	na	0.04†	0.03	3.38	0.35
Groundnut	—	—	0.06	0.83†	0.15	0.43
Groundnut oil	na	na	0.02	0.07	7.00	3.23
Linseed	—	—	—	—	5.54	6.50
Linseed oil	na	na	—	—	0.11	0.09
Olive oil	—	—	—	—		
Palm kernels	—	—	1.36	0.06	16.70	17.80
Palm kernel oil	na	na	0.12†	0.0†1	2.50	0.02
Palm oil	na	na	50.96	3.10	0.37	4.12
Rapeseed	42.70	na	0.36	0.32	0.78	1.00
Rapeseed oil	na	na			1.22	0.48
Sesame seed	—	—	—	—	—	4.60
Soya beans	na	na	42.73	1.26	382.40	65.07
Soyabean oil	na	na	—	—	0.17	—
Sunflower seed	—	—	—	—	0.18	—
Sunflower seed oil	na	na	0.02†	—	1.05	0.61

p flax grown for seed only. *continued*

PRODUCTION, EXPORTS AND IMPORTS *continued*

5. LIVESTOCK‡, ANIMAL PRODUCTS, etc.	Production		Exports		Imports	
Chickens d	23 509.0	24 234.3				
Cattle d	3 321.7	3 133.0				
dairy cows d	1 376.0	2 169.5²				
Goats d	5.0*	5.0²				
Sheep d	75.0	36.3				
Horses d	66.0	355.3				
Pigs d	7 979.0	4 586.7				
Bacon/ham	958.3	686.7²	294.3	351.9	0.1	0.3
Meat: 'A'	130.1	75.7	301.2	225.8	—	—
'B'	157.0	172.7	151.1	80.3	0.6	0.2
Butter	119.3	140.1	107.3	135.8	0.6	0.5
Cheese	98.9	65.0	87.8	29.0	0.5	—
Eggs			29.1	67.0	0.5	0.5
Milk	5 228.7	5 298.7*	360.6	375.8q	213.6	198.4
Fish	853.9		490.7	217.3*	21.6	59.4*
Whale/sperm oil	0.1	1.0	0.7	0.1	8.5	13.2
Hides/skins			17.2	10.7		
Wool	0.1	na	0.7	0.1	2.8	1.6

q no. in thousands. q incl. fish landed by Danish vessels in foreign ports.

6. FIBRES, TEXTILES, etc.	Production		Exports		Imports	
Abaca	—	—	—	—	2.6	2.4
Agaves (sisal etc.)	—	—	—	—	17.1	16.6
Cotton lint	1.3		0.1†	0.1†	8.6	9.2
Flax fibre	—	4.01*	0.8	2.0	0.9	0.5
Hemp fibre	—	—	—	—	0.4	0.3
Jute	—	—	0.4†	—	2.4	2.4
Rubber: natural	—	—	—	—	6.3	6.7
synthetic	—	—	0.6	0.5	4.3	2.9
Cotton: yarn	8.1	8.2	0.6	0.5	5.5	7.6
woven fabrics	6.4	6.3	0.5	0.3†	9.7	2.9
Rayon: fibre/yarn	—	—			5.4	2.6
Non-cellulosic fibre/yarn	—	1.4²	1.0	0.2	5.6	
Wool: yarn	0.9	7.4	0.4	0.2	4.6	2.1
woven fabrics	2.8	3.7	0.7		3.5	2.7

7. FUEL AND POWER	Production		Exports		Imports	
Coal: 'A'‡	—	—	1†	6	3 732	4 584
'B'	—	—	35		168	181
Coke	750	800	50	—	1 169	2 124
Electricity h: total	7 459	3 270¹				
thermal	7 459	3 240¹				
hydro	—	30¹				
Oil, crude	—	—	533	—	2 903	na
Petroleum, refined	2 833	10¹	—	—	6 727	3 150¹

h million kWh.

8. IRON AND STEEL	Production		Exports		Imports	
Iron ore	72	44	143	183	4	5
Pig iron	—	—	—	—	110	58
Steel ingots/castings	389	205	43	22	39	3
Iron/steel scrap	na	na	18	4	163	71
Iron/steel products a	na	na				

9. NON-FERROUS MINERALS AND METALS	Production		Exports		Imports	
Platinum group metals c	—	—	0.16s	0.64†	3.65s	1.14s
Silver k, bullion	—	—	40.67†	40.70†	3 829.70s	2 221.70s
Asbestos: fibre	—	—	0.09†	0.04†	21.15s	9.96s
manufactured	na	na	9.01†	1.75†	0.30	0.99i
Mica	—	—	—	—	43.70	34.91s
Aluminium: bauxite	na	na	3.54†	20.41†n	27.38s	0.66†
aluminium						

continued

---

9. NON-FERROUS MINERALS AND METALS—continued	Production		Exports		Imports	
Antimony, metal	—	—	—	—	0.18	0.14
Cadmium, metal	—	—	—	—	0.22	
Chrome, metal	—	—	—	—	0.36	0.69
Cobalt, metal	—	—	—	—	0.02	
Copper, metal	na	na	6.28	3.44†	32.65s	17.01s
Lead, metal	na	na	4.85†	8.12†	21.19s	20.48s
Magnesium: dolomite	na	na			16.89	7.82
magnesite	na	na			3.97	1.29
metal/salts	na	na			4.19	1.76
Manganese: ore	na	na			7.13	2.74
metal	na	na			2.91	2.93
Mercury f	na	na			27.30	7.30
Molybdenum f, metal	na	na				
Nickel, metal	na	na	0.20	0.17	26.40	0.10
Tin, metal			0.87	4.60	0.71	5.93
Titanium minerals					1.25	2.30²
Zinc, metal			3.10	1.24	5.50	2.30²
					20.63	14.39

f '000 fine troy oz. k '000 fine troy oz. s incl. imports for re-export.

10. CHEMICALS n AND FERTILIZERS	Production		Exports		Imports	
Organic chemicals:						
Benzene	na					0.3
Butadiene	na					na
Ethylene	na					na
Methanol	na		0.1			2.7
Phenol	na		0.3			1.1
Phthalic anhydride	na					1.1
Styrene monomer	na		0.1			10.3
Urea	na					4 493.5²
Inorganic chemicals:						
Ammonia	na		3.2			31.8
Carbon black	na		0.1			1.8
Chlorine	na		0.3			0.5
Nitric acid	na					4.5
Sodium carbonate	3.8		²			31.7
Sodium hydroxide	18.0		7.1			24.6
Sulphuric acid						2.2
Plastics:						
Polyamides	16.5²		9.8			na
Polyethylene			0.6			15.5
Polyvinyl chloride						20.9
Fertilizers:						
Phosphates	na				313.1	254.1
Potash	na				287.4	303.8
Pyrites	na				136.6	128.4
Sulphur	na				12.4	2.9

11. INDUSTRY	Production		Exports		Imports	
Aircraft a	—	—	—	—	11.3	2.8
Alcoholic beverages: beer b	4 920.0	2 876.0*	23.1a	0.6	15.9a	4.1a
spirits b	48.01*b	78.01*q	—	8.3a		
Cement	1 812.3	1 185.7	129.3	325.0	32.3	26.3
Electrical engineering a	287.2²	22.0	87.6a	28.0²	121.5	22.5²
Locomotives c	10.01	—	0.3	—	na	—
Railway vehicles a	22.0	—	na	—	1.1	na
Machine tools a	10.01	142.0	141.0	39.2	13.7	na
Merchant ships g	275.0		10.8a	3.7²a	139.0	37.1
Motor vehicles: commercial d r	7.2	4.4			160.3a	63.5²a
private d r	24.7	6.6				

continued

a million $ U.S. b 1967 figure. c no. of units. d no. in thousands.
g '000 G.R.T. h '000 hectolitres. p production for home consumption in 1961.
q production for home consumption in 1961. q incl. assembly of imported parts.
r assembly of imported parts.

na: data not available. — negligible or nil. ¹ one year only. ² two year average. ‡ see appendix. † re-exports.

na: data not available. — negligible or nil. * estimate. ‡ see appendix. † re-exports.

DENMARK (TERRITORIES)

FAEROE ISLANDS — NORTH ATLANTIC

These 21 volcanic islands have had a certain measure of home rule since 1948; they are represented by two members in the Danish Folketing.

AREA: 1 399 sq. km. (540 sq. miles)

LAND USE: (percentage of total)
Arable and orchard
City areas, waste and other land, including rough grazing

POPULATION: 38 000 (1967 estimate)
Capital city: TÓRSHAVN (Thorshavn): population 14135

Distribution of working population (1960)
Total working population: 14135

U.N. group no.		Percentage
0	Agriculture, forestry, fishing and hunting	34.5
1	Mining and quarrying	0.8
2/3	Manufacturing	18.5
4	Construction	5.4
5	Electricity, gas, water and sanitary services	10.2
6	Commerce	10.3
7	Transport, storage and communications	17.9
8	Services	
9	Others	2.1

		Year(s)
Infant mortality (per '000)	16.9*	1965
Crude birth rate (per '000)	24.0*	1965
Crude death rate (per '000)	7.1*	1965
Population per physician	1 160	1964
Population per hospital bed	150	1966
School enrolment: age 5–19 years (percentage)	104‡	1963–4 av.
age over 19 years (per 100 000 population)	16	1965

FINANCE
Currency unit: The Danish krone

EMPLOYMENT AND TRADE
The main occupations are fishing and sheep-rearing. Exports balanced imports at U.S. $ 26 million in 1965, the exports consisting primarily of fish preparations and some wool products. Denmark and the U.K. were the main trading partners.

PRODUCTION, EXPORTS AND IMPORTS
Years: 1963–5 average and 1953–5 average Units: '000 metric tons unless otherwise indicated

	Production		Exports		Imports	
1. CEREALS, etc.						
Barley	—	—	—	—	0.2	0.5
Maize (corn)	—	—	—	—	0.2	—
Potatoes	—	—	—	—	2.4	1.6
2. FRUIT, etc.						
Apples	—	—	—	—	0.4	0.2
Bananas	—	—	—	—	0.1	—
Dates	—	—	—	—	0.2	—
Oranges	—	—	—	—	0.2	0.2
Raisins	—	—	—	—	0.1	—
Wine b	—	—	—	—	0.3	—
3. BEVERAGES, FOREST PRODUCTS, etc.						
Sugar, raw	—	—	—	—	1.4	1.3
4. VEGETABLE OILSEEDS AND OILS						
Coconut oil	—	—	—	—	0.30	0.28
Cottonseed oil	—	—	—	—	—	0.01
Palm oil	—	—	—	—	—	0.01
Soya bean oil	—	—	—	—	0.14	0.04
5. LIVESTOCK‡, ANIMAL PRODUCTS, etc.						
Sheep‡: A'	72.0*		—		—	
Meat‡: B'	na		—		0.7	0.1
Butter					0.1	—
Cheese					0.2	0.1
Eggs	0.1*				0.2	0.1
Fish	140.3n	94.6n	67.1	39.5*	1.2	na
Milk	na				1.6	0.8
Wool d	na		—		—	—
7. FUEL AND POWER						
Coal, A'‡	45		—		3	—
Electricity h: total	41					
hydro	4					
thermal						
Petroleum, refined	—	—	—	—	40	30¹
11. INDUSTRY						
Merchant ships g	0.8		—		0.9	—

d no. in thousands. n incl. fish landed by Faeroes' vessels in foreign ports.
h million kWh. g '000 G.R.T. b '000 hectolitres.

GREENLAND — NORTH ATLANTIC

In 1953 Greenland became an integral part of the Danish realm, and is represented by two members in the Danish Folketing. Defence agreements have been signed with the U.S.A., and air force bases and weather stations have been established.

AREA: 2 175 600 sq. km. (840 000 sq. miles) of which 341 600 sq. km. (131 900 sq. miles) is ice-free land.

POPULATION: 43 000 (1967 estimate)
Capital city: GODTHAAB; population: 3 179 (1960)

Distribution of working population (1960)
Total working population: 11 800

U.N. group no.		Percentage
0	Agriculture, forestry, fishing and hunting	34.4
1	Mining and quarrying	7.1
2/3	Manufacturing	8.2
4	Construction	1.1
5	Electricity, gas, water and sanitary services	10.3
6	Commerce	7.9
7	Transport, storage and communications	27.6
8	Services	
9	Others	0.5

		Year(s)
Life expectancy at birth (years): male	51.4*	1952–9 av.
female	53.6*	
Infant mortality (per '000)	70.1*	1965
Crude birth rate (per '000)	43.5	1965
Crude death rate (per '000)	8.4	1965
Population per physician	710	1963
Population per hospital bed	60	1965
School enrolment: age 5–19 years (percentage)	110‡	1963–4 av.

FINANCE
Currency unit: The Danish krone

EMPLOYMENT AND TRADE
In recent years fishing has largely replaced fur-trapping, whaling and sealing as the main occupation. Sheep and some cattle are pastured. There are large resources of coal, but it is of low calorific value and it is planned to discontinue coal mining in 1972. Cryolite is mined, but deposits of lead and zinc also proved uneconomic to recover, and production of these ceased in 1962. Denmark has a virtual monopoly of trade although commerce with the U.K. showed a marked increase in 1965.

PRODUCTION, EXPORTS AND IMPORTS
Years: 1963–5 average and 1953–5 average Units: '000 metric tons unless otherwise indicated

	Production		Exports		Imports	
1. CEREALS, etc.						
Barley	—	—	—	—	0.5*	0.1*
Maize (corn)	—	—	—	—	0.1*	0.3*
Wheat	—	—	—	—	1.0	—
2. FRUIT, etc.						
Apples	—	—	—	—	0.5	0.2*
Oranges	—	—	—	—	0.3	0.1*
Raisins	—	—	—	—	0.1	—
Wine b	—	—	—	—	1.5	—
3. BEVERAGES, FOREST PRODUCTS, etc.						
Coffee	—	—	—	—	0.2	—
Sugar, raw	—	—	—	—	1.8	4.51
Softwood j	—	—	—	—	—	—
Hardwood j	0.52*		0.5		0.21	—
4. VEGETABLE OILSEEDS AND OILS						
Soya bean oil	—	—	—	—	0.02	—
5. LIVESTOCK‡, ANIMAL PRODUCTS, etc.						
Chickens d	na		na		na	0.5*
Sheep d: A'	33.7		na		na	0.1*
Meat‡: d B'	2.0	18.7			1.9	1.0
Butter					na	0.3*
Cheese					—	—
Eggs	37.4*	25.2*			0.5	0.2*
Fish			14.5		0.3	0.1*
Milk					1.5	—
7. FUEL AND POWER						
Coal, A'‡	26	38			12	14²
Electricity h‡	20	10¹	0.1			
Petroleum, refined					73	40¹
9. NON-FERROUS MINERALS AND METALS						
Aluminium, cryolite	na	na	59.31	46.82	—	—

d no. in thousands. b '000 hectolitres. j '000 cu. metres of roundwood equivalent. h million kWh. t thermal.

DOMINICAN REPUBLIC — CARIBBEAN SEA

The Dominican Republic was established in 1844. The population, unlike that of neighbouring Haiti, is primarily of European origin. After 30 years' dictatorship ended in 1961, the country suffered considerable political unrest, culminating in civil war four years later. Peace was restored after intervention by U.S. troops, and free elections followed in 1966.

AREA: 48 442 sq. km. (18 700 sq. miles)

LAND USE: (percentage of total)

	1960
Arable and orchard	21.9
Permanent meadow and pasture	17.8
Forest and woodland	45.7
City areas, waste and other land	14.6

POPULATION: 3 889 000 (1967 estimate)
Largest city: SANTO DOMINGO, capital; population: 577 371 (city proper, 1967)

Distribution of working population (1960)
Total working population: 820 710* (based on a 10% sample of census returns)

U.N. group no.		Percentage
0	Agriculture, forestry, fishing and hunting	61.4
1	Mining and quarrying	0.3
2/3	Manufacturing	8.2
4	Construction	0.4
5	Electricity, gas, water and sanitary services	0.7
6	Commerce	2.6
7	Transport, storage and communications	1.1
8	Services	11.1
9	Others	6.8

		Year(s)
Life expectancy at birth (years): male	57.2	1959–61 av.
female	58.6	
Infant mortality (per '000)	72.7*	1965
Crude birth rate (per '000)	46.5*	1960–5 av.
Crude death rate (per '000)	15*	1960–5 av.
Accidental deaths (per 100 000 population)	3.5*	1960
caused by motor vehicles	13.1*	1965
due to other causes		
Population per physician	1 680	1960
Population per hospital bed	350	1965
School enrolment: age 5–19 years (percentage)	166	1962
age over 19 years (per 100 000 population)	65	1964–5 av.

COMMUNICATIONS

		Year(s)
Motor vehicles in use ('000s): private	26.5	1963–5 av.
commercial	9.7	
Railway length (km.)	1 444.a	1963
Telephones (per '000 population)	0.8	1967
Radio receivers (per '000 population)	41	1963–5 av.
Television sets (per '000 population)	10	1963–5 av.
Daily newspapers (per '000 population)	27	1962

a mainly on sugar estates; no passenger services.

FINANCE
Currency unit: The peso oro, at par with the $ U.S. which, prior to 1947, was the only legal tender.

Exchange rates

	1965	1960	1950
Per £ sterling	2.8	2.8	2.8

		Year(s)
National Income (million $ U.S.)	769	1965
G.N.P. per capita ($ U.S.)	250	1966
Rate of increase of G.N.P. per capita	3.2	1960–4 av.
Foreign trade (percentage of G.D.P.)	31	1963–5 av.

TRADING

Total trade (in million $ U.S.)

	1965	1955	1938
Exports (f.o.b.)	126	115	15
Imports (c.i.f.)	87	98	11

Main trading partners (percentage of total value)

Exports	1965	1955		Imports	1965	1955
U.S.A.	80	55		U.S.A.	54	66
Netherlands	3	5		Germany F.R.	6	4
Spain	3	1		Neths. Antilles	6	4
Germany F.R.	2	2		Canada	5	2
Belg./Lux.	2	3		Japan	5	1
Italy	1	1		Netherlands	3	1
				Italy	3	1

Distribution of trade (percentage of total value)

Exports	1965*	1938*
Sugar and molasses	50	60
Coffee	17	10
Bauxite/aluminium concentrates	9	—

Imports	1965	1955
Machinery and transport equipment	24	27
Food	14	7
Fuels	10	8
Chemicals	10	8
Iron and steel	6	13
Edible oils	3	12
Textiles		

continued

145

na: data not available. — negligible or nil. ¹ one year only. ² two year average. * estimate. ‡ see appendix. † re-exports.

DOMINICAN REPUBLIC continued

PRODUCTION, EXPORTS AND IMPORTS
Years: 1963–5 average and 1953–5 average. Units: '000 metric tons unless otherwise indicated

	Production		Exports		Imports	
1. CEREALS, etc.						
Cassava	150.0*	144.0[1]				
Maize (corn)	96.7*	87.0[2]	2.0	22.0	1.3	
Millets/sorghum					—	
Oats					0.2[2]	
Potatoes	2.0*	2.0			0.5	
Sweet potatoes/yams	146.0*	93.0*		0.5	1.9	
Wheat	—	—			25.4*	
2. FRUIT, etc.						
Apples					0.7	
Bananas	352.3	335.0	79.0	41.8		
Coconuts	45.0*e	na	4.6	0.4[2]		
Grapes						
Lemons	3.0*	na	0.6	0.5	0.3	
Oranges	26.0*	15.0*[2]	0.1	0.1	0.2	
Other citrus fruit	2.0*	na				
Pineapples	5.0*	na			3.1	
Raisins						
Wine b						
3. BEVERAGES, FOREST PRODUCTS, etc.						
Cocoa	38.8	31.1	24.1	22.6		
Coffee	39.6	32.1*	28.8	22.7		
Sugar: cane	6 466.7*	5 429.0				
raw	738.0	647.0	607.9	548.1		
Tobacco: leaf	21.8*	17.7*	19.0	11.6	0.6	0.1
cigars	28.0c	33.7c			na	0.4[2]a
cigarettes	1 761.0e	896.7c				
tobacco/snuff			1.4[2]		na	—
Softwood	307.5*[2]	257.0	2.4	3.3[2]	na	2.1[2]
Hardwood	1 692.5*[2]	27.7p			na	1.5[2]
Wood pulp					4.6[1]	5.3[2]
Newsprint	2.0*	—			6.0[1]	
Other paper						
4. VEGETABLE OILSEEDS AND OILS						
Castor oil					0.01	
Copra	6.50[1]	na	6.57	2.23		
Coconut oil	39.6	na	0.52[2]	0.02	0.01[2]	
Cottonseed	3.00*	na			0.23	
Cottonseed oil						
Groundnuts	35.91	21.91*			0.01	
Linseed oil					0.01	
Olive oil					0.28	
Sesame seed	0.20*	na			0.17	

	Production		Exports		Imports	
5. LIVESTOCK‡, ANIMAL PRODUCTS, etc.						
Chickens d						
Cattle d	1 015.0*	1 196.5[2]				
Goats d	250.0*	895.0				
Sheep d	76.3*	27.0[2]				
Pigs d	255.0*	246.0[2]				
Horses d	28.0*	19.0[2]				
Bacon/ham	1 082.0*	917.5[2]				
Meat‡: 'A'	27.3*					
'B'						
Butter	1.0*	1.0[2]				
Cheese	2.5*	na				
Eggs	3.8*	0.7[1]				
Fish	48.0*	2.1[1]			50.3	
Hides/skins						
6. FIBRES, TEXTILES, etc.						
Agaves (sisal etc.)	0.7*	na	0.1			
Cotton lint	2.0*	na	0.6			
Rubber: natural						
Silk f						
Cotton: yarn	1.0[1]	0.3[2]				
woven fabrics					1.3	
7. FUEL AND POWER						
Electricity h: total	485	190[1]				
hydro	61	—				
thermal	434	190[1]				
Petroleum, refined					437	300[1]
8. IRON AND STEEL						
Iron ore	68m	—	96			
9. NON-FERROUS MINERALS AND METALS						
Aluminium, bauxite	825.03	—	1 003.31			
Copper						
11. INDUSTRY						
Alcoholic beverages						
beer b	263.0	77.1	—		2.33[2]a	0.9a
Cement	244.7	177.0	13.3	36.0	2.0	1.7
Electrical engineering a					9.9	6.2[2]
Motor vehicles a			—		11.6	4.7[2]

a '000 cu. metres of roundwood equivalent. b '000 hectolitres. c no. in millions. d no. in thousands. e no. in millions. f metric tons. h million kWh. m metal content. p production for industries only.

TRADING (Dominican Republic)
Total trade (in million $ U.S.)

	1965	1955	1938
Exports (f.o.b.)	178·0a	114	9
Imports (c.i.f.)	152·0a	95	11

Main trading partners (percentage of total value)

Exports	1965	1955		Imports	1965	1955
U.S.A.	59	61		U.S.A.	41	52
Germany F.R.	14	9		Germany F.R.	12	11
Belg./Lux.	4	7		Venezuela	7	—
Colombia	4	4		Japan	6	6
Netherlands	4	3		U.K.	5	5
Italy	3	3		Sweden	3	2
France	2	2		Colombia	3	1

PRODUCTION, EXPORTS AND IMPORTS (Ecuador)
Years: 1963–5 average and 1953–5 average. Units: '000 metric tons unless otherwise indicated

	Production		Exports		Imports	
1. CEREALS, etc.						
Barley	101.3	86.3	—	—[2]		1.5[1]
Cassava	217.3	na				
Maize (corn)	170.7	123.0	0.6	0.1[2]	3.4	1.9[1]
Oats	2.0*	3.0			1.8	0.1[2]
Potatoes	311.7	na				
Rice	171.2	113.0*[1]	14.8	24.3		
Rye	1.7	3.3				
Sweet potatoes/yams	13.7	76.0[2]				
Wheat	65.7	32.7			45.2	48.9*a
2. FRUIT, etc.						
Apples	2.7	na				
Bananas	2 899.3	na	1 286.7*	504.3		0.1[1]
Coconuts	15.7	na				
Lemons	21.3	na			0.2	
Oranges	162.0	39.0*	1.9	2.8[2]		
Other citrus fruit	3.5[2]	na				
Peaches	4.7	na				
Pineapples	57.3	na				
Raisins					0.2	0.2*
Tomatoes	67.7	na				
Wine					2.8	2.5[2]
3. BEVERAGES, FOREST PRODUCTS, etc.						
Cocoa	43.2	26.4*	34.5	25.6		
Coffee	53.0	27.3*	33.9	20.8		
Sugar: cane	7 416.3	1 808.5[2]				
raw	168.1p	62.3p	61.7	4.6*	0.4	9.2*
Tobacco: leaf	1.7	1.92			—	—
cigars	1.0	8.5a			0.9[2]	0.41
cigarettes	762.0c	730.0c			—[2]	—
Softwood	2.7	—*			—[2]	—
Hardwood	2 489.0[1]	1 191.0[2]	14.0[2]	18.0[2]	9.9[2]	3.41
Newsprint					12.2[2]	1.71
Other paper	3.3*	—				
4. VEGETABLE OILSEEDS AND OILS						
Castor seed	21.06	16.26	21.43	8.30		
Castor oil	3.67*	3.70[1]			0.37	0.04[2]
Copra	9.00	4.70*			0.72[2]a	0.18[1]
Coconut oil	7.93	4.55[2]	0.04			
Cottonseed					0.04	0.05[1]
Cottonseed oil					0.28	0.07[2]
Groundnuts	7.00*	6.90[1]			1.16	—[2]
Linseed oil	1.30*	na			6.83	0.01*
Olive oil	1.10	na			0.01	
Palm kernels						
Palm oil						
Sesame seed						
Soya bean oil						
Tung oil						

	Production		Exports		Imports	
5. LIVESTOCK‡, ANIMAL PRODUCTS, etc.						
Chickens d	5 037.0	950.0*				
Cattle d	1 900.0*	na	1.9		0.1[2]	1.4
Goats d	164.0	na				0.9
Sheep d	1 281.0	na			2.2	0.1[1]
Pigs d	1 182.0	na				1.4
Horses d	72.7*	33.0[1]				
Meat‡: 'A'	171.7	18.1*				
'B'	4.1*	na				
Eggs	13.7	na	8.6		0.3	13.6
Fish	50.0	12.2				
Milk	395.3	na				0.1
Wool	0.6[2]	na				
6. FIBRES, TEXTILES, etc.						
Cotton lint	5.0	2.7*			1.4	
Rubber: natural	0.81	0.42*			0.9	
Cotton: yarn	3.3	2.2			0.1	
woven fabrics	0.21	na			1.4	
Wool, yarn						
7. FUEL AND POWER						
Electricity h: total	539	180[1]	50	179*	337	
hydro	245	120[1]			23	
thermal	294	601				
Natural gas						
Oil, crude	370	480[1]				
Petroleum, refined	640	270[1]				
9. NON-FERROUS MINERALS AND METALS						
Gold k, orem	17.00	21.00	na	18.70		0.04
Silver k, orem	103.00	56.70	47.67	na	0.68	0.07
Asbestos: fibre					0.43	0.50
manufactured					1.50	
Aluminium	0.21	0.07			0.31	0.15
Copper, orem	0.15m	0.36m	1.41	0.17		
Lead: ore	0.33					
metal						
Zinc, ore						
10. CHEMICALS n AND FERTILIZERS						
Chemicals a					na	
Fertilizers:						
Sulphur	0.2p	0.6p			0.1	
11. INDUSTRY						
Beer b	382.0	528.7			2.0	6.3
Cement	290.3	111.3				
Electrical engineering a					7.5[2]	5.0[1]
Motor vehicles a					5.8[2]	5.3[1]
Motor oil						

a million $ U.S. b '000 hectolitres. d no. in thousands. h million kWh. j '000 cu. metres of roundwood equivalent. k '000 fine troy oz. m metal content. n incl. pears and quince.

TRADING (Ecuador)
Total trade (in million $ U.S.)

	1965	1955	1930*
Exports	62	41	4
Imports	64	26	17
			34

Distribution of trade (percentage of total value)

Exports	1965	1955*	1930*		Imports	1965	1955*	1930*
Bananas	62	41	4		Manufactured goods	63	67	(32)
Coffee	14	26	17		(machinery and transport equipment)	(32)		
Cocoa	10	21	34		Chemicals	14	10	8
Sugar	4	na	na		Crude materials and fuels	8	7	2
					Food	8	12	

a based on export and import permits granted.

ECUADOR

SOUTH AMERICA

The Republic of Ecuador has always enjoyed democratic civilian government apart from a military junta which took over from 1963–6. The chief economic problems of the country arise from a lack of mineral resources and slow industrial development, and from the dependence for revenue on tropical crops liable to price fluctuations. Data for the Archipiélago de Colón (Galápagos Islands) are included with Ecuador.

AREA: 455 454* sq. km. (175 851* sq. miles)

LAND USE: (percentage of total)

	1961	1953
Arable and orchard	10.7	5.9
Permanent meadow and pasture	54.9	8.1
Forest and woodland		61.0
City areas, waste and other land	26.3	25.0

POPULATION: 5 508 000 (1967 estimate)
Largest city: GUAYAQUIL; population: 651 542 (city proper, 1965)
Capital city: QUITO; population: 401 811 (city proper, 1965)

Distribution of working population (1962)
Total working population: 1 442 590 (excl. Indian jungle population)

U.N. group no.		Percentage
0	Agriculture, forestry, fishing and hunting	55.6
1	Mining and quarrying	
2/3	Manufacturing	14.6
4	Construction	3.3
5	Electricity, gas, water and sanitary services	0.3
6	Commerce	6.7
7	Transport, storage and communications	3.0
8	Services	13.2
9	Others	3.0

		Year(s)
Infant mortality (per '000)	93*	1965
Crude birth rate (per '000)	48.5*	1960–5 av.
Crude death rate (per '000)	14*	1960–5 av.
Accidental deaths (per 100 000 population)	8.8*	1965
caused by motor vehicles	40.2*	1965
due to other causes		1964
Population per physician	5 290	1964
Population per hospital bed	420	1963–4 av.
School enrolment: age 5–19 years (percentage)	59	1966
age over 19 years (per 100 000 population)	168	1963–5 av.

COMMUNICATIONS

		Year(s)
Motor vehicles in use ('000s): private	14.9	1964
commercial	20.0	1964
Railway track (km.)	1 340	1964
Telephones (per '000 urban population)	0.8*	1965
Radio receivers (per '000 population)	104	1963–5 av.
Television sets (per '000 population)	6	1963–5 av.
Daily newspapers (per '000 population)	52	1962

FINANCE

Currency unit: The sucre	1960	1965	1938
Exchange rates $U.S.	15.15	18.18	14.4
Per £ sterling	42.44	50.9	66.24
	1950	1960	Year(s)
National income (million $U.S.)	945		1965
G.N.P. per capita ($U.S.)	190		1966
Per £ sterling	0.8		1960–4 av.
Rate of increase of G.N.P. per capita			1963–5 av.
Foreign trade (percentage of G.D.P.)	27		1963–4 av.

continued

na: data not available. — negligible or nil. [1] one year only. [2] two year average. * estimate. ‡ see appendix. † re-exports.

EL SALVADOR

CENTRAL AMERICA

The Republic of El Salvador suffered for several years frequent changes of leadership, but following elections in 1962 a more stable government was formed. Some progress has recently been made towards industrialization.

AREA: 21 393 sq. km. (8 236 sq. miles)

FINANCE

Currency unit: The colon

Exchange rates	1965	1960	1950a	1938a
Per $ U.S.	2.5	2.5	2.503	2.502
Per £ sterling	7.0	7.0	7.008	11.509

	1965	1960	*Year(s)*
National Income (million $ U.S.)	692	270	1965
G.N.P. per capita ($ U.S.)		48	1963–5 av.
Foreign trade (percentage of G.D.P.)			

a selling rate.

LAND USE: (percentage of total)

	1961	1950
Arable and orchard	30.3	25.4
Permanent meadow and pasture	28.2	32.9
Forest and woodland	23.7	33.7
City areas, waste and other land	17.8	8.0

POPULATION: 3 151 000 (1967 estimate)
Largest city: SAN SALVADOR, capital; population: 315 570 (city proper, 1966)

Distribution of working population (1961)

	Percentage
Total working population:807 092	
U.N. group no.	60.3
0 Agriculture, forestry, fishing and hunting	0.1
1 Mining and quarrying	12.8
2/3 Manufacturing	4.1
4 Construction	0.2
5 Electricity, gas, water and sanitary services	6.4
6 Commerce	2.2
7 Transport, storage and communications	13.0
8 Services	0.9

		Year(s)
Life expectancy at birth (years): male	56.6	1960–1 av.
female	60.4	1960–1 av.
Infant mortality (per '000)	48*	1966
Crude birth rate (per '000)	15*	1960–5 av.
Crude death rate (per '000)	8	1966
Population per physician	4 320	1964
Population per hospital bed	460	1966
School enrolment: age 5–19 years (percentage)	55	1963–4 av.
age over 19 years (per 100 000 population)	127	1963–5 av.

COMMUNICATIONS

		Year(s)
Motor vehicles in use ('000s): private	24.1	1965
commercial	10.8	1965
Railway track (km.)	755	1965
Mail per capita: domestic	2	1963–5 av.
foreign received	2	1963–5 av.
foreign sent	1.2	1963–5 av.
Telephones (per '000 urban population)	137	1967
Radio receivers (per '000 population)	11.3	1963–5 av.
Television sets (per '000 population)		1964
Daily newspapers (per '000 population)	49*	1961

PRODUCTION, EXPORTS AND IMPORTS

Years: 1963–5 average and 1953–5 average   Units: '000 metric tons unless otherwise indicated

1. CEREALS, etc.

	Production		Exports		Imports	
Cassava	8.0*	na				
Maize (corn)	197.3	171.3	0.2	—	39.6	13.7
Millets/sorghum	112.3	117.0	—	—	1.52	—
Potatoes	4.0*	3.01*	1.2	1.1	2.2	0.7
Rice	31.7	17.7	1.2	1.1	1.7	4.3
Wheat	—	—	0.3	—	43.6	3.3

2. FRUIT, etc.

	Production		Exports		Imports	
Apples	na	na	0.1	—	—	—
Bananas	na	na	0.6	—	—	—
Coconuts	na	na	0.62	—	—	—
Oranges	na	na	0.72	—	—	—
Wine b	na	na	0.2	—	1.2	4.7

n no production figures are available, but quantities are known to be small.

3. BEVERAGES, FOREST PRODUCTS, etc.

	Production		Exports		Imports	
Cocoa a	117.8*	69.5*	103.4	66.6	0.4	0.2
Coffee	966.0	268.3p			—	—
Sugar: cane	78.7	34.7q	17.7	1.4	—	—
raw d	1.2*	0.8*		0.1	1.5	1.7
Tobacco: leaf	1 130.0 c	762.7 c			0.3 t	0.62 t
cigarettes	90.01*	21.01			96.12	53.7
Softwood j			2		2	
Hardwood j	2 870.01*	1 053.52			5.91	3.3
Newsprint					13.71	6.0
Other paper	0.42*	—				

d no. in millions. j '000 cu. metres of roundwood equivalent. p for centrifugal sugar only. q in addition, non-centrifugal sugar 22 (1963–5) and 17 (1953–5). r incl. other tobacco products.*

4. VEGETABLE OILSEEDS AND OILS

	Production		Exports		Imports	
Castor seed	na		0.02	—	—	0.01
Castor oil	na				—	—
Coconut oil	na				—	—
Cottonseed	142.70*	34.30	0.55	0.94	0.07	0.04
Cottonseed oil	na	na	11.04		0.96	0.04
Groundnuts	na		3.30		0.01	
Linseed	—	—	0.09		0.01	
Linseed oil	—	—			0.07	0.05
Olive oil	—	—			0.04	0.03
Sesame seed	0.83*	3.152	0.97	2.13	0.02	0.23
Soya bean oil	—	—				

5. LIVESTOCK‡, ANIMAL PRODUCTS, etc.

	Production		Exports		Imports	
Chickens d	1 933.3*	972.0	0.02		0.01	0.04
Cattle d	919.0	803.3			0.07	0.04
dairy cows d	342.7*	na	16.8	28.3	9.3	24.2
Goats d	15.0*	15.3				
Sheep d	74.0*	90.0			41.2	41.2
Horses d	323.0*	280.2	3.5*		0.6	0.1
Pigs d	44.0*	9.52			1.5	0.2
Meat: 'A' d	na	na	3.8		44.0	0.8*
Butter	3.6*	na			0.32	7.2*
Cheese	7.2	na	0.3			
Eggs d	180.52 c	na				
Milk	220.3*	2.01				
Hides/skins						

d no. in millions. r incl. meat equivalent of live imports.

EQUATORIAL GUINEA

WEST AFRICA

Equatorial Guinea, formerly Spanish Guinea, consists of the mainland territory Rio Muni and the island of Fernando Póo together with some smaller islands. A referendum in 1963 resulted in internal self-government, and complete independence from Spain followed in 1968.

AREA: Rio Muni: 26 017 sq. km. (10 045 sq. miles). Fernando Póo: 2 034 sq. km. (785 sq. miles)

LAND USE: (percentage of total)

	1963
Arable and orchard	7.9
Permanent meadow and pasture	3.7
Forest and woodland	81.6
City areas, waste and other land	6.8

POPULATION: Rio Muni: 201 000   Fernando Póo: 76 000 } (1967 provisional estimates)
Largest city: SANTA ISABEL, capital; population: 37 237 (city proper, 1960)

EMPLOYMENT AND TRADE

In Rio Muni, a mountainous jungle area, cocoa and coffee are grown; timber, for veneer, is the only industry. Fernando Póo is also mountainous, with forests of oil palms, ebony, mahogany and oak, and cultivated areas producing cocoa and some coffee, sugar, tobacco and vanilla. Exports are almost entirely to Spain, and in 1965 included in percentages of total value) cacao 32, coffee 15 and wood 13; chief imports were rice 29 and oil products 26.

Total trade (in million $ U.S.):	
Exports (f.o.b.)	5 900
Imports (c.i.f.)	160

		Year(s)
Infant mortality (per '000)	28.1	1965
Crude birth rate (per '000)	22.8	1965
Crude death rate (per '000)	6.3	1965
Accidental deaths (per 100 000 population)	32.5	1965
Population per physician	144	1961
School enrolment: age 5–19 years (percentage)		1963–4 av.

PRODUCTION, EXPORTS AND IMPORTS

Years: 1963–5 average and 1953–5 average   Units: '000 metric tons unless otherwise indicated

1. CEREALS, etc.

	Production	Imports
Cassava	39.3	na
Rice	na	4.82
Sweet potatoes/yams	25.0*	na

2. FRUIT, etc.

	Production	Exports	Imports
Bananas	12.0*	na	2.42
Coconuts b	6.01*	na	
Wine b	—	—	69.7

b '000 hectolitres. c no. in millions.

3. BEVERAGES, FOREST PRODUCTS, etc.

	Production	Exports	Imports
Cocoa a	32.3	21.6*	17.1
Coffee	6.6	6.7*	5.3
Hardwood j	760.7*	140.52	9.41

j '000 cu. metres of roundwood equivalent. n mainly from Fernando Póo.

4. VEGETABLE OILSEEDS AND OILS

	Production	Exports	Imports
Copra	0.43	na	0.25
Olive oil	2.73*	3.04	na
Palm kernels	3.37	2.58	0.22
Palm oil			

5. LIVESTOCK‡, ANIMAL PRODUCTS, etc.

	Production	Exports	Imports
Cattle d	2.3	na	na
Goats d	5.0*	na	na
Sheep d	25.7*	na	na
Pigs d	4.0*	na	na
Eggs d	0.4*	na	na
Fish	0.9*	—	1.22

d no. in thousands.

6. FIBRES, TEXTILES, etc.

	Production	Exports	Imports
Abaca	0.5	—	0.21

7. FUEL AND POWER

	Production	Exports	Imports
Petroleum, refined.	—	—	252

continued

PRODUCTION, EXPORTS AND IMPORTS *continued* (EL SALVADOR)

6. FIBRES, TEXTILES, etc.

	Production		Exports		Imports	
Agaves (letona)	2.9*	1.4*	0.4*	0.1	—	0.8
Cotton lint	78.3*	21.3	67.5	9.8	0.2	0.3
Rubber, natural	—	—	—	—	0.4	—
Cotton: yarn	3.7	0.6	1.32	—	0.21	—
woven fabrics	4.4	1.5	1.01	—	1.8	—
Rayon, woven fabrics	—	—	—	—	0.7	—

7. FUEL AND POWER

	Production		Exports		Imports	
Coal, 'A' ‡.	—		—		—	1
Electricity h: total	379	1401	—			
hydro	340	1301				
thermal	39	101				
Oil, crude	—	—	—		423	na
Petroleum, refined.	423	—	193		60	1501

h million kWh.

8. IRON AND STEEL

	Production		Exports		Imports	
Steel ingots/castings	—		—		2	1

9. NON-FERROUS MINERALS AND METALS

	Production		Exports		Imports	
Gold k, ore.	na	10.00m	na	9.00m	—	—
Silver k, ore m	278.40*		4.80n	259.33h	0.82	0.45
Asbestos: fibre	—	—	—	—	0.11	0.07
manufactured	—	—	—	—	0.28	—
Aluminium	—	—	—	—	0.53	—
Copper, metal	—	—	—	—	0.22	—
Lead, metal	—	—	—	—	—	—

k '000 fine troy oz. m metal content. n bullion.

10. CHEMICALS n AND FERTILIZERS

	Production		Exports		Imports	
Chemicals.					na	
Fertilizers:						
Potash	—		—		1.8	—
Sulphur	—		—		1.2	0.1

n data not available for years 1953–5.

11. INDUSTRY

	Production		Exports		Imports	
Aircraft a	—		—		0.7	0.7a
Alcoholic beverages	133.0		—		0.5a	—
beer b	83.0	46.0	—		59.3	32.3
Cement						
Electrical engineering a	3.7	2.0	3.7		9.9	4.02
Railway vehicles a	—		0.7	0.12	0.1	7.42
Motor vehicles a	—		—		13.6	

a million $ U.S.   b '000 hectolitres.

---

na: data not available. — negligible or nil. … data not available. * estimate. * estimate. 1 one year only. 2 two year average. † re-exports. ‡ see appendix.

ETHIOPIA

Ethiopia, the ancient empire of Abyssinia, was conquered by the Italians in 1936 but liberated five years later. The adjacent Italian colony of Eritrea was federated to Ethiopia in 1952, and in 1962 was incorporated as a province. Data for Eritrea are included in the following.

AREA: 1 023 000 sq. km. (395 000 sq. miles)

LAND USE: (percentage of total)

	1965
Arable and orchard.	10.3
Permanent meadow and pasture	56.4
Forest and woodland	7.3
City areas, waste and other land	26.0

POPULATION: 23 457 000 (1967 estimate)
Largest city: ADDIS ABABA; capital; population: 560 000 (city proper, 1965)

FINANCE
Currency unit: The Ethiopian dollar

Exchange rates	1965	1960	1950
Per $ U.S.	2.5	2.48	2.48
Per £ sterling	7.0	6.96	6.96

		Year(s)
National income (million $ U.S.)	942	1965
G.N.P. per capita ($ U.S.)	60	1966
Foreign trade (percentage of G.D.P.)	19	1963–5 av.

TRADING
Total trade (in million $ U.S.)

	1965	1955
Exports (f.o.b.)	117	62
Imports (c.i.f.)	151	65

Main trading partners (percentage of total value)

Exports	1965	1955	Imports	1965	1955
U.S.A.	55	57	Italy	18	16
Italy,	5	24	Japan	15	16
Saudi Arabia.	5	17	U.S.A.	12	14
Germany F.R.	4	4	U.K.	11	11
U.K.	4	1	Germany F.R.	9	10
France	3	3	France	5	8
Afars/Issas	3	14	Iran	4	—

Distribution of trade (percentage of total value)

Exports	1965	1955*
Coffee	67	56
Hides and skins	8	10
Oilseeds	8	10
Fruit and vegetables	8	na

Imports	1965	1955*
Manufactured goods	74	na
(machinery and transport equipment)	(37)	(20)
(textiles)	(12)	(28)
Crude materials and fuels	11	9
Chemicals	7	2
Food	5	3

EMPLOYMENT AND PRODUCTION

Ethiopia is a mountainous country; the majority of the population avoids the valleys, because of their excessive heat; however some cane sugar and cotton are grown in these lower regions. On the higher land coffee and grain are produced, and livestock are reared by the nomadic population. The forests provide potential wealth in hardwood, but some exploitation of them is increasing. Mineral wealth is as yet unproven, but some salt, potash and gold are mined. With financial assistance from the World Bank, hydro-electric power is being developed, but industry is still small.

COMMUNICATIONS

		Year(s)
Motor vehicles in use ('000s): private	19.8	1963–5 av.
commercial	7	
Railway track (km.)	1015	1965
Radio receivers (per '000 population)	0.1	1967
Television sets (per '000 population)	0.1	1963–5 av.
Daily newspapers (per '000 population)	1.5	1963–5 av.

PRODUCTION, EXPORTS AND IMPORTS
Units: '000 metric tons unless otherwise indicated
Years: 1963–5 average and 1953–5 average

1. CEREALS, etc.	Production		Exports		Imports	
Barley	785.0	633.0*	0.1	1.0		
Maize (corn)	713.0	170.0*	1.3	6.5	0.1	0.1
Millets/sorghum	3 011.3	1 876.0*	1.5	8.8		
Oats	5.0[1]*	na				
Potatoes	138.0	4.0*	2.0[2]	0.1	2.1	0.9
Rice						
Sweet potatoes/ yams	68.0*	25.0*		3.4		
Wheat	279.0	188.0*			2.2	

2. FRUIT, etc.	Production		Exports		Imports	
Bananas	35.0*	21.5*	12.7		1.4*	1.0
Dates	2.0*	1.0				
Lemons						
Oranges	63.0	10.0*	0.4		0.1	0.4
Raisins					0.41	
Tomatoes	9.0*				1.5[2]	2.1
Wine b						1.7

b '000 hectolitres.

3. BEVERAGES, FOREST PRODUCTS, etc.	Production		Exports		Imports	
Coffee	136.0	46.8*	73.0	40.7		
Sugar: cane	750.0	na	7.5			
raw.	69.2	11.7	0.3[2]		0.6	
Tea	1.4	1.5*			0.2[n]	18.4
Tobacco: leaf	404.0q	170.0*			0.5	0.1
cigarettes	1 083.7*	na			0.2[n]	1.7[1]
Softwood j					0.5	
Hardwood j					0.1[2]	0.2[1]
Wood pulp	22 545.7*	na			4.9*	0.2[1]
Newsprint						
Other paper	0.4*	na				na

r no. in millions. j '000 cu. metres of roundwood equivalent. n incl. other tobacco products.

4. VEGETABLE OILSEEDS AND OILS	Production		Exports		Imports
Castor seed	10.57	17.69	6.16	4.40	na
Cottonseed	10.70	7.50	4.63*	na	
Cottonseed oil.	12.60	15.05	4.43[2]	2.20	0.13
Groundnuts	54.00	52.00q	29.16	17.93	

continued

PRODUCTION, EXPORTS AND IMPORTS *continued*

9. NON-FERROUS MINERALS AND METALS	Production		Exports		Imports	
Gold k, cream	26.00	28.00	na	na	na	
Asbestos	na		na		na	
Platinum group metals[f]	0.24*	0.38*	na		na	
Manganese, ore	na		na		—	

k '000 fine troy oz. m metal content.

10. CHEMICALS n AND FERTILIZERS	Production	Exports	Imports
Chemicals.			na
Fertilizers: Potash	na	na	—

n data not available for years 1953–5.

11. INDUSTRY	Production		Exports		Imports	
Aircraft a					1.2p	
Alcoholic beverages: beer b	137.0	13.0	—		0.4a	
Cement b	64.0	12.3	—	0.3	9.0	
Electrical engineering a	—		—		3.8	0.7a	30.7*
Railway vehicles a	—		—		1.4[2]	9.0
Merchant ships a	—		—		7.7	0.8
Motor vehicles a	—		—		3.0	13.8	5.8[2]

a million $ U.S. b '000 hectolitres. g '000 G.R.T. p Eritrea only.

FIJI

The Fiji Islands, previously a British colony, became an independent member of the British Commonwealth in 1970. Nadi Airport provides an important link on the trans-Pacific air route.

AREA: 18 233 sq. km. (7 036 sq. miles)

LAND USE: (percentage of total)

	1960
Arable and orchard.	16.4
Permanent meadow and pasture	44.0
Forest and woodland	38.5
City areas, waste and other land	1.1

POPULATION: 476 727 (1966 census)
Capital city: SUVA; population: 54 900 (city proper, 1966)
Distribution of working population (1956)
Total working population: 93 257

U.N. group no.		Percentage
1	Agriculture, forestry, fishing and hunting	57.1
	Mining and quarrying	2.1
2/3	Manufacturing	6.8
4	Construction	6.9
5	Electricity, gas, water and sanitary services	0.8
6	Commerce	6.7
7	Transport, storage and communications	4.3
8	Services	12.3
9	Others	3.0

		Year
Infant mortality (per '000)	24.4*	1965
Crude birth rate (per '000)	35.9	1965
Crude death rate (per '000)	5.1*	1965
Population per physician	2370	1965
Population per hospital bed	76	1966
School enrolment: age 5–19 years (percentage)		1963

FINANCE
Currency unit: The Fiji dollar replaced the Fiji pound in 1969 at the rate $F1 to £F0.5

Exchange rates	1965a	1960a
Per $ U.S.	0.396	0.396
Per £ sterling	1.11	1.11

		Year
National income (million $ U.S.)	67	1958
G.N.P. per capita ($ U.S.)	280	1966

a Fiji pounds.

TRADING
Total trade (in million $ U.S.)

	1965	1938
Exports (f.o.b.)	50	8
Imports (c.i.f.)	73	7

Main trading partners (percentage of total value)

Exports	1965	1955	Imports	1965	1955
U.K.	45	41	Australia	29	24
U.S.A.	13	19	U.K.	22	37
Canada	7	21	Japan	12	8
New Zealand	3	2	New Zealand	6	5
Japan	3	na	Iran	4	na
Australia	2	2	India	3	6
Tonga					

Distribution of trade (percentage of total value)

Exports	1965a
Sugar	77
Copra and coconut oil	14

Imports	1965a	
Manufactured goods	43	54
(machinery and transport equipment)	(22)	(18)
(textiles)	(6)	(na)
Food	21	20
Crude materials and fuels	12	13
Chemicals	8	6

COMMUNICATIONS

		Year(s)
Motor vehicles in use ('000s): private	6.2	1963–5 av.
commercial	3.4	
Railway track (km.)	708.4[a]	1965
Mail per capita: domestic	5.1	1963–5 av.
foreign received	0.6	
foreign sent	0.8	1967
Telephones (per '000 urban population)	71	1963–5 av.
Radio licences (per '000 population)	17	1963–5 av.
Daily newspapers (per '000 population)	16	1962–4 av.

PRODUCTION, EXPORTS AND IMPORTS *continued*
Units: '000 metric tons unless otherwise indicated

4. VEGETABLE OILSEEDS AND OILS—continued	Production		Exports		Imports
	1960	1955			
Olive oil					0.04
Rapeseed	5.00*	20.00*	1.83[2]	5.27	
Sesame seed	31.67	38.40	11.63*	13.07	
Soya beans	6.00*	5.00*	0.69		
Sunflower seed	29.00*	12.0*			0.02
Tung oil					

q flax grown for seed only.

5. LIVESTOCK‡, ANIMAL PRODUCTS, etc.	Production		Exports		Imports
Chickens d.	41 700.0*n	na			na
Cattle d	25 290.3	21 250.0*	8.0[2]	5.0	
dairy cows d	7 734.3*	na			
Goats d	18 006.0	14 205.0*	14.2	na	
Sheep d	24 611.0	18 900.0*			
Horses d	1 331.0	1 002.0*	0.3*	0.5	
Pigs d	12.0*	12.0*	3.0	0.2	
Meat‡: A	310.7	411.0*	0.1[2]	0.2	0.1
B	53.4	2.0[2]p	0.1[2]q	0.1	
Butter.	35.7*	50.0[2]q	0.2q		0.1
Cheese		5.6[2]	2.1[2]		
Eggs	73.5	607.0	0.7*		
Milk	8.9[2]j	1.62[2]p	9.3a		
Hides/skins	1 517.3*	na	11.8[2]		
Wool	0.2	na			

a million $U.S. d no. in thousands, incl. ducks, geese and turkeys. p excl. Eritrea. q incl. fish landed by foreign vessels.

6. FIBRES, TEXTILES, etc.	Production		Exports		Imports
Agaves (sisal)	1.0*	0.2q	0.6		2.5
Jute	8.3	2.5[2]			5.1
Cotton lint.	6.1	0.8			0.6
Cotton: yarn					0.01
woven fabrics					2.6[1]

q excl. Eritrea.

7. FUEL AND POWER	Production		Exports		Imports
Coal 'A'‡	208	50			6[2]
Electricity‡: total	153	201			
hydro	55	30			
thermal					
Petroleum, refined			167		70[1]

h million kWh.

continued

---

na: data not available. — negligible or nil. * estimate. ‡ see appendix. [1] one year only. [2] two year average. † re-exports.

FIJI continued

PRODUCTION, EXPORTS AND IMPORTS
Years: 1963–5 average and 1953–5 average. Units: '000 metric tons unless otherwise indicated

	Production		Exports		Imports	
	1965	1953–5	1965		1965	
1. CEREALS, etc.						
Cassava	80.0*	51.0	—	—	—	—
Potatoes	20.3	24.5²	—	0.1	4.9	2.5
Sweet potatoes/yams	12.3*	16.0	—	—	6.2	0.6
Wheat	—	—	—	—	0.1	—
2. FRUIT, etc.						
Apples	na	na	—	—	0.3	—
Bananas	228.7²*	na	4.2	11.8	0.1	—
Coconuts	311.1	na	0.1	—	0.1	—
Oranges			—	—	0.6	—
Wine b.			—	—	—	—
3. BEVERAGES, FOREST PRODUCTS, etc.						
Sugar: cane	2 312.0	1 288.0	159.4		0.1	0.2
raw	300.7	165.2			0.4	0.3
Tea			—	—	0.6	—
Tobacco: leaf	294.0*	na	—	—	—	2.0n
cigarettes			—	—	1.4	30.3²
Softwood j			8.0	0.8²	—	—
Hardwood j	103.7	76.0²	4.3	—	0.12	—
Newsprint j					0.15	—
Other paper	21.0	9.0¹	—	—	0.52*	—

e no. in millions. j '000 cu. metres of roundwood equivalent. n incl. other tobacco products.

5. LIVESTOCK, ANIMAL PRODUCTS etc.—continued

	Production		Exports		Imports	
Bacon/ham	2.0	2.0¹	{ —	—	0.1	0.1
Meat‡: 'A'	0.1*	na	{		1.3	0.5
'B'			—	—	0.2	0.1
Butter	1.0	0.4	—	—	0.4	0.3
Cheese		na	—	—	0.1	—
Eggs	10.0*	25.0*	—	—	4.3	na
Fish		na	1.5	1.5	9.7	5.3
Milk			—	—		
Hides/skins			—	—		

d no. in thousands.

6. FIBRES, TEXTILES, etc.

	Production		Exports		Imports	
Cotton, raw			—	—	0.8	0.6
Rayon, woven fabrics			—	—		
woven fabrics			—	—	0.5p	0.3

p incl. synthetic piece goods.

7. FUEL AND POWER

	Production		Exports		Imports	
Coal, 'A' ‡			—	—	5	19
Electricity h‡	91		10†	na†	173	60¹
Petroleum, refined						

h million kWh. t thermal.

9. NON-FERROUS MINERALS AND METALS

	Production		Exports		Imports	
Gold k, ore	105.30m	73.00m	104.982²q 74.29q		0.27‡q 0.04q	
Silver k, ore	56.00m	19.00m	60.452²q 14.92q		0.14q	
Copper, ore	na	na	0.01	—	0.07r	0.01
Lead, metal					0.08	—
Manganese, ore	3.22	9.99	5.34	5.81		
Tin, metal					0.28	—

k '000 fine troy oz. m metal content. r mete‡. q bullion.

11. INDUSTRY

	Production		Exports		Imports	
Alcoholic beverages beer b	25.0		—	—	0.9au	0.9au
Cement v	31.0		—	—	16.3*	17.0*
Railway vehicles a					0.4	—
Motor vehicles a			—	—	3.9	1.21

a million $ U.S. b '000 hectolitres. u beer and spirits only. v incl. data for Gilbert and Ellice Islands and British Solomon Islands.

continued

FINANCE

Currency unit: The new markka, or Finnmark, equivalent to 100 old markkas, was introduced in 1963

Exchange rates	1965	1960	1955	1938
Per $ U.S.	3.22	320.5	230.0	48.95
Per £ sterling	9.016	898.81	644.3	225.17

		Year(s)
National income (million $ U.S.)	6454	1965
G.N.P. per capita ($ U.S.)	1 600	1966
Rate of increase of G.N.P. per capita	4.4	1960–4 av.
Foreign trade (percentage of G.D.P.)	38	1964–5 av.

TRADING

Total trade (in million $ U.S.)	1965	1955	1938
Exports (f.o.b.)*	1 428	787	181
Imports (c.i.f.)*	1 648	769	183

Main trading partners (percentage of total value)

Exports	1965	1955	1938	Imports	1965	1955	1938
U.K.	16	20	22	U.K.	14	11	18 d
U.S.S.R.	16	17	—	Germany F.R.	18	9	18 d
Germany F.R.	11	9	15 d	U.S.S.R.	14	13	—
Sweden	7	6	2	Sweden	13	6	11
U.S.A.	6	4	3	U.S.A.	6	5	10
Netherlands	4	5	4	France	4	4	2
France	4	5	3	Netherlands	4	4	3

Distribution of trade (percentage of total value)

Exports	1965	1955	1938*
Wood products and paper	69	80	80
Machinery and transport equipment	12	12	6
Dairy produce and eggs	3	1	1
Textiles and clothing	—	—	—
Imports			
Manufactured goods (machinery and transport equipment)	60	50	na
Crude materials and fuels (mineral fuels)	19 (35)	22 (23)	na (10)
Chemicals	10 (10)	8 (12)	4
Food	9	19	13

d incl. Germany D.R.

NORTHERN EUROPE

FINLAND

Finland became a republic in 1919. Territorial concessions had to be made to the U.S.S.R. in 1940 and 1944, but the two countries are now linked by a treaty of non-aggression and mutual assistance.

AREA: 337 032 sq. km. (130 129 sq. miles) incl. inland water, 31 557 sq. km.

LAND USE: (percentage of total)
	1965	1955
Arable and orchard	8.1	7.7
Permanent meadow and pasture	0.4	0.8
Forest and woodland	64.6	64.3
City areas, waste and other land	26.9	27.2

POPULATION: 4 664 000 (1967 estimate)
Largest city: HELSINKI capital; population: 651 988 (1965)

Distribution of working population: (1960)
Total working population: 2 033 268

U.N. group no.		Percentage
0	Agriculture, forestry, fishing and hunting	35.5
1	Mining and quarrying	0.3
2/3	Manufacturing	21.6
4	Construction	8.7
5	Electricity, gas, water and sanitary services	0.9
6	Commerce	11.6
7	Transport, storage and communications	6.4
8	Services	14.8
9	Others	0.3

		Year(s)
Life expectancy at birth (years): male	65.4	1961–5 av.
female	72.6	
Infant mortality (per '000)	17.6	1965
Crude birth rate (per '000)	16.9	1965
Crude death rate (per '000)	9.6	1965
Accidental deaths (per 100 000 population) caused by motor vehicles	23.3	1965
due to other causes	34.2	1965
Population per physician	1 300	1965
Population per hospital bed	90	1966
School enrolment: age 5–19 years (percentage)	81	1963–4 av.
age over 19 years (per 100/'000 population)	813	1964–5 av.

COMMUNICATIONS

Motor vehicles in use ('000s): private	387.5	1963–5 av.
commercial	5 363	
Railway track (km.)	79	1964
Mail per capita: domestic	19.2	1963–5 av.
foreign received	326.5	
foreign sent	136.5	
Telephones (per '000 urban population)	359	1967
Radio licences (per '000 population)		1963–5 av.
Television licences (per '000 population)		1963–5 av.
Daily newspapers (per '000 population)		1960

continued

PRODUCTION, EXPORTS AND IMPORTS
Years: 1963–5 average and 1953–5 average. Units: '000 metric tons unless otherwise indicated

	Production		Exports		Imports	
1. CEREALS, etc.						
Barley	454.7	279.3	5.3		22.6	1.1²
Maize (corn)			1.8†		50.4	37.5
Millets/sorghum			1.5†			
Oats	860.7	774.0	9.4		23.6	12.0
Potatoes	1 109.3	1 178.7			2.0*	4.7
Rice					13.4	12.0
Rye	159.0	127.0	2.7		43.7*	96.5
Wheat	453.7	214.3	8.4		174.9³*	240.4
2. FRUIT, etc.						
Apples	26.0	38.3			37.5	13.7
Bananas					14.4	5.1
Dates					0.3	0.1*
Grapes					9.4	0.9
Lemons					2.8	1.3
Oranges					35.8	19.7
Other citrus fruit					1.9	0.7
Pears					5.6	1.4
Raisins					3.7	5.6
Wine b					56.1	30.7
3. BEVERAGES, FOREST PRODUCTS, etc.						
Cocoa					1.3	0.7
Coffee	431.3	289.7			43.2	26.9
Sugar: beet	54.1	31.7				
Tea					0.7	—
Tobacco: leaf	29.0	12.3			140.4	129.3
cigarettes r	25.0	5 476.3			0.5	0.4
tobacco/snuff	0.8	0.5			6.3	5.0
Softwood j	6 415.0	5 896.2	7 458.0	6 900.0*		
Hardwood j	32 556.0	26 166.7	121.3	91.8	542.7	13.3
Wood pulp	5 243.0	2 362.0	2 056.7	1 150.3	25.9	12.9
Newsprint j	990.7	479.7	2 362.0	421.3	3.7	0.3
Other paper	1 887.7	631.7	1 500.7	451.7	8.3	1.5

b '000 hectolitres. j '000 cu. metres of roundwood equivalent. r incl. data for tobacco products.

4. VEGETABLE OILSEEDS AND OILS

	Production		Exports		Imports	
Castor oil					0.09	0.16
Copra					8.71	8.74
Coconut oil			0.03		0.35	0.43
Groundnuts					1.23	0.17
Groundnut oil					0.16	0.17
Linseed	29.0				12.38	5.62
Linseed oil		1.00²*	0.03		0.36	0.36
Olive oil					0.04	0.10
Palm kernels					0.34	
Palm kernel oil			0.15		0.01	0.17
Palm oil					0.04	1.18
Rapeseed	7.70	17.30	0.01	0.23	2.57	0.07
Rapeseed oil	666	89		0.30*	0.05	0.07
Soya beans	347	170		—²	na	19.852
Soya bean oil			6.46		0.01	0.13
Sunflower seed oil					0.55	0.10
Tung oil					0.15	0.41

5. LIVESTOCK‡, ANIMAL PRODUCTS, etc.

	Production		Exports		Imports	
Chickens d					0.1	14.7
Cattle d	1 942.0*	na			1.8	1.0
Goats d	113.7	81.0¹			14.6	0.1
Horses d	24.0*	24.0¹			2.7	0.7
Pigs d	21.0	9.0¹			0.8	3.8
Chickens d	6 869.3	5 930.7				
Cattle d	2 116.3	1 865.3	1.2		3.4*	2.2p
dairy cows d	1 173.0	1 156.3			3.4	2.7q
Goats d	2.0*	4.7		0.1	2.5	1.5²q
Sheep d	219.7	885.0			2.4r	0.2¹
Horses d	203.7	326.0				
Pigs d	597.0	494.3				
Meat‡: 'A'	163.3	128.7	2.6	2.3	4.3	1.9
'B'	24.3	15.9	0.3	0.6	1.5	0.7
Butter	102.7	62.3	19.7	1.1		
Cheese	35.7	22.3	19.5	11.2		
Eggs	50.2	32.6	9.1	0.1*		
Milk	3 782.7	2 914.0	17.1		32.2	13.4*
Fish	73.3	62.7	17.8	2.1²	7.7	1.5*
Hides/skins	9.0²	9.3			1.4	8.4²
Wool	1.0	1.0				1.0

6. FIBRES, TEXTILES, etc.

	Production		Exports		Imports	
Abaca						0.1
Agaves (sisal etc.)						1.0
Cotton lint						0.7
Flax fibre		0.2*				0.3
Hemp fibre						3.8
Jute						
Rubber: natural						
synthetic	17.6	13.6	2.3			2.2p
Cotton: yarn	12.7	9.8	2.8	9.2		2.7q
woven fabrics	25.0	14.8	18.2			1.5²q
Rayon: fibre/yarn	0.1		0.3			0.2¹
woven fabrics						
Non-cellulosic fibre/yarn		7.8				
Wool: yarn	6.0²	5.6*				
woven fabrics	4.4¹		0.1			

p incl. nylon and waste. q incl. rayon, nylon and waste. r cloth of continuous filament yarn only. t excl. blankets.

7. FUEL AND POWER

	Production		Exports		Imports	
Coal			—	—	2 377	1 943
Coke			—	—	690	377
Electricity h: total	13 360	5 970¹				
hydro	8 788	5 350¹				
thermal	4 572	620¹				
Oil, crude					2 500	na
Petroleum, refined	2 193	na			2 397	1 110¹
Uranium	na					

h million kWh.

8. IRON AND STEEL

	Production		Exports		Imports	
Iron ore	331 m	74 m	224	240	622	90
Pig iron	666	89	510	7	57	25
Steel ingots/castings	347	na	61		52	33
Iron/steel scrap	na	na	3	2	121	50
Iron/steel products a	na	na	26	2	102	63

a million $ U.S. m metal content.

continued

149

na: data not available. — negligible or nil. ¹ one year only. ² two year average. * estimate. † re-exports. ‡ see appendix.

FINLAND continued

PRODUCTION, EXPORTS AND IMPORTS continued

9. NON-FERROUS MINERALS AND METALS

	Production		Exports		Imports	
	1964	1953				
Gold, ore m	20.00	18.00	—	—	0.801n	47.90n
Platinum group metals b	—	—	—	—	4.33²	0.48
Silver, k, ore m	590.00	233.30	7.40	3.83	534.33n	256.03n
Asbestos: fibre	10.62	11.66	0.84	0.69	6.77	1.19
manufactured	na	na	0.05†	—	1.10	0.43
Mica	—	—	—	—	0.47	—
Aluminium:						
alumina	—	—	—	—	11.34p	0.06
aluminium	113.81	46.24	145.94	15.39	28.94	21.73
Chrome, metal	—	0.09	1.27i	—	0.95	0.98
Cobalt, ore	1.72m	na	0.08	—	0.02	—
Copper: ore m	31.99	20.52	1.51	—	11.34	2.74
metal	33.83q	21.15	12.47	3.65	10.52	10.35
Lead: ore m	3.11	—	0.02	—	13.44	—
Magnesium: metal	—	—	—	—	1.84	1.13
Magnesite	—†	—†	—†	—	5.14	4.37
Manganese, metal	—	—	—	0.5	2.00	1.54
metal/salts	3.17m	0.16m	2.70	—	31.40	41.60†
Molybdenum, metal	—	—	—	—	69.00	14.20
Nickel: ore m	—	—	77.90²	28.21	0.22	0.28
metal	—	—	—	0.14	0.37	0.43
Tin, metal	—	—	—	0.04	1.40	3.12
Titanium minerals	0.88m	9.62m	—	—	—	—
Tungsten, ore	66.12m	0.09	1.27i	15.39	8.37	8.55
Vanadium	—	—	—	—	—	—
Zinc: ore m	—	—	0.08	—	—	—

f metric tons. k '000 fine troy oz. m metal content. n bullion/coins, etc.
p hydrate. q incl. scrap. r incl. amalgam. t vanadium oxide. x recovered sulphur. z sulphur content.

10. CHEMICALS n AND FERTILIZERS

Organic chemicals:

	Production		Exports		Imports	
Benzene	0.3	—	—	—	—	—
Butadiene	—	—	—	—	—	—
Ethylene	—	—	—	—	na	—
Methanol	—	—	—	—	4.9	—
Phenol	na	—	—	—	3.0	—
Phthalic anhydride	—	—	—	—	0.4	—
Styrene monomer	—	—	—	—	—	—
Urea	—	—	—	—	1.9	—

continued

---

10. CHEMICALS n AND FERTILIZERS—continued

Inorganic chemicals:

	Production		Exports		Imports	
Ammonia	66.8		0.2		0.9	2.2
Carbon black	95.2		0.2		2.2	
Chlorine	4.2		—		0.2	
Nitric acid	0.8²		1.6		70.2	
Sodium carbonate	107.0		—		3.7	
Sodium hydroxide	357.3		—		22.5	
Sulphuric acid						
Plastics:						
Polyamides	—		0.1		na	
Polyethylene	—		—		8.2	
Polyvinyl chloride	—		—		10.5	
Fertilizers:						
Phosphates	—		—		308.5	163.3
Potash	257.4x	115.3x	65.3		170.8	100.6
Pyrites	60.0p	na	53.0		66.4	39.1
Sulphur						

p recovered sulphur. x sulphur content.

n data not available for years 1953–5.

11. INDUSTRY

	Production		Exports		Imports	
Aircraft a	na		—		14.3	0.7²
Alcoholic beverages	1 083.0	905.7	0.2a		6.6a	3.2a
beer b	65.0*h	104.6p				
spirits b	1 577.3	1 026.3				
Cement	1 083.0		54.0	42.0	10.3	3.7
Electrical engineering a	159.7²		3.3²	18.9	98.4	27.6²
Locomotives a	49.0		na		22.4	—
Machine tools a	—		na		19.5	0.6
Railway vehicles a	—		na		na	—
Merchant ships g	—		97.0	44.2	6.8	36.5²a
Motor vehicles d	136.0		44.0		132.8x	—
commercial d	—		—		—	—
private	1.1		1.4*q		—	—

a million $ U.S. b '000 hectolitres. c no. of units. g '000 G.R.T.
p 1960 figure. q incl. assembly of imported parts.

continued

FRANCE

The Fifth Republic was created in 1958 after France had recovered from German occupation during the second world war. This new constitution emphasizes the role of the president. France is a member of the European Economic Community.

AREA: 551 601 sq. km. (212 919 sq. miles)

LAND USE: (percentage of total)

	1964	1953
Arable and orchard	38.1	38.6
Permanent meadow and pasture	24.3	22.7
Forest and woodland	21.8	20.7
City areas, waste and other land	15.8	18.4

POPULATION: 49 890 000 (1967 estimate)

Largest city: PARIS, capital; population: 7 369 387 (1962)

Distribution of working population (1962)
Total working population: 19 711 500

	Percentage
	1966
Agriculture, forestry, fishing and hunting	19.8
Mining and quarrying	1.6
Manufacturing	26.9
2/3 Construction	8.9
4 Electricity, gas, water and sanitary services	1.3
5 Commerce	13.2
6 Transport, storage and communications	5.4
7 Services	20.1
9 Others	3.9

U.N. group no.

		Year(s)
Life expectancy at birth (years): male	68.2	1966
female	75.4	
Infant mortality (per '000)	11.2	1965
Crude birth rate (per '000)		
Crude death rate (per '000)	11.2	1965
Accidental deaths (per 100 000 population)	25.2	1965
caused by motor vehicles	44.2	1965
due to other causes	900	1965
Population per physician	120a	1965
Population per hospital bed	934	1963–4 av.
School enrolment: age 5–19 years (percentage)	93	1963–5 av.
age over 19 years (per 100 000 population)		

a government hospitals only.

EUROPE

COMMUNICATIONS

		Year(s)
Motor vehicles in use ('000s): private	8 784.3	1963–5 av.
commercial	2 062.1	1965
Railway track (km.)	38 180	
Mail per capita: domestic	165	1963–5 av.
foreign sent	na	
foreign received	13.2	1967
Telephones (per '000 population)	309	1963–5 av.
Television licences (per '000 population)	113.3	1963–5 av.
Radio licences (per '000 population)	245	1963
Daily newspapers (per 000 population)		

FINANCE

Currency unit: The franc. The new franc, equivalent to 100 old francs, was introduced in 1960

Exchange rates	1965	1960	1950b	1938b
Per $ U.S.	4.902	4.903	350	38.01
Per £ sterling	13.738	13.743	980	175.00

			Year(s)
National Income (million $ U.S.)	70 240		1965
G.N.P. per capita ($ U.S.)	1 730		1966
Rate of increase of G.N.P. per capita	3.8		1960–4 av.
Foreign trade (percentage of G.D.P.)	21		1963–5 av.
b old francs			

TRADING

Total trade (in million $ U.S.)	1965	1955	1938
Exports (f.o.b.)	10 051	4 911	879
Imports (c.i.f.)	10 338	4 739	1 329

Main trading partners (percentage of total value)

Exports	1965	1955	1938	Imports	1965	1955	1938
Germany F.R.	18	10	7d	Germany F.R.	18	9	7d
Belg./Lux.	10	7	14	U.S.A.	10	11	11
Italy	9	4	4	Belg./Lux.	8	8	11
U.S.A.	6	7	8	Italy	7	5	8
Switzerland	6	5	6	Algeria	6	12	5
Algeria	5	12	4	U.K.	5	5	5
Netherlands	5	3	4	Netherlands	5	4	3

d incl. Germany D.R.

continued

FRANCE continued

TRADING continued

Distribution of trade (percentage of total value)

	1965	1955	1938*
Exports			
Manufactured goods	63	57	na
Machinery and transport equipment	(26)	(16)	(8)
(textiles and clothing)	(9)	(11)	(12)
Food	13	12	11
Crude materials and fuels	10	8	na
Chemicals	10	8	7
Alcoholic beverages	10	3	5
Imports			
Manufactured goods	44	25	na
Machinery and transport equipment	(20)	(10)	(5)
Crude materials and fuels	31	46	na
(mineral fuels)	(15)	(18)	(19)
Food	15	17	16
Chemicals	7	4	4
Alcoholic beverages	2	5	8

PRODUCTION, EXPORTS AND IMPORTS

Years: 1963–5 average and 1953–5 average   Units: '000 metric tons unless otherwise indicated

1. CEREALS, etc.

	Production		Exports		Imports	
	1965		1965		1965	1938*
Barley	7 184.3	2 478.3	1 993.7	32.7	0.9	101.0
Maize (corn)	3 161.3	949.7	679.6	7.6	560.1	342.9
Millets/sorghum	75.3	5.5a	10.2	1.2	54.4	35.8
Oats	2 665.0	3 625.7	41.4	16.0	11.2	7.9
Potatoes	12 921.0	15 671.0	404.6	223.6	209.1	260.7
Rice	112.3	67.3	6.4	1.7	6.4	6.5
Rye	377.7	473.7	19.3	0.5	0.6	6.5
Wheat	12 949.0	9 970.7	3 214.3	1 245.9	684.6	241.4

2. FRUIT, etc.

	Production		Exports		Imports	
Apples	3 496.7	4 134.0	97.6	74.3	104.7	30.3
Apricots	103.7	42.3	na	1.6	na	5.1
Bananas	—	—	2.4	0.7	371.4	266.2
Cherries	119.7	83.3	9.7	8.1	19.3	19.6
Dates	—	—	na	na	7.1	8.6
Figs	4.3	—	30.5	36.7	82.1	48.2
Grapes	9 628.0*	9 239.3	0.3	0.5	733.9	595.4
Lemons						
Oranges	2.7	1.3	1.1	—	37.4	12.2
Other citrus fruit						
Olives	7.3	30.0	na	0.9	na	1.5
Peaches	452.0	160.2	24.6	4.0n	28.2	4.6n
Pears	418.0*	347.3	0.5	0.7	9.9	7.4
Plums	130.3	134.5				
Raisins	—	—				
Tomatoes	510.3	246.3				
Wine b	62 204.0	60 341.0	4 030.4	2 948.0p	10 630.8	15 255.0q

b '000 hectolitres. n excl. pears for perry. p excl. fortified wine 1 232.0.
q excl. fortified wine.

3. BEVERAGES, FOREST PRODUCTS, etc.

	Production		Exports		Imports	
Cocoa	—	—	0.6†	—	62.9	47.5
Coffee	—	—			222.4	172.2
Sugar: raw	15 717.7	10 259.3¹				
beet	2 334.8	1 651.2	842.1	551.7	427.7	351.5
Tea	—	—	1.7	1.0	2.2	1.4
Tobacco: leaf	44.3	55.0			48.6	37.2
cigars	311.0c	97.2c			—	—
cigarettes	52 256.0c	38 240.7c				1.3²
tobacco/snuff	17.9	19.2				
Softwood j	13 870.5	12 442.7	893.0	1 105.1	2 343.2	719.1
Hardwood j	13 159.5	22 874.7	1 084.0	997.5	1 485.5	341.5
Wood pulp j	1 359.3	1 157.3	96.4	10.7	910.3	463.0
Newsprint	450.3	380.0	3.4	13.6	88.7	57.0
Other paper	2 648.3	1 237.0	163.3	82.7	393.7	38.3

c no. in millions. j '000 cu. metres of roundwood equivalent.

4. VEGETABLE OILSEEDS AND OILS

	Production		Exports		Imports	
Castor seed	na	na	0.01†	—	23.75	19.90
Copra	na	na	0.82	0.60	25.82	1.20
Coconut oil	na	na	1.92	3.07	95.33	87.37
Cottonseed	na	na			3.87	4.64n
Cottonseed oil	na	na			1.01	1.13
Groundnuts	5 000	258¹			0.36†	0.31
Groundnut oil	3 063	900¹	3.63†	0.77†	49.17	309.97
Linseed	45 060	21 220¹	16.72*	0.24	143.07	116.07
Linseed oil	1 054n	—	0.92	0.07	73.32	13.80
Olive oil	43.67	17.50²	0.90	1.66	13.60	13.80
Palm kernels	1.00	7.00*	3.03*	7.70a	18.48	30.36*
Palm kernel oil	na	na	0.31	0.06†	78.36	139.23
Palm oil	na	na	0.87†	2.83	3.81	25.54
Rapeseed	239.00	96.67	17.01	7.70*	37.64	2.43
Sesame seed	na	na	105.63	0.07†	105.63	3.13
Soya beans	na	na	1.63†	1.63†	148.08	57.03
Soya bean oil	na	na	3.58	0.31	1.24	0.20
Sunflower seed	28.00	3.67	1.75	—	0.89	—
Sunflower seed oil	na	na	0.04	—	1.35	—
Tung oil	—	—	0.03†	0.07p	2.11	2.64

n incl. palm kernel oil. p incl. other minor vegetable oils.

5. LIVESTOCK‡, ANIMAL PRODUCTS, etc.

	Production		Exports		Imports	
Chickens d	80 000*	75 000¹				3.0
Cattle d	20 226	16 831	185.8	63.9	20.3	
dairy cows d	10 980*	9 077²				
Goats d	1 078	1 273	16.8	na	140.8	na
Sheep d	8 797	7 838				
Horses d	1 370	2 275				
Pigs d	9 030	7 369	62.2	4.4	333.7	70.1
Bacon/ham¹	2 943		84.7	1.1	146.4	0.1
Meat†: A			26.8	37.4	57.8	24.0
B	1 030	805				7.8
Butter	430	301*	35.3	5.3	8.9	9.3
Cheese	529*	323	56.1	5.5	22.0	8.8
Eggs	536*	425²	4.4	18.5	6.3	15.0
Fish	763n	592n	37.3	40.7²a	318.2	113.2*
Milk	25 801	18 167	925.1	60.3	128.5	33.2
Whale/sperm oil	—¹	—	—	—	19.0	—
Hides/skins	—	—	66.3	30.1	133.3	84.4²
Wool	10²	10	18.3	14.7s	90.6	97.9

d no. in thousands. s incl. re-exports.
n incl. fish landed by French vessels in foreign ports.

6. FIBRES, TEXTILES, etc.

	Production		Exports		Imports	
Abaca	—	—	—	—	4.9	
Agaves (sisal etc.)	—	—	0.1†	0.1†	60.7	37.1
Cotton lint	—	—	0.9†	6.4†	265.7	288.1
Flax fibre	72.5	36.2	121.7†	0.6†	2.6	11.5
Hemp fibre	2.5	2.6	0.6	0.3†	98.5	6.0
Jute	—	—	3.0†	0.8†	132.7	94.2
Rubber: natural	125.5	38.3	58.3	123.0r	77.7	128.0
synthetic	5.0	2.0	143.7†		765.7	18.0
Silk f	288.0	194.0h	41.0	17.5	22.4	648.7
Cotton: yarn	218.4	104.4h	45.7	24.3	12.0	1.1
woven fabrics	138.6	104.4	12.9	13.8	8.9	2.8
Rayon/fibre/yarn	47.1	31.0p				0.4
woven fabrics						
Non-cellulosic	87.0	8.5	20.4	17.8	15.5	na
Wool: yarn	145.1	125.7	25.2	4.8	1.8	0.3
woven fabrics	71.3	64.0	6.5		6.5	1.7*

f metric tons. h '000 cu. metres.
p total output of broad woven fabrics by the French silk industry plus the production of rayon and synthetic fibre piece goods by the French cotton industry. s incl. re-exports.

7. FUEL AND POWER

	Production		Exports		Imports	
Coal: A.†: B.†	50 710	55 330	948	9 086	14 675	8 141
	1 477	2 050	28	6	478	521
Coke	94 489	45 550¹	48	316	4 977	3 812
Electricity h: total	41 510	23 610¹				
hydro	632					
nuclear	52 347	21 940¹			63	
thermal	5 000	258¹			50 360	24 900¹
Natural gas i	3 063	900¹	8 123	5 280¹	3 757	730¹
Oil, crude	45 060	21 220¹	280†	189¹	59r	631¹
Petroleum, refined	1 054n				2 030a	
Rare earths/q						
Uranium/f						

f metric tons. h million kWh. i million cu. metres.
q salts of rare earth minerals. r in addition, rare earth minerals 1 316. t in metal content.

8. IRON AND STEEL

	Production		Exports		Imports	
Iron ore	17 978m	14 006m	21 640	12 006	3 711	618
Pig iron	15 304	9 599	364	357	218	110
Steel	18 769	11 010	489	428	628	160
Steel ingots/castings	na	na	1 510	535	552	158
Iron/steel scrap	na	na	877	546	541	71
Iron/steel products a						

a million $ U.S. m metal content.

continued

na: data not available.   — negligible or nil.   * estimate.   ² two year average.   ¹ one year only.   ‡ see appendix.   † re-exports.

PRODUCTION, EXPORTS AND IMPORTS continued

	Production		Exports		Imports	

9. NON-FERROUS MINERALS AND METALS

	Production		Exports		Imports	
Diamonds a	—	—	6.50	5.20	22.48	9.75
Gold k: ore m, etc.	55.00	37.00				
Platinum group metals k	na	na	780.00†	533.70	10 032.00	14 396.30
Silver k: ore m	1 033.00 p	620.00 p	4 347.33	2 334.32	163.59	121.78
bullion			6.70	3.57	25 838.67	9 143.17
Asbestos: fibre	17.51	11.12	42.12	0.42	96.91	40.86
manufactured			0.77 s	0.16†	32.58	0.20
Mica	0.22	na	202.70	315.29	4.77	1.65
Aluminium: bauxite	2 374.51	1 312.34	157.41	72.33	136.40	10.61
alumina	802.14	na	209.44	52.67	85.23	2.31
aluminium	318.29	120.72	0.05		1.74	6.00
Antimony: ore m	na	na	0.13 m	0.13 m	2.40	0.03
metal	0.11 m	na	0.13	0.50	2.40	0.03
Beryl	na	na			0.60	0.03
Cadmium	0.41	0.15	0.08		0.61	0.21
Chrome: ore	na	na			190.45	76.42
Cobalt: ore	—	—	18.80	8.95	1.95	3.28
metal	na	na			10.86	82.00
Copper: ore	0.30 m	0.35 m	0.68	0.75	10.37	0.76
metal	na	na	1.12	0.01	89.99†	13.59†
Lead: ore	12.88 n	11.27 m	2.79	0.90	273.74	142.65
metal	88.59	62.21	25.30	16.66	135.58	87.90
Magnesium: dolomite	1 123.56	na			57.03	56.81
magnesite	na	na	24.50	9.66	182.43	170.03
kieserite	—	—	0.47	0.08	34.87	21.44
metal/salts	1.82 w	1.22 u	4.13 t	4.45 t	38.68	2.26
Manganese: ore q	na	na	1.73	2.20	786.00	509.44
metal	—	—	199.59	68.42	12.61	15.22
Mercury f	na	na	6.70 †	6.50 †	438.70	345.70
Molybdenum f: ore	na	na			4 550.90	na
metal	—	—	613.00	3.50	87.00	6.70
Nickel: ore	na	na	0.65 †	0.07 †	13.59	16.16
metal	na	na	7.61	1.68	35.72	2.04
Tin: ore	0.41 m	0.50 m	0.56	0.46		
metal	—	—	33.70	0.57	11.03	8.60
Titanium minerals	na	na	0.26	0.52 †	122.40	2.89 r
metal	na	1.14	1.98	na		
Tungsten: ore	na	na	0.57	0.37	0.41	0.18
metal	—	—	1.41		327.15	236.22
Vanadium	na	na				
Zinc: ore	18.65 m	12.76 m	24.36	5.71	65.82	35.21
metal	183.79 v	101.33			24.19	
Zirconium minerals	—	—				

a million $ U.S. f metric tons. k '000 fine troy oz. m metal content. d no. of units. u no. in thousands. r 1959/60 figure.
Gold k: bullion. q incl. manganiferous iron ore. r 1965—7 av. p data incomplete. q 1967 figure.
silver refined from imported ore. q incl. s incl. re-exports. t incl. titanium n 1965—7 G.R.T. n 1965—7 av. p '000 hectolitres.
oxide only. s incl. ferro-vanadium. u vanadium oxide. w incl. figure.
dust. w primary magnesium only.

10. CHEMICALS n AND FERTILIZERS

	Production		Exports		Imports	
Organic chemicals:						
Benzene	178.5		6.8		89.0	
Ethylene	22.1 2		3.6		57.9	
Methanol	184.3				10.8	
Phenol	112.4		20.6		5.1 p	
Phthalic anhydride	91.9		2.6 p		3.8	
Styrene monomer	47.6		10.7		44.1	
Urea	58.3		4.5		15.5	
	88.0		104.9			
Inorganic chemicals:						
Ammonia	1 128.6		17.1		36.9	
Carbon black	87.3		33.9		39.3	
Chlorine	532.6		4.3		1.1	
Nitric acid	2 094.3		3.7		0.3	
Sodium carbonate	1 011.0		223.1			
Sodium hydroxide	682.6		119.8		29.4	
Sulphuric acid	2 660.5		59.2		20.6	
Plastics:						
Polyamides	na		9.0		2.7	
Polyethylene	85.1		22.0		45.9	
Polyvinyl chloride	197.7		46.8		15.5	
Fertilizers:						
Phosphates	42.9	103.0	6.5	0.9	2 545.9	1 295.9
Potash	1 805.2 y	1 058.3 y	1 239.9	1 049.5	63.8	6.2
Pyrites	82.0 x	135.8 x	0.7		371.9	482.4
Sulphur: native	—	2.9			198.0	185.5
recovered	1 480.1 r		996.5	12.3		
x sulphur content. y K₂O content.					p incl. phenol salts. r from natural gas.	

11. INDUSTRY

	Production		Exports		Imports	
Aircraft a	1 118.0 n	na	129.0	7.8	58.9	34.1
Alcoholic beverages			274.1 a	146.9 a	220.1 a	228.6 a
beer b	19 299.0	9 915.0 p				
spirits b	2 678.0 z	1 260.0 r				
Cement	20 538.3	9 665.3	878.0	896.3	83.0	10.3
Electrical						
engineering a	3 546.8 2	na	458.7	139.3 2	378.8	61.7 2
Locomotives c	511.0	180.0 2	33.0	42.6	na	1.5
Railway vehicles a	na	na	60.1	12.9 2	94.4	34.5 2
Machine tools a	220.0 †	na	248.0	73.2	25.0	35.9
Merchant ships g	479.0	276.0	684.6 a	228.4 2 a	294.3 a	29.2 a
Motor vehicles						
commercial d	253.6	154.7				
private d	1 402.4	452.9				

a million $ U.S. b '000 hectolitres. c no. of units.
g '000 G.R.T. n 1965—7 av. p data incomplete. r 1965—7 av.
figure.

PRODUCTION, EXPORTS AND IMPORTS

Years: **1963—5 average** and *1953—5 average* — Units: '000 metric tons unless otherwise indicated

	Production		Exports		Imports	

1. CEREALS, etc.

	Production		Exports		Imports	
Cassava	5.7	11.5 2	—	—	—	—
Maize (corn)	—	—	—	—	0.3	0.5
Potatoes	—	—	—	—	0.6	0.6
Rice	—	—	—	—	0.8	—
Sweet potatoes/yams	9.0 *	4.0 2	—	—	—	—

2. FRUIT, etc.

	Production		Exports		Imports	
Apples	—	—	—	—	0.1	—
Bananas	3.7	na	—	—	0.1	—
Oranges	—	—	—	—	12.0	—
Wine b	—	—	—	—	8.7	—

b '000 hectolitres.

3. BEVERAGES, FOREST PRODUCTS, etc.

	Production		Exports		Imports	
Coffee	—	—	—	—	0.1	—
Sugar, raw	—	—	—	—	0.7	0.7
Hardwood j	51.0	32.7	20.4	—	0.2	0.2
Newsprint	—	—	—	—	0.1	—
Other paper	—	—	1.6	—	0.2	—

j '000 cu. metres of roundwood equivalent.

4. VEGETABLE OILSEEDS AND OILS

	Production		Exports		Imports	
Castor oil	—	—	—	—	0.02 †	—
Coconut oil	—	—	—	—	0.01	—
Cottonseed oil	—	—	—	—	0.02	na
Groundnuts	—	—	—	—	0.08	0.15 *

continued

---

4. VEGETABLE OILSEEDS AND OILS — continued

	Production		Exports		Imports	
Linseed oil	—	—	—	—	0.01	—
Palm kernel oil	—	—	—	—	0.02	na
Palm oil	—	—	—	—	—	na
Rapeseed oil	—	—	—	—	0.06	—
Soya bean oil	—	—	—	—	0.17	—

5. LIVESTOCK‡, ANIMAL PRODUCTS, etc.

	Production		Exports		Imports	
Chickens d	37.0 *	6.0 2	—	—	—	1.6
Cattle d	3.0	3.0 2	—	—	—	—
Goats/sheep d	6.0	5.0 2	—	—	1.6	—
Pigs d	—	—	—	—	0.2	—
Meat‡: 'A'	—	—	—	—	0.6	—
B	—	—	—	—	0.2	—
Butter	—	—	—	—	0.2	0.1
Cheese	—	—	—	—	0.1	0.1
Fish	1.5 †	2.0	0.4	—	0.4	0.4
Milk	—	—	—	—	1.4	0.9

d no. in thousands.

7. FUEL AND POWER

	Production		Exports		Imports	
Electricity h	9				10	10 1
Petroleum, refined	—	—	—	—	10	—

h million kWh. t thermal.

9. NON-FERROUS MINERALS AND METALS

	Production		Exports		Imports	
Gold k: ore m	6.0 2	5.0	4.4 n		—	—

k '000 fine troy oz. m metal content. n bullion/coins etc.

11. INDUSTRY

	Production		Exports		Imports	
Cement	—	—	—	—	10.7	4.0

CARIBBEAN SEA

GUADELOUPE

AREA: 1 702 sq. km. (657 sq. miles)

LAND USE: (percentage of total)

	1965	
Arable and orchard	29.2	
Permanent meadow and pasture	9.0	
Forest and woodland	32.6	
City areas, waste and other land	29.2	

POPULATION: 320 000 (1967 estimate)

Capital city: POINTE-À-PITRE; population: 26 160 (1954)
Total working population: 114 267 (1961)

		Year(s)
Life expectancy at birth (years): male	62.5	1959—63 av.
female	66.5	1959—63 av.
Infant mortality (per '000)	42.1 *	1965
Crude birth rate (per '000)	37.1	1965
Crude death rate (per '000)	8.1	1966
Population per physician	2 110	1965
Population per hospital bed	110	1966
School enrolment: age 5—19 years (percentage)	98	1963—4 av.
age over 19 years (per 100 000 population)	79	1963—4 av.

COMMUNICATIONS

		Year(s)
Motor vehicles in use ('000s): private	13.7	1963—5 av.
commercial	8.6	1967
Telephones (per '000 population)	2.4	1963—5 av.
Radio receivers (per '000 population)	1.1	1963—5 av.
Television licences (per '000 population)		
Daily newspapers (per '000 population)	10	1963—4 av.

FINANCE

Currency unit: The French metropolitan franc
Exchange rates—see France

	Year
National Income (million $ U.S.)	1966 140 * 440
G.N.P. per capita ($ U.S.)	

TRADING

Total trade (in million $ U.S.)	1965	1955	1938
Exports (f.o.b.)	38	34	9
Imports (c.i.f.)	85	37	7

Main trading partners (percentage of total value)

Exports	1965	1955	Imports	1965	1955
France	79	78	France	73	78
U.S.A.	16	1	U.S.A.	8	3
Italy	1	na	Germany F.R.	3	2
Morocco	1	—	Neths. Antilles	2	3
			Trin./Tob.	2	2
			Netherlands	1	1
			U.K.	1	1

Distribution of trade (percentage of total value)

Exports	1965	Imports	1965
Sugar	58	Manufactured goods	58
Bananas	30	(machinery and transport equipment)	(22)
Rum	6	Food	21
		Chemicals	9

continued

FRANCE (OVERSEAS DEPARTMENTS)

French Guiana, Martinique, Guadeloupe, and Réunion were each given the status of a French Overseas Department in 1946.

FRENCH GUIANA

AREA: 90 000 * sq. km. (35 000 * sq. miles)

LAND USE: (percentage of total)

	1954	
Permanent meadow and pasture (savannah)	0.6	
Forest and woodland	94.9	
City areas, waste and other land	4.5	

POPULATION: 38 000 (1967 U.N. estimate)

Capital city: CAYENNE; population: 18 235 (1961)
Total working population: 10 415 (1961)

	1963	Year(s)
Infant mortality (per '000)	39.6 *	1965
Crude birth rate (per '000)	33.6 *	1965
Crude death rate (per '000)	11.4 *	1965
Population per physician	1 240	1965
Population per hospital bed	70	1965
School enrolment: age 5—19 years (percentage)	95	1963—4 av.

COMMUNICATIONS

	1963	Year(s)
Motor vehicles in use ('000s): private	1.2	1963—5 av.
commercial	1.0	1963—5 av.
Telephones (per '000 population)	5.2	1967
Radio licences (per '000 population)	132	1963
Daily newspapers (per '000 population)	86	1966

FINANCE

Currency unit: The French metropolitan franc
Exchange rates—see France

	Year
National Income (million $ U.S.)	1966 18 *
G.N.P. per capita ($ U.S.)	1966 500

EMPLOYMENT AND TRADE

French Guiana has about 80 000 sq. km. of tropical forest. Only a small area is cultivated, the main crops being sugar, manioc, cocoa and bananas. Shrimp fishing and gold mining are recent developments. The European Launching Development Organization has a space research station at Kourou. Exports are gold, hardwood and rum. The chief trading partners are France, the U.S.A. and the West Indies Associated States.

continued

SOUTH AMERICA

---

na: data not available. — negligible or nil. — negligible or nil. ‖ one year only. [1] one year only. [2] two year average. 2 two year average. * estimate. * estimate. ‡ see appendix. ‡ see appendix. † re-exports. † re-exports.

151

FRANCE (OVERSEAS DEPARTMENTS) continued

GUADELOUPE continued

PRODUCTION, EXPORTS AND IMPORTS Units: '000 metric tons unless otherwise indicated
Years: 1963–5 average and 1953–5 average

	Production		Exports		Imports	
1. CEREALS, etc.						
Cassava	5.0	12.0[1]	—	—		
Maize (corn)	1.0				1.3	0.3[1]
Potatoes					3.3	2.2[2]
Rice					7.8	7.5
Sweet potatoes/yams	46.3*	30.0[1]	—	—		
2. FRUIT, etc.						
Apples					0.4*	
Bananas	131.0	108.0[1]	79.7	70.9		
Coconuts f	1.0*[1]				0.1	
Grapes					0.1[2]	
Oranges	10.3				2.2	na
Tomatoes[3]	2.0				6.3	2.0*
Wine[4]					73.4	59.3
5. LIVESTOCK‡, ANIMAL PRODUCTS, etc.						
Chickens d	423.3	275.0[2]			0.9	0.3[2]
Cattle d	70.0	26.3				
Goats d	27.0	28.3				
Sheep d	6.3	10.3				
Horses d	2.0	4.0[2]				
Pigs d	31.0	36.0			0.8*	0.1[1]
Bacon/ham					1.1[2]	
Meat‡: 'A'	1.0	1.0[1]			0.6*	0.1[2]
'B'		na			0.3	0.2[2]
Butter					0.4	
Cheese	0.1*	0.1[1]			0.1	
Eggs	3.2[1]	1.8			2.2	na
Fish					6.3	2.0*
Milk	8.3	6.0[1]				

d no. in thousands.

	Production		Exports		Imports	
7. FUEL AND POWER						
Electricity h: total	40	8			70	30[1]
hydro	1					
thermal	39	8				
Petroleum, refined						

h million kWh.

	Production		Exports		Imports	
10. CHEMICALS n AND FERTILIZERS						
Chemicals					na	
Fertilizers:						
Potash					2.3	

n data not available for years 1953–5.

	Production		Exports		Imports	
11. INDUSTRY						
Alcoholic beverages beer b	na	186.0	2.7 p		2.3 a	na
Cement					70.7	30.7
Electrical engineering a					3.0	
Motor vehicles a					6.0	1.6

a million $ U.S. b '000 hectolitres. p rum only.

j '000 cu. metres of roundwood equivalent.

3. BEVERAGES, FOREST PRODUCTS, etc.

	Production		Exports		Imports	
Cocoa	0.1	na	0.1	0.2		
Coffee	0.3	na	0.1	0.2		0.2
Sugar: cane raw j	1 815.0*	na	165.1	104.1		
Tobacco products	184.6	119.7*			0.2	
Softwood j					37.0	
Hardwood j	37.3	12.0			2.1	
Paper					4.6	

4. VEGETABLE OILSEEDS AND OILS

	Production		Exports		Imports	
Castor oil	na	na			0.04	
Groundnuts	na	186.0			0.48	
Groundnut oil	na				1.91*	
Soya bean oil	na					

MARTINIQUE continued

PRODUCTION, EXPORTS AND IMPORTS
Years: 1963–5 average and 1953–5 average Units: '000 metric tons unless otherwise indicated

	Production		Exports		Imports	
1. CEREALS, etc.						
Cassava	3.0*	na				
Maize (corn)					5.7	1.0[1]
Oats					—	0.9
Potatoes					—	2.5[1]
Rice					3.3	2.5[2]
Sweet potatoes/yams	35.0*	59.0[1]				
2. FRUIT, etc.						
Bananas	156.7	na	126.3	50.4		
Coconuts	na	1.0[1] n	0.1			
Oranges	1.0*	6.0[1] n	na			
Pineapples	19.7		na			
Wine[4]					54.5	41.7

n incl. other citrus fruit.

	Production		Exports		Imports	
3. BEVERAGES, FOREST PRODUCTS, etc.						
Cocoa	0.1	0.1[1]	0.1*		—	0.3[1]
Coffee	na	0.2[1]			0.4	
Sugar: cane raw j	757.0	917.0[1]	64.3		32.0	15.3
	71.3	79.7*	65.8		4.4	3.6
Softwood j					7.6	0.1
Hardwood j	17.7	15.9	—2			0.8
Newsprint						
Other paper			0.5[1]†			

	Production		Exports		Imports	
4. VEGETABLE OILSEEDS AND OILS						
Copra	0.30*	na	na			
Groundnut oil					0.12	
Linseed oil					2.1	
Soya bean oil					6.1	

	Production		Exports		Imports	
5. LIVESTOCK‡, ANIMAL PRODUCTS, etc.						
Chickens d	370.0	200.0[1]			7.1	4.0[1]
Cattle d	37.0	53.3				
dairy cows d	17.0	0.9				
Goats d	12.0	15.0				
Sheep d	23.3	25.3				
Horses d	6.0*	5.0[2]			0.8[1]	
Pigs d	35.0	40.0			0.3	0.1*
Meat‡: 'A'	1.9*	na			0.5	0.2*
'B'						
Butter					3.4	na
Cheese	0.4*	0.2[1]			6.1	2.2*
Eggs	2.5[1]	2.8				
Fish						
Milk	10.0	6.0				

d no. in thousands.

	Production		Exports		Imports	
7. FUEL AND POWER						
Coal					1	
Electricity h i	38	20			77	40
Petroleum, refined						

h '000 hectolitres. i thermal.

	Production		Exports		Imports	
10. CHEMICALS n AND FERTILIZERS						
Chemicals					na	
Fertilizers:						
Potash					4.2	

n data not available for years 1953–5.

	Production		Exports		Imports	
11. INDUSTRY						
Alcoholic beverages	4.6 p				na	21.3
Cement					3.0	
Motor vehicles a					6.1	

a million $ U.S. p rum only.

MARTINIQUE

AREA: 1 090 sq. km. (420 sq. miles)

LAND USE: (percentage of total) — 1964
- Arable and orchard .. 29.1
- Permanent meadow and pasture .. 18.2
- Forest and woodland .. 24.5
- City areas, waste and other land .. 28.2

POPULATION: 330 000 (1967 estimate)
Capital city: FORT-DE-FRANCE; population: 60 648 (1954)

Distribution of working population (1961)
Total working population: 92 344

U.N. group no.		Percentage
0	Agriculture, forestry, fishing and hunting	38.7
1	Mining and quarrying	0.1
2/3	Manufacturing	12.1
4	Construction	9.0
5/8	Services, including electricity, gas, water and sanitary services	24.4
6	Commerce	9.2
7	Transport, storage and communications	4.3
9	Others	2.2

		Year(s)
Life expectancy at birth (years): male	62.5	1959–63 av.
female	66.5	
Infant mortality (per '000)	39.5	1955
Crude birth rate (per '000)	33.3	1965
Crude death rate (per '000)	7.4	1965
Population per physician	2 400	1961
Population per hospital bed	100 a	1966
School enrolment: age 5–19 years (percentage)	108‡	1963–4 av.
age over 19 years (per 100 000 population)	181	1963–5 av.

a government hospitals only.

COMMUNICATIONS
		Year(s)
Motor vehicles in use ('000s): private	14.9	1965
commercial	8.1	1963–5 av.
Telephones (per '000 urban population)	3.7	1967
Radio receivers (per '000 population)	165	1963–5 av.
Television licences (per '000 population)	4.7	1963–5 av.
Daily newspapers (per '000 population)	13.5*	1962–4 av.

FINANCE
Currency unit: The French metropolitan franc
Exchange rates—see France

		Year
National Income (million $ U.S.)	160*	1966
G.N.P. per capita ($ U.S.)	520	1966

TRADING
Total trade (in million $ U.S.)	1965
Exports (f.o.b)	38
Imports (c.i.f.)	91

Main trading partners (percentage of total value)

Exports	1965		Imports	1965
France	88		France	71
Italy	4		U.S.A.	7
U.S.A.	2		Neths. Antilles	3
Guadeloupe	1		Germany F.R.	2
			Italy	2

Distribution of trade (percentage of total value)

Exports	1965		Imports	1965
Bananas and plantains	47		Manufactured goods (machinery and transport equipment)	57
Sugar (refined)	27		(textiles and clothing)	(19)
Rum	10		Food	(8)
Pineapples	8		Chemicals	21
			Crude materials and fuels	17

continued

CARIBBEAN SEA

INDIAN OCEAN

RÉUNION

AREA: 2 508 sq. km. (968.5 sq. miles)

LAND USE: (percentage of total) — 1965
- Arable and orchard .. 24.7
- Permanent meadow and pasture .. 8.0
- Forest and woodland .. 38.2
- City areas, waste and other land .. 29.1

POPULATION: 418 000 (1967 estimate)
Capital city: SAINT-DENIS; population: 65 614 (1961)
Total working population: 95 869 (excluding those in compulsory military service) (1954)

		Year(s)
Life expectancy at birth (years): male	54.1	1959–63 av.
female	60.6	
Infant mortality (per '000)	75.3*	1965
Crude birth rate (per '000)	42.7	1965
Crude death rate (per '000)	9.7	1965
Accidental deaths (per 100 000 population) caused by motor vehicles	15.2	1965
due to other causes	31.8	1965
Population per physician	3 020	1965
Population per hospital bed	150	1966
School enrolment: age 5–19 years (percentage)	90	1963–4 av.
age over 19 years (per 100 000 population)	92	1963–5 av.

COMMUNICATIONS
		Year(s)
Motor vehicles in use ('000s): private	14.4	1963–5 av.
commercial	6.9	1967
Telephones (per '000 urban population)	2.6	1963–5 av.
Radio receivers (per '000 population)	10.9	1963–5 av.
Television sets (per '000 population)	6.7	1963–5 av.
Daily newspapers (per '000 population)	63	1964

FINANCE
Currency unit: The franc CFA

Exchange rates	1965	1960	1957
Per $ U.S.	246.85	246.85	210
Per £ sterling	691.18	691.18	590

TRADING
Total trade (in million $ U.S.)	1965	1955	1938
Exports (f.o.b)	34	33	6
Imports (c.i.f.)	97	41	8

Distribution of trade (percentage of total value)

Exports	1965	1955		Imports	1965	1955
France	84	68		France	68	66
Essential oils	11	33		Malagasy R.	6	14
Rum	5	4		Cambodia	5	6 a
				Italy	2	na
				Germany F.R.	na	na

Exports	1965		Imports	1965
Sugar	78		Manufactured goods (machinery and transport equipment)	54 (14*)
Essential oils	11		(textiles and clothing)	28* (9*)
Rum	5		Food	25 (10)
			Crude materials and fuels	5 (9)
			Beverages and tobacco	4
				na (16*)
				na 2*

a incl. Laos and Vietnam.

continued

na: data not available. — negligible or nil. [1] one year only. [2] two year average. * estimate. ‡ see appendix. † re-exports.

FRANCE (OVERSEAS DEPARTMENTS) continued

RÉUNION continued

PRODUCTION, EXPORTS AND IMPORTS
Years: 1963–5 average and 1953–5 average Units: '000 metric tons unless otherwise indicated

	Production		Exports		Imports	
1. CEREALS, etc.						
Cassava	5.0	8.0[1]	—	—	16.1	12.3
Maize (corn)	15.0	5.0[2]	—	—	0.1	—
Millets/sorghum	3.0	—	—	—	—	—
Potatoes	—	—	0.1	—	—	—
Rice	—	—	—	—	42.0	25.7
Sweet potatoes/yams	3.0	2.0[1]	—	—	—	—
2. FRUIT, etc.						
Apples	—	—	—	—	0.5	0.1
Bananas	7.3*	na	—	—	0.1	—
Oranges	—	—	—	—	1.0	—
Pineapples	1.0	—	—	—	—	—
Wine b	—	—	—	—	72.2	47.0
3. BEVERAGES, FOREST PRODUCTS, etc.						
Coffee	—	—	—	—	1.1	0.8
Sugar: cane	1977.7	1591.7	204.0	161.0	—	—
raw	234.0	174.7	—	—	—	0.7
Tobacco: leaf	—	0.2[2]	—	—	0.4	0.2
Softwood j	100.7	93.3	—	—	22.0	11.3
Hardwood j	—	—	—	—	32.3	4.5
Newsprint	—	—	—	—	0.4	0.3
Other paper	—	—	—	—	0.5	0.4
5. LIVESTOCK‡, ANIMAL PRODUCTS, etc.						
Chickens d	1700n	250	—	—	5.4	0.4
Cattle d	32	401	—	—	1.1	na
Goats d	10	251	—	—	—	—
Sheep d	2	6	—	—	—	—
Horses d	—	21*	—	—	—	—
Pigs d	40*	701	—	—	—	—
Bacon/ham	5*	na	—	—	6.7	—
Meat‡: A, B			—	—	0.3	—
					0.8	0.1
Butter	—	—	—	—	0.1	0.1
Cheese	2*	na	—	—	0.3	0.1
Eggs	2[2]	na	—	—	0.3	0.1[2]
Fish	3*	7	—	—	2.7	na
Milk	—	na	—	—	15.2	2.7*
6. FIBRES, TEXTILES, etc.						
Agaves (sisal etc.)	—	—	—	—	0.1	na
7. FUEL AND POWER						
Coal 'A'‡	—	—	—	—	1.1	na
Electricity h: total	31	5	—	—	—	—
hydro	21	5	—	—	—	—
thermal	10	5	—	—	—	—
Petroleum, refined	—	—	—	—	43	10[1]
10. CHEMICALS n AND FERTILIZERS						
Fertilizers: Potash	—	—	—	—	1.7	na
11. INDUSTRY						
Cement	2.5	na	1.6p	—	103.0	21.3
Electrical engineering a	—	—	—	—	2.9	0.9[2]
Motor vehicles a	—	—	—	—	6.5	1.5
4. VEGETABLE OILSEEDS AND OILS						
Castor oil	—	—	—	—	0.01	0.02[2]
Coconut oil	—	—	—	—	0.01	0.07
Groundnuts	—	—	—	—	0.08	0.07
Groundnut oil	—	—	—	—	1.71	0.28
Linseed oil	—	—	—	—	0.01	0.07
Olive oil	—	—	—	—	0.02	0.01[2]
Soya bean oil	—	—	—	—	0.68	0.40[2]

a million $ U.S. b '000 hectolitres. d no. in thousands. n incl. ducks, geese and turkeys. h million kWh. j '000 cu. metres of roundwood equivalent. n data not available for years 1953–5. p rum only.

FRANCE (OVERSEAS TERRITORIES)

NEW HEBRIDES—(Anglo-French condominium)—see page 190

COMORO ARCHIPELAGO

Previously a French colony attached to Madagascar, the Comoro Islands were granted administrative autonomy in 1946, and in 1958 elected, unlike Madagascar, to remain a French Territory.

AREA: 2170* sq. km. (838* sq. miles)

LAND USE: (percentage of total) — 1955
- Arable and orchard: 36.9
- Permanent meadow and pasture: 13.8
- Forest and woodland: 16.1
- City areas, waste and other land: 33.2

POPULATION: 250 000 (1967 U.N. estimate)
Capital city: MORONI; population: 11 515 (1966)

		Year(s)
Crude birth rate (per '000)	20.6*	1964
Population per physician	16 900	1965
Population per hospital bed	470	1965
School enrolment: age 5–19 years (percentage)	19	1963–4 av.

COMORO ARCHIPELAGO continued

PRODUCTION, EXPORTS AND IMPORTS
Years: 1963–5 average and 1953–5 average Units: '000 metric tons unless otherwise indicated

	Production		Exports		Imports	
1. CEREALS, etc.						
Cassava	31.0*	na	—	—	—	—
Rice	—	—	—	—	10.0	—
Sweet potatoes/yams	1.0*	na	—	—	—	—
2. FRUIT, etc.						
Coconuts	57.3*	na	—	—	—	—
Wine b	—	—	—	—	1.5	—
3. BEVERAGES, FOREST PRODUCTS, etc.						
Coffee	na	na	0.1	—	—	—
Sugar: cane raw	na	na	—	—	0.9	—
4. VEGETABLE OILSEEDS AND OILS						
Copra	3.08	15.00[2]	3.08	3.08	—	—
5. LIVESTOCK‡, ANIMAL PRODUCTS, etc.						
Cattle d	24.7*	17.0[2]	—	—	—	—
Goats d	97.0*	87.5[2]	—	—	—	—
Sheep d	4.0*	4.0[2]	—	—	—	—
Fish	1.6	na	—	—	—	—
Milk	2.0	na	—	—	—	—
6. FIBRES, TEXTILES, etc.						
Agaves (sisal etc.)	na	na	1.0	na	—	—
11. INDUSTRY						
Cement	—	—	—	—	8.7	na p

b '000 hectolitres. d no. in thousands. p see Malagasy Republic.

FRENCH POLYNESIA

French Polynesia consists of a series of island groups scattered over a wide area in the Eastern Pacific. They include the Society Islands (of which Tahiti is the most important), the Tuamotu and Gambier groups, the Austral Islands and the Marquezas Islands. These opted in 1958 to become an Overseas Territory within the French Community.

AREA: 4000 sq. km. (1545 sq. miles)

LAND USE: (percentage of total) — 1964
- Arable and orchard: 16.0
- Permanent meadow and pasture: 5.0
- Forest and woodland: 28.8
- City areas, waste and other land: 50.2

POPULATION: 98 400 (1967 census)
Capital city: PAPEETE; population: 37 485 (1967)
Total working population: 26 500 (1962)

		Year(s)
Infant mortality (per '000)	100.3*	1961
Crude birth rate (per '000)	36.1*	1964
Population per physician	1720	1965
Population per hospital bed	120a	1966
School enrolment: age 5–19 years (percentage)	101‡ b	1963–4 av.

a government hospitals only. b incl. pre-school education.

PACIFIC OCEAN

COMMUNICATIONS

		Year(s)
Motor vehicles in use ('000s): private	4.3	1963–5 av.
commercial	1.8	
Telephones (per '000 urban population)	284	1967
Radio receivers (per '000 population)	4.9	1963–5 av.
Daily newspapers (per '000 population)	13	1961

FINANCE
Currency unit: The franc CFP

Exchange rates	1965	1960	1957
Per $ U.S.	89.76	90	76
Per £ sterling	253.33	251	212

		Year(s)
National income (million $ U.S.)	85*	1966
G.N.P. per capita ($ U.S.)	950	1966

PRODUCTION AND TRADE
The coastal plains and most of the low lying islands are covered with coconut palms. Tropical fruits such as bananas, pineapples and oranges are grown for local consumption. Copra is one of the major products for export; others include coffee, vanilla, and mother-of-pearl. Phosphate deposits were exhausted in 1966. Tourism earns almost half as much as visible exports. Main imports are metal manufactures, textiles, petroleum, sugar and flour.

INDIAN OCEAN

FINANCE
Currency unit: The franc CFA

Exchange rates	1965	1960	1957a
Per $ U.S.	246.85	246.85	210
Per £ sterling	691.18	691.18	590

a official rate.

		Year
National income (million $ U.S.)	13	1958
G.N.P. per capita ($ U.S.)	110	1966

EMPLOYMENT, PRODUCTION AND TRADE
The islands are self-sufficient in basic foodstuffs. The chief export crop was originally sugar cane, but now vanilla, copra, sisal, coffee, cloves, ylang and citronella are the main products, many of which are exported. Timber, for building and railway sleepers, is also exported. The majority of the trade is with France.

continued

COMORO ARCHIPELAGO

PRODUCTION, EXPORTS AND IMPORTS
Years: 1963–5 average and 1953–5 average Units: '000 metric tons unless otherwise indicated

	Production		Exports		Imports	
1. CEREALS, etc.						
Cassava	5.0*	3.0[1]	—	—	—	—
Millets/sorghum	—	—	—	—	0.1[2]	0.7
Potatoes	—	—	—	—	1.1[1]	1.1
Rice	1.0*	na	—	—	2.0	—
Sweet potatoes/yams	—	—	—	—	—	—
Wheat	—	—	—	—	0.5[2]	0.2
2. FRUIT, etc.						
Apples	na	na	—	—	0.2[1]	—
Bananas	na	na	—	—	—	—
Coconuts	189.7e	na	0.41n	—	0.1[1]	—
Grapes	—	—	—	—	0.1[1]	—
Wine b	—	—	—	—	26.8	9.7

continued

b '000 hectolitres. e desiccated. n desicated.

---

na: data not available. — negligible or nil. * estimate. 1 one year only. 2 two year average. ‡ see appendix. † re-exports.

FRANCE (OVERSEAS TERRITORIES) continued

FRENCH POLYNESIA continued

PRODUCTION, EXPORTS AND IMPORTS continued

	Production	Exports	Imports
5. LIVESTOCK‡, ANIMAL PRODUCTS, etc.			
Chickens d	133.7* 110.0[1]		
Cattle d	13.7* 15.5[2]		
Goats d	8.0* 6.5[2]		
Sheep d	5.0 4.0[2]		
Horses d			
Pigs d	17.0* 17.0[2]		
Meat‡ ´ B			2.2*
Butter			1.0[1]
Cheese	0.3*		0.5
Eggs	4.5	2.0	0.2
Fish			0.7
Milk			3.4

d no. in thousands.

	Production	Exports	Imports
7. FUEL AND POWER			
Coal ' A '‡			
Electricity h. hydro.	16		
Petroleum. refined			

h million kWh.

	Production	Exports	Imports
10. CHEMICALS n AND FERTILIZERS			
Chemicals			na
Fertilizers:			
Phosphates p	344.0	341.9 233.3	—

n data not available for years 1953-5.   p produced only in Makatea Is.

	Production	Exports	Imports
11. INDUSTRY			
Cement		—	77.7 19.3

FRENCH TERRITORY OF THE AFARS AND THE ISSAS   EAST AFRICA

Formerly French Somaliland, the French Territory of the Afars and the Issas is so named to emphasize its two main ethnic groups. The importance of the region depends largely upon the transit trade from Addis Ababa (Ethiopia) via the railway.

AREA: 23 000 sq. km. (8 900 sq. miles)

LAND USE: (percentage of total)

	1958	1952
Arable and orchard		
Permanent meadow and pasture	11.1	10.6
Forest and woodland	0.4	0.3
City areas, waste and other land	88.5	89.1

POPULATION: 108 000 (1966 estimate)
Capital city: DJIBOUTI; population: 43 200 (1963)

COMMUNICATIONS
Motor vehicles in use ('000s): private
commercial
Railway track (km.)

FINANCE
Currency unit: The Djibouti franc

	1965	1960	1957
Exchange rates			
Per $ U.S.	214	214	214
Per £ sterling	602	602	602

		Year
National Income (million $ U.S.)	48*	1966
G.N.P. per capita ($ U.S.)	570	1966

		Year(s)
Population per physician	5 300	1962
Population per hospital bed	150	1966
School enrolment: age 5-19 years (percentage)	22	1963-4 av.

EMPLOYMENT, PRODUCTION AND TRADE

The raising of goats and other stock is very important, but crop production is small. Minerals thought to exist are gypsum, mica, amethyst and sulphur, but reserves of these are as yet unproven.
The chief items in transit from Ethiopia are hides and coffee. Major imports are fuel, sugar, cement and cotton goods. Trade is mainly with France but a few imports come from neighbouring countries.

	1965	1955
Total trade (in million $ U.S.)		
Exports (f.o.b.)	3.2	1.2
Imports (c.i.f.)	81.5	34.0

PRODUCTION, EXPORTS AND IMPORTS
Years: 1963-5 average and 1953-5 average   Units: '000 metric tons unless otherwise indicated

	Production	Exports	Imports
1. CEREALS, etc.			
Millets/sorghum			
Rice			
Wheat			
2. FRUIT, etc.			
Dates			
Wine b			
3. BEVERAGES, FOREST PRODUCTS, etc.			
Sugar. raw		3.8[2]	3.3 3.5[2]
Softwood j			
Hardwood j	23.0[1]* 4.5[2]		
Newsprint			0.4[2]
Other paper			0.2[2] 0.1[2]

j '000 cu. metres of roundwood equivalent.

	Production	Exports	Imports
5. LIVESTOCK‡, ANIMAL PRODUCTS, etc.			
Cattle d	13.3* 10.0		5.0
Goats d	499.0* 370.0		3.8
Sheep d	85.0* 85.3		
Horses d	2.7 3.0[2]		
Meat‡ ´ A ; B	0.2 2.0[1]p		na
Fish			11.2[2]
Milk	1.0* na	0.7 2.0[1]	
Hides/skins			

d no. in thousands.   p government inspected meat only.

	Production	Exports	Imports
7. FUEL AND POWER			
Coal ' A '‡			
Electricity h. thermal.	19*		2.6
Petroleum. refined			4.2[1]

h million kWh.

	Production	Exports	Imports
11. INDUSTRY			
Cement			12.3 8.0

continued

SOUTH WEST PACIFIC

NEW CALEDONIA

New Caledonia and its dependencies were annexed by France in 1854. The importance of the region has risen greatly with the exploitation of its nickel reserves.

AREA: 19 103 sq. km. (7 374 sq. miles)

LAND USE: (percentage of total)

	1961	1955
Arable and orchard	4.3	1.0
Permanent meadow and pasture	21.4	28.8
Forest and woodland	14.5	13.4
City areas, waste and other land	59.8	58.8

POPULATION: 86 519 (including 33 600 Europeans) (1963 census)
Capital city: NOUMÉA; population: 34 990 (city proper, 1963)
Total working population: 30 471

Distribution of working population (1963)

U.N. group no.		Percentage
1	Agriculture, forestry, fishing and hunting	38.0
2/3	Mining and quarrying	3.9
	Manufacturing	12.2
4	Construction	9.3
5	Electricity, gas, water and sanitary services	0.7
6	Commerce	9.8
7	Transport, storage and communications	5.1
8	Services	19.9
9	Others	1.1

		Year(s)
Infant mortality (per '000)	32.8*	1965
Crude birth rate (per '000)	29.3*	1965
Crude death rate (per '000)	7.3*	1965
Population per physician	1750	1966
Population per hospital bed	70	1966
School enrolment: age 5-19 years (percentage)	110‡	1963-4 av.
age over 19 years (per 100 000 population)	42	1963-4 av.

PRODUCTION, EXPORTS AND IMPORTS
Years: 1963-5 average and 1953-5 average   Units: '000 metric tons unless otherwise indicated

	Production	Exports	Imports
1. CEREALS. etc.			
Cassava	4.0* 16.0[1]		
Maize (corn)	2.0* 1.0[2]		
Millets/sorghum			
Potatoes	1.0* 1.0[1]		0.8
Rice			1.5[1]
Sweet potatoes/yams	4.0* 5.0[1]		2.9

	Production	Exports	Imports
2. FRUIT, etc.			
Coconuts e	12.7* na		
Wine b		41.6	30.0

	Production	Exports	Imports
3. BEVERAGES, FOREST PRODUCTS, etc.			
Coffee	2.3* 1.8*[2]		
Sugar. raw		1.5	1.6
Tea			2.2 0.1
Softwood j	1.9[2] na		
Hardwood j	8.9[2] na		
Paper			294

j '000 cu. metres of roundwood equivalent.

	Production	Exports	Imports
4. VEGETABLE OILSEEDS AND OILS			
Copra	1.73 3.40[2]	1.32	2.77
Groundnut oil			
Olive oil			

	Production	Exports	Imports
5. LIVESTOCK‡, ANIMAL PRODUCTS, etc.			
Chickens d	144.7*n na		
Cattle d	99.0 102.0[2]		
Goats d	19.0 20.0[2]		
Sheep d	3.7 3.0[2]		
Horses d	9.3 na		
Pigs d	19.0 14.0[2]		
Meat‡ ´ B	0.1* na		
Butter			0.3 0.3
Cheese			0.1 0.1
Eggs	0.5* na		0.8
Fish	na na		1.5[1]
Milk	6.0* na	1.0 0.7	3.7 2.4*

d no. in thousands.   n incl. ducks, geese and turkeys.

	Production	Exports	Imports
7. FUEL AND POWER			
Coal ' A '‡			172 83
Coke			
Electricity h: total	337 60		
hydro	334 50		
thermal	3 10		
Petroleum. refined			12

h million kWh.

	Production	Exports	Imports
8. IRON AND STEEL			
Iron ore	164m		30[1]

m metal content.

	Production	Exports	Imports
9. NON-FERROUS MINERALS AND METALS			
Chrome. ore	84.21m	7.98 86.92	
Magnesium. ore			
magnesite	0.59 na		0.08
Manganese. ore	1.86		
Nickel. ore	44.62*m 13.31*m	882.59 238.20	
metal	44.08	11.00n	156

m metal content.   n ferro-nickel of which the nickel content is 32-35%.

COMMUNICATIONS

		Year(s)
Motor vehicles in use ('000s): private	10.5	1963-5 av.
commercial	3.3	3.1
Mail per capita: domestic	21	1963-5 av.
foreign received	10	
foreign sent		
Telephones (per '000 urban population)	5.5	1967
Radio receivers (per '000 population)	149	1963-5 av.
Daily newspapers (per '000 population)	47	1962-4 av.

FINANCE
Currency unit: The franc CFP

	1965	1960	1950
Exchange rates			
Per $ U.S.	90	90	76
Per £ sterling	251	251	212

		Year
National Income (million $ U.S.)	140*	1966
G.N.P. per capita ($ U.S.)	1480	1966

EMPLOYMENT, PRODUCTION AND TRADE

Agricultural products are coffee, copra, maize, vegetables, and livestock. Great mineral resources exist, especially nickel, chrome, iron and manganese. Small industries are developing. The chief exports in 1963 were chrome, iron, nickel and copra, 66% of the total going to France and the franc zone. The chief imports were coal, coke and petroleum products, 56% of the total coming from France and the franc zone.

continued

FRANCE (OVERSEAS TERRITORIES) continued

ST. PIERRE AND MIQUELON — NORTH WEST ATLANTIC

St. Pierre and Miquelon are two small groups of islands off the coast of Newfoundland.

AREA: 242 sq. km. (93.5 sq. miles)

LAND USE: (percentage of total)

Arable and orchard	—
Permanent meadow and pasture	12.5
Forest and woodland	4.2
City areas, waste and other land	83.3

POPULATION: 5 000 (1967 estimate)
Total working population: 1 773 (1962)

		Year
Crude birth rate (per '000)	25.5	1964
Crude death rate (per '000)	8.8	1964

FINANCE
Currency unit: The franc CFA

Exchange rates

	1946	1960	1957
Per $ U.S.		246.85	210
Per £ sterling		691.18	590

EMPLOYMENT AND TRADE

The islands consist mainly of barren rock, and are unsuitable for agriculture. Fishing is the chief occupation and provides the main exports. Imports are textiles, wine, foodstuffs and fuels.

PRODUCTION, EXPORTS AND IMPORTS
Years: 1963–5 average and 1953–5 average   Units: '000 metric tons unless otherwise indicated

	Production	Exports	Imports
1. CEREALS, etc.			
Potatoes		—	0.4*
2. FRUIT, etc.			
Wine b	2.8	—	1.7
3. BEVERAGES, FOREST PRODUCTS, etc.			
Sugar, raw		—	0.2
5. LIVESTOCK‡, ANIMAL PRODUCTS, etc.			
Cattle d	—		
Goats/sheep d	—		
Pigs d	—		
Meat‡ 'A'	—		
Butter	—		
Milk	8.9	—	0.1
Fish	3.0		0.3
7. FUEL AND POWER			
Coal 'A'‡	—		
Electricity h	na		
Petroleum, refined	—		
11. INDUSTRY			
Cement	—		1.0

b '000 hectolitres.   d no. in thousands.   h million kWh.

WALLIS AND FUTUNA — PACIFIC OCEAN

Previously a French Protectorate, the islands became a French Overseas Territory in 1961.

AREA: Wallis: 275 sq. km. (106 sq. miles); Futuna: 150 sq. km. (58 sq. miles)

POPULATION: Wallis: 5 380; Futuna: 3 000* (1965 estimate)

GABON — CENTRAL AFRICA

Formerly a territory of French Equatorial Africa, and from 1958 a member state of the French Community, Gabon became an independent republic in 1960. It has been a member of the Equatorial Customs Union since its foundation in 1959.

AREA: 267 000 sq. km. (103 089 sq. miles)

LAND USE: (percentage of total)

	1962
Arable and orchard	0.5
Permanent meadow and pasture	na
Forest and woodland (including rough grazing)	74.7
City areas, waste and other land	na

POPULATION: 473 000 (1967 estimate)
Capital city: LIBREVILLE; population: 57 000 (1967)

Distribution of working population (1963)
Total working population: 220 000

U.N. group no.		Percentage	Year(s)
0	Agriculture, forestry, fishing and hunting	84.1	1960–1 av.
1	Mining and quarrying	3.4	
2/3	Manufacturing	1.9	
4	Construction	1.7	
5	Electricity, gas, water and sanitary services	0.1	
6	Commerce	3.7	
7	Transport, storage and communications	1.3	
8	Services	3.2	
9	Others	0.6	

		Year(s)
Life expectancy at birth (years): male	25*	} 1960–1 av.
female	45*	
Population per physician	5 860	1964
Population per hospital bed	110	1966
School enrolment: age 5–19 years (percentage)	50	1963–4 av.
age over 19 years (per 100000 population)	17	1964–5 av.

COMMUNICATIONS

	1965	Year(s)
Motor vehicles in use ('000s): private		
commercial		
Telephones (per '000 urban population)	72	
Radio receivers (per '000 population)		
Television sets (per '000 population)		

FINANCE
Currency unit: The franc CFA

Exchange rates

	1965	1960
Per $ U.S.	246.85	246.85
Per £ sterling	691.18	691.18

		Year(s)
National Income (million $ U.S.)	152	1963
G.N.P. per capita ($ U.S.)	400	1966
Foreign trade (percentage of G.D.P.)	76	1963–5 av.

TRADING
Total trade (in million $ U.S.)

	1965	1955
Exports (f.o.b.)	96	28
Imports (c.i.f.)	62	20

Main trading partners (percentage of total value)

Exports	1965		Imports	1965
France	48		France	58
U.S.A.	18		U.S.A.	12
Germany F.R.	11		Germany F.R.	6
U.K.	4		Cameroon	4
Israel	3		U.K.	3

Distribution of trade (percentage of total value)

Exports	1965		Imports	1965
Wood	44		Manufactured goods (machinery and transport equipment)	72
Manganese	28		Food	9
Petroleum	15		Alcoholic beverages	6
Uranium	9			

continued

PRODUCTION, EXPORTS AND IMPORTS

Years: 1963–5 average   Units: '000 metric tons unless otherwise indicated
Note—no data are available for the years 1953–5.

	Production	Exports	Imports
1. CEREALS, etc.			
Cassava	126.7		
Maize (corn)	1.7*		0.1
Potatoes			0.7
Rice	1.0		1.4
Sweet potatoes/yams	2.0*		
2. FRUIT, etc.			
Apples			0.2n
Bananas	10.0*		
Oranges			0.1
Wine b			89.7
3. BEVERAGES, FOREST PRODUCTS, etc.			
Cocoa	3.6	3.3	1.2
Coffee	2.5*	0.8	0.1
Sugar, raw			na
Tobacco: leaf			
products			na
Hardwood j	2 771.0*1	1 245.0	
4. VEGETABLE OILSEEDS AND OILS			
Groundnuts	0.70l*	0.32	0.04
Groundnut oil	na		0.11
Olive oil			
Palm kernels	na	0.20	0.01
Palm kernel oil	na		
Palm oil	na	0.52	
5. LIVESTOCK‡, ANIMAL PRODUCTS, etc.			
Cattle d	4.0*		0.8
Goats d	59.0*		
Sheep d	47.0*		
Pigs d	6.0*		0.4
Meat‡: 'A'; 'B'			0.1

b '000 hectolitres.   n incl. pears and quince.

continued

	Production	Exports	Imports
5. LIVESTOCK, ANIMAL PRODUCTS—continued			
Butter			0.1
Cheese			0.1
Eggs	1.6*		2.1
Fish	1.37p		2.3
Milk	na	0.1	
Hides/skins			
7. FUEL AND POWER			
Electricity h i	37		
Natural gas i	10		
Oil, crude	1 070	1 097	60
Petroleum, refined	445*	1 387u	
Uranium f			

f metric tons.   h million kWh.   i million cu. metres.   t thermal.   u concentrates.

Recent explorations have shown considerable resources of oil, natural gas and uranium, exploitation of which is increasing rapidly.

	Production	Exports	Imports
9. NON-FERROUS MINERALS AND METALS			
Gold, ore m	38.70	32.67n	
Manganese, ore	958.83	878.30	
11. INDUSTRY			
Aircrafta			0.7
Alcoholic beverages a			3.3
Cement a	34.0		34.0
Electrical engineering a			
Railway vehicles a			3.0
Motor vehicles a			0.2
			6.1

d no. in thousands.   p industrial fishing only.
k '000 fine troy oz.   m metal content.   n bullion (may incl. a small quantity from Congo R.).
a million $ U.S.

GAMBIA — WEST AFRICA

The Gambia was a British colony; however, in 1963 full internal self-government was achieved, and it became an independent member of the Commonwealth in 1965. Special arrangements regarding external affairs have been made with Senegal.

AREA: 9 301 sq. km. (3977 sq. miles)

LAND USE: (percentage of total)
Arable and orchard
Permanent meadow and pasture, forest and woodland
City areas, waste and other land

POPULATION: 343 000 (1967 estimate) (excluding seasonal immigrants working on farms)
Capital city: BATHURST; population: 42 800 (1965)

		Year(s)
Life expectancy at birth (years)	43*	1962–3 av.
Infant mortality (per '000)	72.1a	1965
Crude birth rate (per '000)	48.5a	1965
Crude death rate (per '000)	14.1a	1965
Population per physician	22 000b	1966
Population per hospital bed	690b	1963–4 av.
School enrolment: age 5–19 years (percentage)	16	

a in Bathurst only.   b government hospitals only.

EMPLOYMENT AND PRODUCTION

Most of the population is engaged in agriculture, in particular the cultivation of groundnuts. Fishing and livestock production are considerable. No minerals are at present being exploited and groundnut processing is the only industry.

COMMUNICATIONS

	1966	Year(s)
Motor vehicles in use ('000s): private	1.3	1963–5 av.
commercial	1.0	1967
Telephones (per '000 urban population)	111	1963–5 av.
Radio receivers (per '000 population)	5	1959
Daily newspapers (per '000 population)		

FINANCE
Currency unit: The West African pound, at par with the £ sterling

	1965	1960
Exchange rates Per $ U.S.	0.357	0.357

		Year
National Income (million $ U.S.)	20	1958
G.N.P. per capita ($ U.S.)	90	1966

TRADING
Total trade (in million $ U.S.)

	1965	1955	1938
Exports (f.o.b.)	14	7	2
Imports (c.i.f.)	16	10	2

Main trading partners (percentage of total value)

Imports	1965	1955		Exports	1965	1955
U.K.	41	48		U.K.	50	62
Japan	6	7		Italy	21	na
Burma	4	na		Portugal	10	na
China P.R.	3	na		Netherlands	10	3
France		2		Switzerland	4	na

Distribution of trade (percentage of total value)

Exports	1966		Imports	1966
Groundnuts	64		Manufactured goods (textiles and clothing)	37
Groundnut oil	(31)		(machinery and transport equipment)	22
Fodder (derived from groundnuts)	(19)		Food	15
			Alcoholic beverages	7

continued

---

na: data not available.   — negligible or nil.   ¹ one year only.   ² two year average.   * estimate.   ‡ see appendix.   † re-exports.

na: data not available.   — negligible or nil.   ¹ one year only.   ² two year average.   * estimate.   ‡ see appendix.   † re-exports.

GAMBIA continued

PRODUCTION, EXPORTS AND IMPORTS
Years: 1963–5 average and 1953–5 average Units: '000 metric tons unless otherwise indicated

	Production	Exports	Imports
1. CEREALS, etc.			
Cassava d	6.0* na	— —	— —
Maize (corn)	0.7* na	— —	— —
Millets/sorghum	44.0* na	— —	— —
Potatoes d	na	— 0.2	0.1 0.2
Rice	35.0 na	— —	8.0 3.0
2. FRUIT, etc.			
Wine b	— —	— —	— 1.0

b '000 hectolitres.

	Production	Exports	Imports
3. BEVERAGES, FOREST PRODUCTS, etc.			
Coffee	— —	— —	0.1 0.1
Sugar, raw	— —	— —	3.2 —
Tobacco: leaf	— —	— —	0.1 0.1
cigarettes	— —	— —	na na
Softwood j	146.7* na	— —	0.1 0.1
Hardwood j	— —	— —	— —
Other paper	— —	— —	— —

j '000 cu. metres of roundwood equivalent.

	Production	Exports	Imports
4. VEGETABLE OILSEEDS AND OILS			
Groundnuts	81.90* 42.00*	35.15 37.90	— —
Groundnut oil	1.57 na	8.72 0.01	0.01² 0.18
Palm kernels	1.53 na	1.80 1.80	— 0.01
Palm oil	1.60* 2.10¹	— —	0.6² 0.04

	Production	Exports	Imports
5. LIVESTOCK d, ANIMAL PRODUCTS, etc.			
Chickens d	184.7*n 306.0²n	— —	— —
Cattle d	184.0 145.0²	— —	— —
Sheep d	95.0 81.0²	0.2 —	— —
Goats d	55.3 62.5²	— —	— —
Horses d	na na	— —	— —
Pigs d	2.0 4.0	— —	— —
Meat: 'A', 'B'	3.0* na	— —	— —
Eggs	1.1* na	— —	— —
Fish	na na	0.7 0.7	1.2 1.0*
Milk	na na	— —	— —

d no. in thousands. n incl. ducks, geese and turkeys.

	Production	Exports	Imports
6. FIBRES, TEXTILES, etc.			
Cotton, woven fabrics	— —	— —	2.3 1.0
Rayon, woven fabrics	— —	— —	— —
p incl. synthetic piece goods.			

	Production	Exports	Imports
7. FUEL AND POWER			
Electricity h ‡	8 8	— —	— —
Petroleum, refined	— —	— —	2.0 2.0

h million kWh. ‡ thermal.

	Production	Exports	Imports
9. NON-FERROUS MINERALS AND METALS			
Asbestos	— —	— —	0.1 —
Titanium minerals	na na	0.37	— —

	Production	Exports	Imports
11. INDUSTRY			
Alcoholic beverages			
beer b	215.0 na	— —	8.3 4.0
Cement	— —	— —	0.3a
Electrical engineering a	— —	— —	— —
Motor vehicles a	0.18 —	37.90 0.01	0.6 0.2²
a million $ U.S. b '000 hectolitres.	0.04 —	1.80 —	0.6² 0.3

GERMANY: DEMOCRATIC REPUBLIC   EUROPE

On the termination of World War II in 1945 the Eastern Sector of Germany came under the control of the U.S.S.R. and Poland. Separation from the Western Sector was established, and the German Democratic Republic, referred to as East Germany, was declared in 1949; this was not, however, recognized by many countries and there remains some move towards the reunification of Germany.

Germany D.R. is a member of Comecon.
Pre-war statistics refer to both sectors of Germany.

AREA: 108 174 sq. km. (41 766 sq. miles)

LAND USE: (percentage of total)

		1965
Arable and orchard		46.2
Permanent meadow and pasture		13.3
Forest and woodland		22.3
City areas, waste and other land		13.3

POPULATION: 17 011 931 (1964 census) [19 102 000 in 1947]
Largest city: OST-BERLIN (East Berlin), capital; population: 1 073 647 (city proper, 1965)
Total working population: 7 229 140 (1960)

		Year(s)
Life expectancy at birth (years): male 68.5 / female 73.5		1963–6 av.
Infant mortality (per '000)	24.8	1965
Crude birth rate (per '000)	16.5	1965
Crude death rate (per '000)	13.3	1965
Population per physician	750	1966
Population per hospital bed	80	1966
School enrolment: age 5–19 years (percentage)	79	1963–4 av.
age over 19 years (per 100 000 population)	476	1963–5 av.

COMMUNICATIONS

		Year(s)
Motor vehicles in use ('000s): private 583.2 / commercial 282.3		1964
Railway track (km.)	16 108	1964
Mail per capita: domestic 74 / foreign received 5 / foreign sent 2		1963–5 av.
Telephones (per '000 population)	10.1	1967
Radio licences (per '000 population)	337	1963–5 av.
Television licences (per '000 population)	164.1	1963–5 av.
Daily newspapers (per '000 population)	456	1959

FINANCE
Currency unit: The mark (M.D.N.)

Exchange rates a

	1965	1960
Per $ U.S.	2.22	2.22
Per £ sterling	6.22	6.22

		Year(s)
National Income (million $ U.S.)	20 000*	1960–4 av.
G.N.P. per capita ($ U.S.)	1 220	
Rate of increase of G.N.P. per capita	2.4	

a These rates are calculated on a value fixed on gold, but are not recognized by the International Monetary Fund.

PRODUCTION
The Democratic Republic is economically a less diversified area than the Federal Republic; although almost self-sufficient in food, the country lacks industrial raw materials. Agriculture had been collectivized by April 1960, and industry is centrally planned. The main mineral deposits are lignite and copper, and crude steel plants have been erected as steel from the Ruhr ceased to be available when Germany was divided. Industry produced about 65% of the national income in 1964.

TRADING

Total trade (in million $ U.S.)	1965	1960	1936f
Exports (f.o.b.)	3070	2810	1925
Imports (f.o.b.)	2810		1709

Main trading partners (percentage of total value)

Exports	1965	1955	1936f		Imports	1965	1955	1936f
U.S.S.R.	43	43	—		U.S.S.R.	43	36	4
Germany F.R.	10	11	—		Germany F.R.	9	11	6
Czechoslovakia	10	10	—		Czechoslovakia	9	10	3
Poland	9	7	—		Poland	6	5	1
Hungary	4	4	—		Hungary	4	2	1
Bulgaria	3	2	—		Bulgaria	3	2	1
Romania	2	2	—		Yugoslavia	3	—	1

DISTRIBUTION OF TRADE
In 1965, machinery and transport equipment accounted for 46% of the country's exports.

continued

PRODUCTION, EXPORTS AND IMPORTS
Years: 1963–5 average and 1953–5 average Units: '000 metric tons unless otherwise indicated

	Production	Exports	Imports
1. CEREALS, etc.			
Barley	1 448.0 891.5²	2.7*	199.0 17.7*
Maize (corn)	2.3* 7.5²	—	259.7 8.0*
Oats b	780.0 1 356.2²	7.8* 1.5	— —
Oats/sorghum	—	— —	207.5 1.6*
Potatoes	12 871.7 14 294.0	9.4* 2.4*	32.5 17.7*
Rice	—	—	128.0 na
Rye	1 825.0 2 365.5²	2.1 9.0*	— —
Wheat	1 476.7 1 206.5²	—	1 183.7 41.4*
2. FRUIT, etc.			
Apples	201.3 na	—	73.8% 33.3*
Cherries	72.0 72.1	—	— —
Dates	—	—	11.8* 7.3*
Grapes	—	—	38.0* 7.1*
Lemons	—	—	20.0* 6.2*
Oranges	—	—	25.3* 0.5*
Pears	95.3 na	—	0.6² —
Plums	76.7 120.9	—	— —
Raisins	—	—	10.6* 1.6*
Tomatoes	23.0 na	0.3*	— —
Wine b	—	—	634.8 60.7*

b '000 hectolitres.

	Production	Exports	Imports
3. BEVERAGES, FOREST PRODUCTS, etc.			
Cocoa	—	—	14.6 5.4²
Coffee	—	—	35.6 —
Sugar: beet	5 994.3 6 283.0*	168.9 29.4*	— —
raw	721.7 778.0*	—	165.2* 0.2*
Tea	—	—	1.6 6.0*
Tobacco: leaf	6.8 na	—	28.1 —
cigars²	1 844.0	—	800.8 —
cigarettes	—	137.0²	2 139.0 89.0
tobacco/snuff j	17 915.0 17 366.0	²	185.5 11.6
Softwood j	5 209.3* 8 198.0²	—	116.5 16.5
Wood pulp	1 241.3 1 543.5²	—	— —
Newsprint	644.1 534.0²	na	0.1 0.1
Hardwood j	90.3 90.0*	14.7	61.0 19.2¹
Other paper	818.3 561.0*	35.0 32.3¹	— —

j '000 cu. metres of roundwood equivalent.

	Production	Exports	Imports
4. VEGETABLE OILSEEDS AND OILS			
Castor oil	—	—	0.62 —
Coconut oil	—	—	5.91 0.09²
Cottonseed	—	—	— 0.20²
Groundnuts	—	—	10.60² 0.19*
Groundnut oil	—	—	3.13* 0.25²
Linseed	na na	0.13*	8.25* 5.51*
Linseed oil	5.67 22.50²	²	0.32* ²
Olive oil	—	—	0.33* —
Palm kernels	—	—	— —
Palm oil	—	—	— —
Rapeseed	172.70 167.00²	—	0.90* 0.02*
Soya beans	—	—	6.33* —
Soya bean oil	—	0.49²*	70.57* 3.76*
Sunflower seed	—	—	65.48* —
Sunflower seed oil	—	0.99*	— —

	Production	Exports	Imports
5. LIVESTOCK d, ANIMAL PRODUCTS, etc.			
Chickens d	37 805.7n 23 486.3*	—	— —
Cattle d	3 805.7 3 821.7	—	8.9* 13.3*
Goats d	—	4.0*	— —
Cows d	2 393.3	—	— —
Sheep d	1 887.7 1 142.0²	31.7*	— —
Horses d	379.0 1 563.7	—	— —
Pigs d	340.0 724.0	2.5*	7.3* —
Bacon/ham	8 698.0 8 558.3	—	— —
Meat: 'A', 'B'	834.7*	—	— —
Butter	179.3 na	—	34.7 3.6*
Cheese	46.0 13.01p	0.1*	15.7 13.7*
Eggs	214.5 110.6	—	5.5 12.8*
Fish	215.1 64.6	—	140.4 9.7*
Milk	5 897.0 4 998.3	—	— 2.7*
Wool	3.1² 2.0*	2.8¹	23.4 0.1*

d no. in thousands. n incl. ducks, geese, and turkeys. p factory produce only.

	Production	Exports	Imports
6. FIBRES, TEXTILES, etc.			
Agaves (sisal etc.)	—	—	0.7* 2.6*
Cotton lint	—	—	96.4 0.9*
Flax fibre	5.4 9.8²	0.1*	1.3* 0.1*
Hemp fibre	1.6 4.5²	0.4*	4.4 0.1*
Jute	—	—	27.7 —
Rubber: natural	—	—	— —
synthetic	92.7 na	—	— —
Silk	79.2 na	2.8¹	7.31 —
Cotton: yarn	33.5* 26.8*	—	3.61 —
woven fabrics	—	38.1²	— —
Rayon	31.7 22.2	—	— —
Wool: yarn	—	—	— —
woven fabrics	38.3q na	—	— —

q million sq. metres.

	Production	Exports	Imports
7. FUEL AND POWER			
Coal: 'A', 'B' ‡	2 410² 2 600	— 60	9 575 6 308
Coke	76 200 200 670	6 581 4 088	5 485 4 246
Electricity h ‡: total	50 698 26 300¹	120 30	3 248 2 426
thermal	50 075 25 600¹	—	— —
Natural gas i	110	—	— —
Oil, crude	56 30¹	—	4 183 —
Petroleum, refined	3 823 600¹	1 143	540 —

i million kWh. ‡ million cu. metres.

	Production	Exports	Imports
8. IRON AND STEEL			
Iron ore	492m 427*m	—	1 397m 890
Pig iron	2 249 1 304	—	740 248
Steel ingots/castings	4 256 2 334	—	— —
Iron/steel products	—	—	— —

m metal content.

	Production	Exports	Imports
9. NON-FERROUS MINERALS AND METALS			
Aluminium: bauxite	4 800* 4 500*	—	— —
alumina	na na	—	— 5.32r
aluminium	62* na	—	301.51 —
Chrome: ore m	47* 19	—	35.56 —
Cobalt	—	—	26.62 —
Copper: ore m	25* 20*	—	— —
metal	20* 26*	—	— —
Lead: ore m	10* 5*	—	— —
metal	25* 27*	—	— —
Magnesium: metal	na na	22.40 17.64	81.32 —
metal/salts	na na	—	— —
Manganese, ore m	na na	—	— —
Nickel	1 7	—	— —
Tin: ore m	na na	—	— —
metal	1 7	—	— —
Zinc: ore m	10* na	—	— —
metal	10* na	—	— —

k '000 fine troy oz. m metal content. r calcined alumina.

	Production	Exports	Imports
10. CHEMICALS n AND FERTILIZERS			
Organic chemicals:			
Benzene	1 460.6	—	45.3
Butadiene	na	—	na
Ethylene	109.4	—	na
Methanol	na	—	na
Phenol	5.67	—	na
Phthalic anhydride	na	—	na
Styrene monomer	na	—	na
Urea	na	—	na
Inorganic chemicals:			
Ammonia	514.0	—	na
Carbon black	14.1¹	—	0.8
Chlorine	77.9	—	na
Nitric acid	402.3*	—	na
Sodium carbonate	668.8	209.0¹	na
Sodium hydroxide	366.4	368.4	na
Sulphuric acid	833.4	16.0	na
Plastics:			
Polyamides	na	—	na
Polyethylene	3.0*	—	na
Polyvinyl chloride	98.3	31.2	na
Fertilizers:			
Phosphates	1 876.0o 1 377.7*w	17.4 924.3q	298.6p
Potash	42.3*x 46.0*x	12.9	114.1x 199.1
Pyrites	123.2¹ 95.5¹	22.0	— —
Sulphur	—	—	— —

n data not available for years 1953–5. o P₂O₅ content. q in addition, carbonic caustic potash 14.3. r recovered sulphur. w K₂O content. x sulphur content.

	Production	Exports	Imports
11. INDUSTRY			
Alcoholic beverages b			
beer	13 528 10 260	—	— —
spirits	5 770 2 668	275*q	278
Cement	—	—	— —
Electrical engineering a	380¹	115dr	66dr
Locomotives a	—	—	na
Railway vehicles	587	135	na
Machine tools a	165¹	—	na
Merchant ships g	172¹	4¹	na
Motor vehicles			
commercial a	12 20	36a 14a	16a
private d	93 18	—	— *q

a million $ U.S. b '000 hectolitres. c no. of units. d no. in thousands. g '000 G.R.T. h 1965 figure. n 1960 figure. p 1960 figures. q excl. trade with other Comecon countries. r electrical motors, transformers and radio receivers. t tonnage completed for the use of the Democratic Republic only.

---

na: data not available. — negligible or nil. — data not available. ¹ one year only. ² two year average. * estimate. ‡ see appendix. † re-exports.

GERMANY: FEDERAL REPUBLIC

The Federal Republic of, or West Germany, became a sovereign state in 1955 by the fusion of the three western zones of occupation. West-Berlin remains under tri-partite government, but is also a 'Land' (as yet unincorporated) of the Federal Republic.
Germany F.R. is a member of the European Economic Community.
Saarland, incorporated in the French economic union in 1947, was returned to Germany in 1957. For comparative purposes, data for the Saar for 1953–5 have been included in the following tables when available.
Pre-war figures refer to both sectors of Germany.

AREA: 248 542 sq. km. (95 962 sq. miles) including West-Berlin

LAND USE: (percentage of total)	1965	1955
Arable and orchard	33.4	35.4
Permanent meadow and pasture	23.5	22.9
Forest and woodland	29.0	28.6
City areas, waste and other land	14.1	13.1

POPULATION: 59 872 000 (1967 estimate)
Largest cities: WEST-BERLIN; population: 2 190 577 (city proper, 1966)
HAMBURG; population: 1 851 327 (city proper, 1966)
Capital city: BONN; population: 140 482 (city proper, 1966)

Distribution of working population (1965)
Total working population: 27 157 000

U.N. group no.		Percentage
0	Agriculture, forestry, fishing and hunting	10.9
1	Mining and quarrying	2.0
2/3	Manufacturing	37.5
4	Construction	8.1
5	Electricity, gas, water and sanitary services	0.8
6	Commerce	14.1
7	Transport, storage and communications	5.8
8	Services	20.5
9	Others	0.3

	Year(s)
Life expectancy at birth (years): male	67.6 1964–6 av.
female	73.5
Infant mortality (per '000)	23.8 1965
Crude birth rate (per '000)	17.7 1965
Crude death rate (per '000)	11.2 1965
Accidental deaths (per 100 000 population)	4.9 1965
Permanent motor vehicles	26.4 1965
Population per physician	33.0 1966
Population per hospital bed	90 1966
School enrolment: age 5–19 years (percentage)	88 1963–4 av.
age over 19 years (per 100 000 population)	566 a 1963–5 av.

a excl. engineering schools and post-graduate teacher training.

COMMUNICATIONS

		Year(s)
Motor vehicles in use ('000s): private	8012.4	1963–5 av.
commercial	898.6	1964
Railway track (km.)	35511	
Mail per capita: domestic	144	1963–5 av.
foreign received	16	
foreign sent	15.9	
Telephones (per '000 population)	39.5	1967
Radio receivers (per '000 population)	171.2	1963–5 av.
Television licences (per '000 population)	314.7	1963–5 av.
Daily newspapers (per '000 population)		1962–4 av.

FINANCE

Currency unit: The Deutsche mark

Exchange rates	1965	1950	1938
Per $ U.S.	4.006	4.171	2.494
Per £ sterling	11.227	11.699	11.577

	1965	1960	1955
National income (million $ U.S.)	85 452	85 452	17 892
G.N.P. per capita ($ U.S.)	1700		6 135
Rate of increase of G.N.P. per capita			5 793
Foreign trade (percentage of G.D.P.)	30		

TRADING

Total trade (in million $ U.S.)	1965	1955	1936 d
Exports (f.o.b.)	17 892	6 135	1925
Imports (c.i.f.)	17 472	5 793	1709

Main trading partners (percentage of total value)

Exports	1965	1955	1936 d
France	11	7	5
Netherlands	10	9	8
U.S.A.	8	6	4
Belg./Lux.	8	6	4
Switzerland	6	6	5 a
Italy	6	5	4
Austria	5	6	5

Imports	1965	1955	1936 d
U.S.A.	13	13	6
France	11	7	2
Netherlands	10	7	4
Italy	8	6	3
Belg./Lux.	7	6	3
U.K.	5	4	6
Sweden	4	5	5

Distribution of trade (percentage of total value)

Exports	1965	1955
Manufactured goods	77	74
(machinery and transport equipment)	(46)	(40)
(iron and steel)	(8)	(7)
Chemicals	12	11

Imports	1965	1955
Manufactured goods	43	27
(machinery and transport equipment)	(13)	(5)
Crude materials and fuels	24	40 (9)
(mineral fuels)	19	25
Food		

a incl. former Italian Somaliland. d incl. Germany D.R.

PRODUCTION, EXPORTS AND IMPORTS

Years: 1963–5 average and 1953–5 average Units: '000 metric tons unless otherwise indicated

	Production		Exports		Imports	
1. CEREALS, etc.						
Barley	3 613.7	2 030.0	30.5	11.7	1 147.8	844.0
Maize (corn)	69.0	17.0	227.4	2.8	1 905.1	531.2
Millets/sorghum			19.6†	7.8†	276.4	138.4
Oats	2 227.0	2 526.6	40.2	0.5	407.9	92.1
Potatoes	21 510.3	24 983.0	36.8	55.7	518.9	167.6
Rice	3 224.3	3 645.7	5.0	69.9	157.4	84.6
Rye	3 224.3	3 645.7				
Wheat	4 803.3	3 171.0	108.0	6.6	1 684.8	2 548.5

2. FRUIT, etc.						
Apples	1 462.7	1 228.0	5.8	0.3	528.1	262.1
Bananas			3.5†	4.7†	515.8	174.4
Cherries	233.3	174.8	0.7	0.1	8.6	10.8
Dates			0.1†		228.0	4.9
Lemons	779.0*	340.0†	0.3	0.2†	129.5	100.1
Oranges			0.2†	0.1†	42.2	81.5
Peaches/apricots	28.3 n	35.6	0.2		163.3	68.7
Pears	397.3	402.3	0.2†	0.9	45.3	72.7
Plums	458.3	405.1				12.3
Raisins						48.4
Tomatoes	40.7	25.7				
Wine b	5 597.7	2 441.0	181.4	66.7	4 289.8	2 016.0

b '000 hectolitres. n of which olives 3.0.

3. BEVERAGES, FOREST PRODUCTS, etc.						
Cocoa			0.1†	0.3†	148.1	73.7
Coffee			0.9†	1.1†	256.7	100.4
Sugar: beet	12 236.0	8 997.8	6.7	6.2	205.1	192.1
raw	1 915.2	1 340.3	0.4	0.4	8.1	4.7
Tea			1.7		127.4	61.5
Tobacco: leaf	10.1	24.3		0.1²		0.1²
cigars	3 970.0 c	4 692.4 c	348.0	95.0	6 881.0	4 226.8
cigarettes	95 400.0 c	42 826.0 c	73.9	138.2	2 245.0	797.9
tobacco/snuff	8.5	16.7	3.9	61.0	1 054.6	463.3
Softwood j	16 755.3	16 082.0	163.7	60.8	473.3	105.0
Hardwood j	8 719.6*	7 403.7			1 214.7	225.7*
Wood pulp	1 379.6*	1 340.7				
Newsprint	207.7	225.0				
Other paper	3 792.3	2 036.7				

c '000 metres of roundwood equivalent. j '000 cu. metres of roundwood equivalent.

4. VEGETABLE OILSEEDS AND OILS						
Castor seed	na	na	2.86	3.27	29.63	17.17
Castor oil	na	na	0.29†	0.71	4.58	205.70
Copra	na	na	1.64		254.19	55.70
Coconut oil	na	na			48.25	55.88
Cottonseed	na	na	0.29	0.21	72.10	48.90
Cottonseed oil	na	na	0.99†	0.10†	43.11	36.66
Groundnuts						34.57

continued

PRODUCTION, EXPORTS AND IMPORTS *continued*

4. VEGETABLE OILSEEDS AND OILS—*continued*	Production		Exports		Imports	
Groundnut oil	72 246.7	55 314.3	2.27	0.21	46.17	28.54
Linseed	13 141.3	11 672.0	0.48†	1.00	35.07	3.97
Linseed oil		2.67	5.15	2.47	22.07	81.85
Olive oil			0.01†		1.92	129.43
Palm kernels	na	na			128.82	13.54
Palm kernel oil	na	na	4.53	1.37	14.82	4
Palm oil	na	na	3.49†	4.35†	102.04	85.16
Rapeseed	104.00	22.67	2.91	0.17	65.76*	35.30
Rapeseed oil	na	na	17.53	0.11	5.24	16.00²
Sesame seed	na	na			1 260.90	302.87
Soya beans	na	na	1.03	0.17	14.31	27.00
Soya bean oil	na	na	0.40†	1.67	30.94	28.14
Sunflower seed	na	na	4.45	1.51	59.16	6.15
Sunflower seed oil	na	na	0.03†		3.14	4.34
Tung oil	na	na				

5. LIVESTOCK‡, ANIMAL PRODUCTS, etc.						
Chickens d	na	na	94.3	0.7	404.8	244.5
Cattle	6 510.3	6 464.0 n				na
dairy cows d	192.0	1 041.0	28.5		3.6	
Goats d	907.7	1 384.7	3.5	64.1	247.6	249.6
Sheep d	490.0	1 278.6	0.4	5.2	1.5	25.6
Horses d	7 219.0	13 389.0	16.4	5.5	149.8	69.5
Pigs d	2 877.0	1 988.2			237.0	58.4
Bacon/ham			4.9	22.2	18.1	57.7
Meat‡: A	390.0	200.0			127.9	363.6*
B	492.7	331.0			58.4²	53.3
Butter	653.3	248.7	0.2	30.0	301.7	110.4
Cheese	634.7	761.2	117.3	12.2	142.0	116.7²
Eggs	20 915.7	17 012.0			71.1	62.7
Milk			3.8	1.9		
Whale oil	115.4	106.6				
Hides/skins	1.6	2.7				
Wool						

d no. in thousands. n incl. draught cows. p incl. sperm oil.

6. FIBRES, TEXTILES, etc.						
Abaca						4.3
Agaves (sisal etc.)			0.1†		2.7	36.8
Cotton lint			0.5†		54.2	263.1
Flax fibre			15.3†		65.1	12.9
Hemp fibre			0.8†		55.5	89.7
Jute			2.3†		178.1	137.7
Rubber: natural	136.8	8.2	46.1		87.6 a	227.0
synthetic			275.5†		676.3	
Silk f					27.8	4.6
Cotton: yarn	380.3	290.2 p	8.6		30.0	9.2
woven fabrics	245.8*	233.6*	25.4	23.7	33.0	16.9
Rayon: fibre/yarn	285.5	192.1	104.6	41.9	20.4	3.5 q
woven fabrics	114.2	60.0*	21.4	14.1 q		
Non-cellulosic						
fibre/yarn	142.6	8.1	45.5		20.7	13.2
Wool: yarn	117.3	108.5	3.5	2.1	34.0	11.1
woven fabrics	54.7	68.6	4.2	1.9		

f metric tons. p incl. mixtures predominantly of cotton. q rayon staple fibre cloth only. r yarn input to weaving mills. s incl. imports for re-export.

7. FUEL AND POWER						
Coal:' A ‡	140 317	149 140 n	14 836	14 583	7 773	11 282
B ‡	33 167	92 260	1 580	1 635	1 259	769
Coke	169 185	70 740 p	14 909	10 018	13 301	407
Electricity h: total	33 301	10 750 q				
hydro	13					
nuclear	88					
thermal	145 796	59 990 r				
Natural gas i	2 530	284 i	7	na 1	17	
Oil, crude	7 653	3 150 i	4 857	7 901	50 143	7 100 i
Petroleum, refined	49 500	8 250 i			14 350	7 301
Rare earths i					695 u	585 u
Uranium i					10	

f metric tons. h million kWh. i million cu. metres. n of which 17 330 from Saar. p of which 2 040 from Saar. q of which 20 from Saar. r of which 2 020 from Saar. r of which 119 from Saar. u incl. salts of rare earth minerals.

8. IRON AND STEEL						
Iron ore	2 824 n	3 889 n	303	274	34 416	12 686
Pig iron	25 693	16 135	717	330	553	193
Steel ingots/castings	35 252	20 948	1 039	279	365	113
Iron/steel scrap			1 522	584	1 164	633
Iron/steel products d			1 266	376	751	244

d metric tons. n incl. metal content.

9. NON-FERROUS MINERALS AND METALS						
Gold: ore m	105.30	5.00	253.93	195.00²	2 986.00†	834.50²
ore m	na	na				
Platinum group			2.86	3.27		
metal k			209.15†	16.09†	397.04	92.71
Silver‡: ore m						
bullion		2 060.70	2 297.30	18 563.33	7 984.00	47 179.33	13 921.00

continued

PRODUCTION, EXPORTS AND IMPORTS *continued*

9. NON-FERROUS MINERALS AND METALS—*continued*	Production		Exports		Imports	
Asbestos: fibre	na	na	0.28†	0.26†	153.24	43.78
manufactured	na	na	53.08†	1.88	109.07	0.52
Mica	0.01		0.62†	0.13†	6.06	2.46
Aluminium: bauxite	4.06	5.31	0.98†	1.01†	1 592.10	1 020.21
alumina	605.33	124.41	109.80 q	72.73	84.64 q	53.87
aluminium	221.04		69.31	72.82	231.61	1.63
Antimony: ore			0.77²	0.27	2.64	1.59
metal	0.29	0.24	0.06²	0.06	4.69	0.29
Cadmium			1.58	0.37	238.92	181.46
Chrome: ore			0.05	0.61		0.07
metal					0.89	2.78
Cobalt: ore			0.94	4.27	148.53r	154.54² r
metal	1.60 m	1.87 m	1.33	77.03	586.99	248.00
Copper: ore	332.17	235.23	187.90	77.03	119.25	70.83
metal	50.47 m	65.78 m	6.06	0.08	117.12	55.25
Lead: ore	107.26	108.53	41.92	47.23	119.31	15.39
metal	208.21²		73.99	86.12	171.22	165.70
Magnesium: dolomite			5.94	0.81		
magnesite	0.50 u	0.09 u	113.33	47.45	153.44	9.47
kieserite			7.68	2.95	742.04	309.47
Manganese: ore	192.0	1 041.0	76.28	4.50†	998.87	
metal	490.0	1 278.6	100.60†		731.20	586.70
Mercury f			67.10		276.30	3 088.60
Molybdenum f: ore	2 877.0	1 988.2			3.47	0.32
Nickel: ore			5.68	1.12	26.71	13.12
metal			0.08		8.03	0.95
Tin: ore	1.24	0.49²	1.73	2.08	13.43	7.47
metal					3.47	2.46
Titanium minerals			65.80†		357.80	98.18
Tungsten: ore‡					5.00	0.39
metal			0.26		0.29	
Vanadium	109.52 m	92.53 m	41.20	10.03	130.41	68.99
Zinc: ore	106.65	164.88	77.17	85.04	187.83	57.50
Zirconium minerals			1.18†		26.73	

f metric tons. k '000 fine troy oz. m metal content. p incl. cryolite. q hydrate. r excl. burnt cupreous pyrites. u primary magnesium only.

10. CHEMICALS n AND FERTILIZERS						
Organic chemicals:						
Benzene	274.7		31.1		105.7	
Butadiene	260.2†					
Ethylene	694.3†					
Methanol	572.6		65.5		72.1	
Phenol	144.5 p		49.3		21.2	
Phthalic anhydride	93.6		16.1		9.2	
Styrene monomer	na		na		3.0 i	
Urea	123.2 i					
Inorganic chemicals:						
Ammonia	1 535.1		67.1		1.5	
Carbon black	116.0		28.3		36.9	
Chlorine	1 006.0		1.5		0.8	
Nitric acid	2 431.5*		43.6		64.3	
Sodium carbonate	1 109.8²		92.0		26.2	
Sodium hydroxide	1 115.7		54.5		142.8	
Sulphuric acid	2 903.0					
Plastics:						
Polyamides	na		20.3†		5.7 i	
Polyethylene	224.2		85.7		31.4	
Polyvinyl chloride	329.9		73.4		61.5	
Fertilizers:						
Phosphates	2 177.3 g n	1 546.3 u	38.0		2 151.1	806.0
Potash	7 663	196.4 x	1 736.4	1 326.4	35.6	0.7
Pyrites	181.5 x		20.3		1 549.9	1 022.7
Sulphur	80.3 r	72.1 r	26.1	18.2	394.4	36.2

n data not available. p coal tar and synthetic phenol. r recovered sulphur. w K₂O content. x p sulphur content. g '000 G.R.T. n 1965–7 av. g n of which salts of rare earth minerals.

11. INDUSTRY						
Aircraft a	118* n	na	57.6	0.1	119.1	2.8
Alcoholic beverages			37.4 a	17.5 a	102.9 a	30.6 a
beer b	64 372	34 926				
spirits b	2 782 p	1 694 q				
Cement	31 511	17 095	1 068.7	1 684.3	386.3	60.3
Electrical						
engineering a	6 998²	na	1 320.0	408.0²	398.9	36.4²
Locomotives a	1 058	709²	na	22.0		2.1
Machine tools a			92.1	61.8		
Merchantships g	725 i	na	353.5	117.4 i	68.9	na
Motor vehicles			92.1	429.3	7.0	na
commercial a	961	903	629.0		299.6 a	18.5 a
private a	2 599	531	2 175.0 a	482.5² a		

a million $ U.S. b '000 hectolitres. c no. of units. d no. in thousands. † re-exports.
g '000 G.R.T. i 1958/9 figure. ‡ 1967 figure.

na: data not available. — negligible or nil. — not available. * estimate. † re-exports.
² two year average. ¹ one year only. ‡ see appendix.

GHANA

In 1957, the British colony of the Gold Coast united with the British Trusteeship area of Togoland to become Ghana. The country was declared a republic within the Commonwealth in 1960.

AREA: 238 537 sq. km. (92 100 sq. miles)

LAND USE: (percentage of total)

	1954
Arable and orchard	22.3
Permanent meadow and pasture, forest and woodland	63.9
City areas, waste and other land	13.8

POPULATION: 8 143 000 (1967 estimate)
Largest city: ACCRA, capital; population: 600 200 (1966)

Distribution of working population (1960)
Total working population: 2 725 000*

U.N. group no.		Percentage
0	Agriculture, forestry, fishing and hunting	58.0
1	Mining and quarrying	1.8
2/3	Manufacturing	8.6
4	Construction	3.3
5	Electricity, gas, water and sanitary services	0.5
6	Commerce	13.6
7	Transport, storage and communications	2.5
8	Services	5.7
9	Others	6.0

		Year(s)
Life expectancy at birth (years): male	37.1*	1960
female	na	
Infant mortality (per '000)	82.3*[a]	1963
Population per physician	12 000	1963
Population per hospital bed	770	1966
School enrolment: age 5–19 years (percentage)	57	1963–4 av.
age over 19 years (per 100 000 population)	53	1964–5 av.

[a] registration area only.

COMMUNICATIONS

		Year(s)
Motor vehicles in use ('000s): private	27.0	1963–5 av.
commercial	16.6	1960
Railway track (km)	948	
Mail per capita: domestic	15	
foreign received	4	
foreign sent	0.5	1964–5 av.
Telephones (per '000 population)	71	1967
Radio receivers (per '000 population)	0.1	1963–5 av.
Daily newspapers (per '000 population)	30	1962–4 av.

FINANCE
Currency unit: The new cedi, equivalent to 1.2 cedis, was introduced in 1967. The old cedi replaced the Ghana pound in 1965 at the rate ¢1 to £G 0.305.

Exchange rates	1961	1965b	1960c
Per $ U.S.		0.85	0.357
Per £ sterling		3.28	1.0

		Year(s)
National Income (million $ U.S.)	1 893	1965
G.N.P. per capita ($ U.S.)	230	1966
Foreign trade (percentage of G.D.P.)	35	1963–5 av.

b old cedis. c Ghana pounds.

PRODUCTION
Attempts to decrease reliance on cocoa as the main crop have led to diversification of agriculture by the cultivation of rubber, coffee and tobacco. Re-afforestation has been undertaken, and the fishing industry has been modernized. Recent explorations (1969) have revealed large deposits of bauxite.

TRADING

Total trade (in million $ U.S.)	1965	1955	1938
Exports (f.o.b.)	291	243	32
Imports (c.i.f.)	445	246	38

Main trading partners (percentage of total value)

Exports	1965	1955	Imports	1965	1955	1938*
U.S.A.	17	35	U.K.	26	47	72
Netherlands	13	13	Germany F.R.	9	5	2
Germany F.R.	11	11	U.S.A.	9	9	8
Italy	11	15	Netherlands	7	6	14
U.S.S.R.	11	5	Poland	5	4	
Yugoslavia	4	na	Japan	4	4	10

Distribution of trade (percentage of total value)

Exports	1965	1955
Cocoa	66	76
Wood	13	9
Diamonds	7	6
Manganese	5	6

Imports	1965	1955	1938*
Manufactured goods	74	65	(20)
(machinery and transport equipment)	(33)	(17)	(12)
(textiles and clothing)	(15)	(38)	
Food	11	6	na
Chemicals	6	6	na
Crude materials and fuels	5	7	na

PRODUCTION, EXPORTS AND IMPORTS Units: '000 metric tons unless otherwise indicated
Years: 1963–5 average and 1953–5 average

1. CEREALS, etc.	Production		Exports		Imports	
Cassava	1 224.3*	512.0[2]				
Maize (corn)	178.7*	169.0	0.2		1.8	0.7
Millets/sorghum	184.0*	178.0			0.8	1.4
Potatoes		—[2]			31.9	2.8
Rice	39.0*	23.0[1]			0.5	
Sweet potatoes/yams	1 150.3*	481.5[2]				
Wheat					0.5	

2. FRUIT, etc.	Production		Exports		Imports	
Apples					0.3	
Bananas	na	na	2.7		0.4	
Coconuts	68.7*e	na	na		1.0	
Lemons	13.0*	na	0.3n		0.2	
Pineapples	233.0*	na	na			
Tomatoes	15.7*	na				
Wine b					12.6	7.7

b '000 hectolitres. e no. in millions. n incl. oranges.

3. BEVERAGES, FOREST PRODUCTS, etc.	Production		Exports		Imports	
Cocoa	479.0	226.1[1]	433.5	222.4		
Coffee	3.0*	1.3[1]	3.7		0.1	
Sugar, raw	na				49.3	26.0
Tea					0.1	0.6
Tobacco: leaf	0.9*		na		1.2	
cigarettes	1 747.0c				0.2	1.0[p]d
Hardwood j	9 778.0	7 186.5[2]	0.1	1 040.0	637.7	
Newsprint					12.1	1.2
Other paper	0.8*	na			9.4	1.42

d no. in millions. j '000 cu. metres of roundwood equivalent. p incl. other tobacco manufactures.

PRODUCTION, EXPORTS AND IMPORTS *continued*

6. FIBRES, TEXTILES, etc.	Production		Exports		Imports	
Jute					2.3	
Rubber: natural	na		0.3	0.2	1.5[1]	
yarn	12.5[2]q				9.3	
woven fabrics	na		—	—	1.4[r]	
Rayon, woven fabrics	na					

q million metres. r incl. synthetic.

7. FUEL AND POWER	Production		Exports		Imports	
Coal, 'A'	494	240n			38	99[1]
Electricity h: total	36					
hydro	458	240n				
thermal						
Oil, crude	540		—[1]	—[1]	563	
Petroleum, refined			170		143	320[1]

a million kWh. n incl. Togo (former French Togoland).

8. IRON AND STEEL	Production		Exports		Imports	
Steel ingots/castings	—	—	—	—	2	

9. NON-FERROUS MINERALS AND METALS	Production		Exports		Imports	
Diamonds	2 541.0l	2 197.5l	15.13a	12.81a	22.61[p]	0.08[p]
Gold k, ore	847.0m	735.0m	841.30[p]	784.14[p]	2.32	108.34
Silver k, bullion	na	na	2.41[2]	44.15	20.61	20.17

a million $ U.S. g '000 G.R.T. k metal content. l '000 carats. m metal content.

continued

PRODUCTION, EXPORTS AND IMPORTS—*continued*

9. NON-FERROUS MINERALS AND METALS—continued	Production		Exports		Imports	
Aluminium: bauxite	294.32		255.63	137.96	6.01	0.90[2]
aluminium	na	na			0.75	0.37[2]
Copper, metal	na	na			0.31	0.36
Lead, metal	na	na				
Manganese, ore	491.17	591.27	491.31	587.06	0.13	0.04[2]
Tin, metal	na	na			0.40	0.06[2]
Zinc, metal	na	na				

a million $ U.S. k '000 fine troy oz. l '000 carats. m metal content. p bullion.

10. CHEMICALSn AND FERTILIZERS	Production		Exports		Imports	
Chemicals					na	
Fertilizers:						
Potash	—	—	—	—	0.9	0.1[2]

n data not available for years 1953–5.

11. INDUSTRY	Production		Exports		Imports	
Aircraft a	—	—	—	—		—[2]
Alcoholic beverages b	215.0		—	—	4.6	6.4a
beer b	50.0*		—	—	0.9a	
Cement					559.7	261.3
Electrical engineering a	—	—	—	—	26.1	5.4[2]
Railways vehicles a	—	—	—	—	1.8	36.0
Merchant ships a	—	—	—	—	9.0[1]	
Motor vehicles	1.0[p]					
commercial	—	—			24.3a	14.4a

a million $ U.S. b '000 hectolitres. g '000 G.R.T. p assembly of imported parts.

GIBRALTAR

Gibraltar has been a British colony for more than two centuries, but since 1964 has had a large measure of internal self-government. In 1967 a referendum showed that an overwhelming majority of the inhabitants preferred to retain links with Britain rather than pass under Spanish sovereignty.

AREA: 6.5 sq. km. (2.5 sq. miles)

LAND USE: (percentage of total)
City areas, waste and other land

POPULATION: 25 000* (1967 U.N. estimate)
Total working population: 9 008 (1961)

		Year(s)
Infant mortality (per '000)	20.6	1965
Crude birth rate (per '000)	27.3	1965
Crude death rate (per '000)	9.8	1965
Population per physician	1 000	1983
Population per hospital bed	110	1966
School enrolment: age 5–19 years (percentage)	70a	1963–4 av.

a public education only.

COMMUNICATIONS

		Year(s)
Motor vehicles in use ('000s): private	5.7	1963–5 av.
commercial	0.5	1967
Telephones (per '000 urban population)	19.3b	1963–5 av.
Radio licences (per '000 population)	184	1967
Television licences (per '000 population)	174.2	1963–5 av.
Daily newspapers (per '000 population)	300.3	1962–4 av.

b excl. telephone systems of the armed forces.

FINANCE
Currency unit: The pound sterling c

Exchange rates	1965	1960
Per $ U.S.	0.357	0.357

c local notes and U.K. coins in use.

EMPLOYMENT AND TRADE
Gibraltar is a free port and naval base; revenue is received from transit trade and from port dues and refuelling facilities. Small firms are engaged in food processing and clothing manufacture for local needs and export. Tourism is becoming increasingly important.

PRODUCTION, EXPORTS AND IMPORTS Units: '000 metric tons unless otherwise indicated
Years: 1963–5 average and 1953–5 average

2. FRUIT, etc.	Production	Exports	Imports
Wine b		0.3[1]	1.0

b '000 hectolitres.

3. BEVERAGES, FOREST PRODUCTS, etc.	Production	Exports	Imports
Coffee	—		3.3[1]
Sugar, raw	—		1.8[1]

5. LIVESTOCK, ANIMAL PRODUCTS, etc.	Production	Exports	Imports
Meat‡: A	—	—[1]	0.91
B	—		0.1[2]
Cheese	—		0.2[1]
Fish	—		0.2[1]

7. FUEL AND POWER	Production	Exports	Imports
Coal, 'A' ‡	—	—	2 34
Electricity h t	39	20[1]	197 10[1]
Petroleum, refined	na		197

h million kWh. t thermal.

11. INDUSTRY	Production	Exports	Imports
Cement	—	—[1]	12.0 4.7

continued

na: data not available. — negligible or nil. [1] one year only. [2] two year average. * estimate. ‡ see appendix. † re-exports.

GREECE

Following a revolution in 1967 the king went into exile and a nationalist government took over all constitutional and legislative powers.

AREA: 131 944 sq. km. (50 942 sq. miles)
Land area: 129 310 sq. km. (49 927 sq. miles)

LAND USE: (percentage of total)	1954	1964
Arable and orchard	26.5	29.2
Permanent meadow and pasture	39.1	39.0
Forest and woodland	14.8	19.7
City areas, waste and other land	19.6	12.1

POPULATION: 8 716 000 (1967 estimate)
Largest city: ATHINAI (Athens) capital; population: 1 852 700* (1961)

Distribution of working population (1961)
Total working population: 3 638 600

U.N. group no.		Percentage
0	Agriculture, forestry, fishing and hunting	53.9
1	Mining and quarrying	0.6
2/3	Manufacturing	13.4
4	Construction	4.5
5	Electricity, gas, water and sanitary services	0.5
6	Commerce	7.3
7	Transport, storage and communications	4.2
8	Services	12.1
9	Others	3.4

	male	female
Life expectancy at birth (years)	67.5	70.7

	Year(s)
Infant mortality (per '000)	34.3	1960–2 av.
Crude birth rate (per '000)	17.7	1965
Crude death rate (per '000)	7.9	1965
Accidental deaths (per 100 000 population)	10.6	1965
caused by motor vehicles	26.3	1965
due to other causes	680	1966
Population per physician	170	1965
Population per hospital bed	569	1964–5 av.
School enrolment: age 5–19 years (percentage)		
age over 19 years (per 100 000 population)a		
a incl. pre-school education		

COMMUNICATIONS

		Year(s)
Motor vehicles in use ('000s): private	84.5	1963–5 av.
commercial	65.4	1963
Railway track (km.): domestic	2 583	1963
Mail per capita: domestic	25	
foreign received	6	1963–5 av.
foreign sent	6.69	1967
Telephones (per '000 000 population)	99	1963–5 av.
Radio licences (per '000 000 population)	121	1959
Daily newspapers (per '000 000 population)		

PRODUCTION, EXPORTS AND IMPORTS

Years: 1963–5 average and 1953–5 average Units: '000 metric tons unless otherwise indicated

1. CEREALS, etc.	Production		Exports		Imports	
Barley	299.0	238.3	—	—	—	—
Maize (corn)	280.0	282.7	—	—	31.8	5.7
Millets/sorghum	3.3	4.0	—	—	138.5	—
Oats	153.0	158.0	—	—	5.4	—
Potatoes	562.3	430.3	0.1	—	20.3	6.6
Rice	19.7	57.0a	11.4	7.8a	3.2	2.6
Rye	91.3	132.3	2.3	—	—	—
Wheat	1 855.0	1 318.3	—	—	26.9	222.6

2. FRUIT, etc.	Production		Exports		Imports	
Apples	165.7	48.7	13.2	—	—	0.1
Apricots	21.7	8.5	—	—	—	0.22
Bananas	19.3	—	—	—	6.9	—
Cherries		7.5	—	—	—	—
Dates		—	—	—	0.2	—
Figs	121.7	119.7	—	—	—	—
Grapes	1 196.3	1 055.3	15.9	—	—	—
Lemons	153.0	42.7	18.1	—	—	—
Oranges	312.7	146.7	34.9	—	—	—
Olives	976.3	608.3	57.8	9.1	—	—
Peaches	91.3	36.0	—	—	—	—
Pears	64.0	—	—	—	—	—
Plums	24.3*	—	—	—	—	—
Raisins	153.4	114.7	125.8	—	—	—
Tomatoes	499.7	361.0	—	—	—	—
Wine b	3 249.3	3 888.0	358.0	273.3	0.7	0.3

b '000 hectolitres.

FINANCE

Currency unit: The drachma

Exchange rates	1965	1960	1955	1938
Per $ U.S.	30	30	30	118
Per £ sterling	84	84	84	543

		Year(s)
National Income (million $ U.S.)	4 842	1965
G.N.P. per capita ($ U.S.)	660	1966
Rate of increase of G.N.P. per capita	7.9	1963–4 av.
Foreign trade (percentage of G.D.P.)	24	1963–5 av.

TRADING

Total trade (in million $ U.S.)	1965	1955	1938
Exports (f.o.b.)	328	183	90
Imports (c.i.f.)	1 134	382	132

Main trading partners (percentage of total value)

Exports	1965	1955	Imports	1965	1955
Germany F.R.	23	25	Germany F.R.	17	17
U.S.S.R.	8	13	U.S.A.	10	18
U.K.	8	10	Italy	9	11
Italy	6	15	France	8	6
Yugoslavia	4	3	Belg./Lux.	4	4
			Japan	3	—

Distribution of trade (percentage of total value)

Exports	1965	1955	1938*
Tobacco	34	42	na
Food (fruit)	29	22	30
Textiles and clothing	10	13	(na)

Imports	1965	1955	1938*
Manufactured goods (machinery and transport equipment)	57	45	14
Crude materials and fuels	18	26	(11)
Chemicals	9	8	6

3. BEVERAGES, FOREST PRODUCTS, etc.

	Production		Exports		Imports	
Cocoa	—	—	—	—	3.7	1.0
Coffee	—	—	—	—	9.7	5.2
Sugar: beet	509	na	—	—	—	—
raw	69	na	—	—	69.4	83.3
Tea	—	—	—	—	0.2	0.1
Tobacco: leaf	126	75	68.3	52.1	—	—
cigarettes	13 927 e	8 946 g	—	—	—	—
Softwood j	2 271 i	657 j	0.2	0.1 n	581.7	267.3
Hardwood j	2 462 i*	3 335 j	—	—	61.5	3.6
Wood pulp	2*	na	—	—	74.8	30.0
Newsprint	—	—	—	—	38.3	11.3
Other paper	123*	37*	3.0	—	17.4	7.6

e no. in millions. j '000 cu. metres of roundwood equivalent. n incl. other tobacco manufactures.

4. VEGETABLE OILSEEDS AND OILS

	Production		Exports		Imports	
Castor oil	—	—	—	—	0.03	0.02
Copra	—	—	—	—	0.01	0.17
Coconut oil	—	—	—	—	16.85	22.90
Cottonseed	140.70	92.00	—	—	0.40	—
Cottonseed oil	—	—	—	—	0.13	—
Groundnuts	3.97	3.50	0.17	—	0.14	3.63
Linseed	1.00	—	—	—	0.12	0.12
Linseed oil	na	—	2.06	—	1.71	—
Olive oil	194.33	138.67 b	11.44	—	—	0.01
Palm kernels	—	—	—	—	0.07	—
Palm oil	—	—	—	—	0.78	—
Rapeseed	—	—	—	—	21.48	1.28
Sesame seed	7.60	12.90	0.23	—	0.02	—
Soya bean oil	—	—	—	—	—	—
Sunflower seed	3.00	2.30	0.71	0.57	—	—

p incl. oil extracted by solvents.

continued

PRODUCTION, EXPORTS AND IMPORTS *continued*

5. LIVESTOCK‡, ANIMAL PRODUCTS, etc.

	Production	Exports	Imports
Chickens d	17 849	—	—
Cattle d	1 100	—	14.6
Goats d	4 534	—	—
dairy cows d	688	0.1	na
Sheep d	9 231	—	518.4
Horses d	320	—	—
Pigs d	616	0.2	1.9
Meat A	142*	—	50.7
B	60	—	8.7
Butter	9 g	0.9	1.8
Cheese	113	—	6.2
Eggs	85	2.7	0.2
Fish	119	6.9	41.8
Milk	422	—	127.9
Hides/skins	23	—	9.6
Wool	6	—	2.1

d no. in thousands. g incl. butter made from sheep's milk. r butter from cows' and buffaloes' milk.

6. FIBRES, TEXTILES, etc.

	Production	Exports	Imports
Abaca (sisal etc.)	—	—	0.1
Agaves	79.7	44.7	2.9
Cotton lint	0.2	—	0.7
Flax fibre	—	—	0.5
Hemp fibre	—	—	4.5
Jute	—	—	3.1
Rubber, natural	na	—	0.1
Silk t	32.1	92.3	3.5
Cotton: yarn	21.4	3.6	8.6
woven fabrics	2.5	0.5	1.3
Rayon: fibre/yarn	—	—	—
woven fabrics	0.3	0.1	2.4
Non-cellulosic	10.6	0.1 u	1.4
Wool: yarn	6.0	—	3.9
woven fabrics	—	—	—

f metric tons. p incl. artificial cotton. q incl. linters. r pure cotton cloth only. t incl. synthetic piece goods. u excl. blankets.

7. FUEL AND POWER

	Production	Exports	Imports
Coal A	1 373	—	168
B	786	—	162
Coke	—	—	272
Electricity h: total	3 769	—	25
hydro	768	—	1
thermal	3 001	—	55
Oil, crude	—	—	1 850
Petroleum, refined	1 757	23	1 747

h million kWh.

8. IRON AND STEEL

	Production	Exports	Imports
Iron ore	na	62	—
Pig iron	61 m	—	—
Steel ingots/castings	209	—	22
Iron/steel scrap	na	9	47
Iron/steel products a	na	na	20

a million $ U.S. m metal content.

9. NON-FERROUS MINERALS AND METALS

	Production	Exports	Imports
Gold k, ore m	6.00	—	—
Silver k, ore m	138.70	—	—
Asbestos: fibre	0.07	0.46	4.08
manufactured	na	—	4.23
Mica	—	—	0.03

continued

9. NON-FERROUS MINERALS AND METALS—continued

	Production	Exports	Imports
Aluminium: bauxite	1 197.58	1 110.29	—
alumina d	73.00 n	79	1.27 p
aluminium	na	na	9.37
Antimony-ore m	0.22	0.79	—
metal	—	—	0.04
Chrome, ore	53.95 m	22.45	—
Cobalt	na	28.05	—
Copper: ore	29.61 m	—	10.19
metal	0.61	0.06	5.05
Lead: ore	8.87 m	8.98	1.35
metal	4.72	2.77	0.39
Magnesium: dolomite	9 g	0.53	0.12
magnesite	314.21	121.41	0.42
magnesia/salts	na	42.61	3.16
Manganese, ore	39.79	15.81	2.00
Mercury t	na	0.24 q	—
Nickel, metal	—	—	0.25
Tin, metal	—	—	1.60
Titanium minerals	—	—	0.08
Tungsten, metal	—	—	—
Zinc: ore	11.13 m	21.82	9.88
metal	8.98 m	12.19	—

f metric tons. k '000 fine troy oz. m metal content. n 1966 figure. p hydrate. q unwrought.

10. CHEMICALS n AND FERTILIZERS

Organic chemicals:	Production	Exports	Imports
Benzene	na	—	0.1
Butadiene	—	—	na
Ethylene	—	—	na
Methanol	—	—	0.3
Phthalic anhydride	—	—	3.1
Styrene monomer	—	—	0.6
Urea	—	—	—

Inorganic chemicals:			
Ammonia	na	—	6.7
Carbon black	na	—	0.7
Chlorine	na	—	0.3
Nitric acid	17.2	—	0.4
Sodium carbonate	na	—	16.5
Sodium hydroxide	129.0	0.2	11.7
Sulphuric acid	—	—	29.0

Plastics:			
Polyamides	—	—	—
Polyethylene	—	—	—
Polyvinyl chloride	—	—	—

Fertilizers:			
Phosphates	64.4 x	99.0 x	129.2
Potash	na	—	27.7
Pyrites	36.5	142.1	38.4
Sulphur	8.4	—	—

n data not available for years 1953–5. x sulphur content, r content of ore.

11. INDUSTRY

	Production	Exports	Imports
Aircraft a	na	—	0.3
Alcoholic beverages	54*	—	0.1 a
beer b	na	5.0 a	0.7 a
spirits b	na	3.7 a	—
Hardwood j	431.0	240.4	—
Wood pulp	73.81 b	157.7	1.3
Newsprint	2 726.3	896.0	—
Electrical engineering a	—	0.1	57.2
Railway vehicles a	na	—	254.0
Merchant ships g	3.0	—	5.7
Motor vehicles a	na	1.2	—

a million $ U.S. g '000 G.R.T. p 1961 figure.

na: data not available. — negligible or nil. * estimate. 1 one year only. 2 two year average. ‡ see appendix. † re-exports.

159

GUATEMALA

CENTRAL AMERICA

Guatemala is a republic of which the present constitution was promulgated in 1966 on the restoration of civilian government after three years of military rule.

AREA: 108 889 sq. km. (42 042 sq. miles)

LAND USE: (percentage of total)

	1958
Arable and orchard	13.5
Permanent meadow and pasture	5.3
Forest and woodland	44.4
City areas, waste and other land	36.8

POPULATION: 4 717 000* (1967 estimate)

Largest city: CIUDAD DE GUATEMALA (Guatemala City), capital; population: 577 120 (city proper, 1964)

Distribution of working population (1964)

Total working population: 1 292 220* (based on a 5% sample of census returns)

U.N. group no.		Percentage
0	Agriculture, forestry, fishing and hunting	64.7
1	Mining and quarrying	0.2
2/3	Manufacturing	11.5
4	Construction	2.7
5	Electricity, gas, water and sanitary services	0.1
6	Commerce	6.4
7	Transport, storage and communications	2.2
8	Services	11.5
9	Others	0.7

		Year(s)
Life expectancy at birth (years): male	48.3	1963–5 av.
female	43.7	1963–5 av.
Infant mortality (per '000)	92.6	1965
Crude birth rate (per '000)	48*	1960–5 av.
Crude death rate (per '000)	19*	1960–5 av.
Accidental deaths (per 100 000 population)	7.3	1965
caused by motor vehicles	28.5	1965
Population per physician	3 690	1965
Population per hospital bed	410	1966
School enrolment: age 5–19 years (percentage)	39a	1966
age over 19 years (per 100 000 population)	161	1963–5 av.

a incl. evening courses.

COMMUNICATIONS

		Year(s)
Motor vehicles in use ('000s): private	33.5	1963–5 av.
commercial	14.6	
Railway track (km.)	1 159	1962
Telephones (per '000 urban population)	0.7	1962
Television sets (per '000 population)	12.0	1963–5 av.
Daily newspapers (per '000 population)	31	1962

FINANCE

Currency unit: The quetzal

Exchange rates

	1965	1960	1950	1938
Per $ U.S.	1.0	1.0	1.08	1.01
Per £ sterling	2.8	2.8	2.82	4.65

		Year(s)
National Income (million $ U.S.)	1 247	1955
G.N.P. per capita ($ U.S.)	320	1965
Rate of increase of G.N.P. per capita	2.8	1966
Foreign trade (percentage of G.D.P.)	28	1963–5 av.

TRADING

	1965	1960	1955	1938
Total trade (in million $ U.S.)	187		107	18
Exports (f.o.b.)	229		107	21
Imports (c.i.f.)				

Main trading partners (percentage of total value)

Exports	1965	1955	Imports	1965	1955
U.S.A.	37	74	U.S.A.	42	65
Germany F.R.	13	13	El Salvador	10	1
Japan	11	1	Germany F.R.	10	7
El Salvador	11	2	Japan	7	5
Honduras	4	7	U.K.	5	4
Netherlands	3		Venezuela	3	1
Nicaragua	3		Belg./Lux.	3	1

Distribution of trade (percentage of total value)

Exports	1965	1938*
Coffee	49	76
Textiles and clothing	23	30
Fruit and vegetables	4	10*
Sugar	3	1
Essential oils	3	

Imports	1965	1938*
Manufactured goods	64	(29)
(machinery and transport equipment)	(14)	(11)
(textiles and clothing)	(6)	na
Chemicals	17	9
Food	9	5

PRODUCTION, EXPORTS AND IMPORTS

Years: **1963–5 average** and 1953–5 average. Units: '000 metric tons unless otherwise indicated

1. CEREALS, etc.

	Production		Exports		Imports	
Cassava	3.0*	na				
Maize (corn)	614.7*	389.3			11.2	19.9
Millets/sorghum	12.0*	12.3	0.5	1.1	0.2	
Potatoes	18.0*	9.3	8.2[2]		0.3	0.3[2]
Rice	16.0*	10.0	0.1[2]	0.4	0.3	5.6
Wheat	35.0*	17.7			65.1	

2. FRUIT, etc.

	Production		Exports		Imports	
Bananas	122.7*	na	94.4	153.7		
Grapes						0.4
Oranges	30.0*	na			3.1[2]	1.3
Wine[b]						

b '000 hectolitres.

3. BEVERAGES, FOREST PRODUCTS, etc.

	Production		Exports		Imports	
Cocoa	0.5	na	0.4	0.3		
Coffee	108.2*	71.4*	93.5	55.7		
Sugar: cane	1 833.3*	567.7*[n]				
raw	143.7[n]	1.4*	44.4		11.2	
Tobacco: leaf	1.9*	A	0.1[2]	na	0.2[2]	
cigars[e]	69.0					
cigarettes[e]	2 132.0	1 609.7	8.0		0.3[2]	0.8[1]
Hardwood[j]	4 250.0[1]	645.0	11.6[2]		2.0[1]	
Wood pulp		564.0[1]			4.6[1]	2.2[2]
Newsprint	5.32*				2	3.4[1]

e no. in millions. j '000 cu. metres of roundwood equivalent. n incl. some other vegetable oils. panela 31* (1953–5 av.) and 50* (1963–5 av.).

4. VEGETABLE OILSEEDS AND OILS

	Production		Exports		Imports	
Coconut oil					0.28[2]	0.20
Cottonseed	120.30*	12.67	0.01[2]	4.47	1.07[2]	0.08[2]
Cottonseed oil	na	na	15.28		0.39[2]	
Groundnuts			0.01[2]			
Groundnut oil					0.06[2]	0.25[p]
Olive oil					0.14[2]	0.54
Sesame seed	0.50*	0.50	1.18	0.63	0.01	0.04
Rapeseed oil						
Soya bean oil					0.10	
Tung oil					0.01	

b incl. some other vegetable oils.

5. LIVESTOCK‡, ANIMAL PRODUCTS, etc.

	Production		Exports		Imports	
Cattle[d]	5 617.0*	4 211.3				
dairy cows[d]	1 179.3*	1 160.3	0.6[2]	0.1	36.4[2]	35.6
Goats[d]	637.0*					
Sheep[d]	89.0*	103.7				
Horses[d]	694.0*	805.7			7.7[2]	
Pigs[d]	158.3*	176.0	2.6[2]	7.8		
Meat‡: A	417.0*	429.0	5.32[2]		0.12[2]	0.1
B	52.0*	40.0[2]q			0.22[2]	0.4
Butter	3.1*				0.22[2]	0.4
Cheese	2.0*	na	0.2[2]		0.12[2]	0.1
Eggs	9.0*	na	0.1		1.2[2]	0.4
Fish		0.7	1.0		38.3[2]	19.6
Hides/skins	160.0*	175.0[1]			na	0.6a

a million $ U.S. d no. in thousands. q incl. meat equivalent of live animals. r excl. sheepskins.

continued

PRODUCTION, EXPORTS AND IMPORTS continued

6. FIBRES, TEXTILES, etc.

	Production		Exports		Imports	
Abaca	na	3.2		2.4		
Agaves (henequen)	0.6*	na				
Cotton lint	75.0*	8.0	57.7*			
Jute					1.7[2]	0.1
Rubber, natural					1.4[2]	
Cotton: yarn					9.1	
woven fabrics					1.7	

7. FUEL AND POWER

	Production	Exports	Imports
Electricity[h]: total	426		
hydro	117[1]		220[1]
thermal	309		130[1]
Oil, crude			90[1]
Petroleum, refined	206	1	240
			353

h million kWh.

9. NON-FERROUS MINERALS AND METALS

	Production	Exports	Imports
Silver[k], ore[m]	30.70	na	8.00[p]
Asbestos: fibre	361.70		0.58
manufactured			0.14
Aluminium[a]	na	na	
Antimony, ore[m]	na	0.01[n]	
Chrome, ore[m]	0.27		

continued

WEST AFRICA

GUINEA

Guinea, formerly the colony of French Guinea, part of the French West African Community in 1958 and became an independent republic. Links with France, her main trading partner, were severed, and financial and technical aid were replaced by assistance from the U.S.A., Germany F.R., the U.S.S.R., and China P.R.

AREA: 245 857 sq. km. (95 000 sq. miles)

POPULATION: 3 702 000 (1967 estimate)

Largest city: CONAKRY, capital; population: 197 267 (1967)

Total working population: 1 348 000 (1959)

		Year(s)
Life expectancy at birth (years): male	26*[b]	1955
female	28*[b]	
Population per physician	19 000	1962
Population per hospital bed	530[a]	1966
School enrolment: age 5–19 years (percentage)	22	1963–4 av.
age over 19 years (per 100 000 population)	16	1963–5 av.

a government hospitals only. b African population only.

COMMUNICATIONS

		Year(s)
Motor vehicles in use ('000s): private	8.4	1963–5 av.
commercial	12.8	
Railway track (km.)	662	1965
Telephones (per '000 urban population)	0.2*	1967
Radio receivers (per '000 population)	16	1963–5 av.
Daily newspapers (per '000 population)	0.2	1959

FINANCE

Currency unit: The Guinea franc was introduced in 1960 at par with the franc CFA

Exchange rates

	1965	1960
Per $ U.S.	246.85	246.85
Per £ sterling	691.18	691.18

		Year
National Income (million $ U.S.)	241	1958
G.N.P. per capita ($ U.S.)	80	1966

TRADING

		Year(s)
Total trade (in million $ U.S.)		1963
Exports	46	
Imports	56	

PRODUCTION, EXPORTS AND IMPORTS

Years: **1963–5 average** Units: '000 metric tons unless otherwise indicated

Note—no data are available for 1953–5

1. CEREALS, etc.

	Production	Exports	Imports
Cassava	440.0*		
Maize (corn)	67.3*		
Millets/sorghum	142.0*		
Rice	316.7*		
Sweet potatoes/yams	83.3*		

2. FRUIT, etc.

	Production	Exports	Imports
Bananas	86.0*	33.3*	
Oranges	80.7*		
Pineapples	13.0*		

3. BEVERAGES, FOREST PRODUCTS, etc.

	Production	Exports, etc.	Imports
Coffee	11.7*	na	10.8[2]*
Sugar, raw		na	
Tobacco, leaf	1.3	na	0.3[2]
Softwood[j]		na	3.3[2]
Hardwood[j]	2 125.0*[1]	na	0.1[1]
Newsprint			2.1[1]
Other paper	83.3*		

j '000 cu. metres of roundwood equivalent.

4. VEGETABLE OILSEEDS AND OILS

	Production	Exports	Imports
Groundnuts	12.37	na	
Palm kernels	19.50	16.50*	
Palm oil	11.67*	na	

continued

---

9. NON-FERROUS MINERALS AND METALS—continued

	Production	Exports	Imports
Copper, metal	na		0.18
Lead: ore	0.58*[m]	4.68*[m]	6.51
metal	0.08	0.79	4.66
Mercury[f]		0.25*	
Zinc, ore	0.67[m]	6.50[m]	0.10[s]
		1.56	12.67

f metric tons. k '000 fine troy oz. m metal content. n exports to the U.S.A. only. p bullion. s incl. imports for re-export.

10. CHEMICALS[n] AND FERTILIZERS

	Production	Exports	Imports
Chemicals			na
Fertilizers:			
Potash			9.1
Sulphur			0.1

n data not available for years 1953–5.

11. INDUSTRY

	Production	Exports	Imports
Aircraft[a]			1.4	0.5a
Alcoholic beverages	203.0	0.4a	1.3[a]
beer[b]	192.3	25.3*	1.0	4.0
Cement				
Electrical engineering[a]			10.5	
Railway vehicles[a]		1.0	0.3	
Motor vehicles[a]			16.5	5.8

a million $ U.S. b '000 hectolitres.

continued

na: data not available. — negligible or nil. * estimate. * estimate. [2] two year average. [1] one year only. ‡ see appendix. † re-exports.

GUINEA continued

PRODUCTION, EXPORTS AND IMPORTS continued

	Production ANIMAL PRODUCTS, etc.	Exports	Imports
5. LIVESTOCK‡, ANIMAL PRODUCTS, etc.			
Cattle d	1 716.7*	—	—
Goats d	410.0*	—	—
Sheep d	360.3*	—	—
Horses d	1.0*	—	—
Pigs d	15.0*	—	—
Eggs	2.7*	—	—
Fish	na	—	—
Milk	137.3*	—	—

d no. in thousands.

6. FIBRES, TEXTILES, etc.
Agaves (sisal) · 0.1* — — —

7. FUEL AND POWER
| Electricity h | 166 | — | 230 |
| Petroleum, refined | — | — | — |

h hydro and thermal.

	Production	Exports	Imports
8. IRON AND STEEL			
Iron ore	389 m	560	—

m metal content.

9. NON-FERROUS MINERALS AND METALS
Diamonds l	66.00*	na	—
Aluminium: bauxite	1 737.45	205.35	—
alumina	495.51	486.69[1]	—

l '000 carats.

11. INDUSTRY
| Cement | — | — | 87* |
| Merchant ships g | — | — | 4* |

g '000 G.R.T.

GUYANA

SOUTH AMERICA

Guyana, formerly British Guiana, became an independent member of the British Commonwealth in 1966, attaining republican status in 1970.

AREA: 215 000 sq. km. (83 000 sq. miles)

LAND USE: (percentage of total)
	1962	1954
Arable and orchard	0.9	0.6
Permanent meadow and pasture	11.8	5.1
Forest and woodland	84.3	77.0
City areas, waste and other land	3.0	17.3

POPULATION: 680 000 (1967 U.N. estimate)

Largest city: GEORGETOWN (formerly Demerara), capital; population: 148 391 (1960)

Distribution of working population (1960)
Total working population: 174 730

U.N. group no.		Percentage
0	Agriculture, forestry, fishing and hunting	34.2
1	Mining and quarrying	3.5
2/3	Manufacturing	15.1
4	Construction	7.4
5	Electricity, gas, water and sanitary services	0.5
6	Commerce	10.4
7	Transport, storage and communications	4.4
8	Services	16.7
9	Others	7.8

		Year(s)
Life expectancy at birth (years): male	59	1959–61 av.
female	63	
Infant mortality (per '000)	42.3	1965
Crude birth rate (per '000)	39.7	1966
Crude death rate (per '000)	9.5*	1960–5 av.
Accidental deaths (per 100 000 population)	2.7	1962
caused by motor vehicles	41.1	1962
due to other causes		1963
Population per motor vehicle	2 600	1966
Population per physician	170	1963–4 av.
School enrolment: age 5–19 years (percentage)	83 a	1963–5 av.
age over 19 years (per 100 000 population)	53 b	
a public education only. b universities only.		

COMMUNICATIONS
		Year(s)
Motor vehicles in use ('000s): private	9.1	1963–5 av.
commercial	2.9	
Railway track (km.)	151 a	1964
Mail per capita: domestic	59	1963–5 av.
foreign received	na	
foreign sent	37	1967
Telephones (per '000 urban population)	1.7	1963–5 av.
Radio receivers (per '000 population)	114	1963–5 av.
Daily newspapers (per '000 population)	76	1962–4 av.

a excluding about 130 km. of privately owned railway used for the transport of manganese and bauxite.

FINANCE

Currency unit: The Guyana dollar replaced, at par, the British West Indies dollar in 1966.

Exchange rates	1965	1960	1958
Per $ U.S.	1.71	1.71	1.71
Per £ sterling	4.8	4.8	4.8

	Year(s)		
National Income (million $ U.S.)	160	1965	
G.N.P. per capita ($ U.S.)	300	1966	
Foreign trade (percentage of G.D.P.)	92	1963–5 av.	

TRADING

Total trade (in million $ U.S.)	1965	1955	1938
Exports (f.o.b.)	97	53	12
Imports (c.i.f.)	104	55	11

Main trading partners (percentage of total value)
Exports	1965	1955
U.K.	25	36
Canada	23	36
U.S.A.	19	9
Trin./Tob.	na	na
Norway	6	na
Jamaica	5	na
Netherlands	2	1

Imports	1965	1955	1938
U.K.	31	48	na
U.S.A.	24	13	na
Trin./Tob.	11	na	na
Canada	8	6	na
Netherlands	4	6	na
Germany F.R.	3	3	na
Japan	3	2	na

Distribution of trade (percentage of total value)
Exports	1965	1955	1938*
Crude materials (bauxite and concentrates)	46 (41)	32 (28)	(17)
Food	46 (27)	60 (45)	na (63)
(sugar)	(27)	(14)	(5)
(rice)	(3)	(na)	(na)
Diamonds	3	2	3
(shrimps)	(3)		
Rum	3	3	na

Imports	1965	1955	1938*
Manufactured goods (machinery and transport equipment) (textiles and clothing)	60 (27) (11)	60 (22) (11)	(19) (17)
Food	17	21	21
Chemicals	10	8	2
Petroleum products	9	8	4

continued

PRODUCTION, EXPORTS AND IMPORTS

Years: 1963–5 average and 1953–5 average   Units: '000 metric tons unless otherwise indicated

	Production	Exports	Imports
1. CEREALS, etc.			
Cassava	10.0*	—	—
Maize (corn)	1.0*	—	1.3*
Potatoes	na	—	0.4
Rice	239.0	86.4	8.0[2]
Sweet potatoes/yams	5.0*	43.9	—

2. FRUIT, etc.			
Apples	5.0*	0.6[1]	0.4[1]
Bananas	42.3	—	na
Coconuts e	na	—	—
Grapes	2.0*	—	0.1[1]
Oranges	10.3	—	—
Pineapples	1.7	—	0.2[1]
Raisins	na	—	—
Wine b	na	1.5[2]	0.6[1]

b '000 hectolitres. e no. in millions.

3. BEVERAGES, FOREST PRODUCTS, etc.
Coffee	1	0.4[2]	—
Sugar: cane raw	3 246.0	2 771.0[2]	—
Tea	299.7	256.0	0.1[1]
Tobacco: leaf	371.0	280.3	0.1[1]
cigarettes e	na	236.5	0.3[2]
Softwood j	243.7	—	—
Hardwood j	350.3	28.3[2]	3.0[2]
Newsprint	—	—	145.0[2]
Other paper	—	53.2	2.4[2]

j '000 cu. metres of roundwood equivalent.

4. VEGETABLE OILSEEDS AND OILS
Castor oil	5.53	—	0.01
Copra	na	0.03	0.43[1]
Coconut oil	4.53	—	0.44[1]
Groundnuts	na	—	na
Linseed oil	—	—	0.01[1]
Olive oil	—	—	na
Soya bean oil	—	—	1.45[1]

5. LIVESTOCK‡, ANIMAL PRODUCTS, etc.
Chickens d	1 783.3*	0.4	—
Cattle d	23.0*	—	na
Goats d	64.7*	—	—
Sheep d	2.7*	—	—
Horses d	na	—	0.6[1]
Pigs d	4.3*	0.4[1]	0.1
Bacon/ham }	}		
Meat‡: 'A'	0.7*	0.2[1]	—
'B'			

continued

HAITI

CARIBBEAN SEA

Haiti, once a prosperous French colony, has a population primarily of African origin. The country has a long history of political upheavals, and came under U.S. control from 1915 to 1934, with the U.S. control of revenue continuing until 1947. Further unrest led to a period without a government in 1956; and since 1957 the president has ruled with 'absolute power'.

POPULATION: 4 581 000 (1967 estimate)
Largest city: PORT-AU-PRINCE, capital; population: 240 000 (city proper, 1960)

Distribution of working population (1950)
Total working population: 1 747 187

U.N. group no.		Percentage
0	Agriculture, forestry, fishing and hunting	83.2
1	Mining and quarrying	4.9
2/3	Manufacturing	0.6
4	Construction	0.1
5	Electricity, gas, water and sanitary services	3.5
6	Commerce	0.5
7	Transport, storage and communications	0.4
8	Services	4.6
9	Others	2.7

Since 1950 the pattern of employment has been affected by the introduction of copper and bauxite mining and a considerable increase in the number employed in the maintenance of law and order.

AREA: 27 750 sq. km. (10 700 sq. miles)

LAND USE: (percentage of total)
	1950
Arable and orchard	13.4
Permanent meadow and pasture	18.0
Forest and woodland	25.2
City areas, waste and other land	43.4

continued

PRODUCTION, EXPORTS AND IMPORTS, etc.—continued

	Production ANIMAL PRODUCTS, etc.	Exports	Imports
5. LIVESTOCK‡, ANIMAL PRODUCTS, etc.			
Butter	—	—	0.3
Cheese	0.6*	—	0.5[1]
Eggs	10.5	3.1	2.8
Milk	19.0	3.2	29.2
Hides/skins	—	0.2[1]	na

d no. in thousands. excl. animals pastured on sugar plantations.

6. FIBRES, TEXTILES, etc.
Rubber, natural · na 0.3[1] — —

7. FUEL AND POWER
Coal, 'A' ‡	—	—	2
Electricity h: total	177	—	—
hydro	na	—	—
thermal	na	—	—
Petroleum, refined	—	253	170[1]

h million kWh.

8. IRON AND STEEL
Pig iron · — — 1 n
n incl. steel ingots.

9. NON-FERROUS MINERALS AND METALS
Diamonds	107.67[l]	3.00[2a]	4.46[2]
Gold k, ore m	2.30	na	1.56[2]
Silver i, bullion	—	13.59g	—
Asbestos	—	—	0.27
manufactured	2 602.10	2 377.50	0.89[2]
Aluminium: bauxite	1 493.50*	2 769.89p	
alumina	266.99	251.44*	0.52[2]
Copper, metal	—	—	0.05[2]
Lead, metal	143.45	—	0.03[2]
Manganese, ore	164.47	—	—
Tin, metal	—	—	0.02[2]

a million $ U.S. k '000 fine troy oz. l '000 carats. m metal content. p dried and calcined. q bullion.

10. CHEMICALS n AND FERTILIZERS
Chemicals · — — — na

Fertilizers:
Potash · — — 1.7 0.7[1]
n data not available for years 1953–5.

11. INDUSTRY
Alcoholic beverages	na	2.1 aq	0.5 a
beer b	na	1.5 aq	0.8a
Cement	40.0*	—	—
Electrical engineering a	—	30.0*	16.7
Motor vehicles a	4.3*	na	1.6
	0.7*	3.1	1.6

a million $ U.S. b '000 hectolitres. q rum only.

continued

161

na: data not available. — negligible or nil. * estimate. ‡ see appendix. † re-exports. [1] one year only. [2] two year average.

HONDURAS

Honduras became an independent sovereign state in 1838 and adopted a republican constitution. In 1963 the government was overthrown by the armed forces, and military rule continued until 1965 when elections were held for a new civilian government.

AREA: 112 088 sq. km. (43 227 sq. miles)

LAND USE: (percentage of total)

	1963	1954
Arable and orchard	7.3	7.4
Permanent meadow and pasture	30.5	17.8
Forest and woodland	26.9	43.5
City areas, waste and other land	35.3	31.3

POPULATION: 2 445 000 (1967 estimate)
Largest city: TEGUCIGALPA, capital; population: 170 535 (city proper, 1965)

Distribution of working population (1961)
Total working population: 567 988

U.N. group no.		Percentage
0	Agriculture, forestry, fishing and hunting	66.8
2/3	Mining and quarrying	0.3
4	Manufacturing	7.8
5	Construction	2.0
5	Electricity, gas, water and sanitary services	0.4
6		4.8
7	Transport, storage and communications	1.4
8	Services	12.2
9	Others	4.6

FINANCE
Currency unit: The lempira

Exchange rates	1965	1955	1938
Per $ U.S.	2.0	2.0	2.04
Per £ sterling	5.6	5.6	9.4

	1960	1955	Year(s)
National Income (million $ U.S.)	442		1965
G.N.P. per capita ($ U.S.)	220		1956
Rate of increase of G.N.P. per capita	0.7		1960–3 av.
Foreign trade (percentage of G.D.P.)	43		1963–5 av.

TRADING

Total trade (in million $ U.S.)	1965	1955	1937
Exports (f.o.b.)	127	49	24
Imports	122 (c.i.f.)	54 (f.o.b.)	10 (f.o.b.)

Main trading partners (percentage of total value)

Exports	1965	1955	1937
U.S.A.	59	68	47
Germany F.R.	11	5	10
El Salvador	11	8	7
Japan	4	4	6
Netherlands	4	2	5
Jamaica	3	4	4

Imports	1965	1955	1937*
U.S.A.	74	78	50*
El Salvador	(42)	(50*)	(85)
Guatemala	(4)	(18)	(1)
Germany F.R.	20	19	na
Japan	(8)	(11)	(na)
Neths. Antilles	(6)	(4)	(9)
U.K.	(5)		(na)

Distribution of trade (percentage of total value)

Exports	1965	1955	1937*
Food	74	78	na
(bananas)	(42)	(50*)	(85)
(coffee)	(18)	(18)	(1)
(maize)	(4)		(na)
Crude materials	20	19	na
(wood)	(8)	(11)	(na)
(silver, lead and zinc)	(6)	(4)	(9)
(cotton)	(5)		(na)

Imports	1965	1955	
Manufactured goods	68	62	
(machinery and transport equipment)	(25)	(20)	
(textiles and clothing)	(14)	(17)	na
Chemicals	13	15	
Food	10	14	
Petroleum products	5	6	

		Year(s)
Infant mortality (per '000)	41.2*	1965
Crude birth rate (per '000)	48.5*	1960–5 av.
Crude death rate (per '000)	16*	1960–5 av.
Population per hospital bed	630	1966
Population per physician	5400	1965
School enrolment: age 5–19 years (percentage)	107	1963–4 av.
age over 19 years (per 100 000 population)		1964–5 av.

COMMUNICATIONS

		Year(s)
Motor vehicles in use ('000s): private	8.9	1963–5 av.
commercial	7.3	
Railway track (km.)	1152	1963
Telephones (per '000 urban population)		1967
Radio receivers (per '000 population)	59	1963–5 av.
Television sets (per '000 population)	3.3	1963–5 av.
Daily newspapers (per 100 000 population)	19.5	1963–4 av.

PRODUCTION, EXPORTS AND IMPORTS
Years: 1963–5 average and 1953–5 average   Units: '000 metric tons unless otherwise indicated

1. CEREALS, etc.

	Production		Exports		Imports	
Cassava	16.0*	12.5²				
Maize (corn)	356.0*	183.5²	46.8	6.5	1.2	1.6
Millets/sorghum	60.3	50.3	1.3²	0.1	0.2²	0.2
Potatoes	2.0*	2.5²	0.2	0.5	2.7	1.2
Rice	23.7*	14.3*	0.8		1.8	
Sweet potatoes/yams	3.3*	2.0¹			21.7	4.4
Wheat	1.0*	1.0²	—			

2. FRUIT, etc.

Bananas	827.3*	697.3	421.4	282.3		
Coconuts	13.3*e	na	4.5	4.2²	0.7	0.2
Oranges	17.3n	44.5*n	3.8	0.2		
Other citrus fruit	2.7*	15.0²	1.3	0.8		
Pineapples	3.0*	2.0¹				
Tomatoes	2.0*	3.0²	—		1.7	4.3
Wine b						

3. BEVERAGES, FOREST PRODUCTS, etc.

Cocoa	0.2	0.1²				
Coffee	28.5*	17.2*	21.2	10.4		
Sugar: cane	659.0	na				
raw	30.0p	10.0*p	1.0	1.6	3.6	8.0
Tobacco: leaf	4.4	4.1²	0.2		na	0.1
cigars						
cigarettes	9.0*	7.6²				
Softwood j	1189.0cr	826.0cr			na	
Hardwood j	2 200.0¹	1 813.0*	434.0²	265.5²	0.2²	
Newsprint					1.4¹	0.6¹
Other paper	1 060.0¹	1 067.5²	8.1²	4.3²	13.7¹	2.3¹

4. VEGETABLE OILSEEDS AND OILS

	Production		Exports		Imports	
Castor oil	1.50*	na			0.03	0.01
Copra	na		0.05	0.67	0.03²	0.01
Coconut oil	13.30	2.00	0.24²	0.01	1.46	
Cottonseed			13.23		0.78	0.12
Cottonseed oil					0.07	
Groundnuts					0.01	0.03
Olive oil	0.60	0.20¹	0.10	0.02	0.01	0.04
Linseed oil					0.03	
Palm kernels	1.40*	1.40¹*	0.27²	0.20¹	0.31²	0.01
Palm kernel oil	0.50*	0.60²	0.17		0.02	
Seasame seed						
Soya bean oil						

5. LIVESTOCK‡, ANIMAL PRODUCTS, etc.

Chickens d	4 950.0*	5 953.7				
Cattle d n	1 640.7¹	1 180.0				
dairy cows d	563.0*	na	33.8	34.8	0.2¹	
Goats d	47.0	55.5²	0.4			
Sheep d	8.0	14.0²				
Pigs d	273.7*	na	31.5	39.9		
Meat: A	23.7*	23.5¹				
B	6.3*	4.5¹			na	
Butter	4.0	na	1.0	0.2	0.1	
Cheese	12.0	na	0.2	0.2		
Eggs	9.0*	7.6²	0.5		0.6	0.2
Fish	na	2.6	0.8		20.3	8.3
Milk	138.7	114.5²			0.31*	

d no. in thousands. n cattle rearing is becoming increasingly important, and large numbers are exported to neighbouring countries. e no. in millions. ¹ '000 cu. metres of roundwood equivalent, non-centrifugal sugar 19* (1963–5 av.) and 21* (1963–5 av.).

continued

HAITI *continued*

POPULATION *continued*

		(Years)
Crude birth rate (per '000)	47.5*	1960–5 av.
Crude death rate (per '000)	22*	1960–5 av.
Population per physician	14 000	1965
Population per hospital bed	1990a	1966
School enrolment: age 5–19 years (percentage)	26	1963–4 av.
age over 19 years (per 100 000 population)	39	1964–5 av.

a government hospitals only.

COMMUNICATIONS

	1965	1955	1938	Year(s)
Motor vehicles in use ('000s): private	5.4		7	1965
commercial	1.5		8	1965
Railway track (km.)	354a			1967
Radio receivers (per '000 population)	14			1965
Telephones (per '000 urban population)	0.1b			1967
Television sets (per '000 population)	0.9			1963–5 av.
Daily newspapers (per '000 population)	6			1963

a this track (from Port-au-Prince to Verrettes) is closed to public transport but part of it is still used for transporting sugar cane. b much of the internal telephone system is permanently out of order, but external services are normal.

FINANCE
Currency unit: The gourde, which is fixed at the rate 5 to the U.S. dollar. U.S. coins are also in circulation.

Exchange rates	1965	1960	1955	1938
Per $ U.S.	5	5	5	23
Per £ sterling	14	14	14	23

	1965	1955	1938	Year(s)
National Income (million $ U.S.)	353			1965
G.N.P. per capita ($ U.S.)	70	35	7	1966
Rate of increase of G.N.P. per capita	0.4	39	8	1960–2 av.

TRADING

Total trade (in million $ U.S.)	1965	1955
Exports (f.o.b.)	36	49
Imports (c.i.f.)	36	49

Main trading partners (percentage of total value)

Exports	1965	1955
U.S.A.	36	49
Belg./Lux.		14
France	14	14
Neths. Antilles		10
U.K.		3
S. Korea		1

Imports		1955
U.S.A.		66
Canada		6
Germany F.R.		6
U.K.		4
Neths. Antilles		4
France		3
Netherlands		2

Distribution of trade

Coffee accounts for two-thirds of the exports. Sisal, bananas, and sugar are also exported but in decreasing quantities. Exports of bauxite began in 1957 and of copper in 1960. The chief imports are foodstuffs, machinery, cars and chemicals. The tourist trade has decreased, because of the political unrest.

PRODUCTION, EXPORTS AND IMPORTS
Years: 1963–5 average and 1953–5 average   Units: '000 metric tons unless otherwise indicated

1. CEREALS, etc.

	Production		Exports		Imports	
	1965					
Cassava	118.3*	na				
Maize (corn)	242.7*	na				
Millets/sorghum	180.0*	na				
Potatoes		na				
Rice	38.7*	na			0.7*	
Sweet potatoes/yams	100.0*	120.0¹				
Wheat					49.1*	

2. FRUIT, etc.

Bananas	225.0*	13.0¹	1.5*	10.5²		
Coconuts	28.0¹*	na				
Lemons	14.0*	na				
Oranges	6.0*	na				1.3
Wine b						

3. BEVERAGES, FOREST PRODUCTS, etc.

Cocoa	2.4	1.7*	1.8			
Coffee	33.4*	33.7*	22.9*	23.1		
Sugar: cane	500.0*	465.0*n	27.7*	20.1		0.2
raw	66.0	56.7				0.2
Tobacco: leaf	1.1*	na				0.64p
cigarettes	353.0c	301.0a				0.2
Softwood j	495.0¹*	20.0	2.4		2.5²	16.5
Hardwood j	7 730.0¹*	8 880.0			0.3¹	0.4
Newsprint					1.2¹	0.3
Other paper						1.6

4. VEGETABLE OILSEEDS AND OILS

Castor seed	2.0*	na	5.7²			
Cottonseed	2.0	3.0*	na			
Groundnuts	2.1*	na	na			5.0
Soya bean oil						0.5

5. LIVESTOCK‡, ANIMAL PRODUCTS, etc.   Units: '000 metric tons unless otherwise indicated

	Production		Exports		Imports	
Chickens d	5 470.0*q					
Cattle d	682*					
Goats d	882					
Sheep d	64					
Horses d	255					
Pigs d	1143					
Meat: A	18*					
Butter	na		0.1¹		*	0.1²
Cheese	na				0.1*	0.1²
Fish	na	17*			na	7.31*
Milk	na	9*			14.9	3.32*
Whale/sperm oil	na					
Hides/skins	na		0.3²			

d no. in thousands. q incl. ducks, geese and turkeys.

6. FIBRES, TEXTILES, etc.

Agaves (sisal)	18.6	25.7*	16.6*	25.9		
Cotton lint	1.0*	1.3*	na	1.1		9.02*
Silk f						
Cotton, woven fabrics	0.5*		0.3			3.5

f metric tons.

7. FUEL AND POWER

| Electricity h t | 74 | 60¹ | | | | |
| Petroleum: refined | | | | | 97 | 301 |

h million kWh. t thermal.

9. NON-FERROUS MINERALS AND METALS

Gold k, ore m	7.3	na				
Silver k, ore m	92.0	na				
Aluminium, bauxite	401.3	na	413.2p			
Copper, ore	5.0m	na	12.6			

k '000 fine troy oz. m metal content. p exports to the U.S.A. only.

11. INDUSTRY

Alcoholic beverages a	0.2	0.1²			na	0.4
Cement	50.3	20.0*			0.7*	23.3
Electrical engineering a					na	0.4²
Motor vehicles a					na	2.4²

a million $ U.S.

a million $ U.S. e no. in millions. j '000 cu. metres of roundwood equivalent. n cane consumption at crushing mills. p incl. other tobacco products.

continued

---

na: data not available. — negligible or nil. * estimate. ‡ see appendix. † re-exports. ¹ one year only. ² two year average.

HONDURAS continued

PRODUCTION, EXPORTS AND IMPORTS continued

6. FIBRES, TEXTILES, etc.

	Production	Exports	Imports
Abaca	—	—	—
Agaves (letona)	0.1*	—	—
Cotton lint	7.7 7.0*	7.5 0.1	2.0 1.5
Rubber, natural	na	—	—
Silk f	—	—	—
Cotton, woven fabrics	0.4*	0.1	7.0
f metric tons.			

7. FUEL AND POWER

	Production	Exports	Imports
Electricity h: total	133	—	—
hydro	na	—	—
thermal	na	—	—
Petroleum, refined	—	—	120[1]
h million kWh.			

8. IRON AND STEEL

	Production	Exports	Imports
Steel ingots/castings	—	—	2

9. NON-FERROUS MINERALS AND METALS

	Production	Exports	Imports
Gold k, ore m	23.30	—	—
Silver k, ore m	3 351.70 3 623.00	—	—
Asbestos: manufactured	—	—	0.06
Aluminium	—	—	0.20

continued

10. CHEMICALS c AND FERTILIZERS

	Production	Exports	Imports
Chemicals c			
Fertilizers: Potash	—	—	223

11. INDUSTRY

	Production	Exports	Imports
Aircraft a	—	—	—
Alcoholic beverages	70[1]	—	—
Cement	na	—	—
Electrical engineering a	60[1]	—	—
Railway vehicles a	—	—	—
Merchant ships a	—	—	—
Motor vehicles a	—	—	—

PRODUCTION, EXPORTS AND IMPORTS

Years: 1963–5 average and 1953–5 average   Units: '000 metric tons unless otherwise indicated

1. CEREALS, etc.

	Production	Exports	Imports
Barley	—	0.1†	1.3
Maize (corn)	—	19.7† 13.7†	95.8 17.8
Millets/sorghum	—	—	1.7
Oats	—	—	0.6 0.5
Potatoes	—	5.7† 10.5†	21.2 223.7
Rice	16.0	35.2† 4.8†	397.8 227.5
Sweet potatoes/yams	22.7 34.5²	—	—
Wheat	— 14.0²	7.8†	82.5 17.6²

2. FRUIT, etc.

	Production	Exports	Imports
Apples	—	6.8† 1.1†	27.6 7.7
Bananas	—	1.0† 0.1†	15.6 13.8
Grapes	—	0.1† 0.2†	4.5 1.8
Oranges	—	2.9† 7.3†	62.5 29.0
Other citrus fruit	—	2.0†	16.2 na
Pears	—	na† 0.3†	14.9 na
Raisins	—	1.0†	5.9 1.7
Wine b	—	—	—

3. BEVERAGES, FOREST PRODUCTS, etc.

	Production	Exports	Imports
Cocoa	—	12.6† 0.2†	— 0.2
Coffee	—	1.0† 85.0†	123.0 126.1
Sugar, raw	—	0.3† 1.2†	192.8 6.7
Tea	—	—	6.5 3.5
Tobacco: leaf	2z 8 343z	4.9²n 0.6²n	3.7²n 1.9²n
cigarettes	na	—	42.1
Softwood j	na	0.7† 0.8†	15.8 222.4
Hardwood j	na	46.3† 18.6†	545.0 6.0
Wood pulp	—	0.8† 9.2†	33.3 24.7
Newsprint	—	7.4† 18.6†	123.3 43.4
Other paper	—	—	2.10 14.47

4. VEGETABLE OILSEEDS AND OILS

	Production	Exports	Imports
Castor seed	—	1.23† 0.87†	0.45 0.93
Castor oil	—	0.01† 0.06†	0.11 0.08
Copra	—	—	0.86
Coconut oil	—	1.45† 0.41†	0.64 1.32
Cottonseed	—	0.01† 0.13†	1.43 0.03
Cottonseed oil	—	0.01† 2.15†	9.63 9.87
Groundnuts	—	4.66† 2.70†	11.59 14.47
Groundnut oil	—	—	0.01 2.10
Linseed	—	0.01† 2.30†	0.59 0.72
Linseed oil	—	0.51†	0.01 0.02
Olive oil	—	0.02†	0.66
Palm kernels	—	0.44† 0.13†	1.45 0.20
Palm oil	—	1.58†	— 2.26
Rapeseed oil	—	6.17† 14.27†	6.42 15.57
Sesame seed	—	4.47† 28.80†	11.49 25.60
Soya beans	—	1.34† 2.31†	18.73 3.22
Soya bean oil	—	1.32† 7.14†	2.18 8.33
Tung oil	—	—	—

5. LIVESTOCK, ANIMAL PRODUCTS, etc.

	Production	Exports	Imports
Chickens d	2 347.0 480.0[1]		
Cattle a	13.7 10.3	3.4 0.4	141.3 13.7
dairy cows d	3.0 3.0²		
Goats/sheep d	—	—	6.7
Horses d	1.0* 46.7	1.4 0.5	641.7 504.0
Pigs d	290.0	0.2 0.1	3.5 0.6
Bacon/ham	na	—	10.7 3.5
Meat: 'A'	9.0	0.2 0.1	15.8 0.5
'B'	1.7 na	0.1† 0.1†	1.9 0.7
Butter	—	—	0.4 0.2
Cheese	—	—	37.6 21.7
Eggs	0.3* 77.7p	1.0† 4.3†	62.9 27.8
Milk	5.7 51.4p	13.8 9.3	90.2 47.8
Hides/skins	8.0 4.0²	1.7†a 2.3†a	— 3.1²
Wool	—	—	0.6

6. FIBRES, TEXTILES, etc.

	Production	Exports	Imports
Abaca	—	—	0.4 0.6
Cotton lint	—	0.2† 2.5†	129.8 44.3
Hemp fibre	—	1.3†	0.1
Jute	—	—	3.6
Rubber, natural	—	3.3† 0.1†	8.4 5.1
Silk f	—	4.0†	177.3 287.7
Cotton: yarn	119.5 38.2	98.7† 230.7†	177.3 12.8
woven fabrics	66.6q	12.3† 14.4	38.9
Rayon/fibre/yarn	0.1q 7.5*	na† 1.6†	1.5
woven fabrics	6.2	3.2† 7.5	6.4 6.3
Wool, yarn	—	0.2† 1.0†	4.5 1.4
f metric tons. q registered mill production only. s incl. re-exports.			

7. FUEL AND POWER

	Production	Exports	Imports
Coal, 'A' ‡	2 393	—	177 233
Coke	na 640[1]	5†	5 3
Electricity h: total	na 640[1]	—	—
hydro	—	—	—
thermal	30†	—	—
Petroleum, refined	—	—	1 903 810[1]
h million kWh.			

8. IRON AND STEEL

	Production	Exports	Imports
Iron ore	68 58	133 110	8 —
Pig iron	na	—	9 —
Steel ingots/castings	na	142 50z	4 1
Iron/steel scrap	—	—	80 20
s incl. re-exports.			

9. NON-FERROUS MINERALS AND METALS

	Production	Exports	Imports
Diamonds a	—	1.59†	24.84 7.26
Gold k	1 134.93†	1 117.00†	1 142.74† 165.70
bullion/coins etc.	—	—	—
Platinum group metals	—	0.28†a	17.53k 0.34az
Silver k, bullion	2 218.26†	966.00†	157.23 193.33
Asbestos: fibre	—	—	35.12 0.18as
manufactured	0.04†	0.02†	0.40 0.25
Mica	—	—	0.46 0.11²
Aluminium: bauxite	3.39†	0.24†	12.35 2.56
Cobalt, metal	—	0.81†	0.04 0.71
Copper, metal	6.14†	0.44	10.48 0.74
Lead: ore	na	—	—
metal	0.04†	0.33†s	0.62² 0.29
Magnesium: magnesite	na	—	—
metal/salts	—	—	0.19 0.04a
Manganese: ore	—	—	0.42 —
metal	—	0.70†	0.19 1.55z
Mercury f	0.30	—	13.80 3.30z
Molybdenum, ore f	—	—	—
Nickel, metal	0.05†	0.03†	1.25 0.06z
Tin, metal	0.02†	0.25†	0.08 0.15z
Titanium minerals	0.01	0.03 0.70z	2.20 0.87z
Tungsten, metal	0.07	0.04† 2.07z	5.96 4.56
Zinc, metal	—	—	—
a million $ U.S. k '000 fine troy oz. s incl. re-exports or imports for re-export.			

10. CHEMICALS n AND FERTILIZERS

	Production	Exports	Imports
Chemicals c	na	—	na
Fertilizers: Potash	—	0.4†	0.6 0.6
Sulphur	—	—	0.8 0.9
n data not available for years 1953–5.			

11. INDUSTRY

	Production	Exports	Imports
Aircraft a	—	0.2† 1.6a	11.5a 1.1 4.1a
Alcoholic beverages	189.0 224.0	20.0 49.3	989.0 150.7
Cement	na	45.6² 4.6²	80.0² 9.2³
Electrical engineering a	na	—	— 0.4
Railway vehicles a	8.0	—	40.0
Merchant ships a	—	—	—
Motor vehicles a	na	2.8² 1.1²	30.1 7.1²

a million $ U.S. b '000 hectolitres. e no. in millions. j '000 cu. metres of roundwood equivalent. n incl. other tobacco manufactures. f '000 fine troy oz. g '000 G.R.T.

HONG KONG

Hong Kong has been under British administration since 1842 apart from a period under Japanese occupation from 1941 to 1945. The recent rapid industrial development has decreased the island's long-established importance as an entrepôt, but Hong Kong remains the primary link for trade between China P.R. and the Sterling Area.

AREA: 1 013 sq. km. (391 sq. miles)

LAND USE: (percentage of total)

Arable and orchard	12.6
Forest and woodland	9.7
City areas, waste and other land, incl. scrub and grassland	77.7

POPULATION: 3 834 000 (1967 estimate)
Largest city: VICTORIA, capital; population: 674 962 (1961)

Distribution of working population (1961)
Total working population: 1 211 999

U.N. group no.		Percentage
1	Agriculture, forestry, fishing and hunting	7.2
2/3	Mining and quarrying	0.7
	Manufacturing	39.2
4	Construction	8.3
5	Electricity, gas, water and sanitary services	1.6
6	Commerce	10.8
7	Transport, storage and communications	7.2
8	Services	21.9
9	Others	3.1

		Year(s)
Life expectancy at birth (years): male	66.7	1968
female	73.3	1965
Infant mortality (per '000)	22.8	1965
Crude birth rate (per '000)	28.8	1965
Crude death rate (per '000)	4.9	1965
Accidental deaths (per 100 000 population)	6.8	1965
caused by motor vehicles	17.1	1965
Population per physician	2 310	1966
Population per hospital bed	280	1963–4 av.
School enrolment: age 5–19 years (percentage)	85	1963–5 av.
age over 19 years (per 100 000 population)	277	

COMMUNICATIONS

		Year(s)
Motor vehicles in use ('000s): private	52.1	1963–5 av.
commercial	35	1964
Railway track (km.)	34	
Mail per capita: domestic	17	1963–5 av.
foreign received	20	
foreign sent	8	
Telephones (per '000 urban population)	143	1967
Radio receivers (per '000 population)	10.3	1963–5 av.
Television licences (per '000 population)		1963–5 av.
Daily newspapers (per '000 population)	232.5	1962–4 av.

FINANCE

Currency unit: The Hong Kong dollar

Exchange rates	1960	1965
Per $ U.S.	5.714	5.714
Per £ sterling	16.0	16.0

		Year
National Income (million $ U.S.)	1 045	1963
G.N.P. per capita ($ U.S.)	560	1966

TRADING

	1965	
Total trade (in million $ U.S.)	1 143	1965
Exports (f.o.b.)	1 143	1965
Imports (c.i.f.)	1 569	

The adverse balance of trade is offset by 'invisible' exports including insurance, investments, and income from tourists, and by remittances from nationals living abroad. In 1965 re-exports accounted for 25% of the exports.

Main trading partners (percentage of total value)

Exports	1965	1955	Imports	1965	1955
U.S.A.	28	14	China P.R.	(44)	24
U.K.	14	10	Japan	17	14
Germany F.R.	6	6	U.S.A.	11	12
Japan	6	5	U.K.	11	12
Singapore	5	na	Germany F.R.	3	5
Indonesia	3	8	Thailand	3	3
Australia	3	2	Singapore	3	na

Distribution of trade (percentage of total value)

Exports	1965	1938*
Manufactured goods	83	na
(textiles and clothing)		(8)
(toys)	(44)	
(artificial flowers)	(6)	
Food	6	17
Imports		
Textiles and clothing	23	13
Food	13	26
Machinery and transport equipment	7	6
Chemicals		

continued

CHINA SEA

HUNGARY

The Hungarian republic was proclaimed in 1946 and supreme power vested in Parliament three years later. In 1956 anti-Stalinist revolution was suppressed. A Soviet-Hungarian treaty of friendship was renewed for a further twenty years in 1967. Hungary is a member of Comecon.

AREA: 93 030 sq. km. (35 900 sq. miles)

LAND USE: (percentage of total)

	1965	1947
Arable and orchard	60.7	62.1
Permanent meadow and pasture	14.0	17.1
Forest and woodland	15.3	13.5
City areas, waste and other land	10.0	7.3

POPULATION: 10 212 000 (1967 estimate)

Largest city: BUDAPEST, capital; population: 1 960 000 (city proper, 1966)

Total working population: 4 790 050

Distribution of working population (1963)

U.N. group no.		Percentage
0	Agriculture, forestry, fishing and hunting	32.7
1	Mining and quarrying	3.5
2/3	Manufacturing	26.6
4	Construction	6.7
5	Electricity, gas, water and sanitary services	1.3
6	Commerce	7.6
7	Transport, storage and communications	6.8
8	Services	11.8
9	Others	3.4

			Year(s)
Life expectancy at birth (years): male	67.0		1964
female	71.8		
Infant mortality (per '000)	38.8		1965
Crude birth rate (per '000)	13.1		1965
Crude death rate (per '000)	10.7		1965
Accidental deaths (per 100 000 population) caused by motor vehicles	8.8		1965
due to other causes	31.5		1965
Population per physician	630		1965
Population per hospital bed	81		1966
School enrolment: age 5–19 years (percentage)			
age over 19 years (per '000 population)	493		1964–5 av.

COMMUNICATIONS

			Year(s)
Motor vehicles in use ('000s): private	87.8		1963–5 av.
commercial	na		
Railway track (km.)	8 258		1964
Mail per capita	52		1965
Telephones (per '000 population)	5.86		1963–5 av.
Radio licences (per '000 population)	244		1963–5 av.
Television licences (per '000 population)	65.1		1963–5 av.
Daily newspapers (per '000 population)	166.3		1962–4 av.

FINANCE

Currency unit: The forint

Exchange rates	1965	1962	1958
Per $ U.S.	11.7	11.4	11.7
Per £ sterling	32.9	31.9	32.9

		Year(s)
National Income (million $ U.S.)	8 000*	1966
G.N.P. per capita ($ U.S.)	800*	1966
Rate of increase of G.N.P. per capita	4.9	1960–4 av.

TRADING

Total trade (in million $ U.S.)	1965	1955
Exports (f.o.b)	1 510	601
Imports (c.i.f.)	1 521	555

Main trading partners (percentage of total value)

Exports	1965	1955
U.S.S.R.	35	36
Czechoslovakia	12	13
Germany D.R.	9	11
Poland	7	9
Germany F.R.	4	6
Italy	4	7
Switzerland	3	3

Imports	1965	
U.S.S.R.	30	
Czechoslovakia	13	
Germany D.R.	11	
Poland	7	
Germany F.R.	6	
Austria	5	
U.K.	2	

Distribution of trade (percentage of total value)

Exports	1965	
Manufactured goods (machinery and transport equipment)	64	(32)
Food (fruit and vegetables)	20	(6)
Chemicals	7	
Crude materials and fuels	6	

Imports	1965	
Manufactured goods (machinery and transport equipment)	50	(27)
Crude materials and fuels (mineral fuels)	30	(11)
Food	10	

PRODUCTION, EXPORTS AND IMPORTS

Years: 1963–5 average and 1953–5 average — Units: '000 metric tons unless otherwise indicated

1. CEREALS, etc.

	Production		Exports		Imports	
Barley	904.0	690.0²	60.7	188.0*	200.1	15.0
Maize (corn)	3 580.2	2 730.0	1.8	30.5¹	124.3	4.2
Millets/sorghum	12.0	7.0¹	—	19.3¹	1.0	0.7
Oats	85.3	165.0²	1.4	—	1.0	1.1*
Potatoes	2 003.9	2 640.0²	3.1	7.0¹	18.5	3.2*
Rice	0.8	0.3	0.8	—	14.1	0.4*
Rye	267.3	512.0²	na	—	10.1	—
Wheat	2 063.3	1 895.0²	50.6	162.6*	291.7	205.6

2. FRUIT, etc.

	Production		Exports		Imports	
Apples	438.0	188.0*	128.7		8.9	15.0
Apricots	90.3	30.5¹	4.2		10.2	4.2
Bananas	—	—	—		0.7	
Cherries	65.7	19.3¹	9.8²		51.0	1.1*
Dates	—	—	—		1.1*	0.1*
Grapes	696.7	561.0*	21.3	8.4*	4.8	3.2*
Lemons	—	—	—		18.5	3.2*
Oranges	—	—	—		14.1	0.4*
Other citrus fruit	—	—	—		0.1	—
Peaches	38.7	20.3¹	1.8			—
Pears	51.7	7.0¹	1.4		2.5	—
Plums	225.7	80.3¹	na		2.7	0.2*
Tomatoes	327.7		na			
Wine[b]	4 071.0	3 700.0*	565.2	152.0	52.8	134.7*

3. BEVERAGES, FOREST PRODUCTS, etc.

	Production		Exports		Imports	
Cocoa	—	—	—		0.3	1.3*
Coffee	—	—	—		1.9	1.1
Sugar: beet	3 480.0	2 563.3*	—		51.0	53.1*
raw	459.4	325.0*	178.8	9.8²	4.8	5.9*
Tea	—	—	—		0.7	0.2*
Tobacco: leaf	24.6	19.4*	—	0.2*	4.8	3.2*
cigarettes	44†	57.1*	0.2*		0.1*	0.1*
tobacco/snuff	16 894.0	12 481.0	2.9*		38.2	2.3
Softwood[j]	0.9	2.3	na		6.7	
Hardwood[j]	252.0	200.0*	20.0		41.3²	na
Wood pulp	3 938.3		16.9		6.3	1.3*
Newsprint	61.4		7.1		16.0²a	14.7
Other paper	169.3	125.7*	6.5		68.5	14.2

4. VEGETABLE OILSEEDS AND OILS

	Production		Exports		Imports	
Castor seed	—	—	—		0.04	0.05*
Castor oil	0.33	1.02²	0.26	0.05*	1.59	3.25²*
Copra	—	—	—		1.50	0.35*
Coconut oil	—	—	—		0.65	
Cottonseed	—	—	—		1.01	
Cottonseed oil	na	4.67*	—	0.95*	6.39	
Groundnuts	—	—	—		0.20	
Groundnut oil	—	—	—		0.12	
Linseed	6.00	2.00²*	0.47		4.32	2.58²
Linseed oil	na		0.07		0.89	
Olive oil	—	—	0.59		3.16	
Palm kernels	—	—	—		0.49	0.69*
Palm kernel oil	—	—	—		0.97	4.60*
Palm oil	—	—	0.20		1.16	
Rapeseed	7.00	2.00²*	0.91	0.10*	0.09	
Rapeseed oil	na		0.67	0.23*	20.78	33.00²
Sesame seed	—	—	—		1.61	4.78
Soya beans	1.30		4.85²		0.01	
Soya bean oil	na		0.27*		4.28	
Sunflower seed	108.33	186.00²b	35.56		0.29	
Sunflower seed oil	na		17.49*			

b excl. sunflower grown with other crops.

5. LIVESTOCK‡, ANIMAL PRODUCTS, etc. (d no in thousands)

	Production		Exports		Imports	
Chickens[d]	42 266.7	20 725.0²				
Cattle[d]	1 917.3	2 146.3	133.2	17.3*		0.5*
Goats[d]	836.0	160.0²*	319.4		0.2	—
Pigs[d]	3 249.3	1 787.7		126.4*	4.8	12.6
Sheep[d]	3 271.7	692.0²			0.1*	3.2
Horses[d]	6 250.0	5 083.0²				0.1*
Bacon/ham	451.3	na	165.0	14.0	35.6	5.4*
Meat‡: 'A'	192.7		35.7	14.7*	6.7	1.3*
'B'	18.3q	9.0*q	21.7	2.1*	38.2	0.1*
Butter	120.4	na	5.4*		3.2	—
Cheese	22.8	7.2	3.3²		1.0¹	—
Eggs	1 806.0	1 494.0²	0.1		6.3	1.3*
Milk	21.2		1.43a		na	14.7
Hides/skins	4.8	2.0*	0.1		16.00²b	7.9
Wool			0.5		4.1	1.5

d no in thousands. e excl. butter produced on farms.

continued

PRODUCTION, EXPORTS AND IMPORTS continued

6. FIBRES, TEXTILES, etc.

	Production		Exports		Imports	
Agaves (sisal etc.)	—	—	—		—	3.6
Cotton lint	—	—	0.9†		—	68.0
Flax fibre	5.7	1.2*	3.4		1.8	3.2
Hemp fibre	22.3	18.9²*	4.4	0.3	3.2	2.4*
Jute	—	—	0.6		8.6	5.4*
Rubber: natural	—	—	0.9		15.6	13.0*
synthetic	—	—	—		—	4.6²
Silk[f]	—	—	3.3*		na	
Cotton: yarn	25.7	30.0*	na		na	
woven fabrics[r]	67.1	44.9*[r]	21.6		0.2	
Rayon: fibre/yarn	46.0*	31.7*	na		1.1	
woven fabrics[r]	2.6	0.6	1.2		—	
Wool: yarn	16.8	11.2	—		—	
woven fabrics[r]	29.3r	21.0r	—		—	

7. FUEL AND POWER

	Production		Exports		Imports	
Coal[a]: 'A'[‡]	4 067	2 690	117	551	2 833	836
'B'	13 543	19 620	—	—	1 456	1 059
Coke	10 474	4 940	—		—	—
Electricity[h]: total	10 377	4 501	—		—	—
hydro	830	480¹	—		—	—
thermal	10 397	4 890¹	—		207	—
Natural gas[i]	1 787	1 600¹	—		2 036	291¹
Oil, crude	3 010	1 300¹	500	110¹	497	110¹

8. IRON AND STEEL

	Production		Exports		Imports	
Iron ore	184m	118m	—		2 498	1 213
Pig iron	1 496	793	53	—	110	151
Steel ingots/castings	2 420	1 555	—		375	—
Iron/steel products[a]	—	—	99	na	111	na

a million $ U.S. m metal content.

9. NON-FERROUS MINERALS AND METALS

	Production		Exports		Imports	
Asbestos, fibre	—	—	—		13.41	—
Aluminium: bauxite	1 439.40	298.17	663.98	702.80	—	—
alumina	250.64	na	161.70	71.54	32.81²	17.30
aluminium	56.82	32.49	19.37		24.29²	4.88
Antimony, ore	—	—	—		11.78²	6.40
Chrome: ore	—	—	—		3.37	—
Copper, metal	—	—	—		62.50	41.74
Lead: ore[m]	1.20		—		11.73	—
metal	0.27		—		92.80	—
Magnesium:	491.26		—		1.32	—
Manganese: ore	178.85		—		43.24	0.76

continued

9. NON-FERROUS MINERALS AND METALS—continued

	Production	Exports	Imports
Titanium minerals	—	—	0.09²
Vanadium	—	—	0.12u
Zinc: ore	2.90m	—	12.06
metal	1.48		

f metric tons. u metal content. u ferro-vanadium.

10. CHEMICALS AND FERTILIZERS

	Production	Exports	Imports
Organic chemicals:			
Benzene	6.3		na
Butadiene	na	na	na
Ethylene	na	na	na
Methanol	na	na	na
Phenol	0.3	na	na
Phthalic anhydride	1.5	na	na
Styrene monomer	na		4.0
Urea	na		7.0¹
Inorganic chemicals:			
Ammonia	151.9		na
Carbon black	18.0		na
Chlorine	18.0		na
Nitric acid	45.1		na
Sodium carbonate	45.1		na
Sodium hydroxide	322.7		119.7
Sulphuric acid		3.9	33.5
Plastics:			
Polysulphides	na		4.0
Polyethylene	na		7.0¹
Polyvinyl chloride	18.7²		
Fertilizers:			
Phosphates	—	—	405.9	88.6
Potash	—	—	206.8	27.9
Pyrites	—	—	169.0	92.4
Sulphur	3.2u	—	150.3	

w recovered sulphur. n data not available for years 1953–5.

11. INDUSTRY

	Production		Exports		Imports	
Alcoholic beverages: beer[a]	4 249	2 010				
spirits[b]	189¹q	2497¹r				
Cement	2 146	1 394				
Electrical engineering[a]	402.0¹		19.2		43.0²	
Locomotives[c]	176					
Railway vehicles[a]	101.8²	2497¹	65.7¹			
Machine tools[a]	30¹		69.3		15.2	
Merchant ships[g]	11		10.6			
Motor vehicles: commercial	7	6	19.5	4.5	12.2	3.8

a million $ U.S. b '000 hectolitres. c no. of units. d no. in thousands. q production for home consumption in 1967. r production for Comecon countries. g '000 G.R.T. home consumption in 1959. r excl. trade with other Comecon countries.

NORTH ATLANTIC

ICELAND

Formerly a Danish territory, Iceland was proclaimed an independent republic in 1944.

AREA: 103 000 sq. km. (39 770 sq. miles)

LAND USE: (percentage of total)

	1965	1955
Arable and orchard	—	—
Permanent meadow and pasture	na	
Forest and woodland	na	
City areas, waste and other land	na	

POPULATION: 200 000 (1967 U.N. estimate)

Capital city: REYKJAVÍK; population: 90 792 (1966)

Total working population: 63 695

Distribution of working population (1950)

U.N. group no.		Percentage
0	Agriculture, forestry, fishing and hunting	37.0
1/2/3	Mining, quarrying and manufacturing	21.3
4	Construction	9.3
5	Electricity, gas, water and sanitary services	1.2
6	Commerce	9.1
7	Transport, storage and communications	7.9
8	Services	14.2

		Year(s)
Life expectancy at birth (years): male	70.8	1961–5 av.
female	76.2	
Infant mortality (per '000)	15.0	1965
Crude birth rate (per '000)	24.7	1965
Crude death rate (per '000)	6.7	1965
Accidental deaths (per 100 000 population) caused by motor vehicles	13.5	1965
due to other causes	42.6	1965
Population per physician	760	1964
Population per hospital bed	105‡	1963–4 av.
School enrolment: age 5–19 years (percentage)		
age over 19 years (per 100 000 population)	549	1963–5 av.

COMMUNICATIONS

		Year(s)
Motor vehicles in use ('000s): private	25.3	1963–5 av.
commercial	6.7	
Mail per capita: domestic	38	1965
foreign received	14	1965
foreign sent	4	1967
Telephones (per '000 urban population)	29.3	1963–5 av.
Radio licences (per '000 population)	283	1963–5 av.
Daily newspapers (per '000 population)	438.7	1962–4 av.

continued

na: data not available. — negligible or nil. * estimate. † re-exports. ‡ see appendix. ¹ one year only. ² two year average.

INDIA

India, a union of predominantly Hindu states, became a sovereign democratic republic within the British Commonwealth in 1950, three years after its partition from Pakistan. The question of the sovereignty of Jammu and Kashmir still remains in dispute between the two countries, but data for this area are included. The Portuguese territories of Goa, Daman and Diu joined India in 1961; data for 1938 have been added to those of India for the years 1953–5. Data for 1938 include Pakistan.

AREA: 3 268 081 sq. km. (1 261 807 sq. miles)

LAND USE: (percentage of total)

	1955
Arable and orchard	45.7
Permanent meadow and pasture	2.6
Forest and woodland	14.2
City areas, waste and other land	37.5

POPULATION: 511 115 000a (1967 estimate)
Largest city: CALCUTTA: population: 4 764 979 (1967)
Capital city: NEW DELHI: population: 324 283b (city proper, 1967)
Total working population: 188 675 500ac

Distribution of working population (1961)

U.N. group no.		Percentage
0	Agriculture, forestry, fishing and hunting	72.9
1	Mining and quarrying	0.5
2/3	Manufacturing	9.5
4	Construction	0.3
5	Electricity, gas, water and sanitary services	0.1
6	Commerce	4.1
7	Transport, storage and communications	1.6
8	Services	8.8
9	Others	1.2

		Year(s)
Life expectancy at birth (years): male	41.9	1951–60 av.
female	40.6	
Accidental deaths (per 100 000 population) caused by motor vehicles	1.1*	1961
due to other causes	56.5*	1961
Population per physician	5800	1962
Population per hospital bed	1670	1965
School enrolment: age 5–19 years (percentage)	41	1963
age over 19 years (per 100 000 population)	288	1963–5 av.

a excl. the population of the area of Jammu and Kashmir under Pakistani occupation. b New Delhi is part of the urban agglomeration of Delhi, population 2 874 454 (1967). c excl. the unemployed and persons seeking employment for the first time.

COMMUNICATIONS

		Year(s)
Motor vehicles in use ('000s): private	397.3	1963–5 av.
commercial	352.8	
Railway track (km.)	93 946	1964
Mail per capita: domestic	12	1963–5 av.
foreign received	0.2	
foreign sent	0.2	1967
Telephones (per '000 urban population)	0.2	1963–5 av.
Radio licences (per '000 population)	6.15	1962–4 av.
Daily newspapers (per '000 population)		

FINANCE

Currency unit: The rupee

Exchange rates	1965	1960	1950	1938
Per $ U.S.a	4.78	4.77	4.76	2.89
Per £ sterling	13.33	13.33	13.33	13.33

		Year(s)
National Income (million $U.S.)	42 020	1965
G.N.P. per capita ($U.S.)	90	1966
Rate of increase of G.N.P. per capita	0.7	1960–3 av.

a selling rates.

TRADING

Total trade (in million $ U.S.)	1965	1957b	1955b	1938ab
Exports (f.o.b.)	1692	1350	1280	614
Imports (c.i.f.)	2958	2154	1484	576

Main trading partners (percentage of total value)

Exports	1965	1955b	1938ab
U.S.A.	18	15	9
U.K.	18	28	34
U.S.S.R.	12	1	—
Japan	7	5	2
U.A.R.	3	na	1
Canada	3	2	—
Nepal	2	2	—

Imports	1965	1955b	1938ab
U.S.A.	38	13	6
U.K.	11	25	31
U.S.S.R.	6	5	8d
Germany F.R.	6	6	—
Iran	2	2	1
Japan	2	1	—
Canada	2	1	—

Distribution of trade (percentage of total value)

Exports	1965	1957b	1938*ab
Manufactured goods	47	44	na
(textiles)	30 (34)	28 (32)	17 (20)
Food	18	21	na
(tea)	(7)	(8)	(14)
Crude materials and fuels (metalliferous ores)			

Imports	1965	1957b	1938*ab
Manufactured goods	52	60	na
(machinery and transport equipment)	25 (35)	9 (30)	(13)
Food	14	21	na
(cereals)	(23)	(5)	(9)
Crude materials (textile fibres)	(5)	(7)	(6)
(petroleum and petroleum products)	(10)	(5)	(9)

a incl. Pakistan. b year beginning 1 April. d incl. Germany D.R.

PRODUCTION, EXPORTS AND IMPORTS

Years: 1963–5 average and 1953–5 average   Units: '000 metric tons unless otherwise indicated

	Production		Exports		Imports	
1. CEREALS, etc.						
Barley	2327.0	2932.0				0.1
Cassava	2546.0	698.7				
Maize (corn)	4614.3	2652.0			118.2	0.7
Millet/sorghum	16 299.0	15 909.0			16.7	148.31*
Oats					1.8	3.0¹*
Potatoes	3186.0	1876.7	6.7			
Rice	53 268.3	39 442.0	3.1		644.8	371.9
Sweet potatoes/yams	1368.0¹	1177.0¹				
Wheat	10 993.3	8145.3	0.5		5379.3	764.0

n excl. trade overland with Pakistan.

	Production		Exports		Imports	
2. FRUIT, etc.						
Bananas	2657.0	1873.5²				
Coconuts	4843.7e	na	9.6	0.2*		1.7*
Dates	2.0*	na			45.8	80.1
Figs						
Grapes	2.0*	na			1.2	
Lemons			2.2			
Oranges						
excl. citrus fruit			0.1†			

	Production		Exports		Imports	
3. BEVERAGES, FOREST PRODUCTS, etc.						
Cocoa						0.8
Coffee	62.8	29.6	26.7		5.2	
Sugar: cane	114 057.3	53 694.7				
raw	2942.8r	1437.0¹	350.9		5.8	519.4
Tea	361.2	290.5	211.1		32.6	199.7
Tobacco: leaf	364.6	264.0	67.3		4.1	0.6*
cigarettes	1368.0¹	1177.0¹	3.1aq		1.7q	1.72q
Softwood j	46 764.0o	20 360.0e	17.6		5.3	6.3
Hardwood j	14 189.0¹	14 657.0¹				47.9
Wood pulp	25.02*	77.3			71.6	12.0
Newsprint	530.52	161.7	1.6		90.0	77.3
Other paper			13.0		24.8	49.2

	Production		Exports		Imports	
4. VEGETABLE OILSEEDS AND OILS						
Castor seed	103.7	117.9	25.38	31.72		
Castor oil			0.07		0.05	
Coconut oil	264.3n	180.0²*			0.95	55.30
Copra	450.0*	172.3			0.02	23.20
Cottonseed	763.0*	392.0²			0.33	
Cottonseed oil	2135.0	444.7			1.64	
Groundnuts	3529.1	2727.4	20.28	16.70		

continued

a million $ U.S. b '000 cu. metres of roundwood equivalent. n no. in millions. q incl. other tobacco products. r in addition, gur and khandari 6 800*. f in addition, gur 2 524*. e '000 hectolitres. e no. in millions. n excl. Goa.

ICELAND continued

FINANCE

Currency unit: The kronur

Exchange rates	1965	1960	1950	1938
Per $ U.S.	43.06	38.1	16.32	4.76
Per £ sterling	120.57	106.8	45.7	21.91

		Year(s)
National Income (million $ U.S.)	359	1965
G.N.P. per capita ($ U.S.)	1740	1966
Rate of increase of G.N.P. per capita	3.7	1960–4 av.
Foreign trade (percentage of G.D.P.)	59	1963–5 av.

TRADING

Total trade (in million $ U.S.)	1965	1955	1938
Exports (f.o.b.)	129	52	11
Imports (c.i.f.)	137	74	11

Main trading partners (percentage of total value)

Exports	1965	1955	1938
U.K.	20	16	18
U.S.A.	18	12	8
Germany F.R.	8	15	5
Denmark	7	7	2
Sweden	7	5	2
Italy	6	8	—
U.S.S.R.	5	18	—

Imports	1965	1955	1938
U.K.	14	13	22
U.S.A.	13	13	10
Germany F.R.	12	9	14
Denmark	9	9	9
U.S.S.R.	6	6	2
Norway	6	4	—
Sweden	5	5	4

Distribution of trade (percentage of total value)

Exports	1965	1955
Fish	94	76
(meal, bait and waste)	(21)	(na)
(oil)	(14)	(4)

Imports	1965	1955
Manufactured goods	67	64
(machinery and transport equipment)	(32)	(26)
(textiles and clothing)	(11)	(12)
Crude materials and fuels	13	21
(petroleum products)	(9)	(15)
Food	10	11
Chemicals	7	4

PRODUCTION, EXPORTS AND IMPORTS

Years: 1963–5 average and 1953–5 average   Units: '000 metric tons unless otherwise indicated

	Production		Exports		Imports	
	1965	1938			1955	1938
1. CEREALS, etc.						
Barley					0.4	0.1
Maize (corn)					0.2	0.1
Oats					0.1	0.4
Potatoes	10.3				3.3	3.0²
Rice					0.3	0.4
Rye						
Wheat					0.7	0.4
2. FRUIT, etc.						
Apples					1.7	1.0
Bananas	8.0²				0.9	
Dates					0.1	
Grapes					0.2	
Lemons					0.2	
Oranges					1.8	0.4
Raisins					0.3	0.4
Wine b.					4.6	2.3
3. BEVERAGES, FOREST PRODUCTS, etc.						
Coffee					1.9	1.1
Sugar, raw					10.7	7.7
Tobacco products					0.4	0.3²
Softwood j	0.2²*				90.1	71.8
Newsprint					6.3	4.9
Hardwood j					2.2	1.0
Other paper					8.3	4.6
4. VEGETABLE OILSEEDS AND OILS						
Coconut oil					0.51	1.09
Cottonseed oil						0.09
Groundnut oil					0.01	0.01
Linseed oil					0.05	0.15
Palm kernel oil					0.01	0.01
Palm oil					0.02	0.02
Soya bean oil					0.42	0.36

	Production		Exports		Imports	
	1965	1955	1965	1955	1965	1955
5. LIVESTOCK, ANIMAL PRODUCTS, etc.						
Chickens d	103.7	83.3				
Cattle d	57.7	45.0				
dairy cows d	40.7	32.0				
Sheep d	758.3	540.7				
Horses d	30.3	37.6				
Pigs d	13.7	8.7	2.2		6.3	
Meat†: A	8.2	3.7	2.7		0.9a	
B	2.0	7.0	0.5			
Butter						
Cheese						
Eggs	0.7*	0.6				
Fish	985.4n	453.5n	413.8	164.5¹*	0.3	
Milk	123.7	83.3	5.6			
Whale/sperm oil g	3.2	2.0	2.3	2.8²	7.8	
Hides/skins a	2.8	1.7	2.3		8.0	
Wool a	1.3	1.0	0.3	0.2	6.3	
6. FIBRES, TEXTILES, etc.						
Abaca					0.2	
Agaves (sisal etc.)					0.4	
Rubber, natural					0.2	
Cotton: yarn					0.11	
woven fabrics					0.21p	
Rayon, woven fabrics					0.1	
Wool: yarn	0.5²				0.2	
woven fabrics			—¹			
7. FUEL AND POWER						
Coal, 'A'‡					10	51
Coke					1	1
Electricity h: total	682	41¹				
hydro	641	38¹				
thermal	41	30¹				
Petroleum, refined					433	270¹
h million kWh.						
8. IRON AND STEEL						
Iron/steel scrap	na	na	2²			
9. NON-FERROUS MINERALS AND METALS						
Asbestos: fibre					0.01	0.03
manufactured					0.15	0.05
Aluminium a					0.33	
Copper, metal					0.21	0.30
Lead, metal					0.34	0.11
Tin, metal					0.01	
Titanium minerals					0.18	0.21
Zinc, metal					0.11	0.03
10. CHEMICALS n AND FERTILIZERS						
Chemicals a	19.0				na	
Fertilizers:	112.3					
Potash	0.1				8.2	2.9
11. INDUSTRY						
Aircraft a						
Alcoholic beverages					6.3	0.5
beer b					0.9a	0.3a
Cement						
Electrical engineering a						
Merchant ships a			4.0		7.8	3.6²
Motor vehicles a					8.0	2.2
					6.3	5.2

d no in thousands. n incl. fish landed in foreign ports. j '000 cu. metres of roundwood equivalent. b '000 hectolitres. g '000 G.R.T. a million $ U.S.

na: data not available. — negligible or nil. 1 one year only. 2 two year average. * estimate. * see appendix. ‡ see appendix. † re-exports.

SOUTH EAST ASIA

INDONESIA

The republic of Indonesia was formed in 1949 by the union of the states of the Netherlands East Indies with the exception of the western part of New Guinea. This latter, renamed West Irian, joined Indonesia in 1963.

Data for West Irian have been added to those for Indonesia for the years 1953–5.

AREA: 1 900 000 sq. km. (733 600 sq. miles)

LAND USE: (percentage of total)

	1954
Arable, orchard, permanent meadow and pasture	9.3
Forest and woodland	63.8
City areas, waste and other land	26.9

POPULATION: 110 920 000 (1967 estimate)

Largest city: DJAKARTA, capital; population: 2 906 533 (city proper, 1961)

Distribution of working population (1961)

Total working population: 34 578 234 (based on a 1% sample of census returns)

U.N. group no.		Percentage
0	Agriculture, forestry, fishing and hunting	68.0
1	Mining and quarrying	0.3
2/3	Manufacturing	5.4
4	Construction	1.7
5	Electricity, gas, water and sanitary services	0.3
6	Commerce	6.3
7	Transport, storage and communications	2.0
8	Services	9.0
9	Others	7.2

		Year
Life expectancy at birth (years): male	47.5	1960
female	47.5	1960
Infant mortality (per '000)	87.2	1964
Crude birth rate (per '000)	30.6a	1964
Crude death rate (per '000)	9.2*	1964
Population per physician	34 820a	1964
Population per hospital bed	1 450	1965
School enrolment: age 5–19 years (percentage)	44.b	1961
age over 19 years (per 100 000 population)	95.c	1963

a West Irian: 8 500 (1962). *b* excl. West Irian. *c* universities only.

COMMUNICATIONS

		Year(s)
Motor vehicles in use ('000s): private	146.8	1963–5 av.
commercial	104.3	1961
Railway track (km.)	6 640	1963–5 av.
Mail per capita: domestic	0.1	1961
foreign received	0.1	1963–5 av.
foreign sent	0.2	1967
Telephones (per '000 urban population)	0.2	1963–5 av.
Television sets (per '000 population)	0.3	1959
Daily newspapers (per '000 population)	11 a	

a West Irian: 2 (1961).

FINANCE

Currency unit: The rupiah

Exchange rates* *a*	1964 *d*	1960 *b*	1955 *b*	1938 *c·d*
Per $ U.S.	402	45	3.81	1.84
Per £ sterling	1 126	126.2	10.67	8.46

Since 1949 there has been severe devaluation of the rupiah; in 1959 the value was reduced to a tenth of the nominal value, and in 1965 a new rupiah equivalent to 1 000 old rupiahs was introduced.

		Year
National Income (million $ U.S.)	8 909	1965
G.N.P. per capita ($ U.S.)	100	1966

a all rates taken at the end of the year. *b* principal import rate. *c* Dutch guilders, replaced by the rupiah in 1941. *d* basic selling rate.

TRADING (pre-1963 data exclude West Irian)

Total trade (in million $ U.S.)

	1964 *d*	1960	1955	1938
Exports (f.o.b.)			708	379
Imports (c.i.f.)			946	248
			631	

Main trading partners (percentage of total value)

Exports	1965	1955	1938
U.S.A.	22	14	15
Japan	16	18	3
Netherlands	13	16	21
Australia	8	2	4
Germany F.R.	8	4	4a
China P.R.	6	1	2

Imports	1965	1955	1937*
Japan		82	(31)
U.S.A.		(39)	(45)
U.K.		12	(22)
Germany F.R.			10
China P.R.			(17)
Burma			
Thailand			

Distribution of trade (percentage of total value)

Exports	1963	1955	1937*
Crude materials and fuels (rubber)	82	82	
(petroleum and petroleum products)			
Food	12	10	na

Imports	1962	1955	1937*
Manufactured goods (textiles)	67	67	na
(machinery and transport equipment)			
Food		9	na
Chemicals		9	na
Crude materials and fuel		8	

a includes Germany D.R. and Austria.

PRODUCTION, EXPORTS AND IMPORTS

Years: 1963–5 average and 1953–5 average Units: '000 metric tons unless otherwise indicated

4. VEGETABLE OILSEEDS AND OILS

	Production		Exports		Imports	
	1963–5	1953–5	1963–5	1953–5	1963–5	1953–5
Castor seed	2.00*	5.79				
Copra	437.50*	760.90²a	156.80*	290.60	—	9.1
Coconut oil	420.01*	na				0.3
Cottonseed	na	na				
Groundnuts	6.0*	2.30*				
Groundnut oil	299.83	262.70	3.051*	0.03	na	2.8*
Linseed oil	na	na				
Palm kernels	34.23*	42.63a	34.23*	40.93		
Palm oil	157.27	165.60m	122.93*	129.51		
Sesame seed	2.00¹*	na	2.00²a	1.53		
Soya beans	367.00	350.00		3.552		

5. LIVESTOCK‡; ANIMAL PRODUCTS, etc.

	Production		Exports		Imports	
Chickens *d*	101 295.0*	4 825.5				
Cattle *d*	6 357.0*	6 077.0²				
Goats *d*	5 112.0*	6 460.3¹	0.1*	1.2	na	0.4
Sheep *d*	2 380.0*	2 634.0²	79.0*	62.3¹	na	31.2
Horses *d*	720.0*	612.0				
Pigs *d*	680.7*	42.3p	138.8*	167.3	0.7	
Bacon/ham	135.7*	9.22m	12.01	15.2	7.3	
Meat: 'A'				0.3²		
'B'	25 399.0m	16 351.0m	7.0²	na	0.1q	
Butter	20.0		92.2²	197.3	3.0	
Cheese					3.5	
Eggs	124.3*	na			1.1	0.1
Milk	945.8²	641.9	1.4*	6.0*	9.5	0.2
Hides/skins	36.0*	15.01	13.7*		69.7	na

d no. in thousands. *n* from estates. *u* 1962 figure.

na: data not available. — negligible or nil. * estimate. ¹ one year only. ² two year average. ‡ see appendix. † re-exports.

INDIA continued

PRODUCTION, EXPORTS AND IMPORTS continued

4. VEGETABLE OILSEEDS AND OILS continued

	Production	Exports	Imports
Groundnut oil	na	45.10	72.26	0.53
Linseed	438.3	383.3p	0.01	0.62
Linseed oil	na	0.60	27.81	—
Olive oil	na	—	—	0.01
Palm oil	32.10	0.19	0.17	26.67
Rapeseed	620.81	0.31	0.51	4.07
Rapeseed oil	1 221.0	0.63	1.00	0.20
Sesame seed	446.2	—	—	4.14
Soya beans	—	541.3	—	13.68
Soya bean oil	—	—	—	—
Sunflower seed	161	—	—	0.24
Tung oil	472	0.38	—	na

p flax grown for seed only.

5. LIVESTOCK‡; ANIMAL PRODUCTS, etc.

	Production	Exports	Imports
Chickens *d*	121 232*n 97 372pn	—	—
Cattle *d*	185 709n 159 000p	—	—
dairy cows *d*	56 043*n 20 400b	20.1	0.3
Goats *d*	64 628* 56 626b	—	—
Sheep *d*	42 683* 38 700b	—	—
Horses *d*	1 503* 1 503b	—	—
Bison/ham	5 350* 4 700p	0.1	0.1
Meat: 'A'	533*	0.5	—
'B'	—	—	—
Butter	161	—	—
Cheese	—	549p	—
Eggs	88*	17.6	3.7
Fish	1 233	828	31.0*
Milk	10 235* 7 756p	18.0	6.2
Hides/skins	—	19.5a	4.1*
Wool	18*	7.3	422.9
		9.3	269.4

d no. in thousands. *f* metric tons. *g* cows over three years old.

6. FIBRES, TEXTILES, etc.

	Production	Exports	Imports
Abaca	—	—	2.0
Agaves (sisal etc.)	3.0¹*	—	3.8
Cotton lint.	1 067.3	722.8	52.7
Flax fibre	—	—	0.8
Hemp fibre	67.1	120.4	11.2
Jute	1 282.7	620.0n	27.1
Rubber: natural	43.6	22.0	—
synthetic	11.5	—	—
Silk *f*	1 337.5²	985.3*	629.0
Cotton: yarn	932.2	710.1	12.9
woven fabrics	920.9*	525.9p	0.11
Rayon: fibre/yarn	76.2	8.5	6.1
woven fabrics	86.8	19.3q	6.7
Non-cellulosic	—	—	—
fibre/yarn	1.6	9.1²	8.7
Wool: yarn	20.6	na	—
woven fabrics	13.3l	7.11	—

a metric tons. *n* in addition, mesta 174.0. *p* mill production only. *q* continuous filament piece goods only. *r* sea-borne trade only. *l* million metres.

7. FUEL AND POWER

	Production	Exports	Imports
Coal: 'A'	65 187	38 840	1 160
'B'	527	—	—
Coke	33 623	9 780l	2
Electricity *h*: total	14 927	3 300l	28
hydro	5 350*	6 480l	—
thermal	60	—	—
Natural gas *i*	2 307	350l	360
Oil, crude	932.2	2 450l	739
Petroleum, refined	2 346	—	—
Rare earths *j*			
Uranium *f*			

h million kWh. *i* million cu. metres.

8. IRON AND STEEL

	Production	Exports	Imports
Pig iron	12 883m	3 629m	10 904
Iron ore	6 863	1 908	55
Steel ingots/castings	6 128	1 658	427
Iron/steel scrap	—	—	18
Iron/steel products *a*	—	na	—

a million U.S. *m* metal content.

9. NON-FERROUS MINERALS AND METALS

	Production	Exports	Imports
Diamonds	2.33l	—	7.28a
Gold, ore *k*	139.30m 224.00m	—	55
Platinum group	—	—	427
metals *k*	—	na	18

---

9. NON-FERROUS MINERALS AND METALS continued

	Production	Exports	Imports
Silver, ore *k*	149.30m 110.00m	—	67.16n
Asbestos: fibre	3.55	0.85	15.87n
manufactured	—	—	33.85
Mica	32.10	16.93	2.87
Aluminium: bauxite	620.81	76.80	—
alumina	—	—	—
aluminium	59.69	5.34	2.15
Antimony: ore	—	—	20.78
metal	—	—	1.59
Beryl	0.46p	0.43p	0.11
Cadmium	—	—	0.11
metal	—	—	0.89
Chrome: ore	53.23m 67.67m	22.68	49.53¹
Cobalt, metal	—	—	0.03
Copper: ore	10.20m	0.86	0.33
metal	9.47	6.56	65.23
Lead: ore	4.27m	2.32m	0.01
metal	3.36	2.04	35.51
Magnesium:			
magnesite	858.29	na	0.12
metal/salts	227.07	41.47 31.34	0.822
Manganese: ore	—	0.04 0.85	6.15
metal	1 438.13 1 790.24	1 292.24¹ 587.23¹	0.57
Mercury *f*	na	55.50	195.00
Nickel, metal	—	—	2.44
Tin, metal	—	—	4.92
Titanium minerals	24.37	239.41	0.05† 0.46†	3.30
Tungsten, ore	0.01	0.01	0.12
Zinc: ore	5.70m	39.40 200.70	—
metal	—	6.70 4.12	79.59
	—	2.20	35.51

k '000 fine troy oz. *l* '000 carats. *m* metal content. *n* million $ U.S. *f* metric tons. *g* exports to U.S.A. only. *q* in addition, U.S.\$144 800. *n* in addition, U.S.\$1 095 900 *x* ferroginous ore.

10. CHEMICALS *n* AND FERTILIZERS

Organic chemicals:

	Production	Exports	Imports
Benzene	na	0.6	0.7*
Butadiene	na	—	1.32*
Ethylene	na	—	115.0
Methanol	na	—	0.1
Phenol	na	—	65.7
Phthalic anhydride	na	—	22.2
Styrene monomer	na	—	5.7
Urea	19.7	—	94.7

Inorganic chemicals:

	Production	Exports	Imports
Ammonia	na	—	2.0
Carbon black	12.0	—	—
Chlorine	51.0	—	0.11
Nitric acid	11.8	—	0.1
Sodium carbonate	290.0	—	0.2
Sodium hydroxide	187.0	—	—
Sulphuric acid	645.0	—	—

Plastics:

	Production	Exports	Imports
Polyamides	na	na	2 013
Polyethylene	10.2	na	—
Polyvinyl chloride	8.1	na	28

Fertilizers:

	Production	Exports	Imports
Phosphates	8.1b	4.1b	529.0
Potash	—	0.1*	12.9
Pyrites	na	na	68.1
Sulphur	201.9	—	6.7

n data not available for years 1953–5. *b* apatite. *x* sulphur content.

11. INDUSTRY

	Production	Exports	Imports
Aircraft *a*	—	—	2 382
Alcoholic beverages	na	12.6	—
beer *b*	na	—	64
Electrical	na	—	23
engineering *a*	na	—	2
Locomotives *c*	na	43.7	225
Machine tools *a*	147.0	—	—
Merchant ships *a*	9 876.7 4 276.0	—	0.3
Motor vehicles:			
commercial	38.0¹	5.9	—
private	33.1	9.3q	—
Railway vehicles *a*	117.0	—	—

a million $ U.S. *b* '000 hectolitres. *c* no. of units. *d* no. in thousands.

SIKKIM

Sikkim was under British protection until the transfer of power in India in 1947. By a treaty of 1950 Sikkim became a protectorate of the government of India, which is responsible for communications, defence and external affairs. India is also assisting with a plan for economic development.

AREA: 7 298 sq. km. (2 818 sq. miles)

CENTRAL ASIA

SIKKIM

POPULATION: 183 000 (1967 estimate)

Capital city: GANGTOK; population: 6 848 (city proper, 1961)

EMPLOYMENT AND TRADE

Rice, corn, millet and fruit are produced, with potatoes as the main cash crop. The forests, which cover about one-third of the country, are as yet unexploited.

1. CEREALS, etc.

	Production	Exports	Imports
Cassava	11 357.0	9 300.7	—	—
Maize (corn)	3 803.3	2 139.3	—	—
Potatoes	420.01*	na	na	53.3
Sweet potatoes/	12 591.0	11 278.0	9.1	24.0
yams	3 223.0	2 051.4	0.3	247.9

2. FRUIT, etc.

	Production	Exports	Imports
Apples	—	—	11.9
Bananas	na	na	0.8
Coconuts *a*	—	—	2.9a
Dates	5 393.7	na	0.2
Grapes	—	—	6.9
Oranges	—	—	0.3²
Pineapples	—	—	4.4
Wine *b*	—	—	—

a million $ U.S. *b* '000 hectolitres.

3. BEVERAGES, FOREST PRODUCTS, etc.

	Production	Exports	Imports
Cocoa	1.0	1.2	0.1*	0.4	16.7²
Coffee	112.0	62.3¹	79.0*	31.2	3.0
Sugar: cane	8 921.0*	6 460.3n			23.7
raw	680.7*	42.3p	138.8*	167.3	
Tea *w*	135.7*	9.22m	12.01	15.2	187.3²
Tobacco: leaf	27.0*	46.3¹	0.3²		50.6²
cigars	—	—	—	—	—
cigarettes	25 399.0m	16 351.0m	7.0²	na	151.0n
Softwood *j*	84 795.0¹	3 893.9²	92.2²	197.3	73.4²a
Hardwood *j*	—	—	—	—	
Wood pulp *j*	124.3*	na	—	—	
Newsprint	945.8²	641.9	1.4*	6.0*	
Other paper	36.0*	15.01	13.7*		41.01

n no. in millions. *j* '000 cu. metres of roundwood equivalent. *n* from estates only. *p* in addition, non-centrifugal sugar 146* (1963–5 av.) and 250* (1953–5 av.) *q* incl. other tobacco manufactures.

11. NON-FERROUS MINERALS AND METALS

	Production	Exports	Imports
Diamonds	2.33l	—	7.28a	0.34n	0.60a
Gold, ore *k*	139.30m 224.00m	—			2.27n

na: data not available. — negligible or nil. ¹ one year only. ² two year average. * estimate. ‡ see appendix. † re-exports.

continued

INDONESIA continued

PRODUCTION, EXPORTS AND IMPORTS continued

6. FIBRES, TEXTILES, etc.

	Production	Exports	Imports
Abaca	0.3*	—	1.5
Agaves e	3.5*	na	26.5
Cotton lint .	3.0	—	1.0[1]
Jute	4.7*	na	—
Rubber, natural	649.3	665.8*	707.0
Silk f .	na	—	—
Cotton: yarn	—	—	13.6
woven fabrics	—	—	39.2[1]
Rayon: fibre/yarn	2.00[1]	—	0.6
Rare earths f	106r	—	—

f metric tons. g sisal and cantala.

7. FUEL AND POWER

	Production	Exports	Imports
Coal, 'A' ‡ .	437	na	90
Coke	1 489	—	—
Electricity h: total	na	—	—
hydro	na	—	—
thermal .	na	—	—
Natural gas i	2 900	—	—
Oil, crude	23 244	13 930	3 030[1]
Petroleum, refined .	8 640	3 693	5 910[1]

f metric tons. h million kWh. i million cu. metres.

8. IRON AND STEEL

	Production	Exports	Imports
Iron/steel scrap	na	2	75

9. NON-FERROUS MINERALS AND METALS

	Production	Exports	Imports
Diamonds l	—	—	—
Gold, ore km	6.00	—	—
Silver, ore km	277.30	—	—
Asbestos: fibre	0.02	—	0.12
manufactured	—	—	11.85

f metric tons. k '000 fine troy oz. l '000 carats. m metal content.
r monazite.

continued

NON-FERROUS MINERALS AND METALS—continued

	Production	Exports	Imports
Aluminium: bauxite	609.63	656.93	—
aluminium	195.49	224.01	6.70
Antimony, metal	—	—	0.09
Copper, metal	—	—	3.80
Lead, metal	—	na	1.09
Manganese, ore	4.58	—	—
Mercury f	—	—	16.50
Nickel, ore .	2.03m	24.13	—
Tin: ore	14.90m	27.70	—
metal	1.90	34.90m	—
Zinc, metal	106r	46.54	2.37
		21.40[1]	
		0.48	

f metric tons. k '000 fine troy oz. l '000 carats. m metal content.

10. CHEMICALS n AND FERTILIZERS

	Production	Exports	Imports
Chemicals . .	—	—	na
Fertilizers:			
Phosphates	30.5*	—	—
Sulphur .	1.4	—	7.6

n data not available for years 1953–5.

11. INDUSTRY

	Production	Exports	Imports
Aircraft a	—	—	—
Alcoholic beverages	200.0	—	—
Cement	471.7[1]	2	—
Electrical			
engineering a	26.7[2]	—	—
Railway vehicles a	147.3	—	—
Merchant ships g	—	—	—
Motor vehicles	0.4	—	—
commercial a	na	—	—
private d p	na	—	—
	2.7	—	—
	1.8	—	—

a million $ U.S. b '000 hectolitres. d no. in thousands. g '000 G.R.T.
p assembly of imported parts.

continued

PRODUCTION, EXPORTS AND IMPORTS
Years: 1963–5 average and 1953–5 average Units: '000 metric tons unless otherwise indicated

1. CEREALS, etc.

	Production	Exports	Imports
Barley	966.7*	0.9[2]	1.7
Maize (corn)	840.0*	4.2	1.8[2]
Millets/sorghum	14.0*	0.5	—
Potatoes	28.0*	0.2	—
Rice	107.0*	6.5	4.9*
Wheat .	860.0*	6.7*	99.7[2]
	449.3*	5.9*	3.4
	2 866.7* 2 217.7*	0.3*	

2. FRUIT, etc.

	Production	Exports	Imports
Apples	—	—	—
Apricots	31.7* 57.2*	0.4	—
Bananas	—	—	—
Dates	299.3* 122.0*	24.1*	0.3[1]
Figs	5.0*	—	—
Grapes	253.3*	—	1.0
Lemons	40.0* 39.3	—	0.4[2]
Oranges	50.0*	0.1	na
Olives	15.0*	—	—
Raisins	48.0* 52.9	31.3	32.6

3. BEVERAGES, FOREST PRODUCTS, etc.

	Production	Exports	Imports
Coffee .	—	—	0.2[2]
Sugar: beet	1 283.3* 507.3*	—	—
raw (cane)	200.0*	—	393.9*
cane	168.5 76.7*	—	228.4
Tea	25.9	2.0	5.2[2]
Tobacco: leaf	12.4 14.0*	0.6	—
cigarettes	9 214.0e 6 422.0e	—	—
tobacco/snuff	4.4 5.1	—	—
Softwood j	—	0.1	84.6
Hardwood j	1 603.0 8 227.0[2]	5.4[2]	5.0[2]
Newsprint j	—	0.1	8.4[2]
Other paper	5.5[2]	10.1	52.5[2]

e no. in millions. j '000 cu. metres of roundwood equivalent.

4. VEGETABLE OILSEEDS AND OILS

	Production	Exports	Imports
Castor seed	10.0* 8.4	2.40	—
Castor oil	—	0.10	—
Cottonseed	275.7 113.3*	6.77	15.13
Cottonseed oil .	na	—	0.42[2]
Groundnuts	na 3.3*	—	—
Groundnut oil	na	—	—
Linseed	4.0*	5.07	1.21
Linseed oil	na	—	0.49[2]
Olive oil	1.0*	0.02	—
Palm oil	na	—	—
Sesame seed	6.1* 10.0*	2.80	31.31
Soya bean oil	na	—	—

p incl. coconut oil.

5. LIVESTOCK‡, ANIMAL PRODUCTS, etc.

	Production	Exports	Imports
Chickens d	26 700*	—	—
Cattle d	4 900* 5 000[2]*	—	0.1[2]
Goats d	14 500*	—	0.1[2]
Sheep d	31 843* 17 375[2]	—	6.4
Horses d	470* 370[1]*	—	0.5[2]
Pigs d	7*	—	—
Meat‡ ‡: A	239*	—	—
B	19*	—	—
Butter	—	—	—
Cheese	28*	—	—
Eggs	29* 25	0.6	0.1
Milk	8[2]*	4.31*	0.2*
Fish	1 360*	3.8[2]	39.8[2]
Hides/skins	na	12.2	3.7
Wool	na 10*	2.0[2]	1.4[2]

d no. in thousands. q 1962 figure.

6. FIBRES, TEXTILES, etc.

	Production	Exports	Imports
Cotton lint .	125.3* 56.7[2]*	61.4[2]	1.2[2]
Jute	2.7* 4.0[1]*	—	5.8[2]
Rubber, natural	—	—	—
Silk f	109.0*	83.7	—
Cotton: yarn	na	—	—
woven fabrics	na	—	0.8[2]
Rayon, woven fabrics	na	—	0.1
Wool, woven fabrics	4.0r	—	—

d no. in thousands. f metric tons. r million metres.

7. FUEL AND POWER

	Production	Exports	Imports
Coal, 'A' ‡ .	250 230	—	—
Electricity h: total	2 200[2] 570[1]	—	—
hydro	28.0*	—	—
thermal .	na 570[1]	—	—
Natural gas i	1 190	—	—
Oil, crude	84 100 16 360[1]	63 450 8 330[1]	—
Petroleum, refined .	18 876 7 270[1]	11 127 370[1]	6[2]

h million kWh. i million cu. metres.

8. IRON AND STEEL

	Production	Exports	Imports
Iron ore	16 934m	2	14
Pig iron	na	—	6
Iron/steel scrap	na	—	1[1]

m metal content. t incl. steel ingots.

9. NON-FERROUS MINERALS AND METALS

	Production	Exports	Imports
Asbestos: fibre	0.03	—	2.29
manufactured	—	—	1.38
Mica	—	0.07	0.40 0.63[2]
Aluminium	—	—	4.60
Antimony, ore	0.04	—	—
Chrome, ore	123.08*m 25.88m	125.19	4.70 1.73[2]
Copper, metal	—	—	1.17
Lead: ore	13.97m 12.70m	41.45	—
metal	0.42 0.87	—	0.35
Magnesium,	—	—	0.21
metal/salts	—	—	0.20
Manganese, ore	27.00 5.65	24.67	0.25 0.16[2]
Mercury f	—	—	0.30
Nickel, metal	—	—	—
Tin, metal	—	—	—
Titanium minerals	—	—	—
Zinc: ore	13.61*m 5.53*m	65.71	2.09
metal	—	—	0.65

f metric tons. m metal content.

10. CHEMICALS n AND FERTILIZERS

Organic chemicals:

	Production	Exports	Imports
Benzene	na	—	na
Butadiene	na	—	na
Ethylene	na	—	0.2[2]
Methanol	na	—	na
Phenol	na	—	na
Phthalic anhydride	na	—	—
Styrene monomer	na	—	—
Urea	na	—	—

Inorganic chemicals:

	Production	Exports	Imports
Ammonia	na	—	0.1[2]
Carbon black	na	—	—
Chlorine	na	—	0.1
Nitric acid	na	—	6.4
Sodium carbonate	na	—	—
Sodium hydroxide	na	2	0.5[2]
Sulphuric acid	na	—	—

Plastics:

	Production	Exports	Imports
Polyamides	na	—	na
Polyethylene	na	—	na
Polyvinyl chloride	na	—	—

Fertilizers:

	Production	Exports	Imports
Potash	20.3[2]p 18.3[1]p	—	0.7
Sulphur	na	0.2[2]	2.4

n data not available for years 1953–5. p recovered sulphur.

11. INDUSTRY

	Production	Exports	Imports
Aircraft a	74.0	—	2.1
Beer b	801.3* 87.3	—	10.7* 51.7
Cement	—	76.7*	—
Electrical			
engineering a	na	—	41.0 6.0
Railway vehicles a	na	—	0.8 0.4
Merchant ships g	—	—	0.3 0.3
Motor vehicles a	—	—	50.0 5.5

a million $ U.S. b '000 hectolitres. g '000 G.R.T.

---

na: data not available. — negligible or nil. — negligible or nil. * estimate. [1] one year only. [2] two year average. ‡ see appendix. † re-exports.

167

IRAN MIDDLE EAST

Iran, formerly Persia, is a constitutional monarchy. A member of Cento, Iran has also signed agreements for economic development with Turkey, Pakistan and, more recently, the U.S.S.R.

AREA: 1 621 860* sq. km. (626 200* sq. miles)

LAND USE: (percentage of total)

	Percentage
Arable and orchard	54.8
Permanent meadow and pasture	0.4
Forest and woodland (including unstocked land)	13.5
City areas, waste and other land	31.3

POPULATION: 25 781 090 (1966 provisional census)
City areas, waste and other land

POPULATION: 25 781 090 (1966 provisional census)
Largest city: TEHRĀN (Teheran), capital; population: 2 695 283 (city proper, 1966)

Distribution of working population (1956)
Total working population: 6 066 643

U.N. group no.		Percentage
0	Agriculture, forestry, fishing and hunting	54.8
1	Mining and quarrying	0.4
2/3	Manufacturing	13.5
4	Construction	5.5
5	Electricity, gas, water and sanitary services .	0.2
6	Commerce	5.9
7	Transport, storage and communications	3.4
8	Services	10.8
9		16.5

COMMUNICATIONS

		1960	1950
Motor vehicles in use ('000s): private		42.3*	10.3
commercial		6.1*	11.7
			71.9

		Year(s)	
Railway track (km) . .		3 880	1965
Telephones (per '000) .		121.6	1965
		46.1	1965
Radio licences (per '000 population)		3 480	1964
Population per physician		3 880	1964
Population per hospital bed		880	1967
School enrolment age 5–19 years (percentage		40	1963–5 av.
age over 15 years (per 100 000 population)		107	1964–5 av.

		Year(s)	
Crude birth rate (per '000) .		74.0	1963–5 av.
Crude death rate (per '000) .		0.8	1963–5 av.
Population per physician		69	1963–5 av.
Television sets (per '000 population)		4.4	1963–5 av.
Daily newspapers (per '000 population)		15	1961

FINANCE
Currency unit: The rial

Exchange rates	1960	1950
Per $ U.S.	7.0	32.5
Per £ sterling	81.6	91.04

	1965	1960	1950	1938
National Income (million $ U.S.)	75.75	75.75	32.5	17.5
G.N.P. per capita ($ U.S.)	212.1	212.1	91.04	80.96
Rate of increase of G.N.P. per capita	5 221			
Foreign trade (percentage of G.D.P.)	250	0.2		
	31			

TRADING

Total trade (in million $ U.S.)	1965	1960	1955	1937
Exports (f.o.b.) .	1 303	1 303	396	159
Imports (c.i.f.) .	860	860	312	85

Main trading partners (percentage of total value)

Exports	1965	1955	Imports	1965	1955
Japan	16	11	Germany F.R.	20	17
U.K.	13	11	U.S.A. .	18	19
Netherlands	6	6	U.K. .	13	10
France	6	7	Japan	6	8
U.S.A. .	5	4	France	4	4
Southern Yemen	1		Italy	4	3
			Netherlands	3	2

Distribution of trade (percentage of total value)

Exports	1965	1955 a	1938*
Petroleum and petroleum products .	87	74*	74
Carpets	4	4	4
Cotton	3	5	2

Imports	1965	1955 a	1938*
Manufactured goods (machinery and transport equipment)	68 (36)	69 (17)	na
Food	13	10	
Chemicals	5	5	
Crude materials			

a the 1955 figures are percentages of total imports, excluding concessions, which amounted to 65% of the general imports‡ for that year.

continued

---

na: data not available. — negligible or nil. * estimate. [1] one year only. [2] two year average. ‡ see appendix. † re-exports.

IRAQ

Iraq was a monarchy until 1958 when the king was assassinated and the country declared a republic. Further coups d'état introduced a succession of republican governments during the next ten years; there has also been some internal unrest since a revolt by the Kurdish people in 1961. A customs union was formed with the U.A.R. in 1967.

AREA: 438 446 sq. km. (169 280 sq. miles)

LAND USE: (percentage of total)

	1964	1954
Arable and orchard	16.7	12.3
Permanent meadow and pasture (mainly rough grazing)	9.5	4.0
Forest and woodland (incl. some rough grazing)	4.3	2.0
City areas, waste and other land	69.5	81.7

POPULATION: 8 261 527 (1965 census)
Largest city: BAGHDĀD, capital; population: 1 745 328 (city proper, 1965)

Distribution of working population (1957)
Total working population: 1 795 277 a

U.N. group no.		Percentage
0	Agriculture, forestry, fishing and hunting	47.9
1	Mining and quarrying	0.2
2/3	Manufacturing	9.5
4	Construction	0.6
5	Electricity, gas, water and sanitary services	0.6
6	Commerce	5.0
7	Transport, storage and communications	5.0
8		14.2
9	Others	13.0

	1964	Year(s)
Infant mortality (per '000)	23.7*	1965
Crude birth rate (per '000)	15.2*	1965
Crude death rate (per '000)	4.1*	1965
Population per physician	4 760	1964
Population per hospital bed	530	1966
School enrolment: age 5–19 years (percentage)		1963–4 av.
age over 19 years (per 100 000 population)	316	1963–5 av.

a incl. 41 000* nationals working abroad.

COMMUNICATIONS

	1965	1955	1938	Year(s)
Motor vehicles in use ('000s): private	51.9			1965
commercial	27.6			
Railway track (km.)	2019			1961
Telephones (per '000 population)	9.0*			1967
Radio receivers (per '000 population)	158.0	12.3		1963–5 av.
Television sets (per '000 population)	16.3			1963–5 av.
Daily newspapers (per '000 population)	12	13		1963

FINANCE

Currency unit: The Iraqi dinar, at par with the pound sterling until 1968

Exchange rates	1965	1955	1938
Per $ U.S.	0.357	0.357	0.215

	1965	1955
National Income (million $ U.S.)	882	519
G.N.P. per capita ($ U.S.)	451	272
Rate of increase of G.N.P. per capita		
Foreign trade (percentage of G.D.P.)		

TRADING

Total trade (in million $ U.S.)	1965	1955a
Exports (f.o.b.)	882	519
Imports (c.i.f.)	451	272

Main trading partners (percentage of total value)

Exports	1965	1955a		Imports	1965	1955a
U.K.	16	14		U.S.A.	12	15
France	16			U.K.	11	28
Italy	13	5		Germany F.R.	9	8
Netherlands	8	9		Japan	7	na
Germany F.R.	7	13		U.S.S.R.	6	8
Japan	7			Czechoslovakia	6	na
Spain	3			Poland	4	na

Distribution of trade (percentage of total value)

Exports	1965	1955	1938*
Petroleum (crude)	94	91	74
Imports			
Machinery and transport equipment	20	28	17
Food	15	17	20
Textiles and clothing	11	13	na
Vegetable oils	4	—	

a excl. trade in petroleum.

PRODUCTION, EXPORTS AND IMPORTS

Years: 1963–5 average and 1953–5 average   Units: '000 metric tons unless otherwise indicated

1. CEREALS, etc.

	Production		Exports		Imports	
Barley	740.0	1 035.7	65.2	422.7	0.1	0.2
Maize (corn)	3.0*	6.3	—	0.1	—	—
Millets/sorghum	10.3*	18.0	—	15.5	—	—
Rice	175.0	142.0	—	2.8	20.8	7.0
Wheat	766.7	793.3	1.1	34.0	36.6	3.1
					120.0	11.1

2. FRUIT, etc.

	Production		Exports		Imports	
Apples					22.0	2.9
Bananas					6.3	
Coconuts					1.2	0.1
Dates	320.0*	357.0*[1]	298.9	240.0		
Grapes	45.0*[1]					
Lemons					0.1n	
Raisins					1.3	0.7
Tomatoes	174.0	na				
Wine b					0.3	

3. BEVERAGES, FOREST PRODUCTS, etc.

	Production		Exports		Imports	
Coffee					0.8	0.7
Sugar: beet	—					
raw	83.3*				266.1*	120.5
Tea	2.9				18.3	12.7
Tobacco: leaf	12.8*	8.4*a			19.7	
cigarettes	4 761.0	na			113.6	
Softwood j					48.5[2]	55.7
Hardwood j	36.0*	27.0[2]			0.9[2]	
Newsprint					22.7[2]	6.8
Other paper	174.0	na				

b '000 hectolitres.   n mainly dried limes.   j '000 cu. metres of roundwood equivalent.

PRODUCTION, EXPORTS AND IMPORTS *continued*

6. FIBRES, TEXTILES, etc.

	Production		Exports		Imports	
Cotton lint	10.0*	5.3	2.7	1.9	1.4	0.1
Jute	—	—	—	—	3.5	18.0
Rubber, natural	—	—	—	—	0.5	0.3
Silk k	—	—	—	—	1.3	5.0[2]
Cotton: yarn	2.9*	na	—	—	0.9	—
woven fabrics					6.8	
Rayon, woven fabrics					6.9u	
Wool: yarn	0.32	na				
woven fabrics	1.0[2]u	na				

f metric tons.   u incl. synthetic piece goods.   v million metres.

7. FUEL AND POWER

	Production		Exports		Imports	
Coal 'A'‡	—	—	—	—	—	—
Coke	—	—	—	—	—	—
Electricity h‡	1 145	490[1]	—	—	—	—
Natural gas i	750					
Oil, crude	60 923	33 740[1]	58 310	32 750[1]	—	—
Petroleum, refined	2 450	1 700[1]	47		6.9u	5.2[2]

h million kWh.   i million cu. metres.   ‡ thermal.

9. NON-FERROUS MINERALS AND METALS

	Production		Exports		Imports	
Platinum group metals k						
Asbestos: fibre	—	—	—	—	1.81[2]	0.92[2]
manufactured	—	—	—	—	0.21[2]	0.04
Aluminium	—	—	—	—	6.45	2.07
Copper, metal	—	—	—	—	1.14	0.31
Lead, metal	—	—	—	—	0.03[2]	0.06
Tin, metal	—	—	—	—	0.02	0.02
Zinc, metal	—	—	—	—		

k '000 fine troy oz.

10. CHEMICALS n AND FERTILIZERS

	Production		Exports		Imports	
Chemicals	—	—	—	—	na	1.5
Fertilizers: Potash	—	—	—	—	2.3	32.7
Sulphur	—	—	—	—	0.3	
					1.9	

n data not available for years 1953–5.

11. INDUSTRY

	Production		Exports		Imports	
Aircraft a						1.5
Beer b	41.0	17.9	—	—	11.7[2]	32.7
Cement	1 077.7	238.0	383.0	3.7		
Electrical engineering a					10.7	
Railway vehicles a					17.9	11.5[2]
Merchant ships g			na		0.6	1.4
Motor vehicles a					20.3	22.5

a million $ U.S.   b '000 hectolitres.   g '000 G.R.T.

IRISH REPUBLIC

After years of campaigning for home rule, Southern Ireland (or Eire) accepted dominion status in 1921 and left the British Commonwealth in 1949 to become an independent republic. The Irish Republic is a member of the European Free Trade Association and has applied (1971) to join the European Economic Community.

AREA: 68 893 sq. km. (26 600 sq. miles)

LAND USE: (percentage of total)

	1965
Arable and orchard	18.0
Permanent meadow and pasture	49.0
Forest and woodland	2.8
City areas, waste and other land (incl. rough grazing)	30.2

POPULATION: 2 884 002 (1966 census)
Largest city: DUBLIN, capital; population: 650 153 (1966)

Distribution of working population (1961)
Total working population: 1 108 108

U.N. group no.		Percentage
0	Agriculture, forestry, fishing and hunting	35.2
1	Mining and quarrying	0.9
2/3	Manufacturing	17.0
4	Construction	6.6
5	Electricity, gas, water and sanitary services	1.0
6	Commerce	14.8
7	Transport, storage and communications	5.2
8		18.8
9	Services	8.5

		Year(s)
Life expectancy at birth (years): male	68.1	1960–2 av.
female	71.9	
Infant mortality (per '000)	25.2	1965
Crude birth rate (per '000)	22.1	1965
Crude death rate (per '000)	11.5	1965
Accidental deaths (per 100 000 population) caused by motor vehicles	10.7	1965
due to other causes	25.2	1965
Population per physician	950	1961
Population per hospital bed	91	1966
School enrolment: age 5–19 years (percentage)	70	1963–4 av.
age over 19 years (per 100 000 population)	724	1963–5 av.

COMMUNICATIONS

	1965	Year(s)
Motor vehicles in use ('000s): private	258.5	1964
commercial	49.5	
Railway track (km.)	2346	1967
Mail per capita: domestic	93	1963–5 av.
foreign received	30	1963–5 av.
foreign sent	23	1963–4 av.
Telephones (per '000 population)	212	1967
Radio receivers (per '000 population)	92.4	1963–5 av.
Television sets (per '000 population)	35.64	1963–5 av.
Daily newspapers (per '000 population)	242	

r see coconut oil.

FINANCE

Currency unit: The Irish pound, at par with the £ sterling

Exchange rates	1965	1960	1938
Per $ U.S.	0.357	0.357	0.215

	1965	1955	1938
National Income (million $ U.S.)	2 249		
G.N.P. per capita ($ U.S.)	850		
Rate of increase of G.N.P. per capita	4		
Foreign trade (percentage of G.D.P.)	62		

TRADING

Total trade (in million $ U.S.)	1965	1955	1938
Exports (f.o.b.)	620	310	119
Imports (c.i.f.)	1 042	582	203

Main trading partners (percentage of total value)

Exports	1965	1955	1938		Imports	1965	1955	1938
U.K.	72	89	93		U.K.	55	62	(41)
Germany F.R.	5	3	4a		U.S.A.	24	12	(57)
Netherlands	4	1			Germany F.R.	7	8	(3)
France	3	1			Netherlands	3	3	(7)
Canada	3				France	3	3	(14)
Italy	1				Iran	2	na	

Distribution of trade (percentage of total value)

Exports	1965	1955	1938*
Food (livestock and meat)	55	62	72
(dairy products and eggs)	24	12	(57)
Manufactured goods (textiles and clothing)	7	8	(14)
Crude materials and fuels	3	5	(1)
Beer	2	9	
Imports			
Manufactured goods (machinery and transport equipment)	51	43	50
Food	16	18	(19)
Crude materials and fuels	15	23	(12)
Chemicals	9	6	na

a incl. Germany D.R. and Austria.

continued

---

4. VEGETABLE OILSEEDS AND OILS

	Production		Exports		Imports	
Castor oil	—	—	—	—	0.01	0.02
Copra	—	—	—	—	1.21	2.30
Coconut oil	—	—	—	—	0.21	0.94q
Cottonseed	—	—	—	—		
Cottonseed oil	20.00	10.67*	—	—	18.72	0.33
Groundnuts	—	—	—	—	0.27	
Groundnut oil	na	1.502*p	—	—		
Linseed	8.33	na	0.03		0.01	0.02[1]
Linseed oil			5.47		0.04	0.10
Olive oil	—	—	—	—	0.3	na r
Palm oil	—	—	—	—		
Sesame seed	7.80	14.70	0.68	5.53		

p flax grown for seed only.   q incl. groundnut oil and palm oil.   r see coconut oil.

5. LIVESTOCK‡, ANIMAL PRODUCTS, etc.

	Production		Exports		Imports	
Chickens d	4 398.0*	na	—	—	—	—
Cattle d	1 518.3	721.0*	—	—	—	—
Goats d	2 348.0	1 689.0[1]*	—	—	—	—
Sheep d	9 980.0	na	—	—	—	—
Horses d	168.7	na	0.2	4.1	—	—
Meat†: 'A'	86.7	na	0.2		—	—
'B'	5.9	na				
Butter	18.7*	5.41	—	—	0.3	0.2
Cheese	8.3*	na	—	2	0.8	
Eggs	14.3‡	5.41	—	—	0.3	
Fish	190.0*	na	4.6	5.3[2]	27.8*	
Hides/skins	6.6‡	na	2.8	3.6	0.1	
Wool d	7.0*	8.0*				

d no. in thousands.   t incomplete figure.

ISRAEL

Israel was established in 1948 as an independent sovereign state open to immigration by Jews from all countries of the world. The question of border demarcation with neighbouring Arab states led to persistent hostilities around Israel's borders, until in 1967, she was provoked into launching attacks on Jordan, the U.A.R. and Syria. This 'Six Days' War' terminated with a cease-fire negotiated by the U.N., and the territory under Israeli control increased to four times its former size. Sporadic fighting has continued and the area remains under the threat of another war.

AREA: 20 700 sq. km. (7 992 sq. miles) (1967—i.e. area within the boundaries defined by the 1948 armistice)

LAND USE: (percentage of total)

	1964	1955
Arable and orchard	19.9	17.6
Permanent meadow and pasture	33.9	9.7
Forest and woodland	4.6	3.0
City areas, waste and other land	41.6	69.7

POPULATION: 2 669 000 (1967 estimate)

During the period 1948–1967, 1 300 000 Jewish immigrants entered the country, thus doubling the population and creating an acute refugee problem.
Largest city: TEL AVIV-YAFO (Tel Aviv-Jaffa); population: 389 700 (1965)
Capital city: YERUSHALAYIM (Jerusalem); population: 195 700 (1966)

Distribution of working population:
Total working population: 912 400

U.N. group no.		Percentage
0	Agriculture, forestry, fishing and hunting	12.5
1/2/3	Mining, quarrying and manufacturing	24.5
4	Construction	10.1
5	Electricity, gas, water and sanitary services	12.1
6	Commerce	6.6
7	Transport, storage and communications	28.7
8	Services	3.8
9	Others	

		Year(s)
Life expectancy at birth (years): male / female	70.4 / 73.6a	1967
Infant mortality (per '000)	27.4	1965
Crude birth rate (per '000)	25.8	1965
Crude death rate (per '000)	6.3	1965
Accidental deaths (per 100 000 population)	12.3*	1965
caused by motor vehicles	22.5*b	1965
Population per physician	410	1965
Population per hospital bed	130	1966
School enrolment: age 5–19 years (percentage)	83	1963–4 av.
age over 19 years (per 100 000 population)	933c	1963–5 av.

a Jewish population only. b includes homicide and acts of war. c at universities and degree-granting institutions only.

COMMUNICATIONS

		Year(s)
Motor vehicles in use ('000s): private	62.7	1963–5 av.
commercial	35.2	1964
Railway track (km.)	692	1964
Mail per capita: domestic	67	1963–5 av.
foreign received	14	
foreign sent	12	1963–5 av.
Telephones (per '000 urban population)	11.3	1967
Radio receivers (per '000 population)	271	1963–5 av.
Television licences (per '000 population)	2.7	1963–5 av.
Daily newspapers (per '000 population)	145.5	1962–3 av

FINANCE

Currency unit: The Israeli pound

Exchange rates:	1965	1960	1954	1953
Per $ U.S.	3.0	1.8	1.8	1.0
Per £ sterling	8.4	5.01	5.01	2.8

		Year(s)
National income (million $ U.S.)	2736	1965
G.N.P. per capita ($ U.S.)	1160	1966
Rate of increase of G.N.P. per capita	6.5	1960–4 av.
Foreign trade (percentage of G.D.P.)	37	1963–5 av.

TRADING

Total trade (in million $ U.S.)		1965
Exports (f.o.b.)	406	
Imports (c.i.f.)	811	

Main trading partners (percentage of total value)

Exports	1965	1955		Imports	1965	1955
U.S.A.	14	19		U.S.A.	25	29
U.K.	12	21		U.K.	20	18
Germany F.R.	9	4		Germany F.R.	9	10
Netherlands	6	4		France	4	4
Switzerland	5	4		Italy	4	3
Belg./Lux.	4	4		Netherlands	4	2
Hong Kong	4			Belg./Lux.	3	1

Distribution of trade (percentage of total value)

Exports	1965	1955
Manufactured goods	54	
(cut diamonds)	(36)	(23)
(textiles and clothing)	(9)	(5)
Food	25	41
Chemicals	6	2
Imports		
Manufactured goods	62	42
(machinery and transport equipment)	(28)	(13)
Crude materials and fuels	19	31
Food	11	22
Chemicals	5	4

PRODUCTION, EXPORTS AND IMPORTS

Years: 1963–5 average and 1953–5 average   Units: '000 metric tons unless otherwise indicated

1. CEREALS, etc.

	Production		Exports		Imports	
Barley	73.3	65.3	—	—	64.4	26.9
Maize (corn)	5.0	20.0	—	—	176.0	7.9
Millets/sorghum	623.0	15.0	—	—	175.7	45.1
Oats	—	1.3	—	—	—	—
Potatoes	108.3	73.0	7.7	—	4.9*	15.0
Rice	—	—	—	—	14.9	3.8
Rye	—	—	—	—	2.2	9.5
Wheat	110.7	33.3	1.7²	—	224.8	323.5

2. FRUIT, etc.

	Production		Exports		Imports	
Apples	53.7	2.7p	0.3	—	0.1p	—
Bananas	48.3	13.0	16.1	—	—	—
Dates/figs	3.0	5.3q	—	—	0.5	0.3
Grapes	74.0	25.7	0.5	—	12.2	0.2
Lemons	33.0	16.0	12.2	—	4.7	—
Oranges	625.3	362.7	410.1	—	—	—
Other citrus fruit	132.3	59.7	213.8	—	—	—
Olives	3.0	—	81.2	—	40.1	—
Peaches/apricots	9.7	na	—	—	3.1	—

2. FRUIT, etc.—continued

	Production		Exports		Imports	
Plums	11.7	na	—	—	—	—
Raisins	0.4	na	—	—	0.4²	1.0
Tomatoes	102.3	60.3	15.8	3.3	0.4²	—
Wine b	321.0					

b '000 hectolitres.   p incl. pears and quince.   q incl. avocado pears.

3. BEVERAGES, FOREST PRODUCTS, etc.

	Production		Exports		Imports	
Cocoa	—	—	—	—	1.1	1.0
Coffee	—	—	—	—	5.8	1.1
Sugar: beet	267.0	17.0*				
raw	36.5	na			83.4	61.5
Tea	—	—	—	—	2.2	0.7
Tobacco: leaf	0.9	2.8				
cigars	4.0c	1.4c				
cigarettes	2 947.0c	2 003.3c			0.2¹	
tobacco/snuff						
Softwood j	8.8	0.9			468.9	288.6
Hardwood j	36.3	10.8			151.6	27.1
Wood pulp	7.9	0.3*			72.8	9.3
Newsprint	38.0	6.8*			39.2	13.8
Other paper	3.1					

j '000 cu. metres of roundwood equivalent.

continued

PRODUCTION, EXPORTS AND IMPORTS

Years: 1963–5 average and 1953–5 average   Units: '000 metric tons unless otherwise indicated

1. CEREALS, etc.

	Production		Exports		Imports	
Barley	585.3	219.3	24.2	—	28.4	23.3
Maize (corn)	—	—	—	—	103.9	199.1
Millets/sorghum	—	—	—	—	81.3	0.2
Oats	335.0	538.3	0.6	35.2	0.5	1.6
Potatoes	1 714.3	2 397.3	57.8	—	2.4	2.5
Rye	1.0	3.0	—	—	—	—
Wheat	268.7	440.0	19.1	—	244.5	161.6

2. FRUIT, etc.

	Production		Exports		Imports	
Apples	26.7	na	0.1	—	15.2	4.8
Bananas	—	—	—	—	14.2¹	6.8
Dates	—	—	—	—	0.2¹	—
Grapes	—	—	—	—	1.4	0.9
Lemons	—	—	—	—	0.81	0.6
Oranges	—	—	—	—	19.1	14.9
Other citrus fruit	—	—	—	—	1.3¹	1.0
Pears	—	—	—	—	3.5	2.7
Plums	—	—	—	—	2.7	0.6
Raisins	—	—	—	—	7.3	9.6
Tomatoes	11.3	2.0²	—	0.3†	39.9	22.7

b '000 hectolitres.

3. BEVERAGES, FOREST PRODUCTS, etc.

	Production		Exports		Imports	
Cocoa	—	—	—	—	8.2	5.6
Coffee	—	—	—	—	0.4	0.4
Sugar: beet raw	868.0	704.7	19.1	—	45.9	69.8
Tea	134.7	109.7	0.1*	0.3	11.3	10.3
Tobacco: leaf	—	—	—	—	6.0	6.9
cigars	—	0.2²				
cigarettes	5 377.0e	6 169.3e				
tobacco/snuff	0.8	1.1	0.5²		—	0.2²
Softwood j	278.7	112.0	1.3		473.0	352.4
Hardwood j	48.7	123.0	2.1		60.0	34.8
Wood pulp	31.6²	10.0*	0.9		36.1	28.3
Newsprint	8.0*	—			36.3	26.7
Other paper	80.0*	43.8	14.3	32.7*m	48.5	36.5*

j '000 cu. metres of roundwood equivalent.   m metal content.   p scrap.

4. VEGETABLE OILSEEDS AND OILS

	Production		Exports		Imports	
Castor oil	—	—	—	—	0.15	0.10
Coconut oil	na	na	—	—	3.68	6.37
Copra	na	na	—	—	1.03	1.71
Cottonseed	na	na	—	—	1.59	na
Cottonseed oil	na	na	—	—	1.82	3.26
Groundnuts	na	na	0.32	—	2.16	1.00
Groundnut oil	na	na	—	—	1.30	0.83
Linseed	na	na	0.27	—	1.56	1.00
Linseed oil	na	na	—	—	1.18	1.17
Olive oil	na	na	—	—	0.07	0.06†
Palm kernels	na	na	0.14	—	2.68	1.17
Palm kernel oil	na	na	—	—	0.45	1.74
Palm oil	na	na	—	—	3.62	2.24
Soya beans	na	na	—	—	0.39	—
Soya bean oil	na	na	—	—	0.95	—
Sunflower seed oil	na	na	—	—	0.93	—

5. LIVESTOCK; ANIMAL PRODUCTS, etc.

	Production		Exports		Imports	
Chickens d	10 366.0	13 500.0				
Cattle d	5 060.3	4 461.3	684.5	463.6	129.7	0.6
dairy cows d	1 423.3	1 282.0				
Goats d	41.0*	46.0¹				
Sheep d	4 885.0	3 104.0	292.1	na	259.8	na
Horses d	180.7	313.0				
Pigs d	1 159.0	879.7	4.2	0.4	19.7	19.7
Bacon/ham	465.0	341.7	27.3	7.2		
Meat: 'A' / 'B'	61.8	42.3	85.1	46.9		
Butter	62.7	57.0	19.5	1.7	1.8	1.2²
Cheese	15.0	0.2	0.3	0.9	0.2	2.7
Eggs	44.2	54.3	0.3	8.8	—	3.2²
Fish	31.8²	21.4²	10.5	3.7¹*	15.7	4.4¹*
Hides/skins	3 011.3	2 433.7	157.1	20.8	0.8	16.8
Milk	3 019.8	13.0	5.4²			4.3²
Wool	8.0	5.0	7.1	4.9	4.4	3.0

d no. in thousands.   p incl. fish landed by Irish vessels in foreign ports.   p incl. fish landed by Irish

6. FIBRES, TEXTILES, etc.

	Production		Exports		Imports	
Agaves (sisal etc.)	—	—	—	—	6.3	1.1²
Cotton lint	—	—	—	—	5.7	2.7
Cotton: yarn	1.2		1.2		0.7	3.2²
woven fabrics					9.4	6.9
Flax fibre	—	—	—	—	3.9	4.1
Hemp fibre	13.0					
Jute	—	—	—	—		
Rubber, natural	na	na			4.8	4.8
Silk	—	—	—	—	41.6	21.1
Cotton: yarn	5.7	na	1.0²		4.0	1.9
woven fabrics	3.6*	1.6			4.0	2.0

continued

6. FIBRES, TEXTILES, etc.—continued

	Production		Exports		Imports	
Rayon: fibre/yarn	0.8	0.4	—	—	1.0	0.8t
woven fabrics	7.3	5.1	0.8	—	1.6	1.6
Wool: yarn	7.7	6.7t	na	—	2.0	0.9
woven fabrics					0.9·q	0.5q

r metric tons.   g excl. blankets.   r incl. spun yarn.   t incl. spun yarn.

7. FUEL AND POWER

	Production		Exports		Imports	
Coal: 'A' / 'B'	213	200			1 369p	1 745
Electricity: total	3 221	2 110				
hydro	793	1 600†				
thermal	2 428	490†				
Oil, crude	—	—			1 800	1 020¹
Petroleum, refined	1 713	1 110¹	220	—	590	

h '000 kWh.   h incl. imports for bunkering.

8. IRON AND STEEL

	Production		Exports		Imports	
Iron ore	—	—	3	—	1	6
Pig iron	—	—	—	—	20	3
Steel ingots/castings	20	27	36	—	25	—
Iron/steel scrap	48.5		0.3†		39.9	22.7

9. NON-FERROUS MINERALS AND METALS

	Production		Exports		Imports	
Gold k	—	—	—	—	12.93‡	0.70
Silver: bullion k	1.41‡	136.73	1.20‡		76.14‡	1.95
bullion/coins etc.	—	—	—	—	2.03	3.99
Asbestos: fibre/manufactured	—	—	—	—	14.18	5.65
Aluminium	0.04	3.11p	0.04	3.11p	7.49	3.68
Copper: ore/metal	1.28m	1.65m	0.60	2.23	0.57	1.41
Lead: ore/metal	na	na			0.13	0.54
Magnesium, metal	—	—			0.13	0.02
Nickel, metal	—	—			0.06	
Tin, metal	—	—			0.15	
Titanium minerals	—	—			1.97	
Zinc: ore/metal	0.48m	1.97m	3.59	—	3.45	1.66

k '000 fine troy oz.   m metal content.   p scrap.

10. CHEMICALS AND FERTILIZERS

	Production		Exports		Imports	
Organic chemicals:						
Benzene	na				na	na
Butadiene	—	—	—	—	0.1	na
Ethylene	—	—	—	—	na	na
Methanol	—	—	0.32	—	0.83	na
Phenol	—	—	0.27	—	na	na
Phthalic anhydride	—	—	—	—	na	na
Styrene monomer	—	—	0.14	—	0.41	na
Urea	—	—	—	—	na	na
Inorganic chemicals:						
Ammonia	—	—			5.1	na
Carbon black	—	—			2.3	na
Chlorine	—	—			0.4	na
Nitric acid	—	—			0.4	na
Sodium carbonate	—	—			13.9	na
Sodium hydroxide	—	—			3.0	na
Sulphuric acid	189.0¹		2	—	2.7	na

11. INDUSTRY

	Production		Exports		Imports	
Aircraft a	—	—	1.1	0.3	12.2	1.3
Alcoholic beverages: beer b	3 440.0	3 124.7	21.1a	14.8a	9.2a	3.9a
spirits b	47.2¹p	54.6¹q				
Cement	1 077.7	594.7	259.3	29.3	32.3	45.0
Electrical engineering a	—	—	—	—	48.6	17.4²
Railway vehicles a	59.3²	40.1	11.2	1.2²	1.5	3.7
Merchant ships a	—	—	—	—	0.6	9.3
Motor vehicles: commercial a	20.0¹		0.3a	4.7a	56.4a	31.1a
private a	4.8					

a million $U.S.   b '000 hectolitres.   p 1960 figure.   q assembly of imported parts.

continued

na: data not available.   — negligible or nil.   * estimate.   ¹ one year only.   ² two year average.   ‡ see appendix.   † re-exports.   d no. in thousands.   g '000 G.R.T.

ISRAEL continued

PRODUCTION, EXPORTS AND IMPORTS continued

	Production	Exports	Imports
9. NON-FERROUS MINERALS AND METALS			
Diamondsa	—	135.85†p	16.23† 114.18q 14.06
Asbestos, fibre	—	—	8.44
Aluminium	—	—	8.57
Antimony, metal	—	—	0.19 0.38
Copper, ore	7.93m	na	na 3.65²
Lead, metal	—	—	1.00
Magnesium, metal	—	—	4.63
magnesite	—	—	0.08
Tin, metal	—	—	1.27
Zinc, metal	0.1	0.11	0.48 0.01

a million $ U.S. m metal content. p excl. industrial diamonds and dust. q excl. dust.

	Production	Exports	Imports
10. CHEMICALSn AND FERTILIZERS			
Organic chemicals:			
Benzene	4.0	—	na
Butadiene	0.4	—	na
Ethylene	—	—	4.9
Methanol	—	—	na
Phenol	—	—	na
Phthalic anhydride	—	—	0.3
Styrene monomer	—	—	na
Urea	—	—	na
Inorganic chemicals:			
Ammonia	29.5	0.1	19.5
Carbon black	3.0	1.4	0.3
Chlorine	8.7²	0.1	1.1
Nitric acid	12.9	—	0.3
Sodium carbonate	—	—	19.2
Sodium hydroxide	8.6	0.8	81.6
Sulphuric acid	154.7	—	9.1
Plastics:			
Polyamides	2.6	—	1.0
Polyethylene	1.9	0.9	0.3
Polyvinyl chloride	—	—	25.0¹*
Fertilizers:			
Phosphates	309.7	212.2	0.3
Potash	226.2*w	6.7	1.0
Sulphur	—	—	56.4

n data not available for years 1953–5. w K₂O content.

	Production	Exports	Imports
11. INDUSTRY			
Aircrafta	—	—	—
Alcoholic beverages: beerb	264.0 143.0	1.4	6.1t
spiritsb	30.0¹t 38.8¹t	0.1a	1.7
Cement	1 127.3 564.0	125.3	12.3
Electrical engineeringa	—	—	25
Railway vehiclesa	—	1.5	42.7 35.3
Machine toolsa	—	—	1.3 5.0
Merchant shipsg	1.0	—	54.0
Motor vehicles commercial dp	4.3 2.3	1.0a	44.6a 1.3a
private dp	2.8 0.6	—	—

a million $ U.S. b '000 hectolitres. d no. in thousands. g '000 G.R.T. t incomplete figure. p assembly of imported parts. r 1960 data. q 1967 data.

	Production	Exports	Imports
4. VEGETABLE OILSEEDS AND OILS			
Castor seed	na	—	0.28
Castor oil	na	—	0.02
Copra	—	—	4.88
Coconut oil	27.30	1.01	8.57
Cottonseed	2.70*	2.18	na
Cottonseed oil	9.80	3.04	1.05
Groundnuts	8.63	—	0.21
Groundnut oil	na	0.16	3.08
Linseed	—	—	0.09
Linseed oil	2.00* 2.00	—	0.02
Olive oil	—	0.11	0.27
Palm oil	—	—	0.02²
Rapeseed	1.30 0.50	—	1.70²
Sesame seed	—	—	220.70
Soya beans	—	—	16.98
Soya bean oil	na 1.00	23.37	1.19*
Sunflower seed	2.67	—	0.01

	Production	Exports	Imports
5. LIVESTOCK‡, ANIMAL PRODUCTS, etc.			
Chickensd	7 216.7 4 475.0	—	—
Cattled	225.3 94.7	0.3	2.2
Dairy cowsd	119.3 61.0	—	—
Goatsd	158.0 116.7	—	0.3
Sheepd	192.7 83.3	—	—
Horsesd	19.7 12.0*	0.4	19.5
Meatt; A	23.3 3.0†	1.7	0.3
B	74.9 7.0	0.8	1.1
Butter	3.0t	—	0.3
Cheese	21.0	0.4	19.2
Eggs	69.0 23.8	9.7	81.6
Fish	18.6u 9.2a	—	9.1
Milk	335.7 150.0	—	1.0
Wool	0.2	0.2†	—

	Production	Exports	Imports
6. FIBRES, TEXTILES, etc.			
Abaca	—	—	—
Agaves (sisal etc.)	0.6	—	0.3
Cotton lint	17.0	2.5	1.0
Flax fibre	—	—	10.3
Jute	—	—	0.2²
Rubber, natural	—	—	7.1
Cotton: yarn	21.0	7.5	1.2
woven fabrics	9.8	0.1†	—
Rayon, fibre/yarn	—	—	5.4
Non-cellulosic fibre/yarn	1.4	0.4	3.6
woven fabrics	4.2	0.5	0.4
Wool: yarn	1.5¹	—	na

	Production	Exports	Imports
7. FUEL AND POWER			
Coal 'A't	—	—	12
Coke	—	—	8
Electricity ht	3 643	—	—
Natural gasi	40	—	—
Oil, crude	183	—	2 960
Petroleum, refined	3 120	460	360

h million kWh. i excl. aviation spirit. t thermal.

	Production	Exports	Imports
8. IRON AND STEEL			
Pig iron	na	—	28
Iron/steel scrap	na	1	—

d no. in thousands. r government inspected meat only. t factory produce only. u incl. fish landed by Israeli vessels in foreign ports and by foreign vessels in Israeli ports.

*na: data not available. — negligible or nil. ¹ one year only. ² two year average. * estimate. † re-exports. ‡ see appendix.*

ITALY   EUROPE

Italy was declared a republic in 1946 as the result of a national referendum; this terminated a long-established monarchy in which the power of the monarch had already been relinquished. Italy is a member of the European Economic Community.

AREA: 301 224 sq. km. (116 303 sq. miles) including Vatican City

LAND USE: (percentage of total)
		1965
Arable and orchard		50.8
Permanent meadow and pasture		17.1
Forest and woodland		20.2
City areas, waste and other land		11.9

POPULATION: 52 334 000 (1967 estimate)
Largest city: ROMA (Rome), capital: population: 2 484 737 (1965)

Distribution of working population (1965)
Total working population: 19 920 000

U.N. group no.		Percentage
0	Agriculture, forestry, fishing and hunting	25.1
1	Mining and quarrying	0.7
2/3	Manufacturing	28.3
4	Construction	10.6
5	Electricity, gas, water and sanitary services	0.8
6	Commerce	13.9
7	Transport, storage and communications	14.1
8	Services	1.3
9	Others	

	male	female	
Life expectancy at birth (years):	67.2	72.3	1960–2 av.
Infant mortality (per '000)	36		1965
Crude birth rate (per '000)	19.2		1965
Crude death rate (per '000)	10		1965
Accidental deaths (per 100 000 population)	20.8		1965
caused by motor vehicles	22.4		1965
due to other causes			1965
Population per physician	570		1966
Population per hospital bed	100		1963–4 av.
School enrolment: age 5–19 years (percentage)	63		1963–5 av.
age over 19 years (per 100 000 population)	524		1963–5 av.

COMMUNICATIONS
Motor vehicles in use ('000s): private	4 685.4		1963–5 av.
commercial	634.5		1963–5 av.
Railway track (km.)	21 043		1964
Mail per capita: domestic	101		1963–5 av.
foreign received	7		
foreign sent	7		
Telephones (per '000 urban population)	12.4		1967
Radio licences (per '000 population)	199		1963–5 av.
Television licences (per '000 population)	101		1963–5 av.
Daily newspapers (per '000 population)	101		1961

FINANCE

Currency unit: The lira

Exchange rates:	1965	1960	1950	1938
Per $ U.S.	624.7	620.6	625	19.0
Per £ sterling	1750.5	1740	1750	87.4

		Year(s)
National Income (million $ U.S.)	45 549	1965
G.N.P. per capita ($ U.S.)	1030	1966
Rate of increase: G.N.P. per capita	26	1960–4 av.
Foreign trade (percentage of G.D.P.)		1963–5 av.

TRADING

Total trade (in million $ U.S.)	1965	1955	1938
Exports (f.o.b.)	7 200	1 857	553
Imports (c.i.f.)	7 378	2 711	593

Main trading partners (percentage of total value)

Exports	1965	1955	1938
Germany F.R.	21	13	19d
France	10	9	7
U.S.A.	9	7	5
Switzerland	5	7	5
Netherlands	5	5	6
U.K.	4	3	1

Imports	1965	1955	1938
Germany F.R.	15	13	27d
U.S.A.	15	17	12
France	10	5	2
Kuwait	5	5	
U.K.	4	5	6
Netherlands	4	3	1
Argentina		2	2

Distribution of trade (percentage of total value)

Exports	1965	1955	1938*
Manufactured goods	70	55	na
(machinery and transport equipment)	(30)	(20)	(11)
(textile and clothing)	(15)	(15)	(14)
(shoes)	(3)	(1)	(na)
Food (fruit and vegetables)	11	20	23
Crude materials and fuels	9	16	na
Chemicals	8	7	na

Imports	1965	1955	1938
Crude materials and fuels	37	48	na
(mineral fuels)	(16)	(20)	(22)
(textile fibres)	(15)	(21)	(12)
Manufactured goods	33	27	na
(machinery and transport equipment)	(21)	(11)	(na)
Food	21	16	9
Chemicals	7	5	na

d incl. Germany D.R.

PRODUCTION, EXPORTS AND IMPORTS
Years: 1963–5 average and 1953–5 average   Units: '000 metric tons unless otherwise indicated

	Production		Exports		Imports	
1. CEREALS, etc.						
Barley	242.3	294.3	1.3	—	77.4	—
Maize (corn)	3 665.3	3 123.3	333.3	41.7	732.2	—
Millets/sorghum	23.3	—	2.9	1.4	4 097.4	168.7
Oats	513.7	558.7	0.3	—	16.8	3.8
Potatoes	3 919.0	3 244.7	204.3	175.8	164.9	42.2
Rice	565.7	887.3	106.0	203.3	26.5	118.0
Rye					2.6	0.9
Sweet potatoes/yams	34.7	—	33.4	0.5	3.1	111.6
Wheat	8 829.7	8 614.7	—	—	593.4	713.0
2. FRUIT, etc.						
Apples	2 300.7	976.0	447.8	231.5	0.4	0.1
Apricots	65.3	34.6	na	13.8	—	—
Bananas	—	—	—	—	213.8	38.9
Cherries	215.3	125.7	0.4	18.6	5.9	6.7
Dates	1.0*	—	na	0.1	—	—
Figs	269.0	327.0	na	4.4	1.2	1.9
Grapes	9 910.3	8 563.7	197.3	61.4	—	—
Lemons	591.7	342.3	293.0	180.0	0.2	—
Oranges	1 141.3	689.7	199.5	176.9	0.9	0.2¹
Other citrus fruit	—	—	0.5	¹	—	—
Olives	2 323.2	1 631.0	—	—	—	—
Peaches	1 302.0	448.1	107.2	—	0.4	—
Pears	1 001.7	401.3	146.1	59.8	—	—
Plums	128.0	95.5	0.4	18.5	0.4	—
Raisins	1.7	2.1	—	—	9.6	11.9
Tomatoes	3 002.3	1 510.7	—	—	—	—
Wineb	63 126.0	53 809.0	2 274.4	1 190.7	77.5	51.0

b '000 hectolitres.

	Production		Exports		Imports	
3. BEVERAGES, FOREST PRODUCTS, etc.						
Cocoa	—	—	—	—	18.2	—
Coffee	—	—	0.3	—	69.5	—
Sugar: beet	8 309	7 163	3.6	—	23.0	—
raw.	1 080	948*	—	—	426.2	0.9
Tea	—	—	—	—	2.2	—
Tobacco: leaf	73	69	6.7	12.4	20.5	8.4
cigarettes	241e	210e				
cigars	57 783e	36 602e			0.3²	
tobacco/snuff	4	6			0.7	
Softwood	1 438	2 145	12.0	1.6	5 301.0	2 862.9
Hardwood	15 079	9 893	17.7	37.5	1 895.7	277.7
Wood pulp	639	345	24.1	10.6	876.6	277.8
Newsprint	363	129	4.9		9.8	21.7
Other paper	1 697	611	40.0	13.3	263.3	35.3

	Production		Exports		Imports	
4. VEGETABLE OILSEEDS AND OILS						
Castor seed	—	—	0.03	—	9.65	7.07
Castor oil	—	—	—	0.07	0.16	0.05
Copra	—	—	—	—	24.88	7.23
Coconut oil	—	—	3.6	0.63	15.72	25.65p
Cottonseed	8.00	na	—	0.012	—	2.07
Cottonseed oil	7.00	na	0.06	1.30	0.68	0.78
Groundnuts	—	—	0.05	0.04	0.03	18.17
Groundnut oil	4.33	na	0.17	0.10	124.63	3.94
Linseed	—	—	—	—	0.70	23.37
Linseed oil	—	—	—	—	4.52	23.84²
					16.51	

b incl. palm kernel oil.

continued

*na: data not available. — negligible or nil. ¹ one year only. ² two year average. * estimate. p see appendix.*

The Ivory Coast, formerly a territory of French West Africa, became an independent republic in 1960.

AREA: 322 463 sq. km. (124 300 sq. miles)

LAND USE: (percentage of total)

	1965
Arable and orchard	6.4
Permanent meadow and pasture	na
Forest and woodland, including rough grazing	74.4
City areas, waste and other land	na

POPULATION: 4 010 000 (1967 U.N. estimate)
Largest city: ABIDJAN, capital; population: 250 800 (1963)
Total working population: 1 850 000

Distribution of working population (1964)

U.N. group no.		Percentage
0	Agriculture, forestry, fishing and hunting	86.4
1/2/3	Mining and quarrying	0.2
	Manufacturing	0.8
4	Construction	0.9
5	Electricity, gas, water and sanitary services	0.4
6	Commerce	6.8
7	Transport, storage and communications	2.3
8	Services	2.2

		Year(s)
Life expectancy at birth (years)	35	1957–8 av.
Population per physician	19 080	1965
Population per hospital bed	510a	1966
Persons of working age 15–19 years (percentage)	33	1963–4 av.
age over 19 years (per 100 000 population)	37	1963–4 av.

a government hospitals only.

COMMUNICATIONS

	1965	Year(s)
Motor vehicles in use ('000s): private	28.0	1963–5av.
commercial	20.7	1963–5av.
Railway track (km.)	652	1965
Telephones (per '000 urban population)	0.5	1967
Radio receivers (per '000 population)	16	1963–5 av.
Television sets (per '000 population)	0.8	1963–5 av.
Daily newspapers (per '000 population)	3.5	1962–4 av.

FINANCE

Currency unit: The franc CFA

Exchange rates	1965	1960
Per $ U.S.	246.85	246.85
Per £ sterling	691.18	691.18

	Year	
National Income (million $U.S.)	1964	706
G.N.P. per capita ($U.S.)	1966	220

TRADING

Total trade (in million $U.S.)	1965	1955
Exports (f.o.b.)	277	146
Imports (c.i.f.)	236	109

Main trading partners (percentage of total value)

Exports	1965	Imports	1965
France	38	France	62
U.S.A.	16	Germany F.R.	6
Italy	9	U.S.A.	5
Netherlands	7	Italy	3
Germany F.R.	7	Belg./Lux.	3
U.K.	5	Morocco.	2
Algeria	3	Netherlands	2

Distribution of trade (percentage of total value)

Exports	1965	Imports	1965
Food	63	Manufactured goods	68
(coffee)	(38)	(machinery and transport equipment)	(28)
(cocoa)	(18)	(textiles and clothing)	(16)
Crude materials	31	Food	14
(hardwood)	(27)	Crude materials and fuels	7
		(petroleum products)	(5)
		Alcoholic beverages	3

PRODUCTION, EXPORTS AND IMPORTS

Years: 1963–5 average   Units: '000 metric tons unless otherwise indicated
Note—1953–5 data are not available

1. CEREALS, etc.

	Production	Exports	Imports
Cassava	1 120.0	—	—
Maize (corn)	172.7	—	—
Millets/sorghum	82.3	—	—
Potatoes	—	0.22†	na
Rice	236.3	0.2	53.9
Sweet potatoes	—	—	—
yams	1 887.3	—	—
Wheat	—	—	45.6

2. FRUIT, etc.

	Production	Exports	Imports
Apples	—	—	na
Bananas	147.0	129.2	na
Coconuts a	10.0*	na	na
Grapes	—	—	na
Oranges	—	—	na
Pineapples	45.3*	na	325.0
Wine b	—	—	—

3. BEVERAGES, FOREST PRODUCTS, etc.

	Production	Exports	Imports
Cocoa	114.4	116.8	—
Coffee	244.7	190.7	—
Sugar, raw	—	—	29.0
Tobacco: leaf	2.7	0.1	0.9
Hardwood j	7 731.3*	—	0.4
Newsprint	—	—	0.72a
Other paper	—	—	3.12a

j '000 cu. metres of roundwood equivalent.

4. VEGETABLE OILSEEDS AND OILS

	Production	Exports	Imports
Copra	0.12	—	2.7
Coconut oil	na	—	5.7
Cottonseed a	5.08	—	226.7
Cottonseed oil	6.00	—	—
Groundnuts a	1.97	—	12.5
Groundnut oil	0.02	—	0.1
Palm kernels	12.71	—	18.0
Palm oil	0.84	—	—
Sesame seed	1.13a	0.8	na

5. LIVESTOCK‡, ANIMAL PRODUCTS, etc.

	Production	Exports	Imports
Cattle d	316.7	—	na
Goats d	660.0	—	na
Sheep d	527.3	—	na
Horses d	82.3*	—	—
Pigs d	100.0*	—	—
Meat‡: 'A'	7.0	—	—
Butter	—	—	0.6
Cheese	—	—	0.4
Eggs	2.2*	—	na
Fish	51.7	—	2.4
Milk	14.7	1.4	na

d no. in thousands.

6. FIBRES, TEXTILES, etc.

	Production	Exports	Imports
Cotton lint.	3.0	1.3	—
Rubber: natural	2.0	1.6	—
Cotton: yarn	—	—	0.3
woven fabrics	—	—	6.2

7. FUEL AND POWER

	Production	Exports	Imports
Electricity h: total	186		
hydro	115		
thermal	71		
Oil, crude.	—	—	67
Petroleum, refined.	—	7	237

h million kWh.

9. NON-FERROUS MINERALS AND METALS

	Production	Exports	Imports
Diamonds j	192.67*	113.6	1.77a
Manganese, ore	151.75	130.42	—

a million $ U.S.   j '000 carats.

11. INDUSTRY

	Production	Exports	Imports
Aircraft a	—	—	—
Alcoholic beverages a	5.0*	—	—
Cement	—	—	—
Electrical engineering a	—	—	—
Railway vehicles a	—	—	—
Merchant ships g	—	—	—
Motor vehicles a	—	—	—

PRODUCTION, EXPORTS AND IMPORTS *continued*

4. VEGETABLE OILSEEDS AND OILS *continued*

	Production		Exports		Imports	
Olive oil	457.67	271.00n	11.26	10.35	75.31	20.71
Palm kernels	na	na	—	—	1.06	0.10
Palm kernel oil	na	na	0.04	0.07	5.63	—
Palm oil	na	na	0.01	1.80	29.54	18.81
Rapeseed	8.30	9.30	1.31	0.02	95.05	2.60
Rapeseed oil	1.13	0.67	—	—	0.59	3.36
Sesame seed	na	na	—	—	30.20	11.43
Soya beans	na	na	—	—	369.73	—
Soya bean oil	3.33	4.67	0.22	—	3.80	9.31
Sunflower seed	na	na	0.01	0.03	64.00	2.74
Sunflower seed oil	na	na	0.03	0.04q	2.07	1.18q
Tung oil	na	na	—	—	0.97	0.58

n oil extracted by machine only.   q incl. other minor vegetable oils.   r see coconut oil.

5. LIVESTOCK‡, ANIMAL PRODUCTS, etc.

	Production		Exports		Imports	
Chickens d	106 000‡	75 500*				
Cattle d	8 981	9 014‡	—	—	670.5	92.0
Sheep d	4 751	4 912‡				
Goats d	1 247	1 890‡	0.3	—	181.2	na
Pigs d	7 828	9 819‡				
Horses d	352	664‡				
Bacon/ham‡	5 041	4 057²	7.7	0.2	60.1	57.0
Meat‡: 'A'	849	600²	1.3	0.2	1.0	36.0
'B'	500	212	0.8	0.3	298.5	11.9
Butter	69	63			10.8	7.3
Cheese	373	317	23.6	17.9	33.9	22.9
Eggs	447	314²	0.5	0.1	61.8	23.8
Milk	8 982	5 507²u	3.2	1.1*	37.7	112.3†
Wool: fibre	298	254	1.3*	0.7*	288.1*	8.2*
Hides/skins	6	8	2.6	16.6²	4.4	52.3²
			1.1		77.9	45.2

d no. in thousands.   s incl. imports for re-export.   u excl. milk fed to livestock.

6. FIBRES, TEXTILES, etc.

	Production		Exports		Imports	
Abaca	—	—	—	—	0.8	1.3
Agaves (sisal etc.).	4.7	10.7	—	4.5	24.9	6.4
Cotton lint.	0.2	3.0	1.0	0.1	212.8	152.3
Flax fibre	11.2	50.2	0.4	25.0	17.8	2.8
Hemp fibre	—	—	0.1*	—	7.9	0.9
Jute	—	—	0.1†	2	38.2	53.1
Rubber: natural	109.3	—	125.1	345.3	49.0	54.2
synthetic	588.8²	1 311.3	1 121.7		3 546.0	309.3
Silk f	197.5	158.6	21.9	12.7	0.7	0.4
Cotton: yarn	120.3	108.0	7.3	12.0	16.2	2.2
woven fabrics	200.1	120.8	76.7	13.1	7.1	1.2
Rayon: fibre/yarn	25.3	20.9	22.7	14.0	3.8	0.3
woven fabrics						
Non-cellulosic	95.2	6.7	41.9	2.0	6.9	0.3
fibre/yarn	165.3	na	11.0	27.7	1.0	1.0
Wool: yarn	77.1	74.0	56.6		2.7	

f metric tons.   s incl. imports for re-export.

7. FUEL AND POWER

	Production		Exports		Imports	
Coal‡ 'A'‡	483	1 130	10	4	10 732	9 524
'B'‡	593	420	123		40	56
Coke	na	na			437	48
Electricity h: total	75 770	35 380¹				
hydro	42 675	30 510¹	670	402	6 093	734
nuclear	2 078	—	12	9	800	231
thermal	31 017	4 870¹				
Natural gas i	7 580	2 964¹	100	15	992	135
Oil, crude	2 273	2 601¹	3	1	3 864	1 597
Petroleum, refined	53 896	15 470¹	259	43	419	104
Uranium	—	—	11 793	4 990¹	17 000¹	5 90¹

h million kWh.   i million cu. metres.   † incl. geothermal.

8. IRON AND STEEL

	Production		Exports		Imports	
Iron ore	468m	599m			56 330	17 000¹
Pig iron	4 375	1 491			2 317	5 90¹
Steel ingots/steel	10 877	4 367	670	402	6 093	734
castings	31 017	4 870¹	100	15	992	135
Iron/steel scrap	7 580	2 964¹	3	1	3 864	1 597
Iron/steel products a	53 896	15 470¹	259	43	419	104

a million $ U.S.   m metal content.

9. NON-FERROUS MINERALS AND METALS

	Production		Exports		Imports	
Gold k, ore.	—	—	—	—	—	—
Platinum group	—	8.60m			1 763.30†p	9.70r
metals d	—	—	22.11†	0.29†	69.05	4.87
Silver k, ore	—	—	0.33r	3.12	40.87	6 429.30r
Asbestos: fibre	1 061.00m	861.70m	13.71	0.82	16.95	12.00
manufactured	65.86	24.71	44.85	14.84	na	0.82
						continued

9. NON-FERROUS MINERALS AND METALS—*continued*

	Production		Exports		Imports	
Mica	—	—	0.11†	0.01†	2.07	4.04
Aluminium: bauxite	255.03	297.55	1.55	31.86	402.78	100.57
alumina.	259.83q	na	14.40u	13.08	5.63q	0.05
aluminium	110.33	58.16	37.34		95.01	16.96
metal	10.35m	na	0.01	0.16	0.02¹	0.64
Antimony: ore.	—	—	—	—	0.08	0.01
metal	0.28	0.20	1.19†	0.37†	75.13	21.53
Cadmium:	—	—	4.43†		15.66	4.25
metal	—	—	1.89		0.57	2.82
Cobalt, metal	—	—	37.15†	6.02†	246.75	108.10
Copper: ore	2.18m	0.26m	4.84	8.97	21.03	3.35
metal	—	0.40	1.63	0.83	65.54	20.78
Lead: ore	33.89m	44.78m				
metal	41.76	39.04	10.29	4.36	0.87	4.40
Magnesium:	920.00	na	0.09	0.31	44.67	17.80
dolomite	5.55	1.99x	8.74	2.12	9.10	71.35t
magnesite	46.96	48.84	0.82†	0.01	128.83t	3.82
metal/salts	—	—	5.58	0.91	20.50	—
Manganese: ore	1 950.82	1 831.34	2 417.10	666.60	317.10	244.80
metal	—	—			624.90²	215.00
Mercury f: ore	na	na	7.10²		—	—
metal	—	—	0.96†	0.01†	2.22	2.64
Molybdenum f: ore	na	na	0.22†	0.23†	5.68	2.66
Nickel: ore	—	—	15.40†	2.07†	114.50	22.16
metal	—	0.03	—	—	0.05	0.09
Tin, metal	na	na	—	—	0.15	0.08
Titanium minerals	—	—			0.05	0.05
Tungsten: ore	—	—	0.03	0.04	0.44	0.04
metal	—	—	39.45	63.34	3.38	1.44
Vanadium v	111.42m	114.52m			50.88	7.44
Zinc: ore	76.83	66.00	75.83		12.06	1.44
metal						
Zirconium minerals	—	—	—	—	—	—

f metric tons.   k '000 fine troy oz.   m metal content.   b bullion and scrap.   p metal content.   t incl. ferruginous iron ore.   q aluminium oxide content.   r incl. manganiferous iron ore.   x primary magnesium.   v aluminium oxide and ferro-vanadium.   x primary magnesium.   u hydrate.   v vanadium oxide and ferro-vanadium.   x only.

10. CHEMICALS n AND FERTILIZERS

Organic chemicals:	Production		Exports		Imports	
Benzene	89.7				7.1	102.0
Butadiene	na				1.1	8.1
Ethylene	352.11				na	na
Methanol	107.0				19.1	9.8
Phenol	87.9				20.8	1.6
Phthalic anhydride	63.7				4.1	0.2
Styrene monomer	73.3				90.9	23.8
Urea	123.6				167.9	9.3

Inorganic chemicals:	Production		Exports		Imports	
Ammonia	948.0*				12.9	24.7
Carbon black	61.6				23.1	2.4
Chlorine	484.7				13.2	—
Nitric acid	926.6				1.1	8.7
Sodium carbonate	624.8				5.8	1.5
Sodium hydroxide	2 872.4				109.0	0.8
Sulphuric acid.					91.7	—

Plastics:	Production		Exports		Imports	
Polyamides	24.4				0.6	2.2
Polyethylene	159.4*				56.4	7.6
Polyvinyl chloride	285.7				126.3	3.6

Fertilizers:	Production		Exports		Imports	
Phosphates	na	na			95.8	1 616.8
Potash	198.7w	576.5x			67.3	207.0
Pyrites	631.6x	982.0¹				850.6
Sulphur: native	109.4	203.2			5.1	24.2
recovered	1.3	5.1¹*				45.1

n data not available for years 1953–5.   w K₂O content.   x sulphur content.

11. INDUSTRY

	Production		Exports		Imports	
Aircraft a	125.0*p	na			76.3	53.3
Alcoholic beverages					66.5a	9.3
beer b						2.9a
spirits b	4 168.0	1 588.7			6.5	—
Cement	950.0¹r	982.0¹¹			27.4a	—
Electrical	22 009.7	9 292.0			291.7	109.0
engineering a	1 341.3²	na			15.0	216.3
Locomotives c	na	9.0			344.5	286.3
Machine tools a	126.0¹	na			42.0²	—
Motor vehicles	434.0	197.0			33.8	71.1
private d q					8.8	1.4
commercial d q	69.5	35.5			69.8	28.3
	1 079.4	184.9			117.0	25.1
					447.3a	204.4a

a million $ U.S.   b '000 hectolitres.   c no. of units.   d no. in thousands.   q excl. military vehicles.   r 1967 data.   p 1959 data.   p 1965–7 av.

---

na: data not available.   — not available.   — negligible or nil.   ¹ one year only.   ² two year average.   * estimate.   ‡ see appendix.   † re-exports.

a two year average.   ² two year average.   ¹ one year only.   * estimate.   * estimate.   ‡ see appendix.   † re-exports.

JAMAICA
CARIBBEAN SEA

Jamaica, as one of the British West Indies, was granted self-government in 1944, and became a fully independent member of the Commonwealth in 1962.

AREA: 11 525 sq. km. (4 411 sq. miles)

LAND USE: (percentage of total)

	1964	1955
Arable and orchard	21.1	15.2
Permanent meadow and pasture	23.4	20.9
Forest and woodland	17.7	—
City areas, waste and other land	36.3	46.2

POPULATION: 1 876 000 (1967 estimate)
Largest city: KINGSTON, capital: population: 376 520 (1960)

Distribution of working population (1960)
Total working population: 654 582

U.N. group no.		Percentage	Year(s)
0	Agriculture, forestry, fishing and hunting	36.1	
1	Mining and quarrying	0.7	
2/3	Manufacturing	13.7	
4	Construction	7.6	
5	Electricity, gas, water and sanitary services	0.5	
6	Commerce	9.2	
7	Transport, storage and communications	3.0	
8	Services	20.3	
9	Others	8.9	

Life expectancy at birth (years): male 62.6; female 66.6 | 1959–61 av.

		Year(s)
Infant mortality (per '000)	37.4*	1965
Crude birth rate (per '000)	39.5*	1960–5 av.
Crude death rate (per '000)	8.5*	1960–5 av.
Population per physician	2020	1964
Population per hospital bed	260 a	1966
School enrolment: age 5–19 years (percentage)	81	1963–4 av.
age over 19 years (per 100 000 population)	95 b	1963–5 av.

a government hospitals only. b universities only.

COMMUNICATIONS

		Year(s)
Motor vehicles in use ('000s): private	49.5	1963–5 av.
commercial	18.7	
Railway track (km.)	421 a	1964
Mail per capita: domestic	27	1963–5 av.
foreign received	16	
foreign sent	12.8	1967

Radio receivers (per '000 population) 154 | 1963–5 av.
Television sets (per '000 population) 10.7 | 1963–5 av.
Daily newspapers (per '000 population) 71 | 1962

a The Jamaica Railway Corporation also works 31 km. of track on behalf of one of the bauxite companies.

FINANCE
Currency unit: The Jamaican dollar replaced the Jamaican pound in 1969 at the rate J$1 to J£0.5

Exchange rates

	1965 a	1960 a
Per $ U.S.	0.357	0.357
Per £ sterling	1.0	1.0

		Year(s)
National Income (million $ U.S.)	728	1965
G.N.P. per capita ($ U.S.)	460	1966
Rate of increase of G.N.P. per capita	2.3	1960–4 av.
Foreign trade (percentage of G.N.P.)	56	1963–5 av.

a rate for Jamaican pounds.

TRADING

	1965	1955
Total trade (in million $ U.S.)		
Exports (f.o.b.)	220	96
Imports (c.i.f.)	289	128

Main trading partners (percentage of total value)

Exports

	1965 a	1955 a
U.S.A.	38	16
U.K.	16	31
Canada	20	20
Sweden	2	1
Bahamas	2	—
Germany F.R.	1	—

Imports

	1965	1955
U.S.A.	31	27
U.K.	25	35
Canada	11	20
Venezuela	6	—
Japan	3	3
Germany F.R.	2	—

Distribution of trade (percentage of total value)

	1965	1955
Bauxite and alumina	47	—
Sugar and sugar preparations	22	27
Fruit and vegetables	13	35
Petroleum products	4	20
Rum r	2	3

Imports

	1965	1955
Manufactured goods (machinery and transport equipment)	57 (22)	57 (20)
(textiles and clothing)	(8)	(10)
Food (cereals)	20 (7)	20 (9)
Crude materials and fuels (mineral fuels)	12 (9)	13 (9)

a These are percentages of national exports‡ which comprised 95% of general exports in 1955 and 1965.

PRODUCTION, EXPORTS AND IMPORTS
Years: 1963–5 average and 1953–5 average. Units: '000 metric tons unless otherwise indicated

	Production		Exports		Imports	
1. CEREALS, etc.						
Cassava	9.0	17.0	—	—	21.6*	na
Maize (corn)	4.3*	12.0	—	—	1.0*	—
Oats	—	—	—	—	3.2	na
Potatoes	11.0	14.3	—	—	27.9	15.0
Sweet potatoes/yams	214.0*	64.0	—	—	1.0*	0.8
Wheat	—	—	—	—	106.4	54.6^2
2. FRUIT, etc.						
Apples	—	—	—	—	0.6^2	na
Bananas	299.3	249.3	180.8	163.1	—	—
Coconuts	114.7 e	na	0.2	—	0.2^2	na
Grapes	—	—	—	—	—	—
Lemons	10.7	8.7	4.1	2.7	—	—
Oranges	64.0	67.0	6.7	1.4	—	—
Other citrus fruit	32.0	24.0	—	—	—	—
Raisins	—	—	—	—	0.5^2	na
Tomatoes	3.0	4.3	—	—	—	—
Wine f	—	—	—	—	3.2^2	na
3. BEVERAGES, FOREST PRODUCTS, etc.						
Tea	—	—	—	—	1.6	1.7
Tobacco: leaf	2.7*	0.5*	0.3	0.3	2.7	2.7
Coffee	21.0	18.5 e	7.0 e	—	3.7	na
cigars	931.0 c	585.3 c	0.2	0.2	—	—
Sugar: cane	4 833.7*	3 689.7	—	—	—	—
cigarettes	—	—	0.2	0.3	0.2^2	na
raw	490.2	380.0	418.6	298.3	3.3	0.8
Softwood j	4.7*	4.8	—	—	17.0*	40.0^2
Hardwood j	106.4	585.3 c	0.3	0.2	1.5	0.6
Newsprint	16.4	6.1	—	—	0.2	0.3
Other paper	18.7	—	—	—	59.0^2	12.7*

d no. in thousands. e no. in millions. f '000 hectolitres. j '000 cu. metres of roundwood equivalent.

na: data not available. — negligible or nil. * estimate. ‡ see appendix. † re-exports.
1 one year only. 2 two year average. a million $ U.S.

PRODUCTION, EXPORTS AND IMPORTS continued

	Production		Exports		Imports	
4. VEGETABLE OILSEEDS AND OILS						
Castor oil	9.0	17.0	0.10	0.02	0.02^2	0.02
Copra	15.80	8.30	0.02	—	0.21^2	0.08
Coconut oil	na	na	—	—	0.06	—
Groundnuts	3.7	14.3	—	—	0.01^2	—
Linseed	—	—	—	—	0.25^2	—
Linseed oil	na	—	—	—	0.04^2	—
Olive oil	—	—	—	—	—	—
Palm oil	—	—	—	—	0.09^2	—
Soya beans	na	—	—	—	0.04^2	—
Soya bean oil	—	—	—	—	—	—
5. LIVESTOCK†, ANIMAL PRODUCTS, etc.						
Chickens d	2 076.7*	1 900.2^2	—	—	—	—
Cattle d	240.0	248.0	—	—	—	—
dairy cows d	30.3*	na	—	—	2.5^2	—
Sheep d	5.0	13.0	—	—	2.9^2	—
Goats d	269.0*	350.0	0.1	—	3.8^2	—
Horses d	10.0	17.0	—	—	3.3	—
Pigs d	128.0	145.3	—	—	1.5	—
Bacon/ham	—	—	—	—	0.3	—
Meat‡: 'A'	17.0*	16.3	—	—	17.3	—
'B'	8.0*	4.1	—	—	—	—
Butter	—	—	—	—	0.7*	—
Cheese	—	—	—	—	—	—
Eggs	5.0*	na	—	—	1.2^2	—
Milk	15.5	6.0^2	—	—	—	—
Hides/skins	1.3^2	1.6	—	—	—	—

d no. in thousands.

PRODUCTION, EXPORTS AND IMPORTS continued

	Production		Exports		Imports	
6. FIBRES, TEXTILES, etc.						
Abaca	—	—	—	—	—	—
Agaves (sisal etc.)	0.4	0.2	—	—	0.1^2	0.1
Cotton lint	—	—	—	—	0.3^2	—
Jute	—	—	—	—	1.2^2	—
Rubber, natural	—	—	2.3†	—	3.4^2	—
Cotton, woven fabrics	0.8*	—	—	—	0.2^2	—
Rayon, woven fabrics	—	—	—	—	1.3	—
7. FUEL AND POWER						
Coal, 'A'	—	—	—	—	—	—
Coke	—	—	—	—	14	1
Electricity h: total	723	130¹	—	—	1	—
hydro	142	130¹	—	—	1	—
thermal	581	601	—	—	—	—
Oil, crude	—	—	—	—	—	—
Petroleum, refined h	986	150¹†	130	—	1 110	na
					533	350¹

h million kWh.

	Production		Exports		Imports	
8. IRON AND STEEL						
Iron/steel scrap	na	na	3	—	—	—
9. NON-FERROUS MINERALS AND METALS						
Gold k, bullion/coins, etc	—	—	—	—	0.20¹‡	0.10^2
Silver k, bullion	—	—	—	—	1.00	1.13
Asbestos: fibre	—	—	—	—	0.21	0.03^2
Mica	—	—	—	—	0.09	1.39^2
Aluminium: bauxite	7 866.94	1 979.03	6 067.00 b	1 940.90	—	—
alumina	750.07	na	749.95	180.06	—	—
aluminium	—	—	—	—	1.76	2.76^2
Copper, metal	—	—	—	—	0.16^2	0.17
Lead, metal	—	—	—	—	0.22	—
Tin, metal	—	—	—	—	0.17	—
Zinc, metal	—	—	—	—	0.06	—

a million $ U.S. b estimated dry equivalent of actual exports which contain 8–14% free moisture. k '000 fine troy oz.

	Production		Exports		Imports	
10. CHEMICALS n AND FERTILIZERS						
Organic chemicals:						
Benzene	—	—	—	—	0.1^2	na
Butadiene	—	—	—	—	0.3^2	na
Ethylene	—	—	—	—	1.2^2	na
Methanol	—	—	—	—	0.2^2	na
Phenol	—	—	—	—	—	na
Phthalic anhydride	—	—	—	—	—	na
Styrene monomer	—	—	—	—	—	na
Urea	—	—	—	—	2.0¹	na
Inorganic chemicals:						
Ammonia	—	—	—	—	—	na
Carbon black	—	—	—	—	0.1	na
Chlorine	—	—	—	—	—	na
Nitric acid	—	—	—	—	—	na
Sodium carbonate	—	—	—	—	2.1	na
Sodium hydroxide	—	—	—	—	63.0	na
Sulphuric acid	986	na	—	—	0.2	na
Plastics:						
Polyamides	—	—	—	—	—	na
Polyethylene	—	—	—	—	7.9	na
Polyvinyl chloride	—	—	—	—	1.1	na
Fertilizers:						
Potash	—	—	—	—	—	—
Sulphur	—	—	—	—	2.0	—

n data not available for years 1953–5.

	Production		Exports		Imports	
11. INDUSTRY						
Alcoholic beverages beer b	218.0	81.4	3.8 ar	2.6 ar	—	—
spirits b	266.3	102.0	42.3	7.7	—	1.7
Cement	—	—	—	—	1.7	—
Electrical engineering a	—	—	—	—	9.2	4.1^2
Railway vehicles a	—	—	—	—	0.4	—
Motor vehicles a	—	—	—	—	13.1	4.3

a million $ U.S. b '000 hectolitres. r rum only.

JAPAN
EASTERN ASIA

Japan replaced her ancient imperialist regime by a new constitution in 1947. The Emperor remains a symbol of unity but has no powers related to government. After World War II Japan was occupied by the Allies until 1952 when her independence was regained. The Bonin Islands were returned by the U.S.A. to Japan in 1968, and the Ryuku Islands are scheduled for return in 1972.

AREA: 369 662 sq. km. (142 726 sq. miles)

LAND USE: (percentage of total)

	1960	1951
Arable and orchard	16.2	13.8
Permanent meadow and pasture	2.6	3.7
Forest and woodland	68.7	61.0
City areas, waste and other land	12.5	21.5

POPULATION: 98 274 961 (1965 census)
Largest city: TOKYO, capital: population: 11 005 000 (1966)
Total working population: 48 980 000*

Distribution of working population (1965)

U.N. group no.		Percentage	Year(s)
0	Agriculture, forestry, fishing and hunting	26.9	
1	Mining and quarrying	0.8	
2/3	Manufacturing	23.6	
4	Construction	6.2	
5	Electricity, gas, water and sanitary services	19.6	1966
6	Transport, storage and communications	6.2	1965
7	Commerce	15.9	1965
8	Services	0.8	1965
9	Others		

Life expectancy at birth (years): male 68.4; female 73.6 | 1966

		Year(s)
Infant mortality (per '000)	18.5	1965
Crude birth rate (per '000)	18.6	1965
Crude death rate (per '000)	7.2	1965
Accidental deaths (per 100 000 population) caused by motor vehicles	16.5	1965
due to other causes	24.4	1965
Population per motor vehicles	900	1965
Population per hospital bed	86	1966
School enrolment: age 5–19 years (percentage)		1963–4 av.
age over 19 years (per 100 000 population)	1038	1963–5 av.

COMMUNICATIONS

		Year(s)
Motor vehicles in use ('000s): private	1 696.3	1963
commercial	3 561	
Railway track (km.)	27 985	1963
Mail per capita: domestic	92	1963–5 av.
foreign received	1	
foreign sent	2	

COMMUNICATIONS—continued

		Year(s)
Telephones (per '000 urban population)	16.1	1967
Radio licences (per '000 population)	204	1963–5 av.
Television licences (per '000 population)	171.4	1963–5 av.
Daily newspapers (per '000 population)	429.5	1962–4 av.

FINANCE
Currency unit: The yen

Exchange rates

	1965	1960	1950	1938
Per $ U.S.	360.9	358.3	360.8	3.7
Per £ sterling	1010.5	1003.2	1010.7	17.02

		Year(s)
National Income (million $U.S.)		
G.N.P. per capita ($ U.S.)		
Rate of increase of G.N.P. per capita		
Foreign trade (percentage of G.D.P.)		

TRADING

	1965	1960	1955	1938*
Total trade (in million $ U.S.)				
Exports (f.o.b.)	8 452	68 189	2 011	1070
Imports (c.i.f.)	8 170	2 471	1079	

Main trading partners (percentage of total value)

Exports

	1965	1955	1938*
U.S.A.	30	29	16
Liberia	23	31	3
Australia	4	7	3
China P.R.	4	4	34
Hong Kong	3	4	3
Philippines	3	3	1
Thailand	3	1	—

Distribution of trade (percentage of total value)

Exports

	1965		
Manufactured goods	86		
(machinery and transport equipment)	(31)	[16]
(textiles and clothing)	(15)	[41]
Crude materials and fuels			[6]

Imports

	1965		
Crude materials and fuels	59	(16)	[12]
(petroleum and petroleum products)	17	(9)	[10]
Manufactured goods (machinery and transport equipment)	17	(9)	[9]
Food (cereals)			[18]
Chemicals	5		[1]

continued

na: data not available. — negligible or nil. * estimate. 2 two year average. a mainly ships.

JAPAN continued

PRODUCTION, EXPORTS AND IMPORTS continued

10. CHEMICALS AND FERTILIZERS—continued

	Production		Exports		Imports	
Fertilizers:						
Phosphates		0.4 *y*		4.1	2 265.7	1 363.2
Potash	1 755.4 *x*	1 084.2 *x*		12.7	1 077.7	628.9
Pyrites	225.7	193.4			29.4†	0.2
Sulphur: native			0.2	11.9	30.8	
recovered	22.3					

x sulphur content.   *y* K2O content.

11. INDUSTRY

	Production		Exports		Imports	
Aircraft *a*	148.0* *n*			0.1	65.0	9.3
Alcoholic beverages				1.9 *a*		0.8 *a*
beer *b*						
Cement	19 037.0	4 016.7	1 736.7			
Electrical	31 555.0	9 966.7	644.0	974.0		
engineering *a*	4 768.6	na	363.0	27.0	110.0	15.3
Locomotives *c*	363.0	na	38.9	13.0		0.9
Railway vehicles *a*		714.0			71.5	na
Machine tools *a*		1 245.0	2 350.0	309.0	31.6 *a*	21.1 *a*
Merchant ships *d*	305.0	600.0	313.6 *a*	8.4 *a*		
Motor vehicles	3 939.0					
commercial *d*	1 139.8	46.1				
private *d*	561.2	9.6				

a million $ U.S.   *b* '000 hectolitres.   *c* no. of units.   *d* no. in thousands.
g '000 G.R.T.   *n* 1965–7 av.

PRODUCTION, EXPORTS AND IMPORTS continued

10. CHEMICALS *n* AND FERTILIZERS

	Production	Exports	Imports
Organic chemicals:			
Benzene	320.7	0.2	118.0
Butadiene	83.6	—	—
Ethylene	542.5	—	—
Methanol	404.2	43.5	—
Phenol	86.1	0.1	2.3
Phthalic anhydride	92.9	3.8	5.0
Styrene monomer *j*	135.7	0.5	—
Urea	1 126.0	655.9	—
Inorganic chemicals:			
Ammonia	1 927.0	57.8	2.9
Carbon black	104.9	8.0	—
Chlorine	219.3	3.0	0.1
Nitric acid	na	28.3	4.6
Sodium carbonate	714.0	42.7	—
Sodium hydroxide *a*	1 245.0	1.3	—
Sulphuric acid.	5 339.7		
Plastics:			
Polyamides	na	na	na
Polyethylene	303.0	41.6	3.1
Polyvinyl chloride	435.2	56.6	2.3

continued

MIDDLE EAST

JORDAN

Jordan is a constitutional monarchy, recognized in 1946 as a sovereign independent state. Since the Arab–Israeli war of 1967 a portion of Jordanian territory has been occupied by Israel. There has been considerable guerilla extremist activity within the country.

AREA: 97 740 sq. km. (37 730 sq. miles) (pre-1967)

LAND USE: (percentage of total)

	1965
Arable and orchard.	11.6
Permanent meadow and pasture	2.2
Forest and woodland, incl. unstocked land.	0.7
City areas, waste and other land	85.5

POPULATION: 2 145 000 (1967 U.N. estimate)
Largest city: AMMAN, capital; population: 330 396 (city proper, 1967)

Distribution of working population (1961)
Total working population: 389 978

U.N. group no.		Percentage
1	Agriculture, forestry, fishing and hunting	35.3
2/3	Mining and quarrying	2.4
	Manufacturing	10.3
4	Construction	0.4
5	Electricity, gas, water and sanitary services	0.4
6	Commerce	8.0
7	Transport, storage and communications	3.1
8	Services	13.7
9	Others.	18.4

		Year(s)
Life expectancy at birth (years): male	52.6*	1959–63 av.
female	52.0*	
Infant mortality (per '000)	48.1*	1965
Crude birth rate (per '000)	5.6*	1965
Crude death rate (per '000)	na	1965
Accidental deaths (per 100 000 population)	24.2	1965
caused by motor vehicles	4 040	1966
due to other causes	580	1966
Population per physician	71	1963–4 av.
Population per hospital bed	111	1963–5 av.
School enrolment: age 5–19 years (percentage)		
age over 19 years (per 100 000 population)		

COMMUNICATIONS

		Year(s)
Motor vehicles in use ('000s): private	9.7	1963–5 av.
commercial	5.9	
Railway track (km.)	402	1969
Mail per capita: domestic	4	1962–4 av.
foreign received	3	
foreign sent	1.5	1967
Telephones (per '000 urban population)	91	1963–5 av.
Radio licences (per '000 population)	19*	1962
Daily newspapers (per '000 population)		

FINANCE

Currency unit: The Jordan dinar, at par with the pound sterling until 1968

	1965	1960	1958
Exchange rates			
Per $ U.S.	0.357	0.357	0.215

		Year(s)
	1965	1954
National income (million $ U.S.)	339	9.2
G.N.P. per capita ($ U.S.)	220	7.7
Foreign trade (percentage of G.D.P.)	42	77.7

TRADING

Total trade (in million $ U.S.)	1965	1955	1938
Exports (f.o.b.)	28	8	3
Imports (c.i.f.)	157	76	6

Main trading partners (percentage of total value)

Exports	1965	1955		Imports	1965	1955
Lebanon.	26	27		U.S.A.	15	10
Kuwait	13			Germany, F.R.	12	19
Saudi Arabia	12			Lebanon.	7	11
Syria	11	27		Syria	5	7
Yugoslavia	8	3		Japan	5	3
India	7	17		Italy	4	2
Iraq						

Distribution of trade (percentage of total value)

Exports			1965
Food			50
(fruit and vegetables)			(43)
Natural phosphates			31
Manufactured goods	54		
(machinery and transport equipment)	(15*)		
(textiles and clothing)	(12*)		

Imports			1955
Manufactured goods	51		
Food	26		
(cereals)	(18)		
(fruit and vegetables)	(13)		
Crude materials and fuels	10	(7)	1955
Chemicals	11	(6)	
		(2*)	

continued

173

JAPAN continued

PRODUCTION, EXPORTS AND IMPORTS *continued*

Years: 1963–5 average and 1953–5 average   Units: '000 metric tons unless otherwise indicated

1. CEREALS, etc.

	Production		Exports		Imports	
Barley	1 065.3	2 360.7	—	5.4	426.2	682.0
Maize (corn)	87.7	74.0	—	0.8	3 102.7	241.4
Millets/sorghum	44.0*	112.6	—	—	1 110.3	40.2
Oats	135.3	158.3	0.1	—	9.7	0.6
Potatoes	3 793.0	2 688.7	17.5	28.6	534.8	1 252.6
Rice	16 866.0	12 169.3	0.2	1.9	19.5	0.1
Sweet potatoes/	1.7	2.0				
yams	5 831.0	5 932.3		0.6	3 471.8	2 053.7
Wheat.	1 082.3	1 452.7				

2. FRUIT, etc.

	Production		Exports		Imports	
Apples	1 125.7	438.3	16.7	10.1	321.7	—
Bananas	na	na				25.4
Cherries	3 368	65				
Grapes	203.0	58.0	0.2	0.1	13.2	1.3
Lemons/grapefruit	64.3	22.0	14.4	3.7	0.8	2.4
Oranges	1 368.0	540.0				
Peaches	211.7	67.3	5.3	5.0		5.0
Pears	346.7	108.7			na	na
Plums	47.1				16.6	1.3
Raisins						
Tomatoes	500.7	146.0				
Wine *b*	99.7		1.3		5.3	3.3

3. BEVERAGES, FOREST PRODUCTS, etc.

	Production		Exports		Imports	
Cocoa	—	—	—	—	29.2	3.6
Coffee	—	—	—	—	19.3	3.0
Sugar: beet	1 405	313				
cane	648	65	0.2	—		
raw (beet)	190	47				
(cane)	251 *n*	— *n*	6.5	22.4	1 559.2	1 059.8
Tea	81	66	4.0	15.0	2.9	0.7
Tobacco: leaf	188	122	7.1	6.0	23.3	8.2
cigars	2					
cigarettes	164 289 *e*	95 718 *e*				
tobacco/snuff				0.3	6.2 *a*	—
Softwood *j*	34 673	29 337	187.0	146.1	6 703.0	319.3
Hardwood *j*	25 504	24 638	420.2	375.0	8 781.0	557.0
Wood pulp	4 918	1 682	6.2	9.1	501.1	105.7
Newsprint	1 131*	437	217.3	42.5	29.7	5.0
Other paper	5 901				138.0	na

6. FIBRES, TEXTILES, etc.

	Production		Exports		Imports	
Abaca	—	—	—	—	29.7	30.2
Agaves (sisal etc.)	—	—	—	—	13.3	7.6
Cotton lint.	—	—	1.2	—	700.5	471.5
Flax fibre	4.2	5.3			9.9	3.2
Hemp fibre	0.7*	2.6		0.3	0.2	0.1
Jute	0.7	1.3	1.7	0.2*	86.2	30.3
Rubber: natural			18.4		206.0	90.9
synthetic	124.8		3 037.7	4 571.0	53.8 *a*	2.7
Silk *j*	18 881.0	15 964.0	14.3	11.0	1 529.0	90.0
Cotton: yarn	394.1	395.8	130.1	110.0		
woven fabrics	474.1	284.6	68.9	64.4		—
Rayon: fibre/yarn	164.1 *n*	162.2			0.9	—
woven fabrics						
Non-cellulosic						
fibre/yarn	320.2	10.8	38.5	0.8	—	0.4
Wool: yarn	152.1	81.7	8.6	0.3	0.3	0.6
woven fabrics	128.8	141.3 *b*	10.5 *q*	1.4 *q*	—	—

7. FUEL AND POWER

	Production		Exports		Imports	
Coal: A, ‡.	50 837	42 420	76	527 *r*	13 819	6 750
B	240	1 370	18	13	16	3 380
Coke	na	na				
Electricity *h*: total	177 314	59 620				
hydro	71 411	45 070	3	—	61 746	6 790
thermal	105 900	14 550 *i*	613	—	12 447	—
nuclear	3	137 *i*				
Natural gas *i*	1 970	717	310 *i*			
Oil, crude	717	6 790 *i*				
Petroleum, refined	54 570					

8. IRON AND STEEL

	Production		Exports		Imports	
Iron ore	1 406 *m*	890 *m*	29 *m*	77 *m*	32 174	4 918
Steel	24 348	4 943	192	199	2 523	10
Steel ingots/castings	37 487	8 273	3	189	4 365	1 135
Iron/steel products		na	967		136	12

9. NON-FERROUS MINERALS AND METALS

	Production		Exports		Imports	
Diamonds *a*	—	—	1.01†		27.44 *i*	0.91
Gold *k*, ore *m*	470.70 *u*	237.00 *u*				
Platinum group	—	—	—	—	387.14	na
Silver *k*, ore *m*	4.18	1.17	1 064.00	3 777.33	6 117.67	19.86
metals *k*	8 838.70 *u*	6 046.70 *u*				
Asbestos: fibre	15.92	5.55	32.80	1.62	130.35	1.58
manufactured	na		0.06†	—	5.03	7.24
Mica	na	na	0.60†	—	51.23 *p*	295.80
Aluminium: bauxite	575.00	na	105.96 *b*	19.39	52.35	3.44
alumina	261.20	52.04	56.22	0.01	6.75	2.31
aluminium	0.29 *m*	0.30 *m*	na	—	0.55	0.01
Antimony: ore	1.24	1.54	0.75	0.01	0.02	na
metal	43.17 *m*	32.30 *m*	11.85	2.55	2.74	45.83
Cadmium	na	na	0.01†	—	1.55	0.22
Chrome: ore		na		—	327.75	0.10
metal	106.64 *m*	66.05 *m*	2.15	2.75	613.06	5.65
Cobalt: ore	334.19	71.17	33.73	—	189.44	38.06
metal	99.18	22.56 *m*	5.66	0.29	62.53	21.95
Copper: ore		24.30			45.60	15.39
metal						11.24
Lead: ore	1 753.28	186.51	3.31	0.27	12.74	57.92
metal	288.12	3.05 *x*	1.49	26.67	24.54	1.07
Magnesium: ore			39.60	1.20	792.34 *q*	133.37
dolomite	161.06	248.90			1 194.20	127.10
magnesite	296.66 *m*	194.44 *m*			60.30	389.70
metal/salts	na	na	0.27	1.50	934.40	218.72
Manganese: ore					10.26	0.08
Mercury *k*	0.83 *m*	0.80 *m*	0.51	4.41	15.24	5.32
metal	1.88	0.90	34.70	0.16	180.10	34.56
Molybdenum *k*: ore	1.91 *r*	3.31 *r*	0.06	0.11	2.23	0.15
metal	0.79	0.80				
Nickel: ore	na	na	na		0.03	0.05 *z*
metal	211.81	104.89	5.71	2.61	272.10	0.03 *b*
Tin: ore	322.05	97.86	57.02 *t*		28.26	6.97
metal	0.79				25.98 *l*	
Titanium minerals						
Tungsten: ore						
Vanadium: ore						
metal						
Zinc: ore						
Zirconium minerals						

4. VEGETABLE OILSEEDS AND OILS

	Production		Exports		Imports	
Castor seed	—	—	—	0.21	37.28	21.87
Castor oil	—	—	2.31	0.03†	24.54	40.37
Coconut oil	—	—	0.53	0.07	96.01	40.63
Copra	—	0.30	0.02	0.10 *z*	196.93	45.63
Cottonseed	na	27.00 *p*	0.43	0.07	17.89	7.73
Cottonseed oil	96.13		0.14	0.07	98.69	50.87
Groundnuts	2.33	3.30	0.82	0.01	0.36	0.32
Groundnut oil	na	na	0.01	—	24.39	13.20
Linseed	na	na	2.00	—	0.28	na
Linseed oil			0.27†	—	17.10	15.53
Olive oil	123.30	259.67	2.85	0.50	94.98	11.10
Palm kernels	4.33	5.53	0.35	0.63	33.27	12.53
Palm kernel oil	262.70	437.33	0.17	6.87	1 666.33	588.13
Palm oil	na	na	4.31		0.78	0.10
Rapeseed					5.65	na
Rapeseed oil					3.94	3.25
Sesame seed						
Soya beans						
Soya bean oil						
Sunflower seed						
Tung oil						

5. LIVESTOCK‡, ANIMAL PRODUCTS, etc.

	Production		Exports		Imports	
Chickens *d*	108 794	44 287				
Cattle *d*	3 368	2 880 *q*	1.6	2.6	1.2	1.6
dairy cows *d*	1 937					
Goats *d*	397	506 *q*	0.1	—	0.1	—
Sheep *d*	290	735 *q*				
Horses *d*	396	945				
Pigs *d*	3 578	857 *q*	0.8	0.9	2.3	0.7
Meat¹: A‡	622	181	0.1	0.1	65.5	0.1
B‡	184*	*r*	28.2	—	44.6	1.3
Butter *d*	13	7		0.9	1.7	1.0
Cheese	924	324		1.3 *q*	0.1	1.0
Eggs	6 652	4 663	547.5	150.0 *t*	182.6	14.9 *t*
Fish	3 163	663	23.3	2.1	742.5	105.6
Whale oil	152	182 *q*			154.0 *l*	54.3
Hides/skins	44	*r*	0.1	0.3 *q*	140.0	49.7
Wool	na	na				

continued

na: data not available.   — negligible or nil.   * estimate.   * two year average.   ¹ one year only.   ‡ see appendix.   † re-exports.

JORDAN continued

PRODUCTION, EXPORTS AND IMPORTS
Years: 1963–5 average and 1953–5 average · Units: '000 metric tons unless otherwise indicated

1. CEREALS, etc.

	Production	Exports	Imports
Barley	72.0 · 57.3	2.0 · 5.9	14.1 · 2.6
Maize (corn)	8.7 · 17.0[2]	— · 0.1[2]	7.2 · 0.5
Millets/sorghum	13.7 ·	2.1 · 0.9	8.3 · 0.5
Potatoes	19.7 · na	— · 2.2	15.9 · 5.3
Wheat	216.3 · 137.3	0.6 · 1.6[2]	35.2 · 22.4

2. FRUIT, etc.

	Production	Exports	Imports
Apples	5.0 · 4.0[2]	0.1 ·	15.0 · 0.2
Bananas	11.0 · 10.0	3.0 · 3.6	7.2 · 10.2
Figs	1.0 ·	— ·	— ·
Grapes	19.7 · 29.0	0.7 · 0.1	2.6 · 0.3
Lemons	72.0 · 46.5[2]	1.3 ·	5.2 · 0.2[2]
Oranges	8.7 · na	1.4 · 10.2[2]	6.2 ·
Other citrus fruit	30.7 · na	0.3 ·	0.2 ·
Olives	58.0 · 55.0[2]	— ·	— ·
Pears		0.3[2] ·	0.2[2] ·
Raisins	1.2 · 0.92*	— ·	0.1 ·
Tomatoes	230.7 · 46.0[2]		
Wine b			
b '000 hectolitres.

3. BEVERAGES, FOREST PRODUCTS, etc.

	Production	Exports	Imports
Cocoa			0.1 ·
Coffee			1.7 · 0.7
Sugar, raw			54.7 · 25.8
Tea	1.6* · 0.8[2]	0.1[2] · 0.2[2]	0.1 · 0.8
Tobacco: leaf	1 224.0e · 446.0e	0.4[2] ·	0.1an · 0.4
cigarettes			79.6[2] · 31.1[2]
Softwood j	17.7 · 72.7		0.8 · 0.2[2]
Hardwood j			5.1 · 2.5
Newsprint j			
Other paper			
a million $ U.S. e no. in millions. j '000 cu. metres of roundwood equivalent.

4. VEGETABLE OILSEEDS AND OILS

	Production	Exports	Imports
Castor oil			0.03 · 0.02
Coconut oil		— · 2	0.76 · 1.26[2]
Cottonseed oil			0.80 · 0.54
Groundnuts			0.01 ·
Linseed oil	14.33* · 10.67*	0.65 · 3.73	0.76 · 0.08
Olive oil	1.60 · 3.90[2]	0.36 · 1.00	3.99* · 0.10
Sesame seed			6.14* · 2
Soya bean oil			

5. LIVESTOCK‡, ANIMAL PRODUCTS, etc.

	Production	Exports	Imports
Butter	2.0 ·		
Cheese			
Eggs			
Milk			
Hides/skins			
Wool			
d no. in thousands.

6. FIBRES, TEXTILES, etc.

	Production	Exports	Imports
Agaves (sisal etc.)			
Cotton lint			
Rubber, natural			
Cotton: yarn			
woven fabrics			
Rayon, woven fabrics			
Wool: yarn			
woven fabrics			

7. FUEL AND POWER

	Production	Exports	Imports
Coal, 'A'‡			
Electricity h: total	135 ·		
hydro	na ·		
thermal	na ·		
Oil, crude			
Petroleum, refined	310 ·	— · 1	
h million kWh.

8. IRON AND STEEL

	Production	Exports	Imports
Steel ingots/castings			45 ·

9. NON-FERROUS MINERALS AND METALS

	Production	Exports	Imports
Asbestos			
Aluminium			
Copper, metal			
Lead, metal			
Tin, metal			

10. CHEMICALS n AND FERTILIZERS

	Production	Exports	Imports
Fertilizers:			
Phosphates	669.0 · 92.8	529.6 · 77.7	370 ·
Potash		0.01 ·	33 ·
Sulphur			
n data not available for years 1953–5.

11. INDUSTRY

	Production	Exports	Imports
Aircraft a			
Alcoholic beverages			6.8 · 0.21
Cement	302.7 · 194.8	— ·	5.3 ·
Electrical engineering a			
Motor vehicles a			6.5[2] · 1.0
		0.2 ·	10.9 · 1.7
a million $ U.S. b '000 hectolitres.

continued

KENYA

Kenya, formerly a British East African protectorate, became an independent member of the Commonwealth in 1963 and achieved republican status the following year. Grants for development have been received from the U.K. and China P.R. Kenya is a member of the East African Community.

AREA: 582 600 sq. km. (224 960 sq. miles)

LAND USE: (percentage of total)

	1961	1953
Arable and orchard	2.9	2.7
Permanent meadow and pasture	6.7	20.6
Forest and woodland	6.7	
City areas, waste and other land	87.5	74.5

Sixty per cent of the land is unproductive due to lack of water, but revenue is gained from tourist and safari attractions in this area.

POPULATION: 9 948 000 (1967 estimate)
Largest city: NAIROBI, capital; population: 314 760 (1962)

EAST AFRICA

Distribution of working population (1965)
Total working population: 5 940 000

U.N. group no.		Percentage
0	Agriculture, forestry, fishing and hunting	35.3
1	Mining and quarrying	0.4
2/3	Manufacturing	12.0
4	Construction	3.6
5	Electricity, gas, water and sanitary services	0.4
6	Commerce	9.2
7	Transport, storage and communications	6.1
8	Services	32.8
9	Others	0.2

		Year(s)
Life expectancy at birth (years)	42.5*	1962
Infant mortality (per '000)	34.2[a]	1965
Crude birth rate (per '000)	50* b	1965
Crude death rate (per '000)	30* b	1964
Population per physician	12 820	1966
Population per hospital bed	780	1965
School enrolment: age 5–19 years (percentage)	48	1963–4 av.
age over 19 years (per 100 000 population)	22	1963–5 av.

continued

a non-Africans. b Africans.

COMMUNICATIONS

Motor vehicles in use ('000s): private	70.8	1963–5 av.
commercial	10.7	1969
Railway track (km.)	926.0	1967
Telephones (per '000 urban population)	31	1967
Radio receivers (per '000 population)		1963–5 av.
Television sets (per '000 population)	9	1963–4 av.
Daily newspapers (per '000 population)		

FINANCE
Currency unity: The East African shilling

	1960	1965	1938 a
Exchange rates	7.143	7.143	0.215
Per $ U.S.	20.0	20.0	1.0
Per £ sterling			

	1960	1965
National Income (million $U.S.) a	725	
G.N.P. per capita ($U.S.) a	90	
a East African pounds of 20 shillings.

TRADING
Note—trade with Uganda and Tanganyika is excluded.
Total trade (in million $ U.S.)

	1955	1965
Exports (f.o.b.)	78	145
Imports (c.i.f.)	200	249

PRODUCTION, EXPORTS AND IMPORTS
Years: 1963–5 average and 1953–5 average · Units: '000 metric tons unless otherwise indicated

1. CEREALS, etc.

	Production	Exports	Imports
Barley	14.0 · 15.0	— ·	
Cassava	600.0[m] ·		
Maize (corn)	1 125.3 n · 179.7 n	29.5 · 53.3	27.3 · 1.6[2]
Millets/sorghum	320.0[m] · na	0.5 · 0.8	3.4 · 0.6
Oats	1.3 · 10.7		
Potatoes	192.5[2] ·	1.6 · 0.9	2.5 · 6.5
Rice	17.0 · na	0.1 · 0.2[2]	
Sweet potatoes/yams	126.0* ·	— ·	4.8 · 10.9
Wheat	450.0 · 128.0[2]		
n from farms and estates only. s incl. re-exports.

2. FRUIT, etc.

	Production	Exports	Imports
Apples	65.0[e] ·	1.8[1] ·	0.8 · 0.5
Coconuts		— ·	0.3 · 0.9*
Dates			0.1 · 0.1
Grapes			
Citrus fruit	25.3* ·	0.1 · 0.5[2]	0.2 · 0.1[2]
Pineapples			7.3 · 5.3
Raisins			
Wine b			
b '000 hectolitres. e no. in millions.

3. BEVERAGES, FOREST PRODUCTS, etc.

	Production	Exports	Imports
Coffee	45.2* · 18.4[2]	39.4 · 16.0	
Sugar: cane	408.7 n · 7.3		43.9 · 31.5
raw	13.6 · 0.2*	0.3 ·	21.6 s · 0.4
Tea	0.4 · 106.7 h	23.0 · 4.8	6.1 ·
Tobacco: leaf	1 900.0* ·		
cigarettes/snuff	0.1 ·	208.0[2]* · 228.3	0.7 · 0.1[2]
Softwood j	7 553.0[2]* · 130.7	6.2 · 2.9	5.8 · 1.3[2]
Hardwood j	2.5[2]* ·		2.9 · 4.3[2]
Newsprint j			26.6 ·
Other paper			
j '000 cu. metres of roundwood equivalent. b incl. small quantity of cigars. s incl. re-exports.

4. VEGETABLE OILSEEDS AND OILS

	Production	Exports	Imports
Castor seed	3.33* ·	5.88 · 5.37	0.06 · 0.02
Castor oil			0.45 · 0.27
Copra	1.00* · 1.20[2]q	0.11 · 0.83	0.81 · 1.22
Coconut oil	10.70* · 5.00*	0.33 · 0.02	
Cottonseed	2.80 ·	2.07 ·	
Cottonseed oil		0.01 · 0.01	— ·
Groundnuts			
Groundnut oil	1.00 ·	0.88 · na	3.43 ·
Linseed	3.00[m] · 3.00[2]q	1.25 · 2.34[q]	
Linseed oil	326.3[m] ·		0.05 ·
Olive oil			
Palm kernels			
Palm kernel oil			
Palm oil			
Sesame seed	1.7 ·	0.2 ·	0.1 ·
Soya bean oil			
n from farms and estates only. q exports of coconut oil and copra in copra equivalent.

5. LIVESTOCK d, ANIMAL PRODUCTS, etc.

	Production	Exports	Imports
Chickens d	7 251.3[m] d 7 675.0[2]		
Cattle d	6 367.0[m] 3 875.3*		
Goats d	4 984.0 2 692.7*		0.3 · 0.7
Sheep d	2.3 5.3	0.4 · 0.7	0.1 · 0.7
Pigs d	36.0[m] 42.3 n	3.2 · 0.7	
Horses d	32.0* n 16.0 m	0.5 ·	0.1 · 0.1
Bacon/ham d	na 4.7* n	2.1 · 1.2	0.1 · 0.1
Meat†: 'A'	4.7 n 4.7* n	0.1 · 0.1	
Butter	1.0 0.9		
Cheese			
Eggs			
d no. in thousands. n data not available for Uganda.

continued

---

5. LIVESTOCK, ANIMAL PRODUCTS, etc.—continued

	Production	Exports	Imports
Fish	21.4 · 33.5	4.6 · 0.1	1.9 · na
Milk	238.7[m]q · 179.3[m]q	6.5[2] · na	9.6 · 4.5*
Hides/skins	0.6[2] · 5.0	0.7 · 0.5	0.7 · na
Wool			
n on farms and estates only. p incl. ducks, geese and turkeys. q excl. milk fed to livestock.

6. FIBRES, TEXTILES, etc.

	Production	Exports	Imports
Agaves (sisal etc.)	67.8 · 37.7	60.2 · 35.6	2.6 ·
Cotton lint	5.0* · 2.3*	2.8 · 0.1	0.7 ·
Flax fibre			7.5 ·
Jute			0.1 ·
Rubber, natural			
Cotton, woven fabrics			
Rayon, woven fabrics			
Wool, yarn			

7. FUEL AND POWER

	Production	Exports	Imports
Coal, 'A'‡			42 · 19
Coke			1 · 2
Electricity h: total	305 ·		
hydro	191 ·		
thermal	114 ·		
Oil, crude			
Petroleum, refined	1 120 ·	573 ·	1186 · na
			317 · 740[1]
h million kWh.

8. IRON AND STEEL

	Production	Exports	Imports
Iron ore			3 ·
Pig iron			1 · 1
Steel ingots/castings		12 ·	
Iron/steel scrap			

9. NON-FERROUS MINERALS AND METALS

	Production	Exports	Imports
Gold k, ore	11.00[m] · 9.00[m]	11.61[t] · 9.10[t]	4.26[t] · 1.63[t]
Silver k, ore	40.30[m] · 8.30[m]	40.23[t] ·	
Asbestos: fibre	0.13 · 0.16		1.35 · 3.24
Mica	na · 0.01		0.02 · 1.84
Copper, ore			
Aluminium	2.10 · na	3.09[t] · 0.05	1.61 ·
Lead, metal	na ·	3.41[w] ·	
Magnesium			
Tin, metal	0.17 ·		0.32 · 0.64
Zinc, metal			0.14 · 0.03
k '000 fine troy oz. t bullion. w unwrought.

10. CHEMICALS n AND FERTILIZERS
Chemicals · · ·

	Production	Exports	Imports
Fertilizers:			
Potash			0.11 · 0.12
Sulphur			1.37 · 0.08
n data not available for Uganda.

11. INDUSTRY

	Production	Exports	Imports
Aircraft a			na ·
Alcoholic beverages			
beer b	473.0 · 184.0	— ·	0.3 · 0.2
Cement	415.3 · 67.3	314.3 · 7.0	1.1 · 0.1
Electrical engineering a			
Railway vehicles a			4.1 · na
Machine tools a			1.5[2] a · na
Motor vehicles a			0.7 · 127.0
			8.9 · na
			4.7[2] · na
			1.0 · na
			21.4 · na
a million $ U.S. b '000 hectolitres. v incl. data for Uganda.

Main trading partners (percentage of total value)

Exports	1965	1955 a	Imports	1965	1955 a
U.K.	21	28	U.K.	28	44
Germany F.R.	16	12	U.S.A.	10	3
U.S.A.	4	4	Japan	10	9
Netherlands	4	2	Germany F.R.	7	6
Canada	4	—	Iran	5	2
Japan	3		Kuwait	3	3
Sweden			France	3	

Distribution of trade (percentage of total value)

Exports	1965	Imports	1965
Food	55	Manufactured goods, machinery and transport equipment	59
(coffee)	(30)		
(tea)	(13)		
Crude materials and fuel	33	Crude materials and fuels	(26)
(petroleum products)	(10)	(petroleum products)	13
(sisal)	(8)	Food	11
(pyrethrum)	(5)	Chemicals	9
a refers to total trade for Kenya, Uganda and Tanganyika.

---

na: data not available. — negligible or nil. * estimate. 1 one year only. 2 two year average. ‡ see appendix. b '000 hectolitres. v see appendix. m metal content. t bullion. w unwrought.

na: data not available. — negligible or nil. * estimate. 1 one year only. 2 two year average. ‡ see appendix. b '000 hectolitres. v incl. data for Uganda.

KOREA, SOUTH

The Republic of Korea was established in 1948 after three years' occupation by American troops after World War II. The Korean war of 1950–3 was the result of an attempt by North Korea to reunite the two sectors of Korea; the armistice re-established the 38th parallel as the boundary between the two countries.

AREA: 98 431 sq. km. (38 004 sq. miles)

LAND USE: (percentage of total)	1964	1954
Arable and orchard.	22.9	20.6
Permanent meadow and pasture	0.2	
Forest and woodland, incl. rough grazing	67.1	65.4
City areas, waste and other land	9.8	14.0

POPULATION: 29 207 856 (1966 census)
Largest city: SŌUL (Seoul), capital: population: 3 794 959 (city proper, 1966)
Total working population: 9 199 000

Distribution of working population (1965)

U.N. group no.		Percentage
0	Agriculture, forestry, fishing and hunting	54.4
2/3	Mining and quarrying	0.9
	Manufacturing	8.6
4	Construction	0.7
5	Electricity, gas, water and sanitary services	0.2
6	Commerce	10.6
7	Transport, storage and communications	2.0
8	Services	13.0
9	Others.	7.4

		Year(s)
Life expectancy at birth (years): male	51.1	1955–60 av.
female	53.7	
Infant mortality (per '000)	5.0*	1964
Crude birth rate (per '000)	17.7*	1965
Crude death rate (per '000)	5.0*	1965
Population per physician	2 710	1965
Population per hospital bed	2 200	1966
School enrolment: age 5–19 years (percentage)	77	1963–4 av.
age over 19 years (per 100 000 population)	508	1964–5 av.

COMMUNICATIONS

		Year(s)
Motor vehicles in use ('000s): private	14.5	1963–5 av.
commercial	23.3	
Railway track (km.): domestic	4 695	1962
Mail per capita: foreign received	13	1963–5 av.
foreign sent	0.4	
Telephones (per '000 urban population)	1.1	1967
Radio receivers (per '000 population)	65	1963–5 av.
Television licences (per '000 population)	1.3	1963–5 av.
Daily newspapers (per '000 population)	56	1962–3 av.

FINANCE
Currency unit: The won replaced the hwan in 1962 at the rate 1 won to 10 hwan.

Exchange rates	1962	1960a	1950a	1938a
Per $ U.S.	271	650	500*	249
Per £ sterling	759	1820	1400*	300

a hwan.

		Year(s)
National Income (million $ U.S.)	2 497	1965
G.N.P. per capita ($ U.S.)	150	1965
Rate of increase of G.N.P. per capita	3.2	1960–4 av.
Foreign trade (percentage of G.D.P.)	17	1963–5 av.

TRADING

Total trade (in million $ U.S.)	1965
Exports (f.o.b.)	175
Imports (c.i.f.)	463

Main trading partners (percentage of total value)

Exports	1965	1955	Imports	1965	1955
U.S.A.	35	42	U.S.A.	39	35
Japan	25	39	Japan	36	25
S. Vietnam	9	na	Germany F.R.	5	6
Hong Kong	6	11	France	3	na
Thailand	3	na	Philippines	2	na
Netherlands	2	na	Taiwan	2	5
			Hong Kong	14	14

Distribution of trade (percentage of total value)

Exports	1965	1955
Manufactured goods (textiles and clothing)	61 {27}	10 {10}
Crude materials and fuels (plywood)	22 (10)	78 (32*)
Food (fish)	16 (10)	6 (3*)

Imports	1965	1955c
Manufactured goods (machinery and transport equipment)	33 (16)	60 (8)
Crude materials (textile fibres)	30 (13)	4
Chemicals (fertilizers)	22 (14)	17 (na)
Food (cereals)	14 (12)	11 (7*)

a incl. North Korea. b in addition, imports to the value U.S. $233 million financed with foreign aid. c these are percentages of total imports, including those financed with foreign aid.

PRODUCTION, EXPORTS AND IMPORTS Units: '000 metric tons unless otherwise indicated
Years: 1963–5 average and 1953–5 average

	Production		Exports		Imports	
1. CEREALS, etc.						
Barley	768.3	844.3	—	—	169.2	146.5*
Maize (corn)	73.0	12.7	—	—	9.2	60.21
Pellets/sorghum	—	95.7	0.1	—	2.1	28.3*
Potatoes	391.7	310.0²	12.5	—	0.1	104.4
Rice	5 051.3	3 186.3	—	—	39.1	
Rye	19.3	22.7	—	—	—	
Sweet potatoes/Yams	1 317.0	387.3				
Wheat.	136.0	109.7	—	—	583.0	60.9
2. FRUIT, etc.						
Apples	134.0	47.3	—	—	—	
Bananas	—	2.7	—	—	0.3	
Oranges	12.0					
Grapes	36.0	15.2¹				
Peaches	30.7	29.3				
Pears	19.0	7.0			0.1	
Wine b	b '000 hectolitres.					
3. BEVERAGES, FOREST PRODUCTS, etc.						
Sugar, raw	37.9	23.5	7.1†	—	34.2	34.8
Tobacco: leaf	22 470.0	11 828.0	0.7†			
cigarettes¹	9.1	4.6				
tobacco/snuff	1 634.0*	507.3	—	—	144.0	170.3
Softwood¹	186.3*	364.0	—	—	387.0¹	81.4
Hardwood	21.7	4.1	—	—	65.7	4.2
Wood pulp¹	275.0	23.3			16.3	
Newsprint	1.3	1.0				
Other paper	65.3	17.6	0.1	—	3.1	22.0

e no. in millions. f '000 cu. metres of roundwood equivalent.

	Production		Exports		Imports	
4. VEGETABLE OILSEEDS AND OILS						
Castor seed	2.67	na				
Castor oil					0.12	0.12
Copra	8.00	20.67			1.49	1.49
Cottonseed					0.01	0.28
Cottonseed oil	1.63	0.70				
Groundnuts	na		0.01			
Linseed					0.55	0.14
Linseed oil	3.67	1.50			0.13	0.37
Sesame seed	164.36	150.30			5.51	9.17*
Soya beans					0.09	0.052
Soya bean oil						
5. LIVESTOCK‡, ANIMAL PRODUCTS, etc.						
Chickens d	11 745.3	5 544.7				
Cattle d	1 324.3	697.3				
dairy cows d	595.7*	509.3	66.2*	—	0.5*	
Goats d	1.3	1.0				
Sheep d	1 479.0	644.3	0.1		0.1	
Horses d	979.0*	35.6	0.3			
Pigs d; Meat‡, 'A'; 'B'	21.1*				0.2*	
Butter	43.0*	4.5²				
Eggs	589.8	262.5	36.6	na	82.9	75.3
Fish	106.0*	0.3				
Milk	43.3	5.8			0.1	
Hides/skins	65.3	2.5¹			1.1	
Wool	4.51					

d no. in thousands.

continued

KOREA, NORTH

The northern sector of Korea was occupied by Russian troops in 1945 at the end of World War II. In 1948 the People's Republic was established. An attempt to reunite with the southern sector in 1950 resulted in the Korean war and caused great economic hardship to the country; the boundary between North and South Korea returned to the 38th parallel in 1953.

AREA: 121 248 sq. km. (46 814 sq. miles)

LAND USE: (percentage of total)	1960
Arable and orchard.	15.7
Permanent meadow and pasture	na
Forest and woodland, including rough grazing	74.4
City areas, waste and other land	na

POPULATION: 12 700 000 (1967 U.N. estimate)
Largest city: P'YŌNGYANG, capital: population: 653 100 (city proper, 1960)

FINANCE
Currency unit: The won

Exchange rates	1965
Per $ U.S.	2.57
Per £ sterling	7.2

PRODUCTION AND TRADE
After the Korean war, central planning of the economy began, the more recent plans giving priority to heavy industry over agriculture; collectivization had been completed by 1958. Rice accounted for 58% of the agricultural output in 1963; oil drilling started in 1957. Various minerals are found, the most important being coal, lead and graphite. Industries, especially H.E.P., textile, metallurgical and cement production have been intensively developed by the big Japanese concerns.

Trade is mainly with China P.R. The other trading partners are almost exclusively Comecon countries.

PRODUCTION, EXPORTS AND IMPORTS Units: '000 metric tons unless otherwise indicated
Years: 1963–5 average and 1953–5 average

	Production		Exports		Imports
1. CEREALS, etc.					
Barley	250.0*	na		na	—
Maize (corn)	1 613.3*	na	30.3*	na	33.5*
Millets/sorghum	402.1*	na		na	—
Oats	56.0*	na		na	0.44*
Potatoes	948.3*	na		na	—
Rice	2 633.3*	na	14.5*	na	—
Rye	7.0*	na		na	—
Sweet potatoes/Yams	273.3*	na		na	—
Wheat.	85.0*	na		na	80.3*
2. FRUIT, etc.					
Apples	na	na	26.7*	na	—
3. BEVERAGES, FOREST PRODUCTS, etc.					
Sugar, raw	39.3*	na	6.5*	na	22.3
Tobacco, leaf	7.0*	na		na	0.1*
Wood	na				
Newsprint	na				
Other paper	60.0*	na		na	—
4. VEGETABLE OILSEEDS AND OILS					
Coconut oil					
Cottonseed	na			na	—
Groundnuts	na			na	—
Linseed oil					
Sesame seed	na			na	—
Soya beans	215*	na		na	—
5. LIVESTOCK‡, ANIMAL PRODUCTS, etc.					
Cattle d	677				
Goats d	148*				
Sheep d	140*				
Horses d	25*				
Pigs d; Meat‡, 'A'	1 258				
Butter	20*	na		na	—
Eggs	4*				
Fish	500¹	223			0.1*
Milk	54*				

d no. in thousands.

	Production		Exports		Imports
6. FIBRES, TEXTILES, etc.					
Cotton lint.	na			na	na
Hemp fibre	na			na	na
Rubber, natural	—	—	386.3	na	na
Silk f	na			na	na
Cotton: yarn	na			na	na
woven fabrics	na			na	na
Rayon, yarn/fabrics	na			na	na
f metric tons. p 1957 data.					
7. FUEL AND POWER					
Coal	11 700*n	710¹*	na	na	na
Electricity h	12 486	1 010¹*		na	na
n 1961 data. h million kWh.					
8. IRON AND STEEL					
Iron ore	3 500*n	1 100*p	na	na	na
Pig iron	1 317	11.3*	na	na	na
Steel ingots/castings	1 128	67		na	na
n 1961 data. p 1957 data.					
9. NON-FERROUS MINERALS AND METALS					
Gold k, ore m	160.00*			na	na
Silver k, ore m	650.00*			na	na
Copper: ore	8.78*	na		na	na
metal	10.59²q	na		na	na
Lead: ore	45.36	2.00*	na	na	na
metal	54.43m	na		na	na
Manganese, metal	4.14*	7.50*	na	na	na
Tungsten, ore	101.30*m	na		na	na
Zinc: ore	68.00*			na	na
metal				na	na
k '000 fine troy oz. m metal content. q electrolytic.					
10. CHEMICALS n AND FERTILIZERS					
Chemicals n	na			na	na
Fertilizers:					
Phosphates	200.0*p	na		na	—
Potash				na	na
Pyrites	169.7	na		na	—
n data not available for years 1953–5. p apatite.					
11. INDUSTRY					
Cement	2 520.0	265.0¹	na	na	na

Apart from cement, no information on North Korea's industrial production is available.

na: data not available. — not available. — negligible or nil. ¹ one year only. ² two year average. * estimate. † re-exports. ‡ see appendix.

KOREA, SOUTH continued

PRODUCTION, EXPORTS AND IMPORTS continued

(Production columns: 1963–5 average and 1953–5 average. Units: '000 metric tons unless otherwise indicated)

	Production		Exports		Imports	
6. FIBRES, TEXTILES, etc.						
Abaca	—	—	—		—	
Cotton lint	4.0	17.7*	0.1		3.7	14.4
Flax fibre	0.1		—		66.5	
Hemp fibre	5.2	6.3	—	²	0.4	
Jute	—		—	²	—	
Rubber, natural	—		0.3		11.7	2.1
Silk f	757.3	544.0	727.7	189.7	14.7	3.3
Cotton: yarn	64.6	20.2	14.3	3.87¹	8.7	
woven fabrics	27.9	10.8*				
Rayon: fibre/yarn	5.8	6.82*	—		8.6	
woven fabrics	—					
Non-cellulosic	1.3	0.2	—	²	—	
woven fabrics	—					
Wool: yarn	3.5		—		—	
woven fabrics	9.7n	3.2p	—		—	

f metric tons. p million square metres.

	Production		Exports		Imports	
7. FUEL AND POWER						
Coal k, A ‡	9 570	1 310	240	29	130	882
Coke	7		—		28	8
Electricity h: total	3 005	840¹	—		—	
hydro	2 729	461				
thermal	2 276	380¹				
Oil, crude	na	na	—		767	
Petroleum, refined h	700	497¹q	—		647	
Rare earths f	na					

f metric tons. h million kWh. q monazite.

	Production		Exports		Imports	
8. IRON AND STEEL						
Iron ore m	326m	15m	615		—	13
Pig iron	14r	—	—		—	
Steel ingots/castings	173	4	—	10	28	
Iron/steel scrap	na		—		61	

m metal content. r excl. ferro-alloys.

	Production		Exports	Imports	
9. NON-FERROUS MINERALS AND METALS					
Gold k, ore m	76.30	38.00	—	—	
Silver k, ore m	427.30	51.20²	—	—	
Aluminium	1.59	0.09	—	4.01	6.11
Asbestos, fibre	na				
Cobalt	na				
Copper: ore	0.88m	1.16m	—	33.00	
metal	2.63	0.26	—		
Lead: ore	3.23m	0.31m	—	1.67	
metal	0.28	0.03	—	7.69	1.91
Magnesium: metal	na	na			
magnesite	na	na	12.10	1.40	1.78
dolomite	1.6	0.6			
Manganese, ore	5.05	2.71	1.40		

k fine troy oz. m metal content.

	Production	Exports	Imports
10. CHEMICALS AND FERTILIZERS			
Organic chemicals:			
Benzene	na		0.6
Butadiene	na		na
Ethylene	na		na
Methanol	na		7.1
Phenol	na		0.2
Phthalic anhydride	na		na
Styrene monomer	na		na
Urea	na		126.3
Inorganic chemicals:			
Ammonia	na		na
Carbon black	na		2.7
Chlorine	na		—
Nitric acid	na		1.5
Sodium carbonate	6.3		38.0
Sodium hydroxide	13.7		12.0
Sulphuric acid	na		na
Plastics:			
Polyamides	na		na
Polyethylene	—	²	83.1
Polyvinyl chloride	na		2.7
Fertilizers:			
Potash	na		83.1
Pyrites	na	0.1*x	
Sulphur	0.1*x		2.7

x sulphur content. n data not available for years 1953–5.

	Production	Exports	Imports
11. INDUSTRY			
Aircraft a	—	—	—
Alcoholic beverages b	266.0	—	1.0
Cement	1 212.0	52.7	102.7	291.7*
Electrical engineering a	—	—	18.2
Railway vehicles a	—	1.2†	7.4
Merchant ships g	3.0	—	6.0
Motor vehicles: commercial d p	1.6	—	5.2a
private d p	0.8	—	0.6a

b '000 hectolitres. d no. in thousands. g '000 G.R.T. p assembly of imported parts.

continued

PRODUCTION, EXPORTS AND IMPORTS

Years: 1963–5 average and 1953–5 average. Units: '000 metric tons unless otherwise indicated

	Production	Exports	Imports
1. CEREALS, etc.			
Cassava d	10.0	—	—
Maize (corn)	19.0*	—	—
Potatoes	14.3*	—	—
Rice	665.0	—	39.8*
Sweet potatoes/yams	11.7*	—	23.1¹
2. FRUIT, etc.			
Wine b	—	—	—
3. BEVERAGES, FOREST PRODUCTS, etc.			
Coffee	3.0	—	0.2²
Sugar, raw	2.6*	0.2²	2.6²
Tobacco leaf		0.7	0.9²
Softwood j		0.5²	
Hardwood j	204.3	3.0	0.2
Newsprint j	107.3	2.6	0.5
Other paper	na		
4. VEGETABLE OILSEEDS AND OILS			
Cottonseed	0.7	0.3	—
Groundnuts	na	0.71	—
Soya beans	na	na	—
5. LIVESTOCK‡, ANIMAL PRODUCTS, etc.			
Chickens d	10.0	na	—
Cattle d	19.0*	11.02*	—
Goats d		246.0¹	—
Sheep d		na	—
Horses d	11.7*	na	—
Pigs d		177.0¹	—
Meat†, 'A'		na	—
Eggs		5.0n	0.5²
Milk		0.8²	—
Hides/skins			—
6. FIBRES, TEXTILES, etc.			
Cotton: lint	2.0*	—	—
woven fabrics		—	na
7. FUEL AND POWER			
Electricity h, t	12	3¹	57
Petroleum, refined, h		—	10¹
9. NON-FERROUS MINERALS AND METALS			
Tin: ore m	0.32	0.21	0.43	0.09
11. INDUSTRY			
Cement	na	na	na

d no. in thousands. h million kWh. j '000 cu. metres of roundwood equivalent. m metal content. n government inspected meat only. t thermal.

MIDDLE EAST

LEBANON

Lebanon became an independent republic in 1941 after twenty years of French mandatory rule. In 1958 a serious insurrection broke out and rebels captured several towns. The authority of the government was restored only with the help of a considerable force of U.S. troops.

AREA: 8 800* sq. km. (3 400* sq. miles)

LAND USE: (percentage of total)

	1954	1965
Arable and orchard	26.5	28.5
Permanent meadow and pasture	7.9	1.0
Forest and woodland	65.6	9.1
City areas, waste and other land		61.4

POPULATION: 2 520 000 (1967 U.N. estimate)
Largest city: BEIRUT, capital; population: 700 000 (city proper, 1964)

	1965	Year(s)
Crude birth rate (per '000)	32.3*	1965
Crude death rate (per '000)	3.9*	1965
Population per physician	1 390	1966
Population per hospital bed	240	1966
School enrolment: age 5–19 years (percentage)	78	1963–4 av.
age over 19 years (per '000 population)	768	1963–5 av.

EMPLOYMENT AND PRODUCTION

Lebanon is essentially an agricultural country. Ancient cedar forests have suffered from over exploitation, which, with unrestricted grazing of goats, has limited tree growth and led to soil erosion. Iron ore exists, but is difficult to work. Manufacturing is limited, but has doubled in the last ten years. There is a transit trade in gold, and a refinery for oil imported from Iraq and Saudi Arabia.

COMMUNICATIONS

	1965	Year(s)
Motor vehicles in use ('000s): private	86.4	1963–5 av.
commercial	12.7	
Railway track (km)	368	1968
Mail per capita: domestic	15	1962–4 av.
foreign received	10	
Telephones (per '000 population)	4.8	1967
Radio receivers (per '000 population)	113	1963–5 av.
Television sets (per '000 population)	50.3	1963–5 av.
Daily newspapers (per '000 population)	97	1959

FINANCE

Currency unit: The Lebanese pound

Exchange rates	1965	1960	1950a	1938a
Per $ U.S.	3.07	3.15	2.21	1.90
Per £ sterling	8.62	8.82	6.16	8.74

	1965	Year
National Income (million $ U.S.)	408	1958
G.N.P. per capita ($ U.S.)	480	1966

a selling rate.

TRADING

Total trade (in million $ U.S.)	1965	1955
Exports (f.o.b.)	85 (105a)	34 (37a)
Imports (c.i.f.)	182 (582a)	218 (241a)

Main trading partners (percentage of total value) a

Exports	1965	1955	Imports	1965	1955
Saudi Arabia	26	10	France	14	16
Jordan	8	5	U.K.	14	14
Iraq	7	11	U.S.A.	10	13
Syria	—	6	Syria	8	6
Kuwait	5	na	Germany F.R.	6	4
U.S.A.	4	10	Italy	4	

Distribution of trade (percentage of total value)

Exports	1965	1955
Manufactured goods	33	44
Crude materials and fuels	24	36
Food	11	19

Imports	1965	1955
Manufactured goods	27	49
Food	23	27
Crude materials and fuels	12	20
Chemicals	4	4

a value including gold, specie, and banknotes.

continued

SOUTH EAST ASIA

LAOS

Laos, Cambodia and Vietnam, previously states of French Indo-China, became independent states within the French Union in 1949. A rebel invasion of Laos was quashed in 1954 when the Geneva conference called for the withdrawal of foreign forces from Laos, but internal unrest continued and resulted in several changes of government. Rebel movements within the country continue to cause instability, and the proximity to Vietnam has led to some involvement in the Vietnamese war.

AREA: 236 800 sq. km. (91 430 sq. miles)

LAND USE: (percentage of total)

	1964
Arable and orchard	3.4
Permanent meadow and pasture	3.4
Forest and woodland	59.3
City areas, waste and other land	33.9

POPULATION: 2 770 000 (1967 estimate)
Largest city: VIENTIANE, capital; population: 162 297 (1962)

		Year(s)
Crude birth rate (per '000)	47*	1965
Crude death rate (per '000)	23*	1965
Population per physician	20 000	1965
Population per hospital bed	1 650	1966
School enrolment: age 5–19 years (percentage)	24	1963–4 av.
age over 19 years (per 100 000 population)	7	1964–5 av.

COMMUNICATIONS

		Year(s)
Motor vehicles in use ('000s): private	5.4 }	1963–5 av.
commercial		
Radio receivers (per '000 population)	1.8	1963–5 av.
Daily newspapers (per '000 population)	11	1962–4 av.

FINANCE

Currency unit: The kip

Exchange rates	1965	1960	1958
Per $ U.S.	240	80	35
Per £ sterling	672	224	98

		Year
National Income (million $ U.S.)	130	1958
G.N.P. per capita ($ U.S.)	70	1966

EMPLOYMENT AND TRADE

The chief products are rice, maize, and tobacco; much of the land is forested, and the output of teak is considerable; opium also is a source of revenue. Various minerals are found in small quantities, but only tin is mined at present. Industry is limited mainly to weaving and crafts, although there are some saw and rice mills. Exports in 1964 consisted of tin, green coffee and timber; imports consisted of foodstuffs, manufactured goods and machinery, many of which came from the U.S.A. under aid agreements. The chief trading partners were Thailand, the U.S.A., France and the U.K.

continued

---

*na: data not available. — negligible or nil. ¹ one year only. ² two year average. * estimate. ‡ see appendix. † re-exports.*

LESOTHO

Lesotho, formerly the British protectorate of Basutoland, became a republic within the Commonwealth in 1966. The country is surrounded by South African territory and is linked to the South African customs union.

AREA: 30 350 sq. km. (11 720 sq. miles)

LAND USE: (percentage of total)

	1962	1954
Arable and orchard	11.7	12.4
Permanent meadow and pasture	82.2	87.3
Forest and woodland	—	0.3
City areas, waste and otherland	6.1	

POPULATION: 852 459 a (1966 census)
Capital city: MASERU; population: 18 000 (1966)
a excl. absentees working in South Africa (about 12% of the total population).

PRODUCTION, EXPORTS AND IMPORTS
Years: 1963–5 average and 1953–5 average   Units: '000 metric tons unless otherwise indicated

1. CEREALS, etc.

	Production	Exports	Imports
Barley	4.0*	—	—
Maize (corn)	115.0*	—	—
Millets/sorghum	55.0*	—	—
Wheat	41.7†	—	—

FINANCE
Currency unit: The rand was introduced in 1961 at the rate R1 to £0.5 sterling.

Exchange rates

	1965	1960a	1955a	1938a
Per $ U.S.	0.714	0.357	0.357	0.218

		Year
National Income (million $ U.S.)	52*	1966
G.N.P. per capita ($ U.S.)	60	1966

a pounds.

EMPLOYMENT, PRODUCTION AND TRADE
The economy is almost exclusively agricultural, the main crops being wheat, maize, sorghum, barley, oats, and vegetables. Terracing and rotational grazing has improved the pasture for sheep and other livestock.
The main exports are wool and mohair. Remittances from many of the emigrant labourers working in South African mines and industries contribute to the country's income. Trade is mainly with South Africa.

5. LIVESTOCK‡, ANIMAL PRODUCTS, etc.
Units: '000 metric tons unless otherwise indicated

	Production		Exports		Imports	
	1965	1955	1965	1955	1965	1955
Cattle	352.0*	407.0²	—	—	—	—
Goats d	824.0*	599.5²	—	—	—	—
Sheep d	1 450.7	1 311.0²	—	—	—	—
Horses d	87.3*	102.0¹	—	—	—	—
Pigs d	60.0*	na	—	—	—	—
Meat† 'A'	22.0*	na	—	—	—	—
Fish	na	24.7	—	—	—	—
Hides/skins						
Wool	2.1*	2.0	na	na	—	—

LIBERIA

Liberia is an independent republic with a constitution modelled on that of the U.S.A. In 1950 a development programme was initiated and in 1963 the U.S.A. and Germany F.R. granted loans for construction of hydro-electric power units and road systems.

AREA: 111 000 sq. km. (43 000 sq. miles)

LAND USE: (percentage of total)

	1964	1948
Arable and orchard	34.5	16.3
Permanent meadow and pasture	32.5	2.3
Forest and woodland	30.8	34.9
City areas, waste and otherland		46.5

POPULATION: 1 110 000 (1967 U.N. estimate)
Capital city: MONROVIA; population: 80 992 (city proper, 1962)

Distribution of working population (1962)
Total working population: 411 794

U.N. group no.		Percentage
0	Agriculture, forestry, fishing and hunting	80.9
1	Mining and quarrying	3.5
2/3	Manufacturing	2.1
4	Construction	2.9
5	Electricity, gas, water and sanitary services	0.1
6	Commerce	2.8
7	Transport, storage and communications	0.9
8	Services	6.0
9	Others	0.8

		Year(s)
Life expectancy at birth (years): male	36.1*	1962
female	38.6*	
Population per physician	11 570	1965
Population per hospital bed	600	1964
School enrolment: age 5–19 years (percentage)	22	1963–4 av.
age over 19 years (per 100 000 population)	61	1964–5 av.

COMMUNICATIONS

		Year(s)
Railway track (km.)	338	1963
Telephones (per '000 urban population)	10.3	1967
Radio receivers (per '000 population)	113	1963–5 av.
Television sets (per '000 population)	1.5	1963–5 av.
Daily newspapers (per '000 population)	2.8	1962–4 av.

FINANCE
Currency unit: the Liberian dollar, at par with the $ U.S. which is also in circulation.

Exchange rates

	1965	1960	1950	1938
Per £ sterling	2.8	2.8	2.8	4.6

		Year
National Income (million $ U.S.)	154	1964
G.N.P. per capita ($ U.S.)	210	1966

TRADING
Total trade (in million $ U.S.)

	1965	1955	1938
Exports (f.o.b.)	135	43	2
Imports (c.i.f.)	105	26	2

Main trading partners (percentage of total value)

Exports	1965	1955	Imports	1965	1955
U.S.A.	37	87	U.S.A.	48	62
Germany F.R.	27	4	U.K.	12	11
Italy	9	2	Germany F.R.	10	11
U.K.	6	1	Japan	5	na
Belg./Lux.	6		Sweden	4	7
Netherlands	5	5	Netherlands	4	
France	4		Italy	3	

Distribution of trade (percentage of total value)

Exports	1965
Iron ore and concentrates	73
Natural rubber and rubber-like gums	22
Palm nuts and kernels	2

Imports	1965	1955
Manufactured goods	67	63
(machinery and transport equipment)	(24)	(25)
Food	14	17
Crude materials and fuels	9	8
Chemicals	6	6
Beverages and tobacco	3	3

Shipping: The Liberian merchant navy had in 1963 a gross registered tonnage of 10.6 million. The Liberian government requires only a modest registration fee and a nominal annual charge, and maintains no control over the operation of ships flying the Liberian flag.

continued

na: data not available. — negligible or nil. * estimate. ‡ see appendix. † re-exports.

LEBANON continued

PRODUCTION, EXPORTS AND IMPORTS
Years: 1963–5 average and 1953–5 average   Units: '000 metric tons unless otherwise indicated

1. CEREALS, etc.

	Production		Exports		Imports	
Barley	12.7	26.3	4.0	13.2	57.9	22.2
Maize (corn)	10.7	na	0.5	2.8	33.5	13.5²
Millets/sorghum	9.7	10.0	0.2	13.7	3.7	13.8
Oats	2.0*	2.0	—	—	—	0.1
Potatoes	68.0	33.3	28.8	13.0	2.3	5.3
Rice	—	0.7	0.3	—	17.6	10.8
Sweet potatoes/yams	1.0*	na				
Wheat	58.3	56.7	0.6	1.6	205.6	96.5

2. FRUIT, etc.

	Production		Exports		Imports	
Apples	105.0	30.0²	62.4	10.4	0.5	0.8
Apricots	9.7	2.0¹	11.9	0.1	—	—
Bananas	25.0	17.3		7.1	—	3.9
Dates	na	na	7.7	0.5	3.5	
Figs	29.3	75.0²	1.8	8.9	3.6	5.0
Grapes	66.7	29.0	28.8	31.5		
Lemons	153.3	76.7	75.5		1.2	
Oranges	46.3	25.0²	0.4	0.6²	—	0.22
Peaches	7.7	2.0¹	2.2	2.0¹	0.1	0.3
Plums	7.7	11.0²	2.1		0.2	0.3
Raisins	0.3*	0.2¹	0.5		2.7	1.3
Tomatoes	40.3	23.5²				
Wine b						

b '000 hectolitres.

3. BEVERAGES, FOREST PRODUCTS, etc.

	Production		Exports		Imports	
Cocoa	62.3	na			0.5	0.4
Coffee	1.7	1.0¹			3.2	1.4
Sugar: beet	1.4		0.1		53.7	26.0
cane	1 425.0	970.0	2.1	0.4	0.7	0.2
Tea	5.3	2.2			0.2	0.3
Tobacco: leaf	2.4¹	0.3	0.2*			
cigarettes	14.7*	13.0²	1.7*	na		
tobacco/snuff	21.0*	31.0²	3.0²		171.5¹	76.3
Softwood f	8.3*		7.5¹		38.0¹	15.7
Hardwood f			2.2¹		4.3	
Newsprint	0.23	1.43	0.71		27.0¹	7.0
Other paper						

4. VEGETABLE OILSEEDS AND OILS

	Production		Exports		Imports	
Castor oil	—	—	—	—	0.01	1.07*
Copra	na	na	0.05	0.30q	0.64	0.49
Coconut oil	na	0.67	0.35†	1.46	45.44	35.27q
Cottonseed	3.50	1.40²	—	—		
Cottonseed oil	na	na	—	—	0.01	0.01
Groundnuts	na	na	0.01	0.97	0.01	0.09
Linseed oil	9.00*	8.00*	0.54		0.14	0.76
Olive oil					0.1	0.05
Palm oil	0.23	1.43	0.31	0.47	2.3	
Sesame seed					5.4	2.37

q incl. hempseed.

5. LIVESTOCK‡, ANIMAL PRODUCTS, etc.

	Production		Exports		Imports	
Chickens d	11 922.7*	1 640.0¹	0.2*		123.4*	41.0
Cattle d	102.0	30.0	1.7*	na	730.6*	
Goats d	454.0¹	500.0¹				
Sheep d	84.3	60.0			0.1	0.8
Horses d	9.0	2.7	0.1		0.1	1.5
Meat† 'A','B'	57.7*	17.0	0.1		2.3	2.2
Butter	9.00*		0.54			
Cheese	7.0*	4.5²	0.2	0.1	5.4	

continued

5. LIVESTOCK, ANIMAL PRODUCTS, etc.—continued

	Production		Exports		Imports	
Eggs	9.3*	1.5²	3.3	0.4	0.2	1.8
Fish	2.2	na			3.8	na
Milk	9.0*	na			49.4	1.4*
Hides/skins			4.0†	1.4†	9.1	3.3
Wool			2.3†	1.0†	1.7	0.7

d no. in thousands. r incl. ducks, geese and turkeys. t goats registered for taxation only.

6. FIBRES, TEXTILES, etc.

	Production		Exports		Imports	
Cotton lint	na	na	2.5†	1.3†	5.9	3.6
Hemp fibre	na	na			0.9	—
Jute	na	na			6.0	—
Rubber, natural	na	na			0.42	2.17²
Silk f		27.0	4.0	17.7		
Cotton: yarn	3.5¹	3.5²	0.12	na	2.12	0.72²
woven fabrics	na	na	0.12	na	na	na
Rayon, woven fabrics	na	2.9n			0.3	0.4
Wool: yarn	na	0.3¹	0.22p		na	0.8
woven fabrics						

f metric tons. n million metres. p excl. blankets.

7. FUEL AND POWER

	Production		Exports		Imports	
Coal 'A'‡	—	—	—	—	694	1 270
Coke	—	—	—	—	410¹	67
Electricity h: total		190¹	2†			
hydro		170¹	1†			
thermal		80¹				
Oil, crude		860¹		—		
Petroleum, refined	1 226	860¹	143	—¹	890¹	401¹

h million kWh.

8. IRON AND STEEL

	Production		Exports		Imports	
Iron ore		21m	35		9	3
Pig iron	—	—	—	—	35	—
Steel ingots/castings	—	—	1	5	7	1
Iron/steel scrap						

m metal content.

9. NON-FERROUS MINERALS AND METALS

	Production		Exports		Imports	
Gold k: bullion/coins etc.	na		88.50†	2 100.00†	681.30	
Platinum group metals k					3.60	1.81
Silver k, bullion					56.37	0.36
Asbestos: fibre manufactured	19.18	1.91			3.50	1.46¹
Mica					0.54	
Aluminium					2.54	0.57
Copper, metal					0.58	0.37
Lead, metal					0.53	0.01
Tin, metal					0.01	0.01
Zinc, metal					0.87	0.15

k '000 fine troy oz.

10. CHEMICALS n AND FERTILIZERS

	Production		Exports		Imports	
Chemicals					na	
Fertilizers: Potash	—	—	—	—	3.5	0.8
Sulphur	—	—	—	—	12.7	

n data not available for years 1953–5.

11. INDUSTRY

	Production		Exports		Imports	
Aircraft a					na	
Beer b	2.8		—		1.5	2.5
Cement	849.3	366.0	83.3*	38.3	71.7*	6.7
Electrical engineering g					16.0	1.7
Machine tools a					0.1	
Merchant ships a					0.2	
Motor vehicles a					22.9	6.8

a million: $ U.S. b '000 hectolitres. g '000 G.R.T.

e no. in millions. f sawn logs only. j '000 cu. metres of roundwood equivalent. p sawn logs only. n sales.

na: data not available. — negligible or nil. ¹ one year only. ² two year average. * estimate. ‡ see appendix. † re-exports.

LIBERIA continued

PRODUCTION, EXPORTS AND IMPORTS
Years: 1963–5 average and 1953–5 average   Units: '000 metric tons unless otherwise indicated

	Production	Exports	Imports
1. CEREALS, etc.			
Cassava	423.3	—	—
Maize (corn)	na	—	0.1²
Potatoes	na	—	0.8³
Rice	181.3*	—	31.1*n
2. FRUIT, etc.			
Apples	—	—	0.1¹
Oranges	5.0*	—	11.0¹
Wine b	—	—	1.5²
3. BEVERAGES, FOREST PRODUCTS, etc.			
Cocoa	2.7*	1.0¹	0.4
Coffee	3.5*	0.8¹	0.3
Sugar: cane	na	—	3.1*
raw	na	—	0.5¹
Tobacco: leaf	na	—	1.3
Softwood j	na	—	—
Hardwood j	1 706.0¹* 8 700.0²	8.16¹*	2.6¹
Other paper	na	—	0.2
4. VEGETABLE OILSEEDS AND OILS			
Castor oil	1.40*	—	—
Groundnuts	na	—	0.01¹
Groundnut oil	na	—	0.04
Olive oil	na	—	0.14¹
Palm kernels	7.63*	12.07	—
Palm oil	41.20*	0.11	0.05
5. LIVESTOCK‡, ANIMAL PRODUCTS, etc.			
Butter	—	—	0.1²
Cheese	—	—	0.3¹
Eggs	7.8*	0.6p	1.4
Fish	2.0*	na	6.0
Milk	na	—	—
6. FIBRES, TEXTILES, etc.			
Rubber, natural	na	44.4*	34.4
7. FUEL AND POWER			
Electricity h: total	224	—	—
hydro	17	—	—
thermal	207	—	—
Petroleum, refined	na	—	—
8. IRON AND STEEL			
Iron ore	7 708m	959m	11 336
9. NON-FERROUS MINERALS AND METALS			
Diamonds a	na	3.90	0.38
Gold k, ore	2.00*m	1.00*m	0.89q
11. INDUSTRY			
Alcoholic beverages			
beer b	2.0	—	2.31a
Cement	na	—	96.7
Electrical engineering a	na	—	6.81
Railway vehicles a	na	—	2.41
Motor vehicles a	na	—	1 531.0
Motor vehicles a	na	0.1	9.5
Meat: 'A'	na	—	—
'B'	3.0*	na	2.1

d no. in thousands.   *b* incl. fish landed by foreign vessels.   *h* million kWh.   *m* metal content.   *k* '000 fine troy oz.   *m* metal content.   *q* bullion.   *a* million $ U.S.   *b* '000 hectolitres.   *j* '000 cu. metres of roundwood equivalent.   *g* '000 G.R.T.   *p* see note on shipping in Trading section above.

continued

LIBYA

In 1939 Libya, formerly a Turkish and, later, an Italian province, was incorporated into the national territory of Italy. After World War II Tripolitania and Cyrenaica were placed under British, and Fezzan under French Administration until 1949 when Libya became the first independent state to be created by the United Nations. The U.S.A. and the U.K. were granted military facilities, later extended also to the U.S.S.R., in return for economic aid.
The monarchy was overthrown in 1969 and a republic declared.

AREA: 1 759 540 sq. km. (679 358 sq. miles).   Cyrenaica 49%; Tripolitania 20%; Fezzan 31%.
LAND USE: (percentage of total)

	Cyrenaica 1959	Tripolitania 1962	Fezzan 1962
Arable and orchard	0.9	4.9	0.1
Permanent meadow and pasture	0.6	23.4	—
Forest and woodland	0.5	0.1	—
City areas, waste and other land	98.0	71.6	99.9

POPULATION: 1 738 000 (1967 estimate)
Largest city: ṬARĀBULUS (Tripoli), capital; population: 213 506 (city proper, 1964)

Distribution of working population (1964)
Total working population: 405 258

U.N. group no.		Percentage
0	Agriculture, forestry, fishing and hunting	35.7
2/3	Mining and quarrying	3.5
	Manufacturing	7.2
4	Construction	7.8
5	Electricity, gas, water and sanitary services	1.5
6	Commerce	6.6
7	Transport, storage and communications	5.6
8	Services	20.4
9	Others	11.7

Note.—The discovery of oil in 1959 altered completely the pattern of the country's economy, and whereas 80% of the population had previously been engaged in subsistence farming, this figure had been halved by 1964, as the production of crude oil developed into a major industry.

		Year(s)
Crude birth rate (per '000)	37.2*	1966
Crude death rate (per '000)	6.7*	1966
Population per physician	3 160	1966
Population per hospital bed	310	1966
School enrolment: age 5–19 years (percentage)	53	1963–4 av.
age over 19 years (per 100 000 population)	114	1964–5 av.

NORTH AFRICA

COMMUNICATIONS

			Year(s)
Motor vehicles in use ('000s): private	35.3		1963–5 av.
commercial	18.1		
Mail per capita: domestic	8		1963–5 av.
foreign received	7		
foreign sent	1.1		
Telephones (per '000 urban population)	29		1967
Radio licences (per '000 population)	5		1963–5 av.
Daily newspapers (per '000 population)			1962–4 av.

FINANCE
Currency unit: The Libyan pound

Exchange rates	1960
Per $U.S.	0.357
Per £ sterling	1.0

		Year
National Income (million $ U.S.)	1 028	1965
G.N.P. per capita ($ U.S.)	640	1966

TRADING

	1965
Total trade (in million $ U.S.)	
Exports (f.o.b.)	797
Imports (c.i.f.)	320

Main trading partners (percentage of total value)

Exports	1965	1955	Imports	1965	1955
Germany F.R.	28	9	Italy	25	27
Italy	10	39	U.K.	15	25
France	9	2	U.S.A.	15	6
Netherlands	8	na	Germany F.R.	10	4
Spain	3		Japan	4	1
U.S.A.	3		Netherlands	3	5

Distribution of trade (percentage of total value)

Exports	1965
Crude oil	99

Imports	1955	
Manufactured goods (textiles and transport equipment) (textiles and clothing)	74	(36) (15)
Food	13	(10)
Crude materials and fuels (petroleum products)	6	(4)
Chemicals	6	5

continued

PRODUCTION, EXPORTS AND IMPORTS
Years: 1963–5 average and 1953–5 average   Units: '000 metric tons unless otherwise indicated

	Production	Exports	Imports
1. CEREALS, etc.			
Barley	112.0	—	9.8 3.4
Maize (corn)	2.7*p 35.0¹p	—	0.5
Millets/sorghum	1.3 1.02	—	1.7 4.7
Potatoes	11.0 1.5p	—	9.9 3.3
Rice	20.0p	—	10.7 19.8
Wheat	51.0* 19.5*	— 0.1	0.4
2. FRUIT, etc.			
Apples	1.0*	—	4.4
Apricots	na	—	2.8
Bananas	6.3	—	
Cherries	39.3 27.5²	—	
Dates	3.7*	—	
Figs	8.0* 3.0²	—	
Grapes	1.3 0.7*p	—	
Lemons	14.7* 5.0²*p	0.2	0.4
Oranges	100.7p 22.0p	3.1	0.1
Pears	6.7		1.2
Plums	na		
Raisins	114.3	0.6	
Tomatoes	na		
Wine b			1.0¹
3. BEVERAGES, FOREST PRODUCTS, etc.			
Coffee		—	0.6 0.2
Sugar, raw		—	24.5 10.2
Tea	1.0*	—	4.5 2.3
Tobacco: leaf	1.3	1.62*	0.3 0.3²
cigars	843.0a	—	
cigarettes	0.2	—	0.4
tobacco/snuff	26.5²	1.41	86.8 35.0¹
Softwood j	290.0²*	27.0²	5.0¹
Hardwood j			0.3² 0.01
Newsprint	2.8²*	—	2.2 0.8²
Other paper			
4. VEGETABLE OILSEEDS AND OILS			
Castor seed	3.67*p 3.05	3.62	1.85² 0.24
Castor oil			0.37² 0.03
Coconut oil			0.01
Cottonseed oil			0.02
Groundnuts	7.00 5.60¹p	4.31	5.13 1.06
Groundnut oil			1.72
Linseed oil			1.79
Olive oil	9.67p 4.33	2.20²	0.02
Palm kernel oil			0.03
Palm oil			2.11
Soya bean oil			
5. LIVESTOCK‡, ANIMAL PRODUCTS, etc.			
Chickens d	915.0* 283.3u		2.8
Cattle d	121.7* 120.5r	4.2	69.9
Goats d	2 053.0 1 022.5²r		
Sheep d	1 860.0 1 290.3r		
Horses d	37.0 16.7		0.3
Pigs d	4.0p 1.54p	0.2¹	0.4
Meat: 'A'	10.7*		0.3
'B'	2.5*	na	1.1
Butter	—	—	0.1¹²
Cheese	2.7*	0.2	0.3
Eggs	0.32 2.2	0.1 na	17.3 2.2*
Milk	12.3*	2.1	
Hides/skins	na 1.0	0.7 1.1²	
Wool			
6. FIBRES, TEXTILES, etc.			
Cotton, woven fabrics			1.51*
Wool, yarn			0.1²
7. FUEL AND POWER			
Coal/coke	—	—	—
Electricity h t	153 60¹	—	6
Oil, crude	40 750 1	40 660	
Petroleum, refined	na	—	340
8. IRON AND STEEL			
Iron/steel scrap	—	—	—
9. NON-FERROUS MINERALS AND METALS			
Silver k, metal manufactured	108.58	4²	
Asbestos	na		
11. INDUSTRY			
Aircraft a			0.5 0.1
Beer b	28.0		363.3 47.3*
Cement			
Electrical engineering a			22.2 1.3²
Motor vehicles a			43.4 1.7

d no. in thousands.   *p* Tripolitania only.   *r* no. registered for taxation.   *u* Cyrenaica only.
p Tripolitania only.
b '000 hectolitres.   *p* Tripolitania only.
e no. in millions.   *j* '000 cu. metres of roundwood equivalent.
h million kWh.   *t* thermal.
b '000 hectolitres.

LIECHTENSTEIN

Liechtenstein has been a principality for over 500 years. Since 1924 close economic and diplomatic ties have existed with Switzerland.

AREA: 160 sq. km. (61.8 sq. miles)

LAND USE: (percentage of total)

	1953
Arable and orchard	12.5
Permanent meadow and pasture	43.7
Forest and woodland	25.0
City areas, waste and other land	18.8

POPULATION: 20 000 (1967 estimate)
Capital city: VADUZ; population: 3 514 (city proper, 1961)
Total working population: 7 575

		Year(s)
Infant mortality (per '000)	15.2*	1965
Crude birth rate (per '000)	20.6*	1965
Crude death rate (per '000)	3.1*	1965
School enrolment: age 5–19 years (percentage)	103‡	1963–4 av.

FINANCE
Currency unit: The Swiss franc

Exchange rates	1957	1962	1965
Per $U.S.	4.37	4.30	4.318
Per £ sterling	12.24	12.05	12.103

EMPLOYMENT, PRODUCTION, AND TRADE
Liechtenstein has changed during the past thirty years from a predominantly agricultural to a highly industrialized country. The farming population has decreased from 70% in 1930 to 8.7% in 1965. Poultry (40 000), cattle (6 000), pigs (6 000) and sheep (1 000) are the principal livestock reared; crops include potatoes (8 000 tons annually) and maize; timber is also of importance. The rapid changeover to light industries such as textiles, ceramics, precision instruments, canned foods and heating appliances has led to a large-scale immigration of foreign workers.
Exports are sent mainly to Switzerland, Germany F.R., France, Austria and the U.S.A. Tourism has recently been developed. There is a customs union with Switzerland, and general trade data for Liechtenstein are included in the Swiss statistics.

EUROPE

na: data not available.   — not available.   — negligible or nil.   * estimate.   1 one year only.   2 two year average.   ‡ see appendix.   † re-exports.

LUXEMBOURG — EUROPE

In 1921 a fifty-year economic union was formed between Belgium and the Grand Duchy of Luxembourg. Luxembourg became a member of Benelux in 1944, and in 1958 a member of the European Economic Community.

AREA: 2586 sq. km. (999 sq. miles)

LAND USE: (percentage of total)

	1965	1954
Arable and orchard	26.7	30.1
Permanent meadow and pasture	24.7	23.6
Forest and woodland	33.2	33.2
City areas, waste and other land	15.4	13.1

POPULATION: 335 000 (1967 estimate)
Capital city: LUXEMBOURG; population: 78 721 (1965)
Total working population: 129 760 (1960) (excl. those in compulsory military service)

Distribution of working population (1960)

U.N. group no.		Percentage
0	Agriculture, forestry, fishing and hunting	14.9
1	Mining and quarrying	3.5
2/3	Manufacturing	33.3
4	Construction	8.3
5	Electricity, gas, water and sanitary services	0.6
6	Commerce	12.1
7	Transport, storage and communications	6.6
8	Services	21.7
9	Others	1.0

		Year(s)
Life expectancy at birth (years): male	61.7	1946–8 av.
female	65.8	
Infant mortality (per '000)	24	1965
Crude birth rate (per '000)	16	1965
Crude death rate (per '000)	12.3	1965
Accidental deaths (per 100 000 population)	26	1967
caused by motor vehicles	90	1967
Population per physician	1030	1963
Population per hospital bed	90	1966
School enrolment: age 5–19 years (percentage)	65	1963–4 av.
age over 19 years (per 100 000 population)	154	1963–5 av.

COMMUNICATIONS

		Year(s)
Motor vehicles in use ('000s): private	55.7	1963–5 av.
commercial	10.4	1964
Railway track (km.)	338	
Mail per capita: domestic	149	
foreign received	69	1963–5 av.
foreign sent	36	
Telephones (per '000 urban population)	25.8	1967
Radio licences (per '000 population)	347	1963–5 av.
Television sets (per '000 population)	74.3	1963–5 av.
Daily newspapers (per '000 population)	425	1964

FINANCE

Currency unit: The Luxembourg franc, at par with the Belgian franc

Exchange rates	1965	1960	1950	1938
Per $ U.S.	49.64	49.70	50.12	23.74
Per £ sterling	139.15	139.35	140.40	109.20

		Year
National Income (million $ U.S.)	496	1965
G.N.P. per capita ($ U.S.)	1920	1966

PRODUCTION AND TRADE

In 1965 about 20 000 people were employed in agriculture, the principal crops being oats, potatoes and wheat; cattle and pig rearing are widespread.

The mining and metallurgical industries are the most important. Luxembourg has the highest steel production per capita in the world. Engineering is well developed and the production of beer is also of importance.

Trade statistics are included with those for Belgium.

PRODUCTION

Years: 1963–5 average and 1953–5 average   Units: '000 metric tons unless otherwise indicated

Note—trade figures are included with those for Belgium

1. CEREALS, etc.

	Production 1963–5	1953–5	Exports	Imports
Barley	20.7	13.3		
Oats	34.0	39.0		
Potatoes	57.3	133.3		
Rye	7.3	13.7		
Wheat	42.3	40.0		

2. FRUIT, etc.

Apples	11.3	na
Cherries	1.0*	na
Grapes	20.0*	14.7*
Pears	2.7*	na
Plums	1.0	na
Wine b	141.0	105.0

b '000 hectolitres.

3. BEVERAGES, FOREST PRODUCTS, etc.

Softwood j	77.3	68.3
Hardwood j	114.3	81.7

j '000 cu. metres of roundwood equivalent.

5. LIVESTOCK‡, ANIMAL PRODUCTS, etc.

Chickens d	433.7	421.0*
Cattle d	161.0	132.3
b dairy cows d	67.7	54.3
Goats d	0.1	0.3
Sheep d	2.3*	3.0
Horses d	2.7	11.6
Pigs d	100.0	93.7

5. LIVESTOCK‡; ANIMAL PRODUCTS, etc. (Production)

	1963–5	1953–5
Meat‡ 'A'	25.7	18.7
'B'	3.8*	na
Butter	5.0	4.0
Cheese	1.0	1.0*
Eggs	3.6	2.3
Fish	0.6†	0.4†
Milk	194.0	180.7
Hides/skins	1.0	0.9

d no. in thousands.   † sport fishing only.

7. FUEL AND POWER

Electricity h: total	2122
hydro	737
thermal	1385

h million kWh.

8. IRON AND STEEL

	Production	Exports
Iron ore	1 849 m	1 817 m
Pig iron	3 974	2 869
Steel ingots/castings	4 392	2 904

m metal content.

11. NON-FERROUS MINERALS AND METALS

Magnesium, dolomite	239.5

11. INDUSTRY

	1963–5	1953–5
Beer b	501.0	372.3
Spirits b	2.0 p	5.7 t
Cement	210.0	152.0

b '000 hectolitres.   p 1966 figure.   t 1960 figure.

continued

MALAGASY REPUBLIC — INDIAN OCEAN

Malagasy, formerly the French colony of Madagascar, became an independent state within the French Community in 1960. Foreign aid has financed improvements in transport, agriculture, industry and social projects.

AREA: 594 180 sq. km. (229 233 sq. miles)

LAND USE: (percentage of total)

	1964	1954
Arable and orchard	4.9	2.2
Permanent meadow and pasture	52.0	62.7
Forest and woodland	21.7	20.3
City areas, waste and other land	21.4	14.8

POPULATION: 6 200 000 (1966 estimate)
Largest city: TANANARIVE (Antananarivo), capital; population: 335 149 (city proper, 1966)
Total working population: 3 200 000 (1964)

		Year(s)
Life expectancy at birth (years): male	37.5*	
female	38.3*	
Infant mortality (per '000)	65.5*	1966
Crude birth rate (per '000)	32.3*	1965
Crude death rate (per '000)	10.4*	1965
Population per physician	10 540	1965
Population per hospital bed	350	1965
School enrolment: age 5–19 years (percentage)	39	1963–4 av.
age over 19 years (per 100 000 population)	40	1963–5 av.

EMPLOYMENT AND PRODUCTION

The majority of the people are engaged in agriculture. Forest resources are abundant. Mineral products include graphite, chrome, mica, and various rarer ores. Industry includes cotton and silk weaving, metal work, food processing, cement, and the manufacture of soap.

COMMUNICATIONS

		Year(s)
Motor vehicles in use ('000s): private	29.5	1963–5 av.
commercial	26.7	
Railway track (km.)	864	1965
Mail per capita: domestic	4.7	1963–5 av.
foreign received	2.1	
foreign sent	0.3	
Telephones (per '000 urban population)	49	1967
Radio receivers (per '000 population)	9	1963–5 av.
Daily newspapers (per '000 population)		1962

FINANCE

Currency unit: The Malagasy franc, at par with the franc CFA

Exchange rates	1965	1960	1958 a
Per $ U.S.	246.85	246.85	210
Per £ sterling	691.18	691.18	590

a francs CFA.

		Year
National Income (million $ U.S.)	424	1958
G.N.P. per capita ($ U.S.)	90	1966

TRADING

Total trade (in million $ U.S.)	1965	1955	1938 c
Exports (f.o.b.)	92	82	24
Imports (c.i.f.)	138	122	17

Main trading partners (percentage of total value)

Exports	1965	1955	Imports	1965	1955
France	45	65	France	63	73
U.S.A.	27	15	Thailand	6	na
Réunion	6	5	U.S.A.	4	4
Germany F.R.	5	2	Germany F.R.	4	2
U.K.	5	1	Iran	2	na
Italy	3	1	Netherlands	2	1
Comoro Arch.	1	na	Senegal	2	na

Distribution of trade (percentage of total value)

Exports	1965	1954*
Food	72	na
(coffee)	(32)	(43)
(vanilla)	(11)	(5)
(sugar and honey)	(5)	na
Crude materials and fuels	17	na
(sisal)	(6)	(2)
Tobacco	5	7

Imports	1965	1954*
Manufactured goods	64	na
(machinery and transport equipment)	(25)	(20)
(textiles and clothing)	(13)	(19)
Food	15	na
(rice)	(7)	na
Chemicals	9	2
Petroleum products	5	4
Alcoholic beverages	3	6

c includes the Comoro Archipelago.

PRODUCTION, EXPORTS AND IMPORTS

Years: 1963–5 average and 1953–5 average   Units: '000 metric tons unless otherwise indicated

1. CEREALS, etc.

	Production 1963–5	1953–5	Exports 1963–5	1953–5	Imports 1963–5	1953–5
Cassava	850.0	796.0[1]	1.3	7.5		
Maize (corn)	99.7*	64.5[2]	0.3	0.2	0.2	0.5
Millets/sorghum	60.0*	na				
Potatoes	73.3*	65.0[2]			0.3	2.7
Rice	1 237.3	1 013.7	22.0	32.3	28.4	

2. FRUIT, etc.

			Exports
Apples	10.0	na	
Bananas	150.0	na	0.1 n
Coconuts e	15.3	na	14.5
Grapes	2.0*	na	
Lemons	2.0*	na	
Oranges	14.0*	na	
Other citrus fruit	1.0	na	
Peaches	5.0	na	
Pineapples	7.0*	na	4.8[2]
Plums	2.3	na	
Tomatoes	8.0*	na	
Wine b	119.4	293.3	

b '000 hectolitres.   n incl. pears and quince.
e no. in millions.   j '000 cu. metres of roundwood equivalent.

3. BEVERAGES, FOREST PRODUCTS, etc.

	Production 1963–5	1953–5	Exports 1963–5	1953–5	Imports 1965	1955
Cocoa	0.4	0.41	0.4	0.3		0.2
Coffee	51.7	46.7*	44.1	41.7		
Sugar: cane	1 116.7	446.0[1]				
raw	99.8	25.7	57.4	5.7	0.5	0.3
Tea	5.8*	4.6*	4.2	4.2	0.4	0.3
Tobacco: leaf	14.1*	12.5[1]				
cigarettes	41.6	2.6*			1.0	
tobacco/snuff	379.0*	3.1[2]	4.8[2]		21.2	8.7*

3. BEVERAGES, FOREST PRODUCTS, etc.—continued

	Production 1963–5	1953–5	Exports 1963–5	1953–5	Imports 1965	1955
Softwood j	3410.0[1]	2 380.0[1]	3.8[2]	0.1[2]	12.5[1]	
Hardwood j			−2	−2	1.0[2]	
Newsprint j						
Other paper						

4. VEGETABLE OILSEEDS AND OILS

	Production 1963–5	1953–5	Exports		Imports
Castorseed	1.00	na	0.99	0.77	0.37
Castor oil	0.27*	1.00[2]	0.27	1.47	1.30 / 0.41[2]
Copra	na	na	1.09		0.01 / 1.75 / 0.12
Coconut oil	3.00	na			0.09
Cottonseed	na	na			
Cottonseed oil	na	na			
Groundnuts	25.20	16.45	5.32	7.53	0.17 / 0.03 / 0.05
Groundnut oil	na	na		0.04	0.06
Linseed oil					
Olive oil					0.15
Palm oil					
Rapeseed oil					
Tung oil	1.00*	0.51	0.93	0.41	

5. LIVESTOCK‡, ANIMAL PRODUCTS, etc.

	Production 1963–5	1953–5	Exports	Imports
Chickens d	13 428.3*	13 000.0*		
Cattle d	6 418.3*	5 974.0	11.4	5.6
b dairy cows d	2 180.0*	471.0		
Goats d	300.0*	378.3		0.1
Sheep d	300.0	223.7	6.9	1.0
Horses d	450.0	54.0*	3.2	0.1
Meat‡: 'A'	85.7*	na		
'B'	2.1*			
Butter	14.1*	12.5[1]	0.3	5.3
Cheese	41.6	2.6*		
Eggs			0.2	
Fish	379.0*	3.1[2]	0.1	
Milk			0.6	
Hides/skins	2.41	2.8[2]	0.3	1.0*

d no. in thousands.

continued

---

na: data not available.   — negligible or nil.   —— not available.   [1] one year only.   [2] two year average.   * estimate.   ‡ see appendix.   † re-exports.

MALAGASY REPUBLIC continued

PRODUCTION, EXPORTS AND IMPORTS continued

	Production	Exports	Imports
6. FIBRES, TEXTILES, etc.			
Agaves (sisal)	26.1	26.5	—
Cotton-lint	2.0	0.2	8.1
Jute	2.0	—	1.9
Silk f		—	2.7
Cotton: yarn	2.4 f	—	1.2
woven fabrics	2.4	—	4.2
f metric tons.			
7. FUEL AND POWER			
Coal 'A' ‡	—	—	14
Coke	140	—	—
Electricity h: total	80	—	—
hydro	70	—	—
thermal			
Petroleum, refined	—	—	150
Rare earths f:	888	863	—
monazite	22	8	—
bastnaesite			
uranothorianite	518 p	507	—
f metric tons. h million kWh. p containing approx. 60% thorium and 20% uranium.			
9. NON-FERROUS MINERALS AND METALS			
Gold k, ore	1.00 m	—	—
Asbestos			
Mica	0.76	0.92	0.69
Aluminium	0.54	0.59	0.30 r
a million $ U.S. b '000 hectolitres. g '000 G.R.T. k '000 fine troy oz. m metal content. q rum only. r incl. Comoro Archipelago.			

continued

PRODUCTION, EXPORTS AND IMPORTS

Years: 1964–5 average and 1953 Units: '000 metric tons unless otherwise indicated

	Production	Exports	Imports
1. CEREALS, etc.	1964-5 / 1953		
Cassava	137.3*	—	—
Maize (corn)	846.0* / 49.0	13.7 / 35.0	—
Millets/sorghum	40.0* / na	0.3	—
Potatoes	3.0* / na	—	0.2
Rice	5.0* / 4.7	1.3 / 1.4	—
Sweet potatoes/ yams	42.3* / na	—	—
Wheat	— / na	—	0.5
2. FRUIT, etc.			
Apples	5.0* / na	—	0.1
Bananas	— / na	—	—
Wine b			0.7
b '000 hectolitres.			
3. BEVERAGES, FOREST PRODUCTS, etc.			
Coffee	12.4 / 7.2	0.2	—
Sugar, raw	19.2 / 14.0	12.5	14.1*
Tea	11.5* / 7.6	13.3	1.9
Tobacco, leaf	3 348.0* / 5 844.7	5.0	7.0
Softwood j			5.3
Hardwood j			0.1
Newsprint			0.4
Other paper			
j '000 cu. metres of roundwood equivalent.			
4. VEGETABLE OILSEEDS AND OILS			
Castor seed	7.70 / 6.00*	0.03	0.10
Coconut oil	na / na	na	—
Cottonseed	32.00* n / 5.95	0.40	0.44
Cottonseed oil	na / na	17.43	0.19
Groundnuts	na / na	na	—
Groundnut oil	1.47 / 0.71	0.60	—
Soya beans			
Sunflower seed		0.03	0.5
Tung oil		1.65	
n sales only.			
5. LIVESTOCK‡, ANIMAL PRODUCTS, etc.			
Chickens d	2 572.0p* / 2 502.0p	—	—
Cattle d	401.3 / 290.7	—	—
dairy cows d	289.7 / 184.7	—	—
Goats d	451.0* / 314.3	—	—

continued

EAST AFRICA

	Production	Exports	Imports
9. NON-FERROUS MINERALS AND METALS—continued			
Beryl	0.21 / 0.45	0.18 / 0.24	—
Chrome, ore	8.45 m	9.27	0.15
Copper, metal	—	—	0.19
Lead, metal	—	—	0.01
Tin, metal	4.92	—	0.09
Titanium minerals		na	—
Zinc, metal	0.51	—	2
Zirconium minerals		—	—
Graphite production averaged 16 480 metric tons in 1963-5.			
10. CHEMICALS n AND FERTILIZERS			
Chemicals	—	—	na
Fertilizers:			
Potash	—	—	1.2
n data not available for years 1963-5.			
11. INDUSTRY			
Aircraft a	—	0.3 q	7.4 a
Alcoholic beverages			
beer b	32.0	—	0.9
spirits b	na	—	4.6 a
Cement	41.7	*	—
Electrical engineering a			
Locomotives c	1.0	—	78.3 / 121.3 p
Railway vehicles a	na	—	na
Merchant ships g	0.1	—	na
Motor vehicles a			7.8 / 4.9
			na
			0.9
			11.9 / 6.6
a million $ U.S. b '000 hectolitres. c no. of units. g '000 G.R.T. p incl.			

MALAWI

Malawi, formerly Nyasaland, and from 1954 part of the Federation of Rhodesia and Nyasaland, became an independent member of the Commonwealth in 1963 and adopted republican status in 1966.

No independent production and trade statistics are available for the duration of the Federation 1954–1963 inclusive.

AREA: 126 338 sq. km. (48 779 sq. miles)
Land area: 95 450 sq. km. (36 853 sq. miles)

LAND USE: (percentage of total)
Arable and orchard . . .
Permanent meadow and pasture . . .
Forest and woodland . . .
City areas, waste and other land . . .

POPULATION: 4 042 412 a (1966 census)
Largest city: BLANTYRE: population: 109 795 (city proper, 1966)
Capital city: ZOMBA: population: 19 000 (city proper, 1966)

Agriculture is the foundation of the economy, and has seen several important developments since 1967. These include a land reorganization scheme and two cotton development projects, which aim to further the transition from a subsistence agricultural economy to one of commercial crop production.

EMPLOYMENT AND PRODUCTION
a excl. about one third of the adult male African labour force, working abroad in the mines, industries, and farms of Zambia and South Africa.

Population per physician 49 250 (1963)
Population per hospital bed 800
School enrolment: age 5–19 years (percentage) 40
age over 19 years (per 100 000 population) 2

COMMUNICATIONS
Motor vehicles in use ('000s): private 7.8 (1965)
commercial 7.0
Railway track (km.) 450 (1969)
Mail per capita: domestic 3 (1964–5 av.)
foreign received 0.2
foreign sent 3 (1967)
Telephones (per '000 urban population)
Radio licences (per '000 population)

continued

FINANCE

Currency unit: The Malawi kwacha replaced the Rhodesian pound in 1971, at the rate 1 KM to RE0.5

Exchange rates (for Rhodesian pounds)	1965	1960	1950	1938
Per $U.S.	0.357	0.357	0.357	0.215
Per £ sterling	1.0	1.0	1.0	0.215

	1963	Year(s)
National Income (million $ U.S.)	10.7	1965
G.N.P. per capita ($U.S.)	3.4	1966
Rate of increase of G.N.P. per capita	8.8	1960–3 av.
Foreign trade (percentage of G.D.P.)	77.1	1964–5 av.

TRADING

	1955	1938
Total trade (in million $ U.S.)	40	5
Exports (f.o.b.)		4
Imports (f.o.b.)	57	na

Main trading partners (percentage of total value)

Exports	1965	Imports	1965
U.K.	47	Rhodesia	36
Rhodesia	10	U.K.	25
Netherlands	4	Japan	7
South Africa	3	South Africa	5
Irish R.	3	Germany F.R.	3
U.S.A.	3	Australia	3

Distribution of trade (percentage of total value)

Exports	1965	Imports	1965
Tobacco	38	Manufactured goods e	70
Tea	28	(textiles and clothing)	(27)
Groundnuts	12	(machinery and transport equipment)	(21)
Cotton	8	Foods	11
Vegetables	7	Chemicals	7
		Crude materials	6

e excl. trade with Rhodesia and Zambia.

SOUTH EAST ASIA

MALAYSIA

Malaysia, a member of the British Commonwealth, was created in 1963 out of the federation of Malaya (West Malaysia), Sarawak, North Borneo (Sabah) and Singapore. In 1965 Singapore seceded from this Federation of states. The constitution provides for one of the nine rulers of the Malay States to be elected as supreme head of the federation for five years. The aim is to ensure strong federal government with some autonomy for state government.

AREA: 329 600 sq. km. (127 260 sq. miles)
POPULATION: 10 071 000 (1967 estimate)
Capital city: KUALA LUMPUR: population: 316 230 (city proper, 1957)

FINANCE

Currency unit: The Malaysian dollar

Exchange rates	1965	1960	1950	1938
Per $U.S.	3.06	3.06	3.06	1.86
Per £ sterling	8.57	8.57	8.57	8.57

		Year(s)
National Income (million $ U.S.)	2349	1965
G.N.P. per capita ($U.S.)	280	1966
Rate of increase of G.N.P. per capita	2.8	1963–5 av.
Foreign trade (percentage of G.D.P.)	84	1963–5 av.

COMMUNICATIONS		Year(s)
Motor vehicles in use ('000s): private	13.5 a	1963–4 years
commercial	4.4 a	
Railway track (km.)	154	1968
Mail per capita: foreign received	1	
foreign sent	3	
Telephones (per '000 urban population)	1.9*	1967
Radio licences (per '000 population)	20.3*	1967
Television licences (per '000 population)		1965
Daily newspapers (per '000 population)	54.4	1964
School enrolment: age 5–19 years (percentage)	37	1963–4 av.

	1965	1960	1955	1938
Infant mortality (per '000)	36.5*			
Crude birth rate (per '000)	35.7*			
Crude death rate (per '000)	5.5*			
Accidental deaths (per 100 000 population)				
caused by motor vehicles				
due to other causes				
Population per physician	9 740			
Population per hospital bed	360			

SABAH

AREA: 76 115 sq. km. (29 388 sq. miles)

LAND USE: (percentage of total)
Arable and orchard . . .
Permanent meadow and pasture . . .
Forest and woodland . . .
City areas, waste and other land . . .

POPULATION: 588 000 (1967 estimate)
Capital city: KOTA KINABALU (Jesselton): population: 21 719 (city proper, 1960)

Distribution of working population (1960)
Total working population: 176 626

U.N. group no.		Percentage
1	Agriculture, forestry, fishing and hunting	80.5
2/3	Mining and quarrying	0.3
	Manufacturing	3.8
4	Construction	0.2
5	Electricity, gas, water and sanitary services	4.4
6	Commerce	2.6
7	Transport, storage and communications	5.7
8	Services	

FINANCE

		Year
National Income (million $ U.S.)	119	1965

continued

PRODUCTION, EXPORTS AND IMPORTS, etc.—continued

	Production	Exports	Imports
5. LIVESTOCK‡, ANIMAL PRODUCTS, etc.—continued			
Sheep d	81.3* / 62.0	—	—
Pigs d	119.0 / 84.0	—	—
Meat‡, A	6.0*	—	—
B	2.8	—	—
Butter		—	0.2
Cheese	0.9* / na	—	—
Eggs	na	—	0.1
Milk	15.0* / na	—	0.1
Hides/skins	29.3* / na	0.1	3.0
	0.4 / 0.2	—	1.0*
d no. in thousands. p incl. ducks, geese and turkeys.			
6. FIBRES, TEXTILES, etc.			
Agaves (sisal)	0.3* / 0.3	0.4	—
Cotton-lint	3.3* / 2.0	4.1*	7.4
Rubber, natural		0.1*	na
Wool, yarn		—	—
7. FUEL AND POWER			
Coal 'A'‡	na r	—	—
Electricity h: total	45	—	65
hydro	5	—	—
thermal	40	—	57
Petroleum, refined		7†	—
h million kWh.			37
9. NON-FERROUS MINERALS AND METALS			
Asbestos		—	0.67 q
Mica	na	—	0.13
Aluminium		—	0.04
Tin, metal		—	—
q manufactured. r fibre.			
11. INDUSTRY			
Alcoholic beverages a	31.0	—	1.2
Cement		—	0.5
Electrical engineering a	1.0	na	2.1
Motor vehicles a		na	3.5
a million $ U.S.			

continued

SABAH continued

TRADING

Total trade (in million $ U.S.)	1965	1955	1938
Exports (f.o.b.)	100	34	6
Imports (c.i.f.)	109	29	4

Main trading partners (percentage of total value)

Exports	1965	1955
Japan	50	8
West Mal./Sing.	15	15
Philippines	14	6
Taiwan	4	5
Australia	3	4a
Hong Kong	2	10

Imports	1965	1955
U.K.	19	8
Hong Kong	15	20
Singapore	13	13
West Malaysia	12	7
U.S.A.	7	5
Japan	5	3
China P.R.	2	10

Distribution of trade (percentage of total value)

Exports	1965	1955	1938*
Crude materials and fuels	78	84	na
(wood)	(61)		(25)
(rubber)	(11)	(40)	(60)
(oilseeds)	(4)	(14)	(na)
Cigarettes	13	2	5

Imports	1965	1955	1938*
Manufactured goods	48	40	na
(machinery and transport equipment)	(26)	(11)	
(textiles and clothing)	(5)	(9)	
Food	17	26	37
Cigarettes	13	na	7
Crude materials and fuels	12	18	na
Chemicals	4	4	na

a incl. New Zealand.

PRODUCTION, EXPORTS AND IMPORTS

Units: '000 metric tons unless otherwise indicated
Years: **1965** = 1963–5 average and *1955* = 1953–5 average

	Production	Exports	Imports
1. CEREALS, etc.			
Cassava	14.0*	—	5.2¹
Maize (corn)	2.7 / 7.0²	—	0.8¹
Potatoes			15.6* / 6.6
Rice	76.3 / 51.5²	—	32.0⁴ / 0.1
Sweet potatoes/yams	3.3* / 14.0¹	—	5.1²ᵖ / 2.2
			0.4 / 0.6
2. FRUIT, etc.			
Apples			0.3¹
Bananas	9.0* / na	0.2	0.1
Coconuts	182.0* / na	1.4¹ / 1.0²	0.7¹
Oranges	1.0* / na		0.4¹
Wine b			
3. BEVERAGES, FOREST PRODUCTS, etc.			
Cocoa	0.2	0.4²†	na
Coffee		4.0²†	0.3² / 6.6
Sugar, raw	0.1 / 0.3²		15.6* / 0.1
Tea			
Tobacco: leaf	0.1	4.8²† / 0.2¹	5.12ᵍ / 0.3ᵖ
cigarettes	584.7	3412.0m / 380.2	58.2 / 2.2
Hardwood j	3 778.0		0.4 / 0.6
Other paper			
4. VEGETABLE OILSEEDS AND OILS			
Copra	33.00*	33.00*² / 0.01²	16.45 / 7.73
Coconut oil	25.15²		0.09² / 0.10*
Groundnuts	na r		0.22¹
Groundnut oil	na	0.01²† / 0.02	1.95² / 0.63²
Palm oil	na		
Soya beans	na		0.09¹
Tung oil	na		0.01¹
r see West Malaysia.			
5. LIVESTOCK, ANIMAL PRODUCTS, etc.			
Chickens d	1 123.3 / 2 500.0	1.3¹ / 0.9	1.2*
Cattle d	15.0 / 15.3	0.1 / na	0.2¹
Pigs d	14.7 / na	14.7	0.1
Goats d	18.0 / 14.7	2.3	0.1
Horses d	5.0 / 3.0		0.1
Meat‡: A	83.0 / 65.3	0.1² / na	1.9
B	4.0* / na r	0.2¹†	11.6¹
Butter	2.5¹ / 2.5¹		1.2*
Eggs	na / na		0.2¹
Milk	2.0 / na		0.4¹
Hides/skins	na / 0.1		4.2*
r see West Malaysia.			

b '000 hectolitres. e no. in millions.

SARAWAK

AREA: 121 900 sq. km. (47 060 sq. miles)

LAND USE: (percentage of total)
		Year
Arable and orchard	5.6	1962
Permanent meadow and pasture	0.1	
Forest and woodland	73.3	
City areas, waste and other land	21.0	

POPULATION: 903 000 (1967 estimate)
Capital city: KUCHING; population: 50 579 (city proper, 1960)

Distribution of working population (1960)
Total working population: 294 285

U.N. group no.		Percentage
0	Agriculture, forestry, fishing and hunting	81.4
1	Mining and quarrying	0.8
2/3	Manufacturing	3.9
4	Construction	1.6
5	Electricity, gas, water and sanitary services	0.2
6	Commerce	4.7
7	Transport, storage and communications	1.9
8	Services	5.5

		Year(s)
Infant mortality (per '000)	42.6*	1965
Crude birth rate (per '000)	28.0	1965
Crude death rate (per '000)	5.0*	1965
Population per physician	1 290	1966
Population per hospital bed	380	1965
School enrolment: age 5–19 years (percentage)	57	1963–4 av.
age over 19 years (per 100 000 population)	18	1963–5 av.

COMMUNICATIONS

		Year(s)
Motor vehicles in use ('000s): private	13.5a	1963–5 av.
commercial	4.4a	1963–5 av.
Mail per capita: domestic	7	1963–5 av.
foreign received	3	
foreign sent	54a	1967
Telephones (per '000 urban population)	3b	1963–5 av.
Radio licences (per '000 population)	25	1961
Television licences (per '000 population)		
Daily newspapers (per '000 population)		

a incl. Sabah. b incl. Sabah and West Malaysia.

FINANCE

		Year
National Income (million $ U.S.)	162	1965

TRADING

Total trade (in million $ U.S.)	1965	1955	1938
Exports (f.o.b.)	124	156	14
Imports (c.i.f.)	158	144	13

Main trading partners (percentage of total value)

Exports	1965	1955
Singapore	36	49 / 42
West Malaysia	18	5
Japan	13	10 / 10
Australia	13	8 / 14
Philippines		7
U.K.		5
New Zealand		2

Imports	1965	1955
Brunei	39	66
West Mal./Sing.	14	9
U.K.	13	9
China P.R.	8	2
Japan	7	2
U.S.A.	5	2
Thailand	2	4

Distribution of trade (percentage of total value) a

Exports	1965	1955	1938*
Petroleum products (re-exports)	36	44	45
Wood	25	17	na
Rubber	18	17	32
Pepper and pimentos	13	7	3

Imports	1965	1955	1938*
Petroleum and petroleum products	44	68	30
Manufactured goods	27	12	na
Food (cereals)	18	12	18
Chemicals	4	2	na

a these are percentages of national exports† (but incl. ships' bunkers), which comprised 85% of general exports in 1965; 96% in 1955.

PRODUCTION, EXPORTS AND IMPORTS

Units: '000 metric tons unless otherwise indicated
Years: **1965** = 1963–5 average and *1955* = 1953–5 average

	Production	Exports	Imports
1. CEREALS, etc.			
Maize (corn)		0.1†	
Potatoes	104.3 / na		6.8² / 1.0¹
Rice			53.1* / 26.9*
Wheat		0.1²	0.41
2. FRUIT, etc.			
Apples			0.31
Bananas	46.01*a / na	0.1†	na
Coconuts		0.1	0.1 / 0.1²
Grapes			0.3
Oranges			0.2¹
Raisins			0.41
Wine b			0.8 / 1.0
3. BEVERAGES, FOREST PRODUCTS, etc.			
Coffee		0.2†	0.7² / 0.4
Sugar, raw			19.3* / 9.8
Tea			0.2²
Tobacco: leaf			0.6² / 0.2¹
cigarettes	7.0	5.0	0.1 / 2.4a
Hardwood j	2 018.0 / 579.0	1 394.0	7.2 / 0.9
Newsprint			1.9* / 0.1²
Other paper			
4. VEGETABLE OILSEEDS AND OILS			
Copra	10.40 / 2.80	2.09 / 0.61	2.43* / 0.07
Coconut oil	na	0.01²	0.90
Groundnuts	na	0.02²	1.19¹ / 0.76
Groundnut oil	na		0.40* / 0.03
Sesame seed			0.031
Soya beans			0.61¹
5. LIVESTOCK, ANIMAL PRODUCTS, etc.			
Chickens d	33.0* / 30.0¹		0.1
Cattle d	8.3 / 8.3		0.31
Pigs d	9.0 / 6.0¹	0.31	11.0¹
Goats d	284.0 / 20.0¹	0.81	0.1 / 0.31
Butter			0.1 / 0.1
Eggs	0.1*	0.1¹†	1.4²
Milk		0.1¹	5.11
Fish		0.41¹†	11.01
		0.1¹†	13.8²
r see West Malaysia.			

d no. in thousands. r see West Malaysia.

	Production	Exports	Imports
6. FIBRES, TEXTILES, etc.			
Rubber, natural	43.5	28.8¹	1.3 / 0.7
7. FUEL AND POWER			
Electricity h, thermal	58	20¹	50 / 79¹
Natural gas i	50	79¹	3 626 / 5 261¹
Oil, crude	2 463 / 2 390¹	1 310² / 3 230¹ₚ	80 / 20¹
Petroleum, refined p		2 273 / 8 401¹	
9. NON-FERROUS MINERALS AND METALS			
Gold f, ore	3.00m / 0.51*m	0.51q	25.67q / 1.94q
Platinum group metals f			0.89² / 0.39
Silver k, bullion			6.48
Asbestos			3.96 / 0.45
Aluminium: bauxite	151.73	170.25	0.57 / 0.28
manufactured	0.04m	0.04	0.14 / 0.04
Copper, metal			0.10¹
Tin, metal			0.03 / 0.10²
Zinc, metal			0.17 / na r
10. CHEMICALS AND FERTILIZERS			
Chemicals		2.43* / 0.61	0.06 / 0.10*
Fertilizers:		2.09	0.07 / 0.90
Phosphates	na p	0.01¹	1.19¹ / 0.76
Potash		0.02²	0.40* / 0.03
			0.031 / 0.60*
11. INDUSTRY			
Aircraft a	33.0* / 30.0¹		1.1 / 0.7
Alcoholic beverages a	8.3 / 8.3		11.0¹ / 14.5
Cement	9.0 / 6.0¹		0.1 / 0.1
Electrical	284.0 / 20.0¹		0.31 / 0.1²
engineering a			0.1 / 0.9
Motor vehicles a			1.4² / 5.11
	0.1*		13.8² / 1.0²

a million $ U.S. r see West Malaysia.

	Production	Exports	Imports
Aircraft a			0.1² / 0.1²
Alcoholic beverages a			1.7² / na r
Cement			3.9 / 4.2²
Motor vehicles a			0.3²

*na: data not available. — data not available. — negligible or nil. ¹ one year only. ² two year average. * estimate. ‡ see appendix. † re-exports.*

WEST MALAYSIA

AREA: 131 587 sq. km. (50 806 sq. miles)

LAND USE: (percentage of total)

	1964	1950
Arable and orchard	18.9	16.9
Permanent meadow and pasture	na	
Forest and woodland	65.7	73.9
City areas, waste and other land	na	9.2

POPULATION: 8 580 000 (1967 estimate)
Largest city: KUALA LUMPUR, capital; population: 316 230 (city proper, 1957)

Distribution of working population (1957)
Total working population: 2 164 861

U.N. group no.		Percentage
0	Agriculture, forestry, fishing and hunting	57.5
1	Mining and quarrying	2.7
2/3	Manufacturing	6.3
4	Construction	3.1
5	Electricity, gas, water and sanitary services	0.5
6	Commerce	9.0
7	Transport, storage and communications	3.5
8	Services	14.8
9	Others	2.6

		Year(s)
Life expectancy at birth (years): male	62.4	1965
female	64.0	1965
Infant mortality (per '000)	50	1965
Crude birth rate (per '000)	36.7	1965
Crude death rate (per '000)	7.9	1965
Population per physician	5890	1965
Population per hospital bed	280	1963
School enrolment: age 5–19 years (percentage)	58	1963–4 av.
age over 19 years (per 100 000 population)	127	1963–5 av.

COMMUNICATIONS

		Year(s)
Motor vehicles in use ('000s): private	144.5	1963–5 av.
commercial	42.2	
Railway track (km.)	1 667	1968
Mail per capita: domestic	21	1963–5 av.
foreign received	6	
sent	1.4	
Telephones (per '000 urban population)	44	1967
Radio licences (per '000 population)	3a	1963–5 av.
Television licences (per '000 population)		
Daily newspapers (per '000 population)	67	1960

a incl. Sabah and Sarawak.

FINANCE

	1964	1950	Year
National Income (million $ U.S.)	2068		1965

TRADING

Note—These trading figures, representing general trade, include the considerable value of the goods from other countries in transit through West Malaysia and, prior to 1965, Singapore.

Total trade (in million $ U.S.)

	1965a	1955a	1955b	1938b
Exports (f.o.b.)	1014	755	1358	334
Imports (c.i.f.)	852	504	1249	315

Main trading partners (percentage of total value)

Exports	1965	1955b	1938b
Singapore	21	21	
U.S.A.	18	17	30
Japan	13	7	9c
U.S.S.R.	7		14
Germany F.R.	3	6	3d
Italy	3	4	3

Imports	1965	1955b	1938b
U.K.	20	18	19
Japan	12	7	16
Thailand	11	7	6
Singapore	11		
China P.R.	7	3	4
Australia	6	5	4
U.S.A.	5	4	3

Distribution of trade (percentage of total value)

Exports	1965	1955b	1938b
Rubber	44	58	48
Tin and alloys	28	11	17
Metalliferous ores	6	6	10
Food	5	3	1
Palm oil	3		

Imports	1965	1955b	1938b
Manufactured goods (machinery and transport equipment)	48 (22)	29 (8)	(7)
(textiles and clothing)	24 (8)	22 (7)	(13)
Food (cereals)	15 (7)	40 (18)	(na)
Crude materials and fuels (petroleum products)	4	4	
Chemicals	3a		

a West Malaysia. *b* incl. Singapore. *c* incl. Taiwan and Korea. *d* incl. Germany D.R.

PRODUCTION, EXPORTS AND IMPORTS

Years: 1963–5 average and 1953–5 average Units: '000 metric tons unless otherwise indicated
Note—production data are for West Malaysia; data for Singapore are given where applicable. Trade figures apply to West Malaysia and Singapore combined.

1. CEREALS, etc.

	Production		Exports		Imports	
Cassava Sing.	303.3*	na 4.0[1]	6.6	9.8		
Maize (corn) Sing.	7.0*	na			97.1	39.0
Millets/sorghum					6.6	1.0*
Oats					1.8[1]	1.0*
Potatoes			2.0†		39.5	31.7
Rice	851.7	664.0	78.8	49.7	618.6	471.8
Sweet potatoes/ yams Sing.	98.3*	na				
Wheat Sing.	5.0	7.0[2]	2.2†	0.4†	103.6	14.0

2. FRUIT, etc.

	Production		Exports		Imports	
Apples			0.8†	1.3†	13.4	8.3
Bananas Sing.	332.0*	288.0[2]*	0.1			
Coconuts Sing.	732.7e	3.0[1]	9.5	8.5		

3. BEVERAGES, FOREST PRODUCTS, etc.

	Production		Exports		Imports	
Cocoa	0.6		0.2		0.1	
Coffee Sing.	2.0*	na	30.2	10.3	23.1	12.9
Sugar, raw	3.0	2.1	30.2	16.9[2]	283.2	182.2
Tea Sing.	2.4*	1.5*	3.2	7.3	3.7	8.4
Tobacco: leaf Sing.	0.4		0.1	0.2	7.9	0.6

continued

PRODUCTION, EXPORTS AND IMPORTS *continued*

5. LIVESTOCK‡, ANIMAL PRODUCTS, etc.

	Production		Exports		Imports	
Chickens d.	21 000.0*[1]	10 000.0*[1]	1.1	1.9	15.2	11.6
Sing.	10 212.0[1]	4 250.0[2]				
Cattle d.	306.7	274.0				
Sing.	145.0*	48.0				
dairy cows Sing.	5.0*	5.0				
Goats d.	316.0*	277.3		15.3	131.8	na
Sing.	2.0	1.0				
Sheep d.	41.7*	1.0				23.7
Horses d.		26.0				
Pigs d.	476.0	332.0				
Sing.	402.0	244.0				
Bacon/ham			0.1	0.1	0.6	0.6
Meat‡: 'A' Sing.	65.3*	25.3*	0.6		10.0	5.9
'B' Sing.	16.7	15.6[2]	0.4	0.1	4.8	1.3
	19.8*	na				
	3.2*	2.4*				
Butter			0.2†	0.4†	5.4	2.0
Cheese			0.1†	0.5	0.8	0.4
Eggs Sing.	11.5*	9.0[1]	1.6		4.0	8.9
	9.9	8.4[2]				
Fish Sing.	241.7[p]	141.2[p]	72.0	44.1*	124.3	61.41*
Milk Sing.	21.3*	2.0[2]	8.7	13.9	331.5	226.9
Hides/skins Sing.	1.0	na		0.9[2]		

d no. in thousands. *p* incl. Sabah and Sarawak. *r* incl. ducks, geese and turkeys.

6. FIBRES, TEXTILES, etc.

	Production		Exports		Imports	
Abaca	na					0.1
Cotton lint	na		0.3		1.3	
Jute	na		0.2†	0.5†		
Rubber, natural Sing.	840.3	608.9	1 059.9[s]	934.4[s]	175.9	335.2
Cotton: yarn	na				2.0	0.5
woven fabrics					22.4	17.8
Rayon: fibre/yarn				1.2[t]		
woven fabrics Sing.	1.5				9.0n	8.3

s incl. re-exports. *t* incl. spun yarn. *n* incl. synthetic piece goods.

7. FUEL AND POWER

	Production		Exports		Imports	
Coal, 'A' ‡:	na					
Coke	na		0.3†			
Electricity h: total	1 886	1 190[1]				
hydro	483	250[1]				
thermal Sing.	1 403	940[1]				
Sing.	928[i]					
Oil, crude	na				4 132	74
Petroleum, refined Sing.	1 360		187†		6 663	4
	2 337		3 230†[1]			

8. IRON AND STEEL

	Production		Exports		Imports	
Iron ore	3 908[m]	710[m]	6 615	1 243	14[1]*	2s
Pig iron	na	na	1†		10	1s
Steel ingots/castings	na	na			19[1]*	8
Iron/steel scrap Sing.	56*	67				

m metal content. *s* incl. imports for re-export.

9. NON-FERROUS MINERALS AND METALS

	Production		Exports		Imports	
Diamonds a			0.06[1]†	0.07[s]	3.57[1]	0.17s
Gold k, ore m	6.70	21.00		16.19[q]		0.56q
Platinum group metals k						
Silver k, bullion	na	na	636.00[r]	1 084.57[s]	3.06	0.57
Asbestos: fibre					8.67	1.92
manufactured			36.05†	0.03†	14.52	0.31s
Mica	na	na			26.12	0.011
Aluminium: bauxite	593.03	182.87	565.36	190.64[p]	0.04	
alumina	na				0.89	—
aluminium	na	2.4*	4.71†	1.09†	10.83	3.96c
Copper: ore	na		1.78[t]	na[t]	—	—
metal			0.65	0.87†	3.98	1.34s
Lead, metal			0.19†		1.19	0.28p
Magnesium: metal						
dolomite	2.86		1.88[1]†		1.92	—
magnesite			0.59†	na[t]	0.39	1.44s
Manganese, ore			3.57		2.08	1.90s
Mercury/	62.19[m]	60.35[m]	0.8[t]	0.09[t]	12.06[t]	12.52p
Tin: metal	77.16	69.16	74.65	68.62[p]	10.87†	0.14s
Titanium minerals	na		134.70	42.40	0.60†	0.2s
Tungsten, ore	0.01	0.13	0.01	0.13	1.25	0.01s
Zinc: ore	na		0.71	0.22[s]	3.16	2.08p
metal	na		0.34†	0.03†		
Zirconium minerals	na					

a million $ U.S. *f* metric tons. *k* '000 fine troy oz. *m* metal content. *p* incl. Sabah and Sarawak. *q* bullion. *r* '000 re-exports and imports for re-export. *t* zircon.
n data not available for years 1953–5.

10. CHEMICALS n AND FERTILIZERS

	Production		Exports		Imports	
Chemicals a	na				na	
Fertilizers:						
Phosphates			0.1†		88.7[1]	5.1
Potash					33.2	0.2
Sulphur			0.2†		6.1	

11. INDUSTRY

	Production		Exports		Imports	
Aircraft a						
Alcoholic beverages: beer b Sing.	369.0[2]	302.0	6.1a	1.8a	17.4a	0.1 9.2a
Cement Sing.	708.7[p]	74.0	18.3[p]	12.7	468.0[p]	327.0
Electrical engineering a	2.12		19.7†	4.8[2]†	90.2	26.0[2]
Railway vehicles a					2.5	1.7
Merchant ships g			55.7†	6.1†	0.41[p]	na
Motor vehicles a					124.2	22.5

a million $ U.S. *b* '000 hectolitres. *g* '000 G.R.T. *p* incl. Sabah and Sarawak.

3. BEVERAGES, FOREST PRODUCTS, etc.—*continued*

	Production		Exports		Imports	
Tobacco: cigars Sing.	0.7		1.7[s]	2.5[2][s]	3.3	10.0[2]
cigarettes Sing.	0.1					
tobacco/snuff Sing.	1.0		7.0[2]	0.1	0.4[2]	0.1
Softwood j	5 973.0[c]		2 089.5	276.9	1 274.9[n]	114.8
Hardwood j	2 496.0				0.5	9.8
Wood pulp			1.1*		31.0	89.0
Newsprint j	3 403.5[2]	1 936.0		2		
Other paper			0.2*		8.6[2]	0.8[2] 20.7[2]

e no. in millions. *j* '000 cu. metres of roundwood equivalent. *n* sawn wood only. *s* incl. re-exports.

4. VEGETABLE OILSEEDS AND OILS

	Production		Exports		Imports	
Castor oil					0.04	0.45
Copra	127.00	155.70	22.39[s]	59.30[s]	37.22	110.97
Coconut oil	na		28.70	78.73	2.25	0.68
Cottonseed oil			0.84	1.37	0.38	11.83
Cottonseed			1.34	1.13	14.74	11.83
Groundnuts	3.00*[b]	na		0.06†	3.88	2.0
Groundnut oil			0.01†		0.38	0.45
Linseed oil					0.03	0.03
Olive oil					0.03	0.02
Palm kernels	32.03	14.23[p][q]	14.09	13.20	2.50	0.03
Palm kernel oil			0.16	0.43	2.68	1.16
Palm oil	132.10	53.37[p][q]	127.51	51.60	0.05	0.05
Rapeseed oil			0.58†	0.30†	3.15	3.43
Sesame seed			0.84†	0.97†	28.07	18.83
Soya beans					0.05	0.07
Soya bean oil			0.01†		0.15	0.07
Tung oil			0.01†			

p incl. Sabah and Sarawak. *q* estate production only. *s* incl. re-exports. *continued*

MALDIVE ISLANDS

The Maldive Islands were under British protection until they were granted independence in 1965; they became a republic three years later. The U.K. retains an air staging post on Gan Island.

AREA: 298 sq. km. (115 sq. miles)

POPULATION: 100 883 (1966 census)
Capital city: MALE; population: 11 202 (city proper, 1965)

INDIAN OCEAN

		Year
Crude birth rate (per '000)	50.1*	1965
Crude death rate (per '000)	22.9*	1965
Population per hospital bed	5 050	1966

EMPLOYMENT AND TRADE

These low lying coral islands are covered with coconut palms, and some millets and fruit are grown. Fishing is the major occupation and bonito accounts for 95% of the island's exports. Fish catches amounted to some 12 000 metric tons in 1965.

---

na: data not available. — negligible or nil. [1] one year only. [2] two year average. * estimate. ‡ see appendix. † re-exports.

MALI — WEST AFRICA

Mali, formerly French Sudan, a member state of French West Africa, became an independent republic in 1960. In 1968 the regime of the president was overthrown and a National Liberation Committee assumed control.

AREA: 1 204 021 sq. km. (464 875 sq. miles)

LAND USE:
About 95% of the land is barren desert, but agriculture is increasing with collectivization and planned irrigation.

POPULATION: 4 745 000* (1967 provisional estimate)
Largest city: BAMAKO, capital: population: 165 000 (1965)

		Year(s)
Life expectancy at birth (years)	35*	1960
Population per physician	40 000	1964
Population per hospital bed	1340 a	1965
School enrolment: age 5–19 years (percentage)	11	1963–4 av.
age over 19 years (per 100 000 population)	4	1963–5 av.

a government hospitals only.

COMMUNICATIONS
		Year(s)
Motor vehicles in use ('000s): private	3.4	1963–5 av.
commercial	4.6	
Railway track (km)	645	1969
Telephones (per '000 urban population)	0.1	1967
Radio receivers (per '000 population)	4	1963–5 av.
Daily newspapers (per '000 population)	0.5	1962

FINANCE
Currency unit: The Mali franc replaced, at par, the franc CFA in 1962.

Exchange rates	1965	1960a
Per $U.S.	246.85	246.85
Per £ sterling	691.18	691.18

a francs CFA.

		Year
National Income (million $U.S.)	224	1958
G.N.P. per capita ($U.S.)	60	1966

TRADING
Total trade (in million $U.S.)	1965
Exports (f.o.b.)	16
Imports (c.i.f.)	43

Main trading partners (percentage of total value)

Exports	1965	Imports	1965
Ivory Coast	30	France	65
Ghana	24	China P.R.	24
Senegal	12	U.S.S.R.	23
Upper Volta	12	U.A.R.	19
U.S.S.R.	4	Ivory Coast	18
Algeria	1	U.S.A.	9
		Yugoslavia	5

Distribution of trade (percentage of total value)

Exports	1965	Imports	1965
Cattle	29	Manufactured goods (machinery and transport equipment)	(23)
Fish	20	(textiles and clothing)	(22)
Cotton	17	Food (sugar and honey)	18
Oilseeds	16	Crude materials and fuels	9
		Chemicals	5

PRODUCTION, EXPORTS AND IMPORTS
Years: 1963–5 average. Units: '000 metric tons unless otherwise indicated
Note—no data are available for the years 1953–5

	Production	Exports	Imports
1. CEREALS, etc			
Cassava	153.3*		
Maize (corn)	93.0*		
Millets/sorghum	710.3*		
Potatoes	na		
Rice	148.3		1.0
Sweet potatoes/yams	70.0*		
Wheat	4.0*		0.4
2. FRUIT, etc.			
Bananas		0.7	0.3
Dates		0.2†	0.7
Oranges		0.1	0.1
Wine b			3.8
3. BEVERAGES, FOREST PRODUCTS, etc.			
Coffee		0.2†	0.2
Sugar, raw			21.5
Tea	2.4*		0.4
Tobacco: leaf		0.2	0.3
products			2.5²
Hardwood j	2 275.0¹*		
4. VEGETABLE OILSEEDS AND OILS			
Cottonseed	32.30*	3.91	0.21
Groundnuts	100.30*	33.07	0.01
Olive oil			0.27
Palm oil			
5. LIVESTOCK‡, ANIMAL PRODUCTS, etc.			
Cattle d	4281.7	65.0	
dairy cows d	2176.7*		
Goats d	8338.0*n	52.5	
Sheep d	4722.3*		
Horses d	146.3*		
Pigs d	18.0*		
Meat‡, 'A'	17.0*		
Eggs	4.6		
Milk	90.0¹	5.3	2.3*
Wool	642.3*	0.5	
Hides/skins	1.41	0.1	

d no. in thousands. n incl. some sheep.

	Production	Exports	Imports
6. FIBRES, TEXTILES, etc.			
Agaves (sisal)	0.2*		
Cotton: lint	16.0*	6.7	
yarn			0.6
woven fabrics			2.8
7. FUEL AND POWER			
Electricity h p	25		
Petroleum, refined			57
11. INDUSTRY			
Alcoholic beverages a	192.0		
Cement q			34.3*
Electrical engineering q		0.7	0.3
Motor vehicles a			1.6
			3.5

h million kWh. p hydro and thermal. a million $U.S. q incl. data for Mauritania and Senegal.

MALTA — MEDITERRANEAN

Formerly a British protectorate, Malta was granted partial self-government in 1947, and independence within the Commonwealth in 1964. The agreement to British forces remaining until 1974 in return for capital aid to the extent of £51 million over the ten-year period was challenged by Malta in 1971, and was still under negotiation at the end of the year.

AREA: 316 sq. km. (122 sq. miles)

LAND USE: (percentage of total)	1965	1954
Arable and orchard	50.0	59.4
City areas, waste and other land	50.0	40.6

POPULATION: 315 765a (1967 estimate)
Capital city: VALLETTA; population: 17 679 (1965)

Distribution of working population (1957)
Total working population: 94 589 a

U.N. group no.		Percentage
0	Agriculture, forestry, fishing and hunting	10.3
1	Mining and quarrying	0.4
2/3	Manufacturing	22.3
4	Construction	11.0
5	Electricity, gas, water and sanitary services	1.2
6	Commerce	13.2
7	Transport, storage and communications	6.9
8	Services	29.4
9	Others	3.5

		Year(s)
Life expectancy at birth (years): male	67.5	1965–7 av.
female	71.6	
Infant mortality (per '000)	34.8	1965
Crude birth rate (per '000)	17.4	1965
Crude death rate (per '000)	9.4	1965
Accidental deaths (per 100 000 population)	4.4	1965
caused by motor vehicles	12.8	1965
due to other causes		
Population per physician	780	1961
Population per hospital bed	100	1965
School enrolment: age 5–19 years (percentage)	96	1963–4 av.
age over 19 years (per 100 000 population)	337	1963–5 av.

a excl. non-Maltese armed forces.

COMMUNICATIONS
		Year(s)
Motor vehicles in use ('000s): private	20.7	1963–5 av.
commercial	6.8	
Mail per capita: domestic	44	1963–5 av.
foreign received	22	
foreign sent	29	
Telephones (per '000 urban population)	8.1	1967
Radio licences (per '000 population)	229	1963–5 av.
Television licences (per '000 population)	73.1	1963–5 av.
Daily newspapers (per '000 population)	124	1956

FINANCE
Currency unit: The pound sterling a

Exchange rates	1965	1960	1955
Per $U.S.	0.357	0.357	0.357

a Maltese bank notes are issued, but U.K. coins are used.

		Year
National Income (million $U.S.)	137	1965
G.N.P. per capita ($U.S.)	510	1966

TRADING
Total trade (in million $U.S.)	1965	1955	1938
Exports (f.o.b.)	24	7	3
Imports (c.i.f.)	98	59	19

Main trading partners (percentage of total value)

Exports	1965	1955	Imports	1965	1955
U.K.	30	21	U.K.	38	40
Italy	9	12	Italy	12	11
Libya	8	16	Netherlands	6	6
U.S.A.	5	na	France	4	5
Spain	5	2	Australia	4	3
Netherlands	4		Germany F.R.	4	3
Switzerland	3		U.S.A.	2	2

Distribution of trade (percentage of total value)

Exports	1965	1955
Manufactured goods (textiles and clothing)	64	na
Crude materials and fuels	12	32*
Beverages and tobacco	11	
Food	8	38
(potatoes)	(6)	(22)

Imports	1965	1955
Manufactured goods	45	40
(machinery and transport equipment)	(16)	(10)
(textiles and clothing)	29	(6*)
Food	29	43
(cereals, fruit, vegetables)	(12)	(na)
(meat and dairy produce)	(8)	
Crude materials and fuels	12	7
Chemicals	7	5

Note—the large deficit on the balance of trade was offset by receipts from ships' dues, repairs and bunkering, tourism and British government grants.

PRODUCTION, EXPORTS AND IMPORTS
Years: 1963–5 average and 1953–5 average. Units: '000 metric tons unless otherwise indicated

	Production 1963–5	1953–5	Exports	Imports 1963–5	1953–5
1. CEREALS, etc.					
Barley	2.0	3.3		6.5	1.0
Maize (corn)				15.1	0.4
Millets/sorghum			7.4	5.7	9.0
Potatoes	20.0	26.3	9.5	4.2	4.9
Rice				0.9	0.9
Wheat	2.7	3.5²	1.95†	58.6	57.3
2. FRUIT, etc.					
Apples				2.9	1.6
Bananas				1.1	0.5
Figs	2.0*	2.0			
Grapes	3.7	5.0			
Lemons				0.1	0.1²
Oranges	3.6	4.9	0.11		
Pears				0.4	0.2
Raisins				0.3	0.2
Tomatoes	6.7	7.0²	0.3		
Wine b	na	0.9	107.9	8.0	
3. BEVERAGES, FOREST PRODUCTS, etc.					
Coffee				0.4	0.2
Sugar, raw				14.3	11.1
Tea				0.5	0.4
Tobacco: leaf				0.4	0.4²
cigarettes	396.0e		0.11	17.4n	16.6
Softwood j				6.9	3.7²
Hardwood j				0.5²	0.4
Newsprint				0.2	
Other paper				0.7¹	0.4p
4. VEGETABLE OILSEEDS AND OILS					
Cottonseed				0.70	1.67
Cottonseed oil				0.05	0.10
Groundnuts				0.38	0.60²
Groundnut oil				0.10	1.00²
Linseed oil				0.03	0.02
Olive oil			1.95†	4.42	0.50
Soya bean oil					
5. LIVESTOCK‡, ANIMAL PRODUCTS, etc.					
Chickens d	1 293.3	na			
Cattle d	29.7	5.5²		7.5	9.4
Goats d	42.0	42.0²			
Sheep d	10.0	19.5²	0.9		
Horses d	2.0	2.0²			
Pigs d	15.0	23.5²			
Bacon/ham	5.3*	3.7q			
Meat‡, 'A', 'B'	1.2*	na	0.9		
Butter				0.2	0.3*
Cheese	3.2	2.2		1.6	1.1
Eggs	1.4	2.2		0.5	0.4
Fish	15.0	7.0		1.3	0.8
Milk	na	0.4		21.7	20.3
Hides/skins				0.2²	
6. FIBRES, TEXTILES, etc.					
Cotton: lint					
woven fabrics				1.0	0.3
Rayon/fibre/yarn				0.5	0.3
woven fabrics				na	
Non-cellulosic fibre/yarn			0.6	0.2r	
Other paper	0.7¹			1.3¹	

continued

e no. in millions. j '000 cu. metres of roundwood equivalent. n incl. other tobacco manufactures. p printing and writing paper only. q government inspected meat only. r incl. synthetic piece goods.

---

na: data not available. — not available. — negligible or nil. ¹ one year only. ² two year average. * estimate. ‡ see appendix. † re-exports.

MALTA continued

PRODUCTION, EXPORTS AND IMPORTS continued

	Production	Exports	Imports
7. FUEL AND POWER			
Coal, A. ‡	126	—	18
Electricity h i	—	—	—
Petroleum, refined	40[1]	217	130[1]

h million kWh. t thermal. v incl. imports for bunkering.

	Production	Exports	Imports
8. IRON AND STEEL			
Steel ingots/castings	na	8	1
Iron/steel scrap	na	10[2]	—

	Production	Exports	Imports
9. NON-FERROUS MINERALS AND METALS			
Diamonds a	—	—	0.09
Gold k, bullion/coins, etc.	—	0.23†	9.07‡
Silver k, bullion	—	—	8.53
Asbestos	—	—	—
manufactured a	—	—	0.03

continued

PRODUCTION, EXPORTS AND IMPORTS continued

	Production	Exports	Imports
9. NON-FERROUS MINERALS AND METALS—continued			
Aluminium a	—	—	0.21
Copper, metal a	—	—	0.11
Zinc, ore a	—	—	0.03

a million $ U.S. k '000 fine troy oz.

	Production	Exports	Imports
10. CHEMICALS r AND FERTILIZERS			
Chemicals a			na
Fertilizers:			
Sulphur	—	0.3[1]	0.1[2]v

n data not available for years 1953–5. v in addition, flowers of sulphur a million $ U.S. $17,900.

	Production	Exports	Imports
11. INDUSTRY			
Alcoholic beverages a	na	0.9[1]p	1.4[1]p 0.1q
Cement	na	0.2q	63.0 29.7
Electrical a	—	—	—
Engineering a	—	—	6.3[1]
Merchant ships g	—	0.2[1]†	0.1[1]
Motor vehicles a	—	3.1	3.1 1.2

a million $ U.S. g '000 G.R.T. p wine and beer. q beer only.

continued

PRODUCTION, EXPORTS AND IMPORTS

Years: **1963–5 average** Units: '000 metric tons unless otherwise indicated
Note—no data are available for the years 1953–5

	Production	Exports	Imports
1. CEREALS, etc.			
Maize (corn)	4.0*	—	
Millets/sorghum	65.0[1]	—	
Potatoes	—	—	0.1
Rice	—	—	0.1[2]
Sweet potatoes/yams	2.0*	—	
2. FRUIT, etc.			
Dates	6.7*	—	
Wine b	—	—	1.2[2]

b '000 hectolitres.

	Production	Exports	Imports
3. BEVERAGES, FOREST PRODUCTS, etc.			
Hardwood j	126.0[1]	—	6.3[2]

j '000 cu. metres of roundwood equivalent.

	Production	Exports	Imports
5. LIVESTOCK‡, ANIMAL PRODUCTS, etc.			
Cattle d	1733.3*	45.2[2]	
dairy cows d	1023.3*		
Goats d	1998.0*	267.0[2]	
Sheep d	2453.3*		
Horses d	—	—	
Meat: A	10.0*	—	0.1[2]
Butter	2.0*	—	

continued

PRODUCTION, ANIMAL PRODUCTS, etc.—continued

	Production	Exports	Imports
5. LIVESTOCK‡, ANIMAL PRODUCTS, etc.—continued			
Eggs	2.2*	—	6.3[1]
Fish	1.3[1]n	5.9[2]	0.8
Milk	104.0[1]	—	

d no. in thousands. n from marine fisheries only.

	Production	Exports	Imports
6. FIBRES, TEXTILES, etc.			
Cotton, woven fabrics	—	—	1.2
Rayon, woven fabrics	—	—	0.3p

p incl. synthetic piece goods.

	Production	Exports	Imports
7. FUEL AND POWER			
Petroleum, refined	—	—	33
8. IRON AND STEEL			
Iron ore	2863m	3691	

m metal content.

	Production	Exports	Imports
11. INDUSTRY			
Aircraft a	—	—	0.1
Alcoholic beverages a	192.0	0.7	0.2[2]
Cement	—	—	34.3[3]*
Electrical engineering a	na	—	1.6
Railway vehicles a	—	0.1	4.3
Motor vehicles a	—	0.2†	3.0

a million $ U.S. q incl. data for Senegal and Mali.

continued

MAURITANIA   WEST AFRICA

Mauritania, formerly a member state of French West Africa, became an independent republic in 1960. Morocco has laid claim to the territory.

AREA: 1 085 805 sq. km. (419 232 sq. miles)

LAND USE: (percentage of total)

	1964
Arable and orchard	0.2
Permanent meadow and pasture	36.2
Forest and woodland	13.9
City areas, waste and other land	49.7

POPULATION: 1 050 000 (1964 census)
Capital city: NOUAKCHOTT; population: 15 000 (city proper, 1965)

		Year(s)
Life expectancy at birth (years)	40*	1961–2 av.
Infant mortality (per '000)	187*	1964–5 av.
Crude birth rate (per '000)	45.1*	1964–5 av.
Crude death rate (per '000)	28*	1964–5 av.
Population per physician	30 000	1965
Population per hospital bed	3720a	1965
School enrolment: age 5–19 years (percentage)	8	1963–4 av.

a government hospitals only.

COMMUNICATIONS

		Year(s)
Motor vehicles in use ('000s): private	1.3	
commercial	2.5	
Railway track (km.)	675	1969
Telephones (per '000 urban population)	0.1*	1967
Radio receivers (per '000 population)	30	1963–5 av.

FINANCE
Currency unit: The franc CFA

Exchange rates	1965	1960
Per $ U.S.	246.85	246.85
Per £ sterling	691.18	691.18

		Year
National Income (million $ U.S.)	111	1965
G.N.P. per capita ($ U.S.)	130	1966

PRODUCTION
The country's wealth lies mainly in its deposits of iron ore; output increased greatly during the decade 1960–70, the development being supported by large investments from France and the other E.E.C. countries. Copper deposits are also being exploited. Other products include cattle, gum, salt, beans and fish.

TRADING

Total trade (in million $ U.S.)	1965
Exports (f.o.b.)	58
Imports (c.i.f.)	24

Main trading partners (percentage of total value)

Exports	1965	Imports	1965
U.K.	47	France	25
U.S.A.	23	U.S.A.	20
Germany F.R.	14	Germany F.R.	19
China P.R.	4	Italy	16
U.K.	3	Belg./Lux.	8
Canada	2	Netherlands	5
		Congo R.	2

Distribution of trade (percentage of total value)

Exports	1965	Imports	1965
Iron ore	94	Manufactured goods (machinery and transport equipment)	
Fish	4	Food	8
		Crude materials and fuels	5

continued

MAURITIUS   INDIAN OCEAN

Mauritius became an independent state within the British Commonwealth in 1968; previously the island constituted a Crown Colony. The French language is spoken—a legacy of French possession during the eighteenth century.
Data include those for Rodrigues and the lesser dependencies.

AREA: 1 865 sq. km. (720 sq. miles)

LAND USE: (percentage of total)

	1965	1955
Arable and orchard	50.6	45.7
Permanent meadow and pasture	16.1	23.7
Forest and woodland	21.5	19.3
City areas, waste and other land	11.8	11.3

POPULATION: 774 000 (1967 U.N. estimate)
Largest city: PORT LOUIS; capital; population: 132 700 (1966)

Distribution of working population (1962)
Total working population: 187 400

U.N. group no.		Percentage
0	Agriculture, forestry, fishing and hunting	37.9
1	Mining and quarrying	0.1
2/3	Manufacturing	14.6
4	Construction	10.6
5	Electricity, gas, water and sanitary services	1.2
6	Commerce	10.0
7	Transport, storage and communications	6.3
8	Services	18.7
9	Others	0.6

		Year(s)
Life expectancy at birth (years): male	58.7	1961–3 av.
female	61.9	
Infant mortality (per '000)	64.1	1965
Crude birth rate (per '000)	35.4	1965
Crude death rate (per '000)	8.6	1965
Accidental deaths (per 100 000 population) caused by motor vehicles	10.1	1965
due to other causes	17.9	1965
Population per physician	3860	1965
Population per hospital bed	260	1965
School enrolment: age 5–19 years (percentage)	86	1965
age over 19 years (per 100 000 population)	13	1965

COMMUNICATIONS

		Year(s)
Motor vehicles in use ('000s): private	12.3	1963–5 av.
commercial	5.0	
Railway track (km.)	145a	1969
Mail per capita: domestic	11	1963–5 av.
foreign received	4	
foreign sent	3	
Telephones (per '000 population)	139	1967
Radio receivers (per '000 population)	1.9	1963–5 av.
Television sets (per '000 population)	2.4	1963–5 av.
Daily newspapers (per '000 population)	94	1962–3 av.

a mainly sugar estate lines.

FINANCE
Currency unit: The Mauritius rupee

Exchange rates	1965	1960
Per $ U.S.	4.76	4.76
Per £ sterling	13.33	13.33

		Year
National Income (million $ U.S.)	159	1965
G.N.P. per capita ($ U.S.)	210	1966

TRADING

Total trade (in million $ U.S.)	1965	1955
Exports (f.o.b.)	66	53
Imports (c.i.f.)	77	53

Main trading partners (percentage of total value)

Exports	1965	1955	Imports	1965	1955
U.K.	78	82	U.K.	27	40
Canada	9	17	South Africa	10	4
U.S.A.	5		Australia	7	4
South Africa	4	2	Burma	6	7
Mal./Sing.	2		France	6	11
Reunion	1		Thailand	5	1
			Hong Kong	4	
			Germany F.R.	3	

Distribution of trade (percentage of total value) a

Exports	1965	1955	1938*
Sugar	96	99	98

Imports	1965	1955
Manufactured goods	45 (15)	45 (16)
(machinery and transport equipment)		
Food	29 (15)	31 (16)
Chemicals	13	11
Crude materials and fuels	7	7

a percentages are of national exports‡ which comprised 95% of the general exports in 1965, and 96% in 1955.

continued

---

na: data not available. — negligible or nil. — not available. [1] one year only. [2] two year average. * estimate. * see appendix. † re-exports.

na: data not available. — negligible or nil. — not available. [1] one year only. [2] two year average. * estimate. * see appendix. † re-exports.

MAURITIUS continued

PRODUCTION, EXPORTS AND IMPORTS
Years: **1963-5 average** and 1953-5 average   Units: '000 metric tons unless otherwise indicated

1. CEREALS, etc.
(table columns: Production, Exports, Imports)

- Cassava
- Maize (corn)
- Millets/sorghum
- Oats
- Potatoes
- Rice
- Sweet potatoes/yams

2. FRUIT, etc.
- Apples
- Bananas
- Grapes
- Coconuts
- Oranges
- Other citrus fruit
- Tomatoes
- Raisins
- Wine *d*

3. BEVERAGES, FOREST PRODUCTS, etc.
- Sugar: cane
- raw
- Tea
- Tobacco: leaf
- cigarettes
- Softwood *j*
- Hardwood *j*
- Newsprint
- Other paper

5. LIVESTOCK‡, ANIMAL PRODUCTS, etc.
- Bacon/ham
- Meat *d*: 'A'; 'B'
- Butter
- Cheese
- Fish
- Milk
- Hides/skins

6. FIBRES, TEXTILES, etc.
- Agaves (sisal etc.)
- Jute
- Cotton, woven fabrics
- Rayon, woven fabrics

7. FUEL AND POWER
- Coal, 'A' ‡;
- Electricity *h*: total
- hydro
- thermal
- Petroleum, refined

9. NON-FERROUS MINERALS AND METALS
- Asbestos: fibre
- manufactured
- Aluminium
- Copper, metal
- Lead, metal
- Tin, metal

10. CHEMICALS *n* AND FERTILIZERS
- Chemicals
- Fertilizers:
- Phosphates
- Potash
- Sulphur

11. INDUSTRY
- Alcoholic beverages
- Cement
- Electrical
- engineering *a*
- Railway vehicles *a*
- Motor vehicles *a*

a million $ U.S.   *b* '000 hectolitres.

continued

FINANCE

Currency unit: The Mexican peso

Exchange rates
	1965	1960	1950 *b*	1955	1938 *b*
Per $ U.S.	12.49	12.49	8.65	4.92	
Per £ sterling	35.0	35.0	24.23	22.63	

	1965	1960	Year(s)
National Income (million $ U.S.)		17 600	1965
G.N.P. per capita ($ U.S.)	470		1966
Rate of increase of G.N.P. per capita	3		1960-4 av.
Foreign trade (percentage of G.D.P.)	14		1963-5 av.

b selling rate.

TRADING

	1965	1955	1938
Total trade (in million $ U.S.)			
Exports (f.o.b.)	1146	804	159
Imports (c.i.f.)	1560	883	110

PRODUCTION, EXPORTS AND IMPORTS
Years: **1963-5 average** and 1953-5 average   Units: '000 metric tons unless otherwise indicated

1. CEREALS, etc.
(columns: Production, Exports, Imports)
- Barley
- Maize (corn)
- Millets/sorghum
- Oats
- Potatoes
- Rice
- Rye
- Sweet potatoes/yams
- Wheat

2. FRUIT, etc.
- Apples
- Apricots
- Bananas
- Coconuts
- Dates
- Figs
- Grapes
- Lemons
- Oranges
- Other citrus fruit
- Olives
- Peaches
- Pineapples
- Plums
- Raisins
- Tomatoes
- Wine *a*

3. BEVERAGES, FOREST PRODUCTS, etc.
- Cocoa
- Coffee
- Sugar: cane
- raw
- Tobacco: leaf
- cigars
- cigarettes
- tobacco/snuff
- Softwood *j*
- Hardwood *j*
- Wood pulp
- Newsprint
- Other paper

4. VEGETABLE OILSEEDS AND OILS
(columns: Production, Exports, Imports)
- Castor seed
- Castor oil
- Copra
- Cottonseed
- Cottonseed oil
- Groundnuts
- Groundnut oil
- Linseed
- Linseed oil
- Olive oil
- Palm kernels
- Palm oil
- Rapeseed
- Sesame seed
- Soya beans
- Soya bean oil
- Tung oil

p flax grown for seed only.

5. LIVESTOCK‡, ANIMAL PRODUCTS, etc.
- Chickens *d*
- Cattle *d*
- Goats *d*
- Sheep *d*
- Horses *d*
- Pigs *d*
- Bacon/ham
- Meat *d*: 'A'; 'B'
- Butter
- Cheese
- Eggs
- Fish
- Milk
- Hides/skins
- Wool

d no. in thousands.   *q* incl. ducks, geese and turkeys.

6. FIBRES, TEXTILES, etc.
- Abaca
- Agaves (henequen)
- Cotton lint
- Flax fibre
- Jute
- Rubber: natural
- synthetic
- Silk *f*
- Cotton: yarn
- woven fabrics
- Rayon: yarn/yarn
- woven fabrics
- Non-cellulosic
- fibre/yarn
- Wool: yarn
- woven fabrics

f metric tons.   *r* excl. blankets.

na: data not available.   — negligible or nil.   — *r* '000 cu. metres of roundwood equivalent.   *n* in addition,
piloncillo 120 (1963-5 av.) and 130* (1953-5 av.).

185

MEXICO

Mexico is a federal republic of 29 states. The land holds considerable resources of potential mineral wealth. Recent social and industrial development has been rapid, and agricultural output is also increasing.

AREA: 1 967 183 sq. km. (761 530 sq. miles) (excl. inland waters and uninhabited islands)

LAND USE: (percentage of total)
	1960	1950
Arable and orchard	12.1	9.5
Permanent meadow and pasture	40.1	34.2
Forest and woodland	22.1	19.7
City areas, waste and other land	25.7	36.6

POPULATION: 45 671 000 (1967 estimate)
Largest city: CIUDAD DE MEXICO (Mexico City), capital;
3 353 033 (city proper, 1967)

Distribution of working population (1960)
Total working population: 11 332 016 *a*

U.N. group no.		Percentage
1	Agriculture, forestry, fishing and hunting	54.2
	Mining and quarrying	1.2
2/3	Manufacturing	13.7
4	Construction	3.6
5	Electricity, gas, water and sanitary services	0.4
6	Commerce	9.5
7	Transport, storage and communications	3.2
8	Services	13.5
9	Others	0.7

CENTRAL AMERICA

		Year(s)
Life expectancy at birth (years): male	57.6	1959-61 av.
female	60.3	
Infant mortality (per '000)	60.7	1965
Crude birth rate (per '000)	44.5*	1965
Crude death rate (per '000)	10.5*	1965
Accidental deaths (per 100 000 population)	6.4	1965
caused by motor vehicles	41.8	1965
due to other causes	1810	1966
Population per physician	510	1966
Population per hospital bed	70	1963-4 av.
School enrolment: age 5-19 years (percentage)	303	1964-5 av.
age over 19 years (per 100 000 population)		

a incl. children over 8 years of age in employment.

COMMUNICATIONS
		Year(s)
Motor vehicles in use ('000s): private	686.4	1963-5 av.
commercial	376.2	1963-5 av.
Railway track (km.)	23 672	1965
Mail per capita: domestic	19	1963-5 av.
foreign received	4	1967
foreign sent	2.1	1963-5 av.
Telephones (per '000 population)	33.4	1963-5 av.
Radio receivers (per '000 population)	114*	1962-4 av.
Television sets (per '000 population)		
Daily newspapers (per '000 population)		

na: data not available.   — negligible or nil.   *1* one year only.   *2* two year average.   * estimate.   † re-exports.

MONGOLIA

Outer Mongolian independence from China, first proclaimed in 1921, was not recognized by China until 1946, and it was finally guaranteed in 1950 by both China P.R. and the U.S.S.R. Relations with the latter were backed by a 20-year treaty of friendship and economic assistance (1966) and with China P.R. by treaties of economic and cultural co-operation and a border agreement (1962). Since the estrangement between China P.R. and the U.S.S.R., Sino-Mongolian relations have deteriorated. The Mongolian People's Republic is a member of Comecon.

AREA: 1 565 000 sq. km. (604 250 sq. miles)

LAND USE: (percentage of total)

		Year
Permanent meadow and pasture	84.0	1970
Forest and woodland	10.5	
Other land	5.5	

POPULATION: 1 170 000 (1967 estimate)

Largest city: ULAANBAATAR (Ulan Bator), capital; population: 195 300 (city proper, 1962)

		Year
Crude birth rate (per '000)	40.0*	1965
Crude death rate (per '000)	9.7*	1965
Population per physician	730	1965
Population per hospital bed	110	1966
School enrolment: age 5–19 years (percentage)	157	1961
age over 19 years (per 100 000 population)	756	1963

COMMUNICATIONS

		Year
Railway track (km.)	1 427	1965
Telephones (per '000 urban population)	1.2	1965
Daily newspapers (per '000 population)	88	1963

FINANCE

Currency unit: The tugrik replaced, at par, the rouble in 1961

Exchange rates	1965a	1960b	1958b
Per $ U.S.	4.0	4.0	4.0
Per £ sterling	11.2	11.2	11.2

a in 1965 there was a tourist exchange premium of 50% on hard-currency notes. b roubles.

PRODUCTION AND TRADE

The Mongols are traditionally herdsmen, and the sheep population numbers approximately 15 million; goats, cattle, horses and camels are also of importance. Some grain and vegetables are grown, wheat production in 1965 being 300 000 and potatoes 25 000 metric tons. Collectivization of agriculture was completed in 1960. The annual yield of hardwood amounts to some 700 000 cubic metres. Minerals include coal, gold, oil and wolfram. Industry is small, but is increasing with the U.S.S.R. at the front. Electricity production (thermal and hydro) in 1965 was in the region of 200 million kWh.

The principal exports are livestock, animal products, and gold; imports consist mainly of manufactured goods, textiles and cement.

Trade is primarily with the U.S.S.R., Switzerland being the only significant trading partner apart from the Comecon countries and China P.R.

MOROCCO

In 1956 Morocco was formed from the union of the French and the Spanish (northern) protectorates and the international zone of Tangier. The Spanish province of Ifni was incorporated into Morocco in 1969. Ceuta and Melilla and three groups of islands off the north coast remain under Spanish sovereignty.

Note: 1953–5 statistics include data for those areas remaining under Spanish sovereignty, and are therefore not strictly comparable with later figures.

AREA: 500 000* sq. km. (193 000* sq. miles)

LAND USE: (percentage of total)

	1963	1953
Arable and orchard	17.7	20.0
Permanent meadow and pasture	17.2	23.8
Forest and woodland	12.0	10.7
City areas, waste and other land	53.1	45.5

POPULATION: 14 193 000 (1967 estimate)

Largest city: CASABLANCA; population: 1 120 000 (city proper, 1966)
Capital city: RABAT; population: 370 000 (city proper, 1966)

Distribution of working population (1960)
Total working population: 3 254 379

U.N. group no.		Percentage	Year(s)
0	Agriculture, forestry, fishing and hunting	56.3	1962
1	Mining and quarrying	1.8	1965
2/3	Manufacturing	8.7	1963–4 av.
4	Construction	4.1	1963–4 av.
5	Electricity, gas, water and sanitary services	0.3	
6	Commerce	7.3	
7	Transport, storage and communications	2.5	
8	Services	9.9	
9	Others (including unemployed)	12.6	

		Year(s)
Life expectancy at birth (years)	47*	1963
Population per physician	12 120	1965
Population per hospital bed	660a	1963–4 av.
School enrolment: age 5–19 years (percentage)	37	1967
	72	1963–4 av.

a government hospitals only.

COMMUNICATIONS

		Year(s)
Motor vehicles in use ('000s): private	157.2	1963–5 av.
commercial	60.9	1964
Railway track (km.)	1 756	
Mail per capita: domestic	5	1963–4 av.
foreign received	2	
foreign sent	1	
Telephones (per '000 population)	50.1	1967
Radio licences (per '000 population)	1.8	1963–5 av.
Television sets (per '000 population)	17	1963

FINANCE

Currency unit: The dirham replaced the Moroccan franc in 1959 at the rate DH 1 to MF 100

Exchange rates	1965	1960	1950a	1938a
Per $ U.S.	5.06	5.06	350	38.01
Per £ sterling	14.17	14.17	980	175.0

		Year(s)
National Income (million $ U.S.)	2 324	1965
G.N.P. per capita ($ U.S.)	170.6	1966
Rate of increase of G.N.P. per capita		1960–4 av.
Foreign trade (percentage of G.D.P.)	35	1963–5 av.

a Moroccan francs.

TRADING

	1965	1955i	1938i
Total trade (in million $ U.S.)			
Exports (f.o.b.)	430	328	43
Imports (c.i.f.)	445	497	63

Main trading partners (percentage of total value)

Exports	1965	1955i		Imports	1965	1955i
France	44	45		France	38	49
Germany F.R.				Germany F.R.	12	9
Spain				U.S.A.	8	4
U.K.				Cuba	6	5
Belg./Lux.				Taiwan	3	4
Netherlands				China P.R.	3	
U.S.S.R.				Italy	3	3

Distribution of trade (percentage of total value)

Exports	1965	1955e*
Crude materials and fuels (natural phosphates)	45	(19)
(metalliferous ores)	12	(10)
Food (fruit and vegetables)	44	(na)
Manufactured goods	5	4
Wine	4	

Imports	1965	1955e*
Manufactured goods	41	(16)
(machinery and transport equipment)	29	(19)
Food (sugar)	5	(17)
(cereals)	3	(5)
Crude materials and fuels	14	na
Chemicals	5	3

c 1938 and 1955 figures are for French Morocco only, and exclude trade with Spanish Morocco and Tangier.

continued

MEXICO continued

PRODUCTION, EXPORTS AND IMPORTS *continued*

7. FUEL AND POWER

	Production		Exports		Imports	
Coal, A.†	1 147	1 340	—	—	50	43
Coke	15 522	6 330¹	—	—	35	11
Electricity h: total	7 236	2 940¹				
hydro	8 286	3 390¹				
thermal						
Natural gas f	11 100	13 000¹	1 450	—	260¹	558¹
Oil, crude	18 140	13 020¹	1 050	na	301¹	na
Petroleum, refined	17 036	10 740¹	1 677	3 120¹	810	1 460¹

h million kWh. f million cu. metres.

8. IRON AND STEEL

	Production		Exports		Imports	
Iron ore	1 461m	358m	11	191	—	—
Pig iron	1 134	279	—	—	32¹	4
Steel ingots/castings	2 293	636	—	—	10	3
Iron/steel scrap	na	na	—	—	548	193
Iron/steel products a	na	na	21	—	44	7

a metal content.

9. NON-FERROUS MINERALS AND METALS

	Production		Exports		Imports	
Diamonds a					0.41²	0.03
Gold r, ore m	221.30m	417.60m			19.30n	1 363.00n
						507.00m
Platinum group						0.65s
Silver k, ore m	41 602.7	45 242.70	36 679.0	34 372.30		
Asbestos: fibre	na	na			21.85	5.69
manufactured			0.01†		0.72	0.88s
Mica	0.37				0.15	0.04i
Aluminium: bauxite					8.60	
alumina					36.86p	1.59q
aluminium	14.10				12.56	7.88i
Antimony: ore	4.69m	3.90m	11.77	7.46	0.02	0.01s
metal	na	na	0.30	0.89	0.04	
Cadmium	na	na	1.01	0.92	0.64	1.25i
Chrome, metal					0.04	
Cobalt, metal					0.01	
Copper: ore	59.17m	56.54m	6.38	39.99	0.04	0.92
metal	52.64	47.14	19.47	46.19	0.04	0.04a
Lead: ore	178.30m	216.33m	3.06²	7.46	0.02²	0.22³
metal	172.39	205.26	152.13³	209.70	1.63	0.72
Magnesite					106.08	196.68
Magnesium					0.02	0.02
Manganese: ore	130.00	195.10			0.43	0.35i
metal/salts						
Mercury: ore m	552.04	646.71	592.50	634.10	0.63	0.10a
Molybdenum f, ore m	47.62	32.35	89.10	37.50	0.07	
Nickel, metal					0.63	0.10a
Tin: ore	0.87m	na			0.48	0.34s
metal	0.94	0.27			0.10	2.08i
Titanium minerals	0.05	na			0.10	1.25
Tungsten, ore	0.08	0.60				

9. NON-FERROUS MINERALS AND METALS —continued

	Production		Exports		Imports	
Vanadium			4.5¹			7.2
Zinc: ore	233.43m	239.83m	314.75	328.85	0.07r	0.4¹
metal	59.64	54.68	46.91		0.08	0.09

a million $ U.S. f '000 fine troy oz. m metal content. n bullion, etc. p hydrates. q incl. hydrates. r vanadium concentrates. s incl. imports for re-export.

10. CHEMICALS n AND FERTILIZERS

	Production	Exports	Imports
Organic chemicals:			
Benzene	14.6		7.2
Butadiene	7.0		0.4¹
Ethylene	na		na
Methanol	na		6.5
Phenol	0.5		2.1
Phthalic anhydride	na		3.7¹
Styrene monomer	na		9.6¹
Urea	74.2		1.2
Inorganic chemicals:			
Ammonia	140.0		103.8¹
Carbon black	na		1.3¹
Chlorine	44.0		na
Nitric acid	117.7²		na
Sodium carbonate	107.6		105.6
Sodium hydroxide	96.0		19.4
Sulphuric acid	442.9²		68.7
Plastics:			
Polyamides	na		na
Polyethylene	—		36.2
Polyvinyl chloride	15.0¹		0.6
Fertilizers:			
Phosphates	32.7	27.7	210.4
Potash	—	—	29.7
Sulphur: native	1 579.1 180.8¹	—	0.3
recovered	42.5 26.1¹	61.6	7.3

n data not available for years 1953–5.

11. INDUSTRY

	Production	Exports	Imports
Aircraft a			
Alcoholic beverages	14.4	0.2	4.0
	3.0a	0.3a	2.0a
beet b	9 487.0 6 268.3		
Cement	4 212.0 1 831.3	17.3	30.0*
Electrical engineering a		2.1† 0.42†	99.0 35.5²a
Railway vehicles a		1.2†	32.0 10.6
Machine tools a			28.0
Merchant ships g	0.3		5.0 0.2¹
Motor vehicles	29.0 22.2	0.9a	218.8a 80.9²a
private d q	61.1 13.5		

a million $ U.S. b '000 hectolitres. d no. in thousands. g '000 G.R.T. q assembly of imported parts.

continued

MONACO

Monaco, a small principality, has been under French protection since 1861. In 1962 a new constitution was promulgated maintaining the hereditary monarchy but renouncing the principle of divine right of the monarch. New neighbourhood treaties with France were signed in 1963.

AREA: 1.5 sq. km. (0.6 sq. miles)

LAND USE

All available ground is built upon. The only cultivation is in private or public gardens.

POPULATION: 24 000 (1967 U.N. estimate)

		Year
Infant mortality (per '000)	2.1*	1965
Crude birth rate (per '000)	20.5*	1965
Crude death rate (per '000)	16.0*	1965
Population per hospital bed a	53b	1966
School enrolment: age 5–19 years (percentage)		1964

a government hospitals only. b public education only.

COMMUNICATIONS

		Year(s)
Telephones (per '000 urban population)	53.9	1967
Radio receivers (per '000 population)	276	1963–5 av.
Television sets (per '000 population)	558	1963–5 av.

FINANCE

Currency unit: The French franc

TRADE

Monaco's prime source of income is tourism; there are, on average, 650 000 visitors a year. Foodstuffs and manufactured goods are imported.

From 1947 until 1968 Nauru was administered, chiefly by Australia, as a U.N. Trusteeship. Nauru then became an independent republic with a limited form of membership of the British Commonwealth.

AREA: 20 sq. km. (8 sq. miles)

LAND USE: (percentage of total)
Arable and orchard.
City areas, waste and other land

POPULATION: 6 056 (of whom 3 101 were indigenous Nauruans) (1966 census)

Total working population: 2 164 (1961), of whom approx. 1 350 are employed in phosphate mining.

PRODUCTION AND TRADE

The chief product is phosphate rock, of which some 1 600 000 metric tons were exported annually during the years 1963–5, compared with an average of 1 250 000 metric tons for the years 1953–5.

There are some 2 000 cattle and 3 000 chickens on the island, but very little land is cultivated. Annual electricity production averaged 12 million kWh. during 1963–5.

Exports, almost entirely phosphates, go to Australia, New Zealand, and the U.K.

Imports consist of foodstuffs, building materials, and machinery.

Trade for the year 1963/4 amounted to (in million $ U.S.): Exports 9.8   Imports 12.5

	1963
Arable and orchard	15
City areas, waste and other land	85

Before 1950 Nepal was ruled by a series of hereditary prime ministers. A revolutionary movement in 1950/1 restored the monarchy which, after ten unsettled years, gained executive power; and a new constitution was introduced in 1962, with a council of ministers and an indirectly elected parliament.

AREA: 141 400* sq. km. (54 600* sq. miles)

LAND USE: (percentage of total)
	1965
Arable and orchard	13.0
Permanent meadow and pasture	14.2
Forest and woodland (incl. unstocked land)	32.2
City areas, waste and other land	40.6

POPULATION: 10 500 000 (1967 estimate)
Largest city: KATMANDU, capital: population: 121 019 (city proper, 1961)

Distribution of working population (1952–4 av.)
Total working population: 4 153 455

U.N. group no.		Percentage
0	Agriculture, forestry, fishing and hunting	93.5
1	Mining and quarrying	1.9
2/3	Manufacturing	0.2
4	Construction	—
5	Electricity, gas, water and sanitary services	1.4
6	Commerce	0.5
7	Transport, storage and communications	0.3
8	Services	2.3
9	Others	0.2

COMMUNICATIONS
		Year(s)
Railway track (km.)	101	1969
Telephones (per '000 urban population)	0.04	1967
Daily newspapers (per '000 population)	0.8	1962–4 av.

FINANCE
Currency unit: The Nepalese rupee

	1965	1960	1958
Exchange rates			
Per $ U.S.	7.619	7.619	3.66
Per £ sterling	20.333	20.333	10.26

		Year
National Income (million $ U.S.)	665	1965
G.N.P. per capita ($ U.S.)	70	1966

TRADING

The principal exports are cereals, jute, timber, oilseeds, medicinal herbs and cattle products. The main imports are textiles, salt, fuels, sugar, machinery, paper, cereals, iron and steel. India is the main trading partner. Foreign aid and external loans contribute to the balance of trade. The value of imports for the year 1967/8 was about U.S. $ 60 million.

PRODUCTION, EXPORTS AND IMPORTS
Years: 1963–5 average   Units: '000 metric tons unless otherwise indicated
Note—no data are available for the years 1953–5

1. CEREALS, etc.	Production	Exports	Imports
Maize (corn)	853.0	—	0.1*
Millets/sorghum	75.3	0.6*	0.1*
Potatoes	na	0.8*	—
Rice	2 172.0	32.5*	—
Wheat	143.0	—	0.5*

3. BEVERAGES, FOREST PRODUCTS, etc.			
Sugar: cane	185.7	—	—
raw	1.3	—	—
Tea	na	—	3.6*
Tobacco, leaf	na	0.1*	0.3*
Softwood j	146.0	16.0	0.8*
Hardwood j	6 826.7*	146.3	na
Paper	1.0*		

j '000 cu. metres of roundwood equivalent.

4. VEGETABLE OILSEEDS AND OILS			
Castor seed	na	—	—
Linseed	na	0.82*	0.04*
Rapeseed	na	0.62*	—
	na	2.99†	

5. LIVESTOCK‡, ANIMAL PRODUCTS, etc.	Production	Exports	Imports
Cattle d	2 629.3*	—	—
Goats d	2 050.0*	—	—
Sheep d	2 052.0*	5.3*	9.53*
Butter	162.0*	0.8	na
Wool	1.0*		

d no. in thousands.

6. FIBRES, TEXTILES, etc.			
Jute	38.0		
Cotton, woven fabrics	na		40

7. FUEL AND POWER			
Electricity h: total	17²		
hydro	10²		
thermal	7²		
Petroleum, refined			

h million kWh.

8. IRON AND STEEL			
Iron/steel products	—	—	na

na: data not available.   — negligible or nil.   — not available.   ¹ one year only.   ² two year average.   * estimate.   ‡ see appendix.

187

PRODUCTION, EXPORTS AND IMPORTS
Years: 1963–5 average and 1953–5 average   Units: '000 metric tons unless otherwise indicated
Note—The trade figures given for 1953–5 are the sum of the trade figures for the French Zone, the Spanish Zone, and Tangier; thus they include trade between these three states. They are therefore not comparable with the trade figures for 1963–5.

1. CEREALS, etc.	Production		Exports		Imports	
Barley	1 305.7	1 807.0*	76.2	405.3	1.1	2.9*
Maize (corn)	353.3*	285.3	74.9	72.6	3.7*	0.1
Millets/sorghum	37.0*	40.3	40.3	29.4	—	—
Oats	11.0*	60.0²	4.7	33.9	—	0.1†
Potatoes	228.7	70.5¹	91.0	16.5	39.5	40.6
Rice	19.0	30.5²	3.3	12.2	—	0.9
Rye	2.7	4.3²	—	—	—	0.2
Wheat	1 235.3	1 162.3*	5.1	145.8	176.0	29.9

2. FRUIT, etc.						
Apples	6.7*		—	—	2.6	6.5
Apricots	19.0	12.2	—	—	—	—
Bananas			—	—	8.3	7.1*
Coconuts			—	—	0.1	—
Dates	83.3	72.3	—	—	1.5	3.4
Figs	66.7*	53.6²	0.2	na	—	—
Grapes	441.7	245.0	3.0	0.9	—	0.7*
Lemons	8.7	5.7	4.5	2.9	—	0.1*
Oranges	530.0	198.0m	409.1	140.7	—	2.0*
Other citrus fruit	186.0	85.0¹	5.1	3.3	—	—
Olives	9.7	na			—	—
Peaches	9.0		—	—	—	—
Pears	2.0*		—	—	—	0.9
Plums	5.3*	na	—	—	—	0.8
Raisins	1.5*	0.1*	—	—	9	1
Tomatoes	222.0¹	129.0¹	78	138	—	18
Wine b	2 830.0	1 662.0*	800.0	228p	11	9

b '000 hectolitres.   n French Morocco only.

3. BEVERAGES, FOREST PRODUCTS, etc.						
Cocoa			—	—	0.3	0.2
Coffee	242.7	na	—	—	9.6	5.0q
Sugar: beet	17.9	na	—	—	—	—
raw	1.8*	2.1*	10.6	27.3	377.0*	315.1q
Tea			0.1	0.5	10.3	15.5
Tobacco: leaf	4 043.0m	2 940.0¹			4.1	2.3
cigarettes	1.6	na	—	2.72	0.31	—
tobacco/snuff	319.0²	210.2	—	2.8*	339.4	264.3
Softwood j	280.6²	787.3	28.6²	—	74.6	5.83
Hardwood j			—	—	12.7	7.7
Wood pulp			—	—	—	3.0
Newsprint			12.5²	12.3²	25.9²	8.3
Other Paper	40.9²	na				

j '000 cu. metres of roundwood equivalent.   p incl. cigarillos.

4. VEGETABLE OILSEEDS AND OILS						
Castor seed	na	na	0.15	—	—	—
Castor oil	na	na	—	—	0.04	0.03
Copra	na	na	—	—	2.68	0.27
Coconut oil	12.00	3.30	1.14	—	14.69	6.44
Cottonseed			—	—	9.52	5.83
Cottonseed oil			—	—	0.69	3.94*
Groundnuts			—	—	1.24	—
Groundnut oil			0.02	—	—	0.01*
Linseed	10.67²	24.00r	2.37	12.50	0.65	2.10
Linseed oil			1.50	—	0.96	10.23
Olive oil	29.67²	17.00*	4.25	3.19	0.13	1.89
Palm kernels			—	—	0.01	0.81
Palm kernel oil			—	—	—	0.27
Palm oil			—	0.07†	—	0.90
Rapeseed			0.01†	—	0.02	—
Sesame seed	na	na	0.03	1.00*	7.98	3.80*
Soya beans	na	na			31.01	0.03
Soya bean oil	na	na	—	—	0.03	0.01
Sunflower seed	8.33	na	—	—	6.45	1.80
Sunflower seed oil			1.14	2.67		

r flax grown for seed only.

5. LIVESTOCK‡, ANIMAL PRODUCTS, etc.						
Chickens d	10 333.3*	694.0¹	—	4.1t	0.6	1.7*
Cattle d	2 922.3*	2 744.2*	0.8	—	0.1	na
Goats d	7 449.0*	10 574.2a				
Sheep d	15 093.0*	15 112.5*	1.2	—	0.3	—
Horses d	307.7*	241.0*				
Pigs d	48.0*	71.0*	—	—	6.2	0.8
Bacon/ham i	133.7*	119.5*			0.2	0.1
Meat†: A	30.0*	53.4¹	—	—	2.5	3.3
B			—	—	4.5	4.2
Butter	40.0*	50.1*	0.4	—	0.2	3.0*
Cheese	199.5	112.2	76.2	76.1*	52.8	26.7*
Eggs	321.7¹	458.6¹				
Milk			—	—	2.10	—
Hides/skins	28.7¹	26.6¹	0.9	—	—	—
Wool	5.9²	6.5*	0.7²	2.1	0.2²	0.1

d no. in thousands.   t Spanish Morocco only.   u number registered for taxation.

6. FIBRES, TEXTILES, etc.						
Agaves (sisal etc.)	0.3	0.1¹	—	7.6	3.1²	0.8
Cotton lint	6.0	1.7*	5.7	—	4.5	3.5
Hemp fibre	na	0.3²	—	0.1†	—	1.4
Jute			—	—	3.2	1.1
Rubber, natural			—	—	1.0	1.0
Silk f			—	—	1.9	0.2
Cotton: yarn	4.5	2.5	—	—	9.0²	0.7²
woven fabrics	5.9²	2.0	0.1²	—	—	9.9
Wool: yarn	0.5	0.6¹	—	0.1	0.9	0.7
woven fabrics						

f metric tons.

7. FUEL AND POWER						
Coal, 'A' ‡	407	470				
Coke		890¹				
Electricity h: total	1 232	770¹	228p	—	78	121
hydro	1 124	770¹			11	9
thermal	108	7				
Natural gas i	10	100¹				
Oil, crude	123	137				
Petroleum, refined	1 030	85.0¹	—	—	806	na
					137	770¹

h million kWh.   i incl. small quantity of Coal 'B'.

8. IRON AND STEEL						
Iron ore	567m	765m	1 030	1 297	9	na
Pig iron	na	na	30	36	1	1
Iron/steel scrap	4.3	98.7*			—	18

m metal content.

9. NON-FERROUS MINERALS AND METALS						
Gold k, ore m	na	4.00				
Silver k, ore m	658.77m	2 094.70m	35.83p	604.00p	—	0.85
Asbestos: fibre	na	0.55	11.69	0.04	2.34	0.11
manufactured	na	na		0.01	0.23	0.16
Mica	na	0.01	—	—	—	1.03
Aluminium: bauxite					1.99	1.03
alumina					0.12² q	—
aluminium	1.48m	0.58m	0.40†	1.41	3.18	1.66
Antimony: ore	2.08	na	2.08	—	0.01	—
metal	na	na	—	—	0.01	0.02
Beryl	na	0.02	—	0.02	—	0.02
Chrome, ore	na	142.85	—	142.85	—	0.26r
Cobalt, ore	1.63m	0.70m	14.16	3.53		
Copper: ore	1.80m	0.90m	5.66	—	2.60	1.06
metal	na	na	1.30	—		0.43
Lead: ore	74.12m	84.52m	125.63	82.44	0.19	na
metal	18.28	26.94	15.12	27.02	0.43²	na
Magnesium: dolomite	na	na			0.03²	na
magnesite	na	na			0.54	0.21†
metal/salts						
Manganese, ore	350.63	413.64	318.74	373.65	1.40	1.00
Mercury f	na	na				
Nickel, ore	0.32m	0.14m	—	—	—	—
Tin: ore	0.01	0.01m	0.01	—	0.25	0.24
metal	na	na	—	—	0.50²	—
Titanium minerals	na	na	—	0.02	—	—
Tungsten, ore	0.01	0.01¹	—	71.73	—	—
Zinc, ore	42.20m	37.64m	76.25	—	2.62r	2.14r

f metric tons.   k '000 fine troy oz.   p bullion.   q incl. hydrate.   r metal.

10. CHEMICALS n AND FERTILIZERS						
Chemicals	0.60	—	—	—	—	—
Fertilizers:						
Phosphates	9 490.2	4 834.7	9 381.9	4 769.7	na	—
Potash	6.1x	0.7x	5.02	—		
Pyrites	269.0	300.0²	23.6a	6.6a	12.8	10.4
Sulphur	826.0	695.6	27.3	9.7	10.0	12.2
						9.8

n data not available for years 1953–5.   x sulphur content.

11. INDUSTRY						
Aircraft a	na	na	—	—	2.5²	na
Alcoholic beverages b	0.1	—	0.11†	—	1.8²	1.8¹ a
beer b			—	—	14.7	189.3
Cement	268.0	300.0²	1.2a	—	17.8²	13.2
Electrical						
engineering a			—	—	1.8	2.2
Railway						1.9
Machine tools a						
Motor vehicles	1.9	n p	5.3	—	18.9² a	34.4a
commercial d b						
private d p						

a million $ U.S.   b '000 hectolitres.   d no. in thousands.   g '000 G.R.T.

na: data not available.   — negligible or nil.   — not available.   ¹ one year only.   ² two year average.   * estimate.   ‡ see appendix.   † re-exports.   a assembly of imported parts.

NETHERLANDS

The Netherlands is a constitutional and hereditary monarchy. The central executive power rests with the Crown while the central legislative power is vested in the Crown and parliament. The country became a member of Benelux (with Belgium and Luxembourg) in 1944, and in 1961 the three became members of the European Economic Community.

AREA: 40 893 sq. km. (15 789 sq. miles) (excl. inland water)

LAND USE: (percentage of total)

	1965	1955
Arable and orchard	28.8	29.7
Permanent meadow and pasture	38.3	35.9
Forest and woodland	8.6	7.1
City areas, waste and other land	24.3	27.3

POPULATION: 12 597 000 (1967 estimate)
Largest city: ROTTERDAM: population: 1 048 487 (1966)
Seat of Government: 'S GRAVENHAGE or DEN HAAG (The Hague); population: 743 208 (1966)

Distribution of working population (1960)
Total working population: 4 168 626

U.N. group no.		Percentage
		10.7
0	Agriculture, forestry, fishing and hunting	1.5
1	Mining and quarrying	29.9
2/3	Manufacturing	9.7
4	Construction	1.6
5	Electricity, gas, water and sanitary services	6.9
6	Commerce	23.5
7	Transport, storage and communications	0.5
8	Services	
9	Others	

		Year(s)
Life expectancy at birth (years): male	71.1	1966
female	76.1	1966
Infant mortality (per '000)	14.4	1966
Crude birth rate (per '000)	19.9	1965
Crude death rate (per '000)	8.0	1965
Accidental deaths (per 100 000 population)		
caused by motor vehicles	19.7	1965
due to other causes	24.1	1965
Population per physician	860	1965
Population per hospital bed	200	1965
School enrolment: age 5–19 years (percentage)	89	1963–4 av.
age over 19 years (per 100 000 population)	1169	1963–5 av.

COMMUNICATIONS

		Year(s)
Motor vehicles in use ('000s): private	1 707.4	1963–5 av.
commercial	217.4	1963–5 av.
Railway track (km.)	3 238	1964
Mail per capita: domestic	193	
foreign received	11	1963–5 av.
foreign sent	18	
Telephones (per '000 urban population)	201.1	1967
Radio licences (per '000 population)	256	1963–5 av.
Television licences (per '000 population)	151.8	1963–5 av.
Daily newspapers (per '000 population)	258.5	1962–4 av.

FINANCE

Currency unit: The guilder, or florin

Exchange rates	1965	1960	1950	1938
Per $ U.S.	3.611	3.770	3.805	1.839
Per £ sterling	10.120	10.568	10.659	8.459

		Year(s)
National Income (million $ U.S.)	15 544	1966
G.N.P. per capita ($ U.S.)	1 420	1966
Rate of increase of G.N.P. per capita	3.1	1960–4 av.
Foreign trade (percentage of G.D.P.)	75	1963–5 av.

TRADING

Total trade (in million $ U.S.)

	1965	1960	1955	1938
Exports (f.o.b.)	6 393	3 770	2 687	593
Imports (c.i.f.)	7 461		3 208	803

Main trading partners (percentage of total value)

Exports	1965	1955	1938
Germany F.R.	28	24	15d
Belg./Lux.	15	18	10
U.K.	12	14	23
France	8	9	8
Italy	5	6	5
U.S.A.	4	3	6
Sweden	3		3

Imports	1965	1955	1938
Germany F.R.	24	18	14
Belg./Lux.	20	18	11
U.K.	17	9	
France			
Italy			
Sweden			

Distribution of trade (percentage of total value)

Exports	1965	1955	1938
Manufactured goods	47	41	31*
(machinery and transport equipment)	(21)	(15)	(6)
(textiles and clothing)	(9)		
Food	23	30	(na)
(meat)	(6)	(5)	
(dairy produce and eggs)	(6)	(11)	(15*)
(fruit and vegetables)	(5)	(5*)	
Crude materials and fuels	17	18	(na)
(petroleum products)	(7)	(9)	

Imports	1965	1955	1938
Manufactured goods	56	46	(na)
(machinery and transport equipment)	(25)	(18)	(4*)
(textiles and clothing)	(9)	(6)	
Food	21	31	11*
(9)	(8)	(10)	(3)
Crude materials and fuels	12	14	na
(petroleum products)	(7)	(5)	
Chemicals	7	5	na

d incl. Germany D.R.

PRODUCTION, EXPORTS AND IMPORTS Units: '000 metric tons unless otherwise indicated
Years: 1963–5 average and 1953–5 average

1. CEREALS, etc.

	Production		Exports		Imports	
Barley	378.7	250.0	45.0	164.5	242.8	524.1
Maize (corn)	—	30.3	3.0†	64.5	1 870.3	533.8
Millets/sorghum	—	—	28.5†	2.3	710.1	119.5
Oats	402.3	510.3	83.9	3.0†	155.2	203.2
Potatoes	3 739.0	4 024.3	630.1	25.8	28.4	9.9
Rice	—	—	18.0†	504.3	58.3	79.1
Rye	306.3	469.3	17.6	26.1†	182.9	135.7
Wheat	644.3	332.0	173.6	11.1	702.9	768.9

2. FRUIT, etc.

	Production		Exports		Imports	
Apples	382.1	328.0n	78.0	94.0	29.3	4.9
Bananas	—	—	0.2†	0.4	73.9	28.5
Cherries	7.0	15.9			3.4	2.3
Coconuts	—	—			0.5	0.7
Dates	—	—			7.7	0.7
Figs	6.3	12.3	1.4		9.4	5.3
Grapes	6.3		4.5		213.7	108.8
Lemons	—	—	0.1†	0.1†	10.9	3.2
Oranges	—	—	0.1†	0.1†		
Other citrus fruit	1.0*		4.8†	0.7†		
Peaches						
Pears	111.0	131.3	36.1	38.7	4.8	0.7
Plums	11.7	21.7		0.3	21.3	16.4
Raisins	—	—				
Tomatoes	290.0	111.0	356.7			
Wine b	—	—	6.4†	3.7†	99.0	

3. BEVERAGES, FOREST PRODUCTS, etc.

	Production		Exports		Imports	
Cocoa	—	—	0.6†	0.1†	108.9	59.1
Coffee	—	—	4.1†		80.9	29.1
Sugar: beet	3 380.0	3 002.0	9.8	124.7	212.2	231.3
raw	552.3	423.7	0.8†	0.4†	9.9	8.9
Tea	—	—	4.1†	5.1†	44.2	33.9
Tobacco: leaf	1 883.0n	1 112.7e				
cigarettes	16 170.0n	10 687.3e	na	1.9²	—	0.8²
tobacco/snuff	13.7	10.4				
Hardwood j	485.3	332.0	34.0	11.1	4 372.6	2 982.1
Softwood j	240.0	321.7*	38.6	21.5	648.3	403.6
Wood pulp	489.0	421.7*	2.2	21.8	2 714	207.3
Newsprint	168.0	102.3*	41.1	26.7	978.0	24.7
Other paper	1 063.0	664.7	408.0	284.7	359.3	133.7

4. VEGETABLE OILSEEDS AND OILS

	Production		Exports		Imports	
Castor oil	na	na	0.03†	0.36	2.09	3.13
Copra	—	—	0.27	0.53†	2.27	0.51
Coconut oil	na	na	1.86†	5.37†	131.33	141.80
Cottonseed oil	na	na	0.08†	1.66†	2.14	0.72
Groundnut oil	na	na	9.16	4.1†	3.30	26.02
Linseed	111.0	na	12.94	12.40	9.23	5.23
Linseed oil	290.0	111.0	3.74	6.41	69.17	62.47
	25.67	23.67			13.88	12.88

continued

PRODUCTION, EXPORTS AND IMPORTS *continued*

4. VEGETABLE OILSEEDS AND OILS—continued

	Production	Exports	Imports
Olive oil	—	0.28†	0.17
Palm kernels	na	19.70	124.87
Palm kernel oil	na	11.63	86.60
Palm oil	15.30	5.83†	68.93
Rapeseed	na	9.86†	74.52
Rapeseed oil	10.70	0.97	11.93
Sesame seed	na	1.79	0.07
Soya beans	na	—	387.12
Soya bean oil	na	0.23†	0.02
Sunflower seed	na	0.30†	23.02
Sunflower seed oil	na	21.14	1.29
Tung oil	na	10.72	7.67
	na	0.37	4.86
	na	0.02†	4.55
	na		0.99

5. LIVESTOCK‡, ANIMAL PRODUCTS, etc.

	Production	Exports	Imports
Chickens d	44 142.3 / 32 516.7		
Cattle d	3 671.0 / 2 984.7	65.5	76.4
dairy cows d	1 719.3p / 1 514.0	29.9	13.0
Goats d	93.0*	4.5	na
Sheep d	465.0 / 404.0		
Horses d	136.3 / 237.0	39.4	0.1
Pigs d	3 314.0 / 2 097.0	35.3	0.3
Bacon/ham	727.0 / 438.3	188.2	31.0
Meat‡: A	160.1*	10.4	16.3
B		148.1	1.0
Butter	95.7 / 73.3	100.6	0.4
Cheese	214.7 / 165.0	33.7	2.3
Eggs	288.6 / 195.7	114.4	5.8
Milk	375.3 / 334.0	105.9	89.0
Fish	7 036.3 / 5 840.3	198.7	113.1*
		1 587.0	963.8*
Hides/skins	8.2	51.9	15.4
Whale/sperm oil	32.6	20.0²	65.4
Wool	0.9	4.3	11.0
	14.7 / 14.9	7.2	80.31*
	29.9		35.6
	27.3		40.72
	25.0n		50.7r

d no. in thousands. p excl. animals kept on agricultural holdings of less than one hectare. q cattle hides only. r incl. small amounts of other marine oils. s excl. marine oils.

6. FIBRES, TEXTILES, etc.

	Production	Exports	Imports
Abaca	—	—	3.1
Agaves (sisal etc.)	—	12.4†	4.2
Cotton lint	—	2.7†	37.6
Flax fibre	33.3	146.6†	80.0
Hemp fibre	35.8	0.9†	0.2
Jute fibre	—	4.6†	23.8
Rubber: natural	—	81.2†	14.1
synthetic	91.7	2.0†	8.3
Silk†	72.7	12.7	16.9
Cotton: yarn	62.4n	29.9	23.9
woven fabrics	55.1	28.5	7.2
Rayon: fibre/yarn	11.2n	8.7	15.4
woven fabrics			
Non-cellulosic	34.0	25.3	9.3
fibre/yarn	27.7n	6.1	9.4
Wool: yarn			
woven fabrics			

n yarn consumption in licensed mills. p incl. spun rayon piece goods. q incl. tyre cord yarn. r continuous filament piece goods only.

7. FUEL AND POWER

	Production	Exports	Imports
Coal† A†‡	11 480 / 11 890	3 067	8 901 / 7 122
Coke	— / 250	858	371 / 308
Electricity h i	22 990 / 10 460l	52	371 / 368
Natural gas i	1 080 / 419l	1 584	
Oil, crude	2 290 / 1 020l	20	23 570 / 11 700l
Petroleum, refined	22 780 / 12 040l	9 267	7 340 / 2 620l

h million kWh. i million cu. metres. j thermal.

8. IRON AND STEEL

	Production	Exports	Imports
Iron ore	2 007	217†	3 059 / 1 149
Pig iron	489.0	109	78 / 20
Steel ingots/castings	2 714	105	207 / 128
Iron/steel scrap	na	384	207 / 35
Iron/steel products a	na	356	354 / 199

a million $ U.S.

9. NON-FERROUS MINERALS AND METALS

	Production	Exports	Imports
Diamonds a	—	29.79†	29.20
Gold k	—	26.37†‡ / 598.26†	192.70† / 547.30
bullion/coins etc.	—	41.66† / 118.87†	75.16† / 739.37
Cottoned oil	na	1 412.33† / 957.30†	5 691.00 / 681.33
Platinum group metals			
Silver k, bullion			18.13

a million $. b U.S. l 1961 data. w 1966 data.

---

9. NON-FERROUS MINERALS AND METALS—continued

	Production	Exports	Imports
Asbestos: fibre	—	0.08†	19.62 / 10.22
manufactured	—	9.52† / 5.18†	56.11 / 43.82
Mica	—	0.15†	0.83 / 0.48
Aluminium: bauxite	na	0.33†	12.38 / 0.49
alumina	na	—	9.15n / 3.33p
aluminium	na	23.20	60.78 / 25.95
Antimony, metal	na	0.14†	0.27 / 0.85
Cadmium, metal	0.04	1.25†	3.34 / 0.27
Chrome: ore	0.01*	—	1.17 / 1.99
metal	na	—	0.18	
Cobalt, metal	na	0.07†	0.24 / 42.30
Copper, metal	na	45.11†	101.05 / 2.58
Lead: ore	na	22.27†	59.82 / 43.81
metal	18.80†	9.79†	
Magnesium:			
dolomite	na	—	333.16 / 35.92
magnesite	na	1.04†	46.37 / 18.66
kieserite	na	15.61†	10.63
metal/salts‡	na	—	13.61 / 18.91
Manganese: ore	8.14†	0.79	15.44a / 40.57q
metal	na	3.50†q	17.49 / 6.49²
Mercury f	10.60†	—	110.40 / 35.13
Molybdenum, f, ore	82.30†	0.06†	290.60 / 28.40
Nickel, ore	1.54†	—	3.49 / 0.50
Tin: ore	—	—	20.53 / 36.51
metal	13.46	12.67†	2.24 / 3.17
Titanium minerals	27.76	28.36	17.50 / 6.69
Tungsten: ore	—	0.21†	0.11 / 0.04
metal	—	—	0.01
Vanadium, metal	—	—	0.01*
Zinc: ore	38.10	5.95†	89.17 / 64.81
metal	26.56	55.64‡	28.62 / 18.44

a million $ U.S. k '000 fine troy oz. n hydrate. p incl. hydrate.
g no. in thousands. s / metric tons. q incl. manganiferous iron ore. r ferro-vanadium.

10. CHEMICALS n AND FERTILIZERS

	Production	Exports	Imports
Organic chemicals:			
Benzene	47.0²	34.8	1.4
Butadiene	na	na	na
Ethylene	na	2.3	14.1
Methanol	18.8	2.2	48.5
Phenol	11.8	1.8	7.4
Phthalic anhydride	—	11.7	14.4
Styrene monomer	404.0¹	177.1	0.4
Urea			
Inorganic chemicals:			
Ammonia	557.0	3.2	20.2
Carbon black	55.3²*	45.1	9.5
Chlorine	137.5²	3.1	0.3
Nitric acid	145.5²	0.2	1.3
Sodium carbonate	973.3	2.0	9.7
Sodium hydroxide		na	34.4
Sulphuric acid		47.1	50.4
Plastics:			
Polyamides	na	6.0	0.9
Polyethylene	43.7	28.9	18.7
Polyvinyl chloride	18.0	na	43.3
Fertilizers:			
Phosphates	—	1.9	756.4 / 512.1
Potash	—	2.4† / 1.7	516.1 / 502.8
Pyrites	—	—	238.1 / 436.1
Sulphur	30.3p	4.8† / 7.6†	174.1 / 1.3

n data not available for years 1953–5. p recovered from sulphide ores.

11. INDUSTRY

	Production	Exports	Imports
Aircraft a	84.0¹* w	151.4	756.4 / 16.4
	2 043.0	27.6a	4.7a
Alcoholic beverages			
beer b	4 927.0	10.0	10.2
spirits b	223.0† / 320.0¹		18.0a
Cement	2 642.7	553.8	1 768.3 / 343.0
Electrical			
engineering a	1 055.0²	22.3	169.9² / 123.a²
Railway vehicles a		22.2	11.5
Machine tools a	12.0¹	141.0	558.4 / 28.1
Motor vehicles	279.0	152.4	66.0 / 26.0
commercial a		69.6a	14.5a	371.6a / 109.7²a
private a	543.3c		

a no. in thousands. b '000 hectolitres. c '000 G.R.T. g '000 G.R.T.
d no. in thousands. j 1967 data. l 1961 data. u assembly of imported parts. v incl. assembly of imported parts. w 1966 data.

na: data not available. — negligible or nil. * estimate. ‡ see appendix. † re-exports.

NETHERLANDS (TERRITORIES)

NETHERLANDS ANTILLES   CARIBBEAN SEA

The Netherlands Antilles consists of the Leeward Islands (Curacao, Aruba and Bonaire) and the smaller Windward Islands. Since 1954 it has been fully autonomous in domestic affairs although it remains an integral part of the Netherlands realm.

AREA: 1 019 sq. km. (394 sq. miles)

LAND USE: (percentage of total)

	1951
Arable and orchard	5.2
Permanent meadow and pasture	—
Forest and woodland	—
City areas, waste and other land	94.8

POPULATION: 212 000 (1967 estimate)
Capital city: WILLEMSTAD; population: 94 133 (1960)

Distribution of working population (1960)
Total working population: 80 199

U.N. group no.		Percentage
0	Agriculture, forestry, fishing and hunting	1.7
1	Mining and quarrying	1.1
2/3	Manufacturing	25.8
4	Construction	6.8
5	Electricity, gas, water and sanitary services	2.0
6	Commerce	13.7
7	Transport, storage and communications	6.2
8	Services	23.8
9	Others	18.9

		Year(s)
Infant mortality (per '000)	17.6*	1965
Crude birth rate (per '000)	27.3*	1965
Crude death rate (per '000)	5.0*	1965
Population per physician	1450	1964
Population per hospital bed	110	1964
School enrolment age 5–19 years (percentage)	112‡	1963–4 av.

COMMUNICATIONS

		Year(s)
Motor vehicles in use ('000s): private	22.2	1963–5 av.
commercial	4.4	1963–5 av.
Mail per capita: domestic	20	
foreign received	24	1963–5 av.
foreign sent	16	
Telephones (per '000 urban population)	11.1	1967
Radio receivers (per '000 population)	506	1963–5 av.
Television sets (per '000 population)	4.6	1963–5 av.
Daily newspapers (per '000 population)	135	1963–4 av.

FINANCE

Currency unit: The Netherlands Antilles guilder.

Exchange rates	1965
Per $ U.S.	1.886
Per £ sterling	5.281

		Year
National Income (million $ U.S.)	200	1965
G.N.P. per capita ($ U.S.)	1090	1966

TRADING

Total trade (in million $ U.S.)	1965	1955	1938
Exports (f.o.b.)	603	803	188
Imports (f.o.b.)	617	831	214

Main trading partners (percentage of total value)

Exports	1965	1955
U.S.A.	43	26
U.K.	8	14
Canada	4	4
Netherlands	4	na
Germany F.R.	3	2
Japan	2	8
Brazil		

Imports	1965	1955
Venezuela	77	78
U.S.A.	3	3
Netherlands	4	4
Trin./Tob.	2	1
Colombia	1	
Japan	1	

Distribution of trade (percentage of total value)

Exports	1966	1955
Petroleum and petroleum products	95	95

Imports		
Crude materials and fuels (petroleum and petroleum products)	80	88
Manufactured goods (machinery and transport equipment)	12 (79)	6 (88)
(textiles and clothing)	(4)	(2)
	(3)	(1)
Food	4	2

PRODUCTION, EXPORTS AND IMPORTS Units: '000 metric tons unless otherwise indicated
Years: 1963–5 average and 1953–5 average

1. CEREALS, etc.	Production		Exports		Imports	
Maize (corn)					0.7	1.4
Millets/sorghum	5.0*	na				
Potatoes					6.9	6.8
Rice					5.0	2.9

2. FRUIT, etc.						
Apples					1.1	0.7
Bananas					4.3	3.2
Coconuts					0.2	0.2
Grapes					0.2	0.2
Lemons					0.1	0.1
Oranges					2.5	1.9
Other citrus fruit					0.1	0.1
Pears					2.9	2.0
Wine b						

3. BEVERAGES, FOREST PRODUCTS, etc.						
Coffee					0.3	0.1
Sugar, raw					7.0	5.7
Tea					0.1	0.1
Tobacco, leaf					1.1a	0.42
Hardwood j						
Softwood j					11.1a	
Newsprint n					4.1²	
Other paper					0.42²	
					1.5²	

9. NON-FERROUS MINERALS AND METALS						
Asbestos, manufactured					0.3	0.1
					7.0	5.7

10. CHEMICALS n AND FERTILIZERS						
Chemicals			120.9			
Fertilizers: Phosphates	31.5*p	30.0¹p	103.7			
Sulphates	na					

7. FUEL AND POWER						
Electricity h	989	220¹				
Oil, crude			603†	2 950¹†	40 470	42 200¹
Petroleum, refined t	36 960	40 890	35 050	36 810¹	3 463	4 050¹

5. LIVESTOCK‡, ANIMAL PRODUCTS, etc.						
Chickens d	57.7*p	na				
Cattle d	6.0*	na				
Goats d	85.0*	na				
Sheep d	22.0*	na				
Pigs d	4.0*	na				
Bacon/ham						
Meat‡: 'A'	3.0*					
'B'						
Butter						
Cheese	0.5*	na				
Eggs	na					
Fish	0.6					
Milk	2.0*	na				

11. INDUSTRY						
Aircraft a					0.04a	0.04a
Alcoholic beverages a					0.05	0.76²*
Cement					0.76²a	
Electrical engineering a					0.07²a	
Motor vehicles a					1.01*	

4. VEGETABLE OILSEEDS AND OILS						
Coconut oil					0.04	
Groundnuts					0.05	
Groundnut oil						
Linseed oil						
Soya bean oil a	2.21					

a million $ U.S. b '000 cu. metres of roundwood equivalent. n data not available for years 1953–5. p recovered sulphur.

SURINAM   SOUTH AMERICA

Since 1954 Surinam has been fully autonomous in domestic affairs, although remaining an integral part of the Netherlands realm.

AREA: 163 800 sq. km. (63 243 sq. miles)

LAND USE: (percentage of total)

	1954
Arable and orchard	0.2
Permanent meadow and pasture	
Forest and woodland	74.6
City areas, waste and other land	25.2

POPULATION: 363 000 (1967 estimate)
Largest city: PARAMARIBO, capital; population: 110 867 (city proper, 1964)

Distribution of working population (1964)
Total working population: 80 199 (excl. tribal Indians, negroes and the armed forces)

U.N. group no.		Percentage
0	Agriculture, forestry, fishing and hunting	24.8
1	Mining and quarrying	7.0
2/3	Manufacturing	8.9
4	Construction	2.8
5	Electricity, gas, water and sanitary services	1.1
6	Commerce	11.0
7	Transport, storage and communications	2.4
8	Services	29.7
9	Others	12.3

		Year(s)
Life expectancy at birth (years): male	62.5	1963
female	66.7	
Crude death rate (per '000)	7.8	1965
Population per physician	2410	1965
Population per hospital bed	190	1966
School enrolment: age 5–19 years (percentage)	86	1963–4 av.
age over 19 years (per 100 000 population)	229 a	1963–4 av.

a at universities, degree-granting institutions, and teacher-training colleges only.

COMMUNICATIONS

		Year(s)
Motor vehicles in use ('000s): private	6.8	1963–5 av.
commercial	1.9	1963–5 av.
Railway track (km.)	81	1964
Telephones (per '000 urban population)	12.6	1964
Radio receivers (per '000 population)	148.1	1963–5 av.
Television sets (per '000 population)	33	1959

FINANCE

Currency unit: The Surinam guilder.

Exchange rates	1965
Per $ U.S.	1.87
Per £ sterling	5.33

		Year
National Income (million $ U.S.)	96	1964
G.N.P. per capita ($ U.S.)	360	1966

TRADING

Total trade (in million $ U.S.)	1965	1955	1938
Exports (f.o.b.)	58.3	26.8	3.2
Imports (c.i.f.)	95.1	27.3	3.7

Main trading partners (percentage of total value)

Exports	1965	1954
U.S.A.	73	81
Canada	7	6
Netherlands	5	3
Germany F.R.	1	
Japan	1	
Guyana	1	

Imports	1965	1954
U.S.A.	47	39
Netherlands	20	29
U.K.	6	7
Trin./Tob.	6	8
Germany F.R.	4	4
Japan	2	3
China P.R.	—	

Distribution of trade (percentage of total value)

Exports	1965	1955
Bauxite and alumina	80	80
Food	11	8
Wood and wood products	7	9

Imports	1965	1955
Manufactured goods (machinery and transport equipment)	71 (32)	56
Crude materials	9	12
Food	9	18
Chemicals	9	8

PRODUCTION, EXPORTS AND IMPORTS Units: '000 metric tons unless otherwise indicated
Years: 1963–5 average and 1953–5 average

1. CEREALS, etc.	Production		Exports		Imports	
Cassava	2.0	2.3				
Maize (corn)	1.0	1.0²			2.3	1.6
Potatoes						0.1
Rice	84.3	63.3	18.8	8.6		

2. FRUIT, etc.						
Bananas	8.0	2.3	4.7	3.2²		
Coconuts	6.3a	na				
Lemons	0.3	1.0	1.9	1.3		
Oranges	8.7	7.7	2.9	1.2		
Other citrus fruit	5.3	2.3				
Tomatoes	1.0					
Wine b					0.9	0.7

3. BEVERAGES, FOREST PRODUCTS, etc.						
Cocoa	0.2	0.2	0.2			
Coffee	0.4	0.4	0.2			
Sugar: cane raw	193.7	14.5	3.8	0.2		
Tea					0.1	0.1
Tobacco: leaf						
cigars			1.0e			
cigarettes	98.0e	66.4e			0.52a	0.52²
Hardwood j	263.0²	315.7	17.4²	20.5	9.8²	
Newsprint n					0.42²	0.32²
Other paper					1.3²	0.27a

4. VEGETABLE OILSEEDS AND OILS						
Castor oil						
Coconut oil	0.70				0.02	0.04
Copra	45.0b					na
Cottonseed oil					0.10	na
Groundnuts					0.04	0.03
Linseed oil					0.10	na
Olive oil					0.02	
Palm kernels	1.00*				0.29	0.22
Palm kernel oil	na					
Soya bean oil	na					

5. LIVESTOCK‡, ANIMAL PRODUCTS, etc.						
Chickens d	320.3	262.0²				
Cattle d	38.3	33.0¹			0.4	
Goats d	11.0	5.0¹				
Sheep d	5.0	2.0¹			0.1	
Horses d	8.0	7.0¹				
Pigs d	8.0					
Bacon/ham	0.3*				0.1	
Meat‡: 'A'					0.4	0.3
'B'					0.2	0.3
Butter	0.9				0.4	0.2
Cheese	3.9		0.8		1.7	na
Eggs	8.7	2.0p	na		5.7	2.7
Fish	na					
Milk						

d no. in thousands. p incl. shrimps landed by foreign vessels.

6. FIBRES, TEXTILES, etc.						
Rubber, natural			0.2			

7. FUEL AND POWER						
Coal, A'‡						
Electricity h	164a	203				2
Petroleum, refined	20t					100¹

h hydro and thermal. t thermal.

9. NON-FERROUS MINERALS AND METALS						
Gold, ore m	6.00	7.00				
Silver k, ore m						
Asbestos: fibre						
Aluminium: bauxite	3 919.24	3 253.13	3 945.11	3 254.35		
alumina	71.89¹	19.79	4.57			
aluminium	1.25¹	0.42				

11. INDUSTRY						
Beer	45.0b	0.1b			0.2a	0.6a
Cement	na				47.0	16.3
Electrical engineering a					1.9	29.3
Motor vehicles a	0.70	0.85			5.6	9.2²
	na	na			2.9	1.1²

a million $ U.S. b '000 hectolitres. d no. in thousands. e no. in millions. j '000 cu. metres of roundwood equivalent. k '000 fine troy oz. m metal content. n excl. printing and writing paper. p incl. shrimps landed by foreign vessels.

na: data not available.   — negligible or nil.   * estimate.   ¹ one year only.   ² two year average.   † re-exports.   ‡ see appendix.

NEW HEBRIDES

The New Hebrides is administered as a unique Anglo-French Condominium. An economic development plan has been set up for the expansion of agriculture and for improving communications and social services.

AREA: 14 760 sq. km. (5 700 sq. miles)

LAND USE: (percentage of total)

	1955
Arable and orchard	4.8
Permanent meadow and pasture	1.7
Forest and woodland	0.5
City areas, waste and other land	93.0

POPULATION: 77 983 (1967 census)
Capital: VILA; population: 800 (city proper, 1948)

		Year(s)
Crude birth rate (per '000)	45*	1966
Population per physician	3 780	1965
Population per hospital bed	220	1966
School enrolment: age 5–19 years (percentage)	82	1963–4 av.

FINANCE

Exchange rates a

	1965	1950
Per $ U.S.	89.76	76
Per £ sterling	251.33	212

Currency unit: The New Hebrides franc, with the value 100 per Australian dollar (which is also in circulation) replaced, at par, the franc CFP in 1970.
a for francs CFP.

TRADING

Total trade (in million $ U.S.)

	1965	1955
Exports (f.o.b.)	9	4
Imports (c.i.f.)	7	4

Main trading partners (percentage of total value)

Exports	1965
France	53
Japan	20
U.S.A.	10
Australia	6

Imports	1965
Australia	46
France	17
Japan	6
U.K.	5
Hong Kong	5
Fiji	4

Distribution of trade (percentage of total value)

Exports	1965
Copra	58
Manganese	26
Fish	12

Imports	1965
Manufactured goods	42
Food	20
Beverages and fuels	10
Crude materials and tobacco	7
Chemicals	5

PRODUCTION, EXPORTS AND IMPORTS
Years: 1963–5 average and 1953–5 average Units: '000 metric tons unless otherwise indicated

	Production		Exports		Imports	
1. CEREALS, etc.						
Potatoes d	—	—	—	—	0.1²	1.5²
Rice	—	—	—	—		
2. FRUIT, etc.						
Coconuts a	184.7	na	—	—		
Wine b	—		—	—	7.3	3.7

b '000 hectolitres. c no. in millions.

	Production		Exports		Imports	
3. BEVERAGES, FOREST PRODUCTS, etc.						
Cocoa d	0.6	0.6*	0.6	0.8*		
Coffee d	0.2*	0.3	0.2	0.3	2.6	
Sugar, raw						
Tobacco, cigarettes					0.8	0.1*
Hardwood j					6.2¹	

j '000 cu. metres of roundwood equivalent.

	Production		Exports		Imports	
4. VEGETABLE OILSEEDS AND OILS						
Copra	34.00	23.43	34.00	23.40		
Groundnut oil			—	—	0.01	

	Production		Exports		Imports	
5. LIVESTOCK‡, ANIMAL PRODUCTS, etc.						
Cattle d	60.7*	45.0²				
Goats d	6.0*	5.0²				
Sheep d	5.7	3.0²				
Pigs d	1.0*	50.0²			2.6	
Horses d						
Fish	3.1	na				
Milk						

d no. in thousands.

7. FUEL AND POWER
Petroleum, refined …

	Production		Exports		Imports	
9. NON-FERROUS MINERALS AND METALS						
Manganese, ore	50.80p					

p sintered ore.

	Production		Exports		Imports	
11. INDUSTRY						
Alcoholic beverages a					57.66	
Electrical engineering a						
Motor vehicles a						

a million $ U.S.

NEW ZEALAND

New Zealand consists of two main and a number of smaller islands. Dominion status was formally adopted in 1947, with a Governor-General appointed by the British Crown. New Zealand also has responsibility for a large tract of land in the Antarctic.

AREA: 268 680 sq. km. (103 736 sq. miles)

LAND USE: (percentage of total)

	1965
Arable and orchard	3.0
Permanent meadow and pasture	47.8
Forest and woodland	23.2
City areas, waste and other land	26.0

POPULATION: 2 676 919 (1966 census)
Largest city: AUCKLAND; population: 548 239 (1966)
Capital city: WELLINGTON; population: 167 859 (1966)

Distribution of working population (1961)
Total working population: 895 363

U.N. group no.		Percentage
0	Agriculture, forestry, fishing and hunting	14.4
1	Mining and quarrying	0.4
2/3	Manufacturing	25.0
4	Construction	9.6
5	Electricity, gas, water and sanitary services	1.3
6	Commerce	18.2
7	Transport, storage and communications	10.3
8	Services	20.3
9	Others	0.4

		Year(s)
Life expectancy at birth (years): male	68.4	1960–2 av.
female	73.8	
Infant mortality (per '000)	19.5	1965
Crude birth rate (per '000)	22.9	1965
Crude death rate (per '000)	8.7	1965
Accidental deaths (per 100 000 population) caused by motor vehicles	20.9	1965
due to other causes	30.5	1965
Population per physician	670	1964
Population per hospital bed	100	1966
School enrolment: age 5–19 years (percentage)	90	1963–4 av.
age over 19 years (per 100 000 population)	1 884	1963–5 av.

COMMUNICATIONS

		Year(s)
Motor vehicles in use ('000s): private	658.8	1963–5 av.
commercial	149.8	1965
Railway track (km.)	3 617	
Mail per capita: domestic	197	
foreign received	na	
foreign sent	14	1963–5 av.
Telephones (per '000 population)	39.9	1967
Radio licences (per '000 population)	245	1963–5 av.
Television licences (per '000 population)	108.6	1963–5 av.
Daily newspapers (per '000 population)	400	1962–4 av.

continued

190

FINANCE

Currency unit: The New Zealand dollar was introduced in 1967 at the rate N.Z.$1 to N.Z.£0.5

Exchange rates a

	1965	1960	1950
Per $ U.S.	0.357	0.357	0.357
Per £ sterling	1.0	1.0	1.0

		Year(s)
National Income (million $ U.S.)	4 503	1965
G.N.P. per capita ($ U.S.)	1 930	1966
Rate of increase of G.N.P. per capita	1.8	1960–3 av.
Foreign trade (percentage of G.D.P.)	40	1963–5 av.

a for New Zealand pounds.

TRADING

Total trade (in million $ U.S.)

	1965	1960	1955	1938
Exports (f.o.b.)	1 006	725		225
Imports (c.i.f.)	1 052	804		217

Main trading partners (percentage of total value)

Exports	1965	1955	1938
U.K.	47	65	84
U.S.A.	12	5	6
Japan	6	1	1
France	4	3	2
Australia	4	6	2
Germany F.R.	4	5	2 d
Belg./Lux.	3	2	1

Imports	1965	1955	1938
U.K.	35	55	84
U.S.A.	17	12	8
Japan	12	4	1
Canada	6	4	2
Australia	6	4	3
Germany F.R.	5	3	9
Kuwait	3	2	na

Distribution of trade (percentage of total value)

Exports	1965		1955*		1938*	
Food (meat)	55	(28)	55	(27)	70	(28)
dairy products and eggs		(25)		(27)		(40)
Crude materials and fuels	38	(29)	42	(36)	28	(21)
(wool)						
Chemicals	3		1		1	
Manufactured goods	3		—		—	

Imports	1965		1955*		1938*	
Manufactured goods	69	(33)	72	(30)	67	(22)
machinery and transport equipment						
(textiles and clothing)	13	(11)	11	(15)	na	(15)
Crude materials and fuels						
(petroleum products)		(7)		(na)		(5)
Chemicals	10		6		6	
Food	6		8		6	

d incl. Germany D.R.

PRODUCTION, EXPORTS AND IMPORTS
Years: 1963–5 average and 1953–5 average Units: '000 metric tons unless otherwise indicated

	Production		Exports		Imports	
1. CEREALS, etc.						
Barley	110.7	54.7			0.6	2.0
Maize (corn)	19.3	7.0*²			1.6*	
Millets/sorghum						
Oats	30.7	25.7			3.4	2.4
Potatoes	263.0	162.0²	6.7		2.3	2.5
Rice						
Sweet potatoes/yams	3.7	na				
Wheat	257.7	107.0			174.6	213.4
2. FRUIT, etc.						
Apples	88.0	61.3*	36.7	20.6		
Apricots	5.3	3.1				
Bananas					29.1	22.3
Coconuts					1.3n	0.9
Dates					1.5	1.8
Grapes	7.3	na				
Lemons	2.0	2.0			0.2	0.1
Oranges					14.8	13.8
Other citrus fruit	1.0	2.3			0.3	0.5
Peaches	18.0	9.1				
Pears	15.7	11.5²	3.1	0.2		
Pineapples					na	0.2
Plums	3.7	2.7				
Raisins					6.6	5.2
Tomatoes	49.0*	na			11.1	8.3
Wine b	78.5²	na				

b '000 hectolitres. n mainly desiccated.

	Production		Exports		Imports	
3. BEVERAGES, FOREST PRODUCTS, etc.						
Cocoa					3.0	2.6
Coffee					0.6	0.6
Sugar, raw			0.2†	0.3†	123.7	101.7
Tea					7.5	6.5
Tobacco: leaf			na		2.4	3.0
cigarettes	4.3	2.0		0.3r		
tobacco/snuff	1.9	2.5			6.7*r	
Softwood j	3 845.0r	1 953.0r	499.0	116.9	0.3²	
Hardwood j	5 849.0	3 537.7	0.5	0.5	99.7	57.0
Wood pulp	234.3	344.7	62.1	77.1	56.7	6.8
Newsprint	398.5	70.0	111.0	0.1	18.1	39.0
Other paper	138.3	39.7	1.2		32.3	28.6

r no. in millions. j '000 cu. metres of roundwood equivalent. r includes leaf tobacco, in million $ U.S.

	Production		Exports		Imports	
4. VEGETABLE OILSEEDS AND OILS						
Castor oil					0.25	0.15²
Copra					3.51	2.23
Coconut oil						0.01
Cottonseed oil					0.11	1.27
Groundnuts					2.54	0.18
Groundnut oil					0.77²	
Linseed	9.33p	na	0.89	2.80		
Linseed oil					0.112	1.59
Olive oil					0.01²	0.10
Palm oil						

continued

4. VEGETABLE OILSEEDS AND OILS—continued

	Production		Exports		Imports	
Rapeseed oil					0.02	0.1²
Soya beans					0.01	
Soya bean oil					1.14	
Sunflower seed oil					0.03	0.13
Tung oil					0.17	0.27

p flax grown for seed only.

	Production		Exports		Imports	
5. LIVESTOCK‡, ANIMAL PRODUCTS, etc.						
Chickens d	4 440*	4 351¹				0.2
Cattle d	6 729	5 730	0.4			
dairy cows d	3 466q	3 766r				
Goats d	33*	31	1.0	1.1		
Sheep d	51 743	37 774				
Horses d	99	166²	na			0.2
Pigs d	751	660				
Bacon/ham	809	585	0.1			0.4
Meat‡: B	48*	31	0.5			
Butter	235	196	488.8	346.4		
Cheese	101	106	181.1	151.6		
Eggs	45	38	91.9	94.0		
Fish						
Milk	5 718	5 136	4.9	4.41*	2.7	
Whale/sperm oil	1		741.9	485.0		
Hides/skins	56²	na	43.4a	28.5a		0.3
Wool	212	136	189.0	136.6		0.1

a million $ U.S. d no. in thousands. q excl. cows in urban areas. r incl. some beef cows.

	Production		Exports		Imports	
6. FIBRES, TEXTILES, etc.						
Abaca					0.4²	0.1²
Agaves (sisal etc.)					5.1	1.0
Cotton lint					0.2	0.3
Flax fibre	0.2	0.3¹			1.8	0.4²
Hemp fibre					9.3	8.5²
Jute					1.5²	
Rubber, natural					8.1	na
Silk j					0.1	0.9
Cotton: yarn					8.1	4.9
woven fabrics					2.9	1.8
Rayon: yarn					0.3	0.7
woven fabrics						
Wool: yarn					2.7	0.2²a
woven fabrics					0.3	0.1

	Production		Exports		Imports	
7. FUEL AND POWER						
Coal: A ‡	677	800				
B ‡	1 183	1 800			1	2
Electricity h: total	9 753	4 900¹				
hydro	7 731	4 600¹				
thermal	2 022u	300¹				
Oil, crude					1 140	
Petroleum, refined	1 063			227	1 397	1 420¹

h million kWh. u incl. geothermal.

continued

NEW ZEALAND — PACIFIC OCEAN (continued)

TRADING

Total trade (in million $ U.S.)

	1965	1955
Exports (f.o.b.)	0.2	0.4
Imports (c.i.f.)	0.7	

Main trading partners (percentage of total value)

Exports	1965	1955
New Zealand	86	94
Fiji	14	—

Imports	1965	1955
New Zealand	73	78
Australia	6	5
U.K.	5	9
Iran	4	na
U.S.A.	3	1
Japan	2	na
Fiji	2	4

Distribution of trade (percentage of total value)

Exports	1965a	1955
Oilseeds (mainly copra)	51	80
Fruit and vegetables	32	7

Imports	1965a	1955
Manufactured goods (machinery and transport equipment)	53	54
Food	28 (20)	27 (15)
Mineral fuels	7	9
Chemicals	5	6
Beverages and tobacco		

a a percentage of national exports‡ in 1965 which comprised 70% of general exports.

NIUE ISLAND

Niue Island, although geographically one of the Cook Islands, has been under separate administration since 1903. External affairs and defence are administered by the New Zealand government.

AREA: 259 sq. km. (100 sq. miles)

LAND USE: (percentage of total)

	1965	1953
Arable and orchard	77.0	38.5
Permanent meadow and pasture	11.5	38.5
Forest and woodland	11.5	23.0
City areas, waste and other land		

POPULATION: 5194 (1966 census); population: 956 (1965)

Capital: ALOFI; population: 956 (1965)

		Year(s)
Infant mortality (per '000)	10.2*	1965
Crude birth rate (per '000)	38.1*	1965
Crude death rate (per '000)	8.9*	1965
Population per physician	830	1965
Population per hospital bed	170a	1965
School enrolment: age 5–19 years (percentage)	104‡	1963–4 av.

a government hospitals only.

FINANCE

Currency unit: The New Zealand dollar

COOK AND NIUE ISLANDS

PRODUCTION, EXPORTS AND IMPORTS Units: '000 metric tons unless otherwise indicated

Years: 1963–5 average and 1953–5 average

	Production		Exports		Imports	
1. CEREALS, etc.						
Rice	—		—	—	0.1	0.1
2. FRUIT, etc.						
Bananas	na		0.3		0.2	
Coconuts e	16.0*	na	1.7	na	0.9	
Oranges	na		na		0.1	
Other citrus fruit	na		0.1		0.1	
Wine b						

b '000 hectolitres. e no. in millions.

	Production		Exports		Imports	
3. BEVERAGES, FOREST PRODUCTS, etc.						
Sugar, raw					0.9	0.4
Tobacco					na	0.11a
Softwood j					3.9²	1.1²
Hardwood j	49.8*					0.2¹

a million $ U.S. j '000 cu. metres of roundwood equivalent.

	Production		Exports		Imports	
4. VEGETABLE OILSEEDS AND OILS						
Copra: Cook Is.	1.23*	na	1.51 } 1.93			
Niue Is.	na	0.60²	na			

	Production		Exports		Imports	
5. LIVESTOCK‡, ANIMAL PRODUCTS, etc.						
Chickens d	55.0*	64.0¹				
Cattle d	2.0*	0.7				
Goats d	2.0*	2.7				
Horses d	2.0*	2.0²				
Pigs d	12.0*	9.7				
Butter					0.1*	
Fish	na	0.8				
Milk					0.2	

d no. in thousands.

	Production		Exports		Imports	
11. INDUSTRY						
Electrical engineering a					0.1²	

a million $ U.S.

TOKELAU ISLANDS

PACIFIC OCEAN

The Tokelau Islands, geographically part of the Gilbert and Ellice Is. group, became a New Zealand territory in 1949. They consist of three small atolls.

AREA: 10 sq. km. (4 sq. miles)

POPULATION: 1900 (1966 census)

Total working population: 429 (1961)

na: data not available. — negligible or nil. ¹ one year only. ² two year average. * estimate. ‡ see appendix. † re-exports.

NEW ZEALAND continued

PRODUCTION, EXPORTS AND IMPORTS continued

	Production		Exports		Imports	
8. IRON AND STEEL						
Iron ore	na	na	—	—	—	8
Pig iron	na	na	—	—	8	3
Steel ingots/castings	na	na	—	—	1	—
Iron/steel scrap	na	na	—	27	—	

	Production		Exports		Imports	
9. NON-FERROUS MINERALS AND METALS						
Diamonds a	na	na	—	0.74	0.57	0.53
Gold k: ore m	11.70	35.60	—	0.74	—	0.05
bullion/coins etc.	na	11.00†	32.70†	10.82	0.81	
Platinum group metals k.						
Silver k: ore m	0.16*	45.70	—	11.25	2.14	1.22
bullion	0.13	na	0.06	18.00		
Asbestos: fibre	na	na	—		98.38¹	39.18
manufactured	na	na	—	0.01a	6.33	3.17
Mica	na	na	—		1.01a	0.44ap
Aluminium	na	na	—		0.13a	0.05a
Antimony, metal					9.74	3.01
Chrome, metal						0.19
Cobalt, metal					0.07	0.08²
Copper, metal	2.50†	0.47†		13.19	3.30	
Lead, metal	0.90†			6.55	5.32	
Magnesium: dolomite						6.89
magnesite	7.15	na			0.17	0.06
metal/salts	0.75	na			0.68	0.71
Manganese: ore		0.23				
metal	na				0.56	1.70
Mercury f					5.20	0.02
Nickel, metal					0.21	0.47
Tin, metal			6.08q		0.41	2.18
Titanium minerals					4.40	
Tungsten, ore	0.03			0.04		
Zinc, metal					4.27	2.09

a million $ U.S. f '000 fine troy oz. k '000 metric tons. k metres of asbestos cement sheets. m metal content. p in addition, 48 324 sq. metres of asbestos cement sheets. q scrap.

	Production		Exports		Imports	
10. CHEMICALS n AND FERTILIZERS						
Organic chemicals	0.3¹		—		—	
Inorganic chemicals:						
Ammonia	na		—		0.1²	
Carbon black	na		—			
Chlorine	na		—		0.3¹	
Nitric acid	na		—		na	
Sodium carbonate	na		—		16.9	
Sodium hydroxide	na		—		4.8	
Sulphuric acid	na		—		na	
Plastics			—		na	
Fertilizers:						
Phosphates	—		—		764.4	522.9
Potash	—		—		130.3	33.4²
Sulphur	—		—		178.2	118.1

n data not available for years 1953–5.

	Production		Exports		Imports	
11. INDUSTRY						
Aircraft a	—		—		8.2²	na
Alcoholic beverages					7.3a	na
beer b	2712.0	1845.0	—			
spirits b	30.0*b	na	—		2.7	172.0
Cement	778.0	337.0	0.7			
Electrical engineering a	104.1²	na	na	0.5	68.5	36.3
Railway vehicles a					7.0²	na
Machine tools a					6.0	na
Merchant ships g					6.0	na
Motor vehicles d						
commercial d q	9.4	6.9	—		106.1a	50.8²a
private d q	54.8	26.6	—			

a million $ U.S. b '000 hectolitres. b¹ 1967 production for home consumption only. d no. in thousands. g '000 G.R.T. q assembly of imported parts.

NEW ZEALAND (TERRITORIES)

COOK ISLANDS

The Cook Islands have had complete internal self-government since 1965, but certain links of common citizenship, etc., have been maintained with New Zealand. The High Commissioner represents both the British Crown and the New Zealand government.

AREA: 241 sq. km. (93 sq. miles)

LAND USE: (percentage of total)

	1965	1953
Arable and orchard	43.5	52.2
Permanent meadow and pasture		
Forest and woodland	26.1	17.4
City areas, waste and other land	30.4	30.4

POPULATION: 19 251 (1966 census)

Total working population: 5135 (1965)

FINANCE

Currency unit: The New Zealand dollar

TRADING

Total trade (in million $ U.S.)

	1965	1955
Exports (f.o.b.)	2.8	1.2
Imports (c.i.f.)	4.3	1.6

PACIFIC OCEAN

Main trading partners (percentage of total value)

Exports	1965	1955
New Zealand	99	78

Imports	1965	1955
New Zealand	69	74
Japan	7	na
Australia	6	4
U.K.	4	10
Hong Kong	4	na
Fiji	3	4
U.S.A.	2	na
Canada	1	5

Distribution of trade (percentage of total value)

Exports	1965	1955
Fruit and vegetables	57	41
Clothing	24	14
Oilseeds (mainly copra)	13	17

Imports	1965	1955
Manufactured goods (machinery and transport equipment)	60	44
(textiles)	(15)	(9)
Food	23 (13)	32 (14)
Crude materials and fuels	7	12
Chemicals	7	

continued

na: data not available. — negligible or nil. ¹ one year only. ² two year average. * estimate. ‡ see appendix. † re-exports.

NICARAGUA

CENTRAL AMERICA

Nicaragua has a long history of internal political conflict. A period of dictatorship was terminated in 1956 by the introduction of a more democratic form of government.

The U.S.A. has a permanent option on a canal route through the country and a 99-year option on a naval base on the Pacific coast and on Corn Island in the Caribbean Sea.

AREA: 148 000* sq. km. (57 143* sq. miles)

LAND USE: (percentage of total)

	1963
Arable and orchard	6.2
Permanent meadow and pasture	6.6
Forest and woodland	46.2
City areas, waste and other land	41.0

POPULATION: 1 783 000 (1967 estimate); population: 262 047 (city proper, 1965)
Largest city: MANAGUA, capital; population: 474 960

Distribution of working population (1963)
Total working population: 474 960

U.N. group no.		Percentage
0	Agriculture, forestry, fishing and hunting	59.7
1	Mining and quarrying	0.8
2/3	Manufacturing	11.7
	Construction	3.3
4	Electricity, gas, water and sanitary services	0.3
5	Commerce	7.3
6	Transport, storage and communications	2.5
7		
8	Services	14.2
9	Others	0.2

		Year(s)
Infant mortality (per '000)	51.6*	1965
Crude birth rate (per '000)	48.5*	1960–5 av.
Crude death rate (per '000)	15*	1960–5 av.
Accidental deaths (per 100 000 population)		
caused by motor vehicles	17.2*	1965
due to other causes	7.6*	1965
Population per physician	2 560	1965
Population per hospital bed	430	1965
School enrolment: age 5–19 years (percentage)	188	1963–4 av.
age over 19 years (per 100 000 population)		1964–5 av.

a incl. evening courses.

COMMUNICATIONS		Year(s)
Motor vehicles in use ('000s): private	12.2	1963–5 av.
commercial	5	
Railway track (km.)	403	1961
Telephones (per '000 urban population)	0.7	1967
Radio receivers (per '000 population)	65	1963–5 av.
Television sets (per '000 population)	8.1	1963–5 av.
Daily newspapers (per '000 population)	49	1964

FINANCE
Currency unit: The córdoba

Exchange rates	1965	1960	1950	1938
Per $ U.S.	7.05	7.05	7.05	5.04
Per £ sterling	19.76	19.76	19.76	23.18

			Year(s)
National Income (million $ U.S.)		494	1965
G.N.P. per capita ($ U.S.)		330	1966
Rate of increase of G.N.P. per capita		4.8	1960–4 av.
Foreign trade (percentage of G.D.P.)		49	1963–5 av.

a selling rate.

TRADING

Total trade (in million $ U.S.)	1965	1960	1955	1938
Exports (f.o.b.)		144	72	4
Imports (c.i.f.)		160	70	5

Main trading partners (percentage of total value)

Exports	1965	1955
Japan	34	15
U.S.A.	24	35
Germany F.R.	15	18
Portugal	na	
Costa Rica	3	1
El Salvador	2	14

Imports	1965	1955
U.S.A.	48	65
Japan	7	2
Germany F.R.	6	6
Costa Rica	4	4
El Salvador	4	2
Guatemala	4	3
U.K.	4	

Distribution of trade (percentage of total value)

Exports	1965	1955	1938*
Crude materials (cotton)	60	56	na
(oilseeds)	(46)	(43)	(6)
Food (coffee)	34	43	na
(meat)	(8)	(7)	
(sugar)	(18)	(39)	(47)
	(5)	(5)	
	(4)	(1)	

Imports	1965	1955	1938*
Manufactured goods	64	64	na
(machinery and transport equipment)	(30)	(28)	
(textiles and clothing)	(10)	(12)	
Chemicals	19	16	na
Food	9	9	na
Crude materials and fuels	5	9	na

PRODUCTION, EXPORTS AND IMPORTS
Years: 1963–5 average and 1953–5 average   Units: '000 metric tons unless otherwise indicated

	Production		Exports		Imports	
1. CEREALS, etc.						
Cassava	12.3*	6.0[1]				
Maize (corn)	131.7*	117.5	1.0		7.2	4.4
Millets/sorghum	46.3	55.5[2]	1.1		0.6	
Oats					1.3	0.2
Potatoes	2.0*	1.5[2]			1.0	
Rice	31.3*	36.3*	0.7	14.3[2]	7.5	0.4
Wheat	na	na			17.5	0.8
2. FRUIT, etc.						
Apples					0.1	
Bananas	na	na	18.9	10.0		
Coconuts	na	na	0.4	0.1		
Oranges	na	na	0.1			
Other citrus fruit	na	na	0.2			
Wine b.					2.0	
3. BEVERAGES, FOREST PRODUCTS, etc.						
Cocoa d.	0.4		0.3		0.1	0.2
Coffee d.	30.3*	20.2*	25.2	19.6		
Sugar: cane	1 038.0*	720.0[2]				
raw b.	105.8[n]	36.7*[h]	48.7	10.1	0.4	0.3
Tobacco: leaf d.	4.1[3]*				0.4[2]	
cigarettes d.	22*					
Softwood j.	953.6*	718.7				
Hardwood j.	370.0*[1]	327.0	38.6[2]	128.2[2]		
Newsprint	1 905.0*[1]	774.0[2]	38.4[2]	33.8[2]	2.3[1]	1.0[2]
Other paper			0.4[2]		1.1[1]	1.5[1]

d no. in millions.   j '000 cu. metres of roundwood equivalent.   n in addition, non-centrifugal sugar 20* (1963–5 av.) and 23[1] (1953–5 av.).

PRODUCTION, EXPORTS AND IMPORTS continued

	Production		Exports		Imports	
6. FIBRES, TEXTILES, etc.						
Cotton: lint	110.0	33.7*	97.2	26.7	0.6	1.5[2]
yarn	1.4	0.6[2]			1.8[1]	7.5[2]
woven fabrics					0.1	
Rayon, woven fabrics						
7. FUEL AND POWER						
Electricity h: total	281	110[1]				
hydro	98	10[1]				
thermal	183	100[1]				
Oil, crude	203	1[1]			210	
Petroleum, refined.					60	130[1]
h million kWh.						
9. NON-FERROUS MINERALS AND METALS						
Gold k. ore.	209.70m	244.00m	186.01[t]q	240.28q		
Silver k. ore	372.30m	246.30m	179.34q	224.00q		
Asbestos						
Aluminium						
manufactured					0.08	0.41s
Copper, ore	8.90m	na			0.40	0.12[r]

continued

	Production		Exports		Imports	
9. NON-FERROUS MINERALS AND METALS—continued						
Lead, metal					0.09	0.10s
Mercury f.					0.28	
Zinc, metal					0.09	na
10. CHEMICALS n AND FERTILIZERS						
Chemicals					na	
Fertilizers:					1.9	0.1
Potash					2.4	
Sulphur						
11. INDUSTRY						
Aircraft a					1.0	0.7[1]
Beer b.	98.0	35.8			8.7	15.3
Cement	60.3	25.3	0.3			
Electrical						
engineering a					7.4	2.7[1]
Motor vehicles a					8.2	4.2[1]

f metric tons.   k '000 fine troy oz.   m metal content.   r metal.
s incl. imports for re-export.   q bullion.   a million $ U.S.   b '000 hectolitres.
n data not available for years 1953–5.

WEST AFRICA

NIGER

Niger, formerly a state of French West Africa, became fully independent in 1960. The country is still, however, closely associated with France in the fields of defence and industrial expansion.

AREA: 1 188 794 sq. km. (458 996 sq. miles)

LAND USE: (percentage of total)

	1963
Arable and orchard	11.8
Permanent meadow and pasture	2.3
Forest and woodland	12.3
City areas, waste and other land	73.6

The distribution of rainfall divides the country into a southern zone (arable), a central zone (pasture) and a northern zone (desert). In 1965 a ten-year economic plan was initiated, concentrating on the development of water resources.

POPULATION: 3 546 000 (1967 estimate)
Capital city: NIAMEY; population: 60 000 (city proper, 1967)

Distribution of working population (1960)
Total working population: 767 990 a

	Percentage
Agriculture, forestry, fishing and hunting	96.9
Manufacturing and construction (incl. handicrafts)	0.6
Trade	0.8
Transport, storage and communications	0.2
Services	0.9
Others	0.6

		Year(s)
Life expectancy at birth (years)		1965
Population per physician	65 000	1964
Population per hospital bed	1 340	1966
School enrolment: age 5–19 years (percentage)		1963–4 av.

a from a sample survey which excluded the inhabitants of Niamey (30 000 in 1960), some 234 000 nomads, and foreigners.

COMMUNICATIONS		Year(s)
Motor vehicles in use ('000s): private	2.2	1963–5 av.
commercial	4.0	
Mail per capita: domestic	1.0	1964–5 av.
foreign received	0.6	
foreign sent	0.3	
Telephones (per '000 population)	0.1	1967
Radio receivers (per '000 population)	11	1963–5 av.
Daily newspapers (per '000 population)	0.3	1962–3 av.

FINANCE
Currency unit: The franc CFA

Exchange rates	1965	1960
Per $ U.S.	246.85	246.85
Per £ sterling	691.18	691.18

		Year
National Income (million $ U.S.)	259	1965
G.N.P. per capita ($ U.S.)	80	1966

TRADING

Total trade (in million $ U.S.)	1965	1955
Exports (f.o.b.)	25	16
Imports (c.i.f.)	38	8

Main trading partners (percentage of total value)	1965
Exports	
France	56
Nigeria	25
Algeria	2
Ivory Coast	2
Germany F.R.	2
Senegal	2
Imports	
France	53
China P.R.	5
Netherlands	5
Ivory Coast	3
U.S.A.	3
Dahomey	3

Distribution of trade (percentage of total value)

	1965	
Exports		
Oilseeds and oil	64	
Cattle and sheep	16	
Vegetables	4	
Imports		
Manufactured goods:	69	(32)
(textiles and clothing)	16	(21)
(machinery and transport equipment)	10	(6)
Crude materials and fuels	9	
Food	5	
Chemicals		

continued

PRODUCTION, EXPORTS AND IMPORTS continued
Units: '000 metric tons unless otherwise indicated

	Production		Exports		Imports	
4. VEGETABLE OILSEEDS AND OILS						
Castor seed	na					
Castor oil	na		0.07			
Copra	na		0.01		0.02	
Coconut oil	na					
Cottonseed	185.00*	68.00*	0.71		0.44	0.07
Cottonseed oil	na				0.91	0.07
Groundnuts	114.13	38.77			0.01	0.03
Linseed	0.54	0.03				
Linseed oil	0.07					
Olive oil	0.03					
Palm kernels	na				0.01	0.02
Palm oil	0.501*		0.20		0.05	0.05
Sesame seed	10.10		5.79		0.15	
Soya bean oil	5.27		7.97		0.05	

	Production		Exports		Imports	
5. LIVESTOCK‡, ANIMAL PRODUCTS, etc.						
	2 235*	960*	1 000*			
Cattle d	1 281*		3.9	19.7	1.5	0.1
Goats d	7*	na				
Sheep d	1*	na				
Horses d	175*	150*				
Pigs d	423*	500*	11.8	4.5	0.1	
Meat‡, 'A'	22*	na		0.1[2]	0.3	
Butter	na				0.1	
Cheese	4	na			0.6	
Eggs	33.8[2]	na				
Fish	4	na	1.7		16.9	1.4*
Milk	190 b					

d no. in thousands.   p excl. turtles.

continued

na: data not available.   — negligible or nil.   * estimate.   1 one year only.   2 two year average.   3 three year average.   ‡ see appendix.   † re-exports.

NIGER continued

PRODUCTION, EXPORTS AND IMPORTS

Years: 1963–5 average   Units: '000 metric tons unless otherwise indicated

Note—no data are available for the years 1953–5

1. CEREALS, etc.	Production	Exports	Imports
Cassava	145.0	—	—
Maize (corn)	3.3*	—	—
Millets/sorghum	1 267.0*	1.7[2]	0.5[2]
Potatoes	—	—	0.1[2]
Rice	11.0*	—	1.8
Sweet potatoes/yams	24.3*	—	—
Wheat	1.0	—	—

2. FRUIT, etc.			
Bananas	5.0*	0.1[2]	0.1
Dates	—	—	0.7
Wine b.	—	—	10.7

b '000 hectolitres.

3. BEVERAGES, FOREST PRODUCTS, etc.			
Sugar, raw	—	—	6.9
Tea	—	—	0.2
Tobacco: leaf	0.3*	—	0.2
products	—	—	1.1[2]
Hardwood j	1 925.0[*1]	—	0.7[2]n
Paper	—	—	—

j '000 cu. metres of roundwood equivalent.   n excl. newsprint.

4. VEGETABLE OILSEEDS AND OILS			
Cottonseed	4.00*	3.03[2]	0.52
Groundnuts	153.53*	89.87	0.15
Groundnut oil	4.48	0.03	0.01
Palm oil	na	na	—

5. LIVESTOCK‡, ANIMAL PRODUCTS, etc.			
Cattle d	3 666.7	61.8	—
Goats d	5 233.0	—	—
Sheep d	2 033.3	110.0	—
Horses d	136.7	—	—
Pigs d	—	—	—
Bacon/ham	—	—	—
Meat, 'A'	30.3*	0.2	—
Eggs	1.6	0.4	—
Fish	7.7[2]	0.7	—
Milk	165.0*	—	—
Hides/skins	na	0.5	0.6

d no. in thousands.

6. FIBRES, TEXTILES, etc.			
Cotton: lint	5.0*	0.1[2]	0.2
yarn	—	—	—
woven fabrics	2.0*	1.6	4.0

7. FUEL AND POWER			
Electricity h	15	—	30
Petroleum, refined	—	—	—

h million kWh.   t thermal.

9. NON-FERROUS MINERALS AND METALS			
Tin, ore	0.05[2]m	0.04	—

m metal content.

11. INDUSTRY			
Alcoholic beverages a	—	—	0.9
Cement	—	—	11.7
Electrical engineering a	—	—	—
Motor vehicles a	0.1*	0.1*	1.5 2.9[2]

a million $ U.S.

NIGERIA

Nigeria, a federation of four regions which were formerly British colonies, became sovereign and independent in 1960, and a republic in 1963. The northern part of the British (West) Cameroons joined Nigeria in 1961. The Eastern Region, Biafra, attempted to secede from the federation in 1967; fighting ensued until 1970 when the rebellion collapsed.

AREA: 923 773* sq. km. (356 669* sq. miles)

LAND USE: (percentage of total)

	1961	1950
Arable and orchard	23.6	23.1
Permanent meadow and pasture	na	32.0
Forest and woodland	34.2	44.9
City areas, waste and other land	na	

POPULATION: 61 450 000 (1967 estimate)

Largest city: LAGOS, capital; population: 665 246 (city proper, 1963)

Total working population: 14 913 000 (1952–3 av.)

Agriculture is the main occupation, but an increasing number of people are employed in the expanding industrial sector.

COMMUNICATIONS

		Year(s)		Year(s)
Motor vehicles in use ('000s): private	24.6*	1963	50.9	1965
commercial	10.2*	1963	23.8	1965
Railway track (km.)			3 009	1967
Mail per capita: domestic	0.4	1963		
foreign received	0.2*	1967		
foreign sent	0.1*	1967		
Telephones (per '000 urban population)	9	1963–5 av.		
Radio receivers (per '000 population)	9	1963–5 av.		
Television sets (per '000 population)	10	1963		
Daily newspapers (per '000 population)				

FINANCE

Currency unit: The Nigerian pound replaced, at par, the West African pound in 1959.

Exchange rates	1965	1960	1950a	1938a
Per $ U.S.	0.357	0.357	0.357	0.215
Per £ sterling	1.0	1.0	1.0	1.0

continued

PRODUCTION, EXPORTS AND IMPORTS

Years: 1963–5 average and 1953–5 average   Units: '000 metric tons unless otherwise indicated

1. CEREALS, etc.	Production	Exports	Imports
Barley	na	—	0.3
Cassava	7 296.0* / na	0.1	—
Maize (corn)	1 123.3* / na	0.22	0.1
Millets/sorghum	6 483.3* / na	—	—
Potatoes	na	—	1.7
Rice	360.0* / na	0.1	1.2
Sweet potatoes/yams	13 338.0* / na	—	—
Wheat	—	5.4†	46.2

2. FRUIT, etc.			
Bananas	65.0*e / na	80.8	—
Coconuts	na	0.2	—
Oranges	na	—	—
Other citrus fruit	na	—	—
Wine b.	—	—	7.1

e no. in millions.   b '000 hectolitres.

3. BEVERAGES, FOREST PRODUCTS, etc.			
Cocoa	232.4 / 102.8	227.7	0.3
Coffee	na	2.1	68.7
Sugar, raw	na	—	0.6
Tea	—	—	1.9
Tobacco: leaf	11.6* / 10.7*	0.1	30.9[2]
cigarettes		—	1.2[2]
Softwood j	4 470.0a / 2 294.0a	—	5.1
Hardwood j	31 292.3* / 898.0[1]	911.0	18.3
Newsprint	—	—	—
Other paper	—	407.1	—

j '000 cu. metres of roundwood equivalent.

4. VEGETABLE OILSEEDS AND OILS			
Castor seed	0.22	—	—
Castor oil	na	—	—
Copra	6.57	—	—
Cottonseed	6.90 / 6.57	5.80	—
Groundnuts	92.00 / 68.00*	67.13 / 38.13	—
Groundnut oil	973.97* / 620.67*	565.80 / 390.00*	—
Linseed	na	81.23 / 28.08	—
Palm kernels	414.70* / 446.00*	409.27 / 439.47	—
Palm kernel oil	na	0.27	—
Palm oil	518.33 / 413.30*	138.83 / 200.26	0.22*
Rapeseed oil	na	1.98	—
Sesame seed	22.50 / 15.00[2]*	18.08 / 9.20	—
Soya beans	16.70* / 9.00[2]	17.00 / 9.35[2]	—

5. LIVESTOCK‡, ANIMAL PRODUCTS, etc.			
Cattle d	7 401.0* / na	3.5	92.6*
Goats d	20 278.0 / na		—
Sheep d	7 221.7 / na		—
Horses d	289.0 / na		—
Pigs d	165.3* / na	0.3	0.5
Meat, 'A'	na	0.3	0.5
Butter	na	—	—
Cheese	na	—	—
Eggs	43.9* / na	0.1	0.1
Fish	59.0[2] / 42.0[1]	—	40.2
Milk	608.3* / 14.0[1]	8.4	77.7
Hides/skins	na	8.6[2]	21.8a

d no. in thousands.

6. FIBRES, TEXTILES, etc.			
Cotton: lint	45.7 / 29.0	28.7	—
Flax fibre	na	26.0n	—
Rubber, natural	125.1* / na	1.3[2]	0.3
Silk f	na	24.3	2.7
Cotton: yarn	12.3* / na	—	2.8[2]
woven fabrics	na	—	23.2
Rayon, woven fabrics	—	—	2.8p

f metric tons.   n incl. some linters.   p incl. synthetic piece goods.

7. FUEL AND POWER			
Coal, 'A' ‡	673 / 760	5	3
Coke	1 031 / 210[1]	34	—
Electricity h: total	1 125 / 701	44	26[1]
hydro	906 / 140[1]	—	1[1]
thermal	60	—	—
Natural gas f	57	—	—
Oil, crude	7 753	7 620	—
Petroleum, refined	117r	117	1 090
Rare earths f	50r	10*	310[1]

f metric tons.   h million kWh.   i million cu. metres.   r monazite.

8. IRON AND STEEL			
Iron/steel scrap	na	7	2	—

9. NON-FERROUS MINERALS AND METALS	Production	Exports	Imports
Gold k, ore	0.70m	0.21t	0.08t
Platinum group metals k			
Silver k, bullion			6.68
Asbestos: fibre			20.78
manufactured			8.21
Aluminium	0.23m / 0.02m	0.92	4.95
Copper, metal	9.14m / 8.23m	0.07	1.91
Lead: ore	9.19	11.46	0.70
metal		10.43	0.13
Tin: ore	0.46	0.30	0.99
metal			0.06[2]

k '000 fine troy oz.   t bullion/coins, etc.

10. CHEMICALS n AND FERTILIZERS			
Chemicals			na
Fertilizers:			
Phosphates			10.8p
Potash			1.6
Sulphur			0.1

n data not available for years 1953–5.   p incl. superphosphates.

11. INDUSTRY			
Aircraft a			1.4[2]
Alcoholic beverages a			2.8
beer b	522.0	74.3	3.4a
Cement	781.0	277.3	369.3
Electrical engineering a			
Railway vehicles a		38.5	10.8[2]
Merchant ships g		5.8	6.5
Motor vehicles a		0.2[1]	0.8[2]
commercial	3.7p	55.0a	0.9[2]

a million $ U.S.   b '000 hectolitres.   g '000 G.R.T.   p assembly of imported parts.

WEST AFRICA

		Year(s)
National Income (million $U.S.)	3 650	1965
G.N.P. per capita ($U.S.)	80	1966
Rate of increase of G.N.P. per capita	2.5	1960–2 av.

a West African pounds.

TRADING

Total trade (in million $U.S.)	1965	1955	1938
Exports (f.o.b.)	751	371	46
Imports (c.i.f.)	770	381	42

Main trading partners (percentage of total value)

Exports	1965	1955	Imports	1965	1955	1938
U.K.	38	70	U.K.	31	47	
Netherlands	11	9	U.S.A.	12	7	
Germany F.R.	11	3	Germany F.R.	9	7	
U.S.A.	10	2	Japan	5	3	
France	7	4	Italy	4	1	
Italy	4	2	France	4	1	
Belg./Lux.	2		Netherlands	4	3	

Distribution of trade (percentage of total value)

Exports	1965	1938*
Crude materials and fuels	64	na (38)
(oilseeds)	(26)(32)	(26)
(petroleum)	(26)(4)	(1)
(rubber)	(4)(9)	(na)
(cotton)	(4)(2)	
Food	19 (16)	na (17)
(cocoa)	24 (20)	15
Animal and vegetable oils	13	
Tin and alloys	6	

Imports	1965	1938*
Manufactured goods	74 (34)	na (13)
(machinery and transport equipment)	(17)	(23)
(textiles and clothing)	(20)(27)	
Crude materials and fuels	9 (6)	na (4)
(petroleum products)	(4)(5)	
Food	8	15
Chemicals	7	

continued

---

na: data not available.   — negligible or nil.   1 one year only.   2 two year average.   * estimate.   ‡ see appendix.   † re-exports.

NORWAY

Norway is a constitutional and hereditary monarchy, but legislative power is vested in the 'Storting' (parliament). A member of the European Free Trade Association, Norway has applied to join the European Economic Community. Statistics include those for Svalbard (Spitsbergen) and Jan Mayen Islands.

AREA: 323 886 sq. km. (125 051 sq. miles)

LAND USE: (percentage of total)

Arable and orchard	2.6
Permanent meadow and pasture	0.5
Forest and woodland	21.7
City areas, waste and other land	75.2

POPULATION: 3 784 000 (1967 estimate)
Largest city: OSLO, capital; population: 484 479 (1966)

Distribution of working population (1960)
Total working population: 1 406 358

U.N. group no.		Percentage
0	Agriculture, forestry, fishing and hunting	19.5
1	Mining and quarrying	0.6
2/3	Manufacturing	25.5
4	Construction	9.5
5	Electricity, gas, water and sanitary services	0.9
6	Commerce	13.3
7	Transport, storage and communications	11.9
8	Services	18.4
9	Others	

		Year(s)
Life expectancy at birth (years): male	71	1961-5 av.
female	75.5	
Infant mortality (per '000)	16.8	1965
Crude birth rate (per '000)	17.8	1965
Crude death rate (per '000)	9.5	1965
Accidental deaths (per 100 000 population)		
caused by motor vehicles	12.2	1965
due to other causes	35.9	
Population per physician	810	1965
Population per hospital bed	110	1966
School enrolment: age 5–19 years (percentage)	86	1963-4 av.
age over 19 years (per 100 000 population)	494	1964-5 av.

FINANCE
Currency unit: The krone

Exchange rates

	1965	1955	1950	1938
Per $ U.S.	7.15	7.15	7.15	4.30
Per £ sterling	20.02	20.02	20.02	19.76

		Year(s)
National Income (million $ U.S.)	5409	1965
G.N.P. per capita ($ U.S.)	1710	1966
Rate of increase of G.N.P. per capita	4.6	1960-4 av.
Foreign trade (percentage of G.D.P.)	51	1963-5 av.

TRADING

Total trade (in million $ U.S.)

	1965	1955	1938
Exports (f.o.b.)	1443	633	193
Imports (c.i.f.)	2210	1090	293

Main trading partners (percentage of total value)

Exports	1965	1955	1938
U.K.	18	22	25
Sweden	16	11	11
Germany F.R.	14	11	15d
U.S.A.	7	5	4
Denmark	5	4	4
Netherlands	3	5	7
France	3	4	7

Imports	1965	1955	1938
Sweden	21	16	11
Germany F.R.	16	16	18d
U.S.A.	12	20	16
Denmark	5	5	10
Netherlands	5	4	3
France	3	3	3

Distribution of trade (percentage of total value)

Exports	1965	1955	1938
	57	42	na
Manufactured goods (machinery and transport equipment)	(17)	(7)	(5)
(paper and other wood products)	(9)		(10)
Crude materials and fuels	15	22	(13)
Food (fish)	15	21	(15)
Chemicals	9	9	(9)

Imports	1965	1955	1938
Manufactured goods (machinery and transport equipment)	64	63	na
(textiles and clothing)	(38)	(34)	(28)
(petroleum products)	(7)	(7)	(9)
Crude materials and fuels	18	19	(na)
Food	9	12	9
Chemicals	8	4	5

d incl. Germany D.R.

COMMUNICATIONS

		Year(s)
Motor vehicles in use ('000s): private	415.1	1963-5 av.
commercial	128.7	1964
Railway track (km.)	4 360	
Mail per capita: domestic	113	1963-5 av.
foreign received	11	
foreign sent	9	
Telephones (per '000 population)	25.1	1967
Radio licences (per '000 population)	291	1963-5 av.
Television licences (per '000 population)	107	1963-4 av.
Daily newspapers (per '000 population)	384.3	1962-4 av.

PRODUCTION, EXPORTS AND IMPORTS
Units: '000 metric tons unless otherwise indicated
Years: 1963-5 average and 1953-5 average

	Production		Exports		Imports	
1. CEREALS, etc.						
Barley	476.0	213.3	—	—	42.9	55.8
Maize (corn)	—	—	—	—	95.4	81.6
Millets/sorghum	—	—	—	—	40.3	38.8
Oats	117.3	151.3	0.2	—	8.3	0.8
Potatoes	1 052.0	1 120.0	0.8	—	6.2	0.8
Rice	—	—	—	—	5.9	4.8
Rye	2.3	1.3	—	—	443.3	60.3
Wheat	16.7	37.3	—	—	343.4	300.6
2. FRUIT, etc.						
Apples	49.3	48.3	—	—	19.9	1.1
Bananas	—	—	—	—	28.4	6.6
Cherries	3.7	3.7	—	—	0.3	0.2
Dates	—	—	—	—	0.3	1.4
Figs	—	—	—	—	1.2	
Grapes	—	—	—	—	12.8	3.7²m
Lemons	—	—	—	—	2.4	46.2
Oranges	—	—	—	—	54.6	
Other citrus fruit	—	—	0.2†	—	1.6	na
Pears	7.0	6.7	—	—	11.2	0.3
Plums	14.3	11.2	—	—	3.1	4.2
Tomatoes	8.3	8.0	—	—	49.7	39.7

PRODUCTION, EXPORTS AND IMPORTS *continued*

	Production		Exports		Imports	
3. BEVERAGES, FOREST PRODUCTS, etc.						
Tobacco: leaf	—	—	0.1†	—	4.5	3.7
cigars	17.0a	12.8e				
cigarettes	1 217.0a	1 363.3e			32.0	139.0
tobacco/snuff					159.0	133.1
Softwood	7 197.7	8 522.3	273.0	213.7	347.3	133.9
Wood pulp	527.7	1 098.3	0.2	1.9	105.6	68.7
Wood pulp j	1 743.7	1 192.3	840.4	657.3	46.5	24.3
Newsprint	290.0	165.0	234.7	132.7	23.2	8.1
Other paper	665.0	386.0	395.7	203.0		

a million $ U.S. e '000 cu. metres of roundwood equivalent. j '000 cu. metres of roundwood products.

	Production		Exports		Imports	
4. VEGETABLE OILSEEDS AND OILS						
Castor oil	—	—	—	—	0.21	0.20²
Copra	—	—	—	—	23.40	39.30
Coconut oil	—	—	0.02	—	0.18	
Cottonseed oil	—	—	—	—	5.81	15.30
Groundnuts	—	—	—	—	0.23	0.01
Groundnut oil	—	—	—	—	9.75	20.80
Linseed	—	—	1.14	—	1.44	
Linseed oil	—	—	—	—	0.43	1.32 / 0.50
Olive oil	—	—	—	—	0.01	0.04
Palm kernels	—	—	—	—	0.44	
Palm kernel oil	—	—	—	—	3.20	
Palm oil	—	—	0.06	—	0.09	0.04p
Rapeseed	—	—	—	—	107.84	23.73
Rapeseed oil	—	—	0.03	—	0.03	0.01
Soya beans	—	—	—	—	0.20	0.99
Soya bean oil	—	—	—	—		
Sunflower seed oil	—	—	—	—		
Tung oil	—	—	—	—		

b incl. other minor vegetable oils.

continued

PRODUCTION, EXPORTS AND IMPORTS *continued*

	Production		Exports		Imports	
5. LIVESTOCK‡, ANIMAL PRODUCTS, etc.						
Chickens d	4 607.7	5 653.0			—	—
Cattle d	1 095.3n	1 167.3n			—	—
dairy cows d	547.3	825.5²			—	—
Sheep d	1 936.7n	1 953.0n	0.1	0.4	—	—
Goats d	107.0n	119.3n			—	—
Horses d	76.7	159.0			0.1	
Pigs d	539.0n	416.3n	0.1	na		
Bacon/ham	128.0	109.7		0.1		
Meat‡: A	15.9		1.6	1.5	0.1	0.3
B			4.7	2.8	4.0	0.4
Butter	20.0	16.7	11.2	2.1	0.5	0.2
Cheese	43.3p	26.7p	12.2	2.1	0.3	0.3
Eggs	32.1	26.3	0.3	1.5	1.2	—
Milk	1 767.8a	1 812.9q	488.4	511.8*	79.9	33.01*
Hides/skins	1 671.0	1 591.7*	4.7	1.42	4.7	8.5
Whale/sperm oil	41.2	155.4	8.0	6.02	5.4	4.12
Wool	3.4	2.7	1.1	0.6	1.6	0.7

d on farms only. n in thousands. p excl. cheese made from skim milk. q excl. subsistence catches and fish farm production; incl. fish landed by Norwegian vessels in foreign ports.

	Production		Exports		Imports	
6. FIBRES, TEXTILES, etc.						
Abaca	—	—	—	—	2.0	
Agaves (sisal etc.)	—	—	—	—	1.4	
Cotton lint	—	—	—	—	4.9	
Flax fibre	—	—	—	—	1.0*	
Hemp fibre	—	—	—	—	1.1	
Jute	—	—	—	—	5.0	
Rubber: natural	—	—	0.1†	—	3.9	
synthetic	4.7	3.2n	0.1	—	6.4	
Cotton: yarn	4.2p	5.2p	0.1	—	1.2t	
woven fabrics					3.2u	
Rayon: fibre/yarn	22.9	15.6	15.9	11.8		
woven fabrics	1.9u	0.6u	0.2u		na t	
Non-cellulosic fibre/yarn	0.3		0.1		1.7	
Wool: yarn	7.6	6.7	1.0	0.1	1.2	
woven fabrics	3.3	4.8			1.5u	

n incl. mixed yarns predominantly of cotton. p excl. narrow fabrics. spun rayon piece goods. t non-cellulosic fibre/yarns incl. with rayon. synthetic. u excl. blankets.

	Production		Exports		Imports	
7. FUEL AND POWER						
Coal, A ‡	417	320	785r	574r	289	702
Coke	911	132	37		768	357
Electricity h: total	44 117	21 350†				
hydro	43 966	21 190†				
thermal	151	601				
Oil, crude	2 630	40†	1 290	10¹	2 760	2 750†
Petroleum, refined					3 117	81*

h million kWh. r incl. bunkers.

	Production		Exports		Imports	
8. IRON AND STEEL						
Iron ore	1 418m	740m	1 453	1 075	16	4.3
Pig iron	911	293	571	204	11	
Steel ingots/castings	na	132	100	3	80	
Iron/steel scrap	na	na	8	1	41	
Iron/steel products a	na	na	98	36	112	

a million $ U.S. m metal content.

	Production		Exports		Imports	
9. NON-FERROUS MINERALS AND METALS						
Diamonds a	—	—	—	—	0.01	0.01
Gold k						
bullion/coins etc.			0.05†‡		27.40‡	1.25²
Platinum group metals k			0.02	0.02		2.19
Silver k, ore	na	106.30m	15.72	10.65	2.48	2 452.67n / 1 905.00m
metals k	na	na			4.84	3.17
Asbestos: fibre	386.0	132.0	56.0	2.5	15.15	2.50
manufactured			6.2†			39.4²
Mica	3.33*	1.40	3.92	1.11	4.58	1.53

continued

9. NON-FERROUS MINERALS AND METALS—*continued*

	Production		Exports		Imports	
Aluminium: bauxite	14.33*	62.08			31.47	32.02
alumina	253.39	na	243.40	0.01	502.94	113.63
aluminium				54.56	25.27	11.07
Antimony, metal					0.10	0.10
Cadmium, metal	0.10	0.10	0.09	0.06*		
Chrome: ore					72.75	52.40
metal	0.72	na	36.57	17.07		
Cobalt, metal			0.70			
Copper: ore	14.72m	13.54m	12.07	29.28	55.99	34.30
metal	18.50	12.90	22.45	14.87	26.18	14.17
Lead: ore	3.36m	0.65m	5.60	0.98	12.36	10.80
metal			3.60	1.62		
Magnesium: dolomite	339.59	na	73.81	na	11.71	0.44
magnesite					6.35	0.57
metal/salts	23.02	4.98	22.44	0.05	49.45	0.93
Manganese: ore	32.1		182.16r	81.92r	367.85	158.32
metal						
Mercury f					27.70	26.50
Molybdenum f, ore	219.23n	155.89m	417.90	288.50	43.70†	34.39q
Nickel: ore	30.28	15.99			55.99p	0.04
metal	265.48	145.05	284.80	145.99	1.12	0.40
Tin, metal					0.83	
Titanium minerals					5.60	
Vanadium	12.83m	5.74m				
Zinc: ore	48.98	42.93	16.22	3.14	88.91	78.66
metal			39.65	34.70	7.30	2.97

a million $ U.S. f '000 fine troy oz. k '000 metric tons. m metal content. n bullion. p copper-nickel matte. q mainly copper-nickel matte. r ferro-alloys.

	Production		Exports		Imports	
10. CHEMICALS n AND FERTILIZERS						
Organic chemicals:						
Benzene			0.2		na	
Butadiene					na	
Ethylene					21.5	
Methanol			0.3¹		1.4	
Phenol					3.5	
Phthalic anhydride					1.0	
Styrene monomer			13.8		2	
Urea	90.0¹					
Inorganic chemicals:						
Ammonia	390.6		18.7		22.5	
Carbon black	33.4		3.5		2.3	
Chlorine	24.6		10.4		0.5	
Nitric acid	24.7		1.2		17.1	
Sodium carbonate	63.4		11.8		9.3	
Sodium hydroxide	110.5		12.0		2.0	
Sulphuric acid						
Plastics:						
Polyamides	na		na		na	
Polyethylene					16.5	
Polyvinyl chloride	21.7		14.4		3.3	
Fertilizers:						
Phosphates					174.3	84.6
Potash	329.2x	351.4x	621.9	101.7	122.0	407.5
Pyrites		100.5y	2.6	0.2	46.8	81.4
Sulphur						

n data not available for years 1953-5. x sulphur content. y recovered sulphur.

	Production		Exports		Imports	
11. INDUSTRY						
Aircraft a	na	734.7			5.7	2.7
Alcoholic beverages beer b	22.1¹	51.9²p		0.1†		3.2a
spirits b	1 483.7	792.0		0.2a		
Cement	1 071.0		298.7		22.7	143.3
Electrical engineering a	201.9²	na	25.8	3.5²	110.8	40.9²
Railway vehicles a				0.1†		2.1
Machine tools a					8.6	na
Merchant ships a, g				2.5	1 343.0	574.0p
Motor vehicles a			6.2†	0.1†	100.0	39.4²

a million $ U.S. b '000 hectolitres. g '000 G.R.T. n 1957 figure. p production for home consumption in 1960.

continued

na: data not available. — negligible or nil. — data not available. * estimate. ² two year average. ¹ one year only. ‡ see appendix. † re-exports.

PAKISTAN

When India was partitioned in 1947, Pakistan, with a population 88% Muslim, became an independent Islamic dominion of the British Commonwealth; it became a republic nine years later. The country consists of two regions, West Pakistan, containing the seat of government, and East Pakistan, which are separated by 1 000 miles of Indian territory. Pakistan is a member of Cento.

AREA: 946 720 sq. km. (365 529 sq. miles)

LAND USE: (percentage of total)

	1964	1955
Arable and orchard.	27.5	25.8
Permanent meadow and pasture	na	2.7
Forest and woodland	3.8	71.5
City areas, waste and other land	na	

POPULATION: 107 258 000 (1967 estimate)

Capital city: KARĀCHI; population: 2 721 200 (1967)

Largest city: ISLĀMĀBĀD; this proposed new capital is still (1971) under construction; the temporary seat of government is Rāwalpindi, the adjoining city, to which it moved from Karāchi when the new capital was first planned in 1959.

Distribution of working population (1961)
Total working population: 33 706 000* (excl. armed forces and foreigners)

U.N. group no.		Percentage
0	Agriculture, forestry, fishing and hunting	75.0
1	Mining and quarrying	0.1
2/3	Manufacturing	8.1
4	Construction	1.2
5	Electricity, gas, water and sanitary services	0.1
6	Commerce	4.7
7	Transport, storage and communications	2.1
8	Services	8.1
9	Others	0.8

	Year(s)
Life expectancy at birth (years): male	53.7* } 1962
female	48.8*
Infant mortality (per '000)	142	1964–5 av.
Crude birth rate (per '000)	49	1965
Crude death rate (per '000)	18*	1965
Population per physician	6 200	1965
Population per hospital bed	2 820	1966
School enrolment: age 5–19 years (percentage)	31	1963–4 av.
age over 19 years (per 100 000 population)	238	1963–5 av.

COMMUNICATIONS

		Year(s)
Motor vehicles in use ('000s): private	108.4 }	1963–5 av.
commercial	51.2	
Railway track (km.)	11 337	1964
Mail per capita: domestic	6 }	1962–4 av.
foreign received	1	
foreign sent	0.1	
Telephones (per '000 population)	1	1967
Radio licences (per '000 population)	5	1963–5 av.
Daily newspapers (per '000 population)	5	1962

FINANCE

Currency unit: The Pakistani rupee

Exchange rates	1965	1960	1950	1938
Per $ U.S.	4.78	4.78	3.32	2.89
Per £ sterling	13.33	13.33	11.86	13.33

		Year(s)
National income (million $ U.S.)		1964
G.N.P. per capita ($ U.S.)	8 943	1966
Rate of increase of G.N.P. per capita	90	1960–4 av.
Foreign trade (percentage of G.D.P.)	16	1963–5 av.

TRADING

Note—1938 data include India

Total trade (in million $ U.S.)	1965	1955a	1938b
Exports (f.o.b.)	528	401	614
Imports (c.i.f.)	1 043	290	576

Main trading partners (percentage of total value)

Exports	1965	1955a	1938b
U.K.	13	15	34
U.S.A.	8	7	2
China P.R.	8	13	—
India	8	11	9
Japan	5	6	—
Belg./Lux.	4	2	—

Imports	1965	1955a	1938b
U.S.A.	35	14	6
U.K.	14	28	31
Germany F.R.	10	10	8d
Japan	7	3	10
Italy	3	1	2
Canada	2	4	1
India.	—	—	1

Distribution of trade (percentage of total value)

Exports	1955a
Textiles	78	83*
Food	9	9*
(rice)	(5)	(4)

Imports	1965	1955a	1938b
Manufactured goods (machinery and transport equipment)	64	(38)	67*
Food (cereals)	15	(12)	(18*)
Chemicals	9	7	2*
Crude materials and fuels	7	18*
Animal and vegetable oils	5	9*

a excl. trade on government account. b incl. India. c incl. Germany D.R. d incl. India.

PRODUCTION, EXPORTS AND IMPORTS

Years: 1963–5 average and 1953–5 average   Units: '000 metric tons unless otherwise indicated

	Production	Exports	Imports
1. CEREALS, etc.			
Barley	133.0	137.3	0.2
Maize (corn)	534.7	444.3	—
Millets/sorghum	661.0	641.0	—
Oats	—		4.1
Potatoes	504.3		0.1
Rice	17 766.3	12 581.0	0.4	133.7	5.5
Sweet potatoes/yams	440.0*		0.7	125.9
Wheat	4 345.3	3 130.7	1 565.5

2. FRUIT, etc.			
Apples	1 187.3*	na	1.7
Bananas	80.0*	na	0.1†	2.3
Coconuts	61.0*	na	0.7n
Dates	19.7*	na	4.2*
Grapes	31.0*	na	15.7
Lemons	378.3*	na	1.6
Oranges			0.7
Other citrus fruit	0.7*	na	
Pears			0.2²
Raisins			3.0²
Wine/			0.8*

3. BEVERAGES, FOREST PRODUCTS, etc.			
Coffee	65.3²		0.1
Sugar: beet	25 634.3	12 512.3	
raw: beet	5.8		0.3
cane	290.0p	97.1p	83.1	75.4

continued

PRODUCTION, EXPORTS AND IMPORTS *continued*

	Production	Exports	Imports
5. LIVESTOCK†, ANIMAL PRODUCTS, etc.			
Chickensd	na	11 346¹	
Cattled	34 853*	30 678²	0.1²
dairy cowsd	11 505*/	6 017²	
Goatsd	11 983	10 067¹	
Sheepd	10 670*	6 145¹	
Horsesd	497	470¹	
Pigsd	94	104¹	
Bacon/ham	351	264²	0.1
Meatt 'A'	32	2²	0.1
'B'	112	na	0.5
Butter	20	17	0.1
Cheese			0.6
Eggs	362	260	106.4
Fish	2 743*	3 538¹	
Milk	na	na	0.2
Hides/skins	12	8	
Wool			

d no. in thousands. f no. in millions. t figures based on 1960 census.

6. FIBRES, TEXTILES, etc.			
Cotton lint	406.7	283.0	143.8	1.8
Hemp fibre	10.0*		1.5	0.1
Jute	1 068.3	838.7	762.8	6.7
Rubber, natural				1.0
Silk/			22.4	na
Cotton: yarn	224.7		18.9	9.7¹
woven fabrics	85.1*	88.4	0.6²*	
Rayon: fibre/yarn	2.8	38.9		2.5
woven fabrics		1.2		0.1
Non-cellulosic fibre/yarn	0.1¹	na	na	0.2
Wool: yarn	2.6²	na	na	
woven fabrics		na	na₁	

7. FUEL AND POWER			
Coal 'A'‡	917	380	—	986²
Electricity‡: total	3 472	1 000¹		
hydro	1 679	400¹		
thermal	1 793	600¹		
Natural gas i	1 420	42²		2 050
Oil, crude	500	220¹*	—	943
Petroleum, refined.	2 363	2 361¹	87	

h million kWh. i million cu. metres. n incl. coke.

8. IRON AND STEEL			
Pig iron	na	na	—	59²
Steel ingots/castings	na	na	—	288¹
Iron/steel scrap	na	na		1²

9. NON-FERROUS MINERALS AND METALS			
Asbestos	na	1.04¹		
Aluminium: bauxite				0.33²
aluminium	na	na	—	17.10²

continued

PRODUCTION, EXPORTS AND IMPORTS

	Production	Exports	Imports
9. NON-FERROUS MINERALS AND METALS—*continued*			
Antimony, orem	0.05			—
Chrome, ore	14.18m	24.96m	13.36²	18.68
Lead: ore				8.15¹	0.03n
metal	11.983			13.36²	0.28
Magnesium:				3.82²	0.19
dolomite					0.37p
magnesite	0.67			0.19¹
metal/salts	1.13			18.60²	0.54
Manganese, ore					0.10
Mercury/				0.54²	0.12
Tin, metal				5.62²	1.80
Zinc, metal				

f metal content. m metal. p excl. bars, sheets, pipes and tubes.

10. CHEMICALSn AND FERTILIZERS			
Organic chemicals:			
Benzene			na
Butadiene			na
Ethylene			na
Methanol			na
Phenol			na
Phthalic anhydride			na
Styrene monomer			na
Urea	127.2		na
Inorganic chemicals:			
Ammonia			na
Carbon black			na
Chlorine	3.1		na
Nitric acid			na
Sodium carbonate	31.4		na
Sodium hydroxide	8.2		na
Sulphuric acid	19.7		na
Plastics:			
Polyamides			na
Polyethylene			na
Polyvinyl chloride			na
Fertilizers:			
Potash			0.8	1.0
Sulphur			11.0²	0.9

n data not available for years 1953–5.

11. INDUSTRY			
Aircrafta		0.6†	6.4	1.3
Alcoholic beveragesa	17.0	13.6		1.1a
beer b	1 578.3	634.0	26.0*	803.7*	15.3
Cement			8.3	
Electrical engineeringa				61.1	9.9
Railway vehiclesa		0.9†		32.9	1.1
Machine toolsa				9.0	na
Merchant shipsg	1.0²		0.5†	47.2	6.3
Motor vehiclesa				

a million $ U.S. g '000 G.R.T.

PANAMA

The economy of Panama depends largely on the Canal Zone (*see* U.S.A. page 229), although recent attempts have been made to develop and diversify agriculture.

AREA: 75 650 sq. km. (29 201 sq. miles)

LAND USE: (percentage of total)

	1961	1950
Arable and orchard.	7.5	6.0
Permanent meadow and pasture	11.0	7.4
Forest and woodland	80.5	70.8
City areas, waste and other land	1.0	15.8

POPULATION: 1 329 000 (1967 estimate)
Largest city: PANAMÁ, capital: population: 358 200 (city proper, 1967)

Distribution of working population (1960)
Total working population: 336 969 (excl. tribal Indians)

U.N. group no.		Percentage
0	Agriculture, forestry, fishing and hunting	46.2
1	Mining and quarrying	0.1
2/3	Manufacturing	7.6
4	Construction	4.3
5	Electricity, gas, water and sanitary services	0.5
6	Commerce	9.1
7	Transport, storage and communications	3.0
8	Services	20.1
9	Others	9.1

		Year(s)
Life expectancy at birth (years): male	57.6 }	1960–1 av.
female	60.9	
Infant mortality (per '000)	44.7*	1965
Crude birth rate (per '000)	41.5*	1960–5 av.
Crude death rate (per '000)	10.5*	1960–5 av.
Accidental deaths (per 100 000 population)	10.9*	1965
caused by motor vehicles	28.6*	1965
due to other causes	2 260	1964
Population per physician	330	1966
Population per hospital bed	71	1963–4 av.
School enrolment: age 5–19 years (percentage)	529	1963–5 av.
age over 19 years (per 100 000 population)		

COMMUNICATIONS

		Year(s)
Motor vehicles in use ('000s): private	27.4 }	1963–5 av.
commercial	9.5	
Railway track (km.)	111	1964
Telephones (per '000 urban population)	3.7	1967
Radio receivers (per '000 population)	341	1963–5 av.
Television sets (per '000 population)	50.6	1963–5 av.
Daily newspapers (per '000 population)	75.5	1963–4 av.

continued

PRODUCTION, EXPORTS AND IMPORTS

	Production	Exports	Imports
3. BEVERAGES, FOREST PRODUCTS, etc.—*continued*			
Tea	26.9	24.3	9.6	0.3	0.2
Tobacco: leaf	105.0*	95.5		0.6	0.1²
cigars	na	1.2t		
cigarettes	18 914.0c	4 472.3c	1.1	4.9	15.4¹
Softwoodj	22.0¹	149.0¹	0.6	30.3	—¹
Hardwoodj	3 700.0¹	1 374.0¹		21.4	2.3¹
Wood pulp	35.5*²	—¹	8.6	18.0	23.9¹
Newsprint	33.0*	1	0.1	
Other paper	61.3*			

4. VEGETABLE OILSEEDS AND OILS			
Castor seed	8.00*	0.51²	1.11²	—	1.01
Castor oil	na	na	0.01	2.70*	0.05²*
Copra	13.30	666.00	0.30	13.91	4.97
Coconut oil	na			1.59	4.55
Cottonseed	13.33t	13.00*/	0.39	11.78*	—¹
Cottonseed oil	20*	1.07*/	0.05	2.13	0.10²
Groundnuts	na	na	0.18	1.80	0.44
Linseed oil	na	na		0.08	na
Olive oil			1.05²	2.21	—²
Rapeseed	324.00	310.30			
Sesame seed	32.17	37.30		73.72	—¹
Soya bean oil				0.01	
Tung oil					

r flax grown for seed only.

continued

---

na: data not available. — negligible or nil. ¹ one year only. ² two year average. * estimate. ‡ see appendix. † re-exports.

195

PARAGUAY

Paraguay has a long history of dictatorships and conflicts with neighbouring countries which has resulted in one of the poorest economies in South America. In the last thirty years there has been a tendency towards a more democratic type of government.

AREA: 406 752 sq. km. (157 042 sq. miles)

LAND USE: (percentage of total)

	1964
Arable and orchard	2.2
Permanent meadow and pasture (mainly rough grazing)	24.3
Forest and woodland	51.0
City areas, waste and other land	22.5

POPULATION: 2 161 000 (1967 estimate)
Largest city: ASUNCION, capital; population: 305 160 (city proper, 1962)

Distribution of working population (1962)
Total working population: 616 640* (excl. Indian jungle population)

U.N. group no.		Percentage
0	Agriculture, forestry, fishing and hunting	52.2
1	Mining and quarrying	0.1
2/3	Manufacturing	15.2
4	Construction	3.0
5	Electricity, gas, water and sanitary services	0.2
6	Commerce	6.8
7	Transport, storage and communications	2.4
8	Services	16.7
9	Others	3.4

		Year(s)
Infant mortality (per '000)	41.5*	1965
Crude birth rate (per '000)	43.5*	1960–5 av.
Crude death rate (per '000)	1.8*	1960–5 av.
Population per physician	1 850	1965
Population per hospital bed	500	1965
School enrolment: age 5–19 years (percentage)	65	1963–4 av.
age over 19 years (per 100 000 population)	192	1964

COMMUNICATIONS

		Year(s)
Motor vehicles in use ('000s): private	4.8	1963–5 av.
commercial	5.0	1963–5 av.
Railway track (km)	1 147	1964
Mail per capita: domestic		
foreign received	3	
foreign sent	1	1964
Telephones (per '000 urban population)	0.8	
Radio receivers (per '000 population)	86	1963–5 av.
Daily newspapers (per '000 population)	37	1959

FINANCE
Currency unit: The guarani

Exchange rates	1965	1960	1950a	1938
Per $ U.S.	126	126.8	3.12	2.79
Per £ sterling	352.8	352.8	8.74	12.83

		Year(s)
National Income (million $ U.S.)	378	1965
G.N.P. per capita ($ U.S.)	200	1966
Rate of increase of G.N.P. per capita	1	1960–3 av.
Foreign trade (percentage of G.D.P.)	23	1963–5 av.

a principal import rate.

TRADING

Total trade (in million $ U.S.)	1965	1955	1938
Exports (f.o.b.)	57	35	7
Imports (c.i.f.)	47	29	8

Main trading partners (percentage of total value)

Exports	1965	1955	Imports	1965	1955
Argentina	26	25	U.S.A.	21	14
U.S.A.	25	11	Argentina	21	43
U.K.	11	9	Germany F.R.	19	4
Spain	5	1	U.K.	6	7
Netherlands	4	..	Japan	6	na
Uruguay	4	3	Neths. Antilles	6	6

Distribution of trade (percentage of total value)

Exports	1965	1955
Food	43	12
(meat)	(33)	
(coffee)	(6)	
Wood	17	37
Cotton	8	16*
Tobacco	7	5*
Vegetable oils	na	3
Quebracho extract	64	16
Imports		
Manufactured goods	14	(na)
(machinery and transport equipment)		
Food	10	15
Mineral fuels	5	20
Chemicals		

PRODUCTION, EXPORTS AND IMPORTS
Years: 1963–5 average and 1953–5 average Units: '000 metric tons unless otherwise indicated

1. CEREALS, etc.	Production		Exports		Imports	
Cassava	1 320.3	940.0[1]	—	—	0.18[1]	
	160.0	110.0				
Maize (corn)	3.7	na				
Millets/sorghum	7.2					
Oats		0.7[2]				
Potatoes	7.3*	5.0			0.1	
Rice	19.3	19.0*			2.1	
Sweet potatoes/yams	86.7	75.0[1]				
Wheat	8.3	2.0				

2. FRUIT, etc.	Production		Exports		Imports	
Apples	2.7*					
Bananas	197.0*	na				
Lemons	2.7*	na				
Oranges	159.0	200.0*			0.1[2]	
Other citrus fruit	24.3	12.0*				
Pineapples	10.0*					
Wine			3.3		na	

3. BEVERAGES, FOREST PRODUCTS, etc.	Production		Exports		Imports	
Coffee	6.8		5.5			
Sugar: cane	885.3	321.7				
Tobacco: leaf	42.9	15.3	3.2		0.7	
cigars	17.1	6.4e	12.5			
Hardwood[j][q]	1 720.0*[1]	2 905.0[3]	286.0		190.6	
Newsprint	0.72*				1.11	0.81
Other paper					1.41	

b '000 hectolitres. j '000 cu. metres of roundwood equivalent. q Quebracho

4. VEGETABLE OILSEEDS AND OILS	Production		Exports		Imports	
Castor seed	13.00	1.02[2]	12.19			
Castor oil	na	0.08	3.08			
Coconut oil			3.29			
Cottonseed	24.00	23.67				
Cottonseed oil	8.87	7.00[2]				
Groundnuts						

continued

4. VEGETABLE OILSEEDS AND OILS — continued	Production		Exports		Imports	
Olive oil			—	—		0.18[1]
Palm kernels	9.00*	na	—	0.72		
Palm kernel oil			3.13		1.36[2]	
Palm oil	5.43	2.40[1]	0.1	0.54	na	0.1[2]
Soya beans	11.70	na	2.1	4.96	na	
Tung oil	5.17	2.51			2.37	

5. LIVESTOCK‡, ANIMAL PRODUCTS, etc.	Production		Exports		Imports	
Chickens[d]	5 641.0[1]	3 790.0[1]	55.5*			
	5 725.3	4 167.7				
Cattle[d]	53.0*	68.0[1]	73.0		0.12	na
Goats[d]	401.3	220.0[2]				
Sheep[d]	612.0	345.5[2]				
Horses[d]	693.0*[n]	97.0[1]	0.82[n]			
Pigs[d]	133.7*[n]				0.12	na
Meat‡ 'A'						
'B'						
Butter	10.7*	9.21*[n]			0.1	0.1
Cheese	0.71	0.4[2]			0.1	0.1
Eggs	na	0.1[2]				
Milk	81.7	126.0[2]	7.9[p]		11.8	
Fish	na	13.6[2]				
Hides/skins	5.5					

d no. in millions. e no. in thousands. n skins of cattle and wild animals only. p skins of cattle and wild animals only.

6. FIBRES, TEXTILES, etc.	Production		Exports		Imports	
Cotton: lint	13.0	12.7*	9.2		11.6	
yarn	1.22	2.9				
woven fabrics	1.9	na				
Wool, woven fabrics	0.1	na				

7. FUEL AND POWER	Production		Exports		Imports	
Electricity[h][l]	130	60[l]			147	
Petroleum, refined						

h million kWh. l thermal.

11. INDUSTRY	Production		Exports		Imports	
Beer[b]	74.0	53.4	—	—	1.0	4.0
Cement	na	23.7	7.3		0.2	na
Merchant ships[g]	24.00	7.00[2]	*		2.9	na
Motor vehicles[a]	8.87					

a million $ U.S. b '000 hectolitres. g '000 G.R.T.

na: data not available. — negligible or nil. — not available. [1] one year only. [2] two year average. * estimate. † re-exports. ‡ see appendix.

PANAMA continued

FINANCE
Currency unit: The balboa, at par with the U.S. dollar[a]

Exchange rates	1965	1960
Per £ sterling	2.81	2.81

		Year(s)
National Income (million $ U.S.)	530	1965
G.N.P. per capita ($ U.S.)	500	1966
Rate of increase of G.N.P. per capita	4.9	1960–4 av.
Foreign trade (percentage of G.D.P.)	41	1963–5 av.

a The issue of local currency is restricted to subsidiary coinage; the bulk of the money in circulation is U.S. notes and coins.

TRADING

Total trade (in million $ U.S.)	1965	1955	1937
Exports (f.o.b.)	79	36	8
Imports (c.i.f.)	190	76	18

Main trading partners (percentage of total value)

Exports	1965	1955	Imports	1965	1955
U.S.A.	65	95	U.S.A.	42	60
Canada	10	5	Venezuela	19	na
Panama C.Z.	8	na	Japan	5	1
Germany F.R.	4	1	Germany F.R.	4	4
U.K.	4	—	U.K.	3	2
Japan	3	—	Netherlands	2	1

Distribution of trade (percentage of total value)

Exports	1965	1955	Imports	1965	1955
Food	67	89	Manufactured goods	58	59
(bananas)	(51)	(64)	(machinery and transport equipment)	(21)	(17)
(fish)	(10)	(14)	(textiles and clothing)	(11)	(13)
Petroleum products	30	—	Crude materials and fuels	22	11
			(petroleum and products)	(21)	(10)
			Chemicals	10	11
			Food	9	15

PRODUCTION, EXPORTS AND IMPORTS
Years: 1963–5 average and 1953–5 average Units: '000 metric tons unless otherwise indicated

1. CEREALS, etc.	Production		Exports		Imports	
Barley	—	—			—	
Cassava	45.0*	19.0[1]				
Maize (corn)	82.0	78.0			5.2	
Oats	—	—			1.4	1.6
Potatoes	2.7*	1.5[2]			2.7	
Rice	131.7	102.7				
Sweet potatoes/yams						
Wheat	26.0*	6.0[1]			23.7	

2. FRUIT, etc.	Production		Exports		Imports	
Apples	—	—			1.4	0.1
Bananas	463.3*	340.0[2]*	300.0	216.9*		
	50.0*[1][e]	na	2.8		0.5	0.3
Coconuts	25.0*	23.5[2]	0.1			
Oranges					0.1	0.2
Raisins	—	—			0.1	0.1
Tomatoes	5.0	4.0[2]			2.1	2.0
Wine[b]	—	—				

b '000 hectolitres. e no. in millions.

3. BEVERAGES, FOREST PRODUCTS, etc.	Production		Exports		Imports	
Cocoa[d]	1.0	1.7*	2.0	2.0		
Coffee	4.4	2.6	0.8	0.9		
Sugar: cane	1 054.7*	310.0				
raw	45.8[n]	16.7[n]	14.5	5.5		
Tobacco: leaf	1.1	0.3			0.2	0.2
cigarettes	788.0[p]		0.1†	1.4†	0.2[p]	0.4[p]
Softwood[j]			12.0			
Hardwood[j]	1 834.0*[1]	1 744.0[1]		2	11.3	11.1
Wood pulp					0.4	
Newsprint	—	—[2]			3.3	1.9
Other paper	1.0*[2]		0.5		41.1	3.6

e no. in millions. j '000 cu. metres of roundwood equivalent. n in addition, non-centrifugal sugar 4.7* (1963–5 av.) and 9.3* (1953–5 av.). p incl. other tobacco manufactures.

5. LIVESTOCK‡, ANIMAL PRODUCTS, etc.	Production		Exports		Imports	
Chickens[d]	2 362.0	1 924.0			0.1	
Cattle[d]	900.7	575.0				
dairy cows[d]	486.7	na				
Goats[d]	4.00*[e]				5.2	
Horses[d]	160.0*[e]	171.0[1]	5.7		1.4	
Pigs[d]	188.0	227.3			2.7	
Bacon/ham						
Meat‡ 'A'	30.7	19.0			23.7	
'B'	1.5*					
Butter					1.4	0.1
Cheese	4.7	2.8*				
Eggs	26.1	1.9	7.8		0.5	
Fish	50.0*	33.0[1]	0.3		0.1	0.2
Milk						0.1
Whale oil		21.7				

d no. in millions. e no. in thousands.

6. FIBRES, TEXTILES, etc.	Production		Exports		Imports	
Abaca	2.0*		2.0			
Cotton lint					2.1	2.0

7. FUEL AND POWER	Production		Exports		Imports	
Electricity[h]	358[r]	140[1][l]				
Oil, crude						
Petroleum, refined	2 163	—[1]	1 240		2 163	83

h million kWh. r thermal and hydro. l thermal.

9. NON-FERROUS MINERALS AND METALS	Production		Exports		Imports	
Asbestos manufactured					2.0	na
						240[1]

10. CHEMICALS[n] AND FERTILIZERS	Production		Exports		Imports	
Chemicals	0.30	0.76				
Fertilizers: Potash						

n data not available for years 1953–5.

11. INDUSTRY	Production		Exports		Imports	
Alcoholic beverages beer[b]	280.0	155.7			0.7a	1.3a
Cement	144.0	76.7*	266.0	190.6	3.7	1.0
Electrical engineering[a]			1.7	9.7	8.4	2.3[a]
Merchant ships[g]	0.72*				157.0[1]	na
Motor vehicles[a]					11.5	4.5

a million $ U.S. b '000 hectolitres. g '000 G.R.T.

4. VEGETABLE OILSEEDS AND OILS	Production		Exports		Imports	
Castor oil					0.01	0.10
Copra					6.56	0.03
Coconut oil					0.08	0.19
Cottonseed oil					0.13	0.10
Groundnuts					0.15	0.10
Linseed oil					0.06	0.04
Olive oil					0.05	0.10[1]
Palm kernels					0.09	
Palm oil					0.05	0.1
Soya bean oil					0.48	0.50

na: data not available. — negligible or nil. — not available. [1] one year only. [2] two year average. * estimate. † re-exports. ‡ see appendix.

PERU

SOUTH AMERICA

Peru is a republic. The constitution has been frequently amended, and a military junta seized power in 1968. There have been a number of frontier disputes with Ecuador and Bolivia, and guerillas are active.

AREA: 1 285 215 sq. km. (495 733 sq. miles)

LAND USE: (percentage of total)

	1964	1955
Arable and orchard.	2.0	1.4
Permanent meadow and pasture (mainly rough grazing)	21.7	9.6
Forest and woodland (includes unstocked land)	67.7	56.0
City areas, waste and other land	8.6	33.0

POPULATION: 12 385 000a (1967 estimate)

Largest city: LIMA, capital: population: 1 833 700 (1966)

Distribution of working population (1961)
Total working population: 3 124 579a

U.N. group no.		Percentage
0	Agriculture, forestry, fishing and hunting	49.7
1	Mining and quarrying	2.1
2/3	Manufacturing	13.2
4	Construction	3.4
5	Electricity, gas, water and sanitary services	0.3
6	Commerce	9.0
7	Transport, storage and communications	3.5
8	Services	15.3
9	Others.	4.0

FINANCE

Currency unit: The sol

Exchange rates	1965	1950	1938
Per $ U.S.	26.82	14.95	4.7a
Per £ sterling	75.1	41.88	23.05

a official selling rate.

	1960	1965		
National Income (million $ U.S.)	2 536			
G.N.P. per capita ($ U.S.)	320			
Rate of increase of G.N.P. per capita	3.4	1960–4 av.	
Foreign trade (percentage of G.D.P.)	34	1963–5 av.	

TRADING

Total trade (in million $ U.S.)	1965	1955	1938
Exports (f.o.b.)	666	268	76
Imports (c.i.f.)	719	300	59

Main trading partners (percentage of total value)

Exports	1965	1955		Imports	1965	1955
U.S.A.	34	36		U.S.A.	40	50
Germany F.R.	13	7		Germany F.R.	12	9
Japan	9	9		Japan	7	9
Netherlands	6	10		Argentina	5	6
Belg./Lux.	5	1		U.K.	4	5
Italy	3			Canada	3	2
				Italy	3	2

Distribution of trade (percentage of total value)

Exports	1965	1938*	
Non-ferrous ores and metals	36	28	
Sugar	19	25	
Petroleum and products	12	18	

Imports	1965	1955*	
Machinery and transport equipment	43	34	
Food	15	13	
Textiles	17	4	

Life expectancy at birth (years): male	52.6		1960–5 av.
female	55.5		
	95.2*a		1965
	44.5*a		1960–5 av.
	13*a		1960–5 av.
Infant mortality (per '000)	3.5		1964
Crude birth rate (per '000)	24.3		1964
Crude death rate (per '000)			1965
Accidental deaths (per 100 000 population)	1 560		1965
caused by motor vehicles	410		1964
due to other causes			
Population per physician	1 560		1965
Population per hospital bed	68		1964
School enrolment: age 5–19 years (percentage)	423		1963
age over 19 years (per 100 000 population)			

COMMUNICATIONS

			Year(s)
Motor vehicles in use ('000s): private	130		1963–5 av.
commercial	92.6		
Railway track (km.)	2 654		1960
Telephones (per '000 urban population)	184		1967
Radio receivers (per '000 population)			1963–5 av.
Television sets (per '000 population)	15.8		1963–5 av.
Daily newspapers (per '000 population)	47		1959

PRODUCTION, EXPORTS AND IMPORTS Units: '000 metric tons

Years: 1963–5 average and 1953–5 average

1. CEREALS, etc.	Production	Exports		Imports	
Barley	183.0*			16.0	—
Cassava	478.3	214.7	0.8	0.5	
Maize (corn)	504.0*	306.7	0.1	9.3	0.5
Millets/sorghum	—	—		3.9	0.1
Oats	2.3*a	—		1.2	0.1a
Potatoes	1 486.0*a	1 409.0*a		0.8	
Rice	301.7*	253.0*a	18.1	46.9	
Sweet potatoes	—	—			
Yams	165.0*a	82.7		10.1	1.4
Wheat.	148.0	161.3	397.5	7.0	na
				0.1	0.2n

2. FRUIT, etc.					
Apples	na	na		—	1.4
Bananas	na	na	0.4	0.3	
Coconuts	5.0*	na	0.1	—	
Grapes	56.3*	46.5*a		0.1	3.2
Lemons	202.0*	na	0.1	2.7	
Oranges	10.3*	6.0*a	0.1	1.2	0.4
Olives	—	—		0.8	
Pears	—	—			
Raisins	35.3	na		2.2	1.0
Tomatoes	—	101.7			
Wine*j	—	—			

3. BEVERAGES, FOREST PRODUCTS, etc.					
Cocoa	2.7	4.1	0.1	0.7	0.1
Coffee	51.5*	10.4*	39.0	0.5	5.4
Sugar: cane	7 799.7*p	5 955.5*p			
raw	779.7p	650.7*p,b	427.6	442.1	

continued

PRODUCTION, EXPORTS AND IMPORTS *continued*

5. LIVESTOCK‡, ANIMAL PRODUCTS, etc.	Production		Exports		Imports	
Chickensd	21 825.3*q	11 135.0q				
Cattled	3 784.7	3 359.0			82.5	19.3
Goatsd	4 033.0	2 257.7			6.7	na
Sheepd	15 589.0	16 305.0 }				
Horsesd	1 173.7	532.0				
Pigsd	1 727.0*	1 321.7			6.8	5.4
Meat: 'A'	161.0*	105.7			4.8	0.2
'B'	20.3*	na			5.6	1.5
Butter	3.0*	2.02			1.2	0.6
Cheese	8.7*	9.02				
Eggs	20.0	5.6			96.1	0.51*a
Milk	7 885.8	198.0*	1 465.5	31.5*	0.51a	40.4
Whale oil	491.0	388.0*	2			
Hides/skins	na	na	1.21a	1.72a		
Wool*j	6.1*	4.7	2.2	0.8		

a million $ U.S. d no. in thousands. q incl. ducks, geese and turkeys.

6. FIBRES, TEXTILES, etc.						
Agaves (sisal etc.)	142.7	106.7	116.4*	57.4	0.8	—
Cotton lint	3.3*	3.1r			0.3²	—
Jute	2.9*	na		0.4	2.0	—
Cotton: yarn	17.6	na				—
woven fabrics	10.9²*	0.9			4.1	—
Rayon, fibre/yarn	1.5					
Non-cellulosic					2.6	na
fibre/yarn	0.5	na	2			
Wool: yarn	4.4	na	2		0.1²	0.2
woven fabrics	6.0*	na	2			

r from plantations only. t million metres.

7. FUEL AND POWER						
Coal 'A'‡	137	140	11	18	1	r
Coke	3 649	1 480¹			6	
Electricity k: total	2 411	850¹				
hydro	1 238	630¹			1	
thermal	600	77	370	311	93	
Natural gas i	3 153	2 410¹	107	570¹	630	
Oil, crude	2 893	1 910¹				
Petroleum, refined						

k million kWh. i million cu. metres.

8. IRON AND STEEL						
Iron ore	5 424m	1 064m	5 776	1 505	1	—
Pig iron	25¹					
Steel ingots/castings	84					0.6

m metal content. t excl. ferro-alloys.

9. NON-FERROUS MINERALS AND METALS	Production		Exports		Imports	
Cadmium	0.20	0.03				0.11
Chrome, metal	177.08	39.08				1.03
Copper: orem	156.06	27.17	22.54	10.25	2.09	
metal	151.40	114.47	152.40	26.63	0.09	0.20
Lead: orem	85.89	59.04	65.24	47.17		
metal	1.42	na	80.86	59.06	1.06	1.44
Magnesium: metal/salts	na	na	na	0.66	0.38	0.19
magnesite	0.63	2.37	0.67	4.74		
Manganese, ore	3.0*	2.59	93.00	2.40	0.90	0.60
Mercury: metal/orem	108.58	2.27	547.30	1.50		
Molybdenum, f, orem	535.40				0.02	
Tin: orem	0.03		0.03	0.01†	0.16	0.05
metal	na	0.83	na	0.54m	0.60	0.29
Titanium minerals	0.65	0.20	0.41m	0.19		
Tungsten, ore	—	154.58	187.63	104.34		
Vanadium m	59.90	13.78	55.57	14.60	0.66	0.49
Zinc: orem	228.68					
metal	59.90					

f metric tons. k '000 fine troy oz. m metal content.

10. CHEMICALS n AND FERTILIZERS						
Organic chemicals:						
Benzene	na				na	
Butadiene					na	
Ethylene					na	
Methanol	na				na	
Phenol					na	
Phthalic anhydride					0.7	
Styrene monomer						
Urea						
Inorganic chemicals:						
Ammonia	na				1.9²	
Carbon black				0.2¹	na	
Chlorine					0.1	
Nitric acid	32.8				15.1	
Sodium carbonate	8.0				10.5	
Sodium hydroxide						
Plastics:						
Polyamides	na				na	
Polyethylene					na	
Polyvinyl chloride					na	
Fertilizers:						
Phosphates	187.2p	281.4p			9.6	1.0
Potash					4.9	0.6
Sulphur				0.6	13.7	4.1

n data not available for years 1953–5. p guano.

11. INDUSTRY						
Beer b	1 670.0	898.7			—	—
Spirits j	180.0**q			0.7	—	46.7
Cement	864.3	492.3			30.3	
Electrical engineering g	na	na			50.4	18.6
Merchant ships g					35.9¹a	32.1a
Motor vehicles commercial dr	4.0	na				
private r	1.0	na				
	0.6	na				

a million $ U.S. b '000 hectolitres. d no. in thousands. g '000 G.R.T.
q production for home consumption in 1967. r assembly of imported parts.

PHILIPPINES

SOUTH EAST ASIA

The Philippines gained U.S. 'Commonwealth' status in 1934 followed by independence as a republic in 1946. An agreement with the U.S.A. guarantees certain military base facilities until 1974.

AREA: 299 400* sq. km. (115 600* sq. miles)

LAND USE: (percentage of total)

	1963	1953
Arable and orchard	26.4	19.9
Permanent meadow, and pasture	41.2	53.0
Forest and woodland	21.4	23.2
City areas, waste and other land		

POPULATION: 34 656 000 (1967 estimate)

Largest city: MANILA: population: 1 402 000 (city proper, 1966) Manila is the present (1971) capital, but QUEZON CITY, population 501 800 (city proper, 1966), a suburb of Manila, has been designated as the future capital.

Distribution of working population (1965)
Total working population: 10 543 000 (excl. armed forces)

U.N. group no.		Percentage
0	Agriculture, forestry, fishing and hunting	57.4
1	Mining and quarrying	0.3
2/3	Manufacturing	11.6
4	Construction	2.8
5	Electricity, gas, water and sanitary services	0.2
6	Commerce	10.6
7	Transport, storage and communications	3.5
8	Services	13.5
9	Others.	0.1

continued

PRODUCTION, EXPORTS AND IMPORTS *continued*

3. BEVERAGES, FOREST PRODUCTS, etc.	Production		Exports, etc. — continued		Imports	
Tea	1.2*	0.7	0.1		—	0.1
Tobacco: leaf	3.0	3.5			—	0.3
cigars	1 971.0a	1.3a			na	
cigarettes		2 436.3a			na	
tobacco/snuff	0.5	0.70			na	
Softwood j	11.0²	na	0.1	0.1	143.4	126.2
Hardwood j	2 872.0²	1 651.7	10.4²	4.5	1.22	4.5
Wood pulp	—	—		12.8	17.5²	8.8
Newsprint.	—	2	0.1²	2	34.8²	8.5
Other paper	64.9²	24.0*	0.5		0.1	9.2

e no. in millions. f '000 cu. metres of roundwood equivalent. p in addition, chancaca 20* (1963–5 av.) and 27* (1953–5 av.).

4. VEGETABLE OILSEEDS AND OILS						
Castor seed	7.33*	1.02²	0.45		—	0.1
Castor oil	—	—		0.04	—	0.30
Coconut oil	237.70	168.30		0.13	1.27	
Cottonseed	—	—			na	0.40
Cottonseed oil	—	—			na	0.12
Groundnuts	1.40	0.70			—	0.01²
Groundnut oil	—	—			0.12	0.02
Linseed	—	—			0.17	0.29
Linseed oil	—	—			0.15	0.24
Olive oil	—	—			0.01	
Palm kernels	0.20*	—			—	0.01
Palm oil	—	—				
Sesame seed	—	—			7.36	
Soya bean oil	0.1	0.1	2		2.05	
Sunflower seed oil	39.0	5.4			0.01	
Tung oil	—	—				

continued

197

na: data not available. — negligible or nil. * estimate. * estimate. ‡ see appendix. † re-exports. ² two year average. ¹ one year only.

PHILIPPINES continued

POPULATION—continued

		Year(s)
Life expectancy at birth (years): male	48.8*	1946–9 av.
female	53.4*	1946–9 av.
Infant mortality (per '000)	72.9*	1965
Crude birth rate (per '000)	24.6*	1965
Crude death rate (per '000)	7.3*	1965
Accidental deaths (per 100 000 population)		
due to motor vehicles	2.7*	1965
caused by other causes	8.5*	1965
Population per physician	1330	1966
Population per hospital bed	730	1966
School enrolment: age 5–19 years (percentage)	81*	1963–4 av.
age over 19 years (per 100 000 population)	1 315*	1963–4 av.

COMMUNICATIONS

		Year(s)
Motor vehicles in use ('000s): private	130.2	1963
commercial	37.9	1963
Railway track (km.)	1 136.6	1967
Telephones (per 1 000 urban population)	40.6	1963
Television sets (per '000 population)	2.8	1963–5 av.
Daily newspapers (per '000 population)	17.5	1962–3 av.

FINANCE

Currency unit: The Philippine peso

Exchange rates	1965a	1938b
Per $ U.S.	3.92	2.006
Per £ sterling	10.98	9.228

	1960	1950b	1965a	Year(s)
National Income (million $ U.S.)	2 015	2 015	7 091	1965
G.N.P. per capita ($ U.S.)	5 644	5 644	160	1966
Rate of increase of G.N.P. per capita			0.8	1960–4 av.
Foreign trade (percentage of G.D.P.)			30	1963–5 av.

a import rate. b selling rate with tax.

TRADING

Total trade (in million $ U.S.)	1960	1955	1938
Exports (f.o.b.)	794	413	116
Imports (f.o.b.)	835	534	132

Main trading partners (percentage of total value)

Exports	1965	1955	1938	Imports	1965	1955	1938
U.S.A.	48	65	78	U.S.A.	35	65	68
Japan	26	15	7	Japan	24	8	10
Netherlands	10	8	6	Germany F.R.	4	2	3d
Germany F.R.	4	2	1d	U.K.	4	2	2
Taiwan	2	1	—	Burma	4	na	2
Sweden	1	1	—	Canada	3	3	1
South Korea	1	—	—	Netherlands	2	2	2

Distribution of trade (percentage of total value)

Exports	1965	1955	1938*
Crude materials and fuels	55	na	na
(wood)		(30)	(13)
(metalliferous ores)		(19)	(12)
Food	26	(10)	(na)
(sugar)		(19)	(na)
(fruit and vegetables)		(4)	(39)
Coconut oil	8	4	9

Imports	1965	1955	1938*
Manufactured goods	57	59	na
(machinery and transport equipment)	20	19	(15)
(textiles and clothing)		17	(20)
Food	13	7	14
(cereals)		(21)	(4)
Crude materials and fuels	9	11	na
(petroleum products)		(na)	na
Chemicals		8	9

d incl. Germany D.R.

PRODUCTION, EXPORTS AND IMPORTS

Years: 1963–5 average and 1953–5 average. Units: '000 metric tons unless otherwise indicated

1. CEREALS, etc.

	Production		Exports		Imports	
	1965a	1960				
Cassava	618.7	284.02	—	0.1	0.8	0.1
Maize (corn)	1 328.7	810.7	—	—	3.6	—
Millets/sorghum	—	—	—	—	1.4	—
Oats	17.0	7.3	—	—	0.2	2.0
Potatoes	—	—	—	—	2.0	—
Rice	3 969.3	3 219.0	0.1	0.5	371.5	35.7
Sweet potatoes	—	—	—	—	—	—
yams	736.7	768.3	—	—	396.2	273.2n
Wheat.	—	—	—	—	—	—

n incl. wheat flour.

2. FRUIT, etc.

	1965a	1960				
Apples	—	—	—	—	8.8	3.1
Bananas	713.0*	239.3	—	—	—	—
Coconuts	7 124.7s	na	69.5p	47.9	2.3	2.0
Grapes	—	—	—	—	0.1	—
Lemons	—	—	—	—	2.2	3.1
Oranges	9.0	12.7	—	—	0.1	9.8
Other citrus fruit	21.7	16.3	—	—	0.3	0.5
Pears	—	—	—	—	—	—
Pineapples	160.7*	100.7	6 608.0	2 462.9	0.4	0.1
Raisins	—	—	—	—	0.9	0.52
Sultanas	—	—	—	—	—	—
Wine b.	57.7	37.7	—	—	1.3	1.0

b '000 hectolitres. e no. in millions. p desiccated.

3. BEVERAGES, FOREST PRODUCTS, etc.

	1965a	1960				
Cocoa.	3.7	1.7	—	—	5.3	0.9
Coffee	39.1	7.42	—	—	0.4	1.5
Sugar: cane	12 776.7s	12 726.3	—	—	—	—
raw	1 630.8q	1 217.0q	1 110.6	877.5	0.3	0.1
Tea	0.3	0.3	—	—	1.2	9.8
Tobacco: leaf	58.5	32.0	27.6	9.5	—	—
cigarettes	88.0	14 494.3x	—	—	0.4	0.1
tobacco/snuff	23 001.0x	92.0r	0.4	—	21.12	—
Hardwood j	8 591.3*	3 714.0	6 608.0	2 462.9	43.52	23.0
Softwood j	85.0	121.7	—	—	53.42	13.71
Wood pulp j	127.3*	10.0*	—	—		
Newsprint	—	—	—	—		
Other paper	—	—	—	—		

f no. in millions. g in addition, q '000 cu. metres of roundwood equivalent, r '000 metres of roundwood equivalent. x muscovado and panocha 52* (1953–5 av.) and 77* (1953–5 av.).

4. VEGETABLE OILSEEDS AND OILS

	1965a	1960				
Castor seed	—	—	0.07†	762.27	na	0.10*
Castor oil	—	—	—	—	0.06	0.04
Copra	1 462.03	967.13	935.36	762.27	na	—
Coconut oil	—	—	223.00	66.12	—	0.32
Cottonseed	—	—	—	—	0.83	continued

na: data not available. — negligible or nil. — negligible or nil. * estimate. 2 two year average. 1 one year only. q in addition, q selling rate.

PRODUCTION, EXPORTS AND IMPORTS continued

9. NON-FERROUS MINERALS AND METALS

	Production		Exports		Imports	
Gold k: ore m	413.00	438.60	54.80t	22.90		
bullion/coins etc.	—	—	310.41	56.48	—	139.222
Silver k: ore m	893.30	533.70	370.47	39.53	—	0.63
bullion	na	na	0.93		—	1.29
Asbestos: fibre	—	—	—	—	1.51	—
manufactured	0.31	—	—	—	0.28	—
Mica	—	—	—	—	0.06	—
Aluminium	—	—	—	—	9.99	2.552
Antimony, metal	493.91m	517.75m	538.79	486.36	—	0.01
Chrome, ore	62.49m	14.84m	269.232	74.79	4.41	—
Copper: ore	0.09m	2.19m	1.052	2.25	3.06u	0.93u
metal	—	—	—	—		—
Lead, ore	5.15	na	—	—	2.94	—
Magnesium:					0.48	—
dolomite	—	—	—	—	0.33	—
magnesite	—	—	—	—	—	—
salts	—	—	—	—	0.40	0.802
Manganese, ore	22.47	14.27	9.89	18.02	—	—
Mercury	86.54	7.30	64.20	—	0.04	0.13
Molybdenum f, ore	96.31m	—	199.10	—	1.94	0.12
Nickel, ore	—	—	0.02†	—	3.20	—
Tin, metal	—	—	—	—	12.33u	1.02u
Titanium minerals	—	—	—	—		—
Zinc, ore	2.70m	0.25m	6.92	0.48		

f metric tons. k '000 fine troy oz. m metal content. t exports to the U.S.A. only. u metal.

10. CHEMICALS n AND FERTILIZERS

Organic chemicals:

Benzene	na	—	—	—	—	—
Butadiene	na	—	—	—	—	—
Ethylene	na	—	—	—	—	—
Methanol	na	—	—	—	—	—
Phenol	na	—	—	—	—	—
Phthalic anhydride	na	—	—	—	—	—
Styrene monomer	na	—	—	—	—	—
Urea	na	—	—	—	—	—

continued

10. CHEMICALS n AND FERTILIZERS—continued

Inorganic chemicals:

	Production	Exports	Imports
Ammonia	na	—	30.3
Carbon black	na	—	4.6
Chlorine	na	—	—
Nitric acid	na	—	0.2
Sodium carbonate	12.0	—	18.92
Sodium hydroxide	38.0	—	0.1
Sulphuric acid.	—	—	—

Plastics:

Polyamides	—	—	na
Polyethylene	—	—	3.7
Polyvinyl chloride	—	—	3.1

Fertilizers:

Phosphates	3.6p	1.0p	29.6
Potash	—	—	35.2
Pyrites	32.5x	5.5x	—
Sulphur	0.1	1.9*	9.6

n data not available for years 1953–5. p incl. guano. x sulphur content.

11. INDUSTRY

	Production	Exports	Imports	
Beer b.	1 236.02	517.0	166.0*	49.3
Cement	1 243.0*	350.7		
Electrical engineering a	—	—	41.4	17.6
Railway vehicles a.	—	*	2.5	5.61
Merchant ships g	—	—	10.0	15.9a
Motor vehicles	—	—	58.7a	
commercial q	6.2	3.1		
private q	7.0	1.0		

a million $ U.S. b '000 hectolitres. g '000 G.R.T. q assembly of imported parts.

POLAND

Poland was overrun by Germany from the west and the U.S.S.R. from the east in 1939, and liberated, with certain adjustments in territory, in 1945. In 1947 a communist government was established. An uprising in 1956 was quashed, and further unrest in 1968 led to government purges. Poland is a member of Comecon.

AREA: 311 730 sq. km. (120 359 sq. miles)

LAND USE: (percentage of total)

	1965	1955
Arable and orchard.	52.0	52.0
Permanent meadow and pasture	50.3	13.4
Forest and woodland	25.8	23.8
City areas, waste and other land	10.2	10.8

POPULATION: 31 944 000 (1967 estimate)

Largest city: WARSZAWA (Warsaw), capital: population: 1 261 300 (1966)

Distribution of working population (1960)
Total working population: 13 967 442

	Percentage
Agriculture, forestry, fresh-water fishing and hunting	47.7
Mining, quarrying, sea fishing, manufacturing, gas and	23.3
electric services	5.7
Construction	5.8
Commerce.	4.8
Transport, storage and communications	12.7
Services, water and sanitary services, and others	

COMMUNICATIONS

		Year(s)
Life expectancy at birth (years): male	67.5	1963–5 av.
female	72.9	1963–5 av.
Infant mortality (per '000)	41.7	1965
Crude birth rate (per '000)	17.3	1965
Crude death rate (per '000)	7.4	1965
Accidental deaths (per 100 000 population)		
due to motor vehicles	8.0	1965
caused by other causes	30.8	1965
Population per physician	800	1966
Population per hospital bed	130	1963–4 av.
School enrolment: age 5–19 years (percentage)	90	1964–5 av.
age over 19 years (per 100 000 population)	771	1963–5 av.

		Year(s)
Motor vehicles in use ('000s): private	215.0	1964
commercial	173.5	1960
Railway track (km.): domestic	26 886	1967
Mail per capita: domestic	30	1963–5 av.
foreign received	—	1963–5 av.
foreign sent	4.4	1962–3 av.
Telephones (per 1 000 urban population)	184.3	1967
Radio licences (per '000 population)	54.3	1963–5 av.
Television licences (per '000 population)	148	1962–4 av.
Daily newspapers (per '000 population)		continued

EUROPE

FINANCE

Currency unit: The zloty

Exchange rates a	1965	1960	1958
Per $ U.S.	4.0	4.0	4.0
Per £ sterling	11.2	11.2	11.2

	1965	1960	1958	Year(s)
National Income (million $ U.S.)	20 000*	730*		1966
G.N.P. per capita ($ U.S.)				1966
Rate of increase of G.N.P. per capita		4.8		1960–4 av.

a official rates: the tourist rate in 1970 was 24 zloty per $ U.S. (57.4 per £ sterling).

TRADING

Total trade (in million $ U.S.)	1965	1955	1938
Exports (f.o.b.)	2 228	920	225
Imports (f.o.b.)	2 340	932	248

Main trading partners (percentage of total value)

Exports	1965	1955	1938	Imports	1965	1955	1938
U.S.S.R.	35	31	—	U.S.S.R.	35	34	1
Czechoslovakia	7	9	24a	Czechoslovakia	12	13	23a
Germany D.R.	6	14	9	Germany D.R.	10	5	3
U.K.	5	7	18	Hungary	5	3	1
Germany F.R.	4	4	—	U.K.	4	5	1b
Hungary	4	3	—	Germany F.R.	4	4	—
U.S.A.	3	—	5	Mexico	3	—	b

Distribution of trade (percentage of total value)

Exports	1965*	1955*	1938*
Manufactured goods		48	19
(machinery and transport equipment)	30	(34)	(12)
Crude materials, fuels, minerals and metals	18	59	35
Foods	4	16	2

Imports	1965	1955	1938
Manufactured goods		40	35 (20)
(machinery and transport equipment)		39	49 (31)
Crude materials and fuels	13	13	(na)
Foods	8	11	
Chemicals and rubber	3	3	na

a incl. Germany F.R. and Austria. b see Germany D.R.

---

4. VEGETABLE OILSEEDS AND OILS—continued

	Production		Exports		Imports	
Groundnuts	9.80*	12.60	0.12	0.03	1.74	0.54
Linseed oil	—	—	—	—	0.06	0.04
Olive oil	—	—	—	—	0.30	—
Palm kernel oil	—	—	—	—	5.69	2.472
Sesame seed	1.30*	na	—	—	9.51	3.30
Soya beans	14.0*	na	0.88	—	0.55*	—
Soya bean oil	na	na	—	—	0.10	—
Tung oil	—	—	—	—	—	—

5. LIVESTOCK†, ANIMAL PRODUCTS, etc.

	1965	1955				
Chickens d	52 400.3	44 893.0	—	—	—	—
Cattle d	9 380.0	7 793.0	—	—	2.9	3.7
Goats d	144.0	407.0	—	—	—	—
Sheep d	4 544.0	3 876.0	—	—	—	—
Horses d	—	2 742.3	206.0	—	0.3	0.12
Pigs d	6 596.0	5 538.0	—	—	2.1	0.1
Bacon/ham	199.7*	58.0r	—	—	0.2	1.8
Meat† 'A'	33.0	39.7r	—	—	2.6	0.7
Meat† 'B'	64.8	49.2*	—	—	2.1	0.8
Butter	624.9	353.9	0.3	0.81*	—	0.1
Cheese	—	—	—	—	50.5	31.21*
Eggs	—	—	—	—	420.6	229.9
Milk	41.7*	na	—	—	—	—

r government inspected meat only.

6. FIBRES, TEXTILES, etc.

	1965	1955				
Abaca	112.5	116.0*	—	106.4	31.0	—
Agaves (cantala)	2.5*	0.82	—	—	5.6	2.5
Cotton lint	—	—	—	—	6.2	—
Jute	5.7	1.3	—	0.2	10.02*	9.3
Silk f	0.6	0.6	—	—	—	na
Cotton: yarn	10.2	1.6	—	—	—	—
woven fabrics	17.3*	—	—	—	—	—

7. FUEL AND POWER

	1965	1955				
Coal 'A' ‡	130	—	—	—	16	5
Coke	4 596	1 190	—	—	—	—
Electricity k: total	1 500	380	—	—	59	—
hydro	3 096	810	—	—	18	35
thermal	—	—	—	—	4	2
Oil, crude	4 147	600l	133	—	4 123	na
Petroleum, refined.	—	—	—	—	120	1 570l

k million kWh.

8. IRON AND STEEL

	1965	1955				
Iron ore	809m	788m	1 407	1 309	17	72
Pig iron	—	—	—	—	67	—
Steel ingots/castings	—	—	—	2	12	—
Iron/steel scrap	na	na	—	—	na	na

m metal content.

continued

---

na: data not available. — negligible or nil. — negligible or nil. * estimate. ‡ see appendix. † re-exports. 2 two year average. 1 one year only. l one year only. b see Germany D.R.

POLAND continued

PRODUCTION, EXPORTS AND IMPORTS continued

10. CHEMICALS n AND FERTILIZERS—continued

	Production	Exports	Imports
Plastics:			
Polyamides	na	na	na
Polyethylene	22.8	2.5	1.7 2
Polyvinyl chloride			9.5
Fertilizers:			
Phosphates	82.3	na	997.7 b
Potash	na	1.8†	1 011.3
Pyrites	88.7*	56.8*	20.1 2	24.3 1
Sulphur	320.3	172.0	17.9

n data not available for years 1953–5.   p incl. apatite.

11. INDUSTRY

	Production	Exports	Imports
Alcoholic beverages			
beer b	7 523.0 5 131.3	na na	— —, r
spirits b	945.0 1 v 1 474.0 q	na	—
Cement	8 668.7 3 503.3	685.0 1 366.7* r	321.0 1 39.1 1
Electrical			
engineering	...	...	na na
Locomotives c	328.0 1	na	5.8 na
Machine tools c	na	248.0 2	73.0 u 2 938.0 c na
Merchant ships g	5 e na	271.0 1 5.4 1	14.0 na
Motor vehicles			
commercial	260.0 103.8 1 v	24.3 1	21.7 a
private	34.2 12.2	7.1 a	
	21.8 2.4		

a million $ U.S.   b '000 hectolitres.   c no. of units.   d no. in thousands.
G.R.T.   e no. of units.   f 1960 figure. q 1960 figure. r excl.
trade with Eastern Europe, the U.S.S.R. and China P.R.   t excl. narrow gauge.
u freight and passenger cars only.   v 1956 figure.
a data not available for years 1953–5.   p incl. apatite.

POLAND continued

PRODUCTION, EXPORTS AND IMPORTS

Years: 1963–5 average and 1953–5 average   Units: '000 metric tons unless otherwise indicated

1. CEREALS, etc.

	Production		Exports		Imports	
Barley	1 402.7	1 162.0 2	58.9	27.3	401.7	1.1*
Maize (corn)	15.7	na	0.3	1.0*	366.6	4.3
Millet/sorghum	29.0	na	na	na	160.0	na
Oats	2 629.7	2 180.0 2	na	12.5*	17.7	1.0*
Potatoes	45 330.3	31 341.5 2	632.3	7.0*	0.5	0.1*
Rice	0.3	na	—	—	73.8	13.4*
Rye	7 459.0	6 423.5 2	na	*	136.4	397.3
Wheat	3 177.0	2 068.0	—	39.1*	1 764.4	389.0

n in addition, buckwheat 39.3.

2. FRUIT, etc.

	Production		Exports		Imports	
Apples	472.3	123.0 2	17.8	—	4.6	0.4*
Bananas	—	—	na	na	na	—
Cherries	71.3	64.0	na	na	0.9	—
Dates	—	—	—	—	28.4	1.1*
Grapes	—	—	—	—	30.4	2.6*
Lemons	—	—	—	—	13.1	2.6*
Oranges	—	—	—	—	0.7	—
Other citrus fruit	—	—	—	—	1.4	—
Pears	75.0	25.0* 2	0.2	na	—	1.1*
Plums	85.0	41.7	na	na	—	0.4*
Raisins	—	—	—	—	1.8	—
Tomatoes	284.0	na	—	—	—	—
Wine b	—	—	0.4†	—	173.8	6.7*

b '000 hectolitres.

3. BEVERAGES, FOREST PRODUCTS, etc.

	Production		Exports		Imports	
Cocoa	—	—	—	—	14.5 p	2.0*
Coffee	—	—	—	—	11.7	0.9*
Sugar: beet	11 849.7	7 039.0*	422.9	365.0*	45.0	1.7*
raw	1 517.1	1 147.0*	2.8	—	5.1	1.2
Tea	—	—	—	—	17.2	6.4*
Tobacco: leaf	73.3	27.8* 2	na	na	26.82	0.15*
raw	65.0	28.0 1				
cigarettes/cigarettes c	55 606.0	34 154.3				
tobacco/snuff	0.3	0.41	na	na	2.06	1.37
Softwood j	14 228.7	15 656.0 2	1451.0	573.9	198.0	3.4
Hardwood j	2 710.3	1 618.0 2	22.3	27.2	30.4	55.0 2
Wood pulp	496.2	356.0 2	20.7	10.01	136.0	14.01
Newsprint	77.0	70.0*	18.0	7.01	19.3	
Other paper	713.7	357.7*				

j '000 cu. metres of roundwood equivalent.   p incl. cocoa
paste.   r no. in millions.

4. VEGETABLE OILSEEDS AND OILS

	Production		Exports		Imports	
Castor seed	—	—	—	—	0.20	—
Castor oil	—	—	0.02†	—	2.00	3.50*
Copra	—	—	—	—	0.68	1.39*
Coconut oil	—	—	—	—	6.97	—
Cottonseed	—	—	—	—	5.49	—
Cottonseed oil	na	na	0.01†	na	26.82	0.15*
Groundnuts	—	—	0.03†	—	2.82	1.37*
Groundnut oil	64.33	na	0.01†	—	2.82	0.32*
Linseed	14 228.7	na	na	—	14.98	0.01*
Linseed oil	2 710.3	na	na	—	1.53	—
Olive oil	496.2	na	na	—	17.21	2.10*
Palm kernels	77.0	na	na	—	1.86	—
Palm oil	—	—	—	—	8.54	.2
Rapeseed	332.70	126.00*	22.06	0.13*	2.61	—
Rapeseed oil	—	—	1.43	—	3.65	—
Sesame seed	—	—	—	—	29.98	—
Soya beans	—	—	—	—	20.39	—
Soya bean oil	—	—	—	—	2.33	—
Sunflower seed	—	—	—	—	6.74	—
Sunflower seed oil	—	—	0.4†	—	2.62	2.18

5. LIVESTOCK‡ , ANIMAL PRODUCTS, etc.

	Production		Exports		Imports	
Chickens d	124 849	na	68.7*	—	0.6	—
Cattle d	9 909	7 661				
Goats d	222	na	14.1*	na	0.2	—
Sheep d	3 046	3 91				
Horses d	2 589	2 644				
Pigs d	12 783	10 135	89.2*	36.7*	8.4*	*
Bacon/ham	} 1 646	na	51.7	54.8*	38.4	0.2*
Meat: 'A'		612	37.2	0.7*	5.2	2.5*
'B'		11 g	27.3	2.1*	0.4	—
Butter	223	na	1.4	2.1*	—	—
Cheese	163	206 2	19.0	0.1*	—	—
Eggs	338	117	40.2	18.3	67.9	2.0*
Fish	263	9 761 2	16.7	—	32.7	7.5
Milk	12 855	na	20.1	—	16.0	—
Hides/skins	70	na				
Wool d	4	4*				

d no. in thousands.   q factory produce only.

6. FIBRES, TEXTILES, etc.

	Production		Exports		Imports	
Abaca	—	—	—	—	0.4	1.0
Agaves (sisal etc.)	—	—	—	—	9.9	65.3*
Cotton lint	—	—	—	—	139.2	3.1*
Flax fibre	51.8	52.8 2	8.0	0.2*	6.6	6.7
Hemp fibre	16.0	9.8* 1	1.1	0.1*	22.3	15.1*
Jute	—	—	—	—	36.2	17.8*
Rubber: natural	—	—	—	—	na	7.12
synthetic	38.4	na	na	na	na	na
Silk f	na	13.0*	—	—	na	na
Cotton: yarn	175.6	109.3*	16.9	na	na	na
woven fabrics	91.8	64.8*	23.6 r	na	1.4	na
Rayon: fibre/yarn	na	44.6	na	na	na	na
woven fabrics	14.8 r	na			na	na
Wool: yarn	63.0	50.8	na	na	na	na
woven fabrics	88.3 i	72.7 i			na	na

f metric tons.   r incl. natural silk products.   s incl. re-exports.   t million metres.

7. FUEL AND POWER

	Production		Exports		Imports	
Coal: 'A'	116 443	94 480	19 068	24 205	1 276	473*
'B'	5 823	6 040	5 439	4 096* 1	596	712*
Coke	15 063	15 630 1	2 309	1 996		
Electricity h: total	40 449	14 920 1				
hydro	769	701			330	
thermal	39 680	14 920 1			2 116	
Natural gas i	1 200	390 1	—	—	2 463	
Oil, crude	1 297	201	680			
Petroleum, refined	1 820	510 1				

h million kWh.   i million cu. metres.

8. IRON AND STEEL

	Production		Exports		Imports	
Iron ore	925 m	511 m	30	na	9 055	3 869
Pig iron	5 599	2 711	na	na	392	na
Steel ingots/castings	8 555	3 993	na	na	2	na
Iron/steel scrap	na					

m metal content.

9. NON-FERROUS MINERALS AND METALS

	Production		Exports		Imports	
Silver k, ore m	129.00	97.00			25.19	—
Asbestos, fibre	—	—	—	—	0.88	—
Mica	—	—	—	—	89.09	—
Aluminium: bauxite	14.27 m	4.87 m			89.41	—
alumina	34.60	9.03	8.14			
aluminium	39.40 m	38.50* m			119.32	—
Cadmium	0.42	0.23*	0.33		15.96	—
Chrome, ore	—	—	—	—	32.29	—
Cobalt	—	—	—	—	17.97	—
Copper: ore	47.22	11.48* m				
metal	35.53	2.44			135.96 u	—
Lead: ore	—	—†			7.15	—
metal	—	—†			344.07	—
Magnesium:					211.80	—
magnesite	—	—†			226.20	—
kieserite	1.14					
metal/salts	—	—	—	—	2.53	—
Manganese, ore	—	—	—	—	2.47	—
Mercury f, ore	—	—	—	—	153.97	73.63
Molybdenum f, ore	149.96 m	120.35* m	116.71 1	98.79		
Tin, metal	186.15	145.57*				
Titanium minerals						
Tungsten, ore						
Zinc: ore						
metal						

f '000 fine troy oz.   k '000 metal content.   m metal content.   u calcined and caustic.

10. CHEMICALS n AND FERTILIZERS, etc.

	Production		Exports		Imports	
Organic chemicals:						
Benzene	83.8 2	33.3 2			20.0	—
Butadiene	na	na	na	na	na	na
Ethylene	61.4 2	na	na	na	na	na
Methanol	41.2 2	12.5 2				
Phenol	13.0 1	1.8 2			1.3 1	—
Phthalic anhydride	na	na				
Styrene monomer	170.0 1	3.0 2				
Urea						
Inorganic chemicals:						
Ammonia	523.3	na	na	na	6.9 2	—
Carbon black	16.8 2 r	3.5			2.6	—
Chlorine	88.4	1.8				
Nitric acid	765.7	210.7 2 r			16.2	—
Sodium carbonate	605.1 2	14.4 1				
Sodium hydroxide	223.7 1				18.6 1	—
Sulphuric acid	983.3 7					

n data not available for years 1953–5.

continued

na: data not available.   — negligible or nil.   1 one year only.   2 two year average.   * estimate.   — re-exports.   † re-exports.

PORTUGAL

EUROPE

Portugal is a republic and a member of the European Free Trade Association. Data for Madeira and the Azores, which are considered integral parts of Portugal for administrative purposes, are included with statistics for Portugal.

AREA: 91 641 sq. km. (35 383 sq. miles)

LAND USE: (percentage of total)	1963	1939
Arable and orchard	49.2	38.0
Permanent meadow and pasture	6.0	16.7
Forest and woodland	28.1	27.7
City areas, waste and other land	16.7	17.6

POPULATION: 9 440 000 (1967 U.N. estimate)
Largest city: LISBOA (Lisbon), capital; population: 825 800 (city proper, 1966)

Distribution of working population (1960)
Total working population: 3 423 551

U.N. group no.		Percentage
0	Agriculture, forestry, fishing and hunting	42.3
1	Mining and quarrying	0.8
2/3	Manufacturing	20.3
5	Construction	6.7
4	Electricity, gas, water and sanitary services	0.4
6	Commerce	8.0
7	Transport, storage and communications	3.6
8	Services	14.6
9	Others incl. compulsory military service	3.3

		Year(s)
Life expectancy at birth (years): male	60.7	1959–62 av.
female	66.4	
Infant mortality (per '000)	64.9	1966
Crude birth rate (per '000)	22.9	1965
Crude death rate (per '000)	10.3	1965

		Year(s)
Accidental deaths (per 100 000 population)	13.8	1965
caused by motor vehicles	27.7	1965
due to all other causes	1 180	1966
Population per physician	170	1965
Population per hospital bed	66	1963–4 av.
School enrolment: age 5–19 years (percentage)	344	1963–4 av.
age over 19 years (per 100000 population)		

COMMUNICATIONS

		Year(s)
Motor vehicles in use ('000s): private	193.5*	1963–4 av.
commercial	61.8*	1964
Railway track (km.)	3 597	
Mail per capita: domestic	40	
foreign received	8	1963–5 av.
foreign sent	6.3	
Telephones (per '000 population)	123	1963–5 av.
Radio licences (per '000 population)	210.7*	1963–5 av.
Television licences (per '000 population)	16.4*	1962–4 av.
Daily newspapers (per '000 population)	657*	

FINANCE

Currency unit: The Portuguese escudo

Exchange rates	1965	1960	1955	1938
Per $ U.S.	28.83	28.83	28.95	23.67
Per £ sterling	80.82	80.82	81.10	108.9

		Year(s)
National income (million $ U.S.)	3 233	1965
G.N.P. per capita ($ U.S.)	380	1966
Rate of increase of G.N.P. per capita	5.3	1960–3 av.
Foreign trade (percentage of G.D.P.)	38	1963–5 av.

TRADING

Total trade (in million $ U.S.)	1965	1960	1955	1938
Exports (f.o.b.)	576	285	37	50
Imports (f.o.b.)	923	398		101

Main trading partners (percentage of total value)

Exports	1965	1955	1938	Imports	1965	1955	1938
U.K.	18	15	21	Germany F.R.	15	15	17 d
Angola	14	14		U.K.	13	10	15
U.S.A.	11	10	5	U.S.A.	11	10	12
Mozambique	8	8	5	Angola	8	5	12
Germany F.R.	8	8	13 d	France	8	8	6
France	5	5	5	Italy	5	3	6
				Mozambique	5	2	3
				Sweden	3	2	

Distribution of trade (percentage of total value)

Exports	1965	1938*
Manufactured goods	54	na
(textiles and clothing)	(24)	(7)
Food	17	20
(fish)	(6)	(16)
Crude materials and fuels	20	30
(diamonds)	(13)	(12)
Wine	12	20
Chemicals	7	5

Imports	1965	1938*
Manufactured goods	51	na
(machinery and transport equipment)	(27)	(16)
(iron and steel)	(6)	(25)
Crude materials and fuels	26	53
(textile fibres)	(9)	(9)
(petroleum products)	(11)	(11)
Food	11	17
	(7)	(10)

d incl. Germany D.R.

continued

na: data not available.   — negligible or nil.   * estimate.   ‡ see appendix.   † re-exports.

PORTUGAL continued

PRODUCTION, EXPORTS AND IMPORTS

Years: 1963–5 average and 1953–5 average   Units: '000 metric tons unless otherwise indicated

1. CEREALS, etc.

	Production		Exports		Imports	
Barley	59.7	92.7	—	0.1	5.2	0.1
Maize (corn)	526.3	376.3	0.1	21.6	109.7	5.4
Millets/sorghum	—	7.3*	0.1†	—	1.5	45.1
Oats	88.7	122.0	—	0.2†	—	0.1
Potatoes	1 011.7	1 099.3	13.5	8.1	47.7	33.6
Rice	162.0	159.0	1.2	3.9	18.3	0.7
Rye	197.3	177.7	—	—	1.7	na
Sweet potatoes/yams	37.0†	—	—	—	—	—
Wheat	558.7	659.7	—	8.7	257.0	99.0

2. FRUIT, etc.

	Production		Exports		Imports	
Apples	90.7	42.0²	0.3	0.1	—	0.1
Apricots	7.3*	6.1	—	—	—	—
Bananas	32.0	36.6	2.4	—	6.0	0.1
Cherries	na	na	—	—	—	—
Figs	351.3*	na	0.2	3.5	—	2.4
Grapes	1 912.3	1 729.3³ⁿ	0.5	0.6	—	3.5
Lemons	10.3*	na	—	—	—	0.6
Oranges	101.0*	na	0.1	—	0.5	—
Other citrus fruit	2.0*	na	—	—	—	—
Peaches	502.3	na	0.2	—	—	—
Pears	43.7	23.7	—	—	—	—
Pineapples	56.0*	26.0²*	—	1.8p	—	—
Plums	36.7	18.0	0.2	—	—	1.8p
Raisins	0.1*	na	—	—	—	—
Wine b	13 766.0	11 752.0	2 169.8	1 329.7	1.0	1.0

n excl. Madeira and the Azores.   p from the Azores.   b '000 hectolitres.

3. BEVERAGES, FOREST PRODUCTS, etc.

	Production		Exports		Imports	
Cocoa	—	—	—	—	2.0	0.8
Coffee	105.3*	na	0.1†	—	12.5	9.4
Sugar: beet	48.3*	na				
raw (beet)	9.2	9.7			171.2	116.0
(cane)	5.7					
Tea	0.1*	na				
Tobacco: leaf	na	8.7e	0.13	—	6.2	0.1
cigars	na	na	0.04†	—	6.2	5.0
cigarettes	na	na	0.03†	0.03†	0.11	—
tobacco/snuff	6 378.0j	4 402.3j	0.75	0.36		
Softwood j	4 000.6	2 753.2	627.0	46.3	53.3	15.4
Hardwood j	1 933.3	2 256.0	4.7	0.2	70.5	32.9
Wood pulp	148.4	29.7	100.1	30.5	33.6	22.3
Newsprint	15.3	3.3	1.0	—	13.1	13.0
Paper	117.3*	45.0	6.4	4.3	7.1	4.1

e '000 cu. metres of roundwood equivalent.   j '000 cu. metres of roundwood equivalent.

4. VEGETABLE OILSEEDS AND OILS

	Production		Exports		Imports	
Castor seed	—	—	0.07†	—	0.78	2.30
Castor oil	—	—	—	—	—	—
Copra	—	—	—	—	12.03	7.17
Coconut oil	na	na	0.13	—	—	1.10
Cottonseed	na	na	0.04†	—	8.26	—
Cottonseed oil	na	na	0.03†	0.03†	72.53	23.23
Groundnuts	na	na	0.75	0.36	4.65	0.56
Groundnut oil	na	na	0.03	0.02	3.61	0.53
Linseed	na	na	7.92	9.13	0.81	1.28
Linseed oil	74.67	79.67			8.40	—
Olive oil					17.92	18.93
Palm kernels	na	na	0.44	—	0.06	—
Palm kernel oil	na	na	0.01†	—	14.53	8.99
Palm oil	na	na			4.26	1.65²
Rapeseed	na	na			0.25	—
Sesame seed	na	na			0.15	—
Soya bean oil	na	na				
Tung oil	na	na				

5. LIVESTOCK‡; ANIMAL PRODUCTS, etc.

	Production		Exports		Imports	
Chickens d	8 160.0*	na				
Cattle d	1 087.0*	na	0.2	—	0.2	0.5²
Goats d	631.4*	na	33.6	—	—	—
Sheep d	5 051.4*	na				
Horses d	1 694.0*	na	0.2	1.3²	0.1	1.3²
Meat ‡ 'A'	161.7	99.7q	0.2	0.5	13.2	0.3
'B'	32.8*	31.4	0.3	0.5	0.3	—
Butter	20.7	10.09	1.4	—	0.3	0.5
Cheese	32.7	23.1	109.3	54.9¹*	29.8	25.1*
Eggs	565.7	435.0	16.4	1.7*	1.3	—
Fish	356.3	192.7				
Milk	10.0*	3.0	0.2²	0.3	10.5	5.1²
Whale/sperm oil	7.1		1.0		3.6	1.3
Hides/skins	5.0*	5.0	0.5			
Wool b	15.0²					

d no. in thousands.   p factory produce only.   q incl. meat equivalent of live imports.

6. FIBRES, TEXTILES, etc.

	Production		Exports		Imports	
Abaca	—	—	—	—	0.3	0.1
Cotton lint	0.2*	—	0.1†	0.2†	39.8	45.1
Flax fibre	—	—	—	—	79.4	45.0
Hemp fibre	111.2	—	—	—	0.2	0.1
Jute	—	—	0.4†	—	24.0	6.8
Rubber: natural	—	—	—	—	5.9	3.7
synthetic	—	—	—	—	5.7	—
Silk f	—	—	—	—	0.7	—
Cotton: yarn	73.3	39.2	13.9n	1.5n	0.7	0.3
woven fabrics	41.3	30.6	28.1	13.8	9.4	5.9
Rayon: fibre/yarn	4.0	1.4	0.3²	—	0.1¹	—
woven fabrics	6.4p	1.8p	1.5p	0.1		
Non-cellulosic fibre/yarn	0.5	na	0.1	na	6.6	na
Wool: yarn	13.8²	4.7	0.4	0.4	6.2	—
woven fabrics	6.8	5.2	0.5	0.2	—	—

f metric tons.   n incl. sewing and embroidery thread.   p incl. synthetic fabrics.

7. FUEL AND POWER

	Production		Exports		Imports	
Coal 'A'	430	400	—	3	431	499
'B'	53	90	—	—	224	21
Coke	na	na	—	—		
Electricity h: total	4 566	1 640	—	—		
hydro	4 068	1 390	—	—		
thermal	498	250	—	—		
Oil, crude	—	—	—	—	1 680	1 070
Petroleum, refined	1 530	870	190	210¹	1 070	540¹
Uranium	19f	—	—	—	494q	na

h million kWh.   f metric tons.   q radium salts, in milligrams.

8. IRON AND STEEL

	Production		Exports		Imports	
Iron ore	114m	75m	52	190	—	—
Pig iron	262	na	17	—	—	—
Steel ingots/castings	242	na	36	19	3	12
Iron/steel scrap	na	na	6	1	49	3
Iron/steel products a	na	na				32

f metric tons.   m metal content.

9. NON-FERROUS MINERALS AND METALS

	Production		Exports		Imports	
Diamonds d	21.70	21.00			28.16u	12.11u
Gold k; ore m	53.30	57.30				
Silver k: ore m	0.03	0.06	0.03	—	1.58	0.16
bullion	na	na	0.56	—	2.75	2.16
Asbestos: fibre	0.03	0.02	—	—	0.39	0.06
manufactured	na	na	—	—	0.39	0.02
Mica	—	—	—	—	102.88n	3.23
Aluminium: bauxite	0.01m	0.34	0.05	0.31	10.83	0.03p
alumina	0.02	0.07m	—	—	—	0.06p
aluminium	—	—	0.01	—	0.01	0.05
Antimony, ore	—	—	—	—	0.02	0.02
Beryl	4.00m	0.57m	0.79	—	15.01	0.07
Chrome, ore	na	na	1.26	0.16	—	—
Cobalt, metal	0.19m	1.65m	—	—	8.12	2.50
Copper: ore	1.26	1.29	0.15	0.02		
metal	—	—				
Lead: ore	4.09	—	1.22	4.06	0.52	0.21
metal	—	—	0.06	0.81	1.98	1.63
Magnesium: dolomite	—	—	0.25	0.25		
magnesite	na	na	3.19	na		
metal/salts	—	—	0.08	0.07		
Manganese, ore	7.77	8.75	5.83	7.84	14.20	8.11
Mercury f	—	—	—	1.20†	0.15	0.04
Nickel, metal	0.66m	1.38m	0.09	0.73	0.03	—
Tin: ore	0.63	0.66	0.27	0.06	2.40²	0.33
metal	na	na	0.81			
Titanium minerals	1.68	4.77	1.22	4.06		
Tungsten: ore	0.06	0.55	0.25	0.25		
metal	1.36	na	3.19	na		
Zinc: ore	—	—	0.01†	na	8.61	3.72
metal	—	—	0.08	0.07		

a million $U.S.   f metric tons.   k '000 fine troy oz.   m metal content.   n excl.

10. CHEMICALSⁿ AND FERTILIZERS

	Production		Exports		Imports	
Organic chemicals:						
Benzene	—	—	—	—	na	na
Butadiene	—	—	—	—	na	na
Ethylene	na	na	—	—	na	na
Methanol	na	na	—	—	0.1	0.1
Phenol	na	na	—	—	0.2	0.2
Phthalic anhydride	na	na	—	—	0.5	—
Styrene monomer	na	na	—	—	na	—
Urea	15.0²	na	na	—	1.1	—

a million $U.S.   f metric tons.   hydrate.   p metal.   m imports from Angola only.   n data not available for years 1953–5.

PRODUCTION, EXPORTS AND IMPORTS continued

10. CHEMICALSⁿ AND FERTILIZERS—continued

	Production		Exports		Imports	
Inorganic chemicals:						
Ammonia	na		—		5.1	
Carbon black	na		—		4.0¹*	
Chlorine	na		—		na	
Nitric acid	111.2		—		na	
Sodium carbonate	0.3¹		0.1		0.1	
Sodium hydroxide	412.7		0.2		0.1	
Sulphuric acid			6.3			
Plastics:						
Polyamides	na		na		na	
Polyethylene	na		na		na	
Polyvinyl chloride	4.5¹		0.9*		0.3*	
Fertilizers:						
Phosphates	—		0.8†		266.2	239.7
Potash	—		296.4	380.1	28.1	10.4
Pyrites	279.8x	285.9x	0.3		41.7	2.5
Sulphur	10.5p	15.7¹p	0.6			

n data not available for years 1953–5.   p recovered sulphur.   x sulphur content.

11. INDUSTRY

	Production		Exports		Imports	
Aircraft a						
Alcoholic beverages	469.0	168.3	—	0.1	3.0	1.9
beer b	112.3¹ⁿ	80.0¹p	38.1a	23.8a	na	0.3a
spirits b						
Cement	1 638.7	772.3	267.7	152.0	1.0	0.3
Chemical						
Electrical engineering a	29.7²	na	6.8	0.7²	43.2	14.5²
Locomotives c	10.0					
Railway vehicles a				0.2†	1.4	2.2
Machine tools a	4.0¹	na	—			
Merchant ships g	3.0	6.0				
Motor vehicles			1.2a	17.3r	9.0	15.8
commercial q	4.6	na		0.3a	49.3a	24.8a
private q	16.9					

a million $U.S.   c no. of units.   d no. in thousands.   d no. of units.   g '000 incl. G.R.T.   n 1967 figure.   p 1960 figure.   q assembly of imported parts.   s incl. re-exports.

PORTUGAL (TERRITORIES)

In 1951 the former Portuguese colonies of Angola, Cape Verde Islands, Macao, Mozambique, Portuguese Guinea, Portuguese Timor, and São Tomé and Principe were given the status of 'overseas territories' with financial and administrative autonomy. Customs duties with Portugal were abolished in 1961. The former Portuguese territories in India were incorporated into the Indian Union in 1961.

ANGOLA

AREA: 1 246 700 sq. km. (481 351 sq. miles)

LAND USE: (percentage of total)

Arable and orchard	0.7
Permanent meadow and pasture	23.3
Forest and woodland	34.6
City areas, waste and other land	41.4

POPULATION: 5 203 000 (1967 estimate)
Largest city: LUANDA; population: 224 540 (1960)
Luanda is the present (1971) capital, but NOVA LISBOA has been designated as the new capital.

		Year(s)
Life expectancy at birth (years)	35a	1940
Infant mortality (per '000)	15.6*	1965
Crude birth rate (per '000)	22.2	1965
Crude death rate (per '000)	1.7*	1965
Accidental deaths (per 100 000 population)		1965
caused by motor vehicles	2.2*	1965
due to other causes	12.4²	1964
Population per physician	13 140	1965
Population per hospital bed	410	1966
School enrolment: age 5–19 years (percentage)	na	
age over 19 years (per 100 000 population)	na	1963–5 av.

a latest available figure.

EMPLOYMENT

The majority of the working population is engaged in subsistence farming and the processing of agricultural produce. Mining provides alternative employment and a small number are engaged in oil and copper refining.

COMMUNICATIONS

		Year(s)
Motor vehicles in use ('000s): private	39.0	1963–5 av.
commercial	16.2	1964
Railway track (km.)	3 256	
Mail per capita: domestic	} 0.3	1963–5 av.
foreign received	0.2	1967
foreign sent	0.3	1963–5 av.
Telephones (per '000 urban population)	15	1963–5 av.
Radio licences (per '000 population)	8	1962–3 av.
Daily newspapers (per '000 population)		

CENTRAL AFRICA

FINANCE

Currency unit: The Portuguese escudo

	1953	1937
National Income (million $U.S.)	0.7	0.7
G.N.P. per capita ($U.S.)	23.3	23.3
	34.6	50.7
	41.4	25.3

TRADING

	Year		
Total trade (in million $U.S.)	1958		1965
Exports (f.o.b.)	261	200	200
Imports (c.i.f.)	170	195	195

Main trading partners (percentage of total value)

Exports	1965	1955
Portugal	35	23
U.S.A.	23	23
Netherlands	12	9
Germany F.R.	5	8
France	3	3
Belg./Lux.	2	3

Imports	1965	1955
Portugal	48	47
U.K.	11	12
Germany F.R.	9	9
U.S.A.	8	14
Belg./Lux.	4	4
Sweden	2	1

Distribution of trade (percentage of total value)

Exports	1965	1955
Food	61	64
(coffee)		(47)
Diamonds	16	(45)
Sisal	12	16
Oilseeds and vegetable oils	5	7
	3	4

Imports	1965	1955
Manufactured goods	37	32
(machinery and transport equipment)	(13)	(14)
(cotton piece goods)	(7)	(9)
Wine	8	9
Food	6	5

continued

---

na: data not available.   — negligible or nil.   * estimate.   ¹ one year only.   ² two year average.   † re-exports.   ‡ see appendix.

PORTUGAL (TERRITORIES) continued

ANGOLA continued

PRODUCTION, EXPORTS AND IMPORTS
Years: 1963–5 average and 1953–5 average   Units: '000 metric tons unless otherwise indicated

	Production		Exports		Imports	
1. CEREALS, etc.						
Cassava	1 340.0*	na	—	—	—	—
Maize (corn)	386.3*	na	76.3	3.8	0.1²	5.3
Millets/sorghum	—	—	1.9²	0.3²†	—	—
Potatoes	—	—	1.8	1.1	1.5²	31.8
Rice	27.7*	na	—	—	—	—
Wheat	13.0²	na	—	—	—	2.3 / 3.3
2. FRUIT, etc.						
Bananas	na	na	2.8²	0.12	15	26
Oranges	na	na	0.12		5	
Wine b	na	na	0.8²†		417.0	732.7
3. BEVERAGES, FOREST PRODUCTS, etc.						
Cocoa	0.3	—¹	0.3	58.7	—	—
Coffee	174.0*	65.0*	145.3		—	—
Sugar: cane	733.3*	367.5*	27.3	29.4	0.4	0.1²
Sugar: raw	85.1*	44.0*	1.8	0.5		
Tobacco: leaf	3.6*		0.1		—	—
cigarettes	1 540.0d*	645.0d				
tobacco/snuff	0.1					
Hardwood j	6 902.5²*		131.5²	60.0¹	—	—²
Wood pulp	21.8²		18.9²		—¹	
Paper	2.9²		1.53		2.5²	2.27
6. FIBRES, TEXTILES, etc.						
Agaves (sisal etc.)	na	65.0*	56.5	34.7	—	—
Cotton lint	5.3*	5.7*	4.1	3.8	—	—
Jute	2.0*	0.1²	—		4.5	—
Rubber, natural			—		0.22	0.1²
Cotton, woven fabrics	0.9	0.3	—		5.2	3.3
7. FUEL AND POWER						
Coal 'A'‡						
Coke	na				15	
Electricity h: total	264				9	
hydro					40	
thermal					—¹	
Oil, crude	264	—¹	260	80	33	
Petroleum, refined h	783	493				100¹
8. IRON AND STEEL						
Iron ore	511m	—²	825		—	—
9. NON-FERROUS MINERALS AND METALS						
Diamonds	1 129.33j	731.44j	28.16a	12.11a	—	—
Platinum group metals						
Asbestos: fibre	0.19		0.05		0.99	0.63
Aluminium	2.15m		0.02		0.19	0.02
Copper: ore; metal	1.23		1.44		1.54	0.24
Lead, metal			0.08		0.48	0.17
Magnesalts					0.15	0.04
Manganese, ore	43.04		4.47	40.68	0.37	
Mercury	0.01m				4.00	0.03
Vanadium	0.03m				0.14r	
Zinc, ore						0.13r
10. CHEMICALS AND FERTILIZERS						
Fertilizers: Potash					1.1	0.1
Sulphur	na				0.4	
11. INDUSTRY						
Aircraft d			0.8²			0.1
Alcoholic beverages: beer b	305.0	31.7			0.5¹	0.1
Cement	217.7	47.0	55.7	80.7	13.7ap	10.2a
Electrical engineering d					2.1q	2.3*
Railway vehicles d	0.4				—¹	1.3
Motor vehicles g					11.5	7.6²

n no. in millions. j '000 cu. metres of roundwood equivalent.

CAPE VERDE ISLANDS

AREA: 4 033 sq. km. (1 557 sq. miles)

LAND USE
The islands are mountainous and the climate poor, with very high temperatures and low seasonal rainfall. Agriculture is limited to small areas. Occasional earthquakes have been recorded and there is one active volcano.

POPULATION: 232 000 (1967 estimate); population: 13 142* (1960)
Capital city: PRAIA; population: 13 142* (1960)

Distribution of working population (1960)
Total working population: 105 570*

U.N. group no.		Percentage
0	Agriculture, forestry, fishing and hunting	40.2
1	Mining and quarrying	0.2
2/3	Manufacturing	4.0
4	Construction	4.0
6	Commerce	1.3
7	Transport, storage and communications	1.9
8	Services	51.9
9	Others	0.2

ATLANTIC OCEAN

		Year(s)
Infant mortality (per '000)	76.7	1965
Crude birth rate (per '000)	43.0	1965
Crude death rate (per '000)	10.6	1965
Accidental deaths (per 100 000 population)	1.3	1965
due to motor vehicles	20	1965
due to other causes		1964
Population per physician	8 800	1966
Population per hospital bed	490	
School enrolment: age 5–19 years (percentage)	30	1963–4 av.

COMMUNICATIONS

		Year(s)
Telephones (per '000 urban population)	0.3	1967
Radio licences (per '000 population)	15	1963–5 av.

EMPLOYMENT, PRODUCTION AND TRADE
Agriculture and fishing are the main occupations of the people, the chief products being bananas, coffee, nuts, tuna and pozzolana. Trade is mainly with Portugal. Mindelo is an important bunkering station on the South Atlantic route from Europe to South America, and there is an air base on Sal.

continued

PRODUCTION, EXPORTS AND IMPORTS
Years: 1963–5 average and 1953–5 average   Units: '000 metric tons unless otherwise indicated

	Production		Exports		Imports	
1. CEREALS, etc.						
Barley	15.0*¹	na	—	—	—	—
Maize (corn)	15.0*¹	na	0.1²		—	—
Potatoes			0.1		—	—
Rice	3.0		—		—	—
Wheat	0.9		—		—	—
2. FRUIT, etc.						
Bananas			3.0		10.2	5.0
Wine b	na		na			
3. BEVERAGES, FOREST PRODUCTS, etc.						
Coffee			—		—	—
Sugar, raw			—		0.22	—
Wood j			—		3.2	3.0²
4. VEGETABLE OILSEEDS AND OILS						
Castor seed			0.04		0.03	—
Cottonseed oil			0.32		0.07	—
Groundnuts			—		—	—
Linseed oil			—		0.14	0.01 / 0.04*
Olive oil			—		—	—
5. LIVESTOCK‡, ANIMAL PRODUCTS, etc.						
Cattle d	20.0*	9.5²			0.1	1.0
Goats d	3.0*	38.0²			6.9	0.5
Sheep d		2.5²			0.4²	0.2
Horses d	1.0*	1.0²			1.4	
Pigs d	15.0*	11.0²				
Fish d	2.5²h	1.6n			10.2	5.0
Milk			1.5			
7. FUEL AND POWER						
Coal 'A'‡n						
Electricity h t	na				3.2	
Petroleum, refined n	na				3.0²	1.4
11. INDUSTRY						
Cement	8.3				—	—

d no. in thousands. n incomplete figure. h million kWh. t thermal. n for bunkers.

SOUTH EAST ASIA

MACAO

AREA: 16 sq. km. (6 sq. miles)

POPULATION: 169 299 (1960 census)
Largest city: MACAU, capital; population: 161 252 (city proper, 1960)

Distribution of working population (1960)
Total working population: 41 533

U.N. group no.		Percentage
0	Agriculture, forestry, fishing and hunting	5.3
1/2/3	Mining, quarrying and manufacturing	30.1
4	Construction	3.5
5	Electricity, gas, water and sanitary services	1.1
6	Commerce	26.6
7	Transport, storage and communications	23.0
8	Services	23.8
9	Others	

		Year
Crude birth rate (per '000)	14.6*	1965
Population per physician	3 720	1966
Population per hospital bed	160	1963
School enrolment: age 5–19 years (percentage)	93 a	

a incl. pre-school education.

COMMUNICATIONS

		Year(s)
Telephones (per '000 urban population)	1.1	1967
Radio receivers (per '000 population)	21	1963–5 av.
Daily newspapers (per '000 population)	119	1962–3 av.

FINANCE
Currency unit: The Portuguese escudo; also the pataca for which the exchange rate in 1960 was about 5 per $U.S. (14 per £ sterling)

TRADE
Trade is mainly transit trade by Portuguese, British and Dutch ships, and is handled by Chinese merchants. In 1963, 4 322 vessels, totalling 2 753 700 G.R.T., entered the port.

PRODUCTION, EXPORTS AND IMPORTS
Years: 1963–5 average and 1953–5 average   Units: '000 metric tons unless otherwise indicated

	Production		Exports		Imports	
1. CEREALS, etc.						
Maize (corn)			—		1.2	0.01
Millets/sorghum	1.0*		0.1²†	1.9²	0.5	0.02 / 0.02*
Potatoes	84.0*		4.4†	28.4	1.1	0.13 / 0.03
Rice			—		21.0	na
Wheat			—		0.7	0.07
2. FRUIT, etc.						
Wine b			—		3.2	7.01
3. BEVERAGES, FOREST PRODUCTS, etc.						
Coffee			0.2†		0.4	1.5
Sugar, raw	8.9		6.9		3.2	15.1
Tea	4.8		—		0.3	0.1
Tobacco, leaf			—		30.1²	0.6
Hardwood j			0.12†		4.3²	0.2
Paper			na			1.7 / 2.52²
4. VEGETABLE OILSEEDS AND OILS						
Linseed oil			—		0.01	0.02¹
Olive oil			—		1.13	0.10²
Sesame seed			0.16		0.95	0.45*
Soya bean oil			0.152²			
Tung oil			—			
5. LIVESTOCK‡, ANIMAL PRODUCTS, etc.						
Cattle d						0.22
Goats d	1.0*					0.54*
Pigs d	84.0*					
Meat 'A'; 'B'						
Butter						0.1
Eggs						
Fish						
Milk						na
6. FIBRES, TEXTILES, etc.						
Cotton lint						0.1
Rubber, natural						0.1
7. FUEL AND POWER						
Electricity h t	26	3			37	na
Petroleum, refined	na	na				
Groundnut oil						

continued

d no. in thousands. h million kWh. t thermal.

---

na: data not available.   — negligible or nil.   . . . data not available.   * estimate.   ¹ one year only.   ² two year average.   ‡ see appendix.   † re-exports.

PORTUGAL (TERRITORIES) continued

MOZAMBIQUE

AREA: 784 961 sq. km. (303 074 sq. miles)

LAND USE (percentage of total)

	1961	1948
Arable and orchard	3.4	2.6
Permanent meadow and pasture	56.2	57.1
Forest and woodland	24.8	25.1
City areas, waste and other land	15.6	15.2

POPULATION: 7 124 000 (1967 estimate)
Largest city: LOURENÇO MARQUES, capital; population: 177 929 (1960)

Distribution of working population (1950)
Total working population: 1 672 829

U.N. group no.		Percentage
0	Agriculture, forestry, fishing and hunting	75.3
1	Mining and quarrying	0.1
2/3	Manufacturing	4.7
4/5	Construction and electricity, gas, water and sanitary services	1.2
6	Commerce	1.4
7	Transport, storage and communications	1.0
8	Services	6.9
9	Others	9.4

		Year(s)
Life expectancy at birth (years)	45a	1940
Infant mortality (per '000)	100.9*	1965
Crude birth rate (per '000)	2.4*	1965
Crude death rate (per '000)	1.1*	1965
Accidental deaths (per 100 000 population) caused by motor vehicles	2.8*	1965
due to other causes	6.5*	1964
Population per physician	17 990	1964
Population per hospital bed	650	1963–4 av.
School enrolment: age 5–19 years (percentage)	26	1963–4 av.
age over 19 years (per 100 000 population)	6	1963–4 av.

a latest available figure.

COMMUNICATIONS

		Year(s)
Motor vehicles in use ('000s): private	46.1	1963–5 av.
commercial	8.6	
Railway track (km.)	3 621	1963
Mail per capita: domestic	na	
foreign received	2.2	1963–5 av.
foreign sent	0.3	
Telephones ('000 urban population)	44.6	1967
Radio licences (per '000 population)	15	1963–5 av.
Daily newspapers (per '000 population)	6	1963

PRODUCTION, EXPORTS AND IMPORTS

Years: 1963–5 average and 1953–5 average Units: '000 metric tons unless otherwise indicated

1. CEREALS, etc.

	Production	Exports	Imports
Barley	39.7*	—	na
Cassava	145.0*n	—	na
Maize (corn)	25.7*¹	2.2	36.4
Millets/sorghum	137.7*n	—	—
Potatoes	na	0.3	5.2²
Rice	137.7*n	0.3	3.0
Wheat	9.7*n	1.9	44.6

n from farms and villages only.

2. FRUIT, etc.

	Production	Exports	Imports
Bananas	24.7*	18.3	16.0*
Coconuts	423.3*z	0.11	na
Lemons	—	4.0¹	na
Oranges	8.3*	2.11	—
Other citrus fruit	4.0*		na
Tomatoes	1.0*		
Wine b	—	0.1†	215.7

b '000 hectolitres. z no. in millions.
Cashew nuts are also grown and exported.

3. BEVERAGES, FOREST PRODUCTS, etc.

	Production	Exports	Imports
Coffee	1.0*	0.1†	413.7
Sugar: cane	1 533.3*	—	—
raw	165.8	101.0	0.2¹
Tea	9.8	9.2	na
Tobacco: leaf	2.5*	0.7²	0.5²
cigarettes	1 517.0*j	0.1¹	11.5²
Hardwood j	7 470.0*¹	150.1¹²	2.5¹
Newsprint			
Other paper			

j '000 cu. metres of roundwood equivalent. b incl. other tobacco manufactures.

4. VEGETABLE OILSEEDS AND OILS

	Production	Exports	Imports
Castor seed	1.00*	1.28	—
Castor oil	na	0.06	—
Copra	52.47	39.60	49.00*
Coconut oil	64.30*	8.18	58.00²*
Cottonseed	na	9.85	na
Cottonseed oil	17.03*	1.07	76.0
Groundnuts	na	2.45	8.0
Groundnut oil	na	2.87	77.7
Linseed oil	na	1.73	
Olive oil	na	6.09	93.0
Sesame seed	1.60*	1.59	11.7*
Sunflower seed	1.00*	1.83	

5. LIVESTOCK‡, ANIMAL PRODUCTS, etc.

	Production	Exports	Imports
Chickens d	190.0*¹	—	128.0¹
Cattle d	1 131.3	—	801.7
dairy cows d	280.3	—	na
Goats d	423.0*	0.4	371.7
Sheep d	102.0*	—	80.0
Horses d			8.0
Pigs d	93.0	—	
Bacon/ham	11.7*	0.2	5.0²
Meat‡, 'A'	na	0.1	
Butter	na	—	0.2
Cheese	0.3*	0.7	0.5²
Eggs	6.12	4.9	0.7
Milk	51.0*	6.5²	9.4
Fish		0.9	17.2
Hides/skins	na		

d no. in thousands.

6. FIBRES, TEXTILES, etc.

	Production	Exports	Imports
Agaves (sisal)	31.5*	30.9	24.7*
Cotton lint	32.3*	31.8	30.0*
Jute	na		na
Rubber: natural	1.8	—	na
Cotton: yarn	1.41	0.5¹	na
woven fabrics			

continued

FINANCE

Currency unit: The Portuguese escudo

		Year
National Income (million $ U.S.)	253	1958
G.N.P. per capita ($ U.S.)	100	1966

TRADING

Total trade (in million $ U.S.)	1965	1938
Exports (f.o.b.)	108	8
Imports (c.i.f.)	173	22

Main trading partners (percentage of total value)

Exports	1965	1955
Portugal	37	44
India	15	8
South Africa	12	6
U.S.A.	5	8
Angola	4	
Germany F.R.	4	4

Imports	1965	1955
Portugal	35	29
U.K.	11	15
South Africa	11	8
Germany F.R.	8	14
Iraq	5	na
U.S.A.	4	8
Japan	4	1

Distribution of trade (percentage of total value)

Exports	1965	1955
Crude materials and fuels (cotton)	46	(28) (18)
Food (cashew nuts) (sugar) (tea)	37	(19) (9) (7)

Imports	1965	1955
Manufactured goods (machinery and transport equipment) (textiles and clothing)	56	(23) (16) (28) (11)
Crude materials and fuels	9	na
Food	8	na
Beverages	6	na

PRODUCTION, EXPORTS AND IMPORTS continued

7. FUEL AND POWER

	Production	Exports	Imports
Coal: 'A'	253	63q	319
Coke	170	45q	1
Electricity h: total	228²n		226
hydro	50		1
thermal	na		
Oil, crude	na	—¹	483
Petroleum, refined	473	280	77
Uranium minerals f	na	13	90¹

f metric tons. h million kWh. n consumption. q incl. bunkers.

8. IRON AND STEEL

	Production	Exports	Imports
Iron/steel scrap	na	7	2	—

9. NON-FERROUS MINERALS AND METALS

	Production	Exports	Imports
Gold, bullion/coins etc.	1.50²*	0.80	360.33‡ 106.00
Silver k, ore m	1.00²*	na	na na
Asbestos: fibre	0.15	0.12	0.05 0.58
manufactured	na		0.04 0.01
Mica	0.01¹	0.01	0.31
Aluminium: bauxite	6.10	2.73	—
aluminium	—	2.03	0.04

continued

PORTUGUESE GUINEA

AREA: 36 125 sq. km. (13 948 sq. miles)

LAND USE

The clearance of the mangrove swamps in the low deltaic region of the coast has enabled this area to be developed as paddy fields. Savannah vegetation, with coconut and oil palms, is found on the higher ground inland. On the interior plateau millet and groundnuts are grown, and cattle are reared.

POPULATION: 528 000 (1967 estimate)
Capital city: BISSAU; population: 18 309 (1950)
Total working population: 312 031 (1950)

PRODUCTION, EXPORTS AND IMPORTS

Years: 1963–5 average and 1953–5 average Units: '000 metric tons unless otherwise indicated

1. CEREALS, etc.

	Production	Exports	Imports
Cassava	35.7*	na	—
Potatoes	na		—
Rice	130.0*¹	—	0.4²

2. FRUIT, etc.

	Production	Exports	Imports
Wine b	—	—	14.5²

b '000 hectolitres.

3. BEVERAGES, FOREST PRODUCTS, etc.

	Production	Exports	Imports
Coffee	na	—	0.1¹
Sugar raw	na	—	1.4*
Tobacco, leaf	na		0.5²
Hardwood j	460.0*¹	16.6²	—

j '000 cu. metres of roundwood equivalent.

4. VEGETABLE OILSEEDS AND OILS

	Production	Exports	Imports
Groundnuts	45.27*n	24.63	—
Groundnut oil	0.06²¹	16.6²	0.15²
Olive oil	na		

continued

		Year(s)
Infant mortality (per '000)	80.2*	1966
Crude birth rate (per '000)	7.3*	1965
Crude death rate (per '000)	4.3*	1965
Population per physician	15 410	1963
Population per hospital bed	620a	1966
School enrolment: age 5–19 years (percentage)	11	1963–4 av.

a government hospital beds only.

COMMUNICATIONS

		Year
Telephones (per '000 urban population)	0.2	1967
Daily newspapers (per '000 population)	2	1964

TRADE

In 1965 exports amounted to about U.S. $15 million and imports to about U.S. $4 million and the adverse balance being aggravated by expenditure on the maintenance of law and order. Trade is mainly with Portugal; most foodstuffs and virtually all manufactured goods are imported; exports consist of groundnuts and palm kernels, and a little natural rubber.

4. VEGETABLE OILSEEDS AND OILS—continued

	Production	Exports	Imports
Palm kernels	12.03	9.48	8.01*
Palm oil	8.00*	0.08¹	0.60²*
Sesame seed	na	0.14¹	0.41

5. LIVESTOCK‡, ANIMAL PRODUCTS, etc.

	Production	Exports	Imports
Cattle d	230.0*	—	36.2²
Goats d	152.0*	—	
Sheep d	67.3*	—	
Pigs d	1.0*	—	
Meat‡, 'A'	1.0*	—	0.1¹
Fish	0.8	0.5	1.4*
Milk	—	—	0.5²

d no. in thousands.

6. FIBRES, TEXTILES, etc.

	Production	Exports	Imports
Rubber, natural	na	0.1	na

7. FUEL AND POWER

	Production	Exports	Imports
Petroleum, refined	na	—	20

11. INDUSTRY

	Production	Exports	Imports
Cement	na	—	18.0*	13.7*

continued

---

9. NON-FERROUS MINERALS AND METALS—continued (Mozambique)

	Production		Exports		Imports	
Beryl	0.38	0.68	0.45	0.61	0.54	0.14
Copper, metal	na				0.16	0.05
Lead, metal	na				0.04	0.06
Mercury f	na				0.05	0.01
Tin, metal	na				0.10	0.03
Zinc, metal	na					

f metric tons. k '000 fine troy oz. m metal content.

10. CHEMICALS n AND FERTILIZERS

	Production	Exports	Imports
Chemicals			na
Fertilizers: Sulphur	na		0.5	0.6

n data not available for years 1953–5.

11. INDUSTRY

	Production	Exports	Imports
Aircraft a			0.1¹
Alcoholic beverages	126.0	45.8	
beer b	190.3	98.0	
Cement	na	0.7	1.0*
Electrical engineering a			6.4
Railway vehicles a			2.6
Motor vehicles a			9.0

a million $ U.S. b '000 hectolitres.

continued

PORTUGUESE TIMOR — SOUTH EAST ASIA

AREA: 14 925 sq. km. (5 763 sq. miles)

LAND USE
About 60% of the country is under forest; the remainder of the land is not readily cultivable, but subsistence crops of grain and vegetables are grown, and coffee is produced for export.

POPULATION: 570 000 (1967 estimate)
Capital city: DILI; population: 52 158 (city proper, 1960)

		Year
Crude birth rate (per '000)	19*	1965
Crude death rate (per '000)	9.9*	1965
Population per physician	27 150	1964
Population per hospital bed	780	1966
School enrolment: age 5–19 years (percentage)	8	1961

COMMUNICATIONS

		Year(s)
Telephones (per '000 urban population)	0.1	1967
Radio licences (per '000 population)	2	1963–5 av.

FINANCE
Currency unit: The Portuguese escudo

TRADE
Trade is mainly with Portugal, exports being coffee, copra, natural rubber, and wax. All manufactured goods and most foodstuffs are imported.

PRODUCTION, EXPORTS AND IMPORTS Units: '000 metric tons unless otherwise indicated
Years: 1953–5 average and 1953–5 average

1. CEREALS, etc.
	Production		Exports		Imports	
Cassava	15.0*	14.0¹	—	—	—	—
Maize (corn)	21.0*	22.5²	—	—	—	—
Rice	15.7*	7.0¹	0.2	—	—	0.02
Sweet potatoes/ yams	10.0*	3.0¹				

2. FRUIT, etc.
	Production		Exports		Imports	
Coconuts d	12.0*	na		3.6¹	2.0*	
Wine b	—					

b '000 hectolitres. d no. in millions.

3. BEVERAGES, FOREST PRODUCTS, etc.
	Production		Exports		Imports	
Coffee	1.3*	na	2.4		1.2²	
Sugar, raw	—		—		0.4*	3.2
Tobacco, leaf	0.32*		—		—	

4. VEGETABLE OILSEEDS AND OILS
	Production		Exports		Imports
Copra	1.00*	1.00a	1.58		1.27
Groundnuts	—	—	—		—
Olive oil	—	0.70¹			—

5. LIVESTOCK‡, ANIMAL PRODUCTS, etc.
	Production		Exports		Imports
Cattle d	36.0*	9.0			
Goats d	228.0*	173.0			
Sheep d	50.0*	40.7			
Horses d	94.0*	64.0			
Pigs d	225.0*	168.3			
Fish	0.1	na			

d no. in thousands.

6. FIBRES, TEXTILES, etc.
	Production	Exports	Imports
Rubber, natural	0.3*	0.2	—

SÃO TOMÉ AND PRINCIPE — ATLANTIC OCEAN

AREA: 964 sq. km. (372 sq. miles)
POPULATION: 60 000a (1967 estimate)
Capital city: SÃO TOMÉ; population: 5 714 (city proper, 1960)

		Year(s)
Infant mortality (per '000)	76.6	1965
Crude birth rate (per '000)	53.3	1965
Crude death rate (per '000)	15.9	1965
Accidental deaths (per 100 000 population)	na	
Population per physician	3 050	1964
Population per hospital bed	30	1966
School enrolment: age 5–19 years (percentage)	31	1963–4 av.

a incl. 17 000 immigrant labourers under 4-year contracts.

COMMUNICATIONS

		Year(s)
Motor vehicles in use ('000s): private	0.8	1963–5 av.
commercial	0.3	1967
Telephones (per '000 urban population)	0.9	1963–5 av.
Radio licences (per '000 population)	25	

FINANCE
Currency unit: The Portuguese escudo

PRODUCTION AND TRADE
The chief commercial products are cacao, copra, coffee, palm oil and cinchona, cacao providing 80% of the exports in 1964. Manufactured goods and most foodstuffs are imported.

PRODUCTION, EXPORTS AND IMPORTS Units: '000 metric tons unless otherwise indicated
Years: 1963–5 average and 1953–5 average

1. CEREALS, etc.
	Production	Exports	Imports	
Cassava	2.0*	—	—	
Maize (corn)			1.6	3.3
Potatoes			0.6	0.4
Rice			1.3	1.8

2. FRUIT, etc.
	Production		Exports	Imports	
Bananas	4.3*	na			
Coconuts e	46.0*	na		23.2	20.3
Wine b	—				

b '000 hectolitres. e no. in millions.

3. BEVERAGES, FOREST PRODUCTS, etc.
	Production		Exports		Imports	
Cocoa	8.9	na	8.9	7.6*	8.0	
Coffee	0.2	na	0.2	0.3	0.2	
Sugar, raw					0.9²	0.4

Cinchona is also grown, and the bark exported.

4. VEGETABLE OILSEEDS AND OILS
	Production	Exports	Imports	
Copra	5.63*	5.71	—	0.02
Groundnuts	na			
Linseed oil	na			
Olive oil	na			0.10
Palm kernels	3.03*	3.54		
Palm oil	1.47*	0.82		0.06

5. LIVESTOCK‡, ANIMAL PRODUCTS, etc.
	Production	
Cattle d	3.7*	4.7
Goats d	1.0*	2.0*
Sheep d	2.7	4.0*
Pigs d	4.0	7.0*
Fish	0.7	0.4

d no. in thousands.

7. FUEL AND POWER
	Production	
Electricity h, t	6	— thermal

h million kWh. t thermal.

na: data not available. — negligible or nil. ¹ one year only. ² two year average. * estimate. ‡ see appendix. † re-exports.

RHODESIA — CENTRAL AFRICA

Rhodesia, formerly Southern Rhodesia and a member of the Federation of Rhodesia and Nyasaland from 1954–1963, attained the status of a self-governing British Protectorate upon the dissolution of the Federation. The government made a unilateral declaration of independence in 1965, whereupon the U.N. called on all nations to impose economic sanctions on Rhodesia, 1954–1963.

No independent data for Rhodesia are available for the years of the Federation, 1954–1963.

AREA: 390 622 sq. km. (150 820 sq. miles)

LAND USE: (percentage of total)

	1965	1955
Arable and orchard	4.7	4.7
Permanent meadow and pasture	12.5	12.2
Forest and woodland	60.0	64.0
City areas, waste and other land	22.8	19.1

POPULATION: 4 530 000 (1967 estimate)
Largest city: SALISBURY, capital; population: 330 000 (1966)

			Year(s)
Life expectancy at birth (years): Africans		50	1962
Europeans: male		66.9	}1961–3 av.
female		74.0	
Infant mortality (per '000): Asians		34.5	
Africans		34.3*	}1965
Europeans		23.0	
Crude birth rate (per '000): Asians		32.6	
Africans		32.1*	}1965
Europeans		18.3	
Crude death rate (per '000): Asians		5.1	
Africans		4.5*	}1965
Europeans		6.3	
Accidental deaths (per 100 000 population) caused by motor vehicles		39.7b	}1965
due to other causes		21.9b	
Population per physician		7 570	1964
Population per hospital bed		280	1966
School enrolment: age 5–19 years (percentage)		72a	1963–4 av.
age over 19 years (per 100 000 population)		16	1963–5 av.

a Africans only, but excl. those at mission schools. b Europeans only.

EMPLOYMENT AND PRODUCTION
Approximately half the land in Rhodesia is reserved for ownership by the Africans, who constitute 95% of the population. Cereal crops, particularly maize, form the basis of the subsistence agriculture. Tobacco is the principal commercial crop. Industry is becoming increasingly important. In 1967 the largest sources of employment for African labour were (in descending order) agriculture, manufacturing, construction, mining, and domestic service.

COMMUNICATIONS

		Year(s)
Motor vehicles in use ('000s): private	106.8	}1963–4 av.
commercial	31.8	
Railway track (km.)	3 350	1966
Mail per capita: domestic	15	}1964–5 av.
foreign received	15	
foreign sent	4	
Telephones (per '000 urban population)	2.4	1967
Radio licences (per '000 population)	53*	1965
Daily newspapers (per '000 population)	30	1959

FINANCE
Currency unit: The Rhodesian dollar replaced the Rhodesian pound in 1970 at the rate R$1 to R£0.5.

Exchange rates (for Rhodesian pounds)	1965	1950	1938
Per $ U.S.	0.357	0.357	0.215
Per £ sterling	1.0	1.0	1.0

		Year
National Income (million $ U.S.)	877	1965
G.N.P. per capita ($ U.S.)	210	1966

TRADING

Total trade (in million $ U.S.)	1965	1950	1938
Exports (f.o.b.)	442	117	30
Imports (f.o.b.)	335	165	47

Main trading partners (percentage of total value)

Exports	1965	1950	1938	Imports	1965	1950	1938
Zambia	25	8	7	U.K.	30	47	50
U.K.	22	54	73	South Africa	23	27	15
South Africa	11	11	4	U.S.A.	7	5	19
Malawi	9	1	—	Japan	6	1	na
Japan	6	1	2a	Germany F.R.	4	2	1
Netherlands	3	1	—	Zambia	3	na	3a
				Iran	3	1	1

Distribution of trade (percentage of total value) b

Exports	1965	1950*	1938*
Tobacco	34	50	26
Manufactured goods	31		
Food			

Imports	1965	1950	1938
Manufactured goods (machinery and transport equipment)	67	(32)	(19)
(textiles and clothing)		(14)	(13)
Chemicals	11	11	4
Crude materials and fuels	9	8	3
Food	8	5	
Beverages and tobacco	4	4	3

a incl. Germany D.R. and Austria. b % of national exports† which comprised 90% of general exports in 1965, 82% in 1950 and 80% in 1938.

PRODUCTION, EXPORTS AND IMPORTS Units: '000 metric tons unless otherwise indicated
Years: 1964–5 average and 1953

1. CEREALS, etc.
	Production		Exports		Imports	
Barley	1.3*		—		0.8	0.1
Maize (corn)	752.7b	484.0b	172.3	0.5	37.2	0.1
Millets/sorghum	254.0*	147.0	0.5	0.1†	8.6	33.5
Oats	22.3	10.3	2.4	0.2	0.3	0.5
Potatoes	3.0*	na	—	—	3.6	4.5
Rice	—	—	—	—	10.9	
Sweet potatoes/ yams						
Wheat	3.3	1.0	5.9s	—	89.6	50.0

3. BEVERAGES, FOREST PRODUCTS, etc.
	Production		Exports		Imports	
Coffee					0.4	0.1
Sugar: cane raw	167.9	27.5²	172.3	0.5	33.5	
Tea	1.4	0.5	8.0	0.1†	0.5	
Tobacco: leaf	115.3	55.3²	112.4	39.2s	1.0	4.5
products	na		0.1†		2.0	0.9
Softwood j	80.0	88.3	2.6		48.1	
Hardwood j	3 741.0¹	2 386.0	3.0		41.2	
Wood pulp j	4.1				4.2	
Newsprint j	—				1.4	
Other paper	4.4	5.9			25.4	

j '000 cu. metres of roundwood equivalent. s incl. re-exports.

4. VEGETABLE OILSEEDS AND OILS
	Production		Exports		Imports	
Castor seed	6.00	0.30	0.45		0.04	0.03
Castor oil	na				1.37	0.06
Coconut oil	na				1.23	0.18
Cottonseed	78.87*	52.50	2.25		0.27	
Cottonseed oil	na				0.26	
Groundnuts	17.0*	9.0	1.77	1.80	0.22	0.02
Groundnut oil	4.0*	na	2.4†			

continued

na: data not available. — negligible or nil. ¹ one year only. ² two year average. * estimate. ‡ see appendix. † re-exports.

203

RHODESIA continued

PRODUCTION, EXPORTS AND IMPORTS continued

4. VEGETABLE OILSEEDS AND OILS—continued

	Production 1965	Exports 1965	Imports 1965
Linseed oil	778.0* 562.0	0.01†	0.11 0.02
Olive oil	3587.7 3031.0	—	0.01 0.01
Palm kernel oil	841.3p 630.3p	—	0.05 1.58
Palm oil	557.0* 482.0	—	0.49 0.76
Soya beans	391.7* 294.3	0.10	—
Soya bean oil	6.7* 6.0	—	0.31¹
Sunflower seed	133.0 121.3	0.27	0.22
Sunflower seed oil	77.3 55.3q	0.02	0.14
Tung oil	2.00*p 1.00*p		0.01

p from farms and estates only.

5. LIVESTOCK‡; ANIMAL PRODUCTS, etc.

	Production	Exports	Imports
Chickens d.	9.7* 6.3		
Cattle d.	3 097		
dairy cows d	3 764		
Sheep d	3 526		
Goats d	238		
Horses d	143		
Pigs d.	1 488	886	8
Bacon/ham	126	80	1
Meat‡: 'A'	15.8	15.8¹	
Butter	1.0	—	0.1
Cheese	1.5*	1.1	
Eggs	1.8	—	1.1
Fish	104.7* 55.3	—	12.8
Milk		—	
Hides/skins	4.5	8.6	8.6

d no. in thousands. n incl. some beef cows. q government inspected meat only.

6. FIBRES, TEXTILES, etc.

	Production	Exports	Imports
Cotton lint	3.0	—	1.9
Jute	—	—	—
Rubber, natural	—	—	0.2†
Cotton: yarn	2.8	—	0.5
woven fabrics			
Rayon, woven fabrics	—	—	—
Wool, yarn			

7. FUEL AND POWER

	Production	Exports	Imports
Coal: 'A' ‡.	3 097		
Coke	3 764		
Electricity h: total	3 526		
hydro			
thermal	238		
Oil, crude	na		212.0
Petroleum, refined	143	40	170
Uranium †			297

h million kWh.

8. IRON AND STEEL

	Production	Exports	Imports
Iron ore	41m	na	304
Pig iron	268	6²	236
Steel ingots/castings	114	na	29

m metal content.

ROMANIA

In 1947 the king abdicated under political pressure, and the 'People's Republic' (later known as the 'Socialist Republic') was proclaimed. Romania is a member of Comecon.

AREA: 237 500 sq. km. (91 699 sq. miles)

LAND USE: (percentage of total)

	1965	1955
Arable and orchard	44.1	39.2
Permanent meadow and pasture	18.2	14.3
Forest and woodland	26.8	26.6
City areas, waste and other land	10.9	19.9

POPULATION: 19 105 056 (1966 census)
Largest city: BUCUREŞTI (Bucharest), capital: population: 1 518 725 (1966)

Distribution of working population (1956)
Total working population: 10 466 258

U.N. group no.

		Percentage
0/1/2/3	Agriculture and hunting a	69.6
4	Mining, quarrying, forestry, fishing and manufacturing	14.2
	Construction	2.5
5/8	Services, incl. electricity, gas, water and sanitary services.	6.8
6	Commerce	3.3
7	Transport, storage and communications	2.8
9	Others	0.8

a incl. unpaid family workers.

	1965	Year(s)
Life expectancy at birth (years): male	63.4	} 1963
female	70.3	
Infant mortality (per '000)	44.1	1964
Crude birth rate (per '000)	14.6	1965
Crude death rate (per '000)	8.6	1965
Population per hospital bed	760	1965
Population per physician	760	1966
School enrolment: age 5–19 years (percentage)	85	1963–4 av.
age over 19 years (per 100 000 population)	669	1964–5 av.

COMMUNICATIONS

	1965	Year(s)
Motor vehicles in use ('000s): private	na	1963–5 av.
commercial	30.8	
Railway track (km.)	956	1964
Mail per capita	75	1963–5 av.
Telephones (per '000 urban population)	2.7*	1967
Radio licences (per '000 population)	141	1963–5 av.
Television licences (per '000 population)	19.4	1963–5 av.
Daily newspapers (per '000 population)	170	1962–4 av.

continued

FINANCE

Currency unit: The lei

Exchange rates a	1957	1960	1965
Per $ U.S. ...	6.0	6.0	6.0
Per £ sterling	16.8	16.8	16.8

a since 1957 there has been a special tourist rate of 18 per $ U.S. (50.4 per £ sterling).

		Year(s)
National Income (million $ U.S.)	12 000*	1966
G.N.P. per capita ($ U.S.)	650	1966
Rate of increase of G.N.P. per capita	8.2	1960–4 av.

TRADING

Total trade (in million $ U.S.)	1938	1956	1965
Exports (f.o.b.)	157	397	1102
Imports (f.o.b.)	137	352	1077

PRODUCTION, EXPORTS AND IMPORTS

Years: 1963–5 average and 1953–5 average   Units: '000 metric tons unless otherwise indicated

1. CEREALS, etc.

	Production	Exports	Imports
Barley	394.7 415.0²*	0.4	—
Maize (corn)	6197.3 5415.0²*	867.2* 112.1²*	—
Millets/sorghum	109.0 20.62	2.1* 17.1²*	6.5*
Oats	638 365.0²*	—	—
Potatoes	2508.7 2502.0²*	19.2 0.5*	3.3*
Rice	50.3 42.0²*	16.1 5.3*	36.3
Rye	98.3 192.0²	—	—
Wheat	4520.0 2573.0²*	195.8* 77.5*	208.2*² 45.7*

2. FRUIT, etc.

	Production	Exports	Imports
Apples	180.7	26.01* 9.2*	—
Apricots	30.3	8.11	—
Cherries	45.3	39.61	—
Dates		—	0.1*²
Grapes	918.7 942.0²*	51.0	—
Lemons		—	10.4*
Oranges		—	6.7*
Other citrus fruit		—	0.5*
Peaches	7.3	—	—
Pears	45.0 40.01*	—	
Plums	558.7 473.5	—	0.4*²
Raisins		—	
Tomatoes		—	
Wine b.	503.7 4 655.0	375.0	17.0* 5.7*

b '000 hectolitres.

3. BEVERAGES, FOREST PRODUCTS, etc.

	Production	Exports	Imports
Cocoa		—	4.4
Coffee		—	1.5*
raw.	3 080.0 1 541.7*	59.1	16.3
Sugar: beet	376.5 184.3*	5.9*	0.1*
Tea		—	1.6²
Tobacco: leaf	38.7 18.5²*	—	0.2
cigarettes n	22 148.0		1.1
Softwood j	6 215.5²	2 322.0 781.0	14.2
Hardwood j	15 226.0²	1 055.0 54.5	0.5
Wood pulp	217.0²	37.8 1.8	11.2
Newsprint	50.0² 46.0*	4.3	
Other paper	212.0² 30.3*¹	6.5	

e no. in millions. j '000 cu. metres of roundwood equivalent. n incl. cigars.

4. VEGETABLE OILSEEDS AND OILS

	Production	Exports	Imports
Castor seed	12.3 3.1²	2.77	—
Castor oil	na	—	0.95*
Coconut oil	na 15.3*	—	1.79
Cottonseed	25.7	14.50²*	0.57*
Cottonseed oil	na 10.0²*	0.07*	1.79*
Groundnuts	na	—	0.01²*
Linseed	na	—	0.37*
Linseed oil	na 8.0²*	1.33*	0.03*
Palm/kernel oil	na 13.0²*	—	0.37
Palm oil	2.0	0.33*	0.37
Rapeseed	na	—	—
Soya beans	529.3 280.0²*	4.00	0.06*
Sunflower seed	na	35.62	0.51*
Sunflower seed oil			
Tung oil			

5. LIVESTOCK‡; ANIMAL PRODUCTS, etc.

	Production	Exports	Imports
Chickens d.	37 473n 31 250²n		
Cattle d.	4 653 4 715²*	11.6* 0.1*	0.22*
dairy cows d	1 962p	32.0* na	
Goats d	638 345¹*		
Horses d	726 1 097²		
Pigs d.	5 070 4 660²*	40.0 1.6*	0.1*
Meat‡: 'A'	537*	5.6*	0.2*
Butter	19q	1.4*	
Cheese	50	8.8	1.2*
Eggs	111		1.7*
Milk	352		11.0*
Hides/skins	2 727* 1 985²*	1.0*	0.8*
Wool	15 10*		0.7*

d no. in thousands. n incl. ducks, geese and turkeys. p incl. buffalo cows. q factory produced butter only.

6. FIBRES, TEXTILES, etc.

	Production	Exports	Imports
Agaves (sisal etc.)	8.9* 8.0²*	0.3*	1.3*
Flax fibre	13.1* 6.4²*	0.6²	66.3
Hemp fibre	25.4²*		
Jute	na	—	3.8*
Silk f.	na 10.0²*	71.7*	20.2
Cotton: yarn	74.2 45.6²*	5.3²	1.5²
woven fabrics	41.4 37.0²*		
Rayon: fibre/yarn	3.2 1.4¹*	—	—
woven fabrics	40.0²¹ 31.3²¹		
Wool: yarn	23.8 17.71	—	—
woven fabrics			

f metric tons. r million sq. metres.

7. FUEL AND POWER

	Production	Exports	Imports
Coal: 'A' ‡.	4 943 3 350	—	707
'B'.	1 660 2 750	—	931
Coke	14 249 3 810¹	—	—
Electricity h: total	13 540 3 490¹	—	—
hydro	709 320¹	—	—
thermal	13 180 5 660¹	203	—
Natural gas i	12 760 9 660¹	—	—
Oil, crude	11 176	5 533	—
Petroleum, refined			

h million kWh. i million cu. metres.

8. IRON AND STEEL

	Production	Exports	Imports
Iron ore	1 003m	—	2 388
Pig iron	1 883	—	43
Steel ingots/castings	3 057	na	—

m metal content.

continued

Exports	1965		Imports	1965
U.S.S.R.	40		U.S.S.R.	38
Germany D.R.	9		Germany D.R.	10
Italy	6		Czechoslovakia	6
Germany F.R.	6		Italy	5
Poland	4		France	5
Hungary	3		U.K.	4

Distribution of trade (percentage of total value)

Exports	1956*	1965
Crude materials, fuels, metals	63	39
Manufactured goods (machinery and transport equipment)	na (10)	33 (19)
Food	24	21
Chemicals and rubber	na	7

Imports		
Manufactured goods (machinery and transport equipment)	68 (20)	47 (39)
Crude materials, fuels, minerals, metals	na	43
Food	7	6
Chemicals and rubber	3	

RHODESIA continued (non-ferrous minerals)

9. NON-FERROUS MINERALS AND METALS

	Production	Exports	Imports
Gold: ore m	561.70 521.00	1.00¹‡ 4.90	2.20¹‡ 0.13
bullion/coins etc.		505.66	
Silver k, ore	89.40m 81.30m	565.10 89.78n 81.69n	—
Asbestos: fibre	142.69	164.36² 64.98	— 4.96p
manufactured	na na	0.35¹ 0.17	—
Mica	0.12 0.16	—	—
Aluminium: bauxite	2.03	—	1.03
aluminium	na	0.04†	0.04 0.01q
Antimony, ore	0.10m 0.10m	0.20 0.24	—
Beryl	0.16 1.15	0.12 1.49	—
Chrome: ore	462.73m 369.17	545.38	1.03
metal	na na	na	21.98
Copper: ore	17.12m 0.51m	7.06 3.10	na
metal	15.69 na	18.70 0.50	5.31 0.40
Lead: ore	na na	na 0.02	0.80 0.18
metal	na 0.40	—	—
Magnesium: dolomite	na	0.12¹ na	—
magnesite	28.35	28.94 8.62	0.03
Manganese, ore	na 0.40	na 2.26	0.08
Mercury f.	na	—	0.94
Nickel: ore	0.33 na	0.71¹ 0.07	— 3.70
metal	na na	—	—
Tin: ore	0.51 0.19m	0.06 0.02	0.03
metal	0.51 0.02	0.44 0.04	0.08 0.06
Tungsten, ore	0.01 0.29	0.03¹ 0.28	0.94 0.12
Zinc, ore			

a million $ U.S. f metric tons. k '000 fine troy oz. m metal content. n bullion. q metal.
b in addition, asbestos valued at U.S. $ 154 000. p on farms and estates only.

10. CHEMICALS n AND FERTILIZERS

	Production	Exports	Imports
Chemicals a	na	na	na
Fertilizers:			
Phosphates	2.8	2.8	—
Potash	na	—	—
Pyrites	28.5* x 13.5 x	0.5* x	—
Sulphur	na	21.7	—

n data not available for 1953. x sulphur content. y 1963 data; incl. Nyasaland and Northern Rhodesia.

11. INDUSTRY

	Production	Exports	Imports
Aircraft a	na	—	na
Alcoholic beverages a	na	2.4	2.8
Cement	212.0	6.0	2.1
Electrical engineering a	na	—	3.0
Railway vehicles a	na	8.4	15.4
Motor vehicles: commercial a	1.3	—	6.5
private a	5.0	7.6a	29.1a

a million $ U.S. d no. in thousands. r assembly of imported parts.

ROMANIA continued

PRODUCTION, EXPORTS AND IMPORTS continued

9. NON-FERROUS MINERALS AND METALS

	Production	Exports	Imports
Silver k, o r e m	643.00* 643.00*	na na	na na
Aluminium: bauxite	32.8* 15.20*	na	na
alumina	na na	na	na
aluminium	22.80‡ 5.62²*	na	na
Chrome, ore	na na	na	na
Lead: ore m	11.10¹*	na	na
metal	13.55* 10.53*	na	na
Manganese, ore	161.93 281.83	na	na
Mercury j	6.65	—	—
Zinc	na 75.26	na	na

f metric tons. k '000 fine troy oz. m metal content.

10. CHEMICALS n AND FERTILIZERS

Organic chemicals:	Production	Exports	Imports
Benzene	44.0	na	na
Butadiene	na	na	na
Ethylene	na	na	na
Methanol	na	na	na
Phenol	16.6¹	na	na
Phthalic anhydride	na	na	na
Styrene monomer	na	na	na
Urea	na	na	na
Inorganic chemicals:			
Ammonia	154.9²	na	na
Chlorine	35.1	17.9	na
Carbon black	203.0¹	8.0	na
Nitric acid	226.5²*	8.1a	na
Sodium carbonate	337.8	186.6	na
Sodium hydroxide	198.4	102.9	na
Sulphuric acid	434.7		na

continued

10. CHEMICALSn AND FERTILIZERS—continued

	Production	Exports	Imports
Plastics:			
Polyamides	na	na	na
Polyethylene	na	na	na
Polyvinyl chloride	6.4²	na	na
Fertilizers:			
Phosphates	—	—	139.7p
Potash	—	—	9.3*
Pyrites	162.7x	—	na

n data not available for years 1953–5. p P₂O₅ content. x sulphur content.

11. INDUSTRY

	Production	Exports	Imports
Alcoholic beverages			
beer b	2 435.0¹ 1 308.0¹	45.3	—
spirits b	330.0¹*q 500.0r	na	—
Cement	4 842.7 1 829.0	1 538.0¹	—*‡
Electrical engineering a	na	43.2u	31.1u
Railway vehicles c	165.0w	na	na
Machine tools g	38.0¹	na	na
Merchant ships g	—	—	na
Motor vehicles commercial d	15.7	3.7¹v	na

a million $ U.S. b '000 hectolitres. c no. of units. d no. in thousands.
g '000 G.R.T. q production for home consumption in 1966. r 1961 figure.
t trade with Eastern Europe, the U.S.S.R., and China P.R. u electric
machine apparatus. v trucks only. w locomotives only.

continued

PRODUCTION, EXPORTS AND IMPORTS

Years: 1963–5 average and 1953–5 average   Units: '000 metric tons unless otherwise indicated

Note—1953–5 data are for the former Ruanda-Urundi; i.e. include Burundi.

1. CEREALS, etc.

	Production	Exports	Imports
Barley	1 033.0* 1 977.0	—	—
Cassava	1.7	—	—
Maize (corn)	143.3* 136.0	—	—
Millets/sorghum	218.3 211.3	—	—
Potatoes	100.0* 130.7	—	—
Rice	2.7* 1.0	—	—
Sweet potatoes/ yams	966.7* 1 713.0	—	—
Wheat	5.0* 9.3	—	—

3. BEVERAGES, FOREST PRODUCTS, etc.

	Production	Exports	Imports
Coffee	9.1	na	—
Tea	0.3 0.2²*	na	—
Tobacco	1.5*n 1.6n	na	na

n leaf tobacco.

4. VEGETABLE OILSEEDS AND OILS

	Production	Exports	Imports
Castor seed	4.30* 4.67	na	—
Copra	na	na	—
Cottonseed	4.90* 4.20	na	—
Groundnuts	0.20* na	na	—
Palm kernels	1.00* na p	na	na
Palm oil	na 4.00	na	na
Soya beans		—	na

5. LIVESTOCK‡, ANIMAL PRODUCTS, etc.

	Production	Exports	Imports
Cattle d	1 216.7* 928.7	na	—
Goats d	1 890.0¹ 1 303.7	na	—
Sheep d	680.0* 401.7	na	—
Pigs d	56.0* 49.0	na	—
Meat‡; 'A'	10.0*	na	—
'B'	3.0*	na	na

continued

PRODUCTION, EXPORTS AND IMPORTS, etc.—continued

5. LIVESTOCK‡, ANIMAL PRODUCTS, etc.

	Production	Exports	Imports
Eggs	1.9* na	—	—
Fish	5.1	—	—
Milk	55.0* 5.3	—	—
Hides/skins	0.1 1.3	—	—

d no. in thousands.

6. FIBRES, TEXTILES, etc.

	Production	Exports	Imports
Agaves (sisal)	2.3*	—	—
Cotton lint	0.1 2.0	na	—

7. FUEL AND POWER

	Production	Exports	Imports
Electricity h: total	9.1 16.8	—	na
hydro	11	—	—
thermal	1 0.2*	—	—
Petroleum, refined	1.5*n 1.6n	—	17

h million kWh.

9. NON-FERROUS MINERALS AND METALS

	Production	Exports	Imports
Gold k, ore m	0.24 4.67	na	—
Beryl		na	—
Tin ore	1.37m	na p	—
Tungsten, ore	0.15 na p	—	—

k '000 fine troy oz.   m metal content.   p see Congo D.R.

11. INDUSTRY

	Production	Exports	Imports
Beer b	265.0²	0.1a	0.7
Cement p		na	—
Electrical engineering a		—	—
Motor vehicles a		—	11.6

a million $ U.S.   b '000 hectolitres.   p see Congo D.R.

RWANDA

Rwanda and Burundi which together formed the Belgian territory of Ruanda-Urundi, separated in 1959 after a period of inter-tribal friction. Internal self-government was granted to Rwanda in 1962, but the country is still supported by Belgian aid. The customs union with Burundi was broken off in 1964. Pre-1960 data are for the former Ruanda-Urundi.

AREA: 26 330 sq. km. (10 166 sq. miles)

LAND USE: (percentage of total)

	1963
Arable and orchard	37.8
Permanent meadow and pasture	33.0
Forest and woodland	5.9
City areas, waste and other land	23.3

POPULATION: 3 306 000 a (1967 estimate)
Capital city: KIGALI; population: 4 273 (1959)

		Year(s)
Crude birth rate (per '000)	21.3*	1965
Crude death rate (per '000)	4.8*	1965
Population per hospital bed	97 350	1964
Population per physician	750	1963–4 av.
School enrolment: age 5–19 years (percentage)	44	1963–5 av.
age over 19 years (per 100 000 population)	3	

a African population only.

FINANCE

Currency unit: The Rwanda franc, at par with the Belgian franc until April 1966, thereafter at par with the $U.S.

	1965a	1960
Exchange rates		
Per $ U.S.	50	50
Per £ sterling	140	140

		Year
National Income (million $ U.S.)	95	1958
G.N.P. per capita ($ U.S.)	40	1966

a official rate; the free trade rate was about 118 per $ U.S. (330 per £ Sterling).

TRADING

Total trade (in million $ U.S.)	1965a
Exports (f.o.b.)	14
Imports (c.i.f.)	18

Main trading partners (percentage of total value)

Exports	1965a	Imports	1965a
U.S.A.	49	Belg./Lux.	26
Belg./Lux.	38	Uganda	17
Germany F.R.	3	Germany F.R.	11
Congo D.R.	2	Burundi	6
U.K.	2	U.S.A.	4
		Japan	4
		U.K.	4

Distribution of trade (percentage of total value)

Exports	1965	Imports	1965
Coffee	54	Manufactured goods	37
Tin	37	(machinery and transport equipment)	(28)
Pyrethrum	3	(textiles and clothing)	(16)
Tea	2	Crude materials and fuels	10
		Food	8
		Chemicals	7

a for earlier trade figures, see Congo D.R.

continued

RYUKYU ISLANDS · CHINA SEA

The administration of the Ryukyu Islands of which the largest and most important is Okinawa, was assigned to the U.S.A. after the surrender of Japan in 1945. It has been agreed that the islands should revert to Japanese control in 1972.

AREA: 2 196 sq. km. (848 sq. miles)

LAND USE: (percentage of total)

	1964	1955
Arable and orchard	25.5	19.5
Permanent meadow and pasture	0.9	7.3
Forest and woodland	54.5	52.7
City areas, waste and other land	19.1	20.5

POPULATION: 934 176 (1965 census)
Largest city: NAHA, capital; population: 257 177 (city proper, 1965)

Distribution of working population (1965)
Total working population: 417 000

U.N. group no.		Percentage
0	Agriculture, forestry, fishing and hunting	35.7
2/3	Manufacturing	8.9
4	Construction	7.0
5	Electricity, gas, water and sanitary services	} 4.6
6	Transport, storage and communications	
7	Commerce	18.0
8	Services	22.5a
9	Others	3.3

		Year(s)
Life expectancy at birth (years): male	68.0	1960
female	74.6	
Infant mortality (per '000)	9.8	1965
Crude birth rate (per '000)	22.3	1965
Crude death rate (per '000)	5.3	1965
Accidental deaths (per 100 000 population)	8.9	1965
caused by motor vehicles	16.4	1964
due to other causes		
Population per physician	1 940	1965
Population per hospital bed	290 b	1963–4 av.
School enrolment: age 5–19 years (percentage)	130‡	1963–5 av.
age over 19 years (per 100 000 population)	511	1964–5 av.

a 13% of the labour force was employed by U.S. military and naval establishments.   b government hospitals only.

COMMUNICATIONS

		Year(s)
Motor vehicles in use ('000s): private	10.9	1963
commercial	11.0	
Telephones (per '000 urban population)	4.3c	1967
Television sets (per '000 population)	108.3*	1963–5 av.
Daily newspapers (per '000 population)	255*	1964

c excl. telephones of the U.S. armed forces.

FINANCE

Currency unit: The U.S. dollar

		Year
National Income (million $ U.S.)	144	1958
G.N.P. per capita ($ U.S.)	450	1966

continued

na: data not available.   — negligible or nil.   — data not available.   — negligible or nil.   * estimate.   * estimate.   ‡ see appendix.   ‡ see appendix.   † re-exports.   † re-exports.   ¹ one year only.   ¹ one year only.   ² two year average.   ² two year average.

RYUKYU ISLANDS continued

PRODUCTION, EXPORTS AND IMPORTS
Years: 1963–5 average and 1953–5 average Units: '000 metric tons unless otherwise indicated

	Production	Exports	Imports
1. CEREALS, etc.			
Barley	na	—	1.3
Maize (corn)	na	—	—
Potatoes	6.0* 3.0	—	8.1*
Rice	12.0 18.0²	—	5.9
Sweet potatoes/yams	67.0* 261.7	—	93.4
Wheat	na 1.0	—	24.1
2. FRUIT, etc.			
Apples	1.7* 1.0	—	2.2
Bananas	—	0.1	1.5
Grapes	—	—	—
Oranges	—	0.1	0.1
Other citrus fruit	—	—	4.7
Pineapples	47.3 na	—	0.1
Tomatoes	1.3* 1.3	5.1	—
3. BEVERAGES, FOREST PRODUCTS, etc.			
Sugar: cane	1 823.3		
raw	nan 7.0 m	186.9* 17.5	21.1 4.4
Tea	na 0.1		0.7
Tobacco: leaf	0.1* 0.5		1.6* na
Softwood j			na
Hardwood j	69.0		278.0* na
Newsprint			30.3¹ q na
Other paper			9.7¹ na
4. VEGETABLE OILSEEDS AND OILS			
Cottonseed oil	—	—	1.3
Groundnuts	—	—	8.1*
Rapeseed oil	—	—	5.9
Soya beans	na 4.00	—	93.4
Soya bean oil	na na	—	24.1
5. LIVESTOCK‡, ANIMAL PRODUCTS, etc.			
Chickens d	971.7		0.06²† na
Cattle d	18.3 261.0		0.23
Goats d	57.0 16.3		
Horses d	15.7 19.0		0.08
Pigs d	121.0 143.0¹	1.0	3.4
Meat‡ 'A'	9.7 4.0²	0.1	0.5
Eggs	8.8		0.6
Fish	21.0 12.5	5.1	12.0
Milk	1.0* na		30.2*
6. FIBRES, TEXTILES, etc.			
Cotton lint			0.4
Silk f	na 1.0¹	1.5²	—
7. FUEL AND POWER			
Electricity h‡	652		
Petroleum, refined h t	na	na	300
	—	—	na
11. INDUSTRY			
Cement	33.3*	—	273.7* 143.3*

d no. in thousands.

j '000 cu. metres of roundwood equivalent. n in addition, black sugar 18.0 (1963–5 av.) and 19.3 (1953–5 av.). q sawn wood only.

SAN MARINO

San Marino is a small ancient republic surrounded by Italian territory. A long-established treaty of friendship and a customs union with Italy have been preserved.

AREA: 61.2 sq. km. (23.6 sq. miles)
POPULATION: 18 000 (1967 estimate)
Capital city: SAN MARINO; population: 3 817 (1964)

COMMUNICATIONS
		Year(s)
Telephones (per '000 urban population)	9.5	1967
Radio receivers (per '000 population)	169	1963–5 av.
Television licences (per '000 population)	76.5	1963–5 av.

FINANCE
Currency unit: The lira a

	1955	1938
Exchange rates		
Per $ U.S.	625	—
Per £ sterling	1 750	87.4

EMPLOYMENT, PRODUCTION AND TRADE
The principal farm products are cereals, wine and cattle. Industries include quarrying and dressing building stone, ceramics, textiles and paint manufacture. The tourist trade is considerable; 2 400 000 tourists visited the republic in 1964.

a Italian and Vatican City notes are in use, but local coins and postage stamps are issued.

SAUDI ARABIA

The Saudi Arabian Kingdom was so named in 1932, and executive power remained with the king until a cabinet system of government became effective in 1962. Agreements for trade and co-operation were signed with Kuwait in 1942 and Jordan in 1962. Revenue from oil has been used to finance a recent programme of agricultural, social and industrial development.

AREA: 2 100 000* sq. km. (810 000* sq. miles)
POPULATION: 6 990 000 (1967 U.N. estimate)
Largest city: AR RIYĀḌ (Riyadh), capital; population: 225 000 (city proper, 1965)

LAND USE: (percentage of total)
	1965	1952
Arable and orchard	0.2	0.1
Permanent meadow and pasture (mainly rough grazing)	37.7	58.0
Forest and woodland	0.8	0.3
City areas, waste and other land	61.3	41.6

COMMUNICATIONS
		Year(s)
Population per physician	13 000	1964
Population per hospital bed	1 150	1966
School enrolment: age 5–19 years (percentage)	12	1963–4 av.
age over 19 years (per 100 000 population)	24	1963–5 av.
		Year(s)
Motor vehicles in use ('000s): private	44.8	1963–5 av.
commercial	36	
Telephones (per '000 population)	0.4*	1967
Television sets (per '000 population)	3.8	1963–5 av.
Daily newspapers (per '000 population)	2.5	1962–3 av.

FINANCE
Currency unit: The riyal

	1965	1958
Exchange rates		
Per $ U.S.	4.5	3.69
Per £ sterling	12.6	10.34
	Year	
National Income (million $ U.S.)	850	1958
G.N.P. per capita ($ U.S.)	240	1966

Employment: Camels and sheep are reared by the nomadic population of the oases. Some cereal crops and fruit are grown around most of the oases. Nejd plateau. Oil is the most important industry; others include thermal electricity and cement.

TRADING
Note—data are for the Islamic lunar year of 354 days

Total trade (in million $ U.S.)	1955a	1963a	1965a
Exports (f.o.b.)	561	1 326	1 385
Imports (c.i.f.)	186	350	376

Main trading partners (percentage of total value)

Exports	1965	Imports	1965
Japan	20	U.S.A.	12
Italy	9	U.K.	12
U.S.A.	9	Japan	19
Bahrain	7	Lebanon	9
France	7	Germany F.R.	7
Australia	6	Italy	5
	5	Syria	4

Distribution of trade (percentage of total value)

	Exports 1965	Imports 1965
Crude petroleum	84	
Petroleum products	16	
Manufactured goods (machinery and transport equipment)		54 (28)
Food: cereals		28 (10)
Wood		3

a trade including the value of gold, specie and banknotes.

PRODUCTION, EXPORTS AND IMPORTS
Years: 1963–5 average and 1953–5 average Units: '000 metric tons unless otherwise indicated

	Production	Exports	Imports
1. CEREALS, etc.			
Barley	3.0	—	34.0* 5.3¹
Maize (corn)	65.0*	0.2*	22.9² 7.1
Millets/sorghum	75.5²	—	32.5* 8.3¹
Potatoes			6.6*
Rice	2.7		149.4* 20.6
Wheat	136.0		55.9* 27.3¹
2. FRUIT, etc.			
Apples			9.5*
Bananas	299.3*	3.7*	8.9²
Dates			1.4* 10.3*²
Grapes			1.0*
Lemons			1.5*
Oranges			15.3
Other citrus fruit			0.1*
Pears			0.4*
Tomatoes	59.3*		
3. BEVERAGES, FOREST PRODUCTS, etc.			
Coffee	0.1	0.1*	4.1*²
Sugar, raw			55.0* 22.5¹
Tea			3.4
Tobacco: leaf			0.41
cigarettes			0.3²
Wood			—
4. VEGETABLE OILSEEDS AND OILS			
Castor oil			0.01*
Coconut oil			0.23
Cottonseed			—
Cottonseed oil			0.04²
Groundnuts			1.40
Linseed oil			0.02*
Olive oil			0.34
Rapeseed oil			—
Sesame seed oil	0.37*	0.16	1.80²*
Soya bean oil			0.19*
5. LIVESTOCK‡, ANIMAL PRODUCTS, etc.			
Cattle d	67.0*		6.9*
Goats d	2 306.0*		
Sheep d	2 750.0*	8.1	308.4*
Horses d			
Butter	6.6*		0.7*
Cheese			1.5*
Eggs	9.9		0.8
Fish	20.5		
Milk	4.0*	0.1*	38.3*
Wool			
6. FIBRES, TEXTILES, etc.			
Agaves (sisal etc.)			0.1*
7. FUEL AND POWER			
Electricity h‡	149 n 50¹	—	—
Natural gas i	490		
Oil: crude	89 293 47 540¹	75 020 37 470¹	67
Petroleum, refined	13 900 9 740	10 367	—
9. NON-FERROUS MINERALS AND METALS			
Gold k, ore m	39.00		na
Silver k, ore m	71.70		na
11. INDUSTRY			
Aircraft a			na
Cement b	214.7*	—*	1 123.3* 700.0*
Electrical engineering a			13.0
Motor vehicles a			81.5²

d no. in thousands.

h million kWh. i million cu. metres. n incomplete figure, referring to the production in three cities only. t thermal. k '000 fine troy oz. m metal content. a million $ U.S. p incl. data for other Arabian Peninsular States.

SENEGAL

Senegal, formerly a state of French West Africa, and from 1959–60 a partner in the Federation of Mali, became an independent republic in 1960.

AREA: 197 161 sq. km. (76 124 sq. miles)

LAND USE: (percentage of total)
	1963
Arable and orchard	28.0
Forest and woodland	27.1
Permanent meadow and pasture	44.9
City areas, waste and other land	

POPULATION: 3 670 000 (1967 U.N. estimate)
Largest city: DAKAR, capital; population: 374 700 (1961)
Total working population: 1 317 580 (1960/1)

		Year(s)
Life expectancy at birth (years)		1957
Infant mortality (per '000)		1965
Population per physician	18 760	1965
Population per hospital bed	660 b	1966
School enrolment: age 5–19 years (percentage)	26	1963–4 av.
age over 19 years (per 100 000 population)	77	1964–5 av.

COMMUNICATIONS
		Year(s)
Motor vehicles in use ('000s): private	37*	1963–5 av.
commercial	90.2 a	1964
Railway track (km.)		1967
Telephones (per '000 urban population)	390	1963–5 av.
Radio licences (per '000 population)	53*	1963
Daily newspapers (per '000 population)	6	

FINANCE
Currency unit: The franc CFA

	1965	1960
Exchange rates		
Per $ U.S.	246.85	246.85
Per £ sterling	691.18	691.18
	Year	
National Income (million $ U.S.)	519	1965
G.N.P. per capita ($ U.S.)	210	1966

a in Dakar only. b government hospitals only.

Sierra Leone, previously a British protectorate, became a sovereign and independent member of the Commonwealth in 1961.

AREA: 73 326 sq. km. (27 925 sq. miles)

LAND USE: (percentage of total)

	1965	1955
Arable and orchard	51.1	50.6
Permanent meadow and pasture	30.7	30.4
Forest and woodland	4.2	4.2
City areas, waste and other land	14.0	14.8

POPULATION: 2 439 000 (1967 estimate)
Largest city: FREETOWN, capital; population: 148 000 (city proper, 1966)
Total working population: 937 737

Distribution of working population (1963)

U.N. group no.		Percentage	Year(s)
1	Agriculture, forestry, fishing and hunting	74.8	1965
2/3	Mining and quarrying	5.1	1965
4	Manufacturing	4.4	1965
5	Construction	1.2	1965
6	Electricity, gas, water and sanitary services	0.5	1965
7	Commerce	5.7	1963
8	Transport, storage and communications	3.1	1963-4 av.
9	Services	3.3	1964-5 av.
	Others		

COMMUNICATIONS		Year(s)
Infant mortality (per '000)	117.6*	1965
Crude birth rate (per '000)	43.6*	1965
Crude death rate (per '000)	18.6*	1965
Population per physician	16 440	1965
Population per hospital bed	1 210	1963
School enrolment: age 5–19 years (percentage)	16	1963-4 av.
age over 19 years (per 100 000 population)	36	1964-5 av.
Motor vehicles in use ('000s): private	9.2	1963-4 av.
commercial	4.3	
Railway track (km)	500	1964
Mail per capita: domestic	3	
foreign received	2	1963-5 av.
foreign sent	2	
Telephones (per '000 urban population)	44	1967
Radio receivers (per '000 population)	0.3	1963-5 av.
Television sets (per '000 population)	5	1963-5 av.
Daily newspapers (per '000 population)	7.5	1962-4 av.

FINANCE

Currency unit: The leone replaced the West African pound in 1964 at the rate Le1 to WA£0.5

Exchange rates	1965	1954a	1938a	1955
Per $ U.S.	0.714	0.357	0.215	
Per £ sterling	2.0	1.0	1.0	

			Year(s)
National Income (million $ U.S.)		290	1965
G.N.P. per capita ($ U.S.)		150	1966
Foreign trade (percentage of G.D.P.)		55	1963-5 av.

TRADING

Total trade (in million $ U.S.)	1965	1960a	1954a	1938
Exports (f.o.b.)	83	108	29	11
Imports (c.i.f.)	108		48	7

Main trading partners (percentage of total value)

Exports	1965	1955	Imports	1965	1955
U.K.	75	71	U.K.	33	60
Netherlands	11	7	Germany F.R.	14	2
Germany F.R.	7	12	Japan	8	2
Italy	3	—	Netherlands	6	3
France	1	6	France	4	1
U.S.A.	1	6	Germany F.R.	4	2
			Italy	4	2

Distribution of trade (percentage of total value) a

Exports	1965	1955
Diamonds	64	14
Iron ore and concentrates	19	37
Palm kernels	10	25
Coffee and cocoa	4	12
Imports		
Manufactured goods	64	59
(machinery and transport equipment)	(29)	(15)
(textiles and clothing)	(16)	(22)
Food	14	18
Crude materials and fuels	10	7
(petroleum products)	(9)	
Chemicals	5	4

a % of national exports‡ which comprised 91% of general exports in 1965 and 97% in 1955.

PRODUCTION, EXPORTS AND IMPORTS

Years: 1963-5 average and 1953-5 average   **Units:** '000 metric tons unless otherwise indicated

	Production		Exports		Imports	
1. CEREALS, etc.	1963-5	1953-5	1963-5	1953-5	1963-5	1953-5
Cassava	60.7*	37.7	—		—	
Maize (corn)	9.3*		—		—	
Millets/sorghum	23.3*	27.3	—		—	
Potatoes	—		—		1.0	0.5
Rice	324.0*	221.7	0.3		13.6	8.7
2. FRUIT, etc.						
Bananas			—		0.5	
Coconuts			—		0.1	
Oranges	91.0*		—		3.6	21.7
3. BEVERAGES, FOREST PRODUCTS, etc.						
Cocoa	3.6	3.2	3.2	2.0*	1.9	
Coffee	5.4	4.6	4.01a		1.9	
Sugar, raw			17.5			
Tobacco: leaf			1.1			
cigarettes			13.0²m		1.82	0.1²
Hardwood j	419.0 r	13.02 m	1.00m		0.22*	0.3²
Newsprint	2 688.0 l	2 647.3 l				
Other paper						
4. VEGETABLE OILSEEDS AND OILS						
Groundnuts	5.83*	3.97				0.90
Groundnut oil						na
Palm kernels	52.23	21.63m	65.93			0.55
Palm oil	37.67*		0.44			0.20
Sesame seed	na		0.27			0.97
Soya bean oil	na					
5. LIVESTOCK†, ANIMAL PRODUCTS, etc.						
Chickens d	183.3*					0.2
Cattle d	33.0*	100.0				0.2
Goats d	27.3	11.7				0.2
Sheep d	7.0*	5.0				0.1
Pigs d						5.5
Meat‡ 'A'	11.7*					13.3
Bacon/ham						
Butter						
Cheese	30.2					
Fish						
Milk					0.1	
6. FIBRES, TEXTILES, etc.						
Silk f			—		—	
Cotton: yarn			—		3.5	0.1¹
woven fabrics			—		0.3n	na
Rayon, woven fabrics					46.3	
7. FUEL AND POWER						
Coal ‡, A †, i			3n		27	
Electricity h, i	87	30¹	307		307	30¹
petroleum, refined						
8. IRON AND STEEL						
Iron ore	1 358m	716m	1 155		2 110	2 110
9. NON-FERROUS MINERALS AND METALS						
Diamonds	1 437.67 l	6 005.27 l	50.92a		0.48²	4.13²
Gold, ore						
Platinum group						
Silver, bullion					na	
Asbestos						
Aluminium: bauxite	130.39*	108.26	0.39		0.07	1.04²
Chrome, ore	0.93m		2.95		0.06	0.04²
Copper, metal			0.30		0.04	0.01
Lead, metal			19.97			
Titanium minerals						
Zircon						
10. CHEMICALS‡ AND FERTILIZERS						
Fertilizers:						
Potash						
11. INDUSTRY						
Alcoholic beverages a					1.7¹	2.4p
Cement	15.0				68.3	26.0
Electrical engineering a					6.1²	0.4²
Railway vehicles a					1.2²	1.1
Motor vehicles a					7.7²	1.1²

n data not available for years 1953–5.

SENEGAL *continued*

TRADING

Total trade (in million $ U.S.)	1965	1955a
Exports (f.o.b.)	128	92
Imports (c.i.f.)	160	197

Main trading partners (percentage of total value)

Exports	1965	Imports	1965
France	81	France	79
Germany F.R.	3	Germany F.R.	8
Malagasy R.	2		
Japan	1		
U.K. and Irish R.	1		
South Africa	1		

Distribution of trade (percentage of total value)

Exports	1965	1955a	Imports	1965
Groundnuts (incl. oil and cake)	79		Manufactured goods (textiles and clothing)	48	(16)
Natural phosphates	8		(machinery and transport equipment)		(15)
			Food (cereals)	35	(17)
			Crude materials and fuels	8	
			Chemicals	6	

a incl. data for Mali and Mauritania.

PRODUCTION, EXPORTS AND IMPORTS

Years: 1963-5 average   **Units:** '000 metric tons unless otherwise indicated

Note—no data are available for 1953-5

	Production	Exports	Imports
1. CEREALS, etc.			
Barley	—	—	3.2n
Cassava	159.3	—	1.4
Maize (corn)	45.7	—	
Millets/sorghum	536.7	—	16.0
Potatoes	5.3*	0.2	22.3
Rice	108.7	—	11.6
Sweet potatoes/yams	9.7	—	154.7
Wheat	—	0.1†	63.6
2. FRUIT, etc.			
Apples	4.0*	—	3.2n
Bananas	10.0*¹ e	—	1.4
Coconuts			1.4
Dates	—	—	
Grapes	—	—	0.5
Lemons			0.1
Oranges	3.0*	—	6.2
Other citrus fruit			0.1
Wine e	—	0.2†	114.4

b '000 hectolitres. e no. in millions. n incl. pears and quince.

	Production	Exports	Imports
3. BEVERAGES, FOREST PRODUCTS, etc.			
Coffee	—	0.5†	0.4
Sugar, raw	—	—	71.8
Tea	—	—	1.3
Tobacco: leaf	—	0.1p	0.7
cigarettes			na
Softwood j	1 560.0 r	—	6.8
Hardwood j	2 110.0	—	20.3²
Wood pulp			13.0²
Paper			
4. VEGETABLE OILSEEDS AND OILS			
Castor seed	na	0.10	
Castor oil			0.01
Groundnuts	721.70	211.70	0.06
Groundnut oil	na	125.23	
Linseed oil			0.10
Olive oil			0.02
Palm kernels	3.83	4.02	0.20
Palm oil			

	Production	Exports	Imports
5. LIVESTOCK†, ANIMAL PRODUCTS, etc.			
Chickens d	2 881.0*	—	0.3
Cattle d	1 884.7	—	
dairy cows d	949.0*	—	
Goats d	590.0*	—	
Sheep d	500.0*	—	
Horses d	111.0*	—	
Pigs d	42.0	—	0.6
Meat‡: 'A'	31.3*		0.1
'B'			
Butter			0.5
Cheese			2.1
Eggs	9.2*	—	0.2
Fish	124.5	7.1	10.8
Milk	150.7*	1.2	25.6
Hides/skins	0.31*		

d no. in thousands.

	Production	Exports	Imports
6. FIBRES, TEXTILES, etc.			
Agaves (sisal etc.)	—	—	2.0
Rubber, natural	—	—	0.3
Cotton: yarn	0.5	—	6.7
woven fabrics	1.4	—	
7. FUEL AND POWER			
Coal ‡, A	—	—	1
Electricity h, i	192	—	
Oil, crude	—	—	253
Petroleum, refined	237	—	1 010

h million kWh. i thermal.

	Production	Exports	Imports
9. NON-FERROUS MINERALS AND METALS			
Titanium minerals	4.76	5.34	—
Zirconium minerals	1.21	1.10 q	—

q zircon.

	Production	Exports	Imports
10. CHEMICALS‡ AND FERTILIZERS			
Chemicals			na
Fertilizers:			
Phosphates	798.6	582.2	
11. INDUSTRY			
Alcoholic beverages: beer b	102.0	—	2.2a
Cement r	192.0	0.7	34.3*
Electrical engineering a	na	0.4†	6.2
Railway vehicles a	na	0.2	1.0
Merchant ships a			0.1
Motor vehicles a	na	0.7†	7.6

a million $ U.S. b '000 hectolitres. g '000 G.R.T. r incl. data for Mali and Mauritania.
h million kWh. j '000 cu. metres of roundwood equivalent. p incl. other tobacco products.

na: data not available.   — negligible or nil.   ¹ one year only.   ² two year average.   * estimate.   ‡ see appendix.   † re-exports.

SINGAPORE — SOUTH EAST ASIA

Singapore, an independent state since 1959, became a state within Malaysia in 1963 but seceded two years later, regaining its sovereignty, to become an independent member of the British Commonwealth. Agreements for external defence and mutual assistance have been signed with Malaysia. Singapore's economy relies chiefly on the importance of the port as an entrepôt.

AREA: 581* sq. km. (224* sq. miles) (incl. adjacent islets)

LAND USE: (percentage of total)

	1965	1954
Arable and orchard	22.4	21.3
Permanent meadow and pasture		
Forest and woodland	20.7	26.7
City areas, waste and other land	56.9	52.0

POPULATION: 1 956 000 (1967 estimate)
Capital city: SINGAPORE

Distribution of working population (1957)
Total working population: 480 267

U.N. group no.		Percentage
0	Agriculture, forestry, fishing and hunting	8.4
1	Mining and quarrying	0.3
2/3	Manufacturing	13.9
4	Construction	5.1
5	Electricity, gas, water and sanitary services	1.2
6	Commerce	25.3
7	Transport, storage and communications	10.5
8	Services	33.2
9	Others	2.1

		Year(s)
Infant mortality (per '000)	26.3	1965
Crude birth rate (per '000)	31.1	1965
Crude death rate (per '000)	5.6	1965
Accidental deaths (per 100 000 population)	13.6	1966
caused by motor vehicles	15.2	1966
due to other causes		
Population per physician	2 020	1964
Population per hospital bed	290 a	1966
School enrolment: age 5–19 years (percentage)	82	1963–4 av.
age over 19 years (per 100 000 population)	708*	1963–5 av.

a government hospitals only.

COMMUNICATIONS

	1965	1954
Motor vehicles in use ('000s): private	98.9	20.5
commercial	26	20
Railway track (km.)	20	
Mail per capita: domestic	15	
foreign received		
foreign sent	4.9	
Telephones (per '000 urban population)	231	1967
Radio licences (per '000 population)		1963–5 av.
Television licences (per '000 population)	273.3	1963–5 av.
Daily newspapers (per '000 population)	272.3	1962–4 av.

FINANCE
Currency unit: The Singapore dollar, at par with the Malaysian dollar.

Exchange rates	1965	1960	1955
Per $ U.S.	3.06	3.06	3.06
Per £ sterling	8.57	8.57	8.57

		Year
National Income (million $ U.S.)	948	1965
G.N.P. per capita ($ U.S.)	570	1966

TRADING

Total trade (in million $ U.S.)	1965	1955a	1938a
Exports (f.o.b.)	981	583	334
Imports (c.i.f.)	1 244	745	315

Main trading partners (percentage of total value)

Exports	1965	1955a	1938a
West Malaysia	31	23	
U.K.	6	11	14
Sarawak.	6	11	6
Hong Kong	6	6	1
Sabah	4	4	1
U.S.S.R.	4	4	—
U.S.A.	4	17	30

Imports	1965	1955a	1938a
West Malaysia			
Japan			
U.K.			
China P.R.			
U.S.A.			
Sarawak.			
Australia			

Distribution of trade (percentage of total value)

Exports	1965
Crude materials and fuels	42
(rubber)	(23)
(petroleum products)	(14)
Manufactured goods	27
(machinery and transport equipment)	
Food	15
Chemicals	4

Imports	1965
Manufactured goods	38
(machinery and transport equipment)	(14)
(textiles and clothing)	
Crude materials and fuels	32
(rubber)	(15)
(petroleum products)	(13)
Food	20

a incl. West Malaysia. b incl. Taiwan and North and South Korea.

PRODUCTION
Years: 1963–5 average and 1953–5 average Units: '000 metric tons unless otherwise indicated
Note—Trade figures for Singapore are included with Malaysia.

1. CEREALS, etc. — Production
Cassava: 3.0, 4.0¹
Sweet potatoes/yams: 5.0, 7.0²

2. FRUIT, etc.
Bananas: —, 3.0¹
Coconuts e: 11.3, na

3. BEVERAGES, FOREST PRODUCTS, etc.
Tobacco: leaf 0.4
cigars: 0.1
cigarettes e: 2 496.0
e no. in millions.

5. LIVESTOCK‡, ANIMAL PRODUCTS, etc.
Chickens d: 10 212.0 b, 4 250.0² a
Cattle d: 7.0, 5.0
Dairy cows d: 5.0*, 1.0
Pigs d: 402.0, 244.0
Meat†: 'A' 15.7, 15.6²; 'B' 3.2*, 2.4*
Eggs: 9.9, 8.42
Fish: 11.2, 6.1
Milk: 1.0, 2.0²
d no. in thousands. r incl. ducks, geese and turkeys.

6. FIBRES, TEXTILES, etc.
Rubber, natural: 1.53

7. FUEL AND POWER
Electricity h t: 928
Petroleum, refined: 2 337
h million kWh. t thermal.

11. INDUSTRY
Beer b: 302.0, na
b '000 hectolitres.

continued

SOMALI REPUBLIC — EAST AFRICA

Somalia, formerly Italian Somaliland, was united with British Somaliland to form the Somali Republic in 1960.

AREA: 637 660 sq. km. (246 135 sq. miles)

LAND USE: (percentage of total)

	1960*	1955
Arable and orchard	1.5	1.5
Permanent meadow and pasture	32.3	32.3
Forest and woodland	22.6	22.6
City areas, waste and other land	43.6	43.6

POPULATION: 2 660 000 (1967 estimate)
Largest city: MOGADISCIO (Mogadishu), capital: population: 170 000 (city proper, 1966)

Employment: Livestock rearing is the chief industry of the population, 75% of the population being nomadic. The remainder of the population is engaged mainly in the production of subsistence crops.

		Year(s)
Population per physician	30 000	1960
Population per hospital bed	560	1964
School enrolment: age 5–19 years (percentage)	5	1963–4 av.
age over 19 years (per 100 000 population)	3	1963–5 av.

COMMUNICATIONS

		Year(s)
Motor vehicles in use ('000s): private	4.3	1963–5 av.
commercial	6.1	1963–5 av.
Telephones (per '000 urban population)	0.2	1967
Radio receivers (per '000 population)	12	1963–5 av.
Daily newspapers (per '000 population)	2	1964

FINANCE
Currency unit: The Somali shilling was introduced in 1960 to replace, at par, the Italian somalo and the British East African shilling.

Exchange rates	1965	1960	1958a
Per $ U.S.	7.14	7.14	7.2
Per £ sterling	20.2	20.2	20.2

		Year
National Income (million $ U.S.)	96	1958
G.N.P. per capita ($ U.S.)	50	1966

TRADING

Total trade (in million $ U.S.)	1965	1955a
Exports (f.o.b.)	33	10
Imports (c.i.f.)	50	14

Main trading partners (percentage of total value)

Exports	1965	1955a
Italy	49	78
Arab. Pen. States	39	10
U.A.R.	4	na
Kenya b	3	2
U.S.A.	2	3
Afars/Issas	1	—

Imports	1965	1955a
Italy	29	57
U.S.S.R.	8	na
Kenya b	7	16
U.K.	6	na
France	5	na
Japan	5	3
U.S.A.	na	

Distribution of trade (percentage of total value)

Exports	1965	1955a
Bananas and plantains	46	67
Livestock	29	3
Hides and skins	6	10
Wood charcoal	5	1

Imports	1965	1955a
Manufactured goods	52	56
(machinery and transport equipment)	(24)	(21)
(textiles and clothing)	(9)	(16)
Food	26	21
(rice)	(8)	(4)
Crude materials and fuels	10	12
Chemicals	5	6
Vegetable oils	4	1

a former Italian Somaliland only. b incl. Tanzania and Uganda.
a a former Italian Somaliland unless otherwise indicated.
a somalos.

PRODUCTION, EXPORTS AND IMPORTS
Years: 1963–5 average and 1953–5 average Units: '000 metric tons unless otherwise indicated
Note—the trade figures given for 1953–5 are the sum of the trade figures for the former Italian and British Somalilands; thus they include trade between these two regions, and are not, therefore, comparable with the trade figures for 1963–5.

1. CEREALS, etc. — Production | Exports | Imports
Cassava: 18.3* | na
Maize (corn): 38.0*, 36.3 | Exp. 0.3² | Imp. 4.9², 1.4
Millets/sorghum: 54.3*, 67.0 | Imp. 2.0², 3.8²
Oats: | Imp. 0.6¹, 0.5
Potatoes:
Rice: | Imp. 29.8², 6.3
Sweet potatoes/yams: 2.0*
Wheat: | Imp. 0.2²

2. FRUIT, etc.
Bananas: 141.0, 66.0 | Exp. 102.4*, 40.5
Coconuts d: 1.0*¹, 2.4*
Citrus fruit: 4.0*, 3.0 | Exp. 0.3²
Dates: na
Wine b:
e no. in millions.

3. BEVERAGES, FOREST PRODUCTS, etc.
Coffee: | Imp. 1.5², 0.9
Sugar: cane 173.7, 85.5²; refined 13.7, 8.3 | Imp. 13.8*, 1.6²
Tea: | Imp. 0.1, 7.5
Tobacco: leaf 0.1* | Imp. 3.0¹, 0.4
Softwood b:
Hardwood j: 560.3², 41.5²
Newsprint j: | Imp. 0.4²
Other paper: | Imp. 0.2²
j '000 cu. metres of roundwood equivalent. n in addition cigarettes (in millions) 47.4.

4. VEGETABLE OILSEEDS AND OILS
Coconut oil:
Cottonseed: 2.00*, 1.30 | Imp. 0.19, 0.2¹
Cottonseed oil: na | Imp. 0.03, 7.4
Groundnuts: 1.40*, 0.70 | Imp. 0.7
Groundnut oil: na | Imp. 0.62¹, 1.5
Olive oil: 0.62¹ | Imp. 0.34², 4.5
Sesame seed: 5.17*, 3.47 | Exp. 0.02† | Imp. 0.1†, 0.9

5. LIVESTOCK‡; ANIMAL PRODUCTS, etc. — Production | Exports | Imports
Chickens d: 4 000*b, 3 000*
Cattle d: 1 351*, 1 122*
Goats d: 4 565*, 4 374²* | Exp. 50.8*, 8.5
Sheep d: 3 823*, na | Exp. 858.3², na
Horses d: 4*, na
Pigs d: 22*, na
Meat†, A: na, 2* | Imp. 0.12¹, 0.21
Butter: na
Eggs: 13*, na
Fish: 5²*, na
Milk: 77*, na
Hides/skins: | Exp. 3.8², 1.8² | Imp. na, 2²*
d no. in thousands. p incl. ducks, geese and turkeys.

6. FIBRES, TEXTILES, etc.
Cotton: lint 1.0* | Exp. 3.8², 0.3 | Imp. 0.4², 0.7
woven fabrics: | Imp. 0.12¹
b '000 hectolitres.

7. FUEL AND POWER
Electricity h t: 11 | Exp. 3
Petroleum, refined: | Imp. 37, 10¹
h million kWh. t thermal.

10. NON-FERROUS MINERALS AND METALS
Beryl: 0.01 | Exp. 0.01

10. CHEMICALS n AND FERTILIZERS
Chemicals: | Imp. na
Fertilizers:
Phosphates: | Exp. 0.2 b
n data not available for years 1953–5. p guano.

11. INDUSTRY
Aircraft a: | Imp. 0.2¹
Alcoholic beverages a: 2.00*, 1.30 | Imp. 0.4, 7.4
Cement: na | Imp. 38.3
Electrical engineering a: 1.40*, 0.70 | Imp. na
Motor vehicles a: na | Imp. 1.5, 0.4
Beer b: 5.17*, 3.47 | Imp. 0.1†, 4.5, 0.9
a million $ U.S. b beer and wine only.

---

na: data not available. — negligible or nil. * estimate. ‡ see appendix. 1 one year only. 2 two year average. † re-exports.

SOUTH AFRICA

The Union of South Africa withdrew from the British Commonwealth in 1961 to become the Republic of South Africa. In 1966 the U.N. General Assembly terminated South Africa's trusteeship of South West Africa, but South Africa continues to administer the territory.

AREA: 1 221 042 sq. km. (471 445 sq. miles) (excl. South West Africa)
a see South West Africa.

LAND USE: (percentage of total)

	1960	1954
Arable and orchard	9.9	7.5
Permanent meadow and pasture	74.0	75.7
Forest and woodland	1.3	0.9
City areas, waste and other land	14.8	15.9

POPULATION: 18 733 000 (1967 estimate)
Largest city: JOHANNESBURG; population: 1 152 525 (1960)
Administrative capital: PRETORIA; population: 422 590 (1960)
Legislative capital: CAPE TOWN; population: 807 221 (1960)

Distribution of working population (1960)
Total working population: Africans and Asians 4 551 361
Europeans 1 140 469
U.N. group no.

Distribution of working population

		Africans c and Asians	Europeans	Year
0	Agriculture, forestry, fishing and hunting	34.9	10.3	1960
1	Mining and quarrying	11.9	5.5	
2/3	Manufacturing	9.9	20.1	
4	Construction	4.5		
5	Electricity, gas, water and sanitary services	0.6	0.9	
6	Commerce	4.9	20.5	
7	Transport, storage and communications	2.0	10.7	
8	Services	21.4	22.1	
9	Others	9.9	3.6	

	Africans c	Asians	Europeans	Year
Life expectancy at birth (years): male	49.6*	57.7*	64.7*	1960
female	54.3*	59.6*	71.7*	1960
Infant mortality (per '000)	134.0	55.9	24.5	1965
Crude birth rate (per '000)	44.2	32.3	24.0	1965
Crude death rate (per '000)	15.2	7.7	9.0	1965
Accidental deaths (per 100 000 population)	43.8	26.9	38.6	1966
caused by motor vehicles	42.5	19.6	28.0	1963
Population per physician			1900 b	1962
Population per hospital bed			190 b	1963
School enrolment: age 5–19 years (percentage)	69 b		329 a b	1965
age over 19 years (per 100 000 population)				1967

COMMUNICATIONS

		Year(s)
Motor vehicles in use ('000s): private	1 016	1963–5 av.
commercial	262	1962
Railway track (km.)	21 203	
Mail per capita: domestic	53	1964–5 av.
foreign received	6.9	
foreign sent		1967
Telephones (per '000 urban population)	126	1963–5 av.
Radio receivers (per '000 population)	57	1961
Daily newspapers (per '000 population)		

FINANCE

Currency unit: The rand replaced the South African pound in 1961 at the rate R1 to SA £0.5

Exchange rates

	1965	1960 a	1950 a	1938 a
Per $ U.S.	0.714	0.357	0.357	0.215
Per £ sterling	2.0	1.0	1.0	1.0

National Income (million $ U.S.)

	1965		Year(s)
G.N.P. per capita ($ U.S.)	8 900 b		1965
Rate of increase of G.N.P. per capita	550 b		1966
Foreign trade (percentage of G.D.P.)	3.5 b c		1960–4 av.
	36		1963–5 av.

a South African pounds. b incl. South West Africa. c incl. Botswana, Lesotho and Swaziland.

TRADING

Total trade (in million $ U.S.)

	1965	1955	1938
Exports excluding gold (f.o.b.)	1 485	1 033	157
Exports of gold (f.o.b.)	1 074	497	355
Imports (c.i.f.)	2 459	1 350	463

Main trading partners (percentage of total value of total value excl. gold)

Exports	1965	1955	1938	Imports	1965	1955	1938
U.K.	34	34	77	U.K.	28	31	39
U.S.A.	7			U.S.A.	17	9	21
Japan	7	5	2	Germany F.R.	11	6	15 d
Germany F.R.	4	5	1	Japan	6	4	1
Italy	4	5	7 d	Italy	4	4	1
Belg./Lux.	4	4		Canada	4	3	1
France	3	4	3	France	3	1	1

Distribution of trade (percentage of total value excl. gold)

Exports	1965	1955	1938 b
Crude materials and fuels (textile fibres)	34	(13)	(34)
(metalliferous ores)		(10)	(na)
Manufactured goods (textiles and clothing)	34	(13)	(9)
(diamonds)	23	(13)	20	(7*)
(fruit and vegetables)		(11)	27	(12)
Imports			
Manufactured goods (machinery and transport equipment)	73	(42)	(16)
(textiles and clothing)		(9)	(21)
Crude materials and fuels	13	(19*)	na	(9)
Food	7	(13*)	5	4
		5	6

a 1938 figures are percentages of the value excl. gold; government stores and trade with South West Africa and Zambia. b incl. Germany D.R. d incl. Germany D.R.

PRODUCTION, EXPORTS AND IMPORTS

Units: '000 metric tons unless otherwise indicated
Years: 1963–5 average and 1953–5 average

1. CEREALS, etc.

	Production		Exports		Imports	
	1963–5 av.	1953–5 av.				
Barley	35.7	55.0*	2.8	13.9	—	—
Maize (corn)	4 956.7 n	3 409.7	1 410.3	406.2	—	—
Millets/sorghum	337.3*	163.3	103.6	42.0	—	0.1
Oats	120.0	184.0 i	15.0	16.7	—	—
Potatoes	417.3*		4.0	8.8	—	—
Rice	2.0*	8.0 i	0.3	0.3 z	60.2	18.0
Rye	13.3	na	—	—	na	—
Sweet potatoes/yams	61.0*	na	—	—	—	—
Wheat	875.3	657.0	—	0.6	155.0	234.7

2. FRUIT, etc.

	Production		Exports		Imports	
Apples	139.7*	56.0*	79.8	18.4	0.2†	—
Apricots	30.3	21.7*	0.6	0.6	9.7	2.2 q
Bananas	57.7	na	na	0.4	7.3	1.4
Coconuts					2.2 q	1.3
Dates						
Figs	1.0*	1.0 i	28.7	18.2	—	—
Grapes	721.3*	502.3*	247.4	25.6	—	—
Lemons	22.0*	4.0	93.0	43.5	0.4	0.1
Oranges	462.7*	258.0	262.4	173.9	—	—
Other citrus fruit	51.7*	14.3	27.7*	10.9	—	—

continued

2. FRUIT, etc.—continued

	Production		Exports		Imports	
Peaches	122.7*	49.8*	na	1.9	—	—
Pears	60.7*	26.0* p	na	19.6	—	—
Pineapples	111.0*	74.3*	na	3.5	—	—
Plums	12.0*	8.6	3.3	3.2	—	—
Raisins	140.0	na	187.1	128.3	23.9	2.3
Tomatoes	4 008.5 2	2 896.0*				
Wine e	4 215.0²	2 150.0* b				

b '000 hectolitres. e '000 hectolitres. desiccated coconut. p total handled by the Deciduous Fruit Board. q incl.

3. BEVERAGES, FOREST PRODUCTS, etc.

	Production		Exports		Imports	
Cocoa			0.4†		—	—
Coffee	9 668.7	6 532.3	513.4	190.2	3.3	—
Sugar: cane raw	1 259.7	754.0	43.7*	1.2	10.8	—
Tea			7.7		18.7	0.2
Tobacco: leaf	11 535.0	10 038.0²			16.5	1.7
cigarettes	2 468.2²	2 150.0*	1.0		2.4	2.0
tobacco/snuff	204.0	43.7*	9.4	134.6	na	na
Softwood	99.5²	na			318.8	463.7*
Wood pulp	330.5²	85.0*	11.2		464.0	10.8
Newsprint					16.5	0.2
Other paper					23.9	46.3
					52.7	6.5
					153.3	113.0*

continued

PRODUCTION, EXPORTS AND IMPORTS *continued*

4. VEGETABLE OILSEEDS AND OILS

	Production		Exports		Imports	
Castor seed	12.67	5.79	1.37	0.14	0.13	0.23
Castor oil	na	na	—	—	0.11	0.11
Copra	na	na	—	—	0.17	0.17
Coconut oil	26.00*	11.00	—	0.47	7.70	6.87
Cottonseed	157.73	142.80	—	—	0.05	—
Cottonseed oil			55.51	27.60	0.04²	0.04
Groundnuts	55.51		9.50	16.63	0.03²	0.03
Groundnut oil	9.50				5.45	6.11
Linseed	0.17 s		0.17 s	0.05 s	5.11	6.13
Linseed oil					1.91	2.59
Olive oil						1.16
Palm kernel oil					0.05	—
Palm oil	2.70*		3.41	3.76	0.76	0.24 n
Soya beans	84.00	55.67	0.73	0.24		—
Soya bean oil					0.35²	—
Sunflower seed						
Sunflower seed oil						
Tung oil						

s incl. maize oil. s incl. re-exports.

5. LIVESTOCK‡, ANIMAL PRODUCTS, etc.

	Production		Exports		Imports	
Chickens d	11 168.7*	15 840.0*				
Cattle d	12 366.7*	11 629.5²	11.6	26.5	0.6	103.2
dairy cows d	3 805.0*	2 908.0¹ n				
Goats d	5 288.0*	5 482.0²	6.3	na		
Sheep d	38 233.3*	36 567.0²				
Horses d	460.0*	na	0.1	3.9	0.3	2.5
Pigs d	1 440.0*	514.0²	0.6	2.1 p	0.3	2.2
Bacon/ham	663.0*	390.5² q	15.6	5.4		
Meat‡: A	130.8*	98.5² q	1.2	4.3	6.7	2.2
B	42.7	37.3	3.9	1.1	1.5	0.2
Butter	70.4*	40.1²	7.3	75.4*		
Cheese	621.3	363.8	357.8	5.1	5.1	15.2* a
Eggs	2 526.7*	2 058.5	0.9		31.2	1.5
Fish	30.5					
Milk	67.2*	64.7	24.6 a	31.5	1.2 a	4.3
Whale oil			62.8	57.6	3.5	
Hides/skins						
Wool						

d no. in thousands. n on farms and estates only. q government inspected meat only. canned bacon. w canned meat.

6. FIBRES, TEXTILES, etc.

	Production		Exports		Imports	
Abaca						
Agaves (sisal etc.)	1.8*	na	—	—	0.6	1.4* a
Cotton lint	13.0*	5.7	0.6	0.2	5.1	5.3
Flax fibre			—	—	23.9	2.5
Hemp fibre						1.4
Jute	2.7*	na	0.1†		0.6²	16.2*
Rubber: natural			0.3		26.3	27.3
synthetic	7.3	7.7* a	0.1		19.6²	4.1
Cotton: yarn	38.2	1.1*			15.6	4.2
woven fabrics	11.0¹		0.2*†		31.1²	24.1
Rayon: fibre/yarn					8.7	5.8
woven fabrics						16.3
Non-cellulosic fibre/yarn	2.7²	11.4¹	0.1²		9.0	1.3
Wool: yarn	9.8	15.0¹*	0.1²		1.3	11.9
woven fabrics	4.0*					

r million metres.

7. FUEL AND POWER

	Production		Exports		Imports	
Coal, 'A'‡.	45 287	32 150	1 375	1 059 p	57	15²
Coke, 'A'‡.	29 900*	14 770¹	2	6	11	na
Electricity h: total	40	8¹				
hydro	29 860*	14 770¹				
thermal						
Oil, crude						
Petroleum, refined	3 803	850¹	353	80¹	3 903	940¹
Rare earths (monazite) f	3 062	3 353 w	3 765¹ v	45 a	1 813	2 280 p
Uranium¹.						

h million kWh. u 1956 data. v incl. bunkers. f '000 hectolitres.

8. IRON AND STEEL

	Production		Exports		Imports	
Iron ore	3 482 n	1 223 m	1 022	3	—	—
Pig iron	2 973	1 240	555	35	—	—
Steel ingots/castings	3 090	1 417	2	62	1	2
Iron/steel products dr					77	41

dr m metal content. m metal content.

---

9. NON-FERROUS MINERALS AND METALS

	Production		Exports		Imports	
Diamonds	4 590.33¹	2 714.32¹	142.63 a	105.37 a¹	0.42 n	28.72 a
Gold/coins etc.	29 032.70¹	13 259.70¹	—	—	—	—
bullion/coins etc.	29 889.67¹	12 909.70¹	6.13	6.13	—	—
Platinum group metals f			13.68¹ a	301.67	0.29	
Silver k, ore	554.37	346.44	2 050.69 p	0.24 p	47.755 p	169.73 p
Asbestos: fibre	2 928.70 m	1 296.30 m	110.56 q		6.58²	0.722 a
manufactured	200.21¹	97.87	212.94	1.21 a	2.41 a	0.04
Mica	2.51	2.46	0.87 a	3.09	0.63	na
Aluminium: bauxite			2.12	—	8.27	—
alumina			—	—	0.52	—
aluminium			—	—	25.03 r	5.60*
Antimony, ore	12.25 m	8.52 m	1.17² a¹	0.85†	0.321 v	0.18 v
Beryl	0.19	0.26	20.29	14.40	63.87²	
Chrome, ore	861.26 m	635.88 m	0.15	0.26	5.57²	13.94²
Copper ore	58.36 m	41.04 m	648.02	483.73	36.26	na
metal	54.50	39.68	84.32²	37.59		10.96²
Lead: ore	0.02 m	0.39² m	2.75 m	1.11 m		
metal			0.07			
Magnesite	47.97	0.12	47.97	0.12		
Magnesite/salts	89.98	na	3.36	0.08*	31.17²	9.63
Manganese: ore	1 398.43	705.97	943.65	523.07²	0.557²	—
metal	124.33		124.33			0.72
Mercury f	2.63	2.00	—	1.62	25.90	34.90²
Nickel: ore m	1.60 m	1.34 m	0.922	1.21		—
metal	1.00	0.80	1.30	0.51¹	0.61	0.34
Tin: ore	9.80	0.87²	10.40	0.57		
metal	0.01	0.30 u	0.01	0.40 a	—	17
Titanium minerals	1.27 m		2.08 u		—	—
Tungsten, ore			0.18¹		—	—
Vanadium	0.80		0.87	0.08¹	40.09	20.95¹
Zinc, metal						
Zirconium minerals						

a million $ U.S. f metric tons. k '000 fine troy oz. f '000 carats. m metal data for Swaziland and Bechuanaland. r excl. aluminium sulphates. content. n cut and polished diamonds only. p bullion. u vanadium-oxide. w waste. l middlings. v metal. w waste.

10. CHEMICALS‡ AND FERTILIZERS

Organic chemicals:

	Production		Exports		Imports	
Benzene	na	na	—	—	na	na
Butadiene	na	na	—	—	na	na
Ethylene	na	na	—	—	na	na
Methanol	na	na	—	—	0.31	na
Phenol	na	na	—	—	na	na
Phthalic anhydride	na	na	—	—	1.8²	na
Styrene monomer			0.2¹		24.5¹	
Urea	35.01*		0.2¹			

Inorganic chemicals:

	Production		Exports		Imports	
Ammonia	na	na	—	—	—	7.6²
Carbon black			0.4¹		—	—
Chlorine			0.1¹		88.7²	
Nitric acid					10.6	
Sodium carbonate						
Sodium hydroxide	35.01*		7.5¹			
Sulphuric acid						

Plastics:

	Production		Exports		Imports	
Polyamides	na	na	na		na	20.8
Polyethylene	5.0¹		0.1²			8.1²
Polyvinyl chloride			0.6¹			

Fertilizers:

	Production		Exports		Imports	
Phosphates	547.6	103.6	12.0	—	265.6	323.5 z
Potash			—	—	108.3	24.8
Pyrites	172.7 x	88.4 x	3.8²	0.1		
Sulphur	5.0 y	na	—	—	154.2	69.9²

x sulphur content. y recovered sulphur only. z incl. South West Africa. n data not available for years 1953–5.

11. INDUSTRY

	Production		Exports		Imports	
Aircraft a	na	na	—	—	18.0	4.4 a
Alcoholic beverages: beer b	1 422.0	959.0²	7.2 a	8.0 a	7.3 a	na
spirits b	177.0 n	285.0 p				
Cement	3 405.7	2 207.3	41.0	35.0	33.7 q	26.7 q
Electrical engineering a	253.1²	158.0*			133.1	42.3²
Locomotives a			6.4		na	—
Railway vehicles a			1.7		17.3	6.5
Machine tools a			0.1		27.3	—
Merchant ships g			na		20.0	—
Motor vehicles commercial dr	43.5		5.8	13.1²	275.8	7.2²
private dr	130.0					

a million $ U.S. d no. in thousands. dr '000 units. g '000 G.R.T. n assembly of imported parts. q 1962 data. q incl. data for South West Africa.

209

na: data not available. — *negligible or nil.* — *negligible or nil.* ¹ *one year only.* ² *two year average.* * *estimate.* † *re-exports.* ‡ *see appendix.*

a no. in millions. i '000 cu. metres of roundwood equivalent.

SOUTH WEST AFRICA

Since 1920 South West Africa has been administered by South Africa in whose parliament it is represented. In 1968 the U.N. General Assembly proclaimed that South West Africa should in future be known as Namibia, and it urged the immediate termination of the South African administration of the territory, but this has not yet (1971) been effected.

Walvis Bay (980 sq. km.), the main trading port, is an integral part of South Africa, but is administered by South West Africa.

AREA: 824 295 sq. km. (318 261 sq. miles) (excl. Walvis Bay)

LAND USE: (percentage of total)

	1960	1954
Arable and orchard	0.8	0.1
Permanent meadow and pasture	64.2	62.0
Forest and woodland	6.4	
City areas, waste and other land	28.6	31.8

POPULATION: 594 000 (1967 U.N. estimate)
Capital city: WINDHOEK; population: 36 051 (1960)

Distribution of working population (1960)
Total working population: 203 323

U.N. group no.		Percentage
0	Agriculture, forestry, fishing and hunting	58.5
1	Mining and quarrying	5.9
2/3	Manufacturing	4.3
4	Construction	6.1
5	Electricity, gas, water and sanitary services	0.4
6	Commerce	6.1
7	Transport, storage and communications	3.2
8	Services	11.9
9	Others	5.4

COMMUNICATIONS

		Year
Motor vehicles in use ('000s)	41.5	1966
Railway track (km.)	2338	1964
Telephones (per '000 urban population)	4.4	1967
Daily newspapers (per '000 population)	12	1964

FINANCE
Currency unit: The South African rand

TRADE
90% of the trade is with South Africa.

	Africans	Europeans	Year
Infant mortality (per '000)	111.1*	39.1*	1964
Crude birth rate (per '000)	57.3*	23.0	1964
Crude death rate (per '000)	15.2	6.9	1964
School enrolment: age 5–19 years (percentage)	36a		1963

a Africans and Europeans.

PRODUCTION, EXPORTS AND IMPORTS
Years: 1963–5 average and 1953–5 average   Units: '000 metric tons unless otherwise indicated

1. CEREALS, etc.
	Production		Exports		Imports	
Maize (corn)	9.3*	23.0[1]	—		na	
Millets/sorghum	15.0*	17.3	—		na	
Potatoes			—		0.8[1]	0.1[1]
Rice			na		0.1	0.1
Wheat n	1.0*	1.0[2]	0.2†	—2	1.5²†	0.3, 12.3m

n wheat flour.

2. FRUIT, etc.
	Production	Exports	Imports
Apples			0.1
Bananas			0.3
Grapes			0.2
Oranges			0.4
Raisins			0.1
Wine b			4.7

3. BEVERAGES, FOREST PRODUCTS, etc.
	Production	Exports	Imports
Coffee			0.1
Sugar, raw			5.5
Tea			0.1
Softwood j			24.3²
Hardwood j	168.0²		0.1
Newsprint			0.2
Other paper			0.2

j '000 cu. metres of roundwood equivalent.

4. VEGETABLE OILSEEDS AND OILS
	Production	Exports	Imports
Groundnut oil			0.04
Linseed oil			0.02

5. LIVESTOCK‡, ANIMAL PRODUCTS, etc.
	Production		Exports	Imports
Chickens d	314.0*	180.0		
Cattle d	2 291.3	1 550.0	109.0	
Goats d	1 533.0*	533.3		
Sheep d	3 621.0	3 266.7		
Pigs d	19.0*	23.3		3.3
Horses d	64.0*	36.0		
Meat‡, 'A'	3.3	4.3		3.3, 1.7
Butter				0.1
Cheese				0.1*
Eggs	0.1*	0.1		0.1
Fish	634.8 p	259.9 p	76.3*	
Milk	60.0*	115.5²	2.2	1.1
Wool	4.0*			

d no. in thousands. p incl. ducks, geese and turkeys. p incl. fish landed in Walvis Bay.

7. FUEL AND POWER
	Production	Exports	Imports
Coal, 'A' ‡			0.8[1]
Electricity h ‡	188		0.1[2]
Petroleum, refined			1.5²†

h million kWh. t thermal.

8. IRON AND STEEL
	Production	Exports	Imports
Iron ore	na	—2m	—

m metal content.

9. NON-FERROUS MINERALS AND METALS
	Production		Exports		Imports
Diamonds h	1 464.00 l	699.38 l	1 328.67 l	35.91 a	
Silver h, ore m	1 373.30	951.70	474.84	1 279.21	
Asbestos, manufactured					
Mica	0.35	na	0.31		
Aluminium	0.04	0.49	0.02	0.43	
Beryl	0.01	0.64	0.36	0.47	
Cadmium					
Copper: ore m	35.66	15.91	8.87	15.45	
metal	26.33				
Lead: ore m	85.89	73.53	57.22	66.56	
metal	38.55				
Manganese, ore	1.27	35.26	37.74	29.35²	
Mercury f					
Tin, ore	0.45m	0.33m	0.36	0.45	
Tungsten, ore	0.19	0.13	0.88*	0.54	
Vanadium, ore	1.06	0.56	35.13m	18.42	
Zinc, ore	31.74m	17.81m			

a million $ U.S. f metric tons. k '000 fine troy oz. l '000 carats. m metal content.

10. CHEMICALS n AND FERTILIZERS
	Production	Exports	Imports
Chemicals.			0.4
Fertilizers:			
Phosphates	1.07 p	0.5, 1.2	na

n data not available for years 1953–5. p guano. y see South Africa.

11. INDUSTRY
	Production	Exports	Imports
Beer b			3.3
Cement	60.0		

b '000 hectolitres. y see South Africa.

SOUTHERN YEMEN

The Federation of South Arabia was overrun by the forces of the National Liberation Front in 1967 and was declared the Southern Yemen People's Republic. The last of the British troops and civilians left Aden (formerly a British colony) the same year. The name was amended in 1970 to 'The People's Democratic Republic of Yemen'.

AREA: 160 300 sq. km. (61 890 sq. miles)

LAND USE: (percentage of total)

	1965	1945
Arable and orchard	0.9	0.4
Permanent meadow and pasture (rough grazing)	31.3	62.0
Forest and woodland (mainly scrub)	8.9	
City areas, waste and other land	58.9	37.6

POPULATION: 1 170 000 (1967 estimate)
Largest city: ADEN; population: 225 000 (1964)
Capital city: MADINET AL SHAAB (formerly Al Ittihad)

		Year(s)
Infant mortality (per '000)	75.8a	1965
Crude birth rate (per '000)	38.4a	1965
Crude death rate (per '000)	8.2a	1965
Population per physician	2140a	1966
Population per hospital bed	780a	1964
School enrolment: age 5–19 years (percentage)	46a	1963–4 av.

a Aden State only.

COMMUNICATIONS

		Year(s)
Motor vehicles in use ('000s): private	11.8	1963–5 av.
commercial	2.8	1963–5 av.
Telephones (per '000 urban population)	0.7	1967
Radio receivers (per '000 population)	217	1963–5 av.

FINANCE
Currency unit: The South Arabian dinar, at par with the pound sterling, was introduced in 1965.

Exchange rates

	1965	1960a	1956a
Per $ U.S.	0.357	7.14	7.2
Per £ sterling	1.0	20.0	20.0

a East African shillings, used in Aden.

EMPLOYMENT, PRODUCTION AND TRADE

Extensive irrigation in recent years now enables cash crops of fruit and vegetables to be grown, and in particular the Abyan long-staple cotton, which has (1970) become the country's major export. Subsistence grain-crops are also grown in the higher areas. In the drier parts, nomadic communities live by herding livestock.

The importance of Aden as a bunkering station was greatly reduced by the closure of the Suez Canal.

TRADING

Total trade (in million $ U.S.)	1965	1955a	1938
Exports (f.o.b.)	190	177	16
Imports (c.i.f.)	301	198	30

Main trading partners (percentage of total value)

Exports	1965	1955a	Imports	1965	1955a
U.K.	21	17	Iran	11	3
Yemen	7	11	Japan	11	5
Japan	7	11	U.K.	9	9
South Africa	4	11	Kuwait	7	31
Afars/Issas	3	4	India	4	7
Australia	3		Trucial States	4	na
			Qatar	3	na

Distribution of trade (percentage of total value)

Exports	1965	1955a
Crude materials and fuels b (petroleum products)	84	na
Food	9	10*
Manufactured goods	4	7*

Imports	1965	1955a
Crude materials and fuels (petroleum and products)	43 (39)	(44)
Manufactured goods (textiles and clothing)	33 (12)	na
Food	18 (8)	na

a Aden State (former Aden Colony) only. b incl. ships' bunkers.

PRODUCTION, EXPORTS AND IMPORTS
Years: 1963–5 average and 1953–5 average   Units: '000 metric tons unless otherwise indicated

1. CEREALS, etc.
	Production		Exports		Imports	
Barley					0.1	—
Maize (corn)	25.0		6.6	0.4†	12.7	33.7
Millets/sorghum			9.7		7.3	12.9
Potatoes			18.5†	12.0†	29.4	2.7
Rice			14.3	0.5	37.8	16.2
Wheat	8.3	4.7				3.0

2. FRUIT, etc.
	Production	Exports	Imports
Apples			1.8
Coconuts	8.0	0.1†	13.7
Dates			10.9*, 10.5*²
Grapes			
Oranges		0.1†	1.5, 0.3
Other citrus fruit			
Pears			0.3, 0.2
Wine b		0.1†	0.7, 0.6

b '000 hectolitres.

3. BEVERAGES, FOREST PRODUCTS, etc.
	Production	Exports	Imports
Coffee		4.6, 8.0	4.4, 9.3
Sugar, raw		17.6†, 16.9†	53.2, 26.8
Tobacco: leaf		1.5†, 1.6²†	2.0, 1.0
products		0.2†	4.4, 3.7
Hardwood j		20.0†, 0.2²	1.2², 1.1²
Other paper			0.8[1]

j '000 cu. metres of roundwood equivalent.

4. VEGETABLE OILSEEDS AND OILS
	Production	Exports	Imports
Coconut oil		0.07†, 0.04†	0.28, 1.01
Cottonseed	11.70	9.44, 3.75²	
Cottonseed oil	7.00		0.49, 0.26†
Groundnuts		na	0.16, na
Groundnut oil		0.01†, 0.09†	0.68, 0.37
Linseed oil			0.04, 0.08
Olive oil			0.11, 0.02
Sesame seed	0.90	—²	0.12, 0.40²
Soya bean oil	1.20		na

5. LIVESTOCK‡, ANIMAL PRODUCTS, etc.
	Production	
Cattle d	71.7*	68.0
Goats d	802.0*	855.0
Sheep d	202.3*	200.0
Horses d	0.9	333.9

5. LIVESTOCK‡, ANIMAL PRODUCTS, etc.—continued
	Production		Exports		Imports	
Bacon/ham					0.2	0.5
Meat‡, 'A'			1.6†	0.31†	0.2, 0.9	0.2, 1.9
'B'					0.7	0.1
Butter					7.8	0.9
Cheese					0.9	0.2
Eggs			4.7	7.1*	2.4	4.51*
Fish	53.1	54.2	1.5†	0.8†	33.4	4.6
Milk	na	na	3.7²a	6.4²a	2.4a	8.02a

a million $ U.S. d no. in thousands. e no. in millions.

6. FIBRES, TEXTILES, etc.
	Production		Exports		Imports	
Cotton: lint	6.0	5.2	2.7	8.0²	0.1	5.0²
woven fabrics					5.8	9.4
Rayon, woven fabrics					3.7[1]n	1.7

n incl. synthetic piece goods.

7. FUEL AND POWER
	Production		Exports		Imports	
Coal, 'A' ‡						
Coke						
Electricity h	194²	100[1]			1[1]	31
Natural gas i	10					
Oil, crude						
Petroleum, refined	6 640	4 050[1]	4 107	1 930[1]	6 760, 1 487	na, 980[1]

h million kWh. i million cu. metres. t thermal.

8. IRON AND STEEL
	Production	Exports	Imports
Iron/steel scrap		1	—

9. NON-FERROUS MINERALS AND METALS
	Production	Exports	Imports
Asbestos			0.21, na
Aluminium, manufactured			0.23, 1.24
Tin, metal			0.19

11. INDUSTRY
	Production	Exports	Imports
Alcoholic beverages a			
Cement		5.0*†	1.2[1], na
Electrical engineering a			109.0*, 40.7
Motor vehicles a		1.4²†, 1.6[1]	11.8, 8.3²

a million $ U.S.

continued

na: data not available. — negligible or nil. * estimate. † re-exports. ‡ see appendix. [1] one year only. [2] two year average.

SPAIN

The current regime in Spain was established at the conclusion of the Spanish Civil War, in 1939, with General Franco as Head of the Spanish State.
Islas Canarias (Canary Islands), the Islas Baleares (Balearic Islands) and Morocco, and the North African towns Ceuta and Melilla.

AREA: 504 748 sq. km. (194 883 sq. miles)

LAND USE: (percentage of total)

	1965	1955
Arable and orchard.	40.8	39.7
Permanent meadow and pasture	28.1	19.0
Forest and woodland (incl. some rough grazing)	23.0	27.4
City areas, waste and other land	8.1	13.9

POPULATION: 32 140 000 (1967 estimate)
Largest city: MADRID, capital; population: 2 599 330 (1965)

Distribution of working population (1965)
Total working population: 12 183 600a

U.N. group no.		Percentage
0	Agriculture, forestry, fishing and hunting	34.5
1	Mining and quarrying	1.4
2/3	Manufacturing	24.3
4	Construction	7.9
5	Electricity, gas, water and sanitary services	0.8
6	Commerce	11.6
7	Transport, storage and communications	4.8
8	Services	14.3
9	Others	0.4

a based on a labour force sample survey.

		Year(s)
Life expectancy at birth (years): male	67.3	1960
female	71.9	
Infant mortality (per '000)	37.8	1965
Crude birth rate (per '000)	21.3	1965
Crude death rate (per '000)	8.6	1965
Accidental deaths (per 100 000 population)	9.8	1965
caused by motor vehicles	19.9	1965
Population per physician	800	1966
Population per hospital bed	320	1966
School enrolment: age 5–19 years (percentage)	70	1963–4 av.
age over 19 years (per100 000 population)	386	1964–5 av.

COMMUNICATIONS

		Year(s)
Motor vehicles in use ('000s): private	644.2	1963–5 av.
commercial	304.6	1966
Railway track (km.)	18 942	1966
Mail per capita: domestic	68	1963–5 av.
foreign received	8	
Telephones (per '000 urban population)	9.6	1967
Radio receivers (per '000 population)	133.4	1963–5 av.
Television sets (per '000 population)	131.5	1962–3 av.

FINANCE

Currency unit: The peseta

Exchange rates

	1965	1950	1938
Per $ U.S.	59.99	11.22	9.10
Per £ sterling	167.97	31.42	41.86

				Year(s)
National Income (million $ U.S.)		18 765		1965
G.N.P. per capita ($ U.S.)		640		1966
Foreign trade (percentage of G.D.P.)		18		1963–5 av.

TRADING

	1965	1955	1935
Total trade (in million $ U.S.)			
Exports (f.o.b.)	967	446	191
Imports (c.i.f.)	3 004	617	286

Main trading partners (percentage of total value)

Exports	1965	1955	1935		Imports	1965	1955	1935
Germany F.R.	14	15	13d		U.S.A.	18	19	17
U.K.	11	13	16		Germany F.R.	18	19	14d
U.S.A.	11	11	10		France	11	10	6
France	9	8	9		U.K.	11	11	6
Netherlands	6	5	5		Italy	4	3	4
Cuba	4	4	2		Netherlands	4	3	na
Italy	3		3		Saudi Arabia	3	na	

Distribution of trade (percentage of total value)

Export	1965	1955	1935*
Food (fruit and vegetables)	40	45	53 (38)
Manufactured goods	33	18	na (1)
(machinery and transport equipment)		(10)	
Crude materials and fuels	11	8	na
Chemicals	9	5	7
Wine	4	4	na
Imports			
Manufactured goods	49	38	26 (16)
(machinery and transport equipment)	(27)	(25)	(1)
(iron and steel)	(9)	(5)	
Crude materials and fuels	23	40	na (5)
(petroleum and products)	(9)	(15)	
Food (cereals)	14	7	12 (—)
Chemicals	9	5	9 (1*)	13

d incl. Germany D.R.

PRODUCTION, EXPORTS AND IMPORTS Units: '000 metric tons unless otherwise indicated
Years: 1963–5 average and 1953–5 average

	Production		Exports		Imports	
	1963–5	1953–5				
1. CEREALS, etc.						
Barley.	1 800.0	1 800.0	—	—	558.8	41.8
Maize (corn)	1 172.0	691.3	0.1	0.4	1 223.5	27.1d
Millets/sorghum	41.0	41.0	0.3	0.3	30.3	0.9
Oats	408.7	488.7	—	—	0.3	—
Rice	473.0	391.7	124.2	72.2	213.9	56.6
Rye	382.3	394.3	64.7	55.3	0.8	—
Sweet potatoes/yams	75.0	135.3	—	0.2	—	—
Wheat.	4 521.7	3 947.3	—	—	140.1	424.3

2. FRUIT, etc.						
Apples	417.7	246.3	0.1	0.2	0.2	—
Bananas	140.3	60.3	na	12.1	—	—
Bananas	359.0	106.8n	172.5m	—	2.9	67.7
Cherries	54.7	34.9	—	1.1	—	
Dates	14.7	7.0	—	1.1	—	—
Figs	145.0	170.0	—	1.1	—	—
Grapes	4 646.0	3 116.0	92.1	42.4	0.1	—
Lemons	111.3	44.7	34.7	35.9	—	—
Oranges	1 891.3	1 759.0	1 054.0	937.6	0.2	0.1
Other citrus fruit	42.0	2.0	2.8	0.6	—	—
Olives	1 771.3	1 645.3	—	—	—	—
Peaches	151.3	105.0	na	na	—	—
Pears	162.0	77.0	14.9	0.8	—	—
Raisins	75.3	51.8	4.9	5.0	—	—
Tomatoes	1 343.7	816.0	—	—	—	—
Wineb	28 864.1	19 270.0	2 007.6	1 266.7	2.0	0.7

b '000 hectolitres. m produced mainly in the Canary Islands.

EUROPE

PRODUCTION, EXPORTS AND IMPORTS continued

	Production		Exports		Imports	
4. VEGETABLE OILSEEDS AND OILS—continued						
Olive oil	374.67	303.33	65.31	26.52	0.42	0.93
Palm kernels	—	—	—	—	0.17	
Palm kernel oil.	—	—	—	—	0.30	2.42
Palm oil	—	—	—	—	0.11	
Rapeseed oil	—	—	0.10†	—	0.53	
Sesame seed	—	—	—	—	137.20†	7.30*
Soya beans	—	—	0.13†	—	86.85*	1.11*
Soya bean oil	7.30	1.00²	—	—	26.54	
Sunflower seed oil	—	—	—	—	0.44	
Tung oil	—	—	—	—		

5. LIVESTOCK‡, ANIMAL PRODUCTS, etc.						
Chickensd.	39 830.3	28 676.5²				
Cattled	3 692.0	3 097.5²	1.1	2.2	3.0	0.7
Sheepd	19 194.7	16 772.5²	96.7	na	12.2	
Pigsd.	394.0	606.5²				
Horsesd	408.0	3 691.0²				
Bacon/ham.	5 733.0	5 156.0	3.8	1.5	21.0	0.1
Meat‡: A.	615.0	+10.7	0.6		68.5	1.8
B.	252.3*	99.3	0.3		4.0	
Butter.	34.3	7.3*			1.0	0.1
Cheese	47.6	40.7*	0.2		7.4	0.6
Eggs	233.4	690.3	67.0	20.8*	104.1	4.1*
Fish	1 387.3	2 463.3p	0.1	0.9	319.6	26.6†
Milk	1.0					1.7
Whale oil	—	—	—	—	42.0	10.7
Hides/skins	12.8	22.7*	5.5	0.7	5.6	1.6
Wool						

d no. in thousands. p excl. fish fed to livestock. q incl. fish landed by Spanish vessels in foreign ports. r cattle hides only.

6. FIBRES, TEXTILES, etc.						
Abaca	—	—	—	—	0.3	0.4
Agaves (sisal etc.)	—	—	—	—	10.9	3.0a
Cotton lint	—	—	—	—	17.3	66.5
Flax fibre	43.7	26.3	8.4		2.4	0.3
Hemp fibre	4.8*	8.0	0.5	0.2	26.9	17.5
Jute	5.2	10.1			38.1	13.7
Rubber: natural	0.3			0.1†	33.3	4.0
synthetic	—	—		2.4		
Silkf.	56.7	46.7	49.0		0.6	
Cotton: yarn	126.1	55.3	6.5	0.2	3.2	0.3
woven fabrics	99.9	47.7	6.9	3.7	17.3	0.8p
Rayon: fibre/yarn	60.0	39.5	1.6	0.3²	0.5	na
woven fabrics	16.1q	na			1.8	
Non-cellulosic			0.5	0.1	11.8	11.4
fibre/yarn	12.7	0.1	0.5	0.1	2.3	0.2
Wool: yarn	29.7	15.3	0.5	0.3	40.3	0.2
woven fabrics	—	na				na

f metric tons. t incl. carpets. q incl. waste. r incl. synthetic fabrics. t incl. felts. q natural silk fabrics. r incl. natural silk fabrics, excl. felt.

7. FUEL AND POWER						
Coal‡: A‡.	12 683	12 430	4	84	1 783	811
B‡.	1 330	1 830	26	9	99	152
Coke	2	—	1	2		
Electricityh: total	29 396	10 490²	27	na	12 180	3 630²
hydro	20 792	8 110²	1 123	540²	2 353	1 730²
thermal	8 604	2 380²				
Oil, crude	63	30²				
Petroleum, refined	10 503	88²	0.98	0.07		
Uraniumf						

f metric tons. h million kWh.

8. IRON AND STEEL						
Iron ore	2 617m	1 456m	2 090	1 597	180	299
Pig iron	2 120	910	152	30	13	13
Steel ingots/castings	3 053	1 145	50²		456	3
Iron/steel scrap	na	na	16	2	296	50
Iron/steel productsa	na	na			167	26

a million $ U.S. m metal content.

9. NON-FERROUS MINERALS AND METALS						
Gold, orem	21.70	9.00				
Platinum group						
metalsk	64.2	0.8r				
Silverk, orem	121.0	8.9r				
Asbestos: fibre	3 077.00	1 328.00				
manufactured	na	0.05				

continued

---

9. NON-FERROUS MINERALS AND METALS—continued

	Production		Exports		Imports	
Mica	na	0.11	0.01		0.69	9.18
Aluminium: bauxite	7.79	5.77			68.47	13.01
alumina	—	—			102.88	3.55
aluminium	49.01	3.88	9.53		18.70	
Antimony: ore	0.07m	0.18m			0.58	
metal	0.06	0.01			0.41	
Cadmium: metal	—	—			0.01	
Chrome: ore	—	—			21.00	0.02
metal	—	—			2.00	
Cobalt.	—	—				13.30
Copper: ore	25.55m	7.28m	7.19	0.17	20.21	
metal	59.07	57.38m	4.65	25.89	60.44	0.10
Lead: ore	57.96	57.22			8.76	
metal	na					
Magnesium:						
dolomite	92.88		2.39		1.64	
magnesite	—	—†	25.93		5.60	
metal/salts	19 194.7	772.5²			0.23	
Manganese: ore	16.19	37.48			112.89	14.37
Mercury/: ore	—	—			1.58	3.57
metal	2 505.46	1 412.33	2 121.90	1 372.70		
Nickel: ore.	—	—			0.36	
metal	0.12m	1.04m	0.26	0.27	1.85	0.55
Tin: ore	1.64	0.71			2.83	
metal	0.09	0.04	23.80		0.04	0.07
Titanium minerals	42.22	3.14			5.20	
Tungsten, ore	2.28	0.04	2.43			
Zinc: ore	73.15m	88.06m	21.20		—	
metal	60.89	23.42	18.12		0.93	0.66

k '000 fine troy oz. m metal content.

10. CHEMICALS AND FERTILIZERS

Organic chemicals:						
Benzene	7.2				0.8	
Butadiene	—	—			na	
Ethylene	7.5				9.8	
Methanol	2.3				2.3	
Phenol	6.0				0.5	
Phthalic anhydride	—	—	0.3		14.8	
Styrene monomer	30.7		2.4		9.8	
Urea						
Inorganic chemicals:						
Ammonia	205.2²				3.2	
Carbon black	1.2¹		0.6		17.3	
Chlorine	60.5				0.5	
Nitric acid.	153.1				1.8	
Sodium carbonate	196.9				11.8	
Sodium hydroxide	160.5		2.3		2.3	
Sulphuric acid.	1 449.7		1.6		40.3	
Plastics:						
Polyamides	na				1.1	
Polyethylene	—	—			39.5	
Polyvinyl chloride	29.7*		0.1*		4.1*	
Fertilizers:						
Phosphates	358.6u	208.2m	22.7		1 063.3	716.4
Potash	1 072.3x	973.2*x	332.6	245.7	0.4	
Pyrites	8.0*	5.8	1 139.1	1 460.8	31.9	4.4
Sulphur: native	63.2	35.1	0.4			
recovered						

n data not available for years 1953–5. x sulphur content.

11. INDUSTRY

Aircraft	13.0*n					
Alcoholic beverages	6 697.0	452.3	43.5a	24.6a	10.9	2.7
spiritsb	1 200.0*p	782.0q				0.3a
Cement	8 355.7	3 280.0	11.7*	4.0	1 805.3	24.3
Electrical engineeringa	578.5²	na	7.6	1.6	123.2	26.2
Locomotivesa	77	45.0²	na	na	na	na
Railway vehiclesa	na	na	2.1	na	13.2	17.3
Machine toolsa	50.0¹		8.4	0.2a	37.8	10.9
Motor vehicles:	229.0	56.0	98.0	1.0	na	8.2
commerciald			12.7a		52.6a	26.8a
privated						

a no. of units. d no. in thousands. g million $. i 1962 figure. q 1967 figure.

WEST AFRICA

	Year(s)
Crude birth rate (per '000)	3.8* 1964
Crude death rate (per '000)	3.9* 1964
Population per physician	2 530 1964
Population per hospital bed	250 1965
School enrolment: age 5–19 years (percentage)	21 1963–4 av.

Employment and production: The inhabitants are largely nomadic, but there is also some fishing, and a little maize and barley is grown. Rich deposits of phosphates were discovered in 1963.

SPANISH SAHARA

Spanish Sahara is the only African state remaining (1971) as a Spanish Overseas Province. Claims to the territory have been made by both Morocco and Mauritania; 7 000 sq. km. of the land was ceded by Spain to Morocco in 1958.

AREA: 266 000 000 sq. km. (102 680 sq. miles)

POPULATION: 48 000 (1967 U.N. estimate)
Capital city: EL AAIÚN; population: 5 500 (city proper, 1961)

na: data not available. — negligible or nil.

SUDAN

The Sudan was administered jointly by the U.K. and the U.A.R. (then Egypt) until 1956 when it became a sovereign independent republic. There followed several changes of government with a period (1958–1971) under military rule. A 10-year development plan (1961–1971) has led to improvements in industry, irrigation, transport and education.

AREA: 2 505 813 sq. km. (967 500 sq. miles)

LAND USE: (percentage of total)

	1954
Arable and orchard	2.8
Permanent meadow and pasture	9.6
Forest and woodland	36.5
City areas, waste and other land	51.1

POPULATION: 14 355 000 (1967 estimate)
Largest city: UMM DURMĀN (Omdurman): population: 198 000 (city proper, 1966)
Capital city: AL KHURṬŪM (Khartoum): population: 185 000 (city proper, 1966)

Distribution of working population (1956)
Total working population: 4 844 000*

	Percentage
Agriculture, forestry, fishing and hunting	85.8
U.N. group no.	
0	
2/3	0.6
4 Manufacturing	5.0
5 Construction	0.6
6 Commerce	2.1
7 Transport, storage and communications	4.6
8 Services	
9a Others	1.3

FINANCE

Currency unit: The Sudanese pound

Exchange rates	1965	1960	1950	1938
Per $ U.S.	0.348	0.348	0.348	0.210
Per £ sterling	0.975	0.975	0.975	1.007

		Year(s)
National Income (million $ U.S.)	1221	1965
G.N.P. per capita ($ U.S.)	100	1966
Rate of increase of G.N.P. per capita	3.8	1960–2 av.
Foreign trade (percentage of G.D.P.)	34	1963–5 av.

TRADING

Total trade (in million $ U.S.)	1965	1960	1955	1938
Exports (f.o.b.)	196		145	30
Imports (c.i.f.)	208		140	32

Main trading partners (percentage of total value)

Exports	1965	1955	Imports	1965	1955
Germany F.R.	11	9	U.K.	23	30
Italy	10	9	Japan	9	11
U.K.	10	28	India	9	3
China P.R.	8	1	U.S.A.	7	2
Netherlands	7	2	Germany F.R.	5	4
U.S.S.R.	6	—	U.A.R.	4	4
India	6	14	U.S.S.R.	4	11

Distribution of trade (percentage of total value)

Exports	1965	1955
Crude materials (cotton)	84	92*
(oilseeds)	(47)	(62)
(gum arabic)	(23)	(17*)
Food	(11)	(10)
(fodder)	14	8
Imports		
Manufactured goods	58	58
(machinery and transport equipment)	(21)	(11*)
(textiles and clothing)	(20)	(18*)
Food	22	24
(sugar)	(7)	(7*)
(cereals)	(5)	(4*)
Chemicals	10	5*
Crude materials and fuels	7	10

		Year(s)
Life expectancy at birth (years)	40*	1950
Population per physician	30 720	1964
Population per hospital bed	1010	1965
School enrolment: age 5–19 years (percentage)	15	1963–4 av.
age over 19 years (per 100 000 population)	51	1964–5 av.

COMMUNICATIONS

		Year(s)
Motor vehicles in use ('000s): private	21.1	
commercial	18.4	1963–5 av.
Railway track (km.)	5 403.0	1965
Telephones (per '000 urban population)	17	1967
Radio receivers (per '000 population)	0.3	1963–5 av.
Television sets (per '000 population)	0.8	1963–5 av.

PRODUCTION, EXPORTS AND IMPORTS

Years: 1963–5 average and 1953–5 average Units: '000 metric tons unless otherwise indicated

1. CEREALS, etc.	Production	Exports	Imports
Barley	0.3	—	—
Cassava	121.3*	—	—
Maize (corn)	21.0	22.0[1]	5.4
Millets/sorghum	1 525.0	1 201.0[2]	46.5
Potatoes	25.0*	2.0*	—
Rice			
Sweet potatoes/yams	11.0*	na	—
Wheat	41.3	15.0[2]	51.2

2. FRUIT, etc.	Production	Exports	Imports
Apples			2.1
Bananas	10.0*	0.7	—
Dates	42.3	0.5	3.9*
Grapes			0.1
Lemons			0.9
Oranges	1.0*	na	0.4
Raisins			2.9
Wine b			39.3

3. BEVERAGES, FOREST PRODUCTS, etc.	Production	Exports	Imports
Coffee	196.7*		10.9
Sugar: cane	19.3		
raw		0.6†	152.3
Tea			9.9
Tobacco products			0.7
Softwood j			124.9
Hardwood j	21 180.0	13 588.0	
Wood pulp			0.7
Newsprint			1.3
Other paper	17.3*		4.5

b '000 hectolitres. j '000 cu. metres of roundwood equivalent.
Acacia trees are grown and the gum arabic is an important export.

4. VEGETABLE OILSEEDS AND OILS	Production	Exports	Imports
Castor seed	7.67	4.73	0.01
Castor oil	—[2]		0.54
Coconut oil			0.20
Cottonseed	272.70	88.26	0.01
Cottonseed oil	172.30	108.30	
Groundnuts	203.90	3.01	0.01
Groundnut oil	23.70[1]*	4.55	0.03
Linseed oil	na	26.03	0.04
Olive oil		0.04[2]	0.04
Palm kernels		0.72	0.11
Palm oil			
Sesame seed	172.53	74.37	23.17

5. LIVESTOCK‡, ANIMAL PRODUCTS, etc.	Production	Exports	Imports
Cattle	7 030*	14.7	36.9
Goats d	6 762*	5 000[1]*	
Sheep d	8 525*	6 000[1]*	126.8
Horses d	21*	2[2]*	
Pigs d	5*	na	
Bacon/ham			
Meat: A	141*	na	
Butter		0.1	0.1
Cheese			0.2
Eggs	15*	na	0.1
Fish	958*	1.3	na
Milk		na	0.3
Hides/skins		0.5	15.4
d no. in thousands.		5.0	1.6

6. FIBRES, TEXTILES, etc.	Production	Exports	Imports
Cotton lint	138.3	132.6	81.8
Rubber, natural			na
Jute			0.4
Cotton:* yarn	4.5[1]	na	1.42
woven fabrics	4.4[2]	na	11.9
Rayon, woven fabrics			3.4

n incl. synthetic piece goods.

continued

PRODUCTION, EXPORTS AND IMPORTS *continued*

7. FUEL AND POWER	Production	Exports	Imports
Coal, 'A' ‡			8
Coke			1
Electricity h: total	170	10	
hydro	na	10	
thermal	na	10	
Oil, crude		—[1]	
Petroleum, refined	217		243
h million kWh.			420

8. IRON AND STEEL	Production	Exports	Imports
Iron ore		12	—
Pig iron		2	—
Iron/steel scrap	na	na	10

9. NON-FERROUS MINERALS AND METALS	Production	Exports	Imports
Gold k, bullion	na	0.102[2]p	0.23p
Silver k, bullion		—	
Asbestos	1.90m		0.03[2]p 0.30*p
Mica	21.29m	3.83	2.20
Chrome, ore			7.91
Copper, metal			na 0.02
Lead, metal			0.43 1.70
			0.19 0.24 na

k '000 fine troy oz. m metal content. p bullion.
continued

SWAZILAND

Swaziland, formerly a British protectorate, became an independent member of the Commonwealth in 1968, but remains part of the South African customs union.

AREA: 17 400 sq. km. (6 705 sq. miles)

LAND USE: (percentage of total)
Arable and orchard
Permanent meadow and pasture
Forest and woodland
City areas, waste and other land

POPULATION: 374 697 (1966 estimate)
Capital city: MBABANE: population: 8 390 (1962)
Total working population: 54 144 (1956)

		Year(s)
Life expectancy at birth (years)	44a	1966
Population per physician	7 500	1965
Population per hospital bed	420	1966
School enrolment: age 5–19 years (percentage)	66	1963–4 av.

a African population only.

FINANCE

Currency unit: The South African rand was introduced in 1961.

Exchange rates	1965	1960	1950a	1938a
Per $ U.S.	0.714	0.357	0.357	0.215
Per £ sterling	2.0	1.0	1.0	1.0

a South African pounds.

		Year
National Income (million $ U.S.)	100*	1966
G.N.P. per capita ($ U.S.)	290	1966

EMPLOYMENT, PRODUCTION AND TRADE

Forty-five per cent of the land is in European ownership for the exploitation of minerals but the agricultural and grazing rights of the natives are safeguarded and delimited. The chief crops are maize, cotton, tobacco, sugar, fruit, rice and vegetables. Re-afforestation is being undertaken. The largest mineral products are iron ore and asbestos, and the output of coal is increasing. The chief exports are iron, asbestos, sugar and wood. Trade is mainly with South Africa.

PRODUCTION, EXPORTS AND IMPORTS

Years: 1963–5 average and 1953–5 average Units: '000 metric tons unless otherwise indicated

1. CEREALS, etc.	Production	Exports	Imports
Maize (corn)	33.3*	—	na
Millets/sorghum	20.0*1	—	na
Potatoes	1.0*	—	—
Rice	6.7*	—	—
Sweet potatoes/yams	8.0*	—	—

2. FRUIT, etc.	Production	Exports	Imports
Bananas	1.0*	—	—
Oranges	4.7		
Other citrus fruit	2.7		
Pineapples	3.7*		
Tomatoes	3.0*		

3. BEVERAGES, FOREST PRODUCTS, etc.	Production	Exports	Imports
Sugar: cane	866.7*	—	na
raw	119.5*1	37.0	na
Tobacco, leaf	0.2*	0.2	na
Softwood j	424.5*2	2.1[1]	4.3
Hardwood j	115.5*2		
Wood pulp	52.7*		

j '000 cu. metres of roundwood equivalent.

4. VEGETABLE OILSEEDS AND OILS	Production	Exports	Imports
Cottonseed	3.7	—	—
Tung oil	0.3	—	—

5. LIVESTOCK‡, ANIMAL PRODUCTS, etc.	Production	Exports	Imports
Chickens d	311.3	247.3	na
Cattle	529.0	424.7	na
dairy cows d	228.7	137.5[2]	
Goats d	230.0	145.7	
Sheep d	40.0	31.3	
Horses d	2.3	2.0[2]	
Pigs d	9.0	9.3	
Meat: A	12.7*	20.5[2]	
B	14.3*	2.3[2]	
Eggs	2.6*		
Milk	32.0*	21.0[2]	
Hides/skins		0.41	

d no. in thousands.

6. FIBRES, TEXTILES, etc.	Production	Exports	Imports
Cotton lint	2.0	—	—

7. FUEL AND POWER	Production	Exports	Imports
Coal	11		

8. IRON AND STEEL	Production	Exports	Imports
Iron ore	227m		

m metal content.

9. NON-FERROUS MINERALS AND METALS	Production	Exports	Imports
Gold k, troy oz.	2.00	29.08	—
Asbestos, fibre	34.50	28.08	—
Tin, ore		0.03m	

k '000 fine troy oz. m metal content.

COMMUNICATIONS

		Year(s)
Railway track (km.)	220	1964
Telephones (per '000 urban population)	0.9	1967
Radio licences (per '000 population)	17	1963–5 av.

FINANCE

Currency unit: The South African rand was introduced in 1961.

Exchange rates	1965	1960	1950a	1938a
Per $ U.S.	0.714	0.357	0.357	0.215
Per £ sterling	2.0	1.0	1.0	1.0

a South African pounds.

		Year
National Income (million $ U.S.)	100*	1966
G.N.P. per capita ($ U.S.)	290	1966

9. NON-FERROUS MINERALS AND METALS—*continued*

	Production	Exports	Imports
Manganese, ore	3.27	—	0.70
Mercury		—	0.02
Tin, metal		0.16	na
Zinc, metal		0.15	

f metric tons. m metal content.

10. CHEMICALS AND FERTILIZERS

	Production	Exports	Imports
Chemicals.		na	0.1
Fertilizers:		—	
Potash		—	

n data not available for years 1953–5.

11. INDUSTRY

	Production	Exports	Imports
Aircraft			1.6 0.5
Alcoholic beverages			0.6a 1.5a
beer b	71.0		
Cement	79.7		233.0 29.0
manufactured	40.0*	1.7	
Electrical engineering a			1.0[2]
Railway vehicles a			11.5 na
Merchant ships a			7.6 na
Motor vehicles a			3.0 na
			16.7 2.9[2]

a million $ U.S. b '000 hectolitres. g '000 G.R.T.

SWEDEN

NORTHERN EUROPE

Sweden is an hereditary monarchy. Parliamentary government was established in 1917, but executive power remains with the king. Sweden is a member of the European Free Trade Association.

AREA: 449 793 sq. km. (173 665 sq. miles)

Land area: 411 260 sq. km. (158 787 sq. miles)

LAND USE: (percentage of total)

	1965	1955
Arable and orchard	7.1	8.4
Permanent meadow and pasture	1.2	1.6
Forest and woodland	50.0	50.0
City areas, waste and other land	41.7	40.0

POPULATION: 7 765 981 (1965 census)
Largest city: STOCKHOLM, capital; population: 1 262 402 (1966)

Distribution of working population (1960)
Total working population: 3 244 084

U.N. group no.

		Percentage
0	Agriculture, forestry, fishing and hunting	13.8
1	Mining and quarrying	0.7
2/3	Manufacturing	34.2
4	Construction	9.1
5	Electricity, gas, water and sanitary services	1.1
6	Commerce	13.5
7	Transport, storage and communications	7.5
8	Services	19.8
9	Others	0.3

	Year(s)
Life expectancy at birth (years): male	71.6 1961–5 av.
female	75.7 1961–5 av.
Infant mortality (per '000)	13.3 1965
Crude birth rate (per '000)	15.9 1965
Crude death rate (per '000)	10.1 1965
Accidental deaths (per 100 000 population)	17.9 1965
due to other causes	26.1 1965
Population per physician	910 1966
Population per hospital bed	70 1966
School enrolment: age 5–19 years (percentage)	76 1963–4 av.
age over 19 years (per 100 000 population)	794 1963–4 av.

COMMUNICATIONS

		Year(s)
Motor vehicles in use ('000s): private	1 671.5	1963–5 av.
commercial	137.9	1963–5 av.
Railway track (km.)	13 722	1965
Mail per capita: domestic	169	1965
foreign received	11	1965
foreign sent	8	1965
Telephones (per '000 urban population)	47.9	1967
Radio licences (per '000 population)	385	1963–5 av.
Television licences (per '000 population)	255.2	1963–5 av.
Daily newspapers (per '000 population)	398	1962–4 av.

FINANCE

Currency unit: The krona

Exchange rates	1965	1960	1950	1938
Per $ U.S.	5.18	5.18	5.18	4.19
Per £ sterling	14.52	14.54	14.51	19.25

	1965	1960			*Year(s)*
National Income (million $ U.S.)		17 000*			1966
G.N.P. per capita ($ U.S.)		2 270*			1966
Rate of increase of G.N.P. per capita		4.7			1960–4 av.
Foreign trade (percentage of G.D.P.)		42			1963–5 av.

TRADING

Total trade (in million $ U.S.)	1965	1955	1938
Exports (f.o.b.)	3 969	1 726	464
Imports (c.i.f.)	4 375	1 997	525

Main trading partners (percentage of total value)

Exports	1965	1955	1938
Germany F.R.	14	13	18 d
U.K.	13	20	23
Norway	12	9	6
Denmark	9	6	9
Finland	8	5	2

Imports	1965	1955	1938
Germany F.R.	22	22	22 d
U.S.A.	15	10	14
U.K.	13	14	16
Denmark	6	5	3
Netherlands	6	4	4
France	4	4	3

Distribution of trade (percentage of total value)

Exports	1965	1955	1938*
Manufactured goods	66	50	43
(machinery and transport equipment)	(35)	(22)	(14)
Crude materials and fuels	27	44	41
(wood and paper pulp)	(18)	(32)	(27)

Imports	1965	1955	1938
Manufactured goods	63	51	43
(machinery and transport equipment)	(30)	(20)	(16)
(textiles and clothing)	(9)	(9)	(11)
Crude materials and fuels	18	26	24
(petroleum and products)	(10)	(13)	(9)
Food	8	6	9

d incl. Germany D.R.

PRODUCTION, EXPORTS AND IMPORTS

Years: 1963–5 average and 1953–5 average   Units: '000 metric tons unless otherwise indicated

1. CEREALS, etc.

	Production		Exports		Imports	
Barley	1 322.3	412.3	101.4	22.7	15.0	42.7
Maize (corn)	—	—	—	0.5	39.2	43.4
Millets/sorghum	—	—	—	—	6.2	33.9
Oats	1 314.7	801.7	84.3	11.0	2.1	24.0
Potatoes	1 642.3	1 480.3	0.2	1.5	28.3	48.9
Rice	123.7	256.0	—	—	10.7	8.3
Rye	237.0	172.0	11.0	47.3	83.2	13.7
Wheat	933.0	908.3	264.5	268.4	138.4	30.6

2. FRUIT, etc.

	Production		Exports		Imports	
Apples	237.0	172.0	0.8	0.3	47.3	33.6
Bananas	—	—	—	—	47.5	44.3
Cherries	9.3	7.8	—	—	2.0	1.5
Coconuts	—	—	—	—	0.4	0.3
Dates	—	—	—	—	na	—
Figs	—	—	—	—	2.4	11.4
Grapes	—	—	0.5†	—	23.4	4.3
Oranges	—	—	1.0†	—	105.6	92.8
Other citrus fruit	—	—	1.0†	—	43.2	4.5
Peaches	—	—	0.1†	0.1†	na	2.8

PRODUCTION, EXPORTS AND IMPORTS *continued*

2. FRUIT, etc.—*continued*

	Production		Exports		Imports	
Pears	54.3	31.0	0.2	—	17.2	19.5
Plums	23.0	17.6	—	—	3.9	1.5
Raisins	—	—	—	—	na	4.2
Wine b.	—	—	0.1†	—	328.1	92.7

b '000 hectolitres.

3. BEVERAGES, FOREST PRODUCTS, etc.

	Production		Exports		Imports	
Cocoa	—	—	—	—	7.7	6.6
Coffee	—	—	0.3	—	90.1	50.8
Tea	—	—	—	—	na	na
Sugar: beet	1 548.3	1 826.0	4.1	7.7	83.6	66.7
raw.	242.2	266.0	0.1	0.1	1.4	1.1
Tobacco: leaf	—	0.3	—	—	10.1	8.8
cigars a	0.1	0.3	—	—	—	—
cigarettes	12.5 a	17.8 a	—	—	1.6	0.9 b
tobacco/snuff	7 646.0 c	4 741.3 c	—	—	—	—
Softwood j	41 300.0	35 300.0	8 984.0	7 641.5	292.7	368.7
Hardwood j	6 333.3	3 900.0	35.1	28.4	194.6	113.0
Wood pulp	6 297.3	3 578.0	3 438.3	2 232.7	4.4	0.8
Newsprint	646.0	346.7	438.7	196.3	—	0.1
Other paper	2 270.3 a	1 031.3*	1 378.7	574.7	38.8	12.3*

c no. in millions.   j '000 cu. metres of roundwood equivalent.   *continued*

4. VEGETABLE OILSEEDS AND OILS

	Production		Exports		Imports	
Castor oil	—	—	0.06†	0.01†	1.31	0.83
Copra	—	—	—	—	62.60	49.20
Coconut oil	—	—	0.58	3.73	4.04	4.87
Cottonseed	—	—	—	—	0.02	0.03
Cottonseed oil	—	—	0.25†	—	6.11	0.01
Groundnuts	na	na	0.02†	0.15	0.59	0.23
Groundnut oil	na	3.67 n	0.02†	0.70	1.49	0.30
Linseed	0.02 a	0.17 a	—	—	0.46	5.50
Linseed oil	na	na	0.03	0.01	10.53	10.10
Olive oil	—	—	—	—	0.13	0.09
Palm kernel oil	—	—	0.02†	0.03†	0.80	0.13
Palm oil	—	—	0.01†	—	2.04	3.90
Rapeseed	164.70	124.30 p	50.97	39.13	0.73	0.03
Rapeseed oil	na	na	14.71	14.37	1.78	0.10 a
Soya beans	—	—	—	—	0.03	8.06
Soya bean oil	na	na	1.18 s	0.85 s	10.05	0.68
Sunflower seed oil	—	—	—	—	0.05	—
Tung oil	—	—	—	—	0.87	1.12

n flax grown for seed only.   p seed delivered to oil factories.   q incl. other minor vegetable oils.   s incl. re-exports.

5. LIVESTOCK, ANIMAL PRODUCTS, etc.

	Production		Exports		Imports	
Chickens d.	9 657.1	11 735.0 r				
Cattle d.	2 344.0	2 552.3	13.1	0.4	0.9	0.3
dairy cows d	1 529.7	2 039.3				
Goats d	15.0 a	na				
Sheep d	212.3	196.7	1.4	24.8	1.3	
Horses d	132.0	336.0	28.0	3.1	6.9	17.3
Pigs d.	1 855.0	1 534.7	1.8	4.4	8.6	2.1
Bacon/ham	374.3	321.0	8.9	10.1	1.6	17.3
Meat‡: 'A' }			5.2	4.2	149.6	2.1
'B' }			227.4	57.1 a	na	4.2
Butter.	48.8	43.3	46.4	30.0		na
Cheese	81.7	93.3				
Eggs	96.7	83.3	18.0	9.2	25.2	19.1
Fish.	389.0 u	206.6 u	0.6	0.4	4.8	4.2
Whale/sperm oil	3 888.7	4 328.0				
Hides/skins	0.2	na				
Wool						

d no. in thousands.   u excl. freshwater fish.   incl. fish landed by Swedish vessels in foreign ports.   incl. ducks, geese and turkeys.

6. FIBRES, TEXTILES, etc.

	Production		Exports		Imports	
Abaca	—	—	—	—	—	—
Agaves (sisal, etc.)	—	—	—	—	—	—
Cotton lint	—	—	0.1†	0.1†	0.7	0.3
Flax fibre	1.8	2.7	0.3	1.4	5.6	5.9
Hemp fibre	0.6	0.8	0.3†	0.8	20.1	29.0
Jute	—	—	0.3†	0.2†	3.1	2.7
Rubber: natural					5.1	0.4
synthetic	99.4		0.1		26.5	5.3
Cotton: yarn	19.7	25.1 v	0.1	0.1	27.1	22.2
woven fabrics	19.5	22.4	2.5	0.8	9.0	3.5
Rayon: fibre/yarn	34.8	16.0	22.0	7.7	12.2	8.1
woven fabrics	11.7	7.6	2.9 w	0.4	5.7	3.5
Non-cellulosic						3.6
fibre/yarn	0.2	na	0.2	0.1	10.6	2.1
Wool: yarn	11.7	14.4	0.3	0.3	3.9	5.5
woven fabrics	8.0	17.0	0.9	0.6	4.0	

v incl. mixed yarns.   w incl. synthetic fibres.

7. FUEL AND POWER

	Production		Exports		Imports	
Coal, 'A'‡.	57	190	11	2	1 833	3 456 q
Coke	45 053	23 620	10	38	1 554	2 178
Electricity h: total	42 480	21 740				
hydro	2 573	3 060	243		3 340	1 700
thermal	73	110		7	14 227	6 190
Oil, crude	—	—				
Petroleum, refined.						
Uranium	na	na				

h million kWh.   q incl. lignite and brown coal.

8. IRON AND STEEL

	Production		Exports		Imports	
Iron ore	23 359	14 907	16 258 m	9 977 m	433.4	327.1
Pig iron	120	105	2.7†	1.8†	179.7	187.8
Steel ingots/castings	109	9	16.2	12.7	158.9	89.9
Iron/steel scrap	17	na	0.2	3.4	124.6	49.5
Iron/steel products a	284	na				

a million $ U.S.   m metal content.

9. NON-FERROUS MINERALS AND METALS

	Production		Exports		Imports	
Diamonds a	116.30	99.00	0.18	0.08	1.05	1.00
Gold k, ore m			55.70† p	50.70 p	201.30† p	34.47 p
Platinum group						
Silver k, ore m.	3 273.00	2 061.70	698.00 p	540.00 p	470.00 p	2 642.30 p
Asbestos: fibre			0.07		18.25	12.72
manufactured	na	na	20.38	0.03	18.85	1.86
Mica	0.02 a	0.17 a	0.01	0.02	1.19	0.84
Aluminium: bauxite	na	na	—	—	23.67	22.60
alumina	na	na	—	—	59.45	19.48
aluminium	26.42	10.12	21.29	11.34	54.66	22.82
Antimony, metal	0.02		0.03	0.06	0.38	0.36
Beryl			—	—	0.15	0.10
Chrome: ore			— 2	— 1	136.23	59.56
metal					11.98	2.03
Cobalt, metal	1.90 m	14.14 m	20.84	8.66	95.05	1.69
Copper: ore	47.12	17.18	56.19	37.74		52.37
metal	69.15 m	29.13 m	44.19	10.48	83.09	41.49
Lead: ore	40.45	19.16	12.42	6.01	12.12	18.06
metal						
Magnesium:						
dolomite	73.13 i		4.02	0.03	26.65	
magnesite	— i	— †	0.19	0.03	8.06	1.39
metal/salts	12.00 * n	14.51 n	0.16 †	0.87	40.73	16.66
Manganese: ore			8.93	0.88	76.77	32.20
metal			9.30	1.30	22.51	2.81
Mercury i					92.10	52.00
Molybdenum i: ore					2 952.30	1 079.00
metal			338.30	91.00	586.20	59.70
Nickel: ore						
metal			0.96	0.01	0.44	
Tin, metal			0.14	0.05†	12.56	3.43
Titanium minerals	0.09	0.45	0.17	0.13	1.02	0.79
Tungsten: ore			0.17	0.13	16.60	7.84
metal	na	na	0.15†	0.03†	0.50	7.41
Vanadium i			—	—	0.56	0.02
Zinc: ore	80.36 m	54.10 m	148.54	97.78	0.10	0.03
metal	3 886.7	4 328.0	2.23	1.15	39.93	38.10

a million $ U.S.   i metal content.   k '000 fine troy oz.   m metal content.   n low-grade ore.   p bullion.   r ferro-vanadium.   t excl. calcined.

10. CHEMICALS n AND FERTILIZERS

Organic chemicals:	Production		Exports		Imports	
Benzene	0.5 i		na		na	
Butadiene	na		na		na	
Ethylene	na		na		na	
Methanol	2.0 i		1.1		36.6	
Phenol	3.7		0.2		7.9	
Phthalic anhydride			0.1 i		5.6	
Styrene monomer	na				6.9	
Urea					14.3	
Inorganic chemicals:						
Ammonia	99.4		0.1		15.6	
Carbon black					20.1	
Chlorine	199.1		3.2		2.6	
Nitric acid	179.1				6.1	
Sodium carbonate	1.5				103.2	
Sodium hydroxide	231.1		4.1		28.6	
Sulphuric acid.	522.2		17.0		8.9	
Plastics:						
Polyamides	na					
Polyethylene	16.5 2		9.0		1.0	
Polyvinyl chloride	26.9		7.5		30.1	
					13.5	
Fertilizers:						
Phosphates	na		0.2		433.4	327.1
Potash	212.0 x	194.3 x	2.7†	1.8†	179.7	187.8
Pyrites	25.1 q	28.9 q	16.2	12.7	158.9	89.9
Sulphur			0.2	3.4	124.6	49.5

q recovered sulphur.   r incl. phenol alcohols.   x sulphur content.

11. INDUSTRY

	Production		Exports		Imports	
Aircraft a	76.0 † i	na				
Alcoholic beverages						
beer b	3 002.0	2 082.7			19.8	10.8
spirits b	211.0 † u	344.8 b	1.5		26.7 a	12.9 a
Cement	3 550.0	2 414.0	0.4			
Electrical			90.7	325.7	8.0	7.0
engineering a	806.0 2	na				
Locomotives c	69.0	71.0 a	202.6	62.0 2	255.8	70.4 a
Railway vehicles a.			10.3	1.6	na	na
Merchant ships g	461 i	na	22.0	14.3	35.1	4.5
Motor vehicles	1 026.0	518.0	815.0	372.2	167.0	11.6 2
commercial d			205.3 a	30.4 2 a	310.8 a	14.3
private d	22.9	16.1 w				139.2 2 a
	163.3	41.5 w				

a million $ U.S.   c no. of units.   d no. in thousands.   g '000 G.R.T.   i 1965–7 av.   u production for home consumption in 1967.   w '000 hectolitres.   *production for home consumption in 1960.   w incl. assembly of imported parts.

na: data not available.   — negligible or nil.   — not available.   2 two year average.   * estimate.   † re-exports.   1 one year only.

na: data not available.   — negligible or nil.   2 two year average.   1 one year only.   * estimate.   † see appendix.   ‡ see appendix.

213

SWITZERLAND

A long-established democracy, Switzerland has been a republic since 1798, and maintains a policy of political neutrality. Banking, insurance and tourism are all important factors in the economy. Switzerland is a member of the European Free Trade Association.

AREA: 41 288 sq. km. (15 941 sq. miles)

LAND USE: (percentage of total)	1964	1955
Arable and orchard	10.2	10.8
Permanent meadow and pasture	42.2	41.8
Forest and woodland	23.8	23.8
City areas, waste and other land	23.8	23.6

POPULATION: 6 050 000 (1967 U.N. estimate)
Largest city: ZÜRICH; population: 657 400 (1967)
Capital city: BERN; population: 250 600 (1967)

Distribution of working population (1960)
Total working population: 2 512 411

U.N. group no.		Percentage
0	Agriculture, forestry, fishing and hunting	11.2
1	Mining and quarrying	0.3
2/3	Manufacturing	39.7
4	Construction	9.5
5	Electricity, gas, water and sanitary services	0.9
6	Commerce	13.8
7	Transport, storage and communications	5.4
8	Services	19.0
9	Others	0.2

		Year(s)
Life expectancy at birth (years): male	68.7	} 1958–63 av.
female	74.1	
Infant mortality (per '000)	17.8	1965
Crude birth rate (per '000)	18.8	1965
Crude death rate (per '000)	9.3	1965
Accidental deaths (per 100 000 population) caused by motor vehicles	21.2	1965
due to other causes	37.2	1965
Population per physician	760	1965
Population per hospital bed	80	1965
School enrolment: age 5–19 years (percentage)	62p	1963–4 av.
age over 19 years (per 100 000 population)	519p	1963–5 av.

p public education only.

PRODUCTION, EXPORTS AND IMPORTS
Units: '000 metric tons unless otherwise indicated
Years: 1963–5 average and 1953–5 average

1. CEREALS, etc.
	Production	Exports	Imports
Barley	98.7 / 62.7	— / —	272.2 / 779.8
Maize (corn)	17.0 / 4.0	— / 0.3	161.5 / 79.3
Millets/sorghum	— / —	— / —	18.8 / 11.9
Oats	34.0 / 67.3	— / —	140.3 / 115.6
Potatoes	1 152.3 / 1 760.3	37.0 / 0.4†	15.8 / 73.1
Rice	67.0 / 41.0	0.8 / 0.1†	19.3 / 20.6
Rye	347.3 / 304.0	— / —	19.3 / 3.2
Wheat	— / —	— / —	372.0 / 348.5

2. FRUIT, etc.
	Production	Exports	Imports
Apples	335.0 / 413.0	5.2 / 43.8	23.6 / 16.8
Apricots	8.0 / 3.7	0.1† / —	na / 8.4
Bananas	— / —	na / —	54.7 / 18.4
Cherries	42.3 / 54.9	— / —	1.1 / 3.1
Dates	— / —	— / —	1.1 / 1.6
Figs	— / —	— / —	3.1 / 1.6
Grapes	126.3 / 95.3	— / —	31.7 / 15.8
Lemons	— / —	— / —	17.2 / 13.6
Oranges	— / —	— / —	90.6 / 59.9
Other citrus fruit	— / —	— / —	7.7 / 5.4
Peaches	138.7 / 266.7	8.2 / 1.0	8.8 / 13.2
Pears	— / —	— / —	na / 3.4
Pineapples	— / —	— / —	na / 0.4
Plums	39.3 / 39.0	— / —	2.9 / 2.6
Raisins	— / —	— / —	
Tomatoes	20.7 / 9.7	0.1† / 0.1†	
Wine b.	812.3 / 658.7	9.3 / 28.3	1 552.1 / 1 022.3

b '000 hectolitres.

COMMUNICATIONS

	1964	1955	Year(s)
Railway track (km.)	5112		1963
Motor vehicles in use ('000s): private	835.5	}	1963–5 av.
commercial	87.5		1963
Mail per capita: domestic	252		1963–5 av.
foreign received	28		1963–5 av.
foreign sent	34		1963–5 av.
Telephones (per '000 urban population)	39.3		1967
Radio licences (per '000 population)	276		1963–5 av.
Television licences (per '000 population)	84.1		1963–5 av.
Daily newspapers (per '000 population)	369.3		1962–4 av.

FINANCE
Currency unit: The Swiss franc

Exchange rates	1965	1960	1938
Per $ U.S.	4.318	4.305	4.438
Per £ sterling	12.103	12.068	20.415

	1965	1960	1938
National Income (million $ U.S.)	11 460		
G.N.P. per capita ($ U.S.)	2 250		
Rate of increase of G.N.P. per capita	3.1		
Foreign trade (percentage of G.D.P.)	49		

TRADING
Total trade (in million $ U.S.)	1965	1960	1955	1938
Exports (f.o.b.)	2 959		1 307	302
Imports (c.i.f.)	3 697		1 489	366

Main trading partners (percentage of total value)

Exports	1965	1955	1938
Germany F.R.	17	13	16d
France	12	9	7
U.S.A.	8	8	9
U.K.	8	7	11
Austria	4	3	2
Netherlands	4	4	5

Imports	1965	1955	1938
Germany F.R.	30	24	23d
France	15	15	14
Italy	10	8	8
U.K.	7	7	8
U.S.A.	7	6	6
Belg./Lux.	4	5	4
Netherlands	4	4	3

Distribution of trade (percentage of total value)

Exports	1965	1955*	1938*
Manufactured goods (machinery and transport equipment)	72	na	na
(watches)	(30)	(23)	(18)
(textiles and clothing)	(14)	(19)	(18)
Chemicals	20	16	15
Food	4	2	

Imports	1965	1955	1938
Manufactured goods (machinery and transport equipment)	60	na	na
Food	14	16	23 (8)
Crude materials and fuels	13	13	na
Chemicals	9	9	7

d incl. Germany D.R.

3. BEVERAGES, FOREST PRODUCTS, etc.
	Production	Exports	Imports
Cocoa	— / —	0.3† / —	14.8 / 10.8
Coffee	— / —	5.5† / —	38.3 / 18.7
Sugar: beet	319.0 / 214.0		
raw	48.6 / 34.0		230.1 / 172.8
refined	— / 2.1	2.7 / —	1.4 / 0.8
Tea	— / —	0.1† / —	18.6 / 11.8
Tobacco: leaf	1.7 / 2.1		
cigars	652.0x / 499.3x	2.2†r / —	
cigarettes	16 680.0x / 8 026.3x	5.7 / —	
tobacco/snuff			
Wood: softwood	2 780.6 / 2 886.7	87.0 / 29.9	672.0 / 205.0
hardwood	1 146.7 / 845.0	58.7 / 8.5	370.8 / 216.4
Woodpulp	255.7 / 169.0	10.3 / 2.1	145.0 / 67.0
Newsprint	107.7 / 60.0	— / —	6.9 /
Other paper	470.7 / 248.3*	11.7 / 5.7	85.7 / 13.3

r no. in millions. j '000 cu. metres of roundwood equivalent.

4. VEGETABLE OILSEEDS AND OILS
	Production	Exports	Imports
Castor seed	— / —	— / —	0.05² / 0.74
Castor oil	— / —	0.03† / —	1.46 / 26.80
Copra	na / na	— / —	16.91 / 4.63
Coconut oil	na / na	0.41 / —	3.17 / na
Cottonseed oil	na / na	— / —	na /
Groundnuts	na / na	0.03† / —	70.82 / 36.73
Groundnut oil	na / na	0.39 / —	4.49 / 8.50
Linseed	na / na	— / —	3.85 / 5.40
Linseed oil	na / na	0.40* / 2.20p	3.85 / 7.72p

b incl. other inedible oils.

continued

PRODUCTION, EXPORTS AND IMPORTS *continued*

4. VEGETABLE OILSEEDS AND OILS—*continued*
	Production	Exports	Imports
Olive oil	na / na	— / —	4.63 / 1.55
Palm kernels	na / na	— / —	4.98 / 0.30
Palm kernel oil	0.39		0.56 / —
Palm oil	na / na	— / —	2.37 / 0.62
Rapeseed	13.00 / 5.30	— / —	0.90 / 0.50
Rapeseed oil	na / na	— / —	1.52 / 0.11*
Sesame seed	na / na	— / —	0.71 / 1.83
Soya beans	— / —	— / —	0.33 / 0.07
Soya bean oil	— / —	— / —	3.59 / 0.46
Sunflower seed oil	— / —	0.21†	12.28 / 0.28*
Tung oil			0.28*

5. LIVESTOCK‡, ANIMAL PRODUCTS, etc.
	Production	Exports	Imports
Chickens d	5 960.3 / 6 300.7		0.9² / 36.7
Cattle d	1 729.0 / 1 603.7	12.0 / 11.6	27.5 / 9.2
dairy cows d	1 062.3* / 886.7		2.1
Goats d	239.7* / 197.7	0.3 / na	2.4
Sheep d	77.0 / 124.0		7.8
Horses d	1 471.0 / 1 001.7	0.1 / 0.1	6.0 / 0.3
Pigs d	255.7 / 195.0		39.6 / 24.8
Bacon/ham	47.0* / 31.1	0.1	6.6
Meat‡: 'A'	32.7 / 26.3		6.6
'B'	74.7 / 58.7	34.6 / 20.3	23.5
Butter	30.6 / 29.5p	0.7 / 0.31*	61.9
Cheese	2.9 / 2.0	59.6 / 25.2	137.2
Eggs	3 115.7 / 2 757.0	0.4	4.9
Milk	0.3 / 13.1		
Hides/skins			
Wool			

a million $ U.S. d no. in thousands. p excl. eggs for hatching.

6. FIBRES, TEXTILES, etc.
	Production	Exports	Imports
Agaves (sisal, etc.)			2.9 / 41.8
Cotton lint		0.2† / 2.9†	2.1
Flax fibre		0.1† / 5†	1.2
Hemp fibre			2.4
Jute		0.2†	7.8
Rubber: natural			10.1
synthetic			678.7 / 430.3
Silk		154.0† / 46.0†	0.9
Cotton: yarn	37.3 / 29.8	4.3 / 3.6	4.6
woven fabrics	21.4 / 19.4	5.0 / 5.2	5.5
Rayon: fibre/yarn	22.7 / 21.2	14.0 / 16.9	4.1
woven fabrics		4.0 / 2.5	0.7
Non-cellulosic fibre/yarn			
Wool: yarn	18.6 / 1.7	15.8 / 1.7	6.8 / 1.5
woven fabrics	7.2 / 4.5†	1.5 / 1.0	2.5 / 2.3

a million $ U.S. f metric tons. q yarn consumption in weaving mills. r incl. some nylon.

7. FUEL AND POWER
	Production	Exports	Imports
Coal, 'A'‡		1† / 9†	1 722 / 2 011
Coke	23 112 / 22 785	5†	553 / 632
Electricity h: total	14 030 / 13 920		
hydro			
thermal	327 / 707	70	803 / 6 193
Oil, crude			1 790¹
Petroleum, refined			

f metric tons.

8. IRON AND STEEL
	Production	Exports	Imports
Iron ore	41*m / 56*m	83 / 115	3 / 66
Pig iron	34 / 44	14 / 4	74 / 120
Steel ingots/castings	337 / 158	26 / 3	237
Iron/steel scrap	na / na	18 / 3	7
Iron/steel products a	na / na		223 / 97

a million $ U.S. m metal content.

9. NON-FERROUS MINERALS AND METALS
	Production	Exports	Imports
Gold k	—	525.33‡	157.30 / 55.17
bullion/coins etc.	—	34.20	
Platinum group	—		
metals	—	27.59 / 2.08	40.00 / 11.18
Silver k, bullion	—	596.00 / 297.3	8 543.67 / 4 712.67
Asbestos: fibre	na	0.08 / 0.01n	12.86 / 5.02n
manufactured	na	4.32 / 0.46	6.74 / 2.59
Mica	na	0.18 / na	0.94 / na
Aluminium: bauxite			
alumina	—	0.10 / 0.01	2.73 / 60.26
aluminium	63.83 / 28.50	39.00 / 13.94	127.28 / 7.90
Antimony: metal	—		19.59 / 0.29
Copper: ore	—		0.29 / 0.18
metal	—	22.11 / 1.30	61.09 / 1.28
Lead: ore	—	7.56 / 10.82	31.04
metal	—	0.88	22.92 / 15.53
Magnesium: dolomite	—	1.22	
metal/salts	—x		9.59
Mercury f	—		3.05
Nickel, ore	—x	5.50 / 22.30	43.70 / 44.20
Tin, metal	—	1.52 / 0.93	2.08 / 1.08
Titanium minerals	—	0.21 / 0.16	1.00 / 0.06
Zinc, metal	—		6.50
	—	1.21 / 5.21	27.40 / 24.76

f metric tons. k '000 fine troy oz. n mica incl. with asbestos. x primary magnesium only.

10. CHEMICALS n AND FERTILIZERS
Organic chemicals:	Production	Exports	Imports
Benzene	na	na	na
Butadiene	na	na	na
Ethylene	na	na	na
Methanol	na	0.1	17.0
Phenol	na	0.7²	2.9²
Phthalic anhydride	na	3.3	0.4
Styrene monomer			
Urea			
Inorganic chemicals:			
Ammonia	na	0.4	20.9
Carbon black	na	11.1	6.7
Chlorine	na	2.2	0.3
Nitric acid	na	2.1	3.6
Sodium carbonate	na	19.0	5.5
Sodium hydroxide	167.0		0.4
Sulphuric acid			
Plastics:			
Polyamides	na		na
Polyethylene			7.8²
Polyvinyl chloride	10.5²	3.4²	

11. INDUSTRY
	Production	Exports	Imports
Aircraft a	50.0¹		
Alcoholic beverages: beer b	4 371.0 / 2 426.3p	—	32.5 / 6.0
	4 840q / 145.0r		43.2a / 17.3an
spirits b	4 066.7 / 1 829.7	7.3	84.7 / 74.3
Cement	na / na	84.3	
Electrical engineering a	4 066.7	187.5 / 6.8²	190.4 / 12.9²
Locomotives c	120.0*	113.2 / 54.3	36.8 / 19.4²
Machine tools a	121.0¹		0.6 / 5.0
Merchant ships g	17.7	5.0a	241.1a / 69.9a
Motor vehicles: private d	6.5²		36.2 / 24.7*
			116.9 / 78.3
			39.1 /
			66.5 / 56.1

a million $ U.S. b '000 hectolitres. c no. of units. d no. in thousands. p sales by breweries. q '000 G.R.T. n wine only. av. ‡assembly of imported parts.
a 1966/7 figure. r 1956–60.

SYRIA — MIDDLE EAST

Syria, mandated to France after World War I, became an independent republic during World War II. A brief union with Egypt in 1958, forming the United Arab Republic, was broken when Syria seceded three years later.

AREA: 185 680 sq. km. (71 700 sq. miles)

LAND USE: (percentage of total)

	1964	1955
Arable and orchard	35.9	22.2
Permanent meadow and pasture	33.0	34.1
Forest and woodland	2.4	2.4
City areas, waste and other land	28.7	41.3

POPULATION: 5 600 000 (1967 estimate)
Largest city: DIMASHQ (Damascus), capital; population: 618 457 (city proper, 1966)

Distribution of working population (1965)
Total working population: 1 424 267

U.N. group no.		Percentage
0	Agriculture, forestry, fishing and hunting	55.5
1	Mining and quarrying	
2/3	Manufacturing	11.6
4	Construction	5.5
5	Electricity, gas, water and sanitary services	0.7
6	Commerce	9.9
7	Transport, storage and communications	2.9
8		11.2
9	Services	1.2
	Others	

		Year(s)
Infant mortality (per '000)	22.3*	1965
Crude birth rate (per '000)	33.4*	1965
Crude death rate (per '000)	3.4*	1965
Population per physician	5110	1965
Population per hospital bed	900	1966
School enrolment: age 5–19 years (percentage)	50	1963–4 av.
age over 19 years (per 100 000 population)	630	1964–5 av.

FINANCE
Currency unit: The Syrian pound

Exchange rates	1965	1960	1955
Per $ U.S.	3.82	3.58	
Per £ sterling	10.71	10.05	

		Year(s)
National Income (million $ U.S.)	781	1963
G.N.P. per capita ($ U.S.)	180	1966
Rate of increase of G.N.P. per capita	8.2	1960–4 av.

TRADING

Total trade (in million $ U.S.)	1965	1955
Exports (f.o.b.)	168	128
Imports (c.i.f.)	212	179

Main trading partners (percentage of total value)

Exports	1965	1955a	Imports	1965	1955a
Lebanon	22	21	Germany F.R.	12	10
U.S.S.R.	10		U.K.	8	13
China P.R.	10	10	Iraq	8	16
Italy	6		U.S.A.	7	11
Romania	5	21	France	6	10
Saudi Arabia	5	2	Italy	6	10
			Lebanon	5	6

Distribution of trade (percentage of total value)

Exports	1965	1955
Textiles and clothing	56	63*
Food	34	23
(cereals, fruit and vegetables)	(17)	(9*)
Imports		
Manufactured goods	49	60*
(machinery and transport equipment)	(16)	(15*)
(textiles and clothing)	(13)	(13*)
Food	20	16
(cereals, fruit and vegetables)	18	19
Crude materials and fuels	12	4*
Chemicals		

a incl. gold and specie.

COMMUNICATIONS

		Year(s)
Motor vehicles in use ('000s): private	25.0	1963–5 av.
commercial	13.8	
Railway track (km.)	961	1964
Telephones (per '000 population)	1.6	1967
Radio receivers (per '000 population)	297	1963–5 av.
Television sets (per '000 population)	9.2	1963–5 av.
Daily newspapers (per '000 population)	15	1962–4 av.

PRODUCTION, EXPORTS AND IMPORTS
Years: 1963–5 average and 1953–5 average Units: '000 metric tons unless otherwise indicated

1. CEREALS, etc.

	Production 1963–5 av.	1953–5 av.	Exports		Imports	
Barley	703.7	414.7	284.9	204.5	—	0.2
Maize (corn)	6.7	21.3	1.7	2.7	2.9	0.1
Millets/sorghum	59.3	103.3	8.5			
Potatoes	2.3	4.7	0.9	0.9	0.5	8.6
Rice	1.3	15.3		1.0	15.8	11.3
Rye	na			0.2	28.1	7.7
Wheat	1111.3	757.2	133.9	148.7	—	10.4

2. FRUIT, etc.

	Production		Exports		Imports	
Apples	24.7	8.7	1.2	1.1	12.8	2.2
Apricots	22.0	20.3	na	na	8.0	5.5
Bananas	1.0	na	—	0.3†	0.3†	
Cherries	na	na		0.1†	22.1	26.1
Dates	—	—	na	na	0.4	
Figs	55.0	53.0	0.9	4.7	12.5	2.7
Grapes	198.3	235.7	6.1	0.1	57.4	21.8
Lemons	2.0	1.7	na	0.7	0.7	
Oranges	4.7	3.3	0.8	0.8		
Other citrus fruit						
Olives	85.7	38.0	1.2	—		
Peaches	3.0	2.0	na	0.2	0.5	
Pears	6.0	na	0.2	—		
Plums	0.7*	na	0.1	0.1		
Raisins	na	na				
Tomatoes	134.7	67.7	0.4		0.7	1.0

3. BEVERAGES, FOREST PRODUCTS, etc.

	Production		Exports		Imports	
Cocoa	—	—			0.1	—
Coffee	—	—	0.8†		3.3	1.1
Sugar: beet	143.3	44.3*				
cane raw	2.7	—			73.7	31.5
Tea	17.4	5.7*	—	—	3.0	1.0

continued

PRODUCTION, EXPORTS AND IMPORTS *continued*

5. LIVESTOCK‡, ANIMAL PRODUCTS, etc.—continued

	Production		Exports		Imports	
Meat†: 'A'	59.3*	29.7n	0.6	0.8	—	0.1
'B'	4.6*	1.6²n	0.4	1.3	1.0	0.2
Butter	2.3	12.5²p	0.6	1.8	1.1	
Cheese	28.3	15.5²	0.6	0.4*		
Eggs	14.3	9.2	0.9		3.5	0.7*
Fish	na	na			18.5	1.9²*
Milk	56.7*	152.5²*	3.2	1.0	4.1²	3.1
Hides/skins			1.9²	2.9	0.1	0.5
Wool²	5.2²	4.3	4.7			

n government inspected meat only. p factory produce only.

6. FIBRES, TEXTILES, etc.

	Production		Exports		Imports	
Cotton lint	169.0	70.3	138.8	61.7		
Hemp fibre	0.5	2.0	11.7	10.7	0.2	6.7
Rubber: natural			2.6	na	0.7	0.5
Silk f	na	11.0		na	0.8	0.9
Cotton: yarn	17.2	7.2²*			0.6	
woven fabrics	15.7	na			1.7	
Wool: yarn	0.3r	0.7r				
woven fabrics						

f metric tons. r million metres.

7. FUEL AND POWER

	Production		Exports		Imports	
Coal, 'A'‡	—	—	—	—	2	4
Coke	572	270¹			2	1
Electricity h: total	na	101				
hydro	na					
thermal	na	260¹				
Oil, crude	920	—	30	10¹	970	na
Petroleum, refined					293	510¹

h million kWh.

8. IRON AND STEEL

	Production		Exports		Imports	
Pig iron	—	—	—	—	1	1
Iron/steel scrap					2	2

9. NON-FERROUS MINERALS AND METALS

			Imports	
Gold k: bullion/coins etc.			11.80¹	264.30
Asbestos				
Aluminium			4.63	0.79²
manufactured			0.38	0.32²
Lead, metal			0.43	0.22²
Magnesium: metal/salts				
Tin, metal			0.04¹	0.03²
Zinc, metal			0.08	0.15²
Wool			0.66	0.09
				0.43

10. CHEMICALS n AND FERTILIZERS

	Production		Imports	
Chemicals			na	
Fertilizers: Sulphur			0.7	0.6

n data not available for years 1953–5.

11. INDUSTRY

	Production		Exports		Imports	
Aircraft a						4
Alcoholic beverages	25.0	0.9			0.5²	1
beer b	665.0	246.0			0.3²a	
Cement						
Electrical engineering a			0.1†		13.3	39.7
Motor vehicles a			0.3²p		13.6²	3.0
					5.4	9.9

a million $ U.S. b '000 hectolitres. p used.

TAIWAN — CHINA SEA

Taiwan (the Republic of China), also called Formosa, is controlled by the remnant of the Nationalist government of China. The U.S.A. has pledged protection of Taiwan and its off-shore islands. The Chinese seat at the U.N. was occupied by Taiwan until 1971 when the People's Republic of China took its place.

AREA: 35 961 sq. km. (13 885 sq. miles)

LAND USE: (percentage of total)

		1955
Arable and orchard	24.3	24.7
Permanent meadow and pasture	1.7	na
Forest and woodland	49.1	70.9
City areas, waste and other land	24.9	na

POPULATION: 13 383 357* (1966 census)
Largest city: TAI-PEI, capital; population: 1 155 191 (city proper, 1965)
Total working population: 2 993 029

Distribution of working population (1956)

U.N. group no.		Percentage
0	Agriculture, forestry, fishing and hunting	50.1
1	Mining and quarrying	1.5
2/3	Manufacturing	11.9
4	Construction	2.1
5	Electricity, gas, water and sanitary services	0.5
6	Commerce	6.7
7	Transport, storage and communications	3.6
8		14.2
9	Services	10.4
	Others	

		Year(s)
Life expectancy at birth (years): male	65.8	1965
female	70.4	1965
Infant mortality (per '000)	22.7a	1965
Crude birth rate (per '000)	32.2a	1965
Accidental deaths (per 100 000 population)	5.5	1965
caused by motor vehicles		
due to other causes		
Population per physician	7.7	1965
Population per hospital bed	29.5	1965
Population per hospital bed	2 470	1966
School enrolment: age 5–19 years (percentage)	1 030	1963–4 av.
age over 19 years (per 100 000 population)	80	1963–5 av.
	553	

FINANCE
Currency unit: The Taiwan dollar

Exchange rates	1965a	1960
Per $ U.S.	40.1	39.85
Per £ sterling	112.28	111.56

		1960
National Income (million $ U.S.)	2 297	
G.N.P. per capita ($ U.S.)	230	
Rate of increase of G.N.P. per capita	3.6	
Foreign trade (percentage of G.D.P.)	34	

a selling rate.

TRADING

Total trade (in million $ U.S.)	1965	1955
Exports (f.o.b.)	450	123
Imports (c.i.f.)	557	104a

Main trading partners (percentage of total value)

Exports	1965	1955	Imports	1965	1955
Japan	31	59	Japan	40	30
U.S.A.	22	4	U.S.A.	32	48
S. Vietnam	10		Iraq	4	
Germany F.R.	7	1	Germany F.R.	3	2
Thailand	6	5	Philippines	2	1
Morocco	4	4	Australia	2	

Distribution of trade (percentage of total value)

Exports	1965	1955*
Food	51	85
(fruit and vegetables)	(25)	(8)
(sugar and honey)	(13)	(49)
Textiles and clothing	15	
Wood and paper	10	

Imports	1965	1955*
Manufactured goods	46	(9)
(machinery and transport equipment)	(29)	
Crude materials and fuels	31	(12)
(textile fibres and waste)	(10)	
Chemicals	13	16
Food d	(6)	
(cereals)	(7)	

COMMUNICATIONS

		Year(s)
Motor vehicles in use ('000s): private		
commercial		
Railway track (km.)	13.9	1964
Mail per capita: domestic	376.6	1963–5 av.
foreign received		
foreign sent	1.6	
Telephones (per '000 urban population)		
Radio licences (per '000 population)		
Television licences (per '000 population)		
Daily newspapers (per '000 population)		

PRODUCTION, EXPORTS AND IMPORTS Units: '000 metric tons unless otherwise indicated
Years: 1963–5 average and 1953–5 average

3. BEVERAGES, FOREST PRODUCTS, etc.

	Production		Exports		Imports	
Tobacco: leaf	8.0	5.2	0.5		0.4	0.7
cigarettes	2 763.0	1 756.7a			0.2²	0.2²
tobacco/snuff	1.5	1.1	—	—¹		
Softwood j	2.0	350.0¹	1.8¹		168.0²¹	43.6
Hardwood j	78.0*¹	350.0¹		2	27.8²	49.2
Newsprint	—	—			0.6	0.6
Other paper	3.2*	na	—²		19.4²	5.7

j no. in millions. j '000 cu. metres of roundwood equivalent.

4. VEGETABLE OILSEEDS AND OILS

	Production		Exports		Imports	
Castor seed	—	—				
Castor oil	—	—	0.20†		0.03	na
Copra	—	—	—		na	0.01
Coconut oil	—	—			1.22	3.37
Cottonseed	—	—			0.21	0.01
Cottonseed oil	—	—			0.23	0.80
Groundnuts	279.00	123.00	38.06	45.47	0.02	0.03
Linseed	4.20*	2.10	7.44	1.30	1.14	0.07
Linseed oil	—	—	3.89	1.07*	0.21	na
Olive oil	16.00*	8.67			0.21	0.15
Palm kernels	—	—	2.75		2.06	1.78
Palm oil	—	—	0.07		0.99	3.28
Sesame seed	5.53	12.67			0.97	0.87
Sunflower seed						0.02

5. LIVESTOCK‡, ANIMAL PRODUCTS, etc.

	Production		Exports		Imports	
Chickens d	4 092.7	2 986.3			13.9	1.6
Cattle d	454.0	516.0	32.6			
Goats / cows d	330.2	268.6²	420.0		376.6	na
Sheep d	1 352.0*	612.7				
Horses d	4 632.0	3 753.7				
Pigs d	67.7*	100.6	0.4*		—	—

d no. in thousands.

continued

---

na: data not available. — negligible or nil. * estimate. ‡ see appendix. † re-exports.
¹ one year only. ² two year average. a excl. U.S. $82 million aid imports from the U.S.A.
a two year average. ² two year average. ¹ one year only. a excl. U.S. $82 million aid imports from the U.S.A.

TAIWAN *continued*

PRODUCTION, EXPORTS AND IMPORTS
Years: 1963–5 average and 1953–5 average   Units: '000 metric tons unless otherwise indicated

1. CEREALS, etc.
	Production		Exports		Imports	
Barley	0.7	126.7	—	—	7.8	—
Cassava	241.3	—	—	—	—	—
Maize (corn)	39.3	9.3	—	—	23.6	—
Millets/sorghum	9.0	6.0	—	—	4.3	—
Oats	—	—	—	—	0.1	—
Potatoes	15.0	2.0	6.3	—	0.3	—
Sweet potatoes/yams	2 779.0	2 053.0	168.2	88.4	13.4	1.7
Wheat	2 876.0	2 429.7	—	—	349.4	176.1
	20.7	16.0				

2. FRUIT, etc.
	Production		Exports		Imports	
Apples	284.0	93.0	187.1	26.4	2.7	
Bananas	3.0	na				
Grapes	4.7	na	na			
Lemons	84.7	22.0	6.9	1.1		
Oranges	8.7	7.0	—		0.4	
Other citrus fruit	2.3	na				
Olives	0.3	0.1				
Peaches	3.0	na	—		0.3	
Pears	2.0	na				
Pineapples	207.0	68.3				
Plums	17.3	na				
Raisins	27.7	10.3				

3. BEVERAGES, FOREST PRODUCTS, etc.
	Production		Exports		Imports	
Cocoa					0.1	
Sugar: cane	8 465.7*	5 643.0[2]				
raw	891.5[n]	740.7[m]	771.6	673.7		
Tea	20.0	13.2	16.3	11.1	1.8	
Tobacco: leaf	17.7	12.1*	2.0	0.1	0.7	
cigarettes	12 983.0	9 447.7[h]				
tobacco/snuff	0.3	0.1	0.38			
Softwood j	726.3	465.0[1]	123.0		1.2	
Hardwood j	484.0	463.0[1]	71.4		545.1	
Wood pulp	92.7	21.3*	6.9		29.4	
Newsprint	74.1	33.0*	2.2	na	na	
Other paper	171.0*	33.0*	15.0		4.2	

e no. in millions.   *j* '000 cu. metres of roundwood equivalent.   *n* in addition, non-centrifugal sugar 24 (1963–5 av.) and 16 (1953–5 av.).

4. VEGETABLE OILSEEDS AND OILS
	Production		Exports		Imports	
Castor oil	na				0.04	0.02
Copra	na				2.90	
Coconut oil	2.00	3.00[2]				1.38
Cottonseed	77.70	45.01	0.21		3.20	
Groundnuts			0.02		1.06	
Linseed oil	na				0.25	0.19
Rapeseed	21.00	1.00	0.01		1.87	
Sesame seed	2.57	2.00	0.09		1.46	
Soya beans	59.00	20.30			175.23	100.50[2]
Soya bean oil			0.38		3.17	0.64

5. LIVESTOCK‡, ANIMAL PRODUCTS, etc.
	Production		Exports		Imports	
Chickens d	8 262.3	6 368.0				
Cattle d	101.3	75.7			0.2	
Goats d	143.0	161.7			0.2	
Pigs d	2 772.0	2 767.3	10.3		0.1	
Meat‡: A	235.7	81.3*				
B	26.9*	na			0.2	
Butter					0.2	
Eggs	5.0*	3.5	0.3		3.3	
Fish	369.7[r]	154.3[p]	1.6		48.0	
Milk	11.3	2.0			1.7	
Hides/skins	1.5	0.6	0.21*		19.8[1]*	
Wool					12.6	

d no. in thousands.   *p* incl. fish landed by Taiwanese vessels in foreign ports.

6. FIBRES, TEXTILES, etc.
	Production		Exports		Imports	
Abaca					0.2	
Agaves (sisal)	10.9	0.9	1.5		61.8	
Cotton lint	1.0	1.5[2]	1.9			
Flax fibre	2.2	0.2				
Hemp fibre	4.0	na	0.3		2.6	
Jute	12.0	12.3			6.1	1.9*
Rubber, natural			3.0			
Silk f	31.5[1]	106.0[1]	7.2		0.2[1]	
Cotton: yarn	51.2	22.6	13.1	na		
woven fabrics	28.0	19.5	0.3	na	9.9	
Rayon, fibre/yarn	4.6	na			na	
Non-cellulosic					na	
commercial d u	0.7	0.8	1.2	na	5.4	
private d u	3.2	0.8	1.1	na	0.2	
Woven yarn	4.3[f]	1.4[f]	0.1	na		
woven fabrics						

f metric tons.   *g* million metres.

7. FUEL AND POWER
	Production		Exports		Imports	
Coal 'A' ‡	4 963	na	63	120	10	7
Coke	na	na	—		—	
Electricity h: total	5 952	1 970[1]				
hydro	2 258	1 530[1]				
thermal	3 694	440[1]				
Natural gas i	180	30[1]				
Oil, crude	13	—	57		—	
Petroleum, refined	1 420	600[1]			1 520	780[1]
					40	

h million kWh.   *i* million cu. metres.

8. IRON AND STEEL
	Production		Exports		Imports	
Iron ore	63	8			51	11
Pig iron	338	28	7		3	7
Steel ingots/castings	na	na	7			4
Iron/steel scrap	na	na			288	

9. NON-FERROUS MINERALS AND METALS
	Production		Exports		Imports	
Gold k, ore m	27.30	27.00			77.67r	
Silver k, ore m	69.70	48.00	0.06		1.19	0.37
Asbestos: fibre	0.61	0.17	0.36		0.37	0.47
manufactured	na	na			82.54	26.86
Mica	na	0.02				
Aluminium: bauxite	37.00*	7.55[1]	9.00[1]	2.49	0.02	
alumina	16.74	6.35			0.21[2]	
Chrome, ore	1.88[n]	0.59[m]	12.24	5.23	4.54	0.55
Copper, ore	1.85	0.90	0.09		2.87	1.73
Lead, metal						
Magnesium: dolomite	38.06	na				
metal/salts	na	na	0.57		40.70	2.20
Mercury f	na	1.17			0.13	0.17
Nickel, metal					0.17	
Tin, metal					1.20	
Titanium minerals					6.25	3.28
Zinc, metal						

f metric tons.   *k* '000 fine troy oz.   *m* metal content.   *r* bullion.

10. CHEMICALS n AND FERTILIZERS
	Production		Exports		Imports	
Organic chemicals:						
Benzene	na		0.2		0.1	
Butadiene	na				na	
Ethylene	na				0.4[1]	
Methanol	na				0.5	
Phenol	na				na	
Phthalic anhydride	na				na	
Styrene monomer	132.8				na	
Urea					1.3	
Inorganic chemicals:						
Ammonia	131.5[2]		0.3[1]			
Carbon black	9.0		0.1			
Chlorine	38.4				0.5	
Nitric acid	14.7		3.9		0.1	
Sodium carbonate	53.5		0.1		—	
Sodium hydroxide	138.3					
Sulphuric acid						
Plastics:						
Polyamides	na				0.2[2]	
Polyethylene	na		3.4[2]		12.5[2]	
Polyvinyl chloride	2.4[2]				1.8[2]	
Fertilizers:						
Phosphates	0.6					
Potash	1.5					
Sulphur: native	16.9[x]	9.9[x]			77.4	42.6[y]
recovered	2.5	4.8			82.3	17.1

n data not available for years 1953–5.   *x* sulphur content.   *y* apatite.

11. INDUSTRY
	Production		Exports		Imports	
Beer b	169.0	66.6	25.0		21.9	38.0
Cement	2 347.3	548.7			1.4	
Electrical engineering a						
Railway vehicles a	na	na			na	2.2
Machine tools a	na	na			8.0	0.2
Merchant ships g	5.0	na			12.8[a]	0.5[a]
Motor vehicles						

a million $ U.S.   *b* '000 hectolitres.   *g* '000 G.R.T.   *u* assembly of imported parts.

EAST AFRICA

TANZANIA

Tanzania, an independent member of the British Commonwealth, was formed in 1964 of the union of the Trust Territory of Tanganyika and the Protectorate of Zanzibar. Tanzania is a member of the East African Community.

Where data are given separately, T refers to Tanganyika and Z to Zanzibar, including Pemba.

AREA: T 937 060 sq. km. (361 800 sq. miles)
Z   2 640 „   (1 020 „)

LAND USE: (percentage of total)
	1963	1954
Arable and orchard	12.7	11.6
Permanent meadow and pasture	36.9	16.0
Forest and woodland	37.6	38.2
City areas, waste and other land	12.8	34.2

POPULATION: T 11 876 982 } (1967 census)
Z   354 360
Largest city: DAR ES SALAAM, capital; population: 272 515* (city proper, 1967)

Employment: Agriculture and forestry are the principal occupations in Tanganyika. Cash crops of cotton and coffee are grown on plantations, some of which are now owned by Africans. There is some mining, and industry is being developed. In Zanzibar, particularly on the island of Pemba, clove growing is the major occupation; coconuts are also grown, and fishing is important.

continued

		Year(s)
Life expectancy at birth (years)	…	
Infant mortality (per '000)	37.5*	1957
Crude birth rate (per '000)	42.8*	1958
Crude death rate (per '000)	19.9*	1958
Population per physician	26*	1965
Population per hospital bed	120 / 540	1965
	410 a	1966
School enrolment: age 5–19 years (percentage)	21	1963–4 av.
age over 19 years (per 100 000 population)	3	1963–5 av.

a government hospitals only.

COMMUNICATIONS
		Year(s)
Motor vehicles in use ('000s): private	31.4	
commercial	1.6	1963–5 av.
Railway track (km)	9.4	
Telephones (per '000 urban population)	3 792	1969
Radio receivers (per '000 population)	0.2	1967
Daily newspapers (per '000 population)	10*	1963–5 av.
	5*	1962

FINANCE
Currency unit: The Tanzanian shilling replaced, at par, the East African shilling in 1966. Prior to 1960, East African pounds of 20 shillings were used.

Exchange rates	1955b	1960a	1965a	1938b
Per $ U.S.	0.357	7.143	7.143	0.215
Per £ sterling	1.0	20.0	20.0	1.0

		Year(s)
National Income (million U.S.)		
G.N.P. per capita ($ U.S.)	625	1965
Rate of increase of G.N.P. per capita	80	
Foreign trade (percentage of G.D.P.)	1.3	1960–4 av.
	46	1963–5 av.

a East African shillings.   *b* East African pounds.

TRADING: ZANZIBAR
	1965	1955	1938
Total trade (in million $ U.S.)			
Exports (f.o.b.)	69	82	15
Imports (c.i.f.)	23	13	14

Main trading partners (percentage of total value)

Exports	1965	1955	Imports	1965	1955a
Indonesia	22	40	U.K.	14	33
India	14	21	Tanganyika	9	na
China P.R.	11	na	Japan	7	5
U.S.S.R.	7	na	China P.R.	7	na
Pakistan	6	4	Iran	5	14
U.K.	4	4	India	5	—
			U.S.A.	…	…

Distribution of trade (percentage of total value b)

Exports	1965
Cloves and clove oil	69
Copra and coconut oil	23
Imports	1965
Food	40
Manufactured goods	36
Crude materials and fuels	12
Chemicals	2

a refers to the total trade for Kenya, Uganda and Tanganyika.   *b* % of national exports‡ which comprised 83% of general exports in 1965 and 86% in 1955.

TRADING: TANGANYIKA
Note—trade with Kenya and Uganda is excluded

	1965	1955	1938
Total trade (in million $ U.S.)			
Exports (f.o.b.)	176	102	15
Imports (c.i.f.)	140	122	14

Main trading partners (percentage of total value)

Exports	1965	1955a	Imports	1965	1955a
U.K.	30	28	U.K.	32	44
Hong Kong	8	8	Japan	9	4
Germany F.R.	8	10	Germany F.R.	9	4
India	7	15	Italy	8	6
China P.R.	6	12	India	7	3
U.S.A.	6		U.S.A.	6	3
Netherlands	5		Netherlands	4	3

Distribution of trade (percentage of total value)

Exports	1965
Sisal and other agaves	23
Cotton	20
Coffee	14
Diamonds	8
Fruit and vegetables	8
Imports	1965
Manufactured goods (machinery and transport equipment)	78
	(32)
(textiles and clothing)	(19)
Chemicals	8
Food	—

a incl. Kenya and Uganda, *b* % of national exports‡ which comprised 83% of general exports in 1965 and 86% in 1955.

PRODUCTION, EXPORTS AND IMPORTS
Years: 1963–5 average and 1953–5 average   Units: '000 metric tons unless otherwise indicated
Note—data for Tanganyika and Zanzibar are given separately where available; but, where they are combined, the trade figures include internal trade between the two states.

1. CEREALS, etc.
		Production		Exports		Imports	
Cassava	T	1 033.0*	861.0[1]				
	Z	80.0*	87.3			6.3r	17.6[2]
Maize (corn)	T	623.3*		10.7r	14.0	0.7r	0.5
Millets/sorghum	T	1 084.3*	9/5.5[2]	0.5	5.7	1.4*	0.8
Potatoes	T	9.3	3.0[2]	0.1	0.5		0.5
Rice	T/Z	106.7	52.3[2]		4.0	10.2[1]	17.8
Sweet potatoes/yams	T/Z	250.0*	9.0*				
Wheat		23.7	14.0[1]			3.3r	1.2

r data for Zanzibar na.

2. FRUIT, etc.
		Production		Exports		Imports	
Apples		—		—		0.2r	
Bananas	T/Z	12.0*	14.0				
Coconuts	T/Z	110.0*					
		150.0*					
Dates		5.3r	3.5[2]			0.9	
Oranges/lemons						0.1[1]	
Raisins						3.2r	
Wine b						1.0[2]	2.0

b '000 hectolitres.   *r* data for Zanzibar na.

continued

TANZANIA continued

PRODUCTION, EXPORTS AND IMPORTS continued

	Production	Exports	Imports
3. BEVERAGES, FOREST PRODUCTS, etc.			
Coffee . . . . . . T	37.7	18.3	0.1
Sugar: cane . . . . T	800.0*		
raw . . . . . T	59.6	29.5r	18.8
Tea . . . . T	5.2	12.0	0.1
Tobacco: leaf . . . T	3.9	1.6	31.1
cigarettes		2.3	0.3
Softwood j	1516.0r		
Hardwood j	30.3	46.0	0.21
Newsprint	11 414.3 18 924.52		9.4*
Other paper		7.0	5.4
		4.1	4.1
		25.5	5.4
		21.7	0.7
			2.9

e no. in millions. j '000 cu. metres of roundwood equivalent. n Tanganyika data na. r Zanzibar data na.

	Production	Exports	Imports
4. VEGETABLE OILSEEDS AND OILS			
Castor seed . . . . . T	15.67 n	16.93	0.77 0.17
Copra . . . . T	13.47	4.37	
	13.33*	12.43	5.77 0.23
Coconut oil . . . . . T	na	12.80	0.49 0.07
	97.00*	3.40*	
Cottonseed . . . . . T	32.67	4.21	0.03
Cottonseed oil . . . T	na	1.57	0.13
Groundnuts . . . . . T	12.13n	4.67	0.13
Groundnut oil . . . T	9.91*	0.29	0.16
Linseed oil . . . . . T	0.01		0.07
Olive oil . . . . . . T	1.03		0.02
Palm kernels . . . . T	30.3	1.84	0.05
Linseed . . . . . . T	9.30	0.57	
Sesame seed . . . . T	3.50	8.78	
Soya beans . . . . . T		1.82	
Soya bean oil . . . T	8.00		
Sunflower seed . . . T			
Tung oil . . . . . . T		0.01	

n total sales. r Zanzibar data na.

5. LIVESTOCK‡, ANIMAL PRODUCTS, etc.

Zanzibar is important for the production of cloves and clove oil, the greater part of the world's supply being produced here, mainly on the island of Pemba.

	Production	Exports	Imports
Chickens d . . . . . N	166.7*		
Cattle d . . . . . . N	8 423.0	6 676.0r	
dairy cows d q . . .	3 925.7**	0.31u	
Goats d . . . . . . N	4 408.0 3 986.0r		
Sheep d . . . . . . N	2 765.0 2 842.7	5.0	4.4 4.8
Pigs d : 'A' . . . . N	89.0 117.0		
Meat‡: 'B' . . . . T			
Butter . . . . T	1.0* 1.01		
Eggs . . . . T	1.9*	2.0	0.2 0.1
Milk . . . . T	83.52 50.8		0.1
Hides/skins . . . . T	10.1 135.01	1.6	0.1 0.1
Fish . . . . T	189.0		na
	7.11 4.71p	0.1	30.8 0.4
		0.3*	na
		6.42	

d no. in thousands. p of cattle only. q all cows over 3 years old.

THAILAND SOUTH EAST ASIA

Thailand, formerly known as Siam, is an independent sovereign state. The king no longer exercises absolute power, but since 1958 has ruled through the national assembly. Substantial technical and military aid is received from the U.S.A.

AREA: 514 000 sq. km. (198 400 sq. miles)

LAND USE‡: (percentage of total)

	U.N. group no.	Percentage
Arable and orchard . . .	0	82.0
Permanent meadow and pasture	2/3	
Forest and woodland . . .	5	3.4
City areas, waste and other land	6	0.1
	7	5.6
	8	4.7
	9	2.3

POPULATION: 32 680 000 (1967 estimate)
Total working population: 13 836 984

Distribution of working population (1960)

	1954	1964
Agriculture, forestry, fishing and hunting		
Mining and quarrying . . .		
Manufacturing		
Construction		
Electricity, gas, water and sanitary services		
Commerce		
Transport, storage and communications		
Services		
Others		

Largest city: KRUNG THEP (Bangkok), capital: population: 1 608 305 (1963)

FINANCE

Currency unit: The baht

	1954	1964
Exchange rates Per $U.S.		21.9 } 52.8
Per £ sterling		25.3 } 62.8
		22.0

	1965	1960	1960	1938
National Income (million $U.S.)				
G.N.P. per capita ($U.S.)	20.83	21.14	21.14	2.34
Rate of increase of G.N.P. per capita	58.32	59.19	59.19	10.76
Foreign trade (percentage of G.D.P.)				
	3204			
	130			
	34			

COMMUNICATIONS

Motor vehicles in use ('000s): private / commercial

		Year(s)
Railway track (km.)	3519	1964
Mail per capita: domestic		
foreign received	56	1965
foreign sent	180	
Telephones (per '000 population)	0.3	1967
Radio receivers (per '000 population)	54	1963–5 av.
Television sets (per '000 population)	5.8	1963–5 av.
Daily newspapers (per '000 population)	12	1962–4 av.

Life expectancy at birth (years): male / female

		Year(s)
Infant mortality (per '000)	53.6* } 58.7*	1960
Crude birth rate (per '000)	31.2*	1965
Crude death rate (per '000)	36.4*	1965
Population per physician	7.1*	1965
Population per hospital bed	8 820	1966
School enrolment: age 5–19 years (percentage)	1 090	1966
age over 19 years (per 100 000 population)	56	1963–5 av.

	1965	1960
Telephones	63.1	
	80.0	

Production	Exports	Imports	Year(s)

PRODUCTION, EXPORTS AND IMPORTS

Years: 1963–5 average and 1953–5 average Units: '000 metric tons unless otherwise indicated

	Production		Exports		Imports	
	1965	1955	1965	1955	1965	1955
TRADING						
Total trade (in million $U.S.)						
Exports (f.o.b.)	622	337				
Imports (c.i.f.)	771	342				

Main trading partners (percentage of total value)

Exports	1965	1955	Imports	1965	1955
Japan	18	18	Japan	32	18
West Malaysia	14		Germany, F.R.	19	19
Singapore	7 } 24		U.K.	10	19
India	7 }		U.S.A.	9	11
U.S.A.	9		Netherlands	5	
Germany, F.R.	5	30	Hong Kong	3	2
			Taiwan	2	

Distribution of trade (percentage of total value)	1965	1955	1938*
Exports			
Rice (rice)	54 (34)	52 (45)	14 (45)
Rubber	16	16	23
Tin	9	9	
Jute and kenaf			
Imports			
Manufactured goods (machinery and transport equipment)	68 (31)	69 (21)	na (20)
(textiles and clothing)	(11)	(19)	(6)
Crude materials and fuels	11	11	na
Chemicals	10	8	10
Food	6	9	13

1. CEREALS, etc.

	Production		Exports		Imports	
	1965	1955	1965	1955	1965	1955
Barley . . . . . T	na	na	na	na	na	na
Cassava . . . . T	2 003.0	259.01	0.42			
Maize (corn) . . T	931.0	60.0	42.7*			0.012
Millets/sorghum . T	2.0*	23.3			na	na
Potatoes . . . . T	na	na			0.023	0.232
Rice . . . . . . T	9 793.3 7 220.0					
Sweet potatoes/yams T	189.3					
Wheat . . . . . T	1 783.7 1 193.3		7.6*	27.4[1]a n		

a milled wheat.

2. FRUIT, etc.

	Production	Exports	Imports
Bananas . . . . T	763.0*	na	
Coconuts . . . . T	911.3e	5.1	na
Oranges . . . . T	na	na	0.1 na
Other citrus fruit . T	na	na	1.6
Pineapples . . . T	287.7*	169.2	4.8 0.22
Tomatoes . . . . T	12.7*	na	
Wine b . . . . . T			

b '000 hectolitres. e no. in millions.

3. BEVERAGES, FOREST PRODUCTS, etc.

	Production	Exports	Imports
Coffee . . . . . T	4 435.7 2 318.2	na	4.1 2.22
Sugar: cane . . . T	238.1p	43.0*p	
raw . . . . . T			
Tea . . . . . . T	53.1	65.3*	
Tobacco: leaf . . T	3.0 52.8	5.1	0.1 35.52
cigars	10 242.0 7 190.7e	0.62	1.6 1.22
cigarettes . . .	3 802.7 3 305.7	0.2	4.8 2.92
Hardwood d . . .	3.6 2.0	0.32	
Wood pulp . . .	181.0 1.8		6.2 10.4
Newsprint			26.02 17.4
Other paper . . .			24.62

e no. in millions. d '000 cu. metres of roundwood equivalent, crude brown sugar 140* (1963–5 av.) and 26* (1953–5 av.).

4. VEGETABLE OILSEEDS AND OILS

	Production	Exports	Imports
Castor seed . . . T	41.33	17.58	34.81 19.30*
Castor oil . . . . T			0.04* 0.052
Copra . . . . . T	20.93*	5 609.0	0.14 0.33*
Coconut oil . . . T			7.43 0.74
Cottonseed . . . T	14.0*	28.0*	na
Groundnuts . . . T	32.70	16.30	11.63 1.652
Groundnut oil . . T	82.60	61.60	14.32 16.47*
Linseed oil . . . T		0.8e	0.55 0.324*
Olive oil . . . . T	217.7*		2
Palm oil . . . . T	33.1*	na	
Sesame seed . . T	15.53	9.90	3.15* 3.202
Soya beans . . . T	32.30	21.00	3.44 2.602
Soya bean oil . . T	na	na	0.592
Tung oil . . . . T			0.05* 0.01*

5. LIVESTOCK‡, ANIMAL PRODUCTS, etc.

	Production	Exports	Imports
Chickens d . . . . N	30 300.0*	na	
Cattle d . . . . . N	5 341.3 5 509.0	56.3	12.62 0.1
Goats d . . . . . N	na	na	
Sheep d . . . . . N	na	na	2
Horses d . . . . N	na	na	
Pigs d : 'A' . . . N	4 488.0 3 733.3		20.4 13.62
Meat‡: 'B' . . . T			
Butter . . . . . . T	82.0*	na	4.6 2.52
Cheese . . . . . T		na	0.2 18.4*
Eggs . . . . T	536.9	275.9	12.4 0.1
Milk . . . . T	374.0*	na	0.2
Hides/skins . . . T	na	na	5.92

d no. in thousands.

6. FIBRES, TEXTILES, etc.

	Production	Exports	Imports
Cotton lint . . . T	16.3 8.3	0.1 1.62	14.8
Jute . . . . . . T	7.0* 1.02	7.01*	2.8
Silk d . . . . . T	208.4* 177.0	121.2*	
Rayon, woven fabrics .	16.5 19.7	18.01	0.31
woven fabrics . . T	21.8*	0.12	2.11
			0.11

7. FUEL AND POWER

	Production	Exports	Imports
Coal: 'A' . . . . T	40		8.08 8.08
'B' . . . . T			3.20* 3.20
Coke . . . . . . T			0.98*
Pig iron . . . . T			0.55
Electricity‡: total f	1 135.2		12.21 12.21
hydro . . . . f	565.2		9.01 9.01
thermal . . . f	570.2 320.1		
Oil, crude . . . . T			
Petroleum, refined . T	683[1]	67	643 1 547
			440[1]

f million kWh.

8. IRON AND STEEL

	Production	Exports	Imports
Iron ore . . . . T	40		2.00
Pig iron . . . . T			
Steel ingots/castings . T			54
Iron/steel scrap . . T			2

9. NON-FERROUS MINERALS AND METALS

	Production	Exports	Imports
Asbestos: fibre . . T	200m		
manufactured . .		3m	3.08p
Antimony, ore . . T	1.05m	0.11	2.98[1]s
Aluminium . . . . T	0.05m		
Copper, metal . . T	3.83m	4.69m	3.20
Lead, ore . . . . T	17.03	6.63[1]	0.388*
Magnesium, salts . T	14.18		
Manganese, ore . . T	5.61	9.37 7.58	22.7
Mercury f . . . . T	1.45m	10.47	42.1
Tin: ore . . . . . T	0.40	6.63	15.8a
metal . . . . T		10.41	0.4
Titanium minerals . T	0.18 1.40	1.52	
Tungsten, ore . . T		353.7	
Zinc, ore . . . . T			

f metric tons. m metal content. r metal. s incl. imports for re-export.

10. CHEMICALS‡ AND FERTILIZERS

	Production	Exports	Imports
Organic chemicals:			
Urea . . . . . . T			3.5
Other organic chemicals			2.2[1]
Inorganic chemicals:			
Carbon black . . T			3.2
Chlorine . . . . T			
Nitric acid . . . T			9.0[1]
Sodium carbonate . T	1 103.0	112.7	64.7
Sodium hydroxide . T			17.0[2]
Sulphuric acid . . T			
Fertilizers:			
Nitrogenous a . . T			
Phosphatic a . . T			
Potash a . . . . T			
Sulphur . . . . T	7.1		

a data not available for years 1953–5.

11. INDUSTRY

	Production	Exports	Imports
Aircraft a			1.2[1]
Alcoholic beverages a a			1.2
Cement . . . . . T			48.3
Electrical engineering a			
Railway vehicles a .			
Merchant ships a .			
Motor vehicles a .		2.0	2.98[1]

a million $U.S. b '000 G.R.T.

---

na: data not available. — negligible or nil. [1] one year only. [2] two year average. * estimate. ‡ see appendix. † re-exports.

TOGO

Togo, formerly the French trusteeship territory of Togoland, became an independent republic within the French Union in 1960. (the British trusteeship territory elected to be incorporated into Ghana.) Togo has close economic co-operation with Dahomey, has defended and financial agreements with France, and is an associate member of the European Economic Community.

AREA: 56 000 sq. km. (21 600 sq. miles)

LAND USE: (percentage of total)

		1965	1955
Arable and orchard		38.2	37.3
Permanent meadow and pasture		3.5	3.5
Forest and woodland		9.4	8.8
City areas, waste and other land		48.9	50.4

POPULATION: 1 724 000 (1967 estimate)
Largest city: LOMÉ (capital; population: 128 900) (1966)
Total working population: 648 550 (1958–60 av.)

Employment: The majority of the population is employed in agriculture, both in the production of subsistence crops and in the commercial production of coffee, cocoa, groundnuts, and palm kernels. Since the discovery of large phosphate deposits in 1953, the mining of phosphate rock has provided alternative employment.

			Year(s)
Life expectancy at birth (years): male		—	
female		—	
Infant mortality (per '000)	31.6		1961
Crude birth rate (per '000)	38.5		1961
Crude death rate (per '000)	127*		1961
Population per physician	34.2 *a*		1965
Population per hospital bed	7.6 *a*		1965
School enrolment: age 5–19 years (percentage)	36 400 *b*		1965
age over 19 years (per 100 000 population)	740 *b*		1966
	31		1965
	4		1963–4 av.

a African population.   *b* government hospitals only.

COMMUNICATIONS

			Year(s)
Motor vehicles in use ('000s): private	0.4		1963–5 av.
commercial	0.3		1963–5 av.
Railway track (km.)	443		1964
Mail per capita: domestic	1		1963–5 av.
foreign sent	0.2*		1967
foreign received	18		1963–5 av.
Telephones (per '000 population)	7.5		1965
Radio receivers (per '000 population)			
Daily newspapers (per '000 population)			

PRODUCTION, EXPORTS AND IMPORTS
Years: **1963–5 average** and *1953–5 average*   Units: '000 metric tons unless otherwise indicated

	Production	Exports	Imports	Year(s)
1. CEREALS, etc.				
Cassava	963.3	368.3	—	1965
Maize (corn)	91.3	51.3	—	1965
Millets/sorghum	122.7	115.7	—	1965
Potatoes	—	—	—	
Rice	22.7	12.0	—	1965
Sweet potatoes/	—	—	—	
yams	1 002.0*	387.0	—	1965
2. FRUIT, etc.				
Coconuts	32.3*	na	0.4	1963–5 av.
Wine *b*	—	—	—	
3. BEVERAGES, FOREST PRODUCTS, etc.				
Cocoa	14.2	13.6	0.1	1965
Coffee	13.1	11.0	0.1	1965
Sugar, raw	5.5	3.8	0.3	1965
Tobacco: leaf	—	—	2.8	1965
Hardwood/	948.7*	49.0¹	11.22	1967
Newsprint	—	—	0.1	1963–5 av.
Other paper	—	—	0.1	1963–5 av.
4. VEGETABLE OILSEEDS AND OILS				
Castor seed	0.33	0.48	0.30	1963–5 av.
Copra	2.60	2.58	5.90	1964
Cottonseed	4.20	2.67	2.45	1967
Coconut oil	na	9.10	1.53	1967
Groundnuts	12.83	3.10	2.51	1963–5 av.
Groundnut oil	na	0.28	—	1965
Palm kernels	14.23	9.80	9.63	1963–5 av.
Palm oil	1.67	0.10	0.43	1963–4 av.
Soya bean oil	na	0.01²	na	1965

5. LIVESTOCK‡, ANIMAL PRODUCTS, etc.

	Production	Exports	Imports	Year(s)
Chickens *d*	1 260.7	746.0 *p*	—	1965
Cattle *d*	155.0	126.0	0.3*	1965
Goats *d*	84.0*	na	1.4	1965
Sheep *d*	426.0	260.0	—	1965
Horses *d*	0.7	7.0	—	1965
Pigs *d*	200.0	189.3	0.9	1965
Meat	—	4.0	na	
Eggs	—	0.7*	1.5	
Fish	—	4.7	—	
Milk	—	27.7	—	
Hides/skins	—	0.7	—	

d no. in thousands.   *p* incl. ducks, geese and turkeys.

6. FIBRES, TEXTILES, etc.

	Production	Exports	Imports	Year(s)
Cotton: lint	2.7	1.7	2.1	1963–5 av.
yarn	—	—	0.8	
woven fabrics	—	—	—	

7. FUEL AND POWER

			Year(s)
Electricity *h*: total	28		
hydro	2		
thermal	26		1.7
Petroleum, refined	—		

h million kWh.

10. CHEMICALS‡‡ AND FERTILIZERS

				Year(s)
Chemicals	—	—	—	na
Fertilizers:				
Phosphates	753.0	—	na	

FINANCE
Currency unit: The franc CFA

Exchange rates

		1965	1960	1955
Per $U.S.		246.85	246.85	210
Per £ sterling		691.18	691.18	590

TRADING

	1965	1955	Year
Total trade (in million $U.S.)			
Exports (f.o.b.)	135	210	
Imports (c.i.f.)	100		
Gross National Income (million $U.S.)			
G.N.P. per capita ($U.S.)			

Main trading partners (percentage of total value)

Exports	1965	1955	1938
France	43	31	72
Netherlands	12	19	
Germany F.R.	9	14	
Italy	9	6	
Belg./Lux.	4	3	
Japan	4	2	
Australia	4	3	

Imports	1965	1955	1938
France	46	72	
Germany F.R.	33		
Japan	12		
U.K.	4		10
U.S.A.			7
Netherlands			{32} {19}
Ghana		5	5

Distribution of trade (percentage of total value)

Exports	1965	
Coffee and cocoa		
Natural phosphates		
Oilseeds		
Cotton		

Imports	1965	
Manufactured goods (machinery and transport equipment)		
Food, beverages and tobacco (textiles and clothing)		
Crude materials and fuels		
Chemicals		

TONGA

The kingdom of Tonga, or the 'Friendly Islands', previously a British protected state, became an independent member of the Commonwealth in 1970. The group consists of some 150 islands.

AREA: 700 sq. km. (270 sq. miles)

LAND USE: (percentage of total)

		1965	1955
Arable and orchard		68.6	78.5
Permanent meadow and pasture		15.4	15.7
Forest and woodland		2.9	
City areas, waste and other land		14.3	

POPULATION: 77 429 (1966 census)
Capital city: NUKUALOFA; population: 15 545 (city proper, 1966)

		Year(s)
Infant mortality (per '000)	8.7*	1965
Crude birth rate (per '000)	33.6*	1965
Crude death rate (per '000)	33.5*	1965
Population per physician	3 040	1965
Population per hospital bed	370 *d*	1966
School enrolment: age 5–19 years (percentage)	101‡	1963–4 av.
age over 19 years		

a government hospitals only.

FINANCE
Currency unit: The pa'anga, or Tongan dollar, at par with the Australian dollar, replaced the Australian pound in 1967 at the rate T$1 to A£0.5

Exchange rates (for Australian pounds)

	1965	1960	1950	1938
Per $U.S.	0.45	0.45	0.45	0.25
Per £ sterling	1.25	1.25	1.25	1.25

TRADING

			1964
Total trade (in million $U.S.)			4.3
Exports (f.o.b.)			
Imports (c.i.f.)			

Exports consist mainly of copra and bananas.

COMMUNICATIONS

			Year(s)
Telephones (per '000 urban population)	1.1		1967
Radio receivers (per '000 population)	46		1963–5 av.

PRODUCTION, EXPORTS AND IMPORTS
Years: **1963–5 average** and *1953–5 average*   Units: '000 metric tons unless otherwise indicated

	Production	Exports	Imports	Year(s)
1. CEREALS, etc.				
Cassava	19.0*	7.0²	—	
Sweet potatoes/ yams	70.0*	27.7	—	
2. FRUIT, etc.				
Bananas	na	6.7	4.4	
Coconuts	55.7* *c*	na	0.8 *n*	
Lemons	1.0 *n*	na	—	
Oranges	1.7*	na	—	
3. BEVERAGES, FOREST PRODUCTS, etc.				
Sugar, raw	—	—	0.7¹	
4. VEGETABLE OILSEEDS AND OILS				
Copra	10.17	18.83	9.37	

5. LIVESTOCK‡, ANIMAL PRODUCTS, etc.

	Production	Exports	Imports	Year(s)
Chickens *d*	2.7	na	—	
Cattle *d*	3.0	1.7	—	
Goats *d*	27.0	na	—	
Horses *d*	7.0	6.6	—	
Pigs *d*	27.0	30.0	—	
Eggs	0.1*	na	0.3	

d no. in thousands.

TRINIDAD AND TOBAGO

The islands of Trinidad and Tobago, formerly a British colony and a member of the West Indies Federation, became an independent member of the Commonwealth in 1962.

AREA: 5128 sq. km. (1 980 sq. miles)

LAND USE: (percentage of total)

		1961	1953
Arable and orchard		34.1	33.5
Permanent meadow and pasture		1.0	1.0
Forest and woodland		45.0	45.6
City areas, waste and other land		19.9	19.7

POPULATION: 1 030 000 (1967 U.N. estimate)
Capital city: PORT-OF-SPAIN; population: 93 954 (city proper, 1960)

Distribution of working population: 278 147 (1960)
Total working population: 278 147 (1960)

U.N. group no.

	Percentage
0 Agriculture, forestry, fishing and hunting	19.9
1 Mining and quarrying	14.6
2/3 Manufacturing	10.8
4 Construction	1.9
5 Electricity, gas, water and sanitary services	12.6
6 Commerce	5.8
7 Transport, storage and communications	24.0
8 Services	5.7
9 Others	

		Year(s)
Life expectancy at birth (years): male	62.2	1959–61 av.
female	66.3	1959–61 av.
Infant mortality (per '000)	38.1	1965
Crude birth rate (per '000)	38*	1965
Crude death rate (per '000)	8*	1965
Accidental deaths (per 100 000 population) caused by motor vehicles due to other causes	14.4	1965
Population per physician	3820	1965
Population per hospital bed	230 *a*	1965
School enrolment: age 5–19 years (percentage)	87 *b*	1965
age over 19 years (per 100 000 population)	77	1963

a government hospitals only.   *b* public education only.

COMMUNICATIONS

			Year(s)
Motor vehicles in use ('000s): private	51.7		1963–5 av.
commercial	15.4		1963–5 av.
Railway track (km.)	4.2		1964
Telephones (per '000 urban population)	188		1900–5 av.
Radio receivers (per '000 population)	27.6		1960–5 av.
Television licences (per '000 population)	84		1963
Daily newspapers (per '000 population)			

continued

na: data not available.   — negligible or nil.   ¹ one year only.   ² two year average.   * estimate.   ‡ see appendix.   † re-exports.

FINANCE

Currency unit: The Trinidad and Tobago dollar replaced, at par, the British West Indies dollar in 1962.

Exchange rates

	1965	1960a	1958a
Per $ U.S.	1.71	1.71	1.71
Per £ sterling	4.8	4.8	4.8

		Year(s)
National income (million $ U.S.)	488	1965
G.N.P. per capita ($ U.S.)	630	1965
G.N.P. per capita	121a	1965
Rate of increase of G.N.P. per capita	7.3	1960–1 av.
Foreign trade (percentage of G.D.P.)	121	1963–4 av.

a B.W.I. dollars.

TRADING

	1965	1955	1938
Total trade (in million $ U.S.)			
Exports (f.o.b.)	403	166	35
Imports (c.i.f.)	477	172	35

Main trading partners (percentage of total value)

Exports	1965	1955	Imports	1965	1955
U.S.A.	34	3	Venezuela	26	26
U.K.	16	39	U.S.A.	17	29
Sweden	6	5	U.K.	16	38
Netherlands	6	3	Saudi Arabia	16	6
Canada	5	4	Colombia	5	na
France	3	3	Canada	2	1
Guyana	2	3	Guyana	2	2

Distribution of trade (percentage of total value)

Exports	1965	1955
Petroleum and petroleum products	83	76
Sugar	6	11
Chemicals	5	1

Imports	1965	1955
Petroleum and petroleum products	49	28
Manufactured goods (machinery and transport equipment)	33 (16)	45 (17)
Food	6	11
Chemicals	4	5

PRODUCTION, EXPORTS AND IMPORTS

Years: **1963–5** average and *1953–5 average*   Units: '000 metric tons unless otherwise indicated

	Production		Exports		Imports	
	1965	1955	1965	1955	1965	1955
1. CEREALS, etc.						
Cassava	5.0*	na	—	—	16.32	na
Maize (corn)	3.0*	na	—	—	0.62	na
Millet/sorghum	na	na	—	—	1.32	na
Oats	na	na	—	—	12.52	na
Rice	10.3*	na	0.4††	0.1	28.8	17.8
Potatoes	—	—	—	—	na	na
Sweet potatoes/yams	15.0*	na	—	—	na	na
Wheat	—	—	0.22	—	na	na
2. FRUIT, etc.						
Apples	—	—	—	—	1.12	na
Bananas	25.7*	na	2.0	2.0	1.02	na
Coconuts	117.7*a	na	—	—	0.2	na
Grapes	—	—	—	—	na	na
Lemons	2.0*	4.0	2.5	2.0	na	na
Oranges	15.0*	16.7	4.7	5.1	na	na
Other citrus fruit	29.0*	na	2.0†	0.7	na	na
Tomatoes	3.0*	na	0.9	—	na	na
3. BEVERAGES, FOREST PRODUCTS, etc.						
Cocoa	5.4	8.5	5.3	8.5	—	—
Coffee	4.1	3.6	3.6	1.4	—	—
Sugar: cane	2348.3*	*800.3	—	—	—	—
raw	238.8	178.7	202.6	152.1	0.22	na
Tea	—	—	—	—	0.7	na
Tobacco: leaf	765.0	688.3	0.3†	0.2†	0.22	na
cigarettes	131.0¹	169.7¹	0.9	0.7	na	na
Softwood*j*					77.52	56.2
Newsprint*j*					3.41	1.4
Other paper*j*					17.1¹	2.7¹
b Wine*b*					na	14.0
h in millions. *j j* '000 cu. metres of roundwood equivalent.						

6. FIBRES, TEXTILES, etc.	Production		Exports		Imports	
	1965	1955	1965	1955	1965	1955
Agaves (sisal, etc.)	na	na	na	na	na	na
Cotton: lint	—	—	—	—	0.1	na
woven fabrics	na	na	na	na	na	na
Rayon, woven fabrics	na	na	na	na	na	na

7. FUEL AND POWER						
Coal, 'A'‡	—	—	—	—	—	—
Electricity*h*‡	784	280¹	—	—	—	—
Natural gas*i*	1 030	505¹	—	—	—	—
Oil, crude*h*	6 970	3 600¹	5 280¹	3 820¹	11 540	2 590¹
Petroleum, refined	17 360	14 630	1 370	390¹*	20	120¹
h million kWh. *i* million cu. metres. *t* thermal.						

8. IRON AND STEEL						
Iron/steel scrap	na	na	3	11	—	—

9. NON-FERROUS MINERALS AND METALS						
Gold*h*, bullion/coins etc.	—	—	—	—	0.1²	na
Silver*h*, bullion	—	—	—	—	0.22	na
Asbestos	na	na	na	na	—	—
Aluminium manufactured	na	na	na	na	1.18	1.01
Copper, metal	na	na	na	na	18.32	0.57
Lead, metal	na	na	na	na	0.01	0.16
Magnesium, magnesite	na	na	na	na	0.24	0.04
Tin, metal	na	na	na	na	2.19²	1.47
Zinc, metal	na	na	na	na	0.11	0.10
h '000 fine troy oz.					0.03	

10. CHEMICALS*n* AND FERTILIZERS						
Organic chemicals:						
Benzene	na	na	—	—	0.07	—
Butadiene	na	na	—	—	2.56	—
Ethylene	na	na	—	—	0.03	—
Methanol	na	na	—	—	na	na
Phthalic anhydride	na	na	—	—	na	na
Phenol	na	na	—	—	na	na
Styrene monomer	na	na	—	—	na	na
Urea	na	na	—	—	na	na
Inorganic chemicals:						
Ammonia	na	na	—	—	na	na
Carbon black	na	na	—	—	na	na
Chlorine	na	na	—	—	na	na
Sodium carbonate	na	na	—	—	na	na
Sodium hydroxide	0.4	—	—	—	na	na
Sulphuric acid	na	na	na	na	na	na
Plastics	na	na	na	na	na	na
Fertilizers:						
Potash	na	na	7.4	3.0	na	na
Sulphur	5.3r	5.71*r	15.1	na	1.8	na
n data not available for years 1953–5. *r* recovered sulphur.						

11. INDUSTRY						
Aircraft*a*	—	—	—	—	—	—
Alcoholic beverages beer*b*	90.0	26.6	1.8a	1.2a	5.4	3.0
Cement	176.0	48.7	50.7*	22.0	11.3*	2.0a
Electrical engineering*a*	—	—	—	—	na	na
Motor vehicles*a*	—	—	—	—	1.92	2.4a
Railway vehicles*a*	—	—	—	—	2.3	na
b '000 hectolitres.						

4. VEGETABLE OILSEEDS AND OILS						
Castor oil	—	—	0.01²	—	—	0.1
Copra	13.47*	15.50²	1.96	—	—	—
Coconut oil	—	—	0.90	0.22	—	na
Groundnut oil	—	—	0.32²	0.03	—	—
Linseed oil	—	—	0.03²	0.01²	—	—
Olive oil	—	—	0.15²	0.13²	—	—
Palm oil	—	—	0.02²	0.24	—	—
Rapeseed oil	—	—	0.22	0.11	—	—
Soya bean oil	—	—	0.01	0.21²	—	—

5. LIVESTOCK‡ ANIMAL PRODUCTS, etc.						
Chickens*d*	933.3*n	—	—	—	—	—
Cattle*d*	52.7*	38.0¹	—	—	—	—
Goats*d*	30.0*	32.1¹	—	—	—	—
Sheep*d*	5.0*	4.0	—	—	—	—
Horses*d*	1.0*	na	—	—	—	—
Pigs*d*	40.0*	34.0¹	—	—	—	—
Bacon/ham	0.7*	1.7p	—	—	—	—
Meat: 'A' }						
'B' }	2.0*	3.02	2.52	—	—	—
Butter	—	—	0.2	0.6	4.62	na
Cheese	3.0*	na	—	—	3.02	0.6
Eggs	9.6	4.0	0.3	—	1.3	1.0
Milk	0.5*	na	0.1	—	70.8	0.8
d no. in thousands. *n* incl. ducks, geese and turkeys. *p* government inspected meat only.					4.82	42.4*

na: data not available.   — negligible or nil.   ¹ one year only.   ² two year average.   * estimate.   † re-exports.

Tunisia, formerly a French protectorate, became an independent sovereign state in 1956. The following year the monarchy was abolished and the country was declared a republic. A customs union with France has been maintained.

AREA: 164 150 sq. km. (63 362 sq. miles)

LAND USE: (percentage of total)

	Percentage	*Year(s)*
Arable and orchard	34.6	1964
Rough grazing land	45.2	
Forest and woodland	6.7	
City areas, waste and other land	13.5	

POPULATION: 4 457 862 (1966 census)
Largest city: TUNIS; capital; population: 662 000 (1964)

Distribution of working population (1956)
Total working population: 1 327 520* (excl. foreigners)

U.N. group no.

		Percentage	*Year(s)*
0	Agriculture, forestry, fishing and hunting	68.1	1956
1	Mining and quarrying	1.1	
²/3	Manufacturing	6.1	
4	Construction	4.7	
5	Electricity, gas, water and sanitary services	0.7	
6	Commerce	6.4	
7	Transport, storage and communications	2.6	
8	Services	9.2	
9	Others		

			Year(s)
Infant mortality (per '000)	74.3*		1960
Crude birth rate (per '000)	41.9*		1960
Crude death rate (per '000)	11.8*		1960
Population per physician	8 990		1964
Population per hospital bed	390a		1966
School enrolment: age 5–19 years (percentage) age over 19 years (per 100 000 population)	61 107		1953–5 av. 1953–5 av.
a government hospitals only.			

COMMUNICATIONS

		Year(s)
Railway track (km)	2016	1963–5 av.
Motor vehicles in use ('000s): private	48.7	1967
commercial	28.1	1967
Telephones (per '000 population)	0.8*	1967
Radio licences (per '000 population)	72	1963–5 av.
Television sets (per '000 population)	0.8	1963–5 av.
Daily newspapers (per '000 population)	28	1962

FINANCE

Currency unit: The Tunisian dinar, equivalent to 1 000 Tunisian francs, was introduced in 1958.

Exchange rates

	1965	1960	1938a
Per $ U.S.	0.52	0.42	38
Per £ sterling	1.456	1.176	175

		Year(s)
National income (million $ U.S.)	789	1965
G.N.P. per capita ($ U.S.)	200	1966
Rate of increase of G.N.P. per capita	3.3	1960–4 av.
Foreign trade (percentage of G.D.P.)	38	1963–5 av.
a Tunisian francs.		

TRADING

	1965	1950a	1938a
Total trade (in million $ U.S.)			
Exports (f.o.b.)	120	350	39
Imports (c.i.f.)	245	980	45

Main trading partners (percentage of total value)

Exports	1965	1955	Imports	1965	1955
France	31	55	France	39	75
Italy	12	8	U.S.A.	16	2
U.K.	5	11	Italy	7	4
Yugoslavia	4	4	Germany F.R.	6	2
Greece	4	5	U.S.S.R.	4	—
Algeria	4	4	U.K.	4	3
India	4	—	Brazil	2	1

Distribution of trade (percentage of total value)

Exports	1965	1955
Phosphates and phosphatic fertilizers	34	20
Olive oil	21	18
Metalliferous ores and scrap	6	14

Imports	1965	1955
Manufactured goods (textiles and clothing)	66 (31)	(10*) (14*)
Food (fruit and vegetables)	6 (10)	15* (na)
Crude materials and fuels (petroleum and products)	14 (7)	(na) (3*)
Chemicals	na	na

PRODUCTION, EXPORTS AND IMPORTS

Years: **1963–5** average and *1953–5 average*   Units: '000 metric tons unless otherwise indicated

	Production		Exports		Imports	
	1965	1955	1965	1955	1965	1955
1. CEREALS, etc.						
Barley	222.7	143.7	11.6	20.8	25.2	11.6
Maize (corn)	5.0*	2.02	0.1	5.7	0.5	0.2
Millet/sorghum	10.0* }		1.7	0.6	1.7	na
Oats	48.0* }	7.3	3.7	6.2	0.4	na
Potatoes	—	19.0	2.0	na	24.7	na
Rice	628.7	533.0	72.7	168.5	137.5	9.5
Wheat						
2. FRUIT, etc.						
Apples	8.3	2.52	—	—	1.1	2.2
Apricots	14.7	6.11	—	—	2.2	2.4
Bananas	—	—	—	—	2.4	2.4
Dates	42.0	37.0	2.8	2.7	0.2	na
Figs	18.3	13.0	—	—	0.2	na
Grapes	261.3	134.0*	5.0	4.5	0.2	na
Lemons	14.7	7.01	34.8	15.1	0.4	na
Oranges	73.3	41.7*	0.4	—	—	—
Other citrus fruit	1.0*	na	—	—	—	—
Olives	392.3	na	—	—	—	—
Peaches	10.7	na	—	—	—	—
Pears	4.7	7.01	—	—	—	—
Plums	5.3	na	—	—	—	—
Raisins	0.1*	0.1*²	—	—	—	—
Tomatoes	102.7	25.7	—	—	—	—
Wine*b*	1 830.0	944.0*	293.0	449.0	1.8	3.7
3. BEVERAGES, FOREST PRODUCTS, etc.						
Cocoa	—	—	0.3	0.3*		
Coffee	—	—	0.2	0.3		
Sugar: beet	44.0	na	—	—	75.7	62.6
Tea	1.4	1.7*²	0.5	—	4.8	2.3
Tobacco: leaf	3.0*	na	0.1	0.2	3.0	2.3
cigarettes	2 581.0a	1 898.3a				
cigars	0.9	3.0*	0.01	0.2	na	1.3
tobacco/snuff	54.0*a	16.1				
Softwood*j*	1 219.5*²	100.0			67.3	62.6
Hardwood*j*	1 219.5*²	—2			35.8	
Newsprint*j*	na	na	—	—	25.51	
Other paper*j*	na	na	—	—	4.21	
b '000 hectolitres. *j j* '000 cu. metres of roundwood equivalent.						

4. VEGETABLE OILSEEDS AND OILS	Production		Exports		Imports	
	1965	1955	1965	1955	1965	1955
Castor oil	—	—	0.01†	—	0.1	na
Coconut oil	—	—	0.31	—	0.61	na
Cottonseed	—	—	na	—	0.05	0.03
Cottonseed oil	—	—	na	—	0.03†	0.38
Groundnuts	—	—	0.46	—	0.23	0.35
Groundnut oil	90.67	na	43.24	na	0.07	na
Linseed	—	—	—	—	0.43	0.07
Linseed oil	1.00*	1.00²	na	na	0.01	0.83
Rapeseed oil	—	—	58.67	23.72	0.94	0.12
Sesame seed	—	—	—	—	0.2	na
Sunflower seed	—	—	—	—		

na: data not available.   — negligible or nil.   ¹ one year only.   ² two year average.   * estimate.   ‡ see appendix.   † re-exports.   *continued*

TUNISIA continued

PRODUCTION, EXPORTS AND IMPORTS continued

	Production	Exports	Imports	Year(s)
5. LIVESTOCK‡; ANIMAL PRODUCTS, etc.				
Chickens d r	5 406.3*			1966
Cattle d	654.0*			1966
Sheep d	3 689.0*			1966
Goats d	222.3*			1966
Horses d	83.0			1966
Pigs d	4.0			1966
Bacon/ham }	41.7*			1965
Meat‡: B }	8.4*			1965
Butter	1.3*			
Cheese	11.3*			
Eggs	23.3			
Fish	124.0*			
Hides/skins	na			
Milk				
Wool	1.52			
d no. in thousands. *f* incl. ducks, geese and turkeys.				

6. FIBRES, TEXTILES, etc.

7. FUEL AND POWER

8. IRON AND STEEL

9. NON-FERROUS MINERALS AND METALS

10. CHEMICALS AND FERTILIZERS

11. INDUSTRY

TURKEY

Turkey was declared a republic in 1923, and there followed a long process of reform and 'Westernization.'

Turkey is a member of Cento and an associate member of the European Economic Community, agreements for co-operation and development have been signed with Iran and Pakistan.

AREA: 780 576 sq. km. (301 380 sq. miles)

POPULATION: 31 391 421 (1965 census)

Largest city: ISTANBUL; population: 2 052 368 (1965)
Capital city: ANKARA; population: 971 065 (1965)

LAND USE: (percentage of total)

	1965	1955	Percentage
Arable and orchard	33.5	29.0	
Permanent meadow and pasture	36.2	40.3	
Forest and woodland	13.5	13.4	
City areas, waste and other land	16.8	17.3	

Distribution of working population (1960)

Total working population: 12 993 245

U.N. group no.		Percentage
0	Agriculture, forestry, fishing and hunting	75.0
1	Mining and quarrying	0.6
2/3	Manufacturing	6.2
4	Construction	2.4
5	Electricity, gas, water and sanitary services	3.1
6	Commerce	1.9
7	Transport, storage and communications	5.2
8	Services	5.1
9	Others	

COMMUNICATIONS

	Year(s)
Motor vehicles in use ('000s): private	79.7 / 99.0 / 155.7*
commercial	45
Railway track (Km.)	7929 / 7929
Mail per capita: domestic	
foreign received	
foreign sent	
Telephones (per '000 population)	
Radio licences (per '000 population)	
Television sets (per '000 population)	
Daily newspapers (per 1000 population)	

FINANCE

Currency unit: The lira, or Turkish pound
Exchange rates

	1965 a	1960 a	1955 b	1938 b
Per $ U.S.	9.0	9.0	2.83	1.26
Per £ sterling	25.2	25.2	7.91	5.81

		Year/s
National Income ($million $ U.S.)	7593	1965
G.N.P. per capita ($ U.S.)	280	1966
Rate of increase of G.N.P. per capita	1.6	1960–5 av.
Foreign trade (percentage of G.D.P.)	12	1963–5 av.

TRADING

Total trade (in million $ U.S.)

	1965	1955	1938
Exports (f.o.b.)	464	313	115
Imports (c.i.f.)	577	498	119

Main trading partners (percentage of total value)

Exports

	1965	1955	1938
U.S.A.	18	16	12
Germany F.R.	18	16	43 d
U.K.	9	7	8
Italy	5	2	4
Belg./Lux.	4		
Lebanon	4		

Imports

	1965	1955	1938
U.S.A.	28	22	19
Germany F.R.	15	10	47 d
U.K.	8	8	11
Italy	6	4	
France			
Saudi Arabia	na	3	1
U.S.S.R.	3		4

PRODUCTION, EXPORTS AND IMPORTS

Years: 1963–5 average and 1953–5 average   Units: '000 metric tons unless otherwise indicated

1. CEREALS, etc.

	Production	Exports	Imports
Barley	3 596.0 / 3 008.3	46.8²	3.7
Maize (corn)	996.7 / 842.2	101.0 / 10.2³	11.7
Millets/sorghum	57.7 / 94.3	8.5	
Oats	530.0 / 365.7	1.2	40.3
Potatoes	1 600.0 / 1 038.7	0.7	
Rice	200.0 / 242.7	8.2	13.9
Rye	803.3 / 606.7	46.9	0.5²
Wheat	9 069.0 / 6 718.7	577.3 / 405.4	74.2

2. FRUIT, etc.

Apples	342.0 / 136.3	0.3	
Apricots	88.7 / 68.6		
Cherries	57.7 / 41.7		
Figs	208.0 / 104.0	12.6	
Grapes	2 944.3 / 2 447.7	6.0	
Lemons	62.0 / 22.7	7.9	0.1
Oranges	324.3 / 155.7	14.9	
Other citrus fruit	569.0 / 325.3	1.1*	
Olives	143.0 / 203.3		
Peaches	95.0 / 107.7		
Pears	270.0* / 130.8	39.7	17.0
Plums	143.0 / 108.7		
Raisins	270.0* / 130.8	61.4	10.1
Wine b	332.0 / 209.0*	19.1	20.3
b '000 hectolitres.			

3. BEVERAGES, FOREST PRODUCTS, etc.

Cocoa	—	—	1.1
Coffee	—	—	1.1
Sugar: beet	3 802.1 / 1 357.0	—	0.7
raw	624.8 / 224.7	88.8	6.4
Tea	11.0 / 0.71	3.6	2.4
Tobacco: leaf	150.0 / 113.3	56.7	65.4
cigarettes	33 952.0e / 22 095.0e	1.4	
tobacco/snuff		1.5	
Softwood j	5 531.0 / 2 096.7	2.0	452.9
Hardwood j	4 825.3 / 3 619.7	16.2	7.2
Wood pulp	23.5		
Newsprint	76.3	37.4	
Other paper			
j '000 cu. metres of roundwood equivalent.			

4. VEGETABLE OILSEEDS AND OILS

Castor oil	na		0.21
Copra	na	—	0.35
Coconut oil	na	—	0.01
Coconut oil	491.30 / 266.30	—	0.30
Cottonseed	na	11.28	13.10²
Cottonseed oil	na	0.94	0.01
Groundnuts	17.71 / 10.01	0.87	4.15
Linseed	16.67 / 19.00	0.74	
Linseed oil	na		1.13
Olive oil	94.67 / 54.67*	14.13	0.06
Rapeseed	6.70 / 2.30	0.38	
Sesame seed	36.00 / 49.50	0.40	
Soya beans	36.00 / 3.67	1.29	
Soya bean oil	6.30	2.00	
Sunflower seed	137.33 / 124.00	0.39	36.26
		2.50²	0.01

5. LIVESTOCK‡; ANIMAL PRODUCTS, etc.

	Production	Exports	Imports
Chickens d	27 812.3 / 22 970.3		
Cattle d	12 859.0 / 10 774.0	0.4	19.3²
dairy cows d	4 437.7*		
Sheep d	32 182.3 / 26 876.3	714.3	na
Goats d	21 681.0 / 21 029.0		
Horses d	1 206.7 / 1 211.0	4.02	
Pigs d	12.0		
d no. in thousands.			

6. FIBRES, TEXTILES, etc.

7. FUEL AND POWER

8. IRON AND STEEL

9. NON-FERROUS MINERALS AND METALS

---

na: data not available.   — negligible or nil.   1 one year only.   2 two year average.   * estimate.   ‡ see appendix.   † re-exports.

continued

TURKEY continued

PRODUCTION, EXPORTS AND IMPORTS continued

9. NON-FERROUS MINERALS AND METALS—continued

	Production	Exports	Imports
Copper: ore	32.10m	5.51	4.20
metal	25.69	14.46	13.82
Lead: ore	1.95m	23.94	7.11
metal	1.59	3.04	0.07
Magnesium: metal/salts	370.00*p	—	3.00
dolomite	44.19	na	1.55
magnesite	96.66	63.26	2.59
Manganese, ore	13.60	72.66	1.67
Mercury/ metal			
Nickel, metal	—	31.93z	0.04
Tin, metal	15.04	95.30	0.65
Titanium minerals	5.84m	3.41m	4.31r
Zinc, ore		3.54	0.09
Zirconium minerals			0.77

f metric tons. m metal content. p 1966 figure. r metal. z titanium-oxide only.

10. CHEMICALS n AND FERTILIZERS

	Production	Exports	Imports
Organic chemicals:			
Benzene	na	—	6.1²
Butadiene	na	—	na
Ethylene	na	—	0.1
Methanol	na	—	32.1
Phthalic anhydride	na	—	21.4²
Styrene monomer	na	—	26.5¹y
Urea	na	—	

UGANDA

Uganda, formerly a British East African protectorate, became a fully independent member of the Commonwealth in 1962. In 1966 the prime minister suspended the constitution and assumed full powers of government until the following year when the country became a republic and a new constitution was formed. Uganda is a member of the East African Community.

LAND USE: (percentage of total)

	1964
Arable and orchard	16.0
Permanent meadow and pasture	7.0
Forest and woodland	7.1
City areas, waste and other land	81.2

a African population.

Employment: The majority of the population is employed in agriculture. The cash crops produced include cotton, coffee, oilseeds, tea, sugar, and tobacco.

AREA: 243410 sq. km. (93 981 sq. miles)

POPULATION: 7 934 000 (1967 estimate)

Largest city: KAMPALA, capital: population: 123 332 (1959)

		Year(s)
Infant mortality (per '000)	160*	1959
Crude birth rate (per '000)	42*a	1959
Crude death rate (per '000)	20*a	1959
Population per physician	11 600	1966
Population per hospital bed	890	1966
School enrolment age 5–19 years (percentage)	30	1963–4 av.
age over 19 years (per 100 000 population)	15	1963–5 av.

COMMUNICATIONS

		Year(s)
Motor vehicles in use ('000s): private	28.4	1963–5 av.
commercial	5.6	1969
Railway track (km.)	1160	1969
Telephones (per '000 urban population)	18.3	1967
Radio receivers (per '000 population)	18.5	1963–5 av.
Television sets (per '000 population)	5	1964
Daily newspapers (per '000 population)		

EAST AFRICA

10. CHEMICALS n AND FERTILIZERS—continued

	Production	Exports	Imports
Inorganic chemicals:			
Ammonia	na	—	6.1²
Carbon black	na	—	na
Chlorine	na	—	0.1
Nitric acid	na	—	32.1
Potassium	na	—	21.4²
Sodium carbonate	na	—	43.7
Sodium hydroxide	na	—	27.2
Sulphuric acid	22.3	—	
Plastics:			
Polyamides	na	—	na
Polyethylene	na	—	na
Polyvinyl chloride	na	—	na
Fertilizers:			
Phosphates	na	—	103.1
Potash	3.0	—	4.2
Pyrites	52.5x	12.3x*	101.4
Sulphur, native	21.3	10.4	

a data not available for years 1953–5. n data not available for home consumption in 1967. w 1957 figure. x sulphur content. y incl. oleum.

11. INDUSTRY

	Production	Exports	Imports
Aircraft a	—	—	0.7
Alcoholic beverages			
beer b	287.0	275.7	na
spirits b	206.0	119.0w	na
Cement	2 952.7	678.7	0.7
Electrical engineering a	—	—	660.0
Machine tools a			40.6
Merchant ships g			7.3
Motor vehicles a			6.1
Railway vehicles a			

a East African shillings. b East African pounds. g '000 G.R.T. n '000 hectolitres. i production for home

FINANCE

Currency unit: The Uganda shilling replaced, at par, the East African shilling in 1966. Prior to 1960 East African pounds of 20 shillings were used.

Exchange rates	1965 a	1960 a	1950 b	1938 b
Per $ U.S.	7.143	7.143	0.357	0.215
Per £ sterling	20.0	20.0	1.0	1.0

		Year(s)
National income (million $ U.S.)	585	1965
G.N.P. per capita ($ U.S.)	100	1966
Rate of increase of G.N.P. per capita	0.5	1960–4 av.

TRADING

Note—trade with Kenya and Tanganyika is excluded

	1965	1955 a
Total trade (in million $ U.S.)		
Exports (f.o.b.)	179	299
Imports (c.i.f.)	114	417

Main trading partners (percentage of total value)

Exports	1965	1955 a		Imports	1965	1955 a
U.S.A.	22	12		U.K.	38	44
U.K.	17	28		Japan	10	6
Belg./Lux.	11	3		India.	6	4
China P.R.	6			U.S.A.	5	5
India	3	15		Italy	4	3
Canada	3			Germany F.R.	4	3
Germany F.R.	3	10		France		

Distribution of trade (percentage of total value)

Exports	1965		Imports	1965
Coffee	49		Manufactured goods, (machinery and transport equipment)	78
Cotton	27		(textiles and clothing)	(36)
Copper	13		Chemicals	8
			Food	5

PRODUCTION, EXPORTS AND IMPORTS
Years: 1963–5 average and 1953–5 average   Units: '000 metric tons unless otherwise indicated

1. CEREALS, etc.

	Production	Production	Exports	Exports	Imports	Imports
	1963–5	1953–5	1963–5	1953–5	1963–5	1953–5
Cassava	1 447.0*	na	—	—	0.1	—²
Maize (corn)	672.3	490.3	2.3	15.0²	2.3	—²
Millets/sorghum	19.0*	na	0.4		0.4	
Rice	1.7*	na	5.4	6.2	5.4	6.2
Sweet potatoes/	—	na				
Yams						
Wheat.	1 330.0*	na	1.0			

2. FRUIT, etc.

Apples	na	na	—	—	0.1	0.1
Raisins	na	na	—	—	0.1	0.1
Wine b	0.1†	na	0.1†		2.1	
Wine a					1.3	

b '000 hectolitres.

3. BEVERAGES, FOREST PRODUCTS, etc.

Coffee	160.9	50.7²	148.3	52.1		
Sugar: cane	1 530.3*	469.3	2.9		—	—
raw	122.4	69.7	6.1		6.1	
Tea: raw	7.4	2.7	2.0		6.1	
Tobacco: leaf	3.6	1.8*	na		6.1	
cigarettes	1 205.0c	2 961.7c				
tobacco/snuff						
Softwood j	5.4	2.52	6.7	2.6		
Hardwood j	10 747.7†	12 117.3	9.7	0.7	0.7	0.81
Newsprint			2.0	0.5		
Other paper				0.22		

c no. in millions. j '000 cu. metres of roundwood equivalent.

4. VEGETABLE OILSEEDS AND OILS

Castor seed	2.33*	—	2.06			
Coconut oil						
Cottonseed	156.00	130.67	8.77	16.50²		
Cottonseed oil			0.65	1.94	0.60	
Groundnuts	114.10*	119.00¹	1.11	6.00		
Groundnut oil			2.58	0.10		
Linseed				0.03		
Linseed oil			0.10†		0.01	0.01
Olive oil	30.50²	32.00²*	0.89	1.47	0.01	0.01
Palm oil	1.30*	7.00¹	0.15		0.69	0.01
Sesame seed			0.01	2.34²		
Soya beans			4.2²			
Sunflower seed						

5. LIVESTOCK‡; ANIMAL PRODUCTS, etc.

Cattle d	3 529.7	2 896.0				
Goats d	2 001.0	2 577.7				
Sheep d	804.0	1 100.0				
Pigs d	19.0*	13.5*				
Meat, 'A'	121.4*	53.0*	1.11			
Eggs	72.2	28.0	0.1			
Fish	328.0*	234.0²	0.1			
Milk			8.2			
Hides/skins	30.50²	32.00²*	0.10†	6.1		

d no. in thousands. n cattle hides only.

11. INDUSTRY

	Production	Exports	Imports
Aircraft a	—	—	0.4²
Alcoholic beverages			
Cement	150.0	23.3	1.3
Electrical engineering a	86.3	36.3	
Copper: metal			17.21
ore			

a million $ U.S. b '000 hectolitres. m metal content. q incl. oleum.

UNION OF SOVIET SOCIALIST REPUBLICS

The revolution of 1917 terminated the rule of the Russian Empire by the Tsars, and introduced the socialist system of government, with central planning of the economy. The Union consists of fifteen Soviet Socialist Republics, and local and central power is vested in the Working Peoples' Deputies. The U.S.S.R. is the nucleus of Comecon.

LAND USE: (percentage of total)

	1964
Arable and orchard	10.3
Permanent meadow and pasture	16.6
Forest and woodland	40.6
City areas, waste and other land	32.5

POPULATION: 235 543 000 (1967 estimate)

Largest city: MOSKVA (Moscow), capital: population: 6 507 000 (1967)

AREA: 22 400 000 sq. km. (8 650 000 sq. miles)

Distribution of working population (1959)
Total working population: 108 995 013

	U.N. group no.	Percentage
Agriculture, forestry, fishing and hunting	0	35.2
Mining and quarrying	1	
Manufacturing	2/3	33.6
Construction	4	
Electricity, gas, water and sanitary services	5	4.7
Transport, storage and communications	6	13.3
Commerce	7	13.2
Services	8	
Others (incl. armed forces)	9	

		Year(s)
Life expectancy at birth (years)	70	1966–7 av.
Infant mortality (per '000)	27.6	1965
Crude birth rate (per '000)	18.4	1965
Crude death rate (per '000)	7.2	1965
Population per physician	480	1965
Population per hospital bed	100	1963–5 av.
School enrolment: age 5–19 years (percentage)	99	1963–5 av.
age over 19 years (per 100 000 population)	1 570	1963–5 av.

COMMUNICATIONS

		Year(s)
Railway track (km.)	129 300	1965
Mail per capita		
Telephones (per '000 population)	22.6*	1965
Radio receivers (per '000 population)	315.1	1963–5 av.
Television licences (per '000 population)	57.1	1963–5 av.
Daily newspapers (per '000 population)	229	1964

FINANCE

Currency unit: The rouble

Exchange rates	1965 a	1960	1958
Per $ U.S.	0.9	0.9	4.0
Per £ sterling	2.5	2.5	11.2

		Year(s)
National income (million $ U.S.)	200 000*	1965 a
G.N.P. per capita ($ U.S.)	890*	1965 a
Rate of increase of G.N.P. per capita	4.8*	1960–4 av.

a middle estimate.

6. FIBRES, TEXTILES, etc.

	Production	Production	Exports	Exports	Imports	Imports
Agaves (sisal)	0.3	1.0	0.3	1.0	—	—
Cotton lint	212.0*	71.0	64.4	64.8	0.1	—
Rubber, natural	3.2*	na	na	na	na	na
Cotton, woven fabrics			5.22		1.12	
Rayon, woven fabrics						

a incl. data for Kenya.

7. FUEL AND POWER

	Production	Exports	Imports
Electricity, hydro h	530	33†	190
Petroleum, refined			120¹

h million kWh.

9. NON-FERROUS MINERALS AND METALS

	Production	Exports	Imports
Gold b, bullion/coins etc.	0.41	0.03²	0.90
Silver b, bullion	0.07	0.07	0.10²
Asbestos: fibre			2.03
manufactured	na		
Mica	0.32	0.07	0.23
Aluminium	na	na	
Beryl	na	na	
Copper: ore	17.21†	17.21	7.2
metal	0.19m	0.29	13.0
Lead, ore	0.02	0.05	67.3
Tin, ore	0.19m	0.12	na
Tungsten, ore	0.08m	0.03	na
Zinc, metal	0.18	0.15	14.1

b '000 fine troy oz. m metal content. v incl. metal.

10. CHEMICALS n AND FERTILIZERS AND METALS

	Production	Exports	Imports
Chemicals a	—	na	
Fertilizers:			
Phosphates	11.2p	3.7p	0.4
Potash			1.4
Sulphur			3.1

a data not available for years 1953–5. p apatite.

TRADING

Total trade (in million $ U.S.)
Exports (f.o.b.)
Imports (f.o.b.)

	1965	1955	1938
Exports	8174	3427	256
Imports	8058	3061	272

Main trading partners (percentage of total value)

	1965	1955	1938		1965	1955	1938
Exports				Imports			
Germany D.R.	17	14	na	Germany D.R.	16	13	na
Czechoslovakia	11	10	7f	Czechoslovakia	13	13	5f
Poland	9	12	1	Poland	8	10	9
Bulgaria	7	3	na	Bulgaria	7	4	na
Hungary	5	8	1	Hungary	5	5	na
Romania	5	5	na	Romania	6	5	1
Cuba	5	—	na	Cuba	4	1	na

Distribution of trade (percentage of total value)

	1965	1955
Exports		
Manufactured goods (machinery and transport equipment)	44	37*
Raw materials and fuels (petroleum) (wood)	35 (21) (12)	30* (17*) (5*)
Food	7	11* (4*)
Imports		
Manufactured goods (machinery and transport equipment)	61	49
Food, beverages and tobacco	21 (34)	14 (30)
Raw materials and fuels / incl. Germany F.R.	15	32

PRODUCTION, EXPORTS AND IMPORTS
Years: 1963–5 average and 1953–5 average. Units: '000 metric tons unless otherwise indicated

1. CEREALS, etc.

	Production 1965	1955	1938	Exports 1963–5 average	1953–5 average	Imports 1963–5	1953–5
Barley	22 867.0	na	na	—	—	—	—
Maize (corn)	10 930.7	na	na	—	—	—	—
Millets/sorghum	2 546.7*	na	na	—	—	—	—
Oats	5 194.7	na	na	—	—	—	—
Potatoes	84 484.0	na	na	—	—	—	—
Rice	472.7	na	na	7.2	71.9*	264.9	—
Rye	13 865.7	na	na	433.4	—	334.1	—
Wheat	61 229.0n	2 589.6	650.5*	5 569.7	6.5	1 080.0	9.4*

n in addition, buckwheat 724.7.

2. FRUIT, etc.

	Production			Exports		Imports	
Apples	na	na	na	0.8*	—	140.5	0.2*
Bananas	na	na	na	0.2*	—	20.3	1.9*
Dates	na	na	na	—	—	16.7	5.5*
Grapes	2 974.3	na	na	—	—	100.5	15.8*
Lemons	na	na	na	0.1*	—	38.9	28.0*
Oranges	na	na	na	—	—	128.3	26.0*
Pineapples	na	na	na	0.1*	—	12.9	0.6*
Raisins	na	na	na	0.5*	—	70.52	0.2*
Wine d	12 660.3	4 473.0l	na	—	—	—	—

b '000 hectolitres.

Apricots, cherries, peaches, pears, and plums are also grown, but no figures are available.

3. BEVERAGES, FOREST PRODUCTS, etc.

	Production			Exports		Imports	
Cocoa	—	—	—	—	—	69.7	17.5*
Coffee	—	—	—	—	—	30.3	—
Sugar: beet	65 589	24 533	na	—	—	779.7	404.9*
raw	7 774	3 505	na	2g	157.1	30.2	22.1*
Tea	45*	na	na	1.5*	—	108.9	—
Tobacco: leaf	194*	2g	na	—	—	—	—
cigars	na	na	na	—	—	—	—
cigarettes	280 800c	196 270c	na	—	—	—	—
tobacco/snuff	na	na	na	—	—	—	—
Softwood j	305 900a	238 000m	na	—	—	—	—
Hardwood j	51 793.6*	62 750b	na	157.0c	61.0a	2 566.1	494.1
Wood pulp	3 907	2 970*	na	421.9	—	84.0c	172.0c
Newsprint	598c	2 870c	na	254.9c	—	81.6	172.0c
Other paper	3 389c	1 878*	na	122.0c	2.1*	57.0c	0.7*
				70.52	0.2*	129.5c	75.0c

a million $ U.S.   c no. in millions.   d no. in millions.   j '000 cu. metres of roundwood equivalent.

4. VEGETABLE OILSEEDS AND OILS

	Production			Exports		Imports	
Castor seed	46.7	17.3²	na	—	—	1.4	0.2*
Castor oil	na	na	na	0.2*	—	16.6	0.5*
Coconut oil	na	na	na	—	—	11.2	—
Copra	3 530.0*	2 535.0*	na	—	—	na	1.9*
Cottonseed	na	na	na	—	—	25.3	—
Cottonseed oil	na	na	na	—	—	na	0.7*
Groundnuts	na	na	na	—	—	12.4	1.4*
Groundnut oil	430.0*	na	na	2.1*	—	28.6	39.4*
Linseed	na	na	na	—	—	5.2	—
Linseed oil	na	na	na	0.2*	—	3.6	—
Olive oil	na	na	na	—	—	2.4	—
Palm oil	25.3*	na	na	—	—	10.1	—
Palm kernels	na	na	na	—	—	31.1	—
Rapeseed	380.0*	na	na	—	—	2.0	6.1*
Sesame seed	0.5*	na	na	9.6*	—	1.8	12.2*
Soya beans	5 252.7	na	na	53.9*	—	na	—
Sunflower seed	na	na	na	—	—	—	—
Sunflower seed oil	209.2	na	na	—	—	—	—
Tung oil	0.3*	na	na	0.7*	—	—	—

5. LIVESTOCK‡: ANIMAL PRODUCTS, etc.

	Production			Exports		Imports	
Chickens d	485 100j	na	na	—	—	—	—
Cattle d	86 536	67 534	na	—	—	97.0	3.0*
dairy cows d	38 385	30 000*	na	—	—	—	—
Goats d	5 950	15 000*	na	—	—	1 264.0	—
Sheep d	135 360	108 888	na	—	—	—	—
Horses d	8 500	15 270	na	—	—	—	—
Pigs d	54 555	42 406	na	—	—	69.2	29.4*

5. LIVESTOCK‡: ANIMAL PRODUCTS, etc.—continued

	Production			Exports		Imports	
Meat i: 'A'	6 827	na	na	0.1	—	12.8	61.1
'B'	1 075	na	na	44.4	—	4.3	—
Butter	1 007	na	na	44.4	—	4.4	18.3*
Cheese	467*	na	na	4.4	—	4.4	2.5*
Eggs	1 574	na	na	0.1	—	24.3	3.6*
Fish	4 603	2 246	na	206.9	—	24.3	—
Milk	64 113	na	na	60.2	—	93.1	—
Whale oil	118	43	na	—	—	163.0	—
Hides/skins	na	na	na	—	—	—	—
Wool	214	na	na	26.1	0.1*	49.6c	13.6*
						47.2	

e no. in millions.   p incl. ducks, geese and turkeys.

6. FIBRES, TEXTILES, etc.

	Production			Exports		Imports	
Agaves (sisal, etc.)	1 821.3	na	na	390.9	108.1*	5.1	15.9*
Cotton lint	389.7	na	na	28.9	1.4*	184.5	—
Flax fibre	105.0*	na	na	2.5	—	24.4	1.7*
Hemp fibre	60.0*	na	na	23.3†	23.4*s	293.1	9.1*
Jute	na	na	na	—	—	251.9	14.5*
Rubber: natural	na	na	na	5.7	20.0*	23.9	25.4*
Silk f	2 782.5²	na	na	—	—	13.7*	—
Cotton: yarn	1 262.0	na	na	1 500.0	—	10.0	—
woven fabrics	813.3*	na	na	682.1*	—	10.0	—
Rayon: fibre/yarn	239.4	na	na	—	—	1.0	—
woven fabrics	369.0q	na	na	—	—	—	—
Wool: yarn	154.7*	na	na	—	—	—	—
woven fabrics	109.4	na	na	—	—	—	—

f metric tons.   q million square metres.   r may incl. re-exports.

7. FUEL AND POWER

	Production			Exports		Imports	
Coal: 'A'	207 740*	276 640	na	22 164	1 437	5 656	8 664
'B'	213 957*	114 620	na	3 849	2 875*	659	450
Coke	469 343	151 110	na	—	1 617*	—	—
Electricity k: total	78 217	20 320	na	—	—	—	—
hydro	na	na	na	—	—	—	—
nuclear	na	na	na	—	—	—	—
thermal	na	na	na	—	—	—	—
Natural gas i	381 126	130 790	na	—	—	—	—
Oil, crude	108 700	70 790¹	na	327	2 920¹	180	1 580¹
Petroleum, refined	224 187	8 980	na	36 790	5 040¹	1 840	na
Uranium	16 178	67 000¹	na	20 270			na¹

i million kWh.   i million cu. metres.   l metric tons.   q million metres.

8. IRON AND STEEL

	Production			Exports		Imports	
Iron ore	87 448m	38 102m	na	23 573	8 817	na	—
Pig iron	62 417	30 239	na	3 287	1 200	198	588
Steel ingots/castings	85 428	47 600	9 000*	820	186	55	na
Iron/steel scrap	na	na	na	436	521	na	na
Iron/steel products a	na	na	na	691	293	—	—

a million $ U.S.   m metal content.

9. NON-FERROUS MINERALS AND METALS

	Production			Exports		Imports	
Diamonds c	na	na	na	—	—	—	—
Gold k, o e m	4 000l	na	na	—	—	—	—
Platinum group	4 683	na	na	—	—	—	—
Silver k, o e m	1 300*	na	108*	800.0p	126.5p	—	—
Asbestos, fibre	29 300*	25 000*	na	213.6	—	—	—
Mica	735	340	na	—	—	—	—
Aluminium: bauxite	4 403*	966*	na	209.4	67.1*s	0.3	—
alumina	na	na	na	3.4	1.9*	457.2q	—
aluminium	808*	355*	na	—	41.6*s	6.4	7.01*s
Antimony: ore	na	na	na	—	1.6*s	0.3	7.01*s
metal	1*r	na	na	—	—	—	—
Beryl	na	na	na	—	—	0.2	na
Cadmium	6*m	na	na	na	na	na	na

k '000 fine troy oz.   l '000 carats.   m metal content.   p total for available countries.   r cobbed;   s incl. re-exports or imports for re-export.   p only 10–12% BeO.

---

9. NON-FERROUS MINERALS AND METALS—continued

	Production	Exports	Imports
Chrome: ore	1 317*m	544*m	15.8¹*
metal	1	—	—
Copper: ore	717m	na	—
metal	649	101.2	44.8¹*
Lead: ore	na	na	—
metal	332*	103.0	17.6¹
Magnesium: metal/salts	32*x	2.8	1.7¹
Manganese: ore	7 112*	1 007.6¹	866.6¹
metal/salts	1 264	61.3	—
Mercury j/: ore	5 967m*	207.9	191.0¹
metal	83m	na	—
Molybdenum/ j: ore	22*	0.2	2.1¹s
metal	11	na	—
Nickel/: ore	8	na	6.4
metal	4 389.0¹	37.0¹	na
Tin: ore	432*m	122.0	70.1
metal	497¹	35.5¹	47.4¹
Tungsten, ore	na	na	na
Zinc: ore	na	na	na
metal	242*	19.5	na
Zirconium minerals	na	na	na

f metric tons.   m metal content.   x primary magnesium only.   i imports from China P.R. only.

10. CHEMICALS‡ AND FERTILIZERS

Organic chemicals:	Production	Exports	Imports
Benzene	637	120.2	—
Butadiene	na	na	na
Ethylene	na	na	na
Methanol	848²	36.9	—
Phenol	465	14.3	na
Phthalic anhydride	85¹	2.2	na
Styrene monomer	na	na	0.5
Urea	220¹	19.5	na

Inorganic chemicals:	Production	Exports	Imports
Ammonia	na	na	na
Carbon black	145²	13.4	na
Chlorine	442*	16.5	—
Nitric acid	na	na	na
Sodium carbonate	2 719	29.7	190.1
Sodium hydroxide	1 168	23.7	191.0
Sulphuric acid	7 677	79.1	—

Plastics:	Production	Exports	Imports
Polyamides	na	na	na
Polyethylene	na	na	na
Polyvinyl chloride	106¹	—	—

Fertilizers:	Production	Exports	Imports
Phosphates	11 167*p / 4 493*p	2 977.5	988.5¹y
Potash	2 200*w / 1 589*w	857.3	46.0¹
Pyrites	1 714x	1 063.5	—
Sulphur: native	982*m	417*	135.0	29.7¹
recovered	763¹m	—	—

a million $ U.S.   c '000 hectolitres.   d no. of units.   n no. in thousands.   h '000 G.R.T.   n excl. trade with other Comecon countries, China P.R., North Vietnam and North Korea.   p no. in thousands.   p production for home registration only.   p incl. apatite.   u K₂O content.   w data not available for years 1953–5.   y apatite.

11. INDUSTRY

	Production	Exports	Imports
Aircraft a	na	na	na
Alcoholic beverages			
beer b	29 353	18 573	na
spirits	na	na	na
Cement	66 116	19 146	2 016.0¹	140.0n
Electrical: engineering a	2 137	na	na
Locomotives c:	924	na	na
engineering a			
Machine tools a	790¹	34.4	na
Merchant ships g	428p	na	na
Motor vehicles: commercial d	602	125.5a	328.6a
private d	186	300	na
	93		

UNITED ARAB REPUBLIC

NORTH AFRICA

The United Arab Republic was the title given to the short-lived union between Egypt and Syria in 1958; when Syria withdrew from the union, the name was retained by Egypt.

The Egyptian monarchy terminated in 1953, and the country was declared a republic. Colonel Nasser assumed the presidency in 1956, and, with foreign aid, effected flood-control of the Nile thus providing great advances in agricultural efficiency and the development of hydro-electric power. The Six-Days' War in 1967 led to a destructive interruption in the country's progress, the closure of the Suez Canal, and Israeli occupation of the Sinai Peninsula.

AREA: 1 000 000 sq. km. (386 200 sq. miles)

LAND USE: (percentage of total)

	1965	1954
Arable and orchard	2.7	2.6
Permanent meadow and pasture	—	—
Forest and woodland	—	—
City areas, waste and other land	97.3	97.4

POPULATION: 30 083 419 (1966 census)
Largest city: AL QĀHIRAH (Cairo), capital: population: 4 219 853 (city proper, 1966)

Distribution of working population (1960)
Total working population: 7 769 067 a

U.N. group no.		Percentage
0	Agriculture, forestry, fishing and hunting	56.7
1	Mining and quarrying	0.5
2/3	Manufacturing	9.1
4	Construction	2.0
5	Electricity, gas, water and sanitary services	0.5
6	Commerce	8.1
7	Transport, storage and communications	3.3
8	Services	17.3
9	Others (incl. unemployed)	2.7

COMMUNICATIONS

		Year(s)
Motor vehicles in use ('000s): private	91.9	1965
commercial	23.4	1964
Railway track (km)	4 231	1964
Mail per capita: domestic	2	1963–5 av.
foreign sent	1.1*	1967
foreign received		
Telephones (per '000 population)	5.2	1965
Radio receivers (per '000 population)	59.2	1966
Television sets (per '000 population)	15*	1964
Daily newspapers (per '000 population)		

FINANCE
Currency unit: The Egyptian pound

	1965	1960	1950a	1938a
Exchange rates				
Per $ U.S.	0.35	0.35	0.35	—
Per £ sterling	0.98	0.98	0.98	1.01

	1965	1960	1950a	1938a
National Income (million $ U.S.)	2370	—	—	—
G.N.P. per capita ($U.S.)	160	—	—	—
Foreign trade (percentage of G.D.P.)	32	—	—	—

a selling rate.

Life expectancy at birth (years): male / female

		Year(s)
Infant mortality (per '000)	51.6	1960
Crude birth rate (per '000)	113.2*	1965
Crude death rate (per '000)	41.4*	1965
Accidental deaths (per 100 000 population) caused by motor vehicles due to other causes	14.0*	1965
Population per physician	2 380	1963
Population per hospital bed	560 b	1966
School enrolment: age 5–19 years (percentage)	50	1964
age over 19 years (per 100 000 population)	540	1963–5 av.

a excl. nomads and foreigners.   b government hospitals only.

continued

TRADING

Total trade (in million $ U.S.)

	1965	1955	1938
Exports (f.o.b.)	604	419	147
Imports (c.i.f.)	933	525	184

Main trading partners (percentage of total value)

Exports	1965	1955	1938	Imports	1965	1955	1938
U.S.S.R.	22	5	1	U.S.A.	20	12	10d
Czechoslovakia	10	6	na	Germany F.R.	10	12	10
China P.R.	8	6	—	U.S.S.R.	9	4	1
Germany D.R.	6	4	1	India	6	4	2
Italy	4	6	8	Italy	6	8	6
India	4	9	5	France	5	9	8
				U.K.	5	13	23

Distribution of trade (percentage of total value)

Exports	1965	1955	1938*
Crude materials and fuels	65	83	na
(textile fibres and waste)	(57)	(79)	(75)
Manufactured goods	20	6	na
(textile yarn and clothing)	(17)	(4)	(na)
Food	14	10	6

Imports	1965	1955	1938*
Manufactured goods	41	53	na
(machinery and transport equipment)	(23)	(25)	(15)
Food (cereals and preparations)	24	11	10
	(16)	(—)	(—)
Crude materials and fuel	18	18	na
Chemicals	13	12	11

d incl. Germany D.R.

PRODUCTION, EXPORTS AND IMPORTS

Years: 1963–5 average and 1953–5 average   Units: '000 metric tons unless otherwise indicated

	Production			Exports			Imports		
	1965	1955	1938	1965	1955	1938	1965	1955	1938

1. CEREALS, etc.

Barley	135.0	115.3	3.7	—	—	—	0.01	0.08	0.05j
Maize (corn)	1 967.3*	1 711.7	4.1	—	—	—	1.92	1.92	0.28
Millets/sorghum	736.3*	556.0	37.5²	—	—	—	5.41	12.37	3.51
Potatoes	412.3	198.0	—	1.0	1.0	8.1	40.82	1.59	12.37
Rice	2 039.0*	1 026.7	—	247.1	62.9	24.4	0.44	4.76	0.80
Sweet potatoes/				11.9	412.5	20.7	0.08	0.06	0.25
Yams				14.1	77.3	21.7	0.08	0.032	0.22
Wheat	1 531.0	1 575.7*	1.0	0.2		159.0	1 004.1	1 430	1 210¹

(The remaining sections — 2. FRUIT, etc.; 3. BEVERAGES, FOREST PRODUCTS, etc.; 4. VEGETABLE OILSEEDS AND OILS; 5. LIVESTOCK, ANIMAL PRODUCTS, etc.; 6. FIBRES, TEXTILES, etc.; 7. FUEL AND POWER; 8. IRON AND STEEL; 9. NON-FERROUS MINERALS AND METALS; 10. CHEMICALS AND FERTILIZERS; 11. INDUSTRY — contain dense numerical data not fully legible at this resolution.)

na: data not available.   — negligible or nil.   1 one year only.   2 two year average.   * estimate.   ‡ see appendix.   † re-exports.

UNITED KINGDOM   EUROPE

The United Kingdom, comprising England, Scotland, Wales and Northern Ireland, is a constitutional monarchy, but executive and legislative power are vested in the parliament. The U.K. is a member of the European Free Trade Association and has applied (1971) to join the European Economic Community.

AREA: 229 827 sq. km. (88 736 sq. miles)

LAND USE: (percentage of total)

	1965	1955
Arable and orchard	30.7	34.8
Permanent meadow and pasture	49.7	50.1
Forest and woodland	7.4	6.6
City areas, waste and other land	12.2	13.9

POPULATION: 55 068 000 (1967 estimate)

Largest city: LONDON, capital: population: 7 913 600 (1966)

Distribution of working population: 24 855 500 (1966)

U.N. group no.		Percentage
0	Agriculture, forestry, fishing and hunting	2.3
1	Mining and quarrying	2.3
2/3	Manufacturing	34.8
4	Construction	7.7
5	Electricity, gas, water and sanitary services	1.7
6	Commerce	16.0
7	Transport, storage and communications	6.6
8	Services	27.0
9	Others	0.7

FINANCE

Currency unit: The pound sterling

Exchange rates   Per $ U.S.

	1965	1960	1955	1938
	0.357	0.357	0.357	0.213

The pound is an important currency in international monetary transactions. Its devaluation in 1967 affected particularly the countries of the Sterling Area, many of which also devalued so that their currencies should remain pegged to the pound.

	Year(s)
National income (million $ U.S.)	79 213	1965
G.N.P. per capita (\$U.S.)	1 620	1966
Rate of increase of G.N.P.	2.6	1966–4 av.
Foreign trade (percentage of G.D.P.)	31	1963–5 av.

TRADING

Total trade (in million $ U.S.)

	1965	1960	1955	1938
Exports (f.o.b.)	13 723	13 723	8 863	2 741
Imports (c.i.f.)	16 103	16 103	10 029	4 582

Main trading partners (percentage of total value)

Exports	1965	1955	1938*	Imports	1965	1955	1938*
U.S.A.	11	8	6	U.S.A.	12	11	13
Australia	6	10	8	Canada	8	9	11
South Africa	5	6	6	Germany F.R.	6	4	3d
Germany F.R.	5	4	4d	Australia	5	5	3
Canada	4	5	5	Netherlands	5	3	3
Sweden	4	4	4	Sweden	4	4	3
Netherlands	4	3	3	South Africa	3	2	2

d incl. Germany D.R.

Distribution of trade (percentage of total value)

Exports	1965	1955	1938*
Manufactured goods	75	74	73
(machinery and transport equipment)	(27)	(22)	(9)
(textiles and clothing)	(15)	(15)	(18)
Chemicals	9	8	5
Food	5	3	3

Imports	1965	1955	1938*
Manufactured goods	34	20	16
(machinery and transport equipment)	(11)	(4)	(4)
(non-ferrous metals and fuels)	(8)	(9)	(5)
Crude materials and fuels	29	38	41
Food (petroleum and products)	27	34	34
(fruit and vegetables)	(5)	(5)	(5)
Chemicals	5	3	na

a these are percentages of national exports which comprised 97% of the general exports in 1965, 94% in 1955, and 84% in 1938.

(LIVESTOCK, ANIMAL PRODUCTS; COMMUNICATIONS and other sections with dense numerical data follow, not fully legible at this resolution.)

na: data not available.   — negligible or nil.   1 one year only.   2 two year average.   * estimate.   ‡ see appendix.   † re-exports.

continued

UNITED KINGDOM continued

PRODUCTION, EXPORTS AND IMPORTS

Years: 1963–5 average and 1953–5 average   Units: '000 metric tons unless otherwise indicated

(tabular data: sections 1. CEREALS, etc.; 2. FRUIT, etc.; 3. BEVERAGES, FOREST PRODUCTS, etc.; 4. VEGETABLE OILSEEDS AND OILS; 5. LIVESTOCK, ANIMAL PRODUCTS, etc.; 6. FIBRES, TEXTILES, etc.; 7. FUEL AND POWER; 8. IRON AND STEEL; 9. NON-FERROUS MINERALS AND METALS — with Production, Exports, Imports columns)

Footnotes: *a* million $U.S. *b* '000 hectolitres. *d* no. in millions. *e* no. in thousands. *f* metric tons. *g* incl. re-exports. *h* incl. imports for re-export. *i* metric tons. *q* incl. yarn of cotton waste. *r* incl. mixtures. *s* incl. re-exports.

f metric tons. *k* million kWh. *i* million cu. metres. *s* incl. re-exports.
m metal content. *n* radium compounds in grams. *l* compounds only

na: data not available.   — negligible or nil.   1 one year only.   2 two year average.   * estimate.   ‡ see appendix.   † re-exports.

PRODUCTION, EXPORTS AND IMPORTS *continued*

10. CHEMICALS AND FERTILIZERS

(tabular data: Organic chemicals, Inorganic chemicals, Plastics — Production, Exports, Imports columns)

11. INDUSTRY

(tabular data)

10. CHEMICALS AND FERTILIZERS—*continued*

(tabular data: Fertilizers — Production, Exports, Imports)

Footnotes: *a* million $U.S. *b* '000 hectolitres. *c* no. of units. *g* production in England only for 1966/7. *p* production in England only in 1961. *r* excl. parts. *x* sulphur content. *y* recovered sulphur. *n* data not available for years 1953–5. *z* home consumption in England only.

UNITED KINGDOM (TERRITORIES)   PACIFIC OCEAN

BAHAMAS—see page 125
BERMUDA—see page 127
BRITISH HONDURAS—see page 130
BRUNEI—see page 130
GIBRALTAR—see page 158
HONG KONG—see page 163
NEW HEBRIDES—see page 190
WEST INDIES ASSOCIATED STATES—see page 233

BRITISH SOLOMON ISLANDS   PACIFIC OCEAN

The British Solomon Islands Protectorate comes under the jurisdiction of the Western Pacific High Commission, the headquarters of which are at Honiara, on the islands.

PRODUCTION, EXPORTS AND IMPORTS

Years: 1963–5 average and 1953–5 average   Units: '000 metric tons unless otherwise indicated

(tabular data: 1. CEREALS, etc.; 2. FRUIT, etc.; 3. BEVERAGES, FOREST PRODUCTS, etc.; 4. VEGETABLE OILSEEDS AND OILS; 5. LIVESTOCK, ANIMAL PRODUCTS, etc.; 7. FUEL AND POWER; 9. NON-FERROUS MINERALS AND METALS; 11. INDUSTRY — with Production, Exports, Imports columns)

Footnotes: *b* '000 hectolitres. *d* no. in thousands. *j* '000 cu. metres of roundwood equivalent. *u* metal content. *v* bullion.

For cement data see Fiji.

LAND USE: (percentage of total)

	1965	1952
Arable and orchard	4.9	4.9
Permanent meadow and pasture	1.3	1.3
Forest and woodland	89.4	89.4
City areas, waste and other land	4.4	4.4

AREA: 29 785 sq. km. (11 500 sq. miles)

POPULATION: 144 000 (1967 unofficial estimate)

Capital city: HONIARA; population: 4 300 (city proper, 1964)

PRODUCTION AND TRADE

Most of the land is covered with coconut palms and copra accounted for 94% of the exports in 1965. The cultivation of rice is important, and is developing rapidly. Timber, cocoa, sorghum and trochus shell are also exported, and some income is derived from tourism. Imports include foodstuffs, machinery and building materials.

Exports in 1965 amounted to U.S.$638 000; imports, to U.S.$735 000.

FINANCE

Currency unit: The Australian dollar replaced the Australian pound in 1966 at the rate A$1 to A£0.5

	1965	1960	1950	1938
Exchange rates (for Australian pounds)				
Per $U.S.	0.45	0.45	0.45	0.26
Per £ sterling	1.25	1.25	1.25	1.25

na: data not available.   — negligible or nil.   1 one year only.   2 two year average.   * estimate.   ‡ see appendix.   † re-exports.

continued

CAYMAN ISLANDS — CARIBBEAN SEA

The Cayman Islands, which had been administered by the Governor of Jamaica were placed under the jurisdiction of the British Colonial Office when Jamaica became independent in 1962.

AREA: 260 sq. km. (100 sq. miles)

POPULATION: 9 000 (1967 U.N. estimate)
Capital city: GEORGETOWN; population: 2573 (1960)
Total working population: 3 159 (1960)

EMPLOYMENT AND TRADE
The principal occupations are shipping, fishing, and rope-making. Tourism has developed recently. Imports consist of foodstuffs, textiles and building materials, exports are rope, shark skin and turtle.

		Year
Infant mortality (per '000)	39.7*	1961
Crude birth rate (per '000)	26.9*	1965
Crude death rate (per '000)	7.0*	1965
School enrolment: age 5–19 years (percentage)	74.0*	1964

LAND USE: (percentage of total)	1965
Arable and orchard	1.9
Permanent meadow and pasture	8.9
Forest and woodland	25.0
City areas, waste and other land	64.2

CHANNEL ISLANDS — EUROPE

The Channel Islands are a group of islands off the north coast of France, which have belonged to the British Crown since the eleventh century. They consist of Jersey, Guernsey, Alderney, Sark, and several smaller islands. They each have their own legislature; remnants of feudal government survive on Sark.

AREA: 194 sq. km. (75 sq. miles)
(Jersey 115 sq. km.; Guernsey 63 sq. km.; Alderney 8 sq. km.; Sark 4 sq. km.)

POPULATION: 116 000 (1967 U.N. estimate)
(1961 distribution): Jersey 63 345; Guernsey 47 198; Alderney 1 449; Sark 560)

PRODUCTION AND TRADE
The chief commercial crops are early potatoes, flowers, tomatoes and fern; and dairy cattle are reared. Granite is also exported. The tourist trade flourishes, and provides a reliable source of income. Imports consist mainly of fuel, building materials and foodstuffs, trade being primarily with the U.K.

PRODUCTION, EXPORTS AND IMPORTS
Years: **1963–5 average** and *1953–5 average*   Units: '000 metric tons unless otherwise indicated

Note—since 1960 trade with the U.K. has been regarded as 'internal', and, as the greater part of the islands' trade is with the U.K., few trade figures for 1963–5 are available. Those figures shown for this period exclude trade with the U.K.

	Production		Exports		Imports	
1. CEREALS, etc.						
Millets/sorghum	—	—	—	—	0.5	0.8
Oats	—	—	—	na	0.3	3.4
Potatoes	57.0	na	44.2	na	5.0	0.3
Wheat	0.3	na	—	na	2.2	0.7
2. FRUIT, etc.						
Bananas	—	—	—	—	0.5	0.8
Grapes	—	—	—	—	0.6	0.5
Oranges	—	—	0.2	na	0.6	0.5
Tomatoes	69.4	na	na	na	na	0.8
Wine *b*	—	—	—	—	5.4	1.3
3. BEVERAGES, FOREST PRODUCTS, etc.						
Coffee	—	—	—	—	0.2	0.3
Sugar, raw	—	—	—	—	3.8	
Tea	—	—	—	—	0.7	
5. LIVESTOCK‡, ANIMAL PRODUCTS, etc.						
Chickens *d*	133.7	na	0.5	—	na	—
Cattle *d*	13.0	na	—	—	—	
Horses *d*	3.0	na	0.7	na	0.2	0.2

b '000 hectolitres.

	Production		Exports		Imports	
5. LIVESTOCK‡, ANIMAL PRODUCTS, etc.—*continued*						
Bacon/ham	—	—	—	—	na	0.8
Meat: 'A'	—	—	—	—	na	0.3
Meat: 'B'	—	—	—	—	na	0.5
Butter	—	—	—	—	na	0.8
Cheese	—	—	—	—	na	0.5
Eggs	0.3	0.1	—	—	na	na
Milk	23.3	21.8	—	—	1.3	
7. FUEL AND POWER						
Coal, 'A', ‡	—	—	—	—	na	286
Coke	—	—	—	—	na	17
Electricity *h*	15†	158	na	20	6	
Petroleum, refined	na	20	6		60¹	
8. IRON AND STEEL						
Iron/steel scrap	na	na	2	2	—	—
9. NON-FERROUS MINERALS AND METALS						
Asbestos, manufactured	—	—	—	—	2.38	0.84
Lead, metal	—	—	—	—	0.52	—

d no. in thousands.   *h* million kWh.   *t* thermal.

continued

FALKLAND ISLANDS — SOUTH ATLANTIC

The Crown colony of the Falkland Islands is administered by a governor. The population is almost exclusively of British birth or descent.

AREA: 12 000 sq. km. (4 630 sq. miles)

POPULATION: 2 500 (1967 U.N. estimate)
Capital city: STANLEY; population: 1 074 (1962)
Total working population: 1 163 (1962)

		Year(s)
Population per physician	500	1965
Population per hospital bed	60	1966
School enrolment: age 5–19 years (percentage)	93	1963–4 av.

LAND USE: (percentage of total)	1961
Arable and orchard	—
Permanent meadow and pasture	86.6
Forest and woodland	—
City areas, waste and other land	13.4

FINANCE
Currency unit: The Falkland Islands pound, at par with the pound sterling which is also in circulation.
Exchange rates—see U.K.

EMPLOYMENT AND TRADE
The islanders are principally engaged in sheep farming, wool being the chief export; whaling has now declined. Trade is mainly with the U.K.

TRADING (in million $ U.S.)

	1965	1955	1938
Total trade			
Exports (f.o.b.)	7	11	3
Imports (c.i.f.)	2	8	2

Distribution of trade (percentage of total value)

Exports	1965	1938
Crude materials (mainly wool)	43	47
Food	22	
Animal and vegetable oils	14	

Imports	1965	
Manufactured goods (machinery and transport equipment)	19	(13)
Crude materials and fuels	18	
Food		
Beverages and tobacco	9	

PRODUCTION, EXPORTS AND IMPORTS
Years: **1963–5 average** and *1953–5 average*   Units: '000 metric tons unless otherwise indicated

	Production		Exports		Imports	
5. LIVESTOCK‡, ANIMAL PRODUCTS, etc.—*continued*						
Milk	1.0*	na	—	—	—	—
Wool	na	1.3*	1.5	1.3	—	—
7. FUEL AND POWER						
Coal, 'A', ‡	—	—	—	—	20	180¹
Petroleum, refined	—	—	—	—		

d no. in thousands.

continued

GILBERT AND ELLICE ISLANDS — PACIFIC OCEAN

The Crown colony of the Gilbert and Ellice Islands comes under the jurisdiction of the Western Pacific High Commission. Included also in the group are Ocean Island, the Phoenix Islands and all but five of the Line Islands.

AREA: 955 sq. km. (369 sq. miles)

POPULATION: 48 780 (1963 census)
Capital city: TAPIWA; population: 8 953 (city proper, 1967)

LAND USE: (percentage of total)	1964	1965
Arable and orchard	47.1	39.8
Permanent meadow and pasture	—	
Forest and woodland	—	
City areas, waste and other land	2.3 / 50.6	2.2 / 58.0

					Year(s)
Life expectancy at birth (years): male					
female					
Infant mortality (per '000)					
Crude birth rate (per '000)	1965	1960	1950	1938	
Crude death rate (per '000)					
Population per physician	2 360	110	86		1964
School enrolment: age 5–19 years (percentage)					

FINANCE
Currency unit: The Australian dollar replaced the Australian pound in 1966 at the rate A$1 to A£0.5
Exchange rates (for Australian pounds)

	1965	1960	1950	1938
Per $ U.S.	0.45	0.45	0.45	0.26
Per £ sterling	1.25	1.25	1.25	1.25

PRODUCTION, EXPORTS AND IMPORTS
Years: **1963–5 average** and *1953–5 average*   Units: '000 metric tons unless otherwise indicated

	Production		Exports		Imports	
1. CEREALS, etc.						
Rice	—	—	—	—	0.8²	—
2. FRUIT, etc.						
Coconuts *e*	46.7	na	—	—		
3. BEVERAGES, FOREST PRODUCTS, etc.						
Sugar, raw	—	—	—	—	0.3	—
4. VEGETABLE OILSEEDS AND OILS						
Copra	7.40	9.33	6.93*	7.45²	—	—
5. LIVESTOCK‡, ANIMAL PRODUCTS, etc.						
Pigs *d*	11.0	9.0²	—	—	—	
Fish	na	na	na	na	1.25	1.25
10. CHEMICALS AND FERTILIZERS						
Chemicals	—	—	—	—	na	
Fertilizers: Phosphates *p*	351.7	na	351.7	299.2	na	—

e no. in millions.   *d* no. in thousands.
n data not available for years 1953–5.   *p* from Ocean Island.

11. INDUSTRY
For cement data see Fiji.

continued

---

na: data not available.   — negligible or nil.   ¹ one year only.   ² two year average.   * estimate.   ‡ see appendix.   † re-exports.

ISLE OF MAN
IRISH SEA

The Isle of Man is administered by its own Court of Tynwald, and is not, in general, bound by the Acts of the U.K. Parliament.

AREA: 588 sq. km. (227 sq. miles)

LAND USE: (percentage of total)

	1965
Arable and orchard.	40.7
Permanent meadow and pasture	11.9
Forest and woodland	3.4
City areas, waste and other land	44.0

POPULATION: 50 423 (1966 census)

Capital city: DOUGLAS; population: 19 517 (1966)

PRODUCTION AND TRADE

The main source of income is the tourist industry, half a million British tourists visiting the island annually. The main agricultural products are oats, barley, and root crops, small quantities of which are exported.

Distribution of working population (1951)
Total working population: 23 257

U.N. group no.		Percentage
0	Agriculture, forestry, fishing and hunting	10.9
1	Mining and quarrying	1.4
2/3	Manufacturing	12.0
4	Construction	13.2
5	Electricity, gas, water and sanitary services	12.7
6	Commerce	15.8
7	Transport, storage and communications	9.4
8	Services	26.6
9	Others	8.0

		Year
Infant mortality (per '000).	19.7	1965
Crude birth rate (per '000)	14.9	1965
Crude death rate (per '000).	17.7	1965

ST. HELENA
ATLANTIC OCEAN

St. Helena is a rugged, mountainous island in mid-Atlantic which was, before the building of the Suez Canal, a prosperous and important port of call on the route to India. The island is a Crown colony, administered by a governor and legislative council responsible also for the administration of Ascension Island and Tristan da Cunha (see below).

AREA: 121.7 sq. km. (47 sq. miles)

LAND USE: (percentage of total)

	1962
Arable and orchard.	4.8
Permanent meadow and pasture	4.8
Forest and woodland	2.3
City areas, waste and other land	88.1

PRODUCTION, EXPORTS AND IMPORTS
Years: 1963–5 average and 1953–5 average   Units: '000 metric tons unless otherwise indicated

1. CEREALS, etc.

	Production	Exports	Imports
Barley.	3.3 1.0[2]	—	—
Oats	9.0 13.5[2]	—	—
Potatoes	11.7 8.0[2]	—	—
Wheat.	0.3 7.0[2]	—	—

5. LIVESTOCK‡, ANIMAL PRODUCTS, etc.

	Production	Exports	Imports
Chickens *d*.	67.3 67.3	—	—
Cattle *d*.	29.0 26.7	—	—
Sheep *d*.	115.0 82.7	—	—
Horses *d*	0.7 7.0	—	—
Pigs *d*	5.0 7.3	—	—
Fish	14.0 na	—	—
Milk	na 14.0[2]	—	—
Hides/skins	na	—	—

d no. in thousands.

POPULATION: 4 649 (1966 estimate)
Capital: JAMESTOWN; population: 1 475 (1966)
Total working population: 1 898 (1956) (including Ascension Is.)

		Year(s)
Infant mortality (per '000).	17.7*	1965
Crude birth rate (per '000).	24.6	1965
Crude death rate (per '000).	9.2*	1964
Population per physician	1670	1965
Population per hospital bed	70	1966
School enrolment: age 5–19 years (percentage)	114‡	1963–4 av.

ASCENSION ISLAND

Ascension Island is a small island 700 miles north west of St. Helena from which it is administered.

Area: 88 sq. km. (34 sq. miles)

Population: 1 217 (1968 estimate)

Capital: GEORGETOWN

TRISTAN DA CUNHA

Tristan da Cunha is a small group of volcanic islands in the South Atlantic. A volcanic eruption in 1961 led to the evacuation of the islands for two years. A cable station are situated on Grand

Area: 116 sq. km. (45 sq. miles)

Population: 271 (1969)

Only a small portion of the islands is cultivable, the main crop being potatoes. Cattle, sheep and geese are reared, and a small amount of fruit grown. Fish are plentiful.

PRODUCTION AND TRADE

Flax is grown on the island, and flax fibre, tow, rope, and twine are exported. Lace-making is another industry. Rice, sugar and other foodstuffs and most consumer goods are imported.

SEYCHELLES
INDIAN OCEAN

The Seychelles has long been a Crown colony. In 1965 several outlying islands were added as dependencies of the Seychelles under the name 'British Indian Ocean Territory'. Chronic unemployment of 14% has made the islands dependent on British aid and since 1958, and has delayed self-government. There are plans to develop the tourist industry to make the islands more self-reliant.

AREA: 269 sq. km. (100 sq. miles) (including dependencies)

LAND USE: (percentage of total)

	1954	1965
Arable and orchard.	42.1	42.1
Permanent meadow and pasture	41.0	41.0
Forest and woodland	12.4	9.9
City areas, waste and other land	44.5	47.0

POPULATION: 48 000 (1967 estimate)
Capital city: VICTORIA; population: 10 504 (1960)

*Distribution of working population** (1960)
Total working population: 17 665

	Percentage
Agriculture, forestry and fishing	47
Skilled work	13
Domestic service	13
Trade and commerce	19
Public works	2
Public administration	

		Year(s)
Life expectancy at birth (years): male	60.8	1960
female	65.9	1960
Infant mortality (per '000)	58.7*	1965
Crude birth rate (per '000)	37.4*	1965
Crude death rate (per '000)	11.9*	1965
Population per physician	3290	1964
Population per hospital bed	140 *a*	1966
School enrolment: age 5–19 years (percentage)	69	1963–4 av.
age over 19 years (per 100 000 population)	76	1963–5 av.

a government hospitals only.

Distribution of trade (percentage of total value)

		Percentage	Year(s)
Exports	Copra		
	Food (mainly fish and cinnamon)		
Imports			

COMMUNICATIONS

		Year(s)
Telephones (per '000 urban population)	0.8	1967
Radio receivers (per '000 population)	61	1963–5 av.
Daily newspapers (per '000 population)	35.3	1962–4 av.

FINANCE

Currency unit: The Seychelles rupee

Exchange rates

	1955	1960
Per $ U.S.	4.76	4.78
Per £ sterling	13.32	13.33

TRADING

Total trade (in million $ U.S.)

	1938	1955	1965
Exports (f.o.b.)	0.3	1.3	2.1
Imports (c.i.f.).	0.4 *a*	1.9	3.9

a (f.o.b.)

	1965	1965
Exports		*Imports*
Copra	62	Manufactured goods — machinery and transport equipment	40
Food (mainly fish and cinnamon).	25	Food, beverages and tobacco	33 (13)
		Beverages and tobacco	10
		Chemicals	6

TURKS AND CAICOS ISLANDS
WEST ATLANTIC

These islands, which had been administered by the Governor of Jamaica, were placed under the jurisdiction of the British Colonial Office when Jamaica became independent in 1962.

AREA: 430 sq. km. (166 sq. miles)

POPULATION: 6 000 (1967 U.N. estimate)
Capital city: GRAND TURK; population: 2 339 (city proper, 1960)
Total working population: 2 108 (1960)

		Year
Infant mortality (per '000)	114.1*	1965
Crude birth rate (per '000)	23.1*	1965
Crude death rate (per '000)	10.2*	1965

PRODUCTION, EXPORTS AND IMPORTS
Years: 1963–5 average and 1953–5 average   Units: '000 metric tons unless otherwise indicated

1. CEREALS, etc.

	Production	Exports	Imports
Cassava	1.0* 1.0[2]	—	0.8
Maize (corn)	—	—	0.2
Potatoes	—	—	0.1
Rice	—	—	3.4

2. FRUIT, etc.

	Production	Exports	Imports
Coconuts	49.0* na	na	0.9
Wine *b*.	—	—	0.7

b '000 hectolitres.   *e* no. in millions.

3. BEVERAGES, FOREST PRODUCTS, etc.

	Production	Exports	Imports
Sugar, raw	—	1.2	1.0

4. VEGETABLE OILSEEDS AND OILS

	Production	Exports	Imports
Copra	6.07 6.50	6.50 0.10	0.01
Coconut oil	na	na	0.01
Cottonseed oil.	na	na	0.01[2]
Groundnuts	na	na	0.02
Groundnut oil	na	na	—
Linseed oil	na	na	—

5. LIVESTOCK‡, ANIMAL PRODUCTS, etc.

	Production	Exports	Imports
Cattle *d*	3.0	—	na
Goats *d*	2.0*	—	na
Pigs *d*.	3.0	—	na
Fish *d*	1.5* 7.5*	—	na
Milk	na	—	na

d no. in thousands.

9. NON-FERROUS MINERALS AND METALS

	Production	Exports	Imports
Asbestos, manufactured	—	—	0.03[1]

10. CHEMICALS₁₁ AND FERTILIZERS

	Production	Exports	Imports
Chemicals	na	na	0.7*
Fertilizers:			
Phosphates	na	na	na
n guano.			

11. INDUSTRY

	Production	Exports	Imports
Cement	—	—	3.7	1.3

EMPLOYMENT AND TRADE

A U.S. air base and naval facilities, and a cable station are situated on Grand Turk. The tourist industry is developing rapidly. The chief exports are salt (decreasing), sisal, crawfish, and conches. Earnings of the considerable number of islanders working abroad in the Bahamas are another source of income.

continued

UNITED STATES OF AMERICA

The U.S.A. is a federation of 50 states each of which has its own constitution, judicial system, and legislature. The form of federal government laid down in the Constitution gives executive power to a directly elected president whilst legislative power rests with a two chamber Congress. In 1959 Alaska and Hawaii became the 49th and 50th states. For the purpose of comparisons, the 1953–5 data for these two areas have been included with those for the U.S.A.

AREA: 9 191 802 sq. km. (3 548 974 sq. miles)

LAND USE[1]: (percentage of total)

	1959	1954
Arable and orchard	20.1	19.8
Permanent meadow and pasture	34.9	27.4
Forest and woodland	32.2	34.9
City areas, waste and other land	17.6	20.6

POPULATION: 199 118 000 (1967 estimate)

Distribution of working population: 78 357 000* (1966)

Largest city: NEW YORK; population: 11 410 000* (1966)
Capital city: WASHINGTON, D.C.; population: 2 615 000* (1966)

U.N. group no.

Distribution of working population (1965)

U.N. group no.		Percentage
0	Agriculture, forestry, fishing and hunting	6.2
1	Mining and quarrying	6.7
2/3	Manufacturing	25.6
4	Construction	6.4
5	Electricity, gas, water and sanitary services	1.4
6	Commerce	23.0
7	Transport, storage and communications	4.8
8	Services	27.6
9	Others	4.4

		Year(s)
Life expectancy at birth (years): male	67.0	1967
female	74.2	} 1967
Infant mortality (per '000)	19.4	1966
Crude birth rate (per '000)	9.4	1966
Crude death rate (per '000)	25.4	1966
Accidental deaths (per 100 000 population)	30.4	1965
caused by motor vehicles	27.6	1965
Population per physician	670	1965
Population per hospital bed	120	1965
School enrolment: age 5–19 years (percentage)	103‡	1965
age over 19 years (per 100 000 population)	2 709*	1965

COMMUNICATIONS

		Year(s)
Motor vehicles in use ('000s): private	71 743.8	1963–5 av.
commercial	13 511.7	1963–5 av.
Railway track (km.)	344 949	1964
Mail per capita: domestic and foreign, incl. packages	358	1963–5 av.
foreign received	3	}
Telephones (per '000)	1140	1967
Radio receivers (per '000 population)	1340	1965
Television sets (per '000 population)	345.9	1963–5 av.
Daily newspapers (per '000 population)	315.3	1962–4 av.

PRODUCTION, EXPORTS AND IMPORTS

Years: 1963–5 average and 1953–5 average. Units: '000 metric tons unless otherwise indicated

1. CEREALS, etc.

	Production	Exports	Imports
Barley	8 500.7 / 7 424.3	1 379.7	177.9
Maize (corn)	98 114.3 / 80 268.0	12 832.5 / 2 676.5	24.2
Millet/sorghum	18 798.3 / 4 978.3	2 943.1*	na
Oats	13 280.3 / 19 944.0	179.8	1 460.7 / 1 490.3
Potatoes	12 115.3 / 10 207.0	96.7	16.4
Rye	1 358.9s / 190.7s	155.7	89.8
Sweet potatoes[/]	803.3	589.5	10.5
Yams	na	54.2	33.1
Wheat[j]	33 981.3 / 28 015.7	18 586.7s / 5 885.2	76.0
s incl. re-exports.			223.3

2. FRUIT, etc.

	Production	Exports	Imports
Apples	2 910.0 / 2 275.0	92.9s	35.9
Apricots	197.0 / 208.9	na	2.6
Bananas	3.7* / 3.0*	66.5†	1 490.7 / 1 490.3
Cherries	245.0 / 208.3	na	1.3
Coconuts	na	60.7	80.7
Dates	20.3 / 17.3	3.5‡	16.4
Figs	55.0 / 78.3	0.8	16.9
Grapes	3 515.0 / 2 557.0	97s	14.8
Lemons	493.0 / 524.0	52.5	10.1
Oranges	4 748.3 / 5 273.0	194.7s	2.5
Olives	48.7 / 35.0	49.5	49.9
Peaches	1 672.7 / 1 294.1	79.0s	3.2
Other citrus fruit	na	na	2.4
		7.8	1.1

na: data not available. — negligible or nil. [1] one year only.

continued

FINANCE

Currency unit: The U.S. dollar

Exchange rates
Per £ sterling

	1965	1960	1938
	2.8	2.8	4.64

The $ U.S., which since 31 January 1934 has been fixed at $35 per oz. of fine gold, is the world's leading currency. Other currencies are normally quoted in terms of the $ U.S.

TRADING

Total trade (in million $ U.S.)

	1965	1955	1938
Exports (f.o.b.)	27 532	15 556	3 102
Imports (f.o.b.)	21 431	11 568	2 191

Main trading partners (percentage of total value)

Exports	1965	1955	1938	Imports	1965	1955	1938
Canada	21	20	15	Canada	23	23	13
Japan	8	4	3a	Japan	11	4	6a
Germany F.R.	6	4	8	Germany F.R.	7	5	7
Mexico	4	5	3	Venezuela	6	5	3a
Netherlands	4	3	17	Mexico	3	3	1a
France	4	2	4	Italy	3	3	2

Distribution of trade (percentage of total value)

Exports	1965	1955	1938*	Imports	1965	1955	1938
Manufactured goods (machinery)	49	55	32		(14)	(6)	(—)
Food (cereals and preparations)	15	15	11		(10)	(15)	(11)
Crude materials and fuels	14	16	17		(4)	(9)	(7)
Chemicals	9	—	3		(5)	(12)	(na)
				Food (coffee)	26	26	26

a incl. Germany D.R.; also Austria for the period 7 May–31 December.

PRODUCTION, EXPORTS AND IMPORTS *continued*

4. VEGETABLE OILSEEDS AND OILS

	Production	Exports	Imports
Castor seed	27.3	12.9	0.94	47.00
Castor oil	na	0.40s	1.19s	42.17
Copra	na	0.02	0.13	254.53
Coconut oil	na	3.60s	4.66	301.03
Groundnuts	5 607.7 / 5 594.3	142.00	177.17	63.97
Cottonseed	679.9	5.98	0.17	
Cottonseed oil	na	231.11	232.31	
Linseed	769.0 / 1 009.0	43.50	124.23	18.50
Linseed oil	na	120.91	124.90	5.74
Olive oil	na	10.94	102.29	20.91
Palm oil	na	—	—	0.90
Palm kernel oil	na	—	—	0.20
Rapeseed	0.1*	0.0*	—	22.08
Rapeseed oil	na	0.03	—	38.06
Sesame seed	na	0.52	—	22.09
Soya beans	20 372.7 / 9 919.0	5 554.16 / 380.73	5.50	
Soya bean oil	na	541.37	38.81	14.60
Sunflower seed	na	—	—	2.25
Sunflower seed oil	na	—	—	5.93
Tung oil	7.0	13.0	0.88s	0.27

5. LIVESTOCK‡, ANIMAL PRODUCTS, etc.

	Production	Exports	Imports
Chickens[d].	370 735c / 390 965n		
Cattle[d].	105 888 / 95 302q	46.3	20.3
cows[d][p].	49 882r / 2 646r		
Goats[d].	28 135n / 31 625n	26.5	11.9
Sheep[d].	2 869 / 3 011u		
Horses[d].	56 770 / 49 182		
Pigs[d].	14 364 / 11 637		
Meat[1] 'A'	5 679 / 3 466	10.9	2.2
'B'.	645 / 727	13.8s	5.0*
Butter	1 055 / 810	180.0c	25.2
Cheese	3 800 / 3 750	35.4s	10.9
Eggs	57 012 / 55 620	9.1	39.3
Fish	2 716u / 2 748	119.4	109.2[1]
Whale/sperm oil	na	5 208.5 / 1 756.5	1.5s
Hides/skins	64	92.2a / 1 027.8c	75.9a
Wool	61	1.5	91.9

a million $ U.S. d no. in millions. e no. in thousands. f no. in millions. g on farms only. q on farms only. s incl. re-exports. [1] Texas only. u excl. Alaska. w incl. sperm oil‡.

8. IRON AND STEEL

	Production	Exports	Imports
Iron ore	47 077m / 51 818m	3.3	40 909 / 17 055
Gold: ore[v]	1 538.3 / 1 902.0	48.6	336.4² / 181.8
Pig iron	77 954 / 65 382	7 065 / 7 065	473 / 56
Steel ingots/castings	111 218 / 96 845	596 / 224	87 / 246
Iron/steel scrap[a]	na	6 520 / 660	215 / 173
Iron/steel castings[a]	na	na	877 / 194

a million $ U.S. m metal content.

9. NON-FERROUS MINERALS AND METALS

	Production	Exports	Imports
Diamonds[a]	na	na	307.7 / 935.9
Gold: ore[v]	1 538.3 / 1 902.0	18 171.3	1 478.6²
bullion/coins etc.			
Platinum group metals[k].	na	na	44 212.3 / 747.2
Silver[k]: ore[m]	58 677.7 / 2 505.7	27.7	38 467.5²
bullion	na	na	38 402.5 / 450.6
Mica	104.3	3.3	640.3²
Aluminium: bauxite	1 618.9 / 1 876.4	na	10 550.3 / 11.0
alumina	na	266.0†	na

10. CHEMICALS[n] AND FERTILIZERS

	Production	Exports	Imports
Organic chemicals:			
Benzene	2 542.0	344.5	43.4
Butadiene	1 220.0		
Ethylene	na		
Methanol	1 166.9s	na	0.5†
Phenol	468.8*	10.12	1.5
Phthalic anhydride	286.0	10.1	34.6
Styrene monomer	1 136.0	125.3	237.2
Urea	799.5	31.4	
Inorganic chemicals:			
Ammonia	6 919.6	167.0[1]	1.2
Carbon black	1 088.0[1]	103.4	26.3
Chlorine	4 169.2	37.4	
Nitric acid	4 402.0	0.22	
Sodium carbonate	5 686.6	222.6	1.5
Sodium hydroxide	20 633.9	323.8	34.6

na: data not available. — negligible or nil. [1] one year only. [2] two year average. * estimate. ‡ see appendix. † re-exports.

continued

UNITED STATES OF AMERICA (TERRITORIES)

UNITED STATES OF AMERICA continued

PRODUCTION, EXPORTS AND IMPORTS continued

11. INDUSTRY	Production	Exports	Imports
Aircraft a	10 465² w	741.5 n	104.8
Alcoholic beverages	120 860	106 691 p	380.9 a
beer b	4 001 q	10 324 r	—
Cement	60 993	46 863	1 585
Electrical engineering a	37 863	na	1 592.0
Locomotives c	1 524	1 676² q	786.5²

11. INDUSTRY—continued	Production	Exports	Imports
Railway vehicles a	na	131.1	110.1
Machine tools a	1 160	234.2	145.0
Motorcycles g	280	0.8	113.3
Motor ships g	369	1 779.5 t	1 293.6 a
Motor vehicles d			
commercial d	1 585	131.1	110.1
private d	8 232	1 766	6 532

a million $ U.S. b '000 hectolitres. c no. in thousands.
d no. in thousands. e million $ U.S. g '000 G.R.T. n number on order.
p incl. Puerto Rico. q 1967 figure. g 1959 figure. t incl. Puerto Rico's exports. u excl. parts. v excl. imports from Puerto Rico. w 1965–7 av.

AMERICAN SAMOA

RYUKYU ISLANDS—see page 205

American Samoa is an unincorporated territory of the U.S.A. Its indigenous inhabitants are U.S. nationals. In 1952 civilian control replaced the naval administration.

AREA: 197 sq. km. (76 sq. miles)

LAND USE: (percentage of total)

	1964	1965
Arable and orchard	40	30
Forest and woodland	20	60
City areas, waste and other land	40	10

POPULATION: 29 000 (1967 estimate)

Capital: PAGO PAGO; population: 1 251 (city proper, 1960)
Total working population: 5 889 (1960)

PACIFIC OCEAN

FINANCE
Currency unit: The U.S. dollar

		Year(s)
Infant mortality (per '000)	33.6	1965
Crude birth rate (per '000)	42.9	1965
Crude death rate (per '000)	6.1	1965
Population per physician	1 100	1965
Population per hospital bed	140	1966
School enrolment: age 5–19 years (percentage) age over 19 years (per 100 000 population)	124‡	1963–4 av.
National Income (million $ U.S.)	15*	1965
G.N.P. per capita ($ U.S.)	580	1966
	200‡	1965

PRODUCTION AND TRADE
Coconuts, tropical fruit, and copra are the main products of the islands; fishing is also of commercial importance, and some livestock are reared. Trade is mainly with the U.S.A., the chief exports being copra, tuna, and handicrafts.

PRODUCTION, EXPORTS AND IMPORTS
Years: 1963–5 average and 1953–5 average   Units: '000 metric tons unless otherwise indicated

	Production	Exports	Imports
1. CEREALS, etc.			
Rice	—	0.52	—
2. FRUIT, etc.			
Bananas	1.0*	14.7	na
Coconuts e	7.3*	na	na
e no. in millions.			
3. BEVERAGES, FOREST PRODUCTS, etc.			
Sugar, raw	—	—	—
Hardwood j	—	0.52	0.2
j '000 cu. metres of roundwood equivalent.	—	3.12	
4. VEGETABLE OILSEEDS AND OILS			
Copra	0.80	1.57	—
5. LIVESTOCK‡, ANIMAL PRODUCTS, etc.			
Chickens d	80.0*	67.02	—
Cattle d	na	na	—
Pigs d	13.0	13.52	—
Fish	na	3.72	—
d no. in thousands.			
7. FUEL AND POWER			
Electricity h t	211	—	—
Petroleum, refined	—	—	—
h million kWh. t thermal.			

na: data not available. — negligible or nil. — one year only. 2 two year average. * estimate. ‡ see appendix. † re-exports.

continued

GUAM

WEST PACIFIC

Guam, the largest and most southerly of the Mariana or Ladrone islands, is of great strategic importance. It reverted to U.S. control in 1944 after three years' Japanese occupation. In 1950 civilian control replaced the post-war naval administration, and full U.S. citizenship was granted to the inhabitants.

AREA: 540 sq. km. (209 sq. miles)

LAND USE: (percentage of total)

	1960	1965
Arable and orchard	21.8	21.8
Permanent meadow and pasture	14.5	14.5
Forest and woodland	18.2	18.2
City areas, waste and other land	45.5	45.5

POPULATION: 94 000 (1967 estimate)

Capital city: AGANA; population: 1 642 (city proper, 1960)
Total working population: 20 315 (1964)

FINANCE
Currency unit: The U.S. dollar

		Year(s)
Infant mortality (per '000)	32.5	1965
Crude birth rate (per '000)	33.0	1965
Crude death rate (per '000)	4.4	1965
Population per physician	2 500	1966
Population per hospital bed	270	1965
School enrolment: age 5–19 years (percentage) age over 19 years (per 100 000 population)	90	1963–4 av.
	1 864	1964–5 av.

COMMUNICATIONS

Motor vehicles in use ('000s): private	16.4	1963–5 av.
commercial	23.1	1967
Telephones (per '000 urban population)	22.1	
Radio receivers (per '000 population)	364	1963–5 av.
Television sets (per '000 population)	182	1963–5 av.
Daily newspapers (per '000 population)		

EMPLOYMENT, PRODUCTION AND TRADE

Many of the inhabitants are employed by the U.S. Navy or Air Force. There is a little agriculture, producing maize, bananas and coconuts, and some livestock are reared; but most food and all consumer goods and building materials have to be imported. The island is the only American territory to enjoy a large measure of free trade, excise duties being levied only on tobacco, alcoholic beverages and fuel. Income is derived primarily from the U.S. government but a little copra and some tropical fruits and vegetables are exported.

National Income (million $ U.S.) 120* 1966
G.N.P. per capita ($ U.S.) 1550 1966

PRODUCTION, EXPORTS AND IMPORTS
Years: 1963–5 average and 1953–5 average   Units: '000 metric tons unless otherwise indicated

	Production	Exports	Imports
1. CEREALS, etc.			
Maize (corn)	na	na	0.3*²
Potatoes	na	na	0.4
Rice	na	na	4.2²
Sugar, raw	—	—	1.4²
3. BEVERAGES, FOREST PRODUCTS, etc.			
Sugar, raw	—	—	na
5. LIVESTOCK‡, ANIMAL PRODUCTS, etc.			
Pigs d	6.0n	10.5² n	1.9
Meat‡ 'A'	0.1	na	na
'B'	0.5*	na	na
Eggs	0.2	na	0.42
Fish			na
d no. on farms only. n on farms only.			
7. FUEL AND POWER			
Electricity h t	355	—	110
Petroleum, refined	—	—	
h million kWh. t thermal.			

continued

PACIFIC ISLANDS, TRUST TERRITORY OF

PACIFIC OCEAN

The territory, known also as Micronesia, includes the Caroline, Marshall and Mariana Islands (except Guam). Under a U.N. trusteeship agreement the U.S.A. administers these islands which were formerly mandated to Japan.

AREA: 1779 sq. km. (687 sq. miles)

LAND USE: (percentage of total)

	1965
Arable and orchard	29.8
Permanent meadow and pasture	10.1
Forest and woodland	32.5
City areas, waste and other land	37.6

POPULATION: 91 448 (1967 census)

FINANCE
Currency unit: The U.S. dollar

		Year
National Income (million $ U.S.)	24*	1966
G.N.P. per capita ($ U.S.)	270	1966

PRODUCTION AND TRADE
Copra, cacao, black pepper and ramie are the chief products. Commercial tuna fishing has been developed. Copra is the main export, and guano is obtained from some of the smaller islands.

PRODUCTION, EXPORTS AND IMPORTS
Years: 1963–5 average and 1953–5 average   Units: '000 metric tons unless otherwise indicated

	Production	Exports	Imports
1. CEREALS, etc.			
Cassava	5.0*	9.7	—
Rice	na	na	9.7
Sweet potatoes/yams	4.0*	6.0	0.52
2. FRUIT, etc.			
Bananas	3.0*	2.7	—
Coconuts e	82.7*	0.7	—
Pineapples	na	—	—
e no. in millions.			
3. BEVERAGES, FOREST PRODUCTS, etc.			
Sugar, raw	—	—	0.3
4. VEGETABLE OILSEEDS AND OILS			
Copra	12.47	10.93	10.78
	10.202		
5. LIVESTOCK‡, ANIMAL PRODUCTS, etc.			
Chickens d	105.0	77.3	na
Cattle d	5.3	7.3	na
Goats d	3.0	4.01	na
Pigs d	19.0	9.7	na
Meat‡ 'A'	na	na	na
'B'	na	na	na
Eggs	na	na	na
Fish	na	na	na
Milk	na	na	na
d no. in thousands.			
10. CHEMICALS n AND FERTILIZERS			
Chemicals n	—	—	na
Fertilizers: Phosphates	na	90.6 j	na
n data not available for years 1953–5. n from Angaur Is.			

continued

na: data not available. — negligible or nil. — one year only. 2 two year average. * estimate. ‡ see appendix. † re-exports.

CENTRAL AMERICA

PANAMA CANAL ZONE

A treaty of 1903 authorized the U.S.A. to take over the French Canal Co. with sovereign rights over a ten mile wide strip of Panama territory in return for a capital payment and an annuity. In 1965 the status of the Canal Zone changed; a measure of agreement was reached by the U.S.A. and Panama, and the territory is now administered by the Panama Canal Zone Government.

AREA: 1 676 sq. km. (647 sq. miles) (including water area)

LAND USE: (percentage of total)

	1951
Arable and orchard	0.7
Permanent meadow and pasture	7.7
Forest and woodland (including brush-land)	39.2
City areas, waste and other land	52.4

POPULATION: 56 000 a (1967 estimate). Administrative centre: BALBOA HEIGHTS; population: 3 665 (1965) (incl.

a incl. armed forces.

COMMUNICATIONS

		Year/s
Motor vehicles in use ('000s): private	15.0	1963
commercial	0.8*	1963
Railway track (km)	77	1964
Telephones (per '000 urban population)	22.9	1966

TRANSIT TRADE

In 1966, 11 926 ships used the canal, the majority of which were registered in the U.S.A., Norway, the U.K., Germany F.R., or Liberia. The net weight of cargo amounted to 78 918 013 tons.

PRODUCTION, EXPORTS AND IMPORTS

Years: 1963-5 average and 1953-5 average   Units: '000 metric tons unless otherwise indicated

1. CEREALS, etc.	Production	Exports	Imports
Potatoes	—	0.1	3.4*
Wheat	—	0.5	na

2. FRUIT, etc.	Production	Exports	Imports
Apples	—	—	0.2*
Grapes	—	—	0.7*
Raisins	—	—	0.1*

3. BEVERAGES, FOREST PRODUCTS, etc.	Production	Exports	Imports
Sugar, raw	na	na	na

5. LIVESTOCK‡, ANIMAL PRODUCTS, etc.	Production	Exports	Imports
Bacon/ham	—	—	0.4*
Cheese	—	—	0.21*
Eggs	na	na	na
Milk	na	na	3.0²

7. FUEL AND POWER	Production	Exports	Imports
Electricity‡: total	410		
hydro	277		
thermal	133		
Petroleum, refined h	—	180†	2 713

h million kWh.

11. INDUSTRY	Production	Exports	Imports
Cement	na	na	25.0*

CARIBBEAN SEA

PUERTO RICO

Puerto Rico is a self-governing territory under the protection of the U.S.A. The people have U.S. citizenship, and the island has a non-voting representative in the U.S. Congress. The U.S.A. has agreed to grant complete independence when it is requested.

AREA: 8 891 sq. km. (3 435 sq. miles)

LAND USE: (percentage of total)

	1954	1965
Arable and orchard	40.2	30.4
Permanent meadow and pasture	35.3	35.8
Forest and woodland	12.1	13.3
City areas, waste and other land	11.9	21.0

POPULATION: 2 697 000 (1967 estimate)
Largest city: SAN JUAN, capital; population: 754 300 (1966)
Total working population: 819 500

Distribution of working population (1966)

	U.N. group no.	Percentage
Agriculture, forestry, fishing and hunting	0	17.1
Mining and quarrying	1	1.5
Manufacturing	2/3	18.6
Construction	4	9.5
Services, including electricity, gas, water and sanitary services	5/8	28.5
Commerce	6	17.1
Transport, storage and communications	7	6.8
Others	9	0.9

COMMUNICATIONS

		Year/s
Motor vehicles in use ('000s): private	226	1963-5 av.
commercial	48.1	1967
Telephones (per '000 urban population)	8.1	1967
Daily newspapers (per '000 population)	59.5	1962-4 av.

		Year/s
Life expectancy at birth (years): male	67.1 }	1959-61 av.
female	71.9	
Infant mortality (per '000)	41.8	1965
Crude birth rate (per '000)	30.2	1965
Crude death rate (per '000)	6.7	1965
Accidental deaths (per 100 000 population) caused by motor vehicles	16.1	1965
due to other causes	22.6	1965
Population per physician	980	1965
Population per hospital bed	220	1965
School enrolment: age 5–19 years (percentage)	98c	1963-4 av.
age over 19 years (per 100 000 population)	1 583	1964-5 av.

c incl. pre-school education.

FINANCE

Currency unit: The U.S. dollar

		Year/s
National income (million $ U.S.)	2 525	1965
G.N.P. per capita ($ U.S.)	1 090	1966
Rate of increase of G.N.P. per capita	5.9	1960-4 av.

PRODUCTION AND TRADE

The chief crops are sugar (accounting for 60% of the exports), tobacco, coffee, fruit, maize and yams. Trade is mainly with the U.S.A.

continued

PRODUCTION, EXPORTS AND IMPORTS

Note—Trade figures are included with those for the U.S.A., except for the items shown below

1. CEREALS, etc.	Production	Exports	Imports
Cassava	6.0		10.3
Maize (corn)	11.7		16.7
Rice	2.0*¹		2.7
Sweet potatoes/ yams	27.0		37.3

2. FRUIT, etc.	Production	Exports	Imports
Bananas	114.7		138.3
Coconuts	15.0		
Lemons	3.3		2.0²
Oranges	35.7		28.3
Other citrus fruit	15.3		17.7*
Pineapples	64.0		24.0
Tomatoes	20.3		8.3

e no. in millions.

3. BEVERAGES, FOREST PRODUCTS, etc.	Production	Exports	Imports
Coffee	15.0		13.0
Sugar-cane	8 489.3		9 352.3
raw	870.7	1 064.7	
Tobacco: leaf	15.8		14.8
raw	na	120.7	
cigars e	na	3.9²	
cigarettes e	45.1	197.0	
Hardwood j	na	969.4n	

e no. in millions.   j '000 cu. metres of roundwood equivalent.   n all exported

5. LIVESTOCK‡, ANIMAL PRODUCTS, etc.	Production	Exports	Imports
Cattle d	3 624.0		727.0
dairy cows d	502.7p	399.7p	
Goats d	25.0*,p	26.0p	
Sheep d	na	na	
Horses d	23.0*	36.0*	
Pigs d	160.0p	174.0p	
Meat‡, 'A' d	17.5*	15.3	
'B'	12.5	5.7	
Eggs	4.6	2.5	
Fish	336.0	198.7	
Milk			

d no. in thousands.   p on farms only.

7. FUEL AND POWER	Production	Exports	Imports
Electricity‡: total	3 634		1 050¹
hydro	222	210¹	
thermal	3 412	840¹	
Oil, crude			5 340
Petroleum, refined h	5 380	330¹	340

h million kWh.

11. INDUSTRY	Production	Exports	Imports
Beer b	855.0	76.0q	—
Cement	1 274.3	661.0	na

b '000 hectolitres.   q excl. exports to the U.S.A.

PRODUCTION, EXPORTS AND IMPORTS (continued)

5. LIVESTOCK‡, ANIMAL PRODUCTS, etc.	Production	Exports	Imports
Chickens d	20.7		15.5²
Cattle d	7.0	0.4¹	
Goats d	3.0		
Sheep d	3.0	2.0²	
Horses d	2.0	2.0²	na
Pigs d	1.0	1.0¹	

7. FUEL AND POWER	Production	Exports	Imports
Electricity‡: total	81		0.1¹
thermal		10¹	0.1¹
Petroleum, refined h	—		

h million kWh.   f thermal.

continued

CARIBBEAN SEA

VIRGIN ISLANDS (U.S.A.)

The U.S. Virgin Islands were bought from Denmark in 1917 for strategic reasons. The inhabitants were made U.S. citizens in 1927 but the islands are constitutionally an unincorporated territory, and the U.S. Department of the Interior retains full jurisdiction.

AREA: 344.5 sq. km. (133 sq. miles)

LAND USE: (percentage of total)

	1960	1955
Arable and orchard	14.7 }	32.4
Permanent meadow and pasture	20.6	
Forest and woodland	5.9	50.0
City areas, waste and other land	58.8	17.6

POPULATION: 56 000 (1967 U.N. estimate)
Capital city: CHARLOTTE AMALIE; population: 12 880 (city proper, 1960)

FINANCE

		Year
National income (million $ U.S.)	25*	1966
G.N.P. per capita ($ U.S.)	2 320	1966

Distribution of working population (1960)
Total working population: 11 334

	U.N. group no.	Percentage
Agriculture, forestry, fishing and hunting	0	5.4
Mining and quarrying	1	7.7
Manufacturing	2/3	7.7
Construction	4	12.0
Electricity, gas, water and sanitary services	5	18.4
Commerce	6	9.4
Transport, storage and communications	7	43.0
Services	8	4.6
Others	9	

		Year/s
Infant mortality (per '000)	30.0	1965
Crude death rate (per '000)	46.0	1965
Population per physician	1 000	1963
Population per hospital bed	126‡	1966
School enrolment: age 5–19 years (percentage)	908	1963-4 av.
age over 19 years (per 100 000 population)		

PRODUCTION, EXPORTS AND IMPORTS

Years: 1963-5 average and 1953-5 average   Units: '000 metric tons unless otherwise indicated

1. CEREALS, etc.	Production	Exports	Imports
Rice	—	—	2.1²

3. BEVERAGES, FOREST PRODUCTS, etc.	Production	Exports	Imports
Sugar-cane	162.3*		110.7
raw	10.8	9.0	9.9

d no. in thousands.

5. LIVESTOCK‡, ANIMAL PRODUCTS, etc.	Production	Exports	Imports
Meat‡, 'A'	3.0*		1.0²
Cheese			
Eggs	4.7		na
Milk	2.0		1.7

d no. in thousands.

7. FUEL AND POWER	Production	Exports	Imports
Electricity‡: total	87		
Petroleum, refined h	—		

h million kWh.   f thermal.

continued

---

na: data not available.   — negligible or nil.   1 one year only.   2 two year average.   * estimate.   ‡ see appendix.   † re-exports.

UPPER VOLTA
WEST AFRICA

Upper Volta was reconstituted as a separate state of French West Africa in 1947 after fifteen years' partition between the Ivory Coast, Mali, and Niger, and became an independent republic in 1960. Ties with France concerning finance and technical assistance were retained. The army assumed power in 1966 but there was a partial return to civilian government in 1970.

AREA: 274 122 sq. km. (105 839 sq. miles)

POPULATION: 5 054 000 (1967 estimate)
Capital city: OUAGADOUGOU; population: 59 126 (city proper, 1961)

LAND USE: (percentage of total)

	1960
Arable and orchard	9.0
Permanent meadow and pasture	17.9
Forest and woodland	7.3
City areas, waste and other land	na

			Year(s)
Life expectancy at birth (years): male		32.1*	1960–1 av.
female		31.1*	1960–1 av.
Infant mortality (per '000)		182*	1960–1 av.
Population per physician		63 000	1966
Population per hospital bed		1 680a	1964
School enrolment: age 5–19 years (percentage)		8	1963–4 av.

a government hospitals only.

COMMUNICATIONS

		Year(s)
Motor vehicles in use ('000s): private	3.5	1963–5 av.
commercial	3.0	1963–5 av.
Telephones (per '000 urban population)	3.1*	1960–1 av.
Radio receivers (per '000 population)	10.1	1963–6
Television sets (per '000 population)	0.1	1964–5 av.
Daily newspapers (per '000 population)	0.1	1957

FINANCE
Currency unit: The franc CFA
Exchange rates
Per $ U.S.
Per £ sterling

TRADING

		Year
National income (million $U.S.)	145 / 50	1965 / 1958
G.N.P. per capita ($U.S.)	246.85 / 246.85	1960 / 1966
Per £ sterling	691.18 / 691.18	1960 / 1966

Total trade (in million $U.S.)

	1965	1955
Exports (f.o.b.)	14	5
Imports (c.i.f.)	37	na

Main trading partners (percentage of total value)

Exports	1965		Imports	1965
Ivory Coast	52		France	54
Ghana	19		Ivory Coast	6
France	8		Mali	6
Mali	8		Senegal	3
Italy	3		Germany F.R.	3
			Ghana	2
			U.S.A.	2

Distribution of trade (percentage of total value)

Exports	1965	1965
Food (cattle)	70 (42)	54
Crude materials (cotton)	23 (14)(11)	6 (7)

Imports	1965	1965
Manufactured goods (machinery and transport equipment)	53	
(textiles and clothing)	(19)(13)	
Food (sugar)	21 (5)	
Crude materials and fuels	16	(5)

PRODUCTION, EXPORTS AND IMPORTS
Years: 1963–5 average. Units: '000 metric tons unless otherwise indicated

Note—no data are available for the years 1953–5

1. CEREALS, etc.

	Production	Exports	Imports
Cassava	32.0*	—	—
Maize (corn)	118.7*	0.7	0.1n
Millet/sorghum	1 198.3	—	—
Potatoes	31.7*	—	0.2
Sweet potatoes/yams	51.0*	—	3.3

2. FRUIT, etc.

	Production	Exports	Imports
Apples	—	—	0.1n
Bananas	—	—	1.2
Dates	—	—	0.1
Oranges	—	—	0.6
Wineb	—	—	16.1

b '000 hectolitres. n incl. pears and quince.

3. BEVERAGES, FOREST PRODUCTS, etc.

	Production	Exports	Imports
Coffee	—	0.1	9.3
Sugar, raw	—	—	
Tobacco: leaf products	0.4*	—	0.4
Softwoodj	—	—	
Hardwoodj	3 045.0*1	—	12.4²

j '000 cu. metres of roundwood equivalent.

4. VEGETABLE OILSEEDS AND OILS

	Production	Exports	Imports
Cottonseed	8.70*	3.18	0.03
Groundnuts	93.5*	3.50	—
Groundnut oil	na	0.07	0.01²
Palm oil	—	—	—
Sesame seed	5.37	2.20	0.06²

5. LIVESTOCK‡, ANIMAL PRODUCTS, etc.

	Production	Exports	Imports
Chickensd	3 183.0*		
Cattled	1 973.3*	58.9*	
Goatsd	792.0*		
Sheepd	1 900.0*		
Horsesd	63.7*		
Pigsd	110.0*		
Meat: 'A'	32.0*		131.1
Butter	—		
Eggs	11.4		
Fish	3.7*		
Milk	118.3	0.1	0.1
Hides/skins	0.5²	0.5	

d no. in thousands.

6. FIBRES, TEXTILES, etc.

	Production	Exports	Imports
Cotton: lint	3.7*	1.7	1.8
yarn	—	—	0.63²
woven fabrics	na	—	1.8

7. FUEL AND POWER

	Production	Exports	Imports
Electricity/h	18	—	33
Petroleum, refined	—	—	

h million kWh. t thermal.

9. NON-FERROUS MINERALS AND METALS

	Production	Exports	Imports
Gold k: ore	37m	—	—

k '000 fine troy oz. m metal content. p bullion. l 39p

11. INDUSTRY

	Production	Exports	Imports
Alcoholic beverages beerb	35.0	—	0.8²a
Cement	—	—	29.3
Electrical engineeringa	—	—	1.4
Motor vehiclesa	—	0.1	2.9

a million $ U.S. b '000 hectolitres.

na: data not available. — negligible or nil. 1 one year only. 2 two year average. * estimate. ‡ see appendix. † re-exports.

URUGUAY
SOUTH AMERICA

Uruguay has been a republic since 1830. Apart from the years 1952–66, when executive power was vested in a nine-man 'Council of State', there has been a presidential system of government. The country has an advanced social welfare system.

AREA: 186 926 sq. km. (72 172 sq. miles)

POPULATION: 2 783 000 (1967 estimate)
Largest city: MONTEVIDEO, capital; population: 1 158 632 (city proper, 1963)

LAND USE: (percentage of total)

	1961	1954
Arable and orchard	12.0	12.3
Permanent meadow and pasture	74.1	67.8
Forest and woodland	3.2	2.7
City areas, waste and other land	10.7	17.2

FINANCE
Currency unit: The Uruguayan peso
Exchange rates

	1965	1960	1950	1938
Per $ U.S.	59.9a	11.03	1.5	1.84
Per £ sterling	157.72	30.88	4.21	8.46

TRADING

		Year(s)
National income (million $U.S.)	1 458 / 570	1965 / 1960
G.N.P. per capita ($U.S.)		
Rate of increase of G.N.P. per capita (percentage)	1.3	1960–3 av.
Foreign trade (percentage of G.D.P.)	23	1963–4 av.

a official import rate.

Total trade (in million $U.S.)

	1965	1955	1938
Exports (f.o.b.)	191	184	62
Imports (c.i.f.)	150	229	62

Main trading partners (percentage of total value)

Exports	1965	1955	1938	Imports	1965	1955	1938
U.S.A.	17	13	12	U.S.A.	19	19	13
U.K.	16	14	16d	Germany F.R.	14	12	16d
Netherlands	9	23	3	U.K.	12	12.5	*2
Germany F.R.	9	24d	10	Brazil	10	9	20
Spain	8	4	17	Venezuela	9	6	8
Italy	6	4	8	Argentina	6	1	1
France	6	5	1	Kuwait	4	4	—

Distribution of trade (percentage of total value)

Exports	1965	1955	1938
Wool	47	57	44
Animals and meat	32	8	23
Hides and skins	8	—	12

Imports	1965	1955	1938
Machinery and transport equipment	26	17	20
Fuels	17	6	2
Food	6	4	13
Chemicals	4	—	1

d includes Germany D.R.

COMMUNICATIONS

		Year(s)
Motor vehicles in use ('000s): private	112	1963–5 av.
commercial	81.1	1963–5 av.
Railway track (km)	3 102	1964
Telephones (per '000 urban population)	66.9*	1967
Radio receivers (per '000 population)	342	1963–5 av.
Television sets (per '000 population)	66.4	1963–5 av.
Daily newspapers (per '000 population)	249.5	1962–3 av.

Distribution of working population (1963)
Total working population: 1 015 500*

U.N. group no.		Percentage
0	Agriculture, forestry, fishing and hunting	17.9
2/3	Mining and quarrying	0.2
	Manufacturing	20.8
4	Construction	4.8
5	Electricity, gas, water and sanitary services	1.7
6	Commerce	13.0
7	Transport, storage and communications	6.1
8	Services	27.4
9	Others	8.1

		Year(s)
Infant mortality (per '000)	49.8*	1965
Crude birth rate (per '000)	24.5*	1960–5 av.
Crude death rate (per '000)	9*	1960–5 av.
Accidental deaths (per 100 000 population)	75.1	1966
due to motor vehicles	29.1	1966
due to other causes	29.1	1966
Population per physician	850b	1966
Population per hospital bed	200b	1966
School enrolment: age 5–19 years (percentage)	72	1963
age over 19 years (per 100 000 population)	587a	1963–4 av.

a universities and degree granting institutions only.
b government hospitals only.

PRODUCTION, EXPORTS AND IMPORTS
Years: 1963–5 average and 1953–5 average. Units: '000 metric tons unless otherwise indicated

1. CEREALS, etc.

	Production		Exports		Imports	
Barley	27.7*	39.7	0.9	1.7	1.0	
Cassava	—	2.5				
Maize (corn)	120.0	207.5	0.3	1.8	0.6	
Millet/sorghum	2.0*	5.0²				
Oats	77.0*	44.0	0.1			
Potatoes	84.0*	72.3			2.8²	
Rice	71.3	65.3	19.3	14.3		
Sweet potatoes/yams	77.3*	60.7		2.5		
Wheat	434.3*	835.0	43.3	190.9	45.1	

2. FRUIT, etc.

	Production		Exports		Imports	
Apples	27.7	33.0¹				
Bananas	—	—			23.9	17.0
Grapes	122.3*	143.0¹			0.1n	0.1
Lemons	12.7*	6.3*				
Oranges	48.7*	45.0				
Other citrus fruit	1.0*	1.0²				
Olives	1.0*	na				
Peaches	18.7*	na				
Pears	4.0*	3.0¹				
Plums	5.0*	na				
Raisins	21.7	23.0¹			0.3²	0.4
Wineb	730.0¹	830.5²			0.1	1.3

b '000 hectolitres. n desiccated.

3. BEVERAGES, FOREST PRODUCTS, etc.

	Production		Exports		Imports	
Cocoa					0.8	
Coffee					3.5	2.5
Sugar: beet cane (raw)	347.7* / 224.0*	74.3			108.5 / 44.0¹	290.6¹ / 27.5²
Tea						
Tobacco: leaf cigarettes	10.4	3.7*			36.3 / 3.2	72.3 / 4.1
Softwoodj	3.42	65.0¹				
Hardwoodj	1 135.0²	635.0¹				
Wood pulp					14.0¹ / 20.0¹	12.5* / 27.5²
Newsprint	32.0²*				1.5¹	
Other paper						

e no. in millions. j '000 cu. metres of roundwood equivalent.

4. VEGETABLE OILSEEDS AND OILS

	Production		Exports		Imports	
Castor oil	1.00	na			0.04	0.18
Coconut oil					0.15	0.10
Cottonseed	na	na				
Cottonseed oil	3.50	4.20			0.30	0.97
Groundnuts	na	na			0.55	0.022
Groundnut oil	na	na			0.97	0.60p
Linseed	72.33	59.30n			20.13	
Linseed oil	20.02	37.1,32			0.012	

n flax grown for seed only. p incl. palm oil and shea seed oil.

na: data not available. — negligible or nil. 1 one year only. 2 two year average. * estimate. ‡ see appendix. † re-exports.

continued

PRODUCTION, EXPORTS AND IMPORTS continued

4. VEGETABLE OILSEEDS AND OILS—continued

	Production	Exports	Imports
Olive oil	—	—	0.02 0.36
Soya beans	63.00 79.30	1.53² 3.94q	0.05 na
Sunflower seed	na na		na
Sunflower seed oil,			
Tung oil	—	—	0.02
g incl. other minor vegetable oils.			

5. LIVESTOCK‡, ANIMAL PRODUCTS, etc.

	Production	Exports	Imports
Chickens *d.*	7 266.7* 5 672.0*		
Cattle *d.*	8 717.7 7 916.0		
Goats *d.*	18.0 na		
Sheep *d.*	21 869.3 26 227.5²		
Horses *d.*	463.0		
Pigs *d.*	427.0 256.7		
Meat‡: 'A'	370.3* 366.7	—	
'B'	21.7* 29.4ⁱ	—	
Butter *d.*	9.3* 4.0²	5.4 —²	0.1
Cheese	7.0* 1.3	73.7	0.1
Eggs	16.3* 16.7*	1.3²	
Fish	12.0 0.6	35.1	
Milk	719.0 576.0²	1.2 0.1	
Hides/skins	38.2 4.1	30.3²	0.7
Wool *d.*	61.4* 58.3	25.9 43.4	1.5
d no. in thousands.			

6. FIBRES, TEXTILES, etc.

	Production	Exports	Imports
Agaves (sisal, etc.)	—	—	
Cotton lint	0.7 na	—	0.2 8.8
Hemp fibre	—	—	0.1 0.1
Jute	—	—	3.4 1.2
Rubber, natural	—	—	3.0
Cotton, woven fabrics	0.8 0.9		1.5 0.5
Rayon, fibre/yarn	—	—	
Non-cellulosic	—	—	
fibre/yarn	0.7 na	0.3	0.7 na
Wool: yarn	0.2 0.2	0.2	—² na
woven fabrics		0.1	—² na

7. FUEL AND POWER

	Production	Exports	Imports
Coal, 'A'‡	—	—	
Coke	—	—	
Electricity *h*: total	1 650 930		33¹
hydro	992 680¹		2¹ 3
thermal	658 250		86
Oil, crude	—	—	
Petroleum, refined.	1 463 1 100¹	7 239¹*	1 520 1 100¹
h million kWh.			83 190¹

8. IRON AND STEEL

	Production	Exports	Imports
Iron ore	1 —	—	27 17
Steel ingots/castings	11 —	na —	

Venezuela is one of the more economically stable of the South American republics, due mainly to the considerable revenue from oil. In 1958 a democratic form of civilian government was introduced after five years' military rule.

AREA: 912 050* sq. km. (352 143* sq. miles)

LAND USE: (percentage of total)

	1961
Arable and orchard.	5.7
Permanent meadow and pasture	18.3 } on agricultural holdings
Forest and woodland	52.6
City areas, waste and other land	23.4

POPULATION: 9 352 000 (1967 estimate)

Total working population: 2 406 725* *a*

Distribution of working population (1961)

	U.N. group no.	*Percentage*
Agriculture, forestry, fishing and hunting	0	32.1
Mining and quarrying	1	1.9
Manufacturing	2/3	12.3
Electricity, gas, water and sanitary services.	4	1.1
Construction	5	5.3
Commerce	6	12.6
Transport, storage and communications	7	4.4
Services	8	23.8
Others	9	6.5

Largest city: CARACAS, capital: population: 1 764 274 (1966)

		Year(s)
Life expectancy at birth (years).	66.4	1963–5 av.
Infant mortality (per '000).	47.7* *a*	1965
Crude birth rate (per '000)	47.0* *a*	1965
Crude death rate (per '000).	9.5* *a*	1960–5 av.
Accidental deaths (per 100 000 population)		1963–5 av.
caused by motor vehicles		
due to other causes.	22.2*	1966
Population per physician	25.2*	1966
Population per hospital bed	1210	1965
School enrolment: children age 5–19 years (percentage)	310	1966
age over 19 years (per 100 000 population)	83	1966
	498	1963

COMMUNICATIONS

		Year(s)
Railway track (km).	341.3	1963–5 av.
Motor vehicles in use ('000s): private	139.9	1964
commercial	773	1965
Mail per capita: domestic	11	
foreign sent	29	
foreign received	10	
Telephones (per '000 population)	34.4	1967
Radio receivers (per '000 population)	190	1963–5 av.
Television sets (per '000 population)	70.9	1963–5 av.
Daily newspapers (per '000 population)	78	1963

FINANCE

Currency unit: The bolivar

Exchange rates b	*1965*	*1960*	*1955*	*1938*
Per $ U.S.	4.5	3.35	3.35	3.19
Per £ sterling	12.6	9.38	9.38	14.67

TRADING

	1965	*1960*	*1955*	*1938*
National Income (million $ U.S.)	6 497			*Year(s)*
G.N.P. per capita ($ U.S.).	850		1966	
G.N.P. rate of increase per capita	1.5		1960–4 av.	
Foreign trade (percentage of G.D.P.)	47		1963–5 av.	

Total trade (in million $ U.S.)

	1965	*1960*	*1955*	*1938*
Exports (f.o.b.)	2 745		1 873	181
Imports (c.i.f.)	1 297		943	96

Main trading partners (percentage of total value)

Exports	*1965*	*1955*	*1938*	*Imports*	*1965*	*1955*	*1938*
U.S.A.	37	38	51	U.S.A.	51	59	56
Neths. Antilles	24	37		Germany F.R.	9	6	12 *d*
Canada	10	na		U.K.	8	8	7
U.K.	5		4	Italy	4	—	2
Trin./Tob.	4		3	Japan	4	—	
Brazil	2	4	3	France			
Netherlands	3	3					

d incl. Germany D.R.

PRODUCTION, EXPORTS AND IMPORTS
Years: 1963–5 average and 1953–5 average. Units: '000 metric tons unless otherwise indicated

1. CEREALS, etc.

	Production	Exports	Imports
Barley.	—	—	
Cassava.	318.3 201.3		
Maize (corn)	478.5 326.0	—	8.0*
Millets/Sorghum	na	na	
Oats	—	—	
Potatoes	123.7 38.3		68.2 1.0
Rice *d*.	165.7 76.7*		0.62 na
Rye	—	—	10.6 37.5
Sweet potatoes/			1.4 3.3
Yams	99.7 53.5²	na	0.1
Wheat.	1.0 4.5²		502.0

2. FRUIT, etc.

	Production	Exports	Imports
Apples	—	—	
Bananas	1 296.3 50.5²	3.1*	0.1
Coconuts	170.7*e	0.3	0.6¹ 6.1
Grapes	40.0* na		0.2
Oranges	40.0* na	11.0	5.0 na
Pineapples	40.0 na		0.9 0.4*
Raisins	—	—	
Tomatoes	66.3 na		
Wine *b.*			27.3 49.3

3. BEVERAGES, FOREST PRODUCTS, etc.

	Production	Exports	Imports
Cocoa	21.2 15.3*	12.3	16.5
Coffee	57.1 47.0	20.6	36.8
Sugar: cane	3 826.3* 2 134.7		
raw.	317.4*p 143.7*p	19.5	
Tea	—	—	
Tobacco: leaf	8.7 6.0*	2.6	7.3
cigarettes.		1.6	
cigars *r*	5 139.0* 1 349.0		
Hardwood *j*	—*² —²		75.0
Softwood *j*	8 822.0 3 000.0		38.0
Wood pulp *j*			40.0*
Newsprint	131.4		
Other paper			

4. VEGETABLE OILSEEDS AND OILS

	Production	Exports	Imports
Castor oil	—	—	
Copra	15.90 14.95²		0.07* 0.07
Cotton seed	24.30 8.67		44.98 48.90
Cottonseed oil.	na na		0.04
Groundnuts	1.17 1.05²		9.98 9.98
Groundnut oil	na na		0.34 0.03
Linseed	—	—	3.70²
Linseed oil	—	—	0.03²
Olive oil	—	—	0.67 0.94
Palm kernels	—	—	0.52 0.71
Palm oil	1.50* na	9.30	0.03²
Palm kernel oil	na na		0.01
Rapeseed	—	—	
Sesame seed	43.87 7.33		12.36
Soya beans	na na		14.95
Soya bean oil	—	—	0.92²
Sunflower seed	—	—	0.06
Tung oil	—	—	0.07²

5. LIVESTOCK‡, ANIMAL PRODUCTS, etc.

	Production	Exports	Imports
Chickens *d.*	29 163.3g na		0.1
Cattle *d.*	6 618.3 6 230.0¹		
Goats *d.*	1 247.0		
Sheep *d.*	80.3 na		
Pigs *d.*	1 867.0		
Horses *d.*	398.3* na		
Meat‡: 'A'	187.7* na		
'B'	42.3* na	0.5¹ 4.0	6.02 —
Butter	na na		
Cheese	30.0* na		0.4
Eggs	18.0 na		0.2 3.1
Fish	109.0 67.6	0.3†	
Milk	602.7 306.0²	7.3¹*	4.8* 0.7

6. FIBRES, TEXTILES, etc.

	Production	Exports	Imports
Agaves (sisal)	11.9 na		6.5
Cotton lint	14.0 na		2.5
Hemp fibre	—	—	
Rubber, natural	—	—	0.2
Cotton: yarn	—	—	
woven fabrics	15.2 0.9		4.2
Rayon, fibre/yarn	8.0 2.7		3.8
woven fabrics	2.7 2.3		2.7 na
Non-cellulosic	4.1 2.9		
Wool, woven fabrics			0.2² na

7. FUEL AND POWER

	Production	Exports	Imports
Coal, 'A'‡	37	30	
Coke	—	—	
Electricity *h*: total	7 536 1 600¹		167
hydro	1 233 250		
thermal	6 303 1 350¹		
Oil, crude	6 080 2 420¹	5 071	
Natural gas	177 180 115 400¹	887 700¹	
Petroleum, refined.	56 326 26 060¹	44 927 21 470¹	
h million kWh.			

8. IRON AND STEEL

	Production	Exports	Imports
Iron ore	9 609m na	14 740	
Pig iron	320		
Steel ingots/castings	478		79
Iron/steel scrap	—	—	110¹
Iron/steel products *d*	119 930		85

9. NON-FERROUS MINERALS AND METALS

	Production	Exports	Imports
Diamonds *k*	91 671* 107 641	1.90¹ 1.99a	
Gold *k*, ore	28.30m 48.20m		9.00p
Platinum group			17.61
metals *k*	1.90¹	1.99a	
a million carats. *t* '000 carats.			
b bullion.			

na: data not available. — negligible or nil. ¹ one year only. ² two year average. * estimate. ‡ see appendix. † re-exports.

VENEZUELA continued

PRODUCTION, EXPORTS AND IMPORTS continued

9. NON-FERROUS MINERALS AND METALS—continued

	Production	Exports	Imports
Asbestos: fibre	—	0.36	0.40
manufactured	—		—
Aluminium:			
aluminium	3.89	10.29	1.98 2.44s
aluminium	0.28	0.28	0.61s
Antimony, metal			
Copper, metal	17.12		1.60s
Lead, metal	7.18		0.02s
Magnesium:			
metal	3.72		0.75s
metal/salts			
Mercury/	1.21		0.032
Tin, metal	0.50		0.12s
Titanium minerals	6.60		24.60s
Zinc, metal	0.16		0.13s
	3.10		0.93s
	3.79		0.812

a million $ U.S. f metric tons. k '000 fine troy oz. l '000 carats. m metal
content. p bullion. s incl. imports for re-export.

10. CHEMICALS n AND FERTILIZERS

Organic chemicals:	Production	Exports	Imports
Benzene	na		
Butadiene			
Ethylene			
Methanol			
Phenol			
Phthalic anhydride			
Styrene monomer			
Urea			

continued

10. CHEMICALS n AND FERTILIZERS—continued

Inorganic chemicals:	Production	Exports	Imports
Ammonia	na		0.7
Carbon black	3.52		0.9*
Chlorine	na		
Nitric acid	na		
Sodium carbonate	4.00*		26.42
Sodium hydroxide	15.02		14.4
Sulphuric acid	42.02		0.2
Plastics:			
Polyamides	na		na
Polyethylene			na
Polyvinyl chloride	na		na
Fertilizers:			
Phosphates	2.1*		15.2 22.4
Potash			
Sulphur			

11. INDUSTRY

	Production	Exports	Imports
Aircraft a			8.6 8.6a
Alcoholic beverages b			na 7.9a
beer b	2 631.0 1 290.7		
Cement	1 845.7 1 159.0	210.7 1.3*	91.3 29.72
Electrical engineering a			0.7 25.0
Merchant ships a			1.0 15.8
Motor vehicles:			
commercial a n	10.8		120.0a 90.3a
private a n	23.3		

a million $ U.S. b '000 hectolitres. d no. in thousands. g '000 G.R.T.
n data not available for years 1953–5.

VIETNAM, NORTH — SOUTH EAST ASIA

Vietnam, Laos, and Cambodia comprised the former territory of French Indo-China. In 1954 at the Geneva Conference the rift between North and South Vietnam was generally recognized, and the northern zone was established as the Democratic Republic of Vietnam. It has since been the aim of North Vietnam, which now has a centrally planned economy, to work for reunification with the South.

AREA: 164 103 sq. km. (63 360 sq. miles)

LAND USE: (percentage of total)

	1965
Arable and orchard	12.7
Permanent meadow and pasture	na
City areas, waste and other land	49.8
	na

a official rate.

Two-thirds of the cultivated land is under rice, which in good years supplies the needs of the country. The majority of the people are employed in the paddy fields, or in the cultivation of other crops which include sugar cane, root crops, and cotton. Silk is also grown, and anthracite and phosphates are mined.

The chief trading partners are China P.R. and the Comecon countries.

POPULATION: 20 100 000 (1967 estimate)
Largest city: HANOI; capital; population: 643 576 (1960)

COMMUNICATIONS

		Year
Railway track (km.)	901	1967

FINANCE

Currency unit: The dong

Exchange rates	1965b	1960b
Per $ U.S.	3.6	3.6
Per £ sterling	10.08	10.08

		Year(s)
Rate of increase of G.N.P. per capita	2.8	1960–3 av.

b official rate.

EMPLOYMENT, PRODUCTION AND TRADE

PRODUCTION, EXPORTS AND IMPORTS
Years: 1963–5 average Units: '000 metric tons unless otherwise indicated
Note—no data are available for 1953–5

1. CEREALS, etc.

	Production	Exports	Imports
Cassava	841.3*		
Maize (corn)	252.0*	—	25.6*
Rice	4 469.3*	6.9*	16.1*
Sweet potatoes/ yams	820.3*		

2. FRUIT, etc.

	Production	Exports	Imports
Bananas	na	8.4*	—

3. BEVERAGES, FOREST PRODUCTS, etc.

	Production	Exports	Imports
Coffee	1.1*	0.9*	—
Sugar: cane	760.7*	na	
raw	na		
Tea	3.8*	5.5*	32.6*
Tobacco, leaf	4.6*	0.9*	—
Wood	na	0.3*	—

VIETNAM, SOUTH — SOUTH EAST ASIA

South Vietnam became a republic in 1954, and since that date there has been a series of military and civilian administrations. The North Vietnamese attempts to reunite the country are vigorously resisted by the South Vietnamese who fear the enforcement of communist principles. In this resistance South Vietnam has the active support of the U.S.A. and of some other Western nations.

AREA: 171 665 sq. km. (66 280 sq. miles)

LAND USE: (percentage of total)

	1965
Arable and orchard	17.2
Permanent meadow and pasture	16.8
Forest and woodland	32.8
City areas, waste and other land	33.3

Employment: the majority of the population is employed in agriculture; rubber and rice being the most important products; although considerable diversification has been planned, progress to this end has been slow because of the war against North Vietnam.

There has been some industrial development but this, and trends in employment distribution are distorted by the conditions of war.

POPULATION: 16 973 000 (1967 estimate)
Largest city: SAIGON; capital; population: 1 485 300 (1965)
Total working population: 4 760 000

COMMUNICATIONS

		Year(s)
Motor vehicles in use ('000s): private	32.5	1965
commercial	30.3	1965
Railway track (km.)	1 400	1967
Mail per capita: foreign sent	0.2	1967
foreign received	1	1967
Telephones (per '000 population)	3	1963–5 av.
Radio receivers (per '000 population)	58	1967
Daily newspapers (per '000 population)	32.3	1962–4 av.

		Year(s)
Infant mortality (per '000)		
Crude birth rate (per '000)	36.7*	1965
Crude death rate (per '000)	27.7*	1965
Population per physician	6.4*	1965
Population per hospital bed	19 960	1966
School enrolment: age 5–19 years (percentage)	590	1966
age over 19 years (per 10 000 population)	57	1963–4 av.
	152	1963–5 av.

FINANCE

Currency unit: The piastre

Exchange rates	
Per $ U.S.	
Per £ sterling	

		Year(s)
National Income (million $U.S.)	1 828	1965
G.N.P. per capita ($ U.S.)	120	1965
Rate of increase of G.N.P. per capita	0.1	1960–3 av.
Foreign trade (percentage of G.D.P.)	19	1963–5 av.

a trade rate.

TRADING

Total trade (in million $ U.S.)	1965	1955	1938a
Exports (f.o.b.)	35	69	54*
Imports (c.i.f.)	357	263	

Main trading partners (percentage of total value):

Exports	1965	1955	Imports	1965	1955
France	34	31	U.S.A.	45	12
Germany F.R.	16	2	Taiwan	14	13
U.K.	12	2	Japan	13	13
Japan	11	3	South Korea		
West Mal./Sing.	5	4	Malaysia	4	
Hong Kong	5	1	France	3	51
Italy	4		Germany F.R.	2	2

Distribution of trade (percentage of total value)

Exports	1965	1955
Rubber	73	58
Food (tea)	15	15

Imports	1965	1955
Manufactured goods	57	na
(machinery and transport equipment)	(20)	(15*)
(iron and steel)	(13)	(13*)
Chemicals		
(textiles)	(9)	(4*)
Food	14	na
(medicinal and pharmaceutical products)	(5)	(4*)
(dairy products and eggs)	14 (5)	na (5*)
Crude materials and fuels	12	na

a incl. North Vietnam. b mainly rice.

PRODUCTION, EXPORTS AND IMPORTS continued

4. VEGETABLE OILSEEDS AND OILS

	Production	Exports	Imports
Castor seed	2.00*	0.12*	
Castor oil	na	0.02	
Coconut oil	na		1.39
Coconut oil	na		
Cottonseed	4.00*		
Groundnuts	24.27*	2.32	
Groundnut oil	4.00*	0.64*	
Sesame seed	2.77*	0.36*	
Soya beans	8.00*	0.57*	
Tung oil	0.06*	0.501*	0.50*

d no. in thousands.

5. LIVESTOCK‡, ANIMAL PRODUCTS, etc.

	Production	Exports	Imports
Chickens	na		
Cattle d	800.7	0.6*	—
Horses d	30.0*		—
Pigs d	4 226.0	11.5*	—
Eggs d	na	0.2*	—
Fish	na		—
Milk	na		2.7*

6. FIBRES, TEXTILES, etc.

	Production	Exports	Imports
Cotton lint			3.1*
Jute	2.0*		
Rubber, natural	16.0*	60 a 35	1.8*
Silk f	na	0.4*	
	11.7*		

7. FUEL AND POWER

	Production	Exports	Imports
Coal, 'A'‡	na		
Electricity h	504²		na

h million kWh.

10. CHEMICALS AND FERTILIZERS

Fertilizers:	Production	Exports	Imports
Phosphates	1 000*p		na

p apatite.

11. INDUSTRY

	Production	Exports	Imports
Cement	614.7*	100.0*	—

na: data not available. — negligible or nil. 1 one year only. 2 two year average. * estimate. ‡ see appendix. † re-exports.

continued

VIETNAM, SOUTH *continued*

PRODUCTION, EXPORTS AND IMPORTS Units: '000 metric tons unless otherwise indicated
Years: 1963–5 average and 1953–5 average

	Production	Exports	Imports
1. CEREALS, etc.			
Cassava	304.7	—	—
Maize (corn)	42.3	—	14.0
Millets/sorghum	na	—	—
Potatoes	6.7	—	0.3[1]
Rice	5 111.3	1.4[1]	80.6
Sweet potatoes/ yams	293.0	—	—
2. FRUIT, etc.			
Apples	na	—	1.5[1]
Bananas	210.3	0.3	—
Coconuts	144.7‡	0.5[1]	1.9[1]
Dates	—	—	1.9[1]
Grapes	—	—	2.1[1]
Oranges	—	—	—
Pineapples	55.7	0.4[2]	—
Pears	—	—	0.2[1]
Raisins	—	—	0.2[1]
Wine b	—	—	82.0[1]
3. BEVERAGES, FOREST PRODUCTS, etc.			
Coffee	3.5	0.21	0.21
Sugar: raw	1 082.7	—	59.2
Tea	7.0p	—	—
Tobacco: leaf	5.3	0.21	0.21
cigarettes e	7.2	0.71	3.3
Softwood j	8 220.0	—	—
Hardwood j	710.7	0.4	0.3
Wood pulp	16.0	—	11.72
Newsprint a	15.7*	—	26.0*
Other paper	5.5	—	3.2
4. VEGETABLE OILSEEDS AND OILS			
Castor seed	24.83	—	—
Castor oil	—	0.03	0.072
Copra	19.75[2]	0.43	0.07[2]
Coconut oil	na	0.31[1]	0.30[1]
Cottonseed	23.80	—	2.41
Cottonseed oil	11.90[2]	4.32	1.77[1]
Groundnuts	na	0.86	0.01
Groundnut oil	na	—	0.01
Linseed oil	—	—	0.01
Olive oil	0.57	0.27[1]	0.94
Sesame seed	4.30	—	0.94
Soya beans	—	—	1.70[2]
Soya bean oil	—	—	—

	Production	Exports	Imports
5. LIVESTOCK†, ANIMAL PRODUCTS, etc.			
Cattle d	1 050.7	—	—
dairy cows d	39.7*	—	—
Goats d	33.0	—	—
Sheep d	3.7	—	—
Horses d	11.0	—	—
Pigs d	3 313.0	—	—
Meat‡: A	121.3*	—	—
B	na	—	—
Butter.	na	—	—
Cheese	2a*	—	0.2
Eggs	383.5	—	1.4
Fish	1.0	—	1.1
Milk	na	—	0.22
Hides/skins	na	2.9*	—
6. FIBRES, TEXTILES, etc.			
Cotton lint.	—	—	1.02
Jute	3.7	—	66.2
Rubber: natural	71.7	54.41	58.2
Cotton: yarn	7.6	1.32	120.01
woven fabrics	5.6	1.02	—
7. FUEL AND POWER			
Coal, lignite a	60	—	13.8
Electricity h, thermal	430p	70[1]	3.5
Petroleum, refined.	—	—	6.81
h million kWh. p in addition, hydro 33.	—	165[1]	0.91
9. NON-FERROUS MINERALS AND METALS			
Chrome, ore	2.25*m	—	0.2
Tin, ore	—	—	0.2a
m metal content.	—	—	—
10. FERTILIZERS			
Potash	—	—	11.8
11. INDUSTRY			
Aircraft	—	—	—
Alcoholic beverages	—	—	1.62
beer	941.0b	663.3b	—
Cement	na	na	0.2a
Electrical	—	—	—
engineering a	—	—	—
Railway vehicles a.	—	—	—
Motor vehicles a.	—	—	0.22
a million $U.S. b '000 hectolitres.			

WESTERN SAMOA

PACIFIC OCEAN

Western Samoa, previously administered by New Zealand under a U.N. Trusteeship Agreement, became an independent sovereign state in 1962. The island remains within the British Commonwealth, New Zealand acting as a liaison in external affairs.

AREA: 2 842 sq. km. (1 097 sq. miles)

LAND USE: (percentage of total)

	Percentage	Year(s)
Arable and orchard.	68.5	1955
Permanent meadow and pasture	—	—
Forest and woodland	6.1	—
City areas, waste and other land	24.9	—

POPULATION: 131 377 (1966 census)
Capital city: APIA: population: 25 480 (1966)
City areas, waste and other land
Distribution of working population: 27 941

U.N. group no.

		Percentage	Year(s)
0	Agriculture, forestry, fishing and hunting	31.7	1955
1	Mining and quarrying	—	11.3
5/8	Manufacturing and construction	2.1	10.7
	Services, including electricity, gas, water and		
	sanitary services	64.8	63.1
6	Commerce	1.4	24.9
7	Transport, storage and communications		
9	Others		

FINANCE

Currency unit: The tala, at par with the New Zealand dollar, replaced the Western Samoa pound in 1966 at the rate 1 tala to WS£0.5.

Exchange rates (for Western Samoa pound)	1965	1960
Per $U.S.	0.357	0.357
Per £ sterling	1.0	1.0

TRADING

	1965	1955	1938
Total trade (in million $U.S.)			
Exports (f.o.b.)	6	5	1
Imports (c.i.f.)	9	7	1

Main trading partners (percentage of total value)

Exports	1965		Imports	1965
New Zealand	44		New Zealand	29
Netherlands	16		Australia	19
U.K.	15		U.K.	10
Germany, F.R.	12		U.S.A.	10
American Samoa	5		Japan	9

Distribution of trade (percentage of total value)

Exports	1965		Imports	1965
Copra	41		Manufactured goods	43
Bananas and plantains	30		(machinery and trans-	
Cocoa beans	22		port equipment)	(14)
			(textiles and clothing)	(9)
			Food	31
			(meat)	(9)
			(cereals)	(7)
			Crude materials and fuels.	12

continued

WEST INDIES ASSOCIATED STATES

The West Indies Federation, which was established in 1958, was dissolved in 1962 after Jamaica and Trinidad had seceded. In 1967 the West Indies Associated States was established, consisting of the former British colonies of: Antigua, Dominica, Grenada, Montserrat, St. Kitts with Nevis and Anguilla, St. Lucia, St. Vincent and the Virgin Islands (U.K.). These were given self-government in association with Britain who retains powers and responsibilities for the defence and external affairs of these Caribbean islands.

PRODUCTION, EXPORTS AND IMPORTS Units: '000 metric tons unless otherwise indicated
Years: 1963–5 average and 1953–5 average

	Production	Exports	Imports
1. CEREALS, etc.			
Potatoes	—	0.1	0.1
Rice	—	0.4	0.1
2. FRUIT, etc.			
Bananas	na	—	—
Coconuts e	109.0*	11.4	11.4
e no. in millions.			
3. BEVERAGES, FOREST PRODUCTS, etc.			
Cocoa	4.0	3.5*	3.1
Sugar, raw	—	3.9	3.0
Tobacco: leaf	—	—	2.0
Softwood j	56.0*[1]	—	0.1
Hardwood j	na	—	0.3a
a million $U.S. j '000 cu. metres of roundwood equivalent.			
4. VEGETABLE OILSEEDS AND OILS			
Copra	14.87*	14.52	14.27

	Production	Exports	Imports
5. LIVESTOCK†, ANIMAL PRODUCTS, etc.			
Cattle d	19.3	—	—
Horses d	2.7	—	—
Pigs d	36.0*	—	—
Butter.	na	—	0.1
Fish	na	—	0.1
Milk	na	—	—
d no. in thousands.			
7. FUEL AND POWER			
Electricity h: total	7	—	—
hydro	5	—	—
thermal.	2	—	—
Petroleum, refined.	—	—	10
h million kWh.			
11. INDUSTRY			
Alcoholic beverages a	—	—	0.2
Electrical engineering a	—	—	0.42
Motor vehicles a	—	—	0.5
a million $U.S.			

ANTIGUA

AREA: 442 sq. km. (171 sq. miles)

LAND USE: (percentage of total)

	Percentage	Year(s)
Arable and orchard.	54.6	1964
Permanent meadow and pasture	4.5	
Forest and woodland	13.6	
City areas, waste and other land	27.3	

POPULATION: 61 000 (1967 estimate)
Capital city: SAINT JOHNS: population: 21 595 (1960)
Total working population: 18 212 (1960)

	Year(s)
Life expectancy at birth (years): male	60.5 1959–61 av.
female	64.3
Infant mortality (per '000).	45.4 1965
Crude birth rate (per '000)	30.4 1965
Crude death rate (per '000).	8.4 1965
Population per physician	3 750 1964
Population per hospital bed	140 1964
School enrolment: age 5–19 years (percentage)	109‡ 1963–4 av.
age over 19 years (per 100 000 population).	82 1963

Antigua is less hilly and wooded than the other Leeward Is. and sugar cane and cotton are cultivated and exported. Tourism is developing. Parts of the island are leased to the U.S.A. for military and naval bases.

COMMUNICATIONS

	Year
Telephones (per '000 urban population)	57.0 1967
Radio receivers (per '000 population)	59.2 1966
Television sets (per '000 population)	15* 1966
Daily newspapers (per '000 population)	230

FINANCE

	Year
National Income (million $U.S.).	18* 1966
G.N.P. per capita ($U.S.).	300 1956

DOMINICA

AREA: 728 sq. km. (289.5 sq. miles)

LAND USE: (percentage of total)

	Percentage	Year
Arable and orchard.	25.3	1963
Permanent meadow and pasture	1.9	
Forest and woodland	32.9	
City areas, waste and other land	40.5	

POPULATION: 70 000 (1967 estimate)
Capital city: ROSEAU: population: 10 417 (1960)
Total working population: 23 409

Distribution of working population (1960)

U.N. group no.

		Percentage
0	Agriculture, forestry, fishing and hunting	50.0
1	Mining and quarrying	0.1
2/3	Manufacturing	10.8
4	Construction	10.7
5	Electricity, gas, water and sanitary services.	8.3
6	Commerce	2.3
7	Transport, storage and communications	13.6
9	Services	4.0
	Others.	

	Year(s)
Life expectancy at birth (years): male	60.5 1959–61 av.
female	64.3
Infant mortality (per '000)	45.4 1965
Crude birth rate (per '000)	45.4 1965
Crude death rate (per '000).	9.1 1965
Population per physician	5 600 1963
Population per hospital bed	200 1963
School enrolment: age 5–19 years (percentage)	79 1963–4 av.

FINANCE

	Year(s)
National Income (million $U.S.)	18* 1966
G.N.P. per capita ($U.S.).	230 1966

TRADING

	1965	1960	1955
Total trade (in million $U.S.)			
Exports (f.o.b.)	2.1	1.71	1.71
Imports (c.i.f.)	4.8	4.8	4.8

The chief trading partner in 1963 was the U.K.

Distribution of trade (percentage of total value)

Exports	1954		Imports	1954
Food	81		Manufactured goods	43
(Bananas)	(55)		Food	36
Chemicals	9		Chemicals	8
Crude materials and fuels.	8		Crude materials and fuels.	7

continued

FINANCE

Currency unit: The East Caribbean dollar replaced, at par, the British West Indies dollar in 1965

Exchange rates	1965	1960	1955
Per $U.S.	1.71	1.71	1.71
Per £ sterling	4.8	4.8	4.8

GRENADA

AREA: 344 sq. km. (133 sq. miles)

LAND USE: (percentage of total)

	1965
Arable and orchard	47.1
Permanent meadow and pasture	2.9
Forest and woodland	11.8
City areas, waste and other land	38.2

POPULATION: 99 000 (1967 estimate)

Capital city: SAINT GEORGES: population: 7 303 (1960)

Distribution of working population (1960)
Total working population: 27 314

U.N. group no.		Percentage
0	Agriculture, forestry, fishing and hunting	39.9
1	Mining and quarrying	0.2
2/3	Manufacturing	9.5
4	Construction	10.6
5	Electricity, gas, water and sanitary services	0.7
6	Commerce	10.8
7	Transport, storage and communications	3.2
8	Services	17.1
9	Others	8.0

	male / female	Year(s)
Life expectancy at birth (years):	60.1 65.6	1959–61 av.
Infant mortality (per '000)	42.5	1965
Crude birth rate (per '000)	30.5	1965
Crude death rate (per '000)	8.5	1965
Accidental deaths (per 100 000 population)	3.3	1961
Population per physician	4550	1961
Population per hospital bed	160	1961
School enrolment: age 5–19 years (percentage)	22.2	1965

COMMUNICATIONS

		Year(s)
Motor vehicles in use ('000s): private	2.1	1963–5 av.
commercial	0.6	
Radio receivers (per '000 population)	104	1967
Daily newspapers (per '000 population)	16.3	1962–4 av.

FINANCE

		Year
G.N.P. per capita ($ U.S.)	230	1966

TRADING

Total trade (in million $ U.S.)		1964
Exports (f.o.b.)	5	
Imports (c.i.f.)	11	

In 1964 the main exports were cocoa, bananas and nutmegs, while imports consisted of flour, dried fish and hardware. The chief trading partners were the U.K., Canada and the U.S.A.

MONTSERRAT

AREA: 101 sq. km. (39 sq. miles)

LAND USE: (percentage of total)

	1963
Arable and orchard	50.0
Permanent meadow and pasture	12.5
Forest and woodland	25.0
City areas, waste and other land	12.5

POPULATION: 14 000 (1967 U.N. estimate)

Capital city: PLYMOUTH: population: 1 911 (1960)

Total working population: 4 332 (1960)

	male / female	Year(s)
Life expectancy at birth (years):	49.5 54.8	1946
Infant mortality (per '000)	54.8	1965
Crude birth rate (per '000)	27.4	1965
Crude death rate (per '000)	10.5	1965
Population per physician	3500	1964
Population per hospital bed	200	1966
School enrolment: age 5–19 years (percentage)	75	1963–4 av.

FINANCE

		Year
National Income (in million $ U.S.)	15*	1966
G.N.P. per capita ($ U.S.)	260	1966

TRADING

Total trade (in million $ U.S.)		1965
Exports (f.o.b.)	5	
Imports (c.i.f.)	9	

The chief exports are bananas, vegetables and Sea Island cotton.

ST. KITTS, NEVIS AND ANGUILLA

AREA: 400 sq. km. (155 sq. miles)

LAND USE: (percentage of total)

	1962
Arable and orchard	40.0
Permanent meadow and pasture	10.0
Forest and woodland	17.5
City areas, waste and other land	32.5

POPULATION: 60 000 (1967 unofficial estimate)

Capital city: BASSETERRE: population: 15 726 (city proper, 1960)

Distribution of working population (1960)
Total working population: 19 616

U.N. group no.		Percentage
0	Agriculture, forestry, fishing and hunting	46.0
1	Mining and quarrying	0.1
2/3	Manufacturing	10.6
4	Construction	8.8
5	Electricity, gas, water and sanitary services	0.8
6	Commerce	8.8
7	Transport, storage and communications	4.2
8	Services	18.1
9	Others	3.3

	male / female	Year(s)
Life expectancy at birth (years):	58.0 61.9	1959–61 av.
Infant mortality (per '000)	59.1	1965
Crude birth rate (per '000)	32.7	1965
Crude death rate (per '000)	9.8	1965
Population per physician	4290	1966
Population per hospital bed	270	1966
School enrolment: age 5–19 years (percentage)	104‡	1963–4 av.

FINANCE

		Year

Distribution of trade (percentage of total value)

Exports		1965	1964a
Food (sugar)	91	(89)	94 (92)

Imports		1965	1964a
Manufactured goods (machinery and transport equipment)	46		46
Food	31	(15)	27 (22)
Chemicals	9		7
Crude materials and fuels	8		5
Beverages and tobacco	5		5

a St. Kitts and Nevis only.

The chief products of St. Kitts are sugar and cotton; of Nevis, cotton and coconuts sent mainly to Barbados; cattle-rearing and vegetable growing are other activities. The chief product of Anguilla is salt.

continued

ST. LUCIA

AREA: 616 sq. km. (238 sq. miles)

LAND USE: (percentage of total)

	1965
Arable and orchard	33.9
Permanent meadow and pasture	4.8
Forest and woodland	21.0
City areas, waste and other land	40.3

POPULATION: 105 000 (1967 U.N. estimate)

Capital city: CASTRIES: population: 4 353 (city proper, 1960)

Distribution of working population (1960)
Total working population: 31 372

U.N. group no.		Percentage
0	Agriculture, forestry, fishing and hunting	48.3
1	Mining and quarrying	0.1
2/3	Manufacturing	8.3
4	Construction	9.7
5	Electricity, gas, water and sanitary services	0.7
6	Commerce	7.9
7	Transport, storage and communications	7.0
8	Services	12.7
9	Others	9.1

	male / female	Year(s)
Life expectancy at birth (years):	55.1 58.7	1959–61 av.
Infant mortality (per '000)	41.9	1965
Crude birth rate (per '000)	46.4	1965
Crude death rate (per '000)	8.7	1965
Accidental deaths (per 100 000 population) due to motor vehicles	3.1	1963
Population per physician	6800	1963
Population per hospital bed	204	1963
School enrolment: age 5–19 years (percentage)	78a	1964

FINANCE

		Year
G.N.P. per capita ($ U.S.)	190	1966

TRADING

Total trade (in million $ U.S.)		1964
Exports (f.o.b.)	6	
Imports (c.i.f.)	11	

The chief exports are bananas, copra and cocoa, and the imports flour, machinery and textiles. Trade is mainly with the U.K.

a includes pre-school education.

ST. VINCENT

AREA: 389 sq. km. (150 sq. miles)

LAND USE: (percentage of total)

	1964
Arable and orchard	50.0
Permanent meadow and pasture	2.9
Forest and woodland	44.2
City areas, waste and other land	2.9

POPULATION: 91 000 (1967 unofficial estimate)

Capital city: KINGSTOWN: population: 4 308 (city proper, 1960)

Distribution of working population (1960)
Total working population: 24 856

U.N. group no.		Percentage
0	Agriculture, forestry, fishing and hunting	40.1
1	Mining and quarrying	0.5
2/3	Manufacturing	11.0
4	Construction	11.4
5	Electricity, gas, water and sanitary services	0.9
6	Commerce	11.0
7	Transport, storage and communications	3.9
8	Services	14.9
9	Others	6.3

	male / female	Year(s)
Life expectancy at birth (years):	58.5 59.7	1959–61 av.
Infant mortality (per '000)	69.5	1965
Crude birth rate (per '000)	43.0	1965
Crude death rate (per '000)	9.3	1965
Accidental deaths (per 100 000 population) due to motor vehicles	1.4	1961
Population per physician	10000	1961
Population per hospital bed	210a	1962
School enrolment: age 5–19 years (percentage)	96	1963–4 av.

a government hospitals only.

FINANCE

		Year
G.N.P. per capita ($ U.S.)	230	1966

TRADING

Total trade (in million $ U.S.)		1965
Exports (f.o.b.)	4	
Imports (c.i.f.)	9	

Distribution of trade (percentage of total value)

Exports		1965
Food	82	
Crude materials	16	

Imports		1965
Manufactured goods (machinery and transport equipment)	42	
Food	30	(13)
Chemicals	12	
Beverages and tobacco	7	

The main trading partner in 1964 was the U.K.

VIRGIN ISLANDS (U.K.)

Eleven of the forty-two British islands are inhabited, Tortola being the largest of the group.

AREA: 130* sq. km. (59 sq. miles)

LAND USE: (percentage of total)

	1965
Arable and orchard	26.7
Permanent meadow and pasture	13.3
Forest and woodland	6.7
City areas, waste and other land	53.3

POPULATION: 9 000 (1968 U.N. estimate)

Capital city: ROAD TOWN: population: 891 (city proper, 1960)

Total working population: 2 164 (1960)

		Year(s)
Infant mortality (per '000)	66.7	1964
Crude birth rate (per '000)	28.5	1964
Crude death rate (per '000)	8.6	1964
Population per physician	4000	1961
Population per hospital bed	230	1964
School enrolment: age 5–19 years (percentage)	92	1966

TRADING

Total trade (in million $ U.S.)		1964
Exports (f.o.b.)	0.1	
Imports (c.i.f.)	2.4	

The principal exports are livestock, fish, charcoal, vegetables and fruit.

continued

---

na: data not available.   — negligible or nil.   1 one year only.   2 two year average.   * estimate.   ‡ see appendix.   † re-exports.

PRODUCTION, EXPORTS AND IMPORTS

Years: **1963–5 average** Units: '000 metric tons unless otherwise indicated

Note—the trade figures given are the sum of the separate members of the Associated States, and therefore include inter-trade (if any) amongst them. The 1963–5 data for the West Indies Federation are not comparable due to the inclusion of Jamaica and Trinidad, and have therefore been omitted from the tables.

	Production	Exports	Imports
1. CEREALS, etc.			
Maize (corn)	—	—	0.9
Oats	—	—	0.2
Potatoes	—	—	5.6
Rice	—	—	48.7
Sweet potatoes	7.0*	—	—
Yams	—	—	—

b '000 hectolitres. *e* no. in millions.

	Production	Exports	Imports
2. FRUIT, etc.			
Bananas	152.7*	148.6*	—
Coconuts	658.0*c*	0.5	—
Citrus fruit	12.4*	1.1	—
Wine *b*	7.0*	0.3	1.2

	Production	Exports	Imports
3. BEVERAGES, FOREST PRODUCTS, etc.			
Cocoa	3.1	3.0	—
Sugar: cane	534.3		
raw	62.7	59.1	5.9
Hardwood *j*	41.5¹		

j '000 cu. metres of roundwood equivalent.

	Production	Exports	Imports
4. VEGETABLE OILSEEDS AND OILS			
Copra	9.90*	5.78*	—
Coconut oil	na	9.52	0.02¹
Cottonseed	na	0.08¹	—
Groundnuts	—	—	0.06
Olive oil	—	—	0.02

	Production	Exports	Imports
5. LIVESTOCK‡; ANIMAL PRODUCTS, etc.			
Chickens *d*	113.3*m*	0.7	—
Cattle *d*	47.0	0.7	—
dairy cows *d*	7.0		
Goats *d*	56.0	0.9¹	—
Sheep *d*	48.7		
Horses *d*	5.3		
Pigs *d*	60.0	0.4¹	—
Bacon/ham			
Meat‡; "B"			
Butter		0.3	0.1
Cheese		0.2	0.1
Eggs		0.3*	0.2
Fish		3.2*	2.1
Milk		5.0	9.2

d no. in thousands. *h* incl. ducks, geese and turkeys.

	Production	Exports	Imports
6. FIBRES, TEXTILES, etc.			
Cotton: lint	—	0.2	4.8
woven fabrics	na	—	0.6*
Rayon, woven fabrics	—	—	

	Production	Exports	Imports
7. FUEL AND POWER			
Electricity *h,t*	9	—	—
Petroleum, refined	—	—	66

h million kWh. *t* thermal.

	Production	Exports	Imports
10. FERTILIZERS			
Potash	—	—	2.1

YUGOSLAVIA
EUROPE

In 1945 Yugoslavia was proclaimed a republic and two years later the members of the royal family were deprived of their nationality and property. A new constitution in 1953 made the working people the sole authority at all levels of government and in 1963 the name of the country became the Socialist Federal Republic of Yugoslavia.

AREA: 255 804 sq. km. (98 766 sq. miles).

LAND USE: (percentage of total)

	1965
Arable and orchard	32.5
Permanent meadow and pasture	25.6
Forest and woodland	34.4
City areas, waste and other land	7.9

POPULATION: 19 958 000 (1967 estimate)
Largest city: BEOGRAD (Belgrade) capital; population: 585 234 (1961)

Distribution of working population (1961)
Total working population: 8 340 400

U.N. group no.		Percentage
0	Agriculture, forestry, fishing and hunting	57.0
1	Mining and quarrying	1.7
2/3/5	Manufacturing, electricity, gas, water and sanitary services	12.0
4	Construction	13.8
6	Commerce	3.2
7	Transport, storage and communications	8.7
8	Services	3.7
9	Others	10.6

		Year(s)
Life expectancy at birth (years): male	62.4	1961–2 av.
female	65.6	
Infant mortality (per '000)	71.8	1965
Crude birth rate (per '000)	20.9	1965
Crude death rate (per '000)	8.7	1965
Population per physician	1 200	1966
Population per hospital bed	170	1965
School enrolment: age 5–19 years (percentage)	85	1964–5 av.
age over 19 years (per 100 000 population)	916	

COMMUNICATIONS

		Year(s)
Motor vehicles in use ('000s): private	147.4	1963–5 av.
commercial	57.4	1964
Railway track (km.)	11 847	1964
Mail per capita: domestic	52	1963–5 av.
foreign sent	3	1963–5 av.
foreign received	3	1963–5 av.
Telephones (per '000 population)	134	1967
Radio receivers (per '000 population)	85	1963–5 av.
Television licences (per '000 population)	30.5	1963–5 av.
Daily newspapers (per '000 population)	82.5	1962–4 av.

FINANCE

Currency unit: The Yugoslav dinar; the new dinar equivalent to 100 old dinars was introduced in 1966

Exchange rates (for old dinars)	1965*a*	1966*a*
Per $ U.S.	1 250	300
Per £ sterling	3 500	840

	1965*a*	1960*a*	1950	1938
National income (million $ U.S.)	10 000*	510	140	114
G.N.P. per capita ($ U.S.)		7.7		

a official rates.

TRADING

	1965	1955	1938
Total trade (in million $ U.S.)			
Exports (f.o.b.)	1 092	257	117
Imports (c.i.f.)	1 288	441	114

Main trading partners (percentage of total value)

Exports	1965	1955	Imports	1965	1955
Italy	17	17	U.S.A.	15	33
U.S.S.R.	13	13	Germany F.R.	11	10
Germany F.R.	13	13	U.S.S.R.	8	13
Germany D.R.	7	13	Italy	8	2
Czechoslovakia	7	7	Czechoslovakia	5	5
Poland	6	2,3	Germany D.R.	5	
U.S.A.	6	1.1	U.K.	5	5

PRODUCTION, EXPORTS AND IMPORTS

Years: **1963–5 average and 1953–5 average** Units: '000 metric tons unless otherwise indicated

	Production		Exports		Imports	
1. CEREALS, etc.						
Barley	580.0	367.0	16.9	57.8	45.1	49.8
Maize (corn)	6 086.0	3 581.3	0.1	1.9	—	—
Millet/sorghum	31.0	18.3	3.1	—	—	—
Oats	325.3	297.7	0.4	1.0	17.0	—
Potatoes	2 743.3	2 077.3	1.1	1.1	11.5	9.2
Rice	24.3	22.7	—	—	34.1	—
Rye	162.3	254.0	0.1	—	11.2	—
Wheat	3 769.3	2 712.7	0.1	1 080.7	855.0	

	Production		Exports		Imports	
2. FRUIT, etc.						
Apples	191.3	175.3	0.1	5.6	2.0	
Apricots	23.6	16.9	1.2		9.6	
Cherries	82.0	66.0	1.3		0.6	
Dates	—					
Figs	22.3	19.3	6.1			
Grapes	1 236.7	861.0	14.7			
Lemons	—		—		22.1	
Oranges	—		—		22.0	
Other citrus fruit	—		—		2.0	
Olives	33.3	26.7	0.5			
Peaches	34.0	16.9	0.1	0.3		
Plums	645.0	778.3	0.5	8.1		
Raisins	—		—		2.1	
Tomatoes	292.7	135.3	6.1			
Wine *b*	5 633.3	3 992.0	446.0	171.7	0.6	3.7

b '000 hectolitres.

	Production		Exports		Imports	
3. BEVERAGES, FOREST PRODUCTS, etc.						
Cocoa	—		—		10.1	1.4
Coffee	—		—		17.0	1.7
Sugar: beet	2 706.7	1 387.0	—		—	
raw	353.0	155.7	13.5		92.4	29.6
Tea	—		—		0.5	0.5
Tobacco: leaf	56.2	33.4	21.0	9.2	4.5	
cigars	—		—		11.76	1.77
cigarettes	24 369.0*c*	15 006.7*c*	0.1		0.02	
Softwood *j*	4 370.7	5 084.0	600.0	839.0	35.9	1.30²
Hardwood *j*	13 676.0	13 963.3	743.8	469.2	9.8	0.31
Wood pulp *j*	326.8	66.7	46.1	12.0	3.2	0.83
Newsprint	41.3	34.7	1.1	8.1	13.0	
Other paper	335.7	68.7	42.3	3.1	23.9	7.9

e no. in millions. *j* '000 cu. metres of roundwood equivalent.

	Production		Exports		Imports	
4. VEGETABLE OILSEEDS AND OILS						
Castor seed	3.3	2.0	0.51		0.02	1.30²
Castor oil	0.1		0.13		4.20	0.37
Copra	—		—		11.76	
Coconut oil	5.0	4.0*	—		0.02	0.02
Cottonseed	na		na		0.85	0.53
Cottonseed oil	0.7	0.2	—		1.34	
Groundnuts	—		—		24.43	3.36
Groundnut oil	—		—		0.06	
Linseed	6.0	3.7	0.3		0.35	
Linseed oil	—		—		0.30	0.60
Olive oil	6.0		0.3		0.32	0.14
Palm kernels	—		—		2.05	
Palm kernel oil	—		—		0.27	1.80
Rapeseed	3.0	7.7	—		0.24	1.70
Rapeseed oil	na	0.4	—		0.13	
Sesame seed	na	2.0	—		3.00	
Soya beans	na		—		32.35	3.00
Soya bean oil	252.0	113.3	5.46		0.03	0.50
Sunflower seed	na		—		0.51	4.78
Sunflower seed oil	na		—		0.17	
Tung oil	—		—			

	Production		Exports		Imports	
5. LIVESTOCK‡; ANIMAL PRODUCTS, etc.						
Chickens *d*	28 163.3	27 971.0²	55.4	65.1		
Cattle *d*	5 216.0	5 133.7				
dairy cows *d*	2 617.0	2 406.3			1.2	0.6
Goats *d*	200.0*	420.5²				
Sheep *d*	9 731.7	11 830.0	116.1			
Horses *d*	1 141.3	1 187.0				
Pigs *d*	6 003.0	4 541.7				
Bacon/ham	567.3	336.7	7.6	58.7	131.2	1.2
Meat‡; "A"	180.3*	68.3	3.3	11.4		
"B"	180.5	6.8	108.5	2.9		
Butter	15.0	1.0	0.1			
Cheese	82.0	50.6	1.0	1.8	2.4	
Eggs	38.2	23.8	21.9	44.9	3.9	
Milk	2 237.0	1 583.7	—	58.7	188.9	
Hides/skins	50.4²	9.7	—	2.0²	34.3	
Wool	7.5		0.2	8.3	2.0	

d no. in thousands.

	Production		Exports		Imports	
6. FIBRES, TEXTILES, etc.						
Abaca	—		—		0.7	0.2
Agaves (sisal etc.)	—		—		4.9	80.3
Cotton: lint	2.3	2.0	0.2		32.1	
Cotton: yarn	55.0²	49.3*	64.3	9.6	13.6	0.1
woven fabrics	49.5	20.7	34.5	0.7	18.1	
Flax fibre	2.8*q*	1.22*	na	34.3		
Hemp fibre	29.7*q*		4.3		1.0	
Jute	—		—		2.6	
Rubber: natural	—		—		5.2	
synthetic	51.7*q*	21.0*q*	0.6		0.7	
Rayon, woven fabrics	na		1.0		na	
Silk *r*	na		1.2*r*		na	
Wool: raw	na		na		13.5	
woven fabrics	na		0.6		0.4	

q continuous filament. *r* incl. mixtures. *p* predominantly of cotton.

	Production		Exports		Imports	
7. FUEL AND POWER						
Coal 'A'‡	1 240	1 130	94		392	2
'B'‡	13 860	14 070	54	74*	167	14
Coke	2.8*q*		1.0	1.2*r*	17	34
Electricity *h*: total	14 416	3 590			89	22
hydro	8 196	1 970			112	
thermal	6 220	1 620				
Natural gas *l*	260	64				
Oil, crude	1 837	260¹			883	689
Petroleum, refined	2 063	650¹	300	40¹	207	192

h million kWh. *l* million cu. metres.

	Production		Exports		Imports	
8. IRON AND STEEL						
Iron ore	1 050*m*	494*m*	153	6	7	2
Pig iron	1 103	393	28	7	17	14
Steel ingots/castings	1 678	658	9	4	89	34
Iron/steel scrap	na	na	33		112	22
Iron/steel products *a*	na		40¹			

a million $ U.S. *m* metal content.

	Production		Exports		Imports	
9. NON-FERROUS MINERALS AND METALS						
Diamonds *a*	3 992.30*m*	2 953.70*m*	4.89¹	2 092.00²*a*	0.07	
Gold *k,o,m*	98.30	41.00	4.75	0.74		
Platinum group						
Aluminium: bauxite	1 384.20	651.76	561.99	0.82	15.27	0.51
manufactured	8.75	3.63	0.82	0.94		
aluminium *m*	37.33	21.32	9.09		12.21	2.44
Antimony *m*	2.72*m*	1.52*m*	1.92	1.25*m*	0.82	0.27
Chrome: ore	87.33*m*	125.88*m*	20.35	36.19	0.94	3.98
metal	na		0.02		0.01	8.10
Copper: ore	62.61*m*	na	8.14	57.89	15.25	
metal	53.14		2.44		0.01	
Lead: ore	111.08*m*	86.46*m*	1.15²	14.37	0.04	
metal	102.25	77.05	26.23	15.31		
Magnesium *m*	na		62.82	3.19²	0.04	
Manganese: ore	478.44	na	38.64		5.04	
metal	na	—†	0.14	0.10¹	1.63	0.21
Mercury *f,a*	112.79	28.62	28.64		3.40	0.49
Molybdenum *f,a*	8.00	4.57	8.22	3.26	0.09	0.27²
Nickel, metal *f*	na		20.35	40.28	0.04	
Silver *k,o*	569.67*	497.67*	8.22	0.45	6.43	
Tin, metal		500.00*	404.30	435.10	70.00*	3.88
Titanium minerals	0.09					
Tungsten: ore						
Zinc: ore	90.63*m*	58.95*m*	112.79	12.21	1.63	
metal	44.27	13.99	25.89		3.40	
			16.94		0.09	

k '000 fine troy oz. *f* bullion. *m* metal content.

	Production		Exports		Imports	
10. CHEMICALS‡ AND FERTILIZERS						
Organic chemicals:						
Benzene	na		2.2¹		0.04	
Butadiene	na				0.09	
Ethylene	na				0.04	
Methanol	na		1.9		0.09	
Phenol	7.32		1.5		0.06	
Phthalic anhydride	2.82				0.6	
Styrene monomer	1.3¹					
Urea	6.0¹				31.3²	

continued

PRODUCTION, EXPORTS AND IMPORTS *continued*

10. CHEMICALS AND FERTILIZERS—*continued*

Inorganic chemicals:	Production	Exports	Imports
Ammonia	119.0	—	0.1
Carbon black	7.7*	0.7	1.9
Chlorine	31.8	3.9	—
Nitric acid	213.3	0.62	—
Sodium carbonate	108.7	18.0	14.2
Sodium hydroxide	77.2	14.9	14.9
Sulphuric acid	432.8	1.8	18.0
Plastics:			
Polyamides c	5.6	na	na
Polyethylene	8.7	3.1¹	10.2¹
Polyvinyl chloride	na		
Fertilizers:			
Phosphates	158.5*x	89.7*x	552.5
Potash	—	—	297.2
Pyrites	184.0	138.9	60.7
Sulphur	—	—	38.1
	15.6		5.9²

n data not available for years 1953–5.   *x* sulphur content.

ZAMBIA

CENTRAL AFRICA

Zambia, formerly Northern Rhodesia, became an independent republic within the British Commonwealth in 1964 following the dissolution of the Federation of Rhodesia and Nyasaland. Due to the lack of transport facilities and of fuel resources, the economy of the country has been seriously affected by the economic sanctions imposed upon Rhodesia.

No separate production or trade figures are available for Zambia for the duration of the Federation, 1954–63.

AREA: 752 262 sq. km. (290 586 sq. miles)

LAND USE: (percentage of total)

	1963	1955
Arable and orchard.		
Permanent meadow and pasture	2.6	
Forest and woodland	43.8	40.6
City areas, waste and other land	50.0	49.7
	3.6	9.7

POPULATION: 3 947 000 (1967 estimate)

Largest city: LUSAKA, capital: population: 152 000 (1966)

Employment: The mines and associated industries of Zambia, Rhodesia and South Africa provide employment for much of the indigenous population of Zambia. Only about half the adult male population (as well as the women) is engaged in agriculture. The soil is relatively infertile and the tsetse fly, limiting agricultural activities. In 1967 about a third of the country's agricultural production came from farms run by the few (less than 1 500) Europeans farming in Zambia.

FINANCE

Currency unit: The kwacha replaced the Rhodesian pound in 1968 at the rate K1 to R£0.5

Exchange rates (for Rhodesian pounds)

	1965	1960	1950	1938
Per $ U.S.	0.357	0.357	0.357	0.215
Per £ sterling	1.0	1.0	1.0	1.0

	1965	1955e	1950	1938	Year(s)
National Income ($million $U.S.)					1965
G.N.P. per capita ($U.S.)	647				1966
Rate of increase of G.N.P. per capita	180				1960–4 av.
	0.5				

TRADING

Total trade (in million $ U.S.)

	1965	1955e	1950	1938
Exports (f.o.b.)	532	328	140	50
Imports (f.o.b.)	295	na	75	25

Main trading partners (percentage of total value)

Exports	1965	1950	1938	Imports	1965	1950	1938*
U.K.	38	48	40	Rhodesia	34	13	15
Germany F.R.	13	5	32	U.K.	20	40	43
Japan	12	na	na	South Africa	20	28	16
Italy.	8	na	10	U.S.A.	6	7	10
France	7	9	na	Japan	4	2	2
South Africa.	3	2	1	Germany F.R.	3	na	2
Rhodesia				Italy.	1	1	na

Distribution of trade (percentage of total value)

Exports	1965	1950	1938*
Copper	92	87	88
Zinc, lead, and cobalt	4	9	na
Tobacco	1	2	1

Imports	1965	1950	1938*
Manufactured goods	69	92	na
(machinery and transport equipment)	(33)	(30)	(37)
(textiles and clothing)	(12)	(12)	(10)
Crude materials and fuels	12	na	na
Chemicals	10	3	na
Food	8	3	na

continued

11. INDUSTRY

	Production	Exports	Imports
Aircraft a	—	5.1	1.1
Alcoholic beverages			
beer b	2 635.0		
spirits b	506.0*		
Cement	2 971.7	1 411.0	
Electrical engineering a	724.3	10.3a	2.6a
Locomotives c	na	130.0¹	
Railway vehicles a	na	8.0¹	
Machine tools a	na	232.0¹	
Merchant ships g	na		
Motor vehicles			
commercial d	12.8	2.5p	
private d	26.1	0.7q	

a million $ U.S. *b* '000 hectolitres. *c* no. of units. *d* no. in thousands. *g* '000 G.R.T. *p* incl. assembly of imported parts. *q* no. in thousands. *u* production for home consumption in 1966. *n* data not available for years 1953–5.

PRODUCTION, EXPORTS AND IMPORTS
Years: 1964–5 average and 1953
Units: '000 metric tons unless otherwise indicated

1. CEREALS, etc.

	Production	Exports	Imports
Cassava	152.0*	—	—
Maize (corn)	207.3*	24.7	10.7
Millets/sorghum	256.0*	0.5	36.3
Oats			1.1
Potatoes	2.7	2.3	9.5
Rice b	0.2	2.4	0.3
Sweet potatoes/yams	12.0*	1.9	2.2
Wheat	1.0*	—	22.4
			9.1

a produce of farms only.

2. FRUIT, etc.

	Production	Exports	Imports
Apples	—	—	1.0
Bananas	—	—	1.2
Grapes	—	—	0.2
Oranges	1.0*	—	1.0
Other citrus fruit	—	—	0.1
Raisins	—	—	0.1
Wine b	—	—	3.3

b '000 hectolitres.

3. BEVERAGES, FOREST PRODUCTS, etc.

	Production	Exports	Imports
Coffee	0.5	0.2	—
Sugar, raw		22.7	8.2
Tea	10.3	0.4	0.2
Tobacco, leaf	3.92	11.0	—
Softwood j		1.5†	—
Hardwood j	3 824.0*	4.8	42.1¹
Newsprint j	1 409.9	23.0¹	6.7¹
Other paper	—	—	1.0¹
			4.5¹

j '000 cu. metres of roundwood equivalent.

4. VEGETABLE OILSEEDS AND OILS

	Production	Exports	Imports
Castor seed	—	—	0.01
Castor oil	—	—	0.08
Coconut oil			0.16
Cottonseed	—	0.27	
Cottonseed oil			0.80
Groundnuts	25.43*p	1.87	1.33
Groundnut oil		0.90	0.55
Linseed oil		0.36	0.01
Olive oil			0.07
Palm oil			0.49
Palm kernel oil	—	0.30m	—
Sunflower seed	na		0.11²
Sunflower seed oil	na		0.33

n produce of farms and estates only. *p* sales only.

5. LIVESTOCK‡, ANIMAL PRODUCTS, etc.

	Production	Exports	Imports
Cattle a	1 269.0	969.0	
dairy cows d	594.0*	480.3*	0.5
Goats d	157.0*	97.3*	7.6
Sheep d	36.3	9.7	29.2
Pigs d	64.0	43.0	
Bacon/ham	15.7*		0.1
Meat: 'A'.	1.3*	0.5	0.1
'B'		2.5	0.4
Butter	0.7*		2.9
Cheese			1.0
Eggs	40.8	4.2	0.4
Fish	91.0*	5.02	0.2
Milk			0.1
Hides/skins	0.52 a		6.4
			10.9
			6.5

a million $ U.S. *d* no. in thousands. *g* incomplete figure.

6. FIBRES, TEXTILES, etc.

	Production	Exports	Imports
Cotton lint	na	na	0.3
Rubber, natural	—	—	0.1

7. FUEL AND POWER

	Production	Exports	Imports
Coal 'A'‡	709	na	1 069
Coke	297	na	63
Electricity k: total	412		
hydro	na		
thermal	na	na	808
Petroleum, refined. r	na	na	15

h million kWh.

8. IRON AND STEEL

	Production	Exports	Imports
Iron ore	na	na	
Pig iron	982m	na	160

m metal content.

9. NON-FERROUS MINERALS AND METALS

	Production	Exports	Imports
Diamonds d	na	na	
Gold k, ore m	5.00	na	0.34
Silver k, ore	638.7¹m	21.27r	
Asbestos: fibre	1 047.00m	436.30m	2.54¹r
Mica	34.03	na	1.06
manufactured	14.0¹	na	1.20a
Aluminium	— ² m	—	0.26¹
Antimony, metal	44.24m	23.80	0.08¹
Cadmium	0.01 m	0.08	0.27
Chrome, ore	47.87	36.71m	0.06
Cobalt, ore		27.02	0.38
Copper, ore	0.02	45.52	
metal	1.23m	0.87m	0.01
Lead: ore	634.85	376.42m	0.34
metal		367.25	
Magnesite	18.04	14.41	0.65
Manganese, ore	14.52	682.61m	0.09
Tin: ore		378.02	
metal		28.10¹	
Zinc: ore		12.78	1.11a
metal			

a million $ U.S. *k* '000 fine troy oz. *m* metal content. *n* excl. semi-manufactures. *r* bullion.

10. CHEMICALS AND FERTILIZERS

Chemicals:	Production	Exports	Imports
Fertilizers:			na		
Potash	—	—	—
Pyrites	—	—	—
Sulphur	—	—	—

11. INDUSTRY

	Production	Exports	Imports
Aircraft a	—	—	1.2
Alcoholic beverages a	—	—	0.1
Cement	203.0	—	5.4
Electrical engineering a	—	3.0*	5.1¹
Railway vehicles a	—	1.8	na
Motor vehicles a	—	5.5*	na

a million $ U.S.

COMMUNICATIONS

Motor vehicles in use ('000s): private	41.6	1963
commercial	11.2	1963–5 av.
Railway track (km.): domestic	1 005*	1969
foreign received	7	1964–5 av.
foreign sent	5	
Telephones (per '000 urban population)	1	1967
Radio licences (per '000 population)	2	1963–5 av.
Daily newspapers (per '000 population)	6	1964

Life expectancy at birth (years)	40	1963	
Infant mortality (per '000)	269*	1950	
Crude birth rate (per '000)	51.4*a	1963	
Crude death rate (per '000)	19.6*a	1963	
Population per physician	21 820	1964	
Population per hospital bed	380	1966	
School enrolment: age 5–19 years (percentage)	43 a	1963–4 av.	

a Africans only.

---

na: data not available. — negligible or nil. ¹ one year only. ² two year average. * estimate. ‡ see appendix. † re-exports.

Background and summary data

Area

The area given includes that of inland waters. Where this is significantly different from the land area both figures have been given.

Population

The population of a city refers to that of the urban agglomeration unless otherwise stated.

The terms Africans, Europeans, etc. are used where separate statistics are available for countries with ethnically-mixed populations.

The school enrolment percentages, published by UNESCO, are intended to give a rough indication of the development of education in each country and should not be used for direct comparisons between countries. Figures over 100 are due to the actual age range of pupils not corresponding exactly to the age-standardized population.

Communications

Data for mail per capita give the number of letters per annum.

Data for daily newspapers refer to the number printed per day. The figures should be taken as only an approximate indication of the circulation, as they are, in many cases, based on incomplete data.

The number of radio and television receivers is given where possible, but where only the number of licences issued is available, this figure has been given.

Items have been omitted from the standard format of this table where information was not available or the figure was negligible or nil.

Finance

The observation that a currency is tied to the pound sterling does not necessarily apply after the sterling devaluation of 1967.

The currencies of the 'franc zone' include the franc CFA and the franc CFP which are used by the French Union states of the African and Pacific Financial Communities respectively.

Foreign trade (given as a percentage of the Gross Domestic Product) is defined as the sum of exports and imports.

Trading

Trading figures given are for general trade except where footnoted 'national exports'; these are defined as the exports of domestic (or home-produced) merchandise only.

Trade in gold, specie and banknotes is excluded; but where gold is significant in a country's economy, and where the trade distribution percentages are available only for a total figure which includes trade in gold, then the trade data for gold have also been shown.

Commodities

Notes marked P apply to production only; T to trade only

Commodity (Table no.)	Standardized units and definitions
Abaca (6)	'000 metric tons
Agaves (6)	'000 metric tons / sisal, henequen, letona and cantala
Aircraft (11)	million $ U.S. / P data for 1965–7 only
Alcoholic beverages (11)	
beer	P '000 hectolitres
spirits	P '000 hectolitres / available only for year stated / T million $ U.S. / beer, spirits and wine
Aluminium (9)	'000 metric tons
bauxite	T incl. cryolite
alumina	P 1953–5 data not available
aluminium.	T incl. semi-manufactures, alloys, salts and scrap
Ammonia (10)	'000 metric tons / 1953–5 data not available
Anthracite *see* Coal 'A'	
Antimony (9)	'000 metric tons / P metal content of ore and concentrates
ore	P incl. concentrates / T not available
metal	T incl. regulus, alloys, salts, and scrap
Apples (2)	'000 metric tons
Apricots (2)	'000 metric tons
Asbestos (9)	'000 metric tons
fibre	P incl. crude and waste
manufactured	P not available / T incl. asbestos cement products
Automobiles *see* Motor vehicles	
Bacon/ham (5)	'000 metric tons / P not available separately, but included in Meat 'A'
Baddeleyite *see* Zirconium minerals	
Bananas (2)	'000 metric tons / P excl. plantains
Barley (1)	'000 metric tons
Bastnaesite *see* Rare earths	
Bauxite *see* Aluminium	
Beef *see* Meat 'A'	
Beer *see* Alcoholic beverages	
Benzene (10)	'000 metric tons / 1953–5 data not available
Beryl (9)	'000 metric tons / data incomplete
Bituminous coal *see* Coal 'A'	
Brown coal *see* Coal 'B'	
Butadiene (10)	'000 metric tons / 1953–5 data not available
Butter (5)	'000 metric tons
Cadmium (9).	'000 metric tons / P smelter production / T incl. flue-dust, alloys, salts, and scrap
Cantala *see* Agaves	
Carbon black (10)	'000 metric tons / 1953–5 data not available
Cassava (1)	'000 metric tons / T not available
Castor oil (4).	'000 metric tons / P not available (average commercial extraction rate 45%)
Castor seed (4)	'000 metric tons
Cattle (5)	'000 head
dairy cows.	P population / P population of cows and heifers over two years, and heifers (under two years) in calf
Cement (11)	'000 metric tons / T not available
Cerium *see* Rare earths	
Cheese (5)	'000 metric tons
Cherries (2)	'000 metric tons
Chickens (5)	P population in '000 head / T not available
Chlorine (10).	'000 metric tons / 1953–5 data not available
Chrome (9)	'000 metric tons
ore	P chromite / P incl. concentrates
metal	T not available / T incl. salts and alloys
Cigars and cigarettes *see* Tobacco	
Citrus fruit (2)	
lemons	'000 metric tons / T incl. limes
oranges	P incl. clementines and tangerines
other citrus fruit	mainly grapefruit
Clementines *see* Citrus fruit	
Coal (7)	'000 metric tons
'A'	T excl. coal for bunkering / anthracite and bituminous coal
'B'	P weight of hard coal equivalent / lignite or brown coal / weight of hard coal equivalent
Cobalt (9)	'000 metric tons
ore	P metal content of ore, concentrates, matte and salts
metal	P not available / T incl. alloys, salts, and scrap
Cocoa (cacao) (3)	'000 metric tons
Coconuts (2).	P millions (approx. equivalent to '000 metric tons) / 1953–5 data not available / T '000 metric tons / weight in shell unless otherwise stated
Coconut oil (4)	'000 metric tons / P not available (average commercial extraction rate from copra 64%)
Coffee (3)	'000 metric tons
Coke (7)	'000 metric tons
Copper (9)	
ore	'000 metric tons / P metal content of ore / T incl. concentrates and matte
metal	'000 metric tons / P smelter production / T incl. unwrought copper, alloys, salts, scrap, and copper content of copper-gold and copper-lead ores
Copra (4)	'000 metric tons / *see also* Coconut oil
Corn *see* Maize	
Cotton (6)	'000 metric tons
lint	
yarn	
woven fabrics	
Cottonseed (4)	'000 metric tons
Cottonseed oil (4)	'000 metric tons / P not available (average commercial extraction rate 18%)
Cows *see* Cattle	
Cryolite *see* Aluminium	
Currants *see* Raisins	
Dairy cows *see* Cattle	
Dates (2)	'000 metric tons
Diamonds (9)	'000 carats / P '000 carats / T million $ U.S. / T not available / incl. rough, cut and polished, industrial and gem diamonds, bort and dust
Dolomite *see* Magnesium	
Eggs (5)	'000 metric tons / hens' eggs / P hens' eggs in the shell only
Electrical engineering (11)	million $ U.S. / equipment powered by electricity / P 1964 data only
Electricity (7)	million kilowatt hours / T not available
hydro	
nuclear	
thermal	incl. geothermal where stated

Commodities *continued*

Commodity (Table no.)	Standardized units and definitions
Ethylene (10).	'000 metric tons 1953–5 data not available
Figs (2).	'000 metric tons
Fish (5).	'000 metric tons fish and other aquatic animals landed in domestic ports, but excluding landings by foreign vessels
Flax fibre (6).	'000 metric tons incl. straw, tow, and waste
Flaxseed *see* Linseed	
Gas *see* Natural gas	
Gasoline *see* Petroleum	
Geothermal electricity *see* Electricity	
Goats (5).	P '000 head population T '000 head sheep 1953–5 data not available
Gold (9).	'000 fine troy ounces T where reference to the Appendix (‡) is made the trade in gold was recorded by value only, and the weight obtained by dividing this by the official annual average price of gold per fine troy ounce, but no account was taken of the premium
ore	metal content of ore and concentrates bullion/coins, etc.
Grapefruit *see* Citrus fruit	
Grapes (2).	'000 metric tons
Groundnuts (4).	'000 metric tons shelled equivalent (approx. 70% of weight in shell)
Groundnut oil (4).	'000 metric tons P not available (average commercial extraction rate from shelled nuts 46%)
Ham *see* Bacon/ham	
Hardwood (3).	'000 cubic metres of roundwood equivalent
Hemp fibre (6).	'000 metric tons
Henequen *see* Agaves	
Hides/skins (5).	'000 metric tons
Horses (5).	P population in '000 head T not available *see also* Meat 'B'
Hydro-electricity *see* Electricity	
Ilmenite *see* Titanium minerals	
Iridium *see* Platinum group metals	
Iron ore (8).	P metal content of ore T incl. burnt iron pyrites

Commodity (Table no.)	Standardized units and definitions
Iron/steel (8). scrap products	P not available '000 metric tons million $ U.S.
Jute (6).	'000 metric tons
Kieserite *see* Magnesium	
Lamb *see* Meat 'A'	
Lead (9). ore metal	'000 metric tons P metal content of ores and concentrates P smelter production T incl. alloys, salts, scrap and lead content of base bullion
Lemons *see* Citrus fruit	
Letona *see* Agaves	
Lignite *see* Coal 'B'	
Limes *see* Citrus fruit	
Linseed (flaxseed) (4).	'000 metric tons
Linseed oil (4).	'000 metric tons P not available (average commercial extraction rate 34%)
Livestock (5).	'000 head P population
Locomotives (11). metal	P number T incl. with railway vehicles, in million $ U.S.
Machine tools (11).	million $ U.S. P 1953–5 data not available
Magnesium (9). dolomite magnesite kieserite metal/salts	'000 metric tons P 1953–5 data not available P 1953–5 data not available P not available P primary magnesium only
Maize (corn) (1).	'000 metric tons
Manganese (9). ore metal	'000 metric tons
Meat (5). 'A' 'B'	'000 metric tons beef, veal, pork, mutton, and lamb P incl. bacon and ham '000 metric tons incl. edible offals, poultry, horsemeat, etc. P not available
Merchant ships (11).	'000 gross registered tons T the importing country refers to the country of registration
Mercury (9).	metric tons excl. compounds
Methanol (10).	'000 metric tons
Mica (9).	'000 metric tons incl. micanite and phlogopite

Commodity (Table no.)	Standardized units and definitions
Milk (5).	'000 metric tons T evaporated, condensed, and powdered milk in approximate weight of fresh milk equivalent
Millets/sorghum (1).	'000 metric tons
Molybdenum (9). ore metal	P metal content of ores and concentrates P not available T incl. alloys, salts, and scrap
Monazite *see* Rare earths	
Motor vehicles (11).	T million $ U.S. commercial and private vehicles, incl. motor cycles P number in thousands, excl. motor cycles T incl. alloys, salts, and scrap
Mustard seed *see* Rapeseed	
Mutton *see* Meat 'A'	
Natural gas (7).	million cubic metres
Newsprint (3).	'000 metric tons
Nickel (9). ore metal	P metal content of ore, concentrates, and matte P metal content of ore, concentrates and matte T incl. alloys, salts, and scrap
Nitric acid (10).	'000 metric tons
Non-cellulosic (synthetic) fibre/yarn (6).	'000 metric tons T 1953–5 data not available
Nuclear energy *see* Electricity	
Oats (1).	'000 metric tons
Oil, crude (7).	'000 metric tons
Olives (2).	'000 metric tons T not available
Olive oil (4).	'000 metric tons
Oranges *see* Citrus fruit	
Osmiridium and osmium *see* Platinum group metals	
Palladium *see* Platinum group metals	
Palm kernels (4).	'000 metric tons
Palm kernel oil (4).	'000 metric tons P not available (average commercial extraction rate 48%)
Palm oil (4).	'000 metric tons
Paper, other (3).	'000 metric tons incl. paperboard and all paper other than newsprint
Peaches (2).	'000 metric tons
Peanuts *see* Groundnuts	
Pears (2).	'000 metric tons

Commodity (Table no.)	Standardized units and definitions
Petroleum, refined (7).	'000 metric tons T excl. ships' bunkers except where specified
Phenol (10).	'000 metric tons 1953–5 data not available
Phosphates (10).	'000 metric tons incl. apatite and guano where indicated; excl. manufactured and semi-manufactured phosphates P phosphate rock, chalk and dust T incl. compounds
Phthalic anhydride (10).	'000 metric tons 1953–5 data not available
Pig iron (8).	'000 metric tons incl. ferro-alloys
Pigs (5).	P '000 head population
Pineapples (2).	'000 metric tons T 1963–5 data not available
Platinum group metals (9).	'000 fine troy ounces incl. alloys, iridium, osmiridium, osmium, palladium, rhodium, ruthenium and concentrates; excl. platinum sent by post
Plums (2).	'000 metric tons T 1963–5 data not available
Polyamides (10).	'000 metric tons 1953–5 data not available
Polyethylene (10).	'000 metric tons 1953–5 data not available
Polyvinyl chloride (10).	'000 metric tons 1953–5 data not available
Pork *see* Meat 'A'	
Potash (10).	'000 metric tons P K_2O content or equivalent T salts and compounds
Potatoes (1).	'000 metric tons
Poultry *see* Chickens and Meat 'B'	
Pyrites (10).	'000 metric tons P sulphur content T iron and cupreous pyrites *see also* Iron ore
Radium *see* Uranium	
Railway vehicles (11).	million $ U.S. P not available T incl. locomotives *see also* Locomotives
Raisins (2).	'000 metric tons incl. currants and sultanas
Rapeseed (4).	'000 metric tons incl. mustard seed
Rapeseed oil (4).	'000 metric tons P not available (average commercial extraction rate 38%)

Commodities *continued*

Commodity (Table no.)	Standardized units and definitions
Rare earths (7)	metric tons incl. monazite, thorite, bast-naesite, and cerium
Rayon (cellulosic) (6) fibre/yarn	'000 metric tons
woven fabrics *see* woven fabrics	
Rhodium *see* Platinum group metals	
Rice (1)	'000 metric tons T milled equivalent
Rubber (6) natural; synthetic	'000 metric tons
Ruthenium *see* Platinum group metals	
Rutile *see* Titanium minerals	
Rye (1)	'000 metric tons
Scheelite *see* Tungsten	
Sesame seed (4)	'000 metric tons
Sesame seed oil (4)	'000 metric tons P not available (average commercial extraction rate 48%)
Sheep (5)	'000 head P population T incl. goats 1953-5 data not available
Ships *see* Merchant ships	
Silk (6)	metric tons
Silver (9) ore; bullion	'000 fine troy ounces metal content of ore and concentrates T incl. scrap
Sisal *see* Agaves	
Skins *see* Hides/skins	
Snuff *see* Tobacco	

Commodity (Table no.)	Standardized units and definitions
Sodium carbonate (10)	'000 metric tons 1953-5 data not available
Sodium hydroxide (10)	'000 metric tons 1953-5 data not available
Softwood (3)	'000 cubic metres of roundwood equivalent
Sorghum *see* Millets/sorghum	
Soya beans (4)	'000 metric tons
Soya bean oil (4)	'000 metric tons P not available (average commercial extraction rate 18%)
Sperm oil *see* Whale/sperm oil	
Spiegeleisen *see* Manganese	
Spirits *see* Alcoholic beverages	
Steel ingots/castings (8)	'000 metric tons
Steel products and scrap *see* Iron/steel	
Styrene monomer (10)	'000 metric tons 1953-5 data not available
Sugar (3) beet	'000 metric tons T not available
cane	T not available
raw	P raw equivalent of beet or cane, incl. refined
Sulphur (10)	'000 metric tons
Sulphuric acid (10)	'000 metric tons 1953-5 data not available
Sultanas *see* Raisins	
Sunflower seed (4)	'000 metric tons
Sunflower seed oil (4)	'000 metric tons P not available (average commercial extraction rate 35%)
Sweet potatoes/yams (1)	'000 metric tons T not available

Commodity (Table no.)	Standardized units and definitions
Tangerines *see* Citrus fruit	
Tea (3)	'000 metric tons
Thermal electricity *see* Electricity	
Thorite *see* Rare earths	
Tin (9) ore; metal	'000 metric tons P metal content of ore and concentrates T incl. alloys
Titanium minerals (9)	'000 metric tons incl. ilmenite, rutile, alloys, and salts
Tobacco (3) leaf	'000 metric tons
cigars	P number in millions
cigarettes	P number in millions
tobacco/snuff	T '000 metric tons
Tomatoes (2)	'000 metric tons
Tung oil (4)	'000 metric tons T not available
Tungsten (9) ore	'000 metric tons P WO_3 content (estimated as 60% of ore) T incl. wolfram and scheelite ores and concentrates
Uranium (7)	metric tons P metal content of uranium minerals T '000 metric tons ores and concentrates, or radium products, etc. where specified
Urea (10)	'000 metric tons 1953-5 data not available

Commodity (Table no.)	Standardized units and definitions
Vanadium (9)	'000 metric tons P content of ores and concentrates T content of ores and concentrates, or ferro-vanadium, where specified
Veal *see* Meat 'A'	
Whale/sperm oil (5)	'000 metric tons T whale oil only
Wheat (1)	'000 metric tons incl. spelt T incl. meslin, excl. flour
Wine (2)	'000 hectolitres T *see also* Alcoholic beverages
Wolfram *see* Tungsten	
Wood *see* Softwood and Hardwood	
Wood pulp (3)	'000 metric tons
Wool (5) raw	'000 metric tons P clean wool equivalent
yarn (6)	T incl. mixtures predominantly of wool
woven fabrics (6)	T incl. mixtures predominantly of wool
Yams *see* Sweet potatoes/yams	
Zinc (9) ore; metal	'000 metric tons P metal content of ore T smelter production incl. lithopone, salts and scrap
Zirconium minerals (9)	'000 metric tons incl. zircon, baddeleyite, etc. as individually specified